ENCYCLOPEDIA OF SOUTHERN CULTURE

CHARLES REAGAN WILSON
& WILLIAM FERRIS
Coeditors

ANN J. ABADIE
& MARY L. HART
Associate Editors

Sponsored by
The Center for the Study of Southern Culture
at the University of Mississippi

ENCYCLOPEDIA OF SOUTHERN CULTURE

VOLUME 1

Agriculture–Environment

☆☆☆☆☆☆☆☆☆☆☆☆☆☆☆☆☆☆☆☆

ANCHOR BOOKS
DOUBLEDAY
New York London Toronto Sydney Auckland

AN ANCHOR BOOK
PUBLISHED BY DOUBLEDAY
a division of Bantam Doubleday Dell Publishing Group, Inc.
666 Fifth Avenue, New York, New York 10103

Encyclopedia of Southern Culture was originally published in hardcover in one volume by the University of North Carolina Press in 1989. The Anchor Books edition is published by arrangement with the University of North Carolina Press.

Both the initial research and the publication of this work were made possible in part through a grant from the Division of Research Programs of the National Endowment for the Humanities, an independent federal agency whose mission is to award grants to support education, scholarship, media programming, libraries, and museums, in order to bring the results of cultural activities to a broad, general public.

Book design by Chris Welch

Library of Congress Cataloging-in-Publication Data

Encyclopedia of Southern culture / Charles Reagan Wilson & William Ferris, coeditors; Ann J. Abadie & Mary L. Hart, associate editors.
—1st Anchor Books ed.
p. cm.
"Originally published in hardcover in one volume by the University of North Carolina Press in 1989"—T.p. verso.
Includes bibliographical references and index.
Contents: Vol. 1. Agriculture–Environment—v. 2. Ethnic Life–Law—v. 3. Literature–Recreation—v. 4. Religion–Women's Life.
1. Southern States—Civilization—Encyclopedias. 2. Southern States—Encyclopedias. I. Wilson, Charles Reagan. II. Ferris, William R.
F209.E53 1991 975'.003 90-973
CIP

ISBN 0-385-41545-1

PRINTED IN THE UNITED STATES OF AMERICA
1 3 5 7 9 10 8 6 4 2
FIRST ANCHOR BOOKS EDITION: MAY 1991

"Tell about the South. What's it like there.
What do they do there. Why do they live there.
Why do they live at all."

WILLIAM FAULKNER
Absalom, Absalom!

The *Encyclopedia of Southern Culture* was
produced through major grants from the Program
for Research Tools and Reference Works of the
National Endowment for the Humanities, the
Ford Foundation, the Atlantic-Richfield
Foundation, and the Mary Doyle Trust.

The publication of this volume
was made possible by the
Fred W. Morrison Fund of the
University of North Carolina Press.

CONTENTS

Consultants ix
Foreword xi
Acknowledgments xiii
Introduction xv
Editors' Note xxvii
Agriculture 1
Art and Architecture 85
Black Life 221
Education 397
Environment 529
Index of Contributors 677
Index 679
Picture Credits 691

CONSULTANTS

AGRICULTURE
Thomas D. Clark
248 Tahoma Road
Lexington, Ky. 40503

ART AND ARCHITECTURE
Jessie Poesch
Department of Art
Tulane University
New Orleans, La. 70118

BLACK LIFE
Thomas C. Holt
Department of History
University of Chicago
Chicago, Ill. 60637

EDUCATION
Thomas G. Dyer
Associate Vice President for
Academic Affairs
University of Georgia
Old College
Athens, Ga. 30602

ENVIRONMENT
Martin V. Melosi
Department of History
University of Houston
Houston, Tex. 77004

ETHNIC LIFE
George E. Pozzetta
Department of History
University of Florida
Gainesville, Fla. 32611

FOLKLIFE
William Ferris
Center for the Study of
Southern Culture
University of Mississippi
University, Miss. 38677

GEOGRAPHY
Richard Pillsbury
Department of Geography
Georgia State University
Atlanta, Ga. 30303

HISTORY AND MANNERS
Charles Reagan Wilson
Center for the Study of
Southern Culture
University of Mississippi
University, Miss. 38677

INDUSTRY
James C. Cobb
Honors Program
P.O. Box 6233
University of Alabama
Tuscaloosa, Ala. 35487-6322

LANGUAGE
Michael Montgomery
Department of English
University of South Carolina
Columbia, S.C. 29208

LAW
Maxwell Bloomfield
Department of History
The Catholic University of
America
Washington, D.C. 20017

LITERATURE
M. Thomas Inge
Randolph-Macon College
Ashland, Va. 23005

MEDIA
Edward D. C. Campbell, Jr.
Virginia State Library
11th Street at Capitol Square
Richmond, Va. 23219

MUSIC
Bill C. Malone
Department of History
Tulane University
New Orleans, La. 70118

MYTHIC SOUTH
George B. Tindall
Department of History
University of North Carolina
Chapel Hill, N.C. 27599

POLITICS
Numan Bartley
Department of History
University of Georgia
Athens, Ga. 30602

RECREATION
John Shelton Reed
Department of Sociology
University of North Carolina
Chapel Hill, N.C. 27599

RELIGION
Samuel S. Hill
Department of Religion
University of Florida
Gainesville, Fla. 32611

SCIENCE AND MEDICINE
James O. Breeden
Department of History
Southern Methodist University
Dallas, Tex. 75275

SOCIAL CLASS
J. Wayne Flynt
Department of History
Auburn University
Auburn, Ala. 36830

URBANIZATION
Blaine A. Brownell
School of Social and Behavioral Sciences
University of Alabama at Birmingham
Birmingham, Ala. 35294

VIOLENCE
Raymond D. Gastil
48 E. 21st Street
New York, N.Y. 10010

WOMEN'S LIFE
Carol Ruth Berkin
Baruch College
City University of New York
17 Lexington Avenue
New York, N.Y. 10010

FOREWORD

Can you remember those southern elder men who "jes' set" on their favored chair or bench for hours, every day—and a year later they could tell you at about what time of day someone's dog had trotted by? And the counterpart elderly ladies, their hands deeply wrinkled from decades of quilting, canning, washing collective tons of clothing in black cast-iron pots, in which at other seasonal times pork fat was rendered into lard, or some of that lard into soap? These southern ancestors, black and white, have always struck me as the Foundation Timbers of our South, and I think that we who were reared and raised by them, and amongst them, are blessed that we were.

I consider this *Encyclopedia of Southern Culture* the answer to a deep need that we resuscitate and keep alive and fresh the memories of those who are now bones and dust, who during their eras and in their respective ways contributed toward the social accretion that has entered legend as "the southern way of life," which we continue today.

It is a culture resulting from the antebellum mixture of social extremes based on the chattel slavery that supported an aristocratic gentility; in between the slaves and planters a vast majority struggled for their own survival. Centuries of slavery were abolished by an indelible war whose legacies continue to haunt us. The southern memory is of generations of life, of the good and the bad, the humor and the suffering from the past. The southerner does not sentimentalize but only remembers.

Out of the historic cotton tillage sprang the involuntary field hollers, the shouts, and the moanin' low that have since produced such a cornucopia of music, played daily, on every continent, where I have been astounded at how much I heard of the evolved blues, jazz, and gospel—as well as bluegrass and country—all of them of direct southern origin.

Equally worldwide is southern literature. Writers took the oral traditions of the South—the political rhetoric, preaching, conversational wordplay, and lazy-day storytelling—and converted them into art. The latest addition to southern literature is this *Encyclopedia*, no small part of whose greatness, I think, is that it is compiled by many researchers who did not simply read books but who rubbed shoulders with those whom they interviewed and recorded and studied. They walked and talked with the sharecropper farmers, the cooks, the quiltmakers, the convicts, the merchants, the fishermen, and all the others who make these pages a volume of living memories.

The region and its people have undergone dramatic changes in the last decades, overcoming much, although not all, of the poverty of the past, and they are now sharing in the nation's prosperity. Old ways that divided the people have fallen away to be replaced by new dreams. The hard lessons from the past are not forgotten in this *Encyclopedia.* I testify that this *Encyclopedia of Southern Culture* mirrors the very best of what has lately come to be called "the new South." Never before have such volumes been produced by a team so committed to distilling and presenting our southern distinctiveness.

Alex Haley

ACKNOWLEDGMENTS

These volumes could never have been completed without the assistance of countless individuals. The coeditors and associate editors wish to thank our consultants and contributors for their planning, researching, and writing of articles. We should note that Raven McDavid helped to plan the Language section before his untimely death in 1984. Clarence Mohr's work on the early design of the *Encyclopedia* provided the basic organizational structure for the volumes. Many scholars reviewed articles, made suggestions for improvements, and verified factual material. Richard H. Brown, of the Newberry Library in Chicago, advised wisely on *Encyclopedia* matters, as with other projects of the Center for the Study of Southern Culture. Howard Lamar offered sage counsel on the *Encyclopedia* from its earliest planning stages. Research assistants Elizabeth Makowski and Sharon A. Sharp supervised the review and verification of entries, assisted by numerous teaching assistants and volunteers, and also served as staff writers. Editorial assistants Ann Sumner Holmes, Ginna Parsons, and Karen McDearman Cox supervised final production of copy and served as endless sources of good advice and varied skill. Lolly Pilkington read the entire manuscript with a skilled eye. Teaching assistants in the Department of History and the Southern Studies program spent much time in the library checking and rechecking information and reading galley proof. Personnel in the John Davis Williams Library of the University of Mississippi often came to our rescue, and we are grateful to the many archivists and librarians across the nation who assisted us with obtaining illustrations. Special thanks are due the staff of the University of North Carolina Press, especially its director Matthew Hodgson, editor-in-chief Iris Tillman Hill, managing editor Sandra Eisdorfer, and Ron Maner, Pamela Upton, and Paula Wald.

The *Encyclopedia of Southern Culture* was produced with financial support from the National Endowment for the Humanities, the Ford Foundation, the Atlantic-Richfield Foundation, and the Mary Doyle Trust. The Graduate School and alumni and friends of the University of Mississippi donated required funds for a matching NEH grant in 1983, and the editors are grateful for their assistance. Donors include: The James Hand Foundation by Kathleen Hand Carter; Mrs. R. R. Morrison, Jr.; Mrs. Hester F. Faser; David L. May; James J. Brown, Jr.; Lynn Crosby Gammill; First National Bank of Vicksburg, Mississippi; The Goodman Charitable and Educational Trust, Hallie Goodman, Trustee; Dr. F. Watt Bishop; Robert Travis; Mrs. Dorothy Crosby; Christopher Keller, Jr.; Worth I. Dunn; Wiley Fairchild; Mrs. Eric Biedenharn; John S. Callon; Betty Carter; Shelby Flowers Ferris; Mary Hohenberg; Mr. & Mrs. John Kramer; Samuel McIlwain; and Prescott Sherman.

INTRODUCTION

The American South has long generated powerful images and complex emotions. In the years since World War II, the region has undergone dramatic changes in race relations, political institutions, and economic life. Those changes have led some observers to forecast the eventual end of a distinctive southern region. Other scholars and popular writers point to continuities with past attitudes and behavior. The *Encyclopedia of Southern Culture* appears during a period of major transition in the life of the South and is in part a reflection of these changes. It examines both the historical and the contemporary worlds of southern culture. The *Encyclopedia*'s editors have sought to assemble authoritative, concise, thoughtful, substantive, and interesting articles that will give scholars, students, and general readers a useful perspective on the South.

SOUTHERN CULTURE

The *Encyclopedia*'s definition of "the South" is a cultural one. The geographical focus is, to be sure, on the 11 states of the former Confederacy (Alabama, Arkansas, Florida, Georgia, Louisiana, Mississippi, North Carolina, South Carolina, Tennessee, Texas, and Virginia), but this tidy historical definition fails to confront the complexities of studying the region. Delaware, Kentucky, Maryland, and Missouri were slave states at the beginning of the Civil War, and many of their citizens then and after claimed a southern identity. Social scientists today use statistical data covering the "census South," which includes Delaware, Maryland, West Virginia, Oklahoma, and the District of Columbia. The Gallup public opinion polling organization defines the South as the Confederate states plus Oklahoma and Kentucky.

Moreover, the realities of cultural areas require a broadened definition. Cultural areas have core zones, where distinctive traits are most concentrated, and margins, where the boundaries of the culture overlap with other cultural areas. The *Encyclopedia*'s articles explore the nature of both these core areas and margins in the South. The borders of the South have surely varied over time. In the colonial era Delaware was an agricultural slave state with a claim of being southern. Maryland was a southern state, sharing much with its neighbor, Virginia, in a Chesapeake subculture. Maryland did not join the Confederacy, but soldiers from the state fought in the Confederate armies and one finds Confederate monuments in Baltimore. St. Louis was a midwestern city and the gateway to the West, but southerners have also claimed it. The Mississippi River culture tied St. Louis to areas of the Lower South, and southerners have often been associated with it. John F. Kennedy once said that Washington, D.C., was known for its southern efficiency and northern charm. Carved from an area of Maryland as a concession to southerners, Washington was a slaveowning area and was once a center for slave auctions. Later, under Woodrow Wilson, a southern-born president, the nation's capital became a racially segregated bastion reflecting southern regional mores. Washington has also long been a center for southern black migration, an educational mecca for blacks, and a center for black musicians, artists, and writers. Most recently, geographical proximity to Appalachia has made Washington a center for the performance of such other expressions of southern culture as bluegrass music. Contemporary Washington, however, appears to be less and less "southern," and urban historians consequently omit it from the list of regional cities (and thus there is no separate entry on Washington in the *Encyclopedia*.

Contributors to the *Encyclopedia* at times transcend geography and history when examining questions of regional consciousness, symbolism, mythology, and sectional stereotyping. The "South" is found wherever southern culture is found, and that culture is located not only in the Deep South, the Upper South, and border cities, but also in "little Dixies" (the southern parts of Ohio, Indiana, Illinois, and parts of Missouri and Oklahoma), among black Mississippians who migrated to south Chicago, among white Appalachians and black Alabamians who migrated to Detroit, and among former Okies and Arkies who settled in and around Bakersfield, California. This diaspora of southern ethnic culture is also found in the works of expatriate southern artists and writers. Although Richard Wright and Tennessee Williams lived in Paris and New York, respectively, they continued to explore their southern roots in their writing.

The South exists as a state of mind both within and beyond its geographical boundaries. Recent studies of mythology suggest that the New York theater in the late 19th century and Hollywood in the 20th century have kept alive images, legends, and myths about the South in the national consciousness. One can view the American South and its culture as international property. The worlds of *Roots*, *Gone with the Wind*, blues, country music, rock and roll, William Faulkner, and Alice Walker are admired and closely studied throughout the world. The South has nurtured important myths, and their impact on other cultures is a vital aspect of the *Encyclopedia*'s perspective. In the end, then, the *Encyclopedia*'s definition of the South is a broad, inclusive one, based on culture.

These volumes focus specifically on exploring the culture of the South. In the 1950s anthropologists Alfred Kroeber and Clyde Kluckholn cataloged 164 definitions of culture, suggesting the problems then and now of a precise definition. To 19th-century intellectuals culture was the best of civilization's achievements. Matthew Arnold was perhaps the best-known advocate of this Victorian-era ideal, and H. L. Mencken—the South's nastiest and most entertaining critic in the early 20th century—was also a believer in it. Mencken argued in his essay "The Sahara of the Bozart" (1920) that the upper-class, aristocratic southerner of the early 19th century "liked to toy with ideas. He was hospitable and tolerant. He had the vague thing that we call culture." Mencken found the South of his era severely wanting, though, in this ideal of culture. He saw in the South "not a single picture gallery worth going into, or a single orchestra capable of playing the nine symphonies of Beethoven, or a single opera-house, or a single theater devoted to decent plays, or a single public monument (built since the war) that is worth looking at, or a single workshop devoted to the making of beautiful things." Mencken allowed that the region excelled "in the lower reaches of the gospel hymn, the phonograph and the chautauqua harangue."

The South of Mencken's day did trail the rest of the nation in the development of important cultural institutions; but today the South, the nation, and the world celebrate the "lower reaches" of southern culture. This judgment on the value of the sounds and words coming from the region reflects 20th-century understandings of culture. Anthropologists have taken the lead in exploring the theoretical aspects of cultures. Edward Burnett Tylor gave a classic definition of culture as "that complex whole which includes knowledge, belief, art, morals, law, customs, and any other capabilities and habits" acquired by the members of a society. For students of culture, the goal was to study and outline discrete cultural traits, using this definition to convey the picture of a culture. During the 20th century another major anthropological theory of culture emerged. Kroeber, Bronislaw Malinowski, and Ruth Benedict stressed the study of pattern, form, structure, and organization in a culture rather than the simple listing of observed traits. Patterns could include customs associated with food, labor, and manners as well as more complex social, political, and economic systems.

Recently culture has been viewed as an abstraction, consisting of the inherited models and ideas with which people approach their experiences. The theory of social structure, first developed by British anthropologist Alexander Reginald Radcliffe-Brown in the 1930s and 1940s, stressed that culture must include recognition of the persistence of social groups, social classes, and social roles. The structuralist theories of Claude Lévi-Strauss attempt to apply abstract mathematical formulae to society. Although social anthropologists avoid the term *culture*, they have insured that the study of culture not neglect social background.

The theoretical work of Clifford Geertz is especially significant in understanding the definition of culture developed for the *Encyclopedia of Southern Culture*. Geertz defines *culture* as "an historically transmitted pattern of meanings embodied in symbols, a system of inherited conceptions expressed in symbolic forms." Through culture, humans "communicate, perpetuate, and develop their knowledge about and attitudes toward life." This contemporary definition stresses mental culture, expressed through symbol systems, which gives human beings a framework for understanding one another, themselves, and the wider world. Culture patterns, including material, oral, mental, and social systems, are blueprints for organizing human interaction.

The *Encyclopedia of Southern Culture* is not intended as a contribution to the general study of culture theory, although awareness of theories of culture has been useful background in the conceptualization of the volumes and in the selection of topics. The volumes attempt to study within the southern context what 20th-century humanist T. S. Eliot said, in *Notes towards the Definition of Culture*, was culture—"all the characteristic activities and interests of a people." Articles in the volumes deal with regional cultural achievements in such areas as music, literature, art, and architecture. The broader goal of the volumes is to chart the cultural landscape of the South, addressing those aspects of southern life and thought that have sustained either the reality or the illusion of regional distinctiveness. The volumes detail specific cultural traits, suggest the cultural patterns that tie the region together, point out the internal diversity within the South, and explore with special attention the importance of social structure and symbolism. Above all, the volumes have been planned to carry out Eliot's belief that "culture is not merely the sum of several activities, but a *way of life*."

Eliot's definition of culture, then, can be seen as a working definition for the *Encyclopedia of Southern Culture*. In order to foster interdisciplinary communication, the editors have included the full range of social indicators, trait groupings, literary concepts, and historical evidence commonly used by students of regionalism. The criteria for the all-important selection of topics, however, have been consistently to include the characteristic traits that give the South a distinctive culture.

A special concern of the *Encyclopedia* has been to identify distinctive regional characteristics. It addresses those aspects of southern life and thought—the individuals, places, ideas, rituals, symbols, myths, values, and experiences—which have sustained either the reality or the illusion of regional distinctiveness. The comparative method has been encouraged as a way to suggest contrasts with other American regions and with other societies. One lesson of earlier regional scholarship has been the need to look at the South in the widest possible context. The editors of the *Encyclopedia* have assumed that the distinctiveness of southern culture does not lie in any one trait but rather in the peculiar combination of regional cultural characteristics. The fundamental uniqueness of southern culture thus emerges from the *Encyclopedia*'s composite portrait of the South. The editors asked contributors to consider individual traits that clearly are unique to the region. Although some topics may not be uniquely southern in themselves, contributors have been asked to explore particular regional aspects of those topics. Subjects that suggest the internal diversity of the region are also treated if they contribute to the overall picture of southern distinctiveness. The Cajuns of Louisiana, the Germans of Texas, and the Jews of Savannah, for example, contribute to the distinctive flavor of southern life. Their adaptations, and resistance, to southern cultural patterns suggest much about the region's distinctiveness.

The question of continuity and change in southern culture is another central concern of the *Encyclopedia*. Contributors have examined themes and topics in an evolutionary framework. Historians represent by far the largest group of contributors to the project. The volumes do not attempt to narrate the region's history in a systematic way, a task ably achieved in the *Encyclopedia of Southern History* (1979), but contributors from all disciplines have developed material within an appropriate time perspective. As Clifford Geertz has written, culture is "historically transmitted," a fact that is especially relevant for the study of the South, where the apogee of cultural distinctiveness may well have been in an earlier period. Because the *Encyclopedia* focuses on culture rather than history, historical topics were chosen because they are relevant to the origin, development, or decline of an aspect of southern culture. Given the historical shape of southern cultural development, one would expect less material on the colonial era (before there was a self-conscious "South") and increased concentration of material in the Civil War and postbellum eras (perhaps the high points of southern cultural distinctiveness). Nearly all articles include historical material, and each overview essay systematically traces the development of a major subject area. In addition, such selected historical entries as "Colonial Heritage," "Frontier Heritage," and "Civil War" are included with a cultural focus appropriate to the volumes.

STUDY OF SOUTHERN REGIONALISM

The *Encyclopedia of Southern Culture* reflects a broad intellectual interest in regionalism, the importance of which in the United States is far from unique when seen in a global context. The struggle to accommodate regional cultures within a larger nation is an experience common to many Western and Third World peoples. Despite the contemporary developments in transportation and communication that promise the emergence of a "global village," regionalism is an enduring reality of the modern world. The Basques in Spain, the Scots in Britain, the Kurds in the Middle East, and Armenians in the Soviet Union are only a few examples of groups that have recently reasserted their regional interests.

Although public emphasis on the United States as a cultural melting pot has sometimes obscured the nation's enduring regional heritage, the study of regionalism has long been a major field of scholarship involving leading authorities from many academic disciplines both in the United States and abroad. The *Encyclopedia* is part of the broader field of American Studies, which has dramatically evolved in recent years from a focus on such regional types as the New England Yankees, the southern Cavaliers, and the western cowboys and Indians. Since the 1960s studies of black life, ethnic life, and women's life have significantly changed the definition of American culture. In the 1980s the study of American region, place, and community—whether it be a Brooklyn neighborhood or a county in rural Mississippi—is essential to understanding the nation. In the context of this American Studies tradition, the *Encyclopedia* focuses on the American South, a place that has influenced its people in complex and fascinating ways.

Significant bodies of research exist for all major regions of the United States, but by almost any standard the American South has received the most extensive scholarly attention. Since the 1930s virtually all aspects of southern life have come under increasingly rigorous, systematic intellectual scrutiny. The *Encyclopedia of Southern Culture* is a collaborative effort that combines intellectual perspectives that reflect the breadth of Southern Studies. Sociologists, historians, literary critics, folklorists, anthropologists, political scientists, psychologists, theologians, and other scholars have written on the region, and all of these fields are represented by contributors to the *Encyclopedia*. Journalists, lawyers, physicians, architects, and other professionals from outside the academy have also studied the South, and their contributions appear in these volumes as well.

Students of the South operate within a well-developed institutional framework. The proliferation of academic journals that focus on the South has mirrored expanding disciplinary boundaries in regional scholarship. The *Journal of Southern History*, the *Southern Review*, the *Southern Economic Journal*, *Social Forces*, the *Southern Folklore Quarterly*, the *Virginia Quarterly Review*, the *South Atlantic Quarterly*, and the *Southwestern Political Science Quarterly* are only a few of the titles that have specialized in publishing material on the region. The contemporary era has witnessed a dramatic expansion in the publication of books on the South. The University of North Carolina Press was the first southern university press to publish an extensive list of titles on the South, and by the early 1950s the press alone had produced some 200 studies. Works on the region are now published by university presses in every southern state and find a ready market with national publishers as well.

Research on the South has led to greater appreciation of the region's internal diversity, which is reflected in the study of smaller geographical areas or specialized themes. Such recent periodicals as the *Appalachian Journal*, *Mid-South Folklore*, and *South Atlantic Urban Studies* illustrate the narrowing geographical and topical focus of recent scholarship on the South. Overlapping interests and subject matter shared among regional scholars have exerted a steady pressure toward broadening disciplinary horizons. Meaningful cooperation among disciplines is complicated by differences of vocabulary and method, but students of the American South demonstrate a growing awareness that they are engaged in a common endeavor that can be furthered as much by cooperation as by specialization. Such periodicals as *Southern Quarterly*, *Southern Studies*, and *Perspectives on the American South* have established forums for interdisciplinary study.

In recent years regional scholarship has also influenced curriculum development in colleges and universities. Leading institutional centers for the study of the South include the Center for the Study of Southern Culture at the University of Mississippi, the Institute for Southern Studies at the University of South Carolina, the Institute for Southern Studies at Durham, N.C., and the Center for the Study of Southern History and Culture at the University of Alabama. Appalachian study centers are located at, among other places, the University of Kentucky, East Tennessee State University, Appalachian State University, Mars Hill College, and Berea College. The Institute for Texan Cultures is in San Antonio, and Baylor University launched a Texas Studies Center in 1987. The Center for Arkansas Studies is at the University of Arkansas at Little Rock, while the University of Southwestern Louisiana's Center for Louisiana Studies concentrates on Cajun and Creole folk culture. These developments are, again, part of a broader interest in regional studies programs at universities in other regions, including the Center for the Study of New England Culture at the University of Massachusetts at Amherst and the Great Plains Center at the University of Nebraska.

The *Encyclopedia of Southern Culture* grows out of the work of the University of Mississippi's Center for the Study of Southern Culture, which was established in 1977 to coordinate existing university resources and to develop multidisciplinary teaching, research, and outreach programs about the South. The center's mission is to strengthen the university's instructional program in the humanities, to promote scholarship on every aspect of southern culture, and to encourage public understanding of the South through publications, media productions, lectures, performances, and exhibitions. Center personnel administer a Southern Studies curriculum that includes both B.A. and M.A. degree programs; a Ford Foundation–funded, three-year (1986–89) project aimed at incorporating more fully the experiences of blacks and women into the teaching of Southern Studies; an annual United States Information Agency–sponsored project for international scholars interested in regional and ethnic cultures; such annual meetings as the Porter L. Fortune Chancellor's Symposium on Southern History, the Faulkner and Yoknapatawpha Conference, and the Barnard-Millington Symposium on Southern Science and Medicine; and a variety of periodicals, films, and media presentations. The center administers these programs in cooperation with the on-campus departments in the College of Liberal Arts, the Afro-American Studies program, and the Sarah Isom Center for Women's Studies. The University of Mississippi and its Center for the Study of Southern Culture provided the necessary institutional setting for coordinating the diverse needs of the *Encyclopedia*'s hundreds of participants.

Recognizing both the intellectual maturity of scholarship in the American South and the potential role of regional study in consolidating previously fragmented academic endeavors, the *Encyclopedia* planners conceived the idea of an interdisciplinary reference work to bring together and synthesize current knowledge about the South. Scholars studying the South have been served by a number of reference works, but none of these has had the aims and perspective of the *Encyclopedia of Southern Culture*. The 13-volume series, *The South in the Building of the Nation* (1909–13), which attempted a comprehensive survey of the region's history, was the closest predecessor to this encyclopedia. Other major works include the 16-volume *Library of Southern Literature* (1908–13), Howard W. Odum's monumental *Southern Regions of the United States* (1936), W. T. Couch's edited *Culture in the South* (1936), and, more recently, the *Encyclopedia of Southern History* (1978), the *Encyclopedia of Religion in the South* (1984), and the *History of Southern Literature* (1986).

Like any major reference work, the *Encyclopedia* addresses the long-range needs and interests of a diverse reading audience. Before launching the project the editors consulted extensively with leading authorities in all areas of American Studies and Southern Studies and sought additional advice from directors of comparable projects. Planning for the original single-volume edition began in 1978 with the compilation of a working outline of subjects that had received frequent attention in major studies of regional culture. During the fall of 1979 some 270 U.S. and international scholars received copies of the preliminary topical list, together with background information about the project. Approximately 150 of these scholars, representing a variety of disciplines, responded to this mailing, commenting upon the potential value of the proposed volume and making suggestions concerning its organization and content.

In 1980 the Center for the Study of Southern Culture commissioned several scholars to prepare detailed lists of topics for major sections of the volume, and to write sample articles as well. The National Endowment for the Humanities supported the *Encyclopedia of Southern Culture* with a 1980–81 planning grant and grants covering 1981–83 and 1984–86. The Ford Foundation, the Atlantic-Richfield Foundation, and the Mary Doyle Trust also provided major funding. Full-time work on the *Encyclopedia* began in September 1981. The content of the volume was divided into 24 major subject areas, and the editors selected a senior consultant to assist in planning the topics and contributors for each section. During the fall and winter of 1981–82, the consultants formulated initial lists of topics and recommended appropriate contributors for entries. In general, the consultants were actively involved in the initial stages of planning and less involved in later editorial work. Project staff handled the paperwork for assignments. The editors sent each contributor a packet of information on the project, including the overall list of topics, so that contributors could see how their articles fit into the volume as a whole. Authors were encouraged to make suggestions for additional entries, and many of them did so. When contributors were unable to write for the volume, they often suggested other scholars, thus facilitating the reassignment of articles. The editors assumed the responsibility for editing articles for style, clarity, and tone appropriate for a reference book. They reviewed all entries for accuracy, and research assistants verified the factual and bibliographical veracity of each entry. The senior consultants, with their special expertise in each subject area, provided an additional check on the quality of the articles.

ORGANIZATION AND CONTENT OF THE ENCYCLOPEDIA

The *Encyclopedia of Southern Culture* is a synthesis of current scholarship and attempts to set new directions for further research. The *Encyclopedia*'s objectives are fourfold: (1) The volumes provide students and general readers with convenient access to basic facts and bibliographical data about southern cultural patterns and their historical development. (2) By bringing together lucid analyses of modern scholarship on southern culture from the humanities and the social sciences, the *Encyclopedia* is intended to facilitate communication across disciplinary lines and help stimulate new approaches to regional study. It attempts to integrate disparate intellectual efforts and represents an innovative organization and presentation of knowledge. (3) The volumes can serve as a curriculum component for multidisciplinary courses on the American South and provide a model for scholars wishing to assemble similar research tools in other regions. (4) Viewed in its totality, the *Encyclopedia* locates the specific components of regional culture within the framework of a larger organic whole. At this level, the volumes attempt to illuminate the nature and function of regionalism in American culture.

The editors considered an alphabetical arrangement of articles but concluded that organization of information into 24 major sections more accurately reflects the nature of the project and would provide a fresh perspective. Cross-references to related articles in other sections are essential guides to proper use of the *Encyclopedia*, enabling readers to consult articles written on a common topic from different perspectives. Sections often reflect an academic field (history, geography, literature), but at times the academic division has been rejected in favor of a section organized around a cultural theme (such as social class) that has become a central scholarly concern. In general, the sections are designed to reflect the amount and quality of scholarship in particular areas of regional study. Articles within each section are arranged in three divisions. The overview essay is written by the *Encyclopedia*'s consultant in that section and provides an interpretive summary of the field. That essay is followed by alphabetically arranged thematic articles and then by alphabetically arranged, brief topical-biographical sketches.

Although the editors and consultants conceived each section as a separate unit, sections are closely connected to one another through cross-references. The titles of major sections are brief, but the editors have grouped together related material under these simple rubrics. The Agriculture section thus includes rural-life articles, the Black Life section includes articles on race relations, Social Class includes material on social structure and occupational groups, and Industry includes information on commercial activity.

Several sections deserve special comment in regard to their organization and content. The Black Life section (Vol. 1) contains most, though not all, of the separate entries on southern black culture. The editors placed Richard Wright and Ralph Ellison in Literature (Vol. 3) to honor their roles as central figures in *southern* (as well as black) literature, and most blues musicians are similarly found in Music (Vol. 3). But the list of biographies in Black Life is intended to stand on its own, including individuals representing music, literature, religion, sports, politics, and other areas of black achievement. The *Encyclopedia* claims for southern culture such individuals as Mary McLeod Bethune, Ida Wells-Barnett, Arna Bontemps, and James Weldon Johnson, who traditionally have been seen as part of black history but not southern culture. The separate Black Life section is intended to recognize the special nature of southern black culture—both black and southern. Black culture is central to understanding the region and the *Encyclopedia*'s attempt to explore this perspective in specific, detailed topics may be the most significant contribution of these volumes toward understanding the region. Although the terms *Afro-American* and *Euro-American* are sometimes used, *black* and *white* are more often used to refer to the two major interrelated cultures of the South. These terms seem the clearest, most inclusive, and most widely accepted terms of reference.

The Women's Life section (Vol. 4) has similar aims. Many thematic articles and biographies of women of achievement appear in this section, which is designed to stand on its own. Scholars in the last 20 years have explored southern women's cultural values and issues, and their work provides a distinctive perspective on the region. Gender, like race and social class, has set parameters for cultural life in the South. The section includes articles on family life, childhood, and the elderly, reflecting the major responsibilities and concerns of women. The inclusion of these topics in this section is not meant to suggest that family responsibilities were the sole concern of women or that men were uninvolved with family, children, and the elderly. The articles usually discuss both male and female activities within the family. Scholarship on family life has often focused on women's roles, and family matters traditionally have played a significant part in women's lives. Most of the Women's Life section is concentrated, however, on concerns beyond the family and household, reflecting the contemporary scholarship in this area.

The Education section (Vol. 1) presented especially difficult choices of inclusion, and again, a selective approach was adopted. The flagship state public university in each southern state is included, but beyond that, institutions have been selected that represent differing constituencies to suggest the diversity of educational activity in the region. Berea College, Commonwealth College, the University of the South, and Tuskegee Institute each reflect an important dimension of southern education. The inclusion of additional school entries would have departed from the *Encyclopedia*'s overall guidelines and made a four-volume reference work impossible.

The History and Manners section (Vol. 2) contains a mix of articles that focus on cultural and social dimensions of the South. Combining topics in history and manners reflects the editors' decision that in a reference work on cultural concerns, history entries should deal with broad sociocultural history. There are, thus, no separate, detailed entries on Civil War battles, but, instead, long thematic articles on the cultural meaning of battlefields, monuments, and wars. The article on Robert E. Lee discusses the facts of Lee's life but also the history of his image for southerners and Americans.

Overview essays in each section are interpretive pieces that synthesize modern scholarship on major aspects of southern culture. The consultants who have written them trace historical developments and relate their broad subjects to regional cultural concerns. Many specific topics are discussed within overview essays rather than through separate entries, so readers should consult the index in order to locate such material. As one might expect, major subject areas have developed at a different pace. In such fields as literature, music, religion, folklife, and political culture, a vast body of scholarship exists. In these areas, the *Encyclopedia* overview essays provide a starting point for those users of this reference work interested in the subject. Such other fields as law, art, science, and medicine have only recently emerged as separate fields of Southern Studies. In these areas, the overview essays should help define the fields and point toward areas for further research.

Most thematic, topical, and biographical entries fall clearly within one section, but some articles were appropriate for several sections. The Scopes trial, for example, could have been placed in Religion, Law, or Science and Medicine. Consultants in Black Life, Music, and Women's Life all suggested Bessie Smith as an entry in their categories. The article on cockfighting clearly related to the Recreation section but was placed in Violence to suggest how recreational activities reflect a culture of violence. The gospel music articles could have appeared in Religion, but the editors decided that Music was the most appropriate category for them.

Much consideration and consultation with authorities in relevant fields occurred before such decisions were made on topics that did not fit perfectly into any one section. Readers should rely on the index and cross-references between sections to lead them to desired entries.

Biographies focus on the cultural significance of key individuals. The volumes do not claim to be exhaustive in their biographical entries. Rather than attempt to include all prominent people in a subject area, the editors decided to treat representative figures in terms of their contributions to, or significance for, southern culture. In selecting individuals, the goal was to include biographies of those iconic individuals associated with a particular aspect of the region's culture. Consultants identified those major figures who have immediate relevance to the region. The editors and consultants also selected individuals who illuminate major themes and exemplify southern cultural styles. Persons in this category may have made special contributions to southern distinctiveness, to cultural achievements, or to the development of a characteristic aspect of southern life. The Music and Literature categories have been given somewhat fuller biographical attention than other subject areas, a decision that is warranted by southern achievements in those areas. In addition to the separate biographical entries, many individuals are discussed in such thematic articles as "Linguists" or "Historians," which outline contributions of key persons to certain fields. Readers should consult the index in each volume to locate biographical information on southerners who appear in that volume.

The *Encyclopedia* includes biographies of living persons as well as the deceased. It is especially concerned with regional cultural issues in the contemporary South, and the inclusion of living individuals was crucial to establishing continuities between past and present. Entries on Bill Moyers and Charles Kuralt, for example, help readers to understand that the journalistic traditions of the South have been extended into the television age.

Selecting approximately 250 individuals for inclusion in the *Encyclopedia of Southern Culture* was no easy task. The list of potential individuals was widely circulated, and the choices represent the informed judgment of our consultants and contributors, leading scholars in the field of Southern Studies. The selection of biographies was made in light of the *Encyclopedia*'s overall definition of culture. The goal was not to list every cultural trait or include every prominent individual in the South but to explore *characteristic* aspects of the region's life and culture and to show their interrelationships. The biographical entries are not simply descriptive, factual statements but are instead intimately related to the broader thematic and overview essays. Biographical entries were meant to suggest how a representative individual is part of a broader pattern, a way of life, in the American South.

Interdisciplinary study has become prominent in a number of scholarly areas, but in few is it as useful as in the study of region. The interrelatedness of such specific fields as politics, religion, economics, cultural achievement, and social organization becomes especially obvious when scholars study a region. Interdisciplinary study of the South is a means of exploring humanity in all its aspects. The intellectual specialization of the modern world often makes this study difficult, but the editors of the *Encyclopedia* hope these volumes will promote that goal. Scholars exploring various aspects of the South's life now compose a distinct field of interdisciplinary Southern Studies, and the *Encyclopedia* joins those scholars in common effort to extend the present bounds of knowledge about the South.

The Editors
Center for the Study of Southern Culture
University of Mississippi

EDITORS' NOTE

The *Encyclopedia* is divided into four volumes and 24 major subject areas, arranged in alphabetical order. A table of contents listing articles in each section is found at the beginning of the section. An overview essay is followed by a series of alphabetically arranged thematic essays and then brief, alphabetically arranged topical-biographical entries. Readers are urged to consult the index, as well as the tables of contents, in locating articles.

When appropriate, articles contain cross-references to related articles in other sections. Material is cross-referenced only to similar-length or shorter material. Thematic articles, for example, are cross-referenced to thematic articles or to short topical articles in other sections but not to longer overview essays. Topical-biographical entries are cross-referenced to topical-biographical articles in other sections but not to longer overview or thematic essays. Each cross-reference to related material lists the section in small capital letters, followed by the article title. If the entry is a short topical-biographical article, the title is preceded by a slash. The following example is a cross-reference to, first, a thematic article and, then, a topical-biographical entry, both in the Folklife section:

See also FOLKLIFE: Storytelling; / Clower, Jerry

Every effort was made to update material before publication. However, changes in contributors' affiliations, in biographical data because of the death of an individual, and in the names of institutions, for example, could not be made after the book went to press.

AGRICULTURE

THOMAS D. CLARK

Lexington, Kentucky

CONSULTANT

☆ ☆ ☆ ☆ ☆ ☆ ☆ ☆ ☆ ☆

Agriculture 3
Rural Life 8

Agribusiness 17
Country Store 21
Crops 26
Diversification 28
Garden Patch 31
Good Roads Movement 34
Livestock 36
Mechanization 39
Plantations 41
Poultry 44
Sharecropping and Tenancy 46

Agricultural Extension Services 50
Boll Weevil 51

Communal Farms 52
Corn 54
Cotton Culture 55
Dairy Industry 56
Farm Security Administration 57
Fertilizer 58
Fruit Production 59
Grange 61
Knapp, Seaman A. 62
Naval Stores 63
Peanuts 65
Pecans 66
Pest Control 67
Poe, Clarence Hamilton 70
Progressive Farmer 71
Rice Culture 72
Rural Electrification Administration 74
Rural Free Delivery 75
Sears, Roebuck Catalog 76
Soybeans 77
Sugar Industry 78
Tobacco Culture, Flue-cured 80
Truck Farming 82

Overleaf: Sharecropper, Warren County, Mississippi, 1972

AGRICULTURE

The basic and historic industry in the South has been agriculture. This fact has had an enormous bearing on the development of a distinctive regional culture and economy. From the first English settlement at Jamestown in the opening decade of the 17th century to the present the South's principal economic focus has been upon agriculture. Throughout its history agriculture in the South has experienced four or five distinctive phases of change. Each new era made social, cultural, and economic impressions upon the southern people.

Most British emigrants who approached the American shores were ambitious to reestablish in the New World an Old World pastoral society and agricultural economy. Soil and climate conditions, the forest cover, and difficult access to transportation all contributed to the shaping of distinctive agrarian fortunes and fresh ways of life in the early colonial South. Imperative from the outset was the necessity to develop both subsistence farming and commercial planting. For both types of farmers land became the necessary foundation for economic and social well-being. It was the catalyst that spread Anglo-American civilization over the wide expanse of virgin southern hinterlands.

Soon after initial English settlement the great baronial, river valley plantations appeared, with access to water transportation. Almost simultaneously the great land companies came into existence, hoping to encourage immigration and to speculate in almost unlimited claims of backcountry lands. Land policies were a major factor shaping the spreading settlements. With the expansion of the Atlantic coastal civilization a mixture of plantations and yeoman farms came to characterize the economy. Both depended heavily upon four basic staple crops: corn, tobacco, rice, and indigo. The latter was soon succeeded by Sea Island, or black-seeded, cotton. These crops, with the exception of corn, either took a heavy toll on the thin Tidewater lands or were too regionally and environmentally restricted to permit successful transmission to the upcountry. In time, however, tobacco was transported beyond the Appalachians to become an important cash crop in pioneer Kentucky and Tennessee. Short-staple cotton supplanted the Sea Island variety and was ideally suited to the lands of the developing South.

By the mid-18th century an ever-increasing proportion of the southern population shifted their dependence from commercial crops to the subsistence ones. Two exciting chapters in southern agricultural history involve the growing of corn and the rolling back of the cattle- and hog-droving frontiers. The early Anglo-American immigrants developed a fondness for corn and pork products.

The spread of agrarian culture is reflected in modern geographic and economic studies, which materially revise early notions about the maturing of the agricultural economy across the South.

Sam B. Hilliard's recent *Atlas of Antebellum Southern Agriculture* (1984) conveys a dramatic sense of the changing phases of regional farming and labor. This and other recent studies sharply revise earlier ones that did not do justice to the region's production of livestock and foodstuffs.

Advance of Agricultural Frontiers. The opening of the trans-Appalachian frontier in the Upper South in the latter quarter of the 18th century drew a stream of agricultural emigrants away from the depleted Tidewater and lower Piedmont lands of the Atlantic Seaboard. The western rivers and their valleys held fresh promise for farmers. Traditional agricultural patterns were spread across the mountains but were adapted to a distinctive new way of agrarian life. In Kentucky, for instance, commercial, staple-crop farming was devoted to grain, tobacco, hemp, and livestock production. This pattern also prevailed in the Bluegrass region of Tennessee.

During the first half of the 19th century a major migration to the recently vacated Indian lands of the Atlantic and Gulf coastal South occurred. This movement was stimulated by opportunities to exploit the cotton producing lands of the Old Southwest, the quieting of Indian and international claims, and the ready adaptation of staple crops. Cotton became the principal staple cash crop because of both the nature of the land and the recent invention and perfection of the mechanical cotton gin. On this sprawling, fertile southern frontier at least three layers of human economic and pastoral history existed by the time of the Civil War. All across the region herdsmen or cattle grazers and hog drovers pursued a moderately labor-intensive way of life and pastured their herds and droves on the vast virginal domain. Some of these low-caste forerunners of Anglo-American civilization moved on with the expanding frontier until no more public lands remained to be exploited; others settled down to become yeoman farmers or sharecroppers.

As the southern agricultural frontiers advanced, plain dirt farmers laid claim to modest landholdings, peopled the emigrant trails, opened fields and pastures in the virgin forests, built simple dwellings and barns, and established rural communities. All across new regions these yeomen established subsistence farming, created an uncomplicated economy, held fast to family ties and folkways, personified the image of much of the antebellum South, and formed the bulk of the population. Modern statistical charts and illustrative maps portray the pattern of economic and agricultural expansion in the South to 1860 and convey a sense of the vibrant dynamics of the southern agricultural civilization during these formative years.

Plantations and Farms. In sharp contrast to the panorama of the yeoman-farmer background and the limited production of commercial crops were the plantations, with their extensive landholdings and slave labor force. These sprang up principally in areas with more fertile and productive lands. Of necessity the plantation was a staple-crop, slave-labor, semicommercial enterprise. This type of farming in the South generated its own social, economic, and cultural characteristics. To a large extent the way of life on southern cotton, rice, sugar, and tobacco plantations tended to break much of the isolation in the region. In economic terms, the plantation required extensive management, the opening and maintenance of domestic and foreign markets, the organization of both supply and credit systems, and ready access to transportation facilities. The staple crops were readily adaptable to large landholdings, intensive use of labor, and commercial farming methods.

While rice, tobacco, and sugarcane growing were important regionally, short-staple cotton growing was central to most southern plantations after 1890. Highly adaptable to land, climate, and casual methods of cultivation and harvesting, cotton enjoyed the advantage of having both a domestic and an international market. The yeoman farm was also a producer of cotton, a fact that became more central to its operation after the Civil War.

In recent years economists, sociologists, and historians who have reexamined the available contemporary documentary sources have sharply revised older notions about the nature and diversity of antebellum crop production and its bearing upon earlier forms of rural farm life. The most important areas of regional self-sufficiency that have been reconsidered are the production of consumable crops, the volume of livestock, and the importance of the small and middle-sized farmer.

Whatever role the larger plantation and its more affluent owners may have played in regional commerce, politics, and social and cultural life, it was the yeoman farmer who opened large areas of the land, helped create counties and towns, "lived largely at home," and gave body and soul to southern rural life. From backcountry Virginia and the Carolinas to east Texas there sprang up a homogeneity of racial, social, and cultural agrarian organization. Remarkably, the South before 1860 nurtured two systems of agricultural economy and modes of life—the yeoman farm and the plantation.

The Civil War was a historical watershed of southern farming. Slavery was abolished, and the rural labor situation experienced drastic changes. Though plantations survived, they operated on a different scale. Their labor supply was disrupted, as they had to employ wage workers or sharecroppers. Time was required to reclaim the great cotton markets, and dramatic changes occurred in the financing of this type of farming.

Postbellum Agricultural System. In the postwar years the southern yeoman farmer was caught up in what almost amounted to an economic straitjacket. He was forced by a usurious credit-granting system to turn more and more to production of cash crops, especially cotton and tobacco. All farmers, large and small, were severely pressed to secure sufficient operating capital. A new form of agricultural production credit appeared, based upon crop liens and dependent upon merchants who furnished farm supplies. Both farmer and merchant in turn were thrown largely upon the mercy of wholesalers, manufacturers, extraregional grain and meat producers, and fertilizer distributors.

Between 1865 and 1925 most southern farmers were thrust upon a treadmill, producing sufficient staple crops to pay both inflated prices for supplies and the extortionate interest on crop liens. Both white and black farmers rapidly sank into the economic peonage of the staple-crop system of rising debts and falling prices. The farming operations of the individual tenant or sharecropper became almost primitive in nature. This system of southern farming was ultimately disastrous. Cotton was the predominant cash crop, and its days in the Upland South were numbered after 1920. The crop laid a heavy burden upon its impoverished producers and exacted a heavy toll from the land. Within three-quarters of a century the flagrantly careless methods of cotton cultivation destroyed an enormous amount of topsoil and left behind a deeply gullied landscape. So serious was this loss that by 1933 much of the South was a disaster area. Even more serious, however, each year more and more farmers were forced into the ranks of sharecroppers and tenants, a trend that continued until the New Deal.

Tobacco, sugarcane, and rice were more regionally confined. They never equaled financially and socially the importance of cotton for the southern population. They, like cotton, depended upon widespread domestic and foreign markets, and in the case of dark tobacco, farmers were sorely pressed by the dominance of outside buyers. In the opening decade of this century the dark-tobacco farmers resorted to vigilante tactics in an effort to improve marketing conditions of their crops, resulting in the Black Patch War in Kentucky.

Editors of southern country weeklies and the regional farm journals cajoled and scolded farmers for their failure to grow more foodstuffs. They preached monotonous editorial sermons on the themes of increasing crop diversification, halting the wastage of the soil, and eliminating blind dependence upon nonconsumable crops. Stern critics were Charles Otken, George K. Holmes, W. H. Skaggs, and a score of later authors. Farmers themselves attempted to better their lots by creating organizations to exert political and economic pressures in alleviating oppressive conditions. Vain efforts were made by such groups as the "white cappers" of the cotton belt and the nightriders of the dark-tobacco areas.

Change in Southern Farming. The spread of the boll weevil menace across the cotton belt after 1900 raised bitter winds of change. World War I and the sequent depression in 1921 sounded further warnings that the old cash-crop system was a failure. The socially and economically devastating sharecropping system and the Great Depression of the 1930s hastened the demise of southern staple-crop farming.

The problems of sharecropping and ruinous credit granted by general stores and fertilizer trusts are no longer factors in southern farming. The multiplication of banks and savings and loan companies has made credit available on other bases. The introduction of the tractor, mechanical cotton picker, combine, haying machine, and the nonrow system of cultivation along with vastly improved chemical fertilizers has revolutionized southern farming. Added to the chemical and mechanical advances are the genetically improved plants adapted to southern soils and climate. The importation of new varieties of hardy grasses and the conversion of old cotton fields to grazing lands have dramatically reduced cotton production in the South. Following the eradication of the Texas fever tick and the screw worm, the region has become a major cattle producing section. Introduction of large-volume hay balers has eliminated the use of a large labor force, and hay has now become a major southern crop.

After 1930 the southern agricultural economy underwent an almost miraculous change. None of the doomsayers of the old Farm Security days of the New Deal could have envisioned what was about to occur on the eroded acres of impoverished tenant-dredged farms. Never in the history of agriculture had there occurred such a sharp breaking away from the past. The problems of share and tenant farming largely vanished after 1940, and no economic, social, or cultural institution in the South was left untouched by the post-Depression and World War II revolution. The good roads movement, begun in 1916, was fully developed, the increasing influence of the federal aid programs was felt, the extension and experimental services became more effective agencies, and the old furnishing mercantile system gave way to cash grocery and chain-discount stores and to town and city merchants and implement dealers.

At last the great editorial and farm-agent dream of crop diversification in the South became a reality. The general application of the new sciences to farming ushered in a new age of agrarianism and transformed the rural way of life. A fast-growing and highly mobile segment of the southern population now classified by the U.S. Census Bureau as "rural non-farm" appeared, and the southern black population migrated from the farms to towns and cities. Today part-time farmers with the aid of the new machines and genetically improved crops can produce more with far less time and labor than their forebears could with endless toil.

See also EDUCATION: Rural and Agricultural Education; ENVIRONMENT: Land Use; Natural Resources; Soil and Soil Conservation; GEOGRAPHY: Plantation Morphology; / Cotton Gins; Sugar Plantations; HISTORY AND MANNERS: Frontier Heritage; INDUSTRY: Chain and Specialty Stores; SCIENCE AND MEDICINE: Agriculture, Scientific; / Ruffin, Edmund; SOCIAL CLASS: Migrant Workers; Socialism; Tenant Farmers; / Farmers' Alliance; Mitchell, H. L.; Sharecroppers Union; Southern Tenant Farmers' Union

Thomas D. Clark
Lexington, Kentucky

Agricultural History (January 1979); Thomas D. Clark, *Journal of Southern History* (February 1946), *Pills, Petticoats, and Plows: The Southern Country Store* (1944); Pete Daniel, *Breaking the Land: The Transformation of Cotton, Tobacco, and Rice Cultures since 1880* (1985); Gilbert C. Fite, *Cotton Fields No More: Southern Agriculture, 1865–1980* (1984); Lewis C. Gray, *History of Agriculture in the Southern United States to 1860*, 2 vols. (1933); Matthew Brown Hammond, *The Cotton Industry: An Essay in American Economic History*, Part I (1897); Sam B. Hilliard, *Atlas of Antebellum Southern Agriculture* (1984); Charles S. Johnson, Edwin R. Embree, and Will W. Alexander, *The Collapse of Cotton Tenancy: A Summary of Field Studies and Statistical Surveys, 1933–1935* (1935); Jack Temple Kirby, *Rural Worlds Lost: The American South, 1920–1960* (1987); Howard W. Odum, *Southern Regions of the United States* (1936); Charles Otken, *The Ills of the South: Or Related Causes Hostile to the General Prosperity of the Southern People* (1894); Frank L. Owsley, *Plain Folk of the Old South* (1949); Arthur F. Raper, *Tenants of the Almighty* (1943); Ira De A. Reid, *Sharecroppers All* (1941); William H. Skaggs, *The Southern Oligarchy: An Appeal in Behalf of the Silent Masses of Our Country against the Despotic Rule of the Few* (1924); *Statistical Abstract of the United States*, 1900, 1910, 1920, 1960, 1984 (1901, 1911, 1921, 1961, 1985); Rupert B. Vance, *Human Geography of the South: A Study in Regional Resources and Human Adequacy* (1932), *Human Fac-*

Cotton scene on Popular Street, Macon, Georgia, early 1900s

tors in Cotton Culture: A Study in the Social Geography of the American South (1929). ☆

RURAL LIFE

Just as a truly solid South never existed in an overall regional sense, there has never prevailed a hard and fast pattern of rural life across the region. Much of the developing South, and especially that part designated the Old Southwest, spawned and nurtured an arrested form of frontier American culture that reflected the particular environmental influences to which people were exposed. Southerners were not the only Americans set adrift in such a large mass of virgin land; none, however, implanted this experience more indelibly in their folkways and modes of rural life. The availability of a seemingly inexhaustible amount of reasonably fertile land, a wide variety of trees, generous rainfall and water resources, and a benign climate supplied the natural ingredients for the development of a distinctive culture. Rural southerners, as much by individual choice as by circumstance, made dual responses to the land. Some came as land-greedy plantation masters, but more remained yeoman subsistence farmers. Both created an isolated regional folk culture that sustained almost two centuries of social continuity with definite intrasectional variations.

Southern geographical isolation was a central influence in sustaining one of the most pronounced broad-patterned cultural lags in American history. This powerful and pervasive influence shaped folkways by blending old human forms and customs with necessary adaptations mandated in the new country. Though the southern way of rural life for individual families and communities appeared simple and uncomplicated, in fact the regional pattern was highly complex.

Folk Culture. From the beginnings of English settlement to the present, the modes of rural southern life have been compared and measured against those of older, more mature civilizations, nearly all of which were industrially and technologically oriented. Internally the southern rural way of life included social classes with subtle boundaries, but common to all of them was a taste for regional foods, the prevalence of folk customs, the importance of blood relationships, and a sense of Old World origins. Much of the so-called aristocratic or patrician planter class rose from the common yeoman folk masses and brought up with them many of their tastes and manners. Only after the Civil War and the rise of cities, industries, and diversified commercialization did class distinctions become more sharply defined and divisive.

Perhaps it was a tragic lapse in southern history that the rich regional folk culture was denied sufficient time to mature intellectually and economically before its progress was rudely disrupted by war. Few if any of the regional decision makers of the antebellum South truly comprehended, though, the dynamics of their emerging folk society. In large areas of the developing South in 1860, much of the population had only begun to make transitions from the primitive log-cabin frontier stage to a more mature and intensified social and economic pattern of life. In some areas an inordinately long interval prevailed between stages. The stifling barriers of the great landed hinterland had barely been breached with roads, stream channels and crossings, and railroads. The rural population remained almost wholly dependent upon the small yeoman subsistence farm as its main source of livelihood.

Rich natural resources remained only partially explored and exploited. The necessary human talents and skills had not been developed, nor were there facilities, to bring the resources into profitable production. Two primary resources, the great forest belt and the coal and iron seams, had begun to make miniscule contributions to the economic and cultural advancement of the earlier rural South. Of greater significance was the lag in institutional developments. Rural southerners lacked the necessary vision and entrepreneurial leadership to generate ample institutional support to bring into fruitful production the rich natural bounties of the land. Paradoxically, the rural southern population lived frugal, if not impoverished, lives in many places atop some of the richest resources in America. The agrarian population generated insufficient capital to do more than organize and sustain struggling institutions. It developed no important universities, supported no notable libraries, and sustained only a limited number of banks.

The earlier emigrants who pursued with frenetic passion and expectation the public-land frontier in the Lower South moved almost entirely within a virtually impregnable folk culture. They clung tenaciously to blood relationships. Predominantly these people were of Anglo- and Afro-American origins. Yeoman farmer and planter alike transported in their cultural baggage a defined set of folkways and ancient traditions. For instance, a Mississippi countryman would not have felt awkwardly out of place among country folk of rural hinterland Virginia. He would have readily recognized family names and those of country churches and their denominations, the limited nature of rural schools, common tastes in foods, modes of entertainment and sports, and, most of all, the general social customs. Most likely his people had relatives who remained behind in the great migration.

This was even more true in those other wellsprings of southern population, the Carolinas and Georgia.

Religion, Women, Family, Community. No social force had greater or more diverse impact on the rural southern way of life than religion. The Protestant church, whatever denominational label it bore, was a durable institutional bedrock. Within a loosely defined theological context, rural southern Protestants were exposed to a strong folk mix of biblical fundamentalism, sabbatarianism, emotional conversion experiences, and periodic spiritual rejuvenation. The great wave of unbridled emotional revivalism that occurred in Virginia, the Carolinas, and Kentucky in the mid-18th century and the early part of the 19th spread throughout the rural South. No recurring social event in the lives of most southern countrymen became more fixed institutionally than the annual revivals and camp meetings. The sustained spiritual results of these gatherings are hard to measure beyond the general observations that they no doubt served mightily to keep the church and denominational torches aflame. Conversions, backslidings, and spiritual rebirths were frequent and fervent.

The social influence of the annual revivals was more discernible. They were recurrent punctuations between the growing and harvesting seasons when either the bounteous grace of nature was visible or the will of God was evident in crop failure. Both were occasions for earnest supplication. In some vague historical manner the annual southern country revival meetings almost seemed to be a link with Old World pagan harvest festivals—the sometimes unrestrained emotional atmosphere even offered a trace of the ancient Grecian seasonal rites of the Eleusinian Mysteries.

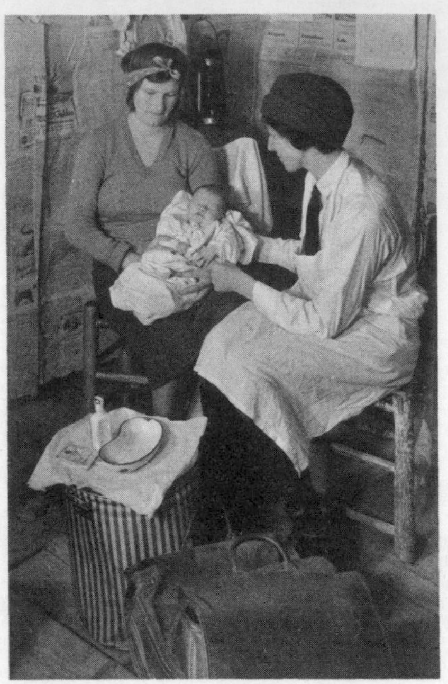

Nurse with new-born baby and mother, Kentucky, early 1900s

Although the ways of rural southern life had a sharply masculine tone, the role of women in regional history has been vital. Homemaking alone involved a multiplicity of onerous tasks for most of two centuries. Not only did the country woman perform all the functions of mother, nurse, family counselor, and spiritual leader, she was as well spinner and weaver, knitter, seamstress, quilter, fruit and vegetable preserver, butcher, and supplemental field hand. She busied herself in soapmaking, tending livestock, and looking after the garden and orchard. No doubt, as many or more women and children worked in the rural South from 1820 to 1920 as in any other section of the United States. As late as 1930 the South had the largest number of women, white and black, engaged in agricultural work of any region in the nation.

In addition to her numerous labors, the country woman kept track of kinships and relatives, remembered ancient folk rhymes, ballads, party games, and the ingredients and applications of folk remedies. She was the main preserver of the Sabbath, lent a softness of tone to the raw frontier, and in a humble way encouraged certain social refinements. However much rural southern women appeared in the background in abstract historical documentation, they provided the solid warping of the social fabric of the rural South in all its ages.

Although the rural southern family was of a strongly patriarchal nature, where the grandfather and father assumed predominant roles in most matters, the mother supplied the human adhesive that held the family together. Generally rural families were close knit and numerous. In the newer areas of the region emigrants moved and settled down as family units, and one still finds southern communities where common family names predominate. Historically, the more isolated neighborhoods were the most cohesive because of family ties, and especially so in the Highland South.

Rural southern families were unified, but members became widely dispersed as they followed the moving frontier westward. Literally hundreds of families in time had members living all across the western part of the country. Travelers repeatedly commented upon the restlessness and constant movement of people in search of new and cheaper lands. Americans are now diligently searching for their blood roots in older settled areas, and southern genealogists, in particular, have produced sizable collections of books, family trees, and guides in tracing an astonishing dispersement of people of common ancestral roots. Throughout the South almost numberless small or private cemeteries dot the landscape, serving as mute repositories of personal historical information that rival the records of county clerks, the census schedules, and collections of family papers. Regardless of the social and economic fortunes of the deceased, in historical perspective they become a vital link in the human history of this age.

Local neighborhoods are just as important an influence in unifying yet dividing the rural South. Modernizing influences such as improved transportation, the introduction of specialized skills and services, the availability of scientific medical care, new types of merchandising, and the rise of urban centers all worked to make the rural southern community a place of both warmhearted, generous neighborliness and of bitter personal strife.

No more appealing nostalgic chapters can be found in the history of the rural South than those describing neighborly common workings such as logrollings, the harvesting and processing of field crops, and the assisting of neighbors fallen victims of misfortunes. Of an even more human nature was communal aid in births, in sickness, and in death and disaster. Whatever country neighbors lacked in skill and sophistication, they made up for in human concern for the welfare of neighbors in need.

Conversely, rural southern neighborhood rifts could be violent, senseless, and irreconcilable, with the old bitterness sometimes lingering on for generations to come. Few, if any, southern communities escaped their fusses and violent incidents. Columns of southern country weekly newspapers and court dockets are filled with accounts of squabbles ranging from disputes over land boundaries and religious beliefs to straying livestock, women, dogs, and politics. The rural southern temper could become overheated with suddenness, and rural memories of injuries were long and brooding.

In a pleasanter vein rural southerners of all ages generated and passed on an impressive body of folklore. Indian-like, they handed down by word of mouth customs, traditions, superstitions, and wild yarns. In a region subjected to serious educational and cultural lags the spoken word was of historical importance, and the folktale of local origin was well adapted to giving a living sense of time and place. In the passing decades it became rich grist for the writers who created a more durable published form of literature. This rural frontier heritage has been important in the development of a regional literature.

Rural Institutions. The southern rural way of life sustained several institutions common to all parts of the South: the local county seat, the country church, the one-room country school, the general store, the weekly newspaper, and the fourth-class post office. The county seat with its court days was at once a center of justice after a fashion and of public administration, a market town, a local gathering place, and a limited professional center. For vast numbers of rural southerners the county seat was the nearest they ever came to visiting an urban community. Country churches were as varied in forms and rituals as they were numerous. Scarcely any community was without at least one church. The southern landscape from the Potomac to the Trinity was dotted with Calvaries, Bethels, Enons, Shilohs, Mt. Sinais, Hebrons, Lebanons, Mount Pleasants, Rocky Hills, Shady Groves, and Campgrounds. These were as much social centers as spiritual founts. Possibly more communicants took home from church notions of crop prospects, cotton and tobacco prices, coon dogs, squirrel hunting, and local news than impressions of what the preachers had said in their interminable sermons on the subject of eternal damnation.

No rural southern institution gathered about itself a warmer aura of human nostalgia than the general or country store. Seated at crossroads all across the South, the stores were combination merchandising and farmers' markets; sources of credit, medicine, and simple bits of luxury; newscenters; resorts for sage advice; and eternal places for gossiping and yarn spinning. Southern crops planted and grown in words around country-store stoves and on their porches far surpassed those actually planted in neighboring fields and ultimately listed in the tables of decennial censuses. Had the store crops ever reached maturity, the South would have made a fabulous showing against the rest of the nation.

In a region largely without access to banks, the general or furnishing store was a life-sustaining source of credit for the maintenance of an informal type of cash flow. Without this, much of the rural southern agricultural system would have been even more seriously handicapped. In large measure general stores in hundreds of isolated rural southern communities shaped the lives of their customers and served as a cardinal link between southern countrymen and the outside world of capital, industry, and contemporary technological and material advances. Stoveside and porch forums were places where every subject of interest to an agrarian society was discussed, and southern mankind's most complex problems were settled with authoritative certainty.

If older southerners have recalled with a certain romantic nostalgia the country store with its heterogeneous mixture of merchandise, smells, and excitement, they have even more fondly recalled one-room country schools and angelic or martinet teachers. For many parts of the South, the primitive schoolroom tucked away in an obscure corner was the only real intellectual gesture people made in a raw country environment. Emphasis on the "three r's" prepared rural youth to function in a plain and unsophisticated society where technical and industrial challenges were absent. Commercial intercourse in most communities seldom was more demanding than simply understanding merchants' accounts at settling-up time at the end of crop seasons. If an individual became literate enough to read the Scriptures, then he had achieved one of the main objectives of an education. There was doubtless reward enough in a countryman's signing his name to a land deed, an application for a marriage license, a mortgage, or any other formal document filed permanently in a county clerk's office. He could also form a vague and partisan political opinion from reading the local country weekly newspaper.

Wherever a new county seat was located, an editor-printer appeared to claim the honor of publishing an official organ. The modest four-page southern weekly was essentially a bulletin of legal notices, the voice of the Democratic county officials, and a broadside for the advertising of worthless proprietary medicines. Nevertheless, the modest news and editorial columns reflected the turnings and workings of the rural southern mind and, almost universally, the partisan and prejudiced opinions of the editors. News columns, especially those called "locals," while astonishingly puerile, reflected the folkways and the sterility of life in rural communities where little of interest happened except birthing and dying. With an authority backed by printer's ink, editors commented on all subjects, upheld public morals, lectured readers on their decorum or lack of it, and discussed politics, religion, and the weather with the certainty that there was only one side to every question. Many of them crusaded effectively for or against public issues. They preached diversification of field crops without being able to suggest solutions to credit, transportation, and marketing dilemmas.

Literary Images. Country weekly papers portrayed rural southerners in their changing moods and in varying social and economic conditions, and they also welcomed them into the world with birth notices and ushered them out of it with eloquent obituaries. Historically, they preserved the countryman's personality and image as raw material for more formal writers. As southern backwoods emigrants pushed deeper inland, they evolved into a new genre of backwoodsmen. Often far removed from the seasoning influences of refining institutions, they regressed culturally. Early regional authors found the country greenhorns captivating subjects for their essays and books. Such natives as Augustus Baldwin Longstreet, William Tappan Thompson, John Jones Hooper, Joseph Glover Baldwin, and George Washington Harris gave immortality to an assortment of southern backcountry types. While these authors distorted descriptions of their fictional characters, they conveyed a strong realistic sense of an important segment of southern life. At the time the genre authors were writing and publishing their books, the country newspapers ran space-filler stories of a kindred nature partly under the guise of semihumorous news items. Foreign and domestic travelers in the antebellum South left accounts of their experiences, many of which were as distorted as the writings of the professed regional humorists.

The rural southerner and his way of life with its crises and triumphs survived the Civil War and Reconstruction as a literary theme. In the writings of George Washington Cable, James Lane Allen, Mary Noailles Murphree, Ellen Glasgow, and Joel Chandler Harris, he appeared in many guises ranging from sophisticated plantation gentry to lowly field hands living close to the footstool of nature and the land. Whatever his role, he exhibited color out of proportion to his condition. Whether it be mountain feudist, sharecropping peasant, tobacco-stained constituent of political demagogues, narrow-minded communicant of a rural evangelical church, or just plain yeoman subsistence farmer, he personified a rural region of the nation floundering against diversity and change, almost always being confronted by the uncertainties of time and fortune.

A later generation of southern writers peopled their books with similar countrymen. William Faulkner gave evidence in his writings that he was conversant with the earlier chroniclers of the backwoods. So did Thomas Wolfe, Erskine Caldwell, Thomas Stribling, and Elizabeth Maddox Roberts. Eudora Welty's characters are rural Mississippians who have direct blood relationship with the pioneers who moved from the Carolinas to settle that state.

In the field of nonfiction, state and local libraries bulge with personal memoirs and regional histories that collectively detail a major portion of the southern rural experience. In a more formal manner Benjamin B. Kendrick and Alex M. Arnett, *The South Looks at Its Past* (1935); Rupert B. Vance, *The Human Geography of the South: A Study in Regional Resources and Human Adequacy* (1932); W. T. Couch, ed., *Culture in the South* (1949); Herman C. Nixon, *Possum Trot: Rural Community, South* (1941); and Howard W. Odum, *Southern Regions of the United States* (1936) are largely about rural southerners. Even the U.S. census reports reveal graphically the unfolding fortunes of the rural South and its people over almost two centuries.

The tempo of life in earlier years was set by recurring crop seasons, plantings, workings, and harvestings, each separated from the other by intervals suggesting a chronic state of laziness and idleness. The agrarian life in its natural rhythms allowed time for neighborliness and the exercise of a distinctive form of rural civility in both social and business intercourse. Even the drawling speech of the rural southerner in some measure reflected the impact of time and the land, the homogeneity of human origins, the cultural lags, racial mixture, geographical isolation, and stubborn resistance to change. These, however, in time were subjected to the inevitable revisions born of lowering old barriers.

Change and Continuity since 1920. The folkways of life in the rural South underwent marked changes in the decade following 1920. Already the boll weevil invasion had shaped the future for one segment of regional agriculture. The rise of towns and industries, the acute depression at the outset of that decade, the impact of consolidated schools and of higher education, the coming of new systems of merchandising, and then the later Great Depression and the New Deal with its various rural problem-solving agencies—all revised, if they did not destroy, the old patterns and customs of southern rural life. Added to these were the scientific breakthroughs in wood-using industries, the spread of modern highway systems, the creation of the Tennessee Valley Authority, the introduction of the Rural Electrification Administration, and the enormous impact of mechanized farming. Within two decades these forces practically erased the bolder outlines of the traditional approaches and patterns of rural life.

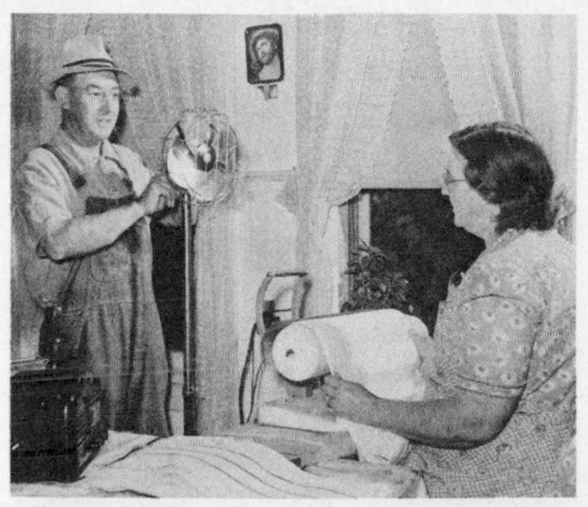

By the 1940s, electricity brought fans, radios, and other conveniences to rural southerners, such as this couple in Knox County, Tennessee

For more than a century the course of rural life in the South was unplanned. After 1920 most of the old rural institutions were caught in the web of failure. The system of sharecropping and tenant farming that had flourished from 1865 to 1920 was on the brink of abject failure. No longer could the South survive this waste of human energy and soils. Both white and black tenants deserted the farm by hundreds of thousands, driven away by biting poverty. In fact one of the most dramatic social and economic changes that occurred in the rural South in this century was the almost complete departure from the land by black farmers.

In reality the cherished dream of a self-sufficient rural America never materialized at any period in southern history. Neither did Henry W. Grady's eloquent oratorical fantasy of a contented agrarian southern population living off the land ever come even remotely near realization. As late as 1930 Howard W. Odum could ask the rhetorical question about the human condition of the rural South: "Are not its white people still more than 90 per cent of the earlier stock? Are they not of Protestant faith, sabbath observing, family loving and patriarchial, of religious intensity, quarreling with the government, individualists taking their politics, their honors, and their drinking hard? Their attitudes toward work and play, toward women and property, toward children and their work, toward the dominant leaders are still much the same as was the early vintage. Both Southeast and Southwest are still frontier folk; the Southeast, parts of which are the oldest of the United States culture, reflecting a sort of arrested frontier pattern of life." This, he thought, still formed a baseline for recovering in the South what might have been.

Southern folk stubbornly held onto cherished standards of conservative Protestant beliefs and personal relationships even in the face of urban modernity. The linkage with frontier political concepts was not broken. Though severely strained, the once viable spirit of obliging neighborliness survived in isolated rural islands in more tentative forms. Change has come most completely, though, in the loss of neighborhood-centering institutions, especially with standardization of the schools at all levels. The crusaders of the late 19th and early 20th centuries who declared war on the lethargic rural ways of life wrought more thoroughly than they knew. The consolidation of schools practically obliterated neighborhood boundaries by removing core centers, and what this revolution in education failed to accomplish the good roads crusade finished.

In this latter quarter of the 20th century, the social, cultural, and statistical patterns of the rural South bear only fading resemblances to the past. Thousands of old and cherished country homesteads have been smashed to earth to make way for pastures and woodlands. Beloved old churches once serving thriving congregations now stand vacant with most of their strict sabbatarian communicants lying in nearby, neglected cemeteries. Sites of the famous campgrounds long ago fell victims to the pines, and few people can now point out the places where country schools, stores, and fourth-class post offices stood. Even villages and towns have succumbed to the ravages of time and progress, forgotten except as names on the pages of local histories.

Nonetheless, southerners strive for continuity. Incessantly searching, blacks and whites on the trail of ancestors have turned genealogy into an important southern industry. Weed-grown and abandoned graveyards, like earlier regional Indian mounds, have become rich informational sources linking present descendants with the past. Four identifiable human interest areas survive from the earlier southern rural way of life: a love of sports, a taste for regional foods and cooking, an all but inerasable streak of religious fundamentalism, and the love of a good folksy yarn.

There lingers on in the southern psyche a yearning to escape into some simplistic air-conditioned and cellophane-wrapped Jeffersonian valhalla, located conveniently near a modern shopping mall, not too far from a football stadium, with free access to a good color television set to relieve the mind of serious concern with social and cultural lags and deficient showings in economic statistical tables. Large areas of the old rural South have fallen victim either to urban sprawl, super highway rights-of-way, airports, or industrial sites. Each year 200,000 more acres of land are gobbled up in this way. The old southern rural pattern of life has been broken beyond hope of restitution. Sunbelt invaders have offered it ruthless competition.

See also ART AND ARCHITECTURE: Farm Buildings; EDUCATION: Rural and Agricultural Education; / *Foxfire*; ENVIRONMENT: Climate and Weather; / Soil and Soil Conservation; FOLKLIFE articles; GEOGRAPHY articles; INDUSTRY: / Chain and Specialty Stores; LANGUAGE: Folk Speech; LITERATURE: Agrarianism in Literature; MYTHIC SOUTH: Plantation Myth; RELIGION: Folk Religion; SCIENCE AND MEDICINE: Health, Rural; / Country Doctor; SOCIAL CLASS: Tenant Farmers; / Farmers' Alliance; Sharecroppers Union; Southern Tenant Farmers' Union; Timber Workers; Tobacco Workers.

Thomas D. Clark
Lexington, Kentucky

John B. Boles, *The Great Revival, 1787–1805: The Origins of the Southern Evangelical Mind* (1972); Thomas D. Clark, *Pills, Petticoats, and Plows: The Southern Country Store* (1944), *The Southern Country Editor* (1948), ed., *Travels in the Confederate States* (1948), *Travels in the New South*, 2 vols. (1962), *Travels in the Old South*, 3 vols. (1959); W. T. Couch, *These Are Our Lives* (1939); Virginius Dabney, *Below the Potomac: A Book about the New South* (1942); Pete Daniel, *Standing at the Crossroads: Southern Life in the Twentieth Century* (1986); James D. B. DeBow, *Statistical View of the United States, Embracing Its Territory, Population—White, Free, Colored and Slave—Moral and Social Condition* (1854); J. Wayne Flynt, *Dixie's Forgotten People: The South's Poor Whites* (1979); Margaret J. Hagood, *Mothers of the South. Portraiture of the White Tenant Farm Woman* (1939); C. Hugh Holman, *Three Modes of Modern Fiction: Ellen Glasgow, William Faulkner, Thomas Wolfe* (1966); Arthur Palmer Hudson, *Humor in the Old Deep South* (1939), *Folklore Keeps the Past Alive* (1961); Benjamin Burks Kendrick and Alex Matthews Arnett, *The South Looks at Its Past* (1935); Jack Temple Kirby, *Rural Worlds Lost: The American South, 1920–1960* (1986); Herman C. Nixon, *Possum Trot: Rural Community, South* (1941); Howard W. Odum, *Folk, Region, and Society: Selected Papers of Howard W. Odum*, ed. Katherine Jocker, Guy B. Johnson, George L. Simpson, and Rupert B. Vance (1964), *Southern Regions of the United States* (1936), *The Way of the South* (1947); Frederick Law Olmsted, *A Journey in the Back Country* (1860); Frank L. Owsley, *Plain Folk of the Old South* (1949); A. E. Parkins, *The South: Its Economic-Geographical Development* (1938); Ben Robertson, *Red Hills and Cotton: An Upcountry Memory* (1942); Theodore Rosengarten, *All God's Dangers: The Life of Nate Shaw* (1975); Louis D. Rubin, Jr., *Writers of the Modern South: The Faraway Country* (1966), with Robert D. Jacobs, *The Southern Renascence: The Literature of the Modern South* (1953); Rupert B. Vance, *Human Factors of Cotton Culture: A Study in the Social Geography of the American South* (1929). ☆

Agribusiness

In the 1930 symposium *I'll Take My Stand* Andrew Lytle criticized southerners who said, "Industrialize the farm; be progressive; drop old fashioned ways and adopt scientific methods." Conversion of farms into scientific, purely commercial endeavors "means the end of farming as a way of life." In the years since Lytle wrote, southern agriculture has been fundamentally restructured, leading to a decline in the number of southerners on the land and the increasing dominance of farming by fewer and fewer large operations. In the spring of 1986 the Congressional Office of Technology Assessment forecast that in the year 2000 about 50,000 large farms would produce 75 percent of America's food and warned that half of the nation's current 2.2 million farmers would be off the land. Contemporary southern agriculture is part of this national trend.

John H. Davis, a former assistant secretary of agriculture, coined the term *agribusiness* in 1955 to describe the vertical integration of agriculture through a company's control of the production, processing, and marketing of farm products. Agribusiness relies heavily on contract farming, whereby an agricultural business contracts with individual farmers for the delivery of produce at a set price. The company then processes the farm commodity and distributes it for sale. The term *agribusiness* gained a new visibility in the early 1970s, with the increasing dominance of American agriculture by corporations. The *Reader's Guide to Periodical Literature* did not use *agribusiness* as a category for indexing until 1971, when national attention was increasingly focused on it.

Southerners have engaged in agriculture as a commercial activity, of course, since the colonial era, when tobacco became North America's leading export. In the antebellum era cotton was not only the centerpiece of the mythic romantic plantation but also a part of the world economy, as Confederates discovered with their failed policy of cotton diplomacy. For generations after 1865, however, southern farmers grew mostly cotton, corn, tobacco, and peanuts on small, relatively inefficient and nonproductive farms. Low income and widespread poverty characterized the system, which required labor-intensive cultivation. Once established, the system held on tenaciously. Markets, transportation, health and educational services, and credit were all inadequate to promote change, despite efforts of reformers.

Chicken "factory"—a major agribusiness enterprise

The southern agricultural system began to change in the 1930s, and especially during and after World War II. By the 1960s a revolution was completed and millions of southerners had left the land. The mid-20th-century transformation of southern agriculture led to the emergence of agribusiness in the contemporary South.

The federal government played a major role in the restructuring of southern agriculture. Farmers fighting the boll weevil welcomed federal government agents and supported Seaman A. Knapp's programs in the early 20th century to discourage the insect. Knapp's demonstration farms, formalized as the Federal Extension Service in 1914, became a source of expertise for farmers interested in change. In the 1930s, government policies reducing crop acreage in exchange for cash payments promoted a reduction in the surplus population of farm workers. Congressional farm policy over the years rewarded large growers, rather than small operators, and made attractive increased capitalization and expansion. During the early 1960s, for example, government payments went to the top producers of major southern crops. Twenty percent of cotton growers in the Southeast gained 61 percent of payments, while 20 percent of Louisiana sugarcane growers received 72 percent of subsidy payments and 20 percent of rice growers got 64 percent of the government money. In the three decades after World War II direct government subsidies represented a major source of corporate farm income; in 1970, almost $5.2 billion was handed out.

The loss of labor during and after the 1930s also promoted fundamental agricultural change. By reducing farm acreage, the federal government had stimulated migration of displaced rural southerners to cities, and World War II was a spur, as the armed services and factories needed workers. After the war, southerners continued to seek opportunities out of the South. Almost a fifth of southerners left the region in the 1940s. More than 1 million blacks alone migrated in that decade. Southern agriculture had traditionally suffered from a labor surplus, according to economic historians, but between 1940 and 1960 the decline of the region's farm population was so drastic, almost 60 percent, that major changes in cultivation patterns occurred. Mechanization of farms also promoted labor decline and the growth of agribusiness. Machines were more efficient on large land acreages than small and reduced the need for human workers. With farm mechanization came the displacement of sharecroppers and tenants. Many sharecroppers were black, and the protests of the civil rights movement provided the last pretext for many landowners to dismiss, without earlier paternalistic concern, former tenants whose families, in some cases, had worked on the land for generations. The displaced tenants scattered, but some remained behind. By the 1970s wide gaps in income and lifestyle existed in southern rural areas between the prosperous agribusiness landowners and managers, on the one hand, and the unemployed or underemployed black poor on the other.

Mechanization laid the basis for agribusiness in the South in other ways as well. Although the first tractors appeared on farms during World War I, most farms in the South were too small or unprofitable for the machines. Southern farmers were comparatively slow to mechanize. In 1940 the value of machinery per Mississippi farm was $138, compared to $795 in the Middle West. International Harvester developed a mechanical picker in the early 1940s, but less than 50 of them were produced during the war years. After the war, the machine, combined with the use of preemergent and postemergent herbicides, helped to change permanently southern farming, allowing farmers to cultivate and harvest the cotton crop with fewer and fewer workers. The tractor, in turn, enabled farmers of many different crops to cultivate larger acreage in a less labor-intensive way. Tractors assisted southern farmers as they switched from cotton and corn to nonrow crops.

Southerners, in fact, increasingly turned from cotton to other farm commodities. By the 1960s much land that once grew cotton was woodland or pasture. By 1970 more than a third of crop acreage in Alabama, Florida, Mississippi, and Virginia was pasture, which promoted the raising of livestock. Cattle, hogs, and poultry assumed greater economic significance. Soybeans, though, were the clear beneficiary of the switch from cotton. Soybeans are extremely versatile in their uses and are not as labor intensive in cultivation as cotton. In 1940 southerners raised 7.6 million bales of cotton and 5.4 million bushels of soybeans, but by 1975 the equivalent figures were 3 million bales and 523 million bushels. The soybean through the 1970s was the centerpiece of southern agribusiness.

The emergence of large farm units made agribusiness possible in the South. The small plots cultivated by sharecroppers and tenants were anathema to centralized farming, but this had changed by the 1960s. In 1950 there were 2.1 million farms in the South, but by 1975 the number was only 720,000.

The average farm size in these decades climbed from 93 to 216 acres. Sharecropper shacks symbolically vanished, and modern centralized operations appeared. Farmowners and part owners became typical agricultural figures. In the 1940s and 1950s the percentage of land operated by *full* owners actually decreased. Many farmers now owned some land and rented additional acreage. Farm management became a crucial factor to success, and capitalization in equipment was more important for some farmers than the amount of land owned.

Geographer Merle Prunty, Jr., has used the term *neo-plantation* to describe this agricultural operation where an owner or manager runs a farm using hired workers. It resembled an antebellum southern plantation in spatial arrangements, but without the earlier paternalistic concern of planters for workers. Large-scale farmers were the only ones who could profit from this scale of operation. The Delta and Pine Land Company plantation at Scott, Miss., embodied these changes. In the late 1930s the plantation's 5,000 tenants raised 16,000 acres of cotton. By 1970 the plantation land area had expanded to 25,000 acres, but the work force of laborers had declined to 500. Cotton grew on 7,000 acres of land, with the rest devoted to soybeans, corn, and grazing land for 3,000 head of cattle.

Changes in government farm policy, the mechanization of southern agriculture, the loss of farm labor, the diversification of farming, the appearance of large farm units all were factors in nurturing agribusiness operations in the South. Vertical integration gradually appeared in new agricultural sectors after World War II, and demographic patterns in the South promoted this. Increasing urbanization and an accompanying mass market for prepared food brought the centralization of food production and distribution. Women were increasingly employed outside the home and households needed new food services. Dairy and poultry producers, among others, in turn, found the delivery of their commodities to consumers concentrated in sometimes far-off cities to be difficult without marketing assistance. Agribusiness offered a valuable economic service, and agribusiness companies made profits, often large, because of economies of scale from the new vertical integration. Critics charged, though, that individual family farmers—once celebrated by Thomas Jefferson as "God's chosen people"—had lost independence and management control, making them subservient to multimillion-dollar corporations.

In the 1970s agribusiness became one of the major foundations for the economic prosperity of the Sunbelt. By the mid-1970s Florida was the nation's second leading producer of fruits and vegetables, and Texas was number one in the size of cattle and sheep herds. Georgia led the nation in the value of its poultry crop, with Arkansas third, and Georgia topped the nation's agriculturalists in peanut production. In 1970 corporate farms were more pervasive in the South than anyplace in the nation except in the western states of California, Nevada, and Arizona. Corporations owned one-fifth of Florida's farm acreage, and 10 companies controlled 119,000 of Florida's 636,000 acres of citrus. Among the leading corporate producers, processors, and distributors in the South during the 1970s were the Coca-Cola Company, Southdown (a Houston sugar corporation), Tropicana (the Florida orange juice giant), Gold Kist (the Atlanta corporation dealing in poultry), and Southland (the Texas convenience store operators). The Associated Milk Producers of Texas was a billion-dollar a year agribusiness firm. Energy producing companies diversified into agribusiness in the early 1970s. Tenneco, for example, was a Houston-based natural gas company whose subsidiaries also produced crops and fertilizers and marketed and distributed agricultural products. Much of agribusiness wealth coming from exploitation of southern resources went out of the South, but, in any event, agribusiness was a key sector of Sunbelt prosperity.

Southern agribusiness operators have faced increasing difficulties in the 1980s. Problems developed in the production of certain southern crops and southerners suffered generally from the national farm crisis. As far back as the 1950s, farmers had faced a cost-price squeeze. In order to increase their efficiency, southern farmers used machinery, fertilizer, gasoline and diesel fuel, hybrid seed, and herbicides, and the costs of large-scale production meant that commodity prices had to keep up with costs. The increased exports of the late 1960s and early 1970s created the best of times. Southerners shared in prosperity as the national net farm income rose from $18 billion to $33 billion in 1973. Optimistic farmers borrowed money to buy more land and more expensive equipment. Declining prices for crops in the mid-1970s and general discontent led to the formation of a protest group—the American Agriculture Movement—in the Great Plains states. Southern farmers who had once aspired to agribusiness success had joined the protest by October of 1977. In November a nine-mile-long parade of tractors drove through President Jimmy Carter's hometown of Plains, Ga., to dramatize the cause. Difficulties grew worse during the 1980s as Ronald Reagan's Administration cut back on federal government aid to farmers. The likely result was the increased dominance of fewer and fewer agribusiness operators and the final end of farming as a southern way of life.

Charles Reagan Wilson
University of Mississippi

William Adams, *Georgia Review* (Winter 1986); *Agricultural History* (January 1979); Pete Daniel, *Breaking the Land: The Transformation of Cotton, Tobacco, and Rice Cultures since 1880* (1985), *Standing at the Crossroads: Southern Life in the Twentieth Century* (1986); Gilbert C. Fite, *American Farmers: The New Minority* (1981), *Cotton Fields No More: Southern Agriculture, 1865–1980* (1984); David R. Goldfield, *Promised Land: The South since 1945* (1987); Jack Temple Kirby, *Rural Worlds Lost: The American South, 1920–1960* (1987); *Progressive Farmer* (February 1986); Ingolf Vogeler, *The Myth of the Family Farm: Agribusiness Dominance of U.S. Agriculture* (1981). ☆

Country Store

From 1865 to 1930 no institution influenced the South's economy, politics, and the daily life of its people more than the crossroads store. Hundreds, maybe thousands, of these stores were scattered throughout the region.

The history of the southern country store begins with the merchant. He was initially an outsider who brought a cost-accounting mentality and objectivity believed to be more or less foreign to the people among whom he settled. In the post–Civil War South he found ways and means of exchanging goods and services with a minimum of cash, for in those times few people had much cash. The storekeeper had to connect with northern and western manufacturers in order to stock his store with goods. The connection ran from alleged Wall Street monied interests through the meat packers, fertilizer manufacturers, wholesale houses, and the feed, grain, and cotton speculators down to the local country-store merchant.

Merchants always existed in the South, but their rise to power came after the Civil War. The storekeeper's fate was linked with that of both whites and blacks. Before the war the slave's needs had been at least minimally met by his owner, the planter, and his labor was coerced, but after 1865 this system of control was ended. Freedom, however, did not bring financial security, and destitute blacks and many poor whites were forced to find food from any source and under any condition. By means of "stomach discipline," through the medium of the commissary on the plantation and the store at the crossroads, it was possible to acquire an effective leverage over black and white labor. The commissary and the store were both political and economic institutions.

One aspect of the legal machinery by which the merchants operated was the strict application of lien laws enacted by state legislatures. The liens were crop liens or mortgages not on land only, as was generally true before the Civil War, but also on livestock and on "all growing crops." But often the crops were not "growing"; liens might be placed on them even before they were planted. These laws originally were designed to give planters security for food and other supplies furnished their freed black tenants and sharecroppers whom they were not now required to support as slaves. But the laws were quickly used by merchants as well as planters. The lien system meant that the purchaser of a crop, usually cotton, was determined at the beginning of the crop year, and often the purchaser came to be the local merchant.

In the post–Civil War period credit was a critical problem throughout the South. Because only a few farmers could borrow money from a bank, if, indeed, there was a bank in the community, and because of the low value of land, the lien laws made it possible for a merchant to offer credit in small amounts to the hundreds and thousands needing it. The system created an interdependence between the storekeeper and both the landed and landless black and white farmers and tenants of the area served by his store. The credit often took the form of coupon books, which were valid for trade only at his store, thus effectively restricting competition for their trade. In addition to his monopoly over trade the merchant charged interest on credit that sometimes ranged as high as 40 percent. On commissary accounts planters often charged as much if not more. Many merchants accumulated large fortunes, but there were great risks involved in merchandising at the crossroads. Merchants had financial obligations to their suppliers, and there were losses incident to weather, depression, crop failures, and overextended credit. When rumors spread that crops were not doing well, merchants often sent out inspectors or went out themselves to the farms to ascertain if their fears were warranted.

Country stores can be found throughout the United States and their counterparts exist in other parts of the world. What, if anything, was especially distinctive and significant about the southern country store? Above all, there was the "furnish" system incident to the lien laws, but beyond this was the central role played by the country store in the social organization of most southern communities outside the mountain areas. It appears to have been the chief community organizer and builder, particularly in the old plantation and biracial areas, for a significant period of time after the Civil War. Probably every village and town community anywhere requires some specific institution that attracts, in the words of sociologist Everett C. Hughes, "a configuration of other institutions about them so that they create a community of a certain kind." Population clusters from hamlets to cities have grown up around fortresses, castles, cathedrals, *cabildos*, and monasteries. A study of such central community institutions might well lead through the marketplace of the Greek city, the forum of republican Rome, the salons of Paris, the coffee and ale houses of old London, the churches of New England, and the schools of the Midwest.

After the Civil War a new series of population concentrations appeared in the South, necessitating new community organizations. Here and there a county courthouse generated a town of lawyers and county officials around it. The southern county seems to have been almost as much a social as a governmental unit. Other communities sometimes emerged around a church, a trading post, an academy, or an inn. Despite the small concentrations of population, in predominantly rural areas a fair number of country stores had been scattered across the South before the war, serving largely white farmers, but their numbers dramatically increased after the war. Towns that grew up around country stores sometimes took the name of the local storekeeper.

In the postbellum South three factors interacted to cause the country store to emerge into a position of much greater strength and significance than it had had in the antebellum South. The first was sheer geographic isolation. Roads were unbelievably poor; to travel five miles from the crossroads over dirt roads almost unpassable in bad weather was a problem for every farmer and sharecropper with his mule and wagon. Not until the coming of the Ford automobile did roads improve much, although many discussions and complaints were heard about them. High railroad freight rates added to the isolation. The second factor was the dominance of cotton in the economy. A botanical annual, cotton so occupied the lives and plans of those on the land that it became in effect an institutional perennial, the crop traditionally, easily, and unskillfully produced, transported, stored, and marketed. Under the circumstances, to have shifted from one crop to another would have required much more credit from money-lending sources than most farmers had access to. The third factor was the biracial structure of a society steadily moving from the racial controls of the antebellum South to the segregation of the postwar era. Whites and blacks came to live in two different but complementary social worlds. It was a situation ripe for trade and for new marketplaces to emerge.

Trade dictates a certain kind of relationship for those involved in it, and this had significance for the biracial agricultural South, especially in the decades following the Civil War. Local churches were divided racially as well as denominationally, and they were used, ordinarily, only one day in the week. Schools were racially segregated and used only seasonally and for limited times during the day and the week. Courthouses were few and far between, and none of these played an important communitywide integrating role. So the full force of the community's population could and did focus on the store, which was open for business every day, except Sunday, throughout the year. Blacks and whites in the postbellum South more nearly approached equality in the store than anywhere else. Never completely equalitarian, it was more so than other institutions where Jim Crow laws and customs effectively separated the races. Blacks patronized the white store along with whites and often were at liberty to try on hats, garments, and shoes as they fancied. A white customer might spend much time in banter with blacks or with whites of lower class than himself at the store, but he would never think of inviting such people to his home. There was an air of familiarity and tolerance at the store rarely matched elsewhere.

The country store also played an important role in meeting daily needs. The store stocked a bewildering variety of items such as hats, corsets, gloves, blouses, stockings, and cheap perfumes for women; blue jeans, overalls, brogans, broad-brimmed hats, and "pridarita" (Pride of Readsville) smoking tobacco for the men; peppermint candy and crackers for the children; and rat cheese for all. Axle grease, lard, kerosene, and other such smelly items gave a characteristic odor to the place. When someone was born, married, or died, the store provided the items needed for these rituals of life and death. The country store was no orderly department store; its goods were not likely to be very systematically arranged and displayed. Almost everything was to be found behind something else.

The country store flourished in the days before the coming of modern brick-store civilization and provided a characteristic feature of the southern landscape. The store was a barnlike wood frame structure to which additions were made as trade expanded. A wing or shed added on one side might be used for machinery, tools, and other heavy items, along with kerosene for home lamps. A wing added on the other side stored seed, fertilizers, stock feed, horse collars, trace chains, and general hardware. A second floor above the main floor was often added. Here among the coffins and caskets the local Masons and Woodmen of the World met on designated evenings. These were rural male fraternities; modern urban service and luncheon clubs, such as Rotary and Kiwanis, had not yet arrived. An office at the rear of the building could be added for desks, account books, and the big iron safe. To this inner sanctum, sharecroppers and tenants, as well as small landowning farmers, were admitted one at a time to go over accounts, to make or receive payments, or to arrange credit against next year's crop. The "drummer," or traveling salesman, representing a jobbing house in Baltimore, Cincinnati, or St. Louis met the store owner at least once a year to take his order for wholesale supplies. The drummer was much more than a salesman; he was a visitor from another world bringing exciting news and opinions from the outside and a fund of racy stories sure to go the rounds and to be repeated many times until he came again.

After the invention of the telephone the store often possessed the only such instrument in the community. The big colorful catalogs of Montgomery Ward and Sears, Roebuck and Company, both of which were national country stores or country-store extensions of sorts, were put to considerable use through the medium of the store. Frequently, the merchant himself mailed or telephoned orders for his customers. The telephone made it possible as never before to get in touch with people in Chicago or any other place in the United States. More important for local people was the opportunity to make quick contact with the local doctor, if there was one, and relatives of a sick member of the family.

In the absence of a local doctor or a drugstore and druggist, who often served as a doctor or medical advisor, the country store reaped much profit from the sale of patent medicines. After food, probably the greatest demand by the rural population was for medicine. Prescriptions came by way of wall, fence, tree, or local newspaper advertising or from the satisfactory experience of neighbors and fellow church members. Historian Thomas D. Clark once noted that the manufacturer of Plantation Bitters claimed an annual sale throughout the South of $5 million worth of the product. Lydia Pinkham's Vegetable Compound for Women made, as Clark puts it, "advanced matronhood a positive joy" and also provided a means of getting one's picture along with a testimonial in a newspaper or an advertising leaflet.

The store operated as a general gathering place every day except Sunday (and sometimes even then if a church service was being held there) and in all seasons of the year. Weather and seasonal conditions nurtured two characteristic scenes played in the country store as theater. One was a summer scene. On the unpaved sidewalk in front men gathered on a hot day to loaf, whittle, play checkers, or pitch horseshoes and to comment on the attractions of passing women. In the winter scene men and boys and sometimes a few women sat around the potbellied stove swapping yarns, arguing politics or religion, and recounting details of farming operations. There was a philosophy present in the assumptions underlying this talk, which would now be called a "cracker-barrel philosophy." The weighty matters under discussion required a sawdust-filled box for the benefit of tobacco chewers. It was a spitting society; everyone spat, even snuff-dipping women, if any were present.

The country store with its southern flavor is still to be found here and there in rural, isolated areas. Certain old-fashioned items of merchandise may still be found there, but now its line of merchandise tends to make it approach the convenience store. A gasoline pump is likely to be found out front along with an opportunity to pick up some trade from passing motorists. Striped candy no longer comes in by the barrel; candy bars and vending machines have been substituted. Cash sales have increased, for banks have taken away the crop-lien credit business. Loafers still gather there consuming quantities of bottled drinks. Between growing towns and cities has come the decline of other towns so that many places, bypassed by the superhighways, are reverting to the level of villages and villages to the level of hamlets. In these villages and hamlets something like the old-time country store tends to hang on, and this accounts, possibly more than any other single institution except the school, for the persistence of such villages and hamlets. In altered form the general store appears to have lasted longer as a pioneer institution in the South than in any other part of the United States.

Edgar T. Thompson
Duke University

Interior of Reganton, Mississippi, country store, 1973

Lewis E. Atherton, *The Southern Country Store, 1800–1860* (1949); Jacqueline P. Bull, *Journal of Southern History* (February 1952); Gerald Carson, *The Old Country Store* (1954); Thomas D. Clark, *Journal of Southern History* (February 1946), *Pills, Petticoats, and Plows: The Southern Country Store* (1944); J. Evetts Haley, *Charles Schreiner: General Merchandise* (1945); Arthur F. Raper, *Preface to Peasantry: The Tale of Two Black Belt Counties* (1936); Francis Butler Simkins, *North Carolina Historical Review* (April 1930); T. S. Stribling, *The Store* (1932); Harold D. Woodman, *King Cotton and His Retainers: Financing and Marketing the Cotton Crop of the South, 1800–1925* (1968). ☆

Crops

Southern culture and commerce have been shaped by a basic dependence upon agricultural production. Cotton, tobacco, corn, peanuts, pumpkins, squash, beans, Irish potatoes, sweet potatoes, chili peppers, and tomatoes are crops indigenous to the United States and were cultivated by Indians and later by colonists in the southern states. These crops continue to be major food and fiber crops. Wheat, rice, indigo, and sugarcane were introduced by Europeans and have become major commercial crops. Seed grain crops, such as soybeans and hybrid sorghums, today surpass all other crops in total acreage and were generally developed in the modern era from European and African stock. Major southern crops now in cultivation, ranked by acreage in production, are soybeans, cotton, rice, tobacco, and sugarcane. Soybean acreage for the past two decades has exceeded acreage in cotton twofold.

During the colonial era, tobacco, rice, and indigo comprised the major commercial crops. However, throughout the colonial and antebellum periods, acreage in corn exceeded that of any other single crop. Most corn never reached the marketplace; instead it provided sustenance for farm families and their animals.

Tobacco was the most valuable colonial crop. John Rolfe, of the Virginia colony, successfully cultivated and cured a West Indian variety of tobacco, which he first shipped to a British market in 1613. Exports from Virginia rose from 20,000 pounds in 1618 to over 500,000 in 1627. By the 1630s overproduction caused a slump in tobacco prices from luxury levels to those of a general commodity. The tobacco market subsequently became a mass market. Exports reached 18 million pounds by 1860. Tobacco farming has historically involved smaller acreages and more intensive labor than other crops. Today, southern farm income from tobacco regularly exceeds $1 billion per year.

Commercial rice production began in South Carolina about 1694 with seed imported from Madagascar. First planted in tidal marshes, rice was soon cultivated along inland river marshes. Cultivation by flooding from ponds and then from tidal rivers employing an ingenious system of locks and dams facilitated rising production within a well-defined coastal region of the Carolinas and Georgia. Antebellum rice production involved large investments in land, mills, and slaves. The Civil War marked the end of a flourishing rice culture in the Carolinas, after which rice cultivation shifted to the Mississippi Delta and to the prairies of southwest Louisiana and Texas.

Rice farming became mechanized in the coastal prairies of Texas and Louisiana where reapers, combines, tractors, hydraulic pumps, rail transportation, cheap land, and improved plant varieties combined to virtually revolutionize the industry. In the 20th century rice growing expanded in Arkansas and Mississippi and developed in Tennessee and California. The 3 million acres of rice in cultivation in 1980 generated approximately $1.3 billion in farm income. Rice ranked sixth in farm value among all U.S. crops. Although the nation's rice production accounts for only 2 percent of the world total, American rice comprises one-third of the total world trade in rice.

Indigo was introduced into the Carolinas from the West Indies by Eliza Lucas about 1739. Parliament exempted indigo from import duties and offered a price subsidy that remained in effect until 1777. The American Revolution and the introduction of chemical dyes terminated this once-profitable industry. Wheat production was commercially significant before the Civil War, with Virginia the leading wheat producer of the southern states. Wheat production and milling continued on a limited basis in most southern states into the 20th century. Texas remains one of the leading wheat producers in the United States.

Cotton became commercially significant after the development of Eli Whitney's gin in 1793. One thousand pounds of cotton were shipped to England in 1789 and 4.5 million bales in 1861. Cotton became synonymous with slavery and the plantation system. The plantation survived the Civil War with the sharecrop and crop-lien systems. Until the 1920s acreage in cotton continued to climb. In 1926 production peaked when the 44.5 million acres in cotton produced 18 million bales. Declining prices, depression, war, government farm programs, and alternative employment opportunities resulted in the rapid demise of the Cotton Kingdom, so that by the 1970s acreage in cotton had declined to about 10 million acres yielding approximately 10 million bales annually, and much of that production was in the irrigated lands of the Southwest, outside the traditional cotton belt.

Children picking cotton at an unidentified location, early 20th century

Corn has been a pervasive crop in the South since frontier days. A large portion of the nation's total corn crop is still grown and consumed on southern farms and in local markets. Commercial production increased appreciably between 1970 and 1980, when U.S. corn production doubled. Kentucky, Georgia, and Texas led in acreage planted in 1980, with the value of the Texas crop $402 million, the Kentucky crop $347 million, and the Georgia crop $188 million.

Despite rapid declines in farm population in the South since World War II, production of most crops has actually increased through the application of scientific farming techniques. Food crops, predominantly those indigenous to the region, continue to be widely produced and consumed. Agriculture and the agrarian heritage continue to play a dominant role in the economic and cultural development of the South.

See also SCIENCE AND MEDICINE: Agriculture, Scientific

Henry C. Dethloff
Texas A&M University

Stuart Bruchey, *Cotton and the Growth of the American Economy* (1967); Pete Daniel, *Breaking the Land: The Transformation of Cotton, Tobacco, and Rice Culture since 1880* (1985); Gilbert C. Fite, *American Farmers: The New Minority* (1981); Paul W. Gates, *The Farmer's Age: Agriculture, 1815–1860* (1960); Duncan C. Heyward, *Seed from Madagascar* (1937); Sam B. Hilliard, *Hog Meat and Hoecake: Food Supply in the Old South, 1840–1860* (1972); Joseph C. Robert, *The Story of Tobacco in America* (1949); John T. Schlebecker, *Whereby We Thrive: A History of American Farming, 1607–1972* (1975); Fred A. Shannon, *The Farmer's Last Frontier: Agriculture, 1860–1897* (1945); J. Carlyle Sitterson, *Sugar Country: The Cane Sugar Industry in the South, 1753–1950* (1953); James H. Street, *New Revolution in the Cotton Economy: Mechanization and Its Consequences* (1967). ☆

Diversification

The history of the American South has been inextricably bound to the agricultural development of the region. In spite of growing industrialization, especially since World War II, the land and farmer have consistently remained among the most influential forces in the shaping of the southern economic, political, and cultural heritage. Almost as pervasive, too, has been the unceasing call for diversification of agricultural activities—a call whose limited success also reveals a significant quality of the southern farmer.

Prior to the Civil War, small, family-owned farms most often typified southern agriculture. These subsistence units were diversified and self-sufficient, producing corn, wheat, dairy products, fruits, sweet potatoes, and livestock. This diversification stemmed mainly from necessity, not from any consciously well-planned effort. Southern farmers toiled long hours to produce what they needed to survive, frequently growing small amounts of the already important cash crops—tobacco or cotton—to supplement their limited incomes. They were, however, generally unaware of (or ignored) calls by agrarian leaders to practice more progressive farming methods. Instead, through trial and error they developed their own farming system—often employing backward methods—which soon became ingrained and handed down from father to son. This system proved difficult to change. Faced with both limited leisure and money, these modest landholders found their cultural opportunities restricted to a basic level, far different from those available to the planter class. They enjoyed quilting bees, corn huskings, family reunions, church events, and traditional folk music sometimes provided by a fiddler. These activities reflected their strong devotion to family, religion, and the land. They were proud, independent, and self-reliant, but lacking in opportunities to learn about more progressive farming methods then being introduced in the 1840s elsewhere in the nation, especially in the North.

Tobacco plantations, with their accompanying slave labor, were self-sufficient in the 17th- and 18th-century South. In the 19th century, also, the great plantations of tobacco and cotton primarily remained self-sufficient. A growing emphasis upon producing more and more of the cash crops, however, proved a detriment to the land and to efforts for diversification. Both farsighted southern agrarian leaders and regional farm publications warned repeatedly of the dangers to the soil and to the overall development of the South in becoming so dependent upon cash crops. Such prominent 19th-century agricultural spokesmen as Edmund Ruffin and John Taylor of Virginia, Dr. Martin W. Phillips of South Carolina, and George W. Jeffreys of North Carolina urged the growing of grain crops, the adoption of fertilizers, the raising of livestock, and other progressive methods to stop the depletion of the southern soil. At the same time the Augusta, Ga., *Southern Cultivator* expressed the concern of many agrarian journals in contrasting the exhausted soil, inefficient methods of production, and general decay of southern farms to the more productive soils, higher land values, and diversification of northern farms. Southern agricultural fairs and societies reiterated that message. Some plantation owners, especially those in Maryland and Virginia, did move to wheat and cattle production but only because tobacco could no longer be economically produced there. Plantation owners generally refused to adopt newer agrarian methods and thereby helped instill a resistance to change that was a portent of darker days for southern farming.

The Civil War and Reconstruction left most southern farmers, black and white, without the capital necessary for economic independence. To secure credit for equipment, food, seed, and other necessities, they pledged in advance to landowners and merchants part of the crops they helped produce. A crop-lien system evolved, with its accompanying tenant and sharecropping farmers, and dominated the South until the 1930s. It marked the nadir of southern agriculture. As decades passed, more and more farmers slipped into the sharecropper-tenant class and destitution dogged their every step. Southern agrarian spokesmen pointed out the obvious—the agricultural system devastated the people and the region. But farmers could do little to change conditions. They lacked, most importantly, the capital to institute basic changes necessary to alleviate their oppression. Because of a lack of schools or inadequate ones illiteracy spread and health conditions deteriorated as balanced diets became as rare as balanced agricultural practices. Stubborn farmers further exacerbated conditions by using backward methods handed down from previous generations. Sometimes they spoke out against their plight. Organizations and political parties including the Farmers' Alliance and the Populists advocated such ideas as agricultural cooperatives where farmers would control production and pricing. Lacking capital and effective leadership, farmers failed to effect changes.

The 20th century witnessed a continuation of these deplorable conditions. Many vigorous attempts to end sharecropping and tenant farming occurred: experiment stations set up by land-grant colleges introduced new farming methods; farm journals such as Clarence H. Poe's *Progressive Farmer* constantly stressed the benefits of diversified plant and animal production; Dr. Seaman A. Knapp did yeoman work by going directly to poor farmers and demonstrating progressive, scientific methods; fairs, agricultural societies, and cooperative extension programs proposed new ways to confront old problems; the U.S. Department of Agriculture blanketed the South with free literature and spokesmen urging diversification—but all of these efforts failed. Conditions remained strikingly similar to those of the 1880s, and southern farmers of the 1920s were the poorest group in the nation. Not surprisingly, their cultural pursuits reflected their meager circumstances and consisted of whatever they could create or imagine in their poor surroundings: self-trained musicians provided accompaniment to homegrown songs that described the plight of the people; the ever-present church and its strong message of eventual salvation provided solace against the bleak economic horizon. Ironically, the southern farmers' inability to change was accompanied by a strange, but bountiful, crop of writers. William Faulkner, Erskine Caldwell, Robert Penn Warren, Flannery O'Connor, Eudora Welty, and others graphically portrayed the farmers' destitution and in so doing established careers that led to international literary acclaim. From a region that wore out soil and soul rose one of the greatest literary blossomings in America.

The Great Depression of the 1930s, along with World War II in the 1940s, ended the crippling economic system that had characterized southern farming since Reconstruction. The federal government, through New Deal enactments, especially the Agricultural Adjustment Act, accomplished crop reduction by paying landowning farmers to restrict their production. These federal payments provided the capital that had been so lacking for decades, and farmers began the slow, steady process of adopting many of the progressive, scientific measures proposed throughout the region's history. World War II and its aftermath witnessed millions of poor farmers leaving the region for better economic opportunities elsewhere in the nation. The events of the 1930s and 1940s effectively eliminated from southern agriculture the small, family farmer who for centuries had played an overwhelmingly important role in the region.

A true revolution became apparent in the region after 1945: farmers acquired larger tracts of land, tractor power replaced animal muscle, livestock production increased dramatically, new crops such as soybeans and peanuts grew where cotton once had grown, and scientific farming became accepted and necessary for survival in the new environment. Rising farm incomes provided a better way of life and decent housing; schools and health facilities now became available to southern farmers.

Outside forces finally reshaped the southern farmer into the modern agricultural producer long yearned for by agrarian leaders.

Diversification came to the South only after all internal attempts failed. This development helps underscore the South's reluctance to change, its tendency to continue with older, more conservative ways, even in the face of viable alternatives. For those farmers who survived the incredible decades of destitution to arrive at a new, better level of life, the most constant of all cultural heritages—the love of the land—still endures.

See also HISTORY AND MANNERS: New Deal; Populism; SCIENCE AND MEDICINE: Agriculture, Scientific; / Ruffin, Edmund; SOCIAL CLASS: Tenant Farmers; / Farmers' Alliance

Joseph A. Coté
University of Georgia Library

Gilbert C. Fite, *Agricultural History* (January 1979), *Cotton Fields No More: Southern Agriculture, 1865–1980* (1984); Lewis C. Gray, *History of Agriculture in the Southern United States to 1860*, 2 vols. (1933); Clarence Hamilton Poe Papers, North Carolina Department of Archives and History, Raleigh; Gavin Wright, *The Political Economy of the Cotton South: Households, Markets, and Wealth in the Nineteenth Century* (1978). ☆

Garden Patch

In addition to maintaining decorative formal gardens, southerners have a tradition of functional gardens providing, especially, vegetables for the table. They are called garden patches, garden plots, kitchen gardens, provision gardens, or simply vegetable gardens. They have been locales for intercultural exchange between the American Indian, European, and African ways of growing.

The first people of the Southeast to keep garden patches were the Indians. As anthropologist Charles Hudson has noted, "In Creek towns, and probably in Indian settlements throughout the Southeast, the women cultivated kitchen gardens in addition to the large fields in the river bottoms, and these were located in and around the town itself." From early times, then, the garden patch was frequently associated with women and with essential provision of food for the table. Corn, beans, and squash, the three principal agricultural crops, were grown in such areas. Land for these garden patches would gradually become exhausted and this sometimes led to relocation of entire towns, in the search for better land for these essential garden areas.

Gardening to colonial European settlers meant not only working on well-planned, formal designs of trees, shrubbery, and flowers, but also the growing of food. The gentry imported plants and seeds from Europe and experimented with native plants. Robert Beverley noted that vegetable gardens were productive in Virginia, where the people had most of the "culinary plants" from England as well as indigenous ones. In North Carolina gardens, said Julia Cherry Spruill, "were parsnips, carrots, turnips, beets, artichokes, radishes, several kinds of potatoes, leeks, onions, shallots, chives, and garlic." Salads included cabbage, savoy, lettuce, fennel, spinach, mint, rhubarb, sorrel, and purslane. Asparagus thrived under natural conditions, and celery, cucumbers, and squash were abundant.

An Afro-American gardening tradition took root in the colonial Southeast as well. Yams, okra, tanniers, collards, benne, and other plants from West Africa all grew in the South in small "provision gardens," which slaveowners sometimes encouraged and other times ignored. Some African plants and growing techniques entered Cherokee agriculture in the 17th century and were adapted by German immigrants in North Carolina and elsewhere and by English settlers. African plant stocks were frequently difficult to transplant, but southerners sometimes imported Caribbean plants or experimented with New World plant substitutes from the Indians.

The techniques of growing vegetables, as well as the plants grown, were another aspect of the Afro-American tradition. A 19th-century planter on the Sea Islands off the coast of Georgia described a slave's garden as "a small patch where arrowroot, long collards, sugar cane, tanniers, ground nuts, beene, gourds, and watermelons grew in comingled luxuriance." The "comingled" look was the key, a form inherited from West Africa and still seen frequently in the American South. The mixture of plant types together, rather than separated out in orderly rows, seems to create an effective "garden climate," explaining the endurance of the form. By layering plants, through planting two or three plants growing to different heights next to each other, the insect population apparently can be reduced, weeds decreased through shading them out, and soil nutrients and water conserved.

The garden patch was a common part of life for blacks and whites on the antebellum southern plantation. The plantation mistress sometimes supervised work on garden plots and kept detailed records of her plantings. One 1834 diary reported that Eliza Mitchell was growing cabbage, strawberries, raspberries, snap beans, corn, cymblings, and sugar beets. Large plantations devoted acreage to the growing of such vegetables, which were used to feed the black work force. Slaveowners, according to most recent studies, let many slaves have garden patches. The bondsmen looked after their crops at the end of the work day, on Saturday afternoon, and on Sunday. Planters often gave slaves some weekend time to work on these and purchased fresh vegetables from their slaves as a way of providing incentive for their work, keeping up morale, and giving the workers extra money for occasional luxuries. If allowed, slaves would market their produce on Saturdays at crossroad stores or in towns. This trade was never as large in the South as in the Caribbean, but it was significant. Most vegetables grown by slaves in their gardens were, however, for consumption by the families that grew them. The ability to control their garden patch and practice gardening skills promoted self-worth among the slaves. This was a family activity, and the family meal of homegrown and prepared vegetables became a simple but significant ritual reinforcing kinship.

Southern tenant farmers after the Civil War and into the 20th century found vegetable garden plots to be especially significant in their lives. Most of their time was devoted to raising cotton or other cash crops, for which they received minimal compensation. The garden plot was widespread among tenants and common among mill town people, whenever the land was available. Some landlords did not want tenants raising vegetables, feeling it took away from their cotton work, but most seem not to have discouraged it. James Agee in *Let Us Now Praise Famous Men* (1941) described an Alabama garden plot. He said it was close to the rear of the house, "about the shape and about two-thirds the size of a tennis court, and is caught within palings against the hunger and damage of animals." The palings were thin slats of pine, which were strung together with wire. Weeds stood outside these fence walls, while inside "the planting is concentrated to the utmost possible, in green and pink-veined wax and velvet butter beans, and in hairy buds of okra." Insects were a continual torment, with beetles and other pests a potential threat to vegetables at every step of the way.

As in earlier times, the fresh vegetables from the garden patch were an important part of the rural southerner's nutrition, especially for the tenants and sharecroppers. By the 1930s government investigations had identified problems with the southern diet, with its heavy reliance on starchy foods and supposed lack of fresh vegetable consumption. Howard W. Odum pointed in 1936 to statistics that showed the South was considerably above the national average and also above every other region in the nation in the amount of farm vegetables raised, suggesting changes in the dietary habits of the people of the region. He concluded that the statistics "indicate the relatively large dependence of the farm folk upon home produce." Novelist Richard Wright, in *Black Boy* (1945), recalled from his Mississippi and Arkansas childhood, "the delight I caught in seeing long straight rows of red and green vegetables stretching away in the sun to the bright horizon."

In the modern South the raising of vegetables, fruits, and other items in small garden plots is a continuing tradition. *New York Times* reporter Wayne King has noted that "one of the pleasures of gardening, particularly in the South, is reading the seed packets. Among radishes, as a mundane example, there are Crimson Giants, Red Princes and Scarlet Globes. One can plant Southland's Louisiana Green Velvet Okra, Mississippi Sunshine Mammoth Edible All-Star Selection Blackeye Peas, Sweet Slice Burpless Hybrid Cucumbers, Dixie Hybrid Crookneck Squash, watermelons called Fat Boy or tomatoes called Big Boy." In addition to a diversity of plants to grow, there is progress on fighting the insects that always plagued the region. Individual gardeners go into their yards with spray tanks of insecticides strapped to their backs, wearing rain slickers, boots, and maybe even goggles, prepared to destroy threats to their summer salads.

Organic gardening has become fashionable in the region today. One practitioner prefers to call it "biologically grown" food, because that phrase conveys the soil-building process and the holistic relationship between the plant and its environment. *Organic farming* generally is defined as farming that uses natural biological methods. It can be more difficult in the South than in the North because the hot climate dries up the organic matter in the soil, making it hard to build it up. The long growing season and mild winters through much of the South mean more insect pests and weeds to fight, lessons learned by every generation and type of southern farmer sooner or later. Southern organic farmers fertilize with natural rock powder, seaweed, fish emulsion, compost, and manure. They plant legumes as crop covering and they believe in crop rotation. Organic farming has become a business in parts of the South, but it is also important in terms of the suburban and city southerners who set aside land in their yard or on their small farms to raise vegetables.

The growth of interest in regional cooking among the middle class has also promoted the growing of vegetable patches. Southerners in the modern South, even those in cities, are not far removed in historical time from the rural farm South, and those southerners who continue to plant their garden patches and grow favorite southern vegetables seem to hold on to a long southern tradition that unites the people of the region.

See also ETHNIC LIFE: Indian Cultural Contributions; HISTORY AND MANNERS: Foodways

Charles Reagan Wilson
University of Mississippi

John B. Boles, *Black Southerners, 1619–1869* (1983); Catherine Clinton, *The Plantation Mistress: Woman's World in the Old South* (1982); Tom Hatley, *Southern Changes* (October–November 1984); Howard W. Odum, *Southern Regions of the United States* (1936); Julia Cherry Spruill, *Women's Life and Work in the Southern Colonies* (1938); Debby Wechsler, *Southern Exposure* (November–December 1983); Peter Wood, *Black Majority: Negroes in Colonial South Carolina from 1670 through the Stono Rebellion* (1974). ☆

Good Roads Movement

The good roads movement in the South was at first primarily an attempt to convince farmers that road improvements would not be detrimental to their interests. Behind the campaign for better roads was the League of American Wheelmen, an organization of bicyclists, which drew its membership almost exclusively from the Northeast. During the late 19th century the league spent considerable time and money attempting to convince farmers in the South, and elsewhere in the country, that good roads would bring them greater economic and cultural rewards. The league also lobbied hard for a federal program aiding road building, and in 1893 Congress earmarked $10,000 as part of an agricultural appropriation bill establishing the Office of Roads Inquiry (ORI).

Limited funding and a need to gain grass-roots support for a good roads movement mandated an investigative and educational role for the new federal agency. Campaigns to survey road conditions, win over opponents of road reforms, and demonstrate the proper techniques in road construction commenced. As part of this effort the ORI launched an assault on the notoriously poor roads in the South. In cooperation with the national Good Roads Association and the Southern Railway, the ORI sponsored a Good Roads Train, which toured the states of Virginia, North Carolina, South Carolina, Georgia, Alabama, and Tennessee during the 1901–2 winter months. At each of 18 stops, southerners listened to speakers explain the advantages of good roads and watched "object-lesson" demonstrations in proper road construction methods. At the train's last stop in Charlottesville, Va., on 3 April 1902, Samuel Spencer, president of the Southern Railway, observed that the train had aroused enthusiasm for an improvement that he regarded "as the most important now before us in the development of the South."

Eighteen local good roads associations were soon located in the six-state area. Members of these vanguard organizations and others that sprang up across the South during the first two decades of the 20th century translated the message of good roads into language that not only farmers but businessmen, educators, ministers, boosters, and politicians could understand. Their efforts were so extensive and unrelenting that historian Francis Butler Simkins considered the good roads movement in the South "the third god [along with industrial and educational projects] in the Trinity of southern progress."

Southern state legislatures were slow, though, to appropriate money for road improvements. Prior to 1906, not one state in the South had started a state aid-for-roads program or established a highway department. Road improvements in the South were made by local good roads organizations, by county bond issues, or occasionally by states like North Carolina, which sponsored "Good Road Days" where citizens actually labored to grade or resurface a stretch of road in their community. There was little understanding of the proper techniques necessary to insure that improvements would last.

When the automobile arrived on the scene, southerners called attention to the poor road conditions in the South by employing reliability runs and interstate tours. In 1909, in conjunction with the Atlanta Automobile Show, the Atlanta *Journal* and the New York *Herald* sponsored a reliability run from Broadway south to Peachtree Street. During the next two years Charles J. Glidden directed two separate tours into the South. These contests received wide attention and gave rise to hundreds of similar efforts in every southern state.

By 1914, when 1,600 good roads delegates assembled in Atlanta at the fourth annual convention of the American Road Congress, it was evident that the question of good roads alone was no longer the single most important issue. Many southerners now envisioned good roads as a means of uniting North and South, bringing money and jobs into the South. The Capital Highway Association (1909), the Dixie Highway Association (1915), the Jackson Highway Association (1915), the Lee Highway Association (1918), the North and South Bee Line Highway Association (1917), and the Bankhead Highway Association (1920), among others, were all organized to promote the construction of new routes between the North and South.

In 1916 Congress passed the Federal Aid Road Act and funds for the first time became available to southern states for road construction. Among its provisions the new law required that all expenditures take place through state highway departments. By 1917 every southern state had a highway department, thus bringing state governments for the first time clearly into the good roads picture. The 1916 law, however, provided money for the construction of post roads only and had little impact on the overwhelming number of miles of ungraded, unpaved roads throughout the South. These tortuous roads hampered the mobility of thousands of soldiers stationed in camps in southern states during World War I, and good roads advocates were quick to point out the national defense benefits of further road improvements. Article after article appeared in the two most widely circulated promotional magazines of the good roads movement in the South, *Dixie Highway*

(1915–20) and *Southern Good Roads* (1910–20). These publications urged Congress to address the problem with additional legislation and more money.

Following the war, Congress passed the Federal Aid Highway Act of 1921. A system of interstate and intercounty roads was designated to constitute the Federal Aid Highway Road System. The Dixie Highway, the Lee Highway, and the Atlantic Coastal Highway became part of this trunk-line system, but federal dollars had to be matched by states on a 50–50 basis, and southern state legislatures rarely appropriated enough money to get the South out of the mud and onto hard-surfaced highways. As late as the 1960s roads in the South remained inferior to those in the North and Midwest. Nevertheless, the efforts of good roads advocates helped not only to increase the urban population of the South but to end much of the sectional isolation southerners had experienced throughout their history.

See also GEOGRAPHY: Roadside; HISTORY AND MANNERS: Automobile; RECREATION: Tourism, Automobile

Howard L. Preston
Spartanburg, South Carolina

John Hollis Bankhead, Sr., Papers, Alabama Department of Archives and History, Montgomery; Cecil K. Brown, *The State Highway System of North Carolina: Its Evolution and Present Status* (1931); Dewey W. Grantham, *Southern Progressivism: The Reconciliation of Progress and Tradition* (1983); Philip P. Mason, *The League of American Wheelmen and the Good Roads Movement, 1880–1905* (1958); Josephine Anderson Pearson Papers, Tennessee State Archives, Nashville; Joseph H. Pratt, *South Atlantic Quarterly* (January 1910). ☆

Livestock

Livestock rivaled cotton in economic importance in the colonial, early national, and antebellum South. Historians, however, have largely ignored the topic. Southern historians and the public have been fascinated with slavery and the Civil War, both of which are closely associated with the cotton culture. Frontier historians remain preoccupied with the cowboy-Indian, rancher-farmer epic enacted on the Great Plains in the post–Civil War era. These topics consequently are richly documented, while data on southern livestock is more elusive.

The first known European to comment on the suitability of the South for stock raising was Cabeza de Vaca, who survived the disastrous 1527 Narvaez expedition to Florida and who eventually made his way across the continent. Throughout the colonial period explorers and settlers constantly noted either the potential for livestock or the manner in which imported animals thrived. Because animals flourished equally well in English, French, and Spanish colonies, the movement of Old World bloodlines from the Atlantic Seaboard into and beyond the Mississippi Valley was multidirectional and continuous through the colonial and early national periods. Spanish beef cattle predominated by the end of the colonial period, but colonists from numerous European nations introduced a variety of breeds. The same applies to the pedigrees of hogs, horses, and sheep, though the latter were not nearly so abundant.

Cattle and pigs were ubiquitous and valuable. From Virginia to Florida this industry—at first unanticipated by founders of the colonies—flourished during the colonial era, though nowhere as extensively as in South Carolina. By the early 18th century vast herds were reported—some numbering in the thousands. Much remains to be discovered about the sale of live animals, meat, and related products. The West Indies provided a lucrative market for stock raisers, and consequently there was an early introduction of Spanish institutions and breeding stock into the English colonies. From the Carolinas cattle raising quickly spread into Georgia, where a further exchange of bloodlines and herding techniques took place along the Florida border.

Meanwhile, a livestock industry was emerging in the Old Southwest. By the second half of the 18th century vast herds of cattle grazed on the luxuriant prairies to the northwest of New Orleans in the Opelousas region. Had not travelers and officials referred so often to the extensive herds of cattle, one might be tempted to question the credibility of their figures, which frequently ranged into the thousands. Spanish census data of the 1780s and 1790s as well as territorial tax records of the early 1900s tend to substantiate the evidence. Indeed, there are strong indications that the raising of cattle and swine accounted for the most prevalent use of the land in the Old South at the turn of the 19th century.

All the tribes of the American Southeast quickly emulated the stock raising of the European intruders. Though Indians owned some pigs, most accounts mention sizable herds of cattle tended by the Native Americans, at times in fenced pastures. Early herdsmen, whose lifestyle kept them in the vanguard of settlement, frequently found themselves in conflict with the tribesmen. Indians resented the destruction of their crops by livestock; whites complained frequently about the theft of stock, especially cattle and horses. Such charges and countercharges were exchanged until the policy of Indian removal was effected. Although all tribes acquired some horses, the Chickasaw and Seminole developed particularly hardy, agile breeds, which were prized by cowboys and cavalrymen. Ironically, stock raising proved to be an important economic activity of the tribes after they were removed to the Indian Territory.

Mounted slaves—some of whom came from African tribes with long herding traditions—tended cattle for generations, often becoming expert horsemen. Though the use of blacks as cattle hunters, or cowboys, first was prevalent in the Carolinas, generations of their descendants watched over livestock as the culture of their masters spread across the South and into Texas. Considering this experience, it is not surprising that free blacks in significant numbers became cowboys in the trans-Mississippi West after the Civil War.

Although cattle raising in the South did not exactly parallel the trans-Mississippi experience, the similarities were surprising. Roundups, branding, long drives, open ranges, and numerous stock regulations all were a part of both the southern and southwestern scene. Most differences related to the ranging of cattle in the pine forests and, farther to the South, among the palmettos. Hence, in many locales the whip either replaced the lariat or was used in addition to it. Long rawhide whips in skillful hands produced a cracking noise that traveled great distances—cracks that most likely are the roots of the appellation "cracker" as in "Georgia cracker."

Though ascertaining accurately the profitability of stock raising prior to the mid-19th century is difficult, ample evidence suggests that cattle, horses, and swine maintained relatively high values. Because both cows and pigs at times roamed out of sight in the piney woods or on stretches of prairie, the wealth of the herders was not readily apparent. However, estate inventories and other manuscripts indicate that the value of stock was surprisingly high, especially in comparison to other property such as slaves. Cattle, horses, and pigs were favorite targets of thieves, suggesting their worth. In addition to the value of animals on the hoof and of fresh or preserved meat, a ready market existed for hides, horns, and tallow. The local, national, and international market for leather was tremendous in a preindustrial society dependent on horses, mules, and oxen for transportation, plowing, and power to operate various machines. Many personal and household items now made of fiber, plastic, or metal were fashioned of leather or horn.

With the invention of the cotton gin and the resumption of a brisk international trade after the War of 1812, cultivation of cotton increased annually until that crop was crowned "king" on the eve of the Civil War. Nevertheless, herding of cattle and swine remained important, although historians widely disagree about just how important. Nor do historians concur on the relationship of herders and planters. Indeed, much remains to be learned about the interdependency of the herdsmen, farmers, and planters. Prior to the War of 1812 many of the so-called planters were in fact ranchers, and their production of livestock—draft animals, beef cattle, and swine—was of sufficient importance to lead them to experiment with the introduction of superior bloodlines of all types of animals, including sheep. (Efforts to improve bloodlines of beef cattle generally proved unsuccessful, probably because of the lack of resistance to "Texas fever," which was endemic among cattle native to the region.) Sheep herding was not a significant factor in the Lower South until the late 19th and early 20th centuries when greater effort was made to market wool. In the Upper South and border states sheep raising was always more important.

In 1860 there were approximately 8 million cattle and 10 million swine in the Lower South. According to some estimates, the value of southern livestock in 1860 was twice that of that year's cotton crop and roughly equal to the combined value of all southern crops. Regardless of the accuracy of these figures, the point is well made; livestock in the South was far more important economically and culturally than heretofore recognized.

Little scholarship exists concerning the status of livestock in the postbellum period. The devastation of meat-producing herds and stables of riding and draft animals during the Civil War is well documented. Historians disagree as to why herding by the plain folk never regained its prewar prominence. Most likely the answer relates to the crop-lien system and the rapid repeal of laws protecting the running of stock on the open range. Nevertheless, stock raising continued to be a way of life in the piney woods and coastal areas. Drives of cattle to the various Gulf Coast ports continued well into the 20th century. With the advances in veterinary science and the development of disease-resistant cattle breeds, cattle raising has reappeared, after a hiatus of a century, as a major industry in the Lower South in the decades since World War II. While many of the herds and feedlots are operated

Farmer in his Sunday best, feeding his pigs, Benton, Mississippi, 1975

under local ownership, some of the largest ranches are in the hands of national and international corporate investors.

See also MYTHIC SOUTH: / "Crackers"

John D. W. Guice
University of Southern
Mississippi

Donald B. Dodd and Wynelle S. Dodd, *Historical Statistics of the South, 1790–1970* (1973); Lewis C. Gray, *History of Agriculture in the Southern United States*, 2 vols. (1933); John D. W. Guice, *Western Historical Quarterly* (April 1977); Sam B. Hilliard, *Hog Meat and Hoecake: Food Supply in the Old South, 1840–1860* (1972); Terry G. Jordan, *Trails to Texas: Southern Roots of Western Cattle Ranching* (1981); Forrest McDonald and Grady McWhiney, *Journal of Southern History* (May 1975), *American Historical Review* (December 1980); Frank L. Owsley, *Plain Folk of the Old South* (1949). ☆

Mechanization

During the antebellum period the institution of slavery, the ignorance of many farmers, the lack of local markets where farmers could inspect and purchase implements, and the reluctance of plantation owners to invest in quality tools retarded the mechanization of southern agriculture. From the colonial period until the early 19th century, local artisans or plantation blacksmiths usually crafted the tools used in southern agriculture, and few implements were standardized. Technological change came slowly, and, prior to the Civil War, the sickle, cradle scythe, and shovel plow remained basic implements for cultivating and harvesting. By the late 1840s, however, more progressive farmers were beginning to use a variety of improved plows, harrows, and cultivators, many of which had been developed and manufactured in the North. By the mid-19th century better farmers also used horse-powered threshing machines, corn shellers, feed mills, and fodder choppers. After the Civil War an abundance of cheap labor, limited capital, inadequate credit institutions, and the large number of small farms limited technological change in the South. Southern farmers did not use the grain drill, corn planter, or reaper extensively until the late 19th century.

By the early 1880s Louisiana and Texas farmers were applying midwestern wheat-growing technology on their rice lands. Although small fields and numerous drainage ditches slowed mechanization, grain binders enabled rice farmers to harvest 15 acres per day. In the late 1890s some rice farmers experimented with steam traction engines for plowing and used elevators for loading rice into railroad cars and storage facilities.

Sugarcane growers replaced the plow with the disc cultivator during the 1890s and doubled the acreage one man could weed per day. The adoption of the disc cultivator was the most important technological change among sugarcane growers during the last half of the 19th century. By the turn of the 20th century growers also were using slings, hooks, and derricks to lift the sugarcane onto wagons and railway cars. On the eve of World War I cane loading machines were in general use throughout the sugar region.

Further technological change lagged until the 1930s when the Great Depression stimulated agricultural mechanization. At that time many landowners preferred to accept government payments from the Agricultural Adjustment Administration for taking land out of production rather than receive rent or cotton from tenants and sharecroppers. Frequently, that money was used to purchase tractors, milking machines, corn pickers, and grain combines. Bankrupt small farmers also sold their lands to larger, more prosperous farmers, and land consolidation enabled more efficient use of mechanized equipment. World War II stimulated mechanization, because industrial jobs and the armed forces drew men and women away from agricultural work. Southern farmers who could afford to do so responded to resulting labor shortages by using more tractors, combines, peanut pickers, hay balers, and dairy equipment.

While southern farmers gradually made technological adjustments during the 1930s and early 1940s, agricultural engineers and tinkerers worked independently or for farm implement companies to solve the most perplexing technological problem in southern agriculture—mechanization of the cotton harvest. During the 1920s Texas and Oklahoma farmers on the southern Plains began using sleds that stripped the cotton bolls from the plants, but mechanical pickers were not efficient until the International Harvester Company built the first practical spindle picker in 1941. Continued labor shortages after the end of World War II and technological improvements during the 1950s made the mechanical picker a commercial success. By the late 1960s mechanical pickers harvested approximately 96 percent of the cotton crop. Because each two-row picker replaced approximately 80 workers, the machine displaced at least a million men and women in the harvest fields after the mid-1940s.

The development of the tractor hastened the mechanization of southern agriculture. Although only 1 percent of the farmers in the 11 cotton states owned tractors in 1920, the later small, general-purpose tractor produced after the mid-1920s was well suited for the southern farm. Great Plains farmers in Texas and Oklahoma adopted the tractor first, and southern farmers gradually turned to it as well. During World War II Arkansas, Mississippi, Alabama, Georgia, and North and South Carolina farmers increased their supply of tractors by 100 percent. Until the end of World War II, however, the adoption of tractors and other mechanized equipment was a response to a declining labor supply rather than a cause of flight from the land. Even so, by 1945 less than 20 percent of the nation's 2 million tractors were located in the cotton states.

By the mid-20th century the most mechanized southern farms were located on the Yazoo Delta or Basin, the Coastal Plain of Texas, and the southern Great Plains in Texas and Oklahoma. In those areas level terrain, large fields, and few obstructions made the farms ideal for the efficient application of mechanization. By the early 1970s southern farmers had begun to use airplanes to dust their crops with pesticides, and the mechanical tobacco

Driver of a combine thrashing oats, Thomastown, Louisiana, 1940

picker was practical in certain limited economic situations. Mechanical pickers also harvested citrus fruits and eight-row planters seeded the cotton crop. By the late 1970s tractors, combines, corn pickers or picker-shellers, pickup balers, and field forage harvesters were common implements on southern farms, and all major aspects of southern agriculture were mechanized.

Technological change has contributed to the decline of the southern farm population and agricultural work force. Mechanization also has encouraged the consolidation of farms, stimulated a neoplantation movement, and enabled southern farmers to produce more food and fiber than ever before. By so doing, mechanization has helped improve the quality of southern farm life.

See also SCIENCE AND MEDICINE: Technology

R. Douglas Hart
State Historical Society of Missouri
Columbia, Missouri

Gilbert C. Fite, *Agricultural History* (January 1950 and January 1980), *Cotton Fields No More: Southern Agriculture, 1865–1980* (1984); Mildred Kelly Ginn, *Louisiana Historical Quarterly* (April 1940); Lewis C. Gray, *History of Agriculture in the Southern United States to 1860*, 2 vols. (1933); J. Carlyle Sitterson, *Sugar Country: The Cane Sugar Industry in the South, 1753–1950* (1953); James H. Street, *The New Revolution in the Cotton Economy* (1957); Bell Irvin Wiley, *Agricultural History* (April 1939). ☆

Plantations

During the 16th and 17th centuries Englishmen established plantations, also called colonies, in Ireland, Virginia, Bermuda, Plymouth, Massachusetts Bay, Jamaica, and elsewhere. During the 17th century, however, the term *plantation* gradually came to mean an extensive agricultural enterprise where proprietors or managers directed large labor forces in the production of export crops. Thereafter plantations remained colonial only in the important sense of their economic relationship to faraway markets.

Plantations of this sort developed first in North America on the Virginia peninsula between the James and York rivers, the first tobacco kingdom, and then spread throughout Tidewater Virginia and Maryland. As white indentured labor gave way to black slavery in the final decades of the 17th century, plantations in the Chesapeake Bay region came to resemble those that Europeans had earlier founded in the Caribbean and northeastern Brazil. South Carolina was from the 1670s a plantation society concentrating on rice and indigo production. Georgia followed suit during the middle of the next century. The plantations of the Carolina-Georgia Low Country fostered the greatest personal fortunes in the North American colonies at the time of the Revolution, and Virginia planters numbered disproportionately among the ranks of the founders of the Republic. George Washington, Patrick Henry, Richard Henry Lee, Thomas Jefferson, James Madison, and George Mason were all planters.

The westward surge of plantations began early. Thomas Jefferson grew tobacco in Virginia's Piedmont before the Revolution. The culture of upland (short staple) cotton, however, was the incentive for expansion both of plantations and black slavery. Eli Whitney's famous gin, invented in 1793, was rapidly duplicated and deployed. Both old and newly made planters pressed into Cherokee and other Indian lands. Andrew Jackson planted cotton and grew wealthy as a pioneer in the Nashville basin. Huge plantations and fortunes were created early in the Mississippi Delta hinterlands and near Natchez. A mature Cotton Kingdom did not appear, however, until the fierce Creeks and Seminoles were subdued and were moved (with the Cherokees and other tribes) farther west. This agricultural empire stretched in a great crescent from south central Virginia, southwesterly around the Appalachians through the central Carolinas, Piedmont Georgia, the Black Belt of south central Alabama and central Mississippi, up and down the wetlands of the lower Mississippi, and westward into eastern Texas. The latter area comprised a cotton frontier during the 1850s. There were also tobacco (and tobacco-cotton) plantations in Virginia and North Carolina, hemp plantations in central Kentucky, rice and Sea Island (long staple) cotton plantations in the Carolina-Georgia lowlands, and enormous sugar estates in southeastern Louisiana. In addition to these great export staples plantations produced, both for consumption and sale, corn, Irish and sweet potatoes, peanuts, and legumes.

Geographers and historians have characterized the plantation as a frontier institution, a flung-out settlement form tied to and dependent upon "metropolitan" capital, industry, and markets. Metropolises for antebellum planters were the textile manufacturing and financial centers of New England, Britain, and Europe. Agents, or factors, arranged sales and shipment of crops and purchases of both durable and luxury consumer goods for planters, their families, and slaves. Frontier estates were sometimes imposing examples of foreign sophistication. The interior walls of Andrew Jackson's Hermitage, for instance, were covered with French wallpaper, and guests drank from expensive, imported crystal. Some riverside mansions in Mississippi and Louisiana were furnished even more lavishly. Most plantation headquarters were more modestly appointed, however. The typical frontier "big house" probably evolved from a simple open-hallway log or board home, which gradually acquired a second story, a prefabricated portico, and columns, all crudely resembling the neoclassical style.

During the three decades before the Civil War a planter was defined by the number of slaves owned—20 or more—rather than by acres of land possessed or pounds of crops grown and shipped. Labor directly affected the amount of land that might be worked and crops that might be grown. Agriculturists believed that 20 or more slaves enabled farmers to achieve certain economies of scale on good, extensive acreage. By this measure there were not many planters or plantations in the Old South. Of

8,039,000 whites living in the 15 slave states in 1850, only 384,884 owned any slaves at all. Of these, 46,274 possessed 20 or more. Only about 2,500 had 30 or more. Only a handful of "great planters" owned 100 or more slaves. Wade Hampton III, the greatest of all and a Confederate general, held about 3,000 blacks in bondage on plantations in South Carolina and Mississippi.

Historians are agreed that, despite their relatively small numbers, planters largely directed antebellum economic, political, and social life. About half of all slaves worked on plantations, and their products dominated southern exports and conferred power upon planters. States adopted the federal ratio method of counting three-fifths of slave populations in determining representation in legislatures, and taxes on slaves were generally low. It is no wonder that the status of planter was the region's *beau ideal* and that the yeomanry and professional men alike aspired to own plantations.

The Civil War destroyed slavery, but not plantations. Ownership of large entailments persisted. Various historians estimate that about half of all plantations were still held by the same families 15 years after Appomattox. The most dramatic changes wrought by emancipation were in the tenure of labor and the occupancy pattern on plantations. Sharecropping replaced legal bondage in much of the South, and sharecroppers, who were former slaves during early postbellum decades, lived in cabins on subdivided tenant farms, instead of in centrally grouped quarters. What geographers term the *fragmented plantation* was born. Sharecroppers, especially blacks, submitted to nearly as much supervision from owners and overseers as during slave times. Sharecroppers had no rights to crops under their care, and, despite technical and legal differences, their situation resembled that of hired laborers. In districts where whites predominated, fragmented plantations were often worked by white tenants who occupied the higher statuses of share tenant or cash renter, and who tolerated less supervision by planters and their agents. From the 1880s until about 1935, however, thousands of white farmowners and tenants fell into the status of sharecropper, while many blacks fled the countryside. By the 1930s most sharecroppers were white.

Fragmented plantations came gradually and painfully to an end between 1935 and 1955. The boll weevil ruined many cotton plantations, particularly in the older regions where the land, owners, and tenants alike were poorer than elsewhere. Laborers fled, and scattered tenant houses were vacated. New Deal crop reduction and subsidy programs for cotton and tobacco had dramatic results: planters evicted thousands of tenants and then began to invest in labor-saving machinery. As mechanical cotton harvesters, herbicides, and pesticides became available during the 1940s, the reconsolidation of plantations gathered momentum. Sharecroppers became hired workers and then were unemployed, as machines and chemicals performed their wonders. Millions fled the countryside in this new American enclosure movement. Bulldozers finally demolished tenant cabins to clear ever-larger fields.

What emerged from this radical transformation was the neoplantation. Superficially it resembled the antebellum model: the owner-manager's power over labor and equipment was centralized once more; and workers (now but a handful on each plantation) once more lived in centrally grouped housing. Neoplantations are more capital-intensive and less labor-intensive than were earlier ones. On the modern plantation there is little reason or opportunity for the paternalism that characterized antebellum plantations and subsequent sharecropper estates. Present agricultural approaches are altogether different. By 1955 the West (especially California and Arizona) had established ascendancy in cotton production, while much of the old plantation South was abandoning the crop. Cotton still grows in the lower Mississippi Delta districts and in Texas, but typical neoplantations are more likely sown with soybeans, grain, sorghum, peanuts, and increased amounts of corn. During the 1960s innovative planters in Mississippi's Delta counties also adopted rice culture from neighboring Louisiana and Arkansas's Grand Prairie and later developed catfish ponds. Many neoplantations produce beef cattle, others are huge dairy operations, and some specialize in pecans. A few score of former fragmented cotton and corn plantations with poor, sandy soil—many of them in southern Georgia and northwestern Florida—have evolved into hunting preserves that also contain timber.

Most neoplantations differ little from large farms in Iowa or California ranches—except, of course, where peculiarly southern crops such as sugar are grown. The term *plantation* remains applicable because neoplantations are concentrated in the historical plantation region and because use of the word persists.

See also GEOGRAPHY: Plantation Morphology; MYTHIC SOUTH: Plantation Myth

Jack Temple Kirby
Miami University of Ohio

P. P. Courtenay, *Plantation Agriculture* (2d ed., 1980); Francis Pendleton Gaines, *The Southern Plantation: A Study in the Development and the Accuracy of a Tradition* (1925); Lewis C. Gray, *History of Agriculture in the Southern United States to 1860*, 2 vols. (1933); Merle C. Prunty, Jr., *Geographical Review* (October 1955); Arthur F. Raper, *Preface to Peasantry: A Tale of Two Black Belt Counties* (1936); Edgar T. Thompson, ed., *The Plantation: An International Bibliography* (1983). ☆

Poultry

Poultry is a common item in the food consumption patterns of southerners today, and the regional taste for southern fried chicken is one that has persisted for many years. Poultry, especially chicken, has served as a regular but supplementary meat to pork, which dominated southern diets during the 1800s and early 1900s.

Chicken was most common in the diets of well-to-do farmers and was regarded among the less affluent population as a semiluxury item. It was a popular Sunday dish and was often served to visitors, including the local preacher. Humorous tales about the preacher's love for chicken abound in both black and white folklore.

Chickens were kept on practically every farm and often ran loose in the barnyard area. As a result farmers virtually lived with their chicken flock. Chickens could be kept on a minimum of feed and were much more convenient to slaughter and prepare for eating than either pork or beef. Predators such as the fox and the hawk were a constant problem for the farmer's barnyard flock, thus requiring the farmer to keep both his dog and shotgun handy.

Since 1900 the per capita rate of consumption of chicken has increased markedly, outstripping the growth in demand for other meats such as beef and pork. During this period, and especially in recent decades, very important changes have occurred in the production of chickens, and these had an effect on both the economy and culture of the South. A few decades ago the rural population of the South was largely self-sufficient in terms of supplying its chicken and egg needs. Farmers maintained small flocks of chickens for their own use. Often the demand by city dwellers for chickens and eggs was met by farmers who sold excess production to town merchants. This trade furnished butter-and-egg money for farm housewives. Today it is rare indeed to find farm families that produce chickens and eggs. In place of this production system have come the large-scale and highly specialized mass production techniques involving the utilization of the latest technological advancements.

This modern era of poultry production dates from the 1930s; its methods had almost totally replaced the previous production techniques by the 1950s. The modern poultry farmer has one or more chicken houses growing 10,000 to 20,000 birds per house. Ordinarily each batch is grown under contract with large agribusiness firms during a period of 7 to 10 weeks. Market-ready chickens are taken to processing plants for slaughtering, dressing, and packing, and are later transported by refrigerated truck to widely dispersed markets. The poultry industry is characterized by a vertical integration in which an agribusiness firm, either through direct ownership or contract, controls the entire production process. Such firms own processing plants, feed mills, and hatcheries, and contract with farmers to raise the chickens. Because of these arrangements the farmer has little voice in the industry. Some observers label this type of poultry farming a modern version of sharecropping. However, one advantage of this production system to the farmer is that it reduces the capital needed to start poultry farming.

Today a large proportion of southern poultry is produced by farmers who derive only a part of their total income from this source. The chief wage earner may have a full-time industrial or commercial job while the family raises chickens as a supplementary source of income, or chicken farming may be ancillary to other agricultural pursuits. Labor needs of poultry farming are minimal because of the automation of the process. The management of two chicken houses of 10,000 to 20,000 chickens each can usually be accomplished during the evenings and on weekends by family members.

Several of the nation's main poultry-growing areas are located in the South. Northeast Georgia was one of the first areas to begin large-scale commercial chicken production, with Gainesville serving as a processing plant center and location of feed mills and hatcheries. Both northeast Georgia and northwest Arkansas began to develop as poultry centers in the late 1930s and early 1940s. They were followed in the 1940s by centers in south central Mississippi and central North Carolina, and in the 1950s by northern Alabama, around Cullman County. Today a trip through these areas provides visible indications of the industry's impact on the landscape with the long, narrow chicken houses on farms and the specialized feed trucks and poultry-transport vehicles that operate between feed mills, farms, and processing plants.

The emergence of chicken production in these areas largely reflects changing conditions of traditional subsistence farming. Many of these regions were from the beginning of settlement poor farm areas. They were populated by low-income farm families who had lost a previous source of farm revenue from cotton in northeast Georgia, northern Alabama, and south central Mississippi; tobacco in North Carolina; and fruit in northwest Arkansas. Any new source of farm income such as chicken raising was welcomed enthusiastically by these farmers. Local entrepreneurs and agricultural officials were largely instrumental in establishing this industry. J. D. Jewell, for instance, played an important role in establishing production in northeast Georgia. He owned a small feed store in Gainesville in the 1930s and encouraged neighboring farmers to grow chickens, affording him a market outlet for feed and other supplies. Because cash with which to buy baby chicks and feed was seriously limited among farmers, Jewell supplied his customers with credit until their chickens were marketed. However, when the chickens reached the proper age and size for marketing, the farmer had no way to get them to market. Jewell provided transportation to haul the live chickens to urban markets. Later his company became one of the major vertical integrators in northeast Georgia, and he became nationally recognized as an industry leader.

Today southern poultry raisers dominate national chicken production, accounting for 61 percent of total output. The five leading states are Arkansas, Georgia, Alabama, North Carolina, and Mississippi. Four of the five most profitable chicken companies (in 1984) are in the South: Tyson Foods in Springdale, Ark.; Gold Kist, a farm-cooperative business in Atlanta; Holly Farms in North Wilkesboro, N.C.; and Perdue Farms Inc., in Salisbury, Md. Chicken has become the fastest-growing part of the fast-food business, profiting such southern companies as Kentucky Fried Chicken, Church's Fried Chicken, Popeyes, and Bojangles.

J. Dennis Lord
University of North Carolina
at Charlotte

J. Fraser Hart, *Annals of the Association of American Geographers* (December 1980); Sam B. Hilliard, *Hog Meat and Hoecake: Food Supply in the Old South, 1840–1860* (1972); Edward Karpoff, *Agricultural Situation* (March 1959); N. R. Kleinfield, *New York Times* (9 December 1984); J. Dennis Lord, "Regional Marketing Patterns and Locational Advantages in the United States Broiler Industry" (Ph.D. dissertation, University of Georgia, 1970), *Southeastern Geographer* (April 1971); Irene A. Moke, *Journal of Geography* (October 1967); Malden C. Nesheim, *Poultry Production* (1979). ☆

Sharecropping and Tenancy

In the post–Civil War years the plantation landlord and the tenant farmer have been among the most prominent figures in the nation's perception of the South. They have been graphic symbols of the region's ruralism, poverty, and cultural backwardness, and have exemplified the paternalism, exploitation,

Sharecropper family at home in Alabama, 1935

and social-class dimensions of southern agriculture. And, indeed, until the mid-20th century these images reflected the reality of several million southerners whose lives were blighted by crop-lien tenancy.

Tenancy was a response to the disorganization and poverty of southern agriculture following the Civil War. Former slaves and landless whites needed access to land and compensation as laborers, but landlords lacked money for wages. To organize production, landowners allowed these workers to farm plots of 20 to 40 acres on a crop-sharing basis. They also undertook the support of their tenants during the crop season by extending credit for food and living necessities, secured by a lien on their portions of the crop. Often this credit was arranged through rural store owners, or furnish merchants, who were also general suppliers of feed, fertilizer, and implements. Landlords with many tenants, however, frequently furnished them directly, through plantation commissaries. This crop-sharing and lien-financing system was necessitated by the South's dearth of farm-production credit. It reflected the limitations of agricultural technology; this system sustained the large force of unskilled labor that was needed as long as cotton and tobacco remained unmechanized.

Although few of the South's landless farmers were independent cash renters, most were share tenants and sharecroppers. These two levels of tenancy were defined by the farmers' contributions to production, their need for subsistence credit, and how closely they were supervised by landlords. Share tenants often owned mules or equipment and might be able to supply some seed or fertilizer. Their furnishing needs varied, as did their supervision. Accordingly,

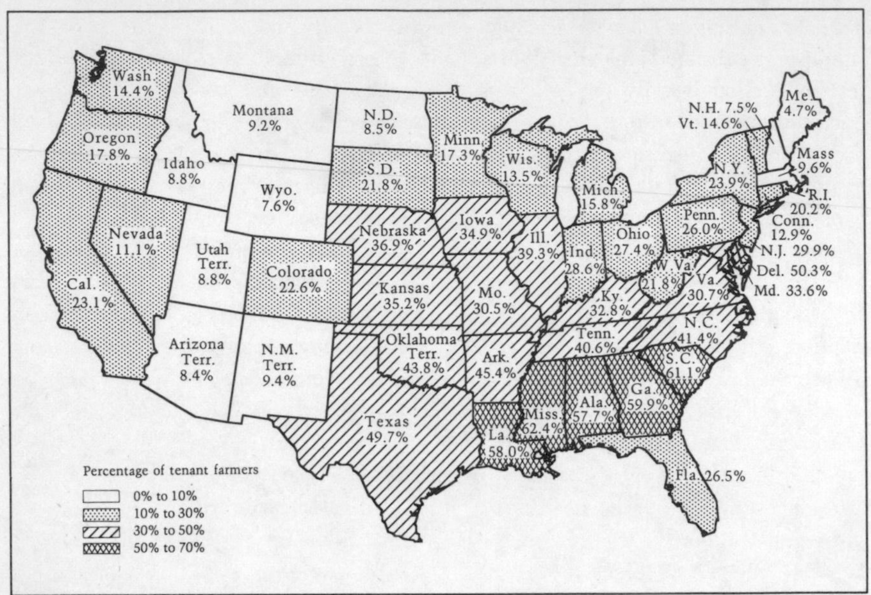

Farm Tenancy, 1890
Source: George B. Tindall, *America: A Narrative History*, 2d ed., vol. 2 (1988).

their portion of the crop could be as much as two-thirds or three-fourths, less, of course, advances and interest. Sharecroppers, on the other hand, usually possessed no workstock or tools and contributed only labor. Dependent on lien credit for nearly all living necessities, and working under much supervision, they ordinarily received no more than half the crop, from which "furnishing" and interest was deducted.

In the chronically depressed southern agriculture of the late 19th century and the early 20th, tenancy increased steadily as many farmers lost their land. It reached its peak in 1930, when the census counted 228,598 cash tenants, 772,573 sharecroppers, and 759,527 other tenants (mostly share tenants) in 13 southern and border states. Tenancy was the dominant pattern in staple-crop production. In 1937 the President's Committee on Farm Tenancy estimated that tenants and croppers were 65 percent of all farmers in the cotton belt and 48 percent in tobacco regions. Approximately two-thirds of southern tenants were white, although among croppers, the lowest tenure group, the numbers of whites and blacks were about equal. Tenants and their families easily comprised nearly half the 1930 southern farm population of 15.5 million.

Southern tenancy was the context for a culture of rural poverty. Tenants and croppers received some of the lowest incomes in America, rarely clearing more than a few hundred dollars per year. Their more common experience, especially in years of low crop prices, was to receive no net income at all because their shares of crops could not cover high-interest furnishing debts. These scant earnings kept rural southerners living right at the bottom of the national scale. Cotton and tobacco tenants lived in the fields they worked in pine-board cabins that lacked window glass, screens, electricity, plumbing, and even wells and privies. Thousands of families were without common household furnishings, stoves, mattresses, or adequate clothing and shoes. The poorest croppers subsisted on a furnish-store diet that relied heavily on salt pork, flour, and meal. Owning no cows or poultry and tending no gardens, they seldom consumed milk, eggs, or fresh vegetables. Malnutrition compounded wretched living conditions to make chronic illness a major feature of rural life, as malaria, pellagra, and hookworm infection stunted the development of children, shortened lives, and lowered the economic productivity of the poor.

Crop-lien tenancy was both exploitive and paternalistic. One of the familiar figures of southern rural lore was the tight-fisted landlord who kept all accounts, charged exorbitant interest on advances, and took over his tenants' cotton for debts. As part of the local power structure, planters were in a position to make whatever settlements they wished, without challenge from poor and illiterate tenants. Perhaps the greatest tragedy of this system was that exploitation was built into it. A landlord who was hard-pressed by mortgage and tax obligations, production costs, and low crop prices, often could not profit without cutting as deeply as possible into his tenants' shares. Moreover, as planters extended credit, they also supervised tenants' farming, leaving the least skilled, especially, with little opportunity to develop competence and self-direction. Tenancy thus bred dependency among the poor.

Tenants had little security on the land. They worked under year-to-year verbal agreements that left landlords free to dispense with their services at settling time. With a great surplus of unskilled labor at hand, planters usually felt little need to hold dissatisfied or unwanted tenants. Most landless farmers were highly mobile, moving as often as every year or two. This transience was socially and economically wasteful; it deprived tenants of any role in their communities and reinforced illiteracy by preventing regular schooling of their children. It destroyed incentives to maintain farm property and contributed greatly to soil erosion.

The southern public's perception of tenancy conformed to traditional American views of poverty, which have been highly judgmental toward the poor. Rural poverty was so pervasive as to be the expected condition of landless farmers. Moreover, tenants and croppers were often seen as unworthy and shiftless people who had neither the ability nor the desire for self-improvement. Yet, at the same time, the assumption frequently expressed in the 1930s was that any ambitious, industrious farmer could work his way up an agricultural ladder, progressing from sharecropping to securer levels of tenancy to small landownership. These persistent views were a major impediment to efforts to reduce rural poverty.

The Great Depression focused national attention on southern tenancy. Ironically this public notice came as the system was beginning to break down. As hard times intensified, many landlords cut their own expenses by abandoning crop sharing, discontinuing furnishing, and converting to wage labor. This trend grew during the New Deal. Under the Agricultural Adjustment Administration (AAA) acreage-reduction contracts decreased labor needs and, in effect, encouraged landlords to dispense with tenants to avoid sharing government payments with them. This impact of the AAA was brought forcefully to public attention after 1935 by the protests of the Southern Tenant Farmers' Union. Tenancy continued as a national issue as the New Deal attempted to alleviate rural poverty through federal relief, the Bankhead Tenancy Act of 1937, and the Farm Security Administration.

In the decades after the 1930s southern agriculture underwent massive changes that swept away tenancy. Mechanization was the most revolutionary development. From the 1930s onward the number of tractors on southern farms increased dramatically, and after World War II the cotton picker came into general use. Landlords employed wage workers to meet their more limited labor needs and discarded outmoded crop-sharing arrangements. Crop and livestock diversification and chemical weed control also made farming less labor-intensive. This transformation of southern agriculture was a major cause of the great postwar exodus of the rural poor from the land and, in many cases, from the region.

See also HISTORY AND MANNERS: New Deal; SOCIAL CLASS: Poverty; Tenant Farmers

Paul E. Mertz
University of Wisconsin
Stevens Point

David E. Conrad, *The Forgotten Farmers: The Story of Sharecroppers in the New Deal* (1965); Charles S. Johnson, Edwin R. Embree, and Will W. Alexander, *The Collapse of Cotton Tenancy: A Summary of Field Studies and Statistical Surveys* (1935); Paul E. Mertz, *New Deal Policy and Southern Rural Poverty* (1978); Arthur F. Raper, *Preface to Peasantry: A Tale of Two Black Belt Counties* (1936); U.S. National Resources Committee, *Farm Tenancy: Report of the President's Committee* (1937); Rupert B. Vance, *Human Factors in Cotton Culture: A Study in the Social Geography of the American South* (1929); Thomas Jackson Woofter, Jr., *Landlord and Tenant on the Cotton Plantation* (1936). ☆

AGRICULTURAL EXTENSION SERVICES

The development of scientific agriculture to increase southern farmer productivity and profits has been crucial. Scientific advancement requires experimentation, which brings both failures and successes, and few southern farmers could afford the risks. In the antebellum period the problem was not serious, however, because the availability of virgin land and cheap labor decreased the costs of soil depletion.

The Civil War marked a turning point in agricultural development. Not only did southern conditions drastically change, but earlier individual and state attempts at scientific agriculture were given a boost by new federal legislation—the Morrill Acts of 1862 and 1890, which provided federal aid to state agricultural colleges, and the Hatch Act of 1887, which funded agricultural experiment stations. In the South much of the early experimentation of the land grant colleges and experiment stations centered on the most important cash crop—cotton.

Researchers soon learned that their work was futile without effective means to communicate their findings to farmers. Thus, a wide variety of extension activities was undertaken, including the publication of bulletins, farmers' institutes and conferences, short courses in agriculture, and agricultural fairs. Such programs still reached only a small number of farmers, usually those who were more literate and in close proximity to agricultural schools.

The spread of the boll weevil and the relative backwardness of agricultural methods increased the need for direct contact with more farmers. The idea of demonstration farms was implemented in 1902 when Seaman A. Knapp was placed in charge of a pilot program that included five model farms in Texas and Louisiana. The effectiveness of taking agricultural instruction to the farmer was recognized in 1914 with the passage of the Smith-Lever Act. This legislation provided the basis for a large-scale, federally sponsored extension program with local farm and home demonstration agents in each county. Significantly, pioneering extension activities at Tuskegee Institute led to the appointment of black agents from the beginning of the program, although they continued to be victims of pay discrimination until the 1960s. By the 1980s the extension network served a declining number of farmers, in part because of U.S. Department of Agriculture policies favoring the growth of agribusiness, but it also administered such programs as 4–H, which reached larger audiences.

Linda O. McMurry
Raleigh, North Carolina

Gladys Baker, *The County Agent* (1939); Jim Hightower, *Hard Tomatoes, Hard Times: The Hightower Report* (1972); H. C. Knoblauch et al., *State Agricultural Experiment Station* (1962); Roy V. Scott, *The Reluctant Farmer: The Rise of Agricultural Extension to 1914* (1970). ☆

BOLL WEEVIL

The cotton boll weevil, *Anthonomous grandis* (Boheman), migrated from Mexico across the Rio Grande River near Brownsville, Tex., in 1892. The weevil's annual fall dispersal carried it to Louisiana in 1903, to Mississippi in 1907, and to the far reaches of the cotton belt in the early 1920s.

By depositing eggs in the cotton square, the boll weevil prevented development of the locks of fiber. Farmers relied on the cultural method—a series of adjustments in growing practices—to reduce the weevil's damage. As farmers adopted parts of this system, especially planting earlier with early maturing varieties, the production figures inched upward, but recovery was usually short of preweevil levels.

During the initial infestation many communities exclusively dependent on cotton underwent boll weevil panics or depressions similar to other economic depressions. When landlords decided not to plant during the coming year, black and white tenants often migrated in advance of the weevil—to the west, north, and east. The weevil, along with industrial opportunities available during World War I, spurred movement to northern cities, as did the severe infestations in Georgia and South Carolina in the early 1920s. The insect, meanwhile, entered southern folklore, as Huddie "Leadbelly" Ledbetter popularized the well-known "Boll Weevil" song, and the town of Enterprise, Ala., in 1919 erected the Boll Weevil Monument to honor the pest that dramatically affected southern life.

Several factors favorable to growing cotton under weevil conditions—drier climate, colder winters, and fertile land—accelerated shifts in cotton production to west Texas, the northern part of the cotton belt, and the Yazoo-Mississippi Delta. Natural and human factors kept some areas out of cotton production long after the weevil's arrival. In Alabama's Black Belt clay-ridden soils prevented early crops. Absentee owners of the old Natchez District no longer wished to risk a cotton crop. The weevil compounded problems of soil erosion and depleted soils in the Piedmont plantation belt of Georgia. The finest of America's cottons, Sea Island, was eliminated.

The agriculturalists who had long summoned the southern farmer to diversify welcomed the weevil as a blessing in disguise. For most farmers, the blessing was indeed well disguised. Basic farm crops, corn and other grains, increased, but supplied little income. The lack of a good marketing system and unfamiliarity with growing, grading, and packing methods beset productive truck farmers. Southerners tried to create markets for peanut oil and sweet potatoes, with little success. Local markets were insufficient for the many who tried dairy farming.

Some boll weevil–induced agricultural developments endured. Farmers of southwest Georgia and southeast Alabama substituted peanuts for cotton. Local plants processed the peanut-fed hogs. Southern farmers converted cotton fields to pasture and upgraded cattle herds—especially in Alabama's Black Belt.

Insecticides, beginning with calcium arsenate in 1919 and followed by a new generation of synthetic ones after World War II, provided some relief. But this increased investment in the crop, along with fertilizers and machinery, brought a shift from extensive planting under the tenant system to planting cotton on the better lands under attentive management.

Cotton continued as an important crop, but the boll weevil destroyed faith in it as a certain source of income and revealed the dangers of reliance on a single crop. Southern farmers and businessmen, mindful that the persistent weevil could strike repeatedly, became more receptive to new crops and industries. Although the boll weevil had some beneficial long-term effects, such present-day interpretations should not overshadow the human plight it caused the tenants and small-farm owners at the bottom of the agricultural ladder.

Douglas Helms
Soil Conservation Service, USDA

Douglas Helms, "Just Lookin' for a Home: The Cotton Boll Weevil and the South" (Ph.D. dissertation, Florida State University, 1977); Walter D. Hunter and Warren E. Hinds, *Mexican Cotton-Boll Weevil*, Bureau of Entomology Bulletin No. 114, S. Doc. 305, 62nd Congress, 2d sess., 1912; Arthur F. Raper, *Preface to Peasantry: A Tale of Two Black Belt Counties* (1936). ☆

COMMUNAL FARMS

Scholarly attention has focused on the large, successful, and well-known communal farms of the Northeast—including those of the Shakers, the Harmony Society, and Oneida. There have been, however, a number of significant communities in the South. The Shakers established Pleasant Hill and South Union in Kentucky in the early 1800s. Nashoba, an interracial Tennessee commune, was founded east of Memphis on the Wolf River in 1825 by Frances Wright, a reformer from Scotland. The name for the community derived from the Indian word for wolf. The experiment lasted until 1828 and was intended as a model society for slaves, whom Wright and her followers purchased and prepared for freedom, and for whites, who lived in a cooperative arrangement based on the ideas of reformer Robert Dale Owen. Wright left Nashoba in 1828 for Owen's New Harmony commune in Indiana, and the Tennessee settlement was gradually phased out. Another notable communal farm was founded by Cyrus R. Teed at Estero, Fla. Its basis was the philosophy of Koreshanity, which claimed to explain the astronomical and religious principles of the universe, and it lasted from about 1900 to 1917.

Clarence Jordon, a Georgia Baptist preacher, conceived the idea for Koinonia Farms, a Christian community that began operations near Americus, Ga., in 1942. The name for the farm came from the Greek word for "fellowship" or "communism," and the intent of its founders was for the community to share its worldly goods. It was to be a religious and a material inspiration to the surrounding impoverished rural areas of south Georgia.

The farm experimented with new scientific techniques for raising poultry and livestock and taught them to other farmers. The farm later successfully grew grapes, pecans, and peanuts, providing an adequate income for the group. Despite its economic success, Koinonia Farms became controversial in the 1950s and 1960s because of the vocal support of its members for racial equality and pacifism. Physical violence and an economic boycott from nearby whites challenged its survival, but it outlasted these threats. The community, which in the early 1980s included about 50 people living at Koinonia, has most recently launched a program to provide low-cost housing to Georgia's rural poor.

In the late 1960s and early 1970s a new wave of community building began. These communal experiments grew out of the counterculture. Many of these latter-day communards were veterans of the civil rights movement, Vietnam War protests, and campus-reform struggles. Of the modern communes in the South, two are especially noteworthy.

The first of these is called Twin Oaks, a commune near Louisa, Va. Inspired by B. F. Skinner's novel *Walden Two* (1948), Twin Oaks was started by eight people committed to the principles of behaviorist psychology. In June of 1967 they moved onto a 123-acre farm purchased from a retired tobacco farmer. Farming supplies food for the group, and their income is supplemented by the sale of handwoven hammocks. Although many other communes have not worked, Twin Oaks is a thriving enterprise in large part because of firm rules on work and cooperation. As of 1983 the community had grown to include some 80 members.

Another intriguing escape from the mainstream of American life is The Farm in Summertown, Tenn., about 80 miles southwest of Nashville. In 1970 Stephen Gaskin led a group of San Francisco hippies from California to this 1,750-acre farm. Like Twin Oaks, The Farm is based on a mixture of idealism and practicality. The Farm has a number of businesses—including a book-publishing company, a mail-order food store, and a CB-repair operation. The Farm has its own international relief organization, called PLENTY, which is recognized by the United Nations. The Farm is organized along the lines of a religious group, following the teachings of Stephen Gaskin, which are based on a combination of Judaeo-Christian ethics and Eastern mysticism. By 1983 The Farm had 950 members in Summertown, making it easily the largest working commune in America. In the future the South may continue to attract more social experiments like communes because of the benign agricultural climate, the relatively low price of land, and the increasingly tolerant attitude of southerners toward alternative life-styles.

See also RELIGION: / Shakers

Angus K. Gillespie
Rutgers University

Stephen Gaskin, *Monday Night Class* (1974); Rosabeth Moss Kanter, *Commitment and Community: Communes and Utopias in Sociological Perspective* (1972); Kathleen Kinkade, *A Walden Two Experiment: The First Five Years of Twin Oaks Community* (1973). ☆

CORN

Corn today has over 500 industrial uses, most of them little known. For nearly three centuries maize or Indian corn had scores of everyday uses in the South, far more than all other crops combined. The area devoted to corn production in the South in 1920 was 46 million acres, the high point in acreage. That represented 44.6 percent of the nation's total. As food it was basic to survival. Southerners, like other rural Americans, ate it as roasting ears, popcorn, hominy grits, cornbread, dodgers, hoecake, johnny cake, pone, mush, fritters, spoon bread, pudding, porridge, parched corn, fish-frying batter, Hoppin' John (with peas), succotash (with beans), cornstarch, and in the Southwest, tamales, tortillas, atole, and posole. They consumed it with meats and sweets and washed it down with corn liquor. This staple grain was on the southern table in some form at practically every meal.

The horses, mules, and oxen that helped to produce crops ate their share of corn, as did the hogs and poultry so vital to southern diets. As animal feed, corn topped all other crops by a wide margin. It was fed green in growing season and as dried grain, fodder, and silage during other months.

Southerners employed corn for nonfood purposes that all but stagger the imagination. They used cobs for pipes, torches, corn shellers, tool handles, jug stoppers, fishing corks, back scratchers, litter, hair curlers, missiles (for the popular corncob fights), salt and pepper shakers (hollowed), knothole plugs, and, above all, kindling. Other Americans certainly used corn products in the same ways, but probably not to the same extent for so long a time as southerners.

Corn, cornmeal, and whiskey served as money to pay millers, weavers, preachers, and taxes, and whiskey was a universal home medicine. Ears of corn were used as darning eggs and as ornaments. Grains served as jewelry and as popcorn Christmas tree strings and were used in games such as bingo and hully gully.

Not to be outdone by the grains they yielded, husks (shucks) had a wide range of uses. They became dolls, dusters, writing paper, weaving material for chair backs, padding for pillows and mattresses, packing for fruits, vegetables, and fragiles, and wrapping for sausages, tamales, ash cakes, and cigarettes. Even silks were useful. Settlers smoked them as tobacco, formed them as hair for dolls, and steeped them to make medicines. Stalks and leaves were adapted for use as scarecrows, bamboo-like fences, thatching, and for erosion stoppage. Fodder became insulation in and outside cabins, and fodder stacks and shocks occasionally served as shelter for families at nights and during bad weather or as places for drunks to sleep off their corn-liquor overdose.

Corn was, without serious rival, the universal plant of the South. Little wonder that southerners fashioned around it a culture of language, literature, poetry, music, art, and humor.

Nicholas P. Hardeman
California State University

Nicholas P. Hardeman, *Shucks, Shoes, and Hominy Blocks: Corn as a Way of Life in Pioneer America* (1981); Sam B. Hilliard, *Hog Meat and Hoecake: Food Supply in the Old South, 1840–1860* (1972); Paul Weatherwax, *Indian Corn in Old America* (1954). ☆

COTTON CULTURE

After the invention of the cotton gin in 1793, cotton spread southwestward. It was cultivated on plantations using slave labor and on small farms. The South produced 2,982,634 bales in 1855 and harvested 4,861,292 in 1859. The Civil War ended slavery, and after a struggle over tenure arrangements, a sharecropping and crop-lien system emerged that absorbed not only former slaves but also increasing numbers of white farmers who had lost their land. Between World War I and the Great Depression, cotton production shifted dramatically to the West. Cotton plantings in the eastern part of the cotton belt declined from 12 million acres in the 1910–14 years to 8.8 million by 1932. Depression and federal acreage-control policies marked the beginning of a new era as planters dismissed sharecroppers, replaced them with wage hands, and later turned to tractors. During World War II the mechanical cotton picker came on the market and pushed millions of farmers off the land. Cotton acreage dropped from 25 million acres in 1940 to 17.5 in 1945. In 1860 approximately two-thirds of all American cotton was produced in the area east of the Mississippi River, but a century later this area was producing only a third of the national total. Currently more cotton is grown west of the Mississippi River than in the old areas of production in the Southeast.

Cotton farmers began their work in the spring, breaking the land, running rows, and planting. After the plants emerged, constant chopping and hoeing continued until lay-by time in midsummer. In the autumn when the bolls matured and opened into fluffy locks, workers picked the seed cotton; then it was ginned for sale. Under slavery, the plantation owner or a white overseer supervised the cultivation of the crop, and a black driver served as field foreman. Some plantations operated a task system that allowed slaves to complete a set amount of work each day, and others used a gang system that required all slaves to work together. After emancipation sharecroppers made verbal contracts during the Christmas season, sometimes received an advance in wages from the landlord, and arranged for credit at a local store. This furnishing arrangement customarily ran only to lay-by time, so sharecroppers had to work at odd jobs to supplement their incomes. At settlement time, much of their share of the crop paid back the exorbitant interest charged by "time" furnishing merchants. Many sharecroppers drifted into a state of peonage, a form of debt bondage that bound them to the land. Croppers moved often, usually within the same community. Most lived in primitive and unsanitary shacks, and the condition of their lives was characterized by illiteracy, poor health, and inadequate food.

In the last decade of the 19th century, the Mexican cotton boll weevil crossed the Rio Grande River and began eating its way northeastward through the cotton belt. All attempts to halt its march failed, but by utilizing cultivation practices developed by the extension service, farmers continued to grow adequate yields. The weevil did not infest western areas as much as the older growing region, and the cost of production in the latter area increased and put farmers in a poor competitive position. As much as any single factor, the weevil hastened cotton's march westward, although mechanization and the lack of a sharecropping system in western areas were also important in the shift.

In the early years of the New Deal, the Agricultural Adjustment Administration (AAA) drastically reduced acreage, and millions of farmers were forced off the land, despite AAA contracts that forbade displacement of tenants. As small owners and sharecroppers attempted to cope with acreage reduction, federal money fueled the drive toward mechanization. Before complete mechanization occurred after World War II, landowners utilized wage laborers to perform the seasonal chopping and picking chores. Many former sharecroppers survived by securing relief from government programs, and large numbers of exfarmers fled to northern cities in search of work and survival.

After 1945, with the perfection of the mechanical picker, there was little need for large numbers of farm workers in the cotton area. The old southern cotton-area farmers could not take advantage of mechanization as well as those of the West. Largely replacing cotton as a southern staple were soybeans, cattle, peanuts, and other crops. Whereas the old cotton culture was highly exploitative, the changes set in motion by the New Deal and by mechanization exacted a high human cost. In some respects it was a mechanical enclosure movement that forced farmers off the land into cities. By 1968 about 94 percent of the cotton crop was machine harvested. The cotton culture that had epitomized the slave and post–Civil War South continued its migration to the West, leaving behind diversified farming on enlarged units. The term *cotton South* became almost solely historical in its meaning.

Pete Daniel
Smithsonian Institution
Washington, D.C

David E. Conrad, *The Forgotten Farmers: The Story of Sharecroppers in the New Deal* (1965); Pete Daniel, *Breaking the Land: The Transformation of Cotton, Tobacco, and Rice Cultures since 1880* (1985); Gilbert C. Fite, *Agricultural History* (January 1980); Eugene D. Genovese, *Roll, Jordan, Roll: The World the Slaves Made* (1974); Donald H. Grubbs, *Cry from the Cotton: The Southern Tenant Farmers' Union and the New Deal* (1971); Henry I. Richards, *Cotton and the Agricultural Adjustment Administration* (1936); Theodore Rosengarten, *All God's Dangers: The Life of Nate Shaw* (1974); James H. Street, *The New Revolution in the Cotton Economy* (1957); Harold D. Woodman, *Journal of Southern History* (November 1977). ☆

DAIRY INDUSTRY

Production of milk and dairy products in the early South differed insignificantly from that in the North. Considerable divergence appeared in the 19th century, though, because of slower urban growth in the South. While the old dairy belt emerged in the North to supply milk for commercially manufactured dairy products in a national market and fluid milk to large cities, southerners haphazardly supplied their towns with fluid milk, made their own butter, and at times bought canned milk and cheese produced in the North.

The dairy picture in the South

changed surprisingly little from the 19th century until about World War II. During that era all across the region many small farmers kept and milked a few, often mixed-breed cows, separated the milk, fed the skim to the hogs, made their own butter, and sold the surplus cream in town or shipped it on the railroad to market. Along with the sale of a few eggs, this trade allowed them a small but steady cash flow. By the 1930s an increasing number of small cheese-manufacturing plants had appeared in the South, and better roads brought motor-truck carriers to pick up whole grade B milk from many small unspecialized producers. Near the towns, dairy specialists milked cows, bottled fluid milk, and sold it to town residents. At the same time, dairymen near larger cities were selling fluid milk to processors who pasteurized it and sold it on the local market.

From World War II onward the growth of highways and urban centers in the South transformed dairy production, processing, and marketing. The small grade B, or manufacturing, milk producer swiftly disappeared, and dairy farming in the South became more specialized than in any place other than California and the Far West. By the 1960s the average cow population of Texas dairy farms was roughly twice that of Wisconsin, a state whose total dairy production dwarfed that of any other state in the Union. During the 1970s efforts toward market rationalization and integration, carried on by large merged milk-producer cooperatives, increasingly blurred distinctions between dairy farming in the South and the rest of the nation.

E. Dale Odom
North Texas State University

Lewis C. Gray, *History of Agriculture in the Southern United States to 1860*, 2 vols. (1933); Thomas R. Pirtle, *History of the Dairy Industry* (1926); John T. Schlebecker, *History of American Dairying* (1967). ☆

FARM SECURITY ADMINISTRATION

During the Great Depression the New Deal administration wrestled with the problem of massive and chronic rural poverty. Between 1935 and 1946 the Farm Security Administration (FSA) was the federal agency that worked to uplift some of America's poorest people.

The FSA began as the Resettlement Administration (RA), created by President Franklin D. Roosevelt's executive order in May 1935. The RA consolidated federal programs for classifying rural land, retiring submarginal farms, and resettling their residents. Also transferred to the RA were rural subsistence homesteads for surplus industrial workers, pilot suburban housing projects, and several cooperative farm communities started with federal relief funds. But the largest responsibility assigned to the new agency was the rural rehabilitation work of the Federal Emergency Relief Administration (FERA). Faced with the urgent needs of destitute farmers, especially southern tenants and sharecroppers, the FERA had attempted to keep them on the land with a combination of production and living credit and close supervision of their farming. Acquiring this rapidly growing program made the RA an antipoverty agency.

The RA's responsibilities expanded in July 1937, when Congress passed the Bankhead-Jones Farm Tenancy Act providing a modest lending program to help tenants buy farms. President Roosevelt assigned this new work to the RA, which was renamed the Farm Security Administration.

Even though the FSA never reached a majority of the poor, and often bypassed the most impoverished, its programs gave substantial aid to many farmers during its peak years of 1937–42. The largest program was always rural rehabilitation. The FSA's 1941 report, for example, indicated loans or grants (typically a few hundred dollars per case) being received by more than 600,000 southern families. County FSA supervisors helped clients write farm- and home-management plans and gave technical advice. At its best this supervision improved the farming skills, self-direction, nutrition, and health of the poor. Among other programs the FSA promoted for low-income farmers were cooperatives for marketing produce and purchasing supplies, joint ownership of breeding livestock or machinery, farm-improvement loans, prepaid health-care plans, and debt-adjustment loans. However, farm-purchase lending under the Bankhead-Jones Act was so poorly funded that the FSA could serve only a few thousand borrowers per year, making little impact on tenancy.

Under southern administrators Will W. Alexander (1936–40) and Calvin B. Baldwin (1940–43), the FSA attempted a comprehensive attack on rural poverty, but its efforts were short-lived. Congress slashed the FSA's funds during World War II and disbanded it in 1946. A few of the FSA's credit functions survive in a successor agency, the Farmers' Home Administration.

Paul E. Mertz
University of Wisconsin
Stevens Point

Sidney Baldwin, *Poverty and Politics: The Rise and Decline of the Farm Security Administration* (1968); Paul E. Mertz, *New Deal Policy and Southern Rural Poverty* (1978). ☆

FERTILIZER

In the 1840s and 1850s an agricultural reform movement occurred in the South as planters and farmers sought some means of restoring their worn-out fields. Farm journals of the period recommended increased use of lime and manures. At the same time superphosphate and Peruvian guano were introduced as commercial fertilizers. By 1860 their use had spread from Maryland and Virginia into the Carolinas and Georgia.

After the Civil War the problems of exhausted land and quick returns on cotton and tobacco crops combined to greatly accelerate the use of fertilizers. To meet this demand the fertilizer industry began to move southward. In 1868 development of the South Carolina phosphate deposits began, and Charleston soon became an important fertilizer

Billboard advertising fertilizer, Laurinburg, North Carolina, 1938

center. In the 1890s new phosphate mines in Florida and Tennessee came into production.

Fertilizer was in most demand for use on cotton, and a mixed product (in 200-pound bags) containing the three principal plant nutrients (nitrogen, phosphorus, and potassium) was popular with southern farmers. Many farmers commonly prepared their own mixtures by combining superphosphate and kainit (a potash salt) with cottonseed meal. The general use of fertilizers had several effects on southern culture. The cotton and tobacco belts were extended into areas where their cultivation was previously unprofitable. The old compost heap was abandoned, and farmers tended to limit cultivation to old upland fields. Commercial fertilizers stimulated intensive farming, particularly in trucking areas, and assured higher yields per acre. Finally, the use of commercial fertilizers was responsible for bringing the fertilizer industry to the South.

During the 1880s the South benefited from the Morrill Act of 1862, which provided for state colleges of agriculture, and later from the Hatch Act (1887), which provided for agricultural experiment stations. Since 1933 the Tennessee Valley Authority (TVA) has operated fertilizer research facilities at Muscle Shoals, Ala., to develop new and improved products and processes. About 64 percent of fertilizers in this nation today are made with technology developed by TVA.

The South continues to supply most of the phosphate, sulfur, and ammonia used in fertilizer production; but vast changes have occurred in the industry during the last 25 years. Consumption of fertilizer, particularly outside the South, has increased greatly. Concentrated fertilizers have replaced traditional low-analysis materials. Bagged fertilizers are being rapidly replaced by fluids and bulk-blended solids. Mechanical handling and custom application is now common. In 1980 southerners used 17.5 million tons of commercial fertilizer (one-third of national consumption), an increase of 83 percent since 1955.

See also ENVIRONMENT: Tennessee Valley Authority

Richard C. Sheridan
Tennessee Valley Authority

Norman L. Haggett and Janice T. Berry, *1980 Fertilizer Summary Data* (1981); Richard C. Sheridan, *Agricultural History* (January 1979); Rosser H. Taylor, *North Carolina Historical Quarterly* (July–October 1953). ☆

FRUIT PRODUCTION

From Florida orange groves to Georgia peach orchards, fruit production has held an important position in the agricultural South. Pecans, tree fruit, citrus, and several types of berries have gained in popularity and status as cash crops, particularly in the past several decades. As row-crop agriculture has become dominated by huge, corporate enterprises, many small-acreage farmers have turned to labor-intensive fruit crops, which yield high returns.

In colonial days wild berries were cultivated and highly prized. Grapes and the native muscadine were used primarily for winemaking, and several hybridized varieties became widely planted. The late 19th century, however, saw a decline in southern vineyards due primarily to the increased competition from California grape production. The industry all but disappeared during the Prohibition era.

With many new "native wine" laws being enacted, a renewed interest in winemaking has appeared in the Southeast, from Virginia all the way to Texas. Government research stations have developed many high-yielding, quality varieties that have replaced the older ones due to their increased sugar content and heavy production. This has, in turn, led to a resurgence in popularity of muscadines for the fresh market, pick-your-own vineyards, and southern wineries.

Bunch grapes, even the French-American hybrids, are highly susceptible to serious insect and disease problems in the Deep South. Much research and interest exist in developing pest-resistant varieties, but, in spite of the good quality of grapes being harvested in the South, no varieties have survived the problems for long. As a result, vinifera and hybrid grapes in the South have yet to become economically competitive with California ones.

Blueberries have become a cash crop in the South. Highbush blueberries generally thrive only as far south as north Arkansas to North Carolina, but many southern research stations have, for several decades, worked with the native rabbiteye blueberries to produce varieties much better adapted and more productive than either highbush or wild plants. Breeding in virtually all southern states has made possible blueberry bushes that have heavy yields of bigger and better-flavored berries. The pick-your-own market has, as with muscadines, helped increase the acreage now planted with blueberries. In addition, blueberry growers' associations in Georgia, Florida, Arkansas, and Mississippi-Louisiana, have begun marketing blueberries by the hundreds of thousands of tons.

A single county in Florida has more acres of oranges than does the entire state of California. By far, most of the oranges, grapefruits, limes, tangelos, and tangerines consumed in the United States (whole or juiced) come from Florida. Until consecutive hard freezes destroyed the last of its citrus groves by the mid-1930s, Mississippi had what was called the "satsuma coast"; the current uppermost limit for citrus has been moved south to the lower half of Florida and south Texas.

Many of the South's citrus groves have been all but ruined by unusually severe freezes in the 1980s, but most of the crops were salvaged through juice processing, and many groves are currently being replanted.

Peaches have been a commercial crop in the South for well over 100 years. Seedling trees were used extensively until such grafted varieties as Belle of Georgia, named in 1875, became available. South Carolina now produces more peaches than Georgia, having sustained less winter damage to its orchards in the last decade. Over 135,000 tons of peaches were harvested from the Southeast in 1984.

Another fruit for the South is the strawberry, with Florida leading its neighbors with over 83 million pounds harvested in 1984. Labor problems are a major limiting factor in strawberry production, with migrant workers performing most of the back-bending harvest work.

Apples and pears have been grown in the mountainous regions of North Carolina, Tennessee, Virginia, and Arkansas for well over half a century. Breeding programs at research stations have produced disease-resistant and mild-climate varieties, which are becoming popular throughout the South. Southern apple production is still concentrated in the cooler regions of the Upper South.

Since the early 1950s small-scale fruit growers have found themselves increasingly under-priced by larger, corporate operations. Migrant workers have constituted the backbone of the large fruit orchards and vineyards, while family farms have had to employ local, seasonal help. Pick-your-own markets, roadside stands, and a general population becoming more interested in the healthful consumption of fresh and processed fruit have all helped develop a stronger fruit industry. With rising long-haul transportation costs and new varieties of fruit adapted for the southern climate, fruit production has become an attractive industry for the South.

Felder Rushing
Mississippi Cooperative
Extension Service

Eugene C. Auchter, *Orchard and Small Fruit Culture* (1929); Norman F. Childers, *Modern Fruit Science: Orchard and Small Fruit Culture* (5th ed., 1975); Economic Research Service, U.S. Department of Agriculture, *Fruit Outlook and Situation* (March 1984); *Fruit South* (1977–79). ☆

GRANGE

In November of 1867 Oliver H. Kelley, the father of the Patrons of Husbandry, returned to Washington, D.C., after a tour of the South and a summer working on a farm in Minnesota. Struck by the despair of southern farmers in South Carolina and Mississippi, Kelley conceived the notion of a national organization for the moral and educational uplift of the agricultural community. The Patrons, commonly called the Grange, pioneered as the first national farm organization and admitted women as equal members. The Grange was also innovative in sending out paid propagandists to spread its gospel. Later radical agrarian organizations in the South admitted women and sent out lecturers.

At first southerners resisted the Grange. Politically, the South was struggling with Reconstruction, and most white farmers feared any organization that originated in the North and especially in Washington, D.C. Moreover, males recoiled at rumors that the Grange advocated women's suffrage. Consequently, the national organization enlisted important men within the southern community to organize the ex-Confederate states and assuage potential white hostility. For example, D. Wyatt Aiken, a well-known southern agriculturalist who edited the *Rural Carolinian* (Columbia, S.C.), served as National Lecturer to the South; John T. Jones of Arkansas, who served as Worthy Master of the National Grange (1876–77), recruited in Texas and Tennessee; and A. J. Vaughan of Mississippi traveled for the Grange in Louisiana, Arkansas, and Mississippi. These organizers, all ex-Confederate officers, were closely identified with the end of Reconstruction and the New South.

The Grange, unlike the later Farmers' Alliance, grew from the top down and was not a grass-roots organization. It entered South Carolina and Mississippi in 1872 and eventually claimed, in 1875, 228,000 members throughout the ex-Confederate states. The organization endorsed typically agrarian aims. In the new state constitutions, after Reconstruction, its members supported such goals as financial retrenchment and railroad regulation. The organization, although technically not political, tended to be composed of traditional Democrats, who feared that a third party would either perpetuate, or bring back, Republican political successes. The Grange leadership supported the Ku Klux Klan and was able to attract few if any black members to its Council of Laborers, a separate organization created for blacks.

The appeal of the Grange to the South was economic and not political. Local and state affiliates formed economic cooperatives throughout the southern states, which extended credit to their members—local stores, warehouses, gins, insurance companies, and individual agents. When the price of cotton did not increase, these overextended and underfinanced cooperatives collapsed. Their demise hastened that of the Grange, and by 1878 the organization was defunct in most of the South.

See also SOCIAL CLASS: / Farmers' Alliance

Robert A. Calvert
Texas A&M University

Solon J. Buck, *The Granger Movement, 1870–1880* (1913); Robert A. Calvert, "Search for Identity: The Grange in the Southwest" (Ph.D. dissertation, University of Texas, 1967); D. Sven Nordin, *Rich Harvest: A History of the Grange, 1867–1900* (1974); Theodore Saloutos, *Farmer Movements in the South, 1865–1933* (1960). ☆

KNAPP, SEAMAN A.

(1833–1911) Agricultural reformer.

Seaman Asahel Knapp brought many experiences to his goal of improving southern agriculture. As editor, college president, essayist, teacher, and organizer, he acquired the skills necessary to secure acceptance of his most important idea—the Farmers' Cooperative Demonstration Work program.

Reared in Essex County, N.Y., Knapp graduated from Union College. Acting upon a physician's advice to seek outdoor activities, he moved to Iowa in 1866 and began a lifelong study of agriculture. As professor and president of Iowa State College (now University), he urged farmers to adopt scientific farming practices. Knapp also edited the *Western Stock Journal and Farmer*, emphasizing the use of better livestock and the diversification of crops. In 1885 he became head of the North American Lumber and Timber Company and moved to Louisiana. For the next decade he convinced farmers that rice could be grown by using modern agricultural practices. In 1898 Knapp joined the U.S. Department of Agriculture, which sent him to Japan where he discovered a rice strain more suitable to America's mechanized demands.

Panic struck Texas cotton farmers in 1903 as the boll weevil devastated wide areas. Knapp's effort to combat this insect gained for him a national reputation and set into motion an agricultural program that promised hope for the South. Backed by financial guarantees from local citizens to compensate for any losses, Knapp persuaded farmers to try methods on their own lands that few had been willing previously to employ. They began using crop rotation, deeper plowing, better livestock, diversification, improved seed selection, and fertilizers. Initially, 7,000 to 8,000 farmers joined the program. The results were impressive. Cotton yields increased 50 to 100 percent over yields on farms using older methods. The boll weevil remained, but Knapp's ideas offset losses from the insect and the Farmers' Cooperative Demonstration Work program was born.

Impressed by Knapp's success, the U.S. Department of Agriculture and later the General Education Board provided funds to spread the program throughout the region. The General Education Board's commitment stemmed from its belief that as the economic status of rural taxpayers increased, better schools would result. Farmers' Cooperative Demonstration projects also contained educational programs including boys' and girls' farm groups—the forerunners of the 4–H clubs.

By the time of Knapp's death in 1911, the Farmers' Cooperative Demonstration Work program was firmly established in the South. A fitting tribute to Knapp's efforts occurred in 1914 with the passage of the Smith-Lever Act, which incorporated the Farmers' Cooperative Demonstration Work ideas into national law.

See also EDUCATION: / General Education Board

Joseph A. Coté
University of Georgia Library

Rodney Cline, *The Life and Work of Seaman A. Knapp* (1936). ☆

NAVAL STORES

The naval stores industry, whose principal products were tar, pitch, and turpentine, derives its name from the use of these products for waterproofing the rigging and hulls of early wooden sailing vessels. The industry was based on the exploitation of the pine woods for resinous juices and is one of the oldest industries in the South. It was developed at Jamestown in 1608 but is associated especially with North Carolina because of the highly resinous long-leaf pine (*Pinus palustris*), whose natural habitat is the approximately 100-mile-wide Coastal Plain from Virginia to Texas.

Until 1835 the people of North Carolina were often referred to, somewhat derisively, as "tar, pitch, and turpentine folk." At the time of the American Revolution, North Carolina produced in value three-fifths of all the naval stores exported from the continental colonies. The naval-stores industry continued throughout the antebellum period, and its uniqueness ultimately bequeathed to the state and its people the nickname "Tar Heels."

Tar was produced by a process of dry distillation in an earthen kiln of pieces of dead long-leaf pine. Lengths of dead wood, called lightwood, omnipresent in the forest, were gathered, split into short pieces, placed in a kiln, covered with earth, and subjected to a slow fire that forced out the resinous matter. The tar was dipped from a pit outside of the kiln and poured into barrels. Pitch was obtained by boiling tar to a thicker consistency.

After 1820 production of tar declined, and by 1835 the production of turpentine and its derivatives, spirits of turpentine and rosin, became the main focus of the industry. This developed from improved processes of distilling and from new uses for spirits of turpentine and rosin. Spirits of turpentine was used as a paint thinner and preserver of wood, but after 1835 it was used also as a solvent in the burgeoning rubber industry, particularly as an illuminant. Camphene lamps were the chief form of light in homes and businesses after the decline of whale oil and prior to the development of kerosene. Camphene (spirits of turpentine mixed with alcohol) provided a bright light, was relatively inexpensive, but was highly inflammable. Rosin, a residue from distilling, found new uses in the manufacture of soap, lamp black, ink, and in sizing paper for printing.

With the development of the second phase of the industry, planters entered the business on a large scale, employing slave labor. Once trained in turpentine operations, blacks preferred turpentining to other forms of farm labor because it was based on the task system and they were somewhat more independent in their work. One man could attend a "crop" of 10,000 boxes spread over 50 to 100 acres of land. The industry required a number of specialized workers: "boxers" cut holes in the base of the tree as a container for the resin; "chippers" periodically reopened the wound in the tree above the box to increase the flow of resin; "dippers" removed the resin from the boxes every 10 days; distillers refined the product at a nearby distillery into spirits of turpentine and rosin; and coopers made barrels for the products.

With the development of this phase of the industry, North Carolina's economy boomed. Until the Civil War the state remained the preeminent naval-stores producer, with production of all forms of naval-stores products valued in 1860 at approximately $12 million.

A turpentine orchard was exhausted in 5 to 10 years of cultivation, and the industry was necessarily migratory. In the post–Civil War period it spread rapidly southward into South Carolina and the Gulf states. The exploitation of the long-leaf pine forest of the Deep South between 1870 and 1920 was one means by which southerners recouped their capital after the war. Factors in Savannah, Jacksonville, Pensacola, and Mobile obtained control of large tracts of pine land and controlled the trade. They leased timber to operators, advanced the capital in the form of goods and tools, and subsequently marketed the products. Savannah became the leading naval-stores port from 1880 to 1920 and continued to set the world price of naval stores until 1950.

In the surge southward North Carolina procedures were followed, and skilled turpentine workers were sought from the Carolinas. Sometimes entire communities of people, plus their household goods, cattle, cats, dogs, chickens, and other property, were transported by train to Georgia, Alabama, or Mississippi. A new community was born in the piney woods of the Deep South, complete with dwellings, distillery, commissary, and a combination church-school. The overseer was operations supervisor, enforcer of law and order, director of the commissary and distillery, and physician. It was a primitive, isolated, lonely, destructive, and unique way of life. In approximately two generations, from 1870 to 1930, most of the original stands of long-leaf pine, covering 130,000,000 acres, were consumed.

The industry underwent little change until the 20th century when the imminent exhaustion of the timber supply prompted the use of clay and metal cups to receive the resin and avoid the premature destruction of the trees. Producers were reluctant to change methods until forced to do so in 1908 by the factors. The federal government attempted to improve techniques and quality by establishing a Naval Stores Experiment Station at Olustee, Fla., in 1932, and by providing a cost-sharing subsidy to producers after 1936.

In the post–World War II period the

development of the sulphate process for making paper led to the production of turpentine and rosin as by-products, and the old man-and-axe turpentine industry fell prey to the more efficient competition of modern chemistry and chainsaw technology. Instead of weekly trips to the woods to chip the trees, the operator removed the entire tree, transported it to the mill, and mechanically and chemically separated it into its component products for subsequent use. Between 1967 and 1972 the federal government liquidated its stocks of naval stores, ceased its subsidy, and in 1973 closed the Olustee Station. Like the village blacksmith, the trail-driving cowboy, and the one-horse shay, the "turpentine man" had had his day.

See also ENVIRONMENT: / Lightwood; SOCIAL CLASS: / Timber Workers

Percival Perry
Wake Forest University

Charles C. Crittenden, *The Commerce of North Carolina, 1763–1789* (1936); Thomas Gamble, ed., *Naval Stores: History, Production, Distribution and Consumption* (1920); Percival Perry, "Naval Stores" (Ph.D. dissertation, Duke University, 1947), *Journal of Southern History* (November 1968). ☆

PEANUTS

Peanuts, *pinders*, *groundpeas*, and *goobers* are names applied to a nutritious food that has been a part of southern culture since colonial times. Groundpea is most descriptive, as the plant is a legume and belongs to the pea family, botanically known as *Arachis hypogaea*. Peanuts were known in South America around 2,800 years ago. Spanish explorers carried them to Spain in the 16th century, and traders carried them to Africa. Peanuts possibly arrived in the South on slave-trading vessels, which carried them as food for slaves. The Congo name for peanuts, *nguba*, became *goober* in the South.

Originally produced by slaves and free blacks for local use and sale, peanuts were exported from South Carolina soon after the Revolution. In the antebellum period they were grown locally in most southern states, but Wilmington, N.C., was the principal commercial market from 1830 to 1860. Nicholas N. Nixon of New Hanover County was the largest producer and promoter of scientific cultivation. Lack of commercial development in other southern areas was due in part to competition from cotton and in part to the tedious hand labor required in peanut production.

The Civil War created a national market for peanuts. Soldiers of both armies fighting in Virginia found locally grown peanuts a portable, nourishing food, confirmed by the Civil War song "Eating Goober Peas." Soldiers who returned home wrote to Virginia for more peanuts, and the commercial industry was born. Between 1865 and 1868 production tripled each year, and the 1869 crop was estimated at over 600,000 bushels. From 1868 to 1900 Norfolk was the peanut capital of the United States and was succeeded after 1900 by Suffolk, Va.

For 30 years after the Civil War peanuts, roasted in the shell, were a treat sold by street vendors. Boiled peanuts were a delicacy associated with cotton-picking and -ginning season. Neighborhood "peanut boilings" were a form of social intercourse in southern communities. Farmers in the Lower South planted peanuts for fall fattening of swine, a practice known in Georgia as "hogging off."

In the decade from 1889 to 1899 commercial production and consumption of peanuts increased over 300 percent. George Washington Carver's research in the 1890s revealed their high nutritional value as food and over 300 uses for peanuts. Devastation to the cotton crop by the boll weevil after 1905 persuaded farmers to change to peanuts. Increased mechanization between 1900 and 1910 reduced labor costs and increased production and consumption.

From 1899 to 1919 peanut production increased eightfold, and World War I established peanuts as a continuing factor in the southern economy. After World War II production became highly mechanized. Peanuts today are the ninth most valuable farm crop in the United States, valued at over $1 billion, with a record 1981 crop of 3.98 billion pounds. Seven states dominate production, with Georgia producing almost one-half, followed by Alabama, North Carolina, Texas, Virginia, Oklahoma, and Florida. Four major types are produced: larger kerneled Virginias, the medium-sized Runner in the Lower South, small Spanish peanuts in Texas-Oklahoma, and Valencias in New Mexico.

The United States makes greater use of peanuts for food than any other country, with annual consumption of nine pounds per person. Two-thirds goes into peanut butter, salted and roasted peanuts, and confectionary products. The remainder is exported or crushed for oil and animal feed. Boiled peanuts are still particularly identified with rural areas of the South, found for sale at roadside stands and eaten as a plain snack. The United States's production of peanuts today is only 10 percent of world production, but accounts for more than one-third of world exports, principally to Canada, Europe, and Japan. Except for the period from 1942 to 1948, production has been controlled since 1934 by various regulations of the U.S. Department of Agriculture.

Percival Perry
Wake Forest University

Frank Selman Arant, ed., *The Peanut, The Unpredictable Legume* (1981); F. Roy Johnson, *The Peanut Story* (1977). ☆

PECANS

Among the various images that summon to mind the South, pecans take first place in the category of edible nuts. When European settlers first arrived in the New World they found black walnuts, hickory nuts, chestnuts, chinquapins, and pecans growing wild in the South. All of these, except the chestnut (killed by a blight around 1920), continue to grow, but only the pecan is commercially important. The pecan is synonymous with the South because its natural habitat is the nine southern states from the Carolinas to Texas. Because of the high quality of the nut meat, the quantity of pecans produced annually, and the relative ease of propagating improved varieties, the pecan has become the "queen of nuts" in the United States. It is, moreover, the fifth most important nut tree in the world, and the southern states are the only substantial producers other than Mexico.

More than one-half the total crop of pecans comes from wild and seedling trees, principally in Texas, Oklahoma, and Louisiana. The region from South Carolina to Louisiana is important for improved varieties, developed since 1890, with Georgia the chief producer. Seedlings are as flavorful as improved varieties, but yield of the latter is twice as great. Production is shifting toward the Southwest (New Mexico) with concentration in larger orchards, increasing mechanization, and preservation by cold storage. Although the number of individual pecan farmers is decreasing, the number of trees bearing and being planted is increasing.

From approximately 1 million pounds in 1900, the pecan crop increased to an average of 10 million in the 1920s; to 20 million in the early 1930s; to 40 million by the late 1930s; and to 60 million around 1945. Since 1960 the average annual crop has approximated 220 million pounds, valued at over $74 million. Great fluctuation in yields and price occur because of the tree's tendency to produce larger crops biennially. Since 1949 the federal government and growers' cooperative associations have attempted to stabilize prices.

Currently 94 percent of pecans are marketed commercially in shelled form. The largest users are bakeries (36 percent of the total), suppliers of unsalted retail packages (24 percent), confectioners (19 percent), and ice cream makers (6 percent). Fewer than 40 firms dominate marketing.

Ground pecan shells have found numerous uses: as mulches for plants and as poultry litter; as filler in feeds and fertilizer; as abrasives in soap and polishes; and as filler in plastic wood, including artistic use in molded figures of birds and animals.

Pecans have a long association with southern life. Many Deep South residents plant pecan trees in the yard because the trees are both ornamental and productive. Pecans have contributed extensively to the culinary aspects of southern life, from pralines, which appeared in Louisiana as early as 1762, to recipes for cakes, notably fruit cakes, for which Claxton, Ga., is famous; in the ubiquitous pecan pie; in cookies; in salad, meat, and bread recipes; as roasted- and salted-nut treats for special occasions; or when consumed directly from the shell around the family hearth at evening, especially as a tradition of the Thanksgiving and Yuletide seasons.

Percival Perry
Wake Forest University

USDA, *Agricultural Statistics* (annual); Jasper G. Woodroof, *Tree Nuts: Production, Processing, Products* (1967). ☆

PEST CONTROL

Temperate climates and continuous planting made staple crops susceptible to numerous pests and diseases. In the 19th century farmers tried any number of means and substances to destroy or repel insect pests. Southerners with a mechanical bent applied their talents to devising machines to collect pests. Under the plantation system, labor-intensive methods were sometimes feasible. To drive rice birds away, slaves stationed on platforms fired old muskets, snapped noisemaking plaited whips of white oak, or laid carrion about the field borders to attract buzzards that the birds mistook for hawks. Cotton growers carried torches through fields to attract and destroy moths of cottonworms. Hand picking crawling insects was a well-known and often-used method where effective. The extensive cultivation of staple crops on low fertility soils generally made labor-intensive pest control unprofitable. Arsenical compounds such as London purple and Paris green were the main insecticides for chewing insects in the late 19th and early 20th centuries, but they were generally too expensive to compensate for the increased production. However, on valuable fruit crops, Bordeaux mixture became a standard poison.

Plant diseases, often soil borne, plagued crops, especially on the Coastal Plain. Tobacco growers found, as had ancient farmers, that rotating crops provided some relief. In 1892 a scientist at the Alabama Agricultural Experiment Station, George F. Atkinson, first described cotton wilt and its transmission. The notion of observing and selecting wilt-resistant varieties of plants probably occurred to many farmers, but some of the first scientific work in selection was done by a U.S. Department of Agriculture scientist, W. A. Orton, on Sea Island cotton in South Carolina beginning in 1899. The first wilt-resistant Sea Island cotton, Rivers, became available in 1902, and the first upland variety, Dillon, followed in 1905. Insect-transmitted diseases such as malaria brought debilitation; yellow fever epidemics brought death and the disruption of trade and social life. In a regional sense, the diseases—or fear of them—contributed to poor land use by discouraging settlement of the river bottoms and deltas in favor of the erosion-susceptible hills. Josiah Nott of Mobile, Ala., recognized that mosquitoes carried yellow fever, but he did not supply the scientific proof. Later discoveries enabled cleanup and spraying activities to eliminate breeding pools.

The 20th-century southern cattle industry rests primarily on eliminating the Texas fever–carrying cattle tick. The tick prevented improvement of southern herds because imported purebreds succumbed to the fever. It deprived cattlemen of northern markets where southern cattle were shunned. In the South cattle brought one-half the price of cattle in tick-free states. When a combination of federal quarantines and state-mandated dipping laws started in 1906, the South was losing an estimated $40 million annually. Of the infested 725,565 square miles, 312,012 had been cleaned and released from quarantine by 1917. The pest was confined to the Texas border by 1943. With the possible exception of fence laws, it was the most pervasive intrusion of state powers into the activities of farmers yet. Some farmers displayed their displeasure by dynamiting dipping vats. Tick riders now patrol the Mexican border to prevent reintroduction.

Alterations in growing methods provided some relief in the early 1900s from the boll weevil, which threatened southern cotton from the 1890s on, but farmers still hoped for an effective insecticide. A University of North Carolina graduate, William C. Piver, formulated calcium arsenate in 1912. It rapidly became the primary boll weevil poison until it was replaced after World War II. Scientists at USDA's Tallulah, La., laboratory pioneered in the use of airplanes for crop dusting. One crop-dusting company based in Monroe, La., evolved into Delta Airlines, and the company's stockholder meetings are still held in Monroe. Yazoo-Mississippi Delta farmers were often receptive to agricultural innovations, and the airplane was no exception. They were the first to use aerial crop dusting on a wide scale. Southern manufacturers provided the animal-drawn equipment for earthbound insect chasers.

World War II accelerated herbicide research that would change agriculture significantly. The South, like other agricultural areas, accepted 2-4D as a herbicide to eliminate weed competition. As more selective herbicides became available, they reduced weed-control costs and gradually eliminated much of the hoeing and chopping. The prospect of control with herbicides made southerners more receptive to introduced grasses for conservation and pasture.

A group of synthetic organic insecticides that killed a broad spectrum of insects became available in the late 1940s and early 1950s. Unlike the arsenical insecticides that had to be ingested, the organochlorine and organophosphate ones killed on contact. As per-acre cotton production increased, the share of insecticide treatment as a cost of production decreased. Insecticides became an integral part of the mechanization of agriculture. Farmers, bankers, and other creditors viewed the pesticides as an umbrella of insurance to protect other investments in the crop—machinery, land, fertilizer, and improved seed. Too often, farmers sprayed on a schedule without regard to insect infestation levels. During the 1970s cotton consumed one-half the insecticides used in the United States. The South accounted for two-thirds of the insecticides used. The South was also the major regional user of nematocides and defoliants.

Cotton insect control has not been without problems and controversies. In the early 1950s the boll weevil became immune to one of the chlorinated hydrocarbon insecticides, benzene hexachloride. Also, the so-called broad-spectrum insecticides killed friend and foe alike. With the demise of natural parasites and predators, incidental cotton pests came to the fore. The most striking example occurred in the Rio Grande Valley in Texas. Predators and parasites controlled the budworm, but the budworm became resistant to the organophosphorous insecticide used on the boll weevil. The insecticide also killed the parasites and predators of the budworm, releasing destructive budworm populations on the valley's cotton crops.

Faced with increasing problems of insect immunity, entomologists looked to eliminating insects from an area as a solution. As in the case of the cattle tick, the life history of an insect occasionally, but not often, provided the opportunity for a single effective control method or the possibility of early elimination. Early destruction of cotton stalks and plowing provided the means to control the pink boll worm in Texas, when farmers chose to use it on a community basis. A method of elimination employed has been sterilizing male insects by irradiation and then releasing them into the insect population. The successful elimination of the cattle screwworm from Curacao in 1954 led to the successful implementation of the technique in the Southeast in 1959. In 1980 the screwworm was eliminated from the United States. Release of sterile males has been utilized as a technique, along with insecticides and lures, in eliminating the Mediterranean fruit fly from Florida. Mississippi and North Carolina hosted USDA pilot projects to eliminate the boll weevil.

Despite these successes insects persisted as an important limitation on crop production. The methods to deal with them moved from being solely the concern of farmers and agriculturalists to matters of public debate and policy. During the two decades since the publication of Rachel Carson's *Silent Spring* (1962) the debates have intensified. The controversy over the areawide programs using insecticides, such as the boll weevil project in North Carolina, and fire ant control with mirex, are but two examples. Traditionally in the South, any agricultural or industrial development that promised to raise incomes and alleviate chronic poverty went unquestioned. Southerners are now more often questioning the balance between benefits and costs in environmental terms.

Early problems with resistance and environmental concerns led to research efforts emphasizing a myriad of complementary control measures that reduced reliance on insecticides. The integrated pest-management approach stressed cultural controls, biological controls, alternate plant varieties, trap plants, insect growth regulators, behavioral-modification chemicals, and timely applications of chemical insecticides. Monitoring of insect populations, or scouting, was essential to reducing unnecessary sprayings.

Some recent developments promised safer and more effective controls: 10 species of sweet potato plants have been selected for resistance to insects; vetch grown under pecan trees harbored predators of pecan pests. After the citrus black fly arrived in Florida, entomologists imported predators from the Rio Grande Valley to control it. Synthetic pyrethoids became the primary cotton insecticide, and residue problems have been lessened because only one-tenth the volume of previous insecticides was required for control.

Douglas Helms
Soil Conservation Service, USDA

Animal Diseases, Yearbook of Agriculture, 1965 (1965); Dale G. Bottrell and Perry L. Adkisson, *Annual Review of Entomology* (1977); Thomas R. Dunlap, *DDT: Scientists, Citizens, and Public Policy* (1981); *Farmer's World, Yearbook of Agriculture, 1964* (1964); Lewis C. Gray, *History of Agriculture in the Southern United States to 1860*, 2 vols. (1933); Douglas Helms, *Agricultural History* (January 1979, January 1980); *Insects, Yearbook of Agriculture, 1952* (1952); John H. Perkins, *Insects, Experts, and the Insecticide Crisis: The Quest for New Pest Management Strategies* (1982); *Plant Diseases, Yearbook of Agriculture, 1953* (1953); John T. Schlebecker, *Whereby We Thrive: A History of American Farming, 1607–1972* (1975). ☆

POE, CLARENCE HAMILTON

(1881–1964) Agricultural journalist.

The life of North Carolina journalist Clarence Hamilton Poe affords insight into the evolution of southern farming from the 1890s into the 1960s. Beginning in 1897 as a "printer's devil" for the Raleigh-based *Progressive Farmer*, he achieved national prominence first as editor, then as owner—positions he held until his death. In the process he built the *Progressive Farmer* into the largest farm journal in the United States. Today it continues to be one of the nation's most significant farm publications.

Using the *Progressive Farmer* as a podium, Poe championed a myth long dominant in southern history—that agrarian life was morally and culturally superior to other types of existence. Poe believed that small, family-owned farms engendered unique cultural and character-building traits. Farm life developed strong, independent individuals with a respect for nature, a sense of community, a dedication to family, a clear understanding of life, a reverence for the earth, and a devotion to God. The farmer tilling the soil, with devoted wife at home rearing the children, created a society superior to that of northern cities where a modern industrial system robbed labor of its dignity and where unrest and half-suppressed rebellion were constant undercurrents.

Poe feared, however, that backward southern farming methods would doom that agrarian lifestyle. Accordingly, he advocated such changes as improved educational facilities, the creation of agricultural cooperatives, and the diversification of farming. With these reforms Poe envisioned idyllic communities "untouched by town influences" where farmers would own and operate grain elevators, livestock associations, and rural credit organizations. Community life would center around educational, religious, social, and intellectual activities. Successful farmers could purchase their own homes and fields and thereby end absentee landlordism. Finally, these communities would remain small, avoiding the problems associated with cities and towns.

Poe's advocacy of the preservation of a supposed superior southern agricultural life underscores one of the region's most persistent myths. Reality, however, was much different. Sharecropping and tenant farming dominated the South throughout the late 19th and early 20th centuries. Eventually southern farming did change, but not because of Poe's influence. Rather, New Deal legislation favored large agricultural farm units, while World War II uprooted untold numbers of farmers. In the 1950s Poe reluctantly concluded that the family farm was a thing of the past—but he still believed in the superiority of rural life.

Joseph A. Coté
University of Georgia Library

Clarence Hamilton Poe, *How Farmers Co-Operate and Double Profits* (1915), Papers, North Carolina Department of Archives and History, Raleigh; *Progressive Farmer*, 1899–1964. ☆

PROGRESSIVE FARMER

The first issue of *Progressive Farmer* appeared 10 February 1886. Colonel Leonidas L. Polk, a former Confederate officer and a farmer from Anson County, N.C., conceived the newspaper, which later became a monthly magazine, as a forum for promoting the goals of a better rural way of life, a more scientific agriculture, and an improved educational system for farm people. The *Progressive Farmer* became a successful North Carolina institution whose efforts led in the early 1890s to a reorganization of that state's department of agriculture and the founding of a new agricultural college, North Carolina State University. Polk, meanwhile, became president of the Farmers' Alliance and North Carolina's first agricultural commissioner.

Polk died in 1892, and Clarence Poe and four colleagues bought *Progressive Farmer* in 1903 for $7,500. Poe was a self-educated farmboy who, as editor of the magazine and a leader in the country life movement, helped to transform southern rural life. Tait Butler, a veterinary medicine professor at Mississippi State University, also contributed to the shape of *Progressive Farmer*. He began publishing a rural life newspaper

Farmer's son in Carroll County, Georgia, 1941

called *Southern Farm Gazette* in 1895, sold it in 1898, and joined Poe's editorial team on *Progressive Farmer* in 1908. Together they purchased *Southern Farm Gazette* and made it the basis for a new western edition of *Progressive Farmer*. The magazine's headquarters moved from Raleigh, N.C., to Birmingham, Ala., in 1911, and the staff was publishing five locally oriented, regional editions by 1928.

Tait Butler's son Eugene became an assistant editor in the Memphis office of *Progressive Farmer* in 1917 and eventually replaced Clarence Poe as president of the Progressive Farmer Company in 1953. Monthly circulation of the magazine hit 1,400,000 in 1959, although it had declined to 850,000 by 1986. The Progressive Farmer Network provides agricultural news to 50 radio stations. Under Butler the magazine's "Country Living" section was expanded into a separate periodical, *Southern Living*. Time Inc. bought Southern Progress Corp., the parent company of *Progressive Farmer*, in 1985.

Charles Reagan Wilson
University of Mississippi

Progressive Farmer, 1899–1964. ☆

RICE CULTURE

As the Carolina and Georgia rice culture made adjustments to post–Civil War labor demands and farmers along the Mississippi River started growing rice using labor-intensive methods, a highly mechanized rice culture developed in the southwest Louisiana prairie. The completion of the transcontinental Southern Pacific Railroad in the early 1880s opened the area, and real estate promoters encouraged midwestern farmers to settle there. These transplanted midwesterners discovered a similarity of Cajun Providence rice to wheat and adapted wheat binders to the soggy rice fields. After several dry years in the early 1890s wilted Providence stands of rice, canal companies organized to furnish water while other farmers dug wells for irrigation. By the turn of the century this highly mechanized rice culture eclipsed the troubled East Coast and Mississippi River growing areas.

The prairie stretched into Texas, and farmers there utilized the same irrigation and growing principles as their Louisiana neighbors. In the early part of the 20th century Arkansas prairie farmers discovered technology and started growing rice. From the beginning these rice farmers utilized the latest machinery, and by World War I many owned binders, tractors, threshers, and irrigation pumps. Unlike many southern crops, rice was capital and machine intensive rather than labor intensive. The tenure system also varied radically from that of other cash crops. Corporations purchased large tracts, sold part, and rented other sections to tenants. A form of sharecropping emerged, and a cropper would pay a portion of his crop to the canal company for water, pay the landlord another portion for rent, and keep the remainder. The tenant furnished all the machinery used in growing and harvesting the crop.

As in farm areas throughout the country, the boom-and-bust cycle of World War I stunted the rice growing industry. During the 1920s the formerly expansive rice culture stabilized as farmers attempted to pay off loans for machinery bought during the war. By this time, tractors had become universal on the prairies, and this varied dramatically from other areas of the South that remained labor intensive.

Rice prices declined, as did those of other commodities, during the early years of the Great Depression. When Congress established the Agricultural Adjustment Administration (AAA) in 1933, rice was included as a basic commodity. Even before a rice program had been set up, prices climbed to a parity level. For the first two years, the rice section of the AAA fumbled with marketing agreements with millers, but in 1935 it set up a program that paralleled other commodity sections. In one important respect the rice section proved innovative; it gave allotments to producers—not to landlords. It reasoned that because tenants had such large investments in machinery, they deserved allotments. Also, crop-rotation customs dictated that often a man farmed his land one year and sharecropped with a neighbor the next.

Throughout the 1930s the rice culture remained stable, and during World War II rice became a valuable food to feed the world. Rice farmers meanwhile turned to combines, making another technological jump. Prosperity continued until the early 1950s, when the end of the Korean War caused a sharp decline in international demand. Rice allotments were cut drastically. The effects in the rice areas of the South paralleled those in the cotton culture 20 years earlier. The allotment system also was changed in parts of Louisiana and Arkansas, for Agriculture Stabilization and Conservation state committees, without calling for a vote from growers, changed rom producer to farm allotments, awarding allotments to landlords.

Louisiana rice farmers felt the forces of change most drastically, but in Arkansas the culture continued to expand. In 1972, the first year since 1956 that no quota was in effect, rice again became an expanding commodity; production increased by 25 percent between 1972 and 1974. With higher prices and no quotas in effect, rice production spread quickly to new lands in Arkansas and the Yazoo-Mississippi Delta. Despite all the changes in the rice culture, many rice farmers continued to lease land or farm on shares. Even as similar crop-sharing practices disappeared in other areas of the South, mechanized rice farmers continued them. The expansive nature of the culture can be seen in the increased farm price that rose from $359 million in 1964 to $1.2 billion in 1973. Because rice culture was highly mechanized by the 1930s, rice farmers suffered much less from the forces of acreage reduction and human displacement than did those in other farm areas of the South. Rice was agribusiness from its origin in the prairies, and new opportunities only meant refinements in the culture—not the agonizing transformation that accompanied mechanization in other areas of the South.

Pete Daniel
Smithsonian Institution
Washington, D.C.

Lawson P. Babineaux, "A History of the Rice Industry in Southwestern Louisiana" (M.A. thesis, University of Southwestern Louisiana, 1967); Pete Daniel, *Breaking the Land: The Transformation of Cotton, Tobacco, and Rice Cultures since 1880* (1985); Henry C. Dethloff, *Arkansas Historical Quarterly* (1970); John N. Efferson, *The Production and Marketing of Rice* (1952); Rudolph Carrol Hammack, "The New Deal and Louisiana Agriculture" (Ph.D. dissertation, Tulane University, 1973); Seaman A. Knapp, *The Present Status of Rice Culture in the United States*, USDA Bulletin No. 22 (1899). ☆

RURAL ELECTRIFICATION ADMINISTRATION

When the Rural Electrification Administration (REA) was created in 1935, less than 4 percent of the farms in the southern states had electricity. Without it, many of the comforts of modern life were unavailable, and for that reason the South enthusiastically welcomed the REA. In 1936, when Congress gave the REA statute authority, southern congressmen were among the agency's most ardent supporters. The Southern Policy Association, a group of southern congressmen anxious to promote southern development, endorsed the REA bill and regarded electrification as an important step in that direction.

As the REA began operation, southern farmers quickly established electric cooperatives, and the percentage of farms with service slowly grew. By 1941 the national average had climbed to 30 percent, and, although the southern percentage was lower, the South moved steadily ahead. At the end of World War II the REA started a massive construction program to finish the job, and by 1955 virtually 90 percent of the South's farmers had electrical service. Although the effects of electrification were evident nationwide, they had the most dramatic impact in the South, owing probably to the region's higher number of substandard homes when the REA started.

By providing running water and indoor toilets, the REA finally helped bring an end to the hookworm that had ravaged the South for over a century. Refrigeration had a similar beneficial effect on diets through the storage of perishable foods. In some small towns cold-storage cooperatives were started. Incandescent lighting improved the quality of life in homes and schools, and radio became a regular feature in southern homes. Electrification stimulated diversification: the Bureau of Agriculture Economics reported an increase in dairy farming, and the South became a major poultry-producing region. Most important, however, was the greater comfort and sense of satisfaction that southerners felt as they began to enjoy the numerous conveniences provided through electricity. Electrification must be considered one of the most significant stimulants for modernization of the rural South.

D. Clayton Brown
Texas Christian University

Erma Angevine, ed., *People. Their Power: The Rural Electric Fact Book* (1980); Marquis William Childs, *The Farmer Takes a Hand: The Electric Power Revolution in Rural America* (1952); Louis J. Goodman, John N. Hawkins, and Ralph N. Love, eds., *Small Hydroelectric Projects for Rural Development: Planning and Management* (1981). ☆

RURAL FREE DELIVERY

Although the free delivery of mail service was commonplace in the nation's cities and towns in 1900, American farmers were still going, usually once a week, to small fourth-class post offices for their mail. That year the farmers in the 11 states of the old Confederacy and Kentucky had nearly 21,000 such post offices, over one-third of all those in the nation, to which the mail was carried from central post offices over more than 94,000 miles of star mail routes.

Slow and inefficient, this mail service offered little relief for the southern farmer's isolation, and in the 1890s, when Postmaster General John Wanamaker suggested delivering mail to farmers, southern members of Congress enthusiastically supported the proposal. In four successive years Leonidas Livingston, Tom Watson, and Charles Moses, all Georgia congressmen, and North Carolina's Senator Marion Butler offered amendments to appropriation bills allocating money for a rural-free-delivery experiment. Finally, in 1896, Postmaster General Wilson L. Wilson, acting upon Senator Butler's amendment, began a rural-delivery experiment in West Virginia with an appropriation of $40,000. During the next six years southern members of Congress labored to keep the experiment alive, and in 1902, following the lead of Congressman Claude Swanson of Virginia, Congress made the rural free delivery of mail a permanent postal service.

In spite of the support southern congressional delegations had given, however, the South never received as much rural-free-delivery mail service as did the midwestern states largely because of postal regulations and politics. According to postal regulations, rural-free-delivery routes were first established where the density and literacy of the population seemed likely to make the route pay for itself, and fewer such places existed in the South than in the Midwest. More importantly, the rural routes were first established when the Republicans controlled the government, and midwestern Republican congressmen found it much easier to secure mail routes for political reasons than did their Democratic counterparts from the South. By 1950, therefore, there was one rural mail route for every 1,278 rural inhabitants in the five midwestern states of Ohio, Illinois, Iowa, Kansas, and Indiana, and only one for every 2,038 people in the 11 Confederate states and Kentucky.

Nevertheless, the rural free delivery of mail revolutionized communication in the South. Daily newspapers became commonplace in southern farm homes, more letters were written and received, more advertising filled the mails, and, more importantly, the rural South was brought into increasing contact with the North. Rural free delivery paved the way for the establishment of a modern parcel post system, which was also supported by southern members of Congress and which helped to break the country storekeeper's monopoly on the southern farmer's trade.

Rural free delivery inspired a good

roads movement throughout the South, led southerners to argue for government aid for building farm-to-market roads, and lured them away from their traditional stand on states' rights.

Wayne E. Fuller
University of Texas at El Paso

Daniel J. Boorstin, *The Americans: The Democratic Experience* (1973); Wayne E. Fuller, *Journal of Southern History* (November 1959), *Mississippi Valley Historical Review* (June 1955), *R.F.D.: The Changing Face of Rural America* (1964). ☆

SEARS, ROEBUCK CATALOG

"Without that catalog," writes Harry Crews in his 1978 autobiography of a Bacon County, Ga., boyhood, "our childhood would have been radically different. The federal government ought to strike a medal for Sears, Roebuck Company for sending all those catalogs to farming families, for bringing all that color and all that mystery and all that beauty into the lives of country people."

A genuine piece of Americana, the "Farmer's Bible" or "Wish Book" had a special impact on the South. Predominantly rural for so much longer than their Yankee counterparts, southerners relied on the Sears catalog for glimpses of urban life or light reading as well as order blanks. In many one-room schoolhouses it served as a primer and reference book. The catalog might even be credited with standardizing material-culture terminology. When a southern farmer needed a new "sling-blade" or "slam-bang," he was forced to order it from Sears as a "weed cutter."

Company policy as well as copy directly affected the region. By locating a major stove supplier in ore-rich Alabama in 1902, Sears became one of the first northern firms to recognize the South's industrial potential. In 1906 Sears's first mail-order branch was established in Dallas, and within the next 20 years both the Atlanta, Ga., and Memphis, Tenn., plants opened regional warehouses stocking items particularly suited to southern trade.

Well into the 19th century country stores provided their rural customers with virtually all their needs. Beginning in the last decades of the century, further extension of the railroads, good roads campaigns, the introduction of rural free delivery (1896), and, eventually, parcel post (1913) dramatically changed conditions that had kept southern farmers isolated and, whatever their dissatisfactions, loyal to the local merchant. Richard Sears's Big Book challenged the retail monopoly.

Sears by no means originated the mail-order business. Rooted in the colonial period (Benjamin Franklin's promotion of his Pennsylvania stoves was one of the original schemes), numerous mail-order firms existed by the end of the Civil War. Montgomery Ward, in operation since 1872 and distributing a wide variety of goods exclusively by mail, had even succeeded in getting his firm named the official supply house for the Grange. Yet by 1900 Sears, Roebuck had become the clear leader in the mail-order world, and it has conceded its edge to none of its competitors since.

Catalogs were designed for hours of fireside reading with woodcuts and flamboyant descriptions to encourage cover-to-cover browsing. Rooted in the principle of "never omitting the obvious" the description of the "Long Range Wonder Double Barrel Breech

Loading Hammerless Shotgun, the World's Wonder" totaled some 3,000 words. If there was not something among the stereoscopes and bicycles, buggies and mackintoshes, dry goods, furniture and gramophones to catch the buyer's fancy, the final testimonials, glowing recommendations of satisfied customers, and most convincingly the famous money-back guarantee usually did.

Sears's successful tactics gave rise to an all-out campaign against the mail-order companies. Shopkeepers lit bonfires in town squares and offered bounties for every new catalog turned in for fuel. Some merchants offered prizes and free admissions to movies in trade for the books. Newspaper editors, dependent on the advertising revenues of local retailers, originated epithets (Monkey Ward, Rears and Soreback, Shears and Sawbuck) and helped circulate accusations about cheap, damaged goods and "sewing machines" that turned out to be a needle and thread. No one had ever *seen* Richard Sears or Ward, so it was not hard to convince many southerners that both men were black—a rumor given added credibility by the later philanthropy of Sears president Julius Rosenwald in the cause of black education.

Ultimately, the automobile, urban growth, and the chain store did more than catalog buying to undermine the economic viability of small local retailers. As urbanization continued and its customers grew more sophisticated, Sears accommodated to the changing market. With the passage of the Pure Food and Drug Act in 1906, highly profitable, if suspect, patent medicines were dropped from the catalog. Gone were the superlatives: "World's Largest," "cheapest," and "America's strongest," unless justified by fact. Catalog vocabulary was simplified ("lachrimal secretions" became tears, "nutrition," food) and descriptions streamlined. In 1976 Sears switched to the "segmented people-oriented approach," to copy that "required the end of any pretension that the catalog is a work of literature."

Little in the 1984 catalog is reminiscent of the extravagant puffery of Richard Sears's "Wish Books"; little about the diversified billion-dollar Sears corporation reflects its humble origins as a watch wholesaler. Yet some fundamentals remain: serviceable, affordable merchandise, a large rural clientele, and loyal customers. In the words of Georgia Governor Eugene Talmadge, "God Almighty, Sears, Roebuck, and Eugene Talmadge" are names to count on.

Elizabeth M. Makowski
University of Mississippi

Louis E. Asher and Edith Heal, *Send No Money* (1942); Lewis E. Atherton, *The Southern Country Store, 1800–1860* (1949); Thomas D. Clark, *Pills, Petticoats, and Plows: The Southern Country Store* (1944); Boris Emmet and John E. Jeuck, *Catalogues and Counters: A History of Sears, Roebuck and Company* (1950); Jack Salzman, ed., *Prospects*, vol. 7 (1982); Sears, Roebuck & Co., *Merchant to the Millions: A Brief History of the Origins and Development of Sears, Roebuck and Co.* (1959); *Time* (20 August 1984); Gordon L. Weil, *Sears, Roebuck U.S.A.* (1977). ☆

SOYBEANS

Soybean production in the United States increased from 13.9 million bushels in 1930 to 2.3 billion bushels in 1982. The acreage devoted to the crop increased from 1 million to 71 million acres in the same period. Introduced as a novelty as early as 1804, the soybean was first used in the United States primarily for forage, beginning about 1900. Although many people saw its potential as a source of oil, less than one-fourth of the planted acreage in the mid-1930s was harvested for beans, which were then pressed for the oil for industrial uses and for meal for livestock feeding. Then a group of German chemists developed refining processes that removed from the oil its unpalatable flavor and odor, making soybean oil usable in products for human consumption.

Since then soybeans have had an impact on every part of the United States, but this impact has been particularly notable in the post–World War II South. As early as 1917 the U.S. Department of Agriculture published bulletins urging southern farmers to consider replacing cotton with soybeans. Not until World War II, though, with its patriotic appeals, high prices, and exodus of labor from southern farms, did many farmers turn from cotton to soybeans. After the war, production declined when farmers found the new crop was highly susceptible to damage from weather and insects. Shifts in cotton production, research, and government policies were among factors bringing soybeans back to prominence.

Cotton production shifted to the West and Southwest where the land and climate were suited to mechanization and where irrigation reduced the chances of crop failure. Research led to the realization that many southern farmers could double crop their land by planting in succession oats or winter wheat and then soybeans. While the development of the solvent extraction of the oil was particularly beneficial to southern farmers, new varieties of soybeans, which were less susceptible to weather and insect damage, were developed by the southern state agricultural experiment stations. The cultural significance of this was clear from the names given to the favorite strains raised in the South—the Davis, Lee, Bragg, Forrest, Pickett, Jackson, and Rebel. E. E. Hartwig, USDA soybean breeder at Stoneville, Miss., deliberately named his varieties after Confederate heroes.

The postwar accumulation of cotton surpluses led the federal government to cut back the acreage of cotton farmers could grow with price supports, leading many southern farmers to turn their land from cotton to soybeans. In 1945 the nine southern and border states of Georgia, Alabama, North Carolina, South Carolina, Tennessee, Mississippi, Missouri, Arkansas, and Louisiana produced 6 million bales of cotton and 18 million bushels of soybeans. In 1982 these same states produced 4.6 million bales of cotton and 757 million bushels of soybeans. A quiet revolution brought about by a single new crop had changed the face of the South.

Wayne D. Rasmussen
U.S. Department of Agriculture

Edward J. Dies, *Soybeans: Gold from the Soil* (1943); Harry D. Fornari, *Agricultural History* (January 1979); W. J. Morse and J. L. Carter, *Yearbook of Agriculture* (1937). ☆

SUGAR INDUSTRY

Cane sugar is a key commodity in international trade and an important component of the modern diet. At one time or another, sugarcane was grown commercially in Alabama, Georgia, South Carolina, Texas, Louisiana, and Florida. However, during the 19th century south Louisiana became the focal point of this dynamic industry.

Between 1880 and 1910 the Louisiana sugar industry experienced a scientific and technological revolution in methods, process apparatus, and scale of operation. The animal-powered mills and open evaporation kettles characteristic of the antebellum period were supplanted by large, technically designed, and scientifically controlled central factories. One commentator of the period, Mark Twain, described the modern sugar factory as "a wilderness of tubs and tanks and vats and filters, pumps, pipes, and machinery." This new industrial world, which emerged in rural Louisiana, was brought about in large part by a variety of local institutions working in alliance with certain agencies of the federal government. They included the Louisiana Sugar Planters' Association (LSPA), the Louisiana Sugar Experiment Station, the Audubon Sugar School, Louisiana State University, and the U.S. Department of Agriculture. These institutions facilitated the introduction of a progressive chemical and engineering technology, derived in part from the European beet-sugar industry, into this traditional plantation culture of the Deep South.

The late 19th-century modernization of the Louisiana sugar industry took place within an international context. Louisiana sugar planters, confronted with competition from the European beet-sugar manufacturers, responded to not only an economic challenge, but a scientific and technological one as well. They met this foreign threat by creating local institutions for coordinating planters' activities, conducting research, and supplying the scientific and technical expertise necessary for the modernization of their industry.

Of these local organizations, the LSPA made the crucial contribution to this agricultural and manufacturing transformation. Established in 1877 and led by many of the wealthiest and most politically powerful sugar planters in Louisiana, the LSPA systematically developed connections with federal government officials, practical engineers, and academic scientists to gain its organizational objectives.

As a result of changes in national party policies concerning the sugar tariff and the concurrent emergence of sugar-producing areas in Hawaii, Puerto Rico, Cuba, and Java, the Louisiana sugar industry entered into a period of decline after 1900. Subsequently, a number of sugar planters and investors channeled their energies and capital into south Florida, where they attempted to apply the practices of the Louisiana industry to the completely different environment found in the Everglades. The economic feasibility of the Florida industry became a reality only after USDA scientists at Canal Point, Fla., and research scientists from the United States Sugar Corporation discovered new varieties of cane, established specific fertilizer requirements, and introduced cultivation techniques appropriate for the region's unique soil, drainage, and climatic conditions. By 1940 Florida's sugarcane industry surpassed Louisiana's not only in terms of yield, but also in quality of raw sugar produced.

The Florida and Louisiana sugar industries supply only a fraction of the sugar consumed in the United States today, but they continue to have a significant impact upon their respective local economies.

John A. Heitmann
University of Dayton

Nöel Deerr, *The History of Sugar* (1949); John A. Heitmann, *The Modernization of the Louisiana Sugar Industry, 1830–1910* (1987); Emile A. Maier, *A Story of Sugar Cane Machinery* (1952); J. Carlyle Sitterson, *Sugar Country: The Cane Sugar Industry in the South, 1753–1950* (1953). ☆

TOBACCO CULTURE, FLUE-CURED

Commercial tobacco production in this country dates to the Jamestown colony in the early 17th century, and the expansion and contraction of plantings varied with international demand and prices. Over the years farmers developed a host of varieties that they cultivated throughout the country. After the Civil War bright tobacco, so called because of its golden color produced by intense heat during curing, became a favorite of manufacturers. As the demand for cigarette tobacco increased in the late 19th century, growers changed the work culture by harvesting several leaves from the stalk at a time instead of cutting the entire stalk, tied bundles of these leaves to a stick, and cured them in barns that had flues. Increased demand set in motion a massive expansion of the flue-cured culture from its northeastern North Carolina seed-bed into eastern North and South Carolina and by World War I to Georgia. Imperialistic growers spread the secrets of flue-curing and cloned tobacco barns, packhouses, and auction warehouses as they conquered new territory.

The flue-cured culture was extremely labor intensive. It was more than a clever saying that it took 13 months to cultivate, harvest, cure, and grade a crop for market. Because of the intense labor requirements of the crop, most tobacco farmers planted only three to six acres, the amount that a family could cultivate. The work routine began in the winter when farmers cut wood to heat the curing barns. In January they cleared land for a plantbed and seeded it before breaking the land and running rows. In May they transplanted seedlings to the fields, plowed, chopped, and as the tobacco grew, picked off hornworms and suckers and broke off the flowery tops. When harvest season arrived in July, they harvested three to four ripe leaves each week, and the process continued for five or six weeks. Harvesters were called "primers," and they put the leaves into sleds pulled by mules that then drew the sleds to a scaffold where women and children handed the leaves to stringers who tied them to sticks. At dusk primers returned from the fields and hung the leaves in the barns for curing. After harvest season each leaf was graded and tied into "hands" for market. It was sometimes Christmas before all the tobacco had been graded and sold.

By 1930 tobacco farmers, like other southern farmers, felt the slump in prices generated by the Great Depression. The Agricultural Adjustment Act (AAA) recognized tobacco as a basic commodity, and growers, warehousemen, manufacturers, and politicians attempted to conclude a marketing agreement with AAA representatives. When the markets opened in 1933, prices remained low, but a marketing agreement that promised parity prices for the 1933 crop in exchange for acreage reduction the next year succeeded. Over 90 percent of flue-cured growers voted for this plan. The AAA stabilized the flue-cured area, and the number of tobacco farms increased during the 1930s and the 1940s. During these years the hand-labor system changed little.

In the 1950s tobacco farmers cut back acreage, and this forced many farmers, especially sharecroppers, out of farming. At the same time, farmers cultivated their land more intensely, increasing production per acre from 922 pounds in 1939 to 2,200 pounds in 1964. Only in the 1960s did the flue-cured tobacco culture mechanize to any extent. In addition to tractors used for plowing and hauling sleds to the scaffold, a mechanical topper covered 20 acres a day and not only removed the tops but at the same time sprayed for suckers and hornworms. By the mid-1960s farmers insisted on intracounty leasing of allotments, and many small-allotment holders leased out acreage to larger growers. In 1968 Congress extended loose-leaf marketing, which had been customary in Georgia, to all areas, ending the labor-intensive grading and tying tasks. By the 1970s farmers were using bulk barns, an innovation that ended the banding and tying tasks at the scaffold. Meanwhile, a mechanical tobacco harvester began cutting out primers. The hand scale ended as machines handled the crop in bulk.

The forces set in motion in the 1950s plus increasing mechanization disrupted the old tenure arrangements in the tobacco area and led to massive displacement of farmers. Because the flue-cured culture mechanized so late, many exfarmers found work in the emerging factories of the area, easing the transition from farming by preserving communities, churches, and schools. In 1982, largely because of the controversy over smoking and health, Congress changed the price-support program, instituting a no-net-cost-to-taxpayers scheme that shifted the cost to tobacco farmers. Also, nonfarm allotment holders such as corporations and educational institutions had until December 1983 to sell their allotments to active farmers.

North Carolina tobacco farmers, Chatham County, 1930s

Like other commodity cultures, tobacco farming became a large-scale and capital-intensive operation that bore little resemblance to the intense hand-and-mule culture that originated in the 19th century.

See also INDUSTRY: / Tobacco Industry; SOCIAL CLASS: / Tobacco Workers

Pete Daniel
Smithsonian Institution
Washington, D.C.

Anthony Badger, *Prosperity Road: The New Deal, Tobacco, and North Carolina* (1980); Pete Daniel, *Breaking the Land: The Transformation of Cotton, Tobacco, and Rice Cultures since 1880* (1985); William R. Finger, ed., *The Tobacco Industry in Transition: Policies for the 1980s* (1981); J. Fraser Hart and Ennis L. Chestang, *Geographical Review* (October 1978); Harold B. Rowe, *Tobacco under the AAA* (1935); Nannie May Tilley, *The Bright-Tobacco Industry, 1860–1929* (1948). ☆

TRUCK FARMING

Truck farming is a form of agriculture that is national in scale, but it has left a significant imprint on the South. It involves the sale of annual fruit crops—as distinguished from orchard crops—and vegetables in commercial markets in fresh condition. This enterprise matured as an agricultural industry because of the development and growth of American cities. During the years following the Civil War, the expansion of the nation's urban population created a year-round demand for fresh produce. Essential to the successful conduct of the industry is the fast and efficient delivery of produce to market by refrigerated transport. During the formative stage following 1865, railroads provided this vital service.

Truck farming emerged as a factor in the economic life of the South during the period of its national evolution. By 1900 it engaged the energies of southerners in scattered segments of the region stretching from the Eastern Shore of Virginia to the lower Rio Grande Valley of Texas. Its spread is attributed to the promotional efforts of railway companies operating in the South, the immigration of northern and European farmers familiar with this type of farming, and low returns from cotton, which prompted some southerners to seek more dependable profits in a new venture. A listing of southern counties containing pockets of intensive production includes Norfolk and Northampton in Virginia, Seminole and Palm Beach in Florida, Copiah in Mississippi, and Cameron and Hidalgo in Texas. By the second half of the 20th century, however, the producing areas in Texas and Florida clearly dominated southern output. Although the southern farmer has produced a wide variety of truck produce, the primary crops have been potato, watermelon, tomato, and cabbage.

In those regions where southerners pursued truck farming energetically a form of agriculture different from that of the prevailing cotton culture emerged. The production of truck crops was not totally free from tenancy, but the landowning small farmer remained the primary producer until the mid-20th century when he was replaced by large agribusiness units. The cultivation of these crops required more intensive and careful effort than that needed for cotton. Migratory workers were often utilized, and extensive use was made of labor furnished by members of the producer's family. In some localities public school schedules were dictated by the planting and harvesting of crops. Distinctive features included packing sheds where local produce was prepared for rail shipment, ice plants that provided refrigeration for the freight cars carrying the produce, and "hot spots" adjacent to the packing sheds where producers and buyers met to transact their business.

In those portions of the South with proper soil and climate conditions in combination with transportation facilities direct to urban markets, truck farming provided the southern farmer with an alternative to dependence on the dominant cash crop.

James L. McCorkle, Jr.
Northwestern State University
of Louisiana

Gilbert C. Fite, *Cotton Fields No More: Southern Agriculture, 1865–1980* (1984); James L. McCorkle, Jr., "The Mississippi Vegetable Industry: A History" (Ph.D. dissertation, University of Mississippi, 1966); Bruce McKinley and W. C. Funk, *An Economic Study of Truck Farming in the Plant City Area, Hillsborough County, Florida* (1926); Wells A. Sherman, *Merchandising Fruits and Vegetables: A New Billion Dollar Industry* (1928). ☆

ART AND ARCHITECTURE

JESSIE POESCH

Tulane University

CONSULTANT

☆ ☆ ☆ ☆ ☆ ☆ ☆ ☆ ☆ ☆

Architecture 87
Visual Arts 92

Architects of Colonial Williamsburg 94
Colonial Revival Architecture 99
Decorative Arts 101
Farm Buildings 106
French Architecture 110
Georgian Revival Architecture 112
German Architecture 116
Gothic Revival Architecture 120
Greek Revival Architecture 125
Historiography of Southern Architecture 129
Industrial 19th-Century Architecture 132

Nonresidential 20th-Century Architecture 135
Painting and Painters, 1564–1790 138
Painting and Painters, 1790–1860 141
Painting and Painters, 1860–1920 144
Painting and Painters, 1920–1960 148
Painting and Painters, 1960–1980 155
Photography and Photographers 157
Queen Anne and Eastlake Styles of Architecture 167
Residential 20th-Century Architecture 169
Resort Architecture 172
Sculpture 180
Vernacular Architecture (Lowland South) 186
Vernacular Architecture (Upland South) 191

Amisano, Joseph 195
Anderson, Walter 196
Art Museums 197
Bearden, Romare 198
Binford, Julien 199
Bottomley, William Lawrence 201
Chapman, Conrad Wise 202
Christenberry, William 203
Cloar, Carroll 203
Dodd, Lamar 205
Douglas, Aaron 207
Eggleston, William 207
Gwathmey, Robert 208
Johnson, William Henry 209
Johnston, Frances Benjamin 210
Koch, Richard 211
Laughlin, Clarence John 212
McCrady, John 213
Mills, Robert 214
Mizner, Addison 215
Southern States Art League 216
Valentine, Edward Virginius 217
West, William Edward 218
Wiener, Samuel G. 219

Overleaf: Carroll Cloar,* Where the Southern Cross the Yellow Dog *(1965)

ARCHITECTURE

Most of the houses in the United States today were probably built after the beginning of World War I. A large number of public buildings, office towers, and industrial structures were also built after that date. What is true of the nation as a whole is equally true of the South, especially in urban centers such as Atlanta, Jackson, Birmingham, Nashville, New Orleans, and others that have greatly expanded in size and population in the last 25 years. We are still perhaps too close in time to this recent rash of building to see it in historical perspective and to see how and if it has distinct regional qualities. A present consensus would probably be that the majority of styles and building types represent national rather than regional choices. Art and architecture are often by their nature national and international in character, but with regional accents. Modern technology and materials (including air-conditioning), modern communication systems, and a highly mobile population have abetted this tendency.

The large hotel with central multistory lobby or atrium is a characteristic modern building type. The spectacular open spaces of hotels of this kind lend a sense of drama and theater to one's visit to a strange city. The Hyatt-Regency Hotel in Atlanta, designed by John C. Portman and Associates and completed in 1967, was the first of this genre. The fashion for and appreciation of a variety of such open, interior public spaces have now spread throughout the land. Though originating in the South (scholars can always identify precedents for each new building type—the much earlier Brown Palace Hotel in Denver is a case in point), one would not identify this fashion as specifically southern. Rather, it seems to represent an innovative impulse in design and form associated with a place undergoing great commercial and economic expansion.

Where once church towers and public buildings, such as schools, county courthouses, or state capitols, were the dominant features of town and city landscapes, now office towers, hotels, and high-rise apartment houses shape the skylines of cities and many towns. Other new building types and new arrangements of buildings and community spaces are changing living patterns. An obvious example is the development of the shopping mall, which is replacing, or has replaced, main street. This is one of many changes brought about by widespread use of the automobile and by population growth.

The advent of air-conditioning, especially from the 1940s onward, when it began to be affordable both in workplaces and in residences even of many poorer people, has done much to cause the built environment of the South to conform even more closely to national patterns. Earlier, the long, hot summers virtually forced the builders of southern homes to find ways of coping with the heat—dogtrots, wide central halls, porches, verandas, piazzas, galleries, cupolas on large houses, attic vents, raised cottages with air circulation underneath, and T-shaped house plans, to name a few. These devices were often concealed so that a given building might appear in shape and detail to conform to a particular style or taste. Although summers are hot in other parts of the country and many of these devices were used elsewhere—the porch, for example, was a ubiquitous feature on houses in the United States during the second half of the 19th century—the porches, swings, hammocks, and other accoutrements were important for longer periods of time in the South. Air-conditioning has thus been a factor in changing the pace of American life and especially life in the South, in ways both overt and subtle. Life in summer is more enclosed and private. New houses seldom have the porches or the overhanging roofs formerly typical. Where once businesses, schools, and colleges closed down or operated at a much slower pace for four months in the summer, they now follow the same schedules as their counterparts throughout the nation.

Despite the fact that a high proportion of the buildings in the South today are relatively new, the survival of older buildings plays an important role both in how southerners interpret their own environment and in how others see and interpret it. Most surviving older buildings are still in use and are therefore part of contemporary life and culture. Some few have been set aside as museums. In both cases they help to give distinctive and particular character to specific places.

Though a few 17th-century structures survive, those older buildings extant and in use date largely from the 18th and 19th centuries. These include the rather sober early Georgian, the more exuberant high Georgian, the neoclassical of the Federal period, the "columnar" style where late Georgian and Greek Revival sometimes blend, the austere "pure" Greek revival, the Gothic, the Italianate of the post-Civil War period, the various picturesque tastes of the late 19th century, and the beaux arts formalism of the early 20th century. Also included now as older and historic are such relatively recent modes as the art deco and moderne of the 1920s and 1930s.

Buildings completed in the modish style of a given time are important not only for the functions they serve but also for the way they demonstrate the shared tastes of an era. They are important symbols or visual statements of what both the owner or patron and the designer or architect conceive to be the role of the building in that time and place. They reflect in turn the status and role of those who live in or use the building. Furthermore, the buildings reflect not only the status of the occupants or users of the building but also the aspirations and achievements of the entire community.

There are conspicuous southern examples in each of the stylistic phases that have enjoyed popularity in this country. Among the most familiar are Drayton Hall in South Carolina, an example of an architectural choice and symbol of the wealthy landed planters on the 18th-century Atlantic Seaboard whose lifestyle had close parallels with English counterparts; the Virginia Capitol in Richmond and the complex of buildings at the University of Virginia, deliberately designed to serve and to symbolize the functions of democratic governance and learning in the new Republic; the Tennessee Capitol, another "temple of democracy" of a slightly later date; and the great columnar houses found in Natchez, Miss., the result of the prosperity of a slaveowning class of cotton planters and merchants in the Deep South. The extraordinary cluster of art deco hotels and residences in Miami is a reminder of that area's spectacular growth in the 1920s and 1930s.

In addition to these conspicuous structures other modest examples exist, less familiar to a wide public but well known within a limited area. The distinctive "Virginia house" developed in the early 17th century and the T-shaped plantation or farm houses found in the Carolinas (which provide an abundance of cross-ventilation) are cases in point. The raised cottages of the Deep South, sometimes called "mosquito" cottages in the Carolinas and "Creole" cottages on the Gulf Coast and in Louisiana, are of several different types and hence different plans but constitute a recognizable genre. They include humble one- or two-room structures lived in by poor blacks and whites as well as cottages of considerably larger scale. Among urban structures the "singles" and "doubles" of Charleston represent particular types, as do the distinctive row houses of Baltimore, the French-influenced cottages of New Orleans, and the long, narrow shotgun houses of the late 19th century. In some cases the consistent or distinctive use of materials identifies, in a general way, other characteristic regional building traditions. The stone houses of Kentucky and the varieties of log structures, particularly in the Upper South, are examples. Many of these were built by frontiersmen as sturdy utilitarian structures in the late 18th and early 19th centuries and have since become symbols of an era.

In some cases different building traditions in different regions developed out of the traditions familiar to the earliest settlers such as the English, French, German, Spanish, and Scottish. Certain construction methods were also assimilated from the Indian and African populations.

A growing body of research into the nature and uses of vernacular structures exists. Such research is fueled by a desire to formulate a more accurate picture of the nature of the built environment and to study more than structural types and architectural modes. Farm buildings and industrial and commercial buildings are, and were, a conspicuous part of the built environment of the South, as elsewhere. Here, too, the study of the variety of forms, tastes, and traditions needs further exploration.

Much of the interest in older structures and the realization of their importance and relevance to understanding ourselves and our past have been stimulated by the movement for historic preservation. Various forces have motivated this interest in architectural preservation. These include respect and love for major historical figures or for buildings associated with historical events; a nostalgia for the past; respect and feeling for distinctive architecture and buildings of a place or period, be it elaborate mansion or simple log cabin or dogtrot; and a desire to preserve the consistent appearance or fabric of a section of a community. In recent years architectural preservation has been seen as a tourist lure for a city, town, or area, and hence an economic asset. Also, the preservation of extant buildings is often economically sensible. Hence old warehouses or factory buildings are being converted into apartment buildings and old railroad stations into restaurants.

The South has actively participated in the historic preservation movement. The earliest successful effort of this kind in the United States is generally identified as the effort to preserve Mount Vernon, the home of George Washington, and to open it to the public, an effort initiated in 1853. The most conspicuous and perhaps most extensive example of historic preservation is Colonial Williamsburg, where an entire community has been restored to its 18th-century ambience. This project was inaugurated in the 1930s. Thanks to relatively little change there during the 19th century, there were 81 intact 18th-century buildings that needed little more than a sprucing up and the removal of additions. At the same time several of the more important buildings, such as the Capitol and the Governor's Palace, both of which had totally disappeared, were reconstructed on the basis of careful study of documents and archaeological research.

The Capitol and the Governor's Palace are among the most impressive buildings at Williamsburg, but the restoration as a whole is significant for its inclusion of a wide range of forms—small and medium-sized houses, outbuildings, shops, and gardens. Increasingly, emphasis has been placed on interpretations of the lifestyle and values of the inhabitants as well as on the physical nature of the built environment. Moreover, although it was once true that only the roles of the political, social, and intellectual leaders of the community were examined, there is now a more evenhanded approach in which the lives of all classes, including slaves and servants, are studied and interpreted. Williamsburg, because of the scale of the restoration and the disciplined research that has characterized the organization, has had a profound effect on the standards of historic preservation and also on the consciousness of both the nation's and the region's architectural history. Other restored areas that have had a similar, if more limited, influence include the Old Salem restoration at Winston-Salem, N.C., which helped to bring to the fore the Germanic heritage of the South, and Westville, near Lumpkin, Ga., a re-creation of the buildings, sights, and smells of a rural mid-19th-century village. Cities with distinct architectural characters in which there have been controlled preservation and restoration include Charleston, Savannah, and New Orleans. They are among the most attractive cities in the country and are seen as emblems of the rich and complex history of the South.

The influence of Williamsburg and the enthusiasm for architecture in a historical idiom go far beyond simple historic preservation. Reinforcing the slightly earlier Colonial Revival architectural style, the Williamsburg work is echoed throughout modern suburbs and in numerous historic architecture projects.

Despite the dicta of early and mid-20th-century architectural theorists and practitioners concerning purity and simplicity of form and the need to build for a machine age, a large number of builders and developers in the South (and elsewhere) opted for modifications of traditional architecture, particularly in residential architecture. In some cases the plans may have changed significantly—front-door access but also side- and back-door access through garages, more "family" rooms, a high proportion of one- or one-and-a-half-story ranch houses—but the surface embellishment is an interpretation of traditional forms, albeit sometimes very free. Among these traditional types in the South is what could be called antebellum revival, that is, the columnar-fronted mansion. More recently, popular magazines have shown examples and plans of vernacular types, such as Louisiana colonial structures with double-pitched sheltering roofs. The recent "postmodern" architectural movement has in a sense taken cognizance of what developers and builders have understood—that a certain amount of ornament and embellishment and playful manipulation of spaces is pleasing to the eye and the spirit. They in turn are trying to create buildings in which some traditional forms and ornament are used in both functional and appealing ways. This is a very self-conscious movement.

Less self-conscious artistically is another new trend that may or may not have an important effect on the nature of architecture and the built environment in the South and elsewhere—the increased awareness of the need for energy conservation. A notable example of the way in which the shape and appearance of the building have been determined by energy and environmental considerations is the Jones Bredge Headquarters of the Simmons Company in Atlanta, Ga., designed by Thompson, Hancock, Witte and Associates and completed in 1975. This building, roughly the shape of a parallelogram, rests on steel trusses (thus it is raised from the ground—a traditional southern practice) and is designed to take advantage of solar and ecological factors. The need to make specific adaptations in order to save energy and materials may reshape, once again, the forms of our shelters.

Whether in vernacular idioms or in more self-conscious architectural styles and designs, whether serving private or public, commercial or industrial needs, buildings are important statements of status, symbols of cultural aspirations, and statements of community pride. Some are personal statements by architect or patron and some now seem to be distinctive period statements. The architecture of the South, as elsewhere, is complex and many layered.

See also BLACK LIFE: Architecture, Black; FOLKLIFE: Aesthetics, Afro-American; Aesthetics, Anglo-American; House Types; / Bungalow House; Dogtrot House; I House; Pyramidal House; Saddlebag House; Shotgun House; T House; GEOGRAPHY: Log Housing; RECREATION: / Colonial Williamsburg

Jessie Poesch
Tulane University

Wayne Andrews, *Pride of the South: A Social History of Southern Architecture* (1979); Edward A. Chappell, "Cultural Change in the Shenandoah Valley: Northern Augusta County Houses before 1861" (M.A. thesis, University of Virginia, 1977); Barbara H. Church, "The Early Architecture of the Lower Valley of Virginia" (M.A. thesis, University of Virginia, 1978); Mary Wallace Crocker, *Historic Architecture in Mississippi* (1973); Henry Glassie, *Folk Housing in Middle Virginia: A Structural Analysis of Historic Artifacts* (1975); Charles B. Hosmer, Jr., *Presence of the Past: A History of the Preservation Movement in the United States before Williamsburg* (1965); John Linley, *The Georgia Catalog: Historic American Buildings Survey, A Guide to the Architecture of the State* (1982); Lewis Mumford, *The South in Architecture* (1941); James Patrick, *Architecture in Tennessee, 1768–1897* (1981); Jessie Poesch, *The Art of the Old South: Painting, Sculpture, Architecture and the Products of Craftsmen, 1560–1860* (1983); Leland M. Roth, *A Concise History of American Architecture* (1979); Kenneth Severens, *Southern Architecture: 350 Years of Distinctive American Buildings* (1981); Dell Upton, "Early Vernacular Architecture in Southeastern Virginia" (Ph.D. dissertation, Brown

Drayton Hall in South Carolina (1738–42), an exemplary Palladian design on the Ashley River

University, 1980), with John Michael Vlach, eds., *Common Places: Readings in American Vernacular Architecture* (1986). ☆

VISUAL ARTS

The works of art created in the South and their creators are part and parcel of the broader national and international artistic milieu but at the same time are rooted in the specific time, place, and person of their creation. In any given period, not just in the recent "modern" era, the arts have seldom reflected regional or national distinctiveness. For example, in the 12th century one finds surprisingly similar sculptural motifs from France to Poland; at the same time an astute scholar can determine the different "hands" in a given sculptural program. In studying the visual arts of the American South, especially the region's 20th-century culture, one gains more by examining and objectively describing what exists than by trying to categorize what is or is not uniquely southern.

Currently interest in the arts is growing in the South. The number of working artists in the region is now in the thousands, and those who support or attend art events surely number in the millions in any given year. Still, a relatively small proportion of the total population is concerned with painting and the visual arts and their role in society. Every city of any size has its museum, its art galleries and dealers, its art classes in institutions of learning or those given by free-lance instructors, its workshops and special exhibitions. Though these activities are still centered in larger cities, the tentacles reach into smaller communities through arts and humanities programs as well as through the media of television, radio, magazines, and newspapers. Whereas artists once felt they could succeed only if their works were shown in New York, more now find a sufficient outlet in their own region. New York is still the center of the art world, but some dealers and museum directors in that city now feel it necessary to keep abreast of what is happening in other regions. Those who are involved in such visual arts as painting and photography may not agree as to what they are all about or what is "good" or what grasps and holds the mind and spirit, yet their numbers are legion.

The emergence and proliferation of the arts, especially during the last 30 years or so, has also to do with the growth of population, the relative affluence of a substantial number of people, the growth of the national economy, the tilt of that economy toward the South, and the growth of a network of museums and schools at all levels. This has made for rich diversification.

Most artists in the South have embraced the tenets of what is loosely called modernism; these tenets include varieties of abstractionism as well as the relatively new realism. The diversity to be found among the works of recent and contemporary artists almost defies description, yet critics have sensed some common elements that have influenced, and are reflected in, the arts in today's South. William A. Fagaly, in a perceptive essay accompanying the exhibit *Southern Fictions*, held at the Contemporary Arts Museum in Houston in 1983, touched upon some of these: a strong sense of place and obsession with the earth; a volatile society given to strong expression and vibrant color; uncontrolled emotional release resulting in violence and tragedy; the mix of cultures—African, English, and Latin; indulgent appetites for indigenous foods and music; a penchant for storytelling and for social interchange; and also a persistent inferiority complex. These "regional" qualities are not necessarily expressed in the work of all artists in the South and, when they are expressed in one way or another, are not necessarily the aspect that most contributes to the success of any given work; nonetheless, they are clearly important. These factors have in fact had more influence on writers and musicians than on productions of the visual arts. Donald Kuspit, in his selection of contemporary paintings for the Virginia Museum of Fine Arts exhibition *Painting in the South: 1564–1980*, which circulated among six museums from 1983 to 1985, sought those works that expressed a southern sensibility. These included works suggesting both southerners' relationship to the land and the conflict between this relationship and such facets of modernization as the streaking highways that cut across this land. He emphasized that regionalism is not necessarily the most relevant element in any single work. Some southern painters' works reflect the influence of popular culture—and the South is one of the nurseries of modern pop culture—the struggle to grasp inherent contradictions in southern culture, the myths that still envelop the South but are dead or dying, a feeling for the absurdities of modern times, and a movement toward decorative abstraction.

Recent historical exhibits and studies of artists in the South reflect a growing sense of the diversity of regional history and of the importance of region itself. Building on the work of William Dunlap in the 1830s, J. Hall Pleasants and Anna Wells Rutledge pioneered in the southern study of art. Pleasants examined the careers of artists who worked in the 18th and 19th centuries in Maryland and produced a series of monographs in the 1940s. A file of his unpublished research is now in the possession of the Maryland Historical Society. Rutledge's 1949 study, *Artists in the Life of Charleston*, is indispensable to anyone interested in the art of South Carolina. Since the work of these and other pioneers, a small but steady flow of regional studies and studies of individual southern artists has appeared. Notable among these is the exhibition mentioned previously, *Painting in the South: 1564–1980*. Its accompanying scholarly catalog is a permanent record of this important exhibition. Even so, the historical study of the visual arts in the South is only in its beginnings.

In the largely agricultural and sparsely settled South, the relatively few who worked in the visual arts often had to struggle for patronage and for opportunities to show and sell their works. Patronage was important in the colonial period, and some of the most distinguished patrons were to be found in the South. The delineation of the flora and fauna of this nation had its roots in the American South—the artists include John White, Mark Catesby, William Bartram, John James Audubon, and Maria Martin—yet development of landscape painting was slow. The hot climate, the great distances, and perhaps even the persistence of a culture whose members preferred to live out-of-doors rather than paint it militated against this. In both the portraits and genre paintings that survive from the 18th and 19th centuries, the biracial, indeed multiracial nature of southern life (and hence American life) is revealed more forcefully than can be discerned from any but the most recent studies of painting in America. What is being done today builds, knowingly or otherwise, on the traditions, practices, and struggles of the past.

See also BLACK LIFE: Art, Black; ENVIRONMENT: Naturalists; / Audubon, John James; FOLKLIFE: Folk Painting; WOMEN'S LIFE: / Martin, Maria

Jessie Poesch
Tulane University

Bruce W. Chambers, *Art and Artists of the South: The Robert P. Coggins Collection* (1984); Corcoran Gallery of Art, *American Painters of the South* (1960); David C. Driskell, *Two Centuries of Black American Art* (1976); Ula Milner Gregory, in *Culture in the South*, ed. W. T. Couch (1935); F. Jack Hurley, Nancy Hurley, and Gary Witt, eds., *Southern Eye, Southern Mind* (1981); James C. Kelly and Estill Curtis Pennington, *The South on Paper: Line, Color and Light* (1985); Donald B. Kuspit, *Art in America* (July–August 1976), *Art Voices South* (January 1979); David Madden, *Southern Quarterly* (Winter 1984); Jessie Poesch, *The Art of the Old South: Painting, Sculpture, Architecture and the Products of Craftsmen, 1560–1860* (1983), in *The Cultural Legacy of the Gulf Coast*, ed. Lucius F. Ellsworth and Linda K. Ellsworth (1976); *Southern Quarterly* (Fall–Winter 1985); Virginia Museum of Fine Arts, *Painting in the South: 1564–1980* (1983). ☆

Architects of Colonial Williamsburg

From its beginning in the late 1920s, Colonial Williamsburg has been conceived as a place where Americans learn about their history. As early as 1932 benefactor John D. Rockefeller, Jr., preferred the motto "That the future may learn from the past," to more esoteric statements of purpose, and few fourth graders or museum administrators have regarded Williamsburg as merely a preservation project since. For more than 50 years, the town has maintained a powerful grip on the national consciousness. Consider for example Lee Iacocca's stated purpose of making the Statue of Liberty and Ellis Island "an ethnic Williamsburg" and modern art curator Henry Geldzahler's somewhat eccentric assessment of Andrew Wyeth as "the Williamsburg of American painting—charming, especially when seen from a helicopter." Such references, as well as countless American buildings carried out in a "Williamsburg" style, reveal that the restored town is widely seen as an expression of American rather than regional culture. Some of the reasons for this lie in its Depression-era origins.

Just how the re-created community of Williamsburg achieved its present evocative condition is worth considering. The essential roles of Rockefeller and the visionary rector of Bruton Parish Church, W. A. R. Goodwin, are well known, but those of the people who most directly created the place are much less so. Chief financial decisions were made by Rockefeller himself, advised by his corporate lieutenants and influenced by Goodwin and restoration architects. Certainly Rockefeller's perception of history and politics affected the emerging museum, but there is little evidence that this perception was not shared by all the principals.

Old courthouse, erected in 1770, Williamsburg, Virginia

In the beginning, design decisions were made on a variety of levels by three groups: partners in the Boston firm of Perry, Shaw, and Hepburn, their representatives in residence at Williamsburg, and an advisory committee. Largely because of a chance meeting between Goodwin and architect William G. Perry in 1926, the Perry, Shaw, and Hepburn firm was hired in 1927 to prepare proposals for restoration of principal parts of the town. The following year, the identity of the benefactor was revealed and Perry, Shaw, and Hepburn began plans for a number of buildings.

The firm had been established in 1922 and had primarily produced relatively modest New England buildings in competent, restrained renditions of historical modes. In 1927, for example, it was involved with a Bulfinch-inspired classroom building for Radcliffe, an Elizabethan or perhaps Jacobean academic building in Brookline, Mass., and a Norman-style Episcopal church in the south end of Boston. At that time, the firm was small (about five draftsmen in addition to the three principals) and the partners were intimately involved in design. As in other architectural offices, varied personalities and talents resulted in the partners' pursuing different parts of the firm's work. Employees remember Perry as a successful promoter, Shaw as a rational space planner, and Hepburn as the talented designer. Nonetheless, surviving drawings show that all three men had some drafting talent, and Perry's story of staying up until 4:00 A.M.

in a New York hotel room doing bird's-eye presentation drawings for Goodwin and the still-anonymous Rockefeller reinforces the impression that he could turn out reasonably convincing images when the situation demanded. Daily management of various projects was carried out by job captains drawn from the drafting room.

With the advent of the Williamsburg restoration, the firm expanded significantly, and much administration and design work shifted to Virginia. In 1928 the firm hired Walter Macomber as "resident architect" and promptly shipped him off to Williamsburg. Largely self-educated through a series of jobs in New England architectural offices and a nearly obsessive recording of traditional buildings, Macomber brought to the project a concern for detail in craftsmanship that long outlived his tenure. For Macomber, the essence of colonial buildings lay in the subtleties of their moldings rather than in their planning, and he encouraged a quickly assembled group of draftsmen to look for design inspiration in the countryside around Williamsburg.

The draftsmen were primarily young, imaginative, hard-drinking men with different backgrounds. Best known today (because of his later publications) is Thomas Waterman, who like Macomber had a nonacademic education. Waterman had worked for Boston ecclesiastical architect Ralph Adams Cram and with William Sumner Appleton, founder of the Society for the Preservation of New England Antiquities. He was on the island of Mallorca preparing measured drawings of Palma Cathedral for Cram in 1928 when the call came from Perry, Shaw, and Hepburn. David Hays, a young draftsman also without memories of college architectural classes, was already working for the partners in Boston, and John Barrows came from a Norfolk firm. They were joined by Sammy MacMurtrie, who was finishing architecture school at MIT, and John Henderson from Georgia Tech. The quality of draftsmanship, as well as the spice of life in Williamsburg, was enhanced by George Campbell, who had recently graduated from a Dublin technical school and had left Ireland because of his antirepublican sentiments. Campbell had a grasp of 18th-century details learned in the streets of Dublin and, when found staying in Boston with William Perry's chauffeur, was sent south. Late in 1928 the group was joined by draftsman Singleton Peabody Moorehead, a young Harvard graduate who had had experience at archaeological sites in the Southwest, had practiced with Macomber's old Boston firm of Strickland, Blodgett, and Law, and had developed skills at sketching old buildings on a grand tour of Europe.

The partners, Macomber, and the draftsmen all expected to have an initial period of time for study and design, but upon arriving they found representatives of the New York construction firm of Todd and Brown already present and anxious for working drawings. Antagonism with Todd and Brown, the necessity of dealing with an astonished but strong-willed Virginia community, and the rapid pace of work in what was largely a new idiom put extraordinary pressure on Macomber and the draftsmen. Early difficulties were exacerbated by the partners' insistence on living in Boston. The development of designs from schematics to final drawings, not to mention the resolution of political issues, was slowed by Perry, Shaw, and Hepburn's general absence.

A stabilizing influence appeared in the autumn of 1929, when the partners sent A. Edwin Kendrew to organize the architectural work. Systematic and eminently reasonable, Kendrew began to bring order out of chaos, and he hired additional staff to deal with the increasing work load. For a majority of them—like Finlay Ferguson, Jr., Francis Duke, Everette Fauber, and Milton Grigg, all from the University of Virginia—this was their first full-time job.

Despite Kendrew's efforts, working conditions contributed to disagreements over professional roles. Thomas Waterman was perhaps the most talented member of the group, and by almost all accounts he became the most aggressive. Drawings show that he produced a large percentage of the designs for reconstruction of the Governor's Palace, Capitol, and Raleigh Tavern, as well as the substantial restoration of the main building at the College of William and Mary. The drawings reinforce suggestions that other draftsmen were sometimes pushed aside to deal with less exciting subjects. Yet everyone present was involved in design development to some degree. Waterman's prominent role in the Palace project notwithstanding, for example, the principal outside elevations were developed from the now-famous Bodleian copperplate by Macomber and John Barrows, most of the paint colors were chosen by Boston interior designer Susan Nash, and the rather lavish entrance hall was designed by Moorehead. Ultimately, Moorehead was the more resilient presence. His tenure at Williamsburg outlasted both Waterman's and Macomber's by 30 years. Kendrew remained even longer; he finally retired, as senior vice president, in 1968.

Arthur Shurcliff, a Boston landscape architect who developed garden and street planting schemes for the historic zone until 1941, further enlivened the hectic early scene. Shurcliff was a dramatic, Wildean character whose independence often overcame his official deference to Perry, Shaw, and Hepburn. Zealous enthusiasm led him to Williamsburg executives Arthur Woods and Kenneth Chorley, or directly to Rockefeller.

From 1928 until 1948 an advisory committee of nationally and regionally prominent architects reviewed projects and helped set architectural standards for the Williamsburg effort. Increasingly this committee came to rely on the local staff for most answers. Initially it helped resolve issues involving the extent of the work and lent support to the architects' efforts. In delicate matters involving the preferences of administrators and donors at the state-run College of William and Mary, for example, the committee occasionally nudged the parties toward a better standard of authenticity. This was particularly helpful in the first several years when the extent of future restorations remained very nebulous. In 1928 only buildings on the main street were considered crucial, and uncertainty existed about how to handle areas that had lost their 18th-century buildings. Even then Goodwin and Rockefeller were thinking in terms of a general environment for the principal buildings—Goodwin called it "the frame of the picture"—but the picture was still much smaller than it ultimately became.

As restoration proceeded, the committee came to rely on the local staff for most answers, because their research at the site had made them more expert than even outspoken committee member Fiske Kimball in evaluating building techniques of colonial Virginia. Somehow between the hours of drafting and drinking, the architects found sufficient time to explore the Tidewater countryside. As Macomber had done earlier in New England and George Campbell in Ireland, they carefully observed the details of traditional buildings and recorded their observations in drawings rather than text. By gradually developing an encyclopedic familiarity with early Virginia design, they were following a 19th-century historicist view that one could become entirely conversant in an ancient style, and thereafter design in it much like its original practitioners did. In many ways, this approach reflected an arts and crafts fascination with local, indigenous character. Old vernacular design was seen as important because it embodied a preindustrial, *regional* personality.

Williamsburg held an appeal for these designers that ran somewhat counter to a vernacular mode. The buildings did not stand in an informal pattern like those in a picturesque English village, but rather were arranged in a precise order along parallel streets broken by public spaces and designed with a strong sense of axis. This simple American Baroque plan brought order to the various vernacular parts, creating a coherent system that seemed very much like the studio projects Moorehead and other students had observed and executed in long, late-night charettes. In many ways, the restored and re-created public buildings and vistas in Williamsburg seemed to offer an American antecedent for grander beaux-arts designs in cities like Chicago and Washington.

The partners in Boston and the respected review committee members, as well as the young draftsmen in Williamsburg, had a shared educational background, formal or not. It emphasized immersion in historical styles and their skillful use for modern buildings. Regional styles were viewed with favor, and modest hand-crafted details were still seen as wholesome. Countering the picturesqueness of vernacular building was a fondness for grand, balanced beaux-arts planning.

All involved were unusually careful in following details of existing buildings and in employing specific evidence when it was available for reconstructions. When direct evidence could not be found, they drew on their understanding of the local style to create plausible reconstructions. They saw life in the 18th-century South as more homogeneous and certainly more genteel than late 20th-century historians do. As a result, their observations among the venerable buildings of Tidewater Virginia were selective, focusing on pleasant, well-resolved design rather than the confusion and cheapness that existed alongside it. The fine products of a slave economy were presented, but the system was romanticized or left unacknowledged. Complex history was thus screened and sanitized and delivered to a nation receptive to its optimistic, patriotic message.

This is not entirely the way it would be done today; provocative economic theory, social history, and the civil rights movement would make that impossible. Yet the grand project that began in 1928 and continued along the same lines for the next 50 years holds an unusual appeal. Substantially the product of a particular time and educational system, Colonial Williamsburg is commonly seen as a graceful effort, a seamless whole. Perhaps it could not have been accomplished at another time. Yet because of its size and complexity, it clearly offers continuing opportunities for development and change.

See also RECREATION: / Colonial Williamsburg

Edward A. Chappell
Williamsburg, Virginia

Charles B. Hosmer, Jr., in *The Colonial Revival in America*, ed. Alan Axelrod (1985), *Preservation Comes of Age: From Williamsburg to the National Trust, 1926–1949* (1981); Fay Campbell Kaynor, *Winterthur Portfolio* (Summer–Autumn 1985); Michael Wallace, *Radical History Review* (1981). ☆

Colonial Revival Architecture

The Colonial Revival subsumes what can be called the "antebellum revival." This would include 20th-century houses built in the Greek Revival or columnar styles of the 1840s and 1850s. By the 1930s and 1940s these original structures had become emblems of the image—real or imagined—of the South's white antebellum "aristocratic" culture, which by this time had gained national acceptance. It had some basis in fact but was considerably nourished by popular novels and films. In England the Queen Anne style revived vernacular English domestic architecture of the medieval period, but in America the style was related to colonial architecture. Beginning roughly in 1867, gathering force in the early 1870s, and growing in favor from 1874 on, the Colonial Revival enjoyed a nostalgic and antiquarian popularity in the South as well as in the rest of the United States.

In 1867 Donald G. Mitchell in his book *Rural Studies* examined old American houses with "a character of their own" that should be respected. However, his proposals for new houses were scarcely influenced by colonial precedents except for his advocacy of half-timbering, which he observed was rarely found in the North but commonly existed in Florida and Louisiana. Illustrated in the book was an old small building that he sketched near New Orleans; he would later propose that Louisiana erect a similar one at the Centennial Exhibition in Philadelphia in 1876.

In 1869 Richard Upjohn, noted architect and the first president of the American Institute of Architects, wrote "Colonial Architecture of New York and the New England States," one of the first such articles in a professional publication. In the 1870s laymen as well as architects enjoyed seaside vacations, which focused attention upon seaside resort towns, many of which had not changed since colonial days. This widespread exposure to colonial architecture helped to promote the style's popularity.

The Colonial Revival, wrote one architect in 1876, is "no feeble copy of foreign styles of questionable fitness and in little sympathy with our institutions but distinctly American." Despite the interest in the American colonial past generated by the 1876 Centennial Exhibition, no structure at that exhibit replicated any colonial structure. The Connecticut State Building came the closest. It was certainly not a strict copy of a Connecticut saltbox but was intended to evoke thoughts of the state's early history, according to architect Donald Mitchell.

In March of 1876 the *American Architect* suggested that architects spend their holidays making notes of colonial architecture because it, "with all its faults of formality and meagerness, was, on the whole, decidedly superior in style and good building, if we may say so, to most that has followed it." The following year noted architects Charles McKim, William Mead, Stanford White, and William Bigelow made a walking tour of colonial New England buildings that were attracting attention in the professional journals (such as the *American Architect*, which published Robert Peabody's "Georgian Homes of New England" in 1877). Sketching their way along the coast of Massachusetts and New Hampshire, they seemed to be searching for a national heritage on which to build an American architectural style. In later years eclectic devotees would claim this trip as the "discovery" of the colonial. The subsequent architectural firm of McKim, Mead, and White would dominate American architecture for years.

The Colonial Revival style began at first as an addition to the Queen Anne vocabulary; details such as Adamesque garlands, classical pilasters, and Palladian windows were common. But by 1879, the style had emerged in its own right. Shingles yielded to clapboards, picturesque massing to symmetry. The playful roof of the Queen Anne was replaced by a standard hipped or gabled roof. At the center of the facade, the symmetrical axis, was an elaborate doorway flanked by big broad windows with a single sheet of plate glass below and many smaller panes above arranged in a pseudo-Georgian pattern. Details and massing in this initial phase were larger than their original colonial counterparts, with many of the elements oversized or exaggerated.

The 20th century brought a more academic approach, perfectly symmetrical, correctly proportioned, and more widely accepted. At first only Georgian and Federal precedents were used; however, as various regions of the country explored their colonial architecture, numerous variations became popular. In the Southwest the mission style (characterized by semicircular arches, low-pitched tiled roofs, and stucco surfaces) and the pueblo style (characterized by massive-looking battered walls with round corners, flat roofs, and projecting roof beams called "viga") evolved. In Florida, Texas, and California the Spanish past was romanticized in the Spanish Colonial Revival style popularized by the 1915 San Diego Exposition. The Mar-A-Lago by Addison Mizner in Palm Beach, Fla., is a superb example of the style. White stuccoed Spanish-style cottages and churches and schools built in the Spanish mission styles are also to be found in Louisiana and Alabama, where the earlier Spanish period of domination was relatively short but nonetheless important. In Louisiana, Mississippi, and Alabama, the Creole colonial heritage was borrowed, while from New York came the Dutch colonial, and from Cape Cod came the style that bore its name. From Virginia came the Williamsburg style after the reconstruction of that capital in the 1930s. Versions of Williamsburg-Georgian houses have appeared throughout the country, North and South, East and West, since the 1930s. Whether these have enjoyed more popularity in the South since that time is difficult to say. Certainly they appear in significant numbers in affluent suburbs and sections of cities from Baton Rouge to Norfolk. Alongside the plans and external architectural features of Williamsburg-Georgian, the interior paneling and the "Williamsburg colors," such as soft muted blues and greens, have been used in numerous interiors.

All of these styles were very popular in the South in early 20th-century neighborhoods, as housing demands created enormous pressures. The strong national sentiment, which resulted in the introduction of variations of what were originally regional forms into all parts of the country, served in part to blur the sense of regional architecture.

Robert J. Cangelosi
New Orleans, Louisiana

Alan Axelrod, ed., *The Colonial Revival in America* (1985); Donald W. Curl, *Mizner's Florida: American Resort Architecture* (1984); Robert B. Harmon, *The Colonial Revival in American Architecture: A Brief Study Guide* (1983); Marian Page, *Historic Houses Restored and Preserved* (1976); William H. Pierson, Jr., *American Buildings and Their Architects: The Colonial and Neo-Classical Styles* (1970); Carole Rifkind, *A Field Guide to American Architecture* (1980); Leland M. Roth, *A Concise History of American Architecture* (1979). ☆

Decorative Arts

In 1949 the American curator at the Metropolitan Museum of Art, speaking at the First Antiques Forum at Williamsburg, noted that "very little of artistic merit was made south of Baltimore." The history of southern decorative art is not, however, one of underachievement but of underappreciation. Much of this neglect was at the hands of native sons and daughters until this century. Well-assembled collections of antiques appeared in New England by 1793, but such collections were largely unknown in the South at that time except for the occasional preservation of inherited family pieces or items belonging to Revolutionary War heroes.

Generally speaking, old furniture in the region was thrown or given away or was stored and forgotten. Heat, humidity, and insects have taken their toll as have fires, earthquakes, hurricanes, tornadoes, and wars. Charleston, S.C., for example, experienced so-called great fires in 1740, 1828, and 1861. Ironically, when the city was under seige in 1863 to 1865, Charlestonians who could moved prized family pieces to Columbia for safekeeping only to see their state capitol torched in 1865. Looting during the war contributed to the dearth of surviving southern-made objects. Economic depression followed the Civil War, forcing some southerners to move away and others to sell heirlooms that had survived the war. Continuing regional poverty in the 20th century discouraged interest in preserving craftsmen's products.

A new era of respect for southern handiwork began in 1952 when the Virginia Museum of Fine Arts at Richmond, the magazine *Antiques*, and Colonial Williamsburg jointly organized a major exhibition, *Southern Furniture, 1640–1820*. It was the first show of its kind and spawned many exhibits and studies thereafter. The Virginia Museum exhibit has been overshadowed by only one development—the founding of the Museum of Early Southern Decorative Arts (MESDA) in 1965 in Winston-Salem, N.C. MESDA has fostered a systematic approach to the study of regional decorative arts. Its 15 period rooms are arranged chronologically from 1690 to 1820, and it has four galleries and an outstanding collection. More ambitious, though not as visible, are MESDA's ongoing, long-range projects such as the survey of regional decorative arts in public and private collections, to be published as the *Catalogue of Early Southern Decorative Arts* and the *Index of Early Southern Artists and Artisans.* The latter contains data on a wide spectrum of individuals from cabinetmakers to silversmiths and addresses questions regarding identification of craftspeople, use of technology, design and materials sources, education, apprenticeship experiences, and social customs. Since 1975 the public has been informed of MESDA's work through its quarterly periodical, the *Journal of Early Southern Decorative Arts.*

The scholarship of the last 30 years has promoted development of a comprehensive picture of the South's decorative arts, which have been geographically widespread and culturally diverse. Though fewer "schools" of artisans have been identified than in the Northeast, distinguishing design and construction techniques have been established.

The dominant influence upon the decorative arts along the southeastern seaboard and in many island areas was English. However, the region's decorative arts are richer because of contributions from Moravians, Shakers, Swiss Protestants, Afro-Americans, and French and Caribbean immigrants. In whatever period craftsmen have been active in the South, they have generally taken contemporary concepts of aesthetics and combined them with ideas remembered or inherited from their homelands, using available materials and tools. This has been true of goldsmiths, carriagemakers, potters, needleworkers, and many other craftspeople.

Valuable discoveries have been made regarding the location and output of individuals and workshops, and we now have a growing tabulation of southern-made objects. This research refutes earlier assumptions that southern production was meager and unrefined or that fine crafted things in the South were imported from Europe in general and England in particular.

Decorative arts are often born more from necessity than from the urge to display. This was true for household items in the early South. After shelter, furniture was the most pressing need. Imported furniture was expensive, and only a limited amount could be brought with colonists by ship. Initially, the simplest of devices passed as furniture—benches, stools, chests, and trunks. These were made by carpenters, joiners, and turners or by homeowners themselves. Resourcefulness was a necessity, and comfort was secondary.

When colonists settled the Tidewater sections of Maryland, Virginia, and the Carolinas, they found abundant hardwoods and soon favored oak and walnut for furniture. Secondary woods included yellow pine, maple, red cedar, and in South Carolina, cypress. The need for storage and the absence of closets dictated the production of cupboards, clothespresses, and blanket chests. More complex but not at all beyond the abilities of turners was the gateleg table particularly popular from 1675 through the early 1700s. Its side leaves could be raised when needed or dropped for placement against a wall, providing more space in modest-sized rooms.

The chair, so common and indispensable today, was less common in the 17th century than stools and benches. No single type of chair in the South may be called typical, but armchairs resembling the Brewster or Great chairs of New England were known. They featured turned architectural elements throughout, caging the sitter upon a rush seat. Beds from the early colonial period are as rare as colonial-era chairs, and when equipped with bedstead curtains and valances, they were valued even then at more than their weight in tobacco.

From the 17th century to the early 18th century southerners' desire for luxury goods was not substantial enough to support specialized artisans, but as farmers and traders began to prosper they sought goods such as table services. Silver pieces, sometimes engraved, survive from the Charleston, S.C., area. They approximate the form and embellishment of contemporary English work. Earthenware pottery from the mid-17th century has been found in Virginia. Utilitarian rather than ornate, it was made from Virginia clay banks, which later yielded good brick for permanent homes and civic buildings.

By the middle of the 18th century dramatic changes had come to southern decorative arts. The colonies of the preceding century survived and stabilized, and some settlements even prospered. Soon some southerners desired to improve personal possessions and had the means to do so. English culture became even more dominant. Colonists, emulating prosperous merchant and manufacturing classes in England who aspired to aristocratic values, constructed imposing homes and purchased generous furnishings.

Baltimore and Annapolis, Md., Norfolk and Williamsburg, Va., Edenton, N.C., and Charleston, S.C., boasted active cabinet production. Colonial furniture workshops usually had English-trained craftsmen who instructed and supervised colonial apprentices or local artisans using English copybooks, the most influential being *The Gentleman and Cabinet-Maker's Directory* (London, 1754) by Thomas Chippendale. Southern artisans soon achieved high levels of stylistic and technical ability. Their work and reputation led to sales in New England and exports to Europe. That success coincided with a proliferation of furniture forms more service- and comfort-oriented—easy chairs, tea tables, and several types of desks/secretaries.

Remarkable information has been pieced together concerning outstanding workshops in Williamsburg where craftsmen like Peter Scott, Anthony Hay, and Benjamin Bucktrout sharpened their skills in the 1700s. They created household furniture and ceremonial pieces using mahogany when possible. Durable and easy to carve, mahogany could be polished, revealing superb graining; and though not a native material, it was easily imported from the Caribbean.

Eighteenth-century furniture from eastern Virginia mixed refinements with sound construction. Especially noticeable on case furniture and otherwise elaborate items were the standard features of full dust boards between drawers, paneled backs, and composite feet. Emphasis upon high-quality construction was a trait of southern furniture and contributed to the long-standing perception of it as "plain but neat." By contrast, northern furniture was more flamboyant. In Virginia and elsewhere Chippendale was followed by furniture resembling English Sheraton, Hepplewhite, and Regency styles. Production increased, yet standards remained high.

If Virginia had an 18th-century rival in the decorative arts, it was indeed Charleston, S.C. Not only was Charleston the commercial, political, legal, and social center of South Carolina, but it rivaled Philadelphia culturally and was deservedly known as the jewel of the Southeast. Furniture had been produced in Charleston since soon after its founding in 1670. High English tariffs (33 percent duty on imports by 1822) on finished products encouraged the resourceful Carolinians in their domestic arts.

Charleston furniture almost presumes mahogany. So much of it came from the West Indies that by 1740 all duties on it were repealed. A Charleston chair, for example, was easily distinguished from English imports by the amount of mahogany, by its thicker rails, and by heavier corner blocks. A Charleston double chest of drawers, a bookcase, or a secretary might be exceptionally tall, scaled to high ceilings. Likewise, Charleston beds sometimes had nine-foot posts and had removable headboards to facilitate nocturnal breezes. By 1810 a Charleston directory listed 81 cabinetmakers, and the city's furniture making was at a high point. It declined in the mid-1820s because of the acceptance of cheaper mass-produced pieces from England and New England.

Furniture making followed settlers as they pushed inland, upland, and over the tall line of mountain ranges. From the Germans in the North Carolina Piedmont to the French in lower Louisiana, national craft traditions were retained at least in spirit. Moravian furniture, for example, redefined the term *spartan*. Sawbuck tables and conservatively designed chairs met the utilitarian needs of a simple lifestyle. French settlements in the lower Mississippi Valley also produced rather austere furniture. Large armoires distinctive to the area were made from fine-grained walnut that responded to polishing and from abundant supplies of cypress. Delicately carved, cloven-hoofed doe's feet supported tables, bedsteads, and case furniture alike. Louisiana furniture has only recently been studied, and few pieces have survived. Its difference from French or French Canadian work has been noted, but its similarity to furniture from the French islands of the West Indies has increasingly been recognized.

Late 18th-century silver from the southern colonies is a rarer commodity than furniture because it could be melted for other purposes. Fighting occurred in Charleston, S.C., and the surrounding countryside during the Revolutionary War, and it is a small miracle that any silver survived at all. The British forcibly took it by the rice barrelful, with one account suggesting 500 rice barrels of silver were taken.

At least 35 silversmiths were active at the time, producing mugs, bowls, tankards, and coffee pots as well as occasional unusual items for the table. Craftsmen of note included Daniel and Thomas You and Alexander Petrie. The work of James Geddy II of Williamsburg is well known, too, and can still be appreciated through his re-created home and workshop at Williamsburg.

By the early 19th century silversmith Charles Burnett of Georgetown in the District of Columbia was forming vessels that reflected the growing identification by the American Republic with ancient Greek institutions and aesthetics. An affinity for things Greek was even more noticeable in American furniture. French Empire styles also gained popularity, and American craftsmen synthesized English Regency and French Empire by looking at imported pieces and poring over fashion books like Thomas Hope's *Household Furniture*.

Baltimore was an active center during this period. Fine work also came from Alexandria, Va. Beyond chairs in the manner of Herculaneum and Pompeii, the most conspicuous changes could be seen in chests of drawers often termed "bureaus" or "consol bureaus." Emblematic features included highly figured mahogany veneers accented by brass hardware, carved scrolls of bold proportion, and columns supporting an overhanging top drawer. Scrolls animated sofas on back rails and writhing arm rests. The scale was generally masculine and vigorously imposing, all compatible with Greek Revival architecture, the best examples of which are in the South. This furniture was remarkably inexpensive.

The pendulum of taste eventually swung from classical to other revival styles by the mid-1800s. Rococo revival was especially represented in the South by the successful New Orleans firm of Prudent Mallard. Mallard was at various times listed as a furniture dealer, cabinetmaker, and upholsterer. Rococo furniture could be fancifully ornate with seemingly endless pierced and carved vinework. Mallard's bedroom sets were eagerly sought by those living great distances upriver from New Orleans. His half-testers featured dowels in the footboard finials that could be raised to support tentlike gauze protection against mosquitoes. Such pragmatic adoption of a high style to local conditions of climate was typical of southern ingenuity.

The Civil War and the Reconstruction period that followed disrupted patronage of most of the decorative arts in the South. But progress did not end altogether, as evidenced by the innovative Newcomb pottery works at Tulane University.

Research into the decorative arts of the South is still in its infancy. Yet current scholarly interest is very encouraging, and the titles of recent studies and exhibition catalogs reveal increased specificity and focus. Valuable resources include *Furniture of Williamsburg and Eastern Virginia, 1710–1790, Furniture of the Georgia Piedmont before 1830; John Shaw: Cabinetmaker of Annapolis; Early Furniture of Louisiana*; and currently in preparation *Mississippi-Made Furniture, 1790–1865*. Magazines such as *Southern Accents* and *Texas Homes* are popular forums for the decorative arts in the South, and national periodicals such as the magazine *Antiques* frequently publish stories on the South.

Secretary, brought to Greene County, Georgia, in 1802, a typical southern antique by the time this photograph was made in 1941

Thomas Dewey
University of Mississippi

E. Milby Burton, *Charleston Furniture, 1700–1825* (1955); George B. Cutten, *Silversmiths of North Carolina, 1696–1860* (2d ed., 1984); Marshall B. Davidson, E. Milby Burton, and Helen Comstock, *South Furniture* (1952); William Voss Elder III and Lu Bartlett, *John Shaw: Cabinetmaker of Annapolis* (1983); Henry D. Green, *Furniture of the Georgia Piedmont before 1830* (1976); William Griffin et al., *Neat Pieces: The*

Plain-Style Furniture of Nineteenth-Century Georgia (1983); Wallace B. Gusler, *Furniture of Williamsburg and Eastern Virginia, 1710–1790* (1979); Jessie Poesch, *The Art of the Old South: Painting, Sculpture, Architecture and the Products of Craftsmen, 1560–1860* (1983), *Early Furniture of Louisiana* (1972); Gregory R. Weidman, *Furniture in Maryland, 1740–1940* (1984). ☆

Farm Buildings

Farm buildings are working buildings. The number, kind, and arrangement of buildings on a farm vary regionally according to the type of agriculture practiced in a given locality and inherited ethnic and traditional ideas. Geographical diversity is complicated by change over time. Alterations in the agricultural system of a locality may result in nearly complete replacement of older farm buildings with newer ones. In some parts of eastern Virginia, for example, the change from tobacco to corn, peanut, and hog farming resulted in the nearly complete destruction of the area's 18th- and early 19th-century farm buildings. More commonly, changes in farming practices have altered the preferred types of farm buildings even though the crop has remained the same. Colonial tobacco-growing practices required different kinds of tobacco barns from those used since the early 19th century, so few tobacco barns survive from before 1800.

The most conspicuous farm building to lay observers is the barn. In English tradition, a barn was a place to store unthreshed grain and to process it by threshing. Its plan consisted of large storage bays alternating with narrower runways fitted with doors at one or both ends for wagon entry and with wooden floors for threshing. The smallest version, consisting of a storage bay on either side of a runway, was known by the 18th century as an English barn. Large examples might extend seven to nine parts, with four to five storage bays alternating with threshing floors and runways. After threshing, the grain might be stored in chests in the barn or in separate granaries. Animals lived not in the barn but in other buildings.

There is little evidence that barns of this sort were built in the earliest Tidewater southern settlements. Little need existed for such large buildings for grain storage; other crops, notably tobacco and maize, or Indian corn, occupied more of the farmers' time and resources. Where they were used, barns tended to be small. Grain was most commonly threshed in the field by horses or on portable threshing floors in the farmyard and only occasionally on permanent threshing floors in the barn.

Early barns are more common in the Upland South, and they have attracted considerably more study. Geographers and folklorists have labeled the most common of them single-crib, double-crib, and transverse-crib barns. All are one-story buildings, commonly augmented by open sheds on one or more sides to shelter animals and equipment. The single-crib barn contains one enclosed space; the double-crib barn has two enclosures, separated by a runway. In form it resembles the traditional English barn, although Terry G. Jordan has associated it with central-runway hay barns in Austria, and Martin Wright believes it has a Scandinavian ancestry. Surviving examples seem to have been built for mixed use, with grain storage in one bay, animal housing in another, and the dirt-floored runway used for vehicle loading and shelter below, with hay storage on poles above. The form is an additive one, and examples with three cribs and two runways exist. Single-crib and double-crib barns normally have gable roofs with their ridges running parallel to the entry facades. The transverse-crib barn, on the other hand, has its entrances on the gable ends, as do other southern farm buildings of all sorts. It consists of three or more adjacent cribs, or enclosures, on either side of a wide runway. There are many theories about the origin of the transverse-crib barn, none conclusively established. Henry Glassie's hypothesis is the simplest; he has suggested that the transverse-crib barn was created in the early 19th-century Tennessee Valley through the construction of two parallel double-crib barns separated to create two runways at right angles. Ultimately one of the runways was filled in, creating the transverse-crib barn. Whatever its origin, it seems likely that the transverse-crib barn is a creation of the Upland South. Like the double-crib barn, it was a mixed-use building, housing animals, hay, and farm implements.

In the eastern uplands between the late 18th and the early 20th centuries, farmers also built forebay (also bank, or Pennsylvania) barns, a hybrid of English and Germanic traditions probably created in Pennsylvania in the 18th century. Others used English barns, bank barns without forebays, and hybrids like the cantilever barns of east Tennessee and western North Carolina. In the latter, an upper level was deeply cantilevered beyond a lower on two or four sides of a double- or transverse-crib barn. Few examples survive and their precise origins are uncertain, but they represent a localized combination of the crib barn with the cantilevered appearance and framing of the forebay barn as a way of increasing hay-storage capacity.

Specialized buildings on southern farms tended to be few and small. Even barns were unnecessary. The most common buildings other than barns were small storage houses for field crops. Granaries about 20 feet wide and 20 to 40 feet long were used in the Tidewater for the storage of grain and field crops. The survivors, few of which date before 1800, tend to contain a single open space, sealed inside with flush boards about waist high to permit bulk storage. Most have gable-end entries. Equally prevalent are small, freestanding "cribs" (not to be confused with the cribs that are parts of a barn) for storing corn. One common form, which can be found all over the United States, is made of log or of frame covered with narrow, widely spaced slats. It is 3 or 4 feet high, about the same width, and 10 feet long. The entry is from the gable, and the sides slant in toward the bottom, giving the ends a pentagonal appearance. Along the Atlantic Coast, somewhat larger, gable-end, vertical-walled buildings, about 10 by 20 feet, were constructed. Usually they could be partitioned with loose boards into three parts for ease of loading. Since the late 19th century, many farmers have preferred tall, thin, slatted structures, loaded from the top. Frequently, "drive-through" cribs are created by placing under a single roof one or more cribs that alternate with wagonways for loading them.

Another important class consists of farm buildings that serve for processing agricultural products. Most common are small square buildings, 8 to 12 feet on a side, used in smoking or chemically curing meat and for storing dairy products and keeping them cool. These are usually included in the domestic complex, standing close to the house. From North Carolina south, cotton gins in large buildings built for that purpose are common. Farther north, small gins can sometimes be found installed in a corner of a granary or storage shed, indicating that cotton had been a minor crop for the farmer.

The most recognizable and carefully studied of the processing and storage buildings found on southern farms are the tobacco "barns" scattered throughout the region. Southern farmers have cultivated tobacco as a market crop since the early 17th century, and a variety of barn forms have been created in response to changing methods of cultivation and curing. Before the early 19th century tobacco farmers in the Tidewater and Piedmont regions prepared and partially dried their tobacco in open sheds before hanging it in long, narrow barns to finish curing. The tobacco leaves were tied in bunches, or "hands," and draped over sticks a little over five feet long. The inside of the barn was fitted with horizontal poles, running front to back, set at intervals of about five feet horizontally and vertically. The sticks carrying the tobacco leaves were draped across these tier poles, which filled the barn from the ridge of the roof to within a few feet of the floor. There the tobacco was left to be dried by the air. Then it was taken down and pressed into enormous barrels, or hogsheads, for sale and shipping.

Methods of curing by heat have been used since the 18th century, when tobacco was exposed to damped open fires whose smoke was allowed to drift out through holes in the barn. Fire curing of dark tobaccos is still common in the Virginia Piedmont and in Kentucky, where square or oblong barns, respectively, are used for the process. About 1820 a technique was developed for curing bright tobaccos, grown in eastern Virginia and North Carolina, in small barns using the heat from enclosed fires. These "flue-cured" barns, which are still widely used, are cubical structures 16 to 24 feet on a side. Many are built of log, though frame and more recently concrete-block structures can also be found. The earliest survivors are heated from long, low, open-topped, floor-level stone furnaces, resembling barbecue pits, which are stoked from the outside. From the far end of the furnace a metal flue protrudes, carried horizontally to the far corner and then up through the roof of the barn. This flue, together with the piece of sheet metal that covers the open top of the furnace, helps to diffuse the heat evenly through the barn, which like its colonial predecessors is filled with tier poles to carry the tobacco sticks. Flue-cured barns are customarily scattered over the farm, convenient to the fields. Open sheds on one or more sides provide shelter for the workers who strip the plants and prepare the tobacco to be hung. In North Carolina one occasionally sees long rows of these barns connected by a continuous arcade of open worksheds, but more often the barns stand singly or in pairs. In the 20th century, fuel-oil furnaces, recognizable by the fuel-oil tanks next to the barn, replaced coal- and wood-fired furnaces as the preferred heating method, and they in turn were supplanted by propane heating devices, identifiable by the sheet-metal monitor on the ridge of the roof. Most recently, "bulk curing" in small, tightly sealed metal boxes resembling trailers has begun to replace flue curing.

Air curing continues to be used for some tobaccos. In southern Maryland, long, narrow barns are used. These are usually covered with vertical-board siding in which every other board is hinged to allow the sides to be opened for greater air penetration when the building is full. In the Appalachian uplands hay barns are often adapted to the purpose simply by pulling off most of their exterior siding.

A farm is an economic entity. Except, perhaps, for a small yard in front of the house, the farm buildings are a unit with the farmhouse, the yards, and the fields. Together, they constitute a continuous group of related spaces carefully designed for the production, processing, and storage of agricultural products. The farmer must decide which necessary tasks require special buildings, which can be performed in multipurpose buildings, and which can be accomplished in the open. Thus, the open sheds that cluster around all southern farm buildings cannot be overlooked in an account of the architecture of the farm. They form transitional spaces between the tightly enclosed farmhouse and farm buildings and the open yards and fields; their use is encouraged by the mild climate of the region, which allows storage, equipment shelter, and even animal housing in sheds rather than fully enclosed buildings.

The largest divisions of the farmstead are the yards and fields themselves. Here space is differentiated by the varied fences and walls that are in many cases the oldest forms to be seen on the southern farm. Picket fences for front yards and gardens and post-and-rail fences for gardens and farmyards were first recorded in the 17th century, and they are still used for these purposes. The snake, or Virginia, fence and its

Outbuilding on a farm, Sharon, Mississippi, 1972

stake-and-rider variants have been used to enclose pastures and fields since the late 17th century. Their advantage is that they can be disassembled and moved as land use changes. Horizontal-board fences, a 19th-century innovation, are also common in prosperous areas of the South. In limestone regions of the Upland South stone, or "rock," fences were popular. A striking form of Kentucky stone wall, in which the horizontal courses are capped by a row of jagged stones set on edge, is known as the Bluegrass fence, but it is a northern European form. As in other parts of the country, wire fencing and electric fencing have replaced wood and stone, particularly for farm fields; but the diligent observer can still find all of the traditional fence types.

See also AGRICULTURE: / Tobacco Culture; FOLKLIFE: / Smokehouse; GEOGRAPHY: Plantation Morphology; / Cotton Gins

Dell Upton
University of California
at Los Angeles

Eric Arthur and Dudley Witney, *The Barn: A Vanishing Landmark in North America* (1972); Ligon Flynn and Roman Stankus, in *Carolina Dwelling: Towards Preservation of Place: In Celebration of the North Carolina Vernacular Landscape*, ed. Doug Swaim (1978); Henry Glassie, *Mountain Life and Work* (Spring 1964, Summer 1965), *Pattern in the Material Folk Culture of the Eastern United States* (1969), *Pennsylvania Folklife* (Winter 1965–66, Summer 1966); J. Fraser Hart and Eugene Cotton Mather, *Annals of the Association of American Geographers* (September 1961); Terry G. Jordan, *American Log Buildings: An Old World Heritage* (1985); Marian Moffett and Lawrence Wodehouse, *The Cantilever Barn in East Tennessee* (1984); Karl B. Raitz, *Landscape* (Spring 1978); Orlando V. Ridout, in *Perspectives in Vernacular Architecture*, ed. Camille Wells (1982); Laura Scism, in *Carolina Dwelling: Towards Preservation of Place: In Celebration of the North Carolina Vernacular Landscape*, ed. Doug Swaim (1978). ☆

French Architecture

Although France's colonial domination of Louisiana lasted only from 1682 to the 1760s, her influence upon the architecture and culture of the region was profound. Encompassing all the territory drained by the Mississippi River, Louisiana was claimed by LaSalle, who in 1682 had descended the river from the French holdings in Canada. Not until 1698, however, did Pierre le Moyne de Iberville sail from France to build the first French outpost on the Gulf Coast. Situated on the eastern shore of Biloxi Bay, Fort Maurepas was a modest example of a system of fortifications developed by the French military engineer Sebastien Vauban (1633–1707). Built entirely of timber, it consisted of a square palisade with pointed bastions at the corners designed to eliminate blind spots on the wall. Thus, the pattern of fortifications was strongly influenced by French military engineering theory. Many other forts followed, all employing the Vauban system to some degree.

In addition to fortifications, military engineers laid out towns (usually on a grid plan) and designed buildings for the crown, often guided by French precedent published in books such as *La Science des Ingenieurs* (Paris, 1729). Their designs were usually simplified adaptations of current Louis XV forms. The larger colonial structures were outwardly symmetrical and generally rectangular, with high-pitched roofs usually hipped at the ends. Moulded stucco details such as quoins at the corners and horizontal bands were often used to imitate stone masonry construction. In massing and detail they were similar to French buildings elsewhere, but the subtropical climate had a marked influence upon the local buildings. Unlike France and Canada, the southern colony had frequent, heavy rains and a long summer. Because traditional French building forms were better suited to northern latitudes, roofed galleries were added to shade the walls and provide sheltered outdoor living space. The gallery roofs were often framed from the tops of the turned or chamfered wood posts to a point about halfway up the slope of the main roof, giving the roof an unusual double pitch (e.g., The Intendance, 1749).

The heavy timber building frame known as *colombage* was brought from France, where it had been in wide use since medieval times. It consisted of squared timbers pinned together at mortise-and-tenon joints. Continuous sills were laid upon the ground, and posts were set at the corners of the building and at the sides of all windows and doors. Across the tops of these posts, horizontal members formed the top of the walls. In order to add stability, diagonal members were added, and to achieve some insulation, the walls were filled with either soft bricks or with *bousillage* (a mixture of mud and moss or straw) and covered on the outside with wide boards or stucco. The roof-framing systems of even small French colonial buildings were usually well-crafted trusses pinned at the joints with wooden pegs. Dormers were small and attics were most often used only for storage.

French influence did not cease when colonial Louisiana was ceded to Spain in 1763. Although the government changed, many of those who designed and constructed the buildings were born of French parents, and they carried on the tradition that had already been established.

The greatest influence that the Spanish had on architecture was their enactment of laws governing building construction in the city of New Orleans. Until then, owners were free to build as they chose, which usually meant frame buildings roofed with flammable wood shingles. In 1788 and again in 1794, catastrophic fires leveled large portions of the city. After the second great fire, the Cabildo, or city government, specified that all roofs be covered with slate or tile, that walls be of brick or brick between posts covered with stucco, and that buildings be built up to the front property line, thus creating a sort of fire wall and giving the city its intensely urban character.

During the Spanish period, Americans began to filter into the former French colony, and many of them continued to build in the adapted French style. By responding to the problems of climate and limited available materials, the "typical" French house became an accepted form that survived long after the Louisiana Purchase of 1803. This type of house was rectangular, usually of two stories, and the rooms opened onto one another without halls. The first story was built entirely of stuccoed brick and was used for utility purposes; the second story was of colombage filled with brick or bousillage and covered on the outside with stucco or wide shiplapped boards. Interior walls were invariably plastered and painted. All wood, except the floors, was painted. Access to the second floor was by exterior stairs under the sheltering gallery roofs. Openings were protected by solid wooden shutters hung on strap hinges, and the first floor was paved with brick if it was paved at all. The second-floor ceiling joists and floorboards formed the ceiling of the first floor. The principal floor was usually well finished, with French doors and casement windows hung on decorative wrought-iron hinges. Top and bottom bolts, slide latches, and knob-operated bar latches completed the door and window hardware. The exposed second-floor ceiling joists (always beaded on the corners) supported the beaded attic floorboards. The plastered walls were usually adorned with a baseboard, chair rail, and cornice (always of wood). Ceilings on the principal floor were generally high (10 to 12 feet) to allow the summer heat to rise so that cross-ventilation could carry it out of the house.

The principal architectural feature of most rooms was the mantel. Fireplaces in buildings of this type were invariably on interior walls, and they were often paired back to back. Consequently, the fireboxes and breasts projected into the rooms. Mantels were paneled on the sides, and the shelf always wrapped around the breast, returning against the wall. Ornament on these "Creole" mantels varied from engaged turned posts to fluted pilasters. The more elaborate gougework on some Creole mantels was probably a result of influence from the American North. Sometimes, the breasts were also encased in paneling and the room cornice was carried out around them.

Variations of this perfectly adapted building form were used in towns and suburbs and in the country until the middle of the 19th century. The popularity of the great national building styles—Greek Revival, Gothic, and Italianate—ultimately overwhelmed the traditional local style, but even these were somewhat affected by the adapted French forms.

Combining as it did elements of Louis XV design and climatic adaptations to the southern latitude, expressed in indigenous materials, French colonial architecture left a unique and enduring impression upon the South—one that exists in no other place in quite the same way.

See also ETHNIC LIFE: / French; Spanish

Frank W. Masson
New Orleans, Louisiana

Jessie Poesch, *The Art of the Old South: Painting, Sculpture, Architecture and the Products of Craftsmen, 1560–1860* (1983); Italo W. Ricciuti, *New Orleans and Its Environs: The Domestic Architecture, 1727–1870* (1938); Samuel Wilson, Jr., *Bienville's New Orleans: A French Colonial Capital, 1718–1768* (1968). ☆

Georgian Revival Architecture

Within the space of a quarter century, from the 1920s to the beginning of World War II, a body of truly distinguished domestic architecture was produced in the South. These Georgian Revival houses, distinctive from those of the early 20th century and those of the post-World War II period, occupy a place in the architectural history of the South—and particularly the Upland South—not unlike that of the houses of the mid-19th-century antebellum period. Both were products of a rapidly developing economy, and both were places on which their owners had lavished money in the creation of a handsome home. Both were also brought to a halt by war: in the first instance, by the Civil War; in the second, by the prolonged economic effects of the Great Depression and then by World War II.

The Georgian Revival of the interwar period was separate and distinct from the Colonial Revival of the early 20th century. At the same time, it grew from many of the same impulses that had fostered the earlier effort and was the final or mature phase of the Colonial Revival. The character of the houses of the period is specific, definable, and discrete; they are also extraordinarily beautiful buildings.

The personality of the houses of the Georgian Revival is dominated by the architecture of the 18th century of Virginia and Maryland, which by a confluence of natural and contrived circumstances, came to be seen as an exemplar of the finest design. This borrowing represents one of the earliest instances in this country of a contemporary adaptation of older indigenous architecture. The upper middle class and the aspiring aristocrats of the early 20th century—some of whom were the descendants of the middle class and aristocracy of the 18th century—were anxious to assume the trappings of their own, or collateral, ancestry and saw the houses of the 18th century as appropriate settings.

The image of the Virginia house was strong and desirable, and its adaptation as a model was a deliberate decision by 20th-century southerners. Much was written about the 18th-century houses of Virginia in the period. They were more celebrated than those of any other southern state. A few books were written about the houses of South Carolina, Charleston, Georgia, and Alabama, and Thomas Tileston Waterman's *Early Architecture of North Carolina* appeared, but none was so exhaustive an investigation of 18th-century houses as Thomas Tileston Waterman's *The Mansions of Virginia*. Published in 1945, it did not influence the designs of the 1920s and 1930s, but it showed the degree of scrutiny applied in that era to 18th-century houses.

An appreciation of the mansions of the James River is well stated and purposefully crafted in remarks that William Lawrence Bottomley (1883–1951), a leading architect of the Georgian Revival country house, made on the topic during an interview in 1929. Speaking principally of the great James River plantations, he said,

> . . . they have a marvelous natural advantage because of their location in a beautiful, in many ways romantic, country; but the point is . . . that this natural advantage has been turned to full account through the development of a splendidly sound architectural tradition . . . the direct outcome of a distinguished civilization, built up in two centuries or more of country life. . . . The Virginia families who maintained this tradition were careful to nourish it and to enrich it as much as possible, by drawing on inspiration outside. . . . But the importations were so thoroughly absorbed into the Virginia tradition that it remained absolutely American—American of the Old South. I believe we should do everything possible to preserve this old southern ideal of country house architecture because it is one of the finest things we have and it is still vital.

Bottomley was foremost among a group of architects, mainly from New York and Philadelphia, who designed buildings—mostly Georgian Revival—for southern clients from 1910 to 1940, mostly in the 1920s. This group included Harrie T. Lindeberg, Robert Rodes McGoodwin, Charles Barton Keene, Aymar Embury, Hobart Upjohn, William Adams Delano, Chester Holmes Aldrich, John Russell Pope, and Dwight James Baum. Each specialized in house types and styles related to the matter of "personality," a frequent topic of architectural writing of the period. The houses of these architects were important in themselves, but their deeper significance lies in their influence. In Richmond, where the largest single group of Georgian Revival houses by William Lawrence Bottomley is located, and throughout Virginia, Bottomley's houses were emulated by local and regionally important architects, including Henry Baskervill (1867–1946) among others. Bottomley designed one of his finest Georgian Revival houses in the 1930s, Tatton Hall in Raleigh, N.C., for N. E. Edgerton. In Winston-Salem, the houses of

Charles Barton Keene were often the particular models for houses by the local architectural firm of Northrup and O'Brien and by C. Gilbert Humphries. In Atlanta and the state of Georgia the work of Neel Reid, distinguished by a lavish hand heavily influenced by an affection for Italy and the classical devices of the Italian Renaissance, saw wide admiration and emulation there and in the states of the Lower South.

Other architects throughout the South also designed in the Georgian Revival style. In Virginia, perhaps the greatest local practitioner of the style, after Bottomley, was Duncan Lee (1884–1954), who took Carter's Grove, one of the landmark houses of the 18th century, and transformed it into one of the landmark houses of the Georgian Revival. He connected the wings to the main block, raised the roof, and added ranges of dormers, one of the hallmarks of the Georgian Revival. Stanhope S. Johnson was another Virginia architect who achieved great acclaim for his Georgian houses, including Galliston Hall in Farmington at Charlottesville.

Interior hallway in a Virginia home designed by architect William T. Bottomley

Architects elsewhere in the South were also specialists in the Georgian Revival. Among them were James R. Edmunds and Herbert G. Crisp, who operated as the Office of Joseph Evans Sperry in Baltimore. One of their landmark houses is located not in Maryland but outside Chapel Hill, N.C. It was designed for David St. Pierre Du Bose, of a distinguished South Carolina family, and his wife who, having lived for some time in Baltimore, chose architects of that city to create a house for their Meadowmont estate. It obviously borrows from Maryland houses, including the Hammond-Harwood House doorway, one of the most frequently copied features of the period, which appears at Meadowmont on the east entrance.

The Georgian Revival houses of these architects were found most commonly in two places in the South. They were located on large multiacre lots in the upper-level suburban developments of the period, such as Windsor Farms in Richmond and Biltmore Forest in Asheville; or they were the seats of large suburban or rural estates, where they were often accompanied by complementary outbuildings that, in Keene's work, create a harmonious assembly. These architects not only designed houses and other buildings that were not only built in the South but that, in numerous ways, reflected the southern climate, geography, society, and strong traditions. Those traditions and their imagery, illusionary or real, accounted for the success of Edmunds and Crisp's work.

The principal Georgian Revival restoration project in the 1920s and 1930s was the restoration of Williamsburg, Virginia's colonial capital. Word of this project spread rapidly among the architectural community, and progress on the various buildings was widely reported in both professional and decorator magazines. Williamsburg was but the largest of many such efforts, including the restoration of Stratford Hall by the Robert E. Lee Memorial Association; of Gunston Hall by the Colonial Dames of America; and of Monticello, on which Fiske Kimball advised. Other projects were Kenmore in Fredericksburg; Wilton in Richmond; and Christ Church, Lancaster County, Va. Among the last of these was the reconstruction of Tryon Palace in New Bern, N.C.

Coinciding with these architectural restorations was an associated and closely related series of garden restorations by one of a series of men, including, principally, Charles Gillette (1886–1969), Arthur Shurcliffe, Umberto Innocenti of New York, or Thomas Sears of Boston. In 1923 the James River Garden Club published a seminal work, *Historic Gardens of Virginia*, which included period and documentary photographs of Virginia gardens, together with restored gardens of the 1910–20 period and the early 1920s. It remains one of the most important works of the period, which also saw the publication of *Carolina Gardens* and *The Garden History of Georgia* (1933).

The success of the Georgian Revival was also influenced and enhanced by developments in brickwork. Herbert Claiborne, Sr. (1886–1957) was an acknowledged historian of Virginia brickwork, and his firm, Claiborne & Taylor, had executed work on a number of restorations. He brought his knowledge of 18th-century Virginia brickwork and his experience in repairing it to the construction of houses in Richmond and other parts of Virginia. As did the architects, Claiborne & Taylor set a high standard of excellence that became a model for emulation.

The people who commissioned Georgian Revival houses in Virginia and elsewhere in the South were of two types. Some, including most of those in Richmond, were prominent individuals in their states and the region, many having second-generation ancestors in Virginia. This group looked back locally to their 18th-century origins and tried to downplay the industrial 19th-century sources of their wealth and any associated Victorian manifestations. Another group of clients during the interwar period included non-southerners or relocated southerners for whom farm seats and hunting boxes were expanded, overbuilt, or designed anew in Virginia, North Carolina, South Carolina, Maryland, and Georgia. Because of the social status of these housebuilders and the professional status of the architects, much of the best work in the Georgian Revival style was published, mainly in the 1920s and 1930s, in such national trade, professional, and related magazines as *House Beautiful*, *Architect*, *Architectural Record*, *House and Garden*, and *Country Life*.

One of the lasting contributions of the Georgian Revival to southern and American architectural history was a publication, *Great Georgian Houses of America*. The Great Depression led to much retrenchment in the architectural profession. The chief response to the rising unemployment of draftsmen and apprentice architects was the organization of Architects Emergency Committee, beginning in 1930. In 1932 trained architects and draftsmen began producing measured drawings of the plans, plats, elevations, and details of America's historic houses, which were published in 1933 in *Great Georgian Houses of America* for the benefit of the Architects Emergency Committee.

Great Georgian Houses was published by subscription, with the names of subscribers listed at the front in the fashion of 18th-century English architectural book publishing, suggesting a parallel to the social status of the subscribers. Forty-four houses, representing 14 states and the District of Columbia, were illustrated in the first volume. Not unexpectedly, more houses were included from Virginia (9 of the 44) than from any other state. Maryland houses were second in number. Sixteen pages were given to Mount Vernon, the largest section devoted to a single building, and their inclusion was the first time that the Mount Vernon Ladies Association had given permission for their publication. Bremo, the Cocke family estate in Fluvanna County, Va., is shown on 11 pages. The prominence of the Virginia and Maryland houses reflected their significance as exemplars of the finest Georgian and Federal work. Volume 2 of *Great Georgian Houses of America* was published in 1937 and included illustrations of six houses in both Virginia and New York; otherwise, no single state was represented by more than three houses.

The seeds of change were, however, already in the wind. For architects who practiced after World War II and for the clients of those architects, *Great Georgian Houses* had a broad appeal and did serve as the inspiration and source book for the design of numerous revival houses. But distinct changes in both the scale and character of these postwar houses set them apart from those of the interwar period. The careers of most of the architects who had designed Georgian Revival houses in the interwar period were largely over by 1937, and few had work of any consequence after 1941. *Great Georgian Houses* is a fitting epitaph for their careers and for the Georgian Revival of the interwar period.

See also HISTORY AND MANNERS: Historic Preservation; RECREATION: / Colonial Williamsburg

Davyd Foard Hood
North Carolina Department of Cultural Resources
Raleigh, North Carolina

Mary Wallace Crocker, *Historic Architecture in Mississippi* (1973); Charles B. Hosmer, Jr., *Presence of the Past: A History of the Preservation Movement in the United States before Williamsburg* (1965); Marian Page, *Historic Houses Restored and Preserved* (1976); William H. Pierson, Jr., *American Buildings and Their Architects: The Colonial and Neo-Classical Styles* (1970); Leland M. Roth, *A Concise History of American Architecture* (1979); Kenneth Severens, *Southern Architecture: 350 Years of Distinctive American Buildings* (1981). ☆

German Architecture

Germanic settlement in the South had two main sources: movement south from Pennsylvania in the 18th century and immigration to Texas in the mid-19th century. The eastern Germans abandoned their distinctive architectural traditions early in the 19th century, while the Texas Germans maintained theirs only until the end of the century. Nevertheless, the diversity of Germanic regional traditions in Europe is reflected in the very different buildings that can still be seen in the two regions.

Germans settled in the South in the 17th century, and their names can be found in the record books from an early date. Architecturally, however, the Germanic groups who settled in Pennsylvania in the 1680s made the first notable marks on the landscape. In the 1720s the descendants of those colonists, augmented by fresh arrivals from Europe, began to migrate down the Shenandoah Valley along the Great Valley Road, which stretches from south-central Pennsylvania through Maryland, Virginia, and Tennessee, with a branch into North Carolina. Although they have been called Germans, they were of diverse central and western European origins, including emigrants from the present-day nations of Germany, Switzerland, the Netherlands, France, Czechoslovakia, and Poland. Scholars and antiquarians have given most attention to the architecture of those groups with origins near the Rhine River. They created a distinctive material legacy.

Central to their traditions was a kind of house, imported by German and Swiss immigrants, called the *Flurkuchenhaus* (hall-kitchen house), or Continental house. It was one or two stories tall and had two to four rooms in the main story. Its distinctive feature was an off-center interior chimney. To one side was a long, narrow kitchen (*Küche*), into which the front and rear outside doors opened. It had a large fireplace for cooking, and the stairs were located in one corner. Sometimes a secondary room was partitioned off at the rear of the kitchen or in an entrance vestibule at the front. On the opposite side of the central chimney a square or nearly square parlor (*Stube*) was heated by a metal or ceramic stove that was attached to the chimney and fed through a stokehole in the rear from the kitchen fireplace. By the end of the 18th century, iron Franklin-type stoves or small fireplaces were more common. Some builders installed a fixed table and benches in the front outside corner of the *Stube*, although none now survive. Often, there was a narrow sleeping and storage room (*Kammer*) behind the *Stube*.

The Continental house was very much a farmhouse: the cellar and the upper floors were as important as the main level. The cellar was devoted to food preparation and storage. Cellars were usually dug under only part of the house and, in large examples, included an outer room and an inner one that might be vaulted or otherwise insulated for use as a cool storage space. If possible, the house was built over a spring to provide a water source. In recognition of the active use of the cellar, the house was frequently located on a bank in such a way that both the main floor and the basement could be entered at grade. The loft area of the *Flurkuchenhaus* was traditionally used for the storage of grain and other farm produce. Loose boards laid over the collar beams of the roof trusses increased the attic's storage capacity, and a fixed stair on one gable end gave access to this uppermost level. Some houses had small pent roofs that sheltered working spaces close to the outside walls, and others had large porches or piazzas in which, according to 19th-century accounts, saddles, bridles, and other equipment were hung. The domestic space might be extended farther into the yard by an outdoor bake oven. As the description suggests, the Germanic house was a rural building, although a few urban examples could be found in the South.

The *Flurkuchenhaus* was not the only dwelling used by Germanic farmers in the 18th-century South. Single-room houses were common but are not as conspicuous to the modern observer. Most of the survivors were sturdily built and bank sited in the customary fashion and had two full stories of living space. At the other extreme, a few very large houses separated the traditional ground-floor rooms with a narrow entry passage that might contain the stair. In the best surviving example, Schiefferstadt (mid-18th century) in Frederick, Md., the passage runs through the middle of the chimney stack. Fireplaces opening onto the passage were used to stoke the iron stoves in the living rooms.

Germanic farmers used distinctive structural systems to create their farmhouses and farm buildings. Among the surviving structures, log walls are most common. Log building was brought to America from central Europe, and Germans in the South maintained the tradition. Early German structures tended to use massive logs with full-dovetail notching, although half-dovetail and V-notched buildings can also be found. Finer buildings employed rubble, sometimes coursed, limestone walls. The German method of framing, or *Fachwerk*, was rare in the South. *Fachwerk* is a timber-framing system distinguished by the use of square posts linked by intermediate horizontal rails about the same size as the posts. No studs are used in *Fachwerk*. The most recognizable feature is the diagonal bracing that connects horizontal members at the top and bottom of the wall rather than running from a vertical to a horizontal timber as in English traditional building. Although the term is usually translated as half-timbering, and the frame might be filled with brick or wattle and daub and exposed to view on the exterior, southern examples were usually covered with weatherboards.

Most Germanic buildings in the 18th-century South were built by individual farmers, yet the largest and most conspicuous groups of survivors are those of the Moravian communalists at Salem and Bethabara in the North Carolina Piedmont. The Moravians arrived at Bethabara in November 1753, but the principal Moravian settlement at Salem was begun in 1766. Although the Moravians carefully regulated building in their communities, traditional structural systems and traditional forms characterized their work. The early buildings were built of *Fachwerk* or log; after the 1780s brick was common. Special plans were devised for the enormous communal dwellings that housed the single men and women, but the smaller 18th-century dwellings used the traditional plans employed by German farmers in Maryland, Virginia, and North Carolina. Eighteenth-century public buildings like the tavern, the boys' school, and the Vorsteher's house used Anglo-American two-room-deep, central-passage plans.

Germanic ideas were also major components of a distinctive barn type brought into the Upland South. Called a bank barn, a forebay barn, a Pennsylvania barn, or a Switzer barn, it combined Continental siting and use with English interior arrangements. In Switzerland a barn with its upper level overhanging the lower along one long side was used to house farm animals below and the hay to feed them above. In Pennsylvania in the 18th century the upper floor of the Swiss barn began to be arranged like an English barn, with openings in the center of both long sides affording access to a central threshing floor flanked by storage bays for grain.

The bank barn was set into a hillside like the Continental house, so that both levels could be approached at grade. In the Upland South the Pennsylvania barn was occasionally built in brick, but more often in log or stone with frame overhangs, or forebays. The heyday of the bank barn in the South was the first half of the 19th century, although it continued to be built until the end of the century.

In the 18th century, Germanic groups in the South were known for avoiding contact with Anglo-Americans; but after the Revolution they were drawn into the larger society, and their architecture began to show signs of assimilation. The forebay barn is the most obvious example of this fusion, although its effects can be observed in Continental houses as well. They were made to appear more like large Anglo-American houses by increasing the number of openings, spacing them regularly, and sometimes moving the door closer to the center either to achieve or to give the impression of symmetry. Other builders moved the chimneys to the ends. Household work was moved out of the house into separate kitchens and other domestic outbuildings. They substituted freestanding meat houses and smokehouses for vaulted cellars, and they built small houses over springs to cool their dairy products instead of constructing their dwellings over the springs. With the importance of the house as a working building reduced, many builders abandoned bank siting and set their houses flat on the ground. The old narrow room that was once the kitchen was now used as a sitting room or dining room. Finally, the Continental plan itself was abandoned. After 1830 it was difficult to recognize any distinctive features in the architecture of those whose ancestors had come from central Europe in the 18th century.

There was a fresh German contribution to southern architecture in the mid-19th century, when emigrants from many parts of present-day Germany came to Texas as part of a larger migration of Germans to the central regions of the United States. The first few arrived in 1831 and began to settle in the region between Austin and Houston. A larger group arrived between 1845 and 1860, settled in east Texas near their predecessors, and also went to the hill country of west-central Texas northwest of San Antonio. Impelled by overpopulation, the mechanization of German agriculture, and crop failures in the 1840s and 1850s, about 30,000 Germans immigrated to Texas before 1860. In Texas they abandoned some distinctive architectural customs, including the building of house-barns, courtyard farmsteads, and tightly clustered agricultural villages, although Fredericksburg and New Braunfels in the hill country were envisioned as traditional farm villages. They tended to settle in dispersed farmsteads similar to other Texans, but their preference for mixed farming led to the construction of capacious barns that distinguished their farmsteads.

The Texas Germans built in log, frame, and stone. Their timber structures used *Fachwerk* frames similar to those found in the eastern South. Many were covered on the exterior with weatherboards, as in the 18th-century examples; but exposed and whitewashed frames, with either a rendered plaster protecting wattle and daub or pieces of limestone between the timbers, were more common than elsewhere in the South. In the hill country limestone construction dominated after the Civil War.

Although the agricultural practices and structural systems of Texas Germans had European origins, this was less true with respect to their house forms. On farms and in towns Germans built one- and two-room houses with central entries and three-opening facades. Often there was a rear kitchen lean-to roof and a gable-end stair to the second story. When German farmers abandoned Fredericksburg to live on their agricultural tracts in the late 19th century, very small versions of these one-room houses were built as "Sunday houses" for use by the family when in town. The plan and appearance of Texas German houses are similar to those of Anglo-American Texans and very different from the postmedieval European farmhouses to which they have been compared.

See also ETHNIC LIFE: / Germans; FOLKLIFE: House Types; GEOGRAPHY: Log Housing; RELIGION: / Moravians

Dell Upton
University of California at Los Angeles

Edward A. Chappell, *Proceedings of the American Philosophical Society* (February 1980); Bernard L. Herman, in *Carolina Dwelling: Towards Preservation of Place: In Celebration of the North Carolina Vernacular Landscape*, ed. Doug Swaim (1978); Terry G. Jordan, *German Seed in Texas Soil: Immigrant Farmers in Nineteenth-Century Texas* (1966), *Texas Log Building: A Folk Architecture* (1978); William J. Murtagh, *Moravian Architecture and Town Planning: Bethlehem, Pennsylvania, and Other Eighteenth-Century American Settlements* (1967); Dell Upton, *Notes on Virginia* (Summer 1979), in *Material Culture of the Wooden Age*, ed. Brooke Hindle (1981). ☆

Gothic Revival Architecture

Despite a preoccupation with classical architecture and culture, the South has always flirted with a Gothic identity. The concepts of chivalry, feudalism, and aristocracy are so deeply embedded in the southern psyche that they remain there today. To truly understand the southern Gothic Revival buildings, one must see them as part of a larger phenomenon, social as well as architectural.

Southern interest in the Middle Ages expressed itself in numerous ways. One was an extravagant admiration for romantic-antiquarian literature such as Sir Walter Scott's Waverley novels. A host of minor southern writers before the Civil War emulated Scott's style, and southern families even named their children after the titles and characters of Gothic novels.

Southerners wrote of themselves as if they were describing heroes of Gothic romance. In contrasting the northern and southern characters, Richmond newspaper editor and historian Edward Pollard spoke of a lack of congeniality between the Puritan colonists who established themselves on the "rugged and cheerless soil of New England" and the colonists of Virginia and the Carolinas who were, he said, "distinguished by their polite manners, their fine sentiments, their attachment to a sort of feudal life, . . . and the prodigal and improvident aristocracy that dispersed its stores in constant rounds of hospitality and gaiety."

Other 19th-century writers were less enthusiastic about the South's Camelot-like self-image. Mark Twain commented caustically on the phenomenon and blamed it on Sir Walter Scott, who "with his enchantments . . . sets the world in love with dreams and phantoms; with decayed and swinish forms of religion; with decayed and degraded systems of government . . . and the sham chivalrys of a brainless and worthless long-vanished society. . . . Most of the world has now outlived a good part of these harms, . . . but in our South they flourish pretty forcefully still." Twain blamed "the Sir Walter disease" for what he considered the worst traits of the southern character and manners, from jejune romanticism to duels, inflated speeches, and inflexible patterns of rank and caste. Twain concluded that but for the influence of Scott, the southern character "would be wholly modern, in place of modern and medieval mixed."

If Twain felt that Scott's romantic-chivalric attitudes had retarded the South, he also did not fail to link Scott with southern Gothic architecture. One building he specifically attacked was the Louisiana State Capitol at Baton Rouge, by architect James Dakin. The Capitol, anathematized by Twain as "this little sham castle," was, in fact, the largest and most conspicuous Gothic public building in the antebellum South. As such, it was probably a more potent symbol than Twain realized. In addition to literary associations, it conjured up the image of a South with fortified castles as statehouses, suggesting decentralized, feudal governments and an individualistic-separatist mentality. Although only two castellated statehouses were built in the United States, both were in the Deep South (Louisiana and Georgia). It is difficult to suppose that southerners—and northerners as well—did not read political as well as literary symbolism into them.

Louisiana state capitol, Baton Rouge, 1847–49

Another context in which medieval imagery might have seemed symbolically appropriate was the southern plantation: the only true nonurban, decentralized, self-sustaining (i.e., "feudal") social unit in 19th-century America. But Gothic plantation houses were a comparative rarity. The image of planters living like feudal lords in Gothic castles surrounded by a class of humans linked in an unending bond to the soil was perhaps too stark to be palatable. The Greek Revival plantation house, with its symbolic ambiguity, seemed to divert notice from the moral problems of a slave economy, whereas the Gothic would have called attention to them. Waverley (1852), near Columbus, Ga., seems to underscore the literary appeal but moral unsuitability of the Gothic castle for plantation architecture. It is a Greek Revival plantation house with a romantic name derived from Scott.

Despite the general reservations, however, a few planters had romantic enthusiasm enough to opt for Gothic. One example is Belmead, in Powhatan County, Va., the castellated villa of

Philip St. George Cocke, whose very name tells us about his family's pretensions to an aristocratic-chivalric ideal (he had a cousin named Richard Ivanhoe Cocke). Belmead, designed in 1845 by New York architect Alexander Jackson Davis, is situated above the James River, from which it is meant to be viewed. More than any other southern Gothic house, it resembles the Gothic villas along the Hudson River in New York State. This resemblance may help to explain the scarcity of Gothic castles in the South. Large Gothic villas may have been stigmatized by wealthy yet socially conservative southerners because of their implied connections to liberal and progressive patrons in New York and the Northeast. Romanticism in the South seemed to be of a nostalgic, backward-looking, Sir Walter Scott type, while northern Romanticism was of a progressive, forward-looking character, expressing itself in transcendentalism, the Hudson River school of painting, and the American park movement.

By choosing castellated Gothic for Belmead, Philip St. George Cocke exhibited a less regional, more cosmopolitan sensibility than most southern planters were willing to evince. Yet despite its architectural cosmopolitanism, Belmead had regional touches, such as window glass decorated with southern plantation crops: cotton, tobacco, wheat, and Indian corn. These, used in place of medieval heraldic devices, made the point that any claims the planter class had to being a "hereditary aristocracy" rested entirely on the land.

A Gothic plantation house of an alternate type was Afton Villa, at St. Francisville, La., built for the Barrow family. Rather than build a castellated villa, an unknown architect skillfully adapted the functional requirements of the plantation house to a vastly expanded version of a Gothic cottage. This symmetrical villa, with its steep overhanging roofs, wooden ornamentation, and inset galleries, was organized behind a regular vertical and horizontal grid not unlike a classical portico and used many of the climate-control devices of the southern Greek villas.

Despite the claim made by some 19th-century critics that Gothic, as a "northern" architectural style, was inappropriate to a southern geography, symmetrical Gothic villas and cottages proved a popular residential type in the South. These "pointed-style" houses were smaller, less expensive, and less "feudal" than the castles and also did not seem to have the negative associations with northern liberalism that the larger villas did. Executed in a variety of sizes and materials, they appealed to a great socioeconomic range and, like Greek country villas, were usually found in rich agricultural regions of the South. Southern builders adapted the cottage designs from northern journals and architectural pattern books such as Andrew Jackson Downing's *The Horticulturist, A Journal of Rural Art and Rural Taste*, or his better-known *The Architecture of Country Houses* (1850). These pattern-book designs were aimed at a rural audience, which explains their popularity in the predominantly agrarian South. Downing, although a New Yorker, was careful not to alienate his southern readers, and his writings on architecture, horticulture, and picturesque landscape became the model for many southern agricultural journals. Aside from these, the early 19th-century South had few architectural publications of its own.

Despite the numerous smaller Gothic

Afton Villa, a Gothic plantation house near St. Francisville, Louisiana, built 1849–early 1850s

residences, it was in ecclesiastical architecture that the South seemed most comfortable with its Gothic identity. Two churches in the South, the Episcopal and the Roman Catholic, had liturgical traditions reaching back to the Middle Ages, and, by reference, to the architectural traditions of the English parish church and the European Gothic cathedral.

Episcopal congregations could look to the resources of the Cambridge Camden Society in England and its bimonthly publication on church building and ritual, *The Ecclesiologist*. The ecclesiological movement was, in one sense, the religious arm of British colonial expansionism, and *The Ecclesiologist* reviewed and criticized new church construction, not only in Britain but in the New World as well. Consequently, the use by the American Episcopal church of "approved" Gothic architecture was an inescapable reality.

Southern Episcopal congregations frequently employed northern architects approved by the New York Ecclesiological Society, the American counterpart of the English ecclesiologists. The two architects who had the most influence on southern Episcopal churches were Richard Upjohn and Frank Wills, both of New York. Of the two, Wills was less well known but was perhaps the more sensitive architect. Among the southern churches Wills designed is Trinity Episcopal Church (1833–53) in Mobile, Ala., a fine version of the English 14th-century parish churches revived by British architect Augustus Welby Pugin and favored as models by the ecclesiologists.

Upjohn, renowned for designs such as Trinity Church in New York, had a major impact on southern Episcopal church building both through commissioned designs and through his 1852 publication, *Upjohn's Rural Architecture*. This church pattern book provided modest wooden designs for rural parishes too poor to afford elaborate masonry structures and the fees of a professional architect. As a result of Upjohn's own designs and his pattern book, there are southern Episcopal churches by him in Alabama, North and South Carolina, Florida, Georgia, Maryland, Mississippi, and Texas.

Unlike the humble models for Episcopal parishes were the Gothic churches designed for southern Catholic congregations. The Catholic churches were larger, grander, cathedral-type structures, usually found in urban settings because of the large numbers of Irish, German, and other European Catholic immigrants who settled in southern cities. Between 1830 and 1850 the number of Catholics in America rose from 600,000 to 3.5 million. This vast increase in the Catholic population was given conspicuous physical expression in southern port cities by such Gothic monuments as James Dakin's St. Patrick's Cathedral in New Orleans. These huge Catholic churches were being erected at a time when antiimmigrant sentiment was at its height. There were anti-Catholic riots in some southern cities, and nativist political parties such as the Know-Nothings sprang up on antiforeign platforms. It was no coincidence that the vast new Catholic cathedrals, often the most conspicuous monuments on 19th-century southern skylines, were raised in the very teeth of this discrimination as impressive statements in brick and stone of the solidarity of Roman Catholicism.

Medieval forms were also used to house southern institutions. Architect James Renwick and Congressman Robert Dale Owen, in their plan for the Smithsonian Institution, Washington, D.C., and Owen in his book *Hints on Public Architecture* (1849) proposed making an amalgam of picturesque Gothic and Romanesque into a "national style" for public buildings. One of Owen's principal arguments for the revival of medieval architecture was its relative economy of construction. Medieval buildings were cheaper on a large scale because they did not require marble, their masonry could be roughly finished, and their walls were a simple two-dimensional "skin" thrown around the interior, with token pointed arches, towers, and crenelations to give "historical style." By contrast, classical public buildings required a high degree of finish, expensive materials, and dozens of carved steps, columns, and capitals.

Trinity Episcopal Church, Mobile, Alabama, 1853–55

The cheapness of castellated Gothic, combined with its planning flexibility, made it popular for large southern institutional structures where cost was a decisive factor. James Dakin cited cost as one of the reasons for his selection of Gothic for the Louisiana statehouse, and the style was used for orphanages, schools for the deaf and mute, military academies, jails, prisons, and lunatic asylums. Frequently to be found in juxtaposition with these great, stripped-down Gothic institutional buildings were grounds landscaped in romantic or picturesque fashion, like English 18th-century parks. The picturesque grounds, in addition to being appropriate to Gothic Revival architecture, may have been seen as having therapeutic value for inmates of such institutions as the Nashville, Tenn., Hospital for the Insane, built between 1851 and 1854, by architect Adolphus Heiman. In any case, "institutional Gothic" was used to house many of 19th-century southern society's disenfranchised: the needy, the deaf, the dumb, the blind, the insane, the penalized, and in the case of picturesque cemeteries, the dead.

Gothic was also used for southern educational institutions, a role that hints at Gothic scholasticism and English medieval campus planning. This trend continued into the 20th century, in such fine examples of collegiate Gothic architecture as those of architect Horace Trumbauer at Duke University, Durham, N.C.

Both Greek and Gothic in the South were aspects of a larger search for an architectural and regional identity. It was a quest not merely to house southern people and institutions but to achieve for southern civilization a parity with the great civilizations of the past, whether classical or medieval. As a southern writer for the Columbia, Tenn., *Guardian* put it in 1842, "We shall have our troubadours and our minstrels—and the banks of our Mississippi will become in song as classic as the Tiber, and in Romance as famous as the Danube."

See also MYTHIC SOUTH: Romanticism

Patrick A. Snadon
University of Kentucky

Francis Kervick, *Architects in America of Catholic Tradition* (1962); Caulder Loth and J. T. Sadler, *The Only Proper Style: Gothic Architecture in America* (1975); James Patrick, *Winterthur Portfolio* (Summer 1980); William H. Pierson, Jr., *American Buildings and Their Architects: Technology and the Picturesque, The Corporate and Early Gothic Styles* (1978); Phoebe B. Stanton, *The Gothic Revival and American Church Architecture: An Episode in Taste, 1840–1856* (1968); David B. Warren and Katherine S. Howe, *The Gothic Revival Style in America, 1830–1870* (1976). ☆

Greek Revival Architecture

In the popular imagination, Greek Revival architecture, especially the great plantation house, is symbolic of the antebellum South. The potency of this image has discouraged not only analysis of its origins but also consideration of its validity. Most frequently, such architecture has been discussed in the context of romantic beauty, as the residue of an aristocratic culture somehow akin to the "Athenian Golden Age." At its best, this myth has created such visions as the neoromantic photographic studies of Clarence John Laughlin—themselves masterpieces of 20th-century southern art. At its worst, the image has obscured the complex forces that were at work in the South in the decades before the Civil War, producing diverse and expressive architectural forms overlaid with rich and often enigmatic meanings.

By the time of the American Revolution, neoclassicism held sway in the countries of western Europe. Highly educated and well-traveled men of the revolutionary generation, such as Thomas Jefferson, employed Federal-style architecture as one means of expressing

An old mansion in Natchez, Mississippi, photographed in 1940

their status as creators of a new nation. Provincial only in its superficial native and patriotic motifs, this style's geometry, planning, and overall articulation reflected forms that had originated in Europe.

As Jefferson and his colleagues were replaced by younger men, the sense of a permanent and self-assured America increased. Americans felt confident enough to take a more myopic view in their search for aesthetic inspiration, with one result being the Greek Revival style in architecture, still attuned to international neoclassicism, but now a more effervescent, innovative, idealistically chauvinistic, and diverse variation on that theme. Buoyant American nationalism was crystallized in the form of templed dwellings, churches, courthouses, and capitols.

This phenomenon was not identical in the North and South, however. The South continued to be agrarian in reality and aristocratic in aspiration; but it also continued to be necessarily international in outlook due to its emphasis on direct European trading connections. The North, on the other hand, looked toward industrialization, egalitarianism, and urbanized self-sufficiency. Furthermore, the South's distinctive agricultural circumstance included regional variation, and it experienced a considerable evolution over the course of time. The 18th century was dominated by the coastal enclaves of tobacco-raising Virginia and rice-growing South Carolina and Georgia, but the 19th century saw the rising importance of sugar-producing Louisiana and later the inland "cotton kingdom." Here, as the frontier moved westward, the boom periods of the early 19th century produced the many great white-columned buildings amidst an even greater number of crude, one-room log cabins and dogtrot houses.

The philosophical differences between North and South were not profound before 1820. Only as southerners felt compelled to defend the institution of slavery did their region become isolated and their position intransigent. The southern mind became progressively sectional, then regionally nationalistic, and finally unilaterally expansionistic, culminating in the Confederacy and plans to annex Mexico, Cuba, and the rest of the Caribbean. As one concrete manifestation of this attitude, there appeared a nationalistic architecture. Slavery, considered by many to be the central theme of antebellum southern culture, upset the equilibrium of southern life, creating an aberration that transfixed both North and South. The architectural parallel was a kind of fetish, what J. Frazier Smith has called the "white-pillared architecture." A paradox was created: the Orders, or columns with entablatures, were the formal basis of classicism and neoclassicism and were physical evidence of the ancient conception of proportion and balance in life as well as in art; in southern, antebellum, columnar architecture, however, that balance proved elusive. Rather than an ordering element, the column became a device of exhibitionism, a sectional emblem, and a symbol of paternalistic and chivalrous society, aristocratic rule, and hierarchical rigidity. This white-columned architecture might well have been exported, along with slavery, to any new lands the South claimed as it fulfilled its belligerent conception of manifest destiny. The Greek Revival style, declining in the North on the eve of the Civil War, remained integral to southern culture when apocalyptic external forces terminated its development.

Columnar plantation houses were being built in the South through the 1850s, although their details were becoming less archaeologically "Grecian" and more "baroque." While competing with other styles such as Gothic and Italian, the concept of the columned facade remained in favor in the South a decade after its demise in the North; and though acquiring a newer, more eclectic, ornamental, and aggressive vocabulary, the basic syntax was still in evidence and perhaps would have survived had the South been the victor in the Civil War.

Southern residential buildings displayed columns as profusely as did public architecture. In a decentralized, agrarian economy the plantation house was as much a symbol of stability and authority as was any seat of religion or government. That southern domestic architecture so universally appropriated the column did not, however, seem to reduce the significance of public buildings. If anything, the societal status of the domestic architecture was elevated well above that prevalent in the North, and that of public architecture was at least equivalent.

In molding public opinion and housing southern institutions, architects and patrons viewed Greek Revival public structures as eminently practical, modern buildings that made virile collective statements about southern cultural and economic attainment. To this end, of the 13 southern states, 8 had capitols planned by legislative fiat (a much higher percentage than in any other region), itself a telling comment on the search for preordained order within the culture. Similarly, 8 of these 13 had one or more capitols in Greek-temple form. Rivaling the capitols in size and importance were such buildings as hotels, which served the same purpose as Roman triumphal arches—to act as symbolic gateways and to impress travelers with the economic progress and cultural accomplishments of southern cities. The temple form was ubiquitous; but alternative Greek building types could serve with at least equal appropriateness—a stoa for a commercial block or a Greek treasury for a bank. Many of the most successful and least archaeological of the southern public buildings, far from being only "Grecian," included imaginative combinations of elements from other architectural vocabularies: Renaissance massing and wall division, Roman vaulting and domes, and more primitive Egyptian forms—all used not to supplant but to elaborate and energize the somewhat limited trabeated vocabulary of the Greeks.

This Greek Revival public architecture has been even less well investigated than domestic work. If this important, monumental neoclassical architecture is to be satisfactorily understood, it must be more carefully assessed within its southern context, and it must be compared to the European models created by such 19th-century classicists as J. N. L. Durrand and Karl Fredrick Schinkel.

The proliferation in recent years of books pretending to address southern domestic architecture, but most often recapitulating pallid myth, has certainly done more harm than good. Even noted scholars have often purveyed anachronistic confusion. William H. Pierson, Jr., in *American Buildings and Their Architects: The Colonial and Neo-Classical Styles* (1970), has written that southern domestic architecture "was dominated almost entirely by the peripteral colonnade"; but this simply was not the case. The three original southern enclaves each developed distinctive domestic schemes. Throughout the 18th century, Virginians preferred the Georgian, two-story, two-room-deep residence having a brick mass of Palladian inspiration covered by a hipped roof and often provided with a two-story central pedimented bay or portico. During the Greek Revival period this form was made more classically correct in both spirit and detail, and the result spread throughout the South as Virginians migrated into newly developing lands. In North Carolina and Georgia a wide, one-room deep, two-story block with a low-pitched, transverse-gabled roof was the most common form, unself-conscious at first, but gradually being furnished with a more pretentious one- or two-story porch or piazza across the long side; this piazza often employed columns with extremely wide intercolumniations to support a deep entablature, typically hiding the sloping roof behind. In Louisiana the Norman French peasant's house, transported to and developed first in the West Indies and possibly in Canada, was enlarged and outfitted with galleries, often, but not always, on all four sides. To these three prototypes must be added the pattern-book buildings and those designed to individual specifications by professionally trained architects. All of these types were then intermingled with one another, producing almost endless variants.

In addition to stylistic developments there were extensive environmental adaptations. Once again, many published materials have created confusion. Wayne Andrews, in his *Pride of the South: A Social History of Southern Architecture* (1979), has suggested that in the South there were "not too many inventions that served the particular demands of Southern climate." This observation could hardly be more inaccurate. The list of sun- and heat-control devices perfected by southern designers and builders was impressive. These included raised first floors, high ceilings, belvederes, and stair-tower plenums to take advantage of air stratification and natural convection; windows, jib-windows, doors, transoms, and longitudinal and transverse halls, all carefully located to encourage cross-ventilation; and roof overhangs, shutters, and latticework positioned to prevent solar heat gain. Such features have been verified, using modern testing procedures, to conform to current scientific energy conservation theory and application. Significantly the Georgian, Federal, and Queen Anne styles, which preceded and followed the Greek Revival, never displayed an equivalent degree of environmental modification; these styles tended to be quite homogeneous in both North and South. And, after all, ancient Greek architecture was created for a hot, sunny climate; it was the North that never came to grips with environmental adaptation.

Some authors have attributed environmental features such as the gallery to the influence of slaves' building experiences in Africa or the West Indies. The effects of slavery on the form of the southern plantation were, however, manifested in a much more calculated fashion. Planters sought to minimize or to conceal architecturally the negative aspects of slavery while calling attention to the number of slaves they owned, the primary indicator of their economic success. This complex pattern of behavioral control was accomplished by means of site planning, landscaping, spatial form and placement, and horizontal and vertical circulation elements, all subtly interconnecting layers and zones of family, guest, and servant spaces. Perhaps the greatest success of the southern Greek Revival plantation was its careful and tenuous accommodation of stressful social and environmental circumstances.

Finally, although southerners rarely spoke explicitly about their architecture, they built prolifically and on a grand scale. If one searches for incisive documentary evidence, especially among published materials, one searches almost in vain. This vacuum suggests not that southerners never thought seriously about architecture, but rather that very subtle attitudes were at work that valued most not a house but a home, not buildings as volumetric space but buildings as stages for human action, not landscape design but land itself, and so on. In the South certain matters pertaining to taste, culture, and manners have traditionally been neither questioned nor spoken about openly, so much so that they may, to an outside observer, appear to have been unimportant or even unknown. The southerner, however, would probably prefer the term unself-conscious behavior—a code of unspoken but ever-present decorum in patterns of thought and personal interaction, ultimately much like the modular regularity of classical architecture itself. Both, however, were systems that allowed adequate flexibility of expression within a carefully defined grammar and syntax. In the end, the resolution of the enigma of southern life and the architecture that reflected and supported it must be sought through an understanding of these peculiar attitudes and institutions that blossomed and faded in the South like a strange, hybrid flower.

See also EDUCATION: Classical Tradition; ENVIRONMENT: Climate and Weather; HISTORY AND MANNERS: Manners; MYTHIC SOUTH: Plantation Myth

Michael W. Fazio
Mississippi State University

Patrick A. Snadon
University of Kentucky

James Robert Bienvenu, "Two Greek Revival Hotels in New Orleans: The St. Charles by James Gallier, Sr., and the St. Louis by J. N. B. de Pouilly" (M.A. thesis, Tulane University, 1961); Talbot Hamlin, *Greek Revival Architecture in America: Being an Accout of Important Trends in American Architecture and American Life prior to the War between the States* (1944); W. Darrell Overdyke, *Louisiana Plantation Homes: Colonial and Antebellum* (1965); William H. Pierson, Jr., *American Buildings and Their Architects: The Colonial and Neo-Classical Styles* (1970); Jessie Poesch, *The Art of the Old South: Painting, Sculpture, Architecture, and the Products of Craftsmen, 1560–1860* (1983); J. Frazier Smith, *White Pillars: Early Life and Architecture of the Lower Mississippi Valley Country* (1941). ☆

Historiography of Southern Architecture

Many historians of southern culture have been at least touched by the heavy air of nostalgia that threatens to stifle the region, but architectural historians have been even less willing or able than scholars in related fields to break through this layer of illusion and expose the reality beneath.

The origins of this tendency can be traced to a group of writers who created a mythical southern kingdom, complete with architectural setting, casting themselves as literary priests without whom an initiation into the mysteries of southern life would have been impossible. Writing before the Civil War, Virginia novelists such as John Pendleton Kennedy (*Swallow Barn*, 1832) and John Esten Cooke (*The Virginia Comedians*, 1854) began the tradition. Subsequently, southern writers developed a rhetoric of reconstruction, using as a forum such popular literary magazines as *Scribner's Monthly* (later *Century Magazine*), *Lippincott's Magazine*, and *Harper's*. Authors like Joel Chandler Harris and Sherwood Bonner fashioned an image of a southern civilization to serve their ends as apologists and propagandists for a prostrate South bent on rehabilitating its reputation. Thomas Nelson Page polished the facets of this southern romantic legend to virtual perfection.

Contemporary with these mythmakers, late 19th-century architectural writer-critics such as Mariana Van Rensselaer, Russell Sturgis, and Montgomery Schuyler (often writing, ironically, in the same literary magazines as Harris, Bonner, and Page) virtually ignored the South in their examinations of American building. Even the first historical studies of the country's architecture, which appeared in the 1920s, ventured only into Virginia and sometimes Charleston and New Orleans. The foremost of these publications were *Domestic Architecture of the American Colonies* (1922) and *American Architecture* (1928), both by Fiske Kimball, *American Colonial Architecture* (1924) by Joseph Jackson, and *The Story of American Architecture* (1927) by Thomas Tallmadge. Fiske Kimball's monograph, *Thomas Jefferson; Architect*, appeared in 1916 and Helen Pierce Gallagher's *Robert Mills* in 1935.

In 1941 the Society of Architectural Historians was founded, and its *Journal* was immediately dominated by American materials—a situation that has changed radically. Subsequently, additional general surveys of American building history were added, each containing sections devoted to the South: Talbot Hamlin's *Greek Revival Architecture in America* (1944), primarily a formal analysis and now badly dated; James Marston Fitch's *American Building: The Historical Forces That Shaped It* (1948), which included a perspective on social and intellectual factors; and Hugh Morrison's *Early American Architecture* (1952). Also appearing were two more studies of nationally renowned architects who practiced in the South—*Benjamin Henry Latrobe* (1955) by Talbot Hamlin and *William Strickland, Architect and Engineer, 1788–1854* (1950) by Agnes Gilchrist.

This same period saw the creation of a type of book that looked to the earlier popular propagandists for its inspiration—the limited-edition picturebook with short, often flowery text. The earliest of these appeared in Virginia, including Robert A. Lancaster, Jr.'s *Historic Virginia Houses and Churches* (1915), Edith Tunis Sale's *Manors of Virginia in Colonial Times* (1909), and Francis A. Christian and Suzanna W. Massie's *Homes and Gardens in Old Virginia* (1930); the latter was assembled for the Garden Club of America, one important supporter of the genre. Similar are the *History of Homes and Gardens in Tennessee* (1935), edited by Robert Seawell Brandau; Archibald Henderson and Bayard Wootten's *Old Homes and Gardens of North Carolina* (1939); Elizabeth Simpson's *Bluegrass Houses and Their Traditions* (1933); and J. Wesley Cooper's *Natchez, A Treasure of Antebellum Homes* (1957). In South Carolina the buildings of Charleston have dominated interest, leading to the production of such specialized titles as Elizabeth Curtis's *Gateways and Doorways of Charleston: South Carolina in the Eighteenth and Nineteenth Centuries* (1926). Louisiana authors have developed a particularly ethereal point of view, the most imaginative being that of Clarence John Laughlin in *Ghosts along the Mississippi* (1948).

A more substantive type of regional work began in South Carolina with *Dwelling Houses of Charleston, South Carolina* (1917) by Alice Ravenel, Huger Smith, and Daniel Elliott Huger Smith, and *Charleston, South Carolina* (1929) by Albert Simonds and Samuel Lapham. Further studies with scholarly aspirations appeared in the subsequent decades. Thomas Tileston Waterman's work is exemplary, including his *Mansions of Virginia, 1706–1776* (1946). Also active in the Tidewater were Henry Chandlee Forman, best known for his *The Architecture of the Old South: The Medieval Style, 1585–1850* (1948), and Frederick Nichols, whose interests extended to Georgia as well. In Kentucky, Clay Lancaster has published widely, primarily in journals, as has Rexford Newcomb, author of *Architecture in Old Kentucky* (1953). Likewise, Samuel Wilson, Jr., has conducted studies of the architecture of New Orleans and nearby parishes in Louisiana, and Samuel Gaillard Stoney and Beatrice St. Julien Ravenel have continued the tradition established earlier in Charleston and its environs with *Plantations of the Carolina Low Country* (1955) and *Architects of Charleston* (1945) respectively.

A more general work of significance is J. Frazier Smith's *White Pillars* (1941) with its emphasis on the Orders, or columns with entablature, as symbols of the southern Greek Revival style. Also cited often is Lewis Mumford's *The South in Architecture* (1941); however, this small volume provides little real insight into regional issues and architectural solutions. The frequent citation of James C. Bonner's "Plantation Architecture of the Lower South on the Eve of the Civil War," in the *Journal of Southern History* (August 1945), a study of forces at cross-purposes with neoclassicism, reflects not so much the absolute quality of that article as the celebrity that has met any imaginative examination of the nature of southern architecture. Also not to be ignored are the state guidebooks produced during the Depression years by the Federal Writers' Project.

Contemporary scholarship has begun to show signs of maturation. Albert Manucy's *The Houses of St. Augustine* (1962) represents a model of its type—a detailed technical analysis of building types in a specific location. John Linley's *Architecture of Middle Georgia* (1972) and Frederick Nichol's more substantive *The Architecture of Georgia* (1976) cover that state reasonably well, if not exhaustively. Much less analytical but still useful are Mary Wallace Crocker's *Historic Architecture in Mississippi* (1973) and D. Gregory Jeane and Douglas C. Purcell's *The Architectural Legacy of the Lower Chattahoochee Valley in Alabama and*

Georgia (1976). Likewise, Thomas Brumbaugh's *Architecture of Middle Tennessee* (1974) is a picture book in the lineage of garden club publications. Arthur Scully has produced the only carefully researched study of a southern practitioner, *James Dakin, Architect* (1973); also noteworthy is the less comprehensive *William Nichols, Architect* (1979) by C. Ford Peatross. An unusual and significant work is Clay Lancaster's extensively documented *Eutaw: The Builders and Architecture of an Antebellum Southern Town* (1979). Wayne Andrews's *Pride of the South: A Social History of Southern Architecture* (1979) has magnificent photography but is more of a social register than a social history. Likewise, Kenneth Severens's *Southern Architecture* (1981) promises in its title much more than it delivers. The groundwork has simply not yet been sufficiently laid for such a sweeping view of southern architecture. Finally, James Patrick's *Architecture in Tennessee, 1768–1897* (1981) contains a thought-provoking text, with overtones of religious philosophy. His work addresses social and aesthetic issues and strives for an understanding of the continuity of southern architectural development.

More such studies are needed, studies that view southern architecture intellectually and analytically and not simply romantically. Researchers must address all stylistic periods and not overemphasize antebellum neoclassicism. Also, more detailed works on specific communities and areas and on specific designers are required before a comprehensive regional history can be successfully compiled.

Michael W. Fazio
Mississippi State University

Industrial 19th-Century Architecture

No cohesive southern industrial architecture emerged during the 19th century. Despite the growth of sectionalism, the ornamentation and construction techniques of southern mills revealed that they were part of a national movement. The millwrights, engineers, and, in a few cases, architects who planned these structures copied earlier northern models and rarely incorporated any innovations. The configuration of many 19th-century factories was dictated by their manufacturing process, so that specific types of industries developed distinctive buildings with little regional variation. A company's wealth usually determined the degree of embellishment. Stone, wood, or brick covered early mills, but over time brick exteriors became nearly universal, and a standardized industrial style became ubiquitous. Bays separated by brick pilasters, windows and doors crowned with segmental arches, and corbelled cornices and gables characterized warehouses, factories, and related buildings throughout the nation. Larger edifices exhibited the influence of current Victorian styles with Romanesque, Gothic, or Second-Empire features.

Given these national forces, most southern factories resembled those of their northern competitors. The construction of blast furnaces in North Carolina, Tennessee, Georgia, and Alabama mirrored that of earlier ones in New England and Pennsylvania. The walls of Richmond's Tredegar Iron Works, one of the region's most significant antebellum industries, showed no southern characteristics. Similar brick structures topped by monitors and flanked by squatty chimneys housed iron foundries in cities throughout the North and South. Tobacco factories in Statesville and Mount Airy, N.C., and in Lynchburg, Va., processed a southern product, but their rectangular, multistoried buildings with embellished stepped-gabled fronts might have sheltered a myriad of other manufactories throughout the nation.

Perhaps the southern economic and physical environment influenced the architecture of some mills. The lack of capital after the Civil War and the abundance of yellow pine caused some southern builders to continue using handhewn timbers with mortise-and-tenon joints after they had been superseded by iron or machined posts. These earlier framing methods were employed in rural grist mills, other small factories, and wooden bridges—both covered ones and deck-truss railroad trestles. In some cases black craftsmen preserved these traditional techniques: Horace King, an exslave, and his sons built such structures in Alabama, Mississippi, and Georgia through the first decade of the 20th century. Climate probably dictated the configuration of the region's open-sided turpentine stills and sawmills.

Larger urban mills displayed more distinctive styling, which tended to reflect local influences; such individuality disappeared with the onslaught of standardization. Richmond's Dunlop Mills structure (1853) rose seven stories above the James River. Its vertical emphasis typified flour mills, but its parapet end walls, with lunettes over each bay, gave the appearance of a late 18th- or early 19th-century Virginia building. Twenty years later, the Piedmont Mills building (c. 1875) in Lynchburg, Va., with its pilasters and arched windows resembled grist mills in any other American city. This uniformity increased as national companies that manufactured milling equipment began designing and constructing complete mills.

Lacking any national models, the architecture of Charleston's three antebellum rice mills evoked the classical mood of the city. The most magnificent of these was Governor Thomas Bennett's Italian Renaissance "palace," which began milling rice in 1844. Its rusticated lower level, large Palladian windows on the front and sides, and the Greek and Roman details on the other fenestration were all copied from various Italian palaces. Its elaborate surface contrasted starkly with the plain, massive timbers that supported it. The interior and exterior bays did not even correspond, and some of the rows of inside columns ended in window openings. Such an exuberant facade might have been an inappropriate screen for a steam engine and milling equipment, and it might have been emblematic of the region's, or Charleston's, hostility toward industry, but its grand style was an appropriate reflection of the importance of rice to the city's economy.

Among the South's—and the nation's—grandest structures were those associated with railroads. Viewed both as a gateway to a community and as a symbol of a town's urban status, railroad stations, train sheds, and shop buildings were conceived with special attention to fanciful details. In Nashville the antebellum Louisville & Nashville depot stood as a fortress with battlements along the roof and the corner towers, and trains entered through Tudor arches. In Savannah's Central of Georgia complex, normally mundane structures—privies, a water tower, and a smokestack—were combined into an ornamental column. The Central of Georgia's depot, offices, warehouses, and shops were built between 1850 and 1890 and contained classical, Gothic, and Italianate components. Despite their stylistic differences, they collectively illustrated the continuing importance of the railroad to the city and asserted, in brick, the goal of making Savannah the leading cotton center. By the turn of the century, railroad stations in major southern cities resembled Romanesque cathedrals, Gothic castles, and Roman "baths." This railroad architecture was national, not southern: it revealed that southern cities shared the urban ethos that pervaded the rest of the nation.

Textile mills became symbolic of the South's drive to industrialize during the 19th century. Early southern entrepreneurs employed northern-trained millwrights, so the first southern factories repeated the characteristics of Rhode Island spinning mills—narrow buildings, three to five stories in height, with a front stair tower capped by a cupola. With exceptions like the Augusta Factory (1847), which resembled the massive structures of Lowell, most antebellum and the initial postbellum mills remained austere in decoration and limited in volume. After 1880 the scale of factories increased substantially because of improvements in motive power and illumination, but few innovations occurred in the system of interior supports; more wooden posts and beams were simply added to span the greater lengths. Mill engineers gave little attention to improving working conditions.

The design emphasis by the 1880s focused on the exterior of these mills. Decorative brickwork embellished many of their features, but especially the cornices and the Romanesque arches of the massive towers that dominated most of these structures. The heavily ornamented mills conveyed a civic dimension by embodying the pride and aspirations of entire communities. The ornamentation, although Victorian in tone and similar to that on northern mills, may also have been an expression of the New South creed (or cotton mill crusade), which promised to transform the region. Ironically, like the corbelled and arched masonry, the impact of industrialism on the South—and its poverty—was superficial.

Stylistically, the most distinctive New South mills appeared in Georgia and especially in Augusta. Having led the region in textile production for four decades, the Georgia corporations had sufficient internal expertise to design their own plants in the 1880s. Probably the South's most imposing industrial facade was Augusta's Sibley Mill (1880). Because of its crenellated parapet and decorative stair towers and pavilions topped with finials, some historians have speculated that it was modeled after the British Houses of Parliament, but it probably was intended to imitate, and thereby memorialize, the Confederate Powder Works, which had earlier stood on the site. At the same time, its exuberance appeared to have been inspired by the optimism of the New South creed.

By contrast, the Carolina and Alabama mills of the 1880s were built by national engineering firms such as Lockwood and Greene with more restrained and more uniform designs. They planned the Columbia (S.C.) Duck Mill (1893), the world's first textile factory to be powered by electricity, but its architecture failed to suggest its uniqueness. It resembled all the other mills along the Atlantic Seaboard. The 1890s publications of Daniel Tompkins, a southern mill engineer, reflected this standardization; his mills varied only in scale. By that decade, the exuberance of the New South was waning; as plants grew in size, windowed areas expanded, and less corbelling appeared on the smaller brick areas of these more utilitarian structures. By 1900 the factory was a permanent part of the southern landscape: the triad of brick smokestack, water tank, and mill tower rising above a pine forest marked the location of a textile factory and its surrounding village. The workers and often their houses remained southern in style, but the architecture of the mill building was national in style. Southern sectionalism had been unable to stem the homogenizing force of the national economy.

See also INDUSTRY: / Textile Industry; MYTHIC SOUTH: New South Myth

John S. Lupold
Columbus College

Keith L. Bryant, Jr., *Journal of Urban History* (February 1976); Stephen Goldfarb, *Industrial Archeology in Georgia* (1978); Samuel Lapham, Jr., *Architectural Record* (August 1924); Theodore A. Sande et al., *Journal of the Society of Architectural Historians* (December 1976). ☆

Nonresidential 20th-Century Architecture

The nonresidential southern architectural styles of the early 20th century can be divided into the same two categories as residential architecture—historic and nonhistoric.

Period revivals were very popular in the conservative South. The same styles that adorned residential structures could also be found on nonresidential ones. The French, Spanish, Dutch, and English Colonial Revival styles, as well as the Federal and Georgian, were very popular, as were the Renaissance, Tudor, and neo-Italianate styles. In addition, four other historical styles were commonly employed for nonresidential structures—the Gothic Revival, neoclassical, stripped-down classical, and beaux arts.

The Gothic Revival style (1900–40) of the early 20th century was primarily used on public buildings, churches in particular. Precedents favored were the English perpendicular and Tudor styles, but the French Gothic was occasionally employed alone or combined with the English style. The silhouettes of these buildings are very complex, although symmetry is common. These Gothic Revival structures are generally built of masonry stone when available. In commercial buildings terra cotta is often used. The most renowned Gothic architects of this period were Ralph Adams Cram and Bertram Grosvenor Goodhue. Cram had developed the theory that Gothic architecture had "not suffered a natural death," therefore, he intended to "take up English Gothic at the point where it was cut off." The Gothic Revival style was particularly popular for southern universities. Loyola of the South in New Orleans and the University of Florida in Gainesville are two such examples.

Neoclassical, stripped-down classical, and beaux arts styles were used for monumental buildings in cities and towns throughout the South. All three are derived from the same source—classical Greek and Roman prototypes—but the manner in which the elements are used distinguishes each style.

Neoclassicism (1900–40) encompassed Greek, Roman, and Renaissance elements and characteristics composed in the classical manner, with a monumental scale. The 1929 New Orleans Criminal Court Building by Diboll & Owen Architects is a typical example of the style.

Stripped-down classicism, sometimes referred to as fascist moderne, employed the same massing and scale as neoclassicism but made little or no use of historically derived details. Many such public structures throughout the South were built as Depression-era projects by the WPA and PWA. The 1939 State Fair Exhibit Museum in Shreveport, La., is a good example of this style.

Beaux arts classicism (1890–1920) employs classical elements in a theatrical or baroque manner. The École des Beaux Arts in Paris was directly responsible for the reemergence of classicism, but exhibitions such as the World's Columbian Exposition (Chicago, 1893), the Louisiana Purchase Exposition (St. Louis, 1904), and the Panama-Pacific Exposition (San Francisco, 1915) propagated the style in the public's mind. Cities of white marble were sought in the national City Beautiful movement.

All three classical styles were popular in the South for governmental and civic buildings, libraries, museums, colleges, theaters, banks, railway terminals, monuments, and memorials.

Nonhistorically inspired styles popular during the early 20th century include the commercial, the decorative brick, storefront modern, art deco, and streamline moderne.

The commercial style (1890–1910) arose out of the ashes of the great Chicago fire to spread across the nation. An anonymous editor of *Industrial Chicago* wrote in 1891, "The Commercial Style is the title suggested by the great office and mercantile buildings now found here. The requirements of commerce and the business principles of real estate owners called this style into life. Light, space, air and strength were demanded by such requirements and principles as the first objects and exterior ornamentation as the second."

Commercial-style buildings were an early development of the high-rise office complex, and at least one example can be found in every southern city. They are generally 5 to 16 stories, with flat skylines, large windows, and an external structural expression. This style was made possible through technological advances such as steel-frame construction, the passenger elevator, fireproofing techniques, and mechanical ventilation. The Mills Building, designed by Trost and Trost Architects in 1910 in El Paso, Tex., and the Wainwright Building, designed by Adler and Sullivan in St. Louis in 1890, are typical examples.

The decorative brick style was an outgrowth of the commercial style. Whereas the commercial style shunned ornamentation, the decorative brick style used masonry products in an innovative decorative manner. Patterns of masonry pinwheels, sinkages, and polychromatic motifs were employed. The spandrels were generally recessed slightly behind the piers, and the skyline was often broken. Terra cotta ornaments were sometimes incorporated. Examples of this style can be found in

New Orleans's Historic Warehouse District. The Woodward-Wright warehouse by Emile Weil is a typical example there.

Many small commercial buildings and stores in small towns are in this idiom. Such buildings are the hallmark of main streets throughout the nation including, of course, the South. In many county seats, such as Oxford, Miss., these are among the buildings that front the streets and the square where the county courthouse is situated. The core of small-town life was once centered here.

The storefront modern style developed simultaneously with strip shopping developments. The style, as its name implies, was one that simply addressed the front of the structure, ignored the unseen rear, and had no sides to contend with, except on corner buildings. Intended to be seen from the passing auto, the style used slick, clean materials with bold details and lots of neon lights. Opaque glass and baked-enamel panels were often used. The versatility and boldness of the style made it perfect for widespread usage by chain stores. By its standardized design of red opaque glass and gold lettering, one recognized a Woolworth store in New Orleans as easily as in Macon.

Art deco (1920–30) was popularly used for high-rise buildings and movie theaters. Stylized ornamentation was perhaps its most recognizable feature. Motifs based on pure geometry, abstracted naturalistic forms, or stripped-down ancient decorative elements manifested themselves in hard-edged, low-relief ornamentation.

As a style of ornamentation, art deco evolved in France during the early 1920s as a reaction to the art nouveau. The 1925 L'Exposition des Arts Decoratif in Paris diffused a sentiment in America that there could be modern ornamentation. This concept bridged the gap between the beaux arts philosophy, which contended historical ornamentation was essential, and the Bauhaus philosophy, which renounced all ornamentation. Art deco structures are alive with bold colors, dramatic massing, picturesque skylines, and an emphasis on the vertical, making this style popular for resort areas such as the Miami Beach Art Deco District.

Streamline moderne (1930–40) developed during a period of rapid social change. The worldwide Depression had caused disillusionment and confusion. The common desire to "get things moving again" demanded drastic solutions. Out of this confusion a new profession emerged—industrial design—which literally reshaped everything in order to stimulate a devastated economy.

Industrial designers promoted streamlining as a symbol of the future—a future that combined art, engineering, design, processing, packaging, and sales. Instead of the applied art of the art deco, streamlining preferred subtle meaningful forms of ornament. Although buildings were static, the principles of fluid dynamics were applied. Architects had to settle for an abstraction of motion, resulting in slick, curved surfaces. The style was very popular for Greyhound bus stations and gas stations throughout the South.

The architect Theodore Flaxman, of Shreveport, La., was among those Americans who early studied and responded to this modern "international" style. A municipal incinerator built in the 1930s in Shreveport, and since destroyed, was cited at the 1937 World's Fair in Paris as one of the best examples of modern architecture in America. The

Mayer House in Shreveport, built in 1930, is a fine surviving example of this genre.

The Louisiana State Capitol Building, designed by the New Orleans firm of Weiss, Dreyfous and Seiferth, was one of two skyscraper capitols in the United States (the other is in Nebraska) built in the early 1930s. The architects called it modern classic, and it used a restrained modern idiom, including symbolic low-relief sculpture on the outside and richly colored marble panels, with echoes of art deco detailing, on the inside. Built while Huey Long was the governor of the state, it is, in a sense, his monument, and a monument to his individual brand of populist politics.

Robert J. Cangelosi
New Orleans, Louisiana

William H. Jordy, *American Buildings and Their Architects*, vol. 3 (1972); Walter C. Kidney, *The Architecture of Choice: Eclecticism in America, 1880–1930* (1974); Carole Rifkind, *A Field Guide to American Architecture* (1980); Leland M. Roth, *A Concise History of American Architecture* (1979); G. E. K. Kidder Smith, *The Architecture of the United States: The South and Midwest* (1981). ☆

Painting and Painters, 1564–1790

The first two important, but unsuccessful, European attempts to establish colonies in that part of North America that is now the United States were in the South. In each of these an artist-draftsman accompanied the expeditions and was charged with recording impressions of the peoples, the flora, and the fauna of the region, as well as with mapmaking. Thus, Jacques Le Moyne de Morgues in 1564 and 1565 accompanied the French expedition that established a short-lived Huguenot settlement on the St. Johns River in Florida, and John White served as cartographer and draftsman to Sir Walter Raleigh's 1585 expedition that established the Roanoke colony. Only one of the original 42 watercolors by Le Moyne survives (in the New York Public Library), while a portfolio of White's work, including 59 watercolors, has survived (British Museum). Among these are delicately rendered depictions of the Indian inhabitants, showing them at tasks such as cooking, fishing, and cultivating crops, as well as renderings of plants and creatures. The Indians are made to appear somewhat Europeanized, but there is nonetheless valuable ethnological information. These works were disseminated in Europe by Théodore De Bry, who published in Germany a series of volumes on the New World, reproducing the drawings of White and Le Moyne as engraved illustrations. De Bry's first volume, *A Briefe and True Report of the New Found Land of Virginia*, published in 1590, had engravings based on White's drawings and was accompanied by Thomas Hariot's narrative, a somewhat optimistic account of a land with a mild climate like Persia. This was followed by German, Latin, and French editions. Between 1590 and 1620 this volume went through 17 printings. The volume with engravings based on Le Moyne's drawings and his text was published in German, French, and Latin some years after the artist's death in 1591. Thus, in the years between 1590 and 1620, when permanent colonies had been established, these volumes and engravings formed the English and European visions of America. Moreover, subsequent books, such as John Smith's *The Generall Historie of Virginia* of 1624, had illustrations based on De Bry's engravings. Images representing America and extending well into the 18th century, such as that on an 18th-century Spanish tile, were drawn from Smith's *Generall Historie*.

Virtually no paintings or drawings survive from the first 60 or so years of permanent settlement in the South, years in which the settlers suffered from disease, high mortality rates, poor planning, inability to adjust to the hot climate, and poor relations with the Indians. It was far from a Persian paradise. Likewise, very few artifacts, such as furniture or silver, survive from this period.

One cannot identify surviving paintings and graphic arts created in the South and find records of artists and their patrons before the early years of the 18th century, which brought the development of the plantation society and the growth of towns. Patrons were largely of the planter and merchant classes, and their choice was for portraits. This preference was shared with fellow colonists in the North and indeed with many English people.

A German-born artist, Justus Engelhardt Kühn (died 1717), recorded the likenesses of several Maryland and Virginia planter families, often showing them posed in elegant settings whose source lay in remembered European scenes or in prints. In Charleston, Henrietta Johnston (died 1728 or 1729) used pastels to render delicate interpretations of her patrons. She was the wife of a minister and supplemented her husband's income with her work. Charles Bridges was an agent for the missionary Society for Promoting Christian Knowledge and earned part of his income by painting portraits of notables in the Williamsburg area. An unidentified artist working in the Jamestown area recorded the likenesses of members of the Brodnax and Ambler families. William Dering also worked in and around Williamsburg.

Another Englishman, John Wollaston, lived in Maryland, Virginia, and South Carolina intermittently from 1753 to at least 1767. His elegant, graceful renditions of his subjects helped to introduce the rococo taste. The Swedish-born artist Gustavus Hesselius (1682–1755) is known to have worked in Maryland, and possibly in Virginia, before settling in Philadelphia. His son, John (1728–78), found patrons in Virginia and in 1763 settled permanently in Maryland. With these three artists one can begin to trace more clearly some of the interactions and interrelationships among artists in the southern colonies. Wollaston appears, for example, to have influenced in part the style of Gustavus Hesselius. The latter no doubt taught his son something of the art and craft of painting. John Hesselius in turn is known to have been the first teacher of Charles Willson Peale (1741–1821), who was born in Maryland and was among the slowly growing number of aspiring young American-born artists who spent a year or more studying in England. Peale was taught, as were a number of his generation, by his fellow American, Benjamin West, only a few years his senior but well established in London. Peale returned and settled for a time in Annapolis; some of his finest portraits show Marylanders and Virginians. He later moved to Philadelphia and made some visits to the southern states. Several of his children and his nieces and nephews, who also became artists, visited the South in search of patrons. His son Rembrandt Peale

(1778–1860) lived for a time in Baltimore, where he established the short-lived Peale Museum in 1797.

In Charleston the artist Jeremiah Theüs (c. 1719–74) enjoyed something of a monopoly of patronage from 1739 until his death in 1774. Born to a Protestant family in Switzerland, he immigrated with them as a youth to South Carolina, to escape religious persecution. There is a certain stiffness in many of his portraits, but this is often redeemed by his skillful use of color and his feeling for elegance of fabrics. During the 18th century southerners living on the Atlantic Seaboard often maintained close business and personal ties with England; young men were sometimes sent there for their education. During visits to the homeland they had their portraits painted, thus carrying artistic patronage beyond the borders of the region.

As one examines these portraits of the 18th century, it is fair to say that patron and artist alike wished for an image that was a likeness and a statement of the status of the sitter. Rich fabrics, satins, velvets, and laces were fashionable and are depicted. Often several members of a family were painted as a group, thus emphasizing the importance and continuity of family ties.

The first renderings of flora and fauna of the present United States, as done by Le Moyne and White, were based on those in the Southeast. Likewise, the first systematic study and publication of natural history in North America, Mark Catesby's two-volume *Natural History of Carolina, Florida, and the Bahama Islands* (published 1731–43), drew upon this verdant region for most of its material. Catesby, an Englishman, first visited the American continent from 1712 to 1719. His interest in the natural history of the New World and his collection of its specimens led a group of naturalists to sponsor a second trip from 1722 to 1725. Upon his return to England, he learned to do engravings and embarked upon publication. His illustrations are among the first to depict animals and birds in their natural habitats. In his engraved depictions he deliberately eschewed shadows, both because he felt they were beyond his competence and because he believed greater accuracy could be achieved without them. To the modern eye his illustrations have an appealing, slightly naive quality. A three-folio collection of his natural history drawings on which his plates are based is now in the Royal Collection at Windsor Castle.

Two other artist-draftsmen who may have hoped to achieve publications such as those given to White, Le Moyne, and Catesby are Alexandre De Batz and Philip Georg Friedrich Von Reck. De Batz was connected with the French military forces in Louisiana, and a small group of his surviving drawings, dated between 1731 and 1735, are in the Peabody Museum in Boston. They include a drawing of a temple and chief of the Acolapissas Indians and one showing Choctaw warriors and children. These are among the earliest surviving visual documents from the Deep South. (The numerous architectural plans and elevations done by the French engineers in connection with the colonies in Mobile, New Orleans, and the adjacent areas represent another group.)

Von Reck's journal and drawings have only recently come to light; they have been stored in the Royal Library of Denmark apparently since the 18th century. A Protestant German, Von Reck accompanied a group of Salzburgers who established a settlement in Georgia in 1734 and again in 1736. He stayed only a few weeks on his first visit and a few months on his second, but during these times he made a number of drawings of flora and fauna found in that region as well as several straightforward drawings of the Yuchi Indians. Some of these drawings are captioned in several languages—Yuchi, Greek, German, and French or English. The works of both Von Reck and De Batz are valuable documentaries of the first encounters of Europeans and the native peoples in the New World.

See also ENVIRONMENT: Naturalists

Jessie Poesch
Tulane University

Francis W. Bilodeau and Mrs. Thomas J. Tobias, eds., *Art in South Carolina, 1670–1970* (1970); Bruce W. Chambers, *Art and Artists of the South: The Robert P. Coggins Collection* (1984); David C. Driskell, *Two Centuries of Black American Art* (1976); James T. Flexner, *First Flowers of Our Wilderness: American Painting, the Colonial Period* (1969); Caroline M. Hickman, *Southern Quarterly* (Fall–Winter 1985); Jessie Poesch, *The Art of the Old South: Painting, Sculpture, Architecture and the Products of Craftsmen, 1560–1860* (1983); Virginia Museum of Fine Arts, *Painting in the South: 1564–1980* (1983); Carolyn J. Weekly, *Antiques* (November 1976, February 1977); Ben F. Williams, *Two Hundred Years of the Visual Arts in North Carolina* (1976). ☆

Painting and Painters, 1790–1860

Portraiture was the most popular art form, both North and South, during the early years of the rapidly expanding new Republic. Portrait painters were legion, and the careers of many have not been examined. Even though the South was less densely populated than the North, many artists practiced their skills in local communities, both large and small. Thomas Cantwell Healy worked in Port Gibson, Miss., in the 1850s, and a number of French-born artists, such as J. J. Vaudechamp and Jacques Amans, established themselves in New Orleans during the 1830s through 1850s. Artists such as Matthew Harris Jouett and Ralph E. W. Earl found their patrons in relatively new communities west of the Appalachians, such as Lexington, Ky., and Nashville, Tenn.

The many portraits reflect changing tastes and values. The 18th-century feeling for elegance is seen in paintings by Thomas Sully's student, Thomas S. Officer, who was in Mobile and Richmond in the 1830s and 1840s. In general, however, painters moved toward the austerity of the neoclassical and an ever-greater emphasis on the very realistic. There was little idealizing. Though some paintings exist of young and beautiful women who might qualify as "southern belles," considerably more are of unpretentious matrons, such as a stern-looking portrait of the wife of Isaac Shelby, a governor of Kentucky, painted in 1827 by Patrick Henry Davenport (Kentucky Historical Society).

During this period one can trace a developing iconography of national and regional heroes. Gilbert Stuart was one of several artists who helped make George Washington's image familiar through the many copies of his portraits. Some of these found their way into the South, adorning county courthouses or city halls. Legislative bodies commissioned portraits. North Carolina commissioned two full-length portraits of Washington from Thomas Sully. A misunderstanding occurred, and Sully produced a dramatic canvas of *Washington Crossing the Delaware* that was too large for the space. It was refused and now is in the Boston Museum of Fine Arts. The city of Charleston still owns a handsome full-length portrait of Washington, which was commissioned from John Trumbull and was completed in 1792. Charleston also has an excellent miniature painting of the Marquis de Lafayette by Charles Fraser. The city of Richmond and the state legislature of Kentucky were among other political bodies that commissioned portraits of the renowned general Lafayette when he made his grand return visit to the United States in 1825. Ralph E. W. Earl became the virtual court painter of Andrew Jackson after he attained fame. Other heroes who were painted a number of times include Jefferson, Calhoun, Clay, and Daniel Boone.

The painting of miniatures—small, intimate portraits in watercolor on ivory—enjoyed a special popularity in the early decades of the 19th century. One of the finest of the practitioners of this art was Charles Fraser of Charleston. In 1857 he was given a retrospective exhibition in his native city, and over 400 of his miniatures were shown. He was particularly adept in painting the elderly, showing them in honest yet sympathetic likenesses.

Several artists, such as Jacob Frymire, Joshua Johnston, and Charles Peale Polk, all of whom worked in the late 18th or early 19th centuries, might be classified as slightly naive painters. Polk and Johnston worked in and around Baltimore. Johnston is important as the first known professional black painter in the European tradition. Both Polk and Frymire traveled in western Maryland and Virginia as itinerant painters.

The biracial and multiracial nature of southern society is visible in a number of paintings from this era. Several portraits of free people of color, such as one attributed to Francois Fleischbein (c. 1860, New Orleans Museum of Art), or the portrait of James Armistead Lafayette by John R. Martin (c. 1824, Valentine Museum, Richmond), show dignified, attractive individuals. George Catlin included Seminole Indians

View of Mount Vernon, looking toward the southwest

among the subjects he recorded in the 1830s. A handsome, full-length portrait of the Creek Indian chief William McIntosh (c. 1820–23, Alabama Department of Archives and History) is attributed to Nathan and Joseph Negus. The Seminole leader Osceola was painted both by Robert R. Curtis of Charleston and by Catlin in 1838. Among the most poignant of paintings of blacks is the large *Plantation Burial* (1860, Historic New Orleans Collection) done by John Antrobus in Louisiana. It is a sympathetic depiction of a moment in the private lives of members of a slave community.

During the late 18th and early 19th centuries landscape painting gained importance as a genre in the United States, particularly in New York State and New England. George Beck painted several picturesque views of Baltimore in the late 1790s (Maryland Historical Society). George Washington was one of his patrons. The meticulously rendered scenes by Francis Guy (c. 1800–05, Maryland Historical Society) qualify more as portraits of cities than as landscapes proper. Both Beck and Guy helped launch the development of landscape painting. In general, however, this development in the South was fitful until after the Civil War. George Cooke, working in the 1830s, and T. Addison Richards were among artists who wrote on the virtues of scenery in the South, and each did some cityscapes and landscapes. Richards, however, candidly admitted that the terrain was difficult, distances too great, transportation poor, and access to urban centers limited. William Charles Anthony Frerichs was one who caught the drama of the North Carolina mountains on his canvasses. James Cameron, working in Chattanooga in the late 1850s, recorded the dramatic terrain of that area. In an impressive painting showing Colonel and Mrs. James A. Whiteside, their children, and their servants, this artist combined group portraiture and landscape (Hunter Museum of Art, Chattanooga). A large and richly detailed painting of the New Orleans waterfront done in 1853 by Hippolyte Sebron (Tulane University) is another that is more cityscape than landscape. Influenced by Daguerre, it has an open-ended "slice-of-life" quality that presages compositional concepts of the Impressionists.

The most famous of all American painters of natural history, John James Audubon, did many of his preliminary studies for his *Birds of America* in the Deep South, particularly in Louisiana, Mississippi, and South Carolina. Outdoor life, sports, and horse racing were popular in the South, so it is no surprise that the most popular animal or horse painter in the United States in the 19th century, Edward Troye, spent most of his time in the South. Troye lived for some time in Kentucky and Alabama and traveled throughout the region. Many of his works, which often include depictions of jockeys and trainers, are still in private collections.

The lives of a number of painters were abruptly changed with the advent of the Civil War. Some left the region, others joined the military forces, and those who remained found few patrons in the years 1860 to 1865.

See also BLACK LIFE: Art, Black; ENVIRONMENT: / Audubon, John James

Jessie Poesch
Tulane University

Bruce W. Chambers, *Art and Artists of the South: The Robert P. Coggins Collection* (1984); Corcoran Gallery of Art, *American Painters of the South* (1960); James H.

Craig, *The Arts and Crafts in North Carolina, 1699–1840* (1965); David C. Driskell, *Two Centuries of Black American Art* (1976); David Moltke-Hansen, *Art in the Lives of South Carolinians: Nineteenth-Century Chapters* (1979); Estill Curtis Pennington, *William Edward West, 1788–1857: Kentucky Painter* (1985); Jessie Poesch, *The Art of the Old South: Painting, Sculpture, Architecture and the Products of Craftsmen, 1560–1860* (1983); *Southern Quarterly* (Fall–Winter 1985); Virginia Museum of Fine Arts, *Painting in the South: 1564–1980* (1983). ☆

Painting and Painters, 1860–1920

The differences in circumstances between the South and its peoples and the rest of the nation were probably felt most acutely by southerners during and after the Civil War, extending until World War I. In many cases these differences lasted until World War II and, in part, still exist. They affected artists and their choices of subject matter in subtle ways and significantly reduced their chances for showing and selling their works. Nevertheless, artists who worked in the South were influenced by the same artistic trends that influenced artists in other parts of the country.

During the Civil War Winslow Homer, Edwin A. Forbes, Henry Mosler, Alfred R. Waud, and William Waud were among artists who followed the troops and recorded day-to-day events for popular journals. Homer also created oil paintings based on his observations in the South at this time, including his *Defiance: Inviting a Shot Before Petersburg, Virginia* (1864) and his *At the Cabin Door* (1865–66). The first suggests the courage and sometimes foolhardiness of soldiers in that conflict; the second indicates the proud, quiet hopes and subtle defiance of blacks at this time. Conrad Wise Chapman joined the Confederate army and, after being wounded, was reassigned to Charleston, S.C., and ordered to illustrate the city's fortifications. The 31 small oil-on-board paintings, though most frequently viewed for their historical content, are noteworthy for their freshness and clarity.

In Richmond, William D. Washington painted the *Burial of Latané* in 1864, recording an incident of 1862 and showing white women and slaves performing a young war hero's burial service, a service attended by white children but by no adult white males. In 1869 Everett B. D. Fabrino Julio painted a large-scale double equestrian portrait showing the imagined conference of General Lee and Stonewall Jackson on the eve of the battle of Chancellorsville—a battle in which Jackson was struck down, dying shortly thereafter. Prints based on these two paintings subsequently enjoyed wide circulation among white southerners and became symbols of the Lost Cause—the death of heroes and the role of women who carried on nobly in the absence of their men. Henry Mosler's painting *The Lost Cause*, first exhibited in 1868, showed a weary infantryman returning to his ruined cabin, thus focusing on the effect of the war on ordinary yeoman farmers of the highlands. This Mosler painting was reproduced in chromolithographs and widely circulated. In the late 1860s John Adams Elder's *Battle of the Crater* and a notable posthumous portrait of Stonewall Jackson (Corcoran Gallery of Art) were well known. In the decades after the war still other artists, among them William Gilbert Gaul and Xanthus R. Smith, painted imaginary episodes of the conflict. Alfred Waud was one of several artists whose drawings record the South during Reconstruction, and Forbes and Waud later contributed illustrations for late 19th-century publications on the war. Thus, a group of now little-known paintings and drawings formed an iconography of noble defeat, an ethos that helped salve the pride of white southerners during years of poverty and reconstruction.

Winslow Homer returned to Virginia in the 1870s and did a group of paintings of southern blacks, all characterized by quiet dignity and forthright depiction. John James Elder, Richard Norris Brooke, and Lucien Whiting Powell were Virginia artists who painted everyday life of blacks in the 1870s and 1880s. Lyell E. Carr did a similar series of rural black Georgia life in the 1890s. The intent of the artists was to show "sober and truthful" depictions of these impoverished peoples. All of these artists were influenced in part by changing European choices of subject matter; the southern black, for example, was equated with the picturesque laboring peasant and thus became an emblem of the South. To the 20th-century eye some of these depictions have a sentimental quality—though they are a far cry from the caricature seen on minstrel-show, music-sheet illustrations. They record blacks as a passive, untroubled people, a view shared by both northern and southern whites. They record the role of blacks in the life of the South, and many are painted with great skill and present their subjects with great dignity. William Aiken Walker's small paintings of blacks and their cabins frequently served as picturesque mementoes, which northern visitors to the southern resorts took home. Less than successful artistically, they too are known for their depictions of black rural southerners and their heritage.

The southern landscape—particularly the quiet, rural life along the bayous and streams of south Louisiana and the Gulf Coast—became the favorite subject matter for artists Richard Clague, Marshall Smith, and William Buck. Joseph Rusling Meeker, who had served with the Union navy, returned again and again to the Deep South to paint the verdure and humid atmosphere of the wetlands. Flavius Fisher, living in Lynchburg, Va., made the open spaces of the Dismal Swamp his theme. Further north, artists such as Carl Brenner and Clarence Boyd painted the characteristic woodlands of Kentucky in a style that has roots both in the Barbizon school of France and in the reverent and meticulous response to nature articulated by Asher B. Durand of New York. Though their paintings were based on the world around them, these artists were not self-consciously regional in the later spirit of the 1930s.

Occasionally their critics expressed a strongly regional attitude. Praising Richard Clague's work on 21 January 1871, a reviewer in the *Commercial Bulletin* of New Orleans spoke of his ability to capture "the characteristics of our peculiar scenery," and, in perhaps an oblique reference to the dramatic works of artists such as Bierstadt, said that "there is no meretricious glare about these fine studies, no straining after effect." In the early 20th century Ellsworth Woodward of New Orleans, following the precepts of the arts and crafts movement and of John Dewey, exhorted artists of the region to draw

Conrad Wise Chapman,* Camp Near Corinth, Mississippi *(1862)

from their own environment for the subjects of their works.

During the 1870s Florida began to attract visitors. It was the "new Eden," the still-unspoiled paradise of the expanding industrial nation. Northern artists such as Winslow Homer, with his brilliant late watercolors of the tropics (including Florida), Thomas Moran, and William Morris Hunt were among those who spent one or more winters there. Martin J. Heade first came to Florida in 1883 and later settled in St. Augustine, where he led a small artists' colony until his death in 1904. His glowing landscapes of the wetlands of Florida show a still-primitive wilderness. George Inness, and then his son, George Inness, Jr., found warmth and a sense of union with nature in Tarpon Springs, Fla. Elliot Daingerfield, a native of North Carolina, was a close friend and associate of the elder Inness in New York. In his mature years he returned regularly to his summer home in Blowing Rock, N.C., where he painted the familiar contours of the land in muted tonalities, which also suggest his deep, religious feeling for the spiritual quality of the natural world.

Knowledge of women artists practicing in America in the late 19th and early 20th centuries is still somewhat limited, but in this period several women artists from the South emerged. Clara Weaver Parrish and Anne Goldthwaite, both of Alabama, were among artists who received their training and spent much of their artistic careers in New York, though each returned to the South with some regularity and included southern subjects in their works. This emergence of women artists coincided with the women's suffrage movement and the slow access to higher education gained by women at this time. Newcomb College of Tulane University, founded in 1886–87, was one of the first women's colleges in the South to have an extensive art training program. Gertrude Roberts Smith, painter, and Mary Sheerer, ceramic designer, were both teachers at Newcomb College and important artists in their own right and helped to shape a generation of women artists after the college's founding.

Artistic organizations, formed from time to time in various southern communities, provided opportunities for meetings among artists, instructed aspiring artists, and provided occasions for exhibits. In New Orleans, for example, the Southern Art Union was organized around 1881 and lasted until sometime after 1883. The Southern Arts League was organized in 1885, changed its name to the Artists' Association of New Orleans, and officially incorporated in 1886; by 1899 it had 63 members. In the late 1890s the Arts and Exhibition Club was founded, and by 1905 merged with the Artists' Association, thus forming the Art Association of New Orleans, a group that still exists but is now one among many art groups in the city. The Arts and Crafts Club of New Orleans was founded in 1922 and continued as an exhibiting and teaching organization until March 1951. Similar organizations were formed in other cities and areas, some short-lived, others surviving for considerably longer times, such as the Nashville Art Association, the Waco Art League in Texas, the Carolina Art Association in Charleston, and the Mississippi Art Association.

One national culmination of this local and regional artistic activity was the formation at a meeting held in Washington, D.C., in May 1909 of the American Federation of Arts, an organization that aimed to include "all institutions, societies, city and village improvement associations, and schools and other organizations in the United States, whose purpose is to promote the study of art, the cultivation of the public taste, and the application of art to the development of material conditions in our country." Though the majority of those attending the founding meeting were from New York, Boston, and Philadelphia, delegates included those from the Art Association of New Orleans, the Carolina Art Association, and the Waco Art League, as well as a number from Maryland organizations and a sizable group from private and public organizations based in Washington, D.C., then still a very southern city. William Woodward, representing both the Art Association of New Orleans and Tulane University, was one of the principal speakers.

Despite the efforts of local and regional organizations, artists in the South still found it difficult to find patrons and exhibit their works. The area was still essentially rural, and the art groups were quite small. Another organization designed to help artists reach a wider audience was the Southern States Art League, founded in 1921. One of its founders, Ellsworth Woodward, bemoaned the fact that so many of the South's best artists had found it necessary to leave the area and had achieved success only in the North. The Southern States Art League regularly sponsored exhibits and meetings until its virtual demise in 1946. Its most successful exhibit was held in Nashville in 1935, when over 12,000 people attended.

Despite many artists' seeming isolation, the influence of the Impressionists and the Symbolists found its way into the South during the last decade of the 19th and the first two decades of the 20th centuries through the network of communication in the artistic world. Evidence of this influence is seen in the works of artists such as Ellsworth and William Woodward, Alexander Drysdale, and Gertrude Roberts Smith, all of New Orleans; Robert Loftin Newman, whose roots were in Tennessee; William Posey Silva, who depicted landscapes of Tennessee and Georgia; J. Gari

Melchers in Virginia; and Julian Onderdonk in San Antonio.

See also BLACK LIFE: Art, Black; ENVIRONMENT: / Homer, Winslow; MYTHIC SOUTH: / Lost Cause Myth

Jessie Poesch
Tulane University

Bruce W. Chambers, *Art and Artists of the South: The Robert P. Coggins Collection* (1984), *Southern Quarterly* (Fall–Winter 1985); Corcoran Gallery of Art, *American Painters of the South* (1960); David C. Driskell, *Two Centuries of Black American Art* (1976); Max Kozloff, *Artforum* (May 1973); David Moltke-Hansen, *Art in the Lives of South Carolinians: Nineteenth-Century Chapters* (1979); Pauline Pinckney, *Painting in Texas: The Nineteenth-Century* (1967); Virginia Museum of Fine Arts, *Painting in the South: 1564–1980* (1983); Ben F. Williams, *Two Hundred Years of the Visual Arts in North Carolina* (1976). ☆

Painting and Painters, 1920–1960

The modern period in southern painting can be said to begin in the early 1920s with the activities of the Fugitive group at Vanderbilt University in Nashville. Although the Fugitives were essentially a literary group, they were also concerned with theories of artistic expression in general, especially with regard to the South. Their importance lies in their cosmopolitan attitude toward creative expression. The four major figures in the movement were Donald Davidson, John Crowe Ransom, Allen Tate, and Robert Penn Warren. Although respecting the new modernism that spanned national boundaries, they regretted that southern culture, as they had known it, appeared to be dissolving under the pressure of the new industrial age. Like the modern artist in general, the Fugitives struggled with the rift between reason and the imagination, between science and faith; they assumed the mantle of the modern sensibility but set out to make it uniquely southern as well. Donald Davidson, always the Fugitive with the strongest sense of his southern roots, wrote an essay for the *Saturday Review* in May 1926 titled "The Artist as Southerner." He felt that any artist who chose his materials exclusively from his surroundings was provincial, not innovative or modern, yet he recognized the peculiar clash between modernism and tradition that marked the dilemma of the southern artist.

The Fugitives were not the only group to recognize that a new period of expression was at hand. The circle of the *Double Dealer* magazine, published in New Orleans from 1921 to 1926, sought to end the artistic backwardness that they, like the Fugitives, had perceived as the South's lot since the end of the Civil War. William Faulkner, who would best exemplify the new southern artist, was among the younger southerners this magazine featured. Another magazine, the *New South*, begun in Chattanooga in 1927, turned matters in its first issue more expressly to art. In a spirited essay on "The South in American Art," a writer extolled the southern artists who painted the local yet American scene. "We must build and maintain schools wherein Southern talent may be educated and trained," he wrote, "and thereby interpret the spirit and traditions of the South, which can only be expressed by native artists."

The call for painters of the southern scene was sparked by the activities of Thomas Hart Benton, who traveled extensively in 1928 and 1929 over the back roads of the Deep South, gathering material for his major mural programs in New York in the early 1930s on American history and culture. The paintings that Benton produced on his trip through the South were prophetic of the kind of work many southern painters would turn to in the 1930s. One southern artist who echoed Benton's activity in the same period was Conrad Albrizio, who completed an important mural cycle in 1930 for the Louisiana State Capitol Building in Baton Rouge. The building was the brainchild of the flamboyant governor Huey P. Long and was one of the most successfully designed and decorated public buildings of its time. Albrizio's cycle of paintings, done for the governor's reception room, has unfortunately been lost; however, complete sketches survive to show that the artist executed a series of narrative scenes of the daily life of the state, including a panel depicting industrial activity.

Likewise, the artist Roderick MacKenzie, working in Birmingham, Ala., completed four large panels depicting the history of that commonwealth for the domed central portion of the statehouse. This kind of artistic activity in the South increased markedly with the onset of the Depression and the art programs of Franklin D. Roosevelt's New Deal. Between January 1933 and April 1939 the social service wings of the New Deal poured nearly $2 billion into the southern states, providing large-scale relief and resulting in many wide-ranging physical improvements. The federal art programs had a direct and profound effect on painting activity in the South. One result was the rapid emergence of an even greater sectional feeling with regard to the development of the arts. By encouraging a regional focus, the New Deal programs had the effect of turning many southern artists and communities inward.

In order to comprehend fully the nature of painting in the South in the 1930s, it is necessary to understand the Agrarian and regionalist movements. The Agrarian philosophy, which grew out of the earlier Fugitive movement in Nashville, had to do with the desire, in Allen Tate's words, for "getting back to the roots" of the southern experience. The Agrarians posited a duality between agrarian and industrial society, with the latter viewed as a threat to southern civilization. However, this movement was far from simplistic; the arguments of its best writers were often impassioned and stimulating. Donald Davidson again set the tone in an article titled "A Mirror for Artists," where he maintained that the duty of the southern artist was first to be an active member of his community. Seen in this context, one can understand the participation of an artist like Conrad Albrizio in a symposium in 1936 titled "The Arts in the Community." Albrizio echoed the aims of other southern painters of this period by calling for work that would "appraise the people of the community, their spirit, and their degree of culture." He went on to execute mural programs in several southern cities throughout the decade, maintaining that the artist's role was to help the average southerner understand that "the real values of everyday life" and "the beauty of simple things" were the keys to lasting artistic expression.

Albrizio's beliefs were typical of the regionalist movement as a whole in the decade of the 1930s. Richard Coe, who painted the Birmingham steel mills in this period, had identical views. He headed the Alabama section of the WPA, saying that "American art for and by the American people is a slogan worth heeding." Another Alabama artist who was equally active along these lines was Kelly Fitzpatrick, who helped establish the Alabama Art League in Montgomery in 1930. Three years later on the banks of the Coosa River in Elmore County he founded the Poka-Hutchi Art Colony, which flourished during the summers until 1948, attracting some of the South's leading artists, many of whom were keenly interested in depicting the lives of the rural people, black or white. Artists like Howard Cook followed Thomas Hart Benton's footsteps and traveled through the region in order to portray the southern worker realistically, yet with sympathy and dignity. In many respects, the concerns of artists like Cook mirrored those of major regionalist thinkers like Howard W. Odum of the University of North Carolina at Chapel Hill, who steered the old southern sectionalism into a constructive investigation of local culture as a part of a larger national picture.

In 1936 a young painter named Lamar Dodd was appointed to the art faculty of the University of Georgia after winning an award at the annual exhibition of the Art Institute of Chicago for a painting depicting a slag dump and railroad cut near Wylan, Ala. Such a subject was typical for Dodd, who preferred to paint things that captured, in his words, "the mood of the place," the everyday South. Like many southern artists in this period, Dodd was trained at the Art Students League in New York before returning to his native area to paint and teach. He soon gained a reputation as the outstanding artist in Georgia, and he was active in many educational, civic, and professional groups, including the Association of Georgia Artists and the Southeastern Art Association. Thus, an energetic artist like Lamar Dodd was able to found a large and important center for art at the University of Georgia, and the South began to have a generation of young artists trained largely in their native region.

Activity was under way in Mississippi as well. The Mississippi Art Association, founded in 1911, was followed by the Gulf Coast Art Association of Biloxi, with William Woodward of New Orleans as president. Individual painters in Mississippi, while not as numerous as in the neighboring states of Alabama and Louisiana, nevertheless mirrored similar social concerns in their work, as in Marie Hull's paintings of sharecroppers that she painted after her return from extensive study in New York and Europe. Again, such depictions were meant to dignify the individual, not demean him. One contemporary newspaper account of Hull's sensitive portraits recognized their "clear sharp eye and indomitable spirit," where the subjects were "slightly stooped by (their) toiling decades but strengthened rather than broken by them." The Mississippi artist who gained greatest recognition in the 1930s was John McCrady, who initially worked in Oxford, where he became friends with William Faulkner. McCrady was vocal about wanting to paint southern subjects and soon set up a studio in New Orleans, where he achieved a national reputation as a regionalist while completing work for the WPA. In 1937 he was featured in *Life* magazine, and the following year he helped found an association of artists called A New Southern Group. In 1939 McCrady and Robert Penn Warren were awarded Guggenheim fellowships; McCrady's intent was to paint a series of works on "The Life and Faith of the Southern Negro."

Clearly, the regionalist movement had an overriding effect on the painting of the South in this period, and just as clearly, regionalism to the artists was less a matter of blind nativism than cultural growth. This was nowhere more apparent than in Dallas, Tex., where strong new artistic activity centered around the events of the Texas State Centennial in 1936. A group of talented younger artists, who were informally labeled "The Nine," rose to prominence and developed what became one of the most notable and original regional schools of southern painting. Dallas stood at the boundary of the Southeast and Southwest, and the paintings of The Nine reflected that duality. The principal artists in the group were Alexandre Hogue, Jerry Bywaters, Otis Dozier, William Lester, and Everett Spruce. All but Spruce, who hailed from Arkansas, had been raised in Texas in rural communities. Their paintings depicted rural and urban subjects, set against the Texas landscape, and were characterized by clarity and openness of space and light. No single artist dominated this important group, and they all were intensely active in community affairs, teaching, writing, and working with local galleries and the newly built Dallas Museum of Fine Arts. This group was active until the events of World War II forced them to go their separate ways; yet they exemplified the enormous impact that a regionalist aesthetic had on the development of southern culture.

Throughout the Depression era many southern painters, including the members of the Dallas Nine, felt compelled to portray the southern black as a way of coming to grips with the reality of their own environment. In a similar way, the decade of the 1930s witnessed the expanding struggles of the Afro-American artist's search for his own roots—roots far deeper and harder to trace. As early as 1921 W. E. B. Du Bois, writing in the *Crisis*, had maintained that "the transforming hand and seeing eye of the artist, white or black," were needed to help in the search for Afro-American identity. Alain Locke's *The New Negro*, published in 1925, began to spur interest in Afro-American folklore and art as a method of turning social disillusionment into racial pride. In 1931 Locke, then professor of philosophy at Howard University, published an article in the *American Magazine of Art* titled "The American Negro as Artist," where he surveyed the work of the major Afro-American artists of the period, many of whom had come from the South. He had warm words of praise for a younger generation of artists who aimed to express in their art the "race, spirit, and background as well as the individual skill and temperament of the artist." One of these artists was William H. Johnson, who was just then beginning his remarkable career. Born in Florence, S.C., but associated with Charleston, he studied at the Art Students League in New York and was awarded a William E. Harmon Foundation Prize for further study abroad. In 1938 he began teaching at the Harlem Community Center in New York and exhibited his works to increasingly wide acclaim; yet it was not to last. His color denied him the opportunity and recognition that he deserved, and his later life was marked by tragic circumstances. However, other artists could turn such prejudices to their advantage. Aaron Douglas, who founded the department of art at Fisk University in Nashville and taught generations of students, is an example. Douglas was trained in New York and was an active member of the Harlem Renaissance; he furnished the illustrations for Locke's book *The New Negro*. With the help of Edwin Harleston, another Afro-American artist from Charleston, Douglas completed a series of highly significant murals depicting the course of "Negro history" for the library at Fisk University. As an artist, Douglas maintained that he wanted to "place himself where the people are," and his selfless contributions to the development of Afro-American art in the South cannot be overemphasized.

A number of young white southern painters were also interested in the sympathetic portrayal of blacks along the lines suggested by Douglas and were committed to change during this period. Charles Shannon, who was born and raised in Montgomery, Ala., studied at the Cleveland School of Art and returned in 1935 to Butler County, where he built a log cabin and proceeded to paint a number of expressionistic works about southern blacks. "I came to love this land," the artist wrote, "the plants and people that grew from it." In 1938 Shannon received a Julius Rosenwald Fellowship "for Southerners who are working on problems distinctive to the South." The following year Shannon and a group of friends organized a cooperative venture in Montgomery that they called New South, which was designed to enrich the cultural life of the area by gathering together artists and artisans to work in a gallery and theater, and to teach workshops and classes.

In Virginia a similar effort was made by Julien Binford, who had returned from his study in New York to buy a piece of land in Fine Creek, where he busily converted the ruins of an old foundry into a house and studio. Binford was one of the first recipients of the Virginia Artist Fellowships instituted by the Virginia Museum of Fine Arts in Richmond, and he used it to conduct classes at the Craig House Negro Art Center. In 1942 he produced a much-heralded mural for the black congregation of the Shiloh Baptist Church near his home. Binford's contemporary, Robert Gwathmey, a native of Richmond, infused social commentary into his work in a more overt fashion. In 1946 he told a writer for *Art News* that he would return to his home every summer after teaching in New York and see anew the deep social problems that affected his native South. Yet his paintings seemed to exude more pathos than hate. As a southern painter he was angry and critical, but he also seemed to shoulder some of the guilt.

The period of World War II activated a broad cycle of change in the South. The region was on the move, shifting, growing, and changing old and seemingly entrenched patterns. Sometimes the change was strongly resisted, often for the sake of an increasingly outmoded sectionalism. Southern painters became more concerned not with a sense of place, but with a sensibility. Romare Bearden, originally from Charlotte, studied and worked in New York and Europe before coming to the realization that his most evocative images came from "the people I knew and remembered down South." His work represents the essence of the migration of the southern black from the rural areas and traditions to postwar urban society. "I paint out of the tradition of the Blues, of call and recall," the artist has written. "I never left Charlotte, except physically."

Remembrances, visions, the mythol-

Walter Anderson,* Walter Anderson Rowing His Boat *(c. 1950s)

ogy of place—these elements underlie much postwar southern painting. Carroll Cloar, an artist originally from Arkansas, moved to Memphis in 1955 and began a series of paintings based on his boyhood in the Arkansas Delta. "There is a joy in the sense of belonging, of possessing and being possessed, by the land where you were born." His meticulous, vibrant works evoke the spirit of folk art yet with a power that derives from sophisticated study of his surroundings. Likewise, Hobson Pittman's paintings seem like dream worlds of southern myths and impressions. Raised on a plantation near Epworth, N.C., Pittman became a noted artist and teacher outside his native South, but the imagery and spirit of the region never left his work. All three of these artists—Bearden, Cloar, and Pittman—have created evocations, dreams, and remembrances of an otherworldly South that seems to exist mostly as fiction.

Some southern artists in the postwar period withdrew to create a world wholly their own yet inextricably part of southern culture. Walter Inglis Anderson, after studying art in Pennsylvania and in Europe, moved to a tiny cottage in Ocean Springs, Miss., where, in virtual seclusion, he painted the local flora and fauna. Throughout the 1950s Anderson spent most of his time on Horn Island, a small, ever-changing sandbar rich in plants and wildlife. He produced thousands of watercolors of this southern version of Walden Pond and kept detailed journals of his feelings and impressions as he explored every inch of its terrain throughout the seasons. Like Anderson, Will Henry Stevens also adopted a uniquely personal vision, but one that embodied two separate styles. He taught at Newcomb College in New Orleans from 1921 until his retirement in 1948 and spent nearly all his summers in western North Carolina, painting the woods and hillsides. His "pastel paintings" of these southern woodlands, using a nonrubbing chalk of his own invention, were praised when they were first exhibited in 1941. Curiously, Stevens also painted in a more nonobjective style and exhibited those works separately. In December 1941 he went so far as to have two simultaneous exhibitions in separate galleries, which may suggest the dilemma that some southern artists faced regarding a search for a meaningful style in a period when southern culture was undergoing profound changes.

Stevens spent his summers close to an enormously influential school that had been founded in 1933 near Black Mountain, N.C. It was an entirely experimental community, with shifting ideas and goals, but it attracted some of the brightest and most fertile artistic minds of the postwar era, including Josef Albers, Walter Gropius, Willem de Kooning, Robert Motherwell, Clement Greenberg, Beaumont Newhall, and Buckminster Fuller. The only southern painter to receive an invitation to teach at this isolated outpost was Robert

Gwathmey; for the most part, the effect of Black Mountain College on the immediate development of painting in the South was minimal. Yet the artistic climate in the South changed drastically in this period, in part because of the influence of the New York School and of the art centers that had been established at southern colleges and universities. For the first time the impetus for artistic change was generated from within the South itself.

The activity of artists like Ralston Crawford, based in New Orleans, is an example of the newer acceptance of modernist styles in the region. Crawford, who had adapted a style of nonrepresentational geometric abstraction, began teaching at Louisiana State University at Baton Rouge in 1949. In his paintings of New Orleans, which were done in a series, he conveyed the hard light and busy rhythms of the city's industrial and maritime activity in color-filled forms and shapes that revealed his passion for jazz. Like Crawford, George Cress developed his art within the new idiom. Cress attended Emory University and then studied art under Lamar Dodd and Jean Charlot at the University of Georgia and was thus a member of the new generation of artists trained within the South. He began teaching at the University of Chattanooga and has served in the Southeastern College Art Conference, as well as the Tennessee Arts Council. His painting style evolved out of the context of the second generation of the New York School, as he depicted the layered bluffs of his region in an abstract pattern of loose patches of color and texture. Cress's contemporary Claude Howell, who has taught at the University of North Carolina in his native Wilmington since 1953, works in a more representational style, painting structured, austere views of his locale. Michael O'Brien, in his stimulating book, *The Idea of the American South*, has written of the artist's need to see "the South itself as an idea, used to organize and comprehend disparate facts of social reality." Certainly the modern southern artist has assumed a southern sensibility in his work and has developed out of that position. Thus, an artist like William Halsey of Charleston could turn from early, representational paintings of his surroundings to ones that became increasingly abstract without relinquishing the uniquely southern sensibility that some have sensed in his work.

Throughout the period herein reviewed, southern artists sought to preserve a regional aesthetic as opposed to a more national one. It was a period of paradox and change, when older sectional desires clashed with national, and eventually international, artistic influences. Artists in the South in the period prior to World War II could not be classified in the avant-garde sense as independent; in the more traditional sense, they thought of themselves as integral members of—even interpreters for—their own southern society. Only after the establishment of a comprehensive cultural network of museums and universities does one find the growth of the independent sensibility, the open acceptance of the broader framework of American culture with the southern artist fully a part of the international art world.

See also BLACK LIFE: Art, Black; EDUCATION: / Black Mountain College; HISTORY AND MANNERS: Modernism; New Deal Cultural Programs; LITERATURE: Agrarianism in Literature; / Davidson, Donald; Ransom, John Crowe; Tate, Allen; Warren, Robert

Penn; MYTHIC SOUTH: Regionalism; / Agrarians, Vanderbilt

Rick Stewart
Dallas Museum of Art

Amon Carter Museum, *Texas Painting and Sculpture: The Twentieth Century* (1971); Bruce W. Chambers, *Art and Artists of the South: The Robert P. Coggins Collection* (1984); Corcoran Gallery of Art, *American Painters of the South* (1960); David C. Driskell, *Two Centuries of Black American Art* (1976); Ralph H. Hudson, *Black Artists / South* (1979); Huntsville Museum of Art, *Contemporary Painting in Alabama* (1980); James C. Kelly and Estill Curtis Pennington, *The South on Paper: Line, Color and Light* (1985); Jack Morris, *Contemporary Artists of South Carolina* (1970); Virginia Museum of Fine Arts, *Painting in the South: 1564–1980* (1983). ☆

Painting and Painters, 1960–1980

In studying contemporary art in the South, one must explore signs and symbols associated with the region in the popular imagination and pay particular attention to how these have emerged in the visual arts.

If one is indeed shaped by the environment, daily life, and early experiences, then the concept of a "southern" type of art is as inevitable as history. The internal characteristics of southern art, especially when it comes to modern and contemporary paintings, present a far from tidy field, partly because the region itself is so heterogeneous. One can distinguish between the Deep South (South Carolina, Georgia, Alabama, Mississippi, and Louisiana) and the Southern Rim (Tennessee, Virginia, North Carolina, Florida, Texas, and sometimes Arkansas and others) on the basis of historical, sociocultural, and economic factors, all of which affect art and artists.

The *American Heritage Dictionary* defines the term *regionalism* in three ways, and art from the Southeast fits all three understandings. The first is of, pertaining to, or characteristic of a large geographical region, and Nellie Mae Rowe, Sam Doyle, Robert Gordy, and Elizabeth Shannon are southern artists who are regional in this sense of the term. The second definition is of, pertaining to, or characteristic of a particular region or localized district, and Donald Roller Wilson, Carroll Cloar, Romare Bearden, and Juan Gonzales represent southern art in this aspect. *Regionalism* can also mean something characterized by a particular language dialect in an area. The religious, social, and ethnic localism of Sister Gertrude Morgan, the Reverend Howard Fenster, Jesse Poimboeuf, and Rise Delmar Ochsner exemplify regional art of this type.

To the extent that distinct regional subcultures exist, some aspects might be used by regional artists to evoke a sense of place, time, and geographical identity, e.g., Sam Doyle's "first black midwife, she was a slave." With respect to such factors in contemporary southern painting, one must look outside the field of art for clues. In *The Enduring South* (1975) John Shelton Reed isolates four influences he considers important in this region: familism, religiosity, localism, and a greater tolerance for violence than the rest of the country. To these one might add the isolationism of the "old folks at home" mentality or what should be classified as the "South of the mind," which holds true in the social localism of such cities as Charleston, Mobile, and Savannah.

In southeastern painting regional imagery abounds, as in the works of Patty Whitty Johnson, Sue Moore, and Douglas Bourgeois. A respect for custom and the past is still prevalent, affecting newcomers in a variety of ways, and a certain inclination remains toward representational images and a decorative unity of form that appears to be a consistent shaping force in the art of such southerners as Jasper Johns, Kenneth Noland, Dorothy Gillespie, and Ida Kohlmeyer. Thus, a basis seems to exist for positing clearly identifiable qualities when it comes to southern art.

In the visual arts the term *regionalism* presents additional problems. According to conventional wisdom, provincials are those people who do not live in or receive artistic truth from New York City. Much of the art produced outside of New York has its own roots, references, and traditions. When outsiders—mainstream critics, artists, and others—are brought in to judge exhibitions of "southern" art, they more often than not ignore these sharp differences, applying their own standards to the art they see. The problem with this, for example, may clearly be seen in the case of south Florida, which is the tropics, the gateway to the Latin Americas and the Caribbean. It is inconceivable that such factors would not exert considerable influence on the art of an impressionable generation of younger creators in the state. To ignore these realities on the grounds of mainstream standards would neither be responsible criticism nor a fair assessment of the surrealist-style art.

Doubtless the setting of the South conjures up pictures in the popular imagination of weeping willows, cypresses, Spanish moss, plantations, and Afro-Americans—not tropical iconography. The overall impression, as noted previously, can be deceptive. The art of this region is undeniably the product, like any serious art, of a search for meaning. Explicit in this definition is a decided concern with irrationality, ineptitude, banality, and deceitful fragility on the one hand, and, on the other hand, a refined literary picturesqueness with a special emphasis on representation and decorative embellishments. To these qualities one might add whimsicality; sly, humorous exaggerations concerning both Christian and pagan themes; and dashes of charm, irony, magic, quaintness, directness, naïveté; a startlingly crude, powerful, and often unexpectedly brutal primitivism.

Clearly, southern artists have been suspicious of established fashions and accepted fundamentals of modern style, i.e., mathematical absolutes, a reliance on science and technology, and rational thought processes. Perhaps in terms of Realism and neo-expressionism, their suspicion of the latter has been prophetic.

While there is at present no definitive southern school of painting, recent exhibitions such as *Black Folk Art in America 1930–1980* (Corcoran Gallery of Art), *More Than Land or Sky: Art from Appalachia* (National Museum of American Art), and *Painting in the South: 1564–1980* (Virginia Museum of Fine Arts) have focused critical attention on southern art. The reality is simply this: before one can begin to discuss southern art, it has to be seen and written about. In this context the efforts of the Southeastern Center for Contemporary Art, the New Orleans Center for Contemporary Art, Nexus, the Atlanta Art Workers Coalition, the Southeast College Art Conference, the Southeastern Women's Caucus for Art, and a host of other art support systems are crucial. Primary among the regional journals is *Art Papers*, which gives serious review to states in the Southeast. These regional resources represent much more than a mere reflection of a mainstream with tributaries that once reached no further than New York, Chicago, and California.

Today's art offers a fascinating array of styles and attitudes, and nowhere more so than in the southeastern region. The problem is that there are not enough trained and motivated critics to pay serious attention to art in the South. Recent issues of *Art News* and *Arts Magazine* have begun to pay some attention, but sweepingly superficial overviews and individual profiles are hardly a remedy for the neglect of regional artists.

See also BLACK LIFE: Art, Black; FOLKLIFE: Folk Painting; HISTORY AND MANNERS: Modernism

Sandra Langer
New York City

Art News (February 1983); Elizabeth C. Baker, *Art in America* (July–August 1976); Bruce W. Chambers, *Art and Artists of the South: The Robert P. Coggins Collection* (1984); Corcoran Gallery of Art, *American Painters of the South* (1960); David C. Driskell, *Two Centuries of Black American Art* (1976); Walter Gabrielson, *Art in America* (January–February 1974); James C. Kelly and Estill Curtis Pennington, *The South on Paper: Line, Color and Light* (1985); Terry Smith, *Artforum* (September 1974); Virginia Museum of Fine Arts, *Painting in the South: 1564–1980* (1983); *Women Artists News* (February 1980). ☆

Photography and Photographers

From 1839, when the first photographic processes were publicly introduced, until the 1880s, photography in the South was virtually indistinguishable from photography practiced elsewhere in America. The daguerreotype, a unique image made upon a sensitized silver plate, was the popular early photographic medium; its first commercial application was for the production of portraits. There was a great deal of mobility among the first daguerreotypists, especially on the Atlantic Seaboard. Realizing the commercial potential of this revolutionary medium, dozens of opportunists labored to make improvements in equipment. Henry Fitz, Jr. (1808–63), a pioneer American telescope manufacturer, developed the lens for Alexander Wolcott's portrait camera, which received the first American photographic patent in May 1840. Fitz operated a portrait gallery in Baltimore, Md., from 1840 to 1842. In New Orleans, Jules Lion (1816–66), a black lithographer, was working with a daguerreotype camera he had brought directly from Paris. Whether or not Lion tried to make portraits at that time is conjectural; he did succeed in making and exhibiting views of the city in March of 1840.

The nation's capital, with its constant parade of statesmen and visiting dignitaries, offered the greatest possibilities for the development of a portrait trade. John Plumbe, Jr. (1808–57), a Welshman, learned daguerreotyping from a student of Wolcott in Washington, D.C., in 1840. His success there led to the establishment of offices in

18 cities by 1846, an unprecedented venture. Plumbe located branches in Baltimore, Md.; Louisville, Ky.; Petersburg, Alexandria, and Richmond, Va.; St. Louis, Mo.; and New Orleans, La.; as well as in other major U.S. cities, Liverpool, and Paris. Understandably, overexpansion and mismanagement led to his financial collapse in 1847. Following the demise of the Plumbe operations, Jesse H. Whitehurst (c.1820–75) dominated the Washington trade. Whitehurst, a native of Virginia, who had opened his first establishment in Norfolk in 1844, added galleries in Richmond and Lynchburg and in Baltimore, Md., to his operations.

During the winter of 1851–52, Marcus A. Root (1808–88), author of *The Camera and the Pencil* (1864) and numerous articles and photographic journals, purchased a Washington gallery in partnership with John Hawley Clarke (1831–1914). James A. Cutting of Boston prepared applications for patents to the collodion processes in Root and Clarke's gallery in 1853 and 1854. These new processes enabled the introduction of the ambrotype, a collodion negative on glass, and the tintype, a collodion negative upon a thin, coated iron sheet. These photos were much cheaper and quicker to produce than daguerreotypes, but the most important use of the collodion process was for the production of glass negatives from which many positives could be made, thus introducing a means of rapid production of inexpensive images.

In 1857 and 1858 a unique opportunity fell to the Washington galleries when a succession of American Indian dignitaries came to negotiate treaties with Congress. The most extensive series of portraits was made in the newly opened studio of James E. McClees, which was operated by Julian Vannerson and Samuel H. Cohen. The tribal chieftains, with their exotic dress, language, and rituals, appealed to the romanticism of the age. The portraits were exhibited in their studio, and copies were offered for sale. Whitehurst and Mathew Brady also made and exhibited Indian portraits that winter. In New York City, Brady had learned daguerreotyping from Samuel F. B. Morse, the inventor and painter who became acquainted with the process directly from Daguerre in Paris.

Another student of Morse was Frederick A. P. Barnard (1809–89), a native of Connecticut. Barnard opened a gallery in October 1841 in Tuscaloosa, Ala., where he was a professor of mathematics at the state university. With his partner William H. Harrington (c. 1810–61), a native of Pennsylvania, he conducted experiments using chlorine as a chemical accelerator, descriptions of which were published in the *American Journal of Science and Arts* (July 1841). Barnard later became the first chancellor of the University of Mississippi and subsequently president of Columbia College in New York City, but he maintained a scientific interest in photography, publishing articles in photographic journals of the day. Harrington relocated in New Orleans, where he maintained a leading daguerreotype gallery until the commencement of the Civil War.

George Smith Cook (1819–1902), also of Connecticut, had a most estimable record in the history of southern photography. Cook learned daguerreotyping in New Orleans about 1843 and remained there until 1845, when he embarked on his four-year odyssey through the South. Cook reportedly spread the art from St. Louis, Mo., to Charleston, S.C., where he finally settled in 1849. He was so renowned that Brady chose him to operate his own New York studio during his absence in 1851 and 1852. Cook moved to Richmond, Va., in 1880, where he operated a gallery until his death.

From historical and sociological standpoints, the most important early galleries were those, like Cook's in Charleston and Richmond, that created a consistent visual chronicle of a developing community, in some instances for a half century. These photographers made thousands of formal studio portraits of prominent and ordinary citizens, their children, and family functions. Some specialized in architectural views, recording the outward and upward growth of the southern cities, or views of commerce along the rivers, especially the great steamboats of the Ohio and Mississippi rivers. Interior and exterior views of these steamboats are beautifully preserved in the glass negatives of J. Mack Moore, who worked in Vicksburg, Miss.

With the advent of the war, the demand for collodion photography accelerated, especially for the manufacture of portraits of departing soldiers and their loved ones. Tintypes and paper prints in the fashionable *carte-de-visite* size, approximately 2½" x 4", were cheap, and multiple images could be made from a single exposure. Even the tintype, when made with a multilens camera, could yield several images on a single plate.

The war gave the photographer a new role—as recorders of the tragic American drama. Wartime photographers who remain famous today, Mathew Brady (c. 1823–96) and Alexander Gardner (1821–82), are remembered particularly for their disturbing views of the scarred battlefields of Maryland and Virginia. In 1866 Gardner published a two-volume *Sketch Book of the War*, which contained over 100 views by 11 photographers. But the volumes were not well received by a public eager to forget the pain and anguish of the war. Similarly, George N. Barnard (1819–1902) offered a portfolio of his war photography without success. Barnard, appointed official photographer for the Chief Engineer's Office, Military Division of the Mississippi in 1863, followed General William T. Sherman's troops on the "march to the sea" through Tennessee, Georgia, and South Carolina. Barnard recorded the aftermath of battle, without the violence of Brady's or Gardner's work but with a disciplined artistic style. Barnard more than any other portrayed the "gentleman's war," as the southerner would prefer to remember it for generations. The photographs that were popular after the war were those of the Confederate commanders. For instance, the most popular photographs of Robert E. Lee were made by Michael Miley (1841–1918), a Lexington, Va., operator. Miley made numerous portraits of Lee, who also lived in Lexington as president of Washington College.

Several more obscure southern photographers were responsible for significant images of the war. Jay D. Edwards (1831–1900), a native of New Hampshire, was a New Orleans operator specializing in view photography at the outset of the war. In the spring of 1861 Edwards went to Pensacola, Fla., where he photographed New Orleans regiments, as well as federal gunboats and fortifications. Edwards, accused of making reconnaissance photos for the Confederacy, had his negatives confiscated.

A traveling photographer in Durham, North Carolina, 1939

Andrew David Lytle was also accused of making spy prints of federal encampments in the occupied city of Baton Rouge, La. William D. McPherson and his partner Mr. Oliver apparently refrained from clandestine activities and allied themselves with the Union. The pair made views of battlesites at Port Hudson, Miss.; in northern Louisiana; and on contract with the Chief Engineer's Office, recorded the ruins of Fort Morgan, Ala., in 1864.

After the war McPherson settled in New Orleans, where he produced an exceptionally fine series of *carte-de-visite* views of the city. About the same time, the D. R. Stiltz Company of Baltimore produced views of public buildings. These pursuits were indicative of an increasing interest in view photographs, which were issued in several formats. The most widely distributed were the stereographic cards, which appeared three-dimensional when seen through a special viewing device. After the war local publishers in the major southern cities began publishing stereographs. A series of stereo cards, forming a panoramic view of a city, was a speciality of these houses. Both Theodore Lilienthal and Samuel T. Blessing offered panoramic series of New Orleans during 1866–1867. J. F. Jarvis and the firm of Bell and Brother produced views of Washington, D.C.; and O. Pierre Havens and J. N. Wilson specialized in views of Savannah, Ga. In 1866 J. Mullen of Lexington, Ky., produced an unusually early series on agriculture and rural life in Kentucky, including pictures of newly emancipated black farmers. C. Seaver, Jr., photographed in Florida, especially in St. Augustine; J. G. Mangold also worked there, "The land of flowers and tropical scenery." The number of stereos printed each year was prodigious, stereographic stores opened in every major city in the South, and every Victorian parlor boasted a viewer of one design or another. The business was soon dominated by firms that published cards in great quantity and sold them cheaply. Eventually the independent southern publishers were put out of business by a succession of large firms with networks for national distribution.

Several technical advances changed the nature of photography about 1880. The dry plate process, developed by an Englishman in 1871, finally gained acceptance with American operators. This process, which used gelatin rather than collodion as the negative support, simplified laboratory work. Secondly, the invention of photolithographic systems for newspapers and journals created new commercial markets for photographs. Agriculture and early industrial communities were photographed for news and promotional services.

At the turn of the century photographers such as J. W. Stephenson of Wilkes County, Ga., focused on the cotton production and sorghum mill operations. Equally important, however, was their documentation of the small southern town: the family reunions, pageants, parades, traveling carnival shows, community baseball teams, bicycle clubs, church meetings, Confederate veterans' parades, and dedications of the ubiquitous memorials. What characterized most of the South between the Civil War and World War I was its agrarian nature. Life for the southerner, both black and white, centered on the family and the church, institutions that nurtured an elemental respect for the cyclical rituals, which gave one a sense of belonging and surviving within his community. Family stories preserved the folk culture, while photographs, neatly tacked in the photo albums, preserved traditions of ancestors and their ceremonies. These became virtually iconic, reinforcing the customs and entrenching the southerner in a romantic conception of the past as he coped with the intrusions of industry and urbanization.

By the turn of the century, northern industrialists were opening factories and mills in southern cities where raw materials and cheap labor were available, and photographers preserved these activities on film. Oscar V. Hunt of Birmingham, Ala., documented the early operations of the U.S. Steel Company at nearby Fairfield, Ala. Caufield and Shook and the Royal Photo Company in Louisville, Ky., photographed the shipbuilding, automobile, and rubber-tire industries from 1903 until the mid-1970s. In Memphis, Tenn., the major inland cotton trade center, J. C. Coovert photographed every aspect of cotton production from the mid-1890s until his death in 1937. About 1900 George Beach and F. J. Schleuter chronicled the early oil and gas operations near Houston, Tex. These firms documented the development of industry and the concomitant prosperity of the communities, the ceremonial openings of banks and stores, the mansions of the businessmen, as well as the storekeepers and clerks on the porches of their "carpenter gothic" cottages.

Railroads expanded into a complicated network connecting the southern market towns, and the rail companies commissioned photographers to depict, in an appealing style, the towns and countryside along their routes, to encourage immigration and travel. The Texas-Ohio Company produced a remarkable folio of sites along the Southern Pacific Line through Texas in 1902. Independent companies, such as the Detroit Publishing Company and the Albertype Company, also specialized in the mass publication of travel views, producing postcards and souvenir books of such picturesque places as Biltmore (the Vanderbilt chateau at Asheville, N.C.), the boardwalks of Florida beaches, or the harbors at Savannah, Ga., and Charleston, S.C.

With the introduction of the box camera and flexible roll film by George Eastman in 1888, inexpensive photographs became available to everyone. Everyday events could be recorded with a new spontaneity. The concept of the amateur was not new. One of the finest early southern amateurs was George Coales of Baltimore, Md., who about 1860 wrote a *Manual on Photography Adapted to Amateur Practice*. Coale made exquisite salt prints of Maryland's waterways and countryside. From the Eastman era, George H. Johnson of Charleston, S.C., recorded events in his city from the earthquake of 1886 to the victory parades of 1918, as well as casual views of his family and genre scenes of black children and sharecroppers, much in the mood of William Aiken Walker's paintings.

With the enthusiasm caused by dry plate photography, camera clubs were formed all over the country. Half a dozen photographic magazines and texts and manuals with instructions for new printing processes were being published at the turn of the century. Some clubs combined the new rage for cycling with the mobility of the box camera. Others took themselves more seriously, renouncing the casual nature of "kodaking," and forming sizable clubs, such as the Kentucky-Tennessee Photographers Association, begun about the turn of the century, which had 140 active members by 1906. Surprisingly, the rage for art also supported a number of schools; one was the Southern School of Photography of McMinnville, Tenn., which claimed in 1906 to have the "Largest Building in the World Devoted to the Teaching of the Art of Photography."

The pictorialist style, as practiced in England, particularly suited the southerner, with his predilection for romance, theatricality, and nostalgia. With a large-view camera, he posed friends or sought picturesque scenes to imitate contemporary paintings or illustrations of Victorian literature. He printed in a technique that resembled a fine art print, each layer more complex than the last.

In Louisville, Ky., Kate Matthews (1870–1957) photographed in the pictorialist style, portraying women and children in ideal domestic settings or posing friends to illustrate novels, such as *The Little Colonel*. Matthews's work was published by *Ladies' Home Journal*, *Vogue*, and *Cosmopolitan* magazines. Arnold Genthe (1869–1942) was primarily known for portraits of celebrities and views of San Francisco's Chinatown. Influenced by the writings of George Washington Cable, Lafcadio Hearn, and Grace King, Genthe photographed the vanishing colonial architecture of New Orleans in the soft-focus manner of pictorialism. His book, *Old New Orleans*, was published in 1926.

A Frances Benjamin Johnston photograph of Edgemont, Albemarle County, Virginia, c. 1935

While some photographers were imitating painting, a few were discovering the camera's ability to record dispassionately. Frances Benjamin Johnston (1864–1952), a native of West Virginia, began her career as a photojournalist within the inner circles of Washington politics in 1889. Johnston's unprecedented course included essays on black education at Hampton Institute in Virginia in 1899, and, periodically from 1902 to 1906, at Tuskegee Institute in Alabama. Her most significant achievement was the survey of southern colonial architecture for the Carnegie Foundation from 1933 to 1940. Johnston made over 6,000 negatives of every aspect of historic buildings and gardens from Maryland to Louisiana.

Lewis Hine compiled the earliest photographic essay for social reform in the South. In 1907 Hine, hired by the National Child Labor Committee to dramatize the tragedy of child labor abuses, photographed in the textile mills of the Carolinas and in the agricultural and fishing industries of the South. In 1933 Hine documented for state and federal agencies the building of the Tennessee Valley Authority dams and nearby communities.

Apart from the photojournalists and social reformers, a succession of documentary photographers have worked in the South, motivated by a respect for the distinctive regional characteristics of the folk cultures, crafts, farming traditions, the storytellers and ballad singers. Doris Ullman (1884–1934), though from a wealthy New York family, was drawn to the qualities of simplicity and devotion she found in the craftsmen of Appalachia and the black people living in isolated rural communities. In contrast to the sentimentalizing manner of some genre photographers, Ullman conveyed the inner strength and religious nature of her subjects. William A. Barnhill, a native of Arkansas, was interested in the handicrafts and local technology of the highlanders of North Carolina. His photographs, taken from 1914 to 1917, though less well known, are of equal significance. Prentice Hall Polk, a black professional photographer, has been recording life at Tuskegee Institute in Alabama since 1927. Polk has created a valuable historical record of the students, educators, and residents of this cultural center for black Americans. A less known, but very important black photographer, Reverend L. O. Taylor of Memphis, photographed and filmed churches, black businesses, and homes of the black middle-class community.

The largest documentary to include the South was that of the Resettlement Administration, later the Farm Security Administration (FSA). From 1935 to 1943 Roy Emerson Stryker directed his staff to gather picture stories, which would persuade Congress to aid the depressed farming communities of America. A significant portion of these photographs was made in the South, where, in some areas, 75 percent of the people were tenant farmers. Dorothea Lange's strong sympathies for the migrant workers and tenant farmers are evident in her photos of the Mississippi River Delta region taken from 1935 to 1938. Marion Post Wolcott and Arthur Rothstein photographed the migrant laborers of the truck farms. Ben Shahn and Russell Lee's forte lay in the portrayal of small-town life and resettlement camps. Walker Evans's disciplined and carefully composed photos portrayed the poverty of the tenant farmers. Evans took a leave of absence to prepare a document on southern sharecroppers for *Fortune* magazine with James Agee. Though *Fortune* rejected the material, it was finally published in 1941 as *Let Us Now Praise Famous Men*, a classic vision of three

Todd Webb photograph of an unnamed Louisiana community, 1940s

tenant families in Alabama, portrayed with dignity and honesty. Eudora Welty made a similar photographic portrait of her home state, Mississippi, while working with the Farm Security Administration. Her work was later published in *One Time, One Place* (1971).

In 1943 Stryker embarked on a project for Standard Oil Company (New Jersey). This time he concentrated not on poverty but on the prosperity that the oil industry was bringing to the country. Because the focus of the ESSO project was upon the largest oil-producing states, much emphasis was placed upon Texas and Louisiana, where Russell Lee and Todd Webb gathered stories of small towns and bayou settlements affected by off-shore exploration and drilling. Edwin Rosskam documented the stories of oil transport along the Mississippi River. In North Carolina, Esther Bubly photographed the towns that lay in the path of the pipeline, and Sol Libsohn produced the story of exploration and drilling off Cape Hatteras.

At the time Stryker's photographers were working in the South, Clarence John Laughlin (1905–85) began exploring his native Louisiana. Laughlin's early fascination with European symbolist writers formalized his reactions against the Depression-era environment and created an enigmatic style that suited his romanticism. Laughlin photographed the plantation houses, the Creole cemeteries, and the streets and characters of New Orleans. Ironically, Laughlin accompanied Edward Weston on the Louisiana portion of his cross-country tour in 1941. Weston's photographs, commissioned for a special publication of Walt Whitman's *Leaves of Grass*, were composed with absolute discipline and in the sharpest focus, while Laughlin's photos were gothic, mystical equivalents of dreams. Laughlin published his work in *Ghosts along the Mississippi* in 1948 and began his long career of lecturing and producing traveling exhibitions.

Photo documentaries of the scope of the FSA and ESSO projects will probably never be attempted again. These are major sociological and historical records of the South in rapid transition from an agrarian to an industrialized society, documents of a people witnessing the collapse of social and religious traditions and experiencing the disintegration of the extended family unit.

Outside of these monumental projects, few have conveyed so forcefully as Roland L. Freeman (b. 1936) the complexity of the urbanization of the South. In the 1960s Freeman, a black photographer and a native of Baltimore, documented the restructuring of a black Maryland tobacco-farming community, following its members from the simple existence in the country to the frustrating anonymous life in city tenements. Like Ullman and Barnhill, Freeman was also inspired by southern folk cultures. In the early 1970s he photographed the black quilters, basketmakers, blacksmiths, and carpenters of southern Mississippi in his own style, celebrating the self-sufficiency of the rural black farmers. Writer Ernest J. Gaines has made similar photographic portraits of his home in rural Louisiana. These photos, like those of Eudora Welty, add an interesting dimension to his craft as a writer of fiction.

Also in the documentary tradition, Alex Harris, a native of Atlanta and an associate of Duke University, has collaborated with psychologist Robert Coles on projects in Alaska and New Mexico, but he has also produced essays on the poor living conditions of tenant families in North Carolina. For several years Debbie Fleming Caffrey has been photographing the resident workers on sugarcane plantations at Franklin, La. With an affection rooted in familiarity, she has recorded them each season with sympathy and dignity.

Recent photography in the South has been called southern only by accident of place. Since the 1930s, southern writing has explored the urbanization of the region and the destruction of its identities. Urbanization was well under way before southern artists became aware of photography's potential for interpreting that experience. When the art did find its proponents on southern campuses in the 1960s, photography there was essentially indistinguishable from the national school. Present education encourages exposure to many visions and techniques, and the highly mobile students of Minor White, Aaron Siskind, and Henry Holmes Smith, to name a few, have spread their diverse talents through the best institutions of the South. John Menapace, at Duke University, transforms the North Carolina landscape into highly disciplined and elegant design abstractions; Jaromir Stephany at the University of Maryland, Baltimore County, uses the *cliché verre* technique to invent nonrepresentational images of dynamic energy; Jerry Uelsmann, at the University of Florida, uses a multiple printing technique to develop mirrors of his imagination. These are photographers whose works are of abstract formalism, of psychic invention, and not of a regional nature. But there are photographers working in the South who have been so moved by the geography, culture, and history of the environment that they have chosen to create art from its raw material.

John McWilliams at Georgia State University produces austerely formal landscapes, some with an underlying outrage against the barbarous intrusions of industry. Emmet Gowin's early work in his native Danville, Va., is presented, not in the symbolism of Uelsmann, but with an immediate and elemental response to the drama of family rituals, celebrations, and tragedies. Gowin's work suggests the theatricality and ambiguity of contemporary storytellers such as Flannery O'Connor. With decidedly greater obscurity and a gently gothic mien, Ralph Eugene Meatyard (1925–72) of Lexington, Ky., enlisted his family and neighbors to devise a private state for his imagined conversations, creating photographs reminiscent of the fiction of Carson McCullers, with its grotesque and symbolic overtones.

William Eggleston (b. 1939), a resident of Memphis, Tenn., uses images from his private experience as a son of a Mississippi Delta farming family to symbolize the erosion of the traditional culture that nurtured him. Eggleston uses the dye transfer method, which produces color of dazzling luminosity, to photograph the incongruous juxtapositions of city and country, suburbia and wilderness. Atlanta photographer Michael Turner evokes the essence of the history of the southern white middle class in his photos of timeworn homes with peeling paint and torn screens. His subjects seem to be the symbols of southern gentility beset by altered economic systems. There is a sense of loss and change. Since 1974, Paul Kwilecki of Decatur County, Ga., has also worked with the landmarks and characters of his immediate surroundings. Kwilecki's intuitive vision is comparable to that of the French masters Atget and Brassai.

Using the camera in a straightforward reportorial manner, Geoffrey L. Winningham (b. 1943) concentrates on the rituals and pastimes of his fellow Texans, expecially the fanatically loyal sportsmen, both participants and spectators. Lyle Bongé of Biloxi, Miss., and New York observes selectively the humor and human foibles and vulnerabilities of Mardi Gras maskers in New Orleans. The portraits of George Dureau of New Orleans and Gay Block of Houston also capture the complex humanity of their subjects. Dureau, a painter, first used photographs as aids to composition but shortly perceived their separate merits. His subjects are the street people of Esplanade Avenue and the lower wards of the city, mostly young blacks photographed against a simple seamless background, creating classical portraits reminiscent of Degas or Velázquez. Amid the largest Jewish community in the South, Block (b. 1942) specializes in photographing middle-class families within their own homes, against the setting of their possessions. She produces portraits of brilliant insight, which enable her subjects to know themselves more clearly.

Several southern women, however, seem dissatisfied with the factual nature of the straight photograph. Though a resident of Rochester, N.Y., Bea Nettles (b. 1946) creates photographs infused with references to her upbringing in Florida, the abundant green of landscapes, dreams and memories of childhood, and a strong attachment to family. Nettles continually experiments with nonsilver processes, reinventing the concept of the photograph. Her highly subjective creations, while unconventional in method, employ constant images of familiarity, which give her work cohesiveness. Rita deWitt of the University of Southern Mississippi and Merri Moor Winnett of North Carolina both print multiple negative montages on paper and fabric, creating highly complex photo-drawings expressing personal experiences. Nancy Rexroth uses an inexpensive plastic Diana camera; her casual approach to her subject, combined with the unpredictable focus of the plastic lens, produces dreamlike snapshots.

One of the most significant southern photographers is William Christenberry (b. 1936), a resident of Washington, D.C., who photographs in color. Each summer he returns to his native Alabama to record familiar places from his youth, compiling a notebook of rural Alabama architecture and social history. Christenberry's exquisitely simple views subtly evoke the presence of former inhabitants.

Christenberry teaches at the Corcoran School of Art in Washington, D.C., one of several schools that nurture photography in the South. Others with strong photographic departments are the University of Maryland, at both its College Park and Catonsville locations, the University of Florida at Gainesville, Georgia State University in Atlanta, and Rice University in Houston, Tex. The Light Factory in Charlotte, N.C., and Nexus, Inc., in Atlanta, Ga., provide workshops of outstanding merit. The finest archival collections in the region are the Gernsheim Collection at the University of Texas, Austin; the Photographic Archives at the University of Louisville (Ky.); and of course, the Photographs and Prints Division of the Library of Congress. Public collections of historical and contemporary interest are located at the Corcoran Gallery in Washington, D.C.; the Museum of Fine Arts in Houston, Tex.; the New Orleans Museum of Art; and the High Museum of Atlanta, Ga.

Mary Louise Tucker
New Orleans, Louisiana

A. D. Coleman, *The Southern Ethic* (1975); F. Jack Hurley, Nancy Hurley, and Gary Witt, eds., *Southern Eye, Southern Mind* (1981); David Madden, *Southern Quarterly* (Winter 1984); Margaret D. Smith and Mary Louise Tucker, *Photography in New Orleans: The Early Years, 1840–1865* (1982); Robert Taft, *Photography and the American Scene: A Social History, 1839–1899* (1938). ☆

Queen Anne and Eastlake Styles of Architecture

The Queen Anne style of architecture was conceived in England by Richard Norman Shaw during the 1860s, though the term is a misnomer. Shaw at first borrowed details from the rural manor houses of Queen Elizabeth's reign, not Queen Anne's. The erroneous designation seems attributable to the English architect J. J. Stevenson in the 1870s.

Shaw's houses were widely published in the architectural press and thus came to be imitated in the United States in the early 1870s. However, the popular acceptance of the Queen Anne in America can be attributed to the Centennial Exhibition of 1876 in Philadelphia. For this fair the British government erected in the Queen Anne style two buildings that received a good deal of critical acclaim.

The style flourished in America during the 1880s and 1890s and represented a renewed interest in the picturesque. The present "epoch of Queen Anne is a delightful insurrection against the monotonous era of rectangular buildings," declared an 1880s magazine. Irregular planning and massing accompanied by a variety of color, texture, and structural expressionism characterized the style.

Americans nationalized the style by the use of Colonial Revival details and regional materials such as shingles and siding. Although the Queen Anne was a mix of architectural details, the main theme was classical and is sometimes called free classic. Frequently the style was combined with Eastlake and Romanesque detailing, creating unique designs. For extra interest, details were sometimes borrowed from Islamic and Oriental precedents.

The impact of the Queen Anne on the southern housing stock was enormous because of the rapid growth of the southern economy during the post-Reconstruction period and because a Queen Anne residence could be erected inexpensively and quickly. The majority of the Queen Anne residences were made of wood, so the developing southern timber industry, such as that in the area around Pensacola, Fla., provided an abundance of materials from which to draw. The Queen Anne house can be found throughout the South, particularly in the Savannah Victorian District, the New Orleans Uptown District, East End Historic District in Galveston, the Historic District of Pensacola, and Atlanta's "Sweet Auburn" Historic District.

Because Queen Anne house designs were often chosen from pattern books of the period such as Holly's *Modern Dwellings*, and details were mass produced thanks to technological advances, a certain consistency in the style was achieved. Externally, Queen Anne houses are massive, irregular, and picturesque. Projecting elements such as cylindrical towers with conical roofs; polygonal turrets with distinctive roofs; tall, elaborate, decorative chimneys with large corbelled tops; and well-detailed entrance porches, verandas, and bay windows are featured elements.

Every surface of the Queen Anne house is textured or has applied ornament, making the house's exterior finishing the dominant decorative element. Windows come in a profusion of shapes but tend to be tall, thin, large, and double-hung. Frequently, the windows have the top sash divided into small colored panes of glass surrounding a larger central field. The lower sash is a single large pane of glass or is divided by a single vertical muntin. This type of window has been designated "Queen Anne window." Stained-glass windows are common, as are Palladian windows and other forms of grouped windows. Doors are usually deeply recessed under porch roofs and vestibules or second-story overhangs and have a large glass area. Roofs are steep and complex with moderate overhangs, polychromatic slates, or patterned metal shingles and elaborate terra cotta ridge tiles. Gables are common and often include a large porch gable, adding to the picturesque effect of the total design.

The floor plans are informal and asymmetrical. The featured room—the "living hall"—was introduced for the style and was designed to impress. This room was generally finished in dark oak or other wood and had an elaborate wooden staircase illuminated by staggered stained-glass windows. Often a large fireplace occupied a place of prominence. The dining room, parlor, and study were connected to the entrance hall by large sliding doors, which permitted a relatively open place that could be divided into private rooms as necessary. The kitchen, with its accessory pantry and storage, opened to the dining room. Projecting and inserted verandas and terraces were integral parts of the total design. Bedrooms and baths were generally relegated to the second story, but were sometimes confined to a rear wing.

The ubiquitous long, narrow cottages of New Orleans, a vernacular form popularly called "shotgun" cottages, were frequently decorated with patterned shingles on their gables and with scroll brackets or courses of turnings supporting the porch roofs. The style is superficial, the plan essentially the same as on earlier structures with Greek Revival porticoes. But even here the builders sometimes achieved a sense of irregular massing by putting small triangular caps over side doors or by adding a small projecting bay on a front porch.

The Eastlake style coexisted with the Queen Anne and shared many of its planning and massing characteristics; but this style is distinguished from the Queen Anne by its detailing, much of which can be traced to the neo-Greco style. Under the auspices of neo-Greco, the round forms and foliated ornament of the Italianate style took on a rectangularity and precision thought to be expressive of an increasingly mechanized and industrial society. Incised ornament was a hallmark. Stylized single-line flowers and long, parallel, narrow channels were favorite details.

The Eastlake style was named after Charles Locke Eastlake, an English architect who is more noted for his books than his architecture. Eastlake's *Hints on Household Taste* was first published in London in 1868 and made its American debut in Boston in 1872. The book was immensely popular, with six editions in the next 11 years. Eastlake promoted a style of furniture and interior detailing that was angular, notched, and carved. He wrote, "It is an established principle in the theory of design that decorative art is degraded when it passes into a direct imitation of natural objects. Nature may be typified or symbolized, but not actually imitated."

Other books, such as *Gothic Forms* by Bruce Talbert, which appeared in America in 1873, helped to formulate the style. While Eastlake concentrated on details, Talbert showed whole interiors.

American architectural designers found their own interpretation of the style. Their ornament was largely the product of the chisel, the gouge, and the lathe. Details were massive, oversized, and robust. Designers placed no limits on the arrangement of forms or the amount of ornamentation on the exterior of the Eastlake house, much to the chagrin of Charles Eastlake, who wrote, "I regret . . . that [I] should be associated . . . with a phase of taste in architecture and industrial art with which I can have no real sympathy and by all accounts seems to be extravagant and bizarre."

The Eastlake style was the product of industrialization, but, ironically, it was named for a leader of the arts and crafts movement who advocated a return to the craftsmanship of the past. Factory-made decorative elements could be ordered by mail from catalogs or bought from local distributors. The Orleans Manufacturing and Lumber Company published one such catalog in 1891. Even entire houses could be ordered prefabricated. The multitude of ornamentations resulted in a wide variety of combinations. Both small cottages in places like Biloxi, Miss., and large houses in New Orleans commonly employed the Eastlake style.

Robert J. Cangelosi
New Orleans, Louisiana

Alan Gowans, *Images of American Living: Four Centuries of Architecture and Furniture as Cultural Expression* (1964); Carole Rifkin, *A Field Guide to American Architecture* (1980); Leland M. Roth, *A Concise History of American Architecture* (1979); G. E. K. Kidder Smith, *The Architecture of the United States: The South and Midwest* (1981). ☆

Residential 20th-Century Architecture

The rapidly expanding middle class and the enormous mobility offered by the automobile created demands for suburban housing. Houses had to be flexible enough to accommodate a changing society and inexpensive enough to be affordable. Consequently, 20th-century houses differed immensely from 19th-century houses in scale and floor plan. Southern housing of the early 20th century can be divided into two categories—those free from historical precedents and those that rely on historical eclecticism.

The most popular nontraditional architectural style of the period was the California style (1900–40), sometimes referred to as the bungalow style. "California" seemed to be the preferred term during the heyday of the style, while "bungalow" simply referred to a small residence. The California style was an honest, bold expression of architecture that synthesized precedents from many sources without mimicking any one. These houses were basically wooden with masonry complements such as porches, chimneys, piers, and retaining walls.

The style is unpretentious and distinguished by its clever use of wooden structural members as ornamentation. Building elements seem to flow from one to the next, with one element being an integral part of that which immediately precedes and follows. The massing of the style is very picturesque, with low lines. Roofs are generous, with broad sloping overhangs. Windows are commonly short and grouped together to take advantage of breezes. The floor plan is very informal, with spaces flowing from one to another, rendering a feeling of openness. Typically, circulation is through the living room, which often has a large fireplace setting the tone of the decor. Interior details reflect a strong "crafts" orientation. Front, side, rear, and sleeping porches are common in order to keep interior spaces cool.

The architects of California formulated the style, giving it its innovative features and design. The Greene brothers, Charles and Henry, were its most influential architects. The style was a builders' style, which was promoted through numerous periodicals, including *Craftsman Magazine*, *Bungalow Magazine*, and *Ladies' Home Journal*. Even the Sears and Roebuck catalog carried California bungalow house plans, "direct from bungalow land," for the meager price of five dollars. With such inexpensive prices, identical houses can be found in widely separated locales.

Southerners eagerly accepted the bungalow, which had been designed for a similar climate, and it was built throughout the region for middle- to low-income housing, in small towns and large. One can readily date the period of growth and expansion of certain sections of cities by the presence of whole groups of these bungalows in a neighborhood. One such subdivision is Gentilly Terrace in New Orleans.

Another popular nonhistorical style was the craftsman style (1900–20). It had its roots in the English arts and crafts movement, as a solution to the "corrupt" values of the Victorian styles. The movement's chief advocate was the English architect turned artist, William Morris. Morris realized that he was unsuccessfully competing with machine art and began to write articles opposing the machine. In 1888 the English Arts and Crafts Exhibition Society was formed, which published articles and held exhibitions extolling the virtues of handcrafted art.

In Boston the first American Society of Arts and Crafts was organized in 1897. But it was from Gustav Stickley's *Craftsman Magazine* and his two *Craftsman Home* books that the movement received its widespread acceptance in the South. Young architects took up the cause, rejecting machine aesthetics as impersonal. Their solution advocated greater honesty and sincerity in architecture with artful attention to every detail. Southern homes using this style tend to be modest in scale. Some of these are found among Gulf Coast cottages and in some summer houses in the mountains of North Carolina, Georgia, and Virginia.

Other early 20th-century nonhistorical styles found in the South include the prairie, art deco, streamline moderne, and international styles. The prairie style (1900–20) evolved on the prairies of the Midwest. It explored new ways of relating building to the landscape and new concepts of interior space. The master of the style was Frank Lloyd Wright, who described the prairie style house as "having sloping roofs, low proportions, quiet skylines, suppressed heavy-set chimneys and sheltering overhangs, low terraces and out-reaching walls sequestering private gardens."

Wright, who has been described as a 20th-century Jeffersonian agrarian, had only one prairie house in the South, the Ziegler House (1909–10) in Frankfort, Ky., but two of his Usonian houses (a variation of the prairie house) are in Falls Church, Va. (the Pope-Leighey House, 1939–41), and Florence, Ala. (the Rosenbaum House, 1939–40).

Art deco (1920–30), which was characterized by a vertical emphasis with highly stylized ornamentation, was commonly employed in commercial architecture but could also be found in large residences and apartment complexes. In the South the style was most popular in southern Florida.

Streamline moderne (1930–40) was inspired by America's love for the machine. Its shapes were guided by the principles of aerodynamics and hydrodynamics. Smooth white curvilinear shapes were used to try to capture the spirit of frozen motion.

The international style (1910–40), which originated in Europe, had limited acceptance in the South, chiefly in metropolitan areas. Henry-Russell Hitchcock and Philip Johnson described it as "first, a new concept of architecture as volume rather than as mass." In addition, "regularity rather than axial symmetry" was the main way of achieving orderly design. The style, finally, "proscribes arbitrary applied decoration." The 1938 Feibleman residence in Metarie, La., is a good example of this style.

Although 20th-century revivals can be found for almost every previous architectural style, the Tudor, neo-Italianate, Renaissance, and Colonial Revival styles have been the most common in the South. The Tudor style (1900–30) was originally based on both English Elizabethan and Jacobean styles and, as a consequence, it is sometimes referred to as the "Jacobethan" style. As the style matured, it began to imitate the English medieval period with greater accuracy. Its most distinguishing feature is half-timbering with stucco or masonry infill. It was used on both modest and expensive houses throughout the South. The Wymond House in Louisville, Ky., is an outstanding example of a large Tudor Revival residence.

The neo-Italianate (1910–30) was a revival of the Italian villas of the Mediterranean, distinguished by shallow brackets and a large umbrella-type roof with barrel roofing tiles. It was very popular for large residences along the Gulf Coast because of its large protective roof and large windows and its air of opulence. The Rostrevor House in Louisville, Ky., is a good example.

The Renaissance revival (1890–1940) developed as an academic reaction to the free spirit of the late 19th-century styles. It borrowed Renaissance elements, details, and composition from England, France, Spain, and Italy. These residences tended to be large and elaborate and were more often than not designed by architects. The style's primary advocate was the New York architectural firm of McKim, Mead, and White. Many such large residences can be found in the Swiss Avenue Historic District in Dallas, Tex.; and Audubon Place in New Orleans. Outstanding individual examples include the Alexander House (1906), Dallas, Tex.; the Hills House (1899), St. Louis, Mo.; and the Armstrong House (1917), Savannah, Ga.

See also FOLKLIFE: / Bungalow House

Robert J. Cangelosi
New Orleans, Louisiana

William H. Jordy, *American Buildings and Their Architects*, vol. 2 (1972); Walter C. Kidney, *The Architecture of Choice: Eclecticism in America, 1880–1930* (1974); Clay Lancaster, *The American Bungalow, 1880–1930* (1985); Leland M. Roth, *A Concise History of American Architecture* (1979); Dell Upton and John Michael Vlach, eds., *Common Places: Readings in American Vernacular Architecture* (1986); Leila Wilburn, *Southern Homes and Bungalows* (1914). ☆

Resort Architecture

Attractive scenery, accessibility, and wealthy clients with leisure time—all the necessary endowments for a resort area —belonged to the South in the 18th century. Many plantation owners in the eastern Tidewater, an area that includes Virginia, Maryland, North Carolina, South Carolina, and Georgia, grew rich planting tobacco, rice, and indigo to trade with England. The Tidewater area consequently emerged as the first part of America to produce wealthy residents with leisure time.

However elegant many of the plantation homes were, they were hot, humid, unhealthy, and uncomfortable during long summers. As transportation developed, the gentry began to escape the unpleasant climate and recurring epidemics by hiding away in the cool mountains of Virginia. Southerners sought resorts that offered simple, close-to-nature living with carefree, healthful, cool environments. Until then, the lack of passable roads actually made it easier for Americans to go to Europe or the West Indies.

Travelers in the 18th and early 19th centuries used inns and taverns located on main highways and toll roads during their journeys. Some of these travelers left descriptive, often derogatory, accounts of their accommodations. Sir August Foster, an Englishman, reported in his travels through Virginia that Gadsby's Tavern in Alexandria "kept the best house of entertainment in America." An inventory of 1802 showed 10 buildings at Gadsby's, including stables, kitchen, and laundry. All of Foster's lodgings were not comfortable, however. He mentioned a few intolerable inns, a wretched log house, and a "mean looking tavern with fare equally so." Phillip Nicklin, under his pseudonym Peregrine Prolix, had a happier stay "at the sign of the Swan" in New Market, Va., on his way back from the springs of Virginia. He wrote that he was "very comfortable . . . fared sumptuously, and lay in fine linen." Equally hospitable inns in Charleston, S.C., often served guests their meals in the summerhouses among the gardens. Taverns and hotels all over the South had ballrooms for community social events.

Tidewater planters and their families endured the crude mountain roads in stagecoaches or on horseback for that singular lure of the resorts—that ancient, mysterious, and magical phenomenon of a natural spring. Since the dawn of history, springs have had widespread appeal. The American Indians believed such waters contained healing qualities and sought springs as they traveled. English colonists brought with them to America a long tradition of using therapeutic waters, as did the German settlers.

A cluster of mineral springs, hot, warm, and tepid, discovered in the early 18th century, developed into America's first resorts. In an area about 75 miles in diameter, the springs bordered what is now the Virginia–West Virginia line. In 1748 George Washington mentioned one, Bath Springs, also known as Alum Springs, in his diary, when he camped in a field near what later became a major resort.

Stagecoach lines began making runs to these resorts, located in "pleasant, accessible mountain valleys, always cool in the summer." Visitors especially liked to tour the "waters"; the whole circuit of the Virginia–West Virginia springs could be made in less than 170 miles. "To the Springs! Leave the heat and the misery behind . . . seek cool air, clean water, relaxing baths, sparkling company!"

The European concept of a spa eventually filtered to these mountain resorts. Primitive resorts quickly offered "hydro-therapy" cures to make guests feel good by bathing and by drinking the water. Springs competed with one another in having a slightly different temperature and mineral content. Water analysis was the focal point for a spring's advertisement in the 19th century. Brochures outlined chemical properties of the waters and listed the diseases that could be cured, documented by testimonials from patrons. In 1846 John J. Moorman, physician-in-residence at White Sulphur Springs, started publishing books on the Virginia springs, other springs in the South, and springs elsewhere in the country. His book, *The Mineral Springs of North America* (1873), is an important source for spring lore, culture, and advertisements for different resorts. He detailed the sundry cures and explained how bottled water sold from many springs produced an important source of revenue.

As the spring resorts rose in prominence, their architecture became more and more sophisticated. The first abodes were tents pitched in fields close to the waters. They gave way to clusters of log cabins gradually replaced by frame buildings. Descriptions from early travelers revealed how similar were the buildings, layouts, and overall plans for the spring resorts, most of which flaunted summerhouses, pavilions, belvederes, kiosks, garden houses, and teahouses amidst their spacious grounds. A 19th-century traveler named Edward Pollard wrote about the ambience of Montgomery's White Sulphur Springs: "The lawn of the springs . . . a large elliptical plain planted with ornamental trees . . . the ground divided by a stream . . . a pleasant architectural effect for the practical designs of comfort."

Early 19th-century architecture of the spring resorts reflected the fashionable Greek Revival style. A classical columned porch, two or three stories high, was common. Spring resort buildings repeatedly used this form, which originated in the 1830s in southern residential architecture. In 1856 when Botetourt Springs resort became Hollins Institute, the forerunner of Hollins College, a dormitory building was built in the Greek Revival style with its plan and porches still in the spring resort manner. Architecture in the later 19th century tended to follow prevalent styles of that time.

The center of attraction of every spring resort was its spring covering, often an octagon with classical columns supporting a dome to make a gazebo form. Rustic touches abounded with branch furniture, log cabins, and informal landscaping, in sharp contrast with the severe Greek Revival architecture.

Southern hospitality played a great part in the ambience of the springs. In the South the absence of large cities left families isolated on their plantations. Resorts, therefore, offered families opportunities for meeting other families and were ideally suited for courting places and marriage markets. Belles arrived with trunks of clothing for summer activities. Genial hosts purposefully tried to create a romantic atmosphere to attract visitors. Ballrooms flourished, as did porches with cozy nooks, bowers, and lover's lanes. The amenities of a good hotel included music, dancing, wine, good company, and the water of the springs.

Alabama Row at the Greenbrier in West Virginia

This aura of southern hospitality at spring resorts continues today, as best exemplified by White Sulphur Springs and its hotel, the Greenbrier. Known from Indian times, these springs attracted development between 1778 and 1783 when tents were first erected on the site. Subsequently, between 1784 and 1786, log cabins were built. By 1800 there were cottages. In 1835 a ballroom and a kitchen were added to a tavern to form the nucleus of a great resort. When Prolix visited in 1835, he reported that the valley had been cleared, except for a few trees left for ornament and shade. He tallied a frame dining room 120 feet long, a kitchen with attached bakery, two large stables with 80 stalls each, a grand ballroom, and rows of cabins built of various materials. All the cabins had porches. Prolix observed that White Sulphur's spring was "covered with a handsome dome supported on columns, and contained in an octagonal marble case . . . the bottom formed of the rock from which the water gushes." Prolix rhapsodized about the charm of the resort and its delightful society that came "to see and be seen, to chat, laugh, and dance."

The most famous buildings at White Sulphur were designed by J. H. B. Latrobe, son of the well-known American architect Benjamin Henry Latrobe. Visiting many of the Virginia springs, he left watercolor sketches that document spring architecture. In 1850 the erstwhile builder designed a row of cottages, today called the Baltimore Cottages. Latrobe noted that they were very up-to-date—"papered, supplied with water, gas, speaking tubes, and all the modern arrangements for comfort."

Each row of cottages had its own social distinction. Bachelors, for example, lived in Wolf Row. Guests walked Lover's Lane, danced in the ballroom, courted on Baltimore Row, heard music from the bandstand in the center of the grounds, ate in the large dining rooms where everyone gathered at mealtime, and attended chapel in the barroom, which was converted for that purpose on Sundays.

In the 19th century the White Sulphur Springs Hotel was renovated with arcades, porticoes, domes, and more guest homes. By 1870 the Chesapeake & Ohio Railroad served the resort. In the 20th century the old main building was torn down and replaced. A central portico, reminiscent of the White House, and a five-story colonnade, reminiscent of a southern mansion, were added after 1922. Today, the Greenbrier survives as one of the most impressive resort complexes left in the South.

The other prime extant example of a spring resort is Hot Springs, Va., with its major hotel, the Homestead. As early as 1766, Thomas Bullitt built a primitive hostel at the Hot Springs. Like the Greenbrier, the Homestead has seen continuous use despite fires, rebuilding, and changing economic conditions. Guests still enjoy the famous hot baths, popular since the 18th century, but their use for hydrotherapy has waned.

The Homestead was rebuilt in "baronial" style after a fire in 1901; a 12-story tower added in 1929 forms "one of America's few Georgian–Colonial Revival high rises." The Cavalier Hotel in Virginia Beach, Va., built in 1927, is another Colonial Revival high-rise structure. The Homestead now has a modern addition in severe geometric forms, as the Cavalier similarly sports a steel frame, glass-walled motel across the street.

The Warm Springs, Ga., resort, like most of its contemporaries, did not flourish in the 20th century, yet it was very popular in the 19th century. Thomas Jefferson visited these springs in 1818 and again in 1825. Prolix stayed in the Warm Springs Hotel, while his two traveling companions stayed in a "most ancient log cabin," consoled by the fact that Jefferson had spent three weeks there. In 1835 Prolix reported that the Warm Springs Hotel was a two-story, brick structure, 100 feet long with a porch on the front. He noted that there was a room for dancing, a parlor, a large and airy eating room, and a tenpin alley. The springs flowed into a wooden, octagonal, men's bathhouse, which was 120 feet in circumference and reputedly built in 1761. A similar women's bathhouse built in 1836 stands nearby. The two bathhouses and a few small cottages are all that remain of this resort.

Careful records of spring architecture and culture in Virginia and West Virginia were left by German artist Edward Beyer, who visited America about 1848 and spent three years drawing and painting. His *Album of Virginia*, printed in Germany, contains 40 lithographs of resorts and other natural attractions in the area. Meticulously drawn "panoramas and accurate architectural projections give details of dress, artifacts, and people." In five of his pictures he added some "future and proposed improvements." Beyer painted not only the big popular springs, but many of the smaller, less fashionable resorts frequented by people who could not afford the big ones.

Each spring possessed some special characteristic. The buildings of Sweet Springs, Va., in Monroe County (now West Virginia), for instance, have always been associated with a Thomas Jefferson design. The "Jefferson" building at Sweet Springs is made of brick with columns and classical detail. It has a 160-foot-long dining room and a 17-foot-wide porch running the length of the building. As yet, no evidence beyond local lore has surfaced to credit the building to Jefferson. The structure today serves as a home for the aged. Rockbridge Alum Springs in Virginia had a central hotel with "Italianate ceilings and a Gothic structure on the grounds." An 1880s description portrayed the atmosphere of this resort in its post–Civil War glory: ". . . lovely skimmed-milk blue bandstand with its crimson touches on the central lawn where brass bands delighted the scattered spectators with marches; the fashionable yellow furniture with black stripes covering the chairs."

Allegheny Springs, Va., featured a remarkable gazebo made of rustic cedar branches, decorated with gnarled, twisted laurel branches and roots. Supposedly built by German immigrants in the 1890s using the art nouveau style, it has been preserved by private owners. In 1872 Yellow Sulphur Springs, Va., erected a building with a French mansard roof, but a year later it burned, to be replaced by a structure in the high Victorian eclectic style with an onion dome tower, which was torn down in 1960. Salt Sulphur Springs Hotel in Monroe County, Va., had a huge dining room in the 1830s, as did most spring resorts, but its distinction was a long line of fans on the ceiling. All the fans were connected to a rope so that they could be pulled by one person. Another Virginia resort, Craig Healing Springs, touted rooms of claw-footed bathtubs filled with spring water.

After the Civil War easy railroad access boosted business at the spring resorts. The southern social elite delighted in staying at the same resorts with former leaders of the Confederacy, but increasing numbers of visitors were northerners. Installation of bathrooms helped revive the popularity of some resorts as the 20th century opened. Yet many hotels were unable to keep up with modern conveniences such as screening, refrigeration, and air-conditioning. Fire continued to take its toll, and many resort structures were not rebuilt after they burned. The 1929 Depression sent numerous resorts into bankruptcy. Rapid transportation by automobile bypassed most of them. The last popular national attention given to a spring resort occurred in the 1940s when President Franklin D. Roosevelt visited Warm Springs in Georgia for hydrotherapy in its 95-degree water. Most of the remaining spring hotels are in a state of decay with the exception of a few that have adapted to new conditions. Religious organizations and similar groups operate some of the survivors.

The deathblow came to the resorts when railroads completely supplanted stagecoach lines. Although railroads first ran to the spring resorts, they later extended to undeveloped areas further south where a warm climate beckoned winter tourists. In the 1880s and 1890s the railroads enhanced resort and real estate development in Florida to such an extent that they created a boom in that state.

Two remarkable railroad men spearheaded the push into Florida. Henry B. Plant went south from his native New England to become president of the Southern Express Company. First laying track for the Atlantic Coast Line into western Florida, he consolidated his railroad business with his land sales. Likewise, Henry M. Flagler developed his railroad lines down the untouched east coast of Florida with accompanying hotel-resorts. Flagler, a partner in Rockefeller, Andrews, and Flagler oil refiners, predecessors of the Standard Oil Company, wanted to develop Florida real estate.

The Tampa Bay Hotel, opened in 1891 on 20 acres of landscaped grounds, best typifies Florida west coast development by Henry B. Plant. At a cost of $3 million, architect J. A. Wood created a hotel in the Moorish style with minarets, domes, wooden horseshoe designs, and crescent-shaped moons "nailed everywhere." A 1917 visitor to the hotel saw it filled with a wildly eclectic collection. It was "the Alhambra . . . furnished in the late Victorian manner." In 1930 the hotel became the University of Tampa, and today it is well preserved. The Tampa Bay Hotel was the architectural wonder of Plant's Florida development, even though his Belleview Hotel in Clearwater, opened in 1895, remained for a long while the largest hotel-resort on Florida's west coast.

On the east coast Henry M. Flagler inaugurated his railroad-resort development with the spectacular Ponce de Leon Hotel in St. Augustine, which had been designed by the New York architectural firm of Carrère and Hastings with the assistance of Bernard Maybeck. According to legend, Flagler looked to Spain for ideas for his Spanish Renaissance-style structure. At a cost of $1.25 million for 540 rooms, he created one of the first buildings in America made of poured concrete. The hotel was later converted to Flagler College.

Moving south from St. Augustine with his railroad and land development schemes, Flagler chose Palm Beach, 70 miles north of Miami, for a new city. "I shall build upon this spot a magnificent playground," he said. With his development of Palm Beach, Flagler also proposed to build churches and private gambling clubs to go with his hotels. In 1894 he set out to build the Royal Poinciana Hotel and raced to complete the railroad to it at the same time. The hotel won! It was the largest wooden structure ever built—six stories high, holding 1,750 guests who were entertained in a park of 32 acres with gardens, tennis courts, and golf courses. The building was a combination of late Victorian eclectic and Queen Anne forms. The Royal Poinciana Hotel was destroyed by the 1934 hurricane, leaving the Breakers, Flagler's other Palm Beach hotel. After an 1893 fire, the Breakers had been rebuilt in 1896 in a Spanish style.

If Flagler and Plant were developers, Addison Cairns Mizner, who also left his mark on Florida, was an adventurer-architect. Moving to Palm Beach in 1918, he quickly stamped his personal interpretation of Spanish architecture on the city and its neighbor, Boca Raton. In 1919 Mizner designed the courtyard for Paris Singer's Everglades Club, a private social club in the city of Palm Beach. Mizner "turned the Spanish style inside out like a glove, making all the openings face a patio." A contemporary description of the club caught the flavor of Mizner's Spanish-Florida style: "Seville, the Alhambra, a dash of Madeira and Algiers, an Italian lagoon and terraced garden and the incomparable Florida sunshine." With many commissions for private homes costing over a million dollars, Mizner used his fake Spanish style to develop Palm Beach architecture. He also developed Worth Avenue, Palm Beach's main shopping street, a rival to Fifth Avenue in New York City. His designs for fake Spanish buildings with little side streets and alleys for shops all served the great hotels and houses at this resort.

Addison Mizner's masterpiece was a resort complex now called the Boca Raton Club. On an inlet on the inland waterway in Boca Raton, he built the first hotel, the Cloister Inn, in a Spanish medieval style. Expanding his concept, he created a scheme for the largest hotel complex in the world. The inn on which he started was executed in Spanish style with pink and white walls surrounded by gardens with thousands of tropical plants and flowers. A dock on the waterway accommodated patrons' yachts. Unfortunately, in 1926 the Florida land-speculation boom ended, leaving only the small inn, completed in February 1926, a few outbuildings, and the docks. Since that time the Boca Raton Club has added a golf course, tennis courts, many other buildings, and a beach club.

Further south, what was to become the city of Miami was reached by the railroad in 1897. The site served as a troop camp during the Spanish-American War. In the 1921–25 Florida land boom automobile access gave the low-lying island considerable prominence and bay-bottom land sold quickly. The boom ended with the 1926 hurricane. Miami's subsequent development slowly gathered momentum until the 1980s. In the 1930s Miami and Miami Beach became fashionable places to escape both the Depression and northern winters. Small hotels in the art deco style were built in a 125-block district of the city. The art deco–Mediterranean Revival style, streamlined and exotic in decoration, was used on more than 800 buildings. Developers of the 1980s, seeking to build high-rise hotels and condominiums, face opposition from these early, small art deco hotels, which are trying to preserve the initial atmosphere of the resort city.

Miami skyrocketed to success as sun-seeking, wealthy tourists and conventioneers descended upon the city. The hotels of Morris Lapidus, whose Fountainbleau Hotel of 1954 is probably the best example of Florida kitsch-baroque architecture, epitomize the extravagance of Miami Beach architecture in the 1950s.

While Flagler and Plant were pushing into Florida to provide seaside resorts, similar resorts sprang up in other areas of the South. Saltwater bathing was never as popular in the 19th century as spring bathing, but by the late 1880s the first cottages opened for business at Virginia Beach, Va., and stilt houses appeared on the Outer Banks of North Carolina.

One of the most unusual island resorts in the South developed on Jekyll Island, a 12-by-2-mile island off the coast at Brunswick, Ga. Organized as a club in 1888 by families like Morgan, Astor, Gould, Vanderbilt, and Rockefeller, Jekyll Island became a winter refuge from January to March for the superrich. A small clubhouse-restaurant was built, and each family had its own house on the island. The club closed in 1942. In 1954 a highway was built to the island, formerly accessible only by boat.

A parallel development took place at Sea Island, Ga., where the Gulf Stream moderates the climate. In 1928 Howard E. Coffin had Addison Mizner build a hotel complex, called the Cloister, in the Mediterranean style. Originally only 46 rooms, the Cloister now occupies the center of a large beach resort. Beautiful beaches also attracted big resort development on Hilton Head Island off South Carolina and at Kiawah Island near Charleston.

Beach resort development continued at Virginia Beach, Va. In the 1930s cottages were built both in residential areas near the water and on stilts along the waterfront. Motels, beginning in the 1920s and the 1930s, supplanted big Victorian hotels of the late 19th century. Today condominiums, with time-sharing arrangements, represent the wave of the future at seaside resorts.

The Gulf Coast of the southern United States has traditionally featured a long saltwater bathing season. Early in the 19th century the Gulf Coast from Mobile to Lake Pontchartrain enjoyed popularity as a resort area for residents from Natchez and New Orleans who wished to escape the heat. Southern plantation architectural styles were transplanted to the beachfront at Biloxi, Ocean Springs, Bay St. Louis, and Pass Christian, Miss. Gulf Coast resort houses rested on brick piers for coolness and floodproofing. Decorative cutout work, often larger than necessary, softened the sunlight and wide verandas provided cross-ventilation. Long wooden piers projecting into the shallow water adjoined the Gulf Coast hotels.

Louis Sullivan, one of America's foremost architects, found inspiration while at Ocean Springs, Miss., vacationing from his Chicago office. He felt so at home that he had a local carpenter build two bungalows between 1890 and 1891. Whether Sullivan or his most famous pupil, Frank Lloyd Wright, actually designed the two vacation cottages is a matter of speculation.

As the 20th century dawned, the great resorts of the 19th century faced doom, precipitated by the economic, social, and transportation revolutions. Transportation, as always, engendered new developments. Private railroad-car sidings were replaced by parking lots. Cheap automobile transportation over interstate highways, with overnight stops in chain motels, became the norm. Resorts in the South gradually adapted to new transportation patterns and sports preferences of the 20th century. Resorts were no longer the domain only of the rich. Wealth became diffused, and new recreational activities gained momentum.

Southern resorts with their moderate climate offer a variety of outdoor sporting activities for long seasons. In the 20th century tennis courts dot many lawns, and ski trails, with the advent of artificial snow, abound along mountain paths. Spectator sports such as horse racing have grown in popularity since 1931, when Hialeah Racetrack in Miami opened, complete with flamingoes. The Tides Inn, started in 1946 on the eastern shore of Virginia, shines as a major resort for yacht owners.

More than any other sport, golf altered the layout of resort complexes. With its need for beautifully manicured courses on expansive tracts, golf changed the look of the 20th-century leisure landscape. By an accident of geology, Pinehurst, in central North Carolina, with its mild, dry climate, sand hills, and piney woods, became the golf capital of the South.

In the late 1800s New England developer James W. Tufts hired landscape architect Frederick Law Olmsted to create a special community. Olmsted laid out a complete village with shopping area, hotel, boardinghouses, some 16 cottages, and a meeting house–chapel based on a New England model. Olmsted's design featured curving streets and lavish landscaping within a protected community. By 1898 Tufts, completing his first course and later adding an appropriate clubhouse in 1899, had introduced the game of golf to Pinehurst. Pinehurst remains a famous southern golfing center with five featured 18-hole championship courses and numerous others in the immediate area. The location of Pinehurst did not depend on water to attract its customers, either for bathing or for drinking. What water was to one generation of tourists, the desire to play a game in a pleasant climate became to the next. Automobiles and airplanes make the contemporary resort easily accessible.

One of the most innovative southern resort communities to be developed in recent years is Seaside, a project near Point Washington, Fla., which has been carefully planned to capture the atmosphere of a small southern town during the late 1800s and early 1900s. Owners Robert and Daryl Davis cooperated with architects to design between 1978 and 1983 a detailed planning and zoning code that not only requires certain structural elements but also encourages such features of southern vernacular architecture as front porches and wood-shingle or metal roofs. Combined with these features are Victorian-style decorative latticework and brackets. The Seaside community further evokes images of small-town life by centering businesses around a town square, incorporating gazebos, and building narrow, tree-lined streets.

Since the early 18th century the spacious layouts and carefully designed environments for leisure in the South have represented the relationship between pleasure-seeking customers and an easy-going atmosphere. Taking advantage of pleasant weather for recreation, southern leisure sites developed innovative environments. Southern craving for socializing spurred a tradition of resort visiting. As transportation and technology opened new areas for leisure pursuits, visitors continued frequenting the great resorts, whose everlasting fame was propagated by southern weather, southern charm, and always "southern hospitality."

See also ETHNIC LIFE: Caribbean Influence; HISTORY AND MANNERS: Automobile; Railroad; / Olmsted, Frederick Law; INDUSTRY: / Flagler, Henry; RECREATION: Tourism; / Hilton Head; URBANIZATION: / Miami

W. L. Whitwell and
Lee Winborne
Hollins College

Cleveland Amory, *The Last Resorts* (1952); Edward Beyer, *Album of Virginia: or, Illustration of the Old Dominion* (1980); Stan Cohen, *Historic Springs of the Virginias: A Pictoral History* (1981); Marshall Fishwick, *Springlore in Virginia* (1978); Sir Augustus John Foster, *Jeffersonian America: Notes on the United States of America, Collected in the Years 1805–6–7 and 1811–12* (1954); Brendan Gill and Dudley Witney, *Summer Places* (1978); Constance M. Greiff, *Lost America: From the Atlantic to the Mississippi* (1971); Andrew Hepburn, *Great Resorts of North America* (1965); James M. Jordan IV, *Virginia Beach* (1974); Louis Joyner, *Southern Living* (June 1984, July 1986); Harnett T. Kane, *The Golden Coast* (1959); Russell Lynes, *The Tastemakers* (1954); Peregrine Prolix, *Letters Descriptive of Virginia Springs* (1835); Perceval Reniers, *The Springs of Virginia* (1941); Ishbel Ross, *Taste in America: An Illustrated History of the Evolution of Architecture, Furnishings, Fashions, and Customs of the American People* (1967); Paul M. Sachner, *Architectural Record Houses 1986* (1986). ☆

Sculpture

The lack of sculpture was one item in H. L. Mencken's indictment of culture in the early 20th-century South, and scholars have generally echoed his sentiments. The South has had, however, a twofold tradition of sculpture—monumental works on the grand scale and folk sculpture on a more humble scale, in the form of stonecarving, woodcarving, ironworking, and other crafts. Although the monumental work in the region is not categorized with the highest artistic achievements, it is a notable reflection of southern cultural values. The folk sculpture of the region is likewise rooted in regional life, and its aesthetic value is increasingly appreciated by critics.

The South has a long tradition of honoring its heroes through monuments. The South Carolina assembly authorized a statue of William Pitt, erected in Charleston in 1766, to commemorate the English hero of the French and Indian War, while Virginia officially honored its governor, Norborne Berkeley, in 1773 in Williamsburg. This tendency was even more pronounced after the American Revolution. Virginia took the lead in honoring heroes from that conflict. The Virginia Legislature commissioned French sculptor Jean Antonine Houdon to do a bust of Lafayette and, later, a marble statue of George Washington dressed in the uniform of the Continental army, which was placed in the Virginia State Capitol Building in Richmond in 1796. In the Old State House in Raleigh, N.C., stands a statue from 1821 by Antonio Canova, depicting Washington in another popular pose of the time—dressed as an ancient Roman, seated on a grand chair. Washington was the very image of Cincinnatus, an image reflecting the early southern, as well as American, attempt to see the new nation's culture in classical terms.

Hiram Powers was not a southerner, but he executed works immortalizing many southern heroes. He did a bust of the aging Andrew Jackson in 1835 and, while living in Washington, D.C., fashioned works of southerners John Marshall and John C. Calhoun. He enjoyed the patronage of southerners, especially the Preston family of South Carolina, who authorized him to do a portrait statue of that state's Calhoun. Henry Clay was the subject of Kentuckian Joel Tanner Hart's full-length statue, completed in 1859, for the Ladies' Clay Association of Virginia.

There are two famed equestrian statues dating from the antebellum era. Clark Mills's bronze monument of Andrew Jackson was unveiled amid much fanfare in Washington in 1853, and replicas were soon ordered for Nashville and New Orleans. It was placed in the heart of New Orleans, in an area known thereafter as Jackson Square. A second equestrian statue was Thomas Crawford's homage to George Washington, placed near the Capitol in Richmond. It was a sculptural group of Washington and other Virginia heroes. Frederick Law Olmsted called it "the highest attainment of American plastic arts."

Many of these works were by nonsouthern artists. John Cogdell (1778–1847), on the other hand, was a Charleston lawyer who exemplified the southerner interested in sculpture as an avocation. Cogdell dabbled in painting but concentrated by the late 1830s on sculpture. He visited Italy for inspiration and later was one of the few native-born Americans to exhibit in the Pennsylvania Academy in Philadelphia and the National Academy of Design in New York. He did busts of Lafayette and Sir Walter Scott. Most aspiring American artists, including a few southerners, lived in Italy, to be near ancient works, a supply of marble, skilled assistants, and the European appreciation of sculpture.

After the Civil War poverty discouraged the commissioning of monumental sculpture. By the turn of the 20th century, however, a movement was under way to honor the Confederacy by erecting monuments to its heroes. For most towns and cities in the region, this meant the erection of a rather standardized monument of a Confederate soldier. These ubiquitous statues represented the idea of sculpture to most southerners. Their artistic merits were few, but culturally they were most significant in using artwork to convey regional values. Typically located on town squares, Confederate monuments were shafts topped by the image of an average soldier. Inscriptions at the base of monuments pledged loyalty to the Lost Cause, "Lest We Forget."

Some monuments to the Confederacy were more artistic than others in conception and execution. Sir Moses Ezekiel and Augustus Lukeman were among the best Lost Cause sculptors, but the most famous was Edward Virginius Valentine, who was born in Richmond in 1838, studied abroad, and then returned to the South in 1865. He became the most renowned artist of the Lost Cause, specializing in sculpting works to honor such Confederate heroes as Robert E. Lee, Thomas "Stonewall" Jackson, Jeb Stuart, and P. G. T. Beauregard. His best-known work is a recumbent statue of Lee in the chapel at Washington and Lee University. Richmond, Va., saw itself as the Rome of the South in nurturing monumental art, with statues to Jeb Stuart, Matthew F. Maury, and Hunter H. McGuire; its Monument Boulevard has statues to Confederate heroes Lee, Davis, and Jackson, as well as one to George Washington. Stone Mountain in Georgia is the most grandiose monument to the Confederacy. The United Daughters of the Confederacy commissioned a carving of the images of Lee, Davis, and Jackson into the mountain, which is a huge granite outcropping. The monument was not completed until 1970.

The South has honored through sculpture cultural heroes other than the Confederates. Elisabet Ney was a German-born artist who came to Texas in the 19th century and produced monuments to such Texas heroes as Sam Houston, Stephen Austin, and Confederate General Albert Sidney Johnston. New Orleans was the home to many monuments, including the Wounded Stag near the Delgado Museum of Art and the symbolic fountain at Audubon Park. Thomas P. Minns executed a series of studies for Nashville honoring blacks, farmers, and rural Tennesseans, while William M. McVey contributed a James Bowie statue in Texarkana and decorative sculpture on the San Jacinto Monument. Clyde Chandler's Sidney Smith Memorial Fountain is in Dallas, and southern gardens provide an attractive setting for much statuary. South Carolina's Brookgreen Gardens have over 300 pieces, by Archer M. and Anna Hyatt Huntington, all in an appropriate southern setting, surrounded by live oaks and Spanish moss. Classical figures were executed for turn-of-the-century expositions at New Orleans, Atlanta, and Nashville; the Parthenon in Nashville is a lasting monument to such fairs.

Fewer monuments have been dedicated to World War I and World War II veterans than to those of earlier conflicts. Needed structures such as roads and bridges have often served as memorials instead. However, one of the region's most original pieces of sculpture was dedicated as a World War I monument on the University of Virginia campus—the McConnell Statue by Gutzon Borglum (the original carver of Stone Mountain and later Mount Rushmore). It is the bronze image of a World War I flying ace, who sits poised on a globe, ready for flight. Charleston's memorial to World War I is a nude male figure adorning Battery Park.

In the contemporary South modern

art, including modern sculpture, is found in cities such as Atlanta, Miami, Dallas, and Houston. There are examples of works by international sculptors such as Alexander Calder, Joan Miró, or Henry Moore. Among the most prominent black sculptors from the South, or those using southern themes, are Richmond Barthé, Francis Marion Marche, Augusta C. Savage, William E. Artis, Selma Burke, Margaret T. Burroughs, Elizabeth Catlett, and Marion Perkins.

In addition to creating a regional tradition of monumental sculpture, black and white southerners have produced a wide variety of folk sculpture. The South has had many craftsmen who produced work that transcended the merely functional to become folk sculpture. They are sometimes called primitive, eccentric, naive, or most commonly, folk artists. This category of sculpture includes commercial art, items with both utilitarian and aesthetic dimensions. It also includes the home sculptor who executes works for pleasure. Home sculpture is seen at craft stores, Christmas fairs, and flea markets.

A frequent southern image in film and literature is the whittler on a porch. Whittling, in fact, has had social, educational, and economic facets that make it a common activity, especially in the rural South. A representative of this tradition, Earnest Bennett (originally from Fairplay, Ky.), was recognized with a National Heritage Award from the National Endowment for the Arts in 1986. The pocketknife, sometimes called a jackknife, was the simple, basic tool needed, and whittling encouraged qualities of resourcefulness and ingenuity in its use. Pocketknives are valued material culture artifacts among carvers, who sometimes collect and trade them. The skill of carving was typically passed from one generation to another, frequently from an elderly family member or neighbor to a young man coming of age.

The inspiration for such folk sculpture comes from the tasks, materials, and skills of everyday life; farmers and carpenters make art while working with wood, quarry workers while working in limestone. Often these are communally shared skills applied to expressive forms, and they enhance the pride and prestige of the maker. A distinctive regional dimension comes also from the use of local materials. Southern folk sculpture has traditionally been in wood, stone, iron, or clay.

Because the South has been a heavily forested area, the use of timber as a material for sculpture was natural, and the skills associated with carving were valued in the southern economy. Sometimes the folk artist used a knife, sometimes a chisel; the wood object might be painted or it might be left unfinished. Some wood carvings were functional, others simply for show, and still others were novelty items. Carved objects included musical instruments, apothecary mortars, barber poles, weathervanes, whirligigs, toys, shop signs, shop carvings, wildfowl decoys, furniture accessories, walking canes, and larger-than-life-size rifles.

Pierre Joseph Landry (1770–1843) was an antebellum southern folk artist who carved in wood apparently as a pastime. He carved works that told stories, especially allegorical ones and those with echoes of religious themes from medieval art. Other antebellum artists carved wooden dolls and toys with movable parts. Religion has served as a prime theme for southern carvers, who have produced many church steeples topped by upward-pointing fingers.

Three-dimensional carved human figures were found in the South, many serving as shop signs. The carved Indian was a nationally popular wooden piece, displayed outside tobacco shops, and was one of the most common full-figured wooden pieces produced in the pre–Civil War South. Matthew S. Kahle, a Lexington, Va., furniture maker, produced a full-figured, standing George Washington for the Washington College Chapel in 1840. A carved black man stood as a symbol outside the New Orleans slave auction. Carved human figures also adorned the bows of ships.

Walking canes have often been carved. They were highly functional products for the elderly and handicapped, and folk artists gave them ornamental touches to make them artistic. Snake canes have been common, with serpents' bodies wrapped around the length of the stick and a head topping off the cane. Three-dimensional animals have also been carved into canes, as have politicians (shops near Monticello in Virginia sell Thomas Jefferson canes). Ceremonial staffs for lodges and fraternal groups have also been produced by folk sculptors.

Carved animals, in the form of domestic pets, livestock, and small animal wildlife, are commonly found in southern homes. They are a modern survival of the traditional southern pastoral ideal. Eagles are popular for interior decoration. Snakes are a favorite image, and the South has its fair share of carved serpents. A common form is a slithering toy—a jointed snake, with carved wooden pieces held together by string or wire. Carving wildfowl decoys began as a folk art by hunters who had a practical use for them. Ned Burgess of Currituck, N.C., for example, turned carving decoys into an art. He made more decoys between 1920 and 1945 than any other North Carolina carver, creating his works for hunters in sportsmen's clubs, for market hunters, and for subsistence hunters. He did many species of local waterfowl, including swans, geese, canvasbacks, redheads, blackheads, pintails, pigeons, black ducks, mallards, ruddy ducks, and coots. Carved ducks are now a ubiquitous presence through much of the South, thanks to commercial marketing.

Among the South's first folk sculptors were the stone carvers who cut gravestones from slate, granite, marble, sandstone, or fieldstone. Limestone seems to have been the most popular rock form. Stone carvers have usually been seen more as craftsmen than as artists, but many gravestones in the region exhibit aesthetic dimensions. Most, to be sure, repeat standard shapes and designs, such as weeping willow trees, cherubic angels, hearts and hands, crosses, skull and bones, flowers, and lambs for children. Scholars have documented, though, the stylized, innovative work of creative stonemasons, such as Laurence Krone, who carved tombstones for customers in southwestern Virginia in the early 19th century. Much stonecarving for graves was, however, anonymous. In the modern South, Nashville, Tenn., carver William Edmondson achieved fame for his stone carvings of animals, angels, flowerpots, religious figures, and garden statuary. He died in 1951, by which time his work had been displayed at the Museum of Modern Art in New York City.

Appalachian folk craftsmen have sometimes carved in a distinctive regional material—coal. Around the turn of the 20th century, for example, a Bell County, Ky., miner created a replica of the Bible from coal. Coal carvings are available at mountain craft fairs and have become a commercialized product for sale at tourist stores.

Ironworkers frequently decorated their practical creations with artistic touches. One type of ironwork in the South involved casting, whereby molten metal was poured into a mold. Not all casting, to be sure, would be classified as sculpture, but the production of a prototype enabled a caster to produce an object for widespread duplication. Iron furnaces turned out a variety of designs for such objects as andirons, stove plates, cast animals, and various household ornaments and cooking utensils. Most cast iron in the South, however, was imported from the North and was more an industrial form than a fine or folk art.

Another form of southern ironwork was wrought iron. Blacksmiths were an essential figure in both rural and city life, and sometimes they embellished their creations with artistic touches. The blacksmith shaped his metal into functional objects of daily living such as andirons, pokers, gates, commercial signs, grave markers, and kitchen implements. Folk sculptors working in both cast and wrought iron used the same themes and designs as other southern sculptors—animal forms, especially snakes, the human form, and scenes of nature and of religious life. The cities of Charleston and New Orleans contain the highest achievements of southern ironwork sculpture—in the lacelike gates and ornamental metal flourishes used in construction. South Carolinian Philip Simmons (b. 1912) is one of the most famous and skilled of many black artisans who invested their utilitarian craft with artistic dimensions.

Sheet metal was another medium for southern metal sculptors. Tin and copper objects were common in southern households, and those with imaginative decorations of design or motif qualify as folk art. Weathervanes, among the most popular of sheet metal objects that have been documented and collected, were common everywhere. In the form of chickens, horses, cows, sheep, or hogs, they topped barns; angels adorned churches; fish and gulls appeared along coastal areas; and arrows, Indians with drawn bows and arrows, and patriotic eagles were frequent.

Stoneware became the dominant form for traditional ceramics in the South by the early 1800s. Potter dynasties—such as those of the Cole, Brown, and Meaders families—provide continuity in the tradition today. Much pottery would not rank as folk sculpture, given that its objects are purely functional or decorated only through painting. Nonetheless, many potters created artistic sculpture in the form of face jugs and highly decorated vessels. Some pots were mainly utilitarian, designed for storing food, churning butter, or watering plants, but potters would decorate even those by incising distinctive designs. Flowerpots and gravemarkers were inscribed with fluted rims and flaring forms. Potters sometimes had stamps with which they made whimsical designs, their signatures, or Masonic or lodge symbols. Potters in the Shenandoah Valley of Virginia were particularly noted for creating molds in the form of animals and birds, fish and flowers, or human figures, and then attaching them to pitchers, bowls, flowerpots, vases, and other vessels to create elaborate, three-dimensional works. Other artists in clay, such as James "Son" Thomas of Leland, Miss., rely on dreams and visions for inspiration. Thomas creates sculptured images of animals and distinctive human skulls.

See also FOLKLIFE articles; HISTORY AND MANNERS: Monuments; / Stone Mountain; MYTHIC SOUTH: / Lost Cause Myth

Charles Reagan Wilson
University of Mississippi

Kate Langley Bosher, in *The South in the Building of the Nation*, vol. 10, ed. Samuel C. Mitchell (1909); Carl Bridenbaugh, *The Colonial Craftsman* (1961); Simon J. Bronner, *Chain Carvers: Old Men Crafting Meaning* (1985), *Grasping Things: Folk Material Culture and Mass Society in America* (1986); John A. Burrison, *Brothers in Clay: The Story of Georgia Folk Pottery* (1983); Charles Camp, ed., *Traditional Craftsmanship in America: A Diagnostic Report* (1983); Allen H. Eaton, *Handicrafts of the Southern Highlands* (1937); John Ezell, *The South since 1865* (2d ed., 1975); William Ferris, ed., *Afro-American Folk Art and Crafts* (1983); Henry Glassie, *Pattern in the Material Folk Culture of the Eastern United States* (1968); Donald Van Horn, *Carved in Wood: Folk Culture in the Arkansas Ozarks* (1979); Cynthia Elyce Rubin, ed., *Southern Folk Art* (1985); Robert Sayers, *Festival of American Folklife 1981*, ed. Jack Santino (1981); Allen Tullos, ed., *Southern Exposure* (Summer–Fall 1977); John Michael Vlach, *The Afro-American Tradition in Decorative Arts* (1977), *Charleston Blacksmith: The Life and Work of Philip Simmons* (1981); Charles G. Zug III, *Turners and Burners: The Folk Potters of North Carolina* (1986). ☆

Vernacular Architecture (Lowland South)

The vernacular, or common, architecture of a region is an indicator of its economic development and changing social values. The realities of life in the 17th-century Lowland South shaped builders' choices of plan types and building technologies, and these have remained at the core of the region's vernacular architecture. The vernacular building system of the Lowland South has been greatly weakened since World War I, but it has never disappeared. Recent historians of the early South have emphasized the area's social instability. A high mortality rate during the first century of settlement, coupled with a high demand for agricultural workers in the labor-intensive tobacco economy, absorbed economic resources and altered social relationships as planters attempted to extract as much labor as possible from their employees. These strains affected southern architectural traditions in two ways.

First, because most early southerners preferred to devote their resources to agricultural production, they developed building systems that capitalized on plentiful supplies of timber to minimize the human investment in building. Crude buildings characterized the beginnings of all the colonies, but in the South they continued to be built long after the Chesapeake and Albemarle settlements were securely under way. The earliest structures were commonly made of rough timbers driven into the ground and covered with split boards nailed to them. Later, 17th-century builders used mortise-and-tenon frames, simplifying them by omitting foundations and sinking the wooden uprights directly into the ground. There were several variations of the "post" building, as recent scholars have called it, ranging from the driven "puncheons" of the first buildings to carefully framed structures set on wooden-block foundations. Post building made it possible to build quickly and cheaply, conserving labor and capital for other uses. It was common even for public structures like churches and courthouses in the 17th-century South. Post building required frequent repairs, and few post-built structures survived more than 20 years after their initial construction. Only two colonial post-built houses—Cedar Park in Anne Arundel County, Md., and Sotterley in St. Mary's County, Md.—still exist, and both owe their preservation to a protective casing of durable materials added early in their existence. In the early 18th century wealthy southerners began to build their homes more substantially, but post-built houses were erected for poor whites and blacks until the end of the colonial period, and post, or "pole," construction is still widely used in southern agricultural buildings.

Although post building was no longer used for finer homes after the 17th century, a distinctive southern framing system grew out of it that embodied the labor-saving intention of post building in the use of a small number of relatively standardized parts, assembled with the simplest of mortise-and-tenon and notch joints. Whereas traditional Anglo-American frames of the type used in New England employ large timbers tied together by complex joints, southern frames consist of pairs of light walls linked at the top. Relatively small major timbers—about four by eight inches in houses—were set at 10-foot intervals, with the spaces between filled by three-by-four-inch studs. Often these were simply nailed into shallow notches chipped into the outer surfaces of the frame. Two long walls constructed in this manner were tilted up, and ceiling joists notched at their undersides were dropped on to hold the walls upright. The roof was most commonly formed of light three-by-four-inch rafters pegged at the top. A light board laid across the ends of the ceiling joists enabled the builder to nail the rafters anywhere along it, eliminating the need for cutting joints to seat the rafters. In the southern frame the parts were relatively unspecialized and could be cut out quickly and in numbers and assembled with equal ease. Yet the system was versatile enough that buildings as small as a smokehouse or as large as a mansion could be built using essentially the same approach. The southern framing system changed little between about 1720 and the Civil War and was used in some areas until the 20th century. It was carried west by southerners into the middle western and south central states, and its influence is apparent in 19th-century buildings as far west as California.

Thus, despite the stereotype of the South as a land of brick buildings, masonry walls have always been rare in the Lowland South, even for large structures; wood has been the characteristic building material. Although timber has most commonly been used in joined frames, log construction entered the Lowland South in the late 17th century. By the end of the 18th century small log houses, often with wooden chimneys, were widely used by poor planters in the Tidewater South—George Washington reported seeing almost nothing else on a trip South through Virginia and North Carolina in 1791—and they were the standard form of slave housing as well. In low-lying sections of east Texas and the Gulf Coast states log construction came with the early settlers and was a common vernacular building technology through the 19th and early 20th centuries. In some parts of the East Coast, however, logs never made much headway, except in small agricultural buildings constructed in the late 19th and early 20th centuries. In those areas the frame tradition was nearly universal and prevailed even where logs were used. For example, late 18th- and early 19th-century builders in northern Maryland were fond of a hybrid log-frame system, in which horizontal logs were tenoned into corner posts.

The 17th century gave the Lowland South its principal domestic plan forms as well as its building technology. At first, immigrants to the Chesapeake and Albemarle regions built many kinds of traditional English houses, but by about 1680 single-story, one-room-deep houses had become the standard. Poorer colonists, constrained by a barebones existence, had no choice about house size. For middling or wealthy people, the choice of small houses was a product of the relation between planters and their workers. Where most English agriculturalists in the 17th century were accustomed to employing familiar locals, who lived and worked in the farmers' own large houses, the presence of a constantly changing labor force of strangers prompted southern planters to abandon the custom and to move their laborers' working and resting areas to outbuildings. Thus, most planters' houses were reduced to one- or two-room dwellings standing at the center of a large domestic complex. From the late 17th century on, this fragmentation of domestic functions into a complex of small buildings was one of the most striking aspects of the southern landscape to outsiders, whose published commentaries repeatedly compared planters' residences to small villages. The creation of the southern domestic complex in the 17th century arose from altered relationships among English people. Although it later became a distinguishing mark of slave society, the separation of house and domestic outbuildings antedated the adoption of slave labor throughout the Lowland South.

A typical domestic complex included a kitchen, usually a building similar in size and appearance to a one-room house; a milkhouse or dairy for the cool storage of dairy products, and a smokehouse for the preservation of meats. Larger complexes in the 18th and 19th centuries contained a laundry, often attached to the kitchen; an office; and, in a few instances, a sunken icehouse, a school, or a small storehouse. Servants lived in the work buildings or in separate houses. In the 17th century cellars were customarily separate from the house and were only moved under the dwelling in the 18th century. Even then they were often thought of as outbuildings and were provided with outside entrances facing the other outbuildings, but with no access from inside the house.

At the core of the complex was the house itself. Two-room, or hall-parlor, houses (the name is a modern one) consisted of a large main room, called the hall by its occupants, which was the principal center of activity. It was used for sitting and eating, and the head of the household sometimes slept there. Off from it was a smaller room, usually called the parlor or chamber, which shared many of the hall's functions. Its more secluded location made it the preferred sleeping room. The parlor often had a door in the end or rear wall leading to the outbuildings at the side or rear of the house. A few very large hall-parlor houses had projecting entry rooms that were called porches, although they were enclosed. Some, like Bacon's Castle (1665) in Surry County, Va., one of the finest houses in the colony when it was built, had a rear tower for the stairs as well.

The relative homogeneity of house size and plan in the late 17th and early 18th centuries dissolved in the mid-18th century. One- and two-room houses remained the staple of the housing stock, but wealthier southerners began to add other spaces to these. A room called the dining room, but serving as many different functions as the earlier hall and parlor, could be found in many large houses. The addition of rooms led many builders in the 18th century to build houses two rooms deep, although others preferred to maintain the traditional single-room depth and to attach the added rooms in ells at right angles to the main house. More important than the use of added rooms and the increased depth of large houses was the use of a passage into which the main door opened. The passage, which usually contained the stair as well, served as a buffer between the outside and the public rooms of the house and allowed circulation to each room of the house without the necessity of passing through any other. Passages made slow headway at first, but by the early 19th century they were common in most houses with more than two rooms and could even be found appended to one-room houses.

The use of passages, extra rooms, and two-room (or double-pile) depths is most striking in the so-called Georgian-plan house, a structure with two rooms on either side of a central passage and usually two stories tall. Georgian plans were first used in the Lowland South in large mansions of the second decade of the 18th century. The smaller houses that used passages or two-room depths have been thought of as derivations of the Georgian form, but, in fact, a more complex process was involved in which traditional builders adapted the new ideas to traditional forms rather than merely imitating upper-class buildings.

Henry Glassie discusses the formal relationships between old and new ideas as they affected an area of Piedmont Virginia in his study *Folk Housing in Middle Virginia*. There were clearly social components to the Georgian idea as well, although these have not received the same attention. Fieldwork suggests, however, that many areas of the South underwent a period of intense experimentation in house forms either just before or just after 1800. During that period, in addition to the traditional forms, houses with odd and unique plans were constructed. At the end of the period of experimentation, each area seems to have selected the same solution to rural housing, based on the central-passage idea. New houses were built with passages, and both older and experimental houses were converted to the newly popular forms. The most conspicuous of the new dwelling types of the early 19th century was a two-story, one-room-deep house with a central passage. Although I houses, as the geographers call them, were built by a few wealthy southerners as early as the 1730s, they were not common until the 1820s. After that, they enjoyed a nationwide popularity, although one-room versions of the same plan were probably more numerous in the Lowland South.

The high visibility of the I house has obscured the continuing presence of single-room and hall-parlor houses. Moreover, the I house is only one of many possible ways to arrange four rooms and a passage. In the Chesapeake–Albemarle region a two-story, double-pile house, one room wide with a passage at the side was popular between 1790 and 1850. In the region stretching

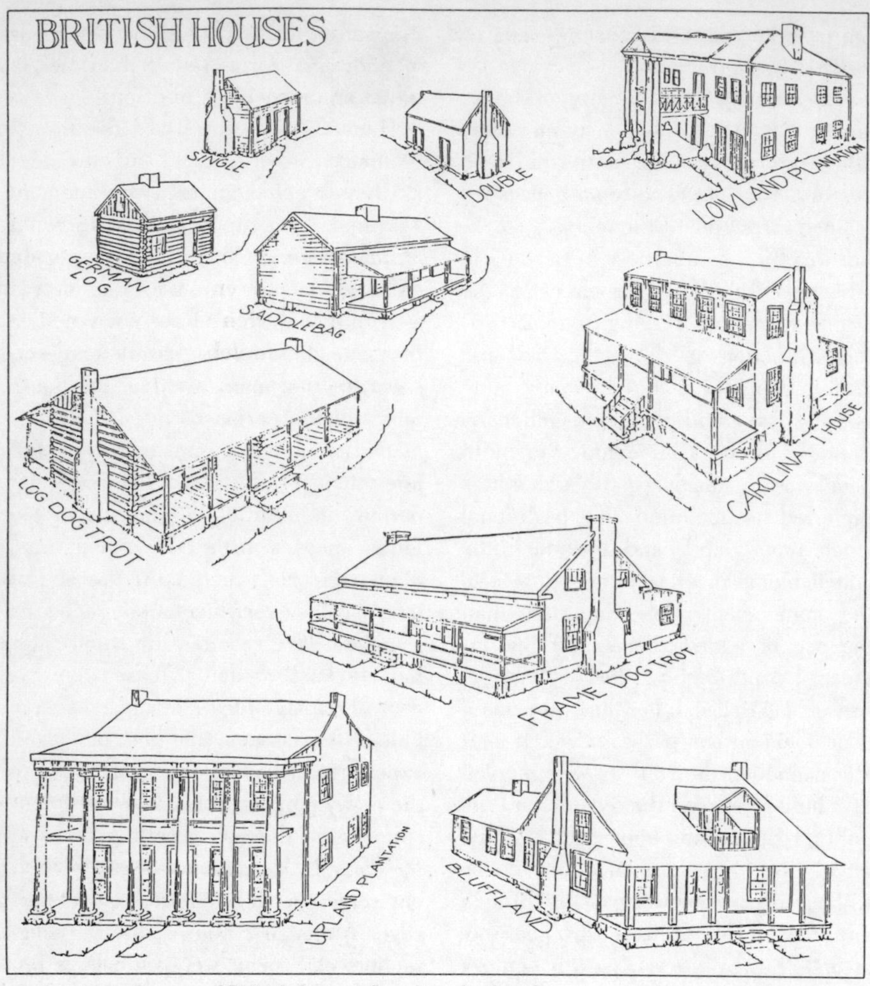

A drawing of types of British houses found in the South

south from southern North Carolina, a one-story house with a central passage and four rooms was built from the mid-19th century into the 20th century. This is often called a Creole cottage in the Gulf Coast states, and in 20th-century hipped-roof versions, a pyramidal cottage. The renowned Charleston single house is in effect an I house turned sideways, although it apparently emerged only after a period of experimentation with traditional urban house plans. All of these houses have been identified as distinctive regional forms, but all incorporate more widespread architectural elements in superficially different ways. Scholars must await an investigation of the reasons such regional choices were made.

In the 19th century southern vernacular builders adopted another nationally popular house form. This was a T- or L-plan building, consisting of two wings set at right angles to one another. One section contained two rooms, one in front of the other, while the other wing contained one room and sometimes an entry passage. This form was adaptable to a large, stylish house or a very modest one. T-plan houses were commonly built in large numbers to house tenants and industrial workers in the late 19th and early 20th centuries. These present another opportunity for study, but their room uses appear to have been traditional; only the picturesque appearance of the perpendicular wings was novel.

See also FOLKLIFE: House Types; / Bungalow House; Dogtrot House; I House; Pyramidal House; Saddlebag House; Shotgun House; T House; GEOGRAPHY: Log Housing

Dell Upton
University of California
at Los Angeles

Cary Carson, in *Material Culture and the Study of American Life*, ed. Ian M. G. Quimby (1978); Cary Carson, Norman F. Barka, William M. Kelso, Garry Wheeler Stone, and Dell Upton, *Winterthur Portfolio* (Summer–Autumn 1981); Brent Glass, in *Carolina Dwelling: Towards Preservation of Place: In Celebration of the North Carolina Vernacular Landscape*, ed. Doug Swaim (1978); Henry Glassie, *Folk Housing in Middle Virginia: A Structural Analysis of Historic Artifacts* (1975), *Pattern in the Material Folk Culture of the Eastern United States* (1969); Lisa Howorth, "Popular Vernacular: The One-Story T House in the South" (M.A. thesis, University of Mississippi, 1984); Dell Upton, in *Material Culture of the Wooden Age*, ed. Brooke Hindle (1981), *Winterthur Portfolio* (Summer–Autumn 1982); Thomas T. Waterman, *The Dwellings of Colonial America* (1950). ☆

Vernacular Architecture (Upland South)

Architecturally, the Upland South can be defined as the area lying between the Ohio River on the north, the Blue Ridge and Smoky Mountains on the east, the northern portions of the Gulf states on the south, and the Ozark Mountains on the west. Since the early 20th century this region has been depicted as a repository of antiquated cultural forms. Students of architecture have tended to concentrate on exotic or archaic forms there, such as log construction, dogtrot-and saddlebag-plan houses, and double-crib barns, and to neglect consideration of more ordinary vernacular buildings and particularly the patterns of architectural change. However, vernacular building in this part of the South, as in the Lowland South, is largely a product of the national popular culture of the 19th century.

Much of the distinctive architecture in the Upland South was brought into the region in the 18th century by the first European colonists, who entered the uplands through the great valley that stretches from central Pennsylvania into Tennessee or who crossed the Blue Ridge and Smoky Mountains from the east. Their architecture included log construction, several small house plans derived from English and Scotch-Irish traditions, and Germanic architectural designs. Popular building types and technologies began in the early 19th century, through new migrants, popular publications, and in rare cases the direct importation of building parts and materials.

The best-known building technology of the Upland South is log construction. The origins of log building in the United States are uncertain. The dominant theory is Fred Kniffen's and Henry Glassie's. They suggest that log construction was brought from Europe to Pennsylvania by Germanic and central European settlers. In Pennsylvania it was rapidly adopted by Anglo-American and

Scotch-Irish builders. More recently, Terry G. Jordan has returned to the earlier 20th-century theory that log construction was introduced into the Delaware Valley by Finns and Swedes in the mid-17th century. Although his argument is not entirely convincing, he has demonstrated that the log architecture of Europe is more varied and its patterns are less clear than Kniffen and Glassie thought. In America the phrase "log building" conceals a complex group of independent traits that must be examined more closely than they have been.

Structurally, the distinctive characteristic of log building is the horizontal courses locking together at the corners to stand up; in the standard form, where there are interstices of several inches between the individual logs, their only vertical support is at the corners. Consequently, log structures are often described according to the shapes of the notches that link them at the corners. The most common notching forms in the Upland South are the V-notch and the full- and half-dovetail notches. Saddle, diamond, square, and half notches are less common. A log structure is really only stable if there are four log sides that brace each other. This four-sided unit is traditionally called a pen or (in farm buildings) a crib and is the basic unit for the analysis of log building plans. Log construction has continued in the Upland South since the first settlement; traditional builders still construct and repair log houses and farm buildings.

Other building methods were equally early, if not as conspicuous. A few frame houses survive from the last quarter of the 18th century. Framing, using pit-sawn and water-mill-sawn materials, was common for large houses throughout the 19th century. In those parts of the uplands where timbering was commercially practiced in the late 19th century, steam-sawn, balloon-framed houses became common after the 1880s. Poorer builders took advantage of cheap mill-sawn materials to build single-wall (box or plank) buildings. These light structures lacked most standard framing members; they were supported by thick, closely set planks. Small horizontal pieces nailed to their inner faces at the top and bottom, and sometimes light vertical sticks at the corners, held the structural planks together. In houses, an outer covering of weatherboards was usually nailed directly to the supporting planks, and any interior finish—whitewash, paper, or plaster—was also applied directly to the structure. Box framing has been studied in Arkansas and Kentucky and undoubtedly was even more widespread, if unreported, in other parts of the South.

Masonry construction was preferred for the largest vernacular structures. Much of the Upland South contains rich stores of easily worked limestone, which was used for chimneys, foundations, and many large houses in the fertile valleys. Large houses and farm buildings built as early as the mid-18th century survive in upland Maryland, Virginia, North Carolina, and Tennessee. Brick structures survive from the 1790s, but they were rare before the second decade of the 19th century.

Vernacular house types were as varied as building technology in the Upland South. Among the earliest surviving houses there are small *cabins*, or houses of a single structural unit, one story high. The definition is Henry Glassie's, but the term was already identified in the 18th century as one favored by the English-speaking settlers in the Upland

South. Glassie distinguishes two types of cabins—one with a gable roof parallel to the front, end chimney, a single front entry, and a square plan that is derived from English traditions; and another that may derive from Scotch-Irish traditions and also has a parallel gable roof and end chimney, but has both front and rear entries and a rectangular plan. The interior is sometimes partitioned into a large room with a fireplace and a smaller one without heat. In addition, some early southerners built traditional Anglo-American hall-parlor (or hall-chamber) houses consisting of a large room, the hall, into which the front door opened, and a smaller room—the parlor or chamber—adjacent to it. Unlike the partitioned rectangular cabin, in the hall-parlor house both rooms were provided with fireplaces.

Other traditional house types are of less certain origin. These include the so-called saddlebag and dogtrot houses, and the double-pen-plan house. The saddlebag house is distinguished by the "draping" of its rooms on either side of a large central chimney like saddlebags on a horse. Unlike central-chimney houses in the Lowland South or the northeastern United States, the rooms on either side form separate structural pens that lean against the chimney, rather than enclosing the stack within a single unified structure. The units may resemble one or more of the simple cabin forms: a saddlebag house might consist of a square unit and a rectangular one, or a square and a two-room rectangular one, or two square or two rectangular units. Many saddlebag houses were built in stages. In the dogtrot house there are also two major sections, built at the same time, and in most cases containing a single room each. They are separated by a passageway that has no front or rear walls, and all three sections are covered by a continuous roof. The enclosed rooms are entered from the passage—the dogtrot proper—rather than from the front of the house. Many dogtrot houses were altered by enclosing the open passage, creating a central-passage plan of a type familiar all over the 19th-century United States. In the third two-part form, the double-pen house, the pens or units are built adjacent to one another without an intervening passage or chimney. Unlike the hall-parlor house, both rooms are approximately equal in size; more striking, each has its own front door. All three of these Upland South plans were most commonly built in one-story or story-and-a-half heights, although two-story dogtrot houses can be found. All are stereotyped as log buildings, though they were built in frame, and occasionally in brick and stone.

The origins of these three distinctive plans remain in dispute. The saddlebag house has been associated with Anglo-American central-chimney traditions as adapted to the exigencies of log-pen building. The double-pen house has similarly been attributed to the peculiarities of the log-pen structure. Another theory is that the double-pen house is an attempt to Anglicize the appearance of a four-bay facade deriving from Germanic building traditions. A third attributes its identical pens to Scandinavian antecedents.

The dogtrot house has been the object of the most speculation. One of the earliest explanations was that of Martin Wright, who argued that, like the double-pen house, the dogtrot derived from Fenno-Scandinavian traditions brought to the Delaware Valley in the 17th century. Others see it as a poor person's version of the Georgian central-passage house. Climatic explanations—that the open "breezeway" is an accommodation to the southern climate—are also popular. Unfortunately, the study of Upland South architecture has concentrated on the indentification of typological examples through often-superficial field examination. No careful study of the physical histories of individual, closely dated examples, of archival sources, and of socioeconomic or room-use patterns has been made, nor has there been direct field study of the proposed precedents. Consequently, scholars do not know how old these Upland South types are or what their history in the region is. All hypotheses about their origins are speculative, and none of the proposed theories seems convincing.

At the same time small house types appeared, several larger vernacular house plans were also imported into the Upland South. These include the so-called Quaker-plan house, another form of uncertain origins. The name derives from a description of an ideal house plan published by William Penn for the benefit of Quaker settlers in Pennsylvania, but no researcher has established any firm link between the 17th-century description and surviving examples, few of which date from before 1790 or after 1830. Quaker-plan houses are similar in plan to hall-parlor houses except that two small square rooms, one in front of the other, take the place of the parlor. These usually share a single chimney with fireplaces set diagonally in the corners of each room.

Central-passage-plan houses, one or two stories high and occasionally two rooms deep, representing the popular culture of the Lowland South and Middle Atlantic source areas, were also introduced to the Upland South in the late 18th century. A few were built in log and limestone, but brick and especially frame were the favored materials. In the 19th century, central-passage, one-room-deep houses—the ubiquitous I houses described by geographers and folklorists—were the most common houses for prosperous farmers and townfolk. As in the Lowland South, the traditional forms continued to be built even as popular house types and new methods of manufacturing building materials and constructing houses and farm buildings spread through the Upland South after 1830.

See also FOLKLIFE: House Types; / Dogtrot House; I House; Pyramidal House; Saddlebag House; Shotgun House; GEOGRAPHY: Log Housing

Dell Upton
University of California
at Los Angeles

Henry Glassie, *Mountain Life and Work* (Winter 1963, Spring 1964, Summer 1965), *Pattern in the Material Folk Culture of the Eastern United States* (1969), in *The Study of American Folklore: An Introduction*, by Jan Harold Brunvand (2d ed., 1978); Terry G. Jordan, *American Log Buildings: An Old World Heritage* (1985); Fred Kniffen, *Annals of the Association of American Geographers* (December 1965), with Henry Glassie, *Geographical Review* (January 1966); Charles E. Martin, *Hollybush: Folk Building and Social Change in an Appalachian Community* (1984); William Lynwood Montell and Michael Lynn Morse, *Kentucky Folk Architecture* (1976); James Patrick, *Architecture in Tennessee, 1768–1897* (1981); Karl B. Raitz, *Landscape* (Spring 1978); Dell Upton and John Michael Vlach, eds., *Common Places: Readings in American Vernacular Architecture* (1986); Thomas T. Waterman, *The Dwellings of Colonial America* (1950). ☆

AMISANO, JOSEPH

(b. 1917) Architect.

Born in New York in 1917, Amisano became a leading designer of modern architecture in the South. He received his architecture degree from Pratt Institute in New York in 1940, was a Fourth Year Design Medalist from that institution, and in 1950 won a Prix de Rome. In 1978 he was elected to the National Academy of Design as an associate member. Before joining the Atlanta firm of Toombs, Amisano, and Wells in 1954, he was associated with the firm of Harrison, Foulhoux, and Abramovitz in New York and in the Canal Zone. Later he joined the New York firm of Walter Sanders, where he met and worked with Buckminster Fuller.

Amisano's first national recognition came in 1942 with his design for proposed row apartments in New York. His major recognition as a designer came with his work in Atlanta in the late 1950s and the early 1960s. He played the major role in the design of Lenox Square, built in Atlanta in 1958 and soon recognized as one of the nation's most successful shopping malls. This "space for people," as Amisano called it, reflected Atlanta's growing importance as a major business center. The mall contained 58 shops, most of them branches of Atlanta's established institutions, including Rich's and Davison-Paxon. The key to the design was the 1,014-foot-long central mall, which provided shoppers with an insulation from automobile traffic. The open mall with its shops seemed to be very much in the spirit of the sunny Italian plazas Amisano had come to know and love during the time he spent in Rome as a Fellow at the American Academy. Spanning the 55-foot width of the mall are arches of white concrete, folded and arched into shapes more sculptural than architectural. Plantings in boxes and pots mask the long perspective of the mall so that shoppers see only four or five storefronts at one time. The design was restrained by its basically stern and classical character and by the economy of the construction. Lavish as the design seemed at the time, the cost was 20 to 25 percent below that of comparable malls.

Amisano's firm designed the Village Shopping Center in Cleveland, Tenn. His design for the Science Center at the University of Georgia in Athens was completed in 1957, and his designs for the Pharmacy Building and the Visual Arts Building on that campus were completed in 1962, the same year Harper High School was built in Atlanta from his design. In 1965 Amisano's plans for the Peachtree Palisades Building, a totally black structure, were completed in Atlanta.

During the period of the late 1960s Amisano designed two distinctive churches in Atlanta. The John Knox Presbyterian Church was completed in 1967 in suburban Atlanta, and the Unitarian Church was completed in 1968. Both were recognized for their distinctive central design. The decade of the 1960s was climaxed, however, by his design for the Atlanta Memorial Arts Center, which was dedicated in October of 1968. The center housed the High Museum of Art, the Atlanta College of Art, Symphony Hall, and the Alliance Theatre. Again the design of the buildings was distinguished by the stern classical character of its massively simple forms. The most important large structure designed by Amisano in the 1970s was the Peachtree Summit Building, completed in 1975.

Amisano's design of the Atlanta University Center Library was completed in the spring of 1983, and his design for the MARTA Peachtree Center station was completed and won a Georgia A.I.A. award in that year. The unique feature of the design is the exposed granite of the tunnel, which was left unfinished as the main decorative element of the station.

Marie Huper Pepe
Agnes Scott College

American Architects Directory (3d ed., 1970); *Antiques* (July 1970); Rob Beauchamp, Atlanta *Journal*/Atlanta *Constitution Weekend* (10 August 1985); *Progressive Architecture* (April 1959). ☆

ANDERSON, WALTER

(1903–65) Painter.

Walter Inglis Anderson was born 29 September 1903 in New Orleans, La., and grew up in the Mississippi Gulf Coast region. Anderson's artistic curiosity, imagination, and love of nature were strongly influenced by his mother's interest in art, music, and literature. His professional art training began at the Parsons Institute in New York City when he was 20. From 1924 to 1928 Anderson studied at the Pennsylvania Academy of the Fine Arts under the supervision of Henry McCarter, an artist who had worked with the impressionists in Paris. The Cressen Award he received from the Academy in 1928 allowed Anderson to travel in France, where he studied the primitive cave paintings at Les Eyzies. McCarter's guidance and these cave paintings contributed to Anderson's strong sense of design and color.

In 1933 Anderson married Agnes Grinstead, and the couple settled down in an antebellum cottage nestled in the woods of Ocean Springs, Miss. The Andersons spent a delayed honeymoon trip canoeing down the Mississippi River two years later. During the mid-1930s he completed a WPA mural in the Ocean Springs High School and produced award-winning pottery for Shearwater Pottery, a business founded by his older brother, Peter, in 1928. Torn between the exacting demands of his job at Shearwater Pottery and his desire to pursue his own artistic career, Anderson suffered a nervous breakdown in 1937. He spent the next three years in and out of mental institutions.

Anderson rejoined his family in 1940 at the Oldfields Plantation near Gautier, Miss., where his father-in-law lived. While at Oldfields, Anderson reread classic books and transformed the texts into a series of block prints and line images. By 1946 his interest in epic illustration had faded, and he left his wife and three children at Oldfields in 1947 to return alone to his cottage in Ocean Springs.

Anderson spent most of the remainder of his life at the cottage fulfilling his fantasy of becoming an "alienado" and revitalized his naturalist painting through numerous jaunts to Horn Island off the Mississippi coast. Anderson often slept on the beach under a small, overturned skiff and sketched in the open. The Brooklyn Museum in New York featured his block prints and children's book illustrations in a 1949 exhibition, but his work entered many public collections as a result of a 1967–68 traveling exhibition organized by the Brooks Memorial Gallery in Memphis.

In 1951 he began one of his most complicated works, *Creation at Sunrise*, a 12-by-14-foot mural painted on the walls of his cottage. The theme of the mural is centered on Psalm 104. The animals, woods, and plants featured in the mural are modeled on those found in the Mississippi Gulf Coast. Light is used impressionistically in several phases of sunrise, morning, storm, noon, sunset, and night. The mural provides art historians with valuable insights into Anderson's often-misunderstood artistic spirit.

Since his death in New Orleans in 1965 Anderson's art has become more visible. Artist, voyager, and naturalist, Anderson created art for art's sake. A great body of his art has yet to be examined or cataloged.

Elizabeth McGehee
Salem College

Susan V. Donaldson, *Southern Quarterly* (Fall–Winter, 1985); Mary Anderson Stebly, *Sea, Earth, Sky: The Art of Walter Anderson* (1980); Redding S. Sugg, Jr., *The Horn Island Logs of Walter Inglis Anderson* (1973), *A Painter's Psalm: The Mural in Walter Anderson's Cottage* (1978), *Walter Anderson's Illustrations of Epic and Voyage* (1980). ☆

ART MUSEUMS

Museums open to the public and displaying a wide range of arts have roots in royal and ecclesiastical collections going back before the Middle Ages. Not until the 18th century, growing out of the educational ideals of the Enlightenment, did museums as known today begin to take shape. Peale's Museum in Philadelphia and the Charleston Museum, both of which display works of art and a variety of natural history objects, are among the earliest of such institutions in the United States. In the second half of the 19th century, however, the great private or quasi-private art museums such as the Metropolitan Museum of Art in New York and the Boston Museum of Fine Arts, both founded in 1870, were established in the United States. Other distinguished art museums in this country founded before 1900 include the Brooklyn Museum (1823), the Albright-Knox Art Gallery in Buffalo (1862), the Philadelphia Museum of Art (1876), the Chicago Art Institute (1879), and the Cincinnati Art Museum (1881). In the South the three museums whose foundations go back to the 19th century are the Gibbes in Charleston (1858), the Telfair Academy in Savannah (1875), and the Valentine in Richmond (1892). (The Smithsonian Institution in Washington, D.C., was founded in 1846, but the subdivisions in which works of art and craft are the major focus mostly date from after 1937, when the National Gallery of Art was founded.)

In the 20th century, museums began to play an important role in the cultural and artistic life of communities in the South; before that time the relatively small size of the cities and the poor economy mitigated against their establishment. Artists, educators, and community leaders were among those who encouraged the founding of such museums. In the early years of this century, and even up to World War II, the opportunities for artists to exhibit their works were few, and they looked to museums as artistic centers where this could take place. Most of the major museums in the South still hold annual or biennial exhibits featuring local or regional artists. With the proliferation of private galleries and art dealers, especially since the 1950s, the need for museums to serve this function is less urgent, but still important.

Both artists and educators were eager for the establishment of museums in which they would be able to see, without traveling great distances, something of the artistic heritage of the past. Artists learn much from other artists, both directly from their teachers and colleagues and indirectly from their study and perception of earlier works of art, and they supported efforts to establish museums. Educators, particularly those who taught art and art history, felt the need for their students and the general public to have the opportunity to see original works of art from other periods and places. Community leaders have shared these desires and have, in addition, perceived art museums as civic assets. Even so, the growth and development of museums in the South were slow and sporadic. Virtually all major southern cities now have a fine arts museum. These include Houston (1900), Dallas (1903), Atlanta (1905), New Orleans (1910), Jackson, Miss. (1911), Memphis (1913), Baltimore (1914), Louisville (1925), San Antonio (1926), Sarasota (1930), Montgomery (1930), Richmond (1934), West Palm Beach (1940), Columbia, S.C. (1950), Birmingham (1951), Columbus, Ga. (1952), Raleigh (1956), Nashville (1957), Little Rock (1960), Fort Worth (1961), and Mobile (1964). In addition to developing permanent collections, most of these museums now have lively educational programs of lectures, films, concerts, special tours, and children's programs. They also host traveling exhibitions, such as the extremely popular one of treasures from King Tut's tomb. New buildings for Atlanta's High Museum of Art, which opened in November of 1983, and Dallas's Museum of Art, which opened in January of 1985, have been hailed as major architectural achievements and as signs of growing public, especially commercial, support for arts in the South. Altogether these varied institutions offer a rich and diverse mix of education and recreation available to young and old alike.

Jessie Poesch
Tulane University

American Association of Museums, *Official Museum Directory* (1986). ☆

BEARDEN, ROMARE

(1914–1988) Painter.

Born 2 September 1914 in Charlotte, N.C., Bearden attended public schools in New York and Pittsburgh but came back south to spend summers with his great-grandparents in Mecklenburg County, N.C. He received a B.S. in mathematics from New York University in 1935, studied at the Art Students League in New York (1936–37), worked on advanced mathematics at Columbia University (1943), served in the U.S. Army (1942–45), and went to Paris after the war to study philosophy and art at the Sorbonne (1951). He worked for the New York Department of Social Services off and on in the late 1930s and late 1940s, and then from 1952 to 1966. He traveled widely and tried his hand at songwriting in the early 1950s. He was art director of the Harlem Cultural Council for years beginning in 1964 and worked with the Alvin Ailey Ballet Company as artistic adviser. His works were exhibited at the Carnegie Museum in Pittsburgh, the Institute of Modern Art in Boston, and the Corcoran Gallery in Washington, D.C., among other places. He is the author of *The Painter's Mind* (with Carl Holty, 1969) and *Six Black Masters of American Art* (with Harry Henderson, 1972). Bearden died March 11, 1988.

Bearden applies cubist techniques to portraying the life of American blacks. He uses large collages and montages, combining African imagery with the spatial dimensions of cubism. Sophisticated and modern in structure, his work also contains a decidedly traditional narrative story line. His themes are not exclusively southern, but many of his paintings treat the South explicitly. Typical subjects are jazz and blues, farm life, the rituals of baptism and voodoo, and perhaps above all, homecoming. His works on the South tend to be lyrical and evocative, to portray mythic characters, and to deal with elemental human concerns. *Sunset-Moonrise with Maudell Sleet* pictures a real-life North Carolina woman from his youth as a godlike figure in her garden. *Miss Bertha and Mr. Seth*, which portrays an elderly black couple posing, is again based on individuals he knew in North Carolina. Critic Ralph Pomeroy has observed that Bearden's thematic interests are so universal that he can "equate a field hand with a god" and mix the races so that "it is no surprise in his work to come upon, say, a hand that has both black and white fingers."

Charles Reagan Wilson
University of Mississippi

Julia Markus, *Smithsonian* (March 1981); Albert Murray, in *Romare Bearden, 1970–1980; An Exhibition Organized by the Mint Museum, Department of Art, Charlotte, North Carolina*, ed. Jerald L. Melbert and Milton J. Bloch (1980); Ralph Pomeroy, *Artnews* (October 1967); John Williams and Bundie Washington, *The Art of Romare Bearden* (1974). ☆

BINFORD, JULIEN

(b. 1908) Painter and sculptor.

Binford, much acclaimed artist of Virginia, was born in Powhatan in 1908, the son of parents who traced their ancestry in America back many generations. At the age of 15 he moved with his family to Atlanta and eventually entered the premedical program at Emory University. He decided to become an artist and found encouragement from Roland McKinney, the newly appointed director of the High Museum of Art. On his recommendation Binford went to Chicago and enrolled in classes at the Art Institute of Chicago under the Russian artist and stage designer Boris Anisfeld, who was known as an expressive colorist. In 1932 Binford won the institute's coveted Ryerson Traveling Fellowship, and after three years of classes in Chicago the young artist was on his way to Paris. There he began experimenting with a variety of mediums and approaches, producing numerous pen-and-ink sketches, as well as a series of evocative gouaches that attracted the favor of French critics. His associates in Paris in this period included the writer Lucien Fabre and the poet Leon Paul Fargue. In 1934 the dealer Paul Guillaume saw the artist's work and declared that Binford possessed "the qualities of a painter and his gouaches show great imagination, spirit, and originality." Binford was subsequently given a one-man show at the Galerie Jean Charpentier and was able to sell some of his work.

Bouyed by his success, Binford ignored the advice of many of his Paris friends and returned to America in 1936. In May of that year he was given a one-man show at the Karl Freund Galleries in New York. One enthusiastic critic wrote that Binford's works displayed a "deep religious spirit, curiosity tinctured, we felt, with satire, their glowing color and extraordinary sensitivity, make them definitely worthy of your attention." Unfortunately, Binford's work attracted no buyers, and he and his French wife, Elizabeth, bought a patch of land in Powhatan, Va., with their savings. The land was verdant with swamp laurel and jewel weed, cedar and sycamore; on the banks of a stream named Fine Creek were the ruins of an old foundry, which the artist would later convert to a studio. He began painting the people and landscape of the area, mostly the black farmers who lived in relative poverty.

In March 1938 the struggling artist signed on with the Federal Arts Project of the Works Progress Administration, which paid him to produce paintings. He completed approximately 40 works prior to his termination with the project in August 1940. That year his work was featured in one of the Virginia Artists Series exhibitions hosted by the Virginia Museum. The artist was lauded for his portrayal of the life of his native state by the museum's director, Thomas Colt. "Return to America has meant a return to realism, which, to him, possesses all the color, all the structure, and all the emotional content of abstraction," he wrote. Binford was awarded the first Senior Fellowship given by the museum, and he established an art class at the Craig House Negro Art Center and taught classes in mural painting at the Richmond School of Art.

During World War II Binford occupied a studio in Hell's Kitchen in New York City and established a lifelong relationship with Midtown Galleries, which subsequently exhibited his work. He was assigned to the navy as a war correspondent for *Life* magazine and executed a number of sketches of New York Harbor in wartime and of convoy activities at sea, which today hang in the Pentagon in Washington, D.C. More significant, however, was his activity as a muralist in the same period. During his WPA tenure he had completed a mural depicting a logging scene in his native South for a post office in Forest, Miss. In 1942 the artist finished a powerful mural titled *The River Jordan* for the Shiloh Baptist Church, a black congregation in his native area. His paintings from this fertile period often portrayed the powerfully expressive gestures of the simple rural people he had grown to appreciate and respect. As one critic tellingly wrote in 1943, "For us it is a record of a people and a time and a place which is part of the heritage of America."

After the war Binford was appointed professor of art at Mary Washington College in Fredericksburg, Va., where he organized a series of exhibitions that helped form the university collection. In 1951 he completed a mural depicting the signing of the Virginia Declaration of Rights for the State Library in Richmond. Since that time the artist has completed several mural commissions and has been given numerous one-man shows. He restored the ruins of the old mill at Fine Creek into a livable structure, where he set up a spacious studio within its three-foot-thick blue granite walls. In his later work he reverted to limpid, yet colorful renditions of the cyclamens, iris, daisies, and violets that abounded around his house in the backwoods country that served as his source of artistic inspiration.

Rick Stewart
Dallas Museum of Art

Art Digest (August 1951); *Artnews* (15 November 1942); Elizabeth Binford, *American*

Artist (April 1953); Virginia Museum of Fine Arts, *Painting in the South: 1564–1980* (1983). ☆

BOTTOMLEY, WILLIAM LAWRENCE

(1883–1951) Architect.

William Lawrence Bottomley made unique contributions to the practice of country house architecture in the South. Through the Georgian Revival houses he designed and through the publication of *Great Georgian Houses of America*, he exerted a distinctive and marked impression on country house design. Bottomley designed houses for clients throughout the South in the states of North Carolina, South Carolina, Florida, Alabama, Louisiana, Maryland, and West Virginia; his reputation was made through his commissioned houses for clients in Virginia.

Bottomley was born on 22 February 1883 in New York City. He received his B.S. in architecture from Columbia University in 1906. For a period he worked in the office of Heins and LaFarge in New York and in July 1907 was awarded the McKim Fellowship in Architecture at the American Academy in Rome. He remained in Rome for just over six months before leaving in March 1908 for Paris, where he succeeded on his entrance exam for the École des Beaux Arts. He returned to the United States in 1909 and married Harriet Townsend, an architectural writer whose mother was from Lexington, Va. Shortly thereafter he formed a partnership, Hewitt and Bottomley, which lasted until 1919, and then had a series of associates, including Edward C. Dean, with whom he worked on the Turtle Bay project. In 1928 he became the principal architect in the firm of Bottomley, Wagner, and White—which was formed largely to handle the design of River House in New York. Bottomley was made a fellow of the American Institute of Architects in 1944. He died on 1 February 1951.

Bottomley's early work had an eclectic flavor (influenced by his travels in Italy, France, and Spain), which can be seen in Turtle Bay Gardens and his stucco-covered houses. Another product of the early 1920s was *Spanish Details* (1924), which included photographs and drawings of portals, courtyards, windows, loggias, doors, ceilings, and ironwork and became a sourcebook for other architects.

His first house in Virginia, designed in 1915, was a classical five-bay house, covered in stucco; its form and organization reflected Georgian principles, which would dominate his work for the next 20 years. The following year he designed a house for H. L. Golsan on Richmond's Monument Avenue, the first of his red-brick Georgian houses in Virginia and the first of seven town houses he would design for this prestigious residential avenue. After these two houses, he gained a series of commissions in Richmond for other country houses and estates, including a beautiful range of houses at Windsor Farms on the hill above the James River, culminating in Milburne, designed in 1934 and completed in 1935.

The Richmond houses became well known in Virginia and helped to secure commissions for Bottomley throughout the state and the South. His designs for farm seats and hunting boxes in the Warrenton-Middleburg area and in Albemarle County, Va., were also published and led to new commissions. Most of the Georgian Revival houses were executed in red brick but notable exceptions included Lockerbie in Birmingham, Ala., and the William E.

Chilton House in Charleston, W.Va., which are distinguished stone buildings. Tatton Hall in Raleigh, N.C., one of his important Georgian Revival houses of the mid-1930s, has a soft salmon-colored brick.

Bottomley's work was a product of early 20th-century interest in the architecture and gardens of the 18th and 19th centuries. His fame rests on the creation of the "ideal" Georgian Revival country house, especially in Virginia. Although the great 18th-century Virginia houses were his models, he reinterpreted them in a manner appropriate to the 20th century. Bottomley also served as chairman of the editorial committee under whose auspices the two-volume *Great Georgian Houses of America* (1933, 1937) was compiled. In the hands of younger architects these two volumes inspired a subsequent generation of houses.

Davyd Foard Hood
North Carolina Department of Cultural History
Raleigh, North Carolina

Davyd Foard Hood, "William Lawrence Bottomley in Virginia: The 'Neo-Georgian' House in Richmond" (M.A. thesis, University of Virginia, 1975); William B. O'Neal and Christopher Weeks, *The Work of William Lawrence Bottomley in Richmond* (1985). ☆

CHAPMAN, CONRAD WISE

(1842–1910) Painter.

Chapman was born in Washington, D.C., where his father, Virginia-born John Gadsby Chapman, painted murals in the Capitol. He grew up in Rome, Italy, where the elder Chapman settled in 1848. His early instruction in art was provided by his father. Fired with devotion to Virginia, young Chapman returned to America with the outbreak of the Civil War in 1861 and enlisted in the Confederate army. He prepared numerous sketches of war scenes, especially in Virginia and South Carolina. In 1863 and 1864 he was assigned to depict the batteries and forts at Charleston, S.C. There he executed his unique and celebrated series of paintings of the Charleston defenses. In 1864 Chapman went briefly to Rome because of his mother's illness. When he returned, he landed in Texas, only to learn that the Civil War had ended.

Chapman joined Confederate General John B. Magruder in supporting Emperor Maximilian in Mexico. Magruder's group, however, soon disbanded. Enamored of the Mexican landscape, Chapman painted an impressive 14-foot-long canvas, the *Valley of Mexico*, a panoramic view of the entire valley. Some critics believe it to be the finest painting by an American of the Mexican landscape and have compared it with works by José Maria Velasco, Mexico's greatest 19th-century landscapist. In later years, Chapman resided in France, Italy, England, New York, and Virginia. Though he lived until 1910 (he died in Hampton, Va.), he completed his most memorable work by the early 1870s.

Conrad Wise Chapman is best known as the principal painter of the Confederacy. His small landscapes of Charleston are some of the most brilliant paintings associated with the Civil War. Each a masterpiece, these paintings—the result of Chapman's private romantic response to the call of sectional patriotism—are characterized by a freshness of color, an excellent use of the effects of light, a deftness of brushstroke, and a skillful use of minute detail. The Charleston paintings also demonstrate a rather extraordinary attitude toward the subject they depict. Though an ardent partisan of the Confederate cause, Chapman revealed in these paintings none of the propaganda elements that dominate many pictorial representations of wartime scenes. For his Charleston work and for his masterpiece, the *Valley of Mexico*, Chapman deserves increased recognition as an important American landscape artist.

L. Moody Simms, Jr.
Illinois State University

Louise F. Catterall, ed., *Conrad Wise Chapman, 1842–1910* (1962); L. Moody Simms, Jr., *Virginia Cavalcade* (Spring 1971). ☆

CHRISTENBERRY, WILLIAM

(b. 1936) Photographer.

Born in Tuscaloosa, Ala., Christenberry's lifelong photographic preoccupation arose from a chance encounter with Walker Evans and James Agee's book, *Let Us Now Praise Famous Men*. Written largely about his native Hale County, Ala., the book, and a subsequent friendship with Evans, motivated Christenberry to make records of places familiar from his childhood: houses, barns, churches, graveyards, general stores, and commercial signs advertising such goods as snuff and cola. Christenberry teaches at the Corcoran Gallery in Washington, D.C., and returns each summer to photograph and to collect remnants of rural buildings, clapboard, rusted tin, and fading signs, which he reassembles into giant collages.

A William Christenberry photograph of a new-made grave, north Mississippi, 1970s

Christenberry photographs in color with subtlety and gentle restraint, as though with a bit of nostalgia for a South that has all but vanished. Christenberry's exquisitely simple views evoke the presence of the inhabitants of 40 years ago.

Mary Louise Tucker
New Orleans, Louisiana

William Christenberry, *Southern Photographs* (1983); Frances Fralin, *Washington Photography: Images of the Eighties* (1982). ☆

CLOAR, CARROLL

(b. 1913) Painter.

As a young boy growing up in Earle, Ark., Carroll Cloar remembered the regional stories and folktales that his parents and others told him. "I could actually remember how I visualized those things when I was told about them, and I painted that way," Cloar later recalled. "I've tried to keep a child's point of view, the simplicity, the wonder."

Cloar graduated from Southwestern College in Memphis, and after two years as a student at the Memphis Academy of Arts, he journeyed to New York and enrolled in the Art Students League, studying under Harry Sternberg and Ernest Fiene. In 1939, after nearly four years of study, he was awarded a MacDowell Traveling Fellowship from the league and used it to travel through Mexico. After service in the air force during World War II, Cloar received a Guggenheim Fellowship for 1946–47 and spent another year in Mexico painting in oil. Afterwards Cloar adopted tempera as his preferred medium, and between 1950 and 1954 he traveled to Central and South America and to Europe, intermittently living and working in New York. The European trip caused a significant change in his career. While there, the artist later recounted, "I just painted, copied things I thought were visually interesting—and then I began to have ideas for my paintings from childhood." Upon his return to America the artist moved to Memphis and began to explore the roots of his upbringing, examining old photographs and reacquainting himself with earlier memories.

Cloar adapted his painting style to one based on the expressive color and linear design of folk paintings, but with very sophisticated results. "I had a whole series of ideas, which I called Childhood Imagery, remembering how I thought of things as a child. The first one was *My Father Was as Big as a Tree.*" The work depicted his father, a burly former logger, standing alongside a stylized tree of similar height, while the artist was shown as a grim-faced child in a soapbox racer, far smaller and distant. Cloar's colors grew luminescent and dreamlike, while natural features were rendered with otherworldly uniformity. He exhibited at the Alan Gallery in New York and was praised by several critics as having a rare gift for observation and imagery. "The fact is, the image in art has neither beginning nor ending," Cloar wrote five years later. "It is a moment in time, isolated from the hours and days that surround it, and the vision comes to the artist whole." Cloar evoked vivid memories of his family and friends, their faces, dress, and customs locked in the eerie stillness of his paintings. Titles such as *Panthers Chasing the Little Girls*, *Brother Hinsley Wrestling with the Angel*, or *Charlie Mae and the Raccoon Tree* are indicative of the rich lore of subject matter that Cloar tapped with his art. In 1959 he purchased an old frame house in Memphis and remodeled part of it into a studio and gallery. Next to the front entrance on the outside of the house the artist created a 14-foot-high mosaic depicting figures of children against a patterned background of flowers, which he titled *A Garden of Love*.

Much of Cloar's work since 1960 has portrayed the inhabitants of his native region in seemingly everyday tasks, such as laboring in a cotton field, killing time in front of a local store, or walking along a narrow country road; they are portrayed in such a way as to make the ordinary become extraordinary. One loses a sense of time, even a sense of specific place in these paintings. The viewer's own senses are sharpened by Cloar's use of rhythmic stroke and pattern, his intensified light and color. Shadows seem as palpable as solid forms, and the scenes take on a visionary resonance. Paintings such as *Where the Southern Cross the Yellow Dog* re-create, in an unforgettable way, the legacy of an incident in southern culture.

In 1969 he was given a priceless hoard of photographs taken by a black photographer in his hometown, and he began to incorporate some of the unidentified, haunting images into his work. All kinds of people, from WPA quilters to anonymous wedding guests, were transposed into the artist's dreamlike vision. "Cloar's real power, and it enables him to transcend mere eclecticism, derives from his feeling for time, especially past time," the painter and critic Sidney Tillim has written. "It is an identification so strong that even contemporary events or portraits, when represented by Cloar in his fastidious style, appear to have occurred long ago or seem to be passing into timelessness." Certainly Carroll Cloar, like William Faulkner, has evoked a South far beyond the mere commonplace and has elevated it to art.

Rick Stewart
Dallas Museum of Art

Catalog of Paintings by Carroll Cloar, Southwestern University Burrow Library Monograph #6 (1963); Paul Cummings, ed., *Dictionary of Contemporary American Artists* (4th ed., 1983); Guy Northrup, *Hostile Butterflies and Other Paintings by Carroll Cloar* (1977). ☆

DODD, LAMAR

(b. 1909) Painter.

Lamar Dodd, one of the preeminent painters of Georgia, was born in Fairburn and received a five-year Certificate of Art and diploma from LaGrange High School in 1926. After a short period as a student in the School of Architecture at the Georgia Institute of Technology, Dodd enrolled in the Art Students League of New York. He studied with Charles Bridgeman and Boardman Robinson and privately with George Luks, who had achieved his reputation as a member of Robert Henri's circle of urban realists. After a year back in LaGrange devoted entirely to painting, Dodd had his first one-man exhibition at the High Museum of Art in Atlanta. He then returned to the Art Students League for a period of further study with Jean Charlot and John Steuart Curry. The young Georgia artist was thus exposed to a range of gifted teachers who worked in traditional representative modes, most of whom believed in an art that depicted and elevated the everyday scene.

Dodd returned to the South in 1934 and spent the next three years honing his abilities, while holding down a job at an art supply store in Birmingham, Ala. His efforts were rewarded when he received an award at the annual national exhibition at the Art Institute of Chicago in 1936. His paintings in this period were portrayals of ordinary things in his environment that most people would overlook. For example, he made sketches of a slag dump, which he transported into evocative paintings that seemed to convey more than just an outward appearance. "I wanted to create a feeling of solid forms," he recalled of this period, "to capture the mood of a place."

In 1937 Lamar Dodd was named to the faculty of the art school at the University of Georgia at Athens. A short time later he was made head of the art department, and he embarked on a distinguished career as a teacher active in many educational, civic, and professional groups. Within a few years he was named one of the outstanding artists in America, with successful one-man exhibitions in New York at the Ferargil Galleries and in Washington at the Corcoran Gallery. He accepted a visiting professorship at the University of Southern California in 1942 and traveled through the Southwest. Similar jaunts in the Midwest followed, and he became president of the Association of Georgia Artists and of the Southeastern Art Association in 1946. Meanwhile, his painting continued to receive high praise. "What he portrays of Georgia is a more elusive and deeper quality, a turn of mind, a design for living, that may seem clannish to outsiders, but is rich in rewards for those born to it," his friend and former teacher Jean Charlot wrote in 1944. In 1948 Dodd was named Regents Professor of Art at the University of Georgia and assumed the presidency of the Southern States Art League. Many painting awards followed, as the artist gained fame as one of the outstanding painters of the South. By 1950 he had been awarded two Carnegie grants and was elected president of the College Art Association of America.

Lamar Dodd's painting had developed from an initial style of realism based on the language of forms to a more abstract version where formal considerations began to predominate. His paintings depicting cotton pickers toiling in a field, for example, conveyed their mood and situation by means of an expressionistic handling of form and color. "Dodd is a realist in that he finds his inspiration in his environing world," one critic wrote in 1949, "but his translation of his personal reactions to it reveal his subtle perception of the character of his visual experiences and of the relation of the things observed to one another." He was cited as a bold and vigorous colorist who achieved "poetry in the plastic language of the paint itself." Dodd continued to exhibit and lecture widely, including a stint in Europe for the United States Information Service in 1956. He was appointed a charter member of the U.S. Advisory Committee in the Arts the following year and participated in the first cultural exchange between the United States and the Soviet Union in 1958.

Perhaps one of the artist's most interesting honors was his appointment in 1963 as an official NASA artist for the Mercury Astronaut project; he covered Gordon Cooper's orbital spacecraft launching at Cape Canaveral. His resulting work was included in the landmark *Eyewitness to Space* exhibition at the National Gallery of Art in 1965. He again served as NASA artist in 1968 and 1969 for the *Apollo 7* and *Apollo 10* launchings. From this experience the artist produced a series of abstract works, some of which indicate his fascination with the idea described by one reviewer as the "poetic experience of men standing many thousands of miles outside the earth and looking back upon it as persons who are at once infinitely detached and yet very much of the earth." Dodd culminated his outstanding career by painting a frontier that is as yet unexplored; he had succeeded in translating his southern environment into the universal language of art.

Rick Stewart
Dallas Museum of Art

Lamar Dodd, *Lamar Dodd: A Retrospective Exhibition* (1970). ☆

DOUGLAS, AARON

(1898–1979) Painter.

Aaron Douglas is widely regarded as one of the most important figures in the history of Afro-American art in the South, but his achievement is part of the larger history of American art as well. Born in Topeka, Kan., Douglas graduated from the University of Nebraska School of Fine Arts in 1925. A short time after that he moved to New York City, where he immediately came under the influence of Winold Reiss, who had done work based on a study of racial and folk types. Illustrations by both men appeared in Alain Locke's pioneering study, *The New Negro*, which was published that same year and among many other things called for the reexploration of African motifs in black art. Douglas's work appeared in many periodicals during the full flower of the Harlem Renaissance, including *Vanity Fair*, *Opportunity*, *Theatre Arts Monthly*, and important but short-lived little magazines like *Fire* and *Harlem*. In 1927 James Weldon Johnson published his book of sermons in verse titled *God's Trombones*, with striking illustrations by Douglas, whose modernist style had been firmly established. The artist reexamined African and Egyptian forms and interpreted them by means of interlocking forms and colors based on a careful study of cubism and other modernist art movements. His paintings frequently depicted symbolic figures intertwined with planes and shafts of modulated light and subdued, yet rich color. Douglas attempted to convey the mystical or spiritual union of American blacks with their ancestral past through formal techniques that were richly evocative.

The most important work Douglas finished in this period was a series of murals, completed in 1934 under the auspices of the Public Works of Art Project, that portrayed the entire Afro-American experience. Four panels that the artist titled *Song of the Towers* depict, in succession, the African heritage, the Emancipation, life in the rural South, and urban dilemma. Douglas had been invited to execute a series of murals on black life for the library at Fisk University in Nashville, Tenn. In 1937 the artist accepted a teaching position there as head of the art department, a post he held until his retirement in 1966. Douglas's previous associations and friendships, as well as his outstanding ability as a teacher, enabled him to enrich the lives of generations of students. Aaron Douglas was one of the most respected, yet self-effacing, artists of the South in the modern period. To date there has been no adequate study or exhibition of his work, leaving a large gap in the art history of the South.

See also BLACK LIFE: / Johnson, James Weldon

Rick Stewart
Dallas Museum of Art

David C. Driskell, Gregory D. Ridley, and D. L. Graham, *Retrospective Exhibition: Paintings by Aaron Douglas* (1971); Nathan I. Huggins, *Harlem Renaissance* (1971). ☆

EGGLESTON, WILLIAM

(b. 1939) Photographer.

Eggleston was born in Memphis, Tenn., where he still resides. Eggleston photographs in color, using the dye transfer method, which produces colors of such richness and density that the subjects seem palpable; the very atmosphere is perceived—the clarity of a sky, dustiness of a country road, the heat of a fire, or the mustiness of a motel room. He is a master of detecting subject matter that will maximize the characteristics of his medium.

Images from his own cultural experiences as a member of a Delta farming family in northern Mississippi portray the encroachment of the urban-industrial spirit upon a community rooted in the habits and values of cotton farming. Eggleston pictures the abrupt boundaries between city pavements and country roads, suburban houses and rolling fields. His photos are about country people living in the city, and the imposition of urban customs upon them. His images also, conversely, affirm the tenacity of the Delta folkways. Eggleston has exhibited widely, including a one-man color show at the Museum of Modern Art, New York, in 1976. Eggleston photographed John Huston's production of *Annie*, and his work appeared in the 1982 book *Annie on Camera*. He also collaborated with David Byrne and the Talking Heads in the production of the film *True Stories*, and Eggleston's photographs will accompany descriptions of the making of the film in a forthcoming book.

Mary Louise Tucker
New Orleans, Louisiana

John Szarkowski, *William Eggleston's Guide with Essay* (1976). ☆

GWATHMEY, ROBERT

(b. 1903) Painter.

Gwathmey is a major exception to the generalization that the 20th-century renaissance in southern culture had little impact on the visual arts. His paintings reflected the same fascination with the South, its people, and its tradition that was found in the writing of novelists, poets, journalists, and historians of the Southern Renaissance. Like many of them, Gwathmey also felt the need to break free of the oppressiveness of the inherited southern culture and social order. Because his art often depicted sharecroppers and white planters in juxtaposition, it was first characterized as merely a southern version of the social realist painting of the 1930s. Only a few southern museums included his works in their collections, compounding the general problem that paintings were not very accessible to most southerners. This created the phenomenon of an artist who was better known and recognized in New York than in his native region.

Gwathmey, however, always considered himself a southerner. He was born in 1903 in Richmond, Va., where he was educated through high school. By the time he began attending North Carolina State in 1924, he had already had several jobs as a laborer. He received his first formal training in art at the Maryland Institute in Baltimore in 1925 and 1926, but he soon transferred to the prestigious Pennsylvania Academy of Fine Arts. While there, he learned art technique well enough to be awarded two European summer study fellowships. He taught at Beaver College and the Carnegie Institute in Pennsylvania and at the Cooper Union in New York City. A Rosenwald Fellowship enabled him to spend part of 1944 living and sketching on a farm in North Carolina. In the late 1930s he destroyed all his previous paintings and began to focus on southern themes. Some, such as *Poll Tax County* (1945), were bitter critiques of the white-controlled caste and political systems. Others, like *Painting of a Smile* (1953), were more subtle examinations of the vitality of black culture and the decadence of the white ruling class.

Robert Gwathmey,* Hoeing *(1943)

Gwathmey believed the South provided an ideal source of inspiration for the visual artist because of the region's colorful vegetation and soil and its striking contrasts of black and white and of past and present. His complex painting *Space* (1964) incorporates commentary on southern involvement in space exploration as well as on the Freedom Rides and a decaying Confederate cannon and monument. Gwathmey's acceptance in the art world of New York led to a comfortable later life on Long Island with his North Carolina-born wife. His political activism brought him under FBI surveillance during the post–World War II period, and he remained a dissenter, particularly during the Vietnam War era. The largest public collection of his works is at the Hirshhorn Museum of the Smithsonian Institution in Washington, D.C.

Charles K. Piehl
Mankato State University

Paul Robeson, *Robert Gwathmey* (1946). ☆

JOHNSON, WILLIAM HENRY

(1901–1970) Painter.

Johnson was an extremely prolific artist whose most important paintings, drawings, and prints concentrated on the history and culture of black people in the United States and especially the South.

Johnson was born in Florence, S.C., the oldest of four children (he had two sisters and a brother). His mother was black and part Sioux Indian, and his father was white. His name was taken from a stepfather, William Johnson, a sharecropper who became infirm while William Henry was still a boy. The young Johnson left school to work and help support his family. His teacher recalled that he was too poor to afford pencils and paper, but he would draw pictures in the dirt.

At age 17 he left Florence against the wishes of his family, determined to become a painter. He arrived in New York City and worked odd jobs, saving his money and sending some home to his family. In 1921 he was the first Afro-American to enroll in the National Academy of Design. During the next five years he won prizes for his achievements while studying with the noted American painter Charles Hawthorne. In 1926 he left for Europe to paint and remained there until 1938, except for one visit to the United States in 1930.

In 1930 he married Halcha Krake, a Danish ceramicist and weaver, and settled in Odense, Denmark. Together, for the next eight years, they worked in their studios and exhibited their artworks throughout Scandinavia and North Africa. By 1938 Johnson felt he had to return home to the United States to paint the history of his people. Living in Europe was becoming more difficult as World War II approached. He and his wife settled in Harlem, where he began to produce his most important body of work. Most of his paintings, such as *Chain Gang* (1939–40), drew on the southern black experience.

In Europe his work was expressionistic, influenced most by the works of Soutine, Van Gogh, Munch, and Gauguin. Once Johnson returned to New York, his style shifted to pseudo narrative, almost cartoonish in its simplicity. Works such as *Jesus and Three Marys* and *Folk Family* particularly distinguish his style at this time, but the public was shocked by this seemingly radical change.

By the time of his wife's death in 1945, Johnson had already begun to show signs of his own illness in his work and in periods of irrational behavior. After his wife's death, he left the United States with all his works and was found wandering on the streets of Oslo, Norway. He was sent home to the United States and hospitalized at Central Islip, Long Island, suffering from syphillis. Johnson died in 1970. His entire collection represents one of the three largest holdings of a single American artist in the Smithsonian Institution, Washington, D.C.

Leslie King-Hammond
The Maryland Institute,
College of Art

Adelyn D. Breeskin, *William H. Johnson, 1901–1970* (1971); Alain Locke, *The American Magazine of Art* (July–December 1931). ☆

JOHNSTON, FRANCES BENJAMIN

(1864–1952) Photographer.

A native of Grafton, W.Va., Johnston studied art in Paris and at the Art Students League in New York but became dissatisfied with the state of academic American art and turned to newspaper illustration. She sensed the potential of photography in journalism, as it was "the more accurate medium." Johnston acquired a camera and studied under the direction of Thomas William Smillie, then in charge of the Division of Photography at the Smithsonian Institution.

Her first essays concerned political events in the capital. She also photographed the Kohinoor coal mines of Pennsylvania, the Mesabe iron ore range on Lake Superior, and female factory workers in Massachusetts. Johnston did not approach her assignments in the spirit of Jacob Riis, the social reformer, but as an objective reporter. In 1899 she was invited by Hampton Institute, an industrial school for blacks, to dramatize the progress of educated, upwardly mobile students and graduates. That public relations and fund-raising project led to an invitation to Tuskegee Institute in Alabama in 1902; she returned there and through 1906 photographed the students and their renowned educators Booker T. Washington and George Washington Carver. While in the area she also photographed, with dignity and sensitivity, poor, rural folk of Alabama. Throughout her career Johnston made portraits of outstanding Americans, such as Susan B. Anthony, Joel Chandler Harris, Theodore Roosevelt and his family, Samuel Clemens, Andrew Carnegie, Alexander Graham Bell, and Jacob Riis.

An interest in architecture and horticulture led to Johnston's greatest commission; she obtained a grant from the Carnegie Foundation to record southern colonial architecture. From 1933 to 1940, when Johnston was in her late sixties and early seventies, she traveled the Atlantic and Gulf Coast states, documenting every aspect of historic buildings and gardens, from mansions to farm buildings in every condition of repair. Her photographs convey a familiarity with the places and an appreciation for the former inhabitants. Several books resulted from the Carnegie survey, *The Early Architecture of North Carolina* (1941) and *Plantations of the Carolina Low Country* (1938) among them. In 1945 Johnston was awarded an honorary membership in the American Institute of Architects. Johnston lived in semiretirement in New Orleans during her last years and died there in 1952.

Mary Louise Tucker
New Orleans, Louisiana

Pete Daniel and Raymond Smock, *A Talent for Detail: The Photographs of Miss Frances Benjamin Johnston, 1889–1910* (1974). ☆

KOCH, RICHARD

(1889–1971) Architectural designer.

During a 55-year career, Koch established a practice diverse in its design approaches and pioneering in its efforts to preserve and adapt the unique architectural heritage of the South. His knowledge of various styles was clearly seen in his reinterpretation of early 19th-century Louisiana building forms. His fusion of then-current ideas of modern design with traditional forms resulted in his being awarded the Silver Medal of the Architectural League of New York in 1938.

Koch was born in New Orleans on 9 June 1889, the son of Anna Frotscher and Julius Koch, an architect-builder from Germany. In 1910 Richard Koch received his architectural degree from Tulane University and then studied at Atelier Bernier in Paris (1911–12). Between 1913 and 1915 he worked in the offices of Aymar Embury II in New York, John Russell Pope, who designed in Washington, D.C., and William Wells Bosworth in Boston. During this period he came to appreciate the architecture of colonial New England and New York.

In 1916 Koch returned to New Orleans and formed a partnership with Charles R. Armstrong, an association that lasted until 1935, interrupted only by Koch's duty as a first lieutenant in the Air Service of the U.S. Army from 1916 to 1918.

Early in his career Richard Koch established a reputation with his sensitive renovations of several important buildings in the Vieux Carré of New Orleans and followed these with work on two noted plantation houses (Shadows-on-the-Teche in 1922 and Oak Alley in 1926). At Le Petit Theatre du Vieux Carré in 1922 he designed a new auditorium in a carefully detailed rendition of an earlier style—one of the first modern buildings in the French Quarter to be designed in this way.

The period 1933 to 1938 seems to have been a watershed in Koch's career; in 1933 he was appointed district officer for the Historic American Buildings Survey in Louisiana. In this capacity he directed teams of architects in making measured drawings of some of the finest early buildings in the state. This close examination of local historic buildings purged his original designs of elements not typical of the Creole and American Federal traditions—notably the Spanish influence seen in much of his work during the 1920s. His sensitivity to the historic environment led him to design quite differently in the Garden District of New Orleans from the way he did in the French Quarter, and to work in the Anglo-American tradition in Mississippi and the French tradition in south Louisiana.

In 1935 Armstrong left the partnership, and in the same year a new associate, Samuel Wilson, Jr., joined his firm; Wilson became a partner in 1955. Together, these two executed many more restorations, renovations, and new designs (some frankly modern, some in Koch's fusion style, and some in strictly historical styles). Koch's practice was always diverse—ranging from fine residences to offices, shops, banks, hospitals, and warehouses.

Koch served as president of the National Architectural Accrediting Board in 1954, and he was made a fellow of the American Institute of Architects in 1938. Koch continued to practice until his death on 20 September 1971.

Frank W. Masson
New Orleans, Louisiana

Hermande de Bachelleseebold, *Old Louisiana Plantation Homes and Family Ties*, vol. 2 (1941); William R. Cullison, *Louisiana History* (Fall 1977); New Orleans *Times-Picayune* (21 September 1971). ☆

LAUGHLIN, CLARENCE JOHN

(1905–1985) Photographer.

Laughlin was born near New Iberia, La., in 1905. Five years later his family moved to New Orleans. Laughlin's early interest in the works of the pre-Raphaelite school led to a stronger intellectual commitment to the French symbolist writers—Baudelaire, Mallarmé, and Bergson. Their works confirmed his disillusion with the state of post-Depression society, an environment of decay, corruption, and poverty of spirit. Remnants of the past grandeur of Louisiana—the plantation houses, the mausoleums and tombs of its cemeteries, the colonial architecture of the city—became the constructs of his imagination and served his preference for an age that had vanished and his reaction against realism in an age of industrialization. Through contemporary magazines, Laughlin became aware of the work of Stieglitz, Strand, Atget, and Man Ray; the latter two artists especially reinforced his impulses for symbolism and surrealism. Laughlin's photographic vision was completely at odds with the popular pictorial style or the straight photography of artists such as Edward Weston or Ansel Adams. But Laughlin gained national recognition when his photographs were exhibited in New York in 1940 with those of Atget. The following year he published *New Orleans and the Living Past.*

During World War II Laughlin worked for the signal corps. After his discharge he returned to photography, working especially as a free-lance architectural photographer. In 1948 he published the monumental *Ghosts along the Mississippi*, began a long career of lecturing, and produced seven traveling photo exhibitions. *Ghosts along the Mississippi* was reissued in 1968.

Prior to his death in 1985, Laughlin remained active with his photography, book collecting, and writing. He did not feel the visual image self-sufficient, and added his own captions to amplify or clarify specific symbolism. Laughlin felt that his images provide clues to the mysterious forces that energize all living things.

Mary Louise Tucker
New Orleans, Louisiana

Mary Louise Tucker, *Modern Photography* (April 1977). ☆

McCRADY, JOHN

(1911–1968) Painter.

John McCrady, best known as a painter of life in the South in the period between the two world wars, was born in the rectory of Grace Church in Canton, Miss. Soon after, his family moved first to Greenwood, Miss., and then to Hammond, La., where his father served as rector of the Episcopal church. In 1928 the family moved to Oxford, Miss., where the young McCrady eventually entered the University of Mississippi. His interest in art was already apparent, and during the summers in 1931 and 1932, he visited his brother in Philadelphia, where he enrolled in courses at the Pennsylvania Academy of Fine Arts. In 1932 he went to New Orleans and prepared for classes in the Arts and Crafts Club. After only a year's study he received a coveted scholarship to the Art Students League in New York City. There he studied very briefly with Thomas Hart Benton and much longer, and with more effect on his art, with Kenneth Hayes Miller. The influence of Miller's weighty figural style can be seen clearly on McCrady's subsequent work, and it was Miller as well who introduced the young southern artist to the multistage technique of painting, which used thin oil glazes over a tempera ground to achieve a brilliance and depth of surface.

McCrady returned to New Orleans in 1934 and within a year exhibited his work at the landmark exhibition *Thirty-Five Painters of the Deep South* at the Boyer Galleries in Philadelphia. The following year he was given his first one-man exhibition at the same galleries and had joined the Federal Arts Project of the Works Progress Administration. In 1937 the artist received national acclaim when his works, including the famous painting titled *Swing Low, Sweet Chariot*, were shown in New York. He was given a five-page spread in *Life* magazine, was praised by Stark Young in the pages of the *New Republic*, and was singled out by *Time* as "the purest example of regional art that turned up during the year." Such praise was high indeed in an age when regionalism was elevated to the status of a national religion, but in terms of southern culture McCrady was one of many talented artists in the period who chose to return to their own surroundings as inspiration for their art. McCrady was instrumental in the formation in 1938 of A New Southern Group, a New Orleans association of painters, sculptors, and graphic artists. He was commissioned by *Life* to paint "the second in a series of dramatic scenes in 20th Century American History," and chose the shooting of Huey

Long. The same year, 1939, he received a Guggenheim fellowship to travel throughout the South to record the life and faith of the southern black, a trip that resulted in many notes and sketches.

In 1942 McCrady opened an art school in the Vieux Carré in New Orleans and began to receive the many commissions that would come to him throughout his artistic life. Although McCrady was praised by the American Institute of Arts and Letters in 1949 for his "warm poetic vision of life in the South," his work did not escape criticism as a "flagrant example of racial chauvinism." To contemporary eyes, McCrady's works do occasionally suffer from an overabundance of stereotype and caricature, but he was a product of his time, wrapped securely in the folk mythology of his native region. In his later years McCrady devoted much of his time to teaching and writing. As late as 1963 he pioneered what was termed the carbon acrylic method of painting, where a carbon sketch on a watercolor board served as the ground, over which were layered a number of acrylic glazes.

Rick Stewart
Dallas Museum of Art

Keith Marshall, *John McCrady, 1911–1968* (1975); *New Republic* (3 November 1937). ☆

MILLS, ROBERT

(1781–1855) Architect.

Born in Charleston, S.C., Robert Mills is often said to be the first native-born American to train specifically for a career in architecture. He served (c. 1799–1801) as an apprentice and draftsman under James Hoban during the construction of the White House, then enjoyed the use of Jefferson's architectural library and executed drawings for the new president. With letters of introduction from Jefferson, Mills toured the seaboard as far north as Boston. In 1803 he entered the office of Benjamin Henry Latrobe and worked in and about Philadelphia until 1809. In that year he married Eliza Barnwell Smith of Winchester, Va., and began his own practice as an architect and engineer in Philadelphia.

While still with Latrobe, Mills proved his competence with the plans for the South Carolina College (Columbia, 1802), the Circular Church (Charleston, 1804), the First Presbyterian Church (Augusta, Ga., 1807), and the Sansom Street Church and wings for Independence Hall (Philadelphia, 1808). His reputation was established in 1812 when he won the design competition for the Monumental Church in Richmond, Va. Here, and in his Burlington Jail (Mount Holly, N.J., 1808), his commitment to fireproof construction was manifest.

His design for the Washington Monument in Baltimore (1814) brought national acclaim. Based upon Trajan's Column, it was the first major monument to George Washington. A depression slowed construction of the monument, and in 1820 Mills moved his family to South Carolina, where he became the civil and military engineer of the state. During the ensuing decade he built canals, published an atlas and a description of the state, worked as a cartographer, and designed the South Carolina Insane Asylum (Columbia, 1821), the fireproof County Records Office (Charleston, 1822), and numerous less notable structures. This interlude in South Carolina may be viewed as a period of preparation for his return to Washington (1830) and his subsequent service to the federal government.

Although busy, he skirted poverty for five years. Then in 1836 the final phase of his career began auspiciously with the design for the U.S. Treasury and his appointment by Andrew Jackson as federal architect, a post he held until 1842. For the federal government he developed a series of customs houses and marine hospitals from Newburyport, Mass., to Mobile, Ala.; he designed the Patent Office (1839) and worked on various modifications of the U.S. Capitol. He also found time for private clients and for writing about municipal waterworks, navigation, railroads, and a route to the Pacific. In 1846 his design for the Washington Monument in Washington, D.C., was published. Despite significant modifications during construction (it was not completed until 1884), this remains his most famous work.

Robert Mills's career mirrored the early evolution of architecture as a profession in America. Aesthetically, his work reflected the growing impact of American pragmatism upon the revival styles of the 19th century. He was a major force in shaping the architectural landscape of the South and, like other southerners in the early Republic, he made vital contributions to the cultural form of the new nation.

John Morrill Bryan
University of South Carolina

John Morrill Bryan, *An Architectural History of the South Carolina College, 1801–1855* (1976), *Robert Mills, Architect, 1781–1855* (1976); Helen Mar Pierce Gallagher, *Robert Mills: Architect of the Washington Monument, 1781–1855* (1935). ☆

MIZNER, ADDISON

(1872–1933) Architect.

Born in Benicia, Calif., Addison Cairns Mizner revived a Spanish-style architecture in Florida and exerted a major influence on the development of Palm Beach. Although he had no formal training in architecture and, in fact, earned no degrees, he did study design in Guatemala and at the University of Salamanca, Spain. More importantly for his architectural career, he acquired practical experience while apprenticed from 1893 to 1896 to the architect Willis Polk in San Francisco and gained a broad knowledge of architecture from his extensive travels in China, Central America, and Europe. While in Guatemala, Mizner began trading in antiques and art. He finally received his license to practice architecture in 1919 from the state of Florida on the basis of the state's grandfather clause.

In 1904 Mizner settled in New York. From his society connections he soon had an active practice consisting principally of additions, renovations, and the design of new residences in New York State and throughout the Northeast. But most of his work, and the part on which his fame rests, was done in the South. In 1918 Mizner went to Florida to convalesce from an accident. That same year he designed the Everglades Club in Palm Beach for Paris Singer. The design of this exclusive club, Spanish-inspired with a flavor of Islam, was a grand architectural success. The club set the style for the rapidly growing winter resort and established Mizner's reputation. During the 1920s Mizner designed more than 100 buildings including clubs, theaters, hotels, entertainment complexes, and some of the grandest estates and mansions in the country. His designs are characterized by the integration of interior rooms with exterior patios and courtyards, richly ornamented interiors, and elaborate portals.

In order to build his designs exactly, Mizner established his own factories for the manufacture of terra cotta, cast-iron, and cast-stone ornament and of new and "antique" furniture. Mizner also ventured into the field of city planning. He was responsible for the layout of the new resort of Boca Raton. These recreational facilities and hotels were finished before the Florida land collapse of 1926, which left Mizner bankrupt. While he continued to receive some commissions, he spent these last years of his life writing *The Many Mizners* (1932), an entertaining biography of his family.

Mizner single-handedly gave form and style to Palm Beach; his theatrical and picturesque architecture embodied the extravagant vacation lifestyle of the famous and wealthy. In the 1920s Mizner ranked as one of the United States's most prominent architects.

Karen Kingsley
Tulane University

Donald W. Curl, *Mizner's Florida: American Resort Architecture* (1984); Addison Cairns Mizner and Ida M. Tarbell, *The Florida Architecture of Addison Mizner* (1928); Anona Christina Orr-Cahall, "An Identification and Discussion of the Architecture and Decorative Arts of Addison Mizner (1872–1933)" (Ph.D. dissertation, Yale University, 1979). ☆

SOUTHERN STATES ART LEAGUE

The Southern States Art League, first named the All Southern Art Association, was created in 1921 to make possible the comprehensive exhibition of art about the South, including the best efforts of southern artists. Those artists judged excellent enough to represent the South did so at annual exhibitions, which were held in major southern cities, and at traveling circuit exhibitions that moved throughout the South.

The goals of the Southern States Art League were to increase public awareness of the talent of southern artists, to improve the artists' status, to encourage patronage and sales of members' works, to educate the public through traveling exhibitions of members' art, to hold a yearly conference to address issues important to the artists, and to publish a monthly newsletter to keep the membership informed. The league hoped to further art education in the South and therefore to assist the southern public in developing a sense of art values. It encouraged the formation of art programs at various southern schools and universities and stressed the need to develop southern art colonies. The league also hoped to enter the political arena and support legislation in Congress that would benefit the artist.

Although the Southern States Art League was chartered in 1921 in Charleston, S.C., administrative offices moved to New Orleans in 1923. Ellsworth Woodward (chairman of the Newcomb College School of Art) was at that time elected president, an office he held until his death in 1939. Ethel Hutson of New Orleans served as secretary until 1947. Membership grew steadily each year, although many members became inactive during the Depression and World War II. The Southern States Art League's records list membership as topping 600 in 1933, but actual names of artists in the records only number 425.

Yearly conventions in major southern cities provided a place for artists to meet, discuss pertinent issues, and exhibit and sell their works, and for the public to view and purchase southern art. The annual convention's exhibition drew increasing numbers of visitors every year, totaling 12,000 at the annual exhibition in Nashville, Tenn., in 1935. The traveling circuit exhibitions were the most effective means of making southern art available to southerners. Two circuits traveled every year, each displaying 30 or so works in large cities and small towns alike. Sales at conventions and traveling circuit exhibitions were usually quite low.

Evaluating the quality of the works shown is difficult; records indicate some titles, but few photographs survive, nor have more than a handful of originals been traced. Landscapes, flower paintings, and genre scenes seem to have dominated. League President Ellsworth Woodward regularly exhorted members to submit only top-quality works of art, but his admonitions often were not heeded.

With the death of Ellsworth Woodward in 1939 the league was weakened. James Chillman, director of the Houston Museum of Fine Arts, became president, but the headquarters remained in New Orleans. When Chillman retired in 1947, Benjamin E. Shute of Atlanta became president. The last conference was held in Richmond, Va., in the same year. Shute resigned within one year, and then Lamar Dodd took over, followed by Joseph Hutchinson of the Mint Museum in Charlotte, N.C. The league was officially dissolved in 1950.

Amy Kirschke
Tulane University

Amy Kirschke, "The Southern States Art League: An Overview" (M.A. thesis, Tulane University, 1983). ☆

VALENTINE, EDWARD VIRGINIUS

(1838–1930) Sculptor.

The son of a prosperous merchant and a member of a family that had lived in Virginia since the middle of the 17th century, Valentine was born in Richmond, where he received his early education from tutors and private schools. He later attended the University of Virginia. Awarded a silver medal for a bust of the Apollo Belvedere in 1855, he began studying anatomy at the Medical College of Virginia the following year. After exhausting the resources of local artists, Valentine went abroad for further study. He studied in London in 1859, in Paris in 1859 and 1860, and in Italy in 1861. In 1861 Valentine went to Berlin, where he studied with the eminent August Kiss until the latter's death four years later. He then returned to Richmond and opened a studio as the Civil War was drawing to an end.

Though Reconstruction Richmond would seem to have been an unlikely place for a sculptor to practice his art, Valentine was successful in obtaining commissions and in selling genre sculptures. After Robert E. Lee's death late in 1870, Valentine received his most inspiring commission—the creation of a recumbent memorial statue of the general for the mausoleum attached to the Lee Chapel at Washington and Lee University. This work is undoubtedly Valentine's finest and most highly acclaimed work.

Valentine's Richmond studio teemed with activity during the 1880s and 1890s. During that period he was the South's best-known sculptor, and numerous examples of his work survive. In addition to his recumbent statue of Lee, among his best are his bronze standing figure of Lee for the Capitol's Statuary Hall in Washington; his statue of Thomas Jefferson for Richmond's Jefferson Hotel; and his bronze statue of Jefferson Davis atop the Davis monument in Richmond. Valentine remained active until his death in Richmond in 1930.

Post–Civil War southerners, by necessity, emphasized the practical and thereby tended to neglect—and sometimes even to smother—the creative spirit. Sculpture especially suffered from this mood and from the poverty that provoked it. Frequently viewed as exotic, sculpture was also expensive. Much of the more elaborate and impressive statuary executed in the postwar South was the work of imported hands. In Edward Virginius Valentine, however, the South produced a native-born sculptor who created works worthy of note. Valentine and his fellow sculptors taught a later generation of southerners that statuary could be an important source of inspiration. Through his sculpture Valentine hoped to give his ideals to the world and to remind southerners of the best of their heritage.

L. Moody Simms, Jr.
Illinois State University

L. Moody Simms, Jr., *Virginia Cavalcade* (Summer 1970); Elizabeth G. Valentine, *Dawn to Twilight: Work of Edward V. Valentine* (1929). ☆

WEST, WILLIAM EDWARD

(1788–1857) Painter.

West was born in Lexington, Ky., on 10 December 1788 to Edward West, Jr., a Virginian who had moved to Kentucky in 1784, and Maria Creed Brown. At an early age William Edward West traveled the Ohio and Mississippi rivers to Natchez and New Orleans and began an association with the Evans and Turner families of the Natchez region, whose relations and friends would provide his most important commissions.

West visited Philadelphia, possibly as early as 1808, where he met Washington Irving and Thomas Sully, two lifelong friends and influences. Although it seems unlikely that he actually studied with Sully, West undoubtedly observed Sully's painting techniques, absorbing those technical aspects of coloration Sully had witnessed in Gilbert Stuart's work. While in Philadelphia, West painted several members of the Gratz family. In the second decade of the 19th century West worked and traveled between Philadelphia and New Orleans. He had studios in Philadelphia (1809–17) and in New Orleans (1817–19) but was most productive in Natchez (1817–19).

West undertook more formal art study in Florence, Italy, and while he was there, George K. Bruen of New York commissioned a portrait of Lord Byron, the English romantic poet, for the American Academy in New York. West went to the poet's villa in Pisa and did the portrait. West lived in Florence until

1825, when he moved to Paris. One of West's best works, an allegorical portrait called *The Muses*, was painted there in 1825, the year West departed Paris for London.

Having gained notoriety as the last portraitist of Byron, West embarked upon a 12-year career as a highly successful Anglo-Saxon painter. He painted many of the most prominent members of the American financial and diplomatic community, and several of the genre or literary paintings that West exhibited at the Royal Academy were well received, especially *Annette Delarbre*, drawn from a story of Washington Irving. West also painted the English poetess Felicia Hemans, with whom he enjoyed a warm correspondence.

From 1832 to 1837 West was involved in financial speculations that left him bankrupt. He returned to Baltimore and opened a studio on Baltimore Street. The young Robert E. Lee, stopping en route to military engineering duties at St. Louis, was painted by West in 1838. West's Baltimore retrenchment was the most productive and successful period in his life. He repaid all his debts in England and amassed enough money to move into semiretirement in New York in 1841.

Throughout the 1840s West lived in New York City, painting various members of the Delano and Astor families and occasionally other New York society figures. He visited and traveled with Washington Irving and exhibited at the American Artist's Union. *The Confessional*, a religious picture, was much admired by Irving and was acquired by Thomas Jefferson Bryan for his "Christian Art" collection. In the late 1840s and early 1850s West painted the last of his Natchez commissions. In 1855 West moved to Nashville, Tenn., to live among his family, and there he died on 2 November 1857. He is buried in the old city cemetery.

West's early work has the spare elegance of the neoclassical portraits of Stuart and Sully. He was a superb colorist, and his portraits were marked by strong characterization and freshness and by deep and richly luminous eyes. A maturing of his style occurred during the years in Italy. An infatuation with mannerist composition revealed itself in his literary and allegorical pictures, especially *The Muses* and *The Present*, two of his finest works. His mature portraits, especially that of Lee, rank among the best work of the 19th century.

Estill Curtis Pennington
Lauren Rogers Museum of Art

William Dunlap, *History of the Rise and Progress of the Arts of Design in the United States* (1834; reprint 1969); Estill Curtis Pennington, *William Edward West (1788–1857): Kentucky Painter* (1985); Henry T. Tuckerman, *Book of the Artists, American Artist Life* (1867; reprint 1940); William Edward West Papers, Catalog of American Portraits, National Portrait Gallery, Smithsonian Institution, Washington, D.C. ☆

WIENER, SAMUEL G.

(1896–1977) Architect.

Wiener was one of the earliest practitioners of modern architecture (the international style) in the United States and introduced the style to the South. Born in Monroe, La., Wiener received his bachelor of architecture degree from the University of Michigan in 1920 and attended the Atelier Gromort, Paris, in 1922 and 1923. He was the Shreveport partner in the Louisiana architectural firm of Jones, Roessle, Olschner, and

Wiener from 1925 to 1940, after which he established a separate practice. Wiener's work of the 1920s employs a wide range of then-fashionable historical styles as well as art deco, of which the Municipal Auditorium, Shreveport (1929), is a particularly splendid example. In 1928 Wiener published *Venetian Houses and Details*. An increasing interest in the new European architecture he saw illustrated in architectural journals inspired a study visit to Europe for several months in 1931. Wiener's work after his return to Shreveport shows a complete break with the past and a total commitment to the ideals and forms of European modernism. During the 1930s Wiener was responsible for all his firm's work in the modern idiom. Wiener also accepted private commissions and sometimes worked in collaboration with his younger brother, William Wiener (1907–81), a 1929 graduate of the University of Michigan with an architectural practice in Shreveport.

Among the residences designed by Sam Wiener are the Wile-Schober House (1934) and the Flesh-Walker-Guillot House (1936), both in Shreveport, and a weekend house on Cross Lake (1933) in collaboration with his brother William. Particularly noteworthy is Sam Wiener's own residence designed in 1937. Other work includes the El Karubah Club on Cross Lake (1931); the Big Chain Store (1940); and several schools, including Bossier High School (1938–40). The very fine Shreveport Orthopedic Clinic (1936) was demolished in the 1970s. Wiener's major work was the Shreveport Municipal Incinerator built in 1935 from Public Works Administration funds. Photographs of the incinerator were exhibited in the U.S. Pavilion at the Paris International Exposition of 1937 as one of the best examples of modern architecture in the United States and in exhibits organized by the Museum of Modern Art, New York. The incinerator photographs, also published extensively in major international and national architectural journals, brought Wiener much acclaim.

Although in startling formal contrast to traditional southern architecture, Wiener's buildings were designed for regional climatic conditions. His use of linear plans and wrap-around corner windows allows cross-ventilation; the light-colored walls have a cooling effect on the buildings; and planar overhangs protect interiors from the sun. Wiener's designs acquired a local character without reducing the ideals and formal qualities of modernism. Although Wiener maintained an active practice after 1940, his later work never matched the originality and boldness of his 1930s designs. Sam Wiener was a major contributor to and advocate of modern architecture in the United States.

Karen Kingsley
Tulane University

Architectural Forum (November 1935); Karen Kingsley, *Modernism in Louisiana: A Decade of Progress, 1930–1940* (1984). ☆

BLACK LIFE

THOMAS C. HOLT

University of Chicago

CONSULTANT

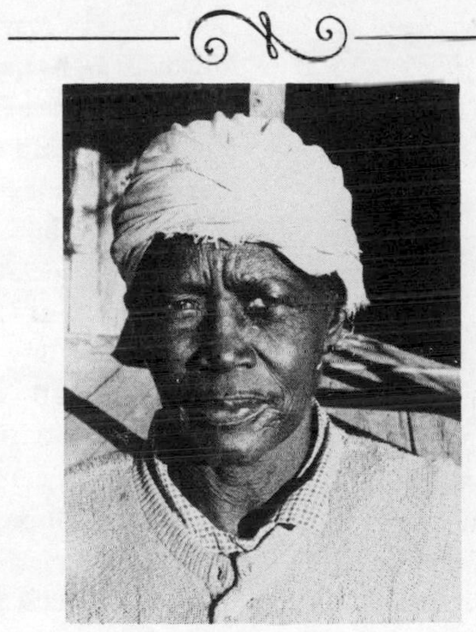

☆ ☆ ☆ ☆ ☆ ☆ ☆ ☆ ☆ ☆

Black Life 223

African Influences 230
Appalachians, Black 231
Architecture, Black 235
Art, Black 239
Business, Black 242
Creolization 245
Dance, Black 248
Education, Black 252
Family, Black 256
Film Images, Black 259
Folklore, Black 262
Fraternal Orders, Black 265
Freedom Movement, Black 267
Funerary Customs, Black 271
Genealogy, Black 273
Health, Black 276

Immigrants and Blacks 279
Indians and Blacks 281
Landownership, Black 283
Literary Portrayals of Blacks 286
Literature, Black 289
Lynching 294
Migration, Black 297
Miscegenation 300
Music, Black 303
Northern Cities, Blacks in 306
Politics, Black 310
Preacher, Black 312
Press, Black 314
Race Relations 318
Religion, Black 323
Slave Culture 326
Speech, Black 329
Sports, Blacks In 333
Theater, Black 335
Towns, Black 337
Workers, Black 339

Bethune, Mary McLeod 342
Bond, Julian 343
Bontemps, Arna 344
Chesnutt, Charles W. 345
Citizens' Councils 346
Commission on Interracial Cooperation (CIC) 347
Congress of Racial Equality (CORE) 349
Douglass, Frederick 350
Du Bois, W. E. B 352
Evers, Medgar 353
Franklin, John Hope 354
Free Southern Theater 355
Gaines, Ernest J. 357
Greensboro Sit-in. *See* LAW: Greensboro Sit-in
Haley, Alex 358
Hamer, Fannie Lou 359
Hancock, Gordon Blaine 361
Hurston, Zora Neale 362
Jackson, Jesse 363
Jim Crow 364
Johnson, Charles S. 365
Johnson, James Weldon 367
Johnson, Robert 368
Juneteenth 369
King, Martin Luther, Jr. 369
Lynch, John Roy 371
Mardi Gras Indians 372
Mason, Charles Harrison 373
Mays, Benjamin 374
Meredith, James 375
Murray, Pauli 376
National Association for the Advancement of Colored People (NAACP) 377
Negro Baseball Leagues 378
Sea Islands 379
Selma March 381
Silas Green Show 381
Southern Christian Leadership Conference (SCLC) 383
Storyville 384
Student Nonviolent Coordinating Committee (SNCC) 385
Toomer, Jean 387
Turner, Nat 388
Walker, Margaret 389
Washington, Booker T. 390
Wells-Barnett, Ida 391
"We Shall Overcome" 393
Williams, Robert F. 394
Woodson, Carter G. 395

Overleaf: Rural Mississippi woman, 1970s

BLACK LIFE

Pre–Civil War Slave-Master Relations. On the eve of the Civil War the overwhelming majority of black Americans were southerners. They were an essential part of the South's labor force, raising its tobacco, cotton, hemp, and rice; mining its coal, salt, and gold; manning its few modern industries, such as textiles and ironworks; and building its railroads. Most performed these jobs as slaves. A minority were free. These free blacks worked in cities of the Lower South as craftsmen and as menial laborers and as owners or hired laborers on the farms of the Upper South. Slavery required a docile and cheap labor force; but at its margins it also permitted skilled black artisans, who claimed a proud, if tenuous, economic independence.

Civil War to World War I: Sharecroppers, Tenants, and Planters. In the decades between the Civil War and World War I, the overwhelming majority of black Americans remained in the rural South, working its farms and mines, while a growing minority labored in its cities. Black farm workers found themselves enmeshed in a system of tenancy and sharecropping that made a mockery of the freedom promised by the abolition of slavery. Black urban dwellers found themselves excluded from many of the crafts their fathers had worked before the war and from the newly developing southern industries. In both the cities and the countryside, blacks were subjected to a virulent racism, excluded from public institutions, denied normal social intercourse, and victimized by racist violence. During the century following emancipation, these economic and social structures of exploitation and exclusion decisively shaped northern as well as southern black life and culture.

Sharecropping and tenancy evolved after the Civil War and tied both blacks and whites to the land until the 1930s, giving way finally under economic and political pressures of New Deal agricultural reforms and war-induced demographic shifts. Well over 80 percent of black Americans lived on farms in the rural South in the late 19th century, and sharecropping touched their social, political, and economic lives.

Sharecropping and tenancy took shape during the first decade after the Civil War as the result of a standoff in the struggle between planters and their former slaves. Planters sought to maintain maximum control over their laborers, a control in which blacks saw uncomfortable similarities to slavery. For their part, the newly freed blacks wanted to escape the plantation, to have a farm and to make their own choices about where, when, and how their families lived and worked. But in order to achieve these goals they needed land.

Unfortunately, all government efforts at land reform for the benefit of the former slaves had failed. During the final months of the war, thousands of 40-acre plots had been distributed to black families along the South Carolina and

Georgia coasts, and Congress passed legislation to facilitate permanent purchases by these settlers. But in the ensuing political struggle between Congress and President Andrew Johnson over Reconstruction policy, the settlers were eventually evicted. In 1866 a homestead law was passed to assist blacks in purchasing public land in the South; but the indifference and incompetence of federal officials charged with administering the law, the poor quality of the land, and the lack of material assistance to the settlers in clearing and developing the plots severely limited the law's effectiveness.

Despite the failure of these governmental initiatives, many blacks were able to purchase farms. Indeed, by 1900 one of every four black farmers owned his land. These successes occurred outside the major plantation areas of the Deep South. For the overwhelming majority of black people just emerging from the rigors of slavery, even the relatively low land prices of the postwar era were beyond their means. Furthermore, those who could scrape together the money experienced great difficulty getting white landowners to sell to them. In fact, black landowners were often targets of racial violence in the 1860s and 1870s.

Following emancipation there was a substantial reduction in the work force—as much as 37 percent by some economists' estimate—primarily because women, children, and the elderly greatly reduced the labor they gave to white estates. There were also collective work stoppages every year between 1865 and 1867. These "job actions," in which workers refused to sign or renew their contracts for the following year, panicked planters and forced wages up and improved working conditions.

Planters, despite their expressed preferences for a wage-and-gang labor system, were hard pressed to actually meet a payroll. Workers complained of not receiving the pay due them or receiving it late. The planters, who had always operated on credit in slavery days, simply did not command the credit to obtain cash for day-to-day operations. After emancipation they lost an important source of wealth and credit, because slaves represented as much as half the value of their property. The value of their other main asset, land, fell to historic lows. The planter—whatever his preferences regarding labor arrangements to replace slavery—found himself in a difficult position. He still had his land, but it was worth less than before the war and, in fact, was worthless if he could not get labor to work it.

Although southerners experimented with a number of other tenure and pay arrangements during the first decade following the Civil War, by the 1880s sharecropping and share tenancy were the dominant practices on tobacco and cotton farms. In this system the planter paid the worker with a share of the crop (usually half) at the end of the year rather than cash every day, week, or month. The worker and his family were assigned a plot of land to till and did not have to work in labor gangs under the direct supervision of the planter or his overseer, a practice they associated with slavery. The situation *looked like* a family farm even though blacks did not own the land.

But appearances were deceiving. In time the sharecropping arrangement came more and more to resemble a wage labor system with wages paid in kind. The planter controlled all matters related to the production and marketing of the crop. Indeed, the cropper could easily recognize his demeaned status by contrasting it with the situation of the share tenant. Southern tenants were mostly white, while black farmers were mostly croppers. Unlike croppers, tenants supplied their own tools, animals, and provisions and paid a share of the crop (usually a fourth of the cotton and a third of the corn) as rent. On rice and sugarcane properties the racial differences were sharper still: blacks worked for wages and tenancy was a status reserved for whites only.

Neither tenants nor sharecroppers prospered under the system. The landowner had solved his immediate credit problems by paying for labor in kind rather than in cash, but the farmer still needed credit to buy food, clothing, fertilizer, and other necessities for himself and his family until the crop came in. He received this credit from local merchants either directly or through the planter, but at an inflated cost. There were high markups on goods purchased on credit as compared to those bought with cash. A recent study found records from the 1880s showing markups, that is credit costs, ranging from 44 percent to 75 percent and averaging 59 percent. This was at a time when short-term interest rates in New York City were between 4 and 6 percent.

Given these extraordinary credit costs, it is easy to see how southern sharecroppers found it difficult to make ends meet. When the system was inaugurated in the 1870s, cotton prices were relatively high—around 30 and 40 cents a pound—but in the 1880s and 1890s the bubble of King Cotton burst on the world market, and by the 1890s depression it was down to 5 cents a pound. Farmers fell deeper in debt, and their debts were simply carried over from one year to another.

The plantation landlord and tenant farmer, historian Paul Mertz writes, became "graphic symbols of the South's ruralism, poverty, and cultural backwardness." They were symbols too of its paternalism, exploitation, and class oppression. The alliance formed between planters and merchants—sometimes cemented by marriages, family ties, or land purchases and defaulted mortgages—achieved a control over black labor and society that even slaveholders might have envied.

The sharecropping system and its attendant institutions imposed white supremacy on rural blacks, but a growing, significant minority of blacks lived in southern cities. Although most were menial day laborers, laundresses, and domestics, others continued prewar traditions of black craftsmanship. In cities like Charleston and New Orleans free blacks had dominated certain trades before the Civil War. Often they had been targets of protests by white workers resenting their competition. In the racial climate of the late 19th century, these protests bore fruit as blacks were increasingly excluded from their traditional trades, like carpentry, and denied access to skilled occupations tied to new technologies such as electricity. Black laborers were also turned away from cotton mills, the hope and symbol of the New South renaissance.

Excluded from the southern economic mainstream, blacks were also denied basic amenities of social life and opportunities for personal development. By the early 1900s public accommodations, transportation, schools, and the ballot box were either inaccessible or were accessible only under degrading and demeaning conditions. Blacks resisted the imposition of this American-style apartheid with bus and streetcar boycotts and court actions and by attempting political and economic alliances with various white dissidents, like the Populists and the Knights of Labor. But most of their traditional allies in the North, influenced by the rising racist tide, had deserted them; the national government was hostile, and the federal courts endorsed the southern system. Black initiatives and challenges brought forth greater violence as race rioters and lynch mobs terrorized black communities. In this setting, men who counseled acquiescence and accommodation, like Booker T. Washington, gained support from blacks and whites; while those insisting upon renewed and militant resistance, like W. E. B. Du Bois and Ida Wells-Barnett, made little headway before the massive demographic changes of World War I and the interwar years set in motion the winds of social change.

Post–World War I Struggles for Racial Equality. The economic opportunities created by World War I and World War II stimulated a dramatic exodus of blacks away from their ancestral roots in the rural South to the cities of the North and West. At the turn of the century, 90 percent of American blacks were southerners, an overwhelming majority of whom lived on farms. By 1960 only one of every two remained in the South, and only one of four lived in rural areas.

In addition to the attractions of industrial jobs and a seemingly more liberal racial climate in the North, blacks were driven out of the rural South by a massive transformation of southern agriculture. The Great Depression brought national attention to the problems associated with sharecropping and tenancy. But government policies intended to solve the problem of depressed commodity prices by reducing production had the effect of encouraging mechanization, farm consolidation, and the reduction of farm labor. Increasingly planters turned to seasonal wage laborers and turned their tenants off the land.

These changes facilitated the greatest political mobilization of black Americans since the Reconstruction era. Freed from the constraints of the rural South, blacks organized in both formal and informal political arenas. Beginning in the North during the 1920s, but spreading to southern cities by the 1940s and 1950s, blacks organized to protest segregation, Jim Crow, and job discrimination. With the advent of the New Deal, blacks became an important factor in national politics, and federal executive and judicial policies reflected the change. These political changes, together with a greatly augmented black intelligentsia and the revival of racial liberalism in the aftermath of Nazism, were essential precursors to the southern civil rights movement, which emerged full-blown in the late 1950s. When that movement had run its course, the face of southern institutions was radically transformed, as blacks voted and held office in unprecedented numbers, decisively influenced presidential politics, and enticed traditional white foes, like Governor George Wallace of Alabama, to recant their earlier racist views.

Cultural Support Systems Among Blacks. The resources for this black militancy were not only in the demographic and geopolitical changes of post–World War II America, but in the inner recesses of the black community—in its institutions and its culture. In "freedom" as in slavery black people depended on cultural support systems provided by community and kin to survive degradation and oppression. In the rural South black families were the essential units embedded within an extended, intergenerational network of kin and friends that embraced secular and religious institutions. Churches, mutual aid associations, and schools were all peopled by parents, grandparents, aunts, cousins, and fictive kinfolk. Even in slavery blacks created customs, ceremonies, and rituals that reinforced their communal values and institutional ties. In freedom these cultural practices multiplied as weddings, funerals, church "homecomings," and family reunions provided occasions for renewing ties between individuals and their communities.

After kinship, religion was the most important value in southern black life. Slaves were not converted to Christianity in significant numbers until the era of the American Revolution and the creation of the Republic. But the specific content of religious doctrine mattered less than the institution of the independent black church. Free blacks established their own churches almost from the outset. Although slaves worshipped with their masters, they also held separate services led by their own slave preachers. With emancipation religious separation became open and formal as former slaves left their masters' churches to establish their own houses of worship. Churches provided venues for self-expression, affirmation of self-worth, and leadership in the black community from Reconstruction to the civil rights movement.

Closely associated with the church, and usually having overlapping membership, was the mutual benefit society. Indeed, a mutual aid association, the Free African Society, had been the precursor of the earliest black church, the A.M.E.'s Mother Bethel in Philadelphia. Fraternal orders and mutual benefit societies complemented the secular mission of the churches, pooling limited individual resources to provide a kind of social safety net. After slavery such organizations multiplied in the South, some of them providing the basis for business enterprises like banking and insurance. Maggie Lena Walker's leadership in the Independent Order of St. Luke, which sponsored a savings bank, a newspaper, and a variety of other community institutions, was one of the more prominent examples of this trend.

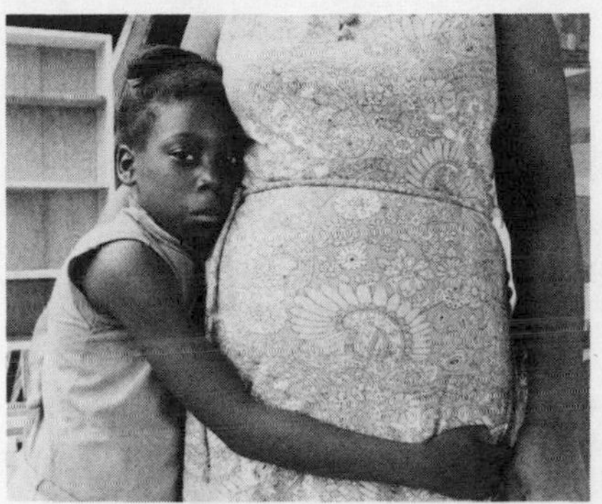

Young girl clinging to mother, 1970s

Creative Expressions of the Black Experience. The traditional black family, churches, and secular organizations provided for black southerners a sense of connectedness, of rootedness, which helps explain certain black cultural values and expressions, a special creativity that thrived despite oppression. There is a tension between tradition and innovation. Throughout black history African patterns of speech have been creolized, mixing features of the Old World with those of the New. The deep structure of an "African grammar," historian-folklorist Charles Joyner suggests, is blended with an English vocabulary to create something that is at once entirely new and yet still familiar.

Evidence of these patterns can be found in such cultural creations as language, religion, music, and folklore. Black aesthetic values, folklorist John Michael Vlach argues, are common in expressive arts as diverse as music, dance, quilting, and ironworking. These values emphasize experimentation, improvisation, and playfulness. Compositions are unbalanced, familiar motifs are combined in novel ways, and the results are often "crazy quilt" patterns that often test or invert the norm.

Performance is also a central feature of black oral tradition. Rapping, toasting, "signifying," and playing "the dozens" are as much a part of that performance tradition as folktales and music. The growth of black literacy in the 20th century created an audience for literary expression. Black poets, novelists, and playwrights drew on traditional oral forms grounded in southern black culture. Poets like Langston Hughes developed blues and jazz idioms, James Weldon Johnson celebrated spirituals and sermons, and Sterling Brown reshaped folklore, tall tales, and history.

Although a majority of black literary works were conceived and published outside the South, the region exerted a powerful influence on their themes, content, and forms. The South provided the cultural template for forms as diverse as jazz and rock and roll, spirituals and gospels, Brer Rabbit and Stagolee. The South provided the essential psychological landscape for a collective memory of suffering and survival. Like Quentin Compson in William Faulkner's *The Sound and the Fury*, black Americans have always had a love-hate relationship with the South. On the one hand, it symbolizes the worst that America has offered to blacks—racism, poverty, and oppression. But it also represents the roots of black culture, history, and "home." It is "down home" to blacks not born there; a "homeplace" for people whose fathers and mothers left decades ago. In community lore and joking it is a place to be escaped from; and yet a place that cannot be escaped. And finally, after the civil rights movement, it became a place to embrace: embraced less in optimism than in pride, because yet another generation had staked a blood-drenched claim to its equivocal legacy; embraced both for a sense of the possibilities it offered and in historical vindication for the many thousands gone.

See also AGRICULTURE: Sharecropping and Tenancy; ART AND ARCHITECTURE: Sculpture; Vernacular Architecture (Lowland South); EDUCATION: Desegregation; / Busing; Fisk University; Jackson State University; Piney Woods School; Tuskegee Institute; FOLKLIFE articles; INDUSTRY: Civil Rights and Business; LANGUAGE: Gullah; LAW: Civil Rights Movement; / Black Codes; *Brown* v. *Board of Education*; Greensboro Sit-in; Little Rock Crisis; *Plessy* v. *Ferguson*; Robinson, Spottswood W., III; Scott, Dred; Scottsboro Case; Slave Codes; MEDIA: Film, Blaxploitation; MUSIC articles; MYTHIC SOUTH: Racial Attitudes; SCIENCE AND MEDICINE: Racism, Scientific; URBANIZATION: Segregation, Residential; VIOLENCE: Literature and Song, Violence in Black; Race Riots; WOMEN'S LIFE: Race Relations and Women

Thomas C. Holt
University of Michigan

Ira Berlin, *Slaves without Masters: The Free Negro in the Antebellum South* (1974); Mary Frances Berry and John Blassingame, *Long Memory: The Black Experience in America*

Martin Luther King, Jr. (in hat), and Stokely Carmichael (right) during civil rights march, Coldwater, Mississippi, 1966

(1981); John W. Blassingame, *The Slave Community: Plantation Life in the Antebellum South* (1972); John B. Boles, *Black Southerners, 1619–1869* (1983); Dan T. Carter, *Scottsboro: A Tragedy of The American South* (1969); Robert Cruden, *The Negro in Reconstruction* (1969); John Hope Franklin, *From Slavery to Freedom: A History of Negro Americans* (1947, 5th ed., 1980); Eugene D. Genovese, *Roll, Jordan, Roll: The World the Slaves Made* (1974); Herbert G. Gutman, *The Black Family in Slavery and Freedom, 1750–1925* (1976); Louis R. Harlan, *The Maryland Historian* (Spring/Summer 1985); Darlene Clark Hine, ed., *The State of Afro-American History* (1986); Thomas C. Holt, *Black over White: Negro Political Leadership in South Carolina during Reconstruction* (1977); Winthrop D. Jordan, *White over Black: American Attitudes toward the Negro, 1550–1812* (1968); Charles Joyner, *Down by the Riverside: A South Carolina Slave Community* (1984); Lawrence W. Levine, *Black Culture and Black Consciousness: Afro-American Folk Thought from Slavery to Freedom* (1976); Sar A. Levitan, William B. Johnson, and Robert Taggart, *Still a Dream: The Changing Status of Blacks since 1960* (1975); Leon F. Litwack, *Been in the Storm So Long: The Aftermath of Slavery* (1979); Rayford W. Logan, *The Negro in American Life and Thought: The Nadir* (1954); Jay Mandle, *The Roots of Black Poverty: The Southern Plantation Economy after the Civil War* (1978); James M. McPherson et al., *Blacks in America: Bibliographical Essays* (1971); August Meier, *Negro Thought in America, 1880–1915* (1963), with Elliot M. Rudwick, *From Plantation to Ghetto* (1966); Howard N. Rabinowitz, *Race Relations in the Urban South, 1865–1900* (1978); Albert J. Raboteau, *Slave Religion: The "Invisible Institution" in the Antebellum South* (1978); Willie Lee Rose, *Rehearsal for Reconstruction: The Port Royal Experiment* (1964); Eileen Southern, *The Music of Black Americans: A History* (1971); Robert Farris Thompson, *Flash of the Spirit: African and Afro-American Art and Philosophy* (1983); John Michael Vlach, *The Afro-American Tradition in the Decorative Arts* (1978); Raymond Wolters, *Negroes and the Great Depression: The Problem of Economic Recovery* (1970); Peter Wood, *Black Majority: Negroes in Colonial South Carolina from 1670 through the Stono Rebellion* (1974); C. Vann Woodward, *The Strange Career of Jim Crow* (1955; 3d ed., 1974). ☆

African Influences

In 1935 Melville J. Herskovits asked in the pages of the *New Republic* "What has Africa given America?" In his answer, a radical response for the time, he briefly mentioned the influence of blacks on American music, language, manners, and foodways. He found most of his examples, however, in the South. Fifty years later the answer to this question could be longer, perhaps less radical, but still surprising to many. Much of what people of African descent brought to the United States since 1619 has become so familiar to the general population, particularly in the South, that the black origins of specific customs and forms of expression have become blurred or forgotten altogether.

Consider, for example, the banjo. Not only is the instrument itself of African origin but so is its name. Although the banjo is encountered today chiefly in bluegrass ensembles where it is considered an instrument of the Appalachians, it was first played by slaves on Tidewater plantations in the 17th and 18th centuries. It was only taken up into the Piedmont and mountains during the 19th century by blacks working on railroad gangs. Although the contemporary banjo is physically quite different from its Afro-American folk antecedent, it retains nonetheless the unique sounds of its ringing high drone string and its drum head. These are the acoustic reminders of the instrument's African origins.

Linguists have noted that southern speech carries a remarkable load of African vocabulary. This assertion is all the more remarkable when we recall that white southerners have often claimed to have little interaction with blacks. Some regional words have murky origins, but there is no controversy for such terms as: *boogie*, *gumbo*, *tote*, *benne*, *goober*, *cooter*, *okra*, *jazz*, *mumbo-jumbo*, *hoodoo*, *mojo*, *cush*, and the affirmative and negative expressions *uh-huh* and *unh-uh*. All are traceable to African languages and usages. The term *guinea* is used as an adjective for a number of plants and animals that were imported long ago from Africa. Guinea hens, guinea worms, guinea grass, and guinea corn, now found throughout the South, are rarely thought of as exceptional, even though their names directly indicate their exotic African origins.

Beyond basic words blacks have created works of oral literature that have become favorite elements of southern folklore. Looking at the whole cycle of folktales with animal tricksters—those put into written form by Joel Chandler Harris and others—some may have European analogies but most appear to have entered the United States from Africa and the West Indies. The warnings they provide concerning the need for clever judgment and social solidarity are lessons taken to heart by both whites and blacks. The legacy of artful language in Afro-American culture is manifested further in other types of performance such as the sermon, the toast, and contests of ritual insult. For people who are denied social and economic power, verbal power provides important compensation. This is why men of words in the black community—the good talkers—are highly esteemed. The southern oratorical style has generally been noted as distinctive because of its pacing, and imagery and the demeanor of the speaker. Some of these traits heard in speeches and sermons are owed to black men of words who of necessity refined much of what is today accepted as standard southern "speechifying" into a very dramatic practice.

In the area of material culture blacks have generally been assumed to have made few contributions to southern life, but such an assessment is certainly in error. There have, over the last four centuries, existed distinctive traditions for Afro-American basketry, pottery, quilting, blacksmithing, boatbuilding, woodcarving, carpentry, and graveyard decoration. These achievements have gone unrecognized and unacknowledged. Take, for example, the shotgun house. Several million of these structures can be found all across the South, and some are now lived in by whites, although shotgun houses are generally associated with black neighborhoods. The first of these distinctive houses with their narrow shapes and gable entrances were built in New Orleans at the beginning of the 19th century by free people of color who were escaping the political revolution in Haiti. In the Caribbean such houses are used both in towns and the countryside; they were once used as slave quarters. Given its history, the design of the shotgun house should be understood as somewhat determined by African architectural concepts as well as Caribbean Indian and French colonial influences. Contemporary southern shotgun houses represent the last phase of an architectural evolution initiated in Africa, modified in the West Indies, and now in many southern locales dominating the cultural landscape.

The cultural expressions of the southern black population are integral to the regional experience. Although the South could still exist without banjos, Brer Rabbit, goobers, and shotgun houses, it would certainly be less interesting. The black elements of southern culture make the region more distinctive.

See also ETHNIC LIFE: Caribbean Influence; FOLKLIFE articles; LITERATURE: / Harris, Joel Chandler; MUSIC: Banjo

John Michael Vlach
George Washington University

J. L. Dillard, *Black English* (1972); Dena J. Epstein, *Ethnomusicology* (September 1975); Melville J. Herskovits, *New Republic* (4 September 1935); Robert Farris Thompson, *Flash of the Spirit: African and Afro-American Art and Philosophy* (1983); John Michael Vlach, *Pioneer America* (January 1976), *The Afro-American Tradition in Decorative Arts* (1978). ☆

Appalachians, Black

Black Appalachians are distinctive within southern culture because their historical and contemporary realities set them apart from other black southerners as well as from the millions of black migrants to northern industrial cities. Moreover, they are among the few blacks in America to have existed as a racial minority in the midst of a cultural minority referred to as part of the culture of persistent poverty in America.

Despite the "discovery" of Appalachian whites by scholars, folklorists, and local color journalists in the late 19th century and the "rediscovery" of their incipient poverty during the Second Reconstruction of Lyndon Johnson's Great Society, little attention has focused on the blacks in their midst. The urbanization and migration of blacks from the South to the North has captured most attention from students of black life, as this became the central theme of the black experience for nearly a century. While Appalachian blacks share the same southern heritage as the millions of black urban migrants, their culture, work history, social homogeneity, and present status amidst considerable white poverty make them distinct from urban blacks and other rural nonfarm blacks in the South. Blacks in Appalachia are unlike other southern blacks for several reasons: (1) their migration was from one rural South area to another; (2) blacks in Appalachia are a very small proportion of the total population; and (3) poverty among black Appalachians is more severe than it is among other blacks—a fact of singular importance in a region characterized as culturally distinct and peripheral to national economic development.

The central and southern highlands of Appalachia cut a diagonal swath from northeast Alabama through Tennessee, Virginia, Georgia, Kentucky, across North and South Carolina, up to West Virginia. In 1980 blacks comprised nearly 9 percent of the estimated 12 million persons in this section of Appalachia. Though the Appalachian Regional Commission established boundaries that extend as far as upstate New York, Pennsylvania, and western Maryland, the central and southern sectors listed are commonly designated as Appalachia.

Black people have been in the southern region of Appalachia since it was colonized by the Scotch-Irish and German immigrants. Though not central to the subsistence agriculture of the highlands, blacks (more slave than free) comprised no less than 15 percent of the regional population between 1800 and 1870. After 1870 the number of blacks in Appalachia grew precipitously (as did the rest of the population) with the industrialization that followed the advent of railroads and the opening of coal mines. Coal mining—with its evolution from a labor-intensive to machine-intensive industry—had the greatest impact on Appalachian blacks in the Cumberland and Allegheny plateaus. Between 1880 and 1930 the growth rate of black populations in the coal-mining region followed the expansion of the industry itself. One study revealed that blacks constituted 53 percent of the miners in Alabama in 1930, and 27 percent in West Virginia, and they numbered nearly 10,000 in Kentucky. The role of blacks in the ranks of the United Mine Workers of America has yet to be clearly delineated, as black participation in antiunion activities during the 1900 to 1930 period overshadowed their strong commitment to labor.

The high emigration from Appalachia since the mid-1950s came in the wake of the decline of coal as an energy source. The mechanization of the industry led to massive loss of jobs, and the rate of black movement away from the region was five times that of the general population. West Virginia blacks, for example, lost more than 15,000 coal-related jobs during the 1950–70 decades, and nearly 50 percent of the black population left the state. Blacks in the Harlan County, Ky., population were reduced by 75 percent during this same period. Although blacks in some

Black coal miners in Appalachia, date unknown

portions of Appalachia, such as the South Carolina, Tennessee, and Alabama urban piedmonts, show stable and growing populations, few blacks in current remigration streams to the South are settling in rural Appalachia. Black emigration from the Allegheny and Cumberland plateaus from 1950 to 1970, then, seems to have had a lasting and final effect: the composition of the remaining black population in the coal regions portends a continuing decline and projection of "no blacks at all" in certain areas of eastern Kentucky, southwestern Virginia, eastern Tennessee, and southern West Virginia within a generation.

Blacks have been moving out of Appalachia steadily since 1930. Over the past half century they have resettled in many of the same cities chosen by the initial wave of blacks moving northward: Cincinnati, Cleveland, and Dayton, Ohio; Indianapolis, Gary, and Fort Wayne, Ind.; Detroit and other areas of employment related to the car industry; and the mills and manufacturing communities around metropolitan Chicago. To a lesser extent, black Appalachians have moved to the northeast corridor between Richmond, Va., and Boston, Mass. Eastern Kentucky's blacks cut a migratory stream to Lexington and Louisville in the state, though more can be found in northern Ohio and Michigan. The same applies to the thousands of West Virginia blacks who left since 1950. Smaller numbers of black Appalachians in the southern highlands left the mountains to seek opportunities in nearby urban areas of Appalachia including Winston-Salem, N.C.; Knoxville, Tenn.; Roanoke, Va.; and Birmingham, Ala.; many went to the dominant city in the area, Atlanta, Ga.

Kinship networks, chronicled as the sustainers of white Appalachian migratory streams, have also been of vital importance to blacks. The long-standing southern extended-family pattern was not generally interrupted in the move into Appalachia (as was the case for blacks moving to the cities at the turn of the century). Its stability has been noted as a life-sustaining link between mountain enclaves and the urban communities of the Midwest. Though generally well adjusted and assimilated in the industrial centers and suburbs, three generations of mountain blacks have developed strong family and community-of-origin networks. One exemplary case, the Eastern Kentucky Social Club, with large chapters in Illinois, Michigan, New York, Ohio, and Indiana sponsors yearly reunions and has hosted an average of 3,500 "homefolk" each Labor Day since 1970. In addition, these sojourners to eastern Kentucky's coalfields practice mutual assistance in the form of providing social and employment contacts for relocating persons and a variety of other civic, educational, and benevolent charities for "members."

Black Appalachians made notable

contributions to mountain culture. Black slaves, for example, introduced an adaptation of an African musical instrument known as a "banjar" (banjo) to mountain life in the highlands as they crossed the Alleghenies with the first wave of white settlers in the 17th century. Clogging, that very popular form of mountain dance, was derived, at least in part, from slave dances such as the "Buck." Piedmont blues have remarkable parallels to the form of country and western music popularized in Nashville. Finally, shape-note singing of hymns was popular among black and white Appalachians as well.

A number of black Appalachians became "persons of note" outside the region. Booker T. Washington is perhaps the best known. Historian Carter G. Woodson, also born in West Virginia, was an early graduate of Kentucky's Berea College. Bill Withers, a popular black balladeer, is from a mountain family in West Virginia, as is television producer Tony Brown. Odetta, the well-known black folk singer, hails from northern Alabama; and black political activist Angela Davis comes from Birmingham. Nikki Giovanni, a prominent writer and poetess during the 1960s, is from Knoxville, which is also home to Sparky Rucker, one of the handful of contemporary black folk artists. Roberta Flack was raised in western North Carolina, and Chicago-based entrepreneur Gloria Proctor was born and raised in Black Mountain, N.C.

Appalachia was the locale for much of the ideological and political brainstorming that led to the momentous changes for blacks in American life. Capron Springs, W.Va., was the site of numerous meetings between northern industrialists-philanthropists and southern missionaries-educators to whom credit is given for carving out the "separate-but-equal" industrial colleges of the South. Sojourner Truth's Underground Railroad had some of its most reliable "stops" in the southern highlands. John Brown's coterie of abolitionists traced their roots to Appalachian emancipationists; the first antislavery newspaper, *The Emancipator*, was founded in Tennessee. Of course, Berea College has the distinction of holding the first biracial educational experiment in the South—the school was predominantly black up to the institutionalization of Jim Crow school systems. On the other hand, sleepy Clinton, Tenn., in the very heart of Appalachia, was the nation's test tube for public school desegregation. Finally, the world-shaking social revolutions sparked by the civil rights movement were begun as a series of community workshops on adult education for black southerners directed by Myles Horton at Tennessee's Highlander Center.

Any comparison of Appalachian blacks with the total Appalachian population shows their socioeconomic plight: they have a higher recent migration rate from the region; higher percentages of dependent persons; a higher percentage of female-headed families with children; lower educational levels; higher unemployment rates; lower job status; and higher incidences of poverty. Since half of all blacks in central and southern Appalachia are urban, they fall between rural blacks and urban blacks on most social indicators. Thus, they are generally "better off" than rural blacks—those concentrated in the Deep South—and are "worse off" than urban blacks. The prospects for blacks in Appalachia's coalfields are not good, although those in the southernmost states may stabilize and insure viable livelihoods.

The experiences of black Appalachians pose intriguing questions in regard to southern culture. How much have they borrowed from Appalachian whites in the form of peculiarly white Appalachian value patterns? How much of what is called Appalachian culture represents white assimilation of traits brought to the mountains by blacks as bondsmen? How much of the southern culture persists among black Appalachians today? Have they evolved a separate, though unrecognized, culture, either from the influence of white Appalachian culture or from isolation from other blacks? In what ways do race relations in Appalachia differ from those in the Deep South and northern industrial cities to which blacks migrated? Whether answers to such questions become important depends on the interest of Appalachian and southern scholars, policymakers, and citizens in examining a most unique case of southern ethnography, demography, and human ecology.

See also ENVIRONMENT: / Appalachian Mountains; ETHNIC LIFE: Mountain Culture; / Appalachians; MYTHIC SOUTH: Appalachian Culture; / Appalachian Myth

William H. Turner
University of Kentucky

Darold T. Barnum, *The Negro in the Bituminous Coal Mining Industry* (1970); David Bellows, "Appalachian Blacks: A Demographic Analysis" (M.A. thesis, Rutgers University, 1974); Michael Bruland, *The Status of Black People in Appalachia; A Statistical Profile* (1971); David A. Corbin, *Life, Work and Rebellion in the Coal Fields: Southern West Virginia Coal Miners, 1880–1922* (1980); Ronald D. Eller, *Miners, Millhands, and Mountaineers: The Modernization of the Appalachian South* (1982); Gloria Jackson and Ester Piovia, *Appalachia and Its Black Population: Selected Social and Economic Characteristics* (1972); Carter G. Woodson, *Journal of Negro History* (April 1916). ☆

Architecture, Black

The African slave brought only the products of his mind to the New World, including the skills of ironworking and woodcarving and proficiency in the use of earth and stone. His innovations in the application of these skills qualified him as an architect alongside many other early American craftsmen.

The colonial plantation system relied upon its slave craftsmen to produce furniture, tools, and often buildings. In 1934, for example, historian Leila Sellers wrote about the Charleston, S.C., area: "Slaves had become proficient in every craft, even that of jeweler . . . the white artisan was virtually eliminated by 1790."

It was slaves who built the 10-room, two-and-a-half-story plantation called Magnolia in Plaquemines Parish, La., in 1795. Records and building technology reveal slave involvement in most early plantation construction throughout Louisiana. A few notable examples include Oakland in Bermuda, Cherokee in Natchez, and Kate Chopin's house, now the Bayou Folk Museum, in Cloutierville. When John Sims's house at Gippy Plantation in South Carolina was destroyed by fire, it was rebuilt in 1852 by slave artisans. Winsor Hall, the oldest landmark in Greenville, Ga., was designed and built in 1836 by Isaiah Wimbush, a slave artisan. Architectural characteristics such as steep, sloping hip roofs, central fireplaces, porches with wide overhanging roofs, and the use of earth and moss to construct walls suggest how elements of African architecture may have been introduced by slave builders.

Plantation records show that these slave artisans were also "hired out" or lent to other plantations. One example was James Bell, a Virginia slave who was brought to Huntsville, Ala., to design and build three spiral staircases for the Watkins-Moore Grayson mansion. Hiring out, however, seems to have been more widely practiced by urban slaveowners.

The papers of 19th-century entrepreneur Robert Jemision, Jr., of Alabama indicate he operated a school for slave artisans. His records of about 1830 show he had in his employ "two slave architects, Horace and Napoleon." Jemision, apparently pleased with Horace's work, introduced a bill in the 1845–46 session of the Alabama legislature to emancipate the slave architect. Horace King, as he became known, built some of Alabama's best constructed covered bridges. His 614-foot bridge spanning the Chattahoochee River was the longest of its type in the United States when it was built in 1873.

A contract drawn up in 1787 between Robin deLogny and "Charles," a free black carpenter, woodworker, and mason, indicated the existence of free black "architects" even before Horace King. The contract empowered Charles to construct Destrehan Plantation in St. Charles Parish, La., and specified that he be paid "one brute Negro, one cow and her calf, 50 quarts corn husks, and upon completion, 100 peastros." Because the contract only specified "a home 60 feet in length by 35 feet in width," we can assume the design was also by the builder Charles.

Besides free black artisans there were also free black planters who, often in efforts to emulate their white counterparts, built large plantation homes. In Louisiana there was Arlington (built in 1850 by Mignon Carlin), Cazelar house (built by Pierre Cazelar), and Parish Plantation (built by Andrew Drumford). After traveling through the 19th-century South, Frederick Law Olmsted wrote that the best houses and the most beautiful grounds that he had visited in Louisiana belonged to a nearly full-blooded black.

It is quite possible that the house Olmsted was referring to belonged to a son of Marie Therese, an exslave who gained her freedom in 1778, received two land grants from the Spanish government, and by 1803 had acquired at least 4,000 acres. Here she established Melrose Plantation, which became the center of the Metoyer landholdings of 13,000 acres, which, in turn, became known as Isle Brevelle, a settlement of "free people of color."

Louis Metoyer, one of Marie's 14 children, studied architecture in Paris and is responsible for the design of the Melrose mansion and many of the later buildings in Isle Brevelle. The main buildings of Melrose and its church, also built by Louis Metoyer, remain standing today. The most unusual of these buildings is the African house, built around 1800. Of purely African design, it is the only structure of its type now standing in the United States and recently was designated a national landmark.

By the end of the Reconstruction period, industrialization, trade unions, racism, and economic depression had dethroned the free black planter class and with it the black craftsman from his domination of the building trades. With the establishment of America's first school of architecture at the Massachusetts Institute of Technology in 1960, architecture began to be professionalized. The distinction between builder and architect was further sharpened in 1897 when Illinois required architects to be licensed by the state.

By 1890 there were 8,090 architects in the United States, 677 of whom were in the South. In 1910 there were 16,613, with 1,462 located in the southern states. Carter G. Woodson, using U.S. census figures, states in his book, *The Negro Professional and the Community*, that in 1890 there were 44 black architects, draftsmen, and inventors and in 1910 there were 54. His list for 1930 contains 45 black architects, none of whom were in southern states. Research has clearly shown that there were black architects in the South prior to 1930, and one can safely speculate that race played a role in determining who was classified as "architect."

In the South, at Booker T. Washington's Tuskegee Institute in Alabama, the first movement of black professional architecture was orchestrated. A closer examination of Washington's "normal school," which had been established to train teachers, reveals a most complete school of architecture within the department of mechanical industries. Tuskegee's early buildings were designed by department faculty members and were built under their supervision by students with student-made bricks. School records indicate that the department was established to make a profit and that it took on design and construction jobs outside the school. Course work included freehand drawing, drafting, and bookkeeping.

Almost without exception, early black architects began at Tuskegee, either as students or faculty members. Booker T. Washington recruited Robert R. Taylor in 1892 to develop the mechanical industries department. Taylor had been among the first blacks to graduate in architecture from MIT, and during his 41 years' tenure at Tuskegee, Taylor designed many of its major buildings, supervised overall campus planning and later became vice president of the Institute. He died suddenly on 13 December 1942, in the Institute's Butler Chapel, his favorite among his own early designs.

John A. Lankford, one of Taylor's earliest pupils, established the first known black professional architectural office in Jacksonville, Fla., in 1899. Prior to opening his office, Lankford had served as superintendent of Shaw University's Mechanical Industries Department, where he was responsible for the design of several buildings. In 1898 he designed and supervised the construction of the $100,000 Coleman Cotton Mill in Concord, N.C. Moving to Washington, D.C., in about 1901, Lankford became one of the leading black architects. He served as the national supervising architect to the A.M.E. church, for which he designed Big Bethel, a landmark of Atlanta's Auburn Avenue, and a church in Capetown, South Africa.

At least three members of Robert Taylor's Mechanical Industries Department faculty at Tuskegee made substantial architectural contributions. Wallace Rayfield, an 1899 graduate of the Pratt School of Architecture, established the first black architectural office in Birmingham, Ala. As with Lankford, much of his work was for churches. He later became the national architect for the A.M.E. Zion church. His designs include Ebenezer Baptist in Chicago and Birmingham's 16th Street Church, the church in which four little girls were killed in the mid-1960s bombing.

William Pittman, also a Tuskegee faculty member under Robert Taylor, moved to Washington, D.C., and worked with John Lankford before establishing his own office there in 1906. Architect Pittman gained the commission to design the Negro Building for the Jamestown Tricentennial in 1907. It was designed and built entirely by blacks and contained exhibits of "progress by the race."

A third Tuskegee faculty member and architect was Vertner A. Tandy. Graduating from Cornell University in 1908, he became the first black architect in New York state and was a leading resident of Harlem's famed Strivers' Row.

Among the black architects who did not attend Tuskegee was Julian Abele, who graduated from the University of Pennsylvania in 1902 and became the chief designer for Horace Trumbauer & Associates in Philadelphia. He was responsible for most of the firm's later work including the design for Duke University and the Duke family mansions in New York and New Jersey.

World War II had a profound effect on the development of black architects in America. In 1941 the War Department awarded a $4.2 million contract to the black architectural, engineering, and construction firm of McKissack & McKissack for the construction of Tuskegee Air Base. Hilyard Robinson, a Washington, D.C., architect, was awarded the architectural design contract. The project is seen today by many senior black architects as a milestone, since it was the only architectural work available to some of them. America's first black fighter squadron was trained at the Tuskegee base, and an organization of the Tuskegee airmen still exists today.

With funds available through the GI bill, black veterans received educational opportunities far exceeding those of previous generations. Racial segregation, however, limited their choices, creating unprecedented high enrollments at such black schools as Howard, Hampton, and Tuskegee, and contributed to the expansion of their faculty and programs.

Many veterans had first been exposed to these schools and their programs while in military training. Thus, John Spencer, AIA (now dean of Hampton's School of Architecture) returned to Hampton to study architecture after his U.S. Navy training there. David Byrd, AIA, president of the Huron Valley, Mich., chapter/AIA, and John Chase, AIA past president of the National Organization of Minority Architects, are also GI bill graduates of Hampton. Most significant, perhaps, was the growth of Howard's program in architecture, which resulted from GI bill enrollments.

The accreditation of Howard's School of Architecture in 1950, taken together with Washington's large black population, made the city the capital of black architects. The most recent AIA listing shows that the District of Columbia is the home of 32 black architects, 21 of whom are members of AIA. Another listing completed in 1971 notes 385 "minority persons" in architecture located in 38 different states and a total of 92 minority-owned firms. This listing shows that 40 percent of black architects and 46 percent of black-owned firms are in California, New York, and the District of Columbia. While there are fewer black architects in the southern states, there are more black-owned firms in the South.

Since 1967 there has been a considerable increase in the involvement of the black architect in AIA. At the 1968 Chicago convention, Taylor Culver was elected president of the Association of Student Chapters/AIA. At the 1970 Boston convention, Robert Nash, FAIA, of Washington, D.C., was elected vice president of the institute and became the first black to hold national office. The National Organization of Minority Architects (NOMA) was established in 1972 in Chicago, and Wendell Campbell, AIA, of Chicago was elected president of the new organization. A forerunner of NOMA was the National Technical Association, which was established in 1925 to bring together various black professionals, including architects and engineers.

Although blacks have inadequate representation in the profession, they are making significant strides toward full participation in America's architecture. There are now seven fully accredited predominantly black schools of architecture, and both black students and black faculty members can be seen at most schools of architecture.

See also ART AND ARCHITECTURE: Sculpture; Vernacular Architecture (Lowland South)

Richard K. Dozier
Tuskegee Institute

Charles A. Brown, *Biography of Wallace Rayfield* (1972); Richard K. Dozier, *Black Enterprise* (September 1976), *Black World* (May 1974), *AIA Journal* (July 1976); *Negro History Bulletin* (April 1940); William Quinn, *Tuesday* magazine (May and June 1972); Anson P. Stokes, *Tuskegee Institute: The First Fifty Years* (1931); Max Bennett Thrasher, *Tuskegee: Its Story and Its Work* (1900); Charles Wesley, *History of Alpha Phi Alpha Fraternity* (1975), *Crisis Magazine* (September 1916). ☆

Art, Black

Many important black artists have come from the South. Some have shown influence of the region in their work, while others have shown no regional or ethnic tendency at all. Black artists were not recorded by name in the South during slavery. However, the works of anonymous craftsmen of that time have long been recognized for their quality. These works were found principally in Louisiana and the Carolinas, where architecture, balconies, wrought-iron gates, stairs, and columns of wood, as well as baskets, were made by blacks. The art of these craftsmen revealed the strong influence of West African imagery and technical skill that African slaves brought and passed down to later generations.

The earliest prominently known black artist in the South was Joshua Johnson. He became a very successful portrait painter in Baltimore soon after 1800 and worked there until at least 1827. Most of Johnson's patrons and subjects were white. His style of painting followed the popular limner tradition of the day: standardized formats, formulas of poses and accessories to which the face of the sitter was added. No other black artist of the time is known to have achieved his success or to have followed in his tradition. He was forgotten after his death and was not rediscovered until the 1940s.

Early in the 20th century black artists of the South became very influential. Because of their limited resources several developed multiple skills as artists, educators, art curators, and art critics. One of the first of these versatile persons was James Herring, who founded the art department at Howard University,

Washington, D.C., in 1925 and the art gallery of the same university in 1930—the first such institutions established by black people. Over the years Howard has provided education for an impressive number of highly regarded black artists. The Howard University Art Gallery also provided exhibiting opportunities for many of the most respected white American artists of the 1930s and 1940s. In 1943 in Washington, D.C., James Herring and curator Alonzo Aden founded the Barnett-Aden Gallery, the first commercial black gallery in America and one of the most important galleries south of New York. Like the Howard Art Gallery, the Barnett-Aden showed an interracial mixture of artists, including some of the most respected white artists in the country. The gallery functioned until Herring's death in 1969.

In 1931 Hale Woodruff, a native of Cairo, Ill., moved from New York to teach at Atlanta University. He established the "Atlanta Annual," a competitive exhibition that was open to black artists throughout the country. The exhibition served as a major source of exposure for black artists, helped to improve black peoples' understanding of their art, and provided the South with another major center of art by blacks. Also in the 1930s Fisk University in Nashville, Tenn., started an art department, where the noted New York painter Aaron Douglas taught for many years.

Although Howard, Atlanta, and Fisk universities provided varying degrees of art education, few other opportunities existed for black artists to develop in the South. Many moved to the North either to begin or to further their study, yet many retained native regional sensibilities in their work in ways that reveal tendencies peculiar to black artists.

One such tendency is the use of satire to describe a black subculture. The tendency might have arisen in slavery as a social code that was permitted by whites who dismissed it as the harmless ways of a simple people. It is a satire that is self-deprecating, embracing insulting stereotypes with irony. Thus, blacks found wry humor in the comical exaggerations of their large lips, bulging eyes, large hands and feet, awkward movement, gaudy clothes, and love of watermelon. They relished this perversity not because they believed it, but because they wearied of escaping its stigma; so a negative definition became a common bond.

One artist who in the 1920s satirized the comical image of blacks through double entendre was Archibald Motley. His grotesque expressions of the stereotypical image of blacks and their life of debauchery created a surreal surface of glitter that camouflaged private loneliness. Motley's popularity declined by 1950, but his work regained attention in the late 1960s when black artists once again became fascinated with satirizing insulting stereotypes that others had created of them. Another painter from the South of Motley's generation whose work was in the same vein was Palmer Hayden. His sensibility was more rural than Motley's, and his art was less witty. Hayden used the stereotypes as a basis for abstraction. In his work large hands and feet, for example, became a basis for a new approach to figurative form. The massive and rough-hewn features Hayden depicted took his art in a direction that was both "naive" and "African"—naive in terms of its structural informality and pictorial inconsistencies, African in terms of its positive translation of West African sculptural character into painting.

Other southern black artists of the time transposed African forms into a black American imagery that played with the stereotypes of black features whites had created. Thus, a black American art began to emerge that was also related to cubism. Black artists of the South came from an environment that caused them to perceive their own bodies as a source of expression and stylization. Further, racial segregation forced their recognition of a cultural and artistic relationship to Africa.

Another artist of the time who discovered a relationship between black America and Africa was Augusta Savage, a realist sculptor whose forms were massive and brooding. A sculptor whose forms and subjects were pronouncedly African in sensibility was Richmond Barthé. Many of the artists who followed them took the black American relationship to African art as a point of departure, moving their ideas further into the realm of a "pan-African abstraction," in which the expressive structure of African art transcended the temporal subject matter to become the essence of their art. The stolid sculptural forms of Selma Burke fit this mold, too, as did the sculpture of Marion Perkins. Elizabeth Catlett's sculpture has been more angular but no less imbued with a feeling of African form. Eldzier Cortor, a painter, developed an elongated figure with African-American facial types in brooding surreal environments.

Some black artists from the South drew ideas from the evolved folk culture of Afro-Americans in the region. One such artist was William H. Johnson, who had become a highly sophisticated painter before moving to Europe in the 1920s. When he returned to the United States in the late 1930s, he abandoned his international style and developed a simplified, two-dimensional form that reflected the vision of a naive. Through this form he explored the black folk experience in America, expressing themes of the family, religion, and war.

Romare Bearden, whose work began to mature around 1940, developed in a similar way. A master of collage, he shapes prismatic, two-dimensional images of black experiences, often reflecting an iconic character of his people's facial types and the psychology of their deprivation. Bearden extends Afro-American associations to Africa through the use of mask-type imagery and African patterns in his compositions. He has created another form of pan-Africanness even though his work has been profoundly affected by modernism, especially cubism and Matisse. Artists like Bearden and Johnson shaped a highly sophisticated art from the iconography of black folk culture.

The unschooled folk artists drew on and depicted folk visions. Because blacks were deprived of formal art training in the South, it is no surprise that many worked outside formal traditions. Each worked from a personal vision and improvised individualistic symbols, forms, and techniques. These artists include David Butler, Minnie Evans, William Edmundson, Clementine Hunter, and Elijah Pierce.

The art of other black artists from the South reveals no conspicuous ethnic tendency. Hughie Lee-Smith's subjects are black and white people set in desolate, surreal environments. Painter-printmaker James Wells is another who has developed a radiant expression and buoyant, figurative forms with which he explores religious themes. Alma Thomas gained international stature in the early 1970s for her abstract forms. In the late 1960s Leo Twiggs developed another range of abstraction through the use of fabrics, while Sam Gilliam extended the modern concept of painting by removing the canvas from the stretcher. Gilliam is credited with developing the concept of draped painting. Martin Puryear's work in wood has inspired a renewed sense of oneness between craftsmanship and the intrinsic expressive potential of the natural material. Other black artists include painters William T. Williams and Joe Overstreet; Merton Simpson has founded an important art gallery in New York. Benny Andrews, the son of sharecroppers in Madison, Ga., attended Ft. Valley State College and the University of Chicago before taking a B.F.A. from the Art Institute of Chicago in 1958. His paintings of the South stress rural living and contrast black and white life.

See also ART AND ARCHITECTURE: Painting and Painters; / Bearden, Romare; Douglas, Aaron; Johnson, William Henry; FOLKLIFE: Folk Painting; / Hunter, Clementine

Keith A. Morrison
University of Maryland

Theresa Dickason Cederholm, *Afro-American Artists: A Bio-bibliographical Directory* (1973); David C. Driskell, *Two Centuries of Black American Art* (1976); Elsa Honig Fine, *The Afro-American Artist* (1971); Lynda Roscoe Hartigan, *Sharing Traditions* (1985); Jane Livingston and John Beardsley, *Black Folk Art in America, 1930–1980* (1982); Keith A. Morrison, *Art in Washington and Its Afro-American Presence: 1940–1970* (1985); James A. Porter, *Modern Negro Art* (1943, reprint 1969); Virginia Museum of Fine Arts, *Painting in the South: 1954–1980* (1983). ☆

Business, Black

West African slaves came from commercial economies and, wherever permitted in the New World, engaged in trade. The "Sunday markets" of the West Indies and South America were often dominated by Africans who filled them with produce from their garden plots. Such commercial activity, although less flourishing in North America, certainly existed, especially in colonial South Carolina. In fact a subeconomy carried on by slaves and free blacks in 18th-century South Carolina became so vigorous that the master class legislated against what it feared could become a political as well as an economic underground.

This tightening of the slave system against communication and assembly, the essence of trading activity, intensified during the 19th century, while simultaneously the number of new Africans became proportionately smaller after the closing of the slave trade in 1807. The tendency, then, was for American slaves to become increasingly socialized and assimilated into a dependent and isolated plantation life, while free blacks were squeezed into the bleakest margins of the southern economy. Unlike Latin America, the American South never had a black majority who out of demographic necessity would come to occupy many of the more favorable niches in the economy.

There were, of course, exceptions. Free blacks in South Carolina, where blacks were a majority, established in Charleston a small elite dealing in goods and services for a white clientele. Skilled craftsmen, especially masons, along with barbers, fishermen, grocers, and caterers constituted this specialized business class not only in Charleston but in New Orleans, Baltimore, Washington, D.C., and other southern cities. After emancipation, only the barbers retained a firm hold on these traditional black occupations. Black artisans, many of them exslaves, found themselves displaced by white workers and closed out of craft unions. Displacement and exclusion, however, did not dim the hopes of a rising class of black professionals and entrepreneurs who represented what Booker T. Washington called the "New Negro for a New Century," casting down their buckets in a New South.

Washington believed that business, above all else, could lift his people up from slavery. Beneath his rhetoric, Washington was no devotee of plantations and paternalism. He was bourgeois to the bone, a historical materialist on the right, who counseled that capitalism would neutralize racism and deliver from slavery all those who would attach themselves to its mighty engine. For black workers this ineluctable force might not work its magic overnight, but in the meantime they were well advised to invest their labor in the development of the New South, while the black middle class would "take advantage of the disadvantages" and build a duplicate black economy behind the walls of segregation.

Racial solidarity and black capitalism became watchwords in the face of an all-powerful Jim Crow. Benjamin J. Davis, a leading black businessman from Atlanta, reminded his colleagues in 1921 that "the white man does nothing with us that he can with a white man. He builds businesses for the employment of white boys and girls; we must build businesses for the employment of black boys and girls. We must have more producers of wealth." For the disciples of Washington, the black business movement amounted to middle-class millenarianism, with Washington presiding as the high priest, and the conventions of the National Negro Business League (founded by Washington in 1900) serving as camp meetings of the faithful testifying to salvation through enterprise.

In retrospect the business movement appears important mostly as myth and symbol, a bittersweet synthesis of two mainstays in American culture—capitalism and racism. But also there was substance. Black doctors, dentists, bankers, lawyers, journalists, and entrepreneurs, many of them educated in black institutions, took their places in black communities and served a black clientele. The highest statement of racial solidarity came from all-black southern towns, over 50 of which existed by 1910, each theoretically connected with the commercial life of the New South, but otherwise separate—each symbolizing a kind of utopian apartheid. By all odds the most famous was Mound Bayou, Miss., "a town owned and operated by our people," exulted a black reporter in 1912, a town where "a black mayor with his black aldermen sit in the council chambers making laws," where "a black marshall carries the billy, a black postmaster passes out the mail, a black ticket agent sells the tickets and the white man's waiting room is in the rear."

Although important ideologically, the black towns could not compete economically or culturally with the "Negro Mainstreets" of southern cities, such as Beale Street in Memphis or "Sweet Auburn" Avenue in Atlanta. In these ethnic enclaves, not unlike those of

European immigrants in northern cities, a vibrant combination of commercial and cultural life gave black business a larger meaning in the everyday lives of the people. Without Booker T. Washington's faith in American capitalism, these black southerners nonetheless affirmed what had come to be theirs in every community large enough to support a commercial district. Business institutions ranged from "mom and pop" stores and juke joints to modern retail stores and essential services, and in the largest cities, newspapers, theaters, hotels, banks, and insurance companies.

The insurance firms deserve special mention because they formed the heart of black financial networks, the cultural beginnings of which can be traced to mutual benefit societies and the church. By the turn of the 20th century the burial insurance offered by the semisacred benefit societies and fraternal lodges increasingly gave way to industrial and ordinary insurance offered by secular enterprises like the North Carolina Mutual (1898) and Atlanta Life (1905). This process of modernization warmed the heart of Washington, and had he lived into the 1920s he would have joined in the celebration of Durham, N.C., as the "Capital of the Black Middle Class," the "Black Wall Street of America." By 1924 the North Carolina Mutual had spawned in Durham a commercial bank, a savings and loan institution, a fire insurance company, and along with a cotton mill and lesser enterprises, a national financial clearinghouse and chamber of commerce, the National Negro Finance Corporation (NNFC).

Symbolically, the failure of the NNFC in 1929 may have marked a turning point in the dream of black capitalism. The onset of the Great Depression, trenchant criticism from a new generation of leftist black academics, continuing black migration out of the South, and the impact of World War II and the civil rights movement on the accommodationist ideas of self help all played a part in the replacement of the dream of Booker T. Washington with the dream of Martin Luther King. The two were not necessarily mutually exclusive, however, and ambivalence on the liberating potential of black capitalism has continued to express itself. Ironically, integration in the South spelled doom for many black businesses whose customers chose to shop in white-owned stores, previously closed to them.

Future case studies may show that black business as culture and history has to be analyzed in subtle, creative ways outside the familiar models of protest and accommodation or neoclassical economics and Marxian theory. From the perspective of women's history, preliminary evidence would suggest that black women, less protected as they were than white women by the Victorian cult of domesticity, may have faced fewer internal barriers to entrepreneurial activity. The best 20th-century example of a black woman who apparently felt no such cultural restraints was Madame C. J. Walker, who took her cosmetics industry North and garnered great fame and fortune. But in the long run scholars may decide that the intimate association between black business and black culture, all within a poignant sense of community, went the way of Beale Street; and that it will be the creative music and the social memory that outlive the commercial meaning of these main streets.

See also INDUSTRY: Insurance; MUSIC: / Beale Street; URBANIZATION: Segregation;

Residential / Charleston; Memphis; New Orleans

Walter B. Weare
University of Wisconsin–Milwaukee

John H. Burrows, "The Necessity of Myth: A History of the National Negro Business League, 1900–1945" (Ph.D. dissertation, Auburn University, 1977); Louis R. Harlan, *Booker T. Washington: The Making of a Black Leader, 1856–1901* (1972), *Booker T. Washington: The Wizard of Tuskegee* (1983); Abram L. Harris, *The Negro as Capitalist: A Study of Banking and Business among American Negroes* (1936); Alexa B. Henderson, "A Twentieth-Century Black Enterprise: The Atlanta Life Insurance Company, 1905–1975" (Ph.D. dissertation, Georgia State University, 1975); August Meier, *Negro Thought in America, 1880–1915* (1963); Howard N. Rabinowitz, *Race Relations in the Urban South, 1865–1890* (1978); Arnold Taylor, *Travail and Triumph: Black Life and Culture in the South since the Civil War* (1976); David M. Tucker, *Lieutenant Lee of Beale Street* (1971); Walter B. Weare, *Black Business in the New South: A Social History of the North Carolina Mutual Life Insurance Company* (1973). ☆

Creolization

Gullah is a creole language developed by the descendants of enslaved Africans in the Low Country and on the Sea Islands of South Carolina and Georgia. The earliest African slaves in these areas did not constitute a speech community as the term is used by sociolinguists. Their various African languages were often mutually unintelligible. The common language that they acquired was an English-based pidgin. Pidgin languages develop as a means by which speakers of diverse languages may communicate with one another. A pidgin has no native speakers: it is a second language by definition. But it became a native tongue when it was passed on to the American-born children of those enslaved Africans. Once a pidgin acquires native speakers, it is no longer considered a pidgin but is said to be a creole language. As a native tongue it must serve not merely the restricted functions of a pidgin, but all the functions of a language.

The process of linguistic change in which two or more languages converge to form a new native tongue is called by students of linguistic change "creolization." The creole language of Afro-American slaves in South Carolina and Georgia, Gullah, continued to develop—both in inner form and extended use—in a situation of language contact. There was reciprocal influence of African and English features upon both the creole and the regional standard. The English contribution was principally lexical; the African contribution was principally grammatical.

The process of linguistic change provides a model for explaining other aspects of the transformation from African to Afro-American culture. What might be called the "creolization of black culture" involves the unconscious "grammatical" principles of culture, the "deep structure" that generates specific cultural patterns. Such "grammatical" principles survived the Middle Passage and governed the selective adaptation of elements of both African and European culture. Herded together with others with whom they shared a common condition of servitude and some degree of cultural overlap, enslaved Africans were compelled to create a new language, a new religion, indeed a new culture.

Not only was the structure of the new language a result of the creolization process, but the structure of language use as well. The African preference for using indirect and highly ambiguous speech—for speaking in parables—was adapted by American-born slaves to a new natural, social, and linguistic environment. This aspect of the creolization process is strikingly evident in their proverbs. By employing the *grammar* of African proverb usage and the largely English *vocabulary* of the new creole language, Afro-Americans were able to transform older African proverbs into metaphors of their collective experience in the New World. Some African proverbs were simply translated into the new vocabulary; others underwent minor changes. Still others retained the semantics of the African proverbs but completely transmuted the rhetoric into metaphors more meaningful to the new environment.

Naming patterns exemplify another way in which Gullah-speaking slaves preserved their African linguistic heritage while also combining aspects of it with English. The traditional African custom of "basket-naming," or bestowing of private names, continued into the 20th century. As late as the Civil War, all seven West African day names, as well as other African basket names, appeared on slave lists in the South Carolina Low Country. But African continuities were not manifested solely in the static retentions of easily recognized African names. On the contrary, behind many of the apparently English names of the slaves were African naming patterns. In many cases African meanings were retained behind direct translation of names into English. Day names, in particular, were frequently translated into their English equivalents. But the creolization process, by which African *means* of using language were applied to a new tongue, produced such fresh seasonal basket names as *Christmas*. Similarly, black names revealed the adaptation to new places of the African pattern of naming after localities.

The creolization process was vividly exemplified in black storytelling. The folk narrative tradition of Afro-Americans, like that of their African ancestors, was eclectic and creative. They took their sources where they found them, remembered what they found memorable, used what they found usable, and forgot the forgettable. Both inherited aesthetic grammars and the realities of the new environment played mediating roles in that process. Animal trickster tales constituted the most numerous type of folk narrative among Afro-Americans as among Africans, but Afro-Americans did not merely retain African trickster tales unchanged. On the contrary, the African narrative tradition was itself creative and innovative both in Africa and in America, where it encountered a strikingly different natural and social environment. Afro-American trickster tales indicate the black response to that new environment and efforts to manipulate it verbally and symbolically. In addition to animal trickster tales, the slaves narrated a cycle of human trickster tales in which the trickster role was not played by a surrogate slave—the rabbit—but by a real slave—John. Both animal and human trickster tales manifested continuities with African themes and with African traditions of indirect speech.

One of the most striking manifestations of the transformation of African cultures into Afro-American culture was in black religion. The slaves did not so much adapt to Christianity (at least not to the selective Christianity preached by their masters) as adapt Christianity to themselves. Just as the masters adapted Christianity to their own culture, so the slaves converted Christianity to theirs. God the judge of human behavior—God the master or overseer—was not the object of worship in Afro-Christianity, but a god more like African deities was: God the transcendent spirit. Blacks worshipped this new Christian deity in traditional African ways, and they made European religious forms serve traditional African religious functions. African religious beliefs and practices continued to flourish, however, in three distinct streams. One stream, including such practices as ecstatic trances and spirit possession as part of religious behavior, merged with Christianity, giving Afro-Christianity a distinctive touch. A second stream, which included belief in hags and witches, as well as in certain malign spirits, continued to exist among slave Christians as a sort of parallel consciousness, neither part of their Christianity nor completely outside of it. A third stream, including conjuration and sorcery, flourished as an underground alternative religious system in ways that ran quite counter to the doctrines of Christianity. What had been a unified religious outlook in Africa, in which virtually all experience was religious, had become fragmented and diversified in the new environment.

Creolization was illustrated as well in both the vocal and instrumental music of Afro-Americans. Their singing of secular songs as well as spirituals remained quite close to West African singing styles, their words often making incisive comments on the world of the local plantations. In instrumental music, the creolization process was exemplified both by continuities in instrumental preference with Africa—the banjo and the drums—and by the adaptation of such European instruments as the fiddle to Afro-American styles. Music, both vocal and instrumental, continued to serve African functions.

Afro-Americans adopted the grains, fruits, vegetables, and meats of the New World environment, but to those foodstuffs they applied an African culinary grammar—methods of cooking and spicing, remembered recipes, ancestral tastes. They added the *soul* ingredients. They not only maintained cultural continuity with West African cuisine, but adapted the African tradition creatively to the opportunities and necessities of a new culinary environment.

The clothing worn by the earliest generations of Afro-Americans, the slaves, served as an outward symbol of group identity and of the individual's place within the group. Just as in a folk community individuals are not completely free to express their individuality in dress, slaves were not completely free to express group consciousness and solidarity in their dress. If clothing is examined in relation to black community life as a whole, then how clothing is worn is seen to be as important as what is worn. A significant function of costume is that of differentiating between the workaday world and the festive world. The rhythmic alteration between work and festivity evident in the temporal life of the community was symbolized in Afro-American costume. For black slaves, that alternation distinguished between weekdays in the plantation fields and the festive air they gave to the weekends—the distinction between the time owed to the master and the time available for their purposes.

They made Sundays the occasion for displaying not merely cleanliness but such finery as they possessed. During the week they might belong to the master, but on Sundays they emerged as self-respecting men and women.

Housing, too, reflected the creolization process. Many surviving slave cabins reflect the convergence of elements of African and European architecture. With facades that exemplify the vocabulary of European symmetry and control, they conceal floor plans marked by African spatial orientations. The long, narrow shotgun house type, which has emerged in the 20th century as a signpost of Afro-American culture, illustrates a similar convergence of cultures.

The creolization process was evident even in Afro-American work patterns. The early technological expertise that made possible rice cultivation on the South Carolina and Georgia coasts had come from Africans rather than Europeans, and numerous African continuities in planting, cultivation, threshing, and winnowing rice underlay the developing Euro-American economic networks and management techniques. The preference of black workers for communal labor, for hoeing in a line to the rhythm of work songs, strikingly exemplified continuity with African tradition. In many cases skilled black plantation craftsmen drew upon highly developed African technologies in metalwork, pottery, woodwork, leatherwork, and weaving. Even house servants played significant roles in the creolization of culture by serving as cultural intermediaries, taking African cultural patterns into the "big house" and European cultural patterns to the quarters. Blacks were not, after all, the only participants in the creolization process in South Carolina and Georgia Low Country, where blacks outnumbered whites by majorities of up to 10 to 1 in some places.

The study of linguistic creolization is a relatively recent phenomenon; the application of creolization theory to the study of Afro-American culture is in its infancy. It is but one explanation of cultural change; it is not the whole story. But it does represent a promising approach to understanding the transformation of diverse African cultures into Afro-American culture.

See also FOLKLIFE: Aesthetics, Afro-American; Clothing; Storytelling; / Proverbs; Shotgun House; HISTORY AND MANNERS: / Soul Food; LANGUAGE: Gullah; Indian Languages; / Indian Trade Languages; MUSIC: Spirituals; / Banjo; Fiddle

Charles Joyner
University of South Carolina—
Coastal Carolina College

Melville J. Herskovits, *The Myth of the Negro Past* (1941); Charles Joyner, *Down by the Riverside: A South Carolina Slave Community* (1984); Lawrence W. Levine, *Black Culture and Black Consciousness: Afro-American Folk Thought from Slavery to Freedom* (1978); Robert Farris Thompson, *Flash of the Spirit: African and Afro-American Art and Philosophy* (1983); John Michael Vlach, *The Afro-American Tradition in Decorative Arts* (1978); Peter Wood, *Black Majority: Negroes in Colonial South Carolina from 1670 through the Stono Rebellion* (1974). ☆

Dance, Black

An enduring expressiveness, even during the oppression of slavery, marks the history of black dance in America, and through dance many aspects of the African heritage of black Americans thrive. As Lynne Fauley Emery in her seminal work *Black Dance in the United States from 1619 to 1970* (1972) explains, "A fundamental element of African aesthetic expression was the dance." When slave-traders plundered Africa, dance assumed new meaning. Aboard slaveships the traders frequently forced their captives to dance either for entertainment for the crew or for exercise (healthy slaves brought higher prices). Even under such conditions the slaveship dances served expressive purposes, too.

Slave couple dancing, as portrayed in* The Century Magazine, *February 1886

A strong African heritage flourished among slaves in the West Indies and spread to plantations of the American South. Among the dances carried over were the Calenda, the Chica, and the Juba or Jumba. The beat of the drum, an integral part of black dance, largely died out in the South after the so-called Stono insurrection in South Carolina in 1739, when escaping slaves beat drums to rally participants. Fearing a secret drum communication system among blacks, slaveowners pressed for prohibitions of slave assemblies and the use of drums. Except in the Georgia Sea Islands and Louisiana, slaves replaced the drum accompaniment to dances by slapping and patting their bodies, stomping their feet, and blowing reed pipes.

On southern plantations slaves danced both freely and under duress. Plantation owners often brought slaves to "the big house" to entertain through dance and music. Many owners prized slaves who danced well, and they sponsored dancing contests. Some owners allowed slave dances on their own plantations, and some gave written passes for slaves to attend dances on other plantations. Whites held conflicting views about black dance, however. Even those who enjoyed the slave entertainment tended to characterize black dances as heathen, lewd, and wild. Black dances, including ones such as the Ring Shout, which were part of religious services, met with particularly strong disapproval from white Protestants.

Occasions for dancing included funerals, weddings, quiltings, corn shuckings, Saturday evenings, and holidays such as Christmas and St. John's Day (June 24). Funeral dances in particular retained African elements, whereas wedding dances (called such despite prohibition of legal slave marriages on plantations) showed stronger European influences. Popular dances included the Buck, the Pigeon Wing, the Jig, the Cake-Walk, the Ring Dance, the Buzzard Lope, Water Dances, and the Juba. Agnes de Mille notes that the rhythm of such dances infused American dance and music with a new lifeblood through the accent on the offbeat or upbeat, a rhythm completely different from European styles. The cotillions, reels, and quadrilles of whites influenced black dances later in the antebellum period.

Black dance in New Orleans had its own character and importance. New Orleans was one of the river-port cities where the Coonjine, or Counjaille, dance sprang up among the slaves who were hired out by their masters as stevedores or roustabouts. In the late 1700s and early 1800s quadroon women—those born to a mulatto mother and white father—sought to become the mistresses of upper-class white men and staged elaborate dances in order to form liaisons. The dances, however, represented white American and European trends rather than black ones. The dances of slaves at Congo Square, an open field "northwest of the city limits," contrasted sharply. Seeking to curb the influence of West Indian immigrants in the early 1800s, the New Orleans city council prohibited assemblies of slaves for dancing and other purposes except on Sundays in an open place. Congo Square, or Congo Plains, became that site. Drums were allowed as accompaniment to such popular dances as the Chica, the Babouille, the Cata, the Voudou, and the Congo. New Orleans blacks also witnessed special, frenzied voodoo ceremonial dances incorporating many African elements, and whites envisioned such dances as cannibalistic rituals. New Orleans's Mardi Gras began as a segregated event, and black participants devised their own festivities and incorporated dances in their parades.

Meanwhile, the minstrelsy tradition spread nationwide. "Even before the Revolutionary War," states Emery, "Americans were being entertained by impersonations of Negroes, and particularly of Negro dancing." In 1828 T. D. Rice, a northern performer, donned blackface and performed as Jim Crow, supposedly mimicking the dance of a crippled, elderly black groom he had seen. Historians generally agree with Emery that "Rice . . . rather than giving audiences a true picture of Negro dance, may have created the first clear-cut, long-lasting caricature of that dance: that grotesque, shuffling, peculiar, eccentric, jumping, loose-limbed, awkward, funny and, of course, rhythmic dance."

One outstanding exception among minstrel performers was the great black dancer William Henry Lane, known as Master Juba, who in his brief lifetime introduced a style that blended Irish and Afro-American dance. In general, though, minstrel shows parodied black life through incorporation of such dances as the Walk-Around and the Cake-Walk. Stereotypes of happy, naturally rhythmic, dancing blacks lingered long afterward. Even black minstrel performers of the 1860s felt compelled to wear wigs and paint exaggerating features to conform to white audiences' views of blacks. Among the black minstrel dancers who achieved great fame were Billy Kersands, member of the Georgia Minstrel troupe and master of the Virginia Essence dance, and Ernest Hogan, member of the Georgia Graduates minstrel troupe and originator of the Pasmala dance step.

In the 1890s increasing numbers of black performers entered the stage. In 1891 dancer Bill Robinson, a native of Richmond, Va., moved from Louisville, Ky., to New York with the popular show *The South before the War*. Robinson, later known as "Bojangles" and "The

King of Tapology," broke barriers as the first black star of the Ziegfeld Follies but gained more recognition—and criticism—for film roles late in his career as the kindly, shuffling servant in scenes with Shirley Temple. Robinson's ability to create rhythmic sound through dance markedly shaped later tap-dancing trends. Throughout the 1920s black tap dancers such as Robinson and Clayton "Peg-Leg" Bates, a native of South Carolina, drew applause. Tap became associated with black dancers despite its origins in Irish and English clogging.

While groundbreaking shows such as *Darktown Follies* and *Shuffle Along* enthralled northern audiences with black song and dance, small black minstrel troupes continued to tour the South, eventually forming a vaudeville circuit called the Theatre Owners' Booking Association (TOBA). After the Civil War blacks in the South turned primarily to the churches as a social center. Many churches strongly disapproved of dance, yet traditions lived on. Emery describes one important trend: "There also developed a peculiar institution called the jook, or juke house. . . . Jook came to mean a Negro pleasure house: either a bawdy house or house for dancing, drinking, and gambling. It is in these jooks that 'the Negro dances circulated over the world' were created. Before being seen on the stage by the outside world, these dances made the rounds of Southern jukes."

Two highly popular dances that had such beginnings were the Black Bottom, which originated in Nashville, Tenn., and the Big Apple, which originated near Columbia, S.C. As masses of southern blacks moved to the North, particularly to Harlem, in the early 1900s, they took or influenced such dances as the Charleston, Ballin' the Jack, the Shimmy, and the Mooche. Other dances with black roots evolved, too, such as "the Lindy Hop, Jitterbug, Shag, Suzi-Q, Camel Walk and Truckin'."

Progress came slowly in concert dance and classical ballet. Black dancers were long scorned because of American and European whites' standards of grace, beauty, and aesthetic purity. On an amateur level, however, The Hampton Institute Creative Dance Group (Hampton, Va.) pioneered in exploring black dance traditions in the South. Its student performers toured the country and emphasized dances based on both African and southern plantation traditions. The Hampton Institute programs both directly and indirectly influenced black dance trends, and Emery notes that "black concert dance companies were formed throughout the segregated institutions of the South, including Spellman College in Atlanta, Fisk University, Howard University, and Tuskegee Institute." Particularly at the South's predominantly black institutions strong programs in black dance still thrive.

In the realm of professional dance, black southerners have faced limited opportunities, though the black southern dance heritage has definitely influenced nationwide trends. By the 1970s black dancers and choreographers had made many inroads across the country. Alvin Ailey, a native of Texas who moved as a youth to Los Angeles, formed in 1958 the Alvin Ailey American Dance Theatre, one of the most highly acclaimed and widely known companies in the United States. Various famous productions have focused on themes of black experiences in the South, such as *District Storyville*, focusing on the early black jazz musicians who played in brothels in New Orleans, and Pearl Primus's *Strange Fruit*, dealing with lynchings of blacks in the South. Currently the South boasts such excellent showcases for dance performance as the Spoleto U.S.A. Festival in Charleston, S.C., and the American Dance Festival in Durham, N.C. Dance companies in the South include some that focus on black dance, such as the African-American Dance Ensemble of North Carolina, and many dance leaders encourage more exploration of forms that uniquely express all realms of black experience.

Blacks continue to influence popular dance styles, and singers such as James Brown often introduce a new dance with an accompanying song. Memphian Rufus Thomas began his musical career on the minstrel circuit and later recorded his "Funky Chicken," the title of both his song and the dance he popularized. Most recently, Michael Jackson has achieved international fame for his music and accompanying dance step, the "Moon Walk," a "postmodern" example of black dance no longer rooted in southern black culture.

See also FOLKLIFE: Voodoo; MUSIC: Dance, Development of; Minstrelsy; RECREATION: Mardi Gras; URBANIZATION: / Charleston; New Orleans

Sharon A. Sharp
University of Mississippi

Barbara N. Cohen-Stratymer, *Biographical Dictionary of Dance* (1982); *Dance Magazine* (May 1984, March 1985); Lynne F. Emery, *Black Dance in the United States from 1619 to 1970* (1972); Jane Goldberg, *Dance Scope* (Summer 1981); Cobbett Steinberg, ed., *The Dance Anthology* (1980); Ellen Switzer, *Dancers! Horizons in American Dance* (1982); Julinda L. Williams, *Dance Scope* (Spring 1980). ☆

Education, Black

Formal education has been of vital importance to the status and aspirations of southern blacks. Denied to all but a few before the Civil War, it later became a barometer of discrimination, subject to successful court action and political protest. To individual black people throughout America it has been a main institutional means to gain personal respect, economic security, and racial progress. Its importance has long made black schooling the focus of much historical research by Carter G. Woodson, Horace Mann Bond, and other black scholars. Recent years have seen a new generation of highly critical scholarship that has placed the South in the context of the national political economy as it has probed reform movements, the southern class structure, and the role of schooling in "social control" by powerful interests, some of which have operated globally.

Beginning with mid-18th-century South Carolina legislation, the years prior to the Civil War witnessed the virtual elimination of formal education and literacy training for southern blacks, both slave and free. Although slavemasters might instruct one or two slaves to read in order to study the Scriptures, the idea of formal schools was another matter. Religious attitudes, some of which portrayed the black as subhuman, rationalized this situation and reinforced attitudes on the potential dangers of educated blacks to southern society, a theme that became a persistent phobia in southern history.

The Civil War spurred the growth of formal education. In 1868 the Hampton Institute was founded with the aid of the Union army. In 1865 the Bureau of Refugees, Freedmen, and Abandoned Lands was established by the federal government to provide general welfare. Within a year its mandate was extended to schooling and it began to provide a wide range of educational opportunities for blacks and poor whites. For five years it attracted teachers from the North and cooperated with missionary and religious organizations, assisting newly founded institutions, including Hampton, Fisk University (1865), Berea College (1855), and Atlanta University (1865). In 1867 Howard University, which was named after General O. O. Howard, the commissioner of the Freedmen's Bureau, was chartered in Washington, D.C., by the federal government. Immediately after the war most states set up school funds, although in many instances blacks had to pay special taxes in addition to those required of all citizens. In sum, there was a widespread black enthusiasm for education and a recognition that it was a key to economic and political power—a belief not usually shared by even those whites interested in black schooling.

Black legislators played an important role in the establishment of public education systems throughout the South, but their influence waned dramatically after the end of Reconstruction. The Ku Klux Klan had found schools a ready target in that era, and afterwards the forces of disfranchisement, discrimination, and segregation soon began to flourish. Attitudes that reinforced black inferiority were institutionalized in the work of Hampton and the Tuskegee Institute (1881), particularly after the 1895 "Atlanta Compromise" address by the latter's principal, Booker T. Washington. An internationally known advocate of industrial education and vocational labor, Washington became a leading symbol of black accommodation to political disfranchisement and exercised considerable influence over the quality of segregated and underfunded black educational institutions and systems throughout the South.

In 1896 the U.S. Supreme Court ruled in favor of "separate-but-equal" facilities for blacks in *Plessy* v. *Ferguson*. This decision legalized segregation and led to increased patterns of underfunding for black education even though white middle-class "progressive" politicians, often in concert with populist allies, soon improved all public education, partly to accommodate and pacify poor whites. Black colleges, which in many cases were little more than secondary schools, received unequal funding from state or, under land-grant provisions, federal sources. Many remained controlled by whites who believed in black inferiority and who consequently administered them in highly authoritarian fashion, a mode of control shared by some black college presidents. Although Hampton, Tuskegee, Fisk, and many other institutions trained black teachers, very few opportunities for graduate study or professional training existed in the South, and only Meharry Medical College (1876) in Nashville and Howard in Washington offered training in medicine, and the latter in law, of a quality comparable to that available in white universities. Black medical education faced the additional burden of a Carnegie Foundation report by Abraham Flexner in 1910, which recommended that medical needs among blacks be treated as community health issues, thereby affecting the quality of training and reinforcing fears about blacks as a "health menace." The legacy of the black medical schools is still very evident. As of 1983 almost half of all black physicians and dentists practicing in the United States had completed their professional training at Meharry.

By the early years of the 20th century protest was under way, expressed through the Niagara Movement and the founding of the National Association for the Advancement of Colored People. W. E. B. Du Bois, a Harvard-trained professor at Atlanta University, visibly opposed black accommodation and Booker T. Washington's "Tuskegee Machine." He encouraged research on black life, challenged black students to demand changes in collegiate conditions, and corrected stereotypes of black people and their African ancestry. Du Bois edited the NAACP's *Crisis*, a journal of signal importance to blacks and to white sympathizers. Consistent with his call for a black "talented tenth," a new generation of leaders, many of whom were trained at Howard University's Law School, used the courts successfully to challenge unequal resources, inferior conditions, disfranchisement, and, in the landmark *Brown v. Board of Education* (1954), de jure segregation itself. The pages of the *Journal of Negro Education*, founded in 1932 at Howard, published the research and political ideas of educators who documented the status of black education throughout the United States and, indeed, in other parts of the world.

The development of a public educational system for southern blacks was plagued by their rural status, inferior facilities, poorly trained teachers and administrators, white hostility, and a new technology that permitted whites to bus their children away from blacks. In cities like Atlanta high schools came very late and their peculiar "vocational" and "industrial" emphasis was of little relevance to an increasingly urbanized industrial economy. To make matters worse, black educators frequently faced discrimination from white counterparts and their unions, which played the race issue to economic advantage.

The 1920s and 1930s saw educational psychology and other manifestations of educational science come to the South. Here, too, blacks faced problems, for they were subjected to culturally biased tests that portrayed them as intellectually deficient and to guidance and counseling programs that slotted them into menial jobs. Black professional associations such as the National Association of Teachers in Colored Schools and the Association of Colleges and Secondary Schools for Negroes strove to improve standards with only mixed results. White philanthropies, including the General Education Board and the Carnegie Corporation, continued to invest disproportionately in the modernization of white education. Blacks were discriminated against by the National Education Association. The American Federation of Teachers, which took a lead nationally in challenging segregation, maintained separate southern chapters. The "progressive" curriculum reform movements that swept the South in the late 1920s and early 1930s kept blacks at a disadvantage, using modern ideas about the differentiated "needs-oriented" course of study to promote nonacademic training. Attempts to gain higher education showed but fitful progress, and economic collapse in the 1930s made blacks suffer inordinately throughout America. Most Depression-era federal programs, including the Tennessee Valley Authority, the Civilian Conservation Corps, and the National Youth Administration, put the New Deal's stamp on segregation and inequality.

Blacks played a visible and important role in fighting racism and totalitarianism through their bravery in World War II and many wartime industries depended on their labor. For these reasons, and because headway was being made in the courts against separate and unequal provisions, southern states began to increase and even equalize expenditures on black schooling. Much of this spending, however, was intended to protect segregation so that even after the 1954 *Brown* decision the regional edifice of legalized segregation failed to crumble. President Eisenhower used federal troops to protect black students who were admitted to Little Rock Central High School in 1957, but the main progress came as the result of protest marches in the early 1960s and from the passage of the Civil Rights Acts of 1957, 1960, and 1964.

Results in the ensuing years have shown the lingering impact of centuries of racism and discrimination. The outer manifestations of legalized racial segregation have disappeared from the South, but integration has contributed to the establishment of an elaborate informal network of private white schools, many of which are Christian academies conducted under fundamentalist religious auspices. Many southern systems of public higher education contain colleges and universities that remain somewhat separate and unequal, while historically black colleges continue their struggle for survival and quality. A generation of black principals and administrators, as well as many teachers, lost their jobs in the reorganization of southern education. In some states, such as Florida, the education of blacks is mired in controversies over competency tests for students and teachers.

Black leaders began to argue in the early 1980s that the main problems facing a majority of blacks were found in deep-seated structural problems of a political and economic nature. Blacks remain grossly underrepresented at all levels of southern government. National income statistics suggest that in spite of the growth of a prosperous middle class, blacks are becoming poorer relative to the rest of the population. Due partly to continued concentration in decayed—northern and southern—urban areas there are disproportionately high unemployment levels, particularly among young people. In Texas and Florida, moreover, blacks face increasing competition from Latin American immigrants, a situation that has spilled over into violence. "Sunbelt" prosperity, which held out much hope, has not been distributed equally, nor is southern economic activity as robust in relation to other parts of the nation as it was in the 1970s.

Other major problems lie in the limited number of blacks who serve as school superintendents or school board members, even when public school systems are predominantly black. As of 1986, Georgia, for example, had only four black school superintendents, although 52 of the 187 school districts were predominantly black. With 32 predominantly black school districts among its total of 128 districts, Alabama had eight black superintendents. Among North Carolina's 141 school districts were four with a black school superintendent and four school boards with a black majority. Tensions have arisen, too, because it is common for white superintendents of predominantly black school systems to send their own children to segregated private schools. The imbalances have arisen for a variety of reasons: whites' control of political and tax structures, and thereby of school boards, low voting rates among blacks, and a shortage of blacks with administrative experience in the schools. In recent years, however, blacks increasingly have pressed for changes, particularly through legal means. Controversy erupted in Indianola, Miss., in 1986 when a white administrator was hired to succeed the retiring superintendent (also white) of the 93 percent black school district. Indianola's black residents boycotted the schools and white-owned businesses for 37 days, leading to a buy out of the new superintendent's contract coupled with his resignation and unanimous approval by the school board of Robert Merritt, a black administrator. Overall, however, assessments show that blacks' strides as administrators and school board members will probably be limited in the near future.

The federal role has been of assistance to blacks, but bureaucratization, persistent antifederal attitudes among conservative whites, and shifting federal priorities have meant a mixed return. National discussion about the overall condition of American education has not included a significant black presence, making it difficult to determine how changes will affect their relative condition, particularly as the national industrial and agricultural bases erode in the face of new technologically based industries. As in the years following the Civil War, black education faces regional and national conditions, most of which may well be beyond the power of the school to influence significantly.

See also EDUCATION articles; LAW: / *Brown* v. *Board of Education*; *Plessy* v. *Ferguson*; SCIENCE AND MEDICINE: Medical Education

Ronald K. Goodenow
Trinity College
Hartford, Connecticut

Horace Mann Bond, *The Education of the Negro in the American Social Order* (1934); Henry A. Bullock, *A History of Negro Education in the South: From 1619 to the Present* (1967); Dudley Clendinen, *New York Times* (23 June 1986); Vincent P. Franklin and James D. Anderson, eds., *New Perspectives on Black Educational History* (1978); Ronald K. Goodenow and Arthur O. White, eds., *Education and the Rise of the New South* (1981); National Alliance of Business, *Directory of Historically Black Colleges and Universities in the United States* (1983); Diane Ravitch, *The Troubled Crusade: American Education, 1945–1980* (1983); Meyer Weinberg, *A Chance to Learn: A History of Race and Education in the United States* (1977); Carter G. Woodson, *The Education of the Negro Prior to 1861* (1919). ☆

Family, Black

In American culture, mention of "the family" suggests the ideal of a nuclear family household, which includes a legally married man and woman and their children. Many Americans might mention other family members, but seldom others beyond primary relatives with whom they have shared a household either as children (parents and siblings) or as adults (children and spouses). This family ideal has been popular in the United States for at least a century and is reflected in most of the family literature, in the media, in public policies regarding the family, and in the philosophy underlying human service programs oriented toward families.

The southern black family includes more than a household of primary relatives. A history of economic and political marginality has made it necessary for southern blacks to depend on support systems beyond the household for their survival. Although friendship bonds and patron-client relationships with whites and other higher status individuals contributed to southern black survival, rights and obligations within these relationships are not usually thought of as being as dependable as kinship bonds during times of need. Thus, early in their history, the concept of family for southern blacks began to extend beyond the residential unit to include not only parents, siblings, and children, but also biologically related kinsmen such as parents' parents and siblings, siblings' children, and children's children, as well as people who are not related at all. Such extension has facilitated survival for blacks in the South by increasing the size and range (including people of different social, ethnic, and racial categories) of the "family."

Although protection, care, instruction, and discipline of children are the primary responsibilities of the parents in the nuclear ideal, southern blacks have utilized shifting residences, fosterage, and informal adoptions to spread these obligations among other "family" members. Children may grow up within a number of households within the family groupings, or they might grow up entirely in a household other than that of their parents. The relatives or friends with whom a child resides might become foster parents of the child, or they might informally adopt the child. In either case, the child's relationship with his biological parents is usually not severed.

As a way to extend the rights and privileges of the family relationship, southern blacks used kinship terms in addressing nonkinsmen. Thus, when someone is addressed with specific kinship terms such as "mother" or "brother," the user of the term is stating that he or she will behave respectively like a son (or daughter) or brother (or sister) in his or her relationship to the person addressed, and that he or she is expecting a motherly or brotherly type of behavior in return. Southern blacks strengthened their links with distant relatives and nonkin relations by upgrading kinship terms, referring, for example, to a third cousin as an aunt or a wife's cousin as a brother-in-law.

In addition to the extended family relationship, the possession of land has given the southern black family a distinctive character. Landownership was a symbol of freedom for the free black during slavery and for the freedman following emancipation. Although land was always difficult for blacks to obtain, many of them did manage to do so. Among blacks in some southern communities, land was not a commodity to be sold but a resource to be used by kinsmen and to be passed down from generation to generation. In some families, the right to land and land use is controlled by one of the oldest and/or the dominant family members. Although black families are rapidly losing their land in the South, family land that resembles small villages with multiple households of related units is still visible in many places.

In an extended black family there is often a dominant dyad or individual, around whom many extended-family activities revolve. One of the family group's oldest couples or persons—often a widow—typically assumes this role. If there is family land, the dominant couple or individual usually lives on it, in many cases controlling its use. If multiple households live on the family land, the dominant person's household is the hub of local extended family activity, and nonlocal family members come first to that household when visiting. When the dominant family figure dies, another family member (usually an offspring) takes this role.

Another key to understanding the southern black family is its relationship to the church. In many rural areas and small towns of the South, churches are made up of a number of extended families. The church also provides rules regarding marriage, male and female behavior, childhood socialization, and respect for the elders. The church provides a community that blacks control. Some churches have "missionary societies" whose primary function is to visit the sick and "shut-in." Churches respond to some of the economic needs of poorer black families through gifts during special times such as Christmas and through special collections of money during Sunday services. Close kinship terms such as father or mother are sometimes used to refer to all elderly people in the church.

Communal occasions reconfirm the extended social support systems of the southern black family. Sunday dinner is a weekly "small feast," which brings together local primary relatives who do not reside together. Large dinners on Thanksgiving and Christmas bring together primary relatives who live in the same area as well as relatives who live elsewhere. Relatives also get together during other holidays such as Memorial Day, the Fourth of July, and Labor Day. "Cookouts," picnics, and barbecues are main events at such occasions. Larger extended family groupings come together at annual family reunions, and even larger groupings come together at church homecomings. Family reunions bring together the descendants of an ancestor or ancestral parents. A church homecoming brings together the present and past membership of a church. The overlapping between kinship and church memberships frequently results in church homecomings resembling large family reunions. Extended family and nonfamily friends also come together for weddings and funerals. These events bring people together and also serve to repay obligations, establish rights to new relationships, and reconfirm old links of rights and obligations.

Although blacks might have wanted to retain African family patterns in their pure form, the slave environment would not allow it. Unilineal descent as it was known in Africa was impossible to maintain because the slavemasters would not allow the development of large corporate groups based on ties as strong as kinship. The slave, in the meantime, needed social support wherever he could get it. Thus, not only did they most likely practice fosterage and adoption at that time, but they also attached kin terms to nonkinsmen and upgraded the kin terms of distant relatives.

By the end of slavery, black family life was becoming stabilized. But emancipation brought new pressures. Because freed slaves knew how to do little else but farm, the lack of opportunities to buy land and to get employment outside the plantation made it difficult for the vast majority of freed slaves to maintain a nuclear family, let alone an extended family. Southern postemancipation problems led to black migration in search of a better life, the emergence of a legal system that imprisoned a disproportionate number of black males, and a host of factors that contributed to the shortened life span of blacks, particularly males. All these factors contributed to an imbalance in local black sex ratios, which in turn affected the structure and function of the southern black family.

One pattern of migration, which accelerated during and after World War I, was to the urban North. For the first one or two generations, black migrants to northern cities maintained their southern kinship systems. They also developed support systems in the North similar to those that they knew in the South. In the absence of kin, they substituted friends. In some cases, supportive friends were treated as kinsmen. Those networks, though, had fewer kin involved than those in the South. After two generations, some urban black families tended to form new extended families. However, the lack of access to land in the urban North prevented black families from organizing themselves around landownership or from residing in multiple households of close proximity as in the South. As a consequence, land eventually lost some of its symbolic significance for northern blacks. When urban heirs sell family land in the South upon the deaths of their parents, the southern black extended family can be affected.

A growing reliance on social services, instead of kin and friends, has taken place in the South, as among southern migrants to the North, particularly with mechanization of southern farms and displacement of farm workers. Southern blacks, however, have managed to maintain to a considerable degree their attachment to the traditional kinship system, family land, and the church.

See also FOLKLIFE: Family Folklore; Funerals; Weddings; MYTHIC SOUTH: Family; WOMEN'S LIFE: / Elderly; Family Reunion

Tony L. Whitehead
University of North Carolina
at Chapel Hill

Allison Davis, Burleigh B. Gardner, and Mary R. Gardner, *Deep South: A Social Anthropological Study of Caste and Class* (1941); K. Y. Day, in *Holding On to the Land and the Lord: Kinship, Ritual, Land Tenure and Social Policy in the Rural South*, ed. Robert L. Hall and Carol B. Stack (1982); John Hope Franklin, *From Slavery to Freedom: A History of Negro Americans* (1947, 5th ed., 1980); E. Franklin Frazier, *Negro Family in the United States* (1939); Herbert G. Gutman, *The Black Family in Slavery and Freedom, 1750–1925* (1977); Melville J. Herskovits, *The Myth of the Negro Past* (1941); Jacqueline Jones, *Labor of Love, Labor of Sorrow: Black Women, Work, and the Family from Slavery to the Present* (1985); E. P. Martin and J. M. Martin, *The Black Extended Family* (1978); D. B. Shimkin, E. M. Shimkin, and Dennis A. Frate, eds., *The Extended Family in Black Societies* (1978). ☆

Film Images, Black

Between World Wars I and II, a small film industry outside the circle of Hollywood studios produced more than 200 "race movies"—feature films intended for a market composed of the black populations in the centers of American cities. Most of these films engaged their audiences depicting situations and characters that reversed the Hollywood portrayal of blacks. Instead of black servants, comedians, and musicians, there were black doctors, policemen, cowboys, judges, gangsters, and soldiers.

During its history from about 1916 through World War II, the race movie industry presented its audiences with a remarkably consistent image of the South as a spiritual home of the most deeply felt values of Afro-American life. This benign vision of life in the South derived from two circumstances. First, race movies usually featured all-black casts and situations, thereby precluding interracial dramatic conflict; and second, many black moviegoers, North and South, shared a memory of the rural South as a family home to be spoken of in only the most sentimental terms.

This black version of southern nostalgia differed from the Hollywood model in that the major studios often sentimentalized not the region but its race relations. Beginning with *Uncle Tom's Cabin* (1903) and extending through *Birth of a Nation* (1915) to *Gone with the Wind* (1939), such films formed a clearly defined genre.

Rarely did Hollywood attempt to present the South from a black perspective. Among the more successful of a handful of departures from cinematic convention were *Hallelujah!* (1929) and *Hearts in Dixie* (1929), both of which exploited a black musical idiom; *The Green Pastures* (1936), based upon Roark Bradford's *Ol' Man Adam an' His Chillun* (1928), a collection of tales told as though from the point of view of a rural black preacher, which, in turn, had been the source of Marc Connelly's Pulitzer Prize play entitled *The Green Pastures* (1929). In 1937 two black collaborators, Clarence Muse and Langston Hughes, contributed to the script of *Way Down South*, a B-movie treatment of the South as a "down-home" source of black virtues. Along with these few features, Hollywood produced occasional short films that ranged from "the usual old southern cabin setting" to the evocative *Yamacraw* (1930), which *Film Daily* characterized as "a jazz symphony of Negro life that is arresting in movement as well as in dramatic idea."

The earliest surviving race movie set in a southern locale was *The Birth of a Race* (1918), an intended antidote to the racial propaganda in D. W. Griffith's *Birth of a Nation*. Originally an ambitious history of mankind that gave due recognition to blacks, it soon passed from the hands of its black creators as costs mounted and grew into a pacifist movie in which blacks had only a small place. Nevertheless, in the last reel blacks are seen as an enduring presence in southern life and as willing volunteers during World War I.

In several black films throughout the 1920s, the southern image was of nurturing, rural permanence, an area in which blacks challenged the reigning social order and promoted racial unity. Among the best were Oscar Micheaux's *Within Our Gates* (1920), which dramatized the lynching of Leo Frank in Atlanta "as witnessed by the author"; *The Brute* (1920), in which the black boxer, Sam Langford, fought against a lynch mob in a film condemned in several southern towns as "a very dangerous picture to show in the South"; Micheaux's *Body and Soul* (1924), an exposé of corrupt preachers and bootleggers in "Tatesville," Ga.; and Micheaux's *Birthright* (1924), a story of a black Ivy Leaguer whose return to the South combined the themes of personal aspiration, racial solidarity, and a return to familial roots.

Several producers of race movies not

only took up southern themes and locales in their films, but actually located in the South. Among them were Cotton Blossom and Lone Star in San Antonio, Ben Strasser in Winston-Salem, C. B. Campbell in Pensacola, and Ker-Mar in Baltimore. During the era of soundfilm, at least two companies established combined production and distribution centers in the South—Ted Toddy's Dixie National Pictures in Atlanta and Alfred Sack's Sackamuse Company in Dallas.

At least two black innovators developed a unique southern genre of visual proselytizing. Eloyce Gist of Washington and Kiefer Jackson of Baltimore were traveling evangelists and lecturers on religious subjects who combined film with oratory. Jackson's show had shots of the Holy Land and reportorial film of ministerial conventions, but Gist included at least one film in her presentation which graphically depicted an allegorical railroad train hurtling toward heaven or hell—depending on whether the passengers decide in time to change their secular ways to live lives of faith and good works.

By the opening of World War II, the black audience had migrated northward, thereby stimulating a trend toward more urbane formulas that emphasized cops-and-robbers "action" rather than homely values. Thereafter, only Spencer Williams, an actor-director-writer who worked for Sack, produced films that catered to southern black audiences. His *Go Down Death*, a film indebted to James Weldon Johnson's poem of the same title, and his *Blood of Jesus* closed out the Depression decade, the latter film earning, in the estimation of Sack's bookkeeper, more than any black film ever made. Both films were shot on southern ground and were deeply rooted in traditional regional values.

Paul Winfield (left) and Kevin Hooks (right) in a scene from* Sounder *(1972)

With the demise of race movies after World War II, Hollywood products ranged over a broad spectrum of attitudes toward the South. *Song of the South* (1946) and *Saratoga Trunk* (1946) celebrated or romanticized traditional white southern values. A spate of movies derived from the works of William Faulkner, Hamilton Basso, and other southerners portrayed the South as sexually repressed and cruel. Still others—*Band of Angels*, *The Foxes of Harrow*, *Drum*, *Mandingo*—were laden with social and political messages that required depicting antebellum times with undisguised rage. In recent years only a handful of black-centered films have treated the South in the warmly sentimental idiom of Spencer Williams's movies. Among them are *Nothing but a Man*, *Sounder*, *Conrack*, and *The Autobiography of Miss Jane Pittman*—the latter a film made for television, a medium that seemed to trade on sentimentality and even to magnify it in such grandiose projects as the incredibly popular *Roots*. Recent films, such as *The Color Purple*

(1985) and *Crossroads* (1986), suggest a renewed interest in southern black life.

See also MEDIA: Film, Blaxploitation; / *Birth of a Nation*; *Color Purple*; *Gone with the Wind*; *Mandingo*; *Roots*; *Uncle Tom's Cabin*

Thomas Cripps
Morgan State University

Donald Bogle, *Toms, Coons, Mulattoes, Mammies, & Bucks: An Interpretive History of Blacks in American Films* (1973); Thomas Cripps, *Slow Fade to Black: The Negro in American Films, 1900–1942* (1977); Phyllis Rauch Klotman, *Frame by Frame—A Black Filmography* (1979); Daniel J. Leab, *From Sambo to Superspade: The Black Experience in Motion Pictures* (1975); Henry T. Sampson, *Blacks in Black and White: A Source Book on Black Films* (1977). ☆

Folklore, Black

The folklore of black southerners is a process of artistic communication, exemplified in recurring performances of music, folktales, and material culture. These performances reflect both continuity with Africa and creativity in the New World.

The oral traditions of black southerners include creole languages such as Gullah and a variety of dialects generally known as "black speech." Southern black folk speech has also included special linguistic forms such as jive talk, with African-derived slang words such as "guy," "jive," "hip," and "dig." Especially notable are such marked forms as rapping and toasting and ritualized linguistic interactions such as signifying and playing the dozens. Black southern proverbs strongly reflect the African preference for speaking by indirection.

Black southern folktales have been told since Africans first arrived in the South. The tales have even influenced the narratives of whites and Native Americans in the region. The tales include legends or folk narratives told as though true. Black southern legends include memorates, or personal experience narratives, as well as local legends and hero tales of such characters as "Old Nat" (Turner), "Moses" (Harriet Tubman), Shine, Jack Johnson, and Joe Louis. Other legends explain why buzzards are bald and why rabbits have long ears and short tails. Southern humor is also exemplified in the outrageous tall tales of black southerners.

The most popular folktales among black southerners have been trickster tales, with their theme of the struggle for mastery between the trickster—a small but sly animal such as Brer Rabbit—and his bigger, more powerful adversary. The trickster defeats his rival not by superior physical strength, but by superior intellect. Folklorists such as J. Mason Brewer and Richard Dorson collected a cycle of trickster stories featuring the never-ending contest of the slave trickster John and Old Marster.

Black southern music had its origins in the field hollers of plantation laborers and the street cries of urban peddlers. A special form of work songs was preserved in southern prisons. John and Alan Lomax collected many such songs from the remarkable Huddie Ledbetter, who after release from prison attained fame as "Leadbelly," the "king of the twelve-string guitar players." From the haunting spirituals of slaves, black gospel music was developed by such singers as Blind Gary Davis and Mahalia Jackson and composers such as Thomas

A. Dorsey and the Reverend Herbert Brewster. The blues evolved from rural performers such as Tommy Johnson, Charley Patton, Mississippi John Hurt, and Blind Lemon Jefferson through female performers like Bessie Smith, Ma Rainey, and Chippie Hill to the modern urban blues of Mississippi Delta expatriates like Muddy Waters (McKinley Morganfield), Howlin' Wolf (Chester Burnett), and B. B. King. The reels and buck dances of slave fiddlers and banjo pickers evolved through fife and drum bands of northern Mississippi, jug bands of Memphis and Charleston, and brass bands of New Orleans into early jazz.

Black southern music has proved enormously influential on white southern musicians. Country music stars Jimmie Rodgers, Hank Williams, Maybelle Carter of the famous Carter Family, Bob Wills (the pioneer of jazz-tinged western swing), and Bill Monroe (the father of bluegrass), all acknowledged the influence of black southern music on them. In the 1950s Elvis Presley stepped into a Memphis recording studio, and out of the integration of white country music and black rhythm and blues ignited the new phenomenon of rock and roll.

Black southern folk belief is strongly influenced by African patterns of folk belief. African folk medicine of both the pharmaceutical and psychological varieties continues to be practiced in the South. Natural phenomena serve as signs foretelling either changing weather or approaching death. Ghosts or haunts—the spirits of the dead—return to trouble the living in the New World as in the Old, and their unwelcome visits can be warded off by various charms. Black religion incorporates the African religious phenomenon of spirit possession, called forth by the black preacher. But other African religious traditions, such as voodoo or hoodoo, exist apart from black Christianity. Many black southerners still take their problems to local conjurers. With the aid of mojo hands, goopher dust, John the Conqueror root, and other substances held to be magical, such conjurers can protect one from misfortune and cast spells upon one's enemies.

Among black southerners, as in cultures around the world, long days of toil alternate with periods of ritual festivity. Harvest time is such an occasion in the rural South; Mardi Gras is another in urban New Orleans. Mamie Garvin Fields in her *Lemon Swamp* recalls the Fourth of July celebrations in Charleston on the Battery, from which blacks were barred the rest of the year. The holiday was marked by barbecue and fried fish, music and speeches, and a recitation of the Emancipation Proclamation. Black southerners, following African tradition, still give a festive air to funerals as well as to weddings and such holidays as Christmas. In antebellum North Carolina (as in Jamaica) the John Canoe festival was an exotic part of slave Christmas celebrations in which bands of dancers, keeping time to the beat of the "gumbo box," triangles, and jawbones, begged donations from spectators.

From slavery to the present, black southern artists have created beautiful folk arts. On rice plantations in South Carolina, men and women made baskets in the African style of coiled basketry. Today black basketmakers in South Carolina are internationally acclaimed for continuing the tradition. Slave potters such as the renowned Dave of South Carolina's Edgefield District produced remarkable alkaline glazed stoneware. Their tradition continues in the clay sculpture of Mississippi's James "Son" Thomas. The gourd fiddles, sheep-hide banjos, beef-rib bones, and willow-stalk quills of slave instrument makers formed a tradition that continues today in Eli Owens's mouth-bows and Othar Turner's cane flutes. Throughout the South the achievements of slave seamstresses and quilters are seen in the cross-stitch embroidery of Mamie Garvin Fields and the quilts of Harriet Powers and Pecolia Warner. Slave blacksmiths not only shod horses and other livestock but also made the striking wrought-iron gates and grilles that were especially prized in South Carolina and Louisiana. Charleston's Phillip Simmons has been nationally recognized for his 20th-century wrought-iron artistry.

From slave cabins to the modern shotgun house, black southerners have made unique contributions to the nation's architectural heritage. In its classic form the shotgun house is small and rectangular, one room wide by three rooms deep, with doors at each end and its gable end to the street.

Black southern foodways also exemplify folk cultural expression. Slaves in the Old South ate the foodstuffs of the plantation environment; but slave cooks applied to them African methods of cooking and spicing, remembered recipes, and ancestral tastes—the *soul* ingredients. They thus maintained cultural continuity with Africa, and introduced African foods—such as okra and yams—to the New World. The fusion of Old World and New World traditions continues in black southern recipes for preparing barbecue, gumbo, and other delicacies.

There were important parallels in the folk culture of southerners whose ancestors came from Africa and that of southerners whose ancestors came from Europe. These parallels fostered widespread cultural exchanges and enriched both groups. Today black southerners have a European folk heritage as well as an African one, and white southerners have an African folk heritage as well as a European one.

The South was the principal arena in which various African cultural traditions were transformed into an Afro-American culture. Black southerners kept alive traditions of their African ancestors and adopted traditions from white southerners. Throughout the South, folklore has been at the center of community life. That folklore has kept alive the shadows and ghosts of the past in the present and expresses a common cultural identity.

See also ETHNIC LIFE: Indian Cultural Contributions; FOLKLIFE articles; HISTORY AND MANNERS: Foodways; MUSIC articles

Charles Joyner
University of South Carolina—
Coastal Carolina College

John Blassingame, *The Slave Community: Plantation Life in the Antebellum South* (1972); Judith Wragg Chase, *Afro-American Arts and Crafts* (1971); W. E. B. Du Bois, *The Souls of Black Folk* (1903); Dena J. Epstein, *Sinful Tunes and Spirituals: Black Folk Music to the Civil War* (1977); William Ferris, *Journal of American Folklore* (April–June 1975); Mamie Garvin Fields and Karen Fields, *Lemon Swamp* (1983); Melville J. Herskovits, *The Myth of the Negro Past* (1941); Charles Joyner, *Down by the Riverside: A South Carolina Slave Community* (1984); Lawrence W. Levine, *Black Culture and Black Consciousness: Afro-American Folk Thought from Slavery to Freedom* (1977); Albert J. Raboteau, *Slave Religion: The "Invisible Institution" in the Antebellum*

South (1978); Eileen Southern, *The Music of Black Americans: A History* (1971); Robert Farris Thompson, *Flash of the Spirit: African and Afro-American Art and Philosophy* (1983); Lorenzo Dow Turner, *Africanisms in the Gullah Dialect* (1949); John Michael Vlach, *The Afro-American Tradition in Decorative Arts* (1978); William Wiggins, *Black People and Their Culture* (1976). ☆

Fraternal Orders, Black

The Afro-American fraternal orders and mutual benefit societies that proliferated throughout the South following emancipation evolved over several generations. They emerged from a rich underground of "invisible" institutions and folkways that slaves had created in their plantation communities; and insofar as they represented a folk culture, they owed their origins and style in part to Africa. They also resembled mutual benefit societies among European immigrants and often began out of purely pragmatic necessity. Melville J. Herskovits possibly exaggerated when he argued for a direct link with African cults and secret societies; and W. E. B. Du Bois probably strained the spiritual connection when he argued for a lineal descent from the West African Obeah worship. During slavery these voluntary associations were doubly clandestine, evolving out of a tradition of secret societies and the need to conceal organized behavior from the master class. As a consequence scholars know very little about the existence of orders and lodges among slaves, although Vincent Harding has identified the Twelve Knights of Tabor as a secret network of 40,000 slaves organized in 1846 with the aim of overthrowing slavery.

Among free blacks a more conspicuous tradition accounted for the formal or "visible" side of institutional development. As early as the 18th century, free blacks formed "African Societies" in the northern and southern urban communities, most notably the Free African Society of Philadelphia, founded in 1787. The Free African Society is more often remembered as the parent organization of the African Methodist Episcopal Church, but its own origins were decidedly secular, designed to provide a system of cooperative social welfare for the struggling black community of Philadelphia. This example of the mutual benefit society preceding the church points to the primacy of these societies and to the hazy distinction between the spiritual and the secular in Afro-American culture.

The program of mutual assistance among urban free blacks, especially the elite of Charleston and New Orleans, often reflected biases of class and color as well as a European orientation. Founded in 1790, Charleston's Brown Fellowship Society, for example, limited its membership to mulattoes, a practice that prompted the darker-skinned free blacks to launch their own equally exclusive society, the Free Dark Men of Color. In other cases, most obviously the black Masons (1787) and the Odd Fellows (1843), separate lodges grew out of their exclusion from the mainstream of white societies. Similar black counterpart groups, like the Elks and the Knights of Pythias, were founded after the Civil War.

Indeed the Civil War and emancipation set off an explosion in the number and variety of Afro-American societies. Four million exslaves seeking social and economic expression valued only the family and possibly the church above the benefit society in their hierarchy of basic institutions. In many cases the mutual aid society, the church, the school, and rudimentary insurance and business enterprises were linked by a common founder and a common set of buildings. Du Bois, writing in 1906 about the social phenomenon as a whole, concluded that "no complete account of Negro beneficial societies is possible, so large is their number and so wide their ramification. Nor can any hard and fast line between them and industrial insurance societies be drawn." Their mixed function, he continued, was "partly social intercourse and partly insurance. They furnish pastime from the monotony of work, a chance for parade, and insurance against misfortune. Next to the church they are the most popular organizations among Negroes."

However pressing the force of discrimination in the drive to establish separate black institutions, it would be a mistake to interpret these expressions of black culture as merely a response to exclusion. Black fraternal and mutual benefit societies took on a life and style of their own, tantamount to a southern folkway in the estimation of anthropologists Hylan Lewis and Hortense Powdermaker. In their respective studies of communities in South Carolina and Mississippi, Lewis and Powdermaker agreed that the "insurance envelope" was an omnipresent feature in humble cabins, and that "insurance" along with "church going, hunting and fishing" was a cultural staple. Doubtless, the vast array of lodges and societies provided an outlet for leadership and an avenue for status, respect, and recreation in compensation for what the larger society denied. In remembering his father as the Grand Marshall of the New Orleans Odd Fellows parade, Louis Armstrong may have caught the essence of this positive function: "I was very proud to see him in his uniform and his high hat with the beautiful streamer hanging down . . . Yes, he was a fine figure of a man, my dad. Or at least that is the way he seemed to me as a kid when he strutted by like a peacock at the head of the Odd Fellows Parade."

Finally it should be emphasized that black women served as role models playing key parts as both members and organizers in black fraternal and benefit societies. Most conspicuous among the leaders was Maggie Lena Walker, who in 1899 assumed leadership of the Independent Order of St. Luke, a Richmond fraternal society founded in 1867 by an exslave, Mary Prout. Under Walker's administration, the Order of St. Luke, like its larger Richmond rival, the Grand United Order of True Reformers, embraced an ideology of self-help and racial solidarity, attempting to organize and uplift the entire black community through a broad range of institutions, including a savings bank, a newspaper (the St. Luke *Herald*), and the St. Luke Emporium. The True Reformers added a utopian vision in its retirement community and cooperative farm. Walker's organization did not survive the Great Depression, but as an illustration of its cultural legitimacy, and hence the cultural depth of black fraternal societies, black women in the final years of the 20th century continue to organize under its banner, even in northern cities.

See also HISTORY AND MANNERS: Fraternal Groups; INDUSTRY: / Insurance; WOMEN'S LIFE: / Walker, Maggie Lena

Walter B. Weare
University of Wisconsin—Milwaukee

W. E. B. Du Bois, *Economic Cooperation among Negro Americans* (1907), *Efforts for Social Betterment Among Negro Americans* (1909); Vincent Harding, in *The Making of Black America*, ed. August Meier and Elliot M. Rudwick (1969); Melville J. Herskovits, *The Myth of the Negro Past* (1941); Lawrence W. Levine, *Black Culture and Black Consciousness: Afro-American Folk Thought from Slavery to Freedom* (1977); Hylan Lewis, *Blackways of Kent* (1955); August Meier, *Negro Thought in America, 1880–1915* (1963); William J. Muraskin, *Middle Class Blacks in a White Society: Prince Hall Freemasonry in America* (1975); Hortense Powdermaker, *After Freedom: A Cultural Study in the Deep South* (1939); Walter B. Weare, *Black Business in the New South: A Social History of the North Carolina Mutual Life Insurance Company* (1973). ☆

Freedom Movement, Black

The series of black protests that began with the Montgomery bus boycott of 1955–56 became during the following decade the most significant southern social movement of the 20th century. Although subsequent studies of this black movement usually stressed its civil rights goals and national leadership, the movement generated its own local institutions and leadership seeking economic and political reforms that went beyond the legislation sought by the major preexisting civil rights organizations. Indeed, black participants often called their movement a freedom struggle in order to express its broad range of goals. Rather than simply continuing long-term civil rights efforts by the National Association for the Advancement of Colored People (NAACP) and other national reform organizations, the southern black freedom movement can best be seen as a tactical and, ultimately, an ideological departure from those efforts. The southern movement was characterized by unconventional and increasingly militant tactics, locally initiated protest activity, decentralized control, and an increasing sense of racial consciousness among participants.

The first major phase of the modern black freedom struggle was the Montgomery bus boycott. Although blacks had protested against racial oppression throughout American history, the Montgomery boycott signaled the beginning of a period during which widely shared racial discontent was expressed through mass movements. Existing civil rights organizations did not initiate the movement, although Rosa Parks, whose arrest prompted the boycott, had been secretary of the local NAACP chapter. Parks's unplanned refusal on 1 December 1955 to give up her bus seat to a white man was both an outgrowth of the gradual rise of black political influence in the city and a stimulus for further mobilization of black community resources. On 5 December a group of local leaders established the Montgomery Improvement Association (MIA) to coordinate the boycott and chose as its leader the Reverend Martin Luther King, Jr., who had come to the city in 1954. King, who had received his divinity doctorate from Boston University, was one of the many new leaders who would reflect the increasing confidence and militancy of the movement, and his inspired oratory, filled with references to Christian and Gandhian concepts of nonviolent resistance, attracted widespread, favorable publicity. Despite the bombing of King's house and other acts of intimidation, the boycott continued until December 1956, when Montgomery officials reluctantly obeyed a Supreme Court order to desegregate the bus system.

The Montgomery bus boycott served as a model for black protest movements in other cities, for it demonstrated the ability of black communities to unite and struggle collectively for change. In 1957 King and his supporters founded the Southern Christian Leadership Conference (SCLC) to provide an institutional framework that would allow blacks to go beyond the NAACP's strategy of litigation and lobbying. As SCLC's leader, King moved cautiously, however, and did not initiate any major protest movements during the next five years. Nevertheless, King's presence in a community often increased black enthusiasm and attracted publicity. In addition, ministers and staff members associated with SCLC played crucial roles in many local movements.

The second major phase of the southern black struggle began on 1 February 1960, when four black college students in Greensboro, N.C., sat at a lunch counter reserved for whites. The students had been affiliated with NAACP youth chapters, but they initiated their protest without consulting adult leaders. Other students in Greensboro and elsewhere soon followed their example, finding that the sit-in tactic offered an appealing way for young blacks without special skills and resources to display their discontent. There had been previous sit-ins, but the Greensboro protest ignited a social movement because it was well publicized and occurred in a region containing many black students. Thousands of students in at least 60 communities, mostly in the Upper South, joined the sit-in movement during the winter and spring of 1960. In a few instances, violent clashes between protesters and white onlookers occurred, but student-led local protest organizations usually succeeded in maintaining nonviolent discipline while also displaying greater militance than the more cautious adult-led organizations. Despite efforts of the NAACP, SCLC, and the Congress of Racial Equality (CORE) to impose some control over the sit-in movement, the student protest leaders typically insisted on maintaining their independence. Even when student leaders formed the Student Nonviolent Coordinating Committee (SNCC) to coordinate the movement, the new civil rights organization was not given authority to set policy for its constituent groups. SNCC would remain the most decentralized, antiauthoritarian, and militant of the major civil rights organizations.

The third phase of the southern struggle, involving the Freedom Rides of 1961, was initiated by a civil rights organization—CORE—but this new form of protest activity did not become a social movement until CORE abandoned its initial campaign. In May 1960 CORE sent 13 riders through the southern states on a bus trip that was designed to expose the extent of segregation in bus terminals. After white mobs viciously attacked the riders near Anniston and at the Birmingham bus station, CORE leaders decided to discontinue their effort. At this point, however, student activists, many of whom had participated in the sit-ins, announced their determination to continue the rides. After encountering further mob violence in Montgomery, a group of riders went to Jackson, Miss., where they were promptly arrested after ignoring Jim Crow rules. Despite Attorney General Robert Kennedy's plea for a "cooling-off" period, other young activists also came to Jackson to join the students already in jail. In addition, the rides into Mississippi encouraged students elsewhere in the South to stage similar protests against segregated transportation facilities during the remaining months of 1961. Participation in the Freedom Rides allowed young students to display their militancy in places distant from their homes and campuses and to form a community of militant activists who saw themselves as the spearhead of the southern movement. This was particularly the case among the several hundred students who spent part of the summer of 1961 in Mississippi jails.

Some of the veterans of the Freedom Rides played important roles in the fourth phase of the southern struggle that began in the fall of 1961. Unlike the previous phases, this one was consciously initiated by civil rights activists who entered communities in order to begin social movements. These activists sought to mobilize poor and working-class blacks who had rarely been involved in previous protests, and during the following two years they were able to increase dramatically the size of the southern struggle. "Freedom songs," often based on traditional religious music, and feelings of racial solidarity that were strengthened through common experiences became the basis of a distinctive movement culture. In the urban and Upper South, activists organized massive demonstrations to achieve desegregation of public facilities, better housing and job opportunities for blacks, and the elimination of discriminatory governmental policies. First in Albany, Ga., during late 1961 and 1962, and then in many other urban areas, marches and rallies were held to demonstrate black resolve and to prod the federal government to intervene on behalf of blacks. Learning from the largely unsuccessful Albany movement, King and other SCLC leaders initiated, during the spring of 1963, a tumultuous protest movement in Birmingham that led President John Kennedy to introduce legislation that became the Civil Rights Act of 1964. The protests of 1963 culminated in August with a march on Washington that attracted over 200,000 participants.

While media attention was focused on the urban demonstrations, the voter registration campaign in the Deep South achieved more gradual gains. Although only a small proportion of eligible black voters had been registered by the end of 1963, local residents had begun to work with a group of full-time civil rights workers (mostly affiliated with SNCC). To coordinate the work of the various national civil rights groups and independent local organizations, Mississippi blacks created the Council of Federated Organizations (COFO), directed by Bob Moses. In 1964 the Mississippi Freedom Democratic party was formed as an alternative to the all-white regular Democratic party. During the summer of 1964 hundreds of northern white volunteers assisted the black organizers and local leaders in the state. Although the MFDP failed in its attempt to unseat the regular delegation at the 1964 national Democratic convention, the summer project and the series of protests the following year in Selma, Ala., publicized the disenfranchisement of blacks in the South and prompted President Lyndon Johnson to introduce voter rights legislation that was enacted during the summer of 1965.

The Selma to Montgomery march was one of the last major demonstrations of the southern struggle. The passage of voting rights legislation, the decline of white support for the black struggle, and the related upsurge in northern urban racial violence made southern blacks more likely to see conventional political tactics rather than mass protest

Police dog attacking civil rights demonstrators, Birmingham, 1963

as the most effective way to achieve their goals. Furthermore, the militant racial consciousness of black activists made some of them less interested in working for civil rights reforms and more determined to achieve political power through building autonomous, black-controlled institutions, such as the Black Panther party in Alabama. Ideological conflict between proponents of "black power," such as SNCC chairman Stokely Carmichael, and more conventional civil rights leaders such as King came into public view during the Mississippi march held in June 1966 after the shooting of James Meredith.

The era of mass demonstrations came to an end in 1965, but the long-term gains of the southern black freedom struggle can be seen in the subsequent rapid growth in the number of black elected officials, the disappearance of humiliating Jim Crow practices, and the increased sense of racial pride and potency felt by many southern blacks. Although most scholarly studies of the southern movement continue to interpret it as an outgrowth of the inexorable trend toward the entry of blacks into the American mainstream, the movement was also a product of Afro-American culture and institutional development and its distinctive emergent ideas have continued to influence black thought and political life.

See also LAW: Civil Rights Movement; MEDIA: Civil Rights and Media; VIOLENCE: Civil Rights, Federal Enforcement; WOMEN'S LIFE: / Parks, Rosa

Clayborne Carson
Stanford University

Clayborne Carson, *In Struggle: SNCC and the Black Awakening of the 1960s* (1981);

William H. Chafe, *Civilities and Civil Rights: Greensboro, North Carolina, and the Black Struggle for Freedom* (1980); Charles W. Eagles, ed., *The Civil Rights Movement in America* (1986); James Forman, *The Making of Black Revolutionaries: A Personal Account* (1972); David L. Lewis, *King: A Critical Biography* (1970); Howell Raines, *My Soul Is Rested: Movement Days in the Deep South Remembered* (1977). ☆

Funeral at Rose Hill Baptist Church, Vicksburg, Mississippi, 1968

Funerary Customs, Black

If the southern way of death has become a remarkable ritual, the funerary customs of black southerners are even more so. While there is some overlap in the way both southern blacks and whites handle the terminal rite of passage, in Afro-American communities a funeral will generally have some distinctive features. Funerals are important social events all across the South, but among blacks funerals assume an especially high level of significance. In black society it would be very bad form for a funeral not to be a lavish, even extravagant, event. The conclusion of one's life is regarded as a highly charged occasion and many blacks make careful plans throughout their lives for the moment of death. Sociologist Hortense Powdermaker noted in her classic study of Indianola, Miss., that "no Negro . . . can live content unless he is assured of a fine funeral when he dies."

Because southern blacks have found themselves chronically held at the lowest economic levels, the custom of elaborate funerals has usually struck outsiders as an unwise use of limited funds or as a peculiar habit. The rationale for giving such a high priority to death rites, however, derives from reasonable political and cultural motives. Before emancipation of slaves in the mid-19th century, the only sure way to acquire one's freedom was to die. In death slaves escaped their masters and attained the dignity of either heavenly salvation if they were Christians or the joy of reconnection with the lost ancestors if they retained African beliefs. While those who lived after them mourned their passing, they also rejoiced in the new status of the deceased. Moreover, although slaves were often closely supervised when working, they were not usually checked carefully when they buried their dead. Funerals came then, over time, to be associated with autonomy and to be regarded as positive, even celebratory, events.

Because slaves were generally free to dispose of their dead as they saw fit, some distinctive beliefs and practices of an African origin were retained. These have over the last century and a half blended with standard Christian ob-

A Mississippi rural life scene, 1968

servance to give southern blacks their own approach to death and funerals. It has been widely held, for example, that the spirit of the deceased does not leave the domain of living but lingers on earth where it may intrude in daily affairs. That spirit must be placated or it might maliciously cause misfortune, pain, or even death. As a consequence of this precept an elaborate system of folk beliefs was developed that offers specific strategies to still an agitated "haint" or ghost. These beliefs follow the general principle that a spiritual being can be dealt with in the same manner as a human being. An expensive funeral thus confers on the spirit of the deceased, by means of a material display, a prominent social status. Another black custom is the so-called second burial, a formal ceremony held several months after interment during which the deceased is eulogized. Such commemorative events are held in part to assure the spirit that his or her family and friends still care. In traditional black graveyards bodies are interred with the objects used by the person in life, and often personal items like razors, lamps, clocks, toys, medicine bottles, glasses, cups, and so forth are clustered on top of the grave mound. These items are placed there to provide the spirits with material comforts so they might "rest easy" and not roam outside the cemetery. While such practice keeps the spirit where it belongs, it also connects the mourners to one they have lost and thus diminishes to a degree their sorrow.

See also FOLKLIFE: Cemeteries; Funerals; Grave Markers

John Michael Vlach
George Washington University

Newbell Niles Puckett, *Folk Beliefs of the Southern Negro* (1926; reprint ed. 1969); Robert Farris Thompson, *Flash of the Spirit: African and Afro-American Art and Philosophy* (1983); John Michael Vlach, *The Afro-American Tradition in Decorative Arts* (1978). ☆

Genealogy, Black

Spurred on by a 1976 bicentennial celebration that called on all Americans to be proud of their immigrant ancestry and by the publication of Alex Haley's immensely popular book *Roots* in 1976, genealogy became the third leading hobby in the United States. Haley's establishment of the African source of his ancestry and the story of his family during the slavery and postslavery periods was a personal achievement in which black Americans took great pride, and they joined white Americans in the passion of ancestor hunting.

Ancestor hunting is filled with many difficulties. The most frequently used records are state and county vital statistics, particularly birth, marriage, and death records, but most states did not begin collecting such records until the latter half of the 19th century, and those providing the information for these records did not always have accurate knowledge. Probate records including wills, estate papers, guardianship records, depositions, records of law suits, and other court actions frequently did not have uniform collection and recording procedures. Moreover, most probate records are simply abstracts with only summary, and sometimes incomplete, information. Deeds, tax lists, and mortgage records are other sources used by genealogists. Such local records are plagued by shifting county and state boundaries over time, and many of them were destroyed by fire, particularly during the Civil War.

Although the difficulties listed above are problematic for all southerners who are interested in ancestor hunting, it is particularly problematic for blacks because of their history of slavery and the persistence of their economic and political marginality. The date sources mentioned above are oriented towards recording life events of citizens and property owners. During the slavery period most blacks in the United States were neither citizens nor property owners. Black ancestor hunters, therefore, cannot approach these records in the same way as their white counterparts.

In the early post-emancipation period, the majority of blacks were not landowners, and those who were rarely made out wills. The practice of dying intestate is still a problem among blacks in many parts of the rural South. As vital statistics began to be collected more systematically, the public recording of most rural, lower-income black (and white) births and deaths was haphazardly done. Birth certificate dates and names of elderly blacks are not always correct. The use of nicknames, the prevalence of illiteracy, and the common practice of giving two or more children within the same generation of an extended family cluster the same name also complicates black ancestor hunting.

Another problem in the search for black genealogy is the traditionally popular practice among southern blacks of informal adoption. To take in children, related and unrelated, was survival strategy for blacks during the slave period and a way of helping needy children in the post-emancipation slave period. Because of this, oral traditions of a family may contain information of an adoption, but not the names of the biological parents of the adoptee. In addition, finding records on a slave's parent now may be difficult because the parents' records could be under a name held when the parent was the property of an owner prior to ownership by the child's master.

Another problem resulting from slave breeding practices was the multiple breeding unions, which contributed to difficulties in establishing biological fatherhood. Historically, when a black woman had children by more than one mate, the child had greater familiarity with maternal relatives while paternal relatives were less well known, if known at all. The high geographical mobility, north and west, by blacks during the latter part of the 19th century and the first half of the 20th century also creates gaps in the genealogical record.

Before going to the records, one must try to exhaust the memories of relatives and, in some cases, family friends, particularly elders who can carry the ancestor hunter back three or four generations. However, older and/or more genealogically knowledgeable family members may be hesistant to provide information, and in some cases may be downright opposed to ancestor hunting, viewing it as "digging up skeletons that should remain buried." These are sentiments found among all racial and ethnic groups, but for some older blacks ancestor hunting is especially problematic because of the concerns about "respectability" and "sin." The symbols of respectability are expressed in family life and include such notions as marital stability, sexual purity on the part of women (of which children by one man is an example), and maternal possessions. Because of the hardships of life in the South, some black families have struggled a long time to achieve these symbols of respectability, but once they are achieved, they try to forget the "sins" of the past.

Ancestor hunting becomes a threat because it might reveal in some cases that "sinful acts" formed the foundation upon which respectability was achieved. For example, higher socioeconomic status might have been achieved through illegal activities (such as selling bootleg whiskey) or illicit sexual activity. One area of sexual activity that may be interpreted as undesirable by some blacks, but at an earlier period provided a foundation upon which family respectability was achieved, is interracial mating. Both black and white family members may be opposed to the documentation of such interracial kinship ties, and they are sometimes kept private.

A devastating revelation is to uncover an incidence of incest within a family cluster, particularly if a child were born from such a union. Uncovering such examples of incest is possible, particularly in rural isolated populations. The probability of unknown incestuous unions is also increased with the instability of black family life that has been fostered by slavery, economic marginality, and residential mobility. There is a strong sentiment that one should not marry one's cousin, but the concept of cousin for some southern blacks is a *classifying kinship term* including not only first cousins (children of parents' siblings) but second, third, and even as distant as seventh cousins. Thus, when a relative opposes ancestor hunting because of a fear of the ancestor hunter's uncovering an ancestral incident of incest, the union may have occurred among persons who would be considered unrelated by most Americans.

The various problems (nonexistent and faulty records and family resistance) have been insurmountable for many a black family historian. But those who have experienced some success state that interviewing relatives has yielded very positive rewards, including becoming better acquainted with relatives beyond the immediate family, broadening the *functional* quality of the family network, and spending more time with older relatives and finding that these people are greater reservoirs of historical information, particularly community and family history, than history books or public documents. They found that Alex Haley was not alone in having older relatives who told stories that were passed down from generation to generation.

Black families not only have oral histories, but some also record their histories as part of family reunion celebrations. One set of North Carolina family reunion records goes back to 1822. In addition to family reunion journals other sources of family information are family Bibles, personal diaries, and mementos such as family albums, scrapbooks, and old letters. In the 18th, 19th, and early 20th centuries, blacks, as well as whites, frequently gave Bibles to newlywed couples. In the covers of these Bibles were written the names of the couple, the date of the marriage, the names and births of each child, and similar genealogical information.

Records kept by various organizations in which family members held membership can also yield significant data for black genealogists. Foremost among such sources are church records of marriage, some of which extend back as much as 150 years. Sources of black genealogical data also include the records of fraternal organizations, professional or occupational associations, and records of organizations that have given awards, honors, and medals to family members. Military organizations are also a good source of records. And, finally, probate records including arrests and convictions have provided genealogical data for some black ancestor hunters.

The records of the Freedman's Bureau have data on thousands of black families. Black genealogists working in the slave period find that it matters whether one's ancestors were slave or free. Some information on free black ancestors might appear in the usual sources of tax lists, marriage records, wills, estate records, and court materials; military records of the Civil and Revolutionary wars contain useful information, and apprentice lists have details on those free blacks who were bound out to learn a trade. Free blacks also appear in the federal census of 1850 and the first census in 1790.

The records of slaveowners are important sources of genealogical data for descendants of slaves. For example, the best (and sometimes only) source of vital statistics on slaves was the property account of the slaveowners. The births and deaths of slaves were important to slaveowners because their labor supply was affected by such events. Most large plantations kept slave birth registers and some also maintained slave death registers as part of their property inventory listings. Some states and territories did not allow slave marriages, but public documentation of preemancipation breeding unions was established by an 1866 cohabitation law. This law allowed exslaves who still cohabitated to acquire a *cohabitation certificate* so as not to be tried for a misdemeanor. These certificates contained preemancipation genealogical data as it recorded the date that the couple started living together.

Other sources of information concerning slaves included bills of sales, manumission records, property inventories, and the tax records, wills, deeds, and various probate records associated with the slaveowner as a person of property. Genealogical materials on blacks also appear in plantation journals and the personal diaries of plantation masters and mistresses and the church records of slave baptisms.

See also FOLKLIFE: Family Folklore; MYTHIC SOUTH: Family; WOMEN'S LIFE: Family, Modernization of; Genealogy

Tony L. Whitehead
Forest Hazel
University of North Carolina
at Chapel Hill

Andrew Billingsley, *Black Families in White America* (1968); Herbert G. Gutman, *The Black Family in Slavery and Freedom, 1750–1925* (1976); Robert B. Hill, *Informal Adoption among Black Families* (1977); Debra L. Newman, *List of Free Black Heads of Families in the United States in 1790* (1973); Minnie K. Peebles, *North Carolina Historical Review* (April 1978); Carter G. Woodson, *Free Negro Owners of Slaves in the United States in 1830 together with a Brief Treatment of the Free Negro* (1925), *Free Negro Owners of Slaves in the United States in 1830 together with Absentee Ownership of Slaves in The United States in 1830* (1924). ☆

Health, Black

In the post–Civil War era white southern physicians noted the rise of disease among newly emancipated blacks and predicted the eventual extinction of blacks from the United States despite all that medicine could do to prevent it. Many white laymen in the South held similar views. In fact, issues of black health have always concerned southern whites. Interest in the subject constitutes a minor theme in the region's history. It is paradoxical that so politically voiceless and socially invisible a group as southern blacks has received so much attention with regard to health, medical care, and disease characteristics. But there are important reasons for this trend, rooted in southern medical, racial, and intersectional history.

First, because southern whites for so long either subjugated or segregated blacks, they have never been able to escape taking at least partial responsibility for black health. Second, because of certain external physical characteristics, especially skin color, blacks in a white-dominated society have been visible and thus easily observed and studied with regard to health. Third, because race has been important in the South and in relations between the South and the rest of the nation, whites have used black medical distinctiveness, real and imagined, for political purposes.

Blacks brought with them from Africa to the New World a heritage of disease and medical care differing in many ways from that of the dominant Euro-American society. Some African health problems (e.g., sleeping sickness) and practices (e.g., use of certain herbs and tribal rites) disappeared for environmental reasons. Yet genetic maladies (sickle-cell anemia), disease susceptibilities (tuberculosis, respiratory diseases) and resistances (malaria, yellow fever), medical treatments (herbs, voodoo), and medical theories (supernatural causes of disease) remained, influencing the lives of both blacks and their white neighbors. White medicine dominated, but slaves, ostensibly not the owners of their bodies, could and did choose to invoke, covertly when necessary, their own medical systems. Some white masters condoned or reluctantly accepted these subtle statements of black independence because they saw no alternatives, felt their slaves should enjoy some freedoms, or noted that the black healing approaches worked. Some of these practices and remedies actually passed from the black to the white medical world.

A number of factors influenced the health status of Afro-Americans during the slavery period (1620–1865). Living conditions played an important role because plantation slave quarters, though located in rural areas, developed many public health characteristics of a village or small town. Infectious disease epidemics, parasitic infestations, and human- and other organic-waste disposal problems resulted from life in slave communities. Nutritionally unbalanced or nutrient-deficient food caused, at the least, weakness and, at worst, death from malnutrition or infection. Hard, unsafe working and living conditions; whipping and other physical punishments; pregnancy, childbirth, and gynecological problems among physically laboring women; and the psychological stresses of a life of servitude also contributed to poor health among slaves.

When slaves needed medical attention, owners usually insisted blacks turn to the Euro-American curing system rather than caring for themselves. Most states required that masters provide for proper maintenance of their human chattel. Some fulfilled this responsibility better than others, depending on widely varying factors including personality, number of slaves, financial status, master-slave relationship, presence or absence of owner, and threat of an epidemic to property (slaves) and to white lives. As a general rule, masters, mistresses, overseers, or overseers' wives used their own medical knowledge and skills on ailing slaves first; then, if these resources failed to reverse the course of disease or injury, they called the local physician. Whites handled illnesses within their own families in a similar manner, applying home remedies before calling in the physician, with one difference. They generally sought professional help sooner for white family members than for slaves.

As southern whites cared for more and more blacks, observed how slaves fared in the southern disease environment, and noted the effectiveness on bondsmen of various medical treatments, they began to notice trends. Blacks seemed much more prone to some diseases, less susceptible or even immune to others, and more or less responsive to one or another remedy. A belief developed, particularly between 1830 and 1860, that the South possessed different health conditions from the North or West, that southern medical care differed from that in the North, that blacks were medically different from whites, and that southern physicians were uniquely suited and trained to handle the region's health problems. Blacks, they further argued, were medically suited for the labor and environment of the South. With mounting antislavery pressure from the North, these observations became political points in the proslavery argument. However, no southern physician ever proved any of these ideas.

Emancipation in 1865 ostensibly released southern whites from the responsibility of providing medical care to blacks. Freedmen were on their own and had to rely on their own resources for the basic necessities of food, clothing, housing, and health. In reality, however, blacks generally did not have the wherewithal to survive without help. White predictions that blacks were doomed as a race because of innate physical inferiority and a dissolute lifestyle now that they were free seemed to be justified. Black health did decline, the result of poor housing, malnourishment, overcrowding, and the psychological stresses of a new environment and lifestyle. Whites noted rises in tuberculosis, syphilis, and insanity. Even federal intervention by the medical department of the Freedmen's Bureau brought only temporary and not always reliable assistance. The bureau's goal was to ease the transition from slavery to freedom for both blacks and whites. Though it employed physicians in key areas to provide hospital and dispensary care, the bureau failed in its medical mission on two counts. It established no mechanisms whereby blacks could either continue to receive medical care or learn to care for themselves. Once the bureau left a state (1868–71), blacks were left to their own devices or to the largess of local white authorities and white physicians. Once again, whites had responsibility for black health, at least in part. Some labor and shareholding contracts contained provisions for medical care paid for by the white landowner. City and county government authorities worried about the spread of infectious diseases from blacks to whites, especially as the black population of cities and towns was rising and their physical movements were less restricted. By the 1890s the larger urban areas established hospitals and clinics to care for both black and white poor. Some northern medical schools and several newly founded black schools (e.g., Meharry, Howard, Leonard) produced a small number of black physicians, many of whom opened practices in southern black communities, but the health and medical care of blacks remained at a lower level than that of whites.

As long as black health was primarily a southern problem, the nation as a whole ignored or remained ignorant of the black's plight. But the post–World War I "great migration" of rural southern blacks in search of better jobs and living conditions to northern and border state cities altered the nation's perception. Now money to study and remedy the poor health situations of blacks came from federal, state, and local governments as well as from private sources like the Rosenwald and Rockefeller foundations. They supported public health campaigns (the annual National Negro Health Week), the building of hospitals, medical education for blacks at white and black institutions, health improvement programs (tuberculosis, child and maternal health, syphilis [including the notorious Tuskegee Syphilis Study]), and overall assessments of black health status and needs (Gunnar Myrdal's classic *An American Dilemma*). The result of all this activity was the desegregation of health facilities, a better awareness of black health problems, the provision of assistance to pay for the high cost of medical care through government programs, the reduction of black mortality rates, and an increase in the number of blacks in the healing professions. Problems remain in the South, where state and local government funds are inadequate to pay for black health needs, rural life and traditional Afro-American healing practices persist, and blacks often cannot afford private medical care.

See also FOLKLIFE: Folk Medicine; Voodoo; HISTORY AND MANNERS: Philanthropy; SCIENCE AND MEDICINE: Health, Public; Education, Medical; Medicine, States' Rights

Todd L. Savitt
East Carolina University

Gaines M. Foster, *Journal of Southern History* (August 1982); James H. Jones, *Bad Blood: The Tuskegee Syphilis Experiment* (1981); *Journal of the National Medical Association* (numerous articles on the history of blacks in medicine in issues from the 1950s to the present); Kenneth F. Kiple and Virginia Himmelsteib King, *Another Dimension to the Black Diaspora: Diet, Disease, and Racism* (1981); Herbert M. Morais, *The History of the Negro in Medicine* (1967); Todd L. Savitt, *Medicine and Slavery: The Diseases and Health Care of Blacks in Antebellum Virginia* (1978). ☆

Immigrants and Blacks

Compared to other regions the South has attracted few immigrants. Whites, already uncomfortable with the large and visible African presence, have generally opposed an influx of strangers from Europe and Asia. Prospective settlers have been deterred from establishing new homes in the area by the image of the South's inhospitable climate and by the prospect of competing with black labor. Yet Cubans, Haitians, and Southeast Asians have migrated to the South in the past generation, and other groups, in fact, came in earlier years.

Black Americans have not been especially receptive to those who looked to the South as a refuge from hunger and oppression. As the least advantaged of native-born Americans, they were the first to experience competition from foreigners for scarce jobs, housing, and education. When newcomers arrived, tensions occasionally erupted into violence; the Miami riot of May 1980, which was caused in part by black resentment at assistance given Cuban refugees, was but one of the latest and worst manifestations of this phenomena.

Whereas in the North immigration was sizable enough to attract public attention and to elicit organized resistance in the generation preceding the Civil War, in the South the reluctance of aliens to compete with slave labor limited the flow of newcomers to negligible numbers. Of those who came, some became slaveowners. More often, they sought work in border state cities such as Baltimore, Louisville, and St. Louis, although New Orleans, Mobile, and Savannah were popular destinations as well. Travelers reported that on occasion slaveowners employed cheap and expendable immigrants to do tasks that might endanger their valuable slave property.

As was to be the case in later years in the North, both slaves and free blacks in the South were sometimes used as "scabs" to destroy early attempts by white workers, many of them recent arrivals from Ireland and Germany, to improve wages and conditions of employment. The difficulty in finding stable and peaceful workers among the immigrants also led many managers of southern industries to prefer native black workers over the newcomers. Yet despite their reputation as unreliable and union prone, white native and immigrant laborers made inroads into a few occupations traditionally dominated by nonplantation slave and free black workers in the 1850s, notably in the textile industry and as longshoremen. In many industries blacks and whites worked alongside each other or in close physical proximity. Although some black employees encountered violence, as did the young Frederick Douglass, who nearly lost his life as a result of attacks by white workers in the Baltimore shipyards in the late 1830s, interracial cooperation rather than hostility was the norm in most integrated industries.

As rural slaves, the bulk of black southerners in the antebellum era had little contact with immigrants. Indeed, not until after emancipation did the issue of immigration receive the attention of large numbers of blacks. And then the subject became important not because of an influx of aliens and heightened competition and conflict, but rather as a result of whites who blamed Afro-Americans for the region's failure to recruit many immigrant workers. Successful recruitment schemes would have imperiled the newly acquired political power of the freedmen and perhaps even their physical survival in their land of birth. Northern blacks who had experienced occupational displacement by immigrants as early as the second quarter of the 19th century and who had roots in the South joined with their southern kin in deploring attempts by white opponents to drive blacks out of the region—and thus intensify economic competition in the North—or to reduce the exslaves to a condition of semiservitude.

Blacks responded to the possibility of massive immigration to the South by exploiting the fears whites held of those who differed in language, values, and religious traditions. They warned that the bulk of newcomers would not be hard-working peasants but the "riffraff" of Europe who would pollute the South with violence, labor discontent, and dangerous ideologies. Rather than expose the region to the evils too readily apparent in Europe and the North, whites would be wise to do as Booker T. Washington counseled in his Atlanta Exposition Address of 1895 and "cast down their buckets" among their familiar, faithful, and devoted black fellow citizens.

Most black leaders were uneasy if not alarmed at the prospect of large-scale immigration, but some professed indifference; they either doubted that aliens would come, saw a possibility of Afro-Americans and disgruntled aliens working together to reform the South, or felt confident that black workers could meet the challenge of greater competition. Indeed, Booker T. Washington and his followers used the specter of immigrant competition to promote the doctrine of racial pride, self-help, landownership, and industrial education. Competition and the example immigrants provided as they overcame adversity in a strange and often hostile environment could actually help in the advancement of the race, they claimed.

Open conflict between blacks and immigrants continued to be rare in postbellum southern society. Instead of expanding, the percentage of southerners born elsewhere actually declined in the late 19th and early 20th centuries. Those foreigners who came were more likely to settle in cities or in agricultural colonies such as Sunnyside, Ark., than to compete directly with black field hands. Afro-Americans could have hardly attributed their persistent plight to the relatively few aliens in Dixie, and they seldom sought to do so. True, they held many of the negative stereotypes of foreigners common among white southerners, especially regarding Italians and

Jews. They also resented newcomers being accorded opportunities and rights denied them. And on occasion, blacks served as handy scapegoats for the frustrations immigrants experienced in their new home. Nevertheless, tension and hostility between blacks and white outsiders in the South have never approached that associated with the North and West. The more overt forms of discrimination from native whites in the South helped blacks remember that it was white racism and not immigration that caused their degradation, whereas in the North and West the larger numbers of aliens and the more subtle forms of discrimination often resulted in Afro-Americans seeing the immigrant as their enemy.

See also ETHNIC LIFE articles; URBANIZATION: / Mobile; New Orleans; Savannah

David J. Hellwig
St. Cloud State University

David J. Hellwig, *The Filson Club History Quarterly* (April 1980), *Mississippi Quarterly* (Fall 1978); James L. Roark, *Masters without Slaves: Southern Planters in the Civil War and Reconstruction* (1977); Arnold Shankman, *Ambivalent Friends: Afro-Americans View the Immigrant* (1982), in "*Turn to the South*": *Essays on Southern Jewry*, ed. N. M. Kagonoff and Melvin I. Urofsky (1979), *The Mississippi Quarterly* (Winter 1977–78); Robert S. Starobin, *Industrial Slavery in the Old South* (1970). ☆

Indians and Blacks

Native Americans first observed Africans in company with the early European explorers, but there was little intensive contact between blacks and Indians until the establishment of Charleston in 1670. The South Carolinians enslaved Indians as well as Africans, but after the Tuscarora War (1711) and the Yemassee War (1715) almost destroyed the colony, the Carolinians changed tactics. Fearful that the enslaved Africans and Indians would unite to overthrow the white minority, they began a divide-and-rule policy to keep the two peoples separated. Indians were paid to capture escaping blacks and punish rebellious slaves; blacks were used to fight against Indians. And, lastly, further enslavement of Indians was discouraged. Most of the enslaved Native Americans were sold to the West Indies. Nevertheless, the considerable previous intermarriage between the two enslaved groups resulted in Afro-Americans having considerable Indian ancestry and absorbing Native American culture.

The southern Indians who had the closest contact with blacks were the Seminoles. This multiethnic people migrated to Florida in the late 1700s to get away from white settlers, and when the United States annexed Florida in 1819, the Seminoles resisted. They welcomed escaping black slaves, whose knowledge of white ways and commitment to freedom made them valuable warriors. Blacks served as interpreters in negotiations with the army, and their advice was respected. Though the Seminole blacks were called "slaves," they had complete freedom to live in their own independent black settlements or to intermarry with Seminoles. They fought fiercely in the Seminole War, as both Indians and blacks resisted removal and reenslavement. White fears of a red-black alliance came true in the 1835–42 war. The United States was forced to accept the Seminole demand that their black allies remain with them before they would move west. The threat to southern slavery, rather than land hunger, was the primary motive for the Seminole conflict. Once the Seminoles were removed to Indian Territory (Oklahoma), however, many of the blacks were kidnapped by slave catchers and sold into slavery in nearby states. In response, during the 1850s many Seminole blacks and Indians migrated to northern Mexico, where their descendants live today.

Chattel slavery was unknown among the aboriginal southeastern Indians, though it may have existed in some of the pre-Columbian Mississippian societies. Among the Cherokees, a captive could be "possessed" by his captor, but such persons were not used for labor purposes. The Cherokees and other Indians who used blacks as plantation slaves clearly adopted the practice from whites. Indeed, many of the earliest and largest Indian slaveholding families were really those with mostly white intermarriage. These mixed-blood families, with their slave-based economy, led in the acculturation of Cherokee, Chickasaw, Choctaw, and Creek. Slavery helped make the previously egalitarian native societies into class-based cash economies, with the nonslaveowning traditionalists on the bottom.

Once they were removed to Indian Territory in the 1830s, class resentments flared up. The slaveowning upper class gained considerable influence in the tribal governments and tightened the slave codes so that the institution became almost as oppressive as among whites. These proslavery factions led the Choctaw, Chickasaw, and Cherokee governments to adopt an alliance of friendship with the Confederate States of America in 1861, and even the Creeks and Seminoles were forced to do likewise. This alliance prompted the antislavery traditionalists to resist. Internal civil war raged in Indian Territory at the same time the national war was going on. The southern tribes were decimated.

Though the antislavery Cherokees got control of their government in 1863 and passed their own Emancipation Act, the victorious United States forced all Indians to end slavery in 1865. Furthermore, before the Union enfranchised blacks in the South, it forced Indian nations to adopt the freed blacks as equal citizens in their tribal governments. This question about whether to agree to adopt their former slaves divided and weakened the Indian governments at a crucial time. The question was complicated by the migration into Indian Territory of more blacks fleeing from white oppression in the South. Though many of the blacks won their fight for recognition of land allotments, both they and their Indian antagonists were largely dispossessed of those lands after the abolition of Indian Territory and the creation of the state of Oklahoma in 1907. Blacks who remained in the state tended to congregate in all-black towns, just as the Indians did in all-Indian areas, so there has not been as much mingling among the two groups as earlier. Their disunity cost them both.

Meanwhile, among the remnant Indians left in the Southeast after the removal era, a new white attitude emerged. Once the major Indian nations were out of the area, Southern whites began trying to lump all non-whites into a subordinate "colored" category. This was especially true if the remnant group was not recognized by treaty and had largely lost its aboriginal culture. The rights of these people defined as "colored" were progressively restricted as the South moved ever more aggressively toward a black-versus-white biracial society. Into the 1870s the Lumbees in North Carolina resisted such trends by guerrilla warfare. But most such groups were too small to resist, and their only option was to isolate themselves from all outsiders, white and black.

Such isolated communities struggled to stay together as land losses and population increases forced them into the cash economy. To establish their Indian identity, they even resisted white attempts at educational integration, accounting for high illiteracy rates among southern Indians. Although both blacks and Indians faced similar discrimination, Indians continued to hope for a less restrictive social status. This allowed whites to formulate a new divide-and-rule policy, and a three-tier segregation policy emerged in counties with Indian communities.

As long as the black community remained powerless, there were no incentives for Indians to identify with it. Intermarriage was discouraged; Indians who did so were generally ostracized and merged into the black community.

Black-Indian relations began to change with the civil rights movement. Not only did black activism provide an inspiring example to dissatisfied Indians, but civil rights legislation sometimes helped Indians as well. As the segregation system began to break down, some Indians considered allying with blacks for further change, especially concerning education. The two groups, however, remain more separated today than in the pre-1840 era.

See also ETHNIC LIFE: Indians; / Cherokees; Chickasaws; Choctaws; Creeks; Lumbees; Seminoles

Walter L. Williams
University of Cincinnati

Daniel F. Littlefield, *Africans and Creeks: From the Colonial Period to the Civil War* (1979), *Africans and Seminoles: From Removal to Emancipation* (1976), *The Cherokee Freedmen: From Reconstruction to American Citizenship* (1978); Theda Perdue, *Slavery and the Evolution of Cherokee Society, 1540–1866* (1979); Walter L. Williams, ed., *Southeastern Indians since the Removal Era* (1979); J. Leitch Wright, Jr., *The Only Land They Knew: The Tragic Story of the American Indians in the Old South* (1981). ☆

Landownership, Black

The evolution of land tenure patterns in the South has shaped the contours of Afro-American life and culture. The acquisition and use of land or real property as a commodity has been a basis for all other forms of wealth. In addition, land has been the physical space on which successive generations of Afro-Americans have organized themselves. Land has thus served an economic and a social role. The link between the use of land to provide food, shelter, and sources of income, and the perception of land as the cornerstone of one's cultural "homeplace" abound in the folkways of southern blacks.

Landownership has translated into economic autonomy, political assertiveness, and social independence for most Americans, and blacks were no exception to this. In the period prior to the Civil War a small number of free blacks acquired a modest amount of real property. It was commonplace for blacks who owned and worked their own farms during this period to have been trained through apprenticeships in other occupations as well. Enslaved blacks were not permitted by law, however, to own or exercise control over property. Though some free blacks owned land they often saw their control over real and personal property abridged by extralegal and illegal practices designed to circumvent black assertiveness and to promote white supremacy.

Still, a sizable number of "quasi-free" blacks remained living and working in the South. Southern free blacks tended to live in urban areas and owned property with an estimated value of $25 million. The Union victory that ended the Civil War emancipated approximately 4 million Afro-American men, women, and children, who joined the ranks of close to a half million free, mostly southern blacks. Most newly freed Afro-Americans knew and understood the significance that the ownership of 40 acres of land, a mule, the acquisition of literacy, and the exercise of the vote held for participation in a "New South," which the demise of chattel slavery offered.

Some blacks who were previously enslaved participated in attempts to demonstrate their serious commitment and expertise in commodities production and land management. During the war almost 800,000 acres of abandoned and confiscated land was amassed under the administration of the Freedmen's Bureau, and much of it was cultivated by blacks with the belief, and sometimes the promise, that following the war they would have the opportunity to own farmsteads. Indeed, many of the 183,000 freedmen, women, and children in contraband camps between 1863 and 1864 cultivated lands producing agricultural settlements such as the ones at Davis Bend, Miss., Port Royal, S.C., and Roanoke Island, N.C.

Although 40 acres and a mule had long been on the black agenda, the events of the Reconstruction era would betray that aspiration for the majority of blacks. Instead of creating independent landowning black family farmers, capable of playing a valuable role in the American economy, the Reconstruction period saw a betrayal of the progressive agenda for social change. Still, despite reactionary white supremacy political campaigns, black codes, vagrancy laws, the Ku Klux Klan, lynchings, and Jim Crow segregation, most black people remained in the South occupied primarily in agriculture.

In the 35 years following the failure of Reconstruction politics to enact a viable land resettlement and purchase plan for the newly emancipated freedmen, one-fourth of the black farmers of the South did acquire land. A relatively small number inherited land from parents who had acquired property either as free blacks or after their emancipation. There are documented instances of land being given to some of the interracial children born of the union of enslaved black women and white men. Clearly, though, the majority of Afro-Americans who acquired land worked to acquire it in parcels. By 1910 this success, which had been achieved against overwhelming odds, culminated in blacks owning more than 15 million acres of land.

About 91 percent of the country's 9.8 million blacks were still in the rural South in 1910. Approximately 890,000 blacks operated farms, 175,000 of which were full owners and another 43,000 of which were part owners. About 218,972 of these farmers were black owner-operators, and 670,000 were tenants who participated in the crop-lien system. The average size of black-owned farms was about 10–20 acres. By 1910 throughout most of the South blacks had been politically disfranchised and the majority were increasingly limited to participation in a cashless debt peonage cycle.

Land's importance as a commodity and as the basis for familial and social organization is reflected in the role it has played in the formation of capital and the creation and maintenance of black institutions. The steady decline in black ownership and the escalating increase in the out-migration of rural Afro-Americans to southern and northern cities between 1910 and 1940, and again from 1950 to most recently, 1975, seriously threatened the work of such black self-help institutions as colleges, churches, lodges, associations, and fraternities and sororities. Clearly, had it not been for the diligent work of blacks who worked in and through the black self-help agricultural experiment stations—such as at Tuskegee Institute—black farm agents, and the cadre of home demonstration agents, much of the multifaceted aid that many black farm families received would have been nonexistent.

"Separate and unequal" describes decades of disproportionate and unequal access to education, banking, credit, and political and legal rights. Black farm families often found themselves obliged to work and where feasible purchase land in areas where the soil was depleted and poor to marginal in quality. Many black farm families could not withstand the combination of these legal and extralegal mechanisms of social control. Gradually, the acquisition of farm acreage, which had steadily increased between 1870 and 1910, began to decline.

The acquisition of black-owned land, which served as the infrastructure supporting the economic stability of southern black rural institutional growth, reached an apex in the early 20th century and has been declining ever since. Consequently, many chose to leave the land and seek a "homeplace" and economic opportunity in other parts of the country. Some were pushed out by poverty, racism, the lack of opportunities, or by the opportunities of urban life.

The persistence of monoculture, or dependency on a single cash crop, continued despite the toll it exacted from both the black and white family farm population. Dependency on nonedible cash crops, malnutrition, low fertility, high infant mortality, pellagra, rickets, nutritional anemia, scurvy, and influenza were but a few of the maladies that, along with the destruction brought on by the boll weevil, cotton boll worm, tobacco bud worm, cattle tick, erosion, under-fertilized and poor soil, low cotton prices, inadequate and often unreasonable credit, governmental policies and tax structures designed to promote large-scale agricultural production, Jim Crow segregation, and often a virulent racism, all contributed to undermining the black presence on the land.

Moreover, except for the relative economic stability of the World War II years, the chronicle of black landownership in the 20th century is captured in a statistical depiction of black land loss, black out-migration, and the high turnover of black-owned land through foreclosures, duress sales, partition sales, or old age liens. In terms of the quality of life, most rural black residents are poor and live at the subsistence scale, survival level for most of their lives.

Between 1910 and 1960 approximately 3 million blacks left the South seeking a new "place" and despite the civil rights movement, between 1960 and 1970 roughly another 1.5 million blacks left the region. However, between 1975 and 1980 this 60-year process of relocating was reversed; about

222,000 blacks left the region while approximately 415,000 blacks moved to the South, though not necessarily as owners of equity in the form of landownership.

Between 1950 and 1970 southern blacks lost control of approximately 6 million acres of land, reducing the number of full and part owners from 193,000 to less than 67,000. Clearly, while not every transaction involving land transfer can be said to have resulted from the oppressive economic and social conditions under which black men, women, and children lived, it would be inaccurate to underestimate the economic consequences of racial oppression in circumventing the expansion of black-owned family farms.

By 1981, 4 percent of the black population lived on farms, representing 222,000 people, whereas 349,000 blacks had lived on farms in 1978. By comparison the white farm population declined 25 percent between 1970 and 1981, while the black farm population dropped 67 percent. Rural population unemployment rates in 1981 for blacks were 11.4 percent and for whites 2.5 percent, while nearly twice as many black farm residents lived in poverty, 30.2 percent versus 16.5 percent of whites.

Black-owned family farms have been a relatively small percentage of the overall black rural and agricultural presence in the South, but their existence has conferred a certain permanence on communities in which black sharecroppers were more easily exploited and at times driven from the land. Landowning blacks have served as a role model for those whose aspirations focused on acquiring land and the security that managing one's own farm generates.

See also AGRICULTURE: Sharecropping and Tenancy; / Agricultural Extension Services; Boll Weevil; HISTORY AND MANNERS: Reconstruction; LAW: / Black Codes; SOCIAL CLASS: Poverty; Tenant Farmers

Marsha Jean Darling
Wellesley College

Marsha Jean Darling, "The Growth and Decline of the Afro-American Family Farm in Warren County, North Carolina, 1910–1960" (Ph.D. dissertation, Duke University, 1982); John Hope Franklin, *From Slavery to Freedom: A History of Negro Americans*, (1947, 5th ed., 1980); Leo McGee and Robert Boone, eds., *The Black Rural Landowner—Endangered Species: Social, Political and Economic Implications* (1979); Claude O. Oubre, *Forty Acres and a Mule: The Freedmen's Bureau and Black Land Ownership* (1978); George B. Tindall, *The Emergence of the New South, 1913–1945* (1967); University of California at Davis, Agricultural History Center, *A List of References for the History of Black Americans in Agriculture* (1981); U.S. Commission on Civil Rights, *The Decline of Black Farming in America* (1982); U.S. Department of Commerce, Bureau of the Census, *Census of Population: 1910, 1920, 1930, 1940, 1950, 1960, 1970, 1980*; *Census of Agriculture: 1910, 1920, 1930, 1940, 1945, 1959, 1969, 1974, 1982*; *The Social and Economic Status of the Black Population in the United States: 1790–1978*, Special Studies, P-23 (1980); *America's Black Population: 1970–1982, A Statistical View* (1983); Monroe Work, ed., *The Negro Yearbook, 1914–1915* (1915). ☆

Literary Portrayals of Blacks

The American South inherited most of its early attitudes toward blacks and its means of portraying them in art and in literature from Europe. The "noble savage" and the "comic servant" had already appeared in European novels. Paintings had included the idea of the exotic primitive long before he appeared in the literature of America.

Following Goldsmith's and Burns's pastoral tradition of happy menials in bucolic settings, such poets as Henry Timrod and Edward Coote Pinkney described dusky peasants happily at work in the cotton patches of the antebellum South, dancing and singing around the campfires at night, delighted with their carefree, childlike existence. Like such religious and political apologists as Albert Taylor Bledsoe and John C. Calhoun, these authors assumed that the "sons of Ham" were appointed by God and fitted by nature to be hewers of wood and drawers of water.

The "peculiar institution" of slavery engendered little artistic expression; following the Civil War, however, Thomas Nelson Page, John Pendleton Kennedy, and others used garrulous old darkies to lament the passing of the old order in sentimental and defensive stories.

This contented slave stereotype was to cast its shadow well into the 20th century. Faulkner used it in *The Unvanquished*, and Margaret Mitchell popularized it in *Gone with the Wind*. Sometimes the figure is a comic young servant, but more often it is a gentle aged retainer. The "mammy" achieved mythic status both as the residual image of loving ties within slavery and as a reflection of continuing historical realities. Over the years, southern whites continued to engage black women to serve as nurses and cooks in white homes. Faulkner's Dilsey is a conscious tribute to his own mammy, Caroline Barr, a person he celebrated for her faith and her love of children. Such moderns as Truman Capote and Carson McCullers show comforting black servants as the mainstays of white children. In their wisdom, they have archetypal qualities; Faulkner even suggests for the role of Nancy in *Requiem for a Nun* a black madonna.

The black male has had a less consistent career in fiction. Uncle Remus, the old narrator of fables, is unusually authentic for the period. Joel Chandler Harris combined an interest in dialect with an ear for Afro-American folktales that shrewdly celebrate rebellion, making Uncle Remus realistic in spite of his sentimental context.

As opposed to this aged and sexless patriarch, the "brute Negro" was a projection of the sexual and political fears that accompanied the Reconstruction. Thomas Dixon, Jr., a violent white supremacist, portrayed blacks as apelike creatures intent on raping innocent young white maidens, thereby justifying the violence of the Klansmen. This image is more than of a rebellious slave, ungrateful and unmanageable. W. J. Cash and others insist that it was part of the spiral of lust and fear that led to the center of the southern psyche. It reflected the myth of the black's sexual potency and the fear of retaliation by black men for white men's use of black women. The myths of southern white womanhood, white supremacy, and racial purity were confronted with the threat of growing black power. The brute Negro is a far cry from the heroic noble savage.

The black male is a less popular subject for southern fiction than the black female because he is less a part of the white community. As farm laborer, butler, or handyman, he is a background figure and an alien. For a time during and after World War I, when blacks migrated in large numbers to northern industrial centers, he was cast as the runaway father or the sharecropper held in peonage.

In the 1920s and 1930s, socially conscious writers such as T. S. Stribling and Erskine Caldwell turned him into a Christ figure. As the Depression deepened and lynchings escalated, sympathy for this victim grew and the heroism of his persecutors disappeared. Redneck whites became the villains.

The self-sufficient black man occasionally emerged as the older, wilder "black prince"—a mythic figure who was magical, footloose, and amoral. Caroline Gordon pictured him as the mystical wanderer; William Styron turned him into a black prophet and rebel. The metamorphosis of the brute Negro into the black prince has been one of the most remarkable indicators of social change in the South. "Uncle Tom," at the same time, has changed from a term of approbation to one of denigration.

Although both male and female victims were at times black in color, the more popular choice has been the "tragic mulatto." This symbol of the perils of miscegenation was guaranteed to win white sympathy in stories as late as *Light in August* and *Band of Angels.* Other authors have used the same figures to signify upward mobility, particularly among the "talented tenth" who became the first professionals from the American black community. They sometimes went north and passed for white, or joined the growing black middle class in urban centers, occasionally returning to the South to help the black folk and to inspire social unrest. This figure sometimes emerges as the "black Anglo-Saxon" who is despised for his mindless aping of white culture or as the "black Babbitt" who is caricatured for his pompous delight in middle-class materialistic values. But in other novels, this "new Negro"—the rebel—uses his education to help his race.

These images have changed with the themes and the language, reflecting the rapid transformation of the black community in the past century. Just as black men and women have moved from illiterate, ragged slaves, to sharecroppers and landowners, to educated business men and women, teachers, lawyers, and doctors, so too the literature has changed. Faulkner portrayed a black veteran of World War I as an ignorant and comic "uppity nigger." He later pictured a black veteran of World War II as a brave and sophisticated politician.

The rise of black authors has also had its impact on the tone and quality of southern white authors. For a time, early in the 20th century, white local colorists affectionately portrayed black cabins filled with quaint folk whose lives were replete with exotic customs. This primitivism broke into more heroic images with Paul Green's Abraham and DuBose Heyward's Porgy. But the "exotic primitives" disappeared as *objects d'art* when black writers like W. E. B. Du Bois, James Weldon Johnson, Jean Toomer, Richard Wright, Ralph Ellison, Zora Neale Hurston, and Alice Walker began publishing.

When William Styron in 1967 tried to incorporate the black point of view into his epic presentation of *The Confessions of Nat Turner*, the black and white liberal community attacked him violently for presuming to speak for blacks. The responses, which addressed issues far more complex than the racial identity of the author or the point-of-view employed, have cast a pall over the creation of or publication of stories by white authors about blacks. Yet the southern writer, black or white, can hardly write about the South without writing about blacks. The slave over the years has gone from "darky" to "nigger" to "Nigra" to "Negro," from "person of color" to "colored" to "black," from "boy" and "gal" to "man" and "woman." The shift is clearly from a stereotype to an individualized human being. The authors have finally moved from defining noun to descriptive adjective in their use of "black."

In the later fiction of Faulkner, Robert Penn Warren, Eudora Welty, Flannery O'Connor, and in the plays of Tennessee Williams and Lillian Hellman, black characters embody human vanity, heroism, comedy, tragedy, and endurance.

See also LITERATURE articles; MYTHIC SOUTH: Plantation Myth; Racial Attitudes; / "Mammy"; "Moonlight-and-Magnolias" Myth; Sambo

Nancy M. Tischler
Pennsylvania State University

Robert A. Bone, *The Negro Novel in America* (1958); John M. Bradbury, *Renaissance in the South: A Critical History of the Literature* (1963); Sterling Brown, *The Negro in American Fiction* (1937); Hugh Gloster, *Negro Voices in American Fiction* (1948); Seymour L. Gross and John Edward Hardy, eds., *Images of the Negro in American Literature* (1966); John Herbert Nelson, *The Negro Character in American Literature* (1926); Nancy M. Tischler, *Black Masks: Negro Characters in Modern Southern Fiction* (1969). ☆

Literature, Black

Over the past century southern black literature has evolved from a relatively sparse body of writings, mainly imitative of Euro-American literary forms and thematically focused on the plight of blacks in the South, to a sophisticated literary canon whose forms and meanings coalesce to give it a distinct identity.

Southern black poetry was basically undistinguished before the 1920s. Slave poet George Moses Horton and abolitionist Frances Ellen Watkins Harper were the most prominent southern black voices in antebellum poetry. Some poets, such as Horton, adopted standard Euro-American poetic techniques and seldom wrote about racial issues. Still others, like Harper, used these standard forms primarily to concentrate on issues germane to southern black life. Post–Civil War poets Albery A. Whitman, George M. McClellan, and Joseph S. Cotter, Sr., at times wrote skillfully about racial and nonracial topics in conventional poetic forms.

Before the 1920s the South produced few black poets who had mastered the art form on a level equal to that of blacks elsewhere in the country. Southern blacks emerged, though, as the dominant voices in the poetry of the Harlem Renaissance of the 1920s, and thereafter they remained in the vanguard of black poets in America. One wing of the Harlem Renaissance arts movement looked to the black South for aesthetic inspiration and artistic direction. Langston Hughes's *The Weary Blues* (1926) and James Weldon Johnson's *God's Trombones: Seven Negro Sermons in Verse* (1927) drew heavily from southern black folk culture and the experiences of the black masses within and outside the South. Hughes tapped an essentially secular component of southern black life—its music. Grounding his poetic technique in musical forms whose origins were southern and black and which, to a large extent, had evolved from the religious orientation of southern blacks, Hughes used blues and jazz to shape the form and meaning of his poetry. Johnson tapped the sacred side of the southern black experience. Choosing the black folk sermon as the embodiment of a southern black world-view and as an indigenous art form, Johnson elevated folk art to the level of high art. Poets, novelists, and playwrights after the 1920s (blacks and whites) followed the example of Hughes, Johnson, and others of the Harlem Renaissance by deriving artistic inspiration from the social and cultural life of the black South.

In the 1920s black poets' use of dialects became more refined as poetic form merged with content. Black dialect gave way to black idiom, and poets made even more extensive uses of features from the southern black oral tradition. Many southern black poets of the Harlem Renaissance also built their poetic canons with forms and themes not exclusively or predominantly black or southern. The lyricism of Jean Toomer's poetry and the intricate patterns of imagery drawn from nature by Anne Spencer revealed that a poetic voice originating from the black South could adopt the Euro-American literary heritage and yet remain relatively free of its constraints.

In the decades following the Harlem Renaissance, southern blacks continued to be major influences on black American poetry. Southerners Sterling Brown, Arna Bontemps, Margaret Walker, and Melvin B. Tolson were among black America's leading poets between the end of the Harlem Renaissance and the 1960s. A native of the District of Columbia, Sterling Brown in his *Southern Road* (1932) captured the spirit of the southern black folk character in the language, form, and personae of his poetry. Between the 1930s and the 1960s Walker and Tolson exhibited in their poetry an intricate blending of the Euro-American and Afro-American heritages. Tolson became one of the best American poets of his time.

As the movement toward a black aesthetic gained impetus in the 1960s, southern black writers, many of them poets, were again among the leaders. During the 1960s and after, the poetry of southern blacks lost many of its more obvious regional qualities and merged with the larger body of black American poetry. The focus shifted from the rural South to the urban North with southern settings, themes, and female personae being replaced by northern settings, themes, and male personae. Nikki Giovanni, Etheridge Knight, Don L. Lee, Naomi Madgett, Sterling Plumpp, and Lance Jeffers are only a few of the widely read contemporary black poets whose origins are southern.

Southern blacks wrote few plays before the 1920s. William Wells Brown's *Escape, or A Leap for Freedom* (1858) and Joseph S. Cotter, Sr.'s *Caleb, the Degenerate* (1903), both dramatic tracts, are notable now chiefly for their historical value. Before the Harlem Renaissance, southern blacks wrote minstrel shows, musical comedies, and a few serious social dramas, but the significance of these works in black American theater arts is also mainly historical. As an outgrowth of the Renaissance, however, Langston Hughes (*Mulatto*, *When the Jack Hollers*, and *Little Ham*), Zora Neale Hurston (*Great Day*), Hal Johnson (*Run, Little Children*), and Arna Bontemps (*St. Louis Woman*) emerged as successful southern black playwrights. In the 1930s the Works Progress Administration's support of black theater arts—plays, playwrights, actors, and actresses—provided for the writing and production of several dramas of social realism by and about southern blacks.

After 1940 the number of southern black playwrights and plays about southern black life declined. Randolph Edmonds, Theodore Ward, and Alice Childress have, however, produced works in this period that rank with the best American plays. From the 1930s through the early 1960s southern black playwrights, like their northern counterparts, used the music, folklore, religion, social history, and other components of southern black life as a major source for their art, but after about 1960 the use of distinctly southern materials decreased sharply in plays by northern and southern blacks. Settings, themes, and characters associated with the urban North became predominant. Still, Alice Childress's *Wedding Band* (1966) and Samm-Art Williams's *Home*, distinctly southern black works, were among the most successful post-1960 plays.

In another genre, southerners were among the earliest (if not the first) black short-fiction writers in America. Until well past 1900 southern black short fiction in the main was thematically about the slave experience and its aftermath and conformed largely to changes and developments in the short story as an American art form. William Wells Brown, Frederick Douglass, Frances W. Harper, and a few other southern blacks wrote various types of short prose fiction during the 19th century. Near the turn of the century Charles Waddell Chesnutt elevated southern black short fiction to the level of literary art. Many of Chesnutt's stories incorporated characteristics of the American local color movement and, regionally, several were classified as plantation literature. The tales of white southerner Thomas Nelson Page and those of Chesnutt exemplified the essential differences between black writers and white writers in approaches to the plantation South. Through characterization, theme, and incident black writers of the South repudiated the romantic image of the plantation. Chesnutt's Uncle Julius, for instance, contradicted the white portrayal of the faithful black servant, epitomized by Page's Sam and Joel Chandler Harris's Uncle Remus. The idyllic portrait of plantation life created by white writers was in stark contrast to the image Chesnutt and other blacks showed of a system infested with greed, inhumanity, deception, and cruelty.

Southern black writers also embellished conventional short-fiction forms by adding features that reflected black life in the South. One such feature was the double entendre, a characteristic of narrative expression rooted especially in the secular and sacred music of the black South. A part of the trickster motif, it helped shape not only characterization but also plot structure, language, and meaning in the different forms of southern black short fiction. Chesnutt's *The Conjure Woman* (1899) exemplified the black writer's skillful use of double entendre.

The Conjure Woman was also an early example of the use of the short-story cycle. The cycle is a fictional narrative that combines techniques of the novel and the short story. Among other collections of short fiction, Langston Hughes's *The Ways of White Folks* (1934) and the Simple series (1950–65); Richard Wright's *Uncle Tom's Children*

(1938) and *Eight Men* (1961); Alice Childress's *Like One of the Family*; James A. McPherson's *Hue and Cry* (1969) and *Elbow Room* (1977); and Ernest J. Gaines's *Bloodline* (1975) demonstrated the consistent expertise of southern black writers' use of the cycle. Hal Bennet, Toni Cade Bambara, and Henry Dumas are among the best contemporary black short-fiction writers of southern origin to have produced superior short-story cycles as well as excellent individual stories.

Between 1900 and the 1970s the novel has been the most widely read and critically acclaimed genre in southern black literature. The manner in which it has concerned itself with the past distinguished it from the general black American novel, the southern white novel, and the Anglo-American novel. The southern white novel has generally dealt with the effects of a real or an imagined past on a present generation, with characters grappling to come to terms with that past. Typically, the southern black novel made the physical and psychological landscapes of the past a living part of the novel; it re-created, repopulated, and critically examined the past as physical setting. Surprisingly, though, southern blacks produced few novels that can be strictly defined as historical novels. Arna Bontemps (*Black Thunder*, 1936), Frank Yerby (*The Foxes of Harrow*, 1946), Waters Turpin (*The Rootless*, 1957), and Margaret Walker (*Jubilee*, 1966) were exceptions.

Those novels concerned with the past, particularly the slave past, used a rather distinct thematic structure. Characteristically, the southern black novel was structurally tripartite—usually beginning in the present, shifting to the recent or remote past, and returning to the present. There were frequent variations: a flight-rejection-return pattern evident in Chesnutt's *The House Behind the Cedars* (1900) and in other novels in the "passing" vein; a South-North-South pattern in Jean Toomer's *Cane* (1923) and in a host of novels that concerned the southern black migrant in the North, from James Weldon Johnson's *The Autobiography of an Ex-Coloured Man* (1912) to Ralph Ellison's *Invisible Man* (1952); a fear-flight-fate pattern in Richard Wright's *Native Son* (1940), William Attaway's *Blood on the Forge* (1941), and several novels whose settings were almost exclusively northern or whose themes were grounded in the violence of living black in America.

Prior to the mid-1970s southern black novels characteristically were concerned with blacks' identity and their process of self-definition. This overarching theme remained prominent over the generations: the 19th-century novels often focused on the plight of the mulatto; the early 20th-century novels that frequently recount the aborted attempts of black characters to "pass" as white; the Harlem Renaissance novels affirmed blackness as a key to identity; the protest-era novels followed in the tradition of *Native Son*; post-1960 novels that dwelt on the effects of black affirmation in a drastically changed, but still white-dominated, society.

For its form and its content, the southern black novel found one of its most influential prose models in the Afro-American slave narrative, which itself was essentially a southern product. Various features of the southern version of the black American novel have their antecedents in the genre: the concentration on generic black experiences and incidents; the tendency toward representative central characters;

the emphasis on the protagonist's process of self-definition; the use of the autobiographical mode and the portrayal of an exemplary life; the analysis of society by an author (or narrator) removed from that society. Indeed, the first black American novelist, William Wells Brown, was himself a fugitive slave, and he cast his first novel, *Clotel* (1853), solidly in the traditions of the slave-narrative genre.

As the southern black novel evolved, from the 19th into the 20th century, its use of narrative voice blended with other features of southern black narrative prose to produce a particularly (but not exclusively) southern point of view in the black novel. For more than a century southern blacks wrote numerous prose narratives, which in their variety conformed to the autobiographical mode. There have been the fugitive-slave narratives and the ex-slave narratives; the spiritual, social, political, and personal autobiographies; the confessionals, exemplary lives, the diary-type and journal-type autobiographies; as well as the autobiographical novel. At times, real-life experiences and incidents were the backdrop for fictional characters; at other times real-life characters become the nucleus around which true-to-life (fictional) experiences and incidents are presented. Southern black prose writers were so attracted to the autobiographical mode that in numerous prose narratives they drew a very thin line between fiction and fact.

One group of prose narratives used the techniques of fiction—a group that includes Richard Wright's *Black Boy* (1945), Will Thomas's *The Seeking* (1953), H. Rap Brown's *Die Nigger Die!* (1970), and Alex Haley's *The Autobiography of Malcolm X* (1965) and *Roots* (1976). In another group the novels (fictional autobiographies) employed nonfiction techniques—Johnson's *The Autobiography of an Ex-Coloured Man* and Ernest J. Gaines's *The Autobiography of Miss Jane Pittman* (1971). Finally, in still another group there are novels such as Toomer's *Cane* and Ellison's *Invisible Man* that contain varying degrees and uses of autobiographical material.

Folktales and aphorisms, sacred and secular music, and the religious orientation or worldview of southern blacks all influenced language, undergirded imagery and symbolism, delineated characterization, and motivated plot structure in the southern black novel. This tendency was evident in the polemical, propagandistic, and apologetic novels that preceded World War I; it increased and became more refined in the novels between World War I and the 1930s; it pervaded such 1930s folk novels as Zora Neale Hurston's *Their Eyes Were Watching God* (1937) and George W. Henderson's *Ollie Miss* (1935); it shaped themes and characterization in the social-protest novels of the 1940s; and it pervaded Ellison's *Invisible Man* and several other novels in the post–World War II period. Southern black novelists as a group have thus made wide and varied uses of the cultural traditions of their region.

The merits of southern black literature have been widely acclaimed nationally and internationally. Ellison's *Invisible Man* won a National Book Award; McPherson's collection of short fiction, *Elbow Room*, was awarded a Pulitzer Prize, as was Alice Walker's novel *The Color Purple* (1982). The numerous awards, prizes, and distinctions accorded to works by blacks of southern origin throughout this century testify to the place they hold within the larger world of American literature.

See also GEOGRAPHY: Expatriates and Exiles; LITERATURE articles

J. Lee Greene
University of North Carolina
at Chapel Hill

Doris Abramson, *Negro Playwrights in the American Theatre* (1969); Richard K. Barksdale and Keneth Kinnamon, eds., *Black Writers of America: A Comprehensive Anthology* (1972); Robert A. Bone, *Down Home: A History of Afro-American Short Fiction from Its Beginnings to the End of the Harlem Renaissance* (1975); Arthur P. Davis and J. Saunders Redding, eds., *Cavalcade: Negro American Writing from 1760 to the Present* (1971); Addison Gayle, *The Way of the New World: The Black Novel in America* (1975); Hugh M. Gloster, *Negro Voices in American Fiction* (1948); James V. Hatch, *Black Playwrights, 1823–1977: An Annotated Bibliography of Plays* (1977); M. Thomas Inge, Maurice Duke, and Jackson R. Bryer, eds., *Black American Writers: Bibliographical Essays*, 2 vols. (1978); Blyden Jackson and Louis D. Rubin, Jr., *Poetry in America: Two Essays in Historical Interpretation* (1974). ☆

Lynching

Lynching is part of the American, especially southern, tradition of vigilante terrorism. Vigilantism has taken several forms, depending on purpose: whitecappers usually flogged, or made threatening night visits, to "regulate" or intimidate their enemies; the charivari was usually a semifestive ritual (such as tar and feathering or merely serenading with "rough music") meant to humiliate transgressors of community standards; lynch mobs killed their victims. Thus lynching is the deadliest form of vigilantism.

Colonel Charles Lynch of Virginia, whose extralegal "court" sentenced Tories to floggings during the American Revolution, apparently provided the origin of the term "lynch-law." Until the 1850s lynch-law (lynching) was commonly associated with corporal and extralegal punishment, but not killing. Then, during the last decade before the Civil War, southern vigilantes, particularly in Louisiana and Texas, routinely inflicted death upon outlaws and on individuals suspected of plotting slave insurrections. That is when lynching took on its lethal connotation.

The Civil War and Reconstruction intensified southern lynching activity. Vigilantism in Texas alone during the war probably accounted for over 150 deaths. Lynching became more widespread in the Reconstruction years and was directed mostly at exslaves, because the free blacks, no longer valued as property, were often viewed as threatening the existence of white civilization. The specter of Haiti, and its bloody slave rebellion of the 1790s, white fear, and predictions of race war helped multiply acts of terrorism.

Not until 1882 were efforts made to gather data on lynching across the United States. During the 70 years from 1882 to the early 1950s, by which time lynching had virtually ended, a total of 4,739 persons reportedly died at the hands of lynch mobs in the United States. (Since these figures were compiled solely from lynching stories printed in leading urban newspapers of each state, it is likely the actual total was nearer 6,000.) Lynching statistics do not, of course, include those blacks or whites who died in race riots; nor would ordinary interracial homicides, where a person of one race killed someone of another race, be listed.

Reported lynchings for the entire United States averaged 150.4 per year during the last 19 years of the 19th century (1882 through 1900). The all-time peak lynch-law year was 1892, with 230. During the first decade of the 20th century (1901–10), lynchings nationally averaged 84.6 per year and dropped further for 1911–20 (to an average of 60.6 annually for the decade). After 1920 reported lynchings continued to decline, with the decade of 1921–30 averaging 27.5 per year. For 1931–40 there were 114 total lynchings (11.4 annual average). The decade of 1941–50 averaged 3 per year. Then lynching virtually ceased. From 1951 to 1985 only 10 lynching deaths were reported in the United States. Approximately 82 percent of all lynchings listed since 1882 took place in the South ("the South" defined here as being the 15 slave states of 1860). Western and midwestern states account for nearly all the remainder. Nationally, 72 percent of all lynch-mob victims have been black; in the South, 84 percent were black. Over 95 percent of the victims, both nationally and regionally, were males. Among the states, Mississippi ranks first in lynching from 1882 to the present, with 581 deaths (539 of them black); Georgia is second with 530 (491 black); Texas third with 493 (352 black); and Louisiana fourth with 391 (335 black). Very few participants in lynch mobs were prosecuted in any state, and prior to World War II almost none ever served time in prison.

Lynch-law was supposed to be, in the blunt words of one advocate of the practice, "the white woman's guarantee against rape by niggers." Ridding society of "black brutes" who violated Caucasian females was indeed the most often mentioned justification for lynching. "Whenever the Constitution comes between me and the virtue of the white women of South Carolina," exclaimed Governor Cole Blease, "then I say 'to hell with the Constitution.' " Since an accused black rapist of Blease's time and place would almost certainly face quick legal execution, why was mob action deemed necessary? Because, according to the rationale of lynching, a ravished white woman must be spared the agony of testifying in court, while the accused presumably would enjoy and be flattered by "the pomp and ceremony of formal justice."

In fact only about one-third of all lynching victims were suspected of rape or attempted rape. Murder or attempted murder was more often the alleged crime. Others who died at the hands of lynch mobs were accused of transgressions of descending importance, such as arson, burglary, slapping a white person, stealing chickens, chronic impudence, or simply being "vagrant and lewd." Whatever the supposed crime, lynching was widely assumed by whites to be a significant deterrent to black criminality. Black males were thought to be more afraid of lynch mobs than anything else. And rape, despite its secondary place in lynch-law statistics, was of prime importance in justifying the concept of vigilante action. Whenever lynching was discussed, rape became the central theme. Whites who objected to lynching ran the risk of being accused of sympathy for black rapists.

Most lynch mobs killed swiftly. The typical victim, after being hoisted with a rope tossed over a tree limb, trestle, or utility pole, would have his death throes ended by a fusillade of bullets. But some lynchings involved prolonged

Lynching of Gus Goodman, Bainbridge, Georgia, 1905

torture and fire. Mississippi, Georgia, and Texas were most likely to witness scenes of medieval horror during the 1890–1920 years. Nearly all torture-lynching victims were blacks accused of both raping and murdering whites. Most were burned at the stake, after preliminary tortures. One accused murderer in Louisiana, a white man, was slowly skinned alive.

Lynch mobs are not easily categorized. The larger throngs were probably made up of people who thought of themselves more as observers than as participants, such as the "hundreds of the best men in Atlanta" who, in 1899, boarded "excursion trains" bound for Newnan, Ga., to see accused rapist-murderer Sam Hose burn at the stake. Sometimes lynch mobs were racially integrated, as were most of the crowds who watched legal executions. Occasionally, black mobs lynched blacks accused of crimes against members of their race. There is one reported case of a white South Carolinian, in jail for molesting and murdering a black child, being handed over to an enraged black mob.

The stereotyped image of poor "redneck" whites making up the mobs who lynched blacks is only partially true. White vigilantes came from all strata of society. Middle- and upper-class participation in lynch mobs was especially common in Louisiana. True, most of the vocal opposition to lynchings came from prominent whites, notably religious leaders, lawyers, and judges. But without the tacit approval of most of the dominant elements in the white community, lynching could not have been so frequent. The South, after all, was essentially a hierarchical society.

Southern newspapers prior to 1920 usually hedged on the question of lynching and seldom condemned it if the mob victim was a black male accused of raping a white female. An outspoken defender of vigilante murder was Henry J. Hearsey (1840–1900), editor-publisher of the New Orleans *Daily States*, the official journal of that city's government. The question of actual guilt, Hearsey admitted, did not really concern him; he was sure lynching deterred black crime, and that was the important thing. Other journalists, not as bloodthirsty, sometimes became so desensitized to lynching that they reported such events with sly humor. As one example, the Port Gibson (Miss.) *Reveille* in 1892 thus described the death of John Robinson, black, who had robbed and killed a white man: "He offered to lead the mob to a railroad trestle under which the money lay buried. John and the money have now exchanged locations."

Antilynching crusaders, both nationally and within the South, began to see public opinion drift in their favor after 1920. Women such as Jessie Daniel Ames and Ida Wells-Barnett and groups such as the Association of Southern Women for the Prevention of Lynching were especially significant. Also, growing fear of legal consequences probably discouraged many would-be lynchers.

See also HISTORY AND MANNERS: Sexuality; MYTHIC SOUTH: / Rednecks; VIOLENCE: Crime, Attitudes Toward; Outlaw-Heroes; / Ku Klux Klan; Mob Violence; WOMEN'S LIFE: / Ames, Jessie Daniel

William I. Hair
Georgia College

Edward L. Ayers, *Vengeance and Justice: Crime and Punishment in the 19th-Century American South* (1984); Ray Stannard Baker, *Following the Color Line* (1908, reprint 1969); Richard Maxwell Brown, *Strain of Violence: Historical Studies of American Violence and Vigilantism* (1975); James H. Chadbourn, *Lynching and the Law* (1933); James E. Cutler, *Lynch-Law: An Investigation into the History of Lynching in the United States* (1905); George C. Rable, *But There Was No Peace: The Role of Violence in the Politics of Reconstruction* (1984); Arthur F. Raper, *The Tragedy of Lynching* (1933); Walter White, *Rope and Faggot* (1929). ☆

Migration, Black

To black southerners, migration has symbolized both the limitations and opportunities of American life. As slaves, many suffered forced migrations with the attendant heartbreaks of separation from family and community. As freed men and women they seized upon spatial mobility as one of the most meaningful manifestations of their newly won emancipation. Subsequently, black southerners sought to better their conditions by moving within the rural South, to southern cities, and finally to northern cities in a frustrating quest for equality and opportunity. Simultaneously, white southerners acted to restrict such movement, because until the mechanization of cotton culture, black geographic mobility—like black social and economic mobility—threatened the racial assumptions and labor relations upon which the southern economy and society rested.

The first significant migration of black southerners followed the American Revolution and the subsequent opening of the trans-Appalachian West to settlement by slaveholders. The enormous expansion of cotton cultivation in the early 19th century, combined with the closing of the foreign slave trade (1808), soon transformed a forced migration dominated by planters carrying their own slaves westward to one increasingly characterized by the professional slave-trader. Although the Chesapeake remained the major source for the interstate slave trade, after 1830 North and South Carolina, Kentucky, Tennessee, Missouri, and eventually Georgia also became "exporters" of slaves. The plantations of Alabama, Mississippi, Louisiana, Florida, Arkansas, and Texas were worked largely by these early black "migrants" and their children. Although it is difficult to determine the volume of the domestic slave trade, one historian has recently estimated that over 1 million black southerners were forcibly relocated between 1790 and 1860.

The forced migrations of the antebellum South were complemented by barriers against voluntary movement. Although each year hundreds of slaves escaped, they represented but a fraction of the southern black population. Even free black southerners were hemmed in, and by the 1830s their movement across state lines was either restricted or prohibited.

During the Civil War white fears and black hopes generated opposing migration streams. Many slaveowners responded to the approach of Union troops by taking their slaves west, either to the western, upcountry areas of the eastern states, or from the Deep South to Texas and Arkansas. Thousands of slaves, on the other hand, fled toward the advancing army.

Ex-slaves continued to move away from plantations after the war ended. For many, like Ernest J. Gaines's fictional Miss Jane Pittman, the act of moving constituted a test of the meaning of emancipation. Others sought to reunite with family separated by antebellum forced migration. Much of the movement grew out of a search for favorable social, political, and economic conditions, especially the chance for "independence," which was closely associated with landownership. The flurry of migration generally involved short distances, often merely to the next plantation or a nearby town or city.

Southern cities offered exslaves the protection of the Freedmen's Bureau and the Union army, higher wages, black institutions, political activity, and freedmen's schools. But under pressure from whites—and often faced with the prospect of starvation—many of the thousands who moved cityward soon returned to the plantations. Urban whites considered the black city dweller a threat to social order, and planters sought to stabilize and reassert dominance over their labor force. Vagrancy laws provided a temporary mechanism, and even after the legislative reforms during Reconstruction, the economic structure of the cities limited the urbanization of the black population. Few jobs outside the service sector were available to blacks, and black men especially found that survival was easier in the countryside. Black southerners continued to migrate to cities in modest numbers; by 1910 less than one-fourth lived in communities larger than 2,500. Some people moved back and forth, mainly between farm and small town, following seasonal labor patterns. This kind of mobility also characterized rural nonfarm labor and established what one historian has called a "migration dynamic," which later facilitated movement to northern cities.

Most black southerners who migrated longer distances in the 19th century headed for rural destinations, generally toward the south and west. During the 1870s and 1880s rumors and labor agents drew blacks living in the Carolinas and Georgia to the Mississippi Delta and other areas in the Gulf states with promises of higher wages and better living conditions. Usually, migrants found social and economic relations similar to what they had left behind. The search for "independence" continued, with black southerners trying Kansas in the 1870s and then Arkansas and Oklahoma between 1890 and 1910. Movement became as central to southern black life as it has been to the American experience in general. Because blacks for so long had been unable to move freely, however, it acquired a special mystique manifested as a major theme in black music and symbolized by the recurrent image of the railroad as a symbol of the freedom to move and start life anew. By the 1890s one black southerner in 12 would cross state lines during the decade in search of the still unfulfilled promise of emancipation. Local moves remained even more frequent.

The direction and historical impact of black migration shifted dramatically during World War I. Northern industrialists, previously reluctant to hire blacks when they could draw upon the continuing influx of white immigrants, turned their attention southward as immigration ceased and production orders began pouring in. Some sent labor agents into the South, but news about opportunities and conditions in the North traveled more often via an emerging black communications network comprising letters from earlier migrants, northern newspapers (especially the Chicago *Defender*), and railroad workers. Observers and subsequent scholars offered various catalogues of "economic" and "social" factors that "pushed" migrants from the South and "pulled" them toward the North. Floods, boll weevil infestations, and credit contractions contributed to the urge to move to northern cities offering higher wages than those available to black southerners. Jim Crow, lynching, disfranchisement, and discrimination in the legal and educational systems contrasted with seemingly more equitable and flexible race relations in the North. Most migrants left because of a combination of motivations, which they often summarized as "bettering my condition." For the first time, however, thousands of black southerners looked to industrial work, rather than landownership, in their hopes to enjoy the prerogatives of American citizenship.

Nearly one-half million black southerners headed north between 1916 and 1920, setting off a long-term demographic shift, which would leave only 53 percent of black Americans in the South by 1970, compared with 89 percent in 1910. Nearly all of these migrants went to cities, first in the Northeast and Midwest, and later in the West. Most followed the longitudinal routes of the major railroads, although by World War II, California was drawing thousands of migrants from Texas, Oklahoma, Arkansas, and Louisiana. At the same time, black southerners moved to southern cities, which by 1970 contained two-thirds of the region's black population. Even the massive urban unemployment of the Great Depression only moderately slowed the continuing flow northward, and movement accelerated to unprecedented levels during World War II and the following decades. Since 1970 migration has leveled off, and there has been some evidence of a return to the South.

Many white southerners initially responded to this "Great Migration" by continuing the tradition of constructing barriers in the paths of black migrants. As always, landlords and employers feared the diminution of their labor supply, a threat that in the 19th century had stimulated the enaction of a corpus of legislation designed to limit labor mobility. As a social movement and a series of individual decisions, however, the Great Migration also constituted a direct—although unacknowledged—threat to the fiber of social and economic relations in the South. The system rested upon the assumption that blacks were by nature docile, dependent, and unambitious. The decision to migrate and the evolution of a "movement" suggested dissatisfaction, ambition, and aggressive action. As they had in the past, white southerners tended to blame the movement on "outside forces" (in this case, labor agents), and localities ineffectively sought to stem the tide by tightening "enticement" laws and forcibly preventing blacks from leaving.

The Great Migration transformed both American urban and Afro-American society, as migrants adapted to urban life while retaining much of their southern and rural culture. It was not unusual for southern communities to reconstitute themselves and their institutions in northern cities. Frequent visiting between relatives in the South and North has contributed to this interchange between regional cultures, and the South is still "down home" to some northern black urbanites.

As a historical process, black migration within and from the South suggests some important continuities suffusing much of southern history: the coercive implications of white dependence on black labor; the refusal of blacks to accept their "place" as defined by whites; and the search for identity and opportunity articulated by black writer Richard Wright, whose personal migration experience began with the hope that "I might learn who I was, what I might be."

See also GEOGRAPHY: Migration Patterns; Population

James Grossman
University of Chicago

Florette Henri, *Black Migration: Movement North, 1900–1920* (1975); Allan Kulikoff, in *Slavery and Freedom in the Age of the American Revolution*, ed. Ira Berlin and Ronald Hoffman (1983); Nell Irvin Painter, *Exodusters: Black Migration to Kansas after Reconstruction* (1976); Arvarh Strickland, *Missouri Historical Review* (July 1975); Carter G. Woodson, *A Century of Negro Migration* (1918). ☆

Miscegenation

This word first appeared in 1863 in an unsigned pamphlet written, it was later learned, by two New York City journalists, David G. Croly and George Wakeman, in collusion with Ohio Congressman Samuel S. Cox. From the Latin words *miscere*, to mix, and *genus*, race, it was created by these three Democrats to be a political weapon to stigmatize the Republican party and the Emancipation Proclamation as promoting sexual mixing of races, particularly of whites and blacks. From 1863 to the present, despite miscegenation's actual infrequency in the United States—especially in comparison with other multiracial societies like Latin America and South Africa—the word has served to conjure a threat to the continuation of white supremacy. Throughout history, racial purity has been more of an idea than a reality. Africans brought to the New World already had mixed with Europeans and Asians. Race mixing has been viewed by Afro-Americans as both a positive symbol of integration and assimilation into a white society and as an undermining of black identity and racial pride.

Well before 1863 the term *racial amalgamation* was commonly used to denote sexual intercourse between members of different races but also could include production of children from this liaison. Although somewhat less pejorative in intent than the word *miscegenation*, it also has reflected widespread negative white American attitudes about black-white sexual relations.

In the Chesapeake Bay area during the 17th century, black male slaves were imported while indentured lower-class single English women came to the colonies as household servants. The shortage of partners of the same race and relatively little prejudice about racial purity among the poorer classes stimulated race mixing.

The Lower South differentiated the status of mulattoes and blacks. Charleston and New Orleans exemplified the racial mixing made possible by urban anonymity. On the other hand, the lack of a large white indentured class on South Carolina plantations, where blacks were both domestic and field slaves, accounts for the absence of racial amalgamation.

In the 17th and early 18th centuries the growth of a relatively free and privileged mulatto class was resisted more in the British colonies than in any other slave society in the Americas. North Carolina and Georgia passed laws opposing racial amalgamation in the 18th century. Pennsylvania and Massachusetts, with relatively small black populations and minimal amounts of slavery, banned intermarriage. The fear of losing a homogeneous white culture in cities like Philadelphia and Boston helps explain the origin of northern laws.

By the beginning of the 18th century the female indentured white servant class diminished throughout the South, and the female-to-male ratio among black slaves became more equal. Although race mixing was less likely to occur between white females and black males, the prohibition of racial amalgamation continued. Laws against racial amalgamation now served to enforce the belief that only blacks could be slaves and that the freedom and independence of whites depended upon this racial distinction.

From the 18th century to the Civil War liaisons between white slave masters and black female slaves did occur, and many of their children were removed from the Lower South. The census of 1850 indicated that the Upper South contained two-thirds of the mulattoes in the entire South.

Except for the time of the American Revolution, when ideas of equality moved some northern states to abolish slavery and rescind their prohibition on racial amalgamation, such laws continued to proliferate in the North up to the Civil War. Both free and slave states entering the Union usually legally prohibited intermarriage, and some of the older states made interracial marriage not merely punishable but null and void. A person was defined as black if he/she had a black or mulatto ancestor in the previous three generations. Not until 1843 did Massachusetts's antislavery sentiment bring the abolition of the state's laws opposing interracial marriage—laws that had not only banned intermarriage but had fined clergymen performing such marriages.

The abolition of slavery, accompanied by the creation of the word *miscegenation* in 1863, raised the specter of increased race mixing—especially between black men and white women. White supremacy under slavery had assumed the childlike, docile quality of male slaves and the aggressiveness of freed blacks; the end of slavery transformed this image of male slaves into one of sexually potent men who wished to rape the daughters of white men. Adding to these deep fears were Victorian images of white women as alternately pure and vulnerable or as creatures of their own uncontrolled sexual passions. Criticism of post–Civil War Radical Reconstruction was replete with this imagery, and the end of Reconstruction brought more state laws against racial intermarriage than ever before. Slavery's abolition ended the relationship of the white master and black female slave, and thus caused a sharp decline in interracial mixing. Less miscegenation occurred than under slavery—a common contrast between slave and free societies. Yet the worst incidents of mob rule and lynching of blacks occurred in the late 19th and early 20th centuries under the guise of preventing racial mixing.

By 1850 a mulatto elite developed, and the importance of this group was dramatically evident in South Carolina during Radical Reconstruction (1868–76) where some 13 percent of the politicians were mulatto. Whether they descended from New Orleans and Charleston mulatto society, from illicit plantation liaisons, or, as a large fraction were, from antebellum free Afro-Americans, mulattoes provided a cadre of race leadership well into the 1920s. But 1880–1920 was also the age of passing, when many light-skinned Afro-Americans chose to identify themselves as whites to avoid the disadvantages of being black in a racist society. Passing and its meaning for black identity were major social and literary concerns in the 1920s for writers and leaders of the Harlem Renaissance.

As recently as 1930, 20 states still outlawed intermarriage between whites and Afro-Americans, and mixed marriages (because of social disapproval) were rare in other states. Despite the 1967 Supreme Court decision *Loving* v. *Virginia*, declaring unconstitutional all laws against intermarriage, the number of marriages between whites and Afro-Americans remains as few as 2 in 1,000. Most mixing has occurred between blacks and mulattoes, and it is estimated that three-fourths of Afro-Americans in the 20th century are of mixed ancestry. White-black intermarriage rates are not likely to exceed soon even 1 percent. In the foreseeable future, miscegenation, therefore, will not bring racial assimilation. Since the 1960s, Afro-Americans mostly have turned toward asserting their racial identity and sense of black pride while seeking equal rights with whites.

Yvonne De Carlo after her character, Amantha Starr, in* Band of Angels *(1957), discovers black ancestry

See also ETHNIC LIFE: Caribbean Influence; Indian Cultural Contributions; HISTORY AND MANNERS: Sexuality; MYTHIC SOUTH: Racial Attitudes

Tilden G. Edelstein
Rutgers University

Ira Berlin, *Slaves without Masters: The Free Negro in the Antebellum South* (1974); Carl N. Degler, *Neither Black nor White: Slavery and Race Relations in Brazil and the United States* (1971); George M. Fredrickson, *White Supremacy: A Comparative Study in American and South African History* (1981); Laurence J. Friedman, *The White Savage: Racial Fantasies in the Postbellum South* (1970); Thomas C. Holt, *Black over White: Negro Political Leadership in South Carolina during Reconstruction* (1977); Winthrop D. Jordan, *White over Black: American Attitudes toward the Negro, 1550–1812* (1968); Joel Williamson, *New People: Miscegenation and Mulattoes in the United States* (1980); Forrest G. Wood, *Black Scare: The Racist Response to Emancipation and Reconstruction* (1970). ☆

Music, Black

Black musical life was never limited to a single style or musical tradition. In the 19th century American popular songs found their way into the repertoire of black folk musicians, European fiddle tunes appeared in medleys performed by itinerant fiddlers, and shape-note singing was adopted by black congregations in imitation of the colonial traditions developed in the North but transplanted to the South in the 1830s. Black musicians were aware of various ethnic musical traditions; and the process of musical acculturation, forced on blacks because of their need to accommodate themselves to a sometimes hostile culture or accepted by them because the other music fitted in so well with their own, led them to learn repertories acceptable to both races.

Two great periods of musical acculturation have been preserved on records. The first occurred during the pre–World War II era when the radio and phonograph made the quick transmission of personal and regional styles possible, the second immediately following the war when Afro-American music was brought to the attention of a larger audience. Some of the evidence needed for studying black southern music comes from those commercial recordings classified as "blues" and marketed as "race records" in the 1920s and 1930s by producers who sought to profit from the sales of phonographs to black families, more of whom owned a record player than a musical instrument. Because those producers and the major record companies limited their "race" catalogs to those items likely to have strong sales among blacks, the other major recordings come from the fieldwork of folklorists employed by the Library of Congress, the Works Progress Administration, and a few major universities, evidence that includes examples dating back to the styles of the Civil War era.

Black musicians created in a variety of forms, from art songs to zydeco music (blues-influenced dance music performed by French-speaking creole blacks). Many black musicians were musically bilingual, capable of absorbing and mastering (1) the Afro-Caribbean rhythms and dance forms brought to the Gulf Coast by emigrants from Haiti, Jamaica, and Cuba; (2) the many ethnic musical styles practiced by Cajun, German, French and Spanish Creole, Mexican, and French performers; and, after emancipation, (3) the new styles of American and European art and popular music from the North. Studies of the Afro-American style tend to emphasize folk music and jazz, but southern blacks also had a repertoire of material that they shared with whites, a "common heritage" known widely throughout the United States.

The multiethnic character of some

Othar Turner playing a black folk instrument, the fife, Gravel Springs, Mississippi, 1971

antebellum southern cities contributed greatly to the opportunities for musical acculturation. Over 40 percent of the population of New Orleans (116,375 in 1850), 24 percent of Mobile (20,515 in 1850), and 30 percent of Charleston (42,985 in 1840) were foreign born. Each of these cities and its various ethnic groups provided music for urban blacks to learn and, through the "hiring out" practice, opportunities for slaves to join free blacks for performances at dances and other social events.

Following the rage for brass band music that began in Europe and spread to the United States in the late 1830s, brasswind ensembles, such as the Richmond Light Infantry Blues (ca. 1840) and Allen's Brass Band (Wilmington, N.C.), were established in the South. Bandbooks of both the pre–Civil War and postbellum periods reveal a repertoire consisting of everything from transcribed fiddle tunes and popular hymns to selections from European operas and American musical theater. The Negro Philharmonic Society of New Orleans (ca. 1838) presented concerts for many years, and one of its directors, Richard Lambert, headed a family that included several generations of famous musicians. Each of the cities of the South seemed to have both slave and free blacks who earned strong vocal reputations for their musicianship. Simeon Gilliat and George Walker were considered the finest musicians in early 19th-century Richmond, and the roster of famous New Orleans musicians at the end of the century features "legends" such as "Klondike," "John the Baptist," Ferdinand "Jelly Roll" Morton, and Anthony Jackson ("the World's Greatest Single-Handed Entertainer").

After 1865 some black artists and composers adopted European aesthetic values and performance traditions. Inspired by the success of the first group of Fisk Jubilee Singers (1871–78), the brilliant career of Mississippi-born Marie Smith Selika, and the many gifted instrumentalists, dancers, and singers who appeared with postbellum minstrel, vaudeville, and tent shows, blacks moved beyond the folk and traditional styles with which they were associated before the war. Trained by such distinguished black educators as John Wesley Work (Fisk University) and Robert Nathaniel Dett (Hampton Institute and Bennett College), many sought professional training for careers as performers or teachers. Few were to realize the dream of international recognition and personal artistic success, but southern-born artists such as Roland Hayes, William Grant Still, W. C. Handy, Leontyne Price, Mahalia Jackson, and many others have made outstanding contributions to the world of music.

The major features of black performance styles are communal singing with call-and-response patterns; polyrhythmic percussive accompaniments to both religious and secular vocal and choral music— foot tapping, hand clapping, and drumming performed in ways similar to known African practices, and the intense, sometimes ecstatic emotional participation of the audience or congregation in the performance.

A number of vocal techniques distinguish Afro-American singing from the popular, operatic, and theatrical styles of the 19th century. Black performers are described in literary sources as capable of producing a wide variety of vocal effects: ascending or descending glides or runs, frequent use of the head or falsetto voice (especially in quick leaps from low robust tones to high piercing ones), vocal imitations of natural and animal sounds. Devices commonly found in reports about and recordings of black storytellers include subtle pitch variations that follow the natural inflections of black speech, changes in pitch and dynamics directly related to the emotional content of a musical phrase, and a sometimes completely arhythmic vocalizing in the manner of an extended free-form sung meditation. Most of these stylistic traits are well-known to black and white audiences today, but they were virtually unknown in the popular music of the North prior to the 1920s, even in the minstrel shows that claimed to be "authentic" imitations of black behavior.

These characteristics can be found in the field cries and hollers, chants, lullabies, ritual songs, ring shouts, and religious songs in which a call-and-response pattern served as a framework for improvising melodies and texts. That ability to spontaneously create texts, tales, and songs has been documented in folklore studies and is a characteristic of almost all Afro-American music such as blues, jazz, and religious song.

Religious institutions, fraternal associations, and traditional seasonal festivals encouraged music making. From the colonial John Canoe or John Conny festivals in North Carolina and Virginia to the regularly scheduled dances in the Place Congo in New Orleans; from the corn shucking parties in Virginia, the Carolinas, and Texas to the cane songs of Mississippi and Louisiana; and from the voodoo ceremonies in Georgia and Florida to the sacred dances of Alabama and Arkansas, music played an important role in black social life. It accompanied dancing and singing and provided a background for an escape from the routines of life.

Three major 20th-century forms of Afro-American music are associated with the South: blues, ragtime piano, and New Orleans jazz. Classic ragtime—the syncopated and carefully structured piano and band music of Scott Joplin, James Scott, and Joseph Lamb—evolved from a combination of the rhythmically irregular Afro-American melodic style and the regular background rhythms of postbellum band music to which should be added the common black folk practice of treating melody, design, and rhythm very flexibly. Ragtime songs and dances were introduced by southern-born blacks who picked up the techniques of ragging tunes by ear, and the wide distribution of various types of rags in southern folk and popular music suggests that blacks and whites shared many musical ideas well before ragtime became popular in the North.

The blues, described by Paul Oliver as "arguably the most significant form of folk music to have emerged in this century," is deeply embedded in the black musical experience. Rich in its use of language and poetic imagery, varied in its multiple attraction to the deepest tragedies and most ribald comedies of human existence, and, musically, the source for the chord structures and harmonic patterns used in much American popular music and jazz, the blues is as important to the musical history of this century as black spirituals were to the 19th. Two major blues forms—urban and rural—are widely recognized by blues scholars. The performance of the blues involves very subtle communications processes. The music is a vehicle for sharing complaints, exorcising sorrow, laughing at the world's absurdities, mocking whites, and maintaining the integrity of black culture.

Dixieland jazz is one of the major forms of ensemble jazz. It was not the exclusive possession of blacks or the South, however, because early New Orleans jazz was played by nearly as many Creoles as blacks, especially after the segregation laws passed by New Orleans in 1894 and 1897 brought Afro-American and Creole cultures together in the uptown section. Still, southern blacks such as Louis Armstrong are inextricably linked with the birth of jazz. The role of black, white, and Creole musicians in creating and developing jazz makes it a classic case of musical amalgamation.

Black southerners, like black Americans elsewhere, adopted many of the same values as whites, but the Afro-American musical style reflects most vividly the inherent dichotomies blacks have faced in being Americans. The tendency to view the style in terms of its various genres—spirituals, blues, ragtime, gospel songs—sometimes obscures the fact that black musicians still treat music as an oral rather than a written art because black culture is still largely an oral culture in both North and South. The real strength of *southern* black music is its diversity, its ability to capture the tensions as well as the achievements of blacks, its indebtedness as well as its contribution to other forms of southern music, and its heritage of preserving older performance practices after the great black exodus from the South. Without southern culture as a stimulant to music acculturation, the Afro-American style would not have produced the unique fusion of traditions that have made it a potent force in this century's popular music.

See also MUSIC articles

William J. Mahar
Pennsylvania State University—
Capitol Campus

Dominique-Rene De Lerma, *Bibliography of Black Music*, 4 vols. (1981–84); Sam Dennison, *Scandalize My Name: Black Imagery in American Popular Music* (1982); Dena Epstein, *Sinful Tunes and Spirituals: Black Folk Music to the Civil War* (1977); David Horn, *The Literature of American Music in Books and Folk Music Collections: A Fully Annotated Bibliography* (1981); Bill C. Malone, *Southern Music—American Music* (1979); Paul Oliver, *Songsters and Saints: Vocal Traditions on Race Records* (1984); JoAnn Skowronski, *Black Music in America: A Bibliography* (1981); Eileen Southern, *Biographical Dictionary of Afro-American and African Musicians* (1982), *The Music of Black Americans: A History* (1971, 2d. ed., 1983); Jeff Todd Titon, *Early Downhome Blues: A Musical and Cultural Analysis* (1977). ☆

Northern Cities, Blacks in

The most distinctive feature of black life in the South in the first half of the 20th century was the crystallization of a distinct Afro-American nationality. The sense of identity among the masses of black people based on a shared culture and common experiences in institutions such as churches provided the matrix sustaining life in the South and laying a foundation that was later transferred to newer settings in the North and West.

Pushed by the ravages of the boll weevil, floods, unemployment after the collapse of an exploitative tenancy-sharecropping system, and surging racism, black people were eager to escape the South. But not until these factors were combined with the pull of better jobs and a better life, especially in the war-stimulated, labor-starved industries of northern cities, did a mass migration begin. The move was facilitated by black newspapers like the Chicago *Defender*, by labor recruiters offering free train tickets, and by word of mouth.

The Afro-American move from the South to the North, from country to city, and from farm to factory is one of the most significant social transformations in the history of the United States. No aspect of the lives of black people was left unchanged. The dynamic interaction of a southern-based, rural Afro-American nationality and northern, urban experiences is key to understanding this process.

In 1900, 9 of every 10 black people lived in the South and about 8 of every 10 lived in rural areas. Although only 170,000 blacks migrated from the South in the first decade of the 20th century, that number increased to 454,000 between 1910 and 1920 and to 749,000 between 1920 and 1930. Between 1930 and 1950 black out-migrants from the South, and mainly *to* the North and cities, totaled 1.9 million. As a result, the percentage of blacks living in the North in 1950 increased to 34 percent, and the percentage living in cities had increased to 62 percent.

In 1940 over a million of the 3 million black people in the North lived in four cities—New York, Chicago, Philadelphia, and Detroit, increasing their black populations from 7 to 30 fold. Between 1910 and 1940, for example, New York's black population increased from 91,709 to 458,444, while Chicago's population grew from 44,103 to 277,731 during the same period.

A definite pattern existed to black migration, with proximity to settlement sites and established transportation routes playing important roles. In 1930, 22 percent of Cleveland's blacks were born in Ohio, but 36 percent came from Georgia and Alabama. In Detroit, more blacks came from Georgia (21 percent) and Alabama (about 14 percent) than were born in Michigan (14 percent). For Philadelphia, 32 percent were born in Virginia and South Carolina while only 30 percent were natives of the state. Finally, almost as many black Chicagoans had been born in Mississippi (17 percent) as in Illinois. Moreover, there was a distinct age and gender selectivity to the migrations: between 1920 and 1930, 45 of every 100 black males between 15 and 34 left Georgia, and between 1940 and 1950, Mississippi lost almost one-half of its young black adults.

The settlement patterns of southern blacks, especially the compactness and segregation of the black community, encouraged the survival of southern culture. Racial segregation existed in the North as well as in the South. A 1940 study of 109 cities using a residential segregation index with 100 as a maximum score, revealed a score of 83.2 for the Northeast (e.g., New York) and 88.4 for the North Central region (e.g., Chicago), as compared to 89.9 for the South. More specifically, the concentration of blacks increased between 1910 and 1950—from 66.8 to 79.7 in Chicago, from 46.0 to 74.0 in Philadelphia, from 64.1 to 80.9 in Boston, and from 60.6 to 86.6 in Cleveland. The result of this concentration was to promote the retention of older southern habits and customs.

The most profound change was in the world of work. Where 60 percent of black men worked in agriculture in 1910, by 1950 only 18.4 percent of blacks were employed as farm workers.

By 1950 also, 38 percent of blacks in general were employed as blue-collar workers in the factories and 34 percent as service workers such as maids and janitors. Although blacks were still on the lowest rungs of the northern economic ladder, and constrained by racially discriminatory "job ceilings," which confined them to "Negro jobs," these low-status jobs were usually higher than those on the upper rungs of southern sharecropping tenancy. They brought higher pay, new skills, greater association with whites, and new organizational participation such as in unions.

In addition, a cultural transformation occurred, necessitated by new conditions and the pace of urban life with its greater freedom. Although racial segregation existed, black life in northern cities was less isolated and intimate than in the rural South. Soul food was commercial, available in numerous restaurants and, as poet Sterling Brown said, "leisurely yarn-spinning" and "slowpaced aphoristic conversation became lost arts."

Religious life underwent profound changes. The rise of the "storefront" church in the city represented the adaptation of the small rural church to city life. In Chicago in the 1940s, 75 percent of the 500 churches in the black community were storefronts. These churches were clustered in the poorer areas of the black community in which migrants were concentrated. Storefronts provided a more intimate context for self-expression and social contacts than the larger, more bureaucratized city churches.

Holiness and spiritualist sects helped solve personal crises and facilitated the adjustment to disruption in family life, loss of social status, and other changes resulting from the transition. Practices such as faith healing were common in some of these churches and similar to practices found in the South. Among the most widely known were the Father Divine Peace Mission Movement and the Moorish Science Temple of America, a forerunner of the Nation of Islam.

While black membership in churches decreased in the urban North and while the significance of the church as a center of social life declined as it competed with other institutions, including movies, concerts, and other forms of recreation, the church nevertheless remained a key institution in the social life of black people in northern cities and provided a context for sustaining other aspects of rural southern life.

Urban life influenced the form, tempo, and lyrics of black music. The blues had long dealt exclusively with "despair and sadness" over wretched rural conditions, both natural and social: "Don't you see how them creatures, now have done me wrong? Boll weevil's got my cotton and the merchant's got my corn." Mirroring the urban reality of Motown (Detroit), the form remained, but the words were appropriately refocused: "Please Mr. Foreman, slow down your assembly line. I don't mind working, but I do mind dying."

The disruptive impact of the migrations and the harshness of the post–World War I and Depression era caused the producers of the new gospel music to consciously incorporate into black church music the sounds and the forms of earlier black musical traditions, including blues and jazz. According to the "Father of Gospel," Thomas A. Dorsey, the music helped "to give [black people] something to lift them out of that Depression . . . out of the muck and mire of poverty and loneliness, of being broke." In the face of dispersal from the black belt South, integration into the urban industrial economy, and racism, black migrants from the South "could go back home" through the blues and other southern musical traditions.

Black family life was affected by the trek north. Initially, urban families retained many of the basic characteristics of their rural counterparts—a larger proportion of children (relative to whites) and more grandchildren living with grandparents (the extended family). Since 1950, however, the number of husband-wife families has declined and the number of divorces increased. The number of female-headed households and the number of black children living in these households increased dramatically. Whether these developments represent the "disorganization" of the black family or show its strength in adapting to a hostile environment is much debated. In moving from the South to the North, from rural to urban, the black family clearly, in any event, changed in both form and function. Compounded by other developments, such as high unemployment among black youth, the problems created by this shift remain unsolved.

One issue that has not been sufficiently researched is the vibrant interchange that goes on between black people in the North and their southern kin. Black newspapers report on visits and reunions in almost every issue.

Social movements among black people in northern cities showed their southern roots. The Universal Negro Improvement Association of Marcus Garvey, one of the largest, is said to have been successful in large measure because of its appeal to newly arrived black southerners who were won over by the movement's emphasis on independent landownership and institutional development, reflecting their nation-like aspirations. Similarly, the increased popularity of the newly organized Communist party in the 1930s was related to its claims that the black belt region of the South was a black homeland and that blacks had the right to national self-determination and a government of their own choosing. More importantly, Communists were active organizers of several key campaigns, which touched the sentiment of transplanted black southerners. One example was the international defense of the Scottsboro (Ala.) boys, nine black youths unjustly accused and given the death sentence for raping two white women who later admitted to false testimony. The appeal of such later leaders as Martin Luther King, Jr., Malcolm X, and other civil rights activists also reflected the sustained interest of northern blacks in conditions in the South—a region defined by Malcolm X as "everything below Canada."

See also GEOGRAPHY: Expatriates and Exiles; Migration Patterns; / Northern Cities, Whites in; SOCIAL CLASS: Communism; LAW: / Scottsboro Case

Ronald Bailey
University of Mississippi

Abdul Alkalimat, *Introduction to Afro-American Studies: A Peoples College Primer* (1986); St. Clair Drake and Horace Cayton, *Black Metropolis: A Study of Negro Life in a Northern City* (1945); E. Franklin Frazier, *The Negro in the United States* (1949); Gunnar Myrdal, *An American Dilemma: The Negro Problem and Modern Democracy* (1944); Joe William Trotter, Jr., *Black Milwaukee: The Making of an Industrial Proletariat, 1915–1945* (1984). ☆

Politics, Black

Black southerners heralded as a second emancipation the momentous 1944 U.S. Supreme Court decision in *Smith* v. *Allwright* outlawing the Texas white primary. In 1923 the Texas Legislature had enacted a law holding that the Democratic party was a private organization possessed of the authority to restrict membership and voting privileges to whites only in Democratic party primary elections. With alacrity, all southern states adopted similar forms of white primary legislation. Although black southerners retained the right to vote in general elections, in the one-party South such participation proved meaningless. Nomination in the primary was tantamount to election because the general elections merely rubber-stamped primary returns.

Few southern blacks enjoyed unfettered access even to general election voting booths. Legislation enacted by southern white politicians in the wake of the collapse of radical Reconstruction (1877) effectively disfranchised the vast majority of the region's black citizens. Poll tax laws, literacy clauses, restrictive voter registration tests, along with fear, intimidation, and violence erected an impenetrable barrier that denied blacks access to both the ballot box and political office. The white primary was a capstone to white supremacy and black powerlessness.

The *Smith* ruling, culminating two decades of litigation and struggle, dealt a shattering blow to black disfranchisement. The U.S. Supreme Court had declared that the right to participate fully in the electoral process could not be "nullified by a state through casting its electoral process in a form which permits a private organization to practice racial discrimination." The Democratic party's exclusion of blacks from voting in primary elections was viewed as a direct violation of the Fifteenth Amendment of the U.S. Constitution.

The *Smith* decision signaled the reentry of hundreds of thousands of blacks into southern politics. Moreover, it established a solid legal foundation through which the National Association for the Advancement of Colored People (NAACP) launched a massive assault on black second-class citizenship, housing segregation, and educational discrimination, giving rise to the modern civil rights movement.

After the landmark Supreme Court decision in *Brown* v. *Board of Education* (1954) prohibiting racial segregation in the schools, the black political revolution was well under way. In 1940 only 5 percent of voting-age black southerners were registered, whereas on the heels of *Smith* black registration increased to 12 percent. Two years after *Brown*, 25 percent of eligible southern blacks were enrolled on voting lists.

This modest growth in black political participation aroused the ire and determined opposition of southern white politicians. Throughout the late 1940s and 1950s Governor Eugene Talmadge of Georgia, Congressman E. C. Boswell of Alabama, Senator Theodore G. Bilbo of Mississippi, and others, initiated strategies designed to thwart black advancement and to preserve white supremacy.

Southern white politicians failed, however, to stem the tide of the political reform impulse unleashed, in part, by a liberal Supreme Court. Indeed, all remaining legal barriers to black voting and office holding fell before the onslaught of subsequent Supreme Court decisions on reapportionment and the strong leadership of Presidents Dwight D. Eisenhower, John F. Kennedy, and Lyndon Baines Johnson. Not to be outdone, the U.S. Congress enacted far-reaching legislation, including the civil rights laws of 1957, 1960, and 1964.

The Voting Rights Act passed by the Congress in 1965 represented a major victory in the black rights quest. It suspended the literacy tests that had been used to bar blacks from the polls, banned the poll tax as a state suffrage requirement, and gave the president the authority to send examiners into the South to register blacks. Not only did black registration and participation in the region's elections increase, but white southerners did also. In 1952 and 1956 fewer than 8 million southerners voted for president, but in 1980 over 20 million voted. Whites made up 9.7 million voters of that increase, blacks 3.1 million.

The significance of the dismantling of voter registration barriers for black political participation in the South cannot be overstated. Of equal importance were the unrelenting pressure and intense voter registration campaigns of civil rights organizations such as the Student Nonviolent Coordinating Committee, the Southern Christian Leadership Conference, the Congress of Racial Equality, and the NAACP.

The increase in black voter registration and office holding during the 1960s altered the South's political landscape. At the beginning of the decade 1,414,052, or 28 percent, of eligible black adults voted. By 1969 a record 64.3 percent participated in the electoral process. The three states registering the greatest percentage of blacks were Tennessee, 92.1 percent; Arkansas, 77.9 percent; and Texas, 73.1 percent.

In 1975 the number of black elected public officials in the South stood at 1,600. Within five years the number had jumped to nearly 2,500, and by January 1985 there were 3,233 black elected officials in the South. For the first time since Reconstruction southern blacks were elected to offices of power in city and county governments, state legislatures, and the U.S. House of Representatives, and they were appointed to prominent positions on the national level. Black mayors have served in scores of small southern towns, such as Tuskegee, Ala.; Fayette, Miss.; and Madison, Ark.; large southern metropolises have also boasted black mayors, including Ernest Morial of New Orleans, La., and Andrew Young of Atlanta, Ga., successor to Maynard Holbrook Jackson, who served as mayor from 1973 to 1982. Blacks now sit as state supreme court justices in Mississippi (Reuben Anderson), South Carolina (Ernest Finney), Virginia (John Charles Thomas), and North Carolina (Henry Frye).

On the national level, southern black politicians have achieved widespread acclaim. Barbara Jordon represented Texas in the Congress. Following Jordon's resignation in 1973, Mickey Leland, a former member of the Texas House of Representatives, was elected to serve. Andrew Young of Georgia was appointed United States ambassador to the United Nations during Jimmy Carter's presidency.

Jesse Jackson's 1984 bid for the presidency of the United States showcased the importance of the black vote in the South and promoted increased voter registration. Jackson's national campaign relied on southern black votes and the organizational power of the black churches in the region. Jackson received over 3 million votes in the primaries and became the central black political figure of the 1980s. The Voter Education Project in Atlanta had registered 750,000 new black voters in the 11 states of the old Confederacy by the summer of 1984.

In spite of impressive gains in black voter registration and office holding, politics has not proven to be a panacea. Persistent inequalities between black and white southerners continue. By 1980 blacks held 3 percent of elected offices in a region where they constituted 20 percent of the population. Over half of the 100 counties in the South with majority black populations still have no black elected officials. Jesse Jackson fought the southern winner-take-all primary system in 1984, pressing for reforms to go beyond the *Smith* decision. The changes wrought since the *Smith* decision indicate significant transformation in black political participation, but the black political revolution is still far from complete, and political parity remains a dream.

See also POLITICS articles

Darlene Clark Hine
Purdue University

Numan Bartley, *The Rise of Massive Resistance: Race and Politics in the South during the 1950s* (1969); Andrew Buni, *The Negro in Virginia Politics, 1902–1965* (1967); Ward E. Y. Elliott, *The Rise of Guardian Democracy: The Supreme Court's Role in Voting Rights Disputes, 1845–1969* (1974); Darlene Clark Hine, *Black Victory: The Rise and Fall of the White Primary in Texas* (1979); William R. Keech, *The Impact of Negro Voting: The Role of the Vote in the Quest for Equality* (1968); Steven F. Lawson, *Black Ballots: Voting Rights in the South, 1944–1969* (1976); Manning Marable, *Black American Politics: From the Washington Marches to Jesse Jackson* (1985); Donald R. Matthews and James W. Prothro, *Negroes and the New Southern Politics* (1966); August Meier and Elliot Rudwick, *CORE: A Study of the Civil Rights Movement, 1942–1968* (1973); Harvard Sitkoff, *The Struggle for Black Equality, 1954–1980* (1981). ☆

Preacher, Black

During the Great Awakening of 1800 and for years after, many itinerant preachers found that their listeners for religious services often numbered in the thousands. To accommodate such large congregations, the camp meeting was institutionalized. These large-scale worship services were especially successful in the border states of Kentucky and Tennessee, where many clergymen from the North traveled. This new form of divine worship, sometimes attracting as many as 20,000 or more at events such as the one held at Cane Ridge, Ky., included black as well as white worshipers. Although this form of worship never caught on in the Northeast, it was highly successful in the South and Southwest. Many black ministers were inspired to preach at such gatherings, though at first only to other blacks, and a characteristic oral style of delivery emerged from this experience.

These sermons were characterized by the preacher's chanting the Word of God rather than delivering it conventionally. The sermon began traditionally enough with a statement of the day's text and its application to contemporary morals. Then, as the preacher got further into the day's message, he began to chant his lines, the metrics and time intervals of the lines became more and more regular and consistent, and as he became further imbued with the Holy Spirit, the preacher's delivery slid into song. The sermons were—and still are—characterized by an increase in emotional and spiritual intensity, expressed by the gradual transition from conventional pulpit oratorical style, through chanting, to highly emotional singing. Many black folk preachers are excellent singers and have had several years' experience with church choirs, if not on the professional stage. Quite a number have been choirmasters, and nearly all these men have from an early age attended church services in which music played a major role. A musical sense has thus been acquired, and its rhythms, intonations, timbres, and verbal phrasing are inextricable parts of the tradition.

Foreign visitors to black church services in the early 19th century remarked not only on the minister's chanting but on the congregation's equally emotional responses. Such witnesses were appalled by the unbridled emotionalism of such services.

The African heritage of black preachers influenced the style of their performances and of the congregations' responses. The African folksong tradition of call-and-response was carried over; not only was the preacher directly in this tradition, but in holy services the congregants felt free to call out to the preacher, or to the other congregants, as the Spirit moved them. The service became, and is still, however, something more than the regulated, orchestrated, and patterned response of one individual or group to another; in black services each member of the congregation actually creates his or her own sacred communion simultaneously with the holy service that is proceeding. Members of the congregation call out spontaneously, and such exclamations may not have been anticipated by the minister.

During a service in which the preacher has been successful in arousing the Spirit of the Lord or in bringing his congregation to a high emotional level, individual cries are frequent, some of the congregation will enter an altered state during which they may lose consciousness or dance seemingly involuntarily, and the preacher will be visibly ecstatic as well. Many people laugh aloud; a few cry unashamedly. When the service is over, they will say that they have had a happy time.

Research on this phenomenon suggests that while much of the sermon cannot possibly be heard distinctly, something is being communicated, and the congregation will feel that it has received God's Word. This may happen because many of the congregation know the Bible almost as thoroughly as does the preacher, and they creatively anticipate his message; also, in these services the congregation participates actively and creatively in the service, and may for long periods be "hearing" their own celebrations.

Both preacher and flock share many common traditions, not only inherited Christianity but also an Afro-American interpretation of that faith flavored by the experience of living in the South. Few preachers have had extensive seminary training; and many of their beliefs, like those of their congregations, are derived from popular traditions. For instance, many preachers prefer to use popular, folk versions of stories and parables in Scripture. Hence, although their Christianity is in the main "official," it is heavily influenced by folkloric elements. In some urban areas these preachers are often known as "old-time country preachers," though many of them have migrated away from the rural South to the urban North. The Reverend C. L. Franklin, for instance, became most famous after he left the South and moved to Detroit.

The ministers do not use manuscripts but believe that when they are in front of congregations the Holy Ghost is using them to communicate His message to the people. This spontaneous preaching style is accurately and movingly reproduced by William Faulkner in the last portion of *The Sound and the Fury*. In those pages the Reverend Shegog from St. Louis delivers a moving sermon in a style indistinguishable from the authentic oral performance. Significantly, this sermon is placed near the novel's conclusion; Faulkner recognized the great emotive and spiritual power that is the potential of this medium and chose to end his book on an affirming note.

Some white preachers also still preach in this mode; the style is not the exclusive property of one ethnic group. But the practitioners are mostly black and usually Methodist or Baptist. The practice is characteristically southern, though many preachers have now moved to the cities of the North and to the Pacific Southwest. These preachers continue to evoke the South in their services. Many professional black singers have vocal qualities that carry heavy echoes of this preaching style. Examples are Aretha Franklin (daughter of the Reverend C. L. Franklin), Sarah Vaughn, and Lou Rawls. Much of the "Motown sound" owes a debt to southern country preaching.

The influence of black folk preachers on the nation extends well beyond the contributions of musical entertainment and the popular arts. The Reverend Martin Luther King, Jr., was a "spiritual" preacher whose "I Have a Dream" speech was in large measure a sermon on racial equality; he is well-known for this oral performance, which profoundly moved his listeners, regardless of their race or ethnic backgrounds. Today, this art is most prominently practiced by Chicago's Jesse Jackson, a southerner by birth and raising. His address to the Democratic National Convention (1984) was a spontaneous sermon, a moving oration delivered by electronic media to the nation and the world.

See also FOLKLIFE: Storytelling; RELIGION: Folk Religion

Bruce A. Rosenberg
Brown University

Richard Allen, in *Black American Literature: 1760–Present*, ed. Ruth Miller (1971); Paul C. Brownlow, *Quarterly Journal of Speech* (December 1972); Gerald L. Davis, *"I Got The Word in Me and I Can Sing It, You Know": A Study of the Performed Afro-American Sermon* (1986); Charles V. Hamilton, *The Black Preacher in America* (1972); Albert J. Raboteau, *Slave Religion: The "Invisible Institution" in the Antebellum South* (1978); Joseph R. Washington, Jr., *Black Religion; The Negro and Christianity in the United States* (1964). ☆

Press, Black

The first black newspaper, *Freedom's Journal*, appeared in New York City 51 years after the Declaration of Independence, 36 years before the Emancipation Proclamation. It was edited by John B. Russwurm and Samuel E. Cornish. In its first editorial, *Freedom's Journal* outlined an objective that is still symbolic of the black press: "We wish to plead our cause. Too long have others spoken for us." Although it had the format of a newspaper this black weekly resembled a magazine more than a newspaper. In the South, the first black newspaper was *L'union*, established in New Orleans, La., on 27 September 1862.

Until the end of the Civil War, black newspapers were published exclusively in northern communities where blacks were literate and had the freedom to publish. But after the emancipation, scores of new newspapers appeared throughout America, particularly in the ex-Confederate states where the majority of blacks lived. The black press had found a new constituency.

After the Civil War, black newspapers such as the Arkansas *Freedman* (1869), the *Colored Tennessean* (1865), the South Carolina *Leader* (1865), the Vicksburg *Colored Citizen* (1867), and the Texas *Freedman's Press* (1868) helped the newly freed slaves to bridge the gap between bondage and freedom by serving as instruments of promotion for suffrage, education, religion, and economic self-help. But overt racism and the increased social restriction of blacks in the South paralleled the return of Democratic rule and indirectly spawned the birth of the Gainesville *New Era* (1873), the Savannah *Tribune* (1875), the Missouri *Negro World* (1875), the Bennettsville (S.C.) *Pee Dee Educator* (1879), and the Galveston *Spectator* (1873). On the other hand, a few of the black papers were not politically active. For example, the North Carolina *Journal of Industry* (1879) in its premiere editorial, "Our Position," promised to "stay clear of politics" and addressed itself to the white people of the South because it viewed the "welfare" of whites and blacks as being inextricably interwoven. Other black newspapers devoted themselves to the "intellectual, moral, and financial interest of colored people."

The themes of land, education, suffrage, race relations, violence and economic self-help characterized the black press after Reconstruction and until the early 1900s. The Baptist *Vanguard* (1882), Gainesville, Fla., *Sentinel* (1887) Jacksonville *Peoples Journal* (1883), Raleigh *Gazette*, North Carolina *Republican and Civil Rights Advocate* (1884), *Star of Zion* (1876), Charleston *Messenger* (1890s), Richmond *Planet*, Petersburg *Lancet* (1882), the Dallas *Express* (1892), and others circulated widely throughout their respective regions and mirrored these themes during this period. They recorded the bitterness, indignation, and disillusionment of the newly freed blacks with the democratic system. At the same time, "they fought to elevate humanity" and to allay the fears of whites. Jesse Duke's Montgomery *Herald* (1886), Mansfield E. Bryant's Selma *Southern Independent* (1886), L. H. Harrison's Birmingham *Wide-Awake* (1888), and R. C. 0. Benjamin's Birmingham *Negro American* (1886) exemplified black protest journalism in the Deep South, whereas John Mitchell's Richmond *Planet* reflected advocacy journalism in the Upper South.

Almost 100 black papers appeared in the 1890s in Alabama alone, followed by more than 70 from 1900 to 1910. But most of them were short-lived weeklies that were prevailingly Republican, financially insecure, and located in urban areas with large black populations. Men, especially ministers, dominated black journalism during the 19th century. A few black women, such as Maggie Lena Walker, Charlotte Hawkins Brown, and Josephine T. Washington, became prominent editors and journalists during this period.

Perhaps the Petersburg *Lancet* and the North Carolina *Republican and Civil Rights Advocate* (1884) best mirrored the advertising, layout, design, and subscription policies of the black press in the post-Reconstruction South. The *Advocate's* motto, "I Take No Step Backward" was carried under the masthead. Subscriptions were 50 cents for 3 months, 90 cents for 6 months, and $1.50 for 12 months. Advertisers included grocers, drug stores, barber shops, hairdressers, butchers, hardware and five-and-dime stores, Sunday school book suppliers, and cigarette and insurance companies. And like the Petersburg *Lancet*, columns were devoted to poems and short stories that dramatized the complexities of marriage and family and the glory of the Old West. The social page was dominated by "brilliant marriages," "large funerals," and "sermons." The black press gave its readers an organic sense of community life.

During the age of Booker T. Washington (1895–1915), the Kansas City *Call*, the Raleigh *Gazette*, the Savannah *Tribune*, the Charleston *Messenger*, the Norfolk *Journal and Guide* (1910), among others, effectively carried Washington's philosophy of economic self-help and racial accommodation, as did the *Colored American* magazine and the New York *Age*, two journals controlled directly by Washington.

On the other hand, however, the Nashville *Globe* (1905) was financially independent and openly contemptuous of Washington's philosophy. The *Globe*, the Richmond *Planet*, and later the Norfolk *Journal and Guide* and the Kansas City *Call* observed that Washington's philosophy was inconsistent with the economic and political realities of life in 20th-century America. The black press was also sensitive to the increased support of the National Association for the Advancement of Colored People (NAACP) among the South's rising black middle class. Black journalist P. B. Young founded the NAACP chapter in Norfolk, Va., in 1917 as an act of "self-preservation."

The event that forced black newspapers to abandon both Washington's philosophy and the Republican party was World War I. The black press supported the war effort, but expressed concern about the disparity between the quest for democracy abroad and the inequities at home. Black editors had hoped that loyalty and patriotism among blacks at home would result in increased political patronage and fair treatment. Instead, the Negrophobes and white supremacists in the South continued racial tyranny through lynching, disfranchisement, and racial segregation.

Although the Great Depression decimated most of the black press, the *Journal and Guide*, the St. Louis *Argus*, the Kansas City *Call*, the Carolina *Times*, the Atlanta *Daily World* (1928), and the Birmingham *World* not only survived but expanded throughout their respective regions. The *Journal and Guide* and the *Call* published national editions as well. Ironically, Mississippi, one of the first states to inaugurate the segregation movement during the 1890s, spawned more black newspapers between 1920 and 1940 than at any other comparable time in its history. Examples include the *Delta Leader* (1929), the *Southern Advocate* (1933), the Mississippi *Enterprise* (1939) and the Jackson *Advocate* (1938). Several publishers, according to historian Julius Thompson, "risked everything and cried out for civil rights," while others sent false signals to the masses and "failed to tell the truth as they saw it."

Collectively, the black press was politically ineffective before World War II. Although the black press complained about the inherent discrimination in many New Deal programs and the discriminatory hiring practices on military bases, A. Philip Randolph's threatened March on Washington in July of 1941 finally prompted President Franklin Roosevelt to issue Executive Order 8802, which banned discrimination in federal employment. The black papers were divided on the infamous Scottsboro case of the 1930s in which nine blacks were charged with the rape of two white females. Although black publisher P. B. Young (*Journal and Guide*), the titular head of the black press, spearheaded a defense fund drive and sought to arouse public sentiment in the South with weekly editorials such as "Darrow, The Communist and Scottsboro," "What Scottsboro Means to America," "Scottsboro vs. Dred Scott," and "The Verdict at Decatur," the Communist International Labor Defense (ILD) actually defended the accused. Locally, however, the *Journal and Guide* was more successful. Young's writings and political acumen saved the life of William Harper, a black man who had been sentenced to death for the crime of rape, and his serialized account of dilapidated schools in several Tidewater Virginia counties led to a state investigation and new schools for blacks.

The themes of equalization, crime, health care, better housing, migration, desegregation of the military, and suffrage predominated in the black press during World War II. The black press supported America's entry into the war and urged blacks to "close ranks," end debate, and suspend bickering. Perhaps the *Journal and Guide* best epitomized the black press when it declared, "We are Americans—we're at war." The *Guide* also reflected the sentiment of the black press when it rejected black activist A. Philip Randolph's proposed March on Washington, noting in a headline, "What Will They Think In Berlin?"

Black newspapers are an invaluable reference if used properly. They sometimes provide the only evidence that a particular incident (especially protest) even occurred. They recorded the births of the most lowly blacks and offered consoling words upon death. How else could families announce the graduation of their children from high school or impending social events? How else could black colleges disseminate information about tuition, schedule of courses, and athletic events? The black press publicized information about communicable diseases and the weather, and it explained controversial racial incidents to the community. Between 1865 and 1945, the black press was a mirror, crusader, advocate, and recorder of black life and culture in the South.

See also MEDIA: Newspapers; / Young, P. B.

Henry Lewis Suggs
Clemson University

Penelope L. Bullock, *The Afro-American Periodical Press, 1838–1909* (1981); Walter C. Daniel, *Black Journals of the United States* (1982); Frederick G. Detweiler, *The Negro*

Press in the United States (1922); Vishnu V. Oak, *The Negro Newspaper* (1948); I. Garland Penn, *The Afro-American Press and Its Editors* (1891); Henry Lewis Suggs, *The Black Press in the South, 1865–1979* (1984); Roland E. Wolseley, *The Black Press, U.S.A.* (1971). ☆

Race Relations

Throughout southern history, from the mid–17th century down to crucial changes in the 1970s, the region's ruling class dedicated itself to one overriding principle—white supremacy. Its large-scale employment of black labor must not be permitted to threaten the South's character as a white man's country. White racism was thus the driving force, the great first cause of southern race relations. Yet the pattern of those relations was complex, changing considerably over the centuries. Although the virulence of racism also grew more or less intense, on the whole it seems most realistic to treat it as a constant. The culture of racism was sufficient to sanction and support the whole range of discrimination that has characterized white supremacy in its successive stages. It follows that those stages themselves cannot be attributed to racism alone. Secondary causes—economic, political, intellectual—must also be considered. So must the fact that southern race relations did not exist in a vacuum. Especially after 1865, the southern ruling class had to operate within broad and changing limits of what the rest of the country would permit.

Under slavery the dominant pattern of white supremacy had been vertical, resting on the use of influence and force. The cruelty of the slave system had been direct, and so had been its sometimes genuinely affectionate paternalism. Black people necessarily developed their personalities, their family relations, their religion, and to an impressive extent their cultural autonomy by exploiting contradictions and opportunities within a complex fabric of dependency. These concessions enabled a profitable and rational economic system to function. There were exceptions to the rule of direct dominance of white over black, notably the free black populations of Charleston, New Orleans, and other southern communities. Moreover, the majority of southern whites had not owned slaves at all, and even fewer whites qualified as plantation owners. Still, the antebellum South's dominant mode of production, the economic foundation that supported its unchallenged planter ruling class, was slavery.

In rural areas, in the sharecropping system that came to replace slavery as the dominant mode of agrarian production after 1865, the dominant means of white control was the crop lien, in which a furnishing merchant (who was often a planter) provided land, seeds, fertilizer, tools, a mule, and credit for purchases of food and clothing in return for a portion (usually half) of the harvested crop. White farmers also engaged in sharecropping, including the crop lien, and a huge literature has examined the extent to which this transitional agrarian system was inherently discriminatory. The verdict seems to be that it was not—indeed, in the circumstances it is hard to conceive of an alternative—but that it provided planters and furnishing merchants who wished to discriminate with abundant opportunities to do so.

In cities, to which blacks as well as whites came in growing numbers, the problem of maintaining a workable system of white supremacy was far more complicated. City blacks were apt to be better educated and less directly dependent on whites. They included merchants, lawyers, teachers, journalists, craftsmen, and funeral directors—what came to be called the black bourgeoisie. Black quarters, where white faces were seldom seen, sometimes stretched for miles. In cities there were more opportunities for contact outside the complex etiquette that governed interracial associations on the plantation. Direct dominance of white over black no longer worked. In urban areas race relations were more impersonal, less paternal, and more competitive.

The 20th-century form of white supremacy was segregation. Although the antebellum and Reconstruction South had certainly known many of its aspects in practice, the usage of the word itself was new. According to the *Oxford English Dictionary*, the relevant "S" volume of which was compiled between 1910 and 1914, *segregation* was not part of the 19th-century vocabulary of race relations. The use of *segregation* as a key word in southern race relations is an indication that white supremacy was moving from one stage to another.

The 1890s were the crucial years when the South moved into this final stage of white supremacy. White southerners in that decade constructed a system and an ideology of race relations that were essentially new.

Why did white southerners create this system and ideology? And why at this time? Many reasons have been proposed, all of which probably have some validity and no combination of which seems quite sufficient. First, the 1890s were a period of political turmoil, centering on the Populist revolt. Everywhere Populists challenged the hegemony of the Democratic party establishment. In several states they worked with Republicans to drive Democrats from power. Equating the maintenance of white supremacy with the survival of their own party, Democrats took the vote away from blacks—and from many poor whites as well. Second, the drive toward segregation centered on cities and industry, which are associated with forces ordinarily considered to be progressive. Without legal segregation, industrialization and urbanization would probably have enabled blacks to threaten white supremacy. Third, this was a period of strong black assertiveness—strikes, boycotts, increased voting—so that to some extent whites were reacting to what they feared or imagined. On the whole the most satisfactory explanation is that the American nation, including the South, was undergoing rapid and massive change. Segregation was a means of placing the race question on hold while substantial parts of the South industrialized and while the nation as a whole modernized, expanded to what it considered its natural limits, and became one of the world's great imperial powers. Not for the first time, nor for the last, black people paid a heavy price for national reconciliation and progress.

Segregation covered the whole range of southern experience. In politics, beginning with the Mississippi plan in 1890, state after state invented or copied various ways—poll taxes, white party primaries, the understanding requirement (in which a prospective voter had to interpret a passage of the U.S. Constitution to the satisfaction of a registrar), as well as the more traditional means of fraud and terror—to exclude all but a tiny minority of black men, and after 1920 of black women, from the franchise. To some degree this was a new departure. Not only during Reconstruction, when federal troops enforced the Fifteenth Amendment, but for more than a decade after the Compromise of 1877, when the North acquiesced in home rule under local conservatives—an event quaintly referred to in southern history books as "Redemption"—blacks had voted in large numbers. Sometimes they had gained political office. More often white politicians and parties had competed for their votes.

In economics, segregation focused not on rural black belt or coastal areas, where the pattern of direct dominance through the crop-lien system largely continued, but on the industrializing Piedmont: the band that stretches from Danville, Va., through Greensboro and Charlotte, N.C., to Greenville, S.C., and Atlanta, Ga., and on to Birmingham, Ala. Black slaves had often worked in the few factories the South possessed before the Civil War. Now they were excluded entirely, as in cotton manufacturing, or restricted to dirty, low-paying jobs that were classified as unskilled, as in tobacco, coal mining, or iron and steel. Throughout the South, which in effect included the nation's capital during the Wilson Administration, blacks in services, retail, or civil administration were not found "above a certain level." The only significant exceptions were in business or industries owned by blacks in the segregated sector—insurance companies, banks, or small manufacturing establishments.

In education, from kindergarten through postgraduate levels, the South provided separate educational streams. According to the classic separate-but-equal argument, which justified segregation and which the Supreme Court accepted in a series of decisions including the landmark *Plessy* v. *Ferguson* (1896), schools were supposed to be equal. In terms of money spent per pupil (the ratio in favor of whites often being 10 to 1 or even higher), available programs, qualifications of teachers, quality of buildings—and not surprisingly, results—the systems were rarely comparable, let alone equivalent.

Segregation, which was called Jim Crow and was the American equivalent of South African apartheid, covered all areas of life, love, work, leisure, and even death. Whenever black people left "their own" areas, they were confronted at every turn by demeaning and often debilitating restrictions. Housing was segregated not only by custom, as it largely remains, but by law. The few blacks whose parents could afford it were born in black hospitals (whose administrators and better-paid doctors and

Street scene, Birmingham, 1940s

even nurses were apt to be white). They went to black schools. When they rode public transportation, they sat in the black section in the rear. If they wanted to drink, eat, or go to the toilet, they might be lucky enough to find facilities reserved for them; otherwise they had to do without. Parks, beaches, golf courses, tennis courts, and swimming pools excluded them; again comparatively rarely they might find separate but undoubtedly inferior facilities. If they ran afoul of the law, they were sworn on separate-but-equal Bibles and, if convicted by usually all-white juries, were sentenced by white judges to segregated jails. When they died, they were embalmed in black funeral parlors (one of the most promising businesses for the black bourgeoisie) and buried in black cemeteries.

The central theme running through much of the discrimination in jobs was the classic southern taboo concerning the mixture of race and sex. White females and black males were simply not supposed to meet, study, or work together except under the most rigid of protocol, lest sexual contact be the result. It has often been remarked that the concern of southern white people about miscegenation increased in inverse proportion to its actual incidence. It was very frequent during slavery, when owners had power over black women; it decreased markedly after 1865, when black men were at last able to protect black women. Perhaps James Baldwin's sarcastic comment to a southern white man reflects this history: "I've been marrying your daughter for centuries."

This vast, complex system of segregation, which covered every aspect of southern life, was built and enforced by white power. Sometimes that power was exercised more or less evenhandedly, according to something approaching a rule of law, albeit a law that was itself discriminatory. Sometimes it was arbitrary and, though rarely punished, exercised outside lawful channels. And it was at times exceedingly violent. Major race riots occurred in Atlanta, New Orleans, Memphis, Wilmington, and many other places. Most of these took place in cities but by no means all, the Phoenix Riot in South Carolina being an important rural example. The ebb and flow of violence followed a curve of real or imagined black "uppitiness": the 1890s when segregation was being established; the years just after World Wars I and II, when black soldiers came home; and the civil rights campaign of the 1960s being the peaks of racial violence. But the valleys were very deep. Hundreds of blacks were lynched, often by mobs transported to the scene by advertised special trains; frequently a town's most "respectable" citizens were unofficially known to have participated. Blacks in the thousands were beaten. At one time or another, all blacks were terrorized.

The rhetoric of racist literature was even more violent than the fact. There seems no useful point in repeating the "black beast" language of the novelist Thomas Dixon or of such prominent politicians as Ben Tillman and Cole Blease of South Carolina, or James Vardaman of Mississippi. As the moderate minister Edgar Gardner Murphy complained, the racial fanatics progressed "from the contention that no negro shall vote, to the contention that no negro shall learn, that no negro shall labor, and (by implication) that no negro shall live." The threat of extermination was by no means always left to implication. Indeed, it is hard to imagine any measure white people might have taken with respect to blacks that would not have been supported and sanctioned by the racist culture that prevailed from 1890 to 1915 and perhaps beyond.

Indeed, if one takes that literature seriously—and the example of Adolf Hitler and the Jewish Holocaust suggests that what fanatics in the 20th century say does indeed have to be taken literally—then segregation was not the worst of all possible "solutions" that white people might have devised. The late 19th century, after all, was the period when the United States brought to a logical and terrible conclusion its campaign of extermination and removal of the American Indians. Black leader Booker T. Washington used that example often in his speeches, as an example of what might happen to people who could not come to terms with the white man's economic and political system.

Segregation was not at first proposed by racial fanatics, but by moderates and liberals. It was not southern racists who developed black colleges, but northern philanthropists; without the latter there would have been none at all. In time segregation would come to be identified with the extreme right of the racial spectrum. In the 1890s, however, segregation was a moderate compromise. So long as there was no social mixing, then blacks could pursue their separate identity at their own pace and in their own way. "Separate but equal" was largely a fiction; but if there had been *nothing* in it, then ordinary people of good conscience, especially in the North, would never have accepted it. And they did.

The violence of the white power that lay behind segregation, as well as the threat of racist literature of the period, explains much about how the system worked. To some extent segregation was self-enforcing. Substantial sections of the black community, notably the much and unfairly maligned black bourgeoisie, had a stake in the system and even benefited from having a protected market in which to operate. They had more to lose from the breakdown of law and order, even when that law was discriminatory. Like any other people faced with power they correctly perceived to be irresistible, blacks created mechanisms through which they collaborated. They also resisted. Sometimes they fought violence with violence. Time and again they employed the methods of peaceful protest—boycotts, strikes, sit-ins, demonstrations—that would ultimately succeed in the 1960s.

Scholars have identified three broad approaches by which black people tried to contend with segregation. The first, associated with Booker T. Washington of Tuskegee Institute in Alabama, was accommodation and economic self-sufficiency. The second, identified with W. E. B. Du Bois of Atlanta University and the National Association for the Advancement of Colored People, was militant and organized resistance, especially in the courts. The third, led by Bishop Henry McNeal Turner of the African Methodist Episcopal church and later by the West Indian Marcus Garvey, was black nationalism and the so-called back-to-Africa movement. All of these approaches combined elements of collaboration and resistance. Even Du Bois accepted that blacks must live with some aspects of segregation, at least for the time being. Despite their often heated controversy, significant interchange took place between these leaders and movements. Their ultimate goal was the same—black power.

Why did the mid-20th-century civil rights movement succeed when others had failed? Partly because blacks of all ages—Rosa Parks, whose refusal to leave her seat in a white section of a bus sparked the Montgomery boycott; the recent graduates of Atlanta and other universities, inspired by such educators as Benjamin Mays, who led the Southern Christian Leadership Conference under Martin Luther King, Jr; the students who sat in at lunch counters in Greensboro and organized voter registration drives in Mississippi—were more numerous and better organized than ever before. As abolitionist Frederick Douglass had said, power concedes nothing without a struggle. Also, discrimination in the South proved increasingly embarrassing to American foreign policy after World War II. Gunnar Myrdal's *An American Dilemma* (1944) argued that Americans could not indefinitely postpone acting to correct such a blatant contradition of the democratic dream. The pivotal Supreme Court decision *Brown* v. *Board of Education* (1954) represented a national judgment on the South's racial system.

But the white South had not been converted. Virtually everywhere it resisted, sometimes violently and massively, sometimes more subtly (and probably more successfully). The civil rights campaign gathered strength and speed, and it would not be denied. Eventually, in place after place, white corporate and political leaders made the decision that though economic, political, and educational discrimination was far from ended, the career of white supremacy as a legal system was over. The South was no longer dedicated to being a white man's domain.

See also EDUCATION: Athletics and Education; Desegregation; / Busing; Christian Academies; HISTORY AND MANNERS: Manners; Sexuality; INDUSTRY: Civil Rights and Business; LAW: Civil Rights Movement; / Black Codes; Slave Codes; MYTHIC SOUTH: Racial Attitudes; RELIGION: Civil Rights and Religion; SCIENCE AND MEDICINE: Racism, Scientific; VIOLENCE: Race Riots; / Mob Violence

John W. Cell
Duke University

John W. Cell, *The Highest Stage of White Supremacy: The Origins of Segregation in South Africa and the American South* (1982); Carl N. Degler, *Neither Black nor White: Slavery and Race Relations in Brazil and the United States* (1971); George Fredrickson, *White Supremacy: A Comparative Study in American and South African History* (1981); Marvin Harris, *Pattern of Race in the Americas* (1964); Winthrop D. Jordan, *White over Black: American Attitudes toward the Negro, 1550–1812* (1968); Edmund S. Morgan, *American Slavery, American Freedom: The Ordeal of Colonial Virginia* (1975); Willis D. Weatherford and Charles S. Johnson, *Race Relations: Adjustment of Whites and Negroes in the United States* (1934); Joel Williamson, *The Crucible of Race: Black-White Relations in the American South since Emancipation* (1985), ed. *The Origins of Segregation* (1968); C. Vann Woodward, *The Strange Career of Jim Crow* (1955; 3d ed. 1974). ☆

Religion, Black

The religious life of the majority of black southerners originated in both traditional African religions and in Anglo-Protestant evangelicalism. The influence of Africa was more muted in the United States than in Latin America, where African-derived theology and ritual were institutionalized in the communities of Brazilian candomblé, Haitian voodoo, and Cuban santeria. Nevertheless, in the United States, as in Latin America, slaves did transmit to their descendants styles of worship, funeral customs, magical ritual, and medicinal practice based upon the religious systems of West and Central African societies.

Although some slaves in Maryland and Louisiana were baptized as Catholics, most had no contact with Catholicism and were first converted to Christianity in large numbers under the preaching of Baptist and Methodist revivalists in the late 18th century. The attractiveness of the evangelical revivals for slaves was due to several factors: the emotional behavior of revivalists encouraged the type of religious ecstasy similar to the danced religions of Africa; the antislavery stance taken by some Baptists and Methodists encouraged slaves to identify evangelicalism with emancipation; blacks actively participated in evangelical meetings and cofounded churches with white evangelicals; evangelical churches licensed black men to preach.

By the 1780s pioneer black preachers had already begun to minister to their own people in the South, and as time went on black congregations, mainly Baptist in denomination, increased in size and in number, despite occasional harassment and proscription by the authorities. However, the majority of slaves in the antebellum South attended church, if at all, with whites.

Institutional church life did not exhaust the religion of the slaves. An "invisible institution" of secret and often forbidden religious meetings thrived in the slave quarters. Here slaves countered the slaveholding gospel of the master class with their own version of Christianity in which slavery and slaveholding stood condemned by God. Slaves took the biblical story of Exodus and applied it to their own history, asserting that they, like the children of Israel, would be liberated from bondage. In the experience of conversion individual slaves affirmed their personal dignity and self-worth. In the ministry, black men exercised authority and achieved status nowhere else available to them. Melding African and Western European traditions, the slaves created a religion of great vitality.

Complementing Christianity in the quarters was conjure, a sophisticated combination of African herbal medicine and magic. Based on the belief that illness and misfortune have personal as well as impersonal causes, conjure offered frequently successful therapy for the mental and physical ills of generations of Afro-Americans and simultaneously served as a system for venting social tension and resolving conflict.

The Civil War, Emancipation, and Reconstruction wrought an institutional transformation of black churches in the South. Northern denominations—black as well as white—sent aid to the freedmen and missionaries to educate and bring them to church. Freedmen, eager to learn to read and write, flocked to schools set up by the American Missionary Association and other freedmen's aid societies. These freedmen's schools laid the foundation for major black colleges and universities such as Fisk, Morehouse, Dillard, and others. Eager to exercise autonomy, freedmen swarmed out of white churches and organized their own. Some affiliated with black denominations of northern origin, others formed their own southern associations.

Black ministers actively campaigned

in Reconstruction politics and in some cases were elected to positions of influence and power. Richard H. Cain, for example, was elected to the U.S. House of Representatives from North Carolina and Hiram R. Revels to the Senate from Mississippi. With the failure of Reconstruction and the disfranchisement of black southerners, the church once again became the sole forum for black politics, as well as the economic, social, and educational center of black communities across the South.

By the end of the century, black church membership stood at an astounding 2.7 million out of a population of 8.3 million. Most numerous were the Baptists who succeeded in 1895 in creating a National Baptist Convention, followed numerically by the black Methodists, as institutionalized in the African Methodist Episcopal church and the African Methodist Episcopal Zion church, both founded in the North early in the century, and the Colored Methodist Episcopal church, formed by an amicable withdrawal from the Southern Methodist Episcopal church, in 1870.

Though too poor to mount a full-fledged missionary campaign, the black churches turned to evangelization of Africa as a challenge to Afro-American Christian identity. The first black missionaries, David George and George Liele, had sailed during the Revolution, George to Nova Scotia and then to Sierra Leone, Liele to Jamaica. Daniel Coker followed in 1820 and Lott Carey and Colin Teague in 1821. But in the 1870s and 1880s the mission to Africa seemed all the more urgent. As race relations worsened, as lynching mounted in frequency, as racism was legislated in Jim Crow statutes, emigration appeared to black clergy like Henry McNeal Turner the only solution. Others saw the redemption of Africa as the divinely appointed destiny of black Americans, God's plan for drawing good out of the evil of slavery and oppression.

Connections between southern black churches and northern ones developed as blacks from the South migrated or escaped north, and as northern missionaries came to the South after the Civil War. Several southern blacks assumed positions of leadership in northern churches. Josiah Bishop, a Baptist preacher from Virginia, became pastor of the Abyssinian Baptist Church in New York, and Daniel Alexander Payne and Morris Brown, both of Charleston, became bishops of the A.M.E. church. Beginning in the 1890s and increasing after the turn of the century, rural southern blacks migrated in larger and larger numbers to the cities of the North. Frequently their ministers traveled with them and transplanted, often in storefront or house churches, congregations from the South.

In the cities, southern as well as northern, black migrants encountered new religious options that attracted some adherents from the traditional churches. Catholicism, through the influence of parochial schools, began attracting significant numbers of blacks in the 20th century. Black Muslims and Jews developed new religio-racial identities for Afro-Americans disillusioned with Christianity. The Holiness and Pentecostal churches stressed the experiential and ecstatic dimensions of worship while preaching the necessity of sanctification and the blessings of the Spirit. They also facilitated the development of gospel music by allowing the use of instruments and secular tunes in church services.

Though urbanization and secularization led to criticism of black religion as accommodationist and compensatory, the church remained the most important and effective public institution in southern black life. The religious culture of the black folk was celebrated by intellectuals like W. E. B. Du Bois and James Weldon Johnson, who acclaimed the artistry of the slave spirituals and black preaching.

In the late 1950s and 1960s the civil rights movement drew heavily upon the institutional and ethical resources of the black churches across the South. Martin Luther King, Jr., brought to the attention of the nation and the world the moral tradition of black religion. Today, black religion is more pluralistic than ever. Although the church is no longer the only institution that blacks control, it still exerts considerable power in black communities.

See also ETHNIC LIFE: Caribbean Influence; FOLKLIFE: Folk Medicine; Voodoo; RELIGION articles

Albert J. Raboteau
Princeton University

Hans A. Baer, *The Black Spiritual Movement: A Religious Response to Racism* (1984); James Cone, *For My People: Black Theology and the Black Church* (1984); W. E. B. Du Bois, *The Souls of Black Folk* (1903); Samuel S. Hill, ed., *Religion in the Southern States: A Historical Study* (1983); C. Eric Lincoln, ed., *The Black Experience in Religion* (1974); Donald G. Mathews, *Religion in the Old South* (1977); Albert J. Raboteau, *Slave Religion: The "Invisible Institution" in the Antebellum South* (1978); Clarence Walker, *A Rock in a Weary Land: The African Methodist Episcopal Church during the Civil War and Reconstruction* (1982); James M. Washington, *Frustrated Fellowship: The Black Baptist Quest for Social Power* (1986); Joseph R. Washington, Jr., *Black Religion: The Negro and Christianity in the United States* (1964). ☆

Slave Culture

Torn from their native land and cast into the caldron of New World slavery, 10 million Africans were brought to the Americas during the four centuries of the Atlantic slave trade. The vast majority of those who survived the squalor and degradation of the "middle passage" and the early years of captivity—what Europeans called "the seasoning process"—suffered physical pain, psychological despair, and mental anguish. Many clung to their traditional languages, values, beliefs, and religions, but everywhere in the New World blacks found that in order to survive they would have to adjust to a new and alien environment.

In the southern colonies (later, states) the cultural transformation among slaves was relatively rapid. A majority of those who arrived in the colonies during the 17th century came from the West Indies and had already spent several years or more in the New World. During the 18th century those who came directly from Africa—called "outlandish" by the colonists—were either separated from the more "assimilated" slaves until they had accommodated themselves to the work routine or, as was the case in Virginia, sold to small slaveholders who worked alongside their bondsmen. Even as the proportion of Africans rose and the number of blacks spiraled upward—from 28,000 in 1700 (11 percent of the total colonial population) to 91,000 in

1730 (14 percent)—slaveowners established procedures to reward those who learned English, acquired new skills, and embraced Christianity. Those who most readily accepted new values, called "New Negroes," and those born on American soil, called creoles, could expect preferential treatment, special privileges, and more prestigious jobs. With the closing of the Atlantic slave trade to the United States in 1808, only a tiny fraction of the total slave population could claim any direct connection with West Africa.

Despite these demographic changes, many aspects of slave culture reflected the influence of Africa. In their family relationships slaves developed broad kinship patterns reminiscent of the familial patterns among various ethnic groups in their ancestral homeland. Even when families were broken by sale, blacks quickly reestablished kin networks whenever possible. Although most children lived with two parents and most adults lived in long-lasting marriages, slaves developed their own, unique family mores. They rarely, if ever, married first cousins; they engaged in sex prior to "marriage," usually with a future partner; they frequently gave their children names of blood kin outside the immediate family; and they had a much broader concept of "family" than most white southerners. "It was months before I learned their family relations," a teacher in South Carolina among the Sea Island slaves observed. "The terms 'bubber' for brother and 'titty' for sister, with 'nanna' for mother and 'mother' for grandmother, and 'father' for all the leaders in church and society, were so generally used I was forced to believe that they all belonged to one immense family."

If most slaveowners showed little interest in slave families, other than encouraging childbearing, they similarly allowed blacks to practice their own brand of Christianity. One of the most distinctive cultural transformations among blacks was their adaptation of various African beliefs and rites to American Protestantism. Slaves dwelt on the Old Testament, not only because they identified with the children, but, as Nathan Huggins points out, "because those books conformed more to their own instincts for tribal and clan deities." In their use of the New Testament they focused on the story of Jesus, the parables, and the Crucifixion. Moreover, slaves ignored the doctrinal disputes between various Protestant sects, believed evil was a force of the universe rather than man's natural condition, and accepted Christianity as fundamentally collective and social rather than individualistic. Revealing their ancestral heritage, slave preachers filled their messages with cosmic imagery and played on the feelings and emotions of the congregation; and, unlike whites (except in a few evangelical sects), slaves actively participated in each religious service, shouting ecstatic prayers, singing deeply felt spirituals, clapping their hands, and fervently entreating, "Come Jesus, Come Lord. Be among us now."

Language, music, and folktales were also important in slave culture. These were, as Lawrence W. Levine indicates, "instruments of life, of sanity, of health, and of self-respect." In communicating with one another slaves sometimes retained elements of speech acquired in West Africa. Along the Sea Island Coast of South Carolina and Georgia blacks spoke Gullah (sometimes known as Geechee), a black dialect that blended various African words, names, and sounds with English. African equivalents were substituted for "tooth," "pregnancy," "alcohol," "sweet potato"; other nouns as well as adverbs, verbs, and adjectives were frequently changed by using groups of words in the African style: *day clean* meant "dawn"; *to sweet mouth* meant to flatter. Blacks also used various forms of ironic or sardonic humor when discussing whites. At the same time a number of slave words crept into the English language—"tote," "banjo," "cooter," "chigger," "yam," "okra," and "juke."

Slave music was an especially distinctive cultural form. Blacks did not draw a clear line between secular and sacred music and, like many of their ancestors in West Africa, sang a great variety of work songs and spirituals. Their lyrics, intonations, and singing style were marked by poetic beauty, emotional intensity, and rich imagery:

Breddren, don' git weary,
Breddren, don' git weary,
Breddren, don' git weary,
Fo d work is most done.

De ship is in de harbor, harbor, harbor,
De ship is in de harbor,
To wait upon de Lord. . . .

'E got 'e ca'go raidy, raidy, raidy,
'E got 'e ca'go raidy,
Fo' to wait upon de Lord.

Passed down from parents to children or from conjurers to other slaves, folktales and folk beliefs were important vehicles for transmitting social values and attitudes. Some stories came directly from Africa; others evolved out of circumstances in the New World; still others were a blending of the two. Almost all the tales involved a lesson of one type or another, lessons about mercy, prestige, patience, greed, wealth, strength, success, honor, and sexual prowess. In most instances slaves used an animal trickster to convey a portrait or to teach a lesson. In the famous Brer Rabbit and the Wolf tale, Rabbit discovers a tar baby at the side of the road (placed there by Wolf). When Rabbit's curiosity gets the better of him, he strikes the tar baby and becomes enmeshed in the tar. Wolf comes to claim his prize. Realizing that Wolf will do exactly what he thinks Rabbit desires least, Rabbit begs not to be thrown into the briar patch, which is, of course, exactly what Wolf does, and wily Rabbit gains his freedom. Such tales were greatly enhanced by the manner of their delivery and the response of the audience. During the telling of a tale slaves chanted, mimicked, acted, and sang. "I don't know how they do it," one observer wrote, "but they will say 'lipity clipity, lipity clipity,' so you can almost hear a rabbit coming through the woods."

Although a distinct slave culture developed in America, relying on extended kinship networks, a different form of Christianity, and a rich folk heritage, many slaves rejected aspects of this culture. Overt resistance to slavery came primarily in two forms—individual acts of violence and running away. A close study of black rebelliousness in Virginia points to how African-born slaves typically ran away in groups and attempted to establish villages on the frontier whereas American-born slaves, who tried to escape in far greater numbers, ran away alone and tried to pass as free persons in the most settled areas of the state. The small number of large-scale revolts—compared to the hundreds of major revolutions in the

Caribbean and South America—reveals the breakdown of West African communalism. Slaves who sought to improve their situation on the plantation and slaves who lived in towns and cities often sought to cast off the manners and attitudes of field hands. They dressed differently, learned to speak and act comfortably around whites, and whenever possible saved money and acquired personal possessions. In addition, as the doors to legal emancipation slowly closed during the antebellum decades, an increasing number of slaves, by one means or another, moved into what contemporaries called "quasifreedom"—halfway between bondage and liberty. While legally enslaved, these blacks lived independent, sometimes completely autonomous lives, securing their own employment, maintaining their own families, and moving about from place to place. At the same time slaves who lived on small plantations or farms, along the frontier, or on plantations owned by French Creoles in Louisiana developed cultural mores and attitudes peculiar to their unique circumstances. In St. Landry Parish, for example, many slaves spoke French. The Civil War and general emancipation did not destroy slave culture, but more and more blacks saw the folkways of the past as a legacy of bondage and sought different values as a symbol of the future and freedom.

See also FOLKLIFE: Aesthetics, Afro-American; / Brer Rabbit; HISTORY AND MANNERS: Colonial Heritage; LANGUAGE: Gullah; LAW: / Slave Codes; MUSIC: Spirituals

Loren Schweninger
University of North Carolina
at Greensboro

John Blassingame, *The Slave Community: Plantation Life in the Antebellum South* (1972); Eugene D. Genovese, *Roll, Jordan, Roll: The World the Slaves Made* (1974); Herbert G. Gutman, *The Black Family in Slavery and Freedom, 1750–1925* (1976); Charles Joyner, *Down By the Riverside: A South Carolina Slave Community* (1984); Lawrence W. Levine, *Black Culture and Black Consciousness: Afro-American Folk Thought from Slavery to Freedom* (1977); Gerald W. Mullin, *Flight and Rebellion: Slave Resistance in Eighteenth-Century Virginia* (1972); Leslie Owens, *This Species of Property: Slave Life and Culture in the Old South* (1976); Albert J. Raboteau, *Slave Religion: The "Invisible Institution" in the Antebellum South* (1978); George Rawick, *From Sundown to Sunup: The Making of the Black Community* (1972); Sterling Stuckey, *Massachusetts Review* (Summer 1968); Thomas Webber, *Deep Like the Rivers: Education in the Slave Quarter Community, 1831–1865* (1978); Peter Wood, *Black Majority: Negroes in Colonial South Carolina from 1670 through the Stono Rebellion* (1974). ☆

Speech, Black

B*lack English* is the term most often used to describe the dialect of lower-class blacks. Although many blacks use varieties of English identical to those used by whites, some linguists suggest that the speech of lower-class blacks is different structurally from any white variety. The relationship of black speech to white speech and the origins of black English are still matters of controversy, but the linguistic features of the dialect are well established. These include such features as invariant *be* (as in *we be working*) for long-term or continuous actions, absence of the *be* verb (as in *they sick*) to convey short-term actions, absence of the suffix *-s* on third-person singular present tense verbs (as in *he run*) and of the suffix *-ed* on past tense verbs (as in *he walk to school yesterday*), among others, and a higher frequency of some processes such as deletion of final consonants (as when *test* is pronounced *tes'*).

Despite the agreement about these features, black English is easily the most controversial topic in the study of southern speech, because attitudes toward it are often bound up with the political and social aspirations of laymen and the scholarly predispositions of linguists. Those who emphasize the essential similarities of all Americans deny that "black English," a dialect with ethnicity as its primary social correlate, exists. Those who emphasize the African heritage of American blacks, on the other hand, stress not only the differences between black and white speech but also the affinities between black speech and Anglophone creoles in the Caribbean and Africa. Linguists who adhere to each position work within different disciplines and use different methodologies, further complicating the problem. Many of the linguists who argue that black and white speech are qualitatively alike are dialect geographers whose primary area of research is English, while many of those who argue that black English is a radically different language are creolists studying Caribbean languages.

Both sides of the controversy, however, are responses to earlier attitudes toward black speech. During the last century, differences between black and white speech were often attributed to differences in physiology and in mental abilities, to the Negro's "thick lips and lazy tongue," and to his childlike mind. Others maintained that black speech was merely an archaic form of English, preserving relic forms that had their origins in rural British dialects but preserving nothing from Africa. More recently, some educators have suggested that the academic difficulties of black children are a consequence of deficiencies in their language. Maintaining that black English lacks grammatical categories such as tense that are necessary for logical thought, these educators claim that the language itself inhibits cognitive operations necessary for academic success. Modern linguistic research on black English confronts and refutes each of these, even as linguists themselves dispute the relationship between black and white speech, especially in the South, and the origins of black English.

Dialect geographers were the first to provide data on black speech, with McDavid and McDavid (1951) the most important of the early studies. Making use of field records of the *Linguistic Atlas of the Middle and South Atlantic States* and of Lorenzo Dow Turner's work on Gullah, the McDavids debunked the myths that black speech is the product of physiology and mental ability and that it preserves nothing of its African heritage. The study documented some two dozen words of African origin (including *okra*, *goober*, and *gumbo*) and suggested that some grammatical tendencies (such as the use of *for* as the sign of the infinitive in *he come for tell you*) and some features of pronunciation (such as a higher frequency of consonant cluster simplification) may reflect African influence, too. Yet the McDavids and other dialect geographers maintained that black and white speech were not radically different—that the range of variants was the same in both varieties, although statistical differences existed.

A decade later creolists such as William Stewart began to challenge the assertion that black and white speech differed only quantitatively. Pointing to similarities between black speech and Caribbean creoles in their use of such features as invariant *be* and zero copula, these creolists suggested that black English differed structurally as well as statistically from white varieties and that the differences were a result of the dialect's peculiar history. Dillard (1972) used literary attestations of creole-like forms and observations of early travelers to support the hypothesis that black English is actually a development of a creole language, much like those spoken in the Caribbean, which had its ultimate origins in a West African pidgin, a simplified admixture of English and a variety of African languages used in the absence of a common tongue. Black English maintains vestiges of its creole history; these account for many of the differences between black and white speech, although Dillard noted that "some Southern white dialects have been strongly influenced by Negro dialect."

Because the creolists lacked solid comparative data to confirm their hypotheses, dialect geographers continued to caution against the notion of "racial" dialects, with ethnicity as the primary social correlate; but these linguists also lacked sufficient data, especially on some crucial grammatical features such as invariant *be*, to establish their conclusion that black and white speech differ only quantitatively. The bitter debate between creolists and dialect geographers over the origin of black English and its relation to white speech became the central focus of scholarship in the field.

The solution to the controversy, however, lay not in polemics but in fieldwork. Sociolinguists using the methods developed by William Labov provided part of the solution. In research that refutes those educators who claim that black English represents a deficient form of English and is itself a barrier to logical thought, Labov and his associates provide extensive data on black speech in New York City, including data on crucial features such as invariant *be* and explicit comparisons with similar white speakers. After examining a number of linguistic features, Labov takes a position somewhere between that of the creolists and the dialect geographers. While he suggests that a number of features are unique to black speech, he concludes that black English is "best seen as a distinct subsystem within the larger grammar of English." Wolfram's (1974) extension of this methodology into the South allows both him and Fasold (1981) to modify Labov's conclusions so that they encompass the relationship between black and white English in the South, where the varieties are much closer than in the North. Both assert that some differences between black and white speech do persist even in the South but that these "by no means indicate widespread deep differences in grammar and phonology." Both also suggest that the creole hypothesis is the most likely explanation for this variation, although they believe that decreolization has eliminated most of the original creole features.

During the last five years, however, work on southern English has challenged even these conclusions. Data from the Linguistic Atlas of the Gulf States project, made available in 1981, provides a much broader range of informants than previous work (Wolfram's sample included primarily children) and suggests that Fasold's conclusions about black-white speech relationships are too restrictive. All the forms that blacks use appear in the speech of at least some whites, although the most stigmatized forms generally are used only by the elderly and most insular. Furthermore, recent work of a number of scholars indicates that the very question of black-white speech relations is too simplistic. For example, Pederson (1972) provides evidence of subregional variation in black English and of the complicated ways in which black speech relates to various dialects spoken by whites, while the essays in Montgomery and Bailey (1985) show that such factors as age, sex, and educational background play as important a role as ethnicity in language variation. The work of Bailey and Maynor (1985) in Texas and Mississippi on the present tense of *be*, particularly the subsystem that includes the features invariant *be* and zero copula, which have generated the most discussion, provides some indication of these complexities. These researchers demonstrate that black and white folk speech structures are quite similar: both varieties use the same forms in the same ways, although differences in the frequency of occurrence of forms do exist. Among younger speakers, however, the situation is quite different, with forms such as invariant *be* disappearing among whites but actually increasing among blacks so that the form is more frequent among children than adults. Moreover, Bailey and Maynor suggest that the speech of black adolescents is structurally different from that of both black and white folk speakers. If black English did not exist as a distinct ethnic dialect in the past, current developments suggest that it certainly may in the future as the speech of lower-class blacks continues to diverge from white varieties.

Even as new research on southern speech has shown the complexities of black-white speech relations, new work in creole studies is providing the kind of knowledge of Caribbean languages that will enable scholars to determine the precise relationship of black English to those creoles. Although most scholars now agree that at least some aspects of black English, including some features incorporated into white speech, show evidence of development from an earlier creole, much of the history of black English is obscure. Reconstructing that history is a major task.

In spite of the fact that these basic questions about black English remain unanswered, two things have been clearly established. First, black English cannot be explained on the basis of physiology, mental ability, or linguistic deficiency. Second, the importance of black English lies not so much in its linguistic features as in the attitudes that the larger society and its speakers have toward it.

Guy Bailey
Texas A&M University

Guy Bailey and Natalie Maynor, *American Speech* (Summer 1985); J. L. Dillard, *Black English: Its History and Usage in the United States* (1972); Ralph W. Fasold, *American Speech* (Fall 1981); William Labov, *Language in the Inner City: Studies in the Black English Vernacular* (1972); Raven I. McDavid, Jr., and Virginia G. McDavid, *American Speech* (February 1951); Michael Montgomery and Guy Bailey, *Language Variety in the South: Perspectives in Black and White* (1985); Lee Pederson, *Studies in Linguistics in Honor of Ravin I. McDavid, Jr.* (1972); Walt Wolfram, *Language* (September 1974). ☆

Sports, Blacks in

Competition has never been simple for the black athlete in the South. Nor has he always had control over his own athletic destiny. Competition traditionally has functioned on two levels, the simplest of which is the competition in the arena of play, the give-and-take between athletes. More difficult and more complex has been the competition to be allowed to compete. In this battle black athletes in the South have been matched against a southern racial policy that emphasized segregation in all areas of life. In some sports the policy occasionally gave way, in others it remained fixed until the second half of the 20th century.

Blacks on the antebellum plantations fished, hunted, and watched cockfights; they boxed in matches promoted by their owners, and they even served as crews for boating regattas. Between 1865 and the 1890s there was no clear policy covering interracial competition in athletics. Although black athletes normally competed on a racially segregated basis, there were times when they vied with whites. In New Orleans, Memphis, and other parts of the South blacks and whites occasionally played baseball together in the 1870s and 1880s. And a few black athletes even gained fortune and fame competing against whites. From 1875 through 1902 black riders won 13 times at the Kentucky Derby. The most famous of the black jockeys, Isaac Murphy, won three times. When Murphy died in 1896, the estimated value of his estate was $50,000.

The most prominent arena of competition, however, was the boxing ring. During the late 1880s and early 1890s, when the national center of boxing was in New Orleans, several important interracial matches were staged. On 6 September 1892 the Olympic Club of New Orleans matched George "Little Chocolate" Dixon, a black, against a white named Jack Skelly. Dixon was the world's featherweight champion and a great boxer. Skelly was unheralded. The result was thoroughly predictable. Dixon administered a brutal beating of his white opponent.

The public reaction to the Dixon-Skelly bout symbolized what was happening to interracial competition throughout the South. A reporter for the Chicago *Tribune* noted that many white spectators "winced every time Dixon landed on Skelly. The sight was repugnant to some of the men from the South. A darky is all right in his place here, but the idea of sitting quietly by and seeing a colored boy pommel a white lad grates on Southerners." Even more to the point, the editor of the New Orleans *Times-Democrat* declared that it was "a mistake to match a negro and a white man, a mistake to bring the races together on any terms of equality, even in the prize ring." After the fight, the Olympic Club announced that it would never again promote an interracial bout.

In the prize ring, the most important area of southern athletic integration, segregation soon became the standard policy. Promoters turned against interracial bouts, and white southerners applauded their action. In one case where an interracial bout was promoted in Mississippi, it was stopped by a man described as "a loyal Southerner" who remarked: "The idea of niggers fighting white men. Why, if that darned scoundrel would beat that white boy the niggers would never stop gloating over it, and, as it is, we have enough trouble with them."

So Jim Crow came to the southern prize ring. He also came to southern baseball diamonds, race tracks, billiard halls, cockpits, and sporting clubs. In most sports Jim Crow was almost as strong above the Mason-Dixon line as below, for athletic segregation was not unique to the South. During the late 19th century professional baseball flirted with an interracial ideal, and a few blacks played on integrated teams. In 1887 the League of Colored Base Ball Clubs was recognized as a minor league under the National Agreement between professional baseball teams, a development that ultimately might have produced a vehicle for black advancement to the major leagues. However, after that year blacks were systematically excluded from "organized" professional baseball, and by 1892 the color line was firmly in place.

Black southern athletes still excelled, although they were hampered considerably by Jim Crow restrictions. Three black southern athletes gained particular fame during the first half of the 20th century. The first was Jack Johnson, the first black heavyweight champion. Born in Galveston, Tex., he was forced to leave the South to practice his trade. In 1908 he defeated Tommy Burns for the championship, but his defiant lifestyle generated only hatred in the white South. Again, white southern attitudes differed little from white northern opinion. In 1913 Johnson was forced to flee the country in order to escape a prison term resulting from a trumped up conviction under the Mann Act.

The other two black southern athletes were Jesse Owens and Joe Louis. They were born only months apart, both sons of Alabama sharecropper parents. Both were also products of the black southern migration to the North. Owens's family moved to Cleveland, Ohio; Louis's to Detroit, Mich. Owens developed into the greatest track-and-field athlete of the first half of the 20th century, achieving his greatest triumphs at the 1936 Olympic Games in Berlin. Louis became the second black to hold the heavyweight boxing title, reigning from 1937 to 1949. Unlike Johnson, both Owens and Louis projected accommodationist images, and thus both were relatively popular in North and South.

Athletes in this era became heroes of black life and folklore. North Carolina blacks sang, for example, of Jack Johnson, "Amaze an' Grace, how sweet it sounds,/Jack Johnson knocked Jim Jeffries down." Joe Louis was especially important in promoting a sense of pride among southern blacks. Writer Maya Angelou has written in *I Know Why the Caged Bird Sings* of the black farmers and workers around Stamps, Ark., gathering in her grandmother's general store to listen to the radio broadcast of a Louis fight, savoring each moment of victory.

After World War II integration became the touchstone in northern sports. In 1945 Branch Rickey, owner of the Brooklyn Dodgers, broke the color line in professional baseball by signing Jackie Robinson. Born in Georgia and raised in California, Robinson admirably responded to the challenge, winning acclaim on and off the playing field. The integration of baseball overshadowed the integration of professional football, which occurred in 1945. Slowly over the next two decades the other major sports followed football and baseball's lead. The National Basketball Association admitted blacks for the first time in 1950, the same year Althea Gibson was allowed to compete at Forest Hills in the U.S. tennis championships. By 1960 the major sports had been integrated in the North.

Integration in the South lagged behind the North. Few professional teams existed in the South, so the major focus of action was in the South's colleges and universities. Some southern states prohibited their universities from competing in athletics with northern schools that had blacks on their teams. As Governor Marvin Griffin of Georgia remarked in 1956, "The South stands at Armageddon. The battle is joined. There is no more difference in compromising the integrity of race on the playing field than in doing so in the classroom. One break in the dike and the relentless seas will rush in and destroy us." As a result of this attitude, the Southeastern Conference (SEC) was the last major intercollegiate conference to integrate its athletic teams.

During the 1960s and 1970s, however, integration came to southern athletics. The major professional and college football, basketball, and baseball teams in the South accepted blacks. The first black athletes in the SEC were signed to scholarships in 1966, and integration of varsity teams began in the 1967–68 season. Even professional golf, the "whitest" of all sports, accepted integration. In 1974 Lee Elder became the first black golfer to participate in the Masters Tournament in Augusta, Ga. By the late 1970s, black athletes had at last won the right to compete in athletics in the South.

Sports, in fact, has come to play a prominent role in recent southern race relations. Participation in high school and college athletics has made black athletes such as Georgia's Herschel Walker into superheroes of whites as well as blacks, has promoted assimilation, and has undoubtedly been important in providing examples of high-achievement blacks. Critics such as sociologist Harry Edwards argue, however, that black involvement in sports has reinforced stereotypical images of blacks as physical performers and caused too many young blacks unrealistically to seek sports stardom at the expense of other career goals.

See also EDUCATION: Athletics and Education; RECREATION: Baseball; Basketball; Boxing; Football; Golf; / Aaron, Hank; Paige, Satchel; Robinson, Eddie; Walker, Herschel

Randy Roberts
Sam Houston State University

William J. Baker, *Jesse Owens: An American Life* (1986); Elliot Gorn, "The Manly Art: Bare Knuckle Prize Fighting and the Rise of American Sports" (Ph.D. dissertation, Yale University, 1983); John A. Lucas and Ronald A. Smith, *Saga of American Sports* (1978); Joan Paul, Richard V. McGhee, and Helen Fant, *Phylon* (December 1984); Randy Roberts, *Papa Jack: Jack Johnson and the Era of White Hopes* (1983); Dale A. Somers, *The Rise of Sports in New Orleans, 1850–1900* (1972); Jules Tygiel, *Baseball's Great Experiment: Jackie Robinson and His Legacy* (1983). ☆

Theater, Black

The theorists and artists of the black arts movement of the 1960s saw the South as the matrix of black culture as well as the place where the struggle for civil rights began. From the days of slavery blacks developed unique forms of entertainment, including satires of slaveowners' society and humorous representations of their own situation that blended storytelling techniques, mimed songs, call-and-response patterns, and that encouraged verbal virtuosity and audience participation. Other rituals emerged at religious gatherings or within the black church, eliciting the involvement of the congregation and assuming a highly dramatized form. All these cultural manifestations were examples of black talent for performance and of the potential for active involvement by black audiences.

These early theatrical activities established both the reputation and the stereotype of blacks as accomplished entertainers, but their political, subversive function has never been properly assessed. Southern blacks were long barred from the legitimate theater as performers. Only free blacks, "free persons of color," were admitted as spectators. When blacks were finally accepted in minstrel troupes, they had to submit to the will of white producers and to the conventions of a genre that perpetuated negative images of their race.

The black renaissance of the 1960s and 1970s brought a theatrical revival to the South. The creation of the Free Southern Theater (FST) in 1963 opened a new era, aiming to develop a black, rural, and urban audience and to support the civil rights movement. The FST participated in the national black theater renaissance of the 1960s and 1970s but nevertheless remained distinctively southern. It was one of the few theaters in the United States (El Teatro Campesino in California is another) that was at one time wholly dedicated to its rural audiences.

The FST emerged as the leading theater troupe, but other groups have also been very active, notably in Louisiana (the Dashiki Project, the Ethiopian Theater, and Dillard and Southern universities in New Orleans) and in Georgia (Carlton Molette at Atlanta University). These groups have reinforced the FST in establishing a strong theatrical tradition; black plays were produced and festivals organized. Black theatrical groups offered workshops on acting and playwriting, and on music and dance, which are now considered essential parts of the theatrical experience.

Recent productions show greater concern for the dramatization of black life and history, a growing interest in folklore and its relationship to African and West Indian oral traditions, and an attention to black women's experience. Plays like *Dark Cowgirls and Prairie Queens*, presented by the Carpetbag Theatre for its 1985–86 season, capture the search of seven black women in the American West for freedom in the pre–Civil War era. Other plays like *Jus' Cumin' Home* and *Sing 'til the Song is Mine*, which were combined in a Jomandi Productions (Florida) tour play called *Voices in the Rain*, explore the interaction of black men and black women. *Junebug Jabbo Jones* by John O'Neal, one of the former directors of the FST, is a celebration of the wealth and diversity of the Afro-American oral tradition. In a long dramatic monologue the storyteller Junebug narrates the happenings of numerous characters and provides his own humorous comments.

Although these groups remain anchored in a tradition of black experience and speech that is distinctively southern, they also maintain contacts with other regions and abroad (John O'Neal's one-man show was presented in a theater festival in Paris at the American Center for Artists and at the Nancy Festival). These productions, imaginative and professional, establish the reputation of a unique southern black theater both regionally and nationally.

See also LITERATURE: Theater

Geneviève Fabre
University of Paris

Tom Dent, Gilbert Moses, and Richard Schechner, *The Free Southern Theatre by the Free Southern Theatre* (1969); Geneviève Fabre, *Drumbeats, Masks, and Metaphor: Contemporary Afro-American Theatre* (1983); Martha Jones, *Black Creation* (Fall 1972); Mance Williams, *Black Theatre in the 1960s and 1970s: A Historical-Critical Analysis of the Movement* (1985). ☆

Towns, Black

The South after 1860 spawned towns with names like New Africa, New Rising Star, Slabtown, Acreville, Promised Land, and others now lost to the historical record. These towns, established by newly emancipated slaves, were uniquely southern. Their origins were rooted in the events of Reconstruction and efforts by freedpeople to claim a complex and multifaceted freedom. All the black towns established during this period were shaped by broad historical forces, a long-standing awareness among blacks that personal freedom was bound inextricably to residential separation from whites, and the policies that emerged from the federal government between 1861 and 1863 that designated slaves as contraband of war.

The antebellum South did not directly foster residential integrity for black people, yet both slaves and free blacks devised strategies for claiming some degree of independence in their living arrangements. Plantation life offered its own kind of residential autonomy and opportunities to forge a folk culture independent of whites. Free blacks established churches, schools for their children, fraternal orders, and mutual aid societies. Institutional structures and collective identities drawn from both experiences were easily adapted to the black town settings of the postwar South.

Slavery decayed wherever invading Union troops solidified their military position, beginning at Fortress Monroe, Va., in June 1861. As blacks deserted the plantations, they sought protection with the Union army. Otherwise preoccupied with military concerns, the army was faced with the problem of feeding, clothing, and housing the human contraband. Specific solutions to this dilemma varied but were guided by two general aims—restoration of the southern economy, primarily its agricultural production, and maintenance of social order.

General Benjamin Butler mobilized the blacks who came to Fortress Monroe as laborers. He set the precedent for federal policy by establishing contraband camps, temporary villages where freedpeople were provided seed and farming tools in return for a portion of their crops as repayment. Brigadier General Rufus Saxon devised a plan to reorganize the cotton economy of the Sea Islands by subdividing plantation lands and thereby establishing the basis for a black peasantry in that location. John Eaton created a black freeholding class at Davis Bend, Miss., parceling out land in his charge in small tracts to be cultivated by individual families. The results of these land experiments were clear. The freedpeople worked harder and the lands were more productive when farmed by families rather than by gang labor. The unintended consequences of the experiments were also clear. Contiguous collections of black-owned land were rapidly elaborated into communities as the freedpeople established the churches, schools, and mutual aid societies that formed the core of community life.

These initial postwar arrangements heightened the expectations of other blacks in the South who were also demanding the opportunity to own land and, in the words of former slave Garrison Frazier, to "live by ourselves rather than scattered among the whites." Economic self-sufficiency, landownership, and community were interconnected and inseparable. As community building continued and blacks found various ways to acquire their own land, the average number of land holdings in the South doubled between 1860 and 1880, and the average size of farm tracts fell from 365 to 157 acres. In some cases these towns began with cooperative purchases of whole plantations, arrangements guided from the outset by principles of mutual aid and reciprocity. In South Carolina, the only state in the defeated Confederacy with a black majority in both its Constitutional Convention and Reconstruction legislature, black land purchases were fostered by the Land Commission. This state agency settled approximately 14,000 black families on farms that they owned. Whatever the strategies used to create the towns during the 1860s and 1870s, they were rarely incorporated political units. Yet, with the institutional structures of church and school firmly entrenched, these stable rural communities survived well into the 20th century.

The intentional land developments of the West that began in the 1870s contrast sharply with the casual black communities of the postwar South. Racial violence, combined with crop failures, instigated a black exodus from the southern states to the West, where inexpensive land was available for homesteading. The establishment of Nicodemus, Kan., in 1877, reflected this movement. Mound Bayou, Miss., which was the easternmost of these towns, was established by Isaiah Montgomery in 1888. Montgomery, with land development and management experience at Davis Bend and business experience in Vicksburg during the mid-1880s, planned the Mound Bayou settlement to coincide with the opening of a new Louisville, New Orleans, and Texas railroad line. One of the early Nicodemus settlers, Edward P. McCabe, who enjoyed a successful career as a Kansas state politician, quit the town when the unassigned lands of Oklahoma were opened for settlement in 1889. McCabe envisioned the creation of an all-black state when he established Langston, Okla., in 1890, and although his dream was not realized, Langston became the home of the state's Colored Agricultural and Normal University.

More than 20 black towns were established in Oklahoma during the late 19th and early 20th centuries. The largest of these was Boley, opened for settlement in 1904. Like Mound Bayou, Boley was created with the intention of capitalizing on the expanding railroad industry and for a time enjoyed a degree of economic prosperity. Boley was a prototype of many other black towns. It adhered to Booker T. Washington's conservative philosophy of moral and economic race development, and it suffered from the predictable disadvantages of marginal capitalism and race discrimination.

Resources in the intentionally developed black towns in the West never matched the expectation of the entrepreneurs who established them. Unable to meet the challenges of change, primarily the mechanization of agriculture and the migration of blacks from rural to urban areas, these towns fell into decline during the first quarter of the 20th century. The heritage of the black towns, the solidarity of race, and the centrality of church and mutual aid in community life were retained and translated into new forms of community in the urban centers of black life by the mid-20th century.

See also URBANIZATION: Segregation, Residential

Elizabeth Rauh Bethel
Lander College

Elizabeth Rauh Bethel, *Promiseland: A Century of Life in a Negro Community* (1981); John Blassingame, *The Slave Community: Plantation Life in the Antebellum South* (1972); Norman L. Crockett, *Black Towns* (1979); Louis S. Gerteis, *From Contraband to Freedman: Federal Policy toward Southern Blacks, 1861–1865* (1973); Edward Magdol, *A Right to the Land: Essays on the Freedmen's Community* (1977); Nell Irvin Painter, *Exodusters: Black Migration to Kansas after Reconstruction* (1976); Hortense Powdermaker, *After Freedom: A Cultural Study in the Deep South* (1939); Willie Lee Rose, *Rehearsal for Reconstruction: The Port Royal Experiment* (1964). ☆

Workers, Black

By 1754 the plantation system, based principally on crops of tobacco, rice, and indigo, was well established in the five southern English colonies—Maryland, Virginia, North Carolina, South Carolina, and Georgia. Over 36 percent of the population in these colonies were black slaves—220,000 out of 609,000.

Many Americans, including some southerners, believed that the spirit of the American Revolution, combined with the economic stagnation in tobacco, rice, and indigo planting, would force slavery to die out in the South, just as it was disappearing in the North. But in 1793 Eli Whitney invented the cotton gin, and planters began to take acreage out of other crops and enter the cotton market. The demand for slaves grew. Not even the prohibition by Congress of the importation of slaves from Africa after 1807 could keep cotton from becoming king. The plantation system spread westward, and slavery became solidly rooted in 15 southern states. By 1860 there were 4 million slaves in these states.

Although the economy of the antebellum South was basically agricultural, by 1861 industrialization had forged ahead to such an extent that the slave states accounted for more than 15 percent of the capital invested in the nation's industry. Some establishments employed both whites and slaves at the same factory, mine, or transportation project. But most of the industrial enterprises in the South employed slave labor almost exclusively. In the 1850s about 200,000 slaves—nearly 5 percent of the total slave population—worked in industry.

In 1860 there were more free blacks in the South than in the North—250,787 against 238,268. The absence of white immigrant artisans in the South and the general shortage of workers in the cities forced southern communities to depend on free black craftsmen. Despite repeated efforts of white workers to drive them out of trades, the needs of the community prevailed, and the free black became an indispensable part of the southern skilled labor force, especially in the Lower South. Unlike free blacks in the North, many in the South were able to work at their trades and to hand on their skills to their children.

A call was issued for a national labor convention of black workers to be held in December 1869 at Washington, D.C. It was issued by a group of black workers headed by Isaac Myers, a Baltimore ship caulker who became the first important black labor leader in America. The call noted that legal freedom had not yet brought economic freedom for the black workers: "Colored Men are excluded from the workshops on account of color." In the South the black worker was "unjustly deprived of the price of his labor," and in areas far from courts of justice, "forced to endure wrongs and oppressions worse than slavery."

The Colored National Labor Union, organized at the convention in Washington, attempted to change the conditions of southern black workers. So, too, did the Knights of Labor, organized in 1869, and the Industrial Workers of the World, founded in 1905. But none of these efforts were successful. The vast majority of black workers in the South lived in communities where even the attempt to unionize often brought wholesale arrests, imprisonments, and lynchings.

In 1914 the vast majority of blacks in the United States still lived in the South and were still the chief cultivators of the South's staple crops, enmeshed in a farm tenantry and sharecropping system that consigned them to a life of tilling the soil under conditions almost as restrictive and pernicious as chattel slavery, in rural isolation and a state of perpetual indebtedness.

Jobs in the new textile, iron, and steel factories in the South fell to the poor whites. There were black miners, especially in Alabama, where 46.2 percent of the coal miners in 1889 were blacks. But many of them worked under the convict-lease system. Blacks were arrested for trivial reasons or for no reason at all and sentenced to work out their penalty in the mines. In other southern states, especially Georgia, the convict-lease system supplied cheap black labor to companies building railroads or cutting timber.

The blacks who gravitated in increasing numbers to southern cities moved into personal and domestic service, traditionally regarded as the province of the black. They found employment in urban districts throughout the South as waiters, saloonkeepers, bartenders, janitors, bellhops, barbers, laundresses, and housekeepers. Black women found domestic work one of the few occupations open to the black.

Blacks in the South were gradually eliminated from skilled positions they had held since slavery. Beginning in the 1890s, white workers, most of them members of the American Federation of Labor (AFL) and the Railroad Brotherhoods, steadily eliminated black labor from jobs in the shipping, railroad, and building industries in the older southern seaboard cities. The jobs of electricians, plumbers, gasfitters and steamfitters, railroad engineers and firemen, stationary engineers, cranemen, hoistmen, machinists, and hundreds of other skilled and semiskilled occupations were labeled "for whites only." Black electricians, plumbers, pipefitters, and carpenters had constituted a fair percentage of those crafts at the turn of the century. A generation later, black building-trades work had become "almost marginal," and by 1950 blacks accounted for only 1 percent of the electricians and 3.2 percent of the carpenters. The figures on black participation in apprenticeship programs were even bleaker: 1 percent for plumbers and pipefitters, and 6 percent for carpenters. In Atlanta the proportion of black carpenters decreased from 36.3 percent in 1890 to 2.5 percent in 1920.

Writing in 1936, George Sinclair Mitchell observed that "the Southern trade unionism of the last thirty-odd years has been in good measure a protective device for the march of white artisans in places held by Negroes." Blacks who had spent years acquiring the skill needed for craftsmen's work were denied membership in white unions, which had signed closed-shop or union-shop agreements with employers, and were forced into menial service at low wages.

The same year that Mitchell's criticism of southern trade unionism was published, a labor organization was emerging that was to change the picture for black workers in the South. This was the Committee for Industrial Organization, which became in 1938 the Congress of Industrial Organizations (CIO). Despite bitter opposition of employers and vicious Red-baiting, in which AFL unions participated, the CIO organized thousands of workers in the South—workers in mining, oil, textiles, tobacco, the pulp and paper industry, transportation, and automobile manufacturing. Several southern industries, especially textiles, were white preserves, and this kept down the number of blacks organized. Still, wherever they were employed, black workers streamed into the CIO. In 1945 Lucy Randolph Mason, who did organizing work for the CIO in the South, noted: "Today CIO unions are found in every Southern state and are growing steadily in the region's basic industries and their by-products. Among the many hundreds of thousands of CIO members there are a vast number of Negroes."

The CIO did little to break down the discriminatory lines in industries where blacks were employed, which made it impossible for blacks to advance into better jobs. Moreover, the CIO's constitutional provisions barring discrimination were sometimes openly flouted in the South. But with all its limitations, the CIO marked a significant step forward for the black worker in the South. Lucy Randolph Mason attended a meeting of black women in Richmond, Va., members of the CIO Tobacco Stemmers' and Laborers' Industrial Union. "I asked the secretary what was the most important thing she gained through the union," she wrote later. " 'Respect,' she replied in a flash. 'The boss can't come out in the plant any more and yell at us, or fire us if we answer him. The union takes care of all that now.' "

See also AGRICULTURE: Plantations; Sharecropping and Tenancy; / Cotton Culture; SOCIAL CLASS articles; VIOLENCE: / Convict Leasing

Philip S. Foner
Philadelphia, Pennsylvania

Horace R. Cayton and George Sinclair Mitchell, *Black Workers and the New Unions* (1939); Philip S. Foner, *History of Black Americans: From Africa to the Emergence of the Cotton Kingdom* (1975), *History of Black Americans: From Emergence of the Cotton Kingdom to the Eve of the Compromise of 1850* (1983), *Organized Labor and the Black Worker, 1969–1981* (1981); Gerald D.

Jaynes, *Branches without Roots: Genesis of the Black Working Class in the American South, 1862–1882* (1986); F. Ray Marshall, *The Negro and Organized Labor* (1965); George Sinclair Mitchell, *Southern Economic Journal* (January 1936); Sterling D. Spero and Abram L. Harris, *The Black Worker: The Negro and the Labor Movement* (1931); Charles G. Wesley, *Negro Labor in the United States, 1850–1925: A Study in American Economic History* (1927); Carter G. Woodson and Lorenzo J. Greene, *The Negro Wage Earner* (1930); Billy Hall Wyche, "Southern Attitudes toward Industrial Unions, 1933–1941" (Ph.D. dissertation, University of Georgia, 1969). ☆

BETHUNE, MARY McLEOD

(1875–1955) Educator.

On 10 July 1875 educator, federal government official, and club woman Mary McLeod Bethune was born near Mayesville, S.C. She was one of 17 children born to former slaves and farm workers, Samuel and Patsy (McIntosh) McLeod. In 1882 Bethune abandoned many of her farm chores to attend the newly opened Presbyterian mission school for blacks near Mayesville. Aided with a scholarship, she left South Carolina in 1888 and continued her education at Scotia Seminary (later Barber-Scotia College) in Concord, N.C., completing the high school program in 1892 and the Normal and Scientific Course two years later. Hoping to become a missionary in Africa, she studied at the Moody Bible Institute in Chicago, but in 1895 the Presbyterian Mission Board turned down her application for a missionary post.

A disappointed Mary McLeod returned to her native South Carolina and began her first teaching job at Miss Emma Wilson's Mission School, where she had once been a student. Shortly thereafter, the Presbyterian Board appointed her to a teaching position at Haines Normal and Industrial Institute, and later transferred her to Kindell Institute in Sumter, S.C.

Following her marriage to Albertus Bethune in May 1898, the Bethunes moved to Savannah, Ga., where their only child, Albert McLeod Bethune, was born in 1899. Later that year, the family relocated in Palatka, Fla., where Mary McLeod Bethune established a Presbyterian missionary school. Five years later, after she separated from her husband, Bethune's lifelong ambition to build a school for black girls in the South led her and her son to Daytona Beach, Fla., where, in October 1904 the Daytona Literary and Industrial School for Training Negro Girls opened with Bethune as its president. Like most black educators in the post-Reconstruction South, Bethune emphasized industrial skills and Christian values, and appealed to both the neighboring black community and white philanthropists for financial support. As a consequence of Bethune's unwavering dedication, business acumen, and intellectual ability, the Daytona Institute grew from a small elementary school to incorporate a high school and teacher training program. In 1923 Bethune's school merged with Cookman Institute, a Jacksonville, Fla., college for men, and became the Daytona-Cookman Collegiate Institute. Six years later, the school's name was changed to Bethune-Cookman College in recognition of the important role that Mary McLeod Bethune had played in the school's growth and development.

As an educator in the South, Bethune had concerns that extended beyond campus life. In the absence of a municipally supported medical facility for blacks, the Daytona Institute, under Bethune's guidance, maintained a hospital for blacks from 1911 to 1927. During much of this same period she also operated the Tomoka Mission Schools for the children of black families working the Florida turpentine camps. Ignoring threats made by members of the Ku Klux Klan, Bethune organized a black voter registration drive in Florida, decades before the voter registration drive of the 1960s. As a delegate to the first meeting of the Southern Conference for Human Welfare, Bethune voiced her opposition to degrading southern racial customs.

Bethune joined and held official positions in a number of organizations, but she is best known among club women and the public at large for her monumental work with the National Council of Negro Women, which she founded at age 60 in 1935. Bethune served as its president until 1949. Dedicated to meeting the myriad needs of blacks in all walks of life, the council grew under Bethune's leadership to become the largest federation of black women's clubs in the United States. Headquartered in Washington, D.C., and with chapters located throughout the country and abroad, this association published the *Aframerican Woman's Journal*, established health and job clinics throughout the South, and educated a number of black youths from poor families in the South.

In 1935 President Franklin D. Roosevelt appointed Bethune as one of his special advisers on racial affairs, and four years later she served as the director of black affairs for the National Youth Administration. In May 1955 at the age of 79, one of the South's most well-known women died. The unveiling of a statue of Bethune in a federal park located in the nation's capital in 1974 and the opening of the Mary McLeod Bethune Museum and Archives for Black Women's History in Washington, D.C. in 1979 are lasting testaments to Bethune's intelligence and determination.

See also SOCIAL CLASS: / Southern Conference for Human Welfare

Sharon Harley
University of Maryland

James J. Flynn, *Negroes of Achievement in Modern America* (1970); Rackham Holt, *Mary McLeod Bethune: A Biography* (1964); Barbara Sicherman and Carol Hurd Green, eds., *Notable American Women: The Modern Period: A Biographical Dictionary* (1980); Emma Sterne, *Mary McLeod Bethune* (1957). ☆

BOND, JULIAN

(b. 1940) Civil rights activist and politician.

Horace Julian Bond was born 14 January 1940 in Nashville, Tenn. Both Bond's parents had graduate degrees; his father, Horace Mann Bond, was a noted educator and administrator and was acquainted with such prominent black leaders as W. E. B. Du Bois. Bond spent his first years with his family in Chester County, Penn., where his father was president of Lincoln University. At the age of 12, Bond transferred to a private Quaker-run school near Philadelphia, a predominantly white school where he made average grades and was an outstanding athlete.

At 17 Bond moved to Atlanta with his family and attended Morehouse College, part of Atlanta University where his father was a faculty member. While in college from 1957 to 1961, Bond developed talents for writing poetry and for activism, particularly in the area of civil rights. In March 1960 he helped organize and participated in the first sit-in in the Atlanta City Hall. This action led to the formation of the Committee on Appeal for Human Rights, which, for a time, maintained a separate identity from a larger group with which it worked closely—the Student Nonviolent Coordinating Committee (SNCC), founded in Raleigh, N.C., in the spring of 1960. Bond proved to be a charismatic leader and activist and was a key figure in many SNCC activities, including voter-registration drives, picketing demonstrations, and boycotts. He also worked as reporter, feature writer, and managing editor for the Atlanta *Inquirer*, a newspaper started by several Morehouse students and faculty members to give the protest movement a voice in the black community.

Bond left school in 1961 and did not earn his B.A. degree until 1971. Since then, he has been the recipient of numerous honorary degrees. After leaving Morehouse, Bond married Alice Clopton and went to work for SNCC on a full-time basis as communications director. In 1965 he ran as a SNCC candidate for the Georgia Legislature from the 136th district in Atlanta and won the seat. Bond was prevented from taking his seat until 1967, however, because of political reaction to his outspoken opposition to U.S. involvement in Vietnam. Following a Supreme Court ruling in his favor, Bond did take his seat and served in the lower house until 1974.

Bond came to national attention at the national Democratic convention in Chicago in 1968, when he was nominated as a vice-presidential candidate after a split in the Georgia delegation. In 1974 he was elected to the Georgia Senate from the fifth district and was reelected in 1980. His bid for a third term ended in September 1986 with his loss in the primary to former city councilman, SNCC chairman, and Bond's ally, John Lewis. Political observers suggested that the district's white minority bloc vote for Lewis (80 percent of white voters supported him) stemmed from their perception of Bond as more militant on racial issues than Lewis and was responsible for Bond's defeat.

Bond remains active on political and social issues and has hinted that he will run for public office again. As of 1987 he was president of the Institute for Southern Studies in Durham, N.C., a research and publication center focused on the South.

Karen M. McDearman
University of Mississippi

W. Augustus Low and Virgil A. Clift, eds., *Encyclopedia of Black America* (1981); John Neary, *Julian Bond: Black Rebel* (1971); *Newsweek* (15 September 1986); Thomas Rose and John Greenya, *Black Leaders: Then and Now* (1984). ☆

BONTEMPS, ARNA

(1902–1973) Writer and scholar.

Arnaud Wendell Bontemps was three years old when his father decided to move his family from his son's birthplace in Alexandria, La., to California. The elder Bontemps hoped to escape the prejudice and intimidation that tormented his and other black families. Trying to protect his son, he later warned Arna never to act black.

Having read *Harlem Shadows*, a book of poems by black author Claude

McKay, Arna Bontemps became aware of the emergence of black voices from Harlem. After he graduated from Union Pacific College in 1923 and with the first publication of one of his own poems, Bontemps moved from Los Angeles to Harlem, where he taught at the Harlem Academy. He continued to write and, subsequently, became identified with the Harlem Renaissance. In 1931 he published his first novel, *God Sends Sunday*, which was later adapted as *St. Louis Woman*, the musical in which Pearl Bailey made her Broadway acting debut.

A few years of teaching and writing in Alabama, a master's degree from the University of Chicago, and work with the Illinois Writers Project marked Bontemps's career until the beginning of his 22-year tenure as librarian at Fisk University in Nashville, Tenn. In 1968 he resumed teaching, first at the University of Illinois and then at Yale, where he served also as curator of the James Weldon Johnson Collection of Negro Arts and Letters. He had moved back to Nashville when he died of a heart attack in 1973.

Bontemps devoted much time to writing about black life, wanting, as he said in *Harper's*, "to write something about the changes I have seen in my lifetime, and about the Negro awakening and regeneration." Short stories portraying southern black life (*The Old South: "A Summer Tragedy and Other Stories of the Thirties"*), historical novels about black uprisings (*Black Thunder*), children's literature about black leaders (*Free at Last: The Life of Frederick Douglass*), and anthologies of works by black authors (*American Negro Poetry*) represent the range of his writings. He also edited W. C. Handy's autobiography, *Father of the Blues*, and collaborated with fellow writers Langston Hughes, Jack Conroy, and Countee Cullen.

Arna Bontemps spent much of his life exploring the culture of his race and his southern black heritage. In doing so, he became a primary force in the development and promotion of black literature in America.

See also EDUCATION: / Fisk University

Jessica Foy
Cooperstown Graduate Program
Cooperstown, New York

Robert A. Bone, *Down Home: A History of Afro-American Short Fiction from Its Beginnings to the End of the Harlem Renaissance* (1975); Arna Bontemps, *Harper's* (April 1965); Arthur P. Davis, *From the Dark Tower: Afro-American Writers, 1900–1960* (1974). ☆

CHESNUTT, CHARLES W.

(1858–1932) Writer.

Charles Waddell Chesnutt, an Afro-American man of letters, was born in Cleveland, Ohio, on 20 June 1858, the son of free blacks who had emigrated from Fayetteville, N.C. When he was eight years old, Chesnutt's parents returned to Fayetteville, where Charles worked part-time in the family grocery store and attended a school founded by the Freedmen's Bureau. In 1872 financial necessity forced him to begin a teaching career in Charlotte, N.C. He returned to Fayetteville in 1877, married a year later, and by 1880 had become principal of the Fayetteville State Normal School for Negroes. Meanwhile he continued to pursue private studies of the English classics, foreign languages, music, and stenography. Despite his successes, he longed for broader opportunities and a chance to develop the literary skills that by 1880 led him toward an author's life. In 1883 he moved his family to Cleveland. There he passed the state bar examination and established his own court reporting firm. Financially prosperous and prominent in civic affairs, he resided in Cleveland for the remainder of his life.

"The Goophered Grapevine," an unusual dialect story that displayed intimate knowledge of black folk culture in the South, was Chesnutt's first nationally recognized work of fiction. Its publication in the August 1887 issue of the *Atlantic Monthly* marked the first time that a short story by a black had appeared in that prestigious magazine. After subsequent tales in this vein were accepted by other magazines, Chesnutt submitted to Houghton, Mifflin a collection of these stories, which was published in 1899 as *The Conjure Woman.* His second collection of short fiction, *The Wife of His Youth and Other Stories of the Color Line* (1899), ranged over a broader area of southern and northern racial experience than any previous writer on black American life had attempted. These two volumes were popular enough to convince Houghton, Mifflin to publish Chesnutt's first novel, *The House Behind the Cedars*, in 1900. This story of two blacks who pass for white in the postwar South revealed Chesnutt's sense of the psychological and social dilemmas facing persons of mixed blood in the region. His second novel, *The Marrow of Tradition* (1901), is based on the Wilmington, N.C., race riot of 1898. Hoping to write the *Uncle Tom's Cabin* of his generation, Chesnutt made a plea for racial justice that impressed William Dean Howells as a work of "great power," though with "more justice than mercy in it." The failure of the book to sell widely forced Chesnutt to give up his dream of supporting his family as a professional author. In 1905 he published his final novel, *The Colonel's Dream*, a tragic story of an idealist's attempt to revive a depressed North Carolina town through a socioeconomic program much akin to the New South creed of Henry W. Grady and Booker T. Washington. The novel received little critical notice.

During the latter years of his life Chesnutt continued to write and publish occasional short stories, but he was largely eclipsed in the 1920s by the writers of the Harlem Renaissance. He was awarded the Spingarn Medal in 1928 by the National Association for the Advancement of Colored People for his pioneering literary work on behalf of the Afro-American struggle. Today Chesnutt is recognized as a major innovator in the tradition of Afro-American fiction, an important contributor to the deromanticizing trend in post–Civil War southern literature, and a singular voice among turn-of-the-century realists who treated the color line in American life.

See also INDUSTRY: / Grady, Henry W.; VIOLENCE: / Wilmington Race Riot

William L. Andrews
University of Wisconsin

William L. Andrews, *The Literary Career of Charles W. Chesnutt* (1980); Helen M. Chesnutt, *Charles Waddell Chesnutt: Pioneer of the Color Line* (1952); Frances Richardson Keller, *An American Crusade: The Life of Charles Waddell Chesnutt* (1978). ☆

CITIZENS' COUNCILS

This group and allied organizations—the Virginia Defenders of State Sovereignty and Individual Liberties, the Tennessee Federation for Constitutional Government, the North Carolina Patriots, and the Georgia States' Rights Council—were formed by white supremacists in the South to resist school desegregation. Appearing first in Mississippi in July 1954, this movement of "white-collar" or "country club" Klans spread rapidly into each of the 11 former Confederate states. Dedicated to "states' rights and racial integrity," the council movement, like the Confederacy itself, failed to overcome southern parochialism and thus never forged a united front. Yet a semblance of regional unity was provided in 1956 by the formation of the Mississippi-based Citizens' Councils of America, an informal confederation of the more viable southern organized resistance groups.

The councils' natural habitats were the old plantation areas of the Lower South, where the black population was most heavily concentrated and where white racial fears were highest. Except in Virginia, where organized resistance was endorsed by the Byrd machine, and Little Rock, where Governor Orval Faubus was a supporter, councils or council-like groups enjoyed little success in the so-called rim-South states. In Florida, North Carolina, Tennessee, and Texas, members of the white power structure rarely became closely identified with the groups. But in the Deep South—in Alabama, Louisiana, Mississippi, and South Carolina—councils won the support of high elected officials and of business and professional leaders. Here, where their power and prestige were greatest, Citizens' Councils officially eschewed violence. Individual members were sometimes implicated in terrorist acts, however, and the movement was instrumental in creating a climate of fear and reprisal in which few whites and even fewer blacks dared challenge the status quo. In Alabama and Mississippi, councils functioned as shadow governments.

There are no reliable membership figures, but the Southwide total probably never exceeded 250,000, though non-dues-paying sympathizers surely numbered many thousands more. Having rapidly expanded in the years immediately after *Brown* v. *Board of Education*, white resistance organizations gradually declined following the federal-state confrontation at Little Rock. In growing numbers whites recognized that some degree of school desegregation was inevitable. Remobilization campaigns in the 1960s failed, and by mid-decade membership even in Mississippi had dwindled to insignificance. Thereafter, diehard movement leaders turned their support to all-white private schools.

See also LAW: / *Brown* v. *Board of Education*; POLITICS: / Byrd machine; Faubus, Orville; VIOLENCE: / Ku Klux Klan

Neil R. McMillen
University of Southern Mississippi

Numan Bartley, *The Rise of Massive Resistance: Race and Politics in the South during the 1950s* (1969); Hodding Carter, *The South Strikes Back* (1959); Neil R. McMillen, *The Citizens' Council: Organized Resistance to the Second Reconstruction* (1971). ☆

COMMISSION ON INTERRACIAL COOPERATION (CIC)

The CIC was founded in Atlanta in 1919 in an effort to ameliorate racial tension growing out of World War I. Seeking to bring "the best" whites and blacks together, the CIC, under the leadership of Executive Director Will W. Alexander, organized some 800 state and local interracial committees throughout the South. By the early 1920s a press service was sending releases concerning black achievements and race relations to about 1,200 newspapers and magazines. Through both local committees and the press service the CIC during its first decade worked to combat the Ku Klux Klan and lynching. In 1930 the organization established the Southern Commission on the Study of Lynching (SCSL) to examine all lynchings in that year and to formulate an effective preventive program. CIC Research Secretary Arthur Raper headed the SCSL's investigations, which were published in 1933 as *The Tragedy of Lynching*. In 1932 CIC Woman's Director Jessie Daniel Ames established the Association of Southern Women for the Prevention of Lynching (ASWPL) as an additional mechanism for opposing the practice.

As a result of the Great Depression of the early 1930s, the commission was forced to modify its program. No longer able to support its field staff, most of the state and local committees (with the exception of North Carolina and Virginia) ceased to maintain active groups. The commission instead, with funding from the Carnegie Foundation, developed a subsidiary group, the Conference on Education and Race Relations (CERR), which sponsored workshops, seminars, and publications to encourage the teaching of race relations in southern colleges. By 1942 CIC records indicated that about 500 southern colleges and 1,000 high schools were utilizing CERR materials. During the 1930s the commission also sought the inclusion of blacks in the various programs of Franklin D. Roosevelt's New Deal. Will W. Alexander headed a CIC committee, funded by the Rockefeller Foundation, which not only persuaded government agencies to hire black advisors on minority affairs but also sponsored several studies concerning the New Deal's impact on blacks. Among these studies were Arthur Raper's *A Preface to Peasantry* and Horace R. Cayton and George Sinclair Mitchell's *Black Workers and the New Unions*. The CIC Committee also was an influential force in bringing passage of the 1937 Bankhead-Jones Farm Tenancy Act, which established the Farm Security Administration (FSA). Will Alexander, though nominally still the CIC director, headed this agency. In Alexander's absence, leadership of the commission largely fell to Jessie Daniel Ames, who began in 1937 to revive state and local interracial committees. In 1940 she established *The Southern Frontier*, a monthly publication designed to keep these groups abreast of race relations news and CIC activities.

Will W. Alexander and other CIC leaders, especially University of North Carolina sociologist Howard W. Odum, concluded by the late 1930s that the commission needed to adopt a new strategy in order to address the South's racial problems. Influenced by Odum's theories of regional development, they envisioned an organization that would confront the inequities of segregation and attack the South's economic problems as a necessary prerequisite to solving its racial difficulties. To carry out their regional plan, they established the Southern Regional Council, with which the commission merged in 1944.

The CIC itself had never attacked the system of segregation, preferring to work within the system to improve the condition of blacks. By 1944 its program seemed conservative and outmoded. In many ways, however, it was, in Arthur Raper's phrase, a "frontier movement," which played an important role in educating southern whites to racial injustice, in examining the economic problems of the South's poor, and in making lynching an unacceptable practice.

See also EDUCATION: / Odum, Howard W.; SOCIAL CLASS: / Southern Regional Council; WOMEN'S LIFE: Ames, Jessie Daniel

Ann Wells Ellis
Kennesaw College

W. E. Cole, *Social Forces* (May 1943); Wilma Dykeman and James Stokely, *Seeds of Southern Change: The Life of Will Alexander* (1962); Ann Wells Ellis, *Atlanta Historical Journal* (Spring 1980). ☆

CONGRESS OF RACIAL EQUALITY (CORE)

Rooted in the 1930s pacifist movements, the Congress of Racial Equality (CORE) was formed in Chicago in 1942 to oppose racial discrimination and encourage integration. For many years the group emphasized interracial membership and Gandhian nonviolent direct action. James Farmer served as CORE's first national chairman and as its dynamic national director from 1961 to 1966.

From 1942 to 1961 CORE focused on integration of public accommodations and in 1946 tested compliance with the Supreme Court's ruling of that year declaring unconstitutional Virginia's laws requiring segregation on interstate motor carriers. To do so, CORE launched the Journey of Reconciliation, an integrated bus trip from Washington, D.C., to Kentucky. The ride elicited little attention, but it boosted CORE morale and served as the model for the Freedom Ride of 1961.

Late-1940s efforts to establish affiliates in the Deep South failed because of fear of brutal reprisals, though in southern border states affiliates slowly grew. After the success of the Southern Christian Leadership Conference's (SCLC) Montgomery bus boycott, CORE increased its southern projects. Its voter registration campaign in Virginia in the late 1950s proved disappointing, but such projects fared better in South Carolina, where in the 1960s CORE also actively supported efforts to integrate lunch counters.

CORE catapulted to national attention in 1961 when it spearheaded the Freedom Ride, an integrated bus trip from Washington, D.C., through the Deep South to test the South's response to the 1960 Supreme Court decision prohibiting segregation in bus- and train-terminal accommodations. Suffering violent reprisals in Anniston and Birmingham, Ala., the CORE riders stopped in Birmingham, where Student Nonviolent Coordinating Committee (SNCC) riders resumed the effort. Further violence occurred in Montgomery, and the CORE-SCLC-SNCC Freedom Ride Coordinating Committee recruited thousands of riders, 360 of whom were arrested and jailed in Jackson, Miss. The campaign resulted in the Interstate Commerce Commission's September 1961 ruling prohibiting segregated facilities in interstate travel. Many Deep South locales ignored the ruling, but a major battle had been won.

Subsequently, CORE's leaders played major roles in the surge of direct action in Mississippi, Alabama, Georgia, and Louisiana. More working-class blacks joined CORE, and attention turned to community development projects. Among civil rights groups CORE's influence waned between 1962 and 1964, partly because CORE-supported activities—such as demonstrations in Gadsden, Ala., and Plaquemine, La.—received little publicity, even when the protesters met with violence.

CORE established a regional office in Louisiana in 1964, but major voter registration campaigns there met with limited success and much harassment. Frustrated black residents armed for self-defense, and CORE accepted such actions as necessary. The murder of CORE workers Michael Schwerner and James Chaney and SNCC vounteer Andrew Goodman in Neshoba County, Miss., in 1964 elicited a national outcry for protection of civil rights workers. Subsequently CORE established "freedom schools" for black youth, community centers, and political programs throughout Mississippi and supported creation of the Mississippi Freedom Democratic party.

Problems and schisms within CORE increased; and by the 1965 CORE convention in Durham, N.C., James Farmer had decided to resign, and CORE's interracial focus had been rejected. Still in operation, CORE now promotes inner-city community-development projects in black neighborhoods.

Sharon A. Sharp
University of Mississippi

Inge Powell Bell, *CORE and the Strategy of Nonviolence* (1968); C. Eric Lincoln, in *The American Negro Reference Book*, ed. John P. Davis (1966); August Meier and Elliott M. Rudwick, *CORE: A Study in the Civil Rights Movement, 1942–1968* (1973). ☆

DOUGLASS, FREDERICK

(1808–1895) Black leader.

Frederick Douglass was the most important black American leader of the 19th century. He was born Frederick Augustus Washington Bailey, in Talbot County, on Maryland's Eastern Shore in 1808, the son of a slave woman, and in all likelihood, her white master. Upon his escape from slavery at age 20, Douglass adopted a new surname from the hero of Sir Walter Scott's *The Lady of the Lake*. Douglass immortalized his formative years as a slave in the first of three autobiographies, *Narrative of the Life of Frederick Douglass, An American Slave*, published in 1845. This and two subsequent autobiographies, *My Bondage and My Freedom* (1855) and *The Life and Times of Frederick Douglass* (1881), mark Douglass's greatest contributions to southern culture. Written both as antislavery propaganda and as personal revelation, they are universally regarded as the finest examples of the slave narrative tradition and as classics of American autobiography.

Douglass's public life ranged from his work as an abolitionist in the early 1840s to his attacks on Jim Crow segregation in the 1890s. Douglass lived the bulk of his career in Rochester, N.Y., where for 16 years he edited the most influential black newspaper of the mid-19th century, called successively *The North Star* (1847–51), *Frederick Douglass' Paper* (1851–58), and *The Douglass Monthly* (1859–63). Douglass achieved international fame as an orator with few peers and as a writer of persuasive power. In thousands of speeches and editorials Douglass levied an irresistible indictment against slavery and racism, provided an indomitable voice of hope for his people, embraced antislavery politics, and preached his own brand of American ideals.

Douglass welcomed the Civil War in 1861 as a moral crusade to eradicate the evil of slavery. During the war he labored as a fierce propagandist of the Union cause and emancipation, as a recruiter of black troops, and on two occasions as an advisor to President Abraham Lincoln. Douglass made a major contribution to the intellectual tradition of millennial nationalism, the outlook from which many Americans, North and South, interpreted the Civil War. During Reconstruction and the Gilded Age Douglass's leadership became less activist and more emblematic. He traveled and lectured widely on racial issues, but his most popular topic was "Self-Made Men." By the 1870s Douglass had moved to Washington, D.C., where he edited the newspaper *The New National Era* and became president of the ill-fated Freedmen's Bank. As a stalwart Republican, he was appointed marshall (1877–81) and recorder of deeds (1881–86) for the District of Columbia, and chargé d'affaires for Santo Domingo and minister to Haiti (1889–91). Douglass had five children by his first wife Anna Murray, a free black woman from Baltimore who followed him out of slavery in 1838. Less than two years after Anna died in 1882, the 63-year-old Douglass married Helen Pitts, his white former secretary, an event of considerable controversy. Thus by birth and by his two marriages, Douglass is one of the South's most famous examples of the region's mixed racial heritage.

Frederick Douglass, abolitionist and black leader, date unknown

Douglass never lost a sense of attachment to the South. "Nothing but an intense love of personal freedom keeps us [fugitive slaves] from the South," Douglass wrote in 1848. He often referred to Maryland as his "own dear native soil." Brilliant, heroic, and complex, Douglass became a symbol of his age and a unique American voice for humanism and social justice. His life and thought will always speak profoundly to the dilemma of being black in America. Douglass died of heart failure in 1895, the year Booker T. Washington rose to national prominence with his Atlanta Exposition speech suggesting black accommodation to racial segregation.

David W. Blight
North Central College
Naperville, Illinois

John Blassingame et al., *The Frederick Douglass Papers*, 2 vols. (1979–1982); Philip S. Foner, *Life and Writings of Frederick Douglass*, 4 vols. (1955); August Meier, *Negro Thought in America, 1880–1915* (1963); Benjamin Quarles, *Frederick Douglass* (1948). ☆

DU BOIS, W. E. B.

(1868–1963) Historian, sociologist, editor, and novelist.

William Edward Burghardt Du Bois was born 23 February 1868 in Great Barrington, Mass. A New Englander in thought and conduct, as he put it, he entered the South in 1885, after a promising high school career, to attend Fisk University in Nashville, Tenn. He found the South deeply humiliating. "No one but a Negro," he wrote, "going into the South without previous experience of color caste can have any conception of its barbarism." Nevertheless, Fisk itself was challenging, even exhilarating, and summer teaching in rural counties sealed his attachment to the black masses and his determination to champion their cause. Graduating in 1888, he trained further at Harvard University (Ph.D. 1895) and the University of Berlin. His doctoral dissertation on the suppression of the slave trade was published in 1896. He held positions briefly with the University of Pennsylvania and Wilberforce in Ohio before returning to the South in 1897 to teach sociology, economics, and history at Atlanta University.

His third book, *The Souls of Black Folk* (1903), was a collection of hauntingly beautiful essays on every important aspect of black culture in the South; perhaps its most famous insight concerned the "double-consciousness" of the black American: "One ever feels his twoness—an American, a Negro; two souls, two thoughts, two unreconciled strivings; two warring ideals in one dark body, whose dogged strength alone keeps it from being torn asunder." With this book he secured preeminence among all Afro-American intellectuals and became the leader of those opposed to the powerful and conservative Booker T. Washington of Tuskegee. His yearly (1897–1914) Atlanta University Studies of black social conditions and a biography of John Brown (1909) added to his reputation.

Increasingly controversial, he moved to New York in 1910 to found and edit *The Crisis*, the monthly magazine of the fledgling NAACP. For 24 years he sustained an assault on all forms of racial injustice, especially in the South. In 1934 he published *Black Reconstruction in America*, a grand Marxist-framed reevaluation of the much-maligned role of blacks in the Civil War and its aftermath. That year he returned to Atlanta University after grave disagreements with the NAACP leadership over strategies during the Depression; Du Bois favored a program of voluntary self-segregation stressing economics that many people found similar to the old program of Booker T. Washington. At Atlanta University he found little support for his projected scheme to organize the study of sociology among black colleges and other institutions in the South. In 1944 he rejoined the NAACP in New York, but soon found himself again at odds with the leadership, this time over his growing interest in radical socialism. He left the NAACP finally in 1948. By this time his attitude toward the South had changed somewhat. Influenced no doubt by the aims of the leftist Southern Negro Youth Congress, he declared in 1948 that "the future of American Negroes is in the South. . . . Here is the magnificent climate; here is the fruitful earth under the beauty of the southern sun; and here . . . is the need of the thinker, the worker, and the dreamer." His Socialist activities culminated in his arrest and trial in 1951 as an unregistered agent of a foreign principal; the presiding judge heard the evidence, then directed his acquittal.

Unpopular and even shunned in some quarters, he turned to fiction to express his deepest feelings. In a trilogy set mainly in the South, *The Black Flame (The Ordeal of Mansart)*, 1957; *Mansart Builds a School*, 1959; *Worlds of Color*, 1961, he told the story of a black southerner, born at the end of Reconstruction, who rises slowly and patiently to the leadership of a small southern school, witnessing in his long lifetime the important events of modern American and world history. In October 1961 Du Bois was admitted to membership in the Communist party of the United States; that month he left his country to live in Ghana at the invitation of Kwame Nkrumah. In February 1963 he renounced his American citizenship and became a Ghanaian. He had made little progress on the task for which Nkrumah had summoned him, the editing of an "Encyclopedia Africana," when he died of natural causes 27 August 1963.

See also EDUCATION: / Fisk University; Tuskegee Institute

Arnold Rampersad
Stanford University

Herbert Aptheker, *Annotated Bibliography of the Published Writings of W. E. B. Du Bois* (1973); Arnold Rampersad, *The Art and Imagination of W. E. B. Du Bois* (1976). ☆

EVERS, MEDGAR

(1926–1963) Civil rights leader.

During the 1950s and 1960s Medgar Wiley Evers dedicated his life to the racial integration of Mississippi. He taught black Mississippians about the power of the ballot and he organized economic boycotts. At his urging, thousands of black customers refused to buy soft drinks, bread, and clothes sold by white-owned businesses that perpetuated segregation in Jackson, Miss. In the guise of a field hand in 1955, he gathered evidence on the lynching of Emmett Till, a black teenager. With force and clarity, Evers spoke out, shaming blacks and whites alike into taking steps to end racial separation.

Born 2 July 1926 Evers grew up in the small, east-central Mississippi town of Decatur. His father worked for a sawmill and on the railroads; his mother was a domestic worker. They raised cows, pigs, chickens, vegetables, and cotton on the small plot of land around their house on the edge of town. As a boy, Medgar learned about self-respect from his father, who did not follow the custom of stepping off the sidewalk when whites approached, and Medgar learned religious values from his mother, who required her children to attend church every Sunday.

Childhood experiences of brutality against blacks embittered Evers, and for a time, after serving in the U.S. Army during World War II, he idolized Jomo Kenyatta of Africa and dreamed of forming a band of fighters, similar to Kenyatta's, who would right the wrongs whites had inflicted on blacks. After the war, he enrolled at Alcorn Agricultural and Mechanical College in southwestern Mississippi. He married Myrlie Beasley on Christmas Eve 1951, and the next year the Magnolia Mutual Life Insurance Company hired him as a salesman. In February 1954, he tried to upgrade his education and break the color barrier at the University of Mississippi Law School, but was rejected. Evers decided not to pursue it, although later, in 1962, he assisted James H. Meredith in becoming the first black to enroll in the university. Evers's volunteer work for the National Association for the Advancement of Colored People turned into a full-time job: he was appointed in late 1954 as the first Mississippi field secretary of the NAACP, a post he held until his death.

He eventually rejected his notions of a Kenyatta-style revolution, though he did name one of his sons after Kenyatta. Evers traveled through Mississippi, inspiring blacks to fight segregation in every nonviolent way possible. Myrlie Evers said her husband amazed the journalists when he would tell them he stayed in Mississippi because he loved it. "It was part of him," she wrote in *For Us, the Living*, a book about their life together. "He loved to hunt and fish, to roam the fields and woods. . . . He had visited many places . . . but always he came back to Mississippi as a man coming home."

This sense of place and Evers's sense of justice led him to fight for change in Mississippi's capital city of Jackson. During the historic spring of 1963 Evers and other civil rights leaders pushed for blacks to be hired on the Jackson police force and as school crossing guards. Evers wanted public facilities and restaurants to be open to everyone, regardless of race. And he sought an end to the signs that segregated white and black races at drinking fountains and restrooms.

Mass meetings, demonstrations at segregated lunch counters, and boycotts of white businesses in Jackson began to force changes. Police arrested black teenagers who demonstrated and corralled them for days at the fairgrounds. Evers remained at the forefront of the city's boycotts, which were attracting national publicity.

On the night of 11 June 1963 President John F. Kennedy told the nation in a televised address that he was sending a bill to Congress to ensure racial justice. The bill was to become the Civil Rights Act of 1964. After seeing Kennedy's speech, Evers drove to his Jackson home. Just after midnight on 12 June a bullet from a high-powered rifle felled him as he stepped from his car. Within an hour, he died at the University of Mississippi Medical Center, three weeks before his 37th birthday. After services in Jackson, Evers's body was flown to the National Cemetery in Arlington, Va., for a military burial.

Berkley Hudson
Providence, Rhode Island

Cleveland Donald, in *Mississippi Heroes*, ed. Dean Faulkner Wells and Hunter Cole (1980); Mrs. Medgar Evers with William Peters, *For Us, the Living* (1967); John R. Salter, Jr., *Jackson, Mississippi: An American Chronicle of Struggle and Schism* (1979). ☆

FRANKLIN, JOHN HOPE

(b. 1915) Historian.

Franklin stands in the first rank of professional historians and also in the first rank of those blacks who work actively on behalf of the modern civil rights movement. Born in Rentiesville, Okla., in 1915, Franklin embodies the ethnic and racial complexities of the South: his family was part Cherokee and part black, and some of its members served as slaves to the Cherokees in the antebellum decades. His father, Buck Franklin, became a successful lawyer in Tulsa and saw his legal offices destroyed in one of the anti-black riots after the Armistice of 1918. Buck Franklin quietly rebuilt his legal practice, for a time actually operating inside a tent, and this experience became vital to the spirit of John Hope Franklin's own protests and achievements.

Given the chance to attend college, young Franklin studied at Fisk (A.B. 1935) and then entered the Harvard graduate program (A.M. 1936, Ph.D. 1941) at a time when there were few black historians in the country. He taught at Fisk University, Howard University, Saint Augustine's College, Brooklyn College, and the University of Chicago. In the field of civil rights, Franklin was instrumental in integrating the Southern Historical Association and the Mississippi Valley Historical Association (now the Organization of American Historians), both of which he eventually served as president; he also contributed background research for the National Association for the Advancement of Colored People in the campaign to integrate the public schools, culminating successfully in the legal case, *Brown* v. *Board of Education* (1954).

In the study of black history Franklin published three major works *From Slavery to Freedom: The History of Negro Americans* (1947; 5th ed., 1980) was an encyclopedic mapping of the path of black progress in America, optimistic in its style; *The Militant South, 1800–1861* (1956) was a bolder, more pessimistic interpretation, which traced both a self-destructive urge among the antebellum southern leaders who produced the Civil War and a continuing tendency to violence after the war; and *Reconstruction after the Civil War* (1963) was one of the early efforts to revise the mythic white view of the horrors of Reconstruction, as embodied in historian William A. Dunning's works, and to focus on black participation and achievement in the post–Civil War period.

See also LAW: *Brown* v. *Board of Education*

John Herbert Roper
St. Andrews Presbyterian College

John Hope Franklin, *Free Negroes in North Carolina, 1790–1860* (1943); Earle E. Thorpe, *Black Historians: a Critique* (1971); and interviews with Franklin, August Meier, C. Vann Woodward, and LeRoy Graf, typescripts filed in Southern Historical Collection, University of North Carolina, Chapel Hill. ☆

FREE SOUTHERN THEATER

The early phase of southern black protest efforts depended heavily on the involvement of whites, including many northerners who served as "freedom riders" and in political action and voter registration projects. The rallying cry of "black and white together" gave way in the mid-1960s to calls for awareness of the unique black experience, which led to the emergence of groups such as the Student Nonviolent Coordinating Committee (SNCC) and its chairman, Stokely Carmichael.

A cultural and artistic complement to the political struggles of the civil rights movement in the early 1960s, the history of Free Southern Theater recapitulates, in most of its essentials, that of the larger movement. Free Southern Theater resulted from the collaboration, in the summer of 1963, of SNCC student directors Gilbert Moses and John O'Neal. O'Neal was a playwright, and Moses had had theatrical experience at Cleveland's Karuma Playhouse and off-Broadway with the Living Theater. Both had come to Mississippi intent on political activity but reluctant to divorce that action from their artistic concerns.

Headquartered at Tougaloo College in Jackson, the Free Southern Theater was an attempt to bridge the gap between art and politics. Its 1963 prospectus emphasized the dual significance of its name: the free development of black talent and self-expression and free-of-cost accessibility to theater, which would present an undistorted image of black society.

With the help of Richard Schechner, then editor of the *Tulane Drama Review*, the New York theater community was tapped for funds. Artistic assistance came from across the country. Training sessions were held at the Guthrie, lighting equipment was loaned by Joseph Papp, and improvisational acting classes were conducted by Second City's Paul Sills. In 1964 the Free Southern Theater moved its base of operations to New Orleans and began a full-time touring schedule, playing 21 towns in 6 states in its first season. With Moses as artistic director, the 25-member company presented plays ranging from Beckett's *Waiting for Godot* to Langston Hughes's *Don't You Want to Be Free*, Ossie Davis's *Purlie Victorious*, and Martin Duberman's documentary drama *In White America*. In addition to workshops in writing and acting, designed to support collective creativity, efforts were made to produce original scripts ("Bogalusa," "Jonesburg Story") that reflected the complexities of local black experience.

Although the goals of the Free Southern Theater were similar to those of other black theater groups throughout the country, the circumstances under which the company worked stamped it as uniquely southern. Bringing plays to rural areas of Mississippi, Louisiana, Georgia, and Alabama, performances were staged by necessity in church auditoriums, schools, and at times in cotton fields. Refused publicity by the local press, unable to find rehearsal or living space, or targeted for violence by police, the performers often had to cancel appearances. Cast members were arrested and charged with vagrancy, evicted from apartments, and otherwise harassed. As late as 1973 an acrimonious debate was sparked by a New Orleans City Council grant of $15,000 to a group that critics claimed "called for the overthrow of the U.S. government," "encouraged violence against whites," and otherwise contributed to racial disharmony.

By the middle 1960s, a period of self-examination, which paralleled the civil rights movement on the national level, led the Free Southern Theater toward a recognition of black consciousness. Questioning the continued relevance of bringing Broadway, off-Broadway, or even radical white theater to the southern black community, some cast members wanted far more emphasis on local forms and idioms. Others doubted the validity of black theater that was not performed and managed exclusively by blacks. The resignation, in 1966, of both Moses and Schechner capped this period of upheaval.

Reorganized (the troup moved its base to the all-black neighborhood of Desire and transferred controlling interest to its black board members) and stabilized financially by grants from the Rockefeller Foundation and the National Endowment for the Arts, the Free Southern Theater continued for more than a decade to mount large-scale productions, offer summer youth workshops, and produce original material. Much of this material was written by cofounder John O'Neal. With plays like *Our Lan'*, *When the Opportunity*

Scratches, Itch It (1974) and the most recent, *Don't Start Me to Talking or I'll Tell Everything I Know* (1980), the Free Southern Theater demonstrated its commitment to theater that distinguished between an audience to be served and a market to be exploited—theater free from the often restrictive aesthetics of the commercial. In the face of decreased financial support and new goals of John O'Neal and other central troupe members, the Free Southern Theater officially ceased operations in November 1985, when a traditional New Orleans funeral service was held to mark its demise.

Elizabeth Makowski
University of Mississippi

Thomas Dent, Richard Schechner, and Gilbert Moses, eds., *The Free Southern Theater by the Free Southern Theater* (1969); Geneviève Fabre, *Drumbeats, Masks, and Metaphor: Contemporary Afro-American Theatre* (1983); James Flannery, *Performing Arts Journal* (October 1985); John O'Neal, *Southern Exposure* (Spring 1981); *Times-Picayune* (27 October 1973; 31 October 1973; 2 November 1983; 6 November 1973); Mance Williams, *Black Theater in the 1960s and 1970s: A Historical Critical Analysis of the Movement* (1985). ☆

GAINES, ERNEST J.

(b. 1933) Writer.

Born in Oscar, near New Roads, La., Gaines lived in the plantation quarters and worked in the fields as a boy. Most of the old people were illiterate, and Augustine Jefferson, the crippled aunt who reared Gaines, encouraged him to read and write letters for them. This was his first literary apprenticeship and started him on a career of bridging the gap between the spoken and the written word. "I came up in a place that was oral," he explains, "we *talked* stories." He has characterized all his books as attempts to capture "the sound of my people talking."

As neither high schools nor libraries were open to blacks in Pt. Coupee Parish, he moved to California in 1948, joining his mother and stepfather in Vallejo, where he finished high school and attended two years of junior college. Homesick, he searched libraries for books about rural life, finding few positive images of blacks in the American South, but responding warmly to accounts of peasant life in the works of Russian writers, particularly Turgenev, and to the lyrics of country blues singers, especially Lightnin' Hopkins.

After serving in the army, he enrolled at San Francisco State College and was graduated in 1957. In 1958 he won a Wallace Stegner Creative Writing Fellowship for graduate study at Stanford.

Six short stories appeared in magazines before Gaines published *Catherine Carmier* (1964), a novel of color-caste discrimination within the black Creole community. *Of Love and Dust* followed (1967), a novel of the convict-lease system in Louisiana, then *Bloodline* (1968), a collection of five stories, including "A Long Day in November," also issued separately as a children's book, and *The Sky Is Gray*, televised in the National Endowment for the Humanities American Short Story series (1980). The novel Gaines characterized as his "folk autobiography," *The Autobiography of Miss Jane Pittman*, was published in 1971 and in 1974 was shown on CBS television in an ambitious production starring Cicely Tyson. *In My Father's House* (1978) is a grim novel exploring future roads open to black

Americans in the years after the civil rights movement. In *A Gathering of Old Men* (1983) Gaines returns to the tragicomic Jane Pittman world of strong, old, enduring, still feisty black plantation folk. Gaines is also a gifted photographer and his photographs of his childhood world in Louisiana have been published in *Callaloo*.

Black oral tradition, the Creole culture, and love between white and black characters are richly portrayed in the fiction of Ernest Gaines. Both black and white characters are treated with sympathy and understanding. Since 1982 Gaines has been Professor of English and Writer in Residence at the University of Southwestern Louisiana, dividing his time between Lafayette and San Francisco.

Patricia K. Rickels
University of Southwestern Louisiana

Michel Fabre, *Callaloo* (May 1978); Patricia K. Rickels, *Southwestern Review* (1979); Charles H. Rowell, *Southern Review* (July 1985). ☆

GREENSBORO SIT-IN

See LAW: / Greensboro Sit-in

HALEY, ALEX

(b. 1921) Writer.

Alexander Palmer Haley was born 11 August 1921 in Ithaca, N.Y. At the time, both of his parents were in graduate school—his mother, Bertha Palmer, at the Ithaca Conservatory of Music and his father, Simon, at Cornell University. When he was six weeks old, Alex and his mother moved to Henning, Tenn., where they lived at her family home (later rejoined by his father) until 1929.

Haley graduated from high school in Normal, Ala., at age 15, enrolled at Alcorn A&M College in Mississippi, and then transferred to Elizabeth City State Teachers College in North Carolina. After two years he left college and enlisted in the U.S. Coast Guard in 1939. He served initially as a mess boy aboard a cargo-ammunition ship in the southwest Pacific. He devoted much of his free time to reading, writing letters, and writing adventure stories. In 1949 the Coast Guard created for him the position of chief journalist, which he held until he retired from military service in 1959 to become a full-time writer.

Haley then moved to New York where he struggled for several years to become a successful writer. Occasionally, magazines would buy his stories, but often they would not. At one low point, Haley says, he had only 18 cents and two cans of sardines. The following day, however, a check for one of his stories arrived in the mail. He kept and framed the 18 cents and cans of sardines as a reminder of the perseverance and determination required for him to achieve the status of an independent writer. In 1962 *Playboy* magazine hired him to conduct a series of interviews. His first was with jazz trumpeter Miles Davis. A subsequent interview with Malcolm X led him

Alex Haley, best-selling author of* Roots, *1980s

to write *The Autobiography of Malcolm X* (1964), which became a best-seller.

Having established himself, Haley embarked upon a 12-year effort to trace the lineage of his mother's family. His search eventually took him to Gambia in West Africa, where his fourth great-grandfather, Kunte Kinte, had been born and then kidnapped in 1767 by slave traders en route to America. Combining fictional dialogue with the factual information he had uncovered, Haley wrote *Roots: The Saga of an American Family*. The novel, published in the fall of 1976, brought the author immediate fame.

By April 1977 nearly 2 million hardcover copies of *Roots* had been sold, a total that has since increased several times. For the novel, Haley received a Pulitzer Prize, a National Book Award, and numerous other honors. Haley's South in *Roots* is not a pleasant one for blacks as is Margaret Mitchell's in *Gone with the Wind*. It portrays instead the harsh aspects of slavery. For many blacks, this story of one family's ancestry captures the essence of their heritage in America.

Early in 1977 the ABC television network broadcast the story in an eight-episode miniseries, of which an estimated 130 million viewers watched at least one episode. A television sequel, *Roots: The Next Generations*, aired in 1979. Although the *Roots* programs had generated much interest in Haley's works, the TV series he created, *Palmerstown U.S.A.*, did not fare well, airing only briefly in 1980 and again in 1981.

See also MEDIA: / *Gone with the Wind*; *Roots*

Jessica Foy
Cooperstown Graduate Program
Cooperstown, New York

Robert Bain, Joseph M. Flora, and Louis D. Rubin, Jr., eds., *Southern Writers: A Biographical Dictionary* (1979); Hans J. Massaquoi, *Ebony* (April 1977); Charles Moritz, ed., *Current Biography* (1977). ☆

HAMER, FANNIE LOU

(1917–1977) Civil rights activist.

Fannie Lou Townsend Hamer was the last of 20 children born to Jim and Ella Townsend, sharecroppers in Montgomery County, Miss. The family moved two years after her birth to Sunflower County, where she worked in the cotton fields from the age of six and attended public school through junior high. In 1945 she married Perry Hamer, a tractor driver on the W. D. Marlon plantation located four miles east of Ruleville. She labored as a field hand on the Marlon plantation until it was discovered that she could read and write. Then she was promoted to timekeeper. She was fired in 1962 because she had attempted to register to vote. Forced to leave the plantation, she received shelter in the home of William Tucker in Ruleville, but had to flee from there after the house was attacked and riddled with bullets.

In 1963 she passed the Mississippi literacy test and became a registered voter. She then became a field secretary for the Student Nonviolent Coordinating Committee, organizing voter registration campaigns and working to obtain welfare and other benefits for underprivileged black families. While returning by bus from a voter registration workshop, she was arrested and severely beaten for attempting to use the restroom in a bus station in Winona. Meanwhile, she had worked with the National Council of Churches in creating Delta Ministry, an extensive community development program in Mississippi.

Because the regular Democratic party of Mississippi refused to accept black members, Hamer joined with black and white protesters in 1964 to form the Mississippi Freedom Democratic party (MFDP). She was a member that year of the MFDP delegation that challenged the seating of the regular Mississippi delegation to the National Democratic Convention, and in her testimony before the credentials committee she vividly described the brutal reprisals she and other blacks had suffered in Mississippi because of their efforts to vote and to exercise other civil rights. Her testimony was dramatically presented to the nation by television. Thereafter, she was in great demand, both as a speaker and as a performer of civil rights songs and spirituals.

The MFDP was unsuccessful in replacing the regular Democratic delegation in 1964, but that convention pledged that no delegation that barred blacks would be seated in future conventions. Hamer became a member of the delegation of the Mississippi Loyalist Democratic party (the successor of MFDP), which unseated Mississippi's regular delegation at the National Democratic Convention. Meanwhile, in 1964 she had attempted to run as the MFDP candidate for the U.S. House of Representatives from Mississippi's Second Congressional District, but her name was not allowed on the ballot. Consequently, she, along with Victoria Gray and Annie Devine, on 4 January 1965, challenged the entire Mississippi delegation in the House of Representatives as unrepresentative of the people of the state. Their challenge failed.

In 1965 Hamer was the plaintiff in a suit that resulted in the U.S. Fifth Circuit of Appeals' setting aside the local elections in Sunflower and Moorhead counties because blacks had not been allowed to vote. She served on the Democratic National Committee from 1968 to 1971. In 1969 she founded and became vice president of Freedom Farms Corporation, a nonprofit venture designed to provide social services, to help needy black and white families produce food, to promote minority business opportunities, and to provide scholarships. She became chairperson of the board of directors of Fannie Lou Hamer Day Care Center founded in Ruleville by the National Council of Negro Women in 1970. She also served as a director of the Sunflower County Day Care and Family Service and the Garment Manufacturing Plant, as chairperson of the Sunflower County Voter's League, as a member of the policy council of the National Women's Political Caucus, as a trustee of the Martin Luther King Center for Social Change, and as a member of the state executive committee of the United Democratic party of Mississippi.

Fannie Lou Hamer received honorary degrees from Tougaloo College, Shaw University, Morehouse College, Columbia College, and Howard University. She also received the Mary Church Terrell Award from Delta Sigma Theta Sorority and the Paul Robeson Award from Alpha Phi Alpha Fraternity. In 1976 the mayor of Ruleville declared a Fannie Lou Hamer Day. She died of cancer in Mound Bayou Hospital the following March 14.

Clifton H. Johnson
Amistad Research Center
New Orleans, Louisiana

Black Enterprise (May 1977); John Egerton, *Progressive* (May 1977); Fannie Lou Hamer Papers, Amistad Research Center, New Orleans, Louisiana; Susan Johnson, *The Black Law Journal* (Summer 1972); June Jordan, *Fannie Lou Hamer* (1972); *Never Turn Back: The Life of Fannie Lou Hamer* (Rediscovery Productions film, 1983); *Sojourners* (December 1982); C. J. Wilson, *New South* (Spring 1973). ☆

HANCOCK, GORDON BLAINE

(1884–1970) Educator and social activist.

Gordon Blaine Hancock, born in Greenwood County, S.C., of exslave parents, attended Benedict College (B.A. 1911, B.D. 1912), Colgate University (B.A. 1919, B.D. 1920), and Harvard University (M.A. 1921). Seneca (South Carolina) Institute principal (1912–18), Virginia Union University professor (1921–52), Richmond's Moore Street Baptist Church pastor (1925–63), and Associated Negro Press columnist (1929–68), he became probably the most peripatetic and popular black spokesman in the Old Dominion and the Upper South during the three decades before the Supreme Court's *Brown* decision in 1954. A politically conscious educator, Hancock is significant as a symbol of black aspiration and dilemma.

Hancock's generation confronted the problem of ending black exclusion and initiating integration without abandoning cultural identity or sacrificing values of self-help and solidarity. Hancock, who offered one of the first courses in race relations at a southern school, merged accommodation and protest ideologies. Doubting that poverty and racism ever would be eliminated through mere militancy, he argued that blacks must seek to advance themselves and try to win white support by learning, saving, and voting. His dual message of autonomous development and interracial cooperation appeared weekly in 114 black newspapers. Throughout the Great Depression and the New Deal, he delivered speeches entitled "Back to the Farm," "Double Duty Dollar," and "Hold Your Job" to hundreds of church, civic, and college groups. Annoyed by what they called his "constant yapping," which allegedly exaggerated racial suffering, critics dubbed Hancock the "Gloomy Dean." Even so, he directed the 1942 Durham conference of black leaders whose far-reaching statement inspired the Southern Regional Council. Disappointed by that body's reluctance to condemn segregation, but less open about it (for fear of alienating liberals) than his fellow educator Benjamin E. Mays, the dean declared: "Like you, I am opposed to further research, and like you I am looking and pressing for action. And, if the Southern Regional Council cannot give this action, like you I want to see it pass. However, let's give it a good chance." After 1954, knowing well the pitfalls of interracialism, the old professor deplored blacks' pursuit of desegregation without a self-help strategy. Aged, infirm, and isolated, unlike the highly visible Mays, he died publicly unheralded.

See also SOCIAL CLASS: / Southern Regional Council

Raymond Gavins
Duke University

Raymond Gavins, *Perils and Prospects of Southern Black Leadership* (1977), *Virginia Magazine of History and Biography* (October 1977). ☆

HURSTON, ZORA NEALE

(1901?–1960) Writer and folklorist.

Born either in 1891 or 1901—the latter is normally given as the date of birth but recent studies suggest an earlier date—in the all-black town of Eatonville, Fla., Hurston became a distinguished novelist, folklorist, and anthropologist. She was next to the youngest of eight children, born the daughter of a Baptist minister who was mayor of Eatonville. Her mother died when Hurston was nine, and she left home at 14 to join a traveling show. She later attended Howard University, where she studied under Alain Locke and Lorenzo Dow Turner, and she earned an A.B. degree from Barnard College in 1928, working with Franz Boas. She became a well-known figure among the New York intellectuals of the Harlem Renaissance in the mid-1920s and then devoted the years 1927 to 1932 to field research in Florida, Alabama, Louisiana, and the Bahamas. *Mules and Men* (1935) was a collection of black music, games, oral lore, and religious practices. *Tell My Horse* (1938) was a similar collection of folklore from Jamaica and Haiti.

Hurston published four novels—*Jonah's Gourd Vine* (1934), *Their Eyes Were Watching God* (1937), *Moses, Man of the Mountain* (1939), and *Seraph on the Sewanee* (1948). Her autobiography, *Dust Tracks on a Road*, appeared in 1948. Married and divorced twice, she worked for the WPA Federal Theatre project in New York (1935–36) and for the Federal Writers' Project in Florida (1938). She taught briefly at Bethune-Cookman College in Daytona Beach, Fla. (1934), and at North Carolina College in Durham (1939), and she received Rosenwald and Guggenheim fellowships (1934, 1936–37).

Hurston was noteworthy for her portrayal of the strength of black life in the South. In her essay "The Pet Negro System," she assured her readers that not all black southerners fit the illiterate sharecropper stereotype fostered by the northern media. She pointed to the seldom-noted black professionals who, like herself, remained in the South because they liked some things about it. Most educated blacks, Hurston insisted, preferred not to live up North because they came to realize that there was "segregation and discrimination up there, too, with none of the human touches of the South." One of the "human touches" to which Hurston referred was the "pet Negro system" itself, a southern practice that afforded special privileges to blacks who met standards set by their white benefactors. The system survived, she said, because it reinforced the white southerner's sense of superiority. Clearly, it was not a desirable substitute for social, economic, and political equality, but Hurston's portrayal of the system indicated her affirmative attitude toward the region, despite its dubious customs.

Hurston had faith in individual initiative, confidence in the strength of black culture, and strong trust in the ultimate goodwill of southern white people, all of which influenced her perceptions of significant racial issues. When she saw blacks suffering hardships, she refused to acknowledge that racism was a major contributing factor, probably because she never let racism stop her. Hurston's biographer, Robert E. Hemenway, notes that "in her later life she came to interpret all attempts to emphasize black suffering . . . as the politics of deprivation, implying a tragedy of color in Afro-American life."

After working for years as a maid in

Miami, Hurston suffered a stroke in early 1959 and, alone and indigent, died in the Saint Lucie County Welfare Home, Fort Pierce, Fla., 28 January 1960. Alice Walker has led a recent "rediscovery" of Hurston, whose works have become inspiration for black women writers.

See also LITERATURE: / Walker, Alice

Elvin Holt
University of Kentucky

Robert E. Hemenway, *Zora Neale Hurston: A Literary Biography* (1977); Zora Neale Hurston, *I Love Myself*, ed. Alice Walker (1979); Alice Walker, *In Search of Our Mothers' Gardens* (1983). ☆

JACKSON, JESSE

(b. 1941) Civil rights activist, minister, politician.

Called "the most famous Black man in America today" by one admiring biographer, a position confirmed by the more scientific conclusions of major national polls, Jesse Louis Jackson was born 8 October 1941 in Greenville, S.C. His mother was Helen Burns, and his father was Noah Louis Robinson, to whom his mother was never married. Charles Henry Jackson became the husband of Jesse's mother, and young Jackson's stepfather provided him with a comfortable home and stable family life.

Jackson grew up in Greenville, where he was sensitive to the racism and segregation of the times and exhibited an inquisitive mind, street savvy, athletic ability, and discipline. He left the University of Illinois after one year when he was told by coaches that a black man could not play quarterback, and he turned down a professional baseball contract when he was offered less than a white counterpart. He became active in the sit-in demonstrations organized by the Congress of Racial Equality (CORE) in Greensboro, N.C., where he had come to enter all-black North Carolina A & T University on a football scholarship. At A & T, he was a star quarterback, honor student, student body president, and fraternity leader. He was elected president of the North Carolina Inter-Collegiate Council on Human Rights, and by his senior year assumed broader responsibilities as the southeastern field director of CORE. Jackson accepted a Rockefeller scholarship to the Chicago Theological Seminary, having decided that the pulpit was a better platform than the courtroom to realize his developing ambitions and commitments.

Jackson's prominence in the civil rights movement is tied to his apprenticeship under Dr. Martin Luther King, Jr. Jackson met King while in college, but he did not join the staff of the Southern Christian Leadership Conference (SCLC) until 1965, helping to organize the Selma marches and demonstrations just prior to King's Chicago campaign. King later appointed Jackson as director of SCLC's Operation Breadbasket, an economic development coalition of ministers and business people using such direct action tactics as boycotts and mass demonstrations.

The assassination of King on 4 April 1968 led Jackson to assume national leadership, an opportunity he seized with vigor. Jackson emerged as the aggressive spokesperson of a movement in disarray. Operation Breadbasket moved away from its parent organization, SCLC, and proclaimed itself the leading civil rights organization in the nation.

After a flurry of boycotts in which "covenants"—agreements to provide jobs, develop businesses, place deposits in black banks, and advertise in the black media—were signed, Operation Breadbasket was renamed Operation PUSH in December 1971. Jackson's tactics were reminiscent of the "Buy Black Campaign" and the "Don't Buy Where You Can't Work" protests of the 1930s in Chicago and other cities.

Jesse Jackson's greatest achievement was his 1984 presidential campaign. Jackson had run for mayor of Chicago in 1971 and had been active in such national political forums as the National Black Political Assembly in 1972 and 1973. He showed himself to be knowledgeable on a wide range of issues, articulate in televised debates, and adept in seizing media attention with such feats as his extrication of a black navy pilot from Syria. Jackson galvanized black community sentiment, and the results were quite unexpected. With a very small campaign war chest, Jackson gathered almost 20 percent of the vote in the Democratic primaries and won 465.5 convention votes. More important, his campaign spurred voter registration, stirred local debate and activity, and challenged Democratic party rules that seemed unfair. His achievement led to an invitation to deliver a keynote to the Democratic National Convention in San Francisco. Looking toward the 1988 campaign, Jackson sought to fashion his "rainbow coalition" into a more viable organization.

Ronald Bailey
University of Mississippi

Rod Bush, ed., *The New Black Vote: Politics and Power in Four American Cities* (1984); Adolph Reed, Jr., *The Jesse Jackson Phenomenon: The Crisis of Purpose in Afro-American Politics* (1986); Barbara A. Reynolds, *Jesse Jackson: America's David* (1985); Hanes Walton, *Invisible Politics: Black Political Behavior* (1986). ☆

JIM CROW

This term used to describe Afro-Americans probably originated in 19th-century minstrelsy. It has also been suggested that the term referred to a slave trader or an escaped slave, but the most generally accepted explanation credits a white minstrel entertainer, Thomas "Daddy" Rice, with popularizing the term. He performed a song-and-dance routine called "Jump Jim Crow" beginning in 1828. With face blackened from burnt cork and dressed in the rags of a beggar, Rice skipped on stage doing a shuffling dance, comically singing "I jump jis' so/ An' ev'y time I turn about I jump Jim Crow." He cited an old Louisville slave belonging to a Mr. Crow as the inspiration for the act, having observed him entertain other workers in a livery stable. By the late 1830s Rice had made "Jim Crow" a part of his promotional name. He helped to put the blackface character into American entertainment and introduced a term to the language.

The story of the term *Jim Crow* is apparently more complicated than this traditional explanation of its origins. Jim Crow was probably first used outside of minstrelsy, to describe segregated facilities in the North. Mitford M. Mathews in *A Dictionary of Americanisms* (1951) cites a reference to a separate railroad car for blacks in Massachusetts in 1841, and Mathews also notes an 1842 item from *The Liberator* referring

Sign at a bus station, Rome, Georgia, 1953

to the "negro pew" and the "Jim Crow car." Leon Litwack in *North of Slavery* (1961) used the term to describe segregated facilities in the pre–Civil War North.

In the late 19th century the name *Jim Crow* took on a new meaning, symbolizing the southern system of legal segregation that emerged after the Civil War. "Jim Crow law" first appeared in the *Dictionary of American English* in 1904, but laws requiring racial segregation had appeared briefly in the South during Reconstruction. They had generally disappeared by 1868, although the persistent custom of segregation did not disappear. Tennessee passed a Jim Crow statute in 1875, and increasingly in the following years blacks and whites were segregated throughout the South on trains, streetcars, steamboats, and port facilities. In the mid-1880s Afro-Americans were barred from white hotels, restaurants, barber and beauty shops, and theaters. By 1885 most states in the South were legally mandating segregated schools. The state constitutional reforms in Mississippi in 1890 and South Carolina in 1895 codified segregation laws, and other southern states soon followed. In 1896 the U.S. Supreme Court upheld the Jim Crow "separate-but-equal" principle in *Plessy* v. *Ferguson.*

These Jim Crow segregation laws were, according to historian C. Vann Woodward, "the public symbols and constant reminders" of the Afro-American's inferior position in the South. "That code lent the sanction of law to a racial ostracism that extended to churches and schools, to housing and jobs, to eating and drinking," concluded Woodward. It separated the races in sport and recreational activities, on all forms of public transportation, in prisons, asylums, orphanages, hospitals, and even in funeral homes and cemeteries. The term *Jim Crow* came to stand for racial segregation and was physically embodied in separate water fountains, eating places, bathrooms, Bibles in courtrooms, and pervasive signs stating "Colored" and "White" that gave the term a concrete meaning for southerners.

See also LAW: / *Plessy* v. *Ferguson*

Charles Reagan Wilson
University of Mississippi

Robert C. Toll, *Blacking Up: The Minstrel Show In Nineteenth-Century America* (1974); William L. Van DeBurg, *Slavery and Race in Popular Culture* (1984); C. Vann Woodward, *The Strange Career of Jim Crow* (1955, 3d ed. 1974). ☆

JOHNSON, CHARLES S.

(1893–1956) Sociologist.

Johnson successfully combined research on southern black life with leadership in the field of race relations. Under Johnson's direction (1928–47) the Fisk University Department of Social Sciences became the focal point for empirical research on the black South. Black scholars beginning with W. E. B. Du Bois made attempts to create a comprehensive body of objective research, but Johnson was the first black academic to secure the funding necessary to undertake ambitious projects. Johnson's vision and resources attracted and gave valuable experience to many young black social scientists including E. Franklin Frazier, Horace Mann Bond, and John Hope Franklin. The recognition given the studies of Johnson and his associates helped to discredit the belief that blacks were unable to undertake objective, scientific research. At the same time, the presence of respected white social scientists such as Robert Park, Eli Marks, and Kenneth Little on the Fisk faculty provided a model of interracial cooperation and reinforced the legitimacy of the Fisk approach to both scholarship and race relations.

Johnson received his sociological training at the University of Chicago (1917–22) where his methods were deeply influenced by the work of Robert Park. However, the fundamental assumption that undergirds Johnson's analysis, and is most fully stated in *The Negro in American Civilization* (1930), was his belief that the problems of blacks were demonstrably socioeconomic and historical in origin and not due to any inherent racial difference. As a consequence of this belief Johnson felt that black status would improve only with the removal of social, economic, and psychological obstacles.

A native southerner who spent only one decade outside the South, Johnson was especially sympathetic to the plight of rural blacks. He used an ethnographic approach to reveal both the isolation and the integrity of the rural black. Among the first to consider the impact of segregation and poverty upon black personality development, Johnson proposed the concept of the "folk Negro" as an alternative to the caste theory of southern race relations. A seemingly indefatigable author, editor, and contributor, Johnson in his most original and enduring contributions, *Shadow of the Plantation* (1934) and *Growing up in the Black Belt* (1941), deftly weaves the striking testimony of rural blacks.

In the history of southern race relations Johnson's only peer in terms of longevity and white confidence was Booker T. Washington. Johnson's nonpolemical approach, which did not sanction segregation, was endorsed and financially supported by the philanthropic and social welfare community beginning with his tenure as director of research and editor of *Opportunity* magazine for the National Urban League (1921–28). Johnson worked closely for three decades with white southern moderates such as Will W. Alexander, Willis Duke Weatherford, and Howard W. Odum to institutionalize the notion of interracial cooperation within the South, and he was the first black to be elected president of the Southern Sociological Society (1945). After he became president of Fisk University (1946–56), Johnson was increasingly called upon to apply his techniques for decreasing racial tensions to international situations, serving as delegate to UNESCO committees and on an American team of advisors on the postwar reorganization of Japan's educational system. But after the 1954 Supreme Court school desegregation decision Johnson was bitterly disappointed in the failure of white southern moderates to forcefully support the early civil rights movement. Shortly before his death in 1956 Johnson made his first public repudiation of white southern racial attitudes, characterizing the southern way of life as antidemocratic and at odds with the national interest.

See also EDUCATION: / Fisk University; Odum, Howard W.

Francille Rusan Wilson
University of Michigan

Patrick Gilpin, "Charles S. Johnson: An Intellectual Biography" (Ph.D. dissertation, Vanderbilt University, 1973); Charles S. Johnson, *New York Times Magazine* (23 September 1956); Richard Robbins, *Journal of Social and Behavioral Sciences* (Fall/Winter 1971–72); Preston Valien, *Sociology and Social Research* (March/April 1958). ☆

JOHNSON, JAMES WELDON

(1871–1938) Writer, civil rights leader, diplomat.

To James Weldon Johnson writing was a serious but secondary interest. Johnson's main concern was the NAACP, and he served from 1916 until 1930 as its field secretary. Johnson also had other interests and even a variety of careers.

Born in 1871 in Jacksonville, Fla., he was the principal of a primary school there. He was the founder of *The Daily American*, the first black daily newsletter, and was admitted to the Florida bar in 1897. Johnson and his brother, Rosamond, wrote successful Broadway musicals; he served as consul to Venezuela and Nicaragua during the administrations of Presidents Roosevelt and Taft. He edited *The Book of American Negro Poetry* (1922) and *The Book of American Negro Spirituals* (with Rosamond, in 1925), created the seven black sermons in verse that make up *God's Trombones* (1927), and wrote his autobiography, *Along This Way* (1933). He also authored *The Autobiography of an Ex-Coloured Man* (1912). In 1930 Johnson was named the Adam K. Spence Professor of Creative Literature at Fisk University, a position he held until his death in 1938.

James Weldon Johnson drew upon both black folklore and his own experiences as a southern black for the subject matter of his writing. Johnson collected spirituals and in *God's Trombones* clearly suggests southern black church speech through his reproduction of the southern black minister's characteristic rhetorical devices—the repetitions, the alliterations, the pauses, the echoes from the King James Bible, and the folk images. Johnson's ability to create the effect of dialect is one of his greatest skills as an artist.

Johnson's fiction evidences a similar skill. Like earlier black and white southern writers—Cable, Twain, Chesnutt—Johnson dramatized the plight of the mulatto. The central issue confronting the hero of *The Autobiography of an Ex-Coloured Man* is his identity in a society where racial caste determines one's identity. In spirit and in form, however, Johnson's work is much closer to Ellison's *Invisible Man* than it is to anything that preceded it. Ellison's conceit of a narrator who is invisible is a logical extension of Johnson's conceit of a narrator who passes for white. Both chronologically and artistically Johnson stands between earlier writers such as Chesnutt, who were beginning to create a black voice, and later writers, such as Ellison, who fully mastered their instrument.

See also EDUCATION: Fisk University; LITERATURE: / Ellison, Ralph

Ladell Payne
Randolph-Macon College

M. Thomas Inge, Maurice Duke, and Jackson R. Bryer, eds., *Black American Writers: Bibliographical Essays*, vol. 1 (1978); Eugene Levy, *James Weldon Johnson: Black Leader, Black Voice* (1973); W. Augustus Low and Virgil A. Clift, eds., *of Black America* (1981). ☆

JOHNSON, ROBERT

(1912–1938) Blues singer.

Robert Johnson was the most celebrated and legendary of the blues artists who emerged from the Mississippi Delta prior to World War II. He was born near Hazelhurst, Miss., in 1912 and raised at a sharecroppers' settlement called Commerce. While still a youngster, he was drawn to the blues he had heard around him, learning to play the music on a harmonica and then a guitar. While still in his teens, he left home to become an itinerant bluesman, traveling throughout the Delta and then up the Mississippi River to Helena, Ark., Saint Louis, Mo., and finally to Chicago, Ill. In the mid-1930s he also traveled to Dallas and San Antonio, Tex., where he made a series of 29 blues recordings that were his legacy to the blues.

Johnson's blues repertoire has proved to be one of the most provocative in the entire history of the music. He was not only a gifted musician, but also a visionary poet. His vision of Afro-American life in the Delta is a haunting one. Songs like "Hellhound on My Trail" and "Me and the Devil Blues" point to his fatalistic assessment of the human condition and the supernatural powers in control of that condition. He saw no way out for blues musicians like himself. Such a choice of vocations necessitated making a pact with the forces of darkness because blues was the Devil's music.

The themes that dominated the landscape of Robert Johnson's blues were erotic, unrequited love, the urge to constantly move and explore new places, and the omnipotent powers of the supernatural. "Love in Vain" was his masterpiece on unrequited love; it was a theme he was obsessed with, appearing in about one-third of his songs. Erotic love was his counterpoint to heartbreak, and in songs like "Traveling Riverside Blues" he portrayed it with graphic and savory delight. Among his best-known travel songs were "Dust My Broom," "Rambling on My Mind," and "Walkin' Blues." The recurring message in these pieces was epitomized in the line—"Travel on poor Bob, just can't turn you 'round."

Robert Johnson's restless spirit reflected the changing social consciousness of the times, especially among the rural black population living in the South. Paradoxically, he was always drawn back to the Delta region he was so obsessed with leaving until, as fate would have it, he was tragically poisoned to death in a Greenwood, Miss., juke joint in 1938. He was in his twenties when he died, and with his passing the legend of Robert Johnson was born. Today he is considered one of the most popular and mysterious bluesmen of the century.

See also ENVIRONMENT: / Delta

Bill Barlow
Howard University

Samuel Charters, *Robert Johnson* (1973); Alan Greenburg, *Love in Vain: The Life and*

Legend of Robert Johnson (1983); Robert Palmer, *Deep Blues* (1981); *Robert Johnson: King of the Delta Blues*, vols. I (CL 1654) and II (C30034), Columbia Records. ☆

JUNETEENTH

Juneteenth is the popular name among black people in Texas for their emancipation day, which they celebrate on 19 June. On that day in 1865 Major General Gordon Granger officially announced the freedom of slaves when he arrived at Galveston to command the District of Texas following the Civil War.

Three black folktales provide other explanations of the date. In one version Texas landowners refused to announce emancipation until the 1865 harvest had been gathered by the slaves. According to a second story, a black man journeyed by mule fromn Washington to Texas and arrived in June 1865 with word of the abolition of slavery. The other legend has the end of slavery declared as late as June because an earlier messenger was killed on the way to Texas.

The celebration of 19 June as emancipation day spread to the neighboring states of Louisiana, Arkansas, and Oklahoma, and later to California as black Texans migrated west. It has appeared occasionally in Alabama and Florida, also as a result of migration.

Large celebrations began in 1866 and continued to be held regularly into the early 20th century, although blacks in some Texas towns honored emancipation on 1 January or 4 July—days favored in some other states. Observations of Juneteenth declined in the 1940s during World War II but revived with 70,000 black people on the Texas State Fair grounds at Dallas during 1950. As school desegregation and the civil rights movement focused attention on the expansion of freedom in the late 1950s and early 1960s, Juneteenth celebrations declined again, although small towns still observed Texas's emancipation day. In the 1970s Juneteenth was revived in some communities, especially after two black members convinced the Texas Legislature to declare Juneteenth an unofficial "holiday of significance . . . particularly to the blacks of Texas."

Typical celebrations over the years included parades, picnics, baseball games or other competitive contests, speeches on freedom and future goals, and dances. Leaders in the black community normally organized the events, although occasionally in the 20th century a business or a black fraternal group assumed that role.

Alwyn Barr
Texas Tech University

Ebony (June 1951); Wendy Watriss, *Southern Exposure* (Number 1, 1977); William Wiggins, " 'Free at Last!': A Study of Afro-American Emancipation Day Celebrations," (Ph.D. dissertation, Indiana University, 1974). ☆

KING, MARTIN LUTHER, JR.

(1929–1968) Minister and civil rights leader.

Born on 15 January 1929 in Atlanta, Ga., Martin Luther King, Jr., came to symbolize the black freedom struggle that dominated the South from 1955 to 1968. He attended Morehouse College and graduated from Crozer Theological Seminary in June 1951. Emerging at the age of 27 as the principal leader of the Montgomery, Ala., bus boycott that initiated a new era of nonviolent protest against racial discrimination, King brought a strong family heritage in the Baptist church and excellent graduate training in philosophy and theology at Boston University to his role as spokesman for a movement that in little more than a decade transformed southern life.

In the early years of his public career King stressed two beliefs: that black southerners had to employ mass action as well as lawsuits if they were to win their constitutional rights as American citizens and that many white southerners would respond positively once they were shown that Christian morality supported the goals of the civil rights cause. The tactics of "direct action" led to protest efforts such as the "sit-ins" of 1960, the Freedom Ride of 1961, and the community-based demonstration campaigns that King's Southern Christian Leadership Conference mounted in Albany, Ga., Birmingham, Ala., St. Augustine, Fla., and Selma, Ala., in the years 1962–65. King's early optimism about the white South, and especially the white church, all but vanished as confrontation after confrontation demonstrated that few white southerners would stand up for racial justice.

Martin Luther King, Jr., as portrayed on a paper fan produced by the Dillion Funeral Homes and Burial Association, Leland, Vicksburg, Greenville, Indianola, and Cleveland, Mississippi, 1968

King's 1963 "I Have A Dream" oration at the March on Washington and his 1964 receipt of the Nobel Peace Prize catapulted him to national and international fame at much the same time that civil rights protests were leading the federal government to enact the landmark Civil Rights Act of 1964 and Voting Rights Act of 1965. Achievement of these milestones and realization of their limitations led King to focus increasingly on the serious problems of his country and world that had not been ameliorated by those racial reform statutes: poverty and economic powerlessness that oppressed many white as well as black Americans, North as well as South; militarism and materialism that led to international violence and economic imperialism. King's desire to attack the former set of problems led him to mount a largely unsuccessful attack upon economic injustice in Chicago's ghettos in 1966; his realization of the need to speak out against international violence and oppression led him in 1967 to denounce America's involvement in Vietnam.

Before his murder, King was articulating a vision far distant from that with which he had begun. America, and the South, required thoroughgoing economic and structural change, and not merely the elimination of racial discrimination, if real human justice were to be attained. That struggle for a more just society would have to employ coercive and disruptive tactics, not simply persuasive ones, for the preceding twelve years had shown that white America was far less interested in social justice than King had imagined in 1956. At the time of his assassination in Memphis on 4 April 1968, Martin Luther King, Jr., believed that the road ahead was still far longer than the road he himself had traveled. As of 1986 the Martin Luther King, Jr., Papers Project, directed by Clayborne Carson at Stanford University, was well underway. The goal of the 15-year project is publication of 12 annotated volumes of selections from the broad range of King's writings, many of which will be available to the public for the first time. Plans are for the first volume to be available in 1990. In January 1986 King's birthday was declared a national holiday, the first such tribute to a black American.

David J. Garrow
City College of New York
CUNY Graduate Center

Gaynelle Evans, *Chronicle of Higher Education* (3 September 1986); David J. Garrow, *Bearing the Cross: Martin Luther King, Jr., and the Southern Christian Leadership Conference, 1955–1968* (1986); Martin Luther King, Jr., *Where Do We Go From Here: Chaos or Community?* (1967); David L. Lewis, *King: A Critical Biography* (1970); Stephen B. Oates, *Let the Trumpet Sound: The Life of Martin Luther King, Jr.* (1982); Kenneth L. Smith and Ira G. Zepp, Jr., *Search for the Beloved Community: The Thinking of Martin Luther King, Jr.* (1974). ☆

LYNCH, JOHN ROY

(1847–1939) Politician and lawyer.

Lynch was born on 10 September 1847 in Concordia Parish, La., the son of an Irishman, Patrick Lynch, and a slave, Catherine White. His father bought and sought to free his whole family, but death and the treachery of a friend intervened, so that Lynch was not freed until 1863 by the Union army in Natchez. Lynch was self-educated, except for four months of formal schooling in 1866. He early became active as a Republican, and in 1869 Governor Adelbert Ames appointed him a justice of the peace. That same year Lynch was elected to the Mississippi House of Representatives. Reelected in 1871, Lynch was chosen as speaker of the House, which he ruled, according to a unanimously passed resolution, "with becoming dignity, with uniform courtesy and impartiality, and with marked ability." The occasion of the resolution was Lynch's departure from the Mississippi House for the U.S. House of Representatives, where he took his seat in December 1873, after handily defeating the Democratic candidate. In all, he served three terms, though his third term was cut short by the necessity of having to contest the election of his Democratic opponent; Lynch was finally declared the winner.

Following defeat for reelection in 1882, Lynch went home to Adams County to run his plantation. Still active as a Republican, he was a delegate to the Republican national conventions of 1884, 1888, 1892, and 1900; earlier, in 1872, while a member of the Mississippi House, he was a delegate to the Republican convention of that year. Democrat Grover Cleveland offered Lynch a minor appointive office, which he turned down; but in 1889 he accepted from Republican President Benjamin Harrison the position of fourth auditor of the Treasury and served until the return of Democrats to national power in 1893.

About this time Lynch began the study of law, and in 1896 he was admitted to the Mississippi bar. From 1893 till 1896, though, Lynch largely busied himself with his Adams County plantation and with real estate speculation in Natchez. From 1896 to 1898 he practiced law in Mississippi and in Washington, D.C., with the firm of Robert H. Terrell. With the outbreak of the Spanish American War in 1898, Republican President William McKinley appointed Lynch as a paymaster of volunteer forces, with the rank of major; in 1901 he was appointed to the same position and rank in the regular army, in which he served till 1911, when he retired.

Lynch then settled in Chicago, where he practiced law and traded in real estate. In 1913 he published his *Facts of Reconstruction*, which is commonly regarded as the best account of Reconstruction by a black participant. His last years were spent writing *Reminiscences of an Active Life*, which was not published till 1970, under the editorship of John Hope Franklin. Lynch was married twice. His 1884 marriage to Ella Somerville, by whom he had one daughter, ended in divorce, and in 1911 he married Cora Williams, who survived him.

Charles E. Wynes
University of Georgia

John Hope Franklin, ed., *Reminiscences of an Active Life: The Autobiography of John Roy Lynch* (1970). ☆

MARDI GRAS INDIANS

The Mardi Gras Indians have the richest of folk rituals associated with Carnival in New Orleans. Groups of blacks, mostly from impoverished neighborhoods, fashion Indian costumes and parade through the streets on Mardi Gras, on the St. Joseph's Day feast on March 19, and in recent years on "Super Sunday," which falls shortly before the late April Jazz and Heritage Festival. For weeks before Mardi Gras the tribes meet in neighborhood bars to rehearse the chants sung on Carnival Day.

The earliest English language reference to the Indians is found in a memoir by Elise Kirsch, who described "a band of men (about 60) desguised as Indians . . . shouting and screaming war hoops." The Mardi Gras mentioned is apparently 1883, which coincides with the time frame fixed by the most reliable informant of the oral tradition, Allison "Tuddy" Montana, chief of the Yellow Pocahontas. Montana's granduncle, a plasterer named Becate Batiste, founded the tribe known as Creole Wild West in the early 1880s. The tribe eventually moved to another neighborhood across town, and the Yellow Pocahontas took its place in the downtown Seventh Ward. Since then tribes have come and gone, but a nucleus of about a dozen gathers annually. They have names such as the Ninth Ward Hunters, Golden Blades, Wild Squatoolas, Black Eagles, White Eagles, and the Red, White, and Blues. Afro-Caribbean dance steps and hand percussions among participants meld with the Indian persona. Similar rituals have long flourished in the carnivals of Haiti, Trinidad, and Brazil.

Until the Depression, tribes often fought with each other and with policemen; however, today's competition is ritualized. Costume making is a point of distinction among the Indians. The costumes are resplendent with billowing os-

The Wild Tchoupitoulas, in Les Blank's film* Always for Pleasure, *(1978)

trich plumes, feathers, beaded vests, and knee pads. Now costumes are usually made each year.

Each tribe is led by a Big Chief, and below him are other chiefs. Women of a Big Chief's entourage in this preponderantly masculine tradition are called Queens. The brave who scouts ahead for each tribe is called Spy Boy. Flag Boy carries the tribal pendant.

In the 1970s street chants moved from the streets into recording studios. Jazz composer Wilson Turbinton arranged the 1973 *Wild Magnolias* LP (Polydor), while *The Wild Tchoupitoulas* (1976, Island) was a collaboration of the Meters, the Neville Brothers, and their uncle, George Landry, who as Big Chief Jolley led the tribe. Landry's warm vocals are the heartbeat of the disc. In addition, two documentaries feature the Wild Tchoupitoulas, *Always for Pleasure* (Les Blank, Flower Films, 1978) and *Up From the Cradle of Jazz* (Davis Frentz, director, Jason Berry and Jonathan Foose, distributors, 1980).

Jason Berry
New Orleans, Louisiana

Jason Berry, Jonathan Foose, and Tad Jones, *Up from the Cradle of Jazz: New Orleans Music since World War II* (1987). ☆

MASON, CHARLES HARRISON

(1866–1961) Minister.

Mason, son of Jerry and Elisa Mason, was born 8 September 1866 on Prior Farm, near Memphis, Tenn. His early education was obtained in the public schools of Memphis, though his attendance at school was infrequent. His major educational experiences, primarily religious, were provided by his mother, replicating her own experiences that followed her conversion to Christianity during the period of American slavery. These experiences were augmented by teachings she received in the Missionary Baptist Church, of which she and her husband were members.

In November of 1878, when Mason was 12 years old, the family moved to Plumersville, Ark., where Mason's education continued in the context of a religious home. A prolonged and intense fever overtook him in 1880, and following a healing experience in September of that year, he was converted and later baptized by his brother, I. S. Nelson, pastor of Mt. Olive Missionary Baptist Church, located near Plumersville.

Mason continued in faithful service in the Baptist church as a layman until 1893, when, at Preston, Ark., he preached his first sermon, which attracted many in attendance to his beliefs. To prepare himself for the ministry, on 1 November of that year he entered Arkansas Baptist College at Little Rock, remaining there for only three months before he left to become a traveling evangelist. In this capacity, he met in 1895 with Charles Price Jones of Jackson, Miss., J. A. Jeter of Little Rock, Ark., and Walter S. Pleasant of Hazelhurst, Miss., and became a member of a small body of Baptist ministers who were seeking a greater spiritual involvement than their church offered. At a meeting in Jackson, Miss., in 1896, they decided to organize churches under their own leadership, and a Church of God in Christ was established at Lexington, Miss., in 1897, "in an old gin on the bank of a little creek." The congregation based its faith on the doctrine of the apostles as recorded on Pentecost (Acts 2:4) and believed that the church's name was revealed to Mason in 1879 from a reference in First Thessalonians 2:14.

In 1906 a report came to the mid-South area that at meetings being conducted by the Reverend William J. Seymour in Los Angeles, Calif., one could receive the baptism of the Holy Ghost, according to Matthew 10:12. Mason, along with J. A. Jeter and D. J. Young of Pine Bluff, Ark., traveled to Los Angeles to the Azusa Street Revival (1906–9), where Mason received the Holy Ghost in March of 1907. They returned to Memphis later that year and began a series of services that attracted a large following. In August of 1907 a General Assembly of the Church of God in Christ was convened in Jackson, Miss., where Mason was elected chief overseer (the term was later replaced by bishop) and D. J. Young was elected editor of their official organ, the *Whole Truth*. By 1934 the denomination had a membership of 25,000, and in 1971 the membership was listed as 425,000, reaching 4.5 million in 1985.

Mason encouraged music and music making in his church and is credited with the composition of several songs, including "I'm a Soldier in the Army of the Lord" and "My Soul Loves Jesus." His congregation is responsible for contributions to black gospel music through such performers as Sister Rosetta Tharpe, Ernestine B. Washington, Andrae Crouch, Edwin and Walter Hawkins, The O'Neal Twins, the Boyer Brothers, and Vanessa Bell Armstrong. The presiding bishop of the Church of God in Christ is J. O. Patterson, with its headquarters in Memphis, Tenn.

Horace Clarence Boyer
Smithsonian Institute

Horace Clarence Boyer, "An Analysis of Black Church Music, with Examples Drawn from Services in Rochester, New York" (Ph.D. dissertation, University of Rochester, 1973); Otho B. Cobbins, *History of Church of Christ (Holiness) U.S.A.* (1966); J. O. Patterson, German R. Ross, and Julia Mason Atkins, *History and Formative Years of the Church of God in Christ with Excerpts from the Life and Works of Its Founder-Bishop C. H. Mason,* (1969); German R. Ross, *Yes, Lord!* (1982). ☆

MAYS, BENJAMIN

(1894–1984) Educator and minister.

Son of Greenwood County, S.C., exslaves, alumnus of Bates College (B.A. 1920) and the University of Chicago (M.A. 1925, Ph.D. 1935), dean of the Howard University School of Religion (1934–40), and president of Morehouse College (1940–62), Benjamin Elijah Mays had become a world-renowned academician and churchman when he eulogized the slain Martin Luther King, Jr., on national television in 1968. Despite his advanced age, he presided over the Atlanta Board of Education during the next decade, as it implemented school desegregation and improved classroom instruction. Recipient of numerous honors—including the recent opening of Atlanta's Benjamin E. Mays High School, induction into the

South Carolina Hall of Fame, and a joint resolution of tribute from the U.S. Congress—Mays is one of the most scholastically decorated southerners of this century.

But his historical importance rests upon more than public visibility since the 1960s. Like others whose names are not as well known, Mays had long been a community leader in the struggle for equality, and he exemplified the courage of politically oriented educators under a legal Jim Crow system. Although he refused Booker T. Washington's call to "Cast down your bucket where you are" and united with W. E. B. Du Bois's post–World War I "talented tenth," hoping "that someday I would be able to do something about a situation that had shadowed my early years and had killed the spirit of all too many of my people," Mays preached familiar ideals. He talked of character, Christianity, education, independence, and pride to blacks, while whites heard his denunciations of caste and his demands for change. Active during the 1930s in antiracist campaigns conducted by the Association of Southern Women for the Prevention of Lynching, Commission on Interracial Cooperation, National Association for the Advancement of Colored People, National Association of Negro Women's Clubs, National Council of Churches, National Urban League, Southern Conference on Human Welfare, and Young Men's Christian Association, he joined the black-liberal coalition that in 1944 formed the Southern Regional Council. A director, he criticized the organization's early failure to oppose segregation. As president of Morehouse College, Mays encouraged the questioning of the segregation system, as individuals such as writer Lillian Smith, a close associate, lectured at the school and criticized laws separating the races. Her largely student audience included several future civil rights crusaders, among them young Martin Luther "Mike" King. Mays's antisegregation views soon created much trouble for the outspoken president, whom witch-hunters labeled a Communist and occasionally picketed. When the council did break its silence, pledging in 1951 to build a segregated South, Mays could already foresee the 1954 *Brown* decision. Fittingly, Atlanta chose the former pioneer to help implement it.

Mays wrote several books, including *The Negro's God as Reflected in His Literature* (1938), *Seeking to be Christian in Race Relations*, with Joseph W. Nicholson (1965), *Negro's Church* (1969), *Born to Rebel* (1971), and *Lord the People Have Driven Me On* (1981). He died 28 March 1984.

See also SOCIAL CLASS: / Southern Regional Council; WOMEN'S LIFE: / Smith, Lillian

Raymond Gavins
Duke University

David L. Lewis, *King: A Critical Biography* (1970); Benjamin E. Mays, *Born to Rebel: An Autobiography of Benjamin E. Mays* (1987); Frank L. Prial, *New York Times* (29 March 1984). ☆

MEREDITH, JAMES

(b. 1933) Civil rights activist.

James Howard Meredith achieved international renown in 1962 when his admission to the University of Mississippi sparked a night-long riot during which two people were killed. Meredith's admission to the all-white university climaxed 18 months of legal and political resistance by both university and state officials, particularly from Governor Ross Barnett, who physically barred Meredith's admission on two occasions. The racial tension that accompanied his admission soon subsided, and Meredith graduated from the University in August of 1963. He described his experiences in *Three Years in Mississippi* (1965).

James H. Meredith's parents, Moses and Roxie Meredith, owned an 84-acre farm near Kosciusko, in Attala County, Miss. Meredith was born on that farm on 25 June 1933. After graduating from a St. Petersburg, Fla., high school, Meredith enlisted in the U.S. Air Force. While in the air force, he conceived a plan to return to his native state to gain admission to the University of Mississippi and break the color barrier in Mississippi.

In the years following his graduation from the university, Meredith pursued a variety of interests and causes. He took graduate courses in economics at the University of Ibadan, Nigeria, in 1964–65 and received a law degree from Columbia University in 1968. In 1966 Meredith was shot and wounded during a walk from Memphis, Tenn., to Jackson, Miss., which he called a "March Against Fear." He has conducted several unsuccessful political campaigns and has served as consultant and lecturer at colleges and universities in America and Africa. Meredith's business interests are as varied as his social and educational pursuits. He owned an apartment building in the Bronx and was a stock broker before returning to Jackson, Miss., in the early 1970s. While in Mississippi, he was self-employed and spent much of his time promoting business ties between American black entrepreneurs and black Africa. Meredith is married to Mary Jane Wiggins and has five children. He served as visiting professor at the University of Cincinnati during the 1984–85 academic year, and in the fall of 1986 he ran unsuccessfully for a position on the Cincinnati, Ohio, school board.

David Sansing
University of Mississippi

James W. Loewen and Charles Sallis, eds., *Mississippi: Conflict and Change* (1974); James H. Meredith, *Three Years in Mississippi* (1965). ☆

MURRAY, PAULI

(1910–1985). Social reformer.

A thirst for learning, the ability to maintain personal directions while setting goals that were greater than she, and "a passion for equality" are the attributes that shaped the life of Pauli Murray, civil rights activist, lawyer, educator, author, and feminist. From early childhood until she entered Hunter College in New York, Murray lived with her aunt, Pauline Fitzgerald Dame, in Durham, N.C. During those years she refined her sense of self-worth and independence and became preconditioned to feminism.

Seeking to return to the "old family ancestral home" in Durham to care for her elderly aunts, Murray became actively involved during the years 1938 to 1941 in the struggle for civil and human rights. According to Murray, her involvement was "me trying to plod along toward some particular, specific objectives." Feeling handicapped with only a B.A. degree, she decided to enroll at the University of North Carolina for graduate studies; her efforts were unsuccessful. Similarly, in 1940, her refusal to sit on a broken seat led to her arrest and conviction for resisting segregation on an interstate bus. Those personal racial confrontations and a national tour in 1941 on behalf of a black man convicted of killing his white landlord prompted her decision to enter Howard University's Law School. Her goal was to become a civil rights lawyer in order to join the legal staff of the NAACP. She continued to protest segregation while a student at Howard by organizing sit-ins against restaurants.

In 1944 she was rejected because of her gender from Harvard's Law School. She attended the University of California School of Law at Berkeley, earning in 1945 the L.L.M. With a J.S.D. from Yale University (1965), Murray had completed her legal training. The sexual and racial barriers she encountered while pursuing her education reinforced her goals to seek better race relations, to eliminate sexism, and to improve the human condition.

She practiced law in New York and California (1946–60), held academic posts in the United States and Ghana (1960–73), was a member of the Committee on Civil and Political Rights of the President's Commission on the Status of Women (1962–63), and cofounded the National Organization for Women (1966). On 8 January 1977 she became one of the first women to be regularly ordained by the Episcopal church.

Murray's book *Proud Shoes: The Story of an American Family* (1956) was a family memoir, a genealogical record of her ancestors in Delaware, Pennsylvania, and North Carolina and especially her grandparents, Robert and Cornelia Fitzgerald. Upon her retirement on 1 January 1983, her first project was to work on a sequel to *Proud Shoes*. She continued to address herself to "the problem of 'psychic violence' in pursuit of the Martin Luther King, Jr., tradition of nonviolence," before her death in July of 1985.

Cynthia Neverdon-Morton
Coppin State College

Pauli Murray interview, Southern Oral History Program, University of North Carolina, Chapel Hill; Pauli Murray, *Southern Exposure* (Winter 1977); *Who's Who among Black Americans* (1980–81). ☆

NATIONAL ASSOCIATION FOR THE ADVANCEMENT OF COLORED PEOPLE (NAACP)

Disheartened by a race riot in 1908 in Springfield, Ill.—the home of President Abraham Lincoln—by the spread of legalized Jim Crow, and by the accommodationist leadership of Booker T. Washington, an interracial group including W. E. B. Du Bois met in New York City in 1910 to establish the NAACP. The organization spent the next few decades in court challenges to the 1896 *Plessy* v. *Ferguson* decision, which sanctioned the separate-but-equal doctrine.

Beginning with *Guinn* v. *the United States* (1915), the NAACP convinced the Supreme Court to outlaw the use of the "grandfather clause" as a means to disfranchise black voters. In 1917 success came in *Buchanan* v. *Warley*, which ended municipal ordinances that sanctioned residential segregation. The NAACP attained further success in the 1930s and 1940s in cases that involved the removal of restrictions on blacks' participation in primary elections and compelled some southern and border states to admit blacks to their law and graduate schools. The culmination of these efforts came in 1954 in *Brown* v. *Board of Education*, which reversed *Plessy* and outlawed racial segregation in public schools.

The NAACP was also an activist organization, especially in its local chapters. In 1915 various NAACP locals picketed theaters showing the racially demeaning movie *Birth of a Nation.* Most major southern cities including Little Rock, Atlanta, Greensboro, and Montgomery had active NAACP chapters, although southern states like Alabama moved to ban the organization during the 1950s. A few southern chapters were especially militant. The president of the Monroe, N.C., NAACP in 1959 vowed self-defense with arms, if necessary, in response to white segregationist violence. The national office suspended him for this breach of policy.

During the civil rights movement, under the leadership of executive director Roy Wilkins and Washington, D.C., representative Clarence Mitchell, the NAACP played a crucial role in the successful lobbying for the 1964 Civil Rights Act and the 1965 Voting Rights Act. A Memphis judge, minister, and Federal Communications Commission member, Benjamin L. Hooks, succeeded Wilkins in 1977.

See also LAW: / *Brown* v. *Board of Education; Plessy* v. *Ferguson;* MEDIA: / *Birth of a Nation*

Dennis C. Dickerson
Rhodes College

John Hope Franklin, *From Slavery to Freedom: A History of Negro Americans* (1947, 5th ed., 1980); Charles F. Kellogg, *NAACP: A History of the National Association for the Advancement of Colored People, Volume I, 1909–1920* (1967); *Records of the NAACP, Branch Files*, Library of Congress, Manuscript Division, Washington, D.C.; B. Joyce Ross, *J. E. Spingarn and the Rise of the NAACP, 1911–1939* (1972); Roy Wilkins with Tom Matthews, *Standing Fast: The Autobiography of Roy Wilkins* (1982). ☆

NEGRO BASEBALL LEAGUES

Under segregation, by custom and sometimes by law, interracial sports encounters were prohibited in the South. As a direct result black southerners developed their own sports world, and baseball was by far the most popular sport of the period.

Each town or rural area had a black baseball team that competed against other local black teams in games that had great cultural importance and entertainment value in those communities. The larger towns had better teams and the very best players became professionals. The top of the black baseball hierarchy was the Negro League—sometimes called the Negro Major Leagues.

Though headquartered in the North for economic reasons, the Negro League had a distinctly southern accent. The league's founder, Rube Foster, was an expatriate Texan; and the majority of players, always southerners, were recruited from southern teams during spring training or during regular Negro League barnstorming forays into the South. In addition, the Negro League contained a smattering of southern teams at various times including the Birmingham Black Barons, Memphis Red

Sox, Atlanta Black Crackers, Jacksonville Red Caps, and Nashville Elite Giants. A Southern Negro League functioned as the strongest Negro minor league. Supplementing the professional and semiprofessional teams of the South were church teams and teams organized around the workplace.

The movement of black athletic talent from South to North mirrored the migration of blacks in general from the South during segregation. Yet the visibility of the black baseball stars and their association with the communities from whence they came provided a unifying influence for all black Americans. Southern blacks were able to follow their baseball heroes through the national black newspapers that circulated throughout the South, and northern black teams appealed to the still strong southern loyalties of the black fans through promotions such as "Texas Day," "Alabama Day," or "North Carolina Day."

The life of the traveling black ball player was difficult. Players were on the road constantly seeking a ball game and a payday, and they augmented the league schedule with exhibitions whenever possible. Sometimes they played three or four games in a single day. At the same time, in an age before television and air-conditioning, the ballplayers provided eagerly sought entertainment and were treated as bona fide celebrities in the black community. When the black players competed against and frequently defeated white major league players during post-season exhibitions in the North and West, they became genuine heroes in black America.

After Jackie Robinson became the first black to enter the major leagues in the 1947 season, black baseball rapidly declined as the black fans deserted their teams to watch integrated baseball. Southern-born Negro Leaguers who achieved prominence in the major leagues after integration include Willie Mays, Hank Aaron, Jackie Robinson, Ernie Banks, and Satchel Paige; but as recounted in the rich folklore that sprang up about Negro baseball, many of the greatest black players never played in the major leagues.

See also RECREATION: / Aaron, Hank; Paige, Satchel

Donn Rogosin
Austin, Texas

John Holway, *Voices from the Great Black Baseball Leagues* (1975); Robert Peterson, *Only the Ball Was White* (1970); Donn Rogosin, *Invisible Men: Life in Baseball's Negro Leagues* (1983). ☆

SEA ISLANDS

The area known as the Sea Islands, or the Low Country, includes all of the southeastern coastal region together with the adjacent islands extending from southern North Carolina to Florida. Apart from the inhabited and arable lands, the islands consist of brackish and salt marshes, beaches, and wooded areas. The three main ethnic groups are Afro-American, Euro-American, and a triethnic (Native American, Afro-American, and Euro-American) mixed group known as "Brass Ankles." Some of the better-known islands are Johns, James, and Wadmalaw (the so-called Bible Islands) near Charleston, S.C.; Edisto, where there is a palm-lined beach; and Ladies and St. Helena islands near Beaufort, S.C., where Penn

Center, founded as a school for the islanders near the end of the Civil War, is located. Daufuskie, known through the photographic work of Jean Moutassamy-Ashe, Sapelo, and St. Mary's in Georgia are three islands still reached only by boat. Jekyll has been developed into a conference center; Ossabaw is a privately owned writers' colony. St. Simon has been suburbanized since the 1950s, and Sea Island, developed as a luxury resort, has been in and out of the news as various prominent people have honeymooned there.

Until the 1930s the Sea Islands were accessible only by boat. Causeways and bridges, which now connect some of the islands to the mainland, have had a major impact on the life of the islanders. Inhabited originally by Yamassee and other Native Americans, the area was invaded, explored, marched through, settled on, and written about successively by the Spanish, English, and French. Africans were brought to work the land, making possible large single-crop economies such as the pre-revolutionary indigo, rice, and cotton and in later years potatoes, tomatoes, soybeans, and cabbage.

During the mosquito season the islands' Euro-American residents moved away to escape malaria, leaving behind the enslaved Africans, many of whom had the sickle-cell gene that protected them from the disease. Because of their isolation, the Afro-Americans preserved many of their African customs in their material folk culture and life, as evident in the distinctive patterning of their quilts, the construction of baskets, women's modes of hair tying, cookery, the making of fishnets, and the practice of fishing. The African influence persists, too, in the Sea Islanders' insurance and burial societies, praying bands, and lodges. The Sea Island creole language (also known as Gullah or Geechee), like the folklore, exudes Africanness, as Lorenzo Dow Turner demonstrated in an epochal study. Much of Turner's work was based on naming customs, some of which are still practiced today.

Books have been written about the area—travel accounts, novels, folklore collections, explorers' journals, educational and religious missionaries' diaries, military records, and studies in history, language, and sociology. Charlotte Forten Grimké, W. F. Allen, Lucy McKim Garrison, Thomas Wentworth Higginson, William Gilmore Simms, Abigail Christensen, Charles Colcock Jones, Elsie Clews Parsons, Julia Peterkin, Guy B. and Guion Griffis Johnson, Guy and Candie Carawan, and many others have written with fascination about the area and its people, whose folkways command attention and respect.

The formerly high concentration of Afro-American residents has changed in recent years for two main reasons: northward migration of the Afro-American islanders in search of better economic opportunity and the influx of Euro-Americans through suburban, resort, and commercial developments. Recent developments on Kiawah, Hilton Head, and Daufuskie islands (S.C.) threaten the serene beauty of the islands as well as the cultural integrity of their Afro-American folkways, which have few defenses against the advance of mainland-originated technology.

See also RECREATION: / Hilton Head

Mary Ann Twining
Buffalo, New York

Edith McBride Dabbs, *Sea Island Diary: A History of St. Helena Island* (1983); Bessie Jones and Bess Lomax Hawes, *Step it Down: Games, Plays, Songs, and Stories from the Afro-American Heritage* (1972); Elsie Clews Parsons, *Folk-lore of the Sea Islands, South Carolina* (1923); Lorenzo Dow Turner, *Africanisms in the Gullah Dialect* (1949); Mary Ann Twining and Keith E. Baird, eds., *Journal of Black Studies* (June 1980). ☆

SELMA MARCH

Throughout the first nine weeks of 1965 Martin Luther King, Jr., and the Southern Christian Leadership Conference (SCLC) helped local civil rights activists in and around Selma, Ala., organize demonstrations to protest discriminatory voter registration practices that had long blocked black citizens from casting ballots. In late February, following the fatal shooting of one protester, Jimmie Lee Jackson, by an Alabama state trooper, civil rights workers proposed a march from Selma to the Alabama state capitol in Montgomery, 54 miles away.

On Sunday, March 7, some 600 civil rights marchers headed east out of Selma on U.S. 80. State and local lawmen blocked the route and attacked the peaceful column with tear gas and billy clubs. News photographers and television cameras filmed the violent scene as the club-swinging lawmen chased the terrified demonstrators back into Selma. National outrage ensued when the film footage and dramatic photographs were featured on television stations and newspaper front pages all across America.

King announced a second march attempt, and civil rights sympathizers from around the nation flocked to Selma to join the effort. Lawmen peacefully turned back that second procession, and SCLC went into federal court seeking government protection for a third, full-scale march to Montgomery. Court hearings delayed a resolution of the question for a week, but on Sunday, March 21, with King and other dignitaries in the lead, 3,200 marchers set out for Montgomery as federal troops and officials furnished careful protection.

Walking some 12 miles a day and camping in fields at night, the marchers' ranks swelled to more than 25,000 when their procession entered Montgomery on Thursday, March 25. The march climaxed with a mass rally at the Alabama state capitol, culminating a three-week set of events that represented the emotional and political peak of the 1960s civil rights era. In the weeks following the march President Lyndon B. Johnson and bipartisan congressional supporters speeded passage of the Voting Rights Act of 1965, a comprehensive statute that remedied most of the injustices the Selma demonstrations had been designed to highlight.

See also URBANIZATION: / Montgomery

David J. Garrow
City College of New York
CUNY Graduate Center

David J. Garrow, *Protest at Selma: Martin Luther King, Jr., and the Voting Rights Act of 1965* (1978). ☆

SILAS GREEN SHOW

"Silas Green from New Orleans" was a traveling minstrel show that was owned, written, managed, and performed by black people. For over a half century (1907–58), the Silas Green Company toured urban and rural communities exclusively in the South and established itself as an institution among its black and white segregated audiences. Approximately 10 months a year, 6 nights a week, the show traveled throughout Florida, Georgia, North and South Carolina, Virginia and West Virginia, Tennessee, Kentucky, Mississippi, Arkansas, Louisiana, and Alabama.

The family-oriented comedy and musical show combined the theatrical traditions of minstrelsy and black musical comedy. White minstrelsy created the "blackface" and the writers of Silas Green retained the use of the burnt cork makeup for the main characters of their show. The comedy, however, *was* acted out in the context of a loosely woven plot that had continuity—a break with minstrelsy that was pioneered by Cole and Johnson in 1898 with *A Trip to Coontown*, the first black musical comedy. The comic story of the Silas Green show was interspersed with several chorus line numbers, one or two blues singers, and specialty acts that displayed a wide range of versatile talents. The musical sounds of "Silas Green from New Orleans" echoed the creative and innovative talents of black Americans. The band played ragtime, jazz, and swing tunes composed by southern and northern blacks, heralding and disseminating the music of its people throughout the South.

During the show's most successful years in the 1930s and 1940s, the troupe numbered up to 75, and the tent in which the production was performed nightly had the capacity to accommodate an audience of more than 2,500 people. Buses, automobiles, and a Pullman car were utilized to transport the troupe, for it was important in the hostile racial environment of the South that the show travel as a unit. Furthermore, most of the local black communities could not provide all of the sleeping and eating facilities for the members of the company; therefore, the Pullman car and trailers fulfilled these necessities.

Throughout its existence, "Silas Green from New Orleans" was black owned and controlled. The first owner of the company was "Professor" Eph Williams, a former circus performer and owner. Eph Williams acquired the show known as the "Jolly Ethiopians" from S. H. Dudley, Sr., and Salem Tutt Whitney and renamed it the Silas Green Company. After Williams's death in 1921, Charles Collier, a protégé of Williams, bought the show and is credited with reorganizing and rejuvenating it. Collier died in 1942; his wife, Hortense maintained the company until 1944 when she sold it to a partnership of Rodney Harris, Charles Morton, and Wilbur Jones. Jones soon bought out his partners and was the sole owner until he took it off the road in 1958. According to Jones the three main factors contributing to the show's demise were increased overhead expenses, the popularity of television, and heightened racial tensions in the South brought on by the 1954 Supreme Court decision in *Brown* v. *Board of Education* declaring segregation in public schools unconstitutional.

"Silas Green from New Orleans" was probably the longest-running black-owned minstrel show in the United States. Noted personalities such as "Ma" Rainey, Bessie Smith, Dewey "Pigmeat" Markham, Mamie Smith, Nipsey Russell, Johnny Huggins, and the comedy team of Butterbeans and Susie were members of the cast for varying lengths of time.

See also MUSIC: / Smith, Bessie

Eleanor J. Baker
Bloomington, Indiana

Chicago *Defender* 2 July 1921, 24 June 1922, 16 April 1932; James W. Johnson, *Black Manhattan* (1968); John Johnson, *Ebony* (September 1954); Major Robinson, *Our World* (April 1949). ☆

SOUTHERN CHRISTIAN LEADERSHIP CONFERENCE (SCLC)

The SCLC was founded in 1957 in Atlanta's Ebenezer Baptist Church, which was pastored by the Reverend Martin Luther King, Sr. Local protest movements, mostly bus boycotts, had occurred between 1953 and 1956 in such southern cities as Baton Rouge, New Orleans, Montgomery, Tallahassee, and Birmingham. Informal meetings took place among local movement leaders, mostly black ministers, including Joseph Lowery of Mobile, Fred Shuttlesworth of Birmingham, and Martin Luther King, Jr., of Montgomery, and among interested northern activists such as A. Philip Randolph, Bayard Rustin, Ella Baker, and Stanley Levison (the only white); the consensus was that a new federated organization could organize and focus growing black militancy in the South. Moreover, the NAACP had been barred legally from some southern states, and SCLC might fill the void left by this activist civil rights group.

Martin Luther King, Jr., largely because of his able leadership of the successful Montgomery bus boycott of 1955–56, became the first president of SCLC. SCLC was synonymous with King. Under the organization's auspices, he became involved in major demonstrations in Albany, Ga. (1961–62), Birmingham, Ala. (1963), St. Augustine, Fla. (1964), and Selma, Ala. (1965). The Birmingham and Selma marches dramatized the need for the Civil Rights Act of 1964 and the Voting Rights Act of 1965. King and SCLC also ventured north to Boston and Chicago to focus attention on racial and urban issues that produced de facto segregation and discrimination for blacks outside the South. He later spoke out strongly against the Vietnam War.

King operated SCLC with able lieutenants including the Reverends Ralph D. Abernathy, Andrew Young, Wyatt T. Walker, and Jesse Jackson. SCLC grew to 275 affiliates in both the North and South, although in many cases these locals were individual Baptist congregations. SCLC also had a Department of Economic Affairs, which for a time operated tutorial centers in 16 Alabama towns and tried to upgrade the occupational status of black steelworkers at an Atlanta plant. A large foundation grant in 1967 established a SCLC-sponsored educational project for black church leaders in 15 selected cities.

Just before King's assassination in 1968 in Memphis, he led that city's black sanitation workers in a fight for better wages and union recognition. King had hoped this effort would precede a massive Poor People's campaign in Washington, D.C. His successor, Abernathy, carried out the plan. Abernathy was eventually succeeded by a black United Methodist clergyman, the Reverend Joseph Lowery.

See also POLITICS: / Young, Andrew; URBANIZATION: / Birmingham; Montgomery; WOMEN'S LIFE: / Baker, Ella Jo

Dennis C. Dickerson
Rhodes College

Southern Christian Leadership Conference Records; Department of Economic Affairs, 1965 folder, 37:2, Martin Luther King, Jr., Center for Nonviolent Social Change Archives, Atlanta, Ga.; Adam Fairclough, *To Redeem the Soul of America: The Southern Christian Leadership Conference and Martin Luther King, Jr.* (1987); Grant Files, Southern Christian Leadership Conference, PA67–580, Ford Foundation Archives, Ford Foundation, New York, N.Y.; David L. Lewis, *King: A Critical Biography* (1970); Aldon D. Morris, *The Origins of the Civil Rights Movement: Black Communities Organizing for Change* (1984); Stephen Oates, *Let the Trumpet Sound: The Life of Martin Luther King, Jr.* (1982). ☆

STORYVILLE

From 1 October 1897 until midnight 12 November 1917 New Orleans had a legally established district for prostitution. Although most often referred to by those who frequented it as "the District," the press called it Storyville for Alderman Sidney Story, who introduced Ordinance Number 13032 that created it.

The boundaries of Storyville were Customhouse (later renamed Iberville) Street, Basin Street, St. Louis Street, and North Robertson Street. This area—today almost totally covered by a federal housing project—lies just east (or downriver) of Canal Street and north (toward Lake Pontchartrain) of the French Quarter. A separate district, meant for blacks, was bounded by Perdido, Gravier, Franklin, and Locust Streets (now covered by government buildings). Storyville itself, however, was inhabited by both blacks and whites.

Prostitution has a long history in New Orleans. French methods of colonization included sending shipments of women from correctional institutions. The French did not stress the importance of sending family groups of settlers, who presumably would have set a higher moral tone. Additionally, the city was first and foremost a port, with the waterfront hell-raising of the usual port city.

Storyville was in some ways the result of a reform movement; unable to eliminate vice, the idea was to control prostitution by organizing it. Storyville could only have flourished, though, in a corrupt environment. Police were underpaid and not well disciplined, and political ward bosses—the Old Regular organization—had great authority to do as they pleased. Above all, the profits were high—for landlords, bar and cafe owners, liquor distributors, and even clothing stores. Storyville, in 1897, seemed to be an idea whose time had come.

In the beginning there were some 230 houses of prostitution and about 2,000 working prostitutes in Storyville. There was a directory, the Blue Book, issued from about 1901 to 1915 in at least 12 editions. The Blue Books listed prostitutes (sometimes divided into blacks and whites, and even Jews and Christians) and carried advertisements: for houses such as Madam Lulu White's Mahogany Hall, for cafes and dance halls, and even for venereal disease cures. Newspapers such as the *Mascot* and the *Sunday Sun* had lurid gossip columns (sometimes detailing peccadillos of New Orleans socialites as well as Storyville regulars). There was an annual Storyville Mardi Gras ball and even a Storyville photographer, Ernest J. Bellocq, whose work has received just praise in recent years and served as the model for Louis Malle's movie *Pretty Baby* (1978).

Storyville may have been many things, but it was not the birthplace of jazz. The main business of the district was prostitution. The pianist, or professor, might entertain the customers in the parlor or play for "naked dances," and the cafes and dance halls did have bands. But jazz, that amalgam of African musical traditions and European instruments and melodies, was evolving before Storyville and was heard at picnics, parades, and dances throughout the city. Jazz fans in New Orleans did not have to go to Storyville to hear it.

Jazz musicians, however, did work there. Tony Jackson (composer of "Pretty Baby") and Ferdinand "Jelly Roll" Morton played piano in houses. Joseph "King" Oliver, Edward "Kid" Ory, Johnny St. Cyr, Freddie Keppard, and Charles "Buddy" Bolden all played there. Louis Armstrong was old enough to sneak in and listen in his youth but not old enough to play in Storyville.

Although Storyville had ornate houses and beautiful women, it was also tough, dirty, and dangerous. The suicide rate was high. Venereal disease was ever present. Opium dens existed and cocaine, or "nose candy," was sold at drugstores. White slavery, child prostitution, lewd performances or "circuses," illegitimacy, and poverty were common. All conceivable crimes of violence—murders, attacks, rapes, robberies, general shoot-outs, poisonings, burnings, knife fights, eye-gougings—were committed in Storyville.

In the last years of the district the population dwindled. Some madams relocated in New Orleans; many moved upriver to Chicago or to other, more fertile economic fields. Finally, with World War I approaching and the morals of sailors at a nearby naval installation in mind, Secretary of the Navy Josephus Daniels suggested and New Orleans Mayor Martin Behrman concurred that Storyville be closed at midnight, 12 November 1917. Only 100 houses and 400 prostitutes remained.

Already dying, Storyville was killed by public opinion. There was a consensus that an officially organized vice district just did not work. As a marketplace, Storyville ceased to exist, but its commodity did not.

"You can make prostitution illegal in Louisiana," Mayor Behrman said, "but you can't make it unpopular."

See also HISTORY AND MANNERS: Sexuality; MUSIC: / Armstrong, Louis; Bolden, Buddy; Morton, Jelly Roll; Oliver, King; URBANIZATION: / New Orleans

Carolyn Goldsby Kolb
New Orleans, Louisiana

Russell Levy, "Of Bards and Bawds: New Orleans Sporting Life before and during the Storyville Era, 1897–1917" (M.A. thesis, Tulane University, 1967); Alan Lomax, *Mr. Jelly Roll* (1950); Al Rose, *Storyville, New Orleans: Being an Authentic, Illustrated Account of the Notorious Red-Light District* (1974); T. Harry Williams, *Huey Long* (1969). ☆

STUDENT NONVIOLENT COORDINATING COMMITTEE (SNCC)

Formed in April 1960, the Student Nonviolent Coordinating Committee (SNCC) drew heavily from Nashville student activists committed to nonviolent direct action. In 1961 Congress of Racial Equality (CORE) leaders asked SNCC to help black students who were waging unsuccessful lunch counter sit-ins in Rock Hill, S.C. Fifteen SNCC members joined the efforts and initiated the "jail-no bail" protest strategy.

SNCC's next major wave of activity came during the CORE-initiated Freedom Ride of 1961. When in the face of violence in Alabama CORE leaders called off the project, SNCC members resumed the trip and traveled to Montgomery, where further violence erupted. SNCC, CORE, and the Southern Christian Leadership Conference (SCLC) formed the Freedom Riders Coordinating Committee, which solicited more participants to extend the rides to Jackson, Miss. Clayborne Carson notes that SNCC workers gained a reputation as the "shock troops" of the civil rights movement.

In 1961 SNCC developed both a protest wing and a voter registration one. Robert Moses headed SNCC's voter registration efforts in Mississippi, and James Forman became the group's new executive secretary. As the Mississippi efforts floundered in the face of resistance, other SNCC staff members launched massive protests of blacks in Albany, Ga., between fall 1961 and summer 1962.

In 1962 and 1963 SNCC staff members became increasingly effective as community organizers, and membership grew. James Forman recruited many notable young black leaders, such as Julian Bond, and activists such as Fannie Lou Hamer joined SNCC's staff. SNCC built support among northerners and expanded its community organization efforts in southwest Georgia and Mississippi. SNCC members increasingly criticized the Kennedy Administration and black groups such as the SCLC and only reluctantly supported the coalition that planned the 1963 March on Washington.

In 1964 SNCC leaders initiated the Mississippi Summer Project, a plan to enlist a massive force of white student volunteers as fieldworkers. All of the other major civil rights organizations supported the plan, and SNCC vied to maintain its leadership role. One 1964 effort was formation of the Mississippi Freedom Democratic party, an alternate Democratic political organization that hoped to challenge the regular party in Mississippi for seating at the Democratic national convention. Through separate voter registration procedures, over 80,000 blacks participated in the SNCC-organized "freedom vote." Though the MFD party challenge gained national support, it ultimately failed. The other major thrust of the Summer Project was establishment of "freedom schools" to educate young blacks in Mississippi. Over 2,000 students attended classes in the 41 schools.

After the murder of SNCC volunteer Andrew Goodman and CORE workers James Chaney and Michael Schwerner in Mississippi in 1964, SNCC moved toward approval of armed self-defense and helped black residents near Selma and Montgomery form the Lowndes County Freedom Organization (LCFO), known as the Black Panther party, headed by Stokely Carmichael.

Ambivalent about SCLC's 1965 voting rights campaign in Selma, Ala., SNCC became active in the Alabama protests after SNCC and SCLC marchers were attacked outside Selma in early spring. Following the Selma to Montgomery march led by Martin Luther King, Jr., SNCC recruited many black college students in Alabama, strengthened its militant focus, and targeted economic reforms and black pride themes. In 1966 Carmichael became chairman, leaders such as Robert Moses and Julian Bond left, and whites were virtually expelled. A tumultuous period followed, and by 1970 SNCC had disintegrated amidst internal conflict and widespread criticism.

Sharon A. Sharp
University of Mississippi

Inge Powell Bell, *CORE and the Strategy of Nonviolence* (1968); Clayborne Carson, *In Struggle: SNCC and the Black Awakening of the 1960s* (1981); James Forman, *The Making of Black Revolutionaries: A Personal Account* (1972); C. Eric Lincoln, in *The American Negro Reference Book*, ed. John P. Davis (1966); Howard Zinn, *SNCC: The New Abolitionists* (1964). ☆

TOOMER, JEAN

(1894–1967) Writer.

The only child of Nina Pinchback and Nathan Toomer, Nathan Eugene Toomer, also known as Jean Toomer, was born in the Washington, D.C., home of his grandparents, Nina Emily Hethorne and P. B. S. Pinchback. Born into a socially and politically prominent family—Pinchback was the first black lieutenant governor of Louisiana during Reconstruction—Toomer enjoyed the advantages and privileges of a middle-class family.

Toomer received his primary and secondary education in the public schools of the District of Columbia. After graduating from M Street High School (now known as Paul Laurence Dunbar High) in 1914, Toomer studied scientific agriculture at the University of Wisconsin, sociology at the University of Chicago, and law at the City College of New York. Toomer's range of interests was impressive, but it revealed not so much the possibilities of an expansive intellect as the workings of an anxious mind in search of what he would later call an "intelligible scheme." The chaotic years between 1914 and 1919, described by Toomer as the "years of wandering," were not completely devoid of order. During this period, Toomer experimented with writing and discovered such writers as Walt Whitman, George Bernard Shaw, and Waldo Frank. These writers exercised an extraordinary influence over Toomer: from Whitman, Toomer sensed the potentialities of ordinary speech; from Shaw, he discovered the didactic uses of art; in Frank, he found a friend and mentor who was instrumental in publishing the single work on which his reputation as an imaginative artist rests—*Cane* (1923).

A collection of verse, prose, and drama, *Cane* was the outcome of a two-month sojourn in the fall of 1921 in Sparta, Ga., where Toomer was acting principal of the Sparta Normal and Industrial Institute. Toomer responded passionately to the black folk culture whose dissolution is the subject of *Cane*. Toomer's sensual portrayal of black life, his emphasis on black folk culture, his experimentation with jazz forms and imagist techniques forged new artistic possibilities for the writers of the New Negro Movement.

Toomer's southern sojourn had personal as well as artistic consequences. Long in search of a sense of wholeness, the young author of *Cane* achieved a unity of art and being while in the South never matched by his conversion to Quakerism, his involvement in Dianectics, and most important of all his work as a teacher of the psychological theories of George I. Gurdjieff. Gurdjieff's theories did not impart to the large body of fiction, verse, and drama written after 1923 the depth of feeling and the complexity of thought so characteristic of *Cane*. This fact explains why so much of the writing after *Cane* remains unpublished and why Toomer died in Doylestown, Penn., in obscurity and isolation.

Rudolph P. Byrd
Los Angeles, California

Brian Joseph Benson and Mabel Mayle Dillard, *Jean Toomer* (1980); Nellie Y. McKay, *Jean Toomer, Artist: A Study of His Literary Life and Work, 1894–1936* (1984); Darwin Turner, *In a Minor Chord: Three Afro-American Writers and Their Search for Identity* (1971). ☆

TURNER, NAT

(1800–1831) Slave.

Born in Southampton County, Va., Turner was a black American slave who led the Southampton insurrection, which has often been seen as the most effective slave rebellion in the South. In recent years, Turner has been a focus of cultural and historical debate.

Turner is the dominant figure among a trio of insurrectionists who led major uprisings, beginning in 1800 with Gabriel Prosser, continuing with Denmark Vesey in 1822, and ending with Turner in 1831. Famous in the folklore and oral history of black Americans, these rebels expressed the powerful urges of blacks to be free. Called "Ol' Prophet Nat" and leader of the most violent of the rebellions, Turner became an especially vivid figure in the underground history of American slavery.

Turner was born to a black woman owned by a plantation aristocrat also named Turner. Transported from Africa in her youth, Nat Turner's mother imbued in him a passion for freedom. Always dreamy and visionary, he learned to read, probably taught by his master's son, and early displayed strong religious feelings. As an adult he became a preacher among the slaves. Sold by the Turner family to a less prosperous farmer and sold again to a Southampton craftsman named Joseph Travis, Turner bitterly withdrew into religious fantasies marked by omens, signs, and visions. Turner burned for his freedom, but he also saw himself as a savior of his people. Following an eclipse of the sun, taken as a sign from the Lord, Turner and four trusted lieutenants embarked upon the bloody insurrection on the night of 21 August 1831, beginning with the slaughter of the Travis family. By 23 August, when the rebellion was thwarted by militia, Turner's rebels had killed almost 60 white men, women, and children. Turner escaped capture for six weeks, but eventually was caught, tried, and executed, as were some 16 others involved with him.

The cultural debate over Turner was sparked in 1967 by the publication of William Styron's novel *The Confessions of Nat Turner*. Though Daniel Panger published *Ol' Prophet Nat* (1967), it was Styron's bestseller that challenged black Americans, historians, and social critics, for it raised questions on Turner, black history, and the "true" character ("Sambo" or "rebel") of the slave in the South. The co-opting of Turner by a white author prompted, for example, a polemical outcry called *William Styron's Nat Turner: Ten Black Writers Respond* (1968). Coming in the midst of the social revolution of the 1960s, Panger's, Styron's, and many others' works devoted to the Southampton Revolt soon made Turner a symbol of "Black Power and social liberation."

See also LITERATURE: / Styron, William

James M. Mellard
Northern Illinois University

John B. Duff and Peter M. Mitchell, *The Nat Turner Rebellion: The Historical Event and the Modern Controversy* (1971); Stephen B. Oates, *The Fires of Jubilee: Nat Turner's Fierce Rebellion* (1975); Henry L. Tragle, *The Southampton Slave Revolt of 1831: A Compilation of Source Material* (1971). ☆

WALKER, MARGARET

(b. 1915) Writer.

One of the first Afro-American writers to return to the region for a career after establishing a national literary reputation, Margaret Walker occupies an important transitional position in the history of southern letters. Born in Birmingham, Ala., on 27 July 1915, Walker left the South to earn her B.A. at Northwestern University (1935) and her M.A. at Iowa (1940). While a student, she worked with the Federal Writers' Project and began work on the poems included in *For My People* (1942), which won the Yale Award for Younger Poets. Pursuing her career in education, Walker taught at Livingstone College (North Carolina) and West Virginia State College before joining the faculty of Jackson State (Mississippi) in 1949. Married and the mother of four children, she has taught English, directed the Institute for the Study of the History, Life, and Culture of Black People, and conducted research for a biography of Richard Wright since that time. Her novel *Jubilee* (1966) solidified her literary reputation and has been translated into numerous languages.

Walker's writing is significant both for its celebration of Afro-American folklife and for its challenge to the romanticized plantation tradition of Thomas Nelson Page and Margaret Mitchell. "For My People," the poem that provided both the title and the central themes for Walker's first collection,

Margaret Walker, Mississippi writer, 1976

traces the history of Afro-Americans from the rural South to the urban North and culminates in a vision of racial assertion and transcendence that anticipated and inspired many younger Afro-American poets. A brilliant reader of her own poetry, Walker draws heavily on the Afro-American oral tradition in poems such as "Kissie Lee" and "Molly Means." Walker's decision to publish two chapbooks—*Prophets for a New Day* (1970) and *October Journey* (1970)—with the black-operated Broadside Press reflects the evolution of Walker's voice evident in poems such as "For Malcolm X" and "Lineage," which has become a minor feminist classic. Similarly, as Walker explains in the monograph *How I Wrote Jubilee* (1971), *Jubilee* relies on materials derived from oral history to counter the romantic image of slavery propagated by works such as *Gone with the Wind.* In addition to presenting an Afro-American vision of the real nature of slavery and Reconstruction, the novel emphasizes the special perspective of the Afro-American woman who must suffer the main effects of violence from whites and blacks. *A Poetic Equation: Conversations between Nikki Giovanni and Margaret Walker* (1974) demonstrates Walker's continuing concern with the racial and sexual issues raised in her poetry and fiction.

See also LITERATURE: / Wright, Richard; MEDIA: / *Gone with the Wind*

Craig Werner
University of Wisconsin

Adrianne Baytop, in *American Women Writers: A Critical Reference Guide from Colonial Times to the Present*, vol. 4, ed. Lina Mainiero (1982); Maxine Block, ed., *Current Biography* (November 1943); Michael L. Edwards, *The Rhetoric of Afro-American Poetry: A Rhetorical Analysis of Black Poetry and the Selected Poetry of Margaret Walker and Langston Hughes* (1980); Elaine M. Newsome, in *Southern Writers: A Biographical Dictionary*, ed. Robert Bain, Joseph M. Flora, and Louis D. Rubin, Jr. (1979). ☆

WASHINGTON, BOOKER T.

(1856–1915) Educator.

Booker Taliaferro Washington was the foremost black educator of the late 19th and early 20th centuries. He also had a major influence on southern race relations and was the dominant figure in black public affairs from 1895 until his death in 1915. Born a slave on a small farm in the Virginia backcountry, he moved with his family after emancipation to work in the salt furnaces and coal mines of West Virginia. After a secondary education at Hampton Institute, he taught an upgraded school and experimented briefly with the study of law and the ministry, but a teaching position at Hampton decided his future career. In 1881 he founded Tuskegee Normal and Industrial Institute on the Hampton model in the Black Belt of Alabama.

Though Washington offered little that was innovative in industrial education, which both northern philanthropic foundations and southern leaders were already promoting, he became its chief black exemplar and spokesman. In his advocacy of Tuskegee Institute and its educational method, Washington revealed the political adroitness and accommodationist philosophy that were to characterize his career in the wider arena of race leadership. He convinced southern white employers and governors that Tuskegee offered an education that would keep blacks "down on the farm" and in the trades. To prospective northern donors and particularly the new self-made millionaires such as Rockefeller and Carnegie he promised the inculcation of the Protestant work ethic. To blacks living within the limited horizons of the post-Reconstruction South, Washington held out industrial education as the means of escape from the web of sharecropping and debt and the achievement of attainable, *petit-bourgeois* goals of self-employment, landownership, and small business. Washington cultivated local white approval and secured a small state appropriation, but it was northern donations that made Tuskegee Institute by 1900 the best-supported black educational institution in the country.

The Atlanta Compromise Address, delivered before the Cotton States Exposition in 1895, enlarged Washington's influence into the arena of race relations and black leadership. Washington offered black acquiescence in disfranchisement and social segregation

Booker T. Washington, black educator, c. 1900

if whites would encourage black progress in economic and educational opportunity. Hailed as a sage by whites of both sections, Washington further consolidated his influence by his widely read autobiography *Up From Slavery* (1901), the founding of the National Negro Business League in 1900, his celebrated dinner at the White House in 1901, and control of patronage politics as chief black advisor to Presidents Theodore Roosevelt and William Howard Taft.

Washington kept his white following by conservative policies and moderate utterances, but he faced growing black and white liberal opposition in the Niagara Movement (1905–9) and the NAACP (1909–), groups demanding civil rights and encouraging protest in response to white aggressions such as lynchings, disfranchisement, and segregation laws. Washington successfully fended off these critics, often by underhanded means. At the same time, however, he tried to translate his own personal success into black advancement through secret sponsorship of civil rights suits, serving on the boards of Fisk and Howard universities, and directing philanthropic aid to these and other black colleges. His speaking tours and private persuasion tried to equalize public educational opportunities and to reduce racial violence. These efforts were generally unsuccessful, and the year of Washington's death marked the beginning of the Great Migration from the rural South to the urban North. Washington's racial philosophy, pragmatically adjusted to the limiting conditions of his own era, did not survive the change.

See also EDUCATION: / Fisk University; Hampton Institute; Tuskegee Institute

Louis R. Harlan
University of Maryland

Louis R. Harlan, *Booker T. Washington*, 2 vols. (1972, 1983), with Raymond W. Smock, eds., *The Booker T. Washington Papers*, 12 vols. (1972–); August Meier, *Negro Thought in America, 1880–1915* (1963). ☆

WELLS-BARNETT, IDA

(1862–1931) Journalist and social activist.

On 16 July 1862, Ida Bell Wells-Barnett, a future journalist, club woman, and militant antilynching crusader, was born a slave in Holly Springs, Miss. The oldest daughter of slave parents James and Elizabeth (Bowling) Wells, she received her public school education in Holly Springs and attended Rust College, which was founded in 1866 as an industrial school for blacks in Holly Springs. A yellow fever epidemic took the lives of Wells's parents, leaving her, at the age of 14, in charge of her younger brothers and sisters. In order to support herself and her siblings, Wells began teaching at a nearby rural school, while attending Rust College.

In 1884 Wells moved her family to Memphis, Tenn., to be near an aunt and to obtain a better-paying teaching position. Before passing the teaching examination for the Memphis public schools, Ida Wells taught at a rural school outside Memphis. In Tennessee she began her lifelong public crusade against injustice and inequality, successfully suing in 1884 the Chesapeake and Ohio Railroad Company for attempting to force her to sit in the smoking car that had been designated for blacks. The lower court decision in Wells's favor was subsequently overruled by the Tennessee Supreme Court.

While in Tennessee, Wells became part owner and editor of a local black newspaper, the Memphis *Free Speech and Headlight* (shortened by Wells to *Free Speech*). Her previous journalistic experience included occasional articles, primarily on race relations in the South, under the pen name "Iola," for religious publications and black newspapers. In 1891 Wells lost her teaching job in Memphis, following the publication in the *Free Speech* of articles critical of the school system's unequal allocation of resources to black schools. The next year a Wells editorial denouncing lynching in general and the lynching of three Memphis blacks in particular resulted in the destruction of the *Free Speech* building and threats on her life.

Although forced thereafter to live outside the South, Wells continued her campaign against racial injustice, especially the lynchings of blacks, as a columnist for the *New York Age*, as an author, and as a prominent lecturer on racial injustice in the United States and abroad. In 1895 she published a pamphlet entitled *A Red Record: Tabulated Statistics and Alleged Causes of Lynchings in the United States, 1892–1893–1894*, which later appeared in London under the title *United States Atrocities*. In her crusade against lynching, the articulate Wells delivered numerous lectures, aided in the formation of antilynching societies in England, and met with President William McKinley in 1898, along with other blacks, to protest the lynchings of blacks. Her fight against injustice also led to the denunciation of black exclusion from the Chicago World's Fair in 1893. She collaborated with Frederick Douglass, Ferdinand L. Barnett (whom she later married), and I. Garland Penn on a publication entitled *The Reason Why the Colored American Is Not in the World's Columbian Exposition—The Afro-American's Contribution to Columbian Literature*.

In 1895 Ida married Ferdinand Lee Barnett, Assistant State's Attorney for Cook County and editor of the Chicago *Conservator*, the first black newspaper in Chicago. Wells then turned her attention to local civic activities. She founded and served as an officer in numerous women's groups, earning the title among some as the "Mother of Clubs." With money provided by some of the organizations she was active in, as well as with her own personal funds, Wells-Barnett traveled to Arkansas and Illinois to investigate race riots during World War I and in the postwar years reported on them for various black newspapers. Up to the time of her death in Chicago on 25 March 1931, Ida B.

Wells-Barnett devoted her life to fighting for full equality for blacks and women throughout the United States, but especially in the South.

Sharon Harley
University of Maryland

Alfreda M. Duster, *Crusade for Justice: The Autobiography of Ida B. Wells* (1970); Ida B. Wells-Barnett, *On Lynchings* (1969). ☆

"WE SHALL OVERCOME"

"We Shall Overcome" began as a labor song and became the anthem of the black freedom movement of the 1960s. The song was first used during a drive by the Congress of Industrial Organizations in the 1940s to organize Piedmont Carolina textile workers. Black tobacco workers in Charleston, S.C., used the song on the picket lines in 1945, and they brought it to the Highlander Folk School in Tennessee. From there it was conveyed to union leaders across the South.

Highlander was a training center in the 1950s for labor organizers and for civil rights workers, especially activists who later founded the Student Nonviolent Coordinating Committee. For six years before the first sit-ins in 1960, blacks and whites had held workshops at Highlander, with singing a part of the activities. "We Shall Overcome" was already identified with Highlander, and Guy Carawan, a white Californian (of southern-born parents), taught the song to the mostly young activists in the late 1950s. The song was copyrighted in 1960, by Ludlow Music, Inc., with words and music credited to Zelphia Horton, Frank Hamilton, Guy Carawan, and Pete Seeger. In fact, "We Shall Overcome" was an adaptation of an old black church tune, "I'll Overcome Someday."

According to Carawan, the first use of "We Shall Overcome" as part of a mass civil rights protest may have been outside the mayor's office in Nashville, Tenn., in the early 1960s. He led a group singing of the song in April 1960, in Raleigh, N.C., as part of a meeting at Shaw University on sit-ins. Jane Stembridge, an activist in the audience, later wrote that the song conveyed an inspiring "common vision" to the protestors. "We Shall Overcome" was widely used during the 1961 protest in Albany, Ga. Bernice Reagon recalled that the song "released a kind of power and required a level of concentrated energy I did not know I had." It was the official theme song of the 1963 March on Washington.

"We Shall Overcome" was the best known of the freedom songs that were a vital part of the black freedom movement. Often based on spirituals or black church music, freedom songs were one of the most emotionally moving aspects of the culture of protest. Civil rights activists testified to the power of those songs to stir the soul and to awaken the power of the black religious tradition and focus it on righteous protest. The SNCC Freedom Singers began touring the nation in 1962, singing freedom songs to raise money, and many freedom songs were later adapted by other protest movements in this nation and overseas.

Charles Reagan Wilson
University of Mississippi

Frank Adams, with Myles Horton, *Unearthing Seeds of Fire: The Idea of Highlander*

(1975); Guy and Candie Carawan, compilers, *Songs of the Southern Freedom Movement: We Shall Overcome!* (1963); Josh Dunson, *Freedom in the Air: Song Movements of the 60's* (1965), *Sing Out* (September 1964); Bernice Reagon, *Sing Out* (January–February 1976). ☆

WILLIAMS, ROBERT F.

(b. 1925) Black activist.

Williams was typical of the generation of southern blacks who launched the civil rights movement in the 1950s. Born in Monroe, N.C., in 1925, Williams grew up in a segregated society, served in the Marines during the Korean War, and after living briefly in Detroit, returned to North Carolina in 1955. He was active in the Monroe black community, and as president of the Union County NAACP led a series of demonstrations against Jim Crow practices and racial discrimination in hiring. In 1957 Williams organized a black rifle club, whose first public activity was to repel an armed Ku Klux Klan attack. When an all-white jury in 1959 acquitted a white man charged with attempted rape of a pregnant black woman, Williams angrily called for blacks to take up arms, to meet "violence with violence" (which he later clarified to mean "the right of armed self-defense against attack"). This outburst resulted in a six-month suspension by the national NAACP office and made him something of a pariah with the civil rights establishment, which then strongly supported Martin Luther King's nonviolent philosophy.

Williams's problems were only beginning. In the summer of 1961 Monroe was on the brink of race war, with the picketing of the public all-white swimming pool triggering armed conflict between the races. In the midst of the melee a white couple drove into a black neighborhood. A crowd of angry blacks marched the whites to Williams's home, where he held them for a few hours before releasing the couple unharmed. Charged with kidnapping, Williams fled the country with his wife and two children.

Williams spent the critical years of the civil rights movement in exile, first in Cuba and later in China. His book, *Negroes with Guns*, appeared in 1962. While in Cuba he broadcast a weekly radio message beamed at the South over "Radio Free Dixie" and edited his newsletter, *The Crusader*. As the movement in this country intensified, so did Williams's militancy; he called for revolution and urged blacks not to fight in Vietnam. While in China he was elected president-in-exile of the separatist Republic of New Africa. Increasingly frustrated by his inability to participate directly in the black struggle, Williams returned to the United States in 1963, living in Michigan while fighting extradition to stand trial in North Carolina. The state finally dropped the kidnapping charges in 1976, allegedly because the surviving white witness was too ill to testify.

Robert Williams's transformation from local NAACP leader to Third World revolutionary underscores the rapid and turbulent evolution of the civil rights movement in the South. His call for blacks to arm themselves, at first so shocking, had by the mid-1960s won support among many southern blacks, who knew from experience that violence had historically defined race relations in their region, and who—like Williams—were now unwilling to turn the other cheek.

John Dittmer
DePauw University

Harold Cruse, *The Crisis of the Negro Intellectual* (1967); James Forman, *The Making of Black Revolutionaries: A Personal Account* (1972); Robert F. Williams, *Negroes with Guns* (1962). ☆

WOODSON, CARTER G.

(1875–1950) Historian.

In 1915 Carter G. Woodson, who was born in New Canton, Va., a son of former slaves, organized the Association for the Study of Negro Life and History. He began publishing the *Journal of Negro History* 1 January 1916 and remained its editor until his 1950 death. Through the *Journal* and through his Associated Publishers, in Washington, D.C., he countered the bias permeating many contemporary accounts of slavery and the black man.

Woodson's 1922 *The Negro in Our History* went through 10 editions and was for many years the most widely used college text on the subject. But as time went on, Woodson turned more and more to racial propaganda in an effort to uplift his people. As one who had risen from a six-year stint in the coalfields of West Virginia to study at Berea College (1896–98), earn B.A. and M.A. degrees at the University of Chicago, take a 1912 Harvard Ph.D. in history, and become dean of liberal arts at Howard University (1919) and West Virginia State College (1920), he had an understandably sure sense of his own abilities. A self-made man, he was successful as an academician and publisher, and he believed in the need to present successful role models to black schoolchildren. As a result he wrote race history, emphasizing examples of individual success. His program for solving the problems of blacks in America was not unlike that of Booker T. Washington, whom he greatly admired.

Woodson became an entrenched member of the "black bourgeoisie." He adopted its mid-19th-century middle-class (white) values. He never learned to think in terms of black power—whether it be labor-union power or mass voting power.

Whatever his shortcomings as a historian and as a theorist, Carter G. Woodson was able to create, through his *Journal* and his Associated Publishers, vehicles for an alternative definition of the black situation to those that dominated American publishing throughout his lifetime.

S. P. Fullinwider
Arizona State University

Frank Klingberg, *Journal of Negro History* (January 1956); Michael Winston, *Journal of Negro History* (October 1975); James O. Young, *Black Writers of the Thirties* (1973). ☆

EDUCATION

THOMAS G. DYER
University of Georgia
CONSULTANT

☆ ☆ ☆ ☆ ☆ ☆ ☆ ☆ ☆ ☆

Education 399

Academic Freedom 408
Adult Education 411
Athletics and Education 413
Black Education. *See* BLACK LIFE: Education, Black
Classical Tradition 416
Desegregation 420
Federal-State Relations 422
Fraternities and Sororities 424
Illiteracy 426
Innovations in Education 429
Learned Societies 431
Legal Education. *See* LAW: Law Schools
Libraries 432
Medical Education. *See* SCIENCE AND MEDICINE: Medical Education

Military Schools 436
Politics of Education 439
Quality of Education 441
Religion and Education 443
Rural and Agricultural Education 448
Teachers 452
Technological Education 453
Urbanization and Education 457
Women's Education. *See* WOMEN'S LIFE: Education of Women

Alabama, University of 459
Arkansas, University of 460
Auburn University 460
Barnard, Frederick A. P. 462
Baylor University 463
Berea College 465
Black Mountain College 465
Bob Jones University 466
Busing 467
Campbell, John C. 469
Chautauqua 470
Christian Academies 471
Citadel, The 472
Clemson University 473
College of William and Mary 474
Commonwealth College 475
Couch, W. T. 477
Curry, J. L. M. 478
Duke University 479
Emory University 480
Fisk University 481
Florida, University of 483
Foxfire 484
General Education Board 485
Georgia, University of 486
Georgia Institute of Technology 487
Gildersleeve, Basil 488
Graham, Frank Porter 489
Hampden-Sydney College 490
Hampton Institute 491
Jackson State University 492
Junior Colleges 493
Kappa Alpha Order 495
Kentucky, University of 496
Key, V. O., Jr. 497
Louisiana State University 497
Mississippi, University of 498
Mississippi State University 500
National Humanities Center 501
North Carolina, University of 502
North Carolina School of the Arts 503
Odum, Howard W. 504
Phillips, U. B. 505
Piney Woods School 506
Randolph-Macon College 508
Rice University 509
Sheats, William N. 510
South Carolina, University of 511
Southern Methodist University 513
Tennessee, University of 514
Texas, University of 515
Texas A&M University 516
Tulane University 517
Tuskegee Institute 518
University of the South 519
Vance, Rupert B. 521
Vanderbilt University 522
Virginia, University of 523
Virginia Military Institute 524
Washington and Lee University 525
Weaver, Richard M. 527
Woodward, C. Vann 527

Overleaf: Schoolbus, Medora School, Southwestern Jefferson County, Kentucky c. 1930

EDUCATION

In recent years a resurgence of interest in the history of American education has yielded a sizable body of scholarship that alters many traditional ideas about the educational process in the South and its relationship to the broader social fabric. Although this research is not extensive enough to permit a thoroughgoing reinterpretation of southern educational history, a foundation has been laid to provide the basis for a broad overview. Scholars and laymen still have no useful modern guide to the evolution of the southern system of education and no interpretation that locates the regional experience within the broader national context.

Education in the American South has been characterized by an incessant quest for equality with educational systems outside the region. In many ways the region has been engaged in an unstinting effort for at least two centuries to develop an educational apparatus of quality comparable to that of the remainder of the nation. This self-conscious quest to obtain educational equality with more progressive systems elsewhere has been strongly inhibited by the region's peculiar values and culture. Furthermore, the most significant changes in schooling processes in the South have occurred in response to nonsouthern influences.

Early Educational Patterns. During the colonial era southerners accepted the English notion of education as a private responsibility. As a result, a stigma surrounded publicly supported education and led to a disparagement of those individuals who were unable to pay for instruction. Sparseness of settlement and a lack of effective governmental apparatus also inhibited the growth of schools in the South. Thus, the socializing effects of education were usually confined to areas where sufficient collective wealth existed to pay tutors for the education of children or where the means of an individual planter or merchant permitted the underwriting of his children's education.

As much interest existed in higher education in the prerevolutionary South as in the lower levels. Some southerners sent their sons to one of the nine colonial colleges located from Virginia northward, while a very few arranged for their education abroad. The attempt to found colleges in the region also reflected interest in higher education. The College of William and Mary, established in 1693, achieved true collegiate status by the third decade of the 18th century, but no other college came into existence in the South prior to the American Revolution. A few other attempts had been made, most notably perhaps the effort mounted by the trustees of Georgia to transfer a college planned for Bermuda to Georgia and a later plan, designed by the evangelist George Whitefield, which pointed toward the establishment of what would have been a denominational, provincial college in Savannah.

The revolutionary era produced significant interest in both common schools and colleges, and the libertarian forces unleashed by the Revolution contributed to a new interest in state systems of education. In several southern states plans evolved for designing unitary systems of education with state universities at the top supported by a system of academies and common schools. Most of these plans failed, although in several southern states universities did emerge prior to 1800, as did a few scattered colleges with no direct ties to the states.

In many respects, the South's educational system for the remainder of the period before the Civil War reflected the region's society and its conservative philosophy. Wealthy southerners hired private tutors for their children's instruction, while the middle class and moderately well-to-do created private contract schools and academies. For much of the period public education, in the contemporary sense of the term, was a foreign concept. The only tax-supported schools were the "poor" schools, which were set aside for those youths who would take a demeaning pauper's oath. Higher education catered to the children of the elite, and the collegiate curricula reflected the fondness of the privileged for classicism and the values of an earlier age. The region also rejected formal schooling for its black population.

This picture of southern education tends to perpetuate stereotypical notions of antebellum society without disclosing the strengths of southern education. Like their northern counterparts, southern primary and secondary schools grew and improved substantially during the pre–Civil War period. Although most of the region's schools remained privately supported, important strides were taken toward establishing tax-supported systems before the Civil War intervened. By 1861 literacy rates among whites had risen to approximately the same level as those of the midwestern states.

In still other ways the South felt the effects of the mid-19th-century educational revival. Southern colleges experimented with the introduction of collateral courses of study in the natural sciences and foreign languages. Colleges also began to admit older students of lower social station who either worked their way through school or received financial aid. Graduates of southern colleges, regardless of their social origins, played influential roles in the region's affairs both before and after the Civil War. The region also succeeded in establishing higher education for women on approximately the same level as that of the region's colleges for men. Although only a few women's colleges emerged, Wesleyan College in Macon, Ga., and several others offered a level of education that was genuinely collegiate. The sectional struggle and the coming of war negated many of these gains, as southern colleges increasingly became tools for the confirmation of regional values.

Civil War and Beyond. The Civil War disrupted education in the South, just as it thoroughly disrupted the activities of other social institutions. After the war, education resumed rather quickly at both lower and higher levels. Colleges that had been forced to close during the war now reopened, as did academies and other lower schools. During Reconstruction some state governments made appropriations for education. Perhaps the most significant question addressed during Reconstruction, however, related to the availability of education for newly freed slaves. Agents of the Freedmen's Bureau and representatives of northern churches began educational efforts in parts of the South even before the close of hostilities. With the coming of peace, large numbers of these groups began to educate the freedmen. Blacks greeted the prospect of education with great enthusiasm, viewing education as a ticket to equality in the white man's society. During radical Reconstruction educational provisions found their way into the new state constitutions, where for the first time in southern history universal education was recognized as a right of all citizens. In addition to the constitutional provisions, state legislators passed laws that established in every southern state a state superintendent of public instruction, made provisions for the training of teachers, and authorized taxes in support of education. The region's poverty, persistent white resistance to educating blacks, and corruption in the management of state government limited the achievements of the educational reforms introduced during Reconstruction. Nevertheless, Reconstruction awakened the region to the concept of universal education and to the hope of state support for public education.

By the turn of the century, southern schools had fallen further and further behind the rest of the nation. In 1900, when the average amount expended per child for education in the United States was slightly less than three dollars, Alabama and North Carolina (at the lower end of the southern scale) provided only 50 cents per child, while Florida and Texas (at the upper end) provided slightly less than $1.50 per child. School terms in the South were less than 100 days in length as opposed to 145 days for the United States. Teachers remained very poorly trained and were pitifully paid, averaging only about one-half the amount paid teachers elsewhere in the nation. Only one southern state required school attendance, and as a result, only about 40 percent of the region's children went to school on a regular basis. Of those who did, only 1 in 10 completed the fourth grade. Schoolhouses were unbelievably primitive in the rural areas and in black areas within the cities. Secondary education throughout the region was virtually nonexistent. Illiteracy rates for the southern states greatly exceeded those in any other part of the nation. Census statistics indicated that at least half of the region's blacks could not read. Undoubtedly, even larger numbers could have been classified as functionally illiterate.

Southern colleges and universities made some progress from the close of Reconstruction until the turn of the century, but by and large they suffered from problems generated by the region's poverty. The Morrill Act of 1862 provided federal funds to designated institutions in the southern states, but state appropriations to public institutions remained quite low and, in some cases, nonexistent, as conservative southern legislators clung to a laissez-faire philosophy toward higher education. Private institutions struggled to survive on gifts from sponsoring denominations and tuition from students. Separate black colleges that opened soon after the close of the Civil War, with assistance from northern agencies like the American Missionary Association, had difficulty surviving in an atmosphere of white hostility.

For the most part, both black and

white colleges adhered to classical liberal arts curricula, although a few state universities and some of the black institutions sought to incorporate agricultural and industrial training into their programs of study. There were a few efforts to introduce modern technological education, most notably at the newly founded Georgia School of Technology. Widespread education of teachers in a collegiate setting would await the second decade of the 20th century.

Reform Efforts. The beginnings of a southern educational reform movement could be discerned during the last two decades of the 19th century. A crusading spirit was brought by state leaders such as Charles B. Aycock and Edwin A. Alderman of North Carolina, Thomas U. Dudley of Kentucky, Charles W. Dabney of Tennessee, James L. Dillard of Louisiana, William N. Sheats of Florida, Oscar Cooper of Texas, J. J. Doyne of Arkansas, Braxton B. Comer of Alabama, Walter B. Hill of Georgia, and William H. Hand of South Carolina.

Funds provided by George F. Peabody, a Massachusetts banker, for the improvement of education at the elementary and secondary levels promoted the establishment of model schools and the improvement of individual schools. J. L. M. Curry, administrator of the Peabody Fund, proselytized throughout the region on behalf of education. Another eastern philanthropist, Robert C. Ogden, with the aid of people like Curry, established a series of educational conferences held throughout the region. These conferences, which coincided with an awakening of Progressivism in the region, brought an outpouring of interest in public education. Progressive southern governors sponsored legislation and constitutional revisions that led to dramatic increases in school revenues, a lengthening of the school terms, increases in the salaries of teachers, and decreases in the illiteracy rate. In addition, consolidation of rural schools followed, and by 1920 important strides had been taken toward establishing widespread public secondary education. During the first three decades of the 20th century, appropriations for education in all the southern states rose dramatically but stayed well below the national average.

Blacks by no means participated fully in the improvements of that era. Black education did benefit somewhat, however, from the introduction of Morrill funds, support of vocational education, and agencies like the Peabody Fund, the General Education Board, the John F. Slater Fund, and the Anna T. Jeanes Fund. In addition, philanthropies like the Rosenwald Foundation contributed millions of dollars toward the construction of black schools.

Despite the improvements in both black and white education during the Progressive era, the region's schools remained woefully inadequate. A few centers of achievement did appear, most notably in higher education, and the South committed an increasingly large percentage of its resources to the support of education. Southern schools, however, made relatively little progress in the game of catch-up, which they would play for decades to come. The agricultural depression of the 1920s and the Great Depression of the 1930s compounded an already difficult fiscal situation. Also, the region's largely rural culture placed a low premium on education for both whites and blacks. Whites refused to acknowledge that blacks should receive equal education, or for that matter be educated beyond

Mother teaching children in a sharecropper home, Transylvania, Louisiana, 1939

even the barest rudiments. State legislators throughout the region saw that black schools received only a fraction of the meager support that flowed to all of education.

Expansion of Education after World War II. As the Depression closed and World War II began, the southern economy entered a period of growth and increasing prosperity. A high birthrate during the war and rapid urbanization helped create a stronger demand for quality education. The growing prosperity of the region promoted increases in funding for education. Consolidation of schools became a hallmark in rural education, while in cities and suburbs massive construction programs were made possible by steadily increasing appropriations from state legislators. In addition to physical growth the region also turned its attention to salaries of teachers and requirements for teacher certification. Libraries and curricula grew, and secondary schools increasingly provided not only college preparatory education but also vocational-technical education.

In addition to the massive infusion of funds into elementary and secondary education, large amounts were also spent on improving the region's public colleges and universities. Long hampered by pitiful support from the states and by inferior facilities and faculties, these institutions now benefited from a growing awareness of the importance of higher education to the modernization of southern society. The appearance of large numbers of veterans on southern campuses following World War II added a much-welcomed source of revenue. The veterans' presence on campus helped to change the orientation of the institutions away from a strict *in loco parentis* posture. Enrollments in many southern institutions more than doubled during the late 1940s as a result of the presence of the veterans.

The southern record in higher education, however, remained well below that of the nation. Institutions such as the University of North Carolina or the University of Texas occasionally achieved national recognition for individual programs, but the achievements of most public and private universities in the region were not compatible with national norms. Indeed, southern *universities* remained little more than large liberal arts *colleges* with a modicum of professional education and little substantial graduate education.

In the early 1950s academicians and politicians developed an enlarged awareness of the importance of research in a university environment. There was a nascent recognition of the availability of federal and foundation funds for the support of research. Accordingly, in the 1950s many state and private institutions hired faculty who had both instructional and research skills. Their research led to a growth in outside funding for university programs during the late 1950s. With the 1958 National Defense

Table 1. *Doctoral Programs at Southern Universities, 1879–1962*

State	University	First Earned Doctorate Awarded	Average Doctorates Per Year 1953–62: Arts and Sciences Only	Including Education
Alabama	Auburn	1955	4	9
	U. Alabama	1952	12	17
Arkansas	U. Arkansas	1953	7	16
Florida	Florida State	1952	31	43
	U. Florida	1934	65	79
	U. Miami	1962	1	1
Georgia	Emory	1948	15	15
	Georgia Inst. of Tech.	1950	10	10
	U. Georgia	1940	5	9
Kentucky	U. Kentucky	1930	23	30
	U. Louisville	1953	6	6
Louisiana	Louisiana State U.	1935	52	58
	Tulane	1887	27	27
Mississippi	Mississippi State U.	1960	1	1
	U. Mississippi	1950[1]	1	5
North Carolina	Duke	1928	69	73
	N.C. State U.	1948	31	31
	U. North Carolina	1883	82	93
Oklahoma	Oklahoma State U.	1948	23	33
	U. Oklahoma	1929	32	49
South Carolina	U. South Carolina	1891[2]	3	4
Tennessee	George Peabody	1919	9	33
	U. Tennessee	1886[3]	33	45
	Vanderbilt	1879	37	37
Texas	Baylor	1954	6	7
	North Texas State U.	1954	1	5
	Rice	1918	20	20

[1]One doctorate was granted in 1893, but none during the next 57 years.
[2]Nineteen doctorates were granted in the 60-year period 1891–1951.
[3]Four doctorates were granted in the 1886–1948 period.

Table 1. *continued*

State	University	First Earned Doctorate Awarded	Average Doctorates Per Year 1953–62: Arts and Sciences Only	Including Education
	Texas A&M	1940	35	35
	Texas Tech U.	1953	3	7
	Texas Women's U.	1953	4	7
	U. Houston	1947	9	19
	U. Texas	1915	125	152
Virginia	U. Virginia	1885	39	45
	Virginia Polytechnic Inst.	1942	13	13
West Virginia	U. West Virginia	1902	6	7
Average		——	23	30
Median		——	13	19

Source: Allan M. Cartter, "Qualitative Aspects of Southern University Education," *Southern Economic Journal* (July 1965).

Education Act, in the wake of the Russian launching of Sputnik, federal support increased exponentially, even though southern institutions did not share in the increased federal funding as greatly as colleges and universities in other parts of the nation.

The new dollars strengthened research and instructional areas of the universities. For the next 30 years southern universities steadily built their research components and worked to achieve the comprehensiveness that had marked the nation's better research universities. Institutions like the University of Florida and the University of Georgia as well as private institutions like Duke and Vanderbilt now appear with increasing frequency in various national rankings of research universities.

The spurt in the growth of southern education after World War II by no means brought the region to parity with other parts of the United States. Without a concomitant move toward establishing equal educational opportunities for blacks and whites, southern education was doomed to remain grossly inferior. During the 1950s southern whites and blacks realized that educational and racial equality were inextricably intertwined. After World War II improvements and increased funds flowed to black schools as white southerners attempted to avert integration through achieving closer approximation of the separate-but-equal formula prescribed in the 1896 Supreme Court decision *Plessy* v. *Ferguson*. Whites' hopes that integration could be avoided were derailed with the *Brown* v. *Board of Education* decision in 1954.

Race Relations and Educational Quality. A program of "massive resistance" and state interposition of federal authority became hallmarks of resistance to racial change in schools. Strong pressures for change came from outside the region as federal officials, the press, and other segments of society pressed for compliance with the court's directive. The schools became a primary focus of civil rights activity as blacks and whites chose to work out many of the region's most serious problems within the schoolroom. White resistance dragged on until the early 1970s when the pressures of legal decisions and federal legislation brought integration of the region's public schools.

White and black southerners finally turned to the problem of bringing the region's schools to a level approximating national norms. Although the region still lagged behind, some progress had been made in the years since the civil rights era had begun. Virtually all areas of educational activity reflected the great increases in funds, and southern spokesmen prophesied that the region would one day become an example to the rest of the nation in the pursuit of academic excellence and equality.

By the early 1980s racial issues had largely taken second place to issues of quality at all levels of southern education. The region now has a full panoply of educational programs ranging from preschool through postsecondary to a wide variety of adult programs. A new awareness of the importance of sound education in attracting business and industry to the region has inspired a resurgence of educational reform efforts. As a result of such efforts most southern schools are now on a par with other systems across the nation. Yet the parity has resulted from a convergence of southern progress and national backsliding in educational quality. Studies such as the 1985 report *A Nation at Risk* have documented a general lowering of national educational standards and thus have provided a new benchmark against which southern educational reforms must be judged.

Beginning in 1983 most southern legislatures inaugurated far-reaching educational reforms aimed at upgrading elementary and secondary education, with special attention given to such quality indicators as teacher salaries and qualifications. So extensive and so thoroughgoing were the reforms that a former U.S. secretary of education offered the judgment that the South might prove to be the leader in a revitalization of American education.

Such reforms depend upon continued economic prosperity in the region and upon the willingness of southerners to tax themselves at higher rates than have been historically acceptable. Whether the region will be able to finance the reforms seems in doubt in some states where growth has slowed and economic recession threatens implementation of reforms. It is not clear, moreover, what effect the reforms will have upon public *higher* education, which has enjoyed considerable progress in the region. The outcome of the reform movement of the 1980s remains in doubt.

Education has been one of the main mechanisms by which southern cultural norms have been maintained and transmitted. In the antebellum era, for example, spokesmen for southern sectionalism saw a continuing struggle against the North for cultural independence, and they attempted to use the southern schools to nurture an explicitly "southern" outlook in the young. Professor J. D. B. De Bow of the University of Louisiana (and editor of *De Bow's Review*) admitted that southern schools were inferior to those elsewhere in scholarly achievement but saw it better that "our sons remained in honest ignorance and at the plough-handle" than full of "doctrines subversive of their country's peace and honor." Delegates to commercial conventions before the Civil War frequently urged the use of native-born southern teachers in schools and a home press publishing textbooks appropriate to southern traditions and interests. The persistent call for a central southern university, training students in regional values, led one group of southerners to found the University of the South at Sewanee, Tenn., in the late 1850s.

American schools have traditionally been seen as institutions of the "melting pot," assimilating children from diverse ethnic backgrounds into the dominant American culture. Studies of mass education in the 20th century now suggest, though, that the process has not worked automatically. Sociologist John Shelton Reed has concluded that the schools have been less powerful in the South than elsewhere. The schools reflect a large degree of community control, "with the culturally conservative function such control implies." Historian Francis Butler Simkins once noted that "among Southerners there is the education which does not educate." Schools have been staffed primarily by southerners who shape the interpretation of educational information in textbooks, and southern students are subject to powerful local influences that make them attuned to receive and believe certain information but not all. Simkins concluded that "the home, not the school, determines the cultural outlook of Southerners," but it is likely, in many cases, that the two reinforced each other.

Elementary school in Warren County, Mississippi, 1962

Certain universities have served as, in effect, regional institutions educating an elite in southern traditions or promoting regional scholarship. The University of the South, Washington and Lee University, the University of North Carolina, and the University of Virginia are only a few examples of schools promoting regionalism in one way or another. Boys' military academies have likely played a similar role at the secondary school level, although much work remains to be done in exploring this topic.

By the mid-1980s it was also unclear how extensively southern cultural norms and beliefs would affect the future course of education in the region. Much evidence existed, however, to suggest that the attenuation of cultural boundaries was proceeding apace and that the South was losing much of its distinctiveness as a result of a significant inmigration, the revolution in race relations, and the systematic exposure of the region through the mass media to dominant national values. The enthusiasm with which political leaders embraced educational reforms as a passport to economic improvement (although in some ways a reenactment of earlier regional flirtations with boosterism) suggested that the region had a stronger commitment to educational improvement than had previously characterized the culture. That southern politicians now longed for a well-trained, educated labor force (as well as a docile one) also offered at least some evidence that the region had embraced national values in that area as well.

See also AGRICULTURE: / Agricultural Extension Services; BLACK LIFE: Education, Black; HISTORY AND MANNERS: Philanthropy, Northern; Progressivism; POLITICS: Segregation, Defense of; SCIENCE AND MEDICINE: Medical Education; Professionalization of Science; / Scopes Trial; SOCIAL CLASS: Poverty; WOMEN'S LIFE: Education of Women

Thomas G. Dyer
University of Georgia

Henry A. Bullock, *A History of Negro Education in the South: From 1619 to the Present* (1967); Thomas D. Clark, *The Emerging South* (1961); Charles W. Dabney, *Universal Education in the South*, 2 vols. (1936); Irving Gershenberg, *History of Education Quarterly* (Winter 1970); Ronald K. Goodenow and Arthur O. White, eds., *Education and the Rise of the New South* (1982); Louis R. Harlan, *Separate and Unequal: Public School Campaigns and Racism in the Southern Seaboard States, 1901–1915* (1958); Diane Ravitch, *The Troubled Crusade: American Education, 1945–1980* (1983); John Shelton Reed, *One South: An Ethnic Approach to Regional Culture* (1982); Charles P. Roland, *The Improbable Era: The South since World War II* (1975); David Tyack, *Managers of Virtue: Public School Leadership in America, 1820–1980* (1982), *Public Schools in Hard Times: The Great Depression and Recent Years* (1984), ed., *Turning Points in American Educational History* (1967); William Preston Vaughn, *Schools for All: The Blacks and Public Education in the South, 1865–1877* (1974); Thomas L. Webber, *Deep Like the Rivers: Education in the Slave Quarter Community, 1831–1865* (1978). ☆

Academic Freedom

Southern culture has presented distinctive problems for academic freedom. Sectional characteristics of religion, race relations, political conservatism, and history have sometimes brought conflicts so violent that physical safety was threatened along with freedom of thought.

More than in any other section, the people of the Bible Belt had a personal and emotional contact with their religion rather than a mere institutional membership. Believers were expected to defend their faith and did so with passions frequently dividing towns, families, and educational institutions into hostile camps. As the mission of the church was to proselytize and to educate its members in its doctrine, so the free exercise of religion demanded the ability to create educational institutions to train preachers and lay readers. The absence of tax-supported public schools in the region motivated the growth of institutes, academies, and colleges with denominational affiliation. As naturally as the churches chose only members of their own religion to be their ministers, they chose only like-minded teachers for their institutions. The proprietary nature of such schools so conflicted with the theory of academic freedom that their character as institutions of higher education has been called into doubt, although many carried on with distinction the development of intellects. The conflicting claim of academics to the right of intellectual freedom and of the churches to the right to establish and maintain colleges is one of the abiding paradoxes of southern culture.

Instances of direct conflict of intellectual freedom with institutional purpose arose when professors changed their beliefs or when they found themselves caught in one of the frequent doctrinal splits in the denominations. The situation could be alleviated if the sect had a powerful central body that could exercise rigid control over the institutions. The upper offices tended to be held by the more liberal elements, which protected the institutions from the radical conservatism sometimes found in the pew. Where government remained on the congregational level, as it did among the Baptists, the Pentecostals, and the Churches of Christ, it was harder for the ecclesiastical hierarchy of the churches to closely supervise the institutions, which sometimes fell under the control of special interests, especially those led by a powerful preacher or those people or factions that could offer large financial incentives. Although many southern colleges and universities continue to have denominational ties, the tendency has been to weaken the sectarian contribution and control so that it is rare to find religious requirements for faculty membership, except in departments such as religion or Bible.

With the rise of the scientific method and the influence of Darwinism, an attempt to accommodate theology to new discoveries became common on religious campuses. In some cases the new theories were so contrary to the older doctrines that charges of heresy could be brought, as in the case of the general assembly's 1888 judgment against James Woodrow in the South Carolina Presbyterian synod. At the same time, and from the opposite direction, a new spirit of hostility toward theological concepts was manifesting itself, tending to claim an exclusive right to the title "intellectualism," and in a few cases going so far as to create a new outlook actively hostile to orthodox Christianity. In a number of cases the men who espoused the new ideas gained control of institutions created under the denominations and separated them from the churches, as at Vanderbilt.

The rise of the public schools in the early 20th century provided a new competition for the church schools, which they were not completely willing or able to face. Tax-supported education would, it was assumed, be religiously neutral because of the separation of church and state mandated by the U.S. Constitution. The new Darwinian theories presented a problem for that neutrality insofar as they dealt directly with the religiously pivotal issues of the nature and origin of man. Moderates in most denominations had already accommodated evolution to the Scriptures by using figurative interpretations of the Old Testament and including a reservation that the human soul, at least, was a special creation of God. They were willing for the tax-supported schools to teach the theories of evolution so long as they handled the matter of human development (and especially the nature of the human soul) with discretion and made no reference to the Bible.

By the 1920s, however, there were reports that a few teachers were using the classrooms to attack the Bible and to inculcate new religious doctrines based upon Darwinism. Such violations of the religious neutrality of the public school motivated appeals to the antiestablishment clause of the First Amendment. Fundamentalists wanted to prohibit all teaching of the evolution of man, while moderates proposed only a clarification of the constitutional infringement involved in a tax-supported assault on some religious beliefs. Proposals in several states were defeated by the divisions between these factions. When a law was proposed in Tennessee, its heading was worded so as to satisfy the fundamentalists while its body prohibited only the teaching that used the theory of the evolution of man in expressed contradiction to the Bible. Even the opponents were mollified, because the wording was so vague that they did not believe it enforceable. The Scopes Trial in June 1925 was supposed to decide the constitutionality of the law, but the tactics of the defense turned it into a contest between the Bible and evolution. The result was that many southerners who had previously accepted both were now convinced the two were mutually exclusive and rejected Darwin to keep God. The South-baiting of the 1920s, so prevalent in the prosecution case and in the reporting of the trial, made many loyal southerners espouse antiintellectualism and made it harder for the moderates to continue to control denominations and institutions; academic freedom thereby suffered. The present attempts in some states to force "creationism" into the classroom or the textbooks have the same roots.

U.S. Supreme Court rulings since the 1950s on Bible reading, prayer, and integration in the public schools have provided new incentives for the formation of church-related primary and high schools, which tend to be under the control of the most conservative local churches and to have associations with the fundamentalist or "religious right" wing of the denominations. The lack of academic freedom in these Christian academies has not received the attention it would in higher education. The main controversies instead are over teacher qualifications, certification, and tuition tax credits.

Political and economic conservatism has created serious problems for academic freedom, especially in the periods of the reinstitution of Democratic control after the Civil War (during the years of Ku Klux Klan domination), the Red Scare, and the McCarthy era. Other sections suffered from the same turmoils, though perhaps not to the same extent.

The most emotional issue for southerners has been that of race relations. Even before the Civil War the controversy had become a struggle for freedom of thought and expression. Almost from the beginning, relations with the slaves and the exslaves took on the volatile mixture of racism, political interests, religious concerns, and sectional pride, and the bloody tragedy engulfed the section for years. After Reconstruction and the reestablishment of white political supremacy, black students and faculty were routinely denied academic freedom as well as civil rights, and the occasional white who defended them was in peril of ostracism, loss of position, and even violence. As the civil rights campaign of the 1950s and 1960s grew, it frequently found its leadership on the campuses. Especially during the integration conflicts, southern campuses witnessed the presence of marshalls, militiamen, tear gas, and even death.

Although not all questions are settled, the basic issues have moved toward resolution so that freedom of thought and expression is no more an issue for the South than for other regions.

See also RELIGION: Civil Rights and Religion; Theological Orthodoxy; SCIENCE AND MEDICINE: Science and Religion; / Scopes Trial

Charles F. Ogilvie
University of Tennessee
at Martin

Clement Eaton, *The Freedom-of-Thought Struggle in the Old South* (1964); Richard Hofstadter and Walter P. Metzger, *Development of Academic Freedom* (1955); James W. Silver, *Mississippi: The Closed Society* (1964). ☆

Adult Education

Historically, adult education has been characterized by the same limitations as public school and postsecondary education in the South. At least three patterns can be distinguished in the analysis of education of adults: the first is provided by the more urbanized trading centers of the interior and coastal areas such as Charleston, Natchez, New Orleans, Memphis, and Savannah; a second pattern, overlaying the first, is derived from the aristocratic plantation society of the East Coast Tidewater and Mississippi Delta areas; finally, the third pattern is developed from the vast interior stretches of the region from the Coastal Plains, the Piedmont, and the mountains that were populated by the relatively isolated, small family farmers.

The education provided to adults in southern trading centers such as Charleston and Natchez was not historically unlike that of the rest of the nation. The second pattern was unique to the region, but only a few thousand people were involved in educating adults on the plantations. In contrast, the distinguishing character of education of adults in the South derived from focusing on small farmers in the southern interior.

The general absence of anything but the most rudimentary provisions for childhood education in a small, often subsistence, farm environment provided little encouragement for many southern adults or children to achieve educationally. Consequently, illiteracy became a pervasive characteristic of thousands of adults in the period from colonial settlement to the Civil War. After the war illiteracy was a problem for more than just newly freed black adults. Thus, for the past one hundred years the battle for literacy has provided a distinctive character to adult education in the states of the old Confederacy.

Responses to the pervasiveness of illiteracy in the 50 years from 1875 to 1925 were diverse and numerous. They included local efforts and external efforts to provide education for adults, black and white. The battle was joined by philanthropists, industrialists, educators, and politicians. They created lay-by schools, moonlight schools, evening schools in textile communities, and a number of socially sensitive educational institutions such as Berea College, the Highlander Folk School, Martha Berry College, Rabun Gap–Nacoochee School, the South Carolina Opportunity School, and Ruskin College.

Rabun Gap–Nacoochee School in Georgia and the South Carolina Opportunity School are two 20th-century institutions that emerged shortly after the turn of the century when the situation concerning adult illiteracy was recognized as being acute. Both institutions continue to this day with modified curricula and missions. Originally, both were designed to provide instruction to families in their areas. The founders of the institutions, Andrew J. Ritchie of the Rabun Gap–Nacoochee School and Wil Lou Gray of the South Carolina Opportunity School, perceived a need to enroll entire families in their programs providing a variety of educational opportunities. In the case of the South Carolina Opportunity School, instruction was limited to a short time during the lay-by period in the summer months. In contrast, families were permitted to move into one of the 21 cottages on the 1,800–acre school farm at Rabun Gap, where they could live for up to 10 years. The heads of each family and all adult children above school age were required to attend school sessions and meetings held for their benefit and improvement. Children of public school age were required to attend a school provided for them for nine months of the year.

By the third decade of the current century, state governments through their systems of public education had begun to make contributions of varying kinds to literacy programs. These programs alternately languished and flourished until 1964 when the federal government, through the Civil Rights Act, began to support adult basic-education programs in the various states. *Adult education* in many southern states is a term now used to refer to adult basic education. The increased prosperity of the southern region has reduced the relative prevalence of adult illiteracy, and a variety of additional provisions exists for meeting other educational needs of adults. Nevertheless, the pressure of approximately 2 million illiterate adults and continuing high levels of attrition in the public schools of the South indicate that, despite various strategies and campaigns and millions of dollars, the problem persists.

Other educational activities for adults exist in varying degrees across the South. Many states now contain at least one university with continuing-education facilities, including programs designed to meet the continuing professional-education needs of various groups from dentists to veterinarians. Technical institutes and community colleges provide a wide range of educational opportunities for adults with different levels of previous educational achievement.

See also BLACK LIFE: Education, Black; SOCIAL CLASS: Poverty; / Highlander Folk School

Huey Long
University of Georgia

Clyde N. Ginn, Frances Karnes, and Beverley B. Maddon, eds., *Issues and Trends in Adult Basic Education: Focus on Reading* (1979); Ronald K. Goodenow and Arthur O. White, eds., *Education and the Rise of the New South* (1981); Malcolm Knowles, *The Adult Learner: A Neglected Species* (1973); Huey Long et al., *Changing Approaches to Studying Adult Education* (1980); Ralph M. Lyon, *The Basis for Constructing Curricular Materials in Adult Education for Carolina Mill Workers* (1937); Joel H. Magisos and Anne E. Stakelon, compilers, *Adult Vocational Education: An Annotated Bibliography of Publications and Projects* (1975); John Ohlinger, *Media and Adult Learning:*

A Bibliography with Abstracts, Annotations, and Quotations (1975). ☆

Athletics and Education

Modern American athletics emerged in the years between 1880 and 1920. Beginning with a concern for nurturing "the strenuous life" in an urban, industrial society, Americans created a highly organized spectator and participant system of athletic activities for the young. These developments began in the Northeast, spread then to the Middle West, and came late to the South. Athletics, though, became an important part of southern education and helped to define a distinctive southern culture.

Americans at the turn of the 20th century articulated a sports ideology that spoke of "muscular Christianity," which stressed the religious significance of manliness and the importance of play for proper physical, spiritual, and mental development. The Young Men's Christian Association, city playground associations, church leagues, business-sponsored community leagues, and the public school athletic leagues all reflected the ideology that had come to the South by the 1920s. The ideology was an urban-centered concern, and the South's relative lack of urban areas in the early 20th century limited the importance of the interest in organized athletics until after 1920. The South's predominantly rural schools, oriented to the seasonal farm cycle, had little interest in, or ability to nurture, extracurricular activities such as athletics. Sports had long been important to rural southerners, but they were in the form of outdoor hunting and fishing. Eventually, though, southerners became convinced of the need for adult management of youthful athletics as a way to nurture cultural values. The emergence of "comprehensive" high schools encouraged adult management of youth sports. Athletics were said to help channel adolescent sexual energy into constructive social and moral habits and to help potentially rebellious students.

High school athletics slowly became an integral part of southern education. Schools, whether urban or rural, have competed since the 1920s in interscholastic leagues designed to allow relatively equal competition between schools of similar enrollment. High school sports in the South helped to give an identity and sense of common purpose to neighborhoods, towns, and cities. Historian Thomas D. Clark has noted that the enthusiasm for school athletics has placed schools "in a curious kind of public domain." "Even hardened old rednecks," Clark notes, "who have wandered in from the cotton fields have caught the fever. Fifty years ago they would have regarded these sports as either effeminate or juvenile. Not so the modern southerner." The emphasis on athletics has brought the general population into close association "with the forms if not the substance of education."

Football is a prime focus for school athletics. Friday night in the autumn is the time for a major southern ritual occasion. Football is the center of a complex cultural event involving more than players on the field. Cheerleaders, baton twirlers, trainers, and marching bands are actively involved, while the stands are filled with students, former players who have graduated and returned to cheer for their team, and parents and friends of parents. As historian Lawrence Goodwyn has written of Texas, schoolboy football "was an instrument of psychic survival and, as such, a centerpiece of the regional culture." When the local high school team was having a bad season, an "uneasiness" settled over the entire community. Journalist James J. Kilpatrick has noted that while high school athletics are also taken seriously in the Midwest, in the South "they're a religion." Local people read in their Saturday papers or their weeklies of "the feats of Panthers, Rebels, Bisons, Rockets, Trojans, Bulldogs, Wildcats, Warriors, Whippets, Raiders, and Tigers."

Basketball was a rallying point for communities whose schools were too poor and/or too small to field football teams. In Kentucky, where basketball so dominates the culture that local storytellers joke that "a Kentucky homosexual is a boy who likes girls more than basketball," many small towns have enjoyed lasting distinction on the basis of their high school team's accomplishments in the state tournament. Girls' basketball was deeply rooted in the schools there long before the recent growth in women's sports.

Although the appearance of comprehensive high schools was an early 20th-century necessity for the development of extracurricular athletic activities, school athletics contributed in more recent times to southern reluctance to accept large, consolidated county high schools. In many rural southern counties a local community maintained its identity as a result of a small school where the boys and girls who comprised the varsity basketball teams were genuine community heroes and heroines. In this setting, the basketball games became the major social activity throughout most of the school year for both the adults and children of the community. These get-togethers provided inexpensive, family-oriented socialization for the rural populace and were carefully scheduled so as not to conflict with church activities—the other focal point of small-town community life.

By the 1960s most rural southern counties contained a "big school"—a county-seat high school with 500 to 2,000 students. However, the county was also still dotted with "country schools," which contained 300 to 600 students in grades 1 through 12. By the late 1960s and early 1970s consolidation and "progress" terminated most of these small, country high schools. The "farmers" rode the big yellow school buses for several hours each day to attend bigger and, ostensibly, better schools. Many of these rural youngsters, who had been "top dog" at their small school, were either too timid or too untalented to participate in extracurricular activities and sports at their new school. Others wanted to be involved but had to ride the bus home in order to assist with daily chores.

In exchange for a broader curriculum and other big-school amenities, many rural youngsters lost an opportunity to build confidence and leadership abilities through participation in sports, clubs, and other extracurricular activities. On the positive side, big-school education unquestionably led more rural youngsters to attend college.

By the 1980s some of the little high schools that once pumped lifeblood into local communities had become grade schools. Many others stood as empty and crumbling monuments to a part of southern life that had been lost forever. The dissolution of the small country high school led to a concomitant disappearance of community spirit and identity and left a rural populace frustrated, disoriented, and nostalgic for the good old days when a last-minute victory over an archrival lit fires of community pride that were rekindled by generations of storytellers. As University of Alabama football coach Paul "Bear" Bryant once observed, "It's hard to rally 'round a math class." For rural southerners, it was hard to rally around an empty building.

The stress on athletics has glorified success on the playing field at the expense of other forms of educational achievement in the South, as across the nation. In the high school social structure the athlete ranks near the top. Texas has led a recent movement to reduce the role of athletics in high schools. In 1984 the state board of education passed a rule, which was authorized by the state legislature, barring students from extracurricular activities if they did not pass every subject they took in the previous six-week examining period. The "no pass, no play" provision was promoted by businessman H. Ross Perot, who headed an advisory committee on educational excellence. The *New York Times* (28 April 1985) said the rule had "stirred about as much emotion in Texas as anything since Santa Anna overran the Alamo." The state's business and political leaders expressed strong commitment to it, but coaches and parents expressed concern over its fundamental challenge to athletic values in Texas schools. The other southern states have recently enacted programs to promote educational improvement, but none at the state level have adopted the Texas model.

Athletics has played a role in the desegregation of southern schools. A particularly skilled black athlete, such as Marcus Dupree in Philadelphia, Miss., can become a hero of the community. The stress on school athletics, however, has channeled black achievement disproportionately into sports at the expense of other activities, according to critics. Moreover, the achievements of black athletes do not always translate into later success for the athletes once they have graduated.

Southern schools have long produced outstanding women athletes, such as Mildred "Babe" Didriksen Zaharias and Wilma Rudolph. The region has a tradition of good girls' basketball, but the culture has only recently encouraged a general interest by girls in organized sports. Victorian ideas on femininity, which stressed passivity and fragility, held on longer in the South than elsewhere in this country and were reinforced by specifically regional notions of the lady and the belle. While the South is above the national average in support of sports such as football and basketball and in the production of talent in those areas, it ranks well below the national average in financial support of women's sports in the schools. Women's sports did expand in the 1920s, thanks to Amateur Athletic Union programs in swimming, track and field, basketball, and gymnastics. Tennis, golf, and swimming were encouraged in the schools rather than more vigorous sports such as softball or basketball. However, industrial sports leagues, which were sponsored by businesses, were important in providing athletic opportunities for women. Bowling is the most popular participant sport among women today in all regions, and the industrial league teams from the South and the Midwest have been strong in that sport and have long dominated in basketball. The late 1960s and 1970s witnessed a revolution in women's sports. Title IX of the Educational Amendments Act of 1972 outlawed sexual discrimination by school districts and institutions of higher learning. The hope was to force improved funding for women's athletics while avoiding the high-pressure, competitive problems of men's sports. Women's sports, though, have developed along the same line as men's, stressing winning, the recruiting of the best high school athletes, the giving of athletic scholarships, and a predominantly spectator orientation.

College and university athletics have reflected many of the same patterns found in the schools. College football, for example, began in the Northeast in the late 19th century, but southern teams earned little national acclaim until the 1920s. The hot climate, regional provincialism, and wide distribution of good players in many small colleges supposedly prevented the emergence of powerful teams. The 1920–45 period witnessed a dramatic change. On 1 January 1926 Coach Wallace Wade's University of Alabama team defeated Washington State in a landmark intersectional game. The University of Georgia defeated Yale three times in a four-year period, and southern teams by the post–World War II years were frequently winning national championships. Southerners responded to these triumphs with an outburst of regional enthusiasm. "Indeed, pride in the strength of sectional football teams took its place along with pride in the valor of the Confederate army as a major source of Southern chauvinism," wrote historians Francis Butler Simkins and Charles Roland in *A History of the South* (1972). The athlete became a glamorous new southern hero and his coach the best-known university figure to the general populace. Athletics was soon a sometimes-consuming affair for students and alumni. Bonfires, cheerleaders, pep bands, and other ingredients of a new ritualism led one writer in 1930 to remark on the football South's "medieval pageantry long forgotten outside the South."

See also BLACK LIFE: Education, Black; Sports, Black; GEOGRAPHY: Sports, Geography of; RECREATION: Basketball; Cheerleading and Twirling; Football; / Bryant, Bear; Manning, Archie; Walker, Herschel

James M. Gifford
Appalachian Development Center
Appalachian State University

Charles Reagan Wilson
University of Mississippi

Jack Berryman, *Journal of Sport History* (Fall 1975); Ellen Gerber et al., *The American Woman in Sport* (1974); James A. Montgomery, "The Development of the Interscholastic Athletics Movement in the United States, 1890–1940" (Ph.D. dissertation, George Peabody College for Teachers, 1960); Tema Okun and Peter Wood, eds., *Southern Exposure* (Fall 1979); Benjamin G. Rader, *American Sports: From the Age of Folk Games to the Age of Spectators* (1983). ☆

Black Education

See BLACK LIFE: Education, Black

Classical Tradition

From its beginnings the intellectual culture of the South reflected the influence of the Greek and Latin classics. In this respect southerners of the 17th and 18th centuries were hardly different from their British and European relatives. New England learning was also based upon a classical curriculum, but—as John Gould Fletcher observed—the Puritans "regarded education primarily as a means of training theological students." The settlers of Virginia and the Carolinas embraced the classics not so much for spiritual and pragmatic reasons but because they were the vehicle of English and European civilization. It is a remarkable coincidence that the first major work of literature produced in the South (or in America, for that matter) was George Sandys's translation of Ovid's *Metamorphoses*. Sandys's version—one of the most influential poetical works of 17th-century England—was composed in Jamestown during the poet's tenure as treasurer (1621–26).

The classical tradition had taken root in all the American colonies by the time of the American Revolution. Students at the College of William and Mary, like their counterparts at Harvard, learned their Latin (still out of Lily's grammar) before matriculation. Greek studies were less the rule than the ideal. This common background provided an important link between sections that had already begun to diverge in other respects. The political thinkers of the Revolution and the Constitution—Jefferson as much as Adams, Madison as much as Hamilton—had constant recourse in their writings to the principles and examples of the ancients. The Greek Revival style of 18th-century public buildings is a vivid testimony to the impact of classical ideals upon the Founding Fathers. Jefferson, in his earlier days, might have deplored the exclusivity of the classical regime, but at his University of Virginia graduates were expected "to be able to read the highest classics in the language with ease, thorough understanding, and just quantity," and Jefferson warned his fellow countrymen against following the example of Europeans, who—in his view—were abandoning Latin and Greek.

The classical tradition did not go unchallenged. The American Revolution bred expectations of a Golden Age in which the shackles of the centuries would be cast aside. The past, it was frequently argued, could not provide useful examples for the American experiment in republican self-government. The classics, which had already been dismissed by Locke and Rousseau as impractical, were now impugned as undemocratic. Northerners like Benjamin Rush and Noah Webster argued that a democratic society should not burden itself with the fripperies of decadent Europe. Such arguments were addressed by the Marylander Samuel Knox in his essay "On Liberal Education" (1799), in which he slyly suggested that opposition to the classics was the result of "vitiated taste and the negligence or indulgence of parents."

In Charleston the battle lines of the ancients and the moderns had been drawn even before the Revolution in debates at the cosmopolitan city's library. In the 1820s Thomas Grimké took up the moderns' case, but Grimké's bold attacks were countered by no less than Roman Catholic Bishop John England and by statesman Hugh S. Legaré. Legaré printed his defense of the classics as the first article of the first issue of his new journal, the *Southern Review*. In the decades to come, the moderns were to have their triumph in the North, but Charleston—like the South as a whole—was to remain devoted to the classics for another century and a half. The College of Charleston maintained a Latin requirement for all arts degrees until 1966. That college's most illustrious student, Basil L. Gildersleeve, became unquestionably the greatest classical scholar America has produced. In 1854—seven years before the war that found the scholar riding with Jeb Stuart—Gildersleeve published an essay on "The Necessity of the Classics." To his defense of classical learning, he added the consideration that classical philology was a good field for southerners because it was "a harvest untouched by the sickle" of northern writers.

The sectionalist note struck by Gildersleeve (half a century before he wrote *The Creed of the Old South*) was one symptom of the growing cultural isolation that the South was imposing upon itself. The lust for modernity was regarded—like Unitarianism and the factory system—as a Yankee invention. Jefferson Davis was one of many prominent southerners who made a plea for keeping southern students at southern colleges. Most of these schools maintained stiff requirements until the turn of the century. Students at the University of Georgia were expected "to read, translate, and parse Cicero, Virgil, and the Greek Testament, and to write true Latin in prose" *before* admission. Similar requirements were imposed by William and Mary, South Carolina College, and Transylvania University (Kentucky), which a young Jefferson Davis attended. Classical requirements did not mean, necessarily, a contempt for more modern disciplines. At the University of Virginia in 1857, 249 students were enrolled in Latin, 248 in chemistry, 168 in Greek, and 171 in natural philosophy. The study of Latin (and Greek) was, however, regarded as necessary instruction. Frederick A. P. Barnard (before becoming president of the University of Mississippi) insisted that students at the University of Alabama needed classical training much more than the usual survey courses in science, even though Barnard was himself a science teacher.

By 1861 the South could be distinguished from the North by its attachment to the classics as much as by its agrarian ideals or its peculiar institution. At a time when the North was priding itself on the progress of the modern age, southern orators were continuing to model their speeches on Cicero and Demosthenes—albeit with the addition of Romantic flourishes—and planters in Mississippi were constructing their houses—not always in the best of taste—on the lines of ancient temples. Even the defense of slavery was justified by classical precedents and argued from ancient authorities. George Fitzhugh discovered, somewhat belatedly, that his *Sociology for the South* (1854) was Aristotelian, while Thomas Roderick Dew was made president of the University of Virginia largely on the strength of his famous proslavery argument, based in large measure on classical sources.

The hundred years following Reconstruction have seen a slow but constant ebbing of classical influences. The New South, envisioned by Henry W. Grady and realized by populists like Ben Tillman, was to be a practical sort of place whose citizens needed engineering and business skills more than the ability to write Latin prose. Southern politics came under the dominion of men who gloried in their identification with the common man and were inclined to hide what learning they possessed as a shameful secret. There were remarkable exceptions, like Sam Ervin of North Carolina, who larded his speeches with allusions to Cicero as well as Burke and Jefferson. Paradoxically, it was the exceptional old-fashioned orators like Ervin or Senator James Eastland of Mississippi who were still regarded as the typical southern statesmen. Even so, despite the South's commitment to modernization, its schools continued to offer Latin, either as a requirement or as a college preparatory elective, into the 1960s, and professional classicists were able to reassure themselves that southern high school graduates were still coming to college able to read a page of Caesar and to tell who fought whom and why under the walls of Troy.

To the extent that the South remains aware of its past, it will remain under the influence of the classics. Most of the major southern writers were schooled in the classics, even though they wrote as men of their own time. Nineteenth-century poets like Poe and Timrod wrote, like their English models, in the Romantic manner, and few attempts were made in a classical or neoclassical idiom. (Louisa McCord's *Caius Gracchus* is a partial exception.) Nonetheless, ancient literature was generally taken for granted by southern writers to an extent that is hard to realize. William Gilmore Simms is the exception that proves the rule: he was always keenly aware of his educational deficiencies. To understand the impact of the classics upon the southern intelligence, one need only browse through the pages of the literary reviews of the last century—*De Bow's Review*, the *Southern Literary Messenger*, and the *Southern Review*—for the countless articles and essays on ancient and modern oratory, classical poets, and even manuscripts of ancient authors. Although only 5 percent of the *Southern Quarterly Review*'s articles were actually devoted to the ancient world, the general impression is of a literary culture that took Greek and Latin for granted.

Indeed, classical themes and allusions abounded in southern literature even until the period after World War II. John Gould Fletcher's contribution to *I'll Take My Stand*, the Agrarian manifesto of 1930, was "Education, Past and Present," a reasoned defense of the old schooling; and the essays and verses of other Agrarians—Allen Tate, Robert Penn Warren, and Donald Davidson—seem to assume the classics as a common ground in a manner quite distinct from the self-conscious allusiveness of Ezra Pound and T. S. Eliot. What the future holds for the classical tradition in southern education and literature is uncertain.

See also: HISTORY AND MANNERS: / Davis, Jefferson; Jefferson, Thomas; Madison, James; INDUSTRY: / *De Bow's Review*; Grady, Henry W.; LAW: / Ervin, Sam; LITERATURE: Agrarianism in Literature; / Davidson, Donald; Poe, Edgar Allan; Simms, William Gilmore; Tate, Allen; Warren, Robert Penn; MYTHIC SOUTH: New South Myth; / Agrarians, Vanderbilt; Fitzhugh, George

Thomas Fleming
McClellanville, South Carolina

Richard Beale Davis, *Intellectual Life in the Colonial South, 1585–1763*, 3 vols. (1978); Clement Eaton, *The Mind of the Old South* (1964); Michael O'Brien, *A Character of Hugh Legaré (1985), ed., All Clever Men Who Make Their Way* (1982); *Southern Humanities Review* (Special Issue 1977); Twelve Southerners, *I'll Take My Stand: The South and the Agrarian Tradition* (1930). ☆

Desegregation

Rigid segregation was the prior condition for southern white acceptance of tax-supported schools, even before the U.S. Supreme Court sanctioned separate-but-equal public accommodations in *Plessy* v. *Ferguson* (1896). With the collapse of two brief, but notable, biracial experiments in the New Orleans public schools (1870–77) and at the University of South Carolina (1873–77), racially dual school systems would be required by law in 17 "southern" states—the 11 former Confederate states, plus Delaware, Kentucky, Maryland, Missouri, Oklahoma, and West Virginia—and the District of Columbia (where Congress had provided separate black schools). Although perceived largely as a southern problem, segregated schools had existed in the North since the early 1800s and increased in reaction to the Great Migration of blacks (1890–1930) in such cities as Chicago, Indianapolis, and Philadelphia, which routinely assigned blacks to separate schools by gerrymandering, transfers, and ability testing.

The desegregation of southern education spanned 50 years and had four phases: (1) 1930–45, inauguration of the NAACP's desegregation campaign, which ended the era of virtually unchallenged Jim Crowism; (2) 1945–54, overturning the separate-but-equal doctrine, first in graduate and professional education and then in elementary and secondary schools; (3) 1955–64, massive southern white resistance countered by escalating federal intervention to enforce court-ordered desegregation and by passage of the 1964 Civil Rights Act; and (4) 1965–85, extensive desegregation of southern school districts by court decisions, civil rights enforcement, and threats of withholding large federal education grants.

Initially, Charles Hamilton Houston and Thurgood Marshall, NAACP Legal Defense and Education Fund attorneys, decided to attack segregation indirectly through lawsuits aimed at equalizing black and white schools in terms of curricula, teachers' salaries, and physical equipment. At the graduate and professional levels, states would be forced either to establish new schools for blacks or to admit them to existing white universities. In 1936 the Maryland Court of Appeals ordered Donald G. Murray admitted to the state university's law school, because none existed for blacks. Two years later, the U.S. Supreme Court ruled that Missouri could not meet the Fourteenth Amendment's equal-protection requirement by giving plaintiff Lloyd Gaines a tuition grant to study law in a nonsegregated state; after Gaines's unaccounted disappearance, Missouri established a Jim Crow law school. Other reverses followed in Kentucky and Tennessee, although West Virginia in 1938 voluntarily admitted blacks to its graduate and professional schools.

To achieve greater returns for the NAACP's time and limited financial resources, Marshall shifted, in 1945, to a direct attack on separate-but-equal education. Between 1948 and 1950 this new strategy opened doors of graduate and/or law schools at the universities of Oklahoma, Kentucky, Texas, Virginia, Missouri, and at Louisiana State University, while Delaware and Arkansas voluntarily admitted blacks. In the pivotal 1950 *Sweatt* v. *Painter* and *McLaurin* v. *Oklahoma State Regents for Higher Education*, the U.S. Supreme

Court unanimously ruled, first, that the University of Texas Law School had to admit Heman Sweatt because the new black law school was inferior in academic traditions and prestige, and it then ordered the University of Oklahoma to accord George McLaurin equal, nonsegregated treatment in the classrooms, cafeteria, and library.

Buoyed by victories and supported by reports of President Truman's Committee on Civil Rights and Commission on Higher Education, the NAACP directly attacked segregated public elementary and secondary schools. On 17 May 1954 the U.S. Supreme Court unanimously ruled in five cases, collectively known as *Brown* v. *Board of Education*, that "separate educational facilities are inherently unequal" and that segregation deprived plaintiffs of equal protection of the laws. The Supreme Court's 1955 implementation decree remanded these cases to federal district courts, which would order desegregation "with all deliberate speed." Such delay did not apply to graduate and professional schools, according to the Supreme Court's decision in a University of Florida Law School case.

Swept up by massive white resistance, southern states enacted a barrage of new laws to prohibit or indefinitely postpone integration: pupil-placement laws, freedom-of-choice amendments, tuition grants, repeal of compulsory attendance laws, modification of teacher tenure, closing of public schools (Norfolk and Prince Edward County, Virginia), state interposition and nullification of the *Brown* decision, and mob violence (University of Alabama, February 1956; Little Rock Central High School, September 1957; University of Georgia, January 1961; and University of Mississippi, September–October 1962). Federal supremacy ultimately triumphed—paratroopers returned nine black students to Little Rock Central High School, while the army secured James Meredith's enrollment at Ole Miss. Both the U.S. Court of Appeals and the Supreme Court refused to allow integration to be suspended.

Where local leadership committed itself to keeping public schools open, integration was peaceful: District of Columbia, St. Louis, Baltimore, Greensboro, Charlotte, Winston-Salem, Dade County, Atlanta, and Dallas. In June 1963, despite Governor George C. Wallace's televised stand in the "schoolhouse door," responsible University of Alabama leadership registered two black students. Heeding the lessons of Mississippi and Alabama, both Clemson and the University of South Carolina integrated with dignity.

Significant desegregation occurred, nevertheless, only after the 1964 Civil Rights Act empowered the U.S. attorney general to bring lawsuits on behalf of black plaintiffs and prohibited, under Title VI, spending federal funds—appropriated under the Elementary and Secondary Education and Higher Education Acts of 1965—in segregated schools and colleges. In *Alexander* v. *Holmes County Board of Education* (1969) the U.S. Supreme Court unanimously ordered all school segregation ended immediately. Methods of creating unitary schools included busing, magnet schools, open enrollments, and rezoning. Meanwhile, traditionally white public colleges and universities in 10 southern and border states, including Oklahoma and Pennsylvania, were required to submit to the Office for Civil Rights comprehensive desegregation plans for increasing the number of black students and faculty, expanding financial-aid and remedial programs, and electing black trustees (*Adams* v. *Richardson*, 1973). Although overwhelmingly black public schools and colleges persist in the South, especially in Alabama, Mississippi, Louisiana, Texas, and the District of Columbia, segregated education is no longer distinctively a southern problem. In many locales new patterns of segregation have evolved as whites, sometimes in large numbers, have left public school settings rather than accept busing and other school-desegregation plans. Various court rulings since the mid-1980s have supported voluntary rather than mandatory efforts to achieve racial balancing in schools, and the implications in the South, as elsewhere in the nation, have yet to be seen.

See also BLACK LIFE: Education, Black; / Meredith, James; National Association for the Advancement of Colored People; LAW: Civil Rights Movement; / *Brown* v. *Board of Education*; Fifth Circuit Court of Appeals; Little Rock Crisis; *Plessy* v. *Ferguson*; POLITICS: Segregation, Defense of

Marcia G. Synnott
University of South Carolina

Russell H. Barrett, *Integration at Ole Miss* (1965); Numan Bartley, *Arkansas Historical Quarterly* (Summer 1966); Augustus M. Burns III, *Journal of Southern History* (Spring 1980); Richard Kluger, *Simple Justice: The History of Brown v. Board of Education and Black America's Struggle for Equality* (1975); Thurgood Marshall, *Journal of Negro Education* (Summer 1952); Gary Orfield, *The Reconstruction of Southern Education: The Schools and the 1964 Civil Rights Act* (1969); J. W. Peltason, *Fifty-eight Lonely Men: Southern Federal Judges and School Desegregation* (1961); President's Commission on Higher Education, *Higher Education for American Democracy: A Report* (1947); President's Committee on Civil Rights, *To Secure These Rights: The Report of the President's Committee on Civil Rights* (1947); Calvin Trillin, *An Education in Georgia: The Integration of Charlayne Hunter and Hamilton Holmes* (1964); Stephen L. Wasby, Anthony A. D'Amato, and Rosemary Metrailer, *Desegregation from Brown to Alexander: An Exploration of Supreme Court Strategies* (1977). ☆

Federal-State Relations

Quality and equality have been dominant themes in the interaction of state and federal governments on the issue of education in the South. The federal government first became substantially involved with southern education when the Freedmen's Bureau allocated over $5 million to private schools that taught former slaves. Though southern state governments founded the first public universities in the United States long before joining the Confederacy, the interaction of state and federal governments following the Civil War assisted in the development of educational opportunities in the South.

At the end of the Civil War the southern states faced challenges to rebuild their society and to educate formerly enslaved citizens. Delegates who met to draft new state constitutions contended with the newly passed Thirteenth, Fourteenth, and Fifteenth Amendments to the U.S. Constitution that confirmed the freedmen's citizenship and mandated that no state could deny equal opportunity to its citizens. The delegates therefore adopted constitutional planks that proclaimed equal educational opportunity.

Despite constitutional language and limited attempts to provide nonsegregated education in some states, southern legislators soon enacted Jim Crow statutes that mandated separate educational facilities for whites and blacks. Motivated by misunderstanding and deepseated prejudices and buoyed by purported scientific evidence that blacks constituted an inferior race, every southern state institutionalized a separate system for blacks and whites by the end of Reconstruction in 1877.

The decades after Reconstruction saw actions by both state and federal governments that legally sanctioned one educational system for whites and another for blacks. The infusion of nearly $2 million as a result of the 1862 Morrill Act helped revive public higher-education institutions in the South. To receive these funds, southern states agreed to provide opportunities for blacks to learn about the agricultural and mechanical arts. Federal authorities, however, acquiesced in state decisions to offer instruction in separate facilities. Federal courts approved these actions when the Supreme Court rendered its infamous 1896 *Plessy* v. *Ferguson* decision that legalized separate-but-equal facilities.

Having chosen to finance two educational systems, southern states offered black citizens schools increasingly inferior to those in other regions of the United States. By 1915 southern states had invested over $145 million in public educational facilities. Of that, however, less than 10 percent was committed to black schools. This investment grew over the years, but the percentage provided black institutions remained proportionately the same. Although white systems of education fared better than black institutions, facilities and support for both lagged behind national standards.

This situation deteriorated steadily until the U.S. Supreme Court reversed itself in 1954 and declared separate-but-equal facilities inherently unequal and therefore unconstitutional. Although the *Brown* v. *Board of Education* decision heralded the demise of dual educational systems in the South, the Court's injunction that states move "with all deliberate speed" to achieve desegregation opened the door for states to stall.

Faced with state intransigence and increasing black unrest, the federal government enacted civil rights laws and education assistance programs in the 1960s that tied receipt of funds to nondiscrimination pledges. Southern states slowly acquiesced. In the 1970s and 1980s progressive state leaders cooperated with federal efforts to remove resistance to desegregation. Finally, blacks and whites began to receive instruction together.

State financing of the single educational system brought significant improvement. By 1985 southern states could boast that per capita expenditures for higher education exceeded the national average. Several states, though, continue under federal orders to eliminate vestiges of segregation in public educational institutions. Nonetheless, state and federal governments now jointly support efforts to expand and improve educational opportunities for all southern citizens.

See also BLACK LIFE: Education, Black; LAW: Supreme Court; / *Brown* v. *Board of Education*; *Plessy* v. *Ferguson*; POLITICS: Segregation, Defense of

Paul S. Baker
Hampden-Sydney College

Frank W. Blackmar, *The History of Federal and State Aid to Higher Education in the*

United States (1890); John S. Brubacher and Willis Rudy, *Higher Education in Transition: A History of American Colleges and Universities, 1636–1976* (3d rev. ed., 1976); Henry A. Bullock, *A History of Negro Education in the South: From 1619 to the Present* (1967); Frederick Mosteller and Daniel P. Moynihan, eds., *On the Equality of Educational Opportunity* (1972); Gary Puckrein, *The Wilson Quarterly* (Spring 1984); Frederick Rudolph, *The American College and University: A History* (1962); Reed Sarratt, *The Ordeal of Desegregation: The First Decade* (1966); Kenneth M. Stampp, *The Era of Reconstruction, 1865–1877* (1965); C. Vann Woodward, *The Strange Career of Jim Crow* (1955; 2d rev. ed., 1966). ☆

Fraternities and Sororities

The first Greek-letter society, Phi Beta Kappa, was founded in Virginia at the College of William and Mary on 5 December 1776 as a secret social organization; only later did it become the nation's leading scholastic honor society. It succeeded the earlier Flat Hat Club at William and Mary, to which Thomas Jefferson had belonged. Phi Beta Kappa members went on to found the original Kappa Alpha at the University of North Carolina in 1812. Before it became defunct in 1855, this fraternity had 12 "circles," all in the South.

Despite these beginnings, progenitors of today's college fraternities are considered to be the three fraternities of the "Union Triad," founded at Union College, Schenectady, N.Y., between 1825 and 1827. By 1850 there were 16 men's fraternities in the country, all founded in the North, but 12 of which had chapters established on southern campuses before secession. First to come south was the Mystical Seven, founded at Wesleyan University in 1837, which established a chapter at the University of Georgia in 1839 and later merged with Beta Theta Pi. The first college fraternity founded in the South was the Rainbow Fraternity, or "W.W.W.," established at the University of Mississippi in 1849. In 1886 it merged with Delta Tau Delta, itself established in 1858 at Bethany College, Va. (now West Virginia). Neither Epsilon Alpha at the University of Virginia nor Alpha Kappa Phi at Kentucky's Centre College survived the Civil War.

The first Greek-letter society founded in Dixie to take permanent root was Sigma Alpha Epsilon, begun in 1856 at the University of Alabama. Sigma Alpha, or the Black Badge Society, founded at Roanoke College in Salem, Va., in 1859, and eventually having eight southern chapters, was disbanded in 1882. The fraternity system flourished in the South before the Civil War, so that at the University of Mississippi, for example, 11 fraternities could be found among a small male student body at the time of secession. When the Civil War began, fraternities folded on nearly every southern college campus as the male students left for battle. However, war did not kill southern Greek-letter societies. During the Atlanta Campaign, five Sigma Chis from various colleges formed the Constantine Chapter of Sigma Chi in Gen. Joseph E. Johnston's Army of Tennessee and initiated two other Confederate soldiers on the night of 17 September 1864 near Jonesboro, Ga., where a monument commemorates the event.

After the Civil War, southern students, mainly Confederate veterans or military-college cadets, organized several new fraternities in the South: Alpha Tau Omega in 1865, Kappa Sigma Kappa (which merged with Theta Xi in 1962) in 1867, and Sigma Nu in 1869 at the Virginia Military Institute; Kappa Alpha Order, at what is now Washington and Lee, in 1865; and Phi Kappa Alpha in 1868 and Kappa Sigma in 1869 at the University of Virginia. Other southern fraternities that appeared later were Sigma Phi Epsilon, founded at the University of Richmond in 1901, and Pi Kappa Phi at the College of Charleston in 1904.

The first Greek-letter women's social organization in the United States was Alpha Delta Pi, begun at Wesleyan College in Macon, Ga., in 1851, closely followed there the next year by Phi Mu. Chi Omega started at the University of Arkansas in 1895. Virginia State Normal School (now Longwood College) in Farmville gave birth to four sororities: Kappa Delta in 1897, Sigma Sigma Sigma and Zeta Tau Alpha in 1898, and Alpha Sigma Alpha in 1901.

Early in this century, black college fraternities and sororities also appeared. The first black men's Greek-letter society was Alpha Phi Alpha at Cornell in 1906, followed by Kappa Alpha Psi at Indiana in 1911. As might be expected, Howard University in Washington, D.C., was the incubator for two black fraternities and three black sororities. For men there were Omega Psi Phi in 1911 and Phi Beta Sigma in 1914, and for women there were Alpha Kappa Alpha in 1908, Delta Sigma Theta in 1913, and Zeta Phi Beta in 1920. Sigma Gamma Rho became a black collegiate sorority at Butler University in Indianapolis in 1929. All these groups are found on southern campuses.

Southern social fraternities and sororities have had their ups and downs, as have others across the nation, in peace as well as in war. Secret societies were eventually suppressed at military colleges, such as VMI and The Citadel. Yet at some southern land-grant colleges once run on military lines there were social organizations such as Lee Guard and George Rifles at Mississippi A&M (now Mississippi State University) that later became chapters of national men's social fraternities. Early in this century, southern Populist governors and legislatures succeeded in banning Greek-letter societies on public campuses, such as in South Carolina from 1897 to 1929 and in Mississippi from 1912 to 1926. However, they continued to exist *sub rosa* in some cases and eventually returned stronger than ever.

Certain southern campuses have long been noted for their hospitality to "the Greeks," most notably the University of Alabama, which in 1963 on the eve of the Vietnam War was the home of 26 men's and 16 women's Greek-letter social organizations. The wave of social protest that swept over American campuses during the 1960s and 1970s was heralded in some quarters as dooming fraternities and sororities. Although the Greek system suffered elsewhere in the country, especially in the Northeast and Far West, it was not damaged noticeably in the South.

The national leadership of Greek organizations has reacted to increasing pressure by parents and college officials concerned about the brutality of certain hazing and initiation rituals. The resistance by Greek organizations to the alteration of these practices stems from the emphasis members place on secrecy of rituals and loyalty, both to each other and to the traditions of their groups. As a result of the recent deaths of some fraternity pledges during hazing rituals and the publicity the deaths received, the campaign against hazing has progressed in the South as elsewhere. The national fraternities, as well as the National Interfraternity Conference, have rules prohibiting hazing, and 18 states have laws against hazing practices. Many campuses, such as the University of Texas at Austin, have taken strong stands against the rituals, expelling students and on occasion suspending fraternity charters for violations of hazing prohibitions.

Fraternity and sorority participation at southern schools appears to be increasing, consistent with the national trend. College students join Greek organizations looking for camaraderie, social status, and the feeling of group unity. The gregariousness, conviviality, and love of ritualistic pomp and hierarchical status usually associated with southerners may account for the seemingly enduring popularity of Greek organizations in the region. Some college students are influenced by members of their families to join a particular Greek society.

Since the 1970s membership in both fraternities and sororities has risen steadily nationwide. In the last five years, national membership has grown by more than 150,000 to about 400,000. The percentage of students in Greek organizations varies widely on southern college campuses, though the percentage involvement is not necessarily indicative of the strength of the Greek system on any given campus. Fraternity participation in the South ranges from 70 percent of male students at Louisiana State University in Baton Rouge and at Centre College in Kentucky, to 5 percent of male students at East Carolina University and Tuskegee Institute. Sorority participation on southern campuses ranges from 65 percent of the female students at Shorter College in Georgia, to 4 percent of females at Tuskegee Institute and at North Carolina State University.

Although a strong Greek system has sometimes been associated with a "party campus" and considered antithetical to a serious academic emphasis, several southern institutions with excellent academic reputations have flourishing Greek organizations, among them Birmingham-Southern College in Alabama, Duke University in North Carolina, Emory University in Georgia, Millsaps College in Mississippi, and Vanderbilt University in Tennessee. Some southern schools have no fraternities and sororities at all. These include Berea College in Kentucky, the University of Dallas, Eckerd College in Florida, and Texas A&M University.

John Hawkins Napier III
Montgomery, Alabama

Allen Cabaniss, *A History of the University of Mississippi* (1949); Clyde S. Johnson, *Fraternities in Our Colleges* (1972); Thomas J. Meyer, *Chronicle of Higher Education* (12 March 1986); John Hawkins Napier III, *The Mississippian* (20 February 1948); John Robson, ed., *Baird's Manual of American College Fraternities* (19th ed., 1977), *The College Fraternity and Its Modern Role* (1966). ☆

Illiteracy

Inability to read and write in any language has been the conventional definition of illiteracy and the basis of most illiteracy statistics. The concept of "functional" illiteracy was advanced during World War II as a result of the U.S. Army experience with soldiers who "could not understand written instructions about basic military tasks." The South has exceeded the rest of the nation in illiteracy, whether defined in functional terms or as the inability to read and write in any language. Information from the U.S. Census of 1870 illustrated the South's heritage of illiteracy. No area of the region had less than 12 percent illiteracy. The cotton-culture subregions, particularly the river-valley and delta areas and the Piedmont and Coastal Plain, were 40 percent or more illiterate. The South was agricultural, and agriculture then depended not upon science but upon traditional practice—learning by doing rather than by reading. The 1870 census found in the nation 4.53 million persons 10 years of age and over unable to read; 73.7 percent of them resided in the South. Four-fifths of blacks were then illiterate.

The agricultural economy rested upon a sparsely distributed population, the use of child labor that discouraged school attendance, and a prejudiced and often fatalistic people who lacked the means for upward mobility in the expanding industrial system of the nation. The church was more important as a social institution than the school; word of mouth, song, and story were prominent means of cultural transmission. Under these conditions illiteracy served to conserve tradition and retard cultural change, whereas a more general literacy would have accelerated adaptation and change. Said a Jasper County, Miss., man: "My grandfather—he raised me—figured going to school wouldn't help me pick cotton any better."

A decline in illiteracy has occurred in the South and the nation. As educational benefits were extended to blacks through both public and private schools (including schools sponsored by religious groups, such as the Congregational church, and by private foundations, such as the Rosenwald Fund), illiteracy rates dropped.

When the education of a generation of children is neglected, the deficiency persists throughout a lifetime. Teaching adults to read has not been as effective in eliminating illiteracy as have mortality and out-migration from the South. The neglect of a generation of school children during the Civil War (those 5 to 14 years of age in 1860) resulted in higher illiteracy rates for the native white population in 1900 (who then were 45 to 54 years of age) than for either the preceding or succeeding generation. The illiteracy rates by age of the black population of Louisiana, from 1890 to 1930, shown in Table 2, illustrate the persistence of the "cohort effect." By tracing the cohort diagonally across the table, one can discern the dogged tenacity of illiteracy, despite mortality and out-migration. The population represented below the diagonal line lived under pre–Civil War conditions. The older the population in 1890, the lower the rate of change in illiteracy to the terminal age group. As time progressed, reductions in illiteracy among the 10 to 14 age group accelerated.

The change in illiteracy in Georgia from 1960 to 1970 illustrates the source of gains and losses of illiterates in a state. The number of Georgia illiterates in 1960 was reduced by 45 percent in 1970. Some 22,530 were estimated to have died during the decade, and 23,840 were lost through out-migration. The Adult Basic Education Program of the state taught 14,380 to read during the period. However, 6,290 new illiterates, aged 14 to 24 years in 1970, entered the illiterate category. This new group testifies to the failure of the family and the school to inculcate literacy skills.

The most extensive recent testing of reading and writing has been conducted by the National Assessment of Educational Progress. In tests of 17-year-olds, the Southeast (which differs from the Census South by excluding Texas, Oklahoma, Maryland, Delaware, and the District of Columbia) scored lower than any other region; the results illustrate functional, rather than conventional, illiteracy. This is especially revealing because the 17-year-old is the product of the present school system.

Although some industrial plants will not hire illiterates, the prevalence of illiteracy in the South apparently has not affected plant location. Following World War II, as more oil, chemical, atomic energy, and other technological industries located in the South, educational requirements for employment rose and, except for common labor, the illiterate worker was less likely to find employment in them (indeed, the unemployment rate of illiterates is higher than that of literate workers). Southern migrants to the North who found jobs in the automobile industry were able to perform the work but often encountered off-the-job difficulties: overextending themselves in credit installment purchases, failing to adjust to city life, or returning home without receiving permission from supervisors. Their absentee rates were higher than those of other workers. Similar employment difficulties evidently plague the Spanish-American in the Southwest.

Table 2. *Illiteracy Rates Among Blacks in Louisiana, by Age, 1890–1930*

Ages	1890	1900	1910	1920	1930
10–14	60.3	49.7	40.0	25.4	7.7
15–24	66.3	54.3	41.5	31.5	14.7
25–34	70.7	58.7	43.9	34.6	21.3
35–44	78.7	65.7	51.0	41.7	26.7
45–54	86.0	76.7	60.5	51.2	34.7
55–64	89.5	84.8	72.4	63.5	45.6
65–up	92.6	89.9	81.4	77.5	64.4

Source: U.S. Bureau of the Census, *Population Reports*, 1900, 1910, 1920, 1930.

In general, illiterates have lower learning capacity, are more likely to be welfare recipients, and have higher rejection rates for military service. If female, they have higher fertility rates, and the instances of infant mortality among illiterates are always higher. There is more illiteracy in rural than in urban areas.

The South has approximately 398,000 illiterates, according to estimates based upon the 1980 census and the November 1979 Current Population Survey. The distribution by color is: white, 44.9 percent; black, 51.4 percent; other nonwhite, 3.7 percent. By age, illiterates are distributed as follows: 14–24 years, 9.2 percent; 25–44 years, 17.0 percent; 45–64 years, 32.2 percent; and 65 years and over, 41.6 percent. These are individuals unable to read and write, according to census definitions; functional illiterates are more numerous.

See also: RELIGION: / Fatalism; SOCIAL CLASS: Poverty

Abbott L. Ferriss
Emory University

Sterling G. Brinkley, *Journal of Experimental Education* (September 1957); John K. Folger and Charles B. Nam, *Education of the American Population* (1967); Eli Ginzberg and Douglas W. Bray, *The Uneducated* (1953); *Historical Statistics of the United States to 1970* (1975); Carman St. John Hunter with David Harman, *Adult Illiteracy in the United States: A Report to the Ford Foundation* (1979); National Assessment of Educational Progress, Report No. 11-R-02 (1982), Report No. 10-W-01 (1980); U.S. Bureau of the Census, *Current Population Reports*, Series P-23, No. 6 (November 1959), No. 8 (February 1963), No. 116 (March 1982); Series P-20, No. 99 (March 1959), No. 217 (March 1971); Sanford Winston, *Illiteracy in the United States* (1930). ☆

Innovations in Education

Education in the South, as in other sections of the United States, is more than schooling. It is, in Bernard Bailyn's words, "the entire process by which a culture transmits itself across the generations," a process that has been deeply and irrevocably influenced by ideas and events originating outside the region. The most prominent shaping forces have been industrialization, urbanization, democratization, and shifts in the class, status, and power structures. Southern educators have had to cope in recent times with such national problems as accelerated rates of social change, greater differentiation in social and occupational roles, the decline of the local community, alterations in the family structure, and increased centralization and bureaucratization of social, political, and economic control. Solutions to these problems have been neither easy nor close at hand.

Throughout the South and the rest of the country individuals and organizations have sought to implement reforms not only in education but also in municipal government, the civil service, capital-labor relations, conservation, and international relations. Industrialization surely created standardized national norms, institutions, and individuals, and education became linked to "human resource development" and "wealth creation." Distinctive differences in education between the South and the rest of the nation have declined under the pressures of creating an efficient industrial state.

The educational responses to industrialization and urbanization nevertheless occurred with different emphases and intensity in the South than in the North. Southern educational reformers used the rhetoric of national educational reformers, but the impulses for change were rooted in southern traditions and some changes were altered to suit regional values and institutions. At least one important result of the southern educational reform movement had no northern equivalent. By the 1950s the South had *two* complete public and segregated school systems, a remarkable organizational achievement. The two systems were gradually and grudgingly fused into one during the 1960s and 1970s.

Alternatives to the modern industrial state and its preferred educational patterns always have been readily available in southern culture. Southern populism, for example, frequently challenged modernism and reaffirmed the values of the local community that were threatened by impersonal and remote forces. Populist theory deplored the erosion of the individual's control over his or her own destiny; it preferred a social order in which power was accessible in close and familiar institutions. Conservative Protestant theology also has helped isolate southern intellectual life and culture from prevailing trends of American society. And the antimodernism exemplified by the Agrarian manifesto *I'll Take My Stand*, which included an essay on education by John Gould Fletcher, persists today in many currents of southern thought.

Contradictions and paradoxes abound in southern educational development. Support for innovations coexisted with a desire for the status quo. Industrialization and urbanization developed along with a longing for an agrarian culture. Commercialism conflicted with religious antimaterialism. Individualism and a striving for liberty contrasted with the values of community and social responsibility. Nationalism was opposed by regionalism. Educators had to hold these conflicting trends in uneasy balance, and innovation was never easy.

When revivals or reactions occur, they are sometimes called innovations, and in these terms the South has frequently been in the forefront. The "New Conservatism" that emerged in the late 1970s addressed such southern political, moral, and social concerns as states' rights, reduced involvement of the federal government in business and educational activities, abortion, gun control, school prayer, and busing. The more recent "back-to-basics" movement in education—a reform of reforms—asserts a position many southern educators never abandoned. It claims the decisive factors in higher levels of academic achievement are pedagogical, not financial: an emphasis in schools on order and discipline, excellence, regular homework, and a high degree of teacher involvement and control. These characteristics are more frequently found in private and parochial schools than in public schools. Paradoxically, this very traditional position may lead to innovations in the use of education vouchers and tuition tax credits, and may dictate the amount of financial support public schools can expect to receive in the future. Similarly, innovative methods and materials for teaching evolution may emerge from religious conservatism.

Innovation occurred within the limits of the three principal models of formal schooling that developed in the South. The *inclusive model* envisions an all-embracing institution providing not only education but a wide variety of social and vocational services as well. This type of school has distinctive roles to play in social, cultural, political, and economic affairs. It is based on the assumptions and proposals of John Dewey.

The *exclusive model* gives the school a severely restricted role. Assigned the task of providing intellectual training for the pupils, the school does not function as a broad social service agency. This kind of institution generally reflects traditionalist assumptions about knowledge, individuals, and society, and is found frequently in the private sector of education.

A *central model* espouses a middle position. It attributes to the school a double role: teaching academic disciplines and arranging for other agencies to provide specialized vocational training and to assist with personal development. This type of institution has gained considerable support since the 1970s.

Innovations in southern education have taken place both within this institutional framework and beyond it throughout the 20th century. Education came to be seen as an ongoing process, flexible in structure, timing, place, and content. In the 1960s a cult of constant innovation appeared, supported nationally by a southern president. Education, health, housing, and other social services were regarded as parts of a whole. There was much easy talk about systems management, designs for change, and change agents; and there was an abundance of educational experiments, movements, reforms, and "breakthroughs." The South has not always led the way in proposing changes in school organization (Head Start and Upward Bound, alternative schools, magnet schools, mainstreaming), use of school personnel (team teaching, collective negotiations, teacher aides), curriculum, (community resources, bilingual education, sex education), and learning techniques (individualized instruction, multimedia centers, computer-assisted instruction), but the region has been profoundly changed by application of such developments.

Higher education in the South did not change dramatically until after World War II, when it was affected by the growth in the number of students, the addition of many new buildings, changes in the balance of subjects, and different emphases on undergraduate, professional, and postgraduate studies. The traditional moderation of higher education was replaced by the less-restrained social service ideology of the multiversity. In the 1960s open admission policies and new study programs were tried (e.g., black and ethnic studies). Distance learning systems were put into operation, with the University of Maryland a member of the vanguard. In general, though, southern universities were not leaders in such developments, and some of the changes adopted in the 1950s, the 1960s, and the 1970s currently are being reassessed.

No single point of view permits easy interpretation of these innovations in southern education. Proponents claimed they would make learning more relevant, or more liberal and humane, or more efficient and cost-effective. Some critics merely said the new ideas and practices did not produce their intended results. Other critics accused the innovators of using the rhetoric of reform for conservative purposes. According to this view, the innovations were intended to increase the school's hold on its pupils and enhance its effectiveness as an instrument of socialization, surveillance, and social control. The cosmetic innovations, these critics said, had the effect of maintaining existing social, political, and economic structures while giving the appearance of changes.

Edgar B. Gumbert
Georgia State University

Bernard Bailyn, *Education in the Forming of American Society: Needs and Opportunities for Study* (1960); Robert Church and Michael W. Sedlak, *Education in the United States: An Interpretive History* (1976); Lawrence A. Cremin, *The Transformation of the School: Progressivism in American Education, 1876–1957* (1961); Henry Ehlers, ed., *Crucial Issues in Education* (6th ed., 1977); Ronald K. Goodenow and Arthur O. White, eds., *Education and the Rise of the New South* (1981); Theodore W. Hipple, ed., *The Future of Education, 1975–2000* (1974); Henry J. Perkinson, *The Imperfect Panacea: American Faith in Education, 1865–1976* (1977); Herbert I. Von Haden and Jean Marie King, *Innovations in Education: Their Pros and Cons* (1971). ☆

Learned Societies

An agrarian region marked by far-flung plantation settlement and hampered by climate, intellectual traditionalism, and, ultimately, a sectional suspicion of northern imports, the antebellum South lagged far behind the rest of the nation in the development of learned societies. Those societies that did exist sprang up in port cities with strong European connections and relatively dense populations. Characterized as "one of the liveliest intellectual centers in colonial America," Charleston supported a Library Society (1748), the Charleston Museum (1773), which was dedicated to providing "an accurate natural history of the province," the South Carolina Literary and Philosophical Society (1813), and the Elliot Society of Natural History (1853).

Drawing little distinction between the theoretical and the practical, and committed to establishing the new nation on a respectable international footing, early organizers both North and South favored the founding of scientific societies that would name and study unique American resources. The two preeminent scientific societies in the Old South, the Elliot Society and the New Orleans Academy of Sciences (1853), attempted to rival their older eastern counterparts and succeeded in attracting the attention of such noted naturalists as John Bachman and Harvard's Louis Agassiz. In 1856 the Elliot Society had a membership comparable to scientific academies in Boston and Philadelphia.

In the late 19th and early 20th centuries the vast majority of national learned societies came into existence, and many of them established branches in the South. The American Philosophical Association, the Modern Language Association, the Society of Biblical Literature, and the American Academy of Religion all formed southern sections. At the same time, societies with a more specifically regional character grew up: the Southern Historical Association (1934), the Southern Society for Philosophy and Psychology (1904), the Southern Sociological Society (1935), and the Southern Speech Communication Association (1930). Since 1947 the Southern Humanities Conference has drawn those scholarly organizations specializing in the humanities into closer association.

Institutes committed to benefiting specific industries or sponsors, commercially oriented research organizations, and traditional learned societies now cover the South. Embracing education (International Studies Association, South Carolina), science (American Society of Biological Chemists, Florida), and the humanities (Pythagorean Philosophical Society, Texas), the list of national societies headquartered, or active, in the southern states reflects New South diversity.

See also HISTORY AND MANNERS: / Southern Historical Association

Elizabeth M. Makowski
University of Mississippi

Joseph C. Kiger, *American Learned Societies* (1963); Alexander Oleson and Sanborn Brown, eds., *The Pursuit of Knowledge in the Early American Republic* (1976); Michael Zils, ed., *World Guide to Scientific Associations* (1982). ☆

Legal Education

See LAW: Law Schools

Libraries

Books came with the first English settlers to the New World. The artist John

White, after returning in 1590 to Roanoke Island off the coast of North Carolina, found little more remaining than, in his own words, "my books torn from the covers." A generation later, when the permanent colonies had been established, books and libraries became integral parts of southern life.

Although printing in the southern colonies was an 18th-century development, individual and even institutional libraries emerged earlier. A substantial supply of devotional titles was imported for these early ventures, but examination of book titles reveals that southern colonists paid less attention to theology than did their New England counterparts. In fact, most titles were in applied science, the need for agrarian and medical practical manuals being imperative from the colonies' earliest days. Literature took second place, with theology and history trailing.

Private libraries were common in the 18th-century South, the most famous being those of the Virginians William Byrd II, John Mercer, and Robert Carter of Nomini Hall. Byrd's was perhaps the first great collector's library in the British colonies developed for purely bibliophilic reasons. The library of Arthur Dobbs, colonial governor of North Carolina, was replete with travel books, natural histories, and works on architecture.

Institutional libraries also appeared in the colonial era. In addition to the collegiate collections at Henrico, the library that began at the College of William and Mary in the 1690s was, by the close of the 18th century, one of the most distinguished in the nation, with approximately 3,000 volumes. Financed by a grant from Princess Anne, the Bibliotheca Provinciales, or Annapolitan Library, was organized in Maryland about 1696, serving as a model for later collections sent to New York, Boston, Philadelphia, and Charleston. At approximately the same time the Reverend Thomas Bray instituted his program for the establishment of parochial and provincial libraries to assist both clergy and laity in their duties. These were established not only in Maryland but at Bath, N.C., and in Charleston. A later development in Charleston, with much more lasting impact, was the formation in 1748 of arguably the most influential of all southern public-club libraries—the Charleston Library Society. In Georgia the most distinguished library by far was that formed by George Whitefield and bequeathed to the Bethesda Orphanage, with the primary goal of transforming that institution into a college.

Libraries in the first two centuries of the South's development were more significant than formal education because reading habits were utilitarian and broadly based. More importantly, the lack of local printing in the South meant that the thirst for reading materials was satisfied by imports. At least until the 1850s, the white southerner had his or her mind, in the words of Richard Beale Davis, "shaped and directed by the world from which he or a recent ancestor had come."

The advent of American independence, the opening of Georgia western lands, the Louisiana Purchase, and the popularization of the cotton gin, all in the decades surrounding the turn of the 19th century, worked to bring additional opportunities to the southern planter. This same period saw the first attempts at establishing state universities in the region in Georgia and North Carolina. Libraries were still, for the most part, considered a private responsibility. Thus, although a number of fine library societies were established, they were rarely free or particularly accessible and hence had little impact on the average rural southerner. Such attitudes became even more apparent as sectional animosities rose. In a survey of 154 American libraries completed in 1849 by Charles Coffin Jewett only 21 were southern and only 7 of those held the national average of 10,580 volumes.

Collections of distinction were formed, however. The library of South Carolina College, one of the most distinguished of all educational institutions in the country, had its own building—an unusual phenomenon for any university of that day. Literary coteries in Charleston and Richmond supported existing library societies in those cities. On most campuses the libraries of strength were those owned by the debating and literary societies, with their holdings oriented toward the political, historical, and theological. Also, Thomas Jefferson played a key role in the creation and support of the Library of Congress, which was established in 1800. After the library's collection was ravaged by fire in 1814, Jefferson contributed his own library, which formed the core of the Library of Congress's collection until its decimation by another fire in 1851.

Bookmobile in Jefferson County, Alabama, early 20th century

The gains made in library services were effectively lost with the onset of war in 1861. New libraries were established at a much lower rate than in the earlier decades. Always a luxury, libraries became virtually unnecessary when simple survival was in question. Private libraries, too, suffered. The distinguished libraries amassed by William Gilmore Simms in South Carolina and Joseph Davis in Mississippi fell under the torch of federal troops. The end of war and the beginning of Reconstruction brought little change immediately. Of the 226 libraries in the United States holding at least 10,000 volumes in 1876, only 29 were in the South. The situation for southern libraries was bleak: personal income was both low and uncertain due to the decreasing agricultural potential; population was sparse and scattered in rural areas, limiting accessibility for the clientele; illiteracy was high; and the race problem affected all aspects of southern life and led to the creation of dual systems of education, as well as other public institutions, when the region lacked resources to provide adequately for even one. Library services remained a low priority when public welfare, health, and education cried for assistance and provided more visible results.

The development of these other programs, however, facilitated the later development of libraries in the region by making governmental projects more acceptable to the populace. Public endeavors in library service were anticipated and better understood. Libraries profited from experiences of agricultural extensionists and others whose public-contact activities provided precedents.

The growth of land-grant colleges and agricultural schools, teacher education, and the general establishment of the public school system led to a more positive image for libraries in the South, lessening elitist tendencies and emphasizing the public responsibility. In 1895 the Cotton States and International Exhibition in Atlanta served to bring into clear focus much of the activity in this regard. Visitors had the opportunity to examine a model library, to view equipment used in libraries, and, most importantly, to see that libraries possessed enough value to be given a place in an exposition calling attention to southern progress. By 1897 Georgia, at the instigation of the staff of the Young Men's Library Association of Atlanta, became the first southern state to establish a statewide library association. Two years later the American Library Association held its first convention in the South, also in Atlanta. This served two significant purposes for the South: local librarians were stimulated by national library concerns, and the visitors to the South were able to realize the seriousness of purpose that characterized southern librarians.

Also in 1899, the first contribution from Andrew Carnegie to a library building in the South was made public. The grant to the city of Atlanta transformed its subscription library, in existence since 1867, into a free public facility. At the same time library apprentice classes, the first in the Southeast, were begun in connection with the Atlanta library, and a later contribution made possible, in 1905, the establishment of the Southern Library School at the Carnegie Library of Atlanta. Library awareness was growing. In 1901 North Carolina enacted a law providing for state support of rural school libraries. Virginia by 1923 had a supervisor of school libraries charged with expanding the number and capabilities of school libraries in that state. With the founding in 1920 of the Southeastern Library Association came an organization for coordinating interests and efforts of librarians within the region. Further developments through the Tennessee Valley Authority and various Works Progress Administration agencies provided opportunities for new buildings and expanded activities.

Since World War II, libraries and library services in the South have dramatically expanded. The concept of "networking"—libraries cooperating to share materials and services—has been quite popular throughout the South, increasing potential for future development. On-line cooperative efforts such as SOLINET in the Southeast and AMIGOS in the Southwest have made sophisticated access tools available even to small regional libraries. In addition, state library operations have benefited from collaborative and cooperative programs of interlibrary loans, multiunit purchasing, and shared costs for on-line searching.

It is, however, in the university library that the greatest growth has occurred. Through the leadership of Harry Ransom and others, the University of Texas and its Humanities Research Center has become one of the premier facilities of its type in the nation. The universities of Virginia, North Carolina, Georgia, Florida, and Texas, plus Louisiana State and Duke universities all have holdings in excess of 2 million volumes. The rapid growth rate of the Sunbelt South and the gradual increase in sophistication in the needs of users made broad-based, extensive information services imperative.

See also HISTORY AND MANNERS: / Byrd, William, II; Jefferson, Thomas

Robert M. Willingham, Jr.
University of Georgia

Mary Edna Anders, *Southeastern Librarian* (Spring 1956); Richard Beale Davis, *Intellectual Life in the Colonial South, 1585–1763*, 3 vols., (1978); John David Marshall, ed., *An American Library History Reader* (1961); Frances Lander Spain, "Libraries of South Carolina: Their Origins and Early History, 1700–1830" (Ph.D. dissertation, University of Chicago, 1944); Louis Round Wilson and Edward A. Wight, *County Library Services in the South* (1935). ☆

Medical Education

See SCIENCE AND MEDICINE: Medical Education

Military Schools

Why are military schools associated with the South, when the most famous of all military preparatory schools is Culver in Indiana? None of the nation's four uniformed service academies is in the South, although Annapolis might demur. Yet popular culture loves southern military-school settings, as in the movie *Taps* (1982), Terence Fugate's 1961 novel *Drum and Bugle*, and Pat Conroy's *Lords of Discipline* (1980), which had as its thinly disguised locale his alma mater, The Citadel, in Charleston, S.C.

The association may be simply the popular perception of the South as America's Sparta, or it may be that the South produces more "Peck's Bad Boys" in need of military discipline. More important is British historian Marcus Cunliffe's argument that military academies have come to be regarded as a feature of "the *idea* of the South," whereas northern military schools are less visible in the culture. Military schools are not just in the South, they are of it as well.

The South has not been famed for its preparatory schools. Aside from Henry Tutwiler's antebellum Green Springs Academy in Havana, Ala., the Webb School at Bell Buckle, Tenn., Episcopal High School in Alexandria, Va., and Woodberry Forest School, also in Virginia, no civilian prep schools readily come to mind, unlike the prestigious ones of the Northeast: Choate, Groton, Hotchkiss, St. Paul's, Middlesex, Hill, and the three Phillipses—Andover, Exeter, and Brooks. Instead, military prep schools thrive, having withstood the reaction against them during the Vietnam War and despite the proliferation of private "segregation" academies in the South, which hurt military-school enrollment in the same period.

Although some military schools have shed uniforms and gone coed, others are still staunch traditionalists. In Alabama's Black Belt, Marion Military Institute is thriving once more with a healthy enrollment, one of only three or four military junior colleges in the United States. Southern military academies, such as Fishburne, Fork Union, and Hargrave in Virginia, Camden in South Carolina, Chamberlain-Hunt in Mississippi, and Riverside in Georgia continue to train boys in hopes of producing soldiers. The Florida Air Academy in Lakeland and the Marine Military Academy in Harlingen, Tex., specialize in training for nonarmy military service. Virginia's Massanutten and Randolph-Macon academies are still military, but have coed day students. Some of the old standbys are gone, though—Mississippi's Gulf Coast Military Academy and Tennessee's Sewanee Military Academy. Tennessee Military Institute is now "TMI Academy," and Georgia Military Academy became the civilian and coed Woodward Academy in 1966.

Montgomery, Ala., once had two private boys' day military prep schools, Starke and Hurt. Both are long since gone, but junior ROTC units are flourishing at all four public high schools, with a choice of army at Sidney Lanier and George Washington Carver, air force at Robert E. Lee, or the marines at Jefferson Davis.

How did all this enthusiasm for military schooling in the South begin? Captain Alden Partridge, a member of the U.S. Military Academy's first graduating class of 1806, founded Vermont's Norwich University on the West Point model in 1819 as the nation's first private military college. He and his Norwich alumni popularized military schooling, founding private and public military academies, institutes, and colleges along West Point lines, both in the North and the South.

These early academies took root and flourished in Dixie at a time of growing sectional consciousness and conflict. The 1831 Nat Turner slave rebellion in Southampton County, Va., and the 1832 nullification crisis in South Carolina, both challenges to southern social order, were followed by the establishment of the Virginia Military Institute (VMI) (1839) and the South Carolina Military Academy at The Citadel in Charleston (1842). In fact, the Palmetto State also supported a second military academy, The Arsenal, in Columbia, until the Civil War. Both these institutions became better known than New England's Norwich and served as exemplars for other southern military schools, as well as furnishing trained officers to their states' militias.

By the time of secession every southern state, except the newest one, Florida, either supported its own military colleges or extended state aid, including arms and accouterments, to private military schools. Federal assistance was also given, as when the U.S. Army detailed a regular officer to teach military theory and tactics at St. John's College in Annapolis in 1824, at Norwich and VMI in the 1830s, and at the University of Tennessee in 1840.

In 1845 Col. Robert T. P. Allen, known affectionately to his cadets as "Rarin' Tarin' Pitchin' Allen," founded the Kentucky Military Institute (KMI). Although it was a private school, that commonwealth's governor was designated its "Inspector," and the state's adjutant general was a member of its board of visitors. It flourished until 1861, when its faculty and students marched off to war, some south and others north.

Major George Alexander founded the Arkansas Military Institute at Tulip in 1850, and it too flourished until its people went to war. Also in 1850 Mississippi's oldest chartered college, Jefferson, founded in 1802 near Natchez and attended by Jefferson Davis, resumed its military program earlier adopted in 1829 after the Alden Partridge plan. The state of Mississippi furnished it with muskets, and thus had its military academy without having to tax itself to maintain it.

In 1851 West Pointer Arnoldus V.

Brumby organized Marietta's Georgia Military Institute, which received state aid until Georgia bought it in 1857 and turned it into a state college. In Tennessee the Western Military Institute at Tyree was merged with the ailing University of Nashville in 1855. Historian John Hope Franklin has written that "no State approached Alabama's feverish interest in military education displayed just before the Civil War." That state extended generous support to two military academies at La Grange and Glenville, providing scholarships to two cadets from each county. Alabama also furnished arms and drill manuals to eight other military schools at various times in the decade of the 1850s and introduced compulsory military training into the University of Alabama in 1860. Texas called Col. R. T. P. Allen from KMI to found the Texas Military Institute at Bastrop.

Not only did these schools produce southern subalterns (VMI had produced more than 400 officers by the time of the Civil War), but some of their faculty gained fame as Civil War generals. Bushrod R. Johnson, the military superintendent at the University of Nashville, became a Confederate major general. Major Daniel H. Hill, later a Confederate lieutenant general, opened the North Carolina Military Institute at Charlotte in 1859, and by the time Fort Sumter surrendered, 150 cadets were enrolled. Incidentally, Citadel cadets claim to have fired the first shot on Fort Sumter, so it was they who began the war. In 1860 the first superintendent of the new Louisiana State Seminary of Learning and Military Academy, now LSU and still known as "the Old War Skule," was that future scourge of the South, William Tecumseh Sherman. The immortal Thomas "Stonewall" Jackson was teaching at VMI during John Brown's raid and commanded a company of cadets that stood guard over the courthouse and jail at Harpers Ferry during Brown's trial and hanging. All these "West Points of the South" (a term VMI has since claimed for itself) established a relationship between military education and southern policy that was proven when the call to arms came. Also, all this time, southern representation at West Point itself remained disproportionately high, and many of its former cadets became Confederate leaders, the most famous being Jefferson Davis, class of 1828, and Robert E. Lee, class of 1829.

After Appomattox and during Reconstruction, practically all southern military schools disappeared, except for VMI and The Citadel. However, during the Civil War, in 1862, the U.S. Congress had passed the Morrill Land Grant Act, which provided for federal land grants to fund the establishment of state agricultural and mechanical colleges that were also required to furnish military instruction. The act did not make such training mandatory, but all the "aggie" schools became military. When such colleges were founded in the defeated and impoverished South, they revived the military-school tradition—at Arkansas in 1871; at Auburn and the Virginia Polytechnic Institute in 1872; at Starkville, Miss., in 1878, where the first president was ex-Confederate Lt. Gen. Stephen D. Lee; at the Georgia Institute of Technology in 1885; at Raleigh, N.C., in 1887; at Clemson, S.C., in 1889; at the revived Louisiana State University, which later boasted the largest barracks in the world; and above all, at Texas A&M, which by World War II had furnished more regular army officers than West Point (seniors there still wear breeches, boots, and spurs). In addition to the land-grant institutions, some of the older state universities began to offer military instruction after the Reserve Officer Training Corps Acts of 1916 and 1920 extended ROTC to other than military institutes and land-grant colleges. At times, it was even compulsory, as at the universities of Mississippi and Alabama and at private colleges such as Davidson. Meanwhile, the southern military preparatory schools began reviving by the 1880s and became fashionable by the Gay Nineties, especially in Virginia's Shenandoah Valley.

Some who argue for the existence of a peculiarly southern martial tradition, such as sociologist Morris Janowitz, suspect that it really came into its own after the Confederacy's defeat; by 1910, 90 percent of the U.S. Army's general officers had southern affiliations. Douglas MacArthur first donned a uniform at a Texas military institute; George Catlett Marshall graduated from VMI to lead the U.S. Army and Air Corps into victory in World War II; the U.S. Marine commander in the Pacific War against Japan, Holland M. "Howlin' Mad" Smith, started his martial career as an Auburn cadet; and General William Westmoreland, commander of U.S. forces in Vietnam, attended The Citadel before receiving an appointment to West Point. During the Vietnam War, when public support for the military reached its nadir, military programs suffered less on southern university campuses than in any other part of America. At Chapel Hill an antiwar protest rally during the Cambodian invasion of 1970 fizzled out, and the following year enrollment applications at VMI and The Citadel rose from previous declines. ROTC programs continued to be maintained on southern civilian college campuses as well. In the 1980s support for military education has increased nationwide, but the South remains the region most committed to it.

See also HISTORY AND MANNERS: Civil War; Military Tradition; Vietnam War; MYTHIC SOUTH: Fighting South

John Hawkins Napier III
Montgomery, Alabama

Army Information Digest (December 1964); William Chapman, *Washington Post* (13 April 1970); Shelby Coffey III, *Washington Post*'s *Potomac Magazine* (9 August 1970); Marcus Cunliffe, *Soldiers and Civilians: The Martial Spirit in America, 1775–1865* (1968), John Hope Franklin, *The Militant South* (1956); Morris Janowitz, *The Professional Soldier: A Social and Political Portrait* (1960); Patricia Linden, *Town and Country* (August 1976); Guy Martin, *Esquire* (June 1985); Drew Middleton, *New York Times* (18 April 1971); John Hawkins Napier III, *Alabama Historical Quarterly* (Fall–Winter 1967), *Alabama Review* (October 1980); William E. Schmidt, *New York Times* (9 April 1984). ☆

Politics of Education

As a vehicle for socializing youth, education is usually seen as a liberalizing and enlightening force. However, education is often a force for oppression, mystification, and enslavement. Any objective evaluation of the historic role of education in the South reveals consistent theoretical and practical examples of the use of education as an oppressive force. Southern educational structure, financing, content, and expansion/development patterns have reflected the region's racist, elitist, patriarchal, paternalistic, and isolationist politics.

In the antebellum period educational policies and practices were woefully inequitable, combining exclusionary education with little or no governmental involvement. In most cases, rich white male children were sent to England for schooling or taught by tutors. Education for blacks was viewed as dangerous for both the slaves and the white elite. Education for women was seen as damaging to their health and to the natural order of society. Women, like slaves, were presumed incapable of, as well as uninterested in, attaining more than minimal academic training. Education for poor white males was rendered problematic because of the exclusive and costly nature of education in the South.

After the Civil War, educational opportunities improved for all groups, especially for those previously excluded. Reconstruction politics led to new educational systems stemming from government involvement in the southern educational process. However, the removal of federal troops from the South heralded the beginning of political segregation, which was reflected in segregated and unequal educational institutions, financing, and opportunities.

Blacks, women, and poor whites were allowed access to academic training, but clearly the education available to them was designed to reinforce their subordinate roles. The black precollegiate and collegiate institutions that began during the period of Reconstruction were forced to function with limited human and material resources. Educational opportunities for women were geared toward gender-biased training and sex-stereotyped careers. Poor white males consistently faced economic barriers to educational goals. The basic theoretical and practical character of southern education continued to reflect a racist, patriarchal, and class-biased political culture.

The civil rights era ushered in some changes, but the basic relationship between the ruling elite and subordinate groups remained. Positive gains such as increased financial support for blacks, women, and poor whites, and less social rigidity—a consequence of minority pressure on the ruling group—must be viewed in conjunction with the reduction in the number of black principals, reduced control over precollegiate educational institutions in the black community, vocational tracking by white counselors and administrators, curricula changes that deemphasized the importance and richness of a distinct black culture, and creation of an illusion of equality that continues to impede positive changes in the South.

Recent political moves toward decentralization, revenue sharing, and block grants to the states provide the South with another opportunity to reimpose and reinforce the political values of the Old South on the New South. Whatever the final outcome, the politics of the South will likely be reflected in the politics of southern education.

See also BLACK LIFE: Education, Black; LAW: Civil Rights Movement; POLITICS: Ideology, Political; SOCIAL CLASS: Politics and Social Class

Shelby Lewis
Atlanta University

Charles W. Dabney, *Universal Education in the South*, 2 vols. (1936); Winifred Green, *New South* (Fall 1970); Patrick McCauley and Edward D. Ball, eds., *Southern Schools: Progress and Problems* (1959); M. Hayes

Mizell, *New South* (Winter 1971); Gary Orfield, *The Reconstruction of Southern Education: The Schools and the 1964 Civil Rights Act* (1969). ☆

Quality of Education

The quality of southern education has improved significantly in the years following racial desegregation of southern schools and colleges. The quality of education is more obvious at all levels of elementary, secondary, and postsecondary schooling. Improvement has been made and continues to be made, but the need for appreciable improvement remains.

The improved quality of education can be attributed in large measure to the growth and expansion of educational opportunity in the southern region as southerners have struggled to achieve the national level of educational quality. Census figures show that southerners now complete more years of formal schooling than they previously did. High school students now graduate at a rate much closer to the national average. College enrollments indicate that southerners now attend college at a rate and in a manner more closely approximating that of the nation and its other regions. Educational statistics at all levels and in all areas suggest convergence with national norms and indices of educational progress. Large differences between the regions existed in 1971, but these had diminished considerably by 1980. For example, in 1971 the Southeast had the largest proportion (36 percent) of nine-year-old students in the lowest achievement group, and the Central States had the smallest proportion (19 percent), a difference of 17 percentage points. By 1980 the Southeast still had the largest proportion in the lowest achievement group (30 percent) and the Northeast had the smallest (21 percent), but the difference was only eight percentage points. The same was true for the 13- and 17-year-old students. The South has accomplished much in its concerted efforts to "catch up."

Significant progress has been made in the preschool and kindergarten years of public education. Among those states with increased rates of participation in preprimary programs, the increase for some was quite dramatic. Eleven states, eight of which were in the Southeast, showed increases of 50 percentage points or more over the period. Arkansas (3 percent in 1971 and 83 percent in 1981) and North Carolina (10 percent in 1971 and 88 percent in 1981) experienced the largest increases. Southern children now generally begin their formal schooling at an earlier age than they did a decade ago, and their chances for success at each subsequent level of education have been appreciably enhanced. Middle schools have replaced junior high schools in most progressive school districts, and opportunities for vocational, technical, or career-related forms of education have greatly expanded at secondary and postsecondary levels. The years of schooling have thus been extended on both ends, while substantive, qualitative changes have been made in the form and content of the education southerners receive.

The improved quality of southern education is evident not only in the quantitative indices of attendance, access, and years completed, but also in the impressions and viewpoints of visitors, the professional judgment of educators, and the national images created by the news media. The location of corporate business and industry in the South remains dependent upon "the quality of the schools" the children of executives, middle managers, and skilled technicians will attend—and upon local schools and colleges as a source of trained, technically competent manpower. Once the prototype of regional branch-office cities, Atlanta enjoys a national reputation as "the nation's most desirable location" for the relocation of national offices; its public schools are depicted nationally as one of education's remarkable success stories.

The South remains a distinctive region educationally by virtue of the composition of its population. Relatively speaking, the South is still younger than other regions and thus has a larger proportion of its population to educate. Between 1950 and 1980 the per capita personal income of southerners increased greatly although it was still only 90 percent of the national figure in 1980. Southerners, despite their belief in education as a means of economic and technological development, continue to tax themselves at a lower rate than other states and regions. Although southerners spend a larger proportion of their tax revenues on higher education, the expenditure per capita falls well below the national average. The salaries of public school teachers and college faculty continue to compare unfavorably with those of their national counterparts.

Other regional differences bearing indirectly on the quality of education include a lower level of urbanization and the South's racial composition. In 1984 only 69 percent of southerners lived in a metropolitan area, as compared to the 76 percent national average. The percentage of blacks in a state's total population ranged from 35.2 percent in Mississippi to 3.3 percent in West Virginia. The combination of the region's urban-rural mix and its racial composition continued in 1985 to produce great tension between schools in the inner city and public schools in suburban areas. The effects on educational quality of establishing private academies in small towns and semirural areas are as yet unclear.

Despite the improved quality of education in the South, there are still lingering, persistent gaps between regional and national achievements. Some gaps may be narrower because of the decline in national standards and norms, and it is distinctly possible that the South did not—or could not—catch up as much as it might have. National efforts to expand educational opportunities for a growing and increasingly pluralistic society have resulted in the side effects of test-score decline, grade inflation, and a crisis in literacy. To many social critics such by-products reflect a genuine decline in the quality of American education and a serious erosion of educational norms and values.

Regional differences in the reading, writing, and computational skills of public school children have been documented by the National Assessment of Educational Progress. Despite noticeable gains by students in the South, National Assessment findings tell an old and embarrassing story of educational deficits. A large proportion of public school students do not meet national expectations in basic learning skills or educational achievement; for most skills and accomplishments the proportion of failing students in the southern region is larger than the proportion reported for other regions of the nation.

Irrespective of lingering regional differences, however, the quality of southern education in the 1980s is directly and immediately affected by national trends and developments. Few questions of quality peculiar to the South have been raised about schools and colleges, and no unique challenge has been identified for southern education. National concerns and issues have focused directly on projected declines in high school and college enrollments, the inadequacies of academic preparation at the secondary school level, and the urgent need for schools and colleges to work more closely on a host of mutual problems. Many southern high schools, like their national peers, have diversified their curricula at the expense of educational substance and content. A large majority have been seeking means of implementing concepts of competency-based education or minimal competency testing mandated by state legislators. The national concern with quality has included a growing dissatisfaction with the last two years of high school and the first two years of college. Colleges have increasingly found it necessary to teach students basic skills not acquired in 12 years of public schooling. National panels and task forces have addressed once again the nation's need for general education, core curricula, and advanced learning skills. Funding priorities and commitments of the federal government have again undergone major shifts or alterations. Education at all levels has been suspected of diminished quality, eroded standards, or loss of integrity. For the first time, southern educators have been able to address questions of quality in a national context of mutual concern and understanding.

See also BLACK LIFE: Education, Black

Cameron Fincher
University of Georgia

Simon S. Johnson, *Update on Education: A Digest of the National Assessment of Educational Progress* (1975); Michael M. Myers, ed., *Fact Book on Higher Education in the South: 1981 and 1982* (1982); National Education Association, *Estimates of School Statistics, 1984–85* (1985). ☆

Religion and Education

Religious institutions and individuals have used education to influence southern culture. Churches have established denominational schools and colleges, interdenominational academies, and theology schools. They have conducted weekly Sunday schools and annual Vacation Bible School classes. All of these institutions have communicated the specific teachings and ways of individual denominations, but they have typically also been standard-bearers of southern regional ways as well. They reflected the dominant evangelical approach of the region's numerically and culturally dominant Protestant groups. The ties between religion, education, and the broader culture were especially apparent in the role of religion in the public schools.

The Anglican church established the College of William and Mary in 1693, and it remained the only religious college in the South until well into the 18th century. Religious groups in the colonial period trained ministers through apprenticeship programs. The number of

Southern Baptist Theological Seminary, Louisville, Kentucky, 1931

denominational colleges, many of which also had theology schools, increased markedly in the late 1700s and early 1800s. Roman Catholics established the South's first school of theology—St. Mary's in 1791 in Maryland. By the early 1800s Catholics operated seminaries in Charleston, St. Louis, New Orleans, and Bardstown, Ky.

After the Great Revival at the turn of the 1800s, evangelical churches—especially the Baptists, Methodists, and Presbyterians—became increasingly prominent in the South and established their own schools. Many congregations and worshipers believed that education was less important than "the call" to the ministry, and many southerners since then have been suspicious of formally trained clergy, favoring religious zeal as the prime criterion for a successful preacher. Nonetheless, the southern churches have not been so antiintellectual that they did not support educational institutions.

Presbyterians have a long tradition of supporting education, and this was reflected in the South. They established Hampden-Sydney in Virginia in 1776, with a seminary added in 1807, and the Union Theological Seminary in Richmond in 1812. They supported Transylvania University in Kentucky, the first college west of the Appalachian Mountains, but withdrew assistance in 1818. Centre College of Kentucky was a cooperative effort of the church and the state; in 1824 the school became fully affiliated with the Presbyterians. Davidson College, which was named for General William Lee Davidson, began near Charlotte in 1836.

In the 1830s the Methodists launched Randolph-Macon in Virginia, Emory in Georgia, Emory and Henry in Virginia, and Holston in Tennessee. The Baptists founded Furman in South Carolina in 1826, Mercer in Georgia in 1833, and Wake Forest in North Carolina in 1834. These were founded by state conventions or regional conferences and assemblies. The University of Richmond in Virginia (1832) was the first attempt of Baptists in the South to establish a school to train their preachers. The Southern Baptist Theological Seminary was set up in Greenville, S.C., in 1859, and moved to Louisville, Ky., in 1877. Some antebellum colleges began as denominational institutions but later became public schools—Auburn University in Alabama started as the Methodist-supported East Alabama Male College (opening in 1859), and the University of Kentucky traces its history back to Kentucky University (1865), a Disciples of Christ school.

The Civil War was as devastating to southern denominational schools as to other aspects of life in the region. The schools and their personnel had assisted in the religious justification of the Old South and offered institutional moral support to the Confederacy. After the war some religious schools became central institutions in tying Christian and southern values together. The University of the South at Sewanee, Tenn., was officially founded in the late 1850s, but it did not offer programs until its resurrection after the war. Washington College became forever identified with southern tradition when Robert E. Lee chose to spend his postwar years there as president, until his death in 1870; the school was soon renamed Washington and Lee.

Following the Civil War large numbers of religiously supported or affiliated black schools emerged. The American Missionary Association was a nondenominational (though mostly supported by Congregationalists) agency that worked among the freedmen during Reconstruction and after. By 1870 it helped to support 170 colleges. The African Methodist Episcopal church, the African Methodist Episcopal Zion church, and other northern Methodist churches also played an important role in religious education in the South after the war. Schools dating from this period include Fisk in Tennessee, Hampton Institute in Virginia, Tuskegee and Talladega in Alabama, Atlanta University in Georgia, and Tougaloo and Rust in Mississippi. Baptists founded Roger Williams University in Nashville in 1863, and the Presbyterian and Reformed churches set up Biddle University in Charlotte in 1867 and Knoxville College in Tennessee in the 1870s. Episcopalians established St. Augustine's in Raleigh, N.C., in 1867.

Church work, especially by evangelical groups, expanded during the late 19th and early 20th centuries as a part of the effort to impose religious values on the South. The Methodists had high hopes for Vanderbilt, which began as that denomination's central college in 1873. The church broke ties in 1914, after the school's governing board became increasingly independent. Emory, Southern Methodist University, and later Duke became important church-supported liberal arts colleges. The Disciples of Christ began financial assistance to the Add-Ran Male and Female College in 1889, and that assistance continued when the school became Texas Christian University in 1902. A closely related religious group, the Churches of Christ, emerged in the early 20th century and now operates 17 schools of higher education, mostly in the South, including David Lipscomb in Nashville, Tenn., Freed-Hardeman in Henderson, Tenn., Harding University in Searcy, Ark., Oklahoma Christian College in Oklahoma City, Lubbock Christian College in Lubbock, Tex., and Abilene Christian University in Abilene, Tex. These institutions are located in areas of the greatest strength of the Churches of Christ.

The South's financial resources could not always match the interest of its religious people in maintaining denominational schools. In 1874 the Methodist Episcopal Church, South, supported 50 colleges, but by 1902 the number had been reduced to 18. A Southern Baptist Convention committee insisted that the "disease of starting Baptist Colleges has been sporadic, endemic, and epidemic." Nonetheless, the churches were not abandoning educational work. Many former colleges were simply reclassified as secondary schools, still under church sponsorship at a reduced cost level. The *Report of the Commissioner of Education, 1899–1900* from the federal government revealed that of 26,237 young people in educational institutions in the 11 former Confederate states plus Kentucky and Oklahoma, 13,859 were attending schools sponsored in some way by churches.

Denominational schools have continued to fulfill a number of vital functions for the churches in the 20th century. The evangelical groups are particularly concerned with missionary activity, and schools are a way to convey that interest to the young. Schools train lay people to work in counseling, publishing, and administration; they provide expertise in adult education, music, and recreational work. Faculties of these institutions are resources for local churches, offering workshops, institutes, and lectures.

The chief concern of denominational schools is the training of the clergy, and major church groups operate important theological schools. The southern Presbyterians maintain four seminaries: Union in Richmond (1823), Louisville in Kentucky (1901), Austin in Texas (1902), and Columbia in Decatur, Ga. (1928). The Cumberland Presbyterian church has Bethel College, McKenzie, Tenn., and the Memphis Theological Seminary. The theological school at Baylor University (established 1901) evolved into the Southwestern Baptist Theological Seminary in Fort Worth (1908). The Baptists also sponsor the Southern Baptist Theological Seminary, which has been in Louisville, Ky., since 1877; the New Orleans seminary (1917); and Southeastern at Wake Forest, N.C. (1951). Important Methodist theological schools are the Perkins School at SMU, the Candler School at Emory, and the Duke Divinity School. The Protestant Episcopal Theological Seminary of Virginia is in Alexandria, and the Episcopal Seminary of the Southwest is in Austin, Tex. St. Luke's School of Theology at the University of the South was the home to one of the South's most accomplished theologians, William Porcher DuBose.

Theological seminaries were rarely well endowed, and they had to face what historian Kenneth K. Bailey has called "a stifling popular distrust of scholarship." When scholarly findings revised traditional beliefs, "ancient myth was often acclaimed over present truth." A writer in the *Southern Methodist Review* in 1887 warned that requiring college training for itinerant preachers would "sound the death-knell of the Church." There were numerous celebrated attempts to remove professors at southern seminaries for teaching "dangerous" ideas—Alexander Winchell at Vanderbilt, James Woodrow at the Presbyterians' Columbia Seminary, Crawford H. Toy and William H. Whitsitt at the Baptist seminary in Louisville, and later, in the 1920s, John A. Rice at Southern Methodist University.

The Fundamentalist movement led to increasing questioning of the teachings of seminary professors during the 1920s. All southern white churches faced conflict over the issue, although the Presbyterian Church in the United States had fewer challenges than did the southern Methodists and the Southern Baptist Convention. Theological seminaries in the South have frequently faced challenges to their academic freedom, but their presidents and faculty have just as often stood up for free intellectual expression. They have represented religious humanism and ecumenicism within denominations that have sometimes not championed those ideas in general.

The relationship between religion and education involves more than the training of preachers and the establishment of denominational schools. A good measure of the influence of southern religion on the overall regional culture is the importance of religion in public education. After the Civil War, southern churches and religious leaders crusaded to impose their moral values on society and also worked to insure religious influence in schools. At first the churches were suspicious of public education. The 1871 General Assembly of the southern Presbyterian church insisted that education was "too dear, too vital to us as a Church, to be remitted to the State." Other church groups agreed, and the Methodists, especially, embarked on an ambitious plan to establish church boarding schools and other institutions for mass education. By the turn of the century the results were disappointing, because few such efforts were adequately supported financially.

The major denominations in the South came to champion the idea of public elementary and secondary schools; they worked to insure religious influences within public education. Vanderbilt University Chancellor James H. Kirkland noted in 1910 that in the South "no unfriendly attitude has been shown to religion either in the lower schools or in the State universities. The Bible is generally read in the public schools, and often school is opened with a song and prayer." In the 1960s historian Francis Butler Simkins wrote that "the implementation of universal education by the southern states bids fair to be the means of making Christianity universal." Schools and colleges across the region "resound with daily prayers, hymns, and Bible reading." University faculty senates began their proceedings with prayers in some places through the 1970s, and sporting events often still begin with invocations (which sometimes are thinly veiled supplications to the gods for assistance to the home team).

Religion's place in public education has become an important issue in the contemporary period because of the church-state relationship. Although national in scope, the debate has focused especially on the South because of the region's tradition of close ties between religion and education. In the 1960 presidential campaign Democratic party nominee John F. Kennedy spoke in Houston before a Protestant ministerial alliance, assuring the preachers that he would not support federal government funds for parochial schools; 20 years later southern fundamentalists were eager to receive tax credits for parents sending children to the Christian academies that increasingly dot the southern landscape.

Challenges to inclusion of prayers in public schools have come from the South. Madalyn Murray O'Hair was in the border South—Maryland—when she filed the lawsuit that led to the 1963 Supreme Court decision outlawing prayer in the public schools. She later moved to Austin, Tex., where she has since established an archive of the American atheist movement and has continued to campaign against church-state ties. In the 1980s a black father in Alabama challenged that state's laws permitting moments of silence in the schools. The South's role in this controversy is complicated. The Southern Baptist Convention has long advocated a strict separation of religion and public education and has generally opposed government aid to schools as well as opposing school prayers. Baylor University has been a leader in studying the issue and has a *Journal of Church and State*. The Virginia-based Moral Majority, on the other hand, has led national efforts to ratify a school-prayer amendment to the Constitution.

Religious leaders and organizations have also played a major role in influencing textbook adoptions in the South. They have testified before state textbook commissions and persuaded many of them to exclude books discussing theories of evolution. Religious leaders and individuals were also prominent in efforts in the early and mid-20th century to adopt only textbooks that positively portrayed southern history and white supremacy. The intimate ties between region and religion were especially clear here.

Finally, the humble Sunday school deserves mention for its role in southern culture. It is not uniquely southern nor even American. Robert Raikes, a printer and publisher in England, is normally considered the founder of the Sunday school movement, which caught on in the United States in the early 1800s. The first Sunday school in the South was apparently established in 1803 in the Second Baptist Church in Baltimore. Many religious people opposed the school idea at first as unbiblical, and Sunday schools were long a local congregational, lay effort more than an official tool of denominations. Sunday schools typically were regarded as missionary work—the Southern Baptist Convention at first included them as part of its Domestic Mission Board; that denomination's present Sunday School Board, headquartered in Nashville, was not set up until 1891. The major denominations embarked on campaigns after World War II to expand their Sunday school work so that it soon involved extensive organization, participation by adults as well as children, increased funding, and elaborate publications. The Sunday schools and related Vacation Bible Schools in the summer may not have been uniquely southern, but they have been fondly remembered institutions of regional life, effectively introducing children not only to the tenets of the region's dominant evangelical churches but also to the dominant cultural attitudes on race relations, child rearing, male-female roles, and countless other topics.

Charles Reagan Wilson
University of Mississippi

Donald S. Armentrout, *The Quest for the Informed Priest: A History of the School of Theology* (1979); Kenneth K. Bailey, *Southern White Protestantism in the Twentieth Century* (1964); Ben C. Fisher, in *of Religion in the South*, ed. Samuel S. Hill (1984); Thomas C. Hunt, James C. Carper, Charles R. Kniker, eds., *Religious Schools in America: A Selected Bibliography* (1986); Charles D. Johnson, *Higher Education of Southern Baptists: An Institutional History, 1826–1954* (1955); Lynn E. May, *Sunday School Leadership* (October 1980); Alan Peshkin, *God's Choice: The Total World of a Fundamentalist Christian School* (1986); Edward J. Power, *Catholic Higher Education in America* (1972); Joe M. Richardson, *Christian Reconstruction: The American Missionary Association and Southern Blacks, 1861–1890* (1986). ☆

Rural and Agricultural Education

When the "Boll Weevil Special" of the Illinois Central Railway pulled into stations throughout the lower Mississippi River Valley, farmers turned out to see the latest in seed, fertilizer, and machinery, all displayed in the boxcars. They turned out, too, to hear lectures from state agriculture agents and university agronomists, who told farmers of the best methods for combating the weevil and other pests. Agents, professors, and displays all traveled in the "Special" during its two-week run through the rural South.

What the farmers got from the "Special" and the other "educational trains" was a continuing agricultural education, delivered in an unusual but fitting way. The trains operated in the South during the first decades of the 20th century and were both a symbolic and practical response by state education officials, state agricultural officials, the U.S. Department of Agriculture, and private interests to the unusual needs and problems of the rural South. During the 19th and early 20th centuries observers from all political points of view agreed that these problems and needs, particularly as they applied to agricultural and rural education, were great.

"Since the war," said Populist L. F. Livingston, "our people have had less opportunity for thought and study than any people in modern history; outside our cities, popular education has largely been a farce." U.S. Commissioner of Education N. H. R. Dawson devoted 50 pages of his *Report of the Commissioner of Education, 1887–88* to chronicling the paucity of educational opportunity in the rural South. Dawson found that in every possible measure of educational progress, the South lagged behind the North and West.

School terms ran 50 to 60 days in the rural South and 100 to 150 in the North and West. Massachusetts spent, in 1880, an average of $14.93 per pupil enrolled in its common schools, the highest in the nation. The lowest level of per capita expenditure by a nonsouthern state was New Jersey's $3.23. Louisiana's $1.53 was the highest in the South and still a princely sum compared to Alabama's $.96 spent for each pupil enrolled in the common schools. This lack of educational opportunity resulted in a staggering rate of adult illiteracy. In 1902 the U.S. Commissioner of Education found a 13.2 percent rate of illiteracy among adult white males living in the rural counties of New Hampshire. In Virginia the comparable rates were 35.4 percent for whites and 65.7 percent for blacks, figures that were typical of the region.

Dawson, in his 1887–88 report, admitted that the idea of the common school, of a schoolhouse in every hamlet and town, had never caught on in the South as it had in the North. Looking back, it is possible to see why this was so. First, settlement patterns in the southern colonies and states created a population more dispersed than in the North and even more dispersed than on the western frontier. The communities that evolved in the rural South were plantation centered, and bonds between families were personal rather than political or legal. In terms of both logistics and custom, the dispersion of the population discouraged the creation of government-sponsored schools.

Second, the South suffered under the double burden of a high population of school-age children and a low level of taxable wealth in the years after the Civil War. For every one child per adult in Massachusetts in 1890, there were two in South Carolina. In the same year, a 1 percent tax in Massachusetts raised five times the revenue as the same tax in the Palmetto State. So southerners were faced with large numbers of children to educate and few financial resources with which to accomplish the task. For rural producers this was asking too much. In times of agricultural depression, the provision of schooling became a near financial impossibility in most communities if left to their own revenue-producing ability.

Third, state political leaders were unwilling to provide centralized support for schooling in the South. Many agreed with the editor of the Scotland Neck *Democrat* who argued in 1887 that "[e]ducation had ruined a great many more men than it has helped." What ruined men, black and white, was the tendency of education to "fire the mind of the ignorant with dreams." "To educate a fellow above the station he moves in," claimed the editorial, "ruins his value as a citizen and destroys his usefulness as a member of society." The experience of Reconstruction, particularly the efforts of the Freedmen's Bureau and of local black school societies, reinforced for many white southerners the dangers of education for any but the elite. The New Orleans *Bulletin* in 1874 railed against northerners teaching in the bureau's schools and argued that under such tutelage blacks would soon demand social and political equality. The *Bulletin* urged its readers not to hire educated blacks, as they were "the most intelligent, therefore the most dangerous." As long as the prevailing view connected education and social instability, white support for schooling for the rural inhabitants of the region remained weak.

Deepening contact between northerners and southerners in the fields of business, education, and politics accompanied the growth of the New South. With that contact came revised notions concerning the social function of education that put agricultural education at the center of a movement to reform rural southern culture.

The model for the "new education" for the New South grew from two sources. In philosophy, the movement to establish schools in the rural South rested on the unlikely example of Samuel C. Armstrong's Hampton Institute. Armstrong, a Freedmen's Bureau agent, founded Hampton in 1868, with assistance from the American Missionary Association, as a white-controlled school for blacks. At Hampton, Armstrong combined training in agriculture with academic courses and rigid discipline to educate blacks to achieve within the narrowly defined limits of their social and economic sphere. The Hampton experiment proved to some southern leaders what northern educators had been saying and practicing for decades: namely, that education could be a powerful force in preserving social stability among blacks and whites alike.

The curriculum of the "new education" owed much to the success of the land-grant colleges, established by the passage of the Morrill Act in 1862. In the South the colleges quickly became centers of research in agriculture. Knowledge of new methods and techniques promised to "readjust agriculture and place it upon a plane of greater profit, reconstruct the rural home, and give attraction and dignity to country life," wrote Seaman A. Knapp, a leader of the "new education." But standing in the way of this revolution in rural living was the illiteracy, the poverty, and the lack of educational means for disseminating the discoveries made in the colleges. Southern educational leaders began in the last decades of the 19th century to push for educational reform based on the Hampton model of skill-centered, "appropriate" education, but with limited success.

Help came in the form of political clout, ideas, organization, and hard cash from the North, and from northern associates of the shapers of the New South. At the center of the northern effort was Robert C. Ogden, New York businessman, philanthropist, and churchman. Ogden had business interests in the South, but his main connection to the region was through his friend Armstrong. Ogden served as a Hampton trustee for 40 years and during that time was instrumental in raising funds for the school. In 1898 he turned his talents and energies to the broader task of organizing a campaign for southern education and, at the urging of J. L. M. Curry, Charles W. Dabney, and others, took the chairmanship of a loose confederation of educational reformers and welded them into the powerful Southern Education Board (1901).

The board began its work as a publicity machine, sending speakers, letters, and circulars to southern politicians, teachers' organizations, and communities. This public campaign sought to encourage support for, and funding of, schools at every level. Ogden recruited able spokesmen to the cause, including Charles B. Aycock, Edwin A. Alderman, Seaman A. Knapp, Albert Shaw, and Charles McIver. Together and separately they canvassed the South, building support for public schooling and the idea of individual and social progress through education.

In 1902 Ogden announced that a generous gift from John D. Rockefeller made it possible for the board to take more direct action. As the General Education Board, Ogden and his group sponsored teachers in rural areas, paid for a regionwide system of rural school inspectors, supported agricultural extension work, funded agricultural experiment stations, helped the "education trains" to carry their message, and managed, through the donation of equipment and supplies, the creation of an agricultural curriculum in southern schools. By 1920 the General Education Board had disbursed over $14 million, most of it raised in the North, in its efforts to build up rural education in the South.

More than simply injecting needed money and manpower into the cause of rural and agricultural education, though, the Campaign for Education in the South recast the idea of education in such a way that it gained the support of southern political leaders and the public in general. To rural producers and their families, education in agricultural methods and the dissemination of new techniques, whether adult education or vocational education for children, promised more productive farms and a better quality of life. To southern policymakers, as Henry W. Grady promised, schools offered "an efficient system of drilling the children to the habits of discipline and the customs of obedience which make for public order."

By the time the "Special" made its last run in 1925, the effort to build schools in the rural South, at least for whites, had succeeded. Southern school reform, in the 1920s, became an element of the national Progressive movement and lost much of its regional tone. Like the "Boll Weevil Special," rural educational development in the South owed much to northern initiative, took education to farmers and their families, and focused on skill training within the agricultural economy of the region. The combination promised a new century of educational growth for the rural South.

See also AGRICULTURE: Diversification; / Agricultural Extension Services; Knapp, Seaman A.; HISTORY AND MANNERS: Philanthropy, Northern; MYTHIC SOUTH: New South Myth

Theodore R. Mitchell
Dartmouth College

James D. Anderson, in *Work, Youth, and Schooling: Historical Perspectives on Vocationalism in American Education*, ed. Harvey Kantor and David Tyack (1982); Charles W. Dabney, *Universal Education in the South*, 2 vols. (1936); Paul Gaston, *The New South Creed: A Study in Southern Mythmaking* (1970); Carl Kaestle, *Pillars of the Republic: Common Schools and American Society, 1780–1860* (1983); A. C. True, in U.S. Department of Agriculture, *Miscellaneous Publications*, no. 15 (1923); C. Vann Woodward, *Origins of the New South, 1877–1913* (1951). ☆

Teachers

Teaching in the South began as an uncertain, insecure, and temporary calling. Most antebellum teachers were men with no special qualifications who taught for irregular terms in scattered rural schools. Ranging from prospective ministers to itinerant ne'er-do-wells, these teachers worked for miserable wages and often "boarded 'round" with the parents of their students. The South's private academies, which sometimes received public funds, offered more stable employment and attracted better-qualified teachers.

The Civil War and Reconstruction devastated public and private education in the region. Black education did advance, thanks to the support of the Freedmen's Bureau and northern philanthropic and religious organizations. Northern teachers came south to assist in many states, but generally southern teachers struggled along in academies or in ill-supported public schools, where conditions were bad for white teachers and students and worse for blacks.

The development of statewide public school systems at the turn of the century changed teaching dramatically. Faced with booming enrollments, school officials hired a new breed of teachers—young, unmarried women. In addition to the belief that they embodied virtue, complacency, and reliability, women were said to make ideal employees because they would work for lower wages. More than in any other region, teaching became stereotyped as "women's work." Today the South has the highest percentage of female teachers in the nation.

Well into the 20th century, many southern teachers could boast of little formal education themselves. School officials built a variety of specialized teacher-education programs using northern models, including teacher institutes, which were periodic "in-service" meetings, and normal schools, which evolved by the 1930s into teachers' colleges and, by the 1950s, into state colleges and universities. Virtually all southern teachers now have college degrees, although urban teachers, white teachers, and high school teachers still go to school longer than their rural, black, and elementary counterparts.

Teacher associations in the South grew up independent of the national organizations with which they are now affiliated. Dominated by male administrators, state and local associations were for many years "teacher" organizations in name only. Teachers joined, not because they wanted to, but because their principals and superintendents demanded it. The associations were friendly to state and local school boards, uninvolved in politics, and indifferent to teachers' salaries and working conditions.

Gradually, the South's teacher organizations underwent three significant transformations. The first occurred after 1920 as they became more responsive to the needs of their members, working in a steady if nonmilitant way to improve teacher welfare. The organizations waged polite campaigns for tenure laws, pension and retirement benefits, and health and sick-leave provisions. During this period they also affiliated with the National Education Association (NEA). Southern teachers continued to think of themselves primarily as members of state and local associations, but gradually they began to see themselves as part of a unified national organization.

The black counterpart of the NEA was the American Teachers Association (ATA), composed of 10 state associations for black teachers. The South's teacher organizations experienced a second transformation with the merger of the ATA and the NEA in 1966. Responding to the civil rights movement, teachers in long-segregated associations joined hands, but often with reluctance and misgivings.

A third transformation occurred during the 1960s and 1970s as teacher associations became militant and politically active, a development in which the South lagged 5 to 10 years behind other regions. Administrators left teacher organizations in droves as they began to behave like teacher unions.

Actually, this was not the South's first experience with teacher unionism. Since the World War I era a very few teachers had joined locals affiliated with the American Federation of Teachers (AFT). Perceived as far too radical by most southern teachers, the AFT caught on only in larger cities, most notably Atlanta and New Orleans, where there was a relatively strong labor movement to lend support.

Collective bargaining for teachers, a common practice in the rest of the country, remains unacceptable to most state legislatures in the South. As of 1985 the average salary of teachers in the South was $20,523 as compared to the national average of $23,500, and the salaries and working conditions are still among the poorest in the nation. Yet southern teachers find their militancy restrained by politics and tradition. The wildcat Mississippi teachers' strike of 1985 signaled a new militancy among the nation's lowest-paid teachers, who gained higher salaries as a result of their protests.

See also BLACK LIFE: Education, Black

Joseph W. Newman
University of South Alabama

Ellwood P. Cubberley, *Public Education in the United States: A Study and Interpretation of American Educational History* (1919); Willard S. Elsbree, *The American Teacher: Evolution of a Profession in a Democracy* (1939); Edgar W. Knight, *Public Education in the South* (1922); Joseph W. Newman, "A History of the Atlanta Public School Teachers' Association" (Ph.D. dissertation, Georgia State University, 1978), *History of Education Quarterly* (Winter 1984), *Journal of Thought* (Fall 1983). ☆

Technological Education

During the 20th century the South, along with the rest of the nation, has become increasingly aware of technology and its impact. Automobiles, computers, and hydroelectric power represent three of the most obvious examples of revolutionary change brought about by technology. Only in recent decades, however, has southern technological education kept pace with these changes or evidenced a high level of achievement.

Southern higher education before the Civil War was little different from that in the North. Focusing on the classical curriculum, a university education prepared the student for life as a cultured gentleman. Training in the sciences and practical fields such as engineering or agriculture had no place in the university experience. Southern education suffered greatly during the Civil War, with almost all institutions closing for the duration. After the war, southern universities continued to stress the traditional liberal arts, but because of the region's economic difficulties, these institutions failed to approach parity with northern schools.

During the 1880s, however, the recovering South began to reevaluate the role of higher education. The success of contemporary businessmen led commentators to stress the importance of practical education as the means to economic enrichment. Latin, Greek, and esoteric sciences were supplanted by curricula designed to prepare the student for a place in the world of business, industry, and agriculture. Many southern states began establishing schools to supply such practical education. Auburn, which was Alabama Polytechnic from 1899 until 1960, Georgia Tech (founded as Georgia School of Technology in 1885), Clemson (1889), Texas A&M (1876), and Virginia Polytechnic Institute (1872) all owed their existence or continuation to the "practical" mentality of state legislators and businessmen, as well as to federal support through the Morrill Act.

The cultural and intellectual change represented by these new schools, however, may have been more apparent than real. As Thomas D. Clark argued in 1965, southern agricultural and mechanical colleges aimed at improving the farming community's way of life. By focusing on land policy and management and agricultural and general engineering, these institutions represented a commitment to the region's agrarian society. The South was apparently not yet ready to mimic the industrial outlook of its northern neighbors.

Another example of cultural inertia in education may be found in the development of separate black schools during the late 19th and early 20th centuries. Both northern philanthropists (guided by the recommendations of George F. Peabody) and state legislators supported the idea of "industrial education" for blacks. Yet this education, even at George Washington Carver's famous experiment station at Tuskegee Institute (1881), was designed to train efficient and contented black laborers for the semiindustrialized southern agricultural economy. Although the region's interest in education had increased markedly by the early 20th century, schools of science and technology to rival northern institutions such as MIT and Rensselaer Polytechnic failed to appear.

The first half of the 20th century witnessed little improvement in southern technological education. The number of institutions providing appropriate instruction grew to include such schools as Louisiana Polytechnic Institute (originally Louisiana Industrial

Institute), Tennessee Polytechnic Institute (founded in 1915, but not a degree-granting school until 1928), and Texas Technological College (chartered in 1923); but few major improvements in curricula or equipment took place. The Great Depression hit state-supported institutions especially hard and further thwarted the growth of southern technological education. With 23 percent of the nation's population, the South in the 1930–31 academic year could claim only 17 percent of American engineering graduates. There had been no change a decade later.

The end of World War II signaled the beginning of a major change in technological education throughout the United States, a change in which the South participated. World War II had been a total technological endeavor, symbolized by the development and use of the atomic bomb. Students entering college after the war (with or without the GI Bill) naturally found engineering and science courses attractive. Compared to prewar levels, engineering enrollments doubled by the end of the decade, even though the number of engineering schools remained virtually constant in both the South and the nation as a whole.

The war experience had emphasized the practical value of government support for research and development, and that value remained substantial during the early years of the Cold War. Defense-related research, whether performed in government or university laboratories, enjoyed generous federal funding. Because of their relative lack of expertise, however, southern schools received little of this federal largesse, preventing significant growth of the region's technological education base. Although large sums flowed from Washington to such southern outposts as Redstone Arsenal (Huntsville, Ala.) and Oak Ridge, Tenn., southern education received few of the benefits.

The national shock of the successful launches of *Sputnik I* and *Sputnik II* in late 1957 precipitated another, and by far the most significant, change in America's educational history. For the next decade the nation focused on improving the scientific and technological base of American culture, with education receiving great attention and massive federal funding. Here, at last, the South began to enter the mainstream of technological and scientific development. The need for improved science education became immediately apparent, with southern schools at every level receiving federal funds to establish new programs and to improve existing ones. Aerospace research facilities, frequently cooperating with local universities, grew rapidly in Georgia, Florida, Alabama, Texas, and Louisiana. Schools such as the University of Alabama-Huntsville, Florida Institute of Technology, and Rice University worked closely with the National Aeronautics and Space Administration to guide the Apollo program to its successful lunar landing.

The flight of *Apollo XI* in July 1969, however, was a crucial turning point. Suddenly federal funding for programs involving science and technology began to evaporate. In part a reaction to growing environmental concerns, this lack of interest in science and technology made itself painfully obvious to undergraduate and graduate students who found it increasingly difficult to secure financial aid. The aerospace industry in the South, which had been the region's major path to its share in the technological renaissance of the Space Age, withered perceptibly, removing employment opportunities in many technical fields. By the early 1970s technological education in the South was in a precarious position.

Within a few years, southern technological education had resumed, but the recovery was due to market pressures and self-sustaining technological developments, rather than government support. The revolution associated with rapid developments in computers led not only to an increased demand for computer programmers and engineers, but also to a heightened appreciation for all technological fields. Although the aerospace industry had not fully recovered from the post-Apollo letdown, almost all other "high-tech" fields enjoyed profound growth. With high salaries available to engineers with undergraduate degrees, schools of engineering found themselves deluged with applications. In the South the region's population growth further reinforced this trend, with undergraduate engineering enrollment during the 1981–82 academic year approaching 100,000 students, distributed among 70 schools.

The rapid growth of southern engineering enrollments, however, was not without difficulties. Beginning in the late 1970s, southern states, as those elsewhere, found it increasingly difficult to fund higher education to any significant level. As a result, faculty strength and salaries rarely kept pace with the growing demands of higher enrollment. Facilities and equipment were similarly difficult to obtain, leading many of the region's technological schools to consider limiting enrollment. A less obvious difficulty concerned the place of traditional programs in those schools with growing technological curricula. Increasingly, English, history, physics, and mathematics departments found themselves pressured to become service departments, providing only those courses required for the engineering program's accreditation.

Despite the current healthy status of technological education in the South, sufficient problems exist to cause concern. Present demand for high-tech training may not be a permanent phenomenon, raising the possibility of an oversupply of trained personnel in the near future. Further, despite legislators' encouragement of practical education, state governments are not, at this time, providing the funds to offer that education. Finally, the emphasis on technological education has frequently led to the atrophy of programs in the arts, humanities, and social sciences. These problems are national, rather than strictly regional, in scope. Until they are addressed by governments and universities alike, the role of technological education in the South will remain an important, but unresolved, issue.

See also BLACK LIFE: Education, Black; HISTORY AND MANNERS: Automobile; Philanthropy, Northern; World War II; SCIENCE AND MEDICINE: Aerospace; Technology; / Carver, George Washington

George E. Webb
Tennessee Technological University

James D. Anderson, *History of Education Quarterly* (Winter 1978); Allan M. Cartter, *Southern Economic Journal* (July 1965); Thomas D. Clark, *Three Paths to the Modern South: Education, Agriculture, and Conservation* (1965); John S. Ezell, *The South Since 1865* (1963); Lawrence P. Grayson, *Engineering Education* (December 1977); Daniel S. Greenberg, *The Politics of Pure Science* (1967); C. Vann Woodward, *Origins of the New South, 1877–1913* (1951). ☆

Urbanization and Education

Scholars have given a variety of explanations for why education in the South differs from education in other regions of the United States. Some have emphasized geography as the causal factor, others economics, others ideology, others social structure, and still others some combination of these factors. Southern differences frequently are attributed simply to the rural nature of life. The urbanization of southern education took place mainly in the New South period and after (roughly 1875 to the present), and this fact provides one more angle from which the South's educational distinctiveness may be considered.

In broad outline, educational developments in southern cities were similar to those in other American cities. Southern cities experienced a progressive reform movement in education in the early 20th century, just as non-southern cities did; city schools in all regions were racked by the Great Depression of the 1930s as well as by the other economic gyrations of the 20th century; and educational institutions have grown more numerous and diverse in this century, both in the South and out of it. Since the 1954 *Brown* v. *Board of Education* decision of the U.S. Supreme Court, southern and non-southern school systems have been faced with the challenge of desegregation. Urban public universities in Charlotte, Birmingham, Tampa, Atlanta, New Orleans, and other southern cities have recently entered the competition for students and funds with nonurban southern public and private colleges and universities, just as newer public universities in Boston, Cleveland, Detroit, Chicago, and Milwaukee have begun to challenge the primacy of their regions' nonurban public universities and private colleges.

Yet, given this overall similarity from region to region, variations in the South's urban educational experience have distinguished it from the experiences of other regions. Changes regarded as innovations elsewhere have different meanings in the South. For example, the school system in Atlanta, Ga., in the late 19th and early 20th centuries selectively adopted educational innovations such as the introduction of technical subjects into the curriculum. Atlantans at first resisted the new subjects and then slowly accepted them, but only as new avenues of preparatory study for higher education. The reformist motive of providing true vocational education as an alternative offering was slow to be realized.

This hesitancy to embrace innovation wholeheartedly was characteristic of urban higher education as well. In the late 19th century and the early 20th, two of the region's urban institutions of higher education, Emory and Vanderbilt, were caught up in a struggle between utilitarian curricular reformers and traditional opponents of that reform. At Emory, which originally was in the small-town setting of Oxford, Ga., the conservatism of President Warren A. Candler (1888–98) undid vocational reforms achieved by his two immediate predecessors. Two decades later, Emory moved from Oxford to the urban setting of Atlanta, a move that was part of a plan by Candler, who by then was a Methodist bishop, to make Emory one of two universities closely tied to the Methodist Episcopal Church, South, and its traditional beliefs and values. Candler and his church had bitterly quarreled with its former affiliate university, Vanderbilt, which under the leadership of Chancellor James H. Kirkland chose secularism over Southern Methodism in order to receive a grant for its medical school from the Carnegie Foundation for the Advancement of Teaching.

At Vanderbilt, even after its divorce from the church and during several decades in which it was led by New South advocates like Kirkland and his successors, opposition to social and educational change was strong. A notable defense of traditional southern values came from the famous Vanderbilt Agrarians who published their manifesto *I'll Take My Stand* in 1930. Ironically, this defense of the values of the rural countryside came from one of the South's preeminent urban universities. One of the Agrarians, Donald Davidson, taught at Vanderbilt for over four decades from the 1910s to the 1950s, defending traditionalism in education and social life during that entire period. Davidson's rabid defense of segregation in the 1950s, however, showed the darker side of southern cultural traditionalism.

The urban South's experience with school desegregation since 1954 has run counter to the prophecies of doom made by Davidson and the antiintegration politicians. Desegregation has taken place with relative success in Florida's major cities—Jacksonville, Miami, and Tampa–St. Petersburg—as well as in other southern cities such as Charlotte, N.C., and Richmond, Va. Thus, by the 1970s most of the images of hate and fear that accompanied desegregation of urban schools came from such northern cities as Boston, Chicago, Buffalo, and Cleveland, rather than from the South. Explanations for this difference vary, but whatever the cause, the South's urban experience clearly contains something that has allowed it to meet the challenge of school desegregation without collapsing into spasms of hate. Nevertheless, the success of desegregation efforts must be interpreted in light of so-called white flight from urban public school systems. For example, in 1985 about 94 percent of Atlanta's public school students were black and in Memphis approximately 77 percent were black. Although some school systems are successfully turning around such trends, the new patterns of segregation will persist in many locales in the foreseeable future.

Comparisons of the southern urban educational experience with that in other regions are almost always made with the Northeast or the Midwest, but southern cities, with the exception of Birmingham and a few others, have little in common with the industrial centers of those areas. As 20th-century commercial, regional, and governmental centers, most of the South's cities have more in common with western cities such as Los Angeles than they do with the older industrial centers. Fruitful results should emerge when southern urban educational development is compared to the situation in western urban centers, as well as to the North and Midwest.

See also MYTHIC SOUTH: / Agrarians, Vanderbilt; URBANIZATION articles

Wayne J. Urban
Georgia State University

Mark K. Bauman, "Warren Akin Candler: Conservative Amidst Change" (Ph.D. dissertation, Emory University, 1975); John

Kohler, "Donald Davidson, a Critique from the Losing Side: The Social and Educational Views of a Southern Conservative" (Ph.D. dissertation, Georgia State University, 1982); William E. Schmidt, *New York Times* (25 May 1985); Twelve Southerners, *I'll Take My Stand: The South and the Agrarian Tradition* (1930); Wayne J. Urban, in *The Age of Urban Reform: New Perspectives on the Progressive Era*, eds. Michael H. Ebner and Eugene M. Tobin (1977), in *Education and the Rise of the New South*, eds. Ronald K. Goodenow and Arthur O. White (1981). ☆

Women's Education

See WOMEN'S LIFE: Education of Women

ALABAMA, UNIVERSITY OF

Chartered in 1820, the University of Alabama opened in 1831 in Tuscaloosa, physically and academically modeled on the University of Virginia. Serious antebellum disciplinary problems turned the university into a military academy by 1860. During the Civil War academic classes and military training continued until federal troops burned the university in 1865.

When only one student registered in 1865, trustees decided to rebuild the school before reopening in 1869. State political turmoil paralyzed the school during Reconstruction, resulting in frequent leadership changes, few students, and little money. Beginning in the mid-1870s when state appropriations rose, student numbers and faculty strength increased, although the university remained a military one. Student unrest returned, now against the military system, which was discontinued in 1903. By the end of the 19th century three of the university's best-known traditions—women students, a flourishing Greek system, and an expanding athletic program—were established.

The 20th century saw the university transformed from a small southern military college to a multicollege university. Programs such as law and medicine that had earlier languished now flourished along with the new graduate school and extension centers. Integration efforts in 1956 failed when a campus riot occurred. Segregation ended in 1963 with the successful enrollment of two black students, and as of 1985 blacks constituted approximately 10 percent of the student body. Student unrest, political instead of racial, returned in 1970 in protests over the killing of four students at Kent State and Jackson State universities.

In 1969 extension centers at Huntsville and Birmingham became autonomous, and in 1975 university trustees combined these two campuses with that at Tuscaloosa to create the University of Alabama system. By the 1970s the medical school in Birmingham achieved international recognition.

The national success of the athletic program in the 1970s overshadowed escalating faculty discontent on the Tuscaloosa campus over administrative neglect of academic programs. The president of that campus resigned after two "no confidence" votes of the faculty. New leadership in the 1980s both in the University of Alabama system and on the Tuscaloosa campus, as well as renewed efforts of university trustees, restored student and faculty confidence and won additional financial support from the state legislature. Joab L. Thomas became president of the university on 1 July 1981, and fall semester 1985 enrollment was 15,163.

See also RECREATION: / Bryant, Bear

Sarah Woolfolk Wiggins
University of Alabama

James B. Sellers, *History of the University of Alabama, 1819–1902* (1953); Suzanne Rau Wolfe, *The University of Alabama: A Pictorial History* (1983). ☆

ARKANSAS, UNIVERSITY OF

The University of Arkansas, located at Fayetteville in the northwest corner of the state, was created by the legislature in 1871 as one of the universities in the land-grant system authorized by Congress in the Morrill Act of 1862. The school's early years were marked by adversity as it struggled to survive inadequate financing, caused in part by the antiintellectualism pervading Arkansas politics in the 1880s.

Like the other land-grant institutions, the University of Arkansas was committed to research and public service as well as teaching. An agricultural experiment station was established in 1888 and an agricultural extension service in 1914. These programs proved to be greatly beneficial to the state's agricultural economy.

In the early 20th century the university began to receive greater support from the citizens and more generous funding from the legislature. The school's "middle period" of development—during the tenures of presidents John C. Futrall, J. William Fulbright, and Arthur M. Harding—was characterized by growth in enrollment, strengthening of the faculty, expansion of the physical plant, and broadening of the curriculum.

At present the university offers degrees in many areas of study, including agriculture, home economics, arts and sciences, business administration, education, engineering, architecture, law, and medical sciences. Graduate instruction was initiated in 1927, and a broad range of programs is now offered leading to master's and doctor's degrees. In the 1984–85 academic year nearly 3,000 undergraduate and graduate degrees were awarded—74 associate's, 1,852 bachelor's, 808 master's, and 124 doctor's degrees. Total enrollment at the Fayetteville campus was 13,773 at the beginning of the fall 1985 semester. In addition to the complex at Fayetteville, the university operates its medical sciences program and the Graduate Institute of Technology at Little Rock; these campuses offer master's and doctor's degrees in a variety of fields. In the 1970s three colleges were merged into the university—the University of Arkansas at Little Rock, the University of Arkansas at Pine Bluff, and the University of Arkansas at Monticello.

See also AGRICULTURE: / Agricultural Extension Services

William Foy Lisenby
University of Central Arkansas

Robert A. Leflar, *First 100 Years: Centennial History of the University of Arkansas* (1972). ☆

AUBURN UNIVERSITY

Auburn began as a Methodist liberal arts college chartered as the East Alabama Male College by the Alabama Legislature over Governor John A. Winston's veto on 1 February 1856. Winston questioned the creation of a second Methodist college since the legislature had just chartered Southern University at Greensboro, which had the support of the Methodist Conference. Both institutions opened in 1859; Auburn had a faculty of 6, a student body of 80 men, and a board of trustees of 51. During the Civil War Auburn closed, but it reopened in 1866. In 1872, with no money to operate the school, the Methodist church transferred ownership to the state, and Auburn became the Agricultural and Mechanical College of Alabama, the first land-grant institution in the South. From this point there was conflict between the traditional and land-grant philosophies. Another continuing problem was the meager or inadequate financing from the state, a situation common in the postwar and, later, the depression South.

Two early presidents, Isaac Taylor Tichenor and William Leroy Broun, led in the development of Auburn's physical plant, scientific curriculum, agricultural education, and experiment stations, but Broun's greater contribution was to recruit a core of brilliant young faculty who shaped the university for 50 years after his death. Two of these dynamic men were George Petrie, a young Johns Hopkins Ph.D. holder, who first came to Auburn in 1887 and who served the university as a history and Latin professor, academic dean, and football coach, and L. N. Duncan, who became president in 1935 and guided the university out of debt to financial stability. In 1899 the school's expanding academic program influenced the legislature to rename the college the Alabama Polytechnic Institute, and in 1960, in recognition of the name by which it had been commonly known and to emphasize the diversity and breadth of its academic programs, the school officially became Auburn University.

Students at Auburn University, 1930s

Auburn University's accomplishments must begin with its agricultural research and extension service contributions, which have improved the economy of the state of Alabama and helped to feed people everywhere, especially in Third World countries. Auburn's superior ROTC program has produced many outstanding officers, and its School of Engineering has graduates all over the world, particularly in the aerospace industry.

A second campus was created by the legislature in 1967 in Montgomery, and by the 1980s the Auburn campus had more students than any other university campus in Alabama. Auburn's athletic teams compete as "Tigers" to a cheer of "War Eagle," and the student newspaper is "The Plainsman"—a reference to the name "Auburn," which came from a line by poet Oliver Goldsmith, "Sweet Auburn, loveliest village of the plain." Although Auburn has attracted a large group of foreign and out-of-state students, the majority remain Alabama

Baptists and Methodists with conservative political views and traditional values. The first black student enrolled in 1964, yet despite a vigorous minority recruitment program and scholarships, blacks remain a small but well-integrated part of the student body and a high percentage of the athletes. James E. Martin became president in 1984. The fall 1985 enrollment was 19,056 students.

See also AGRICULTURE: / Agricultural Extension Services

Leah Rawls Atkins
Auburn University

The College Blue Book, Narrative Descriptions (20th ed., 1985); Ralph B. Draughon, *Alabama Polytechnic Institute* (1954); Mickey Logue and Jack Simms, *Auburn: A Pictorial History of the Loveliest Village* (1981); Malcolm McMillan and Allen Jones, *Auburn University through the Years, 1856–1973*, Auburn University Bulletin, No. 68 (May 1973). ☆

BARNARD, FREDERICK A. P.

(1809–1889) Educator and scientist.

Born in Sheffield, Mass., Frederick Augustus Porter Barnard spent half of his professional life in the South. Barnard received his A.B. degree from Yale in 1828 and, suffering from increasing deafness, he taught mathematics and geography at institutions for the deaf from 1831 to 1837. In 1838 he accepted a teaching position at the University of Alabama, where he hoped to pursue his developing interest in the sciences, especially astronomy, and higher mathematics.

Barnard taught mathematics, natural philosophy, and chemistry at Alabama. He was instrumental in the establishment of an observatory at the university, although he had to struggle with the board of trustees, the administration, and the state government for the funds. While in Alabama, Barnard cultivated an interest in early photographic techniques. He learned daguerrotypy from Samuel F. B. Morse and opened a gallery in Tuscaloosa in 1841. He maintained a scientific interest in photography and published articles in photographic journals throughout his career. During the years 1853–54 Barnard opposed a reorganization of the Alabama curriculum that would have implemented the same type of broad elective system used at the University of Virginia and Brown University. Barnard favored retaining a traditional discipline-oriented system in which the student would be allowed a few elective courses. The board of trustees, as well as Basil Manly, the president of the university, supported the Virginia plan and it was adopted. Barnard refused to work under the new system and resigned in 1854.

Frederick A. P. Barnard, educator and scientist, c. 1860

Barnard then went to the University of Mississippi, which had opened in 1848. The university badly needed instructors, and Barnard taught courses in mathematics, chemistry, physics, civil engineering, and astronomy. An ordained Episcopal minister, he also accepted a job as rector of the Oxford church. In 1856, only two years after his arrival, Barnard became president of the university. As president, his work was hampered by local residents, who saw no practical purpose for the university and regarded it with varying degrees of suspicion and dislike. Barnard was somewhat successful in his efforts to improve instruction and to acquire more sophisticated equipment for the school. Barnard's main interest at the University of Mississippi, as at Alabama, was the sciences, and his critics charged that he emphasized the study of science too heavily, to the exclusion of more traditional studies. As sectional differences intensified, suspicion of Barnard's northern roots pursued him. In March 1860 he was tried by the board of trustees on the charge of being "unsound on the slavery question." His supporters rallied behind him, however, and Barnard was cleared of the charges. Although Barnard was increasingly unhappy with his situation and attempted several times to secure positions elsewhere, poverty kept him from leaving Mississippi.

After Mississippi seceded from the Union early in 1861, university business was interrupted by the enlistment of many students in the military. Barnard left Mississippi in late 1861 and lived in Norfolk, Va., until Union troops captured that city in May 1862. Confederate president Jefferson Davis offered to hire Barnard to conduct a survey of the natural resources of the Confederacy, but Barnard refused because of his Union sympathies.

After working for two years with the U.S. Coastal Survey, Barnard was elected president of Columbia College, now Columbia University. During his 25 years at Columbia (1864–89), Barnard instituted standard entrance exams, introduced the concept of elective courses, and strengthened and enlarged the graduate and professional schools. His interest in science continued, and he was instrumental in founding the National Academy of Sciences in 1863.

Although Barnard later said that his years in Mississippi were among his worst, he seems to have genuinely loved the South and its people. His influence at the southern universities where he worked was felt long after his departure, especially in the area of science, and his hopes for upgrading the quality of education at Alabama and Mississippi were eventually fulfilled.

Karen M. McDearman
University of Mississippi

William J. Chute, *Damn Yankee!: The First Career of Frederick A. P. Barnard* (1977); John Fulton, *Memoirs of Frederick A. P. Barnard* (1896). ☆

BAYLOR UNIVERSITY

Chartered by the last Congress of the Republic of Texas on 1 February 1845, Baylor University is the oldest institution of higher education in Texas and is the world's largest Baptist university. Eponym and one of the chief founders was District Judge Robert Emmett Bledsoe Baylor, who also was an ordained minister. Twenty-four young men and women comprised the opening class of the school at Independence, Tex., on 18 May 1846. The first president, Henry Lee Graves, resigned in 1851 and was followed by Rufus C. Burleson, whose 10-year tenure saw 55 students graduate, including the first graduate, Stephen Decatur Rowe, in 1854. The Civil War years were naturally lean for Baylor, especially during the two-year administration of George W. Baines, great-grandfather of U.S. President Lyndon B. Johnson. Baines was followed by William Carey Crane, who led the institution from 1864 until his death in February 1885.

The Baptist State Convention voted in 1886 to consolidate Baylor and Waco universities at Waco, with the new home to be Baylor University at Waco. Rufus C. Burleson was named president of the unified school, and Reddin Andrews became vice president. Burleson opened the new Baylor University in the facilities of the former Waco University, but within two years new facilities were constructed on a 23-acre site given the institution by the city of Waco. At first the university's degrees for females, who pursued a slightly different curriculum from males, carried the title of "maid" while the men received "bachelor's" degrees. Before the turn of the century all courses were offered to both sexes and all undergraduate degrees were designated "bachelor." Graduate degrees were also available by 1894.

Samuel Palmer Brooks assumed operational control of the university in 1902. A former faculty member and a graduate of both Baylor and Yale, Brooks initiated programs to move the university from its regional parochial level to a complete university status. During Brooks's 29 years as president, several different schools were established as well as a college of arts and sciences. In addition, the university opened a theological seminary (which moved to Fort Worth in 1910 to become Southwestern Baptist Theological Seminary) and began to offer medical degrees through a college of medicine. That college was given independent status in 1969.

Upon Brooks's death in 1931, Pat M. Neff, a former Texas governor (1920–24) was elected president. The Depression caused numerous hardships on the faculty and staff, but the stringent operational measures of Neff enabled the institution to emerge from the period debt free. In 1948 Neff was replaced by William R. White, who immediately embarked upon a building program to meet the post–World War II boom. This was continued and greatly enlarged with the coming of Judge Abner V. McCall to the helm of the institution in 1961. During McCall's 20-year administration, Baylor's campus expanded from 40 acres to 350 acres and the physical structures increased to total more than 50. Enrollment reached the 10,000 mark with students from all 50 states and numerous foreign countries. In June 1981 Dr. Herbert H. Reynolds became president.

The university currently has a college of arts and sciences and schools of law, music, business, education, nursing, and graduate studies. It also operates the Baylor University Medical Center in Dallas and has an affiliate degree program with the United States Army Academy of Health Sciences in San Antonio. The 10,990–member student body (1984–85) has a 22:1 student-teacher ratio, and national fraternities and sororities are among the approximately 200 social, service, honorary, and professional student organizations. Baylor is one of six Texas schools with a

Phi Beta Kappa chapter, and the percentage of National Merit Scholars enrolled is among the highest in the country.

Eugene W. Baker
Baylor University

Eugene W. Baker, *Nothing Better Than This* (1985); Lois Smith Murray, *Baylor at Independence* (1972). ☆

BEREA COLLEGE

In 1853 Kentucky politician Cassius Marcellus Clay and others persuaded abolitionist John Fee to preach a series of sermons in the Cumberland foothills of Madison County. The following year Fee built a home there on a ridge he called Berea, after the town cited in Acts 17:10. The next year a one-room school was built, which doubled as an antislavery church. Fee hoped to create a college that would educate "all colors, classes, cheap and thorough." Some of their neighbors resented and feared farsighted educational leaders such as Fee. The inflammatory effect of John Brown's raid caused armed men to drive Fee and the other Berea leaders out of the state in January 1860. However, the intrepid group returned after the war and incorporated Berea College. The Reverend Henry Fairchild of Oberlin became its first president in 1869, and college classes began in 1870.

For the next century, under the presidential leadership of Henry Fairchild (1869–89), William B. Stewart (1890–92), William G. Frost (1892–1920), William J. Hutchins (1920–39), Francis J. Hutchins (1939–67), and Willis D. Weatherford, Jr. (1967–84), Berea College emerged as an institution with major commitments to educating poor Appalachian youth, to providing a liberal arts education in an atmosphere of Christian service, to maintaining the early founder's goals of interracial education, and to continuing a labor program that allows all students "to work their way through school." Berea's educational philosophy has paid rich dividends to southern Appalachia. Almost 50 percent of Berea's graduates have returned to their mountain homeland to provide significant service in many professional and business fields. Its enrollment in the 1984–85 academic year was 1,554 students.

James M. Gifford
Appalachian Development Center
Morehead State University

Richard B. Drake, *One Apostle Was a Lumberman: John G. Hanson and Berea's Founding Generation* (1975); William Goodell Frost, *For the Mountains: An Autobiography* (1937); Elizabeth Peck, *Berea's First Century, 1855–1955* (1955); John A. R. Rogers, *Birth of Berea College* (1903). ☆

BLACK MOUNTAIN COLLEGE

Thoroughly southern in its origins, though less so in its style, Black Mountain College was founded in 1933 by the volatile South Carolina classics scholar John Rice. The college began in buildings rented from the Blue Ridge Assembly of the Baptist church three miles outside Black Mountain, N.C.; in 1941 it moved a few miles to its permanent site at Lake Eden, N.C. Black Mountain became one of the least orthodox but most influential institutions in American educational history—influential out of all proportion to its short life and the size of its enrollment, which never went above 75. The history of the college breaks down into three periods: the first concluding with Rice's resignation in 1940; the second concluding with the 1949 departure of the painter Josef Albers, a powerful figure in the college after 1933 and especially so after Rice left; the third concluding with the closing of the college in 1956. Many documents charting this history are preserved in the state archives in Raleigh, N.C.

Prophetic of many of the experimental social and educational communities of the 1960s, Black Mountain College from its beginning broke with tradition. The community was largely self-supporting, performing much of its own labor and raising its own livestock and crops. The arts occupied the center of an unprecedentedly flexible curriculum; the college had no requirements, minimal bureaucracy, and never received accreditation. Contrary to the legalized segregation of the 1940s and 1950s, it admitted blacks. The Black Mountain community was probably more diverse than historian Martin Duberman's description of it as "a Yankee island in a Southern sea" suggests, but the college community's members were outside the mainstream of both national and regional culture and politics because of their lifestyles and views of education.

Black Mountain College saw its most creative years, those for which it is best known, under the direction of the poet Charles Olson. Between Olson's arrival in 1951 (after a short visit in 1949) and the school's closing in 1956 because of falling enrollment, lack of faculty, and financial problems, Black Mountain had as students or instructors people who have since become recognized as major innovators in virtually every art: Olson, Robert Creeley, Robert Duncan, and Edward Dorn in poetry; Merce Cunningham in dance; John Cage and David Tudor in music; Robert Rauschenberg in painting. The school also sponsored one of the most important avant-garde literary journals of the post–World War II period, the *Black Mountain Review*, of which seven issues appeared between 1954 and 1957. Black Mountain College survived only 23 years—in late 1954 its enrollment had plunged to nine students—but its impact on the arts in America is still being felt and measured.

Alan Golding
University of Mississippi

Fielding Dawson, *The Black Mountain Book* (1970); Martin Duberman, *Black Mountain: An Exploration in Community* (1972); *OLSON: A Journal of the Charles Olson Archives* (Spring 1974–Fall 1978). ☆

BOB JONES UNIVERSITY

Bob Jones University (BJU) is a nondenominational fundamentalist institution that styles itself "the world's most unusual university." Founded in 1927 by itinerant Methodist evangelist Robert Reynolds Jones, Sr. (1883–1968), the school outgrew early facilities near Panama City, Fla., and moved in 1933 to Cleveland, Tenn., and then, in 1947, to its present 200-acre campus in Greenville, S.C.

Still directed by the Jones family, BJU refuses to seek accreditation by regional or state agencies, fearing outside interference with its ability to stand "without apology for the old-time religion and the absolute authority of the Bible." The university's approximately 5,000-member student body (4,287 students in 1984–85) comes from virtually every state and many foreign countries for studies in Bible, missions, preaching, literature, foreign languages, education, business, and cinematography. BJU boasts a large collection of religious art and stages elaborate Shakespearean productions, seeking to combine the best of Western culture with strict Christian orthodoxy.

Graduates constitute a significant element in America's fundamentalist community. Known for their rigorous separatism, many serve as pastors and teachers in a myriad of independent (mostly Baptist and Bible) churches throughout the United States. They usually maintain close ties with the university and often carry BJU's fervent "Americanism" and conservative politics with them. Several graduates achieved prominence in the early 1980s as leaders of the New Christian Right.

Perhaps the university is best known for its rigid student code, largely unchanged since the 1920s. Students must dress conservatively, avoid off-campus dating, refrain from "griping," not patronize stores where liquor is sold, and observe other stringent regulations. A provision proscribing interracial dating became the subject of prolonged litigation in the 1970s, as the Internal Revenue Service challenged the school's tax-exempt status, claiming that the rule discriminated against minorities. This issue resulted in a Supreme Court case in 1982 and a national controversy over the Reagan Administration's effort to restore the exemption. The university lost the case yet has remained unbending in its commitment to the "old-time religion."

James Guth
Furman University

Gregory Jaynes, *New York Times* (14 January 1982); Melton Wright, *Fortress of Faith: The Story of Bob Jones University* (1960). ☆

BUSING

During the 1970s busing achieved more urban desegregation in the South, especially in Florida, Kentucky, North Carolina, and Tennessee, than it did in the North and the West. Legally, southern cities were more vulnerable to court-ordered remedies because of their past records of school segregation. Administratively, it was easier to implement metropolitan busing in southern communities, where the county was the "basic educational unit" (Florida and Kentucky), the number of school districts was relatively small, and "white flight" to suburbia had not undermined the possibility of creating reasonable black-white pupil ratios in city schools.

In the first major and decisive southern busing case, *Swann* v. *Charlotte-Mecklenburg Board of Education* (1971), the U.S. Supreme Court upheld an extensive busing order—of more than 43,000 children—for the largest school system in the Carolinas and the 43d largest in the nation. Under a proportional plan, black pupils would be transported from central-city to suburban schools, so that each school in the consolidated system would have a balanced black-white ratio. Busing between noncontiguous zones, the Supreme Court ruled, was a permissible remedy, if the school closest to home was racially segregated.

Although metropolitan solutions were implemented in Florida (statewide) and in Charlotte-Mecklenburg, Nashville-Davidson, and Louisville-Jefferson, busing was legally stopped at the city line in Richmond (by a divided Supreme Court) and exchanged in Atlanta for the appointment of more—over half—black school administrators (compromise of 1973).

The Supreme Court extended to northern and western communities (*Keyes* v. *School District No. 1, Denver, Colorado*, 1973), *Swann*'s school-desegregation requirement, but Detroit and similar cities thwarted metropolitan busing plans. In the absence of proof of prior official discrimination and its "inter-district effect" on suburban areas, "an inter-district remedy" was not legally justified (*Milliken* v. *Bradley*, 1974).

Opposition to busing became a heated political issue in the 1972 presidential campaign, when antibusing candidate Governor George C. Wallace of Alabama won the Florida and Michigan Democratic primaries. The Nixon Administration championed the neighborhood school concept and opposed busing. During the past decade, opponents repeatedly argued that busing neither improved the educational achievements of minority pupils nor increased racial tolerance. A 1982 Senate bill (#5951) proposed to prohibit the round-trip busing of pupils in excess of 10 miles or 30 minutes and to allow the attorney general to seek the dissolution of busing orders at the request of local school boards. The measure died in the House, but the debate continues.

Various southern cities have reformulated busing plans that they instituted in the 1970s. For example, in Memphis in 1982 the city and the NAACP Legal Defense and Education Fund, Inc., reached an agreement that allowed the city to limit busing and restore neighborhood status to a number of schools, though as of May 1985 approximately 16,000 black students and 3,500 white students were still being bused to achieve racial balance. The revamped busing plans coupled with aggressive school-improvement efforts enabled the Memphis public schools between 1981 and 1985 to lure back some 3,500 students who had fled the city system in the wake of earlier desegregation plans. Supported by the Reagan Administration, many southern cities are emphasizing alternatives to busing such as magnet schools, which are supposed to offer enriched public school opportunities and encourage voluntary integration. Such approaches may be used increasingly as court requirements for busing are eased or reversed. In 1986, for example, the Fourth Circuit Court of Appeals ruled that Norfolk, Va., could curtail the court-ordered busing that had been instituted in 1971 to achieve integration of the public schools. Throughout the South and the nation busing remains a highly controversial issue as efforts are made to achieve and maintain both racial balancing and educational quality.

Marcia G. Synnott
University of South Carolina

Thomas J. Cottle, *Busing* (1976); Ellie McGrath, *Time* (6 February 1984); Nicolaus Mills, *The Great School Bus Controversy* (1973), ed., *Busing U.S.A.* (1979); *Newsweek* (17 December 1984); Gary Orfield, *Must We Bus?: Segregated Schools and National Policy* (1978); Andy Paztor, *Wall Street Journal* (10 February 1986); William E. Schmidt, *New York Times* (25 May 1985). ☆

CAMPBELL, JOHN C.

(1867–1919) Educator.

John Charles Campbell was born in LaPorte, Ind., 14 September 1867. He attended Williams College and Andover Newton Theological Seminary, graduating from the latter institution in 1895. That same year he married Grace Buckingham and moved to Joppa, Ala., where he headed a mountain academy. After serving there three years, he taught in the public schools of Stevens Point, Wis., and then in 1900 moved to Tennessee, where he served as principal of the Pleasant Hill Academy. From 1901 to 1907 he was superintendent of secondary education, dean, and president of Piedmont College, Demorest, Ga. In 1905, during his tenure at Piedmont, Campbell's wife died. Two years later, in 1907, he married Olive A. Dame of Medford, Mass., and spent several months traveling with her in Sicily and Italy.

In 1908 Campbell attended a meeting of the National Conference of Charities and Correction in Richmond, one session of which was devoted to benevolent work in Appalachia. This led directly to the work for which he is now best remembered. Inspired by a paper at the conference, Campbell approached Mary Glenn, a prominent figure in social work circles, with a proposal to conduct a survey of the social, industrial, educational, and religious problems of the Appalachian mountaineers, which would aid in ascertaining what resources were needed or available. Campbell's proposal was presented to the trustees of the Russell Sage Foundation on 25 May 1908. Funding for the survey was approved annually until October 1912, when he was appointed secretary of a newly established Southern Highland Division of the foundation. Campbell then carried out his plans for Appalachia. In an effort to foster cooperation among agencies working in Appalachia, he helped organize the Conference of Southern Mountain Workers (later known as the Council of the Southern Mountains) and for many years served as the group's leader. At Campbell's suggestion the southern Presbyterian church centralized its school work in the mountains and formed the Synod of Appalachia in 1914—the first formal acknowledgement by that denomination that Appalachia formed a natural, distinctive unit of organization.

Campbell worked for years on a book utilizing the information gathered in his survey of mountain problems, but *The Southern Highlander and His Homeland* (1921) did not appear until two years after his death. Although polemical, it is generally considered the best early study of Appalachia. Campbell's greatest difficulty in finishing the volume was that Appalachia was not a coherent region with a uniform culture and a homogeneous population, but was instead a complex portion of America that could not be easily generalized.

Campbell died in Asheville, N.C., 2 May 1919. With his passing the Russell Sage Foundation's work in the mountains came to an end, although for several years the organization continued to fund the annual meeting of the Conference of Southern Mountain Workers. Campbell's widow, herself a major figure in Appalachian cultural work, helped establish the John C. Campbell Folk School at Brasstown, N.C., in honor of her husband, who was one of the early American advocates of the Scandinavian folk school as an alternative to the traditional rural school. This school is still in existence.

W. K. McNeil
Ozark Folk Center
Mountain View, Arkansas

Isaac Messler, *Mountain Life and Work* (April 1928); Henry D. Shapiro, *Appalachia on Our Mind: The Southern Mountains and Mountaineers in the American Consciousness, 1870–1920* (1978); David E. Whisnant, *All That Is Native and Fine: The Politics of Culture in an American Region* (1983), *Modernizing the Mountaineer: People, Power and Planning in Appalachia* (1979). ☆

CHAUTAUQUA

From its start in 1874 at a Methodist Sunday school assembly in Lake Chautauqua, N.Y., this movement had a southern flavor, and its felicitously packaged blend of semiclassical culture, popular religion, and self-improvement was widely welcomed in the Bible Belt. One cofounder, John Heyl Vincent, a Methodist minister born in Tuscaloosa, Ala., hailed the Chautauqua as a way to "mitigate sectional antipathies" in the post–Civil War years.

Although the circuit or tent Chautauquas still made their rounds of the southern hinterlands until the early 1930s, the independent Chautauquas, which met annually at the same site, had the most lasting influence. Independent Chautauquas were founded at Hillsboro, Va., 1877; Purcell, Va., 1878; Mountain Lake Park, Md., 1883; Monteagle, Tenn., 1883; DeFuniak Springs, Fla., 1884; Siloam Springs, Ark., 1886; Lexington, Ky., 1887; and the Piedmont Chautauqua at Lithia Springs (then Salt Springs), Ga., 1888. The spectacular Piedmont Chautauqua was the brainchild of Henry W. Grady, who called it the "Saratoga of the South." With the assistance of Marion C. Kiser and the Atlanta business community, an 8,000-seat tabernacle, two Italian Renaissance-style hotels, and a summer college building were constructed in about a month by an army of workers. In its heyday, the Piedmont Chautauqua's Summer College was headed by W. R. Harper, dean at Yale College, and included faculty from Harvard, Johns Hopkins, and the University of Virginia.

The circuit Chautauquas began in the Midwest in 1903 and soon spread to the South, where two systems, Alkahest of Atlanta and Radcliffe Attractions of Washington, D.C., handled most of the bookings. Alkahest, boasting that it "covered Dixie like the dew," had a principal seven-day circuit that played 40 towns per year. Radcliffe had three circuits that were scheduled for weeks and split weeks in well over 200 towns. The onset of the Depression and the popularity of radios combined to bring on the demise of the circuit Chautauqua.

The programs in both the independent and circuit Chautauquas were similar, offering something for all tastes and ages. Most popular were the inspirational addresses by such well-known speakers as Russell H. Conwell and William Jennings Bryan, but also widely enjoyed were the dramas, marching music, symphonic concerts, lectures on science, Gilbert and Sullivan operas, Cossack choirs, and magic shows. Many southerners remember the tent shows fondly for first bringing "culture" and entertainment to rural areas.

Benjamin W. Griffith
West Georgia College

Victoria and Robert O. Case, *We Called It Culture: The Story of Chautauqua* (1948); Benjamin W. Griffith, *Georgia Historical Quarterly* (Summer 1971), *Georgia Review* (Spring 1972); Theodore Morrison, *Chautauqua* (1974); Hugh A. Orchard, *Fifty Years of Chautauqua* (1923). ☆

CHRISTIAN ACADEMIES

Because of their central role in the socialization process, public schools have often been a focus of conflict in the United States. The gradual but inexorable application of the Bill of Rights to the states in matters of education, race, and religion since the 1940s prompted many white southerners to create alternate school systems.

The late 1960s saw the courts and the Internal Revenue Service finally demand compliance with *Brown* v. *Board of Education* (1954). One immediate reaction was the creation of secular private segregated (white) schools, often calling themselves "Christian academies."

As the Supreme Court turned its attention from basically Catholic issues (state aid to parochial schools) to more general religious questions (prayer and devotional Bible reading), the character of the "Christian" school changed. By the mid-1970s, integration became much less a factor than secularism, and a bona fide evangelical Christian school movement was born. These private schools are primarily, but not exclusively, white. They are attached to a wide variety of conservative Protestant churches, but particularly to those that identify themselves as independent and fundamentalist. Virtually all the churches that have played a leading role in the "New Christian Right" (such as the Moral Majority) of the 1980s run their own schools. Their philosophy is based upon the claim that churches and parents exclusively have the right and responsibility of education. The schools see themselves preserving *the* Christian and American way of life based upon the moral absolutes found in the Bible.

Curriculum designed specifically for Christian schools stresses providential guidance of American history and the necessity of moral purity in order to retain God's blessing. Some materials display a decidedly (almost caricatured) southern evangelical viewpoint. Slavery is seen in some as an accidental development resulting more from the actions of the North than of the South. Fervent anticommunism characterizes all, while a few display blatant anti Catholicism as well. Some offer little information about the Civil War other than the fact that revivals took place among the Confederate troops. The civil rights movement of the 1950s and 1960s may be discussed in terms of its attending violence, to the exclusion of almost every other topic. Although all the texts affirm the separation of church and state, a vision of America as a Christian nation under assault by the forces of secularism, humanism, and anti-Christianity predominates.

Christian schools have become a crucial ingredient in the evangelical resurgence and its attempt to define and maintain an American Christian civilization. These schools provide many of the leaders and issues that have mobilized the New Christian Right.

See also LAW: / *Brown* v. *Board of Education*; RELIGION: / Moral Majority

Dennis E. Owen
University of Florida

David Nevin and Robert Bills, *The Schools That Fear Built: Segregationist Academies in the South* (1976), *Southern Exposure* (Summer 1979); Alan Peshkin, *The Total World of a Fundamentalist Christian School* (1986); John Whitehead, *The Separation Illusion: A Lawyer Examines the First Amendment* (1977). ☆

CITADEL, THE

The origins of The Citadel may be traced to the alleged plot by Denmark Vesey, a free black, and 34 slaves to murder the white population of Charleston and set fire to the city in 1822. The accused conspirators were tried, convicted, and executed. Real or imagined, the specter of an insurrection terrified white Charlestonians. The city government petitioned the South Carolina Legislature to establish an arsenal or "citadel" to "insure domestic tranquility." The state provided the funds, and by 1825 a "citadel" was under construction at a site bounded by King, Boundary (later Calhoun), Meeting, and Inspection streets. A municipal guard was assigned to oversee the care and disposition of the arms and ammunition. The Citadel was only one of several local agencies established to provide racial and social control.

By an act of the legislature in 1841 a corps of young men assumed the duties of the guard while undertaking "a broad and practical education" at The Citadel, or South Carolina Military Academy. An imposing two-story brick, fortresslike building with turrets was designed and constructed. Over time two additional stories and wings were added. The highly visible, heavily armed cadets who frequently drilled on the parade ground were conducive to the "public order." The cadets and institution reflected the white southerners' liking for military trappings, guns and horses, camaraderie, and ceremony.

In early January 1861 the federal government sent the *Star of the West* to reinforce Fort Sumter in Charleston harbor. Hidden among the sand dunes on nearby Morris Island, cadets from The Citadel directed howitzer fire at the vessel. These were the opening salvos of the American Civil War. The vessel turned about, its mission aborted. In July 1863 The Citadel closed so that the cadets could take up military duties around Charleston.

In February 1865 the commander of the 21st First Colored Troops of the Union army accepted the surrender of the city and established his headquarters at The Citadel. The federal government released the institution to the state in 1882 and the school reopened. In 1922 The Citadel was relocated in the northwestern section of the city along the banks of the Ashley River. The architectural models for the new buildings were those of the old.

Today, the state-supported four-year college is flourishing. In the 1984–85 academic year The Citadel enrolled 3,001 male students in a corps of cadets. Black cadets were admitted for the first time in the 1960s, but to date no women have been accepted into the corps. Perhaps more than any other institution of higher education, The Citadel best reflects the cultural values of the Old South.

A special relationship has developed between Charleston and The Citadel. On Friday afternoons the cadets stage a weekly parade for townspeople and tourists. With unit flags fluttering and cannons booming, the cadets, dressed in uniforms of pre–Civil War design, step out to bagpipers and their band playing tunes like "Scotland the Brave." Invariably they conclude with "Dixie." When a Confederate flag painted on the institution's water tower was painted over in the late 1970s, students and alumni alike were outraged.

The Citadel's mission is to educate the "whole man" within a military setting. The rigors of the "knob," or plebe year, are supposed to foster a camaraderie that lasts a lifetime. Pat Conroy, the school's best-known graduate, is infamous in the eyes of some alumni for his characterization of The Citadel in his *The Lords of Discipline* (1980). Conroy writes that "the plebe system gave cruelty a good name." But for those like Conroy who become seniors, the ceremony of the ring is their most memorable experience. The ring binds them "to the brotherhood" of Citadel men and represents "passage through the system." There are chivalric overtones during graduation ceremonies when a ring is awarded to the cadet selected by his classmates as "the manliest, purest and most courteous."

In 1979 Admiral James B. Stockdale, neither a graduate of the institution nor a southerner, was selected by The Citadel's board of visitors as president. He was a winner of the Medal of Honor for heroic resistance during eight years as a prisoner of war in Hanoi; he was also a scholar. As president of the Naval War College, Admiral Stockdale had instituted electives in the humanities and had taught a course in moral philosophy.

For nearly a year Admiral Stockdale sought to minimize hazing during the plebe year at The Citadel, to change the school's "macho image," to attract scholarly students, and to reorganize the command structure. The board of visitors, however, all Citadel graduates, thought that the admiral was "moving too fast." In September 1980 Stockdale resigned, saying in dismay, "The place is locked in pre–Civil War concrete." The new president, Major General James A. Grimsley, a native South Carolinian, Citadel graduate, and retired U.S. Army major general, promised upon taking office that he planned no changes. That was the wish of the board of visitors, the students, and most of the faculty.

See also URBANIZATION: / Charleston

Walter J. Fraser, Jr.
Georgia Southern College

Oliver James Bond, *The Story of The Citadel* (1936); Pat Conroy, *The Lords of Discipline* (1980); *Newsweek* (1 September 1980). ☆

CLEMSON UNIVERSITY

Clemson began as Clemson Agricultural College, 27 November 1889. Founded by the will of Thomas Green Clemson (1807–88), first Superintendent of Agricultural Affairs and John C. Calhoun's son-in-law, it is the land-grant university of South Carolina. The campus encompasses Fort Hill, the Calhoun-Clemson home, which is located in the Piedmont. The school has, since its inception, been governed by 13 trustees, of whom seven are life trustees. The original seven were named by Thomas Clemson. Upon the death of one of the seven, the remaining six select the successor. Six other trustees are elected by the legislature.

Clemson opened 7 July 1893, on 854 acres with a main building, a chemical laboratory, machine hall, heating and lighting plant, one dormitory to house the 446 students, an infirmary, residences for the 15 faculty, two barns, and six silos. By 1986 the main campus consisted of 1,400 acres, and the total university land, including forests, experiment stations, and other tracts totaled 33,700 acres. There were 1,100 faculty, and student enrollment had grown to 12,926 (including 2,500 graduate students). About 65 percent of the students were from South Carolina, and the remainder were from 46 states, the District of Columbia, Puerto Rico, the Virgin Islands, and 79 countries.

Like many of its land-grant counterparts, Clemson Agricultural College began as a male-only military college and remained so until 1955. After that and until 1971 male students spent the first two years in ROTC; in 1971 the ROTC program became optional. Female students were first housed on campus in 1963. Clemson's racial integration was accomplished with dignity in the winter of 1963.

With the addition of undergraduate programs in most fields in arts and humanities, and master's and doctoral degrees in most scientific and technological areas, the school's name was changed to Clemson University on 1 July 1964. In 1986 nine colleges (Agricultural Sciences, Architecture, Commerce and Industry, Education, Engineering, Forest and Recreation Resources, Liberal Arts, Nursing, and Sciences) and the Graduate School made up the university. In keeping with its mission of public service and through its extension and experimental work, Clemson is involved in every county of South Carolina.

Jerome V. Reel, Jr.
Clemson University

The College Blue Book, Narrative Descriptions (20th ed., 1985). ☆

COLLEGE OF WILLIAM AND MARY

The second college begun in British North America, William and Mary received a royal charter in 1693. Although some Virginia planters continued to educate their children in England, an increasing percentage economized by sending their sons to the less expensive Williamsburg institution, which included grammar and Indian schools in addition to a liberal arts college modeled on the British universities where most of the professors had studied. With a faculty that included such intellectuals as legal scholar George Wythe and the poet Goronwy Owen, William and Mary emerged in the late colonial period as a thriving intellectual center.

The Revolution was disastrous for William and Mary, which suspended classes for almost two years. In 1781 the school suffered a devastating fire. More important, the separation from England deprived the school of crucial income from British sources. There followed a century-long cycle of decline during which William and Mary failed to win even minimal assistance from a state government that turned its attention to the new university in Charlottesville. Although the pre–Civil War faculty included such luminaries as scientist John Millington and jurist St. George Tucker, the presidency of Thomas R. Dew from 1836 to 1846 offered the only hint of true resurgence.

The Civil War very nearly destroyed William and Mary, which again suspended classes as faculty and students alike rushed to join the southern forces. In 1862 the school once more suffered the ravages of fire when Union troops looted and burned the Main Building.

College of William and Mary, Williamsburg, Virginia, c. 1840

President Benjamin S. Ewell returned from the war determined to reopen the college and managed to keep it in operation until it closed for want of funds in 1881. In 1888 the legislature provided a small sum to reopen William and Mary as an institution to train public school teachers. Ewell's successor, Lyon G. Tyler, then undertook the imposing task of reviving the school as a state-supported college. By the time he stepped down as president in 1919, William and Mary was an undistinguished institution, but it was also in no immediate danger.

During the 1920s John D. Rockefeller, Jr., became interested in restoring the town of Williamsburg to its 18th-century character. The college's location beside Colonial Williamsburg fostered interest in the school's heritage and helped to usher in a dramatic renaissance on the Williamsburg campus. Approaching the end of its third century, the College of William and Mary has regained the standard set when Thomas Jefferson was a student there in the 1760s. Its full-time enrollment in the 1984–85 academic year was 6,640.

See also HISTORY AND MANNERS: / Jefferson, Thomas; RECREATION: / Colonial Williamsburg

James P. Whittenburg
College of William and Mary

Herbert Baxter Adams, *The College of William and Mary: A Contribution to the History of Higher Education* (1887); Jack Eric Morpurgo, *Their Magesties Royall Colledge: William and Mary in the Seventeenth and Eighteenth Centuries* (1976); Lyon Gardiner Tyler, *The College of William and Mary in Virginia: Its History and Work, 1693–1907* (1907). ☆

COMMONWEALTH COLLEGE

One of the South's few attempts at resident labor education, Commonwealth was established in 1923 at Newllano Cooperative Colony near Leesville, La. After one turbulent year at Newllano, the faculty moved the tiny school to Polk County, Ark. The director of the college was utopian Socialist William E. Zeuch, who supported theoretical labor education and communal living rather than active participation in radical reform movements. Zeuch established as Commonwealth's original mission the production of sophisticated, literate, and idealistic leaders for the labor movement. Given its southern location and avowed aims, the school was remarkably devoid of controversy.

This placid scenario changed abruptly with the Great Depression, however, when in June 1931 a student-staff revolt headed by longtime Commoner Lucian Koch seized control of the college, ousted Zeuch, and plunged Commonwealth into aggressive labor activity. Delegations of Commoners were sent to Harlan, Ky., and Franklin County, Ill., to support coal miners in their strikes for union recognition. Other Commoners involved themselves in farm-labor organization, supporting the National Farmer's Holiday Association and participating in strike activities in Corinth, Miss., and Paris, Ark. College faculty and staff were prominent in the formation of a new Socialist party in Arkansas in 1931, and Clay Fulks, an instructor, was the party's nominee for governor in 1932. All this activity generated a new reputation for the tiny school, with charges of atheism, free love, and, most frequently, communism being heard around the South.

In spite of the change in direction, Commonwealth always maintained the same pattern of day-to-day existence on campus. Located in rural Polk County, Ark., the school strove to be self-sufficient by requiring four hours of labor per day from staff and students in return for subsistence and, in the case of students, instruction. Faculty were not paid and were expected to participate in every campus activity, including farm work, maintenance, and anything else necessary to escape from "bourgeois interests." Women worked primarily in the kitchen, the library, the laundry, and the school office; men completed chores on the wood crew, carpentry crew, farm crew, masonry crew, or hauling crew.

Classes began at 7:30 each morning and were usually held in the instructor's cottage. The unvarying format was group discussion—occasionally heated. The college operated on a vague quarter system, and students were limited to three courses per quarter. Commonwealth assigned no grades, conferred no degrees, and had no class-attendance requirements. Classes seldom exceeded 6 students, and the total student body never numbered more than 55. The college community, though small, was extremely cosmopolitan and included Americans from various ethnic groups, all geographic sections, and every educational level. The only entrance requirements were intelligence and dedication to the labor movement.

The last five years of Commonwealth's existence were hallmarked by a frequently acrimonious association with the Southern Tenant Farmers' Union. Organizational activities on behalf of the union focused a considerable amount of unwelcome attention on the school; the old charges of free love and communism were revived in the press. In 1936 the union attempted to reorganize the college, oust the radicals, and make it a legitimate place to train labor leaders. The Communist faction was not dislodged, however, and after two stormy years the STFU and other labor groups withdrew their support; this was a fatal blow to the little college. Commonwealth ceased to operate in September of 1940.

See also SOCIAL CLASS: / Southern Tenant Farmers' Union

William H. Cobb
East Carolina University

William H. Cobb, *Arkansas Historical Quarterly* (Summer 1964, Summer 1973); Donald H. Grubbs, *Cry from the Cotton: The Southern Tenant Farmers' Union and the New Deal* (1971). ☆

COUCH, W. T.

(b. 1901) Publisher.

"I have found it necessary to compromise and to be cautious, but I do not compromise or exercise caution merely to avoid criticism." Writing to Walter Lippmann in 1927, on the heels of publishing a controversial edition of the *Congaree Sketches*, William Terry Couch summed up a philosophy that would guide his editorial decisions throughout a 20-year tenure at the University of North Carolina Press.

Born in 1901 in Pamplin, Va., to a Baptist country preacher and the daughter of erstwhile planters, Couch spent his childhood in a variety of small southern towns. When he was 17 the family settled in Hope Creek, a few miles from Chapel Hill, N.C., and Couch worked at part-time and summer jobs to supplement their farming income. Entering the University of North Carolina, he became editor of the student magazine and attracted the attention of Louis Round Wilson, then director of the university press. At 25 Couch became his assistant and in 1932 assumed directorship.

Couch regarded argument and criticism as essential to scholarship. He departed from the guarded, conservative policies of the press and felt that the publication of "nice inoffensive books" did not fulfill the promise of the new social science research that addressed substantive issues like religion, race, and economics.

Of the 450 titles brought out under Couch's direction, 170 dealt primarily with southern topics. A core list included studies such as Arthur F. Raper's *The Tragedy of Lynching* (1933) and Duane McCracken's *Strike Injunctions in the New South* (1931) issued by Howard W. Odum's Institute for Research in Social Science. Such classics as *These Are Our Lives* (1939) and Virginius Dabney's *Liberalism in the South* (1932) appeared, and in 1934 the symposium *Culture in the South*, edited and contributed to by Couch, ambitiously surveyed "the broad stream of southern life" in order to "sound its depths, measure its strengths, discover its complexity and ultimately find ways to remove the debris which now infests its waters."

Couch underscored the need for southern publishing, claiming that "any people that leaves its thinking . . . to minds elsewhere is doomed to subservience." He repeatedly stressed that scholarship was not a frill to be jettisoned in hard times; it was as fundamental to the region's educational process as up-to-date machinery was to farming. As an antidote to what he saw as the failure of southerners to look to books for information and entertainment from an early age, he also published elementary and high school texts, a book for adult illiterates, and work on farming techniques, gardening, and local architecture.

By producing books designed to be of regional interest and by creating a tolerance for diverse and often critical studies of the South, Couch turned the University of North Carolina Press into a prime force for intellectual growth in the region. By 1934 the press was receiving national recognition for its pioneering work, and university presses throughout the country changed directions to follow its lead, producing high-quality books aimed at the general reader in conjunction with specialized scholarship.

A New Deal liberal, in the vanguard of progressive thought on questions of race, Couch had encouraged candid studies on race, and the press maintained a consistent policy of publishing the work of black authors. Nevertheless, he was troubled, as his introduction suggests, by the demand for an end to segregation in Rayford Logan's *What the Negro Wants*. In 1945, a year after its publication, Couch resigned to take up the directorship of the University of Chicago Press. From 1952 to 1959 he served as editor-in-chief of *Collier's*. His most recent book, *The Human Potential*, was published in 1974.

Elizabeth M. Makowski
University of Mississippi

W. T. Couch, *Sewanee Review* (Winter 1945), *Southwest Review* (Winter 1934); Daniel J. Singal, *The War Within: From Victorian to Modernist Thought in the South, 1919–1945* (1982). ☆

CURRY, J. L. M.

(1825–1903) Educator, minister, and politician.

A transitional figure between Old South and New, Jabez Lamar Monroe Curry displayed elements of both cultural traditions in his versatile public career. Born into a socially prominent, economically secure family and steeped in John C. Calhoun's constitutional doctrines, Curry studied law at Harvard. Horace Mann's example impressed upon him the value of universal education, and from his first term in the Alabama Legislature in 1847 to his final role in the Conference for Education in the South at the end of his life, Curry forcefully articulated the essential social, moral, and political functions of public education.

Elected to the U.S. House of Representatives in 1857, Curry resigned to defend secession and to serve in the Confederate Congress, but after 1865 he accepted emancipation when he embraced the racial paternalism of the New South. An ordained Baptist minister, he briefly assumed the presidency of Howard College in Alabama before joining the faculty of Virginia's Richmond College. In 1881 the Peabody Fund, established through the generosity of George Peabody of Massachusetts, named him general agent for its southern education campaign. Except for a three-year period (1885–88) as U.S. minister to Spain, Curry held the position until his death and became the incomparable orator-administrator of the late-19th-century education awakening.

Prodigious traveler, prolific correspondent, and author of numerous reports, he repeatedly addressed southern legislatures and citizens' groups to appeal for tax-supported schools. After 1890 he also represented the Slater Fund, endowed by John F. Slater of Connecticut to educate southern blacks. Because he defined universal education to include blacks and women, Curry championed coeducation, industrial education, teachers' institutes, and normal schools for teacher training.

In spite of his states' rights principles, Curry advocated enactment of the unsuccessful Blair education bill, a measure sponsored in the 1880s by Senator Henry Blair of New Hampshire to appropriate federal funds to fight illiteracy. Curry artfully identified enhanced literacy with the promotion of personal independence, the preservation of limited government, and the protection of individual liberties. Although he remained committed to black advancement, he grew increasingly pessimistic about it, and his inherent white-supremacist racism triumphed over his sense of noblesse oblige. More derivative than original in his ideas, Curry personified southern implementation of northern philanthropy and energetically crusaded for education as the paramount force of social and cultural stability.

See also POLITICS: / Calhoun, John C.

Betty Brandon
University of South Alabama

J. L. M. Curry Papers, Manuscripts Division, Library of Congress and Alabama Department of Archives and History, Montgomery; Merle Curti, *The Social Ideas of American Educators* (1935); Jessie Pearl Rice, *J. L. M. Curry: Southerner, Statesman, and Educator* (1949). ☆

DUKE UNIVERSITY

Duke University in Durham, N.C., traces its origins to a local academy organized by a group of Methodists and Quakers under the leadership of Brantley York in Randolph County, N.C., in 1838. Known initially as Union Institute, it was reorganized in 1851 for the training of teachers and named Normal College before it became affiliated with the Methodist church in North Carolina and was renamed Trinity College in 1859. Continuing to operate during the harrowing years of the Civil War, the college, long presided over by Braxton Craven, acquired a northern-born, Yale-trained president, John F. Crowell, in 1887. In 1892, inspired by generous support offered by Durham Methodists grown prosperous in the tobacco industry, particularly Washington Duke and Julian S. Carr, Trinity College moved to Durham.

A spellbinding Methodist preacher and dynamic administrator, John C. Kilgo, succeeded Crowell as president in 1894 and greatly increased the interest of the Duke family in Trinity. In 1896 Washington Duke offered an endowment of $100,000 provided that Trinity admit women "on equal footing with men," and the college, which even earlier had some women students, quickly accepted the offer. Other gifts from the Duke family followed, with Benjamin N. Duke, Washington Duke's son, serving as a leading benefactor and the principal liaison between the college and the family.

Thanks to support from the Dukes and to an able, relatively young, and ambitious faculty recruited from the new graduate schools at Johns Hopkins, Columbia, and other northern universities, Trinity College had developed by the time of World War I into one of the leading liberal arts colleges in the South. Despite the clamor of powerful Democrats in North Carolina, the trustees of the college refused in 1903 to oust historian John Spencer Bassett, who had publicly deplored the racist politics of the "White Man's Party." Trinity thus achieved one of the pioneering victories for academic freedom in the United States and strengthened its belief in and reputation for independent thought and scholarship.

Dreams of a university organized around Trinity College dated back to Crowell and the 1890s, but President William Preston Few launched a serious effort to realize the dream in the early

1920s. Because Benjamin N. Duke was in failing health after about 1915, Few began with Duke's blessings and assistance to focus his efforts on James B. Duke, Benjamin Duke's younger brother and by far the richest member of the family. In 1919 and again in 1921 Few sketched out his plans to James B. Duke and proposed that, because several educational institutions in the United States were already named Trinity, if and when funds became available to enlarge the institution in Durham it should be named Duke University. James B. Duke was not ready to go along in 1921, but by December 1924, he was.

Naming Duke University as one of the prime beneficiaries of the perpetual philanthropic foundation he then established as the Duke Endowment, James B. Duke also provided around $19 million for the rebuilding of the old Trinity campus, for the creation of a new campus with Tudor Gothic buildings, and for the acquisition of some 8,000 acres of adjoining forest land. In 1930, when the first buildings on the new campus were completed, the old Trinity campus became the site of the coordinate Woman's College, which in 1972 was merged back into Trinity College as the liberal arts college for both men and women. Training in engineering was available in Trinity College after 1903, and in 1939 a separate School of Engineering was organized. In addition to Divinity and Law schools, the Medical School and Hospital were opened in 1930 and a School of Nursing in 1931. What eventually became the School of Forestry and Environmental Studies was established in 1938, and the School of Business Administration opened in 1969.

Chapel at Duke University, Durham, North Carolina

With 9,285 students enrolled in degree programs in the 1984–85 academic year, Duke University continues by choice to be one of the smaller, voluntarily supported, major universities in the nation. Terry Sanford, former governor of North Carolina, became its sixth president in 1970 and served until his retirement in 1984. As of 1986 Keith H. Brodie served as president.

See also INDUSTRY: / Duke, James B.; Tobacco Industry

Robert F. Durden
Duke University

Nora C. Chaffin, *Trinity College, 1839–1892: The Beginnings of Duke University* (1950); Earl W. Porter, *Trinity and Duke, 1892–1924: Foundations of Duke University* (1964); University Archives, Duke University Library. ☆

EMORY UNIVERSITY

Emory College, chartered by the Georgia Methodist Conference in 1836, admitted students in 1838 to its Oxford, Ga., campus. Except when closed briefly during the Civil War, Emory strove through its traditional classical curriculum—in the words of an early president, Augustus Baldwin Longstreet—"to raise up a race of men who shall be fitted for the pulpit or the plow, the court or the camp, the Senate or the shop."

When the General Conference of the Methodist Episcopal Church, South, lost the power to control selections to the trustees of Vanderbilt University in 1913, the conference decided it needed a new university in the Southeast. A former Emory president, Warren A. Candler, now a bishop, persuaded the church commission to make Emory College the nucleus of such a university. The bishop's brother Asa, wealthy from promoting Coca-Cola, would provide a million-dollar endowment and a new campus, a wooded and hilly 75-acre tract northeast of Atlanta.

Chartered in 1915, Emory University first opened theology and law schools on the new campus, with the undergraduate college moving from Oxford in 1919. Later, business, dental, graduate, library, medical, and nursing schools were added. In 1953 the trustees opened college enrollment to women on equal terms with men. In 1962 Emory took the initiative to end racial restrictions by asking the courts to declare unconstitutional provisions in the Georgia constitution and statutes that denied tax-exempt status to private universities and colleges that integrated their student bodies; the state supreme court decided in Emory's favor.

Emory deliberately refrained from intercollegiate competition in major sports, instead emphasizing student participation in an intramural setting. From the 1920s onward, Emory's "athletics for all" program gained national renown and spurred much imitation. Other extracurricular activities of strength included debate, journalism, and choral singing.

Doctoral study began in 1946. Emory's steady strengthening of graduate and professional education, with a strong interdisciplinary thrust, received impetus from the gifts of its most generous benefactor, Robert W. Woodruff, a former student who took over the helm of Coca-Cola in the 1920s. His endowment gift of over $100 million, announced in 1979, was the largest benefaction at one time to a single educational institution in the history of American philanthropy. During the 1984–85 academic year, 8,533 students were enrolled. By its sesquicentennial in 1986, Emory had been accorded a role of increasing national stature in higher education.

See also INDUSTRY: / Coca-Cola; RELIGION: / Methodist Episcopal Church, South

James Harvey Young
Emory University

Mark K. Bauman, *Warren Akin Candler: The Conservative as Idealist* (1981); Henry Morton Bullock, *A History of Emory University* (1936); Charles Howard Candler, *Asa Griggs Candler* (1950); Thomas H. English, *Emory University, 1915–1965* (1966); James Harvey Young, "A Brief History of Emory College," *Emory College 1982/1983* [catalog]. ☆

FISK UNIVERSITY

Fisk University, a leading black educational institution for more than a century, opened in Nashville, Tenn., in 1866. A private, coeducational, liberal arts school, Fisk offers the bachelor's and master's degrees. Fisk began with commendable and lofty—some thought impractical—aims. Its founders, E. M. Cravath, John Ogden, and E. P. Smith, proposed to provide a free school of grades from primary to normal based upon a "broad Christian foundation." Fisk was designed to supply desperately needed, qualified black teachers and ultimately to become a first-class college giving black youth the same educational opportunities and advantages enjoyed by whites.

At first, all students were in primary grades, but a normal class was enrolled in 1867. In 1871 four students were accepted into the college department. Nevertheless, the college preparatory and college classes remained the smallest in the school for several years. Because public schools for black children were generally poor, Fisk was compelled to prepare its own students for advanced training.

The period 1870 to 1915 was critical for Fisk. Black poverty, white indifference, and the popularity of vocational education threatened Fisk's aspiration of becoming a major liberal arts college. But, with the $150,000 earned by the Fisk Jubilee Singers, President E. M. Cravath, supported by a determined faculty and loyal students, built a new campus, improved the faculty, and developed a solid college department.

When students joined alumni in 1925 to oust Fayette A. McKenzie, a white president whom they considered dictatorial, a new era began in Fisk history. Under the leadership of President Thomas E. Jones and noted scholar Charles S. Johnson, who was to become Fisk's first black president in 1946, the university experienced unprecedented growth. By the 1940s it had an endowment of several million dollars and had become an outstanding center of scholarship and culture. Faculty members Charles S. Johnson, James Weldon Johnson, Arna Bontemps, and John W. Work, Jr., all achieved international recognition in their fields. In 1931 Edwin R. Embree, president of the Rosenwald Fund, claimed that Fisk was probably the finest black college in the land. It had the "pick of the country" for its faculty and student body.

One mark of a great university is the degree to which its students are equipped to cope with the demands of life. Judging by their successes, Fisk students have been unusually well prepared. The alumni have distinguished themselves in almost every field of endeavor. Hundreds of Fiskites have become physicians, college presidents, professors, writers, statesmen, and community leaders. Physician George Sheppard Moore, scholar W. E. B. Du Bois, historian John Hope Franklin, and poet Nikki Giovanni are just a few of the famous graduates of Fisk University.

Since the early 1980s, however, Fisk has grappled with the specter of bankruptcy. Under the leadership of Henry Ponder, who became president in 1984, the university reduced its debt from approximately $4 million in 1985 to $600,000 as of May 1986, primarily through financial support from alumni and philanthropies. Nevertheless, Fisk's enrollment has declined steadily in recent years (550 in fall 1984, 506 in fall 1985), and in 1984 President Reagan appointed a special advisory board to evaluate the university's future. Released in May 1986, the board's report, *A Future for Fisk—A Fisk University Five-Year Strategic Plan 1986–*

1991, recommended that the institution decrease its reliance on federal funds, strengthen retention efforts, and broaden its recruitment strategies to encourage attendance by whites as well as blacks.

See also BLACK LIFE: / Bontemps, Arna; Du Bois, W. E. B.; Franklin, John Hope; Johnson, Charles S.; Johnson, James Weldon; MUSIC: / Fisk Jubilee Singers

Joe M. Richardson
Florida State University

Chronicle of Higher Education (21 May 1986); Lester C. Lamon, *Journal of Southern History* (May 1974); *New York Times* (29 April 1986); Gustavus D. Pike, *The Jubilee Singers, and Their Campaign for Twenty Thousand Dollars* (1873); Joe M. Richardson, *A History of Fisk University, 1865–1946* (1980). ☆

FLORIDA, UNIVERSITY OF

The University of Florida is the oldest unit of the Florida university system of higher education. Located in Gainesville in the north-central part of Florida, it traces its roots to the East Florida Seminary, founded in 1853 in Ocala, and the Florida Agricultural College, which began in Lake City in 1884. The first baccalaureate degrees were awarded at the East Florida Seminary in 1882. In 1905 the Florida Legislature passed the Buckman Act consolidating higher-education facilities in the state. The legislation established a college for women (now Florida State University) and a university for men (now the University of Florida). The university began holding classes on the Gainesville campus in September 1906 with an enrollment of 102, and it remained largely a men's school until 1947.

All academic programs are located on a single campus, so that the professional skills represented in the various departments can be combined for interdisciplinary studies. The university includes colleges of agriculture, architecture, building construction, business administration, dentistry, education, engineering, fine arts, forest resources and conservation, health-related professions, journalism and communications, law, liberal arts and sciences, medicine, nursing, pharmacy, physical education, health and recreation, and veterinary medicine. The J. Hillis Miller Health Center includes a teaching hospital, Shands, whose physicians also staff the Veterans' Hospital in Gainesville. The health center is noted for its community-health program, which provides medical and nursing services for a 16-county area.

The university library has more than 3 million volumes, in addition to large collections of manuscripts, maps, rare books, documents, and newspapers. The major special collections relate to Florida and Spanish borderlands history and Latin American and Caribbean studies. The famous Howe Collection on early American literature is at the university, together with the papers and manuscripts of Marjorie Kinnan Rawlings, Zora Neale Hurston, and other noted novelists, poets, and playwrights from Florida and the South. The library also has the largest collection—some 60,000 volumes—of Judaica in the South. The Florida State Museum contains a large collection of North American Indian material and artifacts of the prehistoric period in Florida and the Caribbean. A television station and three radio stations are also located on campus.

The university is governed by a president appointed by the Board of Regents. Marshall M. Criser is president of the University of Florida. There were 35,496 students enrolled as of the 1984–85 academic year.

Samuel Proctor
University of Florida

A. H. Adams, "Public Higher Education in Florida, 1821–1961" (Ph.D. dissertation, Florida State University, 1962); *The College Blue Book, Narrative Descriptions* (20th ed., 1985); Samuel Proctor, "University of Florida, 1853–1906" (Ph.D. dissertation, University of Florida, 1958). ☆

FOXFIRE

In March 1967, 600 copies of an offset magazine named *Foxfire* appeared on the streets of rural Clayton, Ga., the end result of three months of work by 9th- and 10th-grade students and their English teacher, B. Eliot Wigginton. Paid for by $440 in donations collected by the students from merchants and parents in the area, the magazine would certainly have passed from the scene virtually unnoticed had it not been that embedded in the collection of juvenile poetry and short stories were several pages of traditional Appalachian home remedies and superstitions that the Rabun Gap–Nacoochee School students had collected from their older relatives at home. Included, too, was one magical tale (related into a used tape recorder) by Luther Rickman, the retired county sheriff, about the 1936 robbing of the Bank of Clayton by the Zade Sprinkle gang. Transcribed by the four students and their teacher who conducted the interview one evening after school, the story appeared, word for word, in the magazine, and the demand for copies of "that magazine that's got Luther's story in it" was such that all 600 copies disappeared within days, and a second printing of 600 more was ordered to meet the demand.

As reactions to that issue came in, the students, with the support of the principal, decided to keep the magazine going, focusing on the local customs and traditions the readership obviously wanted. By 1971 a large body of material had been collected, and Doubleday offered to publish a book bringing the best of that material together for a broader audience. *The Foxfire Book*, published in March 1972, sold over 3 million copies—more than any book in that company's publishing history. It was followed by the numbered series of *Foxfire* volumes, the latest being *Foxfire 8* (1984), which covers topics ranging from folk pottery to mule swapping. All of the books are compilations of high school students' work and all have been enormously successful—an authentic publishing phenomenon.

The royalty money flowed into the nonprofit, tax-exempt corporation that had been set up in 1968 to solicit donations in support of the project. Wigginton, with the permission of the principal and school board, began to hire other adults (many of whom were former students who had since graduated from college) to work with him inside the public school system to broaden the number of community-based, experiential offerings available to new generations of high school students. By 1982 students were operating a television studio, a record company, a publishing company, a photography division, and a major environmental education program that included both a log home built on campus as a classroom and a full-scale experimental passive solar home. Schools across the country were copying the curricular designs. One hundred and ten acres had been purchased on which students and community carpenters reconstructed 27 historic log structures to serve as a working base of operations. It included staff and guest housing, an archive, a museum, offices, and a recreation area for community celebrations. A scholarship program was initiated that gave over $35,000 a year in college-scholarship assistance. In the fall of 1982 the play *Foxfire*, based on materials from the books and starring Hume Cronyn, Jessica Tandy, and Keith Carradine, became a hit on Broadway.

The staff, regarding all this as prelude, was, by 1982, preparing to play an even larger role in the educational and economic picture of Rabun County—a rural county that had seen a $440 investment pay off. It was an investment that linked the public school curriculum and the area's traditions and culture together in powerful and magical ways.

B. Eliot Wigginton
Foxfire

Richard M. Dorson, *North Carolina Folklore Journal* (November 1973); *Newsweek* (12 April 1982); B. Eliot Wigginton, *Moments: The Foxfire Experience* (1975), *North Carolina Folklore Journal* (May 1974), *Sometimes a Shining Moment: The Foxfire Experience* (1985), ed., *The Foxfire Book* (1972). ☆

GENERAL EDUCATION BOARD

After a tour of southern black schools led by Robert C. Ogden, John D. Rockefeller, Jr., convinced his father to make a financial contribution to education in the South. The following year the Rockefellers pledged $1 million to be spent over a 10-year period and created the General Education Board (GEB). Chartered by the U.S. Congress in 1903 for "the promotion of education in the United States of America, without distinction of race, sex, or creed," the GEB by 1964 had appropriated more than $325 million, approximately 20 percent of which was earmarked for black education.

At the turn of the century the poverty of the post–Civil War period still restricted education in the South, and the region supported two school systems—one for black children and one for white. Because many rural areas were without schools, the GEB designated much of its initial support to developing rural schools. One of its first grants was to Berea College, located in an impoverished area of Kentucky. Berea was also the recipient of the GEB's last appropriation when, in 1964, the board contributed to the establishment of a Special Student Aid Program. The GEB funded training in agricultural economics and community development, believing that the southern economy had to improve before educational advancements could develop.

The GEB worked nationally to raise teachers' salaries, to support natural science and humanities studies, to provide research fellowships, and to improve medical school facilities and staffs. Its continuing focus, however, was on the South, and from 1940 to 1964 the GEB concentrated its work there. Universities such as Atlanta, Duke, and Tulane benefited, as did black students aspiring to teach and black educators who received GEB fellowships for further training.

The GEB strengthened black education enormously. Black universities such as Fisk and Dillard received millions of dollars in GEB grants. Rather than attacking the South's system of school segregation, the board tried to improve the quality of education by working through the predominantly white structure. Because the GEB was a northern institution, its members believed they had to proceed cautiously if their efforts were to succeed. The General Education Board raised the level of education for both blacks and whites by fighting the inequality of education, not between the races, but between the South and other regions of the United States.

Jessica Foy
Cooperstown Graduate Programs
Cooperstown, New York

Raymond B. Fosdick, Henry F. Pringle, and Katharine D. Pringle, *Adventure in Giving: The Story of the General Education Board* (1962); *General Education Board: An Account of Its Activities, 1902–1914* (1915); *General Education Board Review and Final Report, 1902–1964* (1964). ☆

GEORGIA, UNIVERSITY OF

The University of Georgia became America's first state-chartered university in 1785. After prolonged debate the campus was built in Athens, Ga., approximately 65 miles from Atlanta. Franklin College, as it was then called, opened in 1801, under the direction of several Yale graduates including Josiah Meigs, its first president.

The school attempted to remain open during the Civil War, but was forced to close when the Union seizure of Chattanooga early in 1864 caused most of the university community to join the military. After reopening in 1866 Franklin College became the University of Georgia in 1869 under Chancellor Andrew A. Lipscomb.

Through World War II the university was plagued by the same problems that retarded the growth of other southern state schools. The university received inadequate financial support and competed with other state schools for recognition and programs. In 1919 the University of Georgia admitted women, whose presence immediately boosted the College of Agriculture's Department of Home Economics and the Peabody School of Education. The Georgia university system was reorganized in 1932 under the governance of a board of regents.

Since World War II the university's teaching staff, research programs, and public service function have been expanded. The growth of both professional schools and graduate programs rapidly escalated during the 1960s. The first black students were admitted to the university in 1961. By the fall of 1984, 24,371 students were enrolled, 13 schools and colleges existed within the university, and the campus had expanded to cover 3,500 acres. As of 1984 Georgia's president was Frederick C. Davison. In 1986 the university drew national attention when one of its professors, Jan Kemp, won a lawsuit against school administrators accused of compromising academic standards for athletes.

Karen M. McDearman
University of Mississippi

Robert Preston Brooks, *The University of Georgia under Sixteen Administrations*

(1956); E. Merton Coulter, *College Life in the Old South* (1928); Thomas G. Dyer, *The University of Georgia: A Bicentennial History, 1785–1985* (1985). ☆

GEORGIA INSTITUTE OF TECHNOLOGY

Georgia Tech was chartered in 1885 and opened its doors in 1888. Interest in a school of technology in Georgia had been stimulated by the campaign for southern industrialization led by men like Henry W. Grady, editor of the Atlanta *Constitution*. In 1883 a legislative committee settled on the Worcester Free Institute in Massachusetts as an appropriate model. Worcester had pioneered the "commercial shop" system of technical education, in which students shared time between academic studies and work in the shops producing goods for sale.

When the school opened in Atlanta in 1888, it offered degrees only in mechanical engineering. The first professor of that subject, John Saylor Coon, was a founding member of the American Society of Mechanical Engineers. The rapid addition of programs in electrical and civil engineering, industrial chemistry, and textiles reflected both the development of modern engineering practice in America and the economic needs of the state. After the turn of the century architecture and commerce were added to the curriculum. Although the commercial shop system was scrapped in the 1890s, Tech retained a heavy emphasis on practical application.

Football began to play a major role in the school in 1904, when Tech hired its first full-time coach, John Heisman. Under Heisman and his successors, W. A. Alexander and Bobby Dodd, Tech for over half a century enjoyed a reputation as a national powerhouse.

Georgia Tech first won national recognition in engineering in 1930 when it received one of six awards made by the Guggenheim Foundation—and the only one in the South—to support a program in aeronautical engineering. World War II radically transformed Georgia Tech, as it did other colleges. Under the leadership of President Blake Van Leer, Tech responded to the need for a more science- and mathematics-based engineering program and for postgraduate training by shifting its curriculum decisively away from the shop approach, by strengthening programs in the sciences and mathematics, and by establishing its first Ph.D. programs. In 1948 Tech's name was changed from Georgia School of Technology to the Georgia Institute of Technology. It remained part of the university system of Georgia.

The post–World War II era also witnessed the growth of applied research, particularly in the electronics field, with most of the work being done through the Engineering Experiment Station (renamed in 1984 the Georgia Tech Research Institute). Research and development in electronics have in more recent years provided a base for high-technology "spin-off" firms in and near Atlanta.

In 1972 Joseph Mayo Pettit, then dean of engineering at Stanford University, became Georgia Tech's eighth president. Under his leadership Tech continued to move forward in research and graduate education in engineering, science, and related fields.

As of 1984–85 Georgia Tech's total enrollment was 10,958 students. Its campus had grown from the original two buildings to 128 buildings situated on over 310 acres near downtown Atlanta. Among its alumni are numerous presidents of major corporations and leading practitioners in Tech's areas of expertise. Former President Jimmy Carter, who attended Tech before enrolling in the Naval Academy, is recipient of the only honorary doctorate awarded by the Institute.

See also INDUSTRY: / Grady, Henry W.; POLITICS: / Carter, Jimmy

Robert C. McMath, Jr.
Georgia Institute of Technology

Marion L. Brittain, *The Story of Georgia Tech* (1948); Robert C. McMath, Jr., et al., *Engineering the New South: Georgia Tech, 1885–1985* (1985); Robert B. Wallace, Jr., *Dress Her in White and Gold: A Biography of Georgia Tech and of the Men Who Led Her* (1969). ☆

GILDERSLEEVE, BASIL

(1831–1924) Classical scholar.

Born 23 October 1831 in Charleston, S.C., Basil Lanneau Gildersleeve became the most renowned American classicist of the late 19th century. Founder of the *American Journal of Philology* in 1880, Gildersleeve taught classics at Johns Hopkins for almost four decades and became a central figure in the professionalization of Greek and Latin studies in the American university.

Gildersleeve grew up in a home of pronounced southern loyalties. His father, Benjamin, was a northerner by birth but adopted the southern antebellum sectional cause with enthusiasm. A Presbyterian minister and editor of a denominational paper, Benjamin Gildersleeve supervised his son's early education and introduced him, somewhat unsystematically, to the classics. Basil Gildersleeve went on to attend the College of Charleston, Jefferson College in Pennsylvania, and Princeton, where he graduated in 1849. He taught classics at a private academy in Richmond and then spent 1850 to 1853 in Germany at Berlin, Göttingen, and Bonn, before taking his Ph.D. at Göttingen. He spent three years in Charleston writing and teaching. He became a professor at the University of Virginia in 1856, staying there until he went to Johns Hopkins in 1876. His service in the Confederate army left him with a crippling leg injury received in fighting in the Shenandoah Valley campaign. He died 9 January 1924.

Gildersleeve's *The Creed of the Old South* (1915) was a work celebrating the antebellum South. Southerners after the war produced many apologies for the romanticized plantation society, but Gildersleeve's stood out for its perspective on southern history. Although proud of the South's wartime heroism and unquestioning of southern ideals, he did not portray the South as the center of the universe. He did compare the Civil War to the Peloponnesian War—the North was Athens, the South, Sparta—but he knew the ultimate judgment of southern history would come far in the future. His long perspective on history enabled him to escape the anger and bitterness so prevalent in the first generation of southern intellectual life after the war.

Gildersleeve was also significant as a representative of southern intellectual ties with German culture. Gildersleeve inherited a dislike for British culture, stemming from family memories of the British occupation of Charleston during the War of 1812, and his reading of the Scottish Carlyle reinforced the aversion to the English and pointed Gildersleeve toward an interest in Goethe. Gildersleeve called the German author "the most important of all the teachers I ever had." He studied Goethe endlessly for a time when young. "This was the era of my Teutomania," he recalled later. His youthful interest in Germany proved to be enduring. German philology—and that nation's system of university education and scholarly research—became his model for the United States. He hoped, particularly, to give studies of Greece and Rome a new vigor through application of rigorous scholarly methods pioneered in Germany.

Charles Reagan Wilson
University of Mississippi

Basil Gildersleeve, *Forum* (February 1891); Fred Hobson, *Tell about the South: The Southern Rage to Explain* (1983); C. W. E. Miller, *American Journal of Philology* (January 1924); *Selections from the Brief Mention of Basil Lanneau Gildersleeve*, ed. C. W. E. Miller (1930). ☆

GRAHAM, FRANK PORTER

(1886–1972) Educator and statesman.

Professor and president of the University of North Carolina, U.S. senator, and United Nations mediator, Frank Porter Graham was born in Fayetteville, N.C., in 1886. He received both undergraduate and law degrees from the University of North Carolina and a master's degree from Columbia, afterwards studying at the University of Chicago, the London School of Economics, and elsewhere. He left a position as instructor in history at the University of North Carolina for service in the Marine Corps during World War I but returned to rise to the rank of professor by 1927.

In 1930 Graham became president of the University of North Carolina; and in 1932, when that institution was consolidated with the North Carolina College for Women and North Carolina State College, he became president of the larger institution, the Consolidated University of North Carolina. Graham worked diligently during the period of economic depression to increase the university's scholarship funds for needy students and often was involved in intense controversy over political, social, and economic policies. All the while he defended the freedom of the university to seek, learn, believe, speak, and publish. Sometimes he was the object of personal attacks for his support of unpopular causes or persons, yet he never wavered in his faith in the young and in the future of a free, democratic society.

Beyond the university Graham was concerned with the needs of the poor and underprivileged, and he supported racial justice. Twice he was president of the North Carolina Conference for Social Service, and at President Franklin

Frank Porter Graham, president of the University of North Carolina (1930–49)

D. Roosevelt's appointment he served on federal boards and commissions, including the National Advisory Council on Social Security, of which he was chairman. During World War II he served on the National Defense Mediation Board and the National War Labor Board. President Harry Truman appointed him to the President's Committee on Civil Rights, for which Graham made a historic report on the country's racial problems and presented proposals for their solution. At Truman's request he served as the representative of the United States on the United Nations committee on the Dutch-Indonesian dispute. He also helped organize, and was the first president of, the Oak Ridge Institute of Nuclear Studies. In 1949 he was appointed by the governor of North Carolina to fill an unexpired term in the U.S. Senate, but in a bid for nomination for reelection he failed to win a majority in the primary. In a second primary the racial issue was injected to Graham's disadvantage, and he was rejected by his party.

Service on the President's Committee on Civil Rights and his well-known commitment to human rights and association with liberal causes contributed to Graham's defeat. Nevertheless, he continued his public service: as defense manpower administrator for the U.S. Department of Labor, as United Nations representative to mediate the dispute between India and Pakistan over Kashmir, and as assistant secretary general of the United Nations. Graham, a deeply religious man, worked diligently for human betterment not only at home but also throughout the world. He died in Chapel Hill, N.C., in 1972.

William S. Powell
University of North Carolina
at Chapel Hill

Frank P. Graham Papers, Southern Historical Collection, University of North Carolina, Chapel Hill. ☆

HAMPDEN-SYDNEY COLLEGE

A private liberal arts college enrolling some 750 young men as of the 1984–85 academic year, Hampden-Sydney is situated on a 566-acre rural campus in Virginia's tobacco-growing southside, that part of the Old Dominion most reminiscent of the Old South. The college has been in continuous operation since January of 1776 and is the country's 10th-oldest institution of higher learning. Hanover Presbytery founded the college "as a southern replica of Princeton," according to historian Lawrence A. Cremin, intending both to nurture an educated commitment to public service and to promote the Presbyterian faith in the heavily Scotch-Irish counties of south-central Virginia. The name Hampden-Sydney was apparently chosen as symbolic proclamation of the founders' devotion to the principles of political and religious liberty for which John Hampden and Algernon Sydney had struggled in 17th-century England. The college's first board of trustees included such revolutionary luminaries as James Madison and Patrick Henry; and the school colors, garnet and gray, derive from the uniform of purple hunting shirts (dyed with the juice of pokeberries) and gray trousers, which the students' militia company wore while helping to defend Williamsburg and Petersburg during the late 1770s. At the outbreak of the Civil War the student body organized another company of militia, and the "Hampden-Sydney Boys" fought for the Confederacy in a losing effort at Rich Mountain on 10 June 1861.

The college has always drawn the overwhelming majority of its students from Virginia and the neighboring states of the Upper South. Although since 1980 increasing numbers of freshmen have come from both the Deep South and the Northeast, Virginians made up 60 percent of the student body in the 1984–85 academic year. Today Hampden-Sydney is most distinguished for an ambience that blends latter-day preppiness with gentlemanly traditions that hearken back to the 19th-century South. Prominent facets of that ambience, wrote Zöe Ingalls in 1985, are "the prevalence on campus of late-model BMW's and crudely laundered khaki trousers"; a strict student-run honor system; a social life dominated by fraternities; and a liberal arts curriculum that has made, in the words of one faculty member, "few adaptations to the fashion of vocationalism," although far and away the most popular major—economics—is one that students consider likely to facilitate success in the business world.

The most obvious aspect of the college's traditionalism is its firm commitment to continuing as all-male, Hampden-Sydney being the oldest of this country's few remaining all-male colleges. Entering freshmen receive copies of a booklet entitled "To Manner Born, To Manner Bred: A Hip-pocket Guide to Etiquette for the Hampden-Sydney Man," which exemplifies the college's partiality for traditional standards of genteel deportment that strike some observers as elitist or anachronistic. At the same time, however, Hampden-Sydney has been strongly affected by the dramatic changes in technology and race relations that have transformed much of the South and America at large in recent years. The college is integrating a computer laboratory and an audiovisual "International Communications Center" into its academic program; and the second Rhodes Scholar in the school's history, selected in December of 1985, is a black student from southside Virginia, who was also elected president of the student government.

See also ETHNIC LIFE: / Scotch-Irish; HISTORY AND MANNERS: / Madison, James

Shearer Davis Bowman
Hampden-Sydney College

Herbert C. Bradshaw, *History of Hampden-Sydney College, Volume I: From the Beginnings to the Year 1856* (1976); Lawrence A. Cremin, *American Education: The Colonial Experience, 1607–1783* (1970), *American Education: The National Experience, 1783–1876* (1980); Zöe Ingalls, *Chronicle of Higher Education* (18 September 1985). ☆

HAMPTON INSTITUTE

In the mid-1800s northern missionary teachers worked vigorously to establish permanent educational institutions for free blacks, and in 1868 the American Missionary Association and the Freedmen's Bureau provided funding for establishment of the Hampton Normal and Agricultural Institute at Hampton, Va. Samuel C. Armstrong, the school's founder and first principal, developed a lifelong interest in education for blacks after commanding black regiments in the Civil War. Armstrong viewed blacks as intellectually inferior to whites, however, and emphasized "industrial works" programs, a widely accepted stance. The school's elementary-through college-level students received training in agriculture and skilled trades, and many pursued teaching careers in black schools, though opportunities were limited. Commitment to moral virtues, respect for discipline in the military tradition, and compromise and accommodation toward whites were emphasized. Such an approach clashed sharply with the growing demand in the 1890s for black liberal arts programs and drew scathing criticism from leaders such as W. E. B. Du Bois.

The rift between Du Bois and Booker T. Washington stemmed in large part from Washington's dedication to the traditions of Hampton Institute, his alma mater. Washington and Robert R. Moton, another Hampton Institute graduate and Washington's successor at Tuskegee Institute, championed the emphasis on vocational education for blacks. Nevertheless, Hampton Institute gradually phased out its elementary and secondary programs, deemphasized its vocational component, and began offering courses leading to a bachelor of science degree in 1922. By 1933 it received accreditation as a four-year college, and its graduate programs began in 1956. Weathering the strife of a white-supremacist "racial purity" campaign in Virginia in the 1920s and 1930s, the institute finally obtained black leadership when Alonzo G. Moron assumed the presidency from 1947 through 1959.

For many reasons Hampton Institute is recognized, according to Mary F. Berry and John W. Blassingame, as "one of the most influential schools in the history of black education." One of the first colleges to accept Native Americans and to invite African students, the institute has also had world-renowned choirs, a dance company focusing on black traditions, research projects to preserve black folklore, training programs in Africa, and a variety of publications and conferences on issues important to blacks. Its library houses an outstanding collection of materials on black history. The private, coeducational, independent institution currently combines liberal arts, teacher education, and vocational curricula. Both its faculty and student body are interracial and intercultural. Its 1984–85 enrollment was 4,260 students.

See also BLACK LIFE: / Du Bois, W. E. B.; Washington, Booker T.

Sharon A. Sharp
University of Mississippi

Mary Frances Berry and John W. Blassingame, *Long Memory: The Black Experience in America* (1982); W. Augustus Low and Virgil A. Clift, eds., *of Black America* (1981); August Meier and Elliott Rudwick, *From Plantation to Ghetto* (1966); Alrutheus A. Taylor, *The Negro in the Reconstruction of Virginia* (1926); Raymond Wolters, *The New Negro on Campus: Black College Rebellions of the 1920s* (1975). ☆

JACKSON STATE UNIVERSITY

Founded in Natchez, Miss., as a private church school by the American Baptist Home Missionary Society in 1877, Jackson State was established to serve the people of the Mississippi Valley between Memphis and the Gulf Coast. Twenty students were enrolled when the school opened on 23 October. Its first president, Charles Ayer of New York, resigned in 1894, and Luther G. Barrett succeeded him. In that same year the school relocated in Jackson and in

1903 moved to its present location in the city.

Zachary Taylor Hubert of Atlanta became the institution's first black president in 1911. His administration broadened the course of study and awarded the first college-level degree (B.A.) in 1924 to Annie Mae Brown Magee. Major educational activities during this time were directed toward teacher education. The Home Missionary Society withdrew its support in 1938, and the college moved from private control into the state system of higher education.

Jacob L. Reddix became president in 1940. Initially, the state assumed support of the college for the purpose of training rural and elementary schoolteachers, and in 1942 the Board of Trustees raised the curriculum to a four-year teacher's education program. A division of graduate studies and a program of liberal arts was organized in 1953.

On 2 March 1967 John A. Peoples, Jr., became the sixth president and the first alumnus to serve in that capacity. The academic program of the university was greatly expanded and the entire curriculum was reorganized with a newly established Graduate School, and schools of Liberal Studies, Education, Science and Technology, and Business and Economics. Margaret Walker became director of the Institute for the Study of the History, Life, and Culture of Black People in 1968. Since that time the Institute has sponsored distinguished lectures, readings, and symposia on the black experience. Upon the completion of Peoples's tenure in April 1984, the physical plant had also undergone significant change with the construction of six major buildings.

Jackson State received national publicity on 14 May 1970 when 2 students were killed and 12 wounded on campus as local authorities and national guardsmen confronted students during civil rights demonstrations. The incident occurred 10 days after the death of students at Kent State University.

James A. Hefner became the seventh president of Jackson State on 1 May 1984. Jackson State University's special mission as an urban university has sensitized the faculty to increased involvement in services to the community, serving the citizens of Mississippi with a broad array of public service, continuing education, and research programs.

Lelia C. Rhodes
Jackson State University

Lelia G. Rhodes, *Jackson State University: The First Hundred Years, 1877–1977* (1978). ☆

JUNIOR COLLEGES

One of the most notable developments in American higher education in this century has been the explosion in the number of two-year or junior colleges. The forces that spawned this movement in the North and West were also at work in the South.

William Rainey Harper, first president of the University of Chicago, is usually credited with being the founder of the movement when, at the turn of the century, he encouraged Chicago-area high schools to offer college courses that could be transferred to that university. But it was Alexis F. Logan, dean of the School of Education at the University of California, and David Starr Jordan, president of Leland Stanford

Junior University, who seized upon Harper's concept and set the pattern for a junior college movement, not only for California but for the rest of the nation. The motives of these early pioneers centered less on the democratization of American higher education than on preserving the integrity of existing universities. By channeling the less-able student into two-year colleges, they hoped to reserve the universities for only the brightest secondary school graduates.

Logan, Jordan, and other proponents of the movement were heavily influenced by German educational institutions. They saw the two-year college as an extension of the high school, an American counterpart to the German *gymnasium*, rather than as an additional component of higher education. Ironically, with these elite objectives, one of the most vigorous instruments for the democratization of American higher education in this century emerged.

Although the roots of the community college movement are generally considered to be in the North, with its puritan passion for literacy and 19th-century emphasis on expansion of educational opportunity, it was a southerner, Thomas Jefferson, in the late 18th century, who envisioned something similar to the two-year college. He certainly spoke for its later advocates when he wrote: "If a nation expects to be ignorant and free in a state of civilization, it expects what never was and never will be." Yet for the South the transition was not always an easy one. The rural way of life and the remnants of a tradition that saw education as a prerogative of the elite retarded state involvement. Consequently, the weaker private colleges and the manual or trade schools were the first to see the advantages of a two-year college program. Many found that by dropping the junior and senior years, they could prevent or delay impending financial disaster.

With the exception of Texas, which became an early national leader in state support for the two-year college, private two-year colleges were the rule in the South until after World War II. Afterwards, the demands of a new and increasingly urban South resulted in growing community pressure for the establishment of more public two-year institutions.

Educational leaders who argued for an expansion of two-year college programs drew support in 1947 from the report of President Truman's Commission on Higher Education and in 1956 from President Eisenhower's Committee on Education Beyond the High School. As a result, the decades of the 1950s and 1960s saw the establishment of dozens of state-supported two-year colleges throughout the region.

Today, the two-year colleges of North Carolina, Texas, and Florida are among the most numerous and progressive in the nation. Other southern states are also making substantial gains in their attempts to make the first two years of college available to all. Approximately 33 percent of the nation's two-year colleges were located in the 13 southern states (the 11 states of the Confederacy plus West Virginia and Kentucky) as of 1983.

Gerald L. Cates
Truett McConnell College

American Association of Junior Colleges, *Junior College Directory* (1965, 1969, 1971, 1981); Thomas Jefferson, *The Writings of Thomas Jefferson*, 10 vols., ed. Paul Leicester (1892–99); Charles R. Monroe, *Profile* of the Community College (1972); Southern Association of Colleges and Schools, *Proceedings* (1895–1975); Roger Yarrington, ed., *Junior Colleges: 50 States/50 Years* (1969). ☆

KAPPA ALPHA ORDER

Kappa Alpha Order, a national social fraternity for men, preserves in its basic principles and traditions the southern ideal of character its early members feared might perish with the society that existed in the South prior to the Civil War. Founded in the immediate aftermath of war, on 21 December 1865 at Washington College (now Washington and Lee University) in Lexington, Va., Kappa Alpha Order refined its ideals beginning in 1866. Samuel Zenas Ammen, a member of the order and later editor of the Baltimore *Sun*, realized that the initial ideals of the fraternity were too vague and weak. In an effort to establish a strong foundation for the continuing existence of Kappa Alpha Order, the members under the guidance of Ammen began a reformation and elaboration of the Order's principles that resulted in a clearly southern-oriented fraternity.

The Order's outlook drew on the idea of the southern gentleman. The ideal of a gentleman, wrote Ammen, is "that of the chivalrous warrior of Christ, the knight who loves God and country, honors and protects pure womanhood, practices courtesy and magnanimity of spirit and prefers self-respect to ill-gotten wealth." Ammen and early members considered these virtues and graces to be distinctively southern. General Robert E. Lee, who was president of the college during the Order's formative period (1865–70), was perceived by them to be the perfect expression of the southern gentleman, and the members looked to him as the spiritual founder of Kappa Alpha Order.

In perpetuating southern traditions of gentlemanly conduct, Kappa Alpha Order distinguishes itself from all other college social organizations. Although at first the Order preferred to remain exclusively in the South, it exists today with chapters on university and college campuses from coast to coast. The group has initiated about 100,000 members since its founding, and there are now 114 active undergraduate chapters. The characteristics of the southern gentleman preserved by the Order appeal to men across the nation. The Kappa Alpha Order today celebrates its southern heritage on college campuses through spring festivities known as Old South, which includes a week of parties, cookouts, movies, parades, lawn parties, and the annual Old South Ball.

See also HISTORY AND MANNERS: / Lee, Robert E.

Newell Turner
New York, New York

Samuel Z. Ammen, *History of the Kappa Alpha Fraternity, 1865–1900* (1900); William K. Doty, *Samuel Zenas Ammen and the*

Plaque commemorating the founding of the Kappa Alpha Order, Washington College, Lexington, Virginia, 1865

Kappa Alpha Order (1922); Gary T. Scott, "The Kappa Alpha Order, 1865–1897; How It Came to Be and How It Came to Be Southern" (M.A. thesis, University of North Carolina, Chapel Hill, 1968). ☆

KENTUCKY, UNIVERSITY OF

Founded in 1865 in Lexington, the state's land-grant agricultural and mechanical college was at first an uneasy component of the Disciples of Christ's Kentucky University. The college was separated in 1878 from the faction-torn university, and in 1882 James K. Patterson, president since 1869, led students and faculty across town to the new campus donated by the city. Patterson persuaded a divided legislature to retain a state property tax for the college.

In 1908, noting the coeducational enrollment of 500, the legislature renamed it State University, Lexington, Kentucky, thereby initiating a collegiate infrastructure, including Arts and Science, Agriculture, Law, three engineering colleges, and the existing Agriculture Experiment Station. His mission accomplished, Patterson resigned in 1910, and Judge Henry Stites Barker left the bench to become president. Renamed the University of Kentucky in 1916, the institution underwent an investigation that demanded drastic reforms and replacement of Barker. In August 1917 Frank LeRond McVey, an experienced outside academic, accepted the presidency though warned against Kentucky's "damnedest politics." He retired in 1940 from an academically improved university with 6,000 students, 500 staff, and an annual income of $3 million. The university awarded 791 degrees in that year. Morale was good despite discouragements suffered during the Depression.

Compared with similar institutions, the university under Herman L. Donovan (1941–56) and Frank G. Dickey (1956–63) gained no academic ground even with its greater emphasis upon research, publication, and graduate study; the creation of a complete medical center; and development of an unusual university-administered community college system (which by 1985 included 13 colleges). A 1960 state 3 percent sales tax promised adequate funding; the promise was fulfilled for the first (and last) time during the presidency of John W. Oswald (1963–68), and the institution grew in academic reputation as emphasis upon research and graduate and professional education imparted a university character.

Student unrest, energy crises, and inflation have clouded Otis A. Singletary's (1969–) administration. An overgrown state system of higher education has overburdened a poor state whose regionalisms, traditional indifference toward education, and "damnedest politics" have, according to critics, held back the university. It meets the physical criteria of greatness, though, with 20,421 students and 1,842 faculty in Lexington as of fall 1985 and approximately 24,000 students and 600 faculty in the community colleges. The university has achieved prominence in local and regional studies, where the university library has collected purposefully, the university press publishes fruitfully, and sociologists and historians have made significant contributions.

Carl Cone
Lexington, Kentucky

Charles G. Talbert, *The University of Kentucky: The Maturing Years* (1965). ☆

KEY, V. O., JR.

(1908–1963) Political scientist.

A leading scholar of American politics, Valdimer Orlando Key, Jr., was a prolific writer who greatly influenced the study of political science in the 20th century. He was born in Austin, Tex., and spent his childhood in west Texas, where his father was involved in local politics. Key learned a great deal from observing his father's political dealings and developed a sensitivity to political processes that he employed in his studies.

Key attended McMurray College in Abilene, Tex., from 1925 to 1927, received his A.B. degree from the University of Texas in 1929, and studied under Charles E. Merriam at the University of Chicago, where he earned a Ph.D. in 1934. He taught at UCLA, Johns Hopkins, and Yale and in 1951 became Jonathan Trumbull Professor at Harvard, where he remained until his death in 1963. His most important work was *Southern Politics in State and Nation* (1949), which won the Woodrow Wilson Foundation Award. He also authored a widely used textbook, *Politics, Parties, and Pressure Groups* (1942).

Key's work is regarded as significant because he linked the empirical study of politics to the larger issues of democratic government, thereby shifting the traditional focus of students of political processes. He stressed the importance of American politics in determining many other aspects of life. Key's research dealt with three areas of political science: party politics, public administration, and public opinion. His *Southern Politics* is a well-researched analysis of regional political evolution. It relies on legal and statistical data, as well as extensive field interviews, which Key supervised closely. Because of Key's influential work, the discipline of political science became more specialized and empirical, elements that were tempered in Key's own studies by a recognition of politics essentially as an effective *human* activity.

Karen M. McDearman
University of Mississippi

Merle Black and John Shelton Reed, eds., *Perspectives on the American South*, vol. 2 (1984). ☆

LOUISIANA STATE UNIVERSITY

The Louisiana State Seminary of Learning, forerunner of Louisiana State University, opened on 2 January 1860 near the central Louisiana village of Pineville and admitted only male students. Its first superintendent was William Tecumseh Sherman, of later Civil War fame, who reluctantly departed for the North after Louisiana's secession in 1861. After several abortive attempts were made to keep the institution open, classes were suspended for the duration in 1863 as federal forces approached during an invasion of the Red River Valley. The seminary reopened in 1865 with four students under the superintendency of David French Boyd, a prewar faculty member and ex-Confederate colonel who was to remain at the helm for 17 of the next 21 years.

Despite financial stresses typical of the Reconstruction era, the seminary was beginning to flourish when fire destroyed the main building in October 1869 and brought it close to extinction; Boyd presided over its transfer to Baton Rouge, where the seminary shared until 1886 a large structure housing the State Institute for the Deaf, Dumb, and Blind. During his long tenure David Boyd presided over two watershed events: the legislatively mandated merger in 1877 with the Louisiana A&M College, previously located in New Orleans, and the move in 1886 to the former grounds of the U.S. Arsenal in Baton Rouge—LSU's first permanent home in 17 years and the springboard for its eventual development into a large modern university.

David Boyd's younger brother, Thomas Duckett Boyd, was elected president in 1896 and his 31-year tenure—longest of any LSU president—was to encompass several further historical landmarks: the admission of women to the student body in 1906; the utilization by the state of oil severance taxes during the 1920s to provide the university with a solid, permanent support base; and the move to the present campus, beginning in 1925 and pointing the way to the university's most spectacular period of growth. During the decade of the 1930s Governor, later Senator, Huey P. Long adopted LSU as a pet project and channeled state funds into construction and faculty expansion at a time when most universities were retrenching; one result was a quadrupling of enrollment before World War II, making LSU at the time the second-largest university in the former Confederate states. The university became a major center of southern literary and scholarly activity in the 1930s, focused on the *Southern Review*, which was established by Robert Penn Warren and Cleanth Brooks in 1935.

During the post–World War II era LSU expanded into a statewide system including eight separate administrative entities in five cities, with the "flagship" campus in Baton Rouge attaining an enrollment of more than 30,000 students before a leveling off in the mid-1980s. Its 1984–85 enrollment was 28,979 students. Court-ordered desegregation brought the first black graduate student to LSU in 1950, and all levels have been desegregated since the 1960s. In 1978 LSU was awarded status as the nation's 13th sea-grant university, matching its land-grant status of long standing. The current president of the LSU system is Allen Copping, who assumed the office on 15 March 1985. The chancellor of the Baton Rouge campus is James H. Wharton, who has been in the position since 1981.

See also LITERATURE: / Brooks, Cleanth; Warren, Robert Penn; POLITICS: / Long, Huey P.

Jack Fiser
Louisiana State University

Vergil L. Bedsole and Oscar Richard, eds., *Louisiana State University: A Pictorial Record of the First Hundred Years* (1959); Germaine M. Reed, *David French Boyd, Founder of Louisiana State University* (1977). ☆

MISSISSIPPI, UNIVERSITY OF

Located at Oxford in the north-central section of Mississippi, the University of Mississippi was chartered by the legislature in 1844 and opened in 1848. As Mississippi's only state-supported institution of higher learning, the university offered both undergraduate liberal arts degrees and professional degrees. Early presidents included author Augustus Baldwin Longstreet (1849–56) and his successor Frederick A. P. Barnard, who initiated pioneering scientific research and teaching programs. Even after specialized colleges and universities were established in the state, the University of Mississippi continued to offer a comprehensive program including graduate and undergraduate degrees. Currently the university encompasses both the main campus at Oxford and a school of medicine, which opened in 1903 in Oxford and moved to Jackson in 1955.

In 1861 the entire student body withdrew to enroll in the Confederate army. The university suspended operation during the Civil War but reopened in the fall of 1865, becoming coeducational in 1882 and adding its first woman faculty member, Sarah Isom, in 1885. In addition to the normal trials any southern state university might experience, the University of Mississippi suffered two significant crises in its troubled history. In 1928 Governor Theodore G. Bilbo urged the legislature to relocate the state university from Oxford to Jackson, the state capital. His plans called for a gigantic increase in the state appropriation (from $1 million to $25 million), a restructuring of the university's curriculum, and sweeping personnel changes. All the governor's plans went awry, and in the process the university lost its accreditation for two years. Recent scholarship has somewhat tempered the criticism of Governor Bilbo, whose motives were less political and punitive than formerly believed.

Barnard Observatory, University of Mississippi, c. 1859

A second major crisis came in 1962 when James Howard Meredith became the first black student to enroll at the university. Governor Ross Barnett led the state's white power structure in resisting Meredith's admission and delayed his enrollment for nearly 18 months by a series of legal maneuvers. When the courts at last ordered his admission, legal proceedings gave way to violence. Throughout the night of 31 September 1962 rioters surged across the university campus in a vain effort to prevent his enrollment. James Meredith did enroll and graduated from the university in August 1963.

The University of Mississippi is known universally as Ole Miss. This name became associated with the university during the 1896–97 academic year when the student body began publishing an annual, which was styled *The Ole Miss*. Within less than a decade alumni, students, and the media routinely referred to the university as Ole Miss. Although it has never been formally or officially adopted, the name Ole Miss has become a synonym for the University of Mississippi.

The university provides an institutional focus for interdisciplinary study of the American South through its Center for the Study of Southern Culture (established in 1977), Afro-American Studies program, Sarah Isom Center for Women's Studies, and the resources of the John Davis Williams Library, which includes a comprehensive William

Faulkner collection and the Blues Archive. Annual conferences include the Faulkner Conference (since 1974) and the Chancellor's Symposium on Southern History (since 1975).

R. Gerald Turner assumed the office of chancellor in 1984. Enrollment at the Oxford campus as of fall 1985 was 9,004 students.

See also BLACK LIFE: / Meredith, James; POLITICS: / Barnett, Ross; Bilbo, Theodore

David Sansing
University of Mississippi

Allen Cabaniss, *The University of Mississippi: Its First Hundred Years* (2d ed., 1971). ☆

MISSISSIPPI STATE UNIVERSITY

Mississippi State University is located in the eastern part of north-central Mississippi near the town of Starkville. It was chartered by the legislature in 1878 as the Agricultural and Mechanical College of the state of Mississippi to serve as the land-grant institution for white youths. The legislation establishing the college passed after considerable pressure from state Grange leaders who had agitated for several years to have the land-grant education function moved from its original location, the University of Mississippi at Oxford. Grangers preferred a separate institution, one that would better fulfill the mission of the Morrill Act, an 1862 federal law providing college training in scientific agriculture and industrial technology for the children of farmers.

Classes began in October 1880 under the presidency of former Confederate General Stephen D. Lee. Enrollment the first year totaled 354 men; female students were admitted two years later. The college awarded its first baccalaureate degrees in 1883 to eight students. Enrollment now totals 11,663; nearly 10,000 of these students study on the main campus. On-campus enrollment is the largest in the state. There are three off-campus branches; two of these are degree-granting centers located in Meridian and Jackson.

In 1932 the legislature renamed the college Mississippi State College, and it became Mississippi State University in 1958. By then it had developed into a comprehensive, doctoral-degree-granting university committed to fulfilling the land-grant college functions of instruction, research, and service. The university includes 11 academic units: the Graduate School; the schools of Accountancy, Architecture, and Forest Resources; the Division of Continuing Education; and the colleges of Agriculture and Home Economics, Arts and Sciences, Business and Industry, Education, Engineering, and Veterinary Medicine. The Agricultural and Forestry Experiment Station, the Cooperative Extension Service, and numerous specialized units such as the John C. Stennis Institute of Government and the Center for International Security and Strategic Studies are also integral components of the university.

The university's library houses valuable collections of manuscripts, documents, maps, newspapers, and periodicals. A Special Collections department devoted to collecting materials of local, state, regional, and general histories also houses the papers of distinguished Mississippians such as Senator John C. Stennis, Congressman G. V. "Sonny"

Montgomery, and newspaper editors Hodding Carter and Turner Catledge.

Donald Zacharias became the university's 15th chief executive officer when he assumed its presidency in August 1985.

Robert L. Jenkins
Mississippi State University

John K. Bettersworth, *People's College: A History of Mississippi State* (1953); Dean W. Colvard, *The "Land Grant" Way in Mississippi: The Story of Mississippi State University* (1962); James D. McComas, *Mississippi State University: A New Century, a New Dimension* (1978). ☆

NATIONAL HUMANITIES CENTER

In an essay on "Education and the Southern Potential" (1966) sociologist Rupert B. Vance observed, "Beyond the level of graduate training, a new pattern in American intellectual life has been the emergence of centers for advanced study, such as the Institute for Advanced Study at Princeton and the Center for Advanced Study in the Behavioral Sciences at Stanford. There is no comparable institution in the South and none in sight." In 1976, however, the American Academy of Arts and Sciences in Boston, after considering more than 15 potential sites across the United States, accepted the invitation of the Triangle Universities Center for Advanced Studies, Inc. (TUCASI), a consortium of Duke University, the University of North Carolina at Chapel Hill, and North Carolina State University, to locate the newly conceived National Humanities Center in the Research Triangle Park of North Carolina. TUCASI raised funds from North Carolina corporations and foundations for a 30,000-square-foot building, and it assured library support and partial administrative funding for the new center from the three universities. Among the North Carolinians who formed TUCASI and helped establish the National Humanities Center were John Caldwell, Archie K. Davis, William Friday, C. Hugh Holman, and Terry Sanford.

The Center opened in 1978 and each academic year admits as fellows 40 to 50 scholars in the humanities to pursue individual research and to exchange ideas in daily conversation, lectures, interdisciplinary seminars, and conferences. A class of fellows includes young scholars (3 to 10 years beyond the doctorate), scholars in mid-career, and distinguished senior scholars; fellows have private studies and are given fellowship stipends, library assistance, and manuscript typing. Most fellows are chosen in an open competition, for which the Center receives applications from all parts of the United States and also from other nations. Scholars of southern history and culture who have been fellows of the Center include Cleanth Brooks, Richard Beale Davis, John Hope Franklin, Dewey Grantham, and John Shelton Reed. The Center also publishes a quarterly newsletter and produces a weekly radio program on the humanities. A 35-member national board of trustees, composed of leaders from education, the professions, and public life, oversees the Center, and a director is in charge of its administration. Directors have been Charles Frankel (1977–79), William J. Bennett (1979–81), and Charles Blitzer (1983–). Support for the Center has come from private foundations, corporations, the National Endowment for the Humanities and other federal agencies, the Triangle Universities, the state of North Carolina, individual donors, and an endowment fund. The Center's stated purpose is "to encourage scholarship in the humanities and to enhance the influence of the humanities in the United States."

See also BLACK LIFE: / Franklin, John Hope; LITERATURE: / Brooks, Cleanth

Kent Mullikin
National Humanities Center

Terry Eastland, *Change* (April 1980); Melvin Maddocks, *Time* (14 May 1979); Peter Riesenberg, *Christian Science Monitor* (7 May 1979); Malcolm G. Scully, *Chronicle of Higher Education* (28 April 1980). ☆

NORTH CAROLINA, UNIVERSITY OF

The University of North Carolina at Chapel Hill was authorized by the state constitution of 1776 and chartered by the General Assembly in 1789. The cornerstone of Old East Building, today the oldest state-university building in America, was laid on 12 October 1793. The first student arrived on 12 February 1795, and the first class was graduated in 1798. The university survived sectarian and political attacks, public apathy, and continued poverty. It began its slow emergence from obscurity as it strengthened its faculty and liberalized its curriculum. The natural sciences gained equal status with classical studies. After constitutional reforms of 1835 and the success attained by many alumni in state and federal government, a more favorable political climate for the university was accompanied by greater emphasis on education for public service. Three 18th-century and five 19th-century buildings, still standing, met campus needs before 1861 when it was second only to Yale in number of students enrolled. Although the university remained open through the Civil War, it was forced by general economic ruin and political bitterness to close from 1870 to 1875.

First to open a summer "normal school" for teachers (1877), the university introduced regular courses in education as early as 1885. Other guideposts to the future included the beginning of medical and pharmaceutical studies (1879), the first regular legislative appropriation (1881), announcement of graduate studies leading to degrees (1876), organization of scientific laboratories and discoveries of major significance in industrial chemistry (1880–1900), administrative integration of the semiindependent School of Law (1894), and admission of the first women students (1897).

The period before World War I was marked by significant gains in academic standards and productive scholarship of the faculty, reorganization and orderly expansion of library services, and increased emphasis on the applied and social sciences. During the 1920s the state successfully met the needs of the university through enlargement of its physical plant. The University Press was incorporated in 1922, the Institute for Research in Social Science was organized in 1924, and the Southern Historical Collection was established in 1930. From 1930 to 1949 the university was led by former history professor (1915–30) Frank P. Graham, who gained national recognition as an educator, statesman, and social activist. Expansion was halted by the Depression and by World War II but since 1947 has continued apace. A Division of Health Affairs was created that year and has resulted in greatly expanded schools of Medicine, Pharmacy, and Public Health, while new schools of Dentistry and Nursing and the North Carolina Memorial Hospital were established. A planetarium and astronomical observatory, a museum of art, a new library building, enlarged chemistry laboratories, and an indoor sports arena are among later additions to the campus. As of fall 1985 its full-time enrollment was 22,066 students.

William S. Powell
University of North Carolina
at Chapel Hill

R. D. W. Connor, ed., *Documentary History of UNC, 1776–1799*, 2 vols. (1953); William S. Powell, *First State University: A Pictorial History of the University of North Carolina* (1972); Phillips Russell, *These Old Stone Walls* (1972); Louis Round Wilson, *University of North Carolina, 1900–1930* (1957). ☆

NORTH CAROLINA SCHOOL OF THE ARTS

The North Carolina School of the Arts in Winston-Salem, N.C., is a state-supported school designed to train performing artists. Programs of study range from seventh grade through graduate school. The institution incorporates schools of Dance, Design and Production, Drama, and Music. All schools include an undergraduate program; the schools of Dance and Music and the Visual Arts program of the School of Design and Production provide training on the secondary level as well. In addition, a program leading to the Master of Fine Arts degree is offered in the School of Design and Production. There is also a complementary academic program at both the secondary and undergraduate levels. The current enrollment of 787 students represents 54 of North Carolina's counties, 48 states, and 13 foreign countries. The school employs 100 faculty, many of whom are recognized professional artists, and guest artists.

The enabling legislation establishing the school was passed by the North Carolina General Assembly in 1963, with the strong support of Governor Terry Sanford. Winston-Salem was chosen as the site of the campus because an existing structure, the Gray High School building, and the surrounding 40 acres were available, and because Winston-Salem had a reputation for audience and financial support of the arts. Vittorio Giannini, a Juilliard composer, was chosen as the first president of the school, which opened in 1965 with 226 students.

Upon the death of Giannini in 1967, Robert Ward, Pulitzer Prize–winning composer, was selected as president of the school. In the 1972–73 academic year the school became one of the 16 components of the reorganized University of North Carolina system, and in 1974 Robert Suderburg, also a composer, became the chancellor of the school. Jane Elizabeth Milley succeeded him as chancellor in September 1984.

Besides the 40-acre Gray High School campus, which has undergone much renovation, the school has restored the old Carolina Theater in downtown Winston-Salem. The theater has been renamed the Roger L. Stevens Center for the Performing Arts and has been important in the revitalization of downtown Winston-Salem.

The school also has several professional affiliates, including the North Carolina Dance Theater, the North Carolina Shakespeare Festival, the North

Carolina Scenic Studios, and the Piedmont Opera Theatre.

Elaine Doerschuk Pruitt
North Carolina School of the Arts

Gary D. Ford, *Southern Living* (October 1983); Frank Getlein, *Smithsonian* (March 1981); Selwa Roosevelt, *Town and Country* (March 1981). ☆

ODUM, HOWARD W.

(1884–1954) Sociologist.

Howard Washington Odum (born in Georgia in 1884, died in North Carolina in 1954) was the South's best-known social scientist in the first half of the 20th century. In more than 20 books and 200 articles he assessed the level of the region's economic and cultural achievements, explored the forces that inhibited progress, and exhorted his fellow southerners to use their material, intellectual, and spiritual resources to rebuild their region. Odum's work was well known beyond academic circles, and he became an important symbol of the movement to use science and scientific open-mindedness as tools to unlock the region's potential and inspire a new sectional self-confidence.

Odum was educated during the height of the Progressive era. He received his bachelor's degree in 1904 from Emory University, a master's degree in classics from the University of Mississippi in 1906, and Ph.D. degrees from Clark University (psychology) in 1909 and Columbia University (sociology) in 1910. As a young man he absorbed the spirit of the great Progressive-era teachers and orators who believed that science could reveal the secrets of social phenomena and pave the way for major leaps forward in the human condition. Odum brought

Howard W. Odum, renowned sociologist, c. 1930s

this spirit to the University of Georgia, where he was on the faculty in the School of Education from 1913 to 1919. During this period he campaigned actively to improve rural education in Georgia and began a lifelong effort to encourage diversification of southern agriculture by developing the dairy industry (Odum later received national awards as a breeder of Jersey cows). In 1919 Odum became the dean of Emory College, but his vision of Emory as an instrument of social services clashed with the philosophy of the school's conservative chancellor. When the University of North Carolina offered Odum a post as chair of the sociology department and dean of the School of Public Welfare, he moved to Chapel Hill, where he remained for the duration of a remarkably productive career.

At Chapel Hill Odum concentrated on using the resources of social science to study the South's problems and to suggest solutions. Toward these ends he founded the *Journal of Social Forces* and the Institute for Research in Social Science. Between 1924 and 1954 Odum persuaded northern philanthropists to contribute hundreds of thousands of dollars to support institute studies of regional economic conditions, labor relations, race problems, welfare programs, and penal reforms. The most notable of the many products of this work was a massive statistical portrait of the South that Odum published in 1936 under the title *Southern Regions of the United States*. This book was used extensively by contemporary journalists and political leaders in campaigns for regional self-improvement.

Over the course of his career Odum also made major contributions to preserving the cultural history of southern blacks. He published collections of black folksongs in 1911 (in the *Journal of American Folklore*) and in 1925 and 1926 (in book form, with Guy B. Johnson), and between 1928 and 1931 he wrote a trilogy of books based on the life of a wandering black laborer.

Howard W. Odum also participated directly in many social service programs. He helped lead three penal-reform movements in North Carolina, served as assistant director of President Hoover's Commission on Recent Social Trends, was a director of the North Carolina Welfare Commission, and helped found the Southern Regional Council. During the last two decades of his life Odum worked to develop a theory of regionalism that would encourage holistic analysis of all aspects of the South's condition and to devise means to ease the transition to a racially integrated society.

See also SOCIAL CLASS: / Southern Regional Council

Wayne D. Brazil
Hastings College of the Law

Katherine Jocher, Guy B. Johnson, George L. Simpson, and Rupert B. Vance, eds., *Folk, Region, and Society: Selected Papers of Howard W. Odum* (1964); Howard W. Odum, *American Regionalism* (1938), *An American Epoch* (1930), *Cold Blue Moon* (1931), *Rainbow Round My Shoulder* (1928), *Southern Regions of the United States* (1936), *The Way of the South* (1947), *Wings on My Feet* (1929). ☆

PHILLIPS, U. B.

(1877–1934) Historian.

Ulrich Bonnell Phillips has recently been described by historian Eugene D. Genovese as perhaps the greatest historian America has produced. Author of six major works and 55 factual articles, Phillips almost singlehandedly directed the social and economic history of the antebellum South from pietistic antiquarianism to many of the major concerns of contemporary historians. An indefatigable discoverer and user of primary sources, especially plantation records, Phillips was undoubtedly the preeminent historian of the South in the first half of the 20th century. Still, his pervasive, if paternalistic, racism and his insistence that the plantation system was *the* social/economic system of the antebellum South caused his work to be virtually unread until his recent rediscovery.

Phillips was born 4 November 1877 in the small upland Georgia town of LaGrange. He received both his B.A. and M.A. from the University of Georgia and then went to Columbia, where he took his doctorate in 1902 under William Dunning. Phillips taught for short periods at both Wisconsin and Tulane and from 1911 to 1929 at the University of Michigan. On 21 January 1934, four years after leaving Michigan for Yale, Phillips died.

Phillips had four major ideas about the antebellum South: (1) its environment was an essential contributing factor to its development and Frederick Jackson Turner's hypothesis of the frontier worked perfectly for the South of prewar years; (2) the region's political economy was a combination of geography, economics, politics, social structure, race, and ideology and dominated all aspects of southern life; (3) the key to antebellum political economy was the plantation, which was not a mere economic institution but an entire way of life; and, finally, (4) the plantation was primarily a method of social control of a "stupid," genetically inferior race and the necessary first step in what Phillips unabashedly regarded as the continuing, essential task of preserving the South as "a white man's country."

Phillips incorporated Turner's regionalism into his 1902 dissertation "Georgia and States Rights," ostensibly a history of Georgia political thought. During the early 1900s he further developed the frontier thesis in numerous articles in major journals, the 13-volume *The South in the Building of the Nation*, and his introduction to the documentary collection *Plantation and Frontier*. Phillips's first attempt to view political economy as an interrelated system was his 1908 study of the development of the railroad industry, *A History of Transportation in the Eastern Cotton Belt to 1860*, which showed how the needs of the planter class created the type of railroads built in the South. Phillips then concentrated largely upon a systematic study of the plantation economy and produced two classic and highly influential works, *American Negro Slavery* (1918) and *Life and Labor in the Old South* (1929). In the late 1920s Phillips related his ideas of black social control to political history in such essays as "The Central Theme of Southern History" and was preparing a book on the subject at the time of his death.

Mark Smith
University of Texas at San Antonio

Merton Dillon, *Ulrich Bonnell Phillips: Historian of the Old South* (1985); Richard Hofstadter, *Journal of Negro History* (April 1944); John Herbert Roper, *U. B. Phillips: A Southern Mind* (1984). ☆

PINEY WOODS SCHOOL

Piney Woods Country Life School is a private boarding institution in Rankin County, Miss. The campus is surrounded by a 2,000-acre pine forest along Highway 49 between Jackson and Hattiesburg. It was founded in 1909 by a Missourian, Laurence Clifton Jones (1882–1975). After graduating from the University of Iowa in 1907 and teaching at Utica Institute in Mississippi, he decided to start his own school. One day as he sat on the end of a log, a teenage male came and sat on the other end. Jones discovered that the youth could not read because his family had bound him out to work. Each day as Jones taught him to read, more children came.

By the time of the first high school graduating class in 1918, Piney Woods had become known for the opportunity that it provided Afro-American boys and girls who had no money. They made bricks for buildings, worked in the office, and did carpentry, cooking, laundering, cleaning, and farming. In the past as well as today, the work program emphasized educating the head, the heart, and the hand. Students acquired three skills that were to help them earn a living or further their education.

After the 1920s the Piney Woods

School included a school for the blind, which was moved to Jackson under the control of the state in the 1950s. Its musical programs included the Rays of Rhythm, Sweet Hearts of Rhythm, a marching band, a stage band, and a glee club. Visitors were treated with the best of black spirituals as they enjoyed southern hospitality on the Piney Woods campus.

In 1931 the school's elementary and secondary curriculum was enhanced by a junior college that focused on secretarial and teacher training. Numerous graduates from these programs have gone on to receive terminal degrees in their chosen fields. A positive work ethic is instilled in the students not only by the work program but by mottos posted on campus, such as "Will prepare myself and maybe my chance will come," "Devote yourself to a worthy task [and] you can't fail to have a worthy life," and "Work is the mother of contentment."

From the very beginning, Piney Woods has been a success story of interracial cooperation. Black and white citizens from Mississippi and the nation have given their time, talents, and financial resources to the institution. Also, in the early days Jones's wife, Grace Allen Jones (1876–1928), initiated the traveling singers who spent summers on the road introducing Piney Woods to the nation and soliciting funds. In 1953 Jones appeared on the *This Is Your Life* television program. The program and its successive showings helped the school establish the largest endowment of any high school for Afro-Americans in the nation.

Today the school provides an accredited curriculum for approximately 300 students in kindergarten through the 12th grade. In 1985 Charles Beady succeeded James S. Wade as its third president. An integrated board of trustees manages the school and plans for its future.

Alferdteen Harrison
Jackson State University

Alferdteen Harrison, *Piney Woods School: An Oral History* (1982). ☆

Story hour at the Piney Woods School, Mississippi, c. 1940s

RANDOLPH-MACON COLLEGE

Randolph-Macon College began with the desire of the Virginia Conference of the Methodist Episcopal church to have a clergy educated in the liberal arts and the desire of the leading citizens of Mecklenburg County to have a college. Fund-raising began in 1825, and a charter was acquired from the legislature of Virginia on 3 February 1830. The eponymous John Randolph and Nathaniel Macon, both well-known politicians, had no connection with the institution. The college was erected west of Boydton, Va., near the North Carolina border, then at the center of the conference.

At first the curriculum of Randolph-Macon followed the unique elective system of the University of Virginia, but the first formal president, Stephen Olin, persuaded the faculty in 1834 to adopt the rigid curriculum common to colleges at the time. In 1859 Randolph-Macon reverted to the elective system. The college achieved financial stability under President William A. Smith (1846–66). Smith taught a formal course defending slavery, and the college at one time owned two slaves. He and board of trustees chairman John Early, Methodist ministers both, were principals in the formation of the Methodist Episcopal Church, South.

The Civil War cut off the supply of students and forced the brief closing of the school. More damaging was the investment of much of the endowment in Confederate and southern municipal bonds. The war wrecked the regional transportation system and devastated the segment of the population that supported the school and sent sons to it. The board of trustees, pushed by the college president, Thomas Johnson, moved the college in 1868 to Ashland, Va., which had the virtue of being on a railroad line connecting the college with the Maryland Conference of the Methodists.

The college remained small, with 100 to 200 students, but pioneered educational reforms in the teaching of English literature (1870) and physical education (1886). Under the leadership of the college president, William Waugh Smith, the board of trustees established Randolph-Macon Woman's College in Lynchburg, Va., and three preparatory schools (at Bedford, Front Royal, and Danville, Va.), thus forming the Randolph-Macon system.

Modernizing the college in Ashland took more money than its rural, Methodist supporters could afford, and there was an appeal to northern financiers, especially Andrew Carnegie. When the Woman's College met the exacting standards of his pension fund (the first school in the South to do so), the money came with a stipulation that meant the board would cease to be entirely Methodist. This stipulation raised the question, voiced by alumnus James Cannon, of whether the board or the Virginia Conference would own and control the system. After a protracted, debilitating quarrel, the Virginia courts supported the trustees, but the moral victory was with the church. Very little changed at the college until after World War II.

Many of the subsequent improvements at the college reflect the growing prosperity of Virginia. In the postwar presidency of J. Earl Moreland, the college expanded its student body from 300 in the 1930s to 900, with concomitant increases in buildings, curricula, and faculty. In 1964 the college decided to admit students regardless of race and in 1971, during the presidency of Luther W. White III, began to admit residential women students. The student body of nearly 1,000 (964 as of the 1984–85 academic year) is drawn primarily from Virginia (65 percent) and Maryland. The college resolutely emphasizes the liberal arts but also embraces the sciences, including computer science. Its graduates frequently move into the professions (especially law and medicine) and business.

See also RELIGION: / Cannon, James; Methodist Episcopal Church, South

James Edward Scanlon
Randolph-Macon College

Richard Irby, *History of Randolph-Macon College, Virginia* (1898); James Edward Scanlon, *Randolph-Macon College: A Southern History* (1983). ☆

RICE UNIVERSITY

Rice University, a private, independent, coeducational university located in Houston, Tex., opened its doors to students in 1912 as the William Marsh Rice Institute. It was chartered in 1891 by former Houston merchant William Marsh Rice with a $200,000 interest-bearing note payable to the institute upon his death. Subsequently Rice made other gifts to the institute, all payable after his death. When the estate was settled in 1904, approximately $3 million was given to the institute as a separate capital fund, added to the original endowment that had grown to almost $3.3 million. At the time the institute opened in 1912, the endowment stood at approximately $9 million, allowing all students to attend without paying tuition—a privilege not ended until 1965.

The Board of Trustees in Houston appointed mathematician and astronomer Edgar Odell Lovett of Princeton University as president in 1907 with directions to plan the new institution. After worldwide travel, discussions, and faculty recruitment, Lovett oversaw the opening in 1912 marked by an international convocation of scholars. The entering class of 77 students had an international faculty of 10 (Julian Huxley was the first professor of biology), one major academic building (with an elaborate plan for additional buildings by the Boston architectural firm of Cram, Goodhue, and Ferguson), and a large endowment. The honor code, a cherished Rice tradition, was adopted by the student body in 1916. By 1924 the entering freshman class was limited to approximately 450, and undergraduate enrollment has been carefully controlled ever since. In 1985 it was approximately 3,800. The graduate enrollment has grown gradually to almost 1,200.

Under Lovett's direction the Rice Institute first developed major strength in the sciences and engineering, though distinguished instruction was offered from the beginning in the humanities and architecture. The curriculum broadened and the faculty increased greatly in size after World War II under the administration (1946–60) of physicist William V. Houston, as the name change in 1960 to Rice University acknowledged. Moral, social, and economic imperatives drove the university successfully to seek legal authority in 1964 to break the founder's charter in two regards: permission to admit students without regard to race and to charge (a modest) tuition. Further expansion, especially in the humanities and social sciences, came in the 1960s and 1970s during the administrations of chemists Kenneth S. Pitzer (1961–68) and Norman Hackerman (1970–85). In 1961 the National Aeronautics and Space Administration located the Manned Space Flight Center (now Johnson Space Center) on land made available by Rice, and in 1962 the university established the nation's first department of space science. The *Journal of Southern History* has been published at Rice since 1959; *Studies in English Literature* was founded at Rice in 1961; and the *Papers of Jefferson Davis* project has been headquartered at Rice since 1963. In July 1985 *Rice University Studies* (formerly *Rice Institute Pamphlet*) became Rice University Press. The Sheperd School of Music and the Jones School of Administration were added in 1973 and 1976, respectively.

In 1985, the year theologian George E. Rupp of Harvard Divinity School became Rice's fifth president, the endowment passed the half-billion-dollar mark, the largest of any private university in the South. The small undergraduate student body (3,813 enrollment in the 1984–85 academic year) is among the nation's most select, with average SAT scores over 1300 and one of the highest percentages of National Merit Scholarship winners.

See also URBANIZATION: / Houston

John B. Boles
Rice University

Stephen Fox, *The General Plan of the William M. Rice Institute and Its Architectural Development* (1980); Fredericka Meiners, *A History of Rice University: The Institute Years, 1907–1963* (1982); Andrew Forest Muir, in *William Marsh Rice and His Institute*, ed. Sylvia Stallings Morris, *Rice University Studies* (Spring 1972). ☆

SHEATS, WILLIAM N.

(1851–1922) Educator.

During his lifetime William N. Sheats became variously known as Florida's "Little Giant of Education," "Florida's Progressive Educator," and the "Father of Florida's Public School System." His fame grew during more than two decades as superintendent of public instruction, and his efforts set the foundations for a modern state system of public education.

Born 5 March 1851 on a small cotton farm in the red clay foothills of the Appalachians near Auburn, Gwinnett County, Ga., Sheats was proud of his roots and often referred to himself as a Georgia cracker. His inspiration in life was his widowed mother, who though beaten down by sickness and poverty made every effort to get her children to school. Adopting her creed, Sheats worked his way through Emory College, eventually attaining a master's degree, and, while principal of a Georgia high school, he completed by correspondence an accounting course from Moore's Business College. Believing that Florida had a healthful climate, he accepted an offer as vice principal of the East Florida seminary at Gainesville in 1876.

A very popular teacher, Sheats was induced to run for superintendent of Alachua County Schools. He developed his philosophy of administration during three terms as county school superintendent. Reading journals, consulting with educators, and touring school facilities convinced Sheats to emphasize centralization of authority and uniformity of procedure. He revoked all teaching licenses, forcing teachers to take his examination based on a series of textbooks. Facing reexamination every one, two, or three years, teachers flocked to Sheats's institutes on pedagogy. He led the county school board in adopting a rigorous code of conduct for teachers, uniformity of textbooks, and consolidation of schools. He believed so strongly in the separate-but-equal doctrine that he provided excellent teacher training for blacks and attempted to establish for them an industrial training school comparable to Booker T. Washington's Tuskegee Institute. After 12 years of his leadership Alachua County schools went from near the bottom in school quality to near the top.

Sheats gained statewide recognition at the 1885 constitutional convention. The only school man present, he dominated debates that shaped the education article destined to remain in effect for 84 years. The document included provisions that special tax districts be developed for high school education, that the state superintendent of public instruction be elected, that racial integration in the public schools be prohibited, and that the state organize teacher training colleges, one for each race.

In 1892 Sheats became Florida's first elected state superintendent of public instruction. He soon showed the same passion for centralization and regimentation that had characterized his earlier work. He shocked teachers by revoking their licenses as a means to get them to sit for his long and difficult examination. He proposed a uniform course of study, an effort at consolidating schools into larger units, and a state-aid formula for high schools. In black education he caused a national sensation by having the sheriff close a Congregationalist school and arrest the teachers for instructing blacks and whites in the same school.

Educators from around the nation read about "Mr. Sheats" in a *National Education Association* article on the ideal chief state school officer, but his opponents, referring to "Tsar Sheats," schemed for his election defeat. They succeeded in 1904 by portraying him as too liberal on the race question. He was turned out by the voters, even though during his administration 32,000 additional children registered in school, raising the proportion of registered children from 66 percent in 1892 to 71 percent in 1904, and per student expenditures had increased from $4.25 to $8.10.

Sheats made an election comeback in 1912, and during his last years he put a personal stamp on Florida's compulsory attendance law and administered one of the South's most effective uniform textbook laws. On 19 July 1922 he died in office.

Arthur O. White
University of Florida

William N. Sheats, "Journal," William N. Sheats Papers, Southern Historical Collection, University of North Carolina, Chapel Hill; Arthur O. White, *One Hundred Years of State Leadership in Florida Public Education* (1979). ☆

SOUTH CAROLINA, UNIVERSITY OF

Founded in 1801 as the South Carolina College, the University of South Carolina opened in 1805. The college received financial appropriations from the state government, enabling it to build a physical plant, which included the first separate college library building in the United States. The school attracted a faculty that included Francis Lieber, perhaps the most distinguished scholar in the antebellum South. The classical curriculum reached its peak in the 1850s during the presidency of James Henley Thornwell, who declared that the college existed "for Latin and Greek." At that time there were approximately 200 students, with eight professors on the faculty.

Although the era from 1801 to 1861 was prosperous, the next 60 years brought disaster, and the institution was closed on two occasions and reorganized six times. The Civil War forced it to suspend operations in June 1862, and the physical plant was converted into a Confederate military hospital, a status that saved it from the fire that destroyed much of Columbia when Sherman's army occupied the city in February 1865. In January 1866 the school was reopened as a university, but economic distress following the war prevented the state government from providing adequate support. The situation was further complicated when the Radical Republicans gained control of the state government in 1868 and two blacks were elected to the board of trustees. During Reconstruction several blacks were awarded A.B. and LL.B. degrees, and one, Richard T. Greener, became a member of the faculty.

Whites were appalled by events at the "Reconstruction University," and Governor Wade Hampton promptly closed it when the Democrats regained control in April 1877. The school remained closed until October 1880, when it reopened as the South Carolina College of Agriculture and Mechanic Arts. In 1890 Benjamin R. Tillman directed scathing attacks at the institution as the "seedbed of the aristocracy" and led his agrarian followers in a political revolution, which resulted in the founding of rival Clemson and Winthrop colleges.

After Tillman's attacks in 1890, 30 lean years followed during which the school was plagued by economic hardships, Tillmanite legislators, and hostile governors, such as Cole L. Blease. In 1906 it was again allowed to assume the name of university, and in the 1920s under the vigorous leadership of President William D. Melton, appropriations increased sufficiently to place the university in a position of equality with its state rivals. The same was true of enrollment, which grew from 600 to 1,800.

The post–World War II years brought tremendous growth, as the university became by far the largest institution in the state. Enrollment, which was 2,000 in 1940, has increased on the Columbia campus to 23,000, of which almost one-half are women and 8,000 are graduate students. There are also nine regional campuses with an enrollment of 12,000 undergraduates. The doctorate is offered in 50 fields and the master's degree in 104. Blacks were readmitted in 1963, peacefully, and approximately 14 percent of current students are black. The new Thomas Cooper Library is a major research center, while the South Caroliniana Library has become an outstanding repository of materials pertaining to state history.

In the 1980s President James B. Holderman has launched an ambitious program in international studies that operates through the James F. Byrnes International Center. The Institute for Southern Studies sponsors conferences, workshops, publications, and research on the region and especially the state of South Carolina.

Daniel W. Hollis
University of South Carolina

E. L. Green, *History of University of South Carolina* (1916); Daniel W. Hollis, *University of South Carolina*, 2 vols. (1951, 1956); Thomas T. Jones, *The University of South Carolina: Faithful Index to the Ambitions and Fortunes of the State* (1964). ☆

SOUTHERN METHODIST UNIVERSITY

Celebrating its 75th year of founding in 1986, Southern Methodist University (SMU) in Dallas, Tex., has grown from a college with a theology school to a university of 9,000 students in four undergraduate and two graduate professional schools. Its denominational but nonsectarian nature early led to a liberal arts orientation. At the same time, the needs of Dallas led to the creation of schools of law, engineering, business, and the arts as well as theology and to SMU's early embrace of big-time football.

SMU was established in 1911 by a special educational commission of the five annual conferences of the Methodist Episcopal Church, South, in Texas, and it is now owned by the South Central Jurisdiction of the United Methodist Church. Vanderbilt University had severed its connection with the church in the early 20th century, and SMU became the sole Methodist-affiliated institution of higher learning west of the Mississippi River. Both Dallas and Fort Worth were under consideration as sites; the gift of a 133-acre campus and the promise of sustaining funds by Dallas citizens brought SMU to Dallas. It opened its doors in 1915, with 706 students, 35 faculty, and $279,178 in endowment.

The first president was a Georgian and graduate of Emory College, Robert S. Hyer, who came from another Methodist college, Southwestern of Georgetown, Tex. A physicist who had early experimented with wireless communication, he had a vision for SMU. He chose *veritas liberabit vos* as its motto, selected Harvard's and Yale's colors, and borrowed from the University of Virginia the neo-Georgian architectural pattern that still unifies SMU's 80-building campus.

Other SMU leaders, Umphrey Lee (1938–54) and Willis M. Tate (1954–72), were both SMU graduates. Lee, a minister and scholar who had been dean of Vanderbilt's School of Religion, steered SMU through World War II and toward research and scholarship as well as teaching. Tate was a genius at interpreting a university to the business leadership of Dallas and a strong defender of SMU as a "free marketplace of ideas." For his defense of academic freedom he was awarded the Alexander Meikeljohn award of the American Association of University Professors in 1967. Among those whom SMU invited to speak on campus during the times of McCarthyism and of 1960s social unrest were John Gates and Martin Luther King, Jr.

SMU began publishing the *Southwest Review* in 1925. It became respected through the contributions of John H. McGinnis, Henry Nash Smith, J. Frank Dobie, Lon Tinkle, and others. For a brief time just before the founding of the *Southern Review*, the *Southwest Review* was edited jointly by McGinnis at SMU and Cleanth Brooks and Robert Penn

Warren at LSU. The SMU Press was established in 1937.

SMU integrated several of its schools in the 1950s, ahead of most other universities in the region, and was the first Southwest Conference school to have black athletes on its teams. The faculty of Perkins School of Theology had a key leadership role in integration in Dallas.

Marshall Terry
Southern Methodist University

Mary Martha Thomas, *Southern Methodist University: Founding and Early Years* (1974). ☆

TENNESSEE, UNIVERSITY OF

The University of Tennessee enrolls more than 40,000 students on four campuses: the major campus at Knoxville, the Center for the Health Sciences at Memphis, and the predominantly undergraduate campuses at Chattanooga and Martin.

Established in 1794 as Blount College, a private, nonsectarian, coeducational school, it was rechartered by the Tennessee Legislature in 1807 as East Tennessee College, a male-only institution, and endowed with a land grant of 50,000 acres. Often condemned by frontier politicians as a school for rich men's sons, it was a small, struggling institution with never more than 169 students in the antebellum period.

During the Civil War the faculty generally supported the Union, while the loyalties of the students were divided. The university buildings were badly damaged in the conflict. The Confederate army occupied the campus first; later it was used as a military hospital by northern troops.

In 1869, largely because of the Union sentiments of trustees and faculty, it was designated the land-grant university under the Morrill Act. For the next generation a debate ensued within the university over the significance of the land-grant designation. Most of the faculty and the president looked upon agricultural and mechanical arts as merely a branch of the university; the trustees generally supported its transformation into a predominantly agricultural and scientific institution. The victory of the agricultural forces was completed in 1887 with the election of President Charles W. Dabney. Until then the university had been an all-male military school with drills, military government, and mandatory uniforms patterned after West Point. Military government was abandoned in 1890, and women returned in 1892.

From 1901 to 1917 the university was a leading institution in support of campaigns in behalf of universal public schooling in the South. With the aid of the Southern and General Education boards it conducted the Summer School of the South for teachers from throughout the region from 1902 to World War I, with 22,000 teachers attending during the first decade.

The university experienced phenomenal growth after World War II with veterans entering under the GI Bill, followed soon after by their sons and daughters. The first black students enrolled—under court order—in 1952. In 1968, shortly after the University of Chattanooga merged with the university, it was reorganized into a university system with a president as the highest officer and a chancellor over each campus.

Clinton B. Allison
University of Tennessee

Clinton B. Allison, in *Three Schools of Education: Approaches to Institutional History*, ed. Agnes Bagley (1984); James Riley Montgomery, Stanley J. Folmsbee, and Lee Seifert Green, *To Foster Knowledge: A History of the University of Tennessee, 1794–1970* (1984); The University of Tennessee Office of Management Services, *A Graphic View of the University of Tennessee* (7th ed., 1985). ☆

TEXAS, UNIVERSITY OF

For many years Texas lawmakers considered the establishment of a state university. Finally, the Constitutional Convention of 1875 decided that "the Legislature shall, as soon as practicable, establish, organize and provide for the maintenance, support and direction of a university of the first class, to be located by a vote of the people of this State, and styled, 'The University of Texas,' for the promotion of literature, and the arts and sciences, including an agricultural and mechanical department." On 28 March 1881 the legislature passed a bill establishing the university, and Governor Oran M. Roberts signed the measure on 30 March. Later that year, Texans voted to locate the school in Austin. In November 1882 the cornerstone of the west wing of the original main building was laid in place on 40 acres of land one mile north of the Capitol; and in September 1883 the first students began classes in the temporary Capitol at the corner of Congress Avenue and Eleventh Street. Until 1895 the university was without a president, the chairman of the faculty serving as the chief executive officer. President William L. Prather (1899–1905), in addressing the students, uttered the now-famous words, "The eyes of Texas are upon you." Later the words were matched to the tune of "I've Been Working on the Railroad" and became the school song.

At the cornerstone ceremony, Ashbel Smith declaimed prophetically, "Smite the earth, smite the rock with the rod of knowledge, and fountains of unstinted wealth will gush forth." In 1923 oil was discovered on UT's west Texas lands. The money generated goes into the Permanent University Fund, which in 1982 was worth approximately $1.7 billion. UT receives two-thirds of the income from this fund and Texas A&M University one-third. Although still referred to as "the Forty Acres," the present campus occupies 300 acres and has more than 110 buildings. There were 47,838 students enrolled in the fall of 1985. UT has been merged with 13 other institutions to form the University of Texas system.

UT is the only southwestern member of the Association of American Universities. The latest assessment of doctoral education ranked the school 14th among the nation's universities in over-

Tower, University of Texas at Austin, c. 1940s

all academic quality. Graduate programs in law, education, and business rank in the top 10 among public institutions. UT has long been a world leader in energy-related education and research.

The Lyndon Baines Johnson Presidential Library is located on the campus. The UT library, with almost 5 million volumes, is the eighth-largest academic library in the United States and is internationally known for its collection in Latin American history and culture and 20th-century British and American literature.

Norman D. Brown
University of Texas at Austin

Margaret Berry, *The University of Texas: A Pictorial Account of Its First Century* (1980); Ronnie Dugger, *The Invaded Universities: Form, Reform and New Starts* (1974); Roger A. Griffin, *Southwestern Historical Quarterly* (October 1982). ☆

TEXAS A&M UNIVERSITY

Texas Agricultural and Mechanical (A&M) University was the first public institution of higher education in Texas. The Texas Legislature authorized the establishment of the institution under the terms of the Morrill Act in November 1866. The act organizing the Agricultural and Mechanical College of Texas was approved on 17 April 1871; it appropriated $75,000 for the erection of buildings and bound the state to defray all expenses of the college exceeding the annual interest from the endowment. Proceeds from the sale of 180,000 acres of land, located in Colorado and authorized under the Morrill Act, were invested in $174,000 of gold frontier defense bonds of Texas. A locating commission accepted the offer of 2,146 acres of land from Brazos County, and the college opened on 4 October 1876. With an initial enrollment of some 50 students in the fall term of 1876, the institution grew to an enrollment exceeding 37,000 students in the mid-1980s.

The college began as an all-male agricultural and mechanical college with required military training and enrollment in the Corps of Cadets. Participation in military training and membership in the Corps of Cadets became voluntary in 1965. Although fewer than 10 percent of the students are now in the Corps of Cadets, the school continues to furnish more reserve officers than any other institution in the United States and offers ROTC programs leading to commissions in all four branches of the service. Women attended intermittently as special students over the years, but the institution officially admitted women students on a qualified basis after 1963 and adopted an open admissions policy in 1971. The 58th Legislature of Texas, on 23 August 1963, changed the name of the Agricultural and Mechanical College to Texas A&M University.

Texas A&M University offers graduate study in most fields, with a doctorate in many. It supports a College of Veterinary Medicine, established in 1916, and a College of Medicine, authorized in 1971, which graduated its first class in 1981. The Texas A&M University system, whose present chancellor is Arthur G. Hansen, provides administrative direction for Texas A&M University at Galveston, Prairie View A&M University, Tarleton State University, Texas Forest Service, Texas Agricultural Extension Service, Texas Agricultural Experiment Station, Texas

Engineering Experiment Station, Texas Engineering Extension Service, Texas Transportation Institute, Texas Veterinary Medical Diagnostic Laboratory, and numerous other agencies and divisions. In 1971 Texas A&M University became one of the first four sea-grant designated institutions. Its current president is southern historian Frank E. Vandiver.

The university offers leadership in many of the newer technological areas, including space, nuclear research, computers, oceanography, chemistry, and the traditional areas of agriculture, engineering, architecture, education, geosciences, business, and liberal arts. Research expenditures first exceeded $100 million in 1982, and Texas A&M University now ranks in the top 20 universities in research expenditures. Under the authority of the Texas Constitution of 1876, Texas A&M is a branch of the University of Texas, which was established in 1883, and participates in the Permanent University Fund of the State of Texas. Texas A&M University aspires to preeminence in teaching, research, and public service.

Henry C. Dethloff
Texas A&M University

Henry C. Dethloff, *A Centennial History of Texas A&M University, 1876–1976*, 2 vols. (1975), *The Pictorial History of Texas A&M University, 1876–1976* (1975); George Sessions Perry, *The Story of Texas A. and M.* (1951). ☆

TULANE UNIVERSITY

Tulane University was founded in 1834, when seven New Orleans physicians, alarmed by the lack of a local medical school in those times of cholera and yellow fever epidemics, pooled their expertise to found the Medical College of Louisiana at New Orleans. A few years later it became the medical department of the newly established, state-supported University of Louisiana. In 1847 a law department was added; continuing progress, however, was interrupted by the closing of the university during the Civil War. After it reopened in 1878, a liberal arts department was added, later called the Academic Department, now the College of Arts and Sciences.

In 1822 Paul Tulane, a bachelor from Princeton, N.J., arrived in New Orleans to embark upon what would become a highly successful career as a merchant. He remained in New Orleans off and on for more than 50 years before returning to Princeton and retirement. Always a secretive, private person, Tulane in 1881 disclosed to General Randall Lee Gibson of New Orleans that he had for years been contemplating the creation of an institution of higher education. Tulane and Gibson went over the details involved in such an endeavor with the result that Gibson was asked to present the idea to 17 prominent New Orleans men whom Tulane wished to comprise his university's governing body. (The first board of administrators of the Tulane Educational Fund included such notables as Gibson himself, Charles Erasmus Fenner, the Reverend Benjamin Morgan Palmer, Edward Douglass White, and others of similar stature.)

As the specifics of Tulane's gift were completed, officials of the University of Louisiana let it be known that they would welcome inclusion in the plans for the new university. Because it was common knowledge that the older institution had fallen upon lean years, they invited James McConnell, Paul Tulane's New Orleans attorney and himself a member of the board of administrators, to meet with their board to discuss the possible advantages of such an arrangement. After careful investigation, it was agreed that the public University of Louisiana would henceforth be the private "Tulane University of Louisiana," and its doors were opened in 1884.

In 1886 Josephine Louise Newcomb, a native of Baltimore but a resident of New Orleans, sent a letter to the board of administrators expressing her desire to establish an appropriate memorial to her daughter, Harriott Sophie, who had died at the age of 15. Newcomb donated $100,000 to establish the H. Sophie Newcomb Memorial College—the first women's coordinate college in the United States. At her death Newcomb bequeathed to the college the residue of her estate, a sum in excess of $2 million.

In 1894, the year that the College of Technology (later the College of Engineering) was added, Tulane University moved from its downtown campus to its present location on more than 100 acres in uptown New Orleans. The medical department (later school) remained downtown and added schools of dentistry and pharmacy, these last two being closed for lack of students in 1928 and 1934, respectively. Today the Tulane Medical Center encompasses the School of Medicine, the School of Public Health and Tropical Medicine, outpatient clinics, and a full-service teaching hospital. Rounding out the academic components of the university on the uptown campus there followed the School of Architecture, the School of Commerce/Business Administration, the Graduate School, the School of Social Work, and the University College (evening division).

Although both Paul Tulane and Josephine Newcomb specified that the student body was to be composed of young white men and women, in 1962 a federal judge ruled that while the university could not be forced to integrate, it was no longer bound by the racial restrictions of the original gifts, and in 1963 Tulane University voluntarily admitted black students.

The W. R. Hogan Jazz Archive is now a premiere collection on a southern musical form, and the Amistad Collection is a world-renowned archives on black life. In the 1984–85 academic year Tulane had a full-time enrollment of 10,232 students, and Newcomb College of Tulane had 1,737 female students.

Doris H. Antin
Tulane University

John Percy Dyer, *Tulane, 1825–1950* (1954), *Tulane: The Biography of a University, 1834–1965* (1966). ☆

TUSKEGEE INSTITUTE

Tuskegee was founded in 1881, the result of an accommodation between local blacks and whites after white political control of Macon County, Ala., was secured. Booker T. Washington, its first principal, established at the secondary level a curriculum of industrial and agricultural education modeled after his alma mater, Hampton Institute. Unlike Hampton and other new black schools, Tuskegee was staffed entirely by blacks. Washington's growing fame and influence attracted both northern philanthropic and southern conservative support.

George Washington Carver, its most famous teacher, brought national acclaim through his peanut experiments. Monroe N. Work edited the *Negro Year Book* and compiled the annual Tuskegee lynching report, both efforts to combat the images of blacks that whites held in the early 20th century. At the time of his death in 1915, Washington was the most influential American black and Tuskegee Institute the best-known black school in the country.

Robert R. Moton, the second principal, continued the accommodationist approach, though he was conciliatory to Washington's critics in the NAACP. He brought a veterans' hospital to Tuskegee in 1923 and stood firm against pressure for a white hospital staff, thus preserving the Tuskegee tradition of blacks controlling the institution. Recognizing that most Tuskegee graduates became teachers, professionals, and businessmen rather than farmers or tradesmen, Moton oversaw the development of a college department in 1927. Frederick D. Patterson succeeded Moton in 1935 and obtained substantial state support in the establishment of a graduate program (1943) and schools of veterinary medicine (1945) and nursing (1953). Patterson was also instrumental in establishing the Tuskegee Army Air Field in 1941 for the segregated training of black pilots for World War II, an action that brought him scorn from the NAACP.

Luther H. Foster followed Patterson in 1953 and steered the school through the civil rights movement, consistently supporting the voting rights efforts led by Charles G. Gomillion, a faculty member. In 1965 students vigorously protested segregation in the town and administration policies on campus, and students took members of the board of trustees hostage briefly in 1968. Benjamin F. Payton became president in 1981 and oversaw the change in the school's name to Tuskegee University in 1985, at which time its enrollment was approximately 3,500.

See also BLACK LIFE: / Washington, Booker T.; SCIENCE AND MEDICINE: / Carver, George Washington

Robert J. Norrell
University of Alabama

Pete Daniel, *Journal of Southern History* (August 1970); Louis R. Harlan, *Booker T. Washington: The Making of a Black Leader, 1856–1901* (1972), *Booker T. Washington: The Wizard of Tuskegee, 1901–1915* (1983); Linda O. McMurry, *George Washington Carver: Scientist and Symbol* (1981), *Recorder of the Black Experience: A Biography of Monroe Nathan Work* (1985); Robert J. Norrell, *Reaping the Whirlwind: The Civil Rights Movement in Tuskegee* (1985). ☆

UNIVERSITY OF THE SOUTH

The University of the South at Sewanee, Tenn., is the product of an educational thrust by 25 dioceses of the Episcopal church in 12 states south of Virginia. Its name connotes the intention of its founders in 1857 to provide a higher level of graduate education for the entire South, based on Oxford University as its model. Its site on nearly 10,000 acres at a height of 2,000 feet on the Cumberland Plateau was central to the South, healthful, and isolated enough for establishment of its own culture. War intervened before permanent buildings were erected or classes begun, and the principal founder, Bishop and Lt. Gen. Leonidas Polk, was killed in 1864 near Atlanta.

The university is a child of two eras—the prosperous pre–Civil War South and postwar Reconstruction. The donation of land by the Sewanee Mining Company in 1858 required opening the institution within 10 years. English churchmen contributed £2,500 to enable the school to open in September 1868 with nine students and four professors, a week before the deadline. The early faculty were of a caliber ordinarily unobtainable by a struggling college. Generals Josiah Gorgas, Francis A. Shoup, and Edmund Kirby Smith, other Confederate officers, bishops, and great ladies moved to the wilderness to provide a high standard of culture for students from all over the South.

Theology became a distinct department in 1878 and continues. Engineering degrees were awarded from 1875 to 1911. For nearly two decades (1892–1910) professional schools offered degrees in medicine (including dentistry and nursing) and law. Although most colleges abandoned preparatory education many years ago, the Sewanee Academy continued until 1981, when it was merged with St. Andrew's School nearby. Since 1892 the university has published in southern Appalachia, an area of low literacy, the *Sewanee Review*, now the oldest literary-critical quarterly in America, with international circulation and contributors. The School of Theology publishes the quarterly *St. Luke's Journal.*

The College of Arts and Sciences has an enrollment of 1,000 men and women (females were first admitted in 1969), with 75 students in the School of Theology. Total enrollment in the 1984–85 academic year was 1,158 students. Less than 25 percent of the college students come from Tennessee. A characteristic of the Sewanee student body is the kinship of present students to former ones. Fourth-generation students are now taking degrees, and a survey five years ago showed that 20 percent of the college students had been preceded, or were then accompanied, by one or more family members. Sewanee's 20 Rhodes Scholars are a per-capita-of-enrollment record in the region, with other national and regional records in the production of Fulbright and Woodrow Wilson scholars and NCAA scholar-athletes. In a region devoted to subsidized athletics, Sewanee took the lead in 1946 in abandoning athletic scholarships.

Special programs include Education for Ministry, in which 4,000 students here and abroad have enrolled for training of laity. A summer graduate program in theology awards the Doctor of Ministry degree in association with Vanderbilt University. Two hundred students each summer attend the Sewanee Summer Music Center to play in three symphony orchestras. A medieval colloquium, an economics symposium, political science internships, and overseas study involve an area broader than the campus itself.

Owned and controlled by the Episcopal church, with All Saints' Chapel and its 56-bell carillon at the center of the domain, the university retains a character essentially unchanged since its conception. English influence continues in architecture, nomenclature, and academic gowns worn daily by students and professors. The English tutorial system never became the major model of instruction, but individual instruction is available. Latin and Greek are still studied, though no longer required for a degree. The Old South contributed a mixture of grace and gallantry and a dress code that survived the 1960s. Now absent from the campus is a military influence, which, though not a part of the founders' plans, persisted more than a century.

One hundred and twenty-five years after its founding, the University of the South has not reached the heights envisioned by its founders, but it has not lost their intention to serve an entire region.

See also RELIGION: / Protestant Episcopal Church; SCIENCE AND MEDICINE: / Gorgas, Josiah

Arthur Ben Chitty
University of the South

Donald S. Armentrout, *Quest for the Informed Priests: The Centennial History of the School of Theology of the University of the South* (1979); Arthur Ben Chitty, *Reconstruction at Sewanee: The Founding of the University of the South and Its First Administration, 1857–1872* (1954); Moultrie Guerry, with Arthur Ben Chitty and Elizabeth N. Chitty, *Men Who Made Sewanee* (1981). ☆

VANCE, RUPERT B.

(1899–1975) Sociologist.

During his 40-year tenure as a scholar, author, and lecturer at the University of North Carolina at Chapel Hill (UNC), Rupert Bayless Vance sought to unravel the threads weaving the South's people and land into a tapestry of poverty, an effort that became a personal struggle both to understand his own ties to the South and to help break the vicious cycle of dependence and despair inherent in the South's cotton-based economy. With pioneer sociologist Howard W. Odum—founder of the Institute for Research in Social Science and of the department of sociology at UNC, the first sociology department created at a southern university—Vance developed the study of "regional sociology." His experience of living in the South shaped the forms of his scholarship and of his reform efforts.

Born at the turn of the century in Plummerville, Ark., Vance grew up in an area whose wounds from the Civil War had yet to be healed. His early life was filled with hardships. Contracting polio when he was three, Vance lost the use of both of his legs; through physical therapy at an orthopedic clinic in St. Louis, he eventually was able to walk with crutches and was able to enter elementary school when he was 10. In the depths of the 1920s agricultural depression Vance's father lost his farmland and went bankrupt. Vance later utilized the image of his father's failure to represent the general condition of the South. A love of reading, a bachelor's degree in English from Henderson Brown College in Arkadelphia, Ark., and contact with writers such as Edwin Mims and the Agrarians at Vanderbilt University, where he received his master's degree in economics, fostered the clear, descriptive, and humanistic style of his essays. The close relationship that developed between Vance and Howard Odum when Vance joined UNC's fledgling sociology department in 1926 encouraged the young sociologist to pursue his desire for social and economic reforms in the South.

Vance's studies of southern life were interdisciplinary, covering the topics of southern politics, culture, history, demographics, the transformation of the South from a rural area into an urban area, societal conflict, and cotton tenancy. In *Human Factors in Cotton Culture: A Study in the Social Geography of the American South* (1929), *Human Ge-*

ography of the South: A Study in Regional Resources and Human Adequacy (1932), the coauthored (with Nadia Danilevsky) *All These People: The Nation's Human Resources in the South* (1945), and in other studies Vance advocated the theory that the South's problems were man-made, that history—not geography—had arrested the South in a frontier stage of development. The social and economic patterns of the South had been shaped by the plantation. Locked into a rural economy based on the production of cotton while the North grew more urban and industrial, the South retained (until the mid-1940s) a colonial economy—an economy that necessitated the exploitation of natural resources and labor in order to afford goods manufactured in another region. Overpopulation, an unstable cotton market, Jim Crow laws, and parasitic diseases such as hookworm and malaria, Vance argued, had only worsened the South's problems.

As a scholar, government consultant, southerner, and as president or founder of several important sociology societies (including the Southern Sociological Society, the Population Association of America, and the American Sociological Association), Vance lobbied for social reforms such as the 1938 Bankhead-Jones Farm Tenant Bill and constructive urban and industrial planning in the South. Over a decade after his death in Chapel Hill in 1975, Vance's search for reform and his southern cultural studies remain relevant.

Elizabeth McGehee
Salem College

Rupert B. Vance, in *Regionalism and the South*, ed. John Shelton Reed and Daniel J. Singal (1982). ☆

VANDERBILT UNIVERSITY

Vanderbilt University in Nashville, Tenn., emerged after a protracted birth presided over by disparate midwives. These included Bishop Holland N. McTyeire of the Methodist Episcopal Church, South, and "Commodore" Cornelius Vanderbilt, the New York shipping and railroad baron. The early Vanderbilt blended denominational educational goals, northern hopes for sectional reconciliation, and southern needs for quality higher education in the post–Civil War years. Its founders conceived of Vanderbilt as a great university, a rival to such established northern private institutions as Harvard and Princeton. Yet, from the beginning, Vanderbilt was a captive to its geographic setting and the orthodoxy of its Methodist founders. Vanderbilt's story is one of growth from a Methodist to a southern and, finally, to a national university.

The Methodist Episcopal Church, South, granted a charter for the "Central University" in 1872, Cornelius Vanderbilt gave money for an endowment to it in 1873, and Vanderbilt University was dedicated in 1875. It remained a Methodist institution until an acrimonious separation from the church in 1914. While the majority of the first faculty and nearly all of the students were Methodists, Vanderbilt owed its existence to the financial largesse of the benefactor whose name it bore. In the beginning, Vanderbilt's endowment of $1 million made it southern Methodism's wealthiest institution, with greater financial resources than any other southern college except Johns Hopkins. Under Chancellor Landon C. Garland

(1875–93), Vanderbilt faced the challenge of ministering to an educationally benighted South. Vanderbilt pioneered in establishing academic standards at the secondary level by way of entrance examinations held throughout the Southeast and a system of certifying the better preparatory and public high schools.

Under its second chancellor, James H. Kirkland (1893–1937), Vanderbilt grew further away from its Methodist origins. It gained a more cosmopolitan and less Methodist faculty and student body, and foundation money became more important to university budgets. Poised between the parochialism of its Methodist ties and a longing for national stature, Vanderbilt under Kirkland went through a severance of church ties and into an era of munificent gifts from the Carnegie Corporation and the Rockefeller-funded General Education Board. Such philanthropies funded a new Medical School and Nursing School, which, in the 1920s, rivaled the best in the nation. Vanderbilt's other claim to distinction rested on the intellectual flowering of the Fugitives and Agrarians.

From World War II to the present, through three successive chancellors, Vanderbilt has striven for national eminence; Vanderbilt saw its role as more than educational uplift to an impoverished South. Indeed, both the South and Vanderbilt benefited from the postwar economic boom. Vanderbilt's better-qualified students were recruited from a national pool, its faculty became more distinguished and pluralistic, and its graduate programs and research facilities greatly expanded. Yet accompanying Vanderbilt's emergence from a regional cocoon has been the need to comply with national norms.

The strains of modernity became acute after the mid-1950s. Chancellor Harvie Branscomb and President of the Board of Trustees Harold S. Vanderbilt, a major benefactor of the university, led Vanderbilt slowly to a policy of full racial integration in 1963. Branscomb's successor, Alexander Heard, faced the student turbulence of the 1960s and women's demands for equity beginning in the 1970s. Today, Vanderbilt functions in a national arena; it has grown outward from the confines of its Methodist and southern origins. The total enrollment in the 1984–85 academic year was 8,993.

See also MYTHIC SOUTH: / Agrarians, Vanderbilt; RELIGION: / Methodist Episcopal Church, South

Patricia Miletich
Vanderbilt University

Paul K. Conkin, *Gone with the Ivy: A Biography of Vanderbilt University* (1985); Edwin Mims, *Chancellor Kirkland of Vanderbilt* (1940), *History of Vanderbilt University* (1946). ☆

VIRGINIA, UNIVERSITY OF

Founded in Charlottesville by Thomas Jefferson, who designed its classically beautiful buildings, planned its trail-breaking curriculum, and recruited its mostly European faculty, the University of Virginia opened its doors in 1825.

The curriculum was divided into separate schools and offered courses in mathematics, the sciences, and modern languages. It included a novel elective system and rejected any organized religion or theological dogma. No honorary degrees have ever been conferred.

Established in 1842, the honor system is student operated and controlled. It has undergone modifications over the years, but the single sanction, under which lying, cheating, or stealing is punished by permanent expulsion, is still in full force by repeated vote of the students. The university in the 19th century gained its enduring renown as a center of upper-class southern gentility, a place to produce gentlemen.

Until the early 1900s the university never had a president, preferring to operate with a chairman of the faculty, a system instituted by Jefferson. Every other important university in the country had a chief executive officer, and the Board of Visitors finally decided to follow suit. In 1904 it elected Edwin Anderson Alderman, then president of Tulane University, to the presidency of the University of Virginia. Under him there were significant advances in curriculum, faculty, endowment, and enrollment.

Alderman was succeeded in 1933 by John Lloyd Newcomb, dean of the School of Engineering. It was the nadir of the Great Depression, but genuine progress was made. Upon Newcomb's retirement, Colgate W. Darden, Jr., former governor of Virginia, was elected, and served from 1947 to 1959. This was the beginning of the university's impressive forward surge, which has carried the institution to its highest levels of academic achievement and prestige. The impetus created by Darden was greatly enhanced by Edgar F. Shannon, Jr., a member of the English faculty and a Rhodes Scholar, who succeeded him. He served until 1974, when Frank L. Hereford, Jr., former vice president and provost, and an internationally known physicist, became president. Under Hereford the institution made further spectacular advances. A campaign for a $90,000,000 additional endowment had raised $145,900,000 by mid-1985. Hereford was succeeded in 1984 by Robert M. O'Neil, former president of the University of Wisconsin system.

With a fall 1985 enrollment of 17,417 full-time students, including hundreds of blacks and thousands of women, the University of Virginia has entered a new era. Nationally ranked academically, it is especially noteworthy for its Law School, Medical School, Graduate School of Business Administration, and several academic departments, especially English.

Famous alumni include Edgar Allan Poe; Woodrow Wilson; Walter Reed, the conqueror of yellow fever; Julien Green, the only non-Frenchman ever elected to the French Academy; and two judges of the Court of International Justice, John Bassett Moore and Hardy Cross Dillard.

See also HISTORY AND MANNERS: / Jefferson, Thomas; Wilson, Woodrow; LITERATURE: / Poe, Edgar Allan; SCIENCE AND MEDICINE: / Reed, Walter

Virginius Dabney
Richmond, Virginia

Thomas P. Abernethy, *Historical Sketch of the University of Virginia* (1948); Philip Alexander Bruce, *History of the University of Virginia, 1819–1919*, 5 vols. (1922); Virginius Dabney, *Mr. Jefferson's University: A History* (1981). ☆

VIRGINIA MILITARY INSTITUTE

Since its founding in 1839 on the site of a state arsenal at Lexington, the Virginia Military Institute has held a unique position in the educational system of Virginia and the South. It was the nation's first state military college, and the success of VMI, which was patterned on the models of West Point and the École Polytechnique in France, influenced the establishment of military schools throughout the southern states in the 1800s.

VMI is a fully accredited, four-year, state-owned, undergraduate military college for men. It is a college dedicated to the total development of its students' academic excellence, military discipline, physical fitness, and high moral character, and to the founders' concept of educated and responsible citizen-soldiers, men prepared for chosen careers in civilian life but trained and ready for military leadership in time of national need.

While rigorous military training is required of every cadet, VMI's first emphasis has always been on the academic program. Civil engineering, a subject rarely taught in colleges before 1839, became the cornerstone of the academic program, which also offered, in 1846, the first industrial chemistry course in the South and, by 1868, modern courses in physics and meteorology. Today's approximately 1,300 cadets (1,338 in the 1984–85 academic year) pursue bachelor's degree programs in the general fields of engineering, science, and liberal arts, and all participate in Reserve Officer Training Corps (ROTC) programs leading to reserve or regular commissions in the nation's armed forces.

VMI's place in history was enhanced during the Civil War by the great number of its graduates and faculty, including Thomas "Stonewall" Jackson, who served in high command with the Confederacy, and by the Corps of Cadets, which at the 1864 Battle of New Market, Va., won lasting fame as the only college student body in the nation's history to fight as a unit in pitched battle. Notable among alumni of the institute is the late General of the Army George C. Marshall, a 1901 graduate who won the Nobel Prize for Peace in 1953 for the Marshall Plan.

Although VMI began as a military college for Virginians, cadets now come from states across the nation and several foreign countries, and all are part of an enduring "Brother Rat" fraternity that begins in the "rat" or freshman year. Cadets live by an honor code that is deeply rooted in their system of self-government, and the historic cadet barracks, which house the entire corps, are the landmark in VMI's designation as a National Historic District.

See also HISTORY AND MANNERS: / Jackson, Stonewall

Julia Martin
Virginia Military Institute

William Couper, *One Hundred Years at VMI*, 4 vols. (1939); Diane B. Jacob and Judith Morehead Arnold, *A Virginia Military Institute Album, 1839–1910* (1982); Henry A. Wise, *Drawing Out the Man: The VMI Story* (1978). ☆

WASHINGTON AND LEE UNIVERSITY

Washington and Lee University traces its origins back to the mid-18th century when Scotch-Irish Presbyterian settlers in the valley of Virginia established a small classical academy. In 1776 another generation, fired by a zeal for independence and education, changed its name to Liberty Hall and began college-level studies based on John Witherspoon's Princeton curriculum. In 1782 the Commonwealth of Virginia chartered the school, which granted its first bachelor's degrees in 1785. In 1803 it moved to nearby Lexington. It was distinctive among southern colleges, having no official connection with either a church or state.

In 1796 the trustees convinced George Washington to endow the college with canal stock valued at $50,000. The saving legacy still pays a part of each student's costs. In honor of Washington's gift the school became Washington Academy and later Washington College. Until the Civil War it remained a typical, southern classical college training lawyers, doctors, and preachers for regional leadership, particularly in newly opened lands in the South and West.

By 1865 the Civil War had deprived the college of students, decimated its alumni association, and depleted its endowment. Union raiders had wrecked the campus. That year the trustees offered General Robert E. Lee the presidency. He revitalized the place. He raised needed funds, recruited able teachers, and attracted talented students. Under Lee's leadership, the honor system began to take its modern form.

In 1860 all but 1 of 95 students had been Virginians. In 1869, a year before Lee's death, the student body numbered 400 strong from 20 states and one foreign country. Lee hoped to heal the nation's wounds by having boys from North and South studying together. Lee, the pragmatist, also strove to provide leaders in law, medicine, engineering, business, and journalism to rebuild a shattered South. Lee transformed the curriculum before his death in 1870. In 1871 the school, now Washington and Lee University, included a law school and pioneering collegiate courses in business instruction and journalism.

Washington and Lee struggled during the last two decades of the 19th century. During the 20th century, however, the school grew stronger with each generation. The School of Law, enrolling some 350 students, became coeducational in 1972. The first women undergraduates enrolled in September 1985.

Two undergraduate divisions, the College and the School of Commerce, Economics, and Politics, comprise some 1,400 students from throughout the nation and abroad, who choose from nearly 800 courses, 40 percent of which enroll fewer than 10 students. Since 1970 the college has averaged a Rhodes Scholar every third year. Freshmen, numbering about 350, are selected from more than 2,300 applicants.

John D. Wilson, Washington and Lee's president since 1983, guides a southern institution with a national mission, stressing academic excellence and leadership development in an atmosphere of courtesy, friendliness, student self-government, and honor, long the hallmarks of Washington and Lee. This small, independent school combines the intimacy of a college with the broad offerings of a university.

See also HISTORY AND MANNERS: / Lee, Robert E.; Washington, George

Taylor Sanders
Washington and Lee University

Ollinger Crenshaw, *General Lee's College: The Rise and Growth of Washington and Lee University* (1969); Charles Bracelen Flood, *Lee: The Last Years* (1981); William W. Pusey III, *The Interrupted Dream: The Ed-*

ucational Program at Washington College (Washington and Lee University), 1855–1880 (1976). ☆

WEAVER, RICHARD M.

(1910–1963) Intellectual.

Richard Malcolm Weaver, Jr., was born in Asheville, N.C., in a region first settled by his ancestors at the end of the 18th century. He was educated in the public schools of Asheville and Lexington, Ky., then attended the University of Kentucky, where he took the A.B. degree in 1932, and Vanderbilt University, where he finished his M.A. in English in 1934.

Weaver left Vanderbilt in 1936 without completing the terminal degree and took a teaching job in Texas. But the heady experience of studying in Nashville, at the time when activities of the Agrarians centered on the Vanderbilt campus, forever marked Weaver's intellectual development and compelled him to resume his studies at Louisiana State University, another institution under Agrarian influence during this period. Weaver's 1943 LSU dissertation, "The Confederate South, 1865–1910: A Study in the Survival of a Mind and a Culture," is at the heart of his intellectual development as a southern conservative and served as a grounding for his distinguished career as intellectual historian, rhetorician, and political philosopher.

Weaver's dissertation was finally published (posthumously) in 1968 under the title of *The Southern Tradition at Bay: A History of Postbellum Thought*. Before it appeared, he had issued the classic *Ideas Have Consequences* (1948), *The Ethics of Rhetoric* (1953), and *Visions of Order* (1964). Other posthumous collections include *Life without Prejudice and Other Essays* (1965) and *Language Is Sermonic* (1970). While producing this mass of scholarship, Weaver taught on the faculty of the University of Chicago and served as an editor for William F. Buckley's *National Review* and for *Modern Age*. Weaver brought to the revival of conservative intellectual thought an emphasis on traditional southern values and stress on the connection between language and ideology. He remains to this day an influence in rhetoric, history, and political philosophy. At the heart of his conviction was an unwavering devotion to the politics of principle and the tradition of limited government. At Chicago he spoke of himself as an "Agrarian in exile," but at the time of his death, he was preparing to return south (to Vanderbilt) in 1964.

See also MYTHIC SOUTH: / Agrarians, Vanderbilt

M. E. Bradford
University of Dallas

M. E. Bradford, *Modern Age* (Summer–Fall 1970); George H. Nash, *The Conservative Intellectual Movement in America since 1945* (1976). ☆

WOODWARD, C. VANN

(b. 1908) Historian.

Born 13 November 1908 in Vanndale, Ark., to Hugh Allison and Bess Vann Woodward, Comer Vann Woodward has been the most influential historian of the modern South. Educated at Emory University (A.M., 1932), and the University of North Carolina (Ph.D., 1937), Woodward taught at the Georgia Institute of

Technology, the University of Florida, Scripps College, Johns Hopkins University, and Yale University, where he is now Sterling Professor of History Emeritus.

Woodward has shown an unusual blend of activism and detachment, of aristocratic provenance and fascination with the masses, of great privilege conferred by family and friend and iconoclastic rebelliousness, of professional specialization and an eclectic training. Evoking irony in his writing, he has also lived a life of considerable irony, demonstrating what David Minter has called "deep reciprocities" between experiences of his personal life and the history he has written.

Growing up in Arkansas during a period of racial violence and of grinding regional poverty, Woodward was nurtured by a family of devout Methodists committed to moderate social reform. Forsaking this life, he left an Arkadelphia Methodist college for Emory University, studying philosophy there with LeRoy Loemker, who taught him German existentialism and demonstrated to him a life that successfully combined scholarly excellence with social activism. After brief "careers" teaching literature at the Georgia Institute of Technology and studying political science at Columbia University, Woodward entered the University of North Carolina, studying with Howard Kennedy Beale; there he developed a historical interpretation based on class analysis and economic determinism, writing a dissertation that became his first book and his only biography, a celebration of Georgia Populism entitled *Tom Watson: Agrarian Rebel* (1938). In subsequent years, during World War II, he began to integrate his understanding of literature with this economic history, producing his most enduring scholarship, *Origins of the New South, 1877–1913* (1951), and his most influential study, *The Strange Career of Jim Crow* (1955), which the Reverend Martin Luther King, Jr., called "the Bible of the civil rights movement."

After distinguishing himself as a professor at Johns Hopkins University and as a visiting professor at Oxford University, he became Sterling Professor at Yale University, where he directed excellent graduate students who have made their own impact on the study of southern history. At Yale he became an essayist and an editor, turning out the collections of poignant essays, *The Burden of Southern History* (1960) and *American Counterpoint: Slavery and Racism in the North-South Dialogue* (1971), while editing the Pulitzer Prize–winning *Mary Chesnut's Civil War* (1981). His work has also received the Bancroft and Sydnor awards; and he has served as president of the Southern Historical Association, the American Historical Association, and the Organization of American Historians. His interpretation of history, a subtle melding of lyric determinants, has been criticized for underestimating the force of racism and the longevity of segregation; and many others have scorned him for overestimating the reformism inherent in agrarian movements at the turn of the century. He will be long recognized as the starting point for the major debates about the character of the New South.

John Herbert Roper
St. Andrews Presbyterian College

Sheldon Hackney, *Journal of Southern History* (May 1972); Michael O'Brien, *American Historical Review* (June 1973); David M. Potter, in *Pastmasters*, ed. Marcus Cunliffe and Robin Winks (1969). ☆

ENVIRONMENT

MARTIN V. MELOSI

University of Houston

CONSULTANT

☆ ☆ ☆ ☆ ☆ ☆ ☆ ☆

Environment 531

Air-Conditioning 542
Animals 545
Climate and Weather 552
Endangered Species 556
Energy Use and Development 560
Environmental Movements 562
Flood Control and Drainage 568
Forests 571
Gardens and Gardening 574
Indians and the Environment 577
Insects 579
Land Use 581
Natural Disasters 583
Naturalists 586

Natural Resources 591
Parks and Recreation Areas 592
Plants 596
Plant Uses 598
Pollution 601
Reclamation and Irrigation 604
River Life 607
Rivers and Lakes 608
Roads and Trails 612
Soil and Soil Conservation 616
Streams and Steamboats 619
Tennessee Valley Authority (TVA) 622
Trees 625
Water Use 627
Wetlands 634
Alligators and Crocodiles 637
Appalachian Coal Region 638
Appalachian Mountains 639
Armadillo 640
Atchafalaya Basin Swamp 641
Audubon, John James 642
Azalea 643
Big Thicket 644
Blue Ridge 645
Catfish 645
Chesapeake Bay 647
Collard Greens 649
Cypress 650
Everglades 651
Great Smoky Mountains 652
Homer, Winslow 654
Kudzu 655
Lightwood 656
Live Oak 657
Magnolia 658
Mississippi River 659
Mockingbird 661
Natchez Trace 662
Nuclear Pollution 663
Oil Pollution 665
Opossum ("Possum") 666
Outer Banks 668
Palm Trees 669
Red River Expedition 670
Shellfish 671
Shenandoah Valley 673
Spanish Moss 674
Tennessee-Tombigbee Waterway 675

Overleaf:* *John Leon Moran*, Natural Bridge, *Virginia (1985)

ENVIRONMENT

In *The Colonial Search for a Southern Eden* (1953), historian Louis B. Wright noted, "The notion that the earthly paradise, similar to if not the veritable site of the Scriptural Eden, might be found in some southern region of the New World was widely held in the seventeenth and early eighteenth centuries." Some explorers claimed that God had placed Eden on the 35th parallel of north latitude, along a line from New Bern, N.C., to Memphis, Tenn. In more recent times, the idea of a southern Eden has faded, but the post–World War II "Sunbelt" phenomenon has restored a little piece of the myth and raised the esteem for the South as a land of opportunity.

Although the South may not represent a scriptural or a temporal Eden, its history has been influenced nonetheless by environmental factors. Indeed, a longstanding dispute over the relative importance of environment and culture permeates the study of the region. Some view geography as the key variable in its development. Others cite ideology and cultural factors. The issue of environment versus culture also has found its way into the debate over whether the South is best viewed as a "region" or as a "section." As a section, the South can be perceived as a cultural entity, a state of mind, an idea. This perspective is most useful for understanding the social, cultural, and political currents that run through southern history. Viewing the South as a region or a geographic area directs attention to the physical characteristics of the South and especially to its relationship to the rest of the nation.

Climate and the Sectional South. Environmental factors have frequently been used in a deterministic way to reinforce cultural stereotypes about the South as a region. No environmental issue was more influential than the notion of climate as a determining factor in southern culture.

Clarence Cason's *90° in the Shade* (1935) fused climate and culture into stereotypical clichés: "If snow falls infrequently on the southern land, the sun displays no such niggardly tendencies. In Mississippi there is justification for the old saying that only mules and black men can face the sun in July. Summer heat along the middle Atlantic coast and on the middle western plains causes more human prostrations than it does in the South. The difference lies partially in the regularity of high summer temperatures in the South but mainly in the way the southerner takes the heat." Much of the South surely suffers through oppressively hot and humid summers and enjoys mild winters, but to what degree has the climate actually influenced southern history? Historian Carl N. Degler has suggested that the climate has had "a passive, if not active, influence" in shaping the region's past. The commitment to agriculture, especially the opportunity to grow commercial crops such as cotton and tobacco, was made possible by a favorable climate.

Cotton, for instance, requires a growing season of 200 frost-free days, a condition that can be duplicated in few regions outside the South. Rice and sugarcane also require long growing seasons. Degler asserts, "That the climate permitted the growth of these peculiarly southern crops goes a long way to explaining why the South is the only region of the United States that developed plantation agriculture. Certainly the plantation did not spread in the South because of the climate; but without a climate favorable to tobacco, cotton, sugar, and rice southern agriculture would probably have been like that of the North in both crops and organization."

Climate has been a controlling influence in the development of the southern economy and even in the South's social organization. But as a rationalization for such stereotypic traits as laziness, emotionalism, and volatility, climate can be a misleading explanation. As historian Jack Temple Kirby noted in *Media-Made Dixie: The South in the American Imagination* (1978), "southern laziness has long implied more than veranda-sitting (the gentry) and catfishing (blacks and white trash). It has meant the absence of thinking, too."

At its least appealing, climate has been used as a justification for slavery and the persistence of a social order associated with plantation life. The climatic theory of the plantation, in other words, was used to justify the resistance to social change in the South. According to sociologist Edgar T. Thompson, a critic of the climatic theory of the plantation, "a theory which makes the plantation depend upon something outside the processes of human interaction, that is, a theory which makes the plantation depend upon a fixed and static something like climate, is a theory which operates to justify an existing social order and the vested interests connected with that order. Under such a conception the problems of a plantation society can be looked upon as concerning only God who alone can control the climate, and the climatic theory turns out to be really a sort of divine-right theory of the plantation."

Relying on only one variable to evaluate the history of the South serves environmental history badly. However, discounting the importance of environment in understanding the regional and sectional Souths is equally limiting. To fully comprehend the impact of the physical environment on southerners requires an appreciation of the common physical characteristics, as well as the diversity, of the southern states and a comprehensive view of southern physiography, ecology, and the extent of human modification of natural patterns.

Physiography of the South. In popular usage, the Old South is often divided into a "Lower" South—the land of cotton and slavery, the heart of the Confederacy—and an "Upper" South—an area dominated by slaveless farmers with more ambiguous allegiances. Not only has there been an Old South, but a Deep South and several "New" Souths as well. All these designations, despite the imagery they evoke, are rather imprecise renderings of the physical South, because the region has never been a clearly defined geographical unit. This is a key to the difficulty of specifying the precise nature of the South along its borders—Delaware and Maryland to the east, West Virginia, Kentucky, and Missouri to the north, Oklahoma and Texas to the west. However, two features dominate the physical South, whether the boundaries are drawn along the Coastal Plains or the Appalachian Mountains. These landscape features are also competing influences, which often have divided rather than unified the region.

The South's coast is its most dominant physical feature. Stretching more than 3,000 miles, it falls within the Atlantic and Gulf Coastal Plains. Most of the harbors are drowned river mouths that are shallow and subject to silting. The shore is composed of sandy beaches abutted in some cases by swamps, such as Dismal Swamp in Virginia and North Carolina. Along the Mississippi River run several muddy flats. The Coastal Plain, from the Potomac River to the Rio Grande, is an elevated sea bottom with low topographic relief and many marshy tracts. Therefore, coastal altitudes are mostly below 500 feet and more than half are below 100 feet. The Coastal Plains are widest at Texas—about 300 miles—and narrow to 100 miles as they wind eastward. They comprise about one-third of the South.

A major feature of the Coastal Plains is the Mississippi River Valley, which originates in the Central Lowlands of the United States and meanders to the sea. Traditionally the South's greatest "artery of commerce," the Mississippi continually changes the landscape along its route. Wide and marshy, with muddy and sandy banks, the Mississippi has long been an economic lifeline in the South, but it has also been a physical barrier and an environmental threat because of flooding.

Before reaching the higher elevation of the mountains, the Coastal Plains connect with the Piedmont Plateau. Extending from central Alabama northward, the Piedmont Plateau is really a plain of denudation with only a few hills rising about the gently rolling landscape. The western border of the Piedmont Plateau is formed by the Blue Ridge Mountains.

West and north of the Coastal Plains lies the Appalachian system, which begins in Newfoundland and extends to central Alabama. The southern section of the system is formed by two parallel

Flavius J. Fisher*, Dismal Swamp *(1858)

belts and includes the Appalachian Mountains themselves. Historically, this range was the major barrier to east-west movement in what became the United States. The Cumberland Gap was one of very few routes through the mountains. The Appalachians gave the impression of a single geological system because of their formidable nature. In truth, the landscape varies considerably. For example, the southern Appalachians in western North Carolina and northern Georgia are various short ridges and isolated peaks separated by basins and valleys. In or near the Great Smoky Mountains and the Blue Ridge are the highest peaks of the system, including Mount Mitchell (6,684 feet), Cattail Peak (6,609 feet), Mount Guyot (6,620 feet), Mount Le Conte (6,593 feet), and Clingman's Dome (6,640 feet). Unlike the rugged and jagged Rockies, the Appalachians are rounder and substantially lower. Due in part to high humidity, weathering and erosion have shaped the Appalachian skyline. Winters are milder in the Appalachians than in the Rockies.

The northwestern and western reaches of the South—part of the Upper South and east Texas—fall within the Central Lowlands. The Central Lowlands are essentially a vast plain between the Appalachian Plateau and the Rockies. At the eastern edge, where the Lowlands join the Appalachians, the elevation is about 1,000 feet, sloping westward to an altitude of about 500 feet along the Mississippi, then rising again westward. The most distinctive feature of the Lowlands within the South is the Ozark-Ouachita section. Sometimes referred to as the Interior Highlands, this group of low mountains interrupts the monotony of the Lowland landscape. The Ozark Mountains have a drainage pattern and landscape similar to the Appalachian Plateau. South of the Ozarks, beyond the Arkansas River, lie the Ouachita Mountains. The highest point is 2,700 feet, whereas the Ozarks' peak is about 2,000 feet.

An examination of the physiography of the South suggests its diversity and uniqueness. The contrast between the Coastal Plains and the Appalachian system helps explain many of the historical differences between the Upper and Lower South. And although three-fourths of the South has an elevation of less than 1,000 feet above sea level, barriers to east-west movement in the form of the Appalachians and the Mississippi have played an important role in determining regional settlement patterns. The South's geography, however, also demonstrates the important physical connection of the region to the rest of the nation. The Coastal Plains link the South with the Atlantic Seaboard, the Appalachians with the Northeast, and the Lowlands with the Midwest and Southwest. In no way has the South been geographically isolated from the other regions of the nation.

Ecology of the South. The great majority of the South lies within the Temperate Deciduous Forest Biome (natural community), which extends from the Great Lakes to the Gulf of Mexico. It also covers a large portion of the Florida peninsula and extends west to the Ozarks. Broadleaf trees dominate the biome, but evergreens are plentiful to the extreme southern reaches. The shedding of leaves by the deciduous trees in the autumn produces dramatic changes in light conditions and provides shelter for animals. The annual rainfall in the biome ranges from 28 to 60 inches, with the greatest amount near the Gulf.

The Temperate Deciduous Biome is composed of the oak-hickory region and the magnolia-maritime region. The oak-hickory region extends along a line from New Jersey to Alabama, westward into Arkansas and Texas, and then northward to central Illinois. The magnolia-maritime region begins in the southeastern corner of Virginia and extends southward to the magnolia forest near Charleston and then continues along the coast to Houston. A southeastern pine forest runs along the Coastal Plains from North Carolina to Texas. By contrast, the low, wet outer portion of the Coastal Plains is dominated by savannas, everglades, and flatwoods. Despite human modification of the southern forests over the years, forest cover is an important endowment of the South. It has approximately 40 percent of the nation's commercial forests, including the largest portion of its hardwood reserves.

Within or adjacent to the Temperate Deciduous forest are several other natural communities in the regional South. The Mississippi River floodplain sports light-colored cottonwoods along the riverbank. To the extreme west desert or mesquite grassland of a temperate grassland biome extend into the lowlands of west Texas. The southern boundary of the warm temperate magnolia forest is near Palm Beach on the Florida east coast. The vegetation of Florida is transitional between the tropics and the temperate regions with palms, mangroves, tall grass, sedge, rubber trees, hammocks, banyans, pine, and Spanish moss.

Southern soils reflect the significance of the forest cover. The region is blanketed largely by forest soils (podzols). Lime-rich brown soils are found in the bluegrass areas and the Great Valley of Virginia. In most other areas red and yellow soils are common. Along the coast are water podzols and marsh soils, and along the river valleys dark, fertile soils brought by floods are typical. Because the South escaped the last glaciation, southern soils lack the minerals ground by the ice. Heavy rains have leached the soil of its nutrients as well, leaving large deposits of clay throughout the South. Organic material is often vaporized by the heat and the absence of sustained ground freezing traps nutrients above the ice. In large measure the South has medium- or low-grade soils, subject to erosion because of the considerable slope of the land. It is unlikely that most of the South ever had deep, fertile, heavy soils like those in the Midwest.

Despite its mediocre soils, the region possesses other important resources. Large quantities of bauxite are to be found in Arkansas; hematite iron ore near Birmingham; phosphate south of Nashville; titanium in Virginia; manganese, copper, and chromite in the mountains of eastern Tennessee and in the Carolinas. By far the most significant mineral resources are found along the fringes of the South: coal in the Appalachians and oil and natural gas in Texas, Oklahoma, and Louisiana. Sources of water have been crucial to the region. Blessed with several good waterways for inland navigation, fine ports from Houston-Galveston to the Chesapeake, and many lakes and streams, the South in recent times has faced diminishing surface-water supplies because of increased use, rapid economic growth, and pollution. The major rivers, especially the Mississippi and the Tennessee, are among the most significant natural forces for ongoing physical change in the region.

Although the climate and weather of the South vary more than popular lore would suggest, distinctive climatic features do exist. In general, the climate is rainy (except in the Southwest), the summers are hot, and the winters are mild. Compared to the rest of the nation, tornadoes, hurricanes, and fog are frequent.

East of the Rockies the climate of North America is the product of the interaction of two air masses—the continental air mass in the northern portions of Canada and the tropical maritime air mass in the Atlantic/Gulf of Mexico area. In the summer the latter is associated with high temperatures and especially high humidity. In the winter the tropical maritime air mass produces mild spells with rain and fog. Because of the interaction of these air masses, two of the three parts of North America with the most precipitation lie in the South—the southern Appalachians and the southeastern states. In the Southeast and as far west as central Texas, humid subtropical or warm temperate weather is typical. Rainfall tends to be evenly distributed among the seasons. The South does not necessarily produce "hotter" highs than other portions of the nation, but the hot spells are of greater length. About three-fourths of the South has more than 30 inches of rainfall in an average year. The hottest section in the summer is the northern half of the Gulf Coast states. Although considerable variance occurs in the climate, especially between the Coastal Plains and the Appalachian system, no part of the South is subject to prolonged cold. That fact has been vital to its emergence in recent years as an important focus of human migration.

Human Modification of the Environment. Southerners have long exhibited a fierce pride in their section and its heritage. Indeed, this pride has some environmental roots. As writer James Seay noted, "The traditional concept of the southerner as one possessing a strong attachment to the land—and, by extension, a predilection for outdoor sports, especially hunting and fishing—has not diminished appreciably."

The South's agrarian tradition—at least in days past—has accounted for much of the southern affinity for the outdoors. Unintentionally or otherwise, however, human modification of the southern environment over the years has changed the South dramatically, and not always for the better. Human modification, as much as the natural heritage, has shaped the sectional and regional South. The exploitation of forests and the impact of the agricultural system, the Civil War, urbanization, and industrialization have had major roles in transforming a once unspoiled wilderness into a complex modern society. William Faulkner's image of a wilderness South in short stories like "The Bear" is more a literary convention today than a reality in much of the South. Contemporary writers, such as James Dickey in *Deliverance*, portray the modern southerner searching for a wilderness that has vanished.

Exploitation of Forests. As late as 1600 the forests of the south Atlantic and Gulf states were probably less modified than those of the Northeast, with the exception of Virginia where the Indian population was large. In the Lowland region Indians burned forests to facilitate hunting or to favor certain game. The burning produced savanna-type vegetation in the valleys.

Settlers in the southern colonies adopted Indian burning practices. Especially in the piney woods, remote hills, and in areas of sandy soils, where hunting and herding persisted, woodburning practices endured for many years. Woodburning was first practiced not for purposes of forestry, but for hunting, grazing, and the eradication of pests. According to historian Stephen J. Pyne, "fire practices were incorporated into the fabric of frontier existence. What made the South special, however, was the confluence of economic, social, and historical events that worked to sustain this pattern of frontier economy long after it disappeared elsewhere in the United States, a pattern that created a socioeconomic environment for the continuance of woodburning." Given the persistence of using fire for pasturage and game, efforts to stop or reduce burning were slow to develop in the South.

Firing of land was also extremely important in the development of southern agriculture. Here, too, Indian methods were adopted. Agricultural fires were used to prepare sites, to manage fallow fields, to eradicate pests, and to dispose of debris. And because plantation owners acquired the best agricultural lands, smaller farmers found themselves cultivating inferior sites, including piney woods, sandy barrens, and worn-out cotton fields, where annual firing kept the pines from overtaking them. An important result of firing for agricultural purposes was the replacement of many hardwood stands with pines.

Commercial logging did not spread through the South much before the 1880s. Some harvesting of pines and hardwoods had occurred in the antebellum South, but the Appalachian hardwood region generally remained inaccessible until railroad lines were extended into the region. Forests were also spared early commercial development because of the extensive cutting taking place in the Northeast, but after 1880 commercial logging grew by leaps and bounds. The national timber industry moved in, and logging in the southern Appalachians reached its peak. By 1920 the virgin pine forests were gone and little regeneration had occurred. Not until after 1930 did most southern states give any real attention to preserving the remaining virgin forests. As professional foresters entered the region to encourage the development of new crops of timber, they met resistance from the owners of rangelands. Southern forests were too intricately woven into the fabric of the southern economy to be easily protected by modern conservation laws and practices. Clearcutting forestry methods have, since World War II, in fact, decimated the southern hardwood population, introducing a new southern monoculture—pine farms.

Mississippi timber worker, Warren County, Mississippi, 1968

Wildlife was often a casualty of the

use and abuse of southern forests. In the colonial South deer were hunted heavily as an essential source of meat. Numbers increased again after the several Indian expulsions and when cattle replaced deer in the leather trade. Hunting game for sale, however, persisted. White settlement also led to the extermination of bison east of the Mississippi. Among birds, turkey and quail were plentiful, but passenger pigeons were hunted eventually to extinction and parakeets were killed by farmers as pests or turned into pets. Predators such as wolves and black bear had bounties placed on them for threatening humans, livestock, or corn crops. Although the destruction of wildlife was not systematic, by the late 19th century many species were either declining rapidly or nearing extinction, namely the eastern elk, cougar, timber wolf, red wolf, bison, Labrador duck, Carolina parakeet, whooping crane, and ivory-billed woodpecker. However, as historian Albert E. Cowdrey has noted, "the destruction was much more than a regional phenomenon. These were, after all, the times when New Yorkers ate game shot in Minnesota, and when processing centers in Kansas City and Chicago received every week trainloads of 'ducks, geese, cranes, plovers, and prairie chickens'—a continental spoil." A revival of interest in wildlife conservation spread to the South in the 1870s, but was slow in developing over the years. When economic interests were threatened, as in the case of commercial fishing, state governments were quicker to act.

Agricultural System. Southern agriculture is generally thought of as a combination of monocultures. Although this is an overly simplistic view of a region that also practiced stockraising and mixed farming, the environmental implications of southern agriculture were most significant with respect to the staple-crop economies that emerged over the centuries. The long, hot summers in most of the South have made the growing of shallow-root crops difficult. Fodder crops, especially, have been hard to grow, limiting the effective combination of livestock and food crops that encouraged the profitability of small farms.

The notion that several staple crops—especially tobacco, sugar, rice, and cotton—were "ideal" for the southern clime ignores the pervasive problems, such as soil exhaustion and erosion, that resulted from the widespread development of these monocultures. Commercial dependence on these crops meant that immediate profit rather than long-term planning dominated the rise of the plantation system and its consequent dependence on slave labor. Commercial production of tobacco led to wasteful clearing of forests. Acreage of Tidewater plantations was increased in an attempt to counteract the low productivity of the poor soil. Exacerbating the problem of widespread and incessant planting was the draining of nitrogen and potassium. Planters were largely ignorant of the repercussions of their planting activity—and were unaware that the typical wooden plows did not cut deep enough to bring the necessary nutrients to the surface—or, at least, they exhibited little concern for their impact on the land because of the availability of new lands farther inland.

The use of fertilizers and the switch to other crops, such as wheat, eventually improved farming in Tidewater Virginia. But in the Atlantic Piedmont erosion was more likely in the weathered soil. Soil exhaustion was a chronic problem beyond the Piedmont—and not just from the planting of tobacco but also from the cultivation of corn. Overall, the South had the ignominious honor of sustaining the first large-scale soil erosion in the country, centered in the tobacco-growing regions of Virginia, Maryland, and North Carolina. The pattern continued as settlers moved west.

The cultivation of cotton and the emergence of the great cotton belt from the Carolinas to east Texas did little to reverse the pattern of soil erosion and soil exhaustion throughout the South. Over the years the cotton belt shifted, spreading westward in the 19th century as areas in the Southeast were infested with boll weevils or the soil was worn out by years of monoculture. After spreading into Texas the belt contracted again, and the western portion of cotton country was revitalized. The early cultivation of cotton in the Piedmont regions resulted in tens of thousands of gullies. Some of the gullies in Georgia were more than 150 feet deep. The long process of erosion in the Piedmont climaxed in 1920. In the years since the Civil War massive quantities of topsoil had disappeared, some estimates reaching as high as six cubic miles or more.

Both large and small landholders abused their soils, although smaller farmers may have done more damage because they had less land in reserve for rotation or lying fallow. Land policy was largely nonexistent. Nonetheless, until about 1945 cotton was still the agricultural byword in the South, and soil conservation was an unappreciated idea. Eventually extension workers, soil conservationists, and some private individuals began a slow process of educating southern farmers to terracing, contour plowing, and other techniques to avoid soil exhaustion and to improve yields.

In more recent times southern agriculture has changed dramatically. Cotton and corn areas contracted as new and localized special crops, such as soybeans and peanuts, appeared. The total area under cultivation declined as grazing returned to the South. Those staple crops that remained were grown under rotation systems as mechanization increased. Agricultural productivity returned to the South but often in new guises, such as in the fruit and truck belt of the Atlantic Coast and in the subtropical crop belt of the Gulf of Mexico. The memories of the old monocultures endure as a reminder of the hasty and shortsighted practices of the past.

Civil War. The environmental impact of war is often overlooked by scholars and other observers. It was difficult to forget that more than 600,000 people lost their lives in the Civil War, but memories soon faded about the physical devastation that the South suffered from 1861 to 1865. As John Brinckerhoff Jackson noted in his historical tour through the United States during its centennial years, the post–Civil War Reconstruction era required "the almost total reorganization of the Southern landscape—an undertaking scarcely less arduous than the creating of a brand-new landscape in the West."

The Civil War left southern cities in ruins, railroad lines ripped from the ground, plantations burned, factories and mills gutted, and it made itinerants of many southerners. Visitors were struck by the absence of fences—burned as firewood by raiding Yankees or trampled by Confederates searching for food. Other signs of human construction—bridges, trestles, even roads—were destroyed, creating an eerie sense of stillness and emptiness. Woodlands appeared in the deserted countryside where they had not existed for years; other forested areas were barren in the aftermath of battle. The urban South presented an equally depressing picture, be it the smoldering remains in Atlanta and Richmond or the deserted wharves of Charleston.

Recovery came more quickly in the major cities than in the countryside in the postwar South. In time, the physical scars of the war would disappear, but the ravages were a constant reminder that devastation need not come in the form of a hurricane, flood, or tornado. Of all human modifications on the physical environment, war was clearly the most frightening.

Industrialization and Urbanization. The slow transformation of the agrarian South into a region with a mixed economy and thriving cities may very well represent the most dramatic human modification of all. Until the 1870s southern industrialism was largely restricted to tobacco processing, textiles, and iron production. As late as World War I many southern cities had little more than regional influence. The "Sunbelt" phenomenon of the post–World War II era, however, dramatically points to the transformation made in the last 100 years.

In the New South era industrial growth was marked, especially after 1880, but it was not similar in kind or scale to what was taking place in the Northeast. The processing of agricultural goods, the manufacture of furniture, and the production of textiles were small, labor-intensive activities. Only in the manufacture of iron and steel and in the extracting of minerals did the South truly emulate northern industrial practices. Yet statistics bear out the change that was taking place in the postwar South. Even as early as the 1860s, industrial growth showed signs of change. The number of manufacturing enterprises increased 80 percent, the number of workers 30 percent, and the value of products 28 percent. Unfortunately capital investment (increase of 3 percent) and wages (up 8 percent) did not keep pace with this growth, but after the disruptions of Reconstruction had subsided, by the late 1870s, manufacturing again made an upturn.

Although this industrial growth was not impressive by the national standards of the time—in 1904 the South had about 15 percent of the nation's manufacturing establishments and 11 percent of capital invested in manufacturing—the activity could not help but provide a bridge between the monocultural activity of the past and the economic diversity of the present. In the Southeast in the 1960s, nonagricultural employment increased 45 percent, from 8.6 million jobs to 12.5 million. A good portion of this growth, however, did not come in manufacturing but in the professions, technical fields, and in the clerical area, suggesting the emergence of a vital white-collar sector in the economy. Also characteristic of nonagricultural economic growth was the dispersal rather than heavy concentration of industry. Few southern areas, therefore, physically resembled the industrial Northeast even after the infusion of an industrial capacity.

This is not to say that the physical South was little influenced by industrialization. The desire to improve inland navigation led to the transformation of the Mississippi River. The Tennessee Valley Authority virtually remade a gigantic portion of the Upper South. Greater exploitation of natural resources led to strip-mining, squandering of oil and gas resources, and all manner of pollution. Oil spills, effluents in major waterways, smoke, and smog were reminders of a newly emerging South. The creeks and rivers of much of the South were already polluted by cotton mill effluent in the 1920s and 1930s, before anyone talked of a "Sunbelt."

Urbanization of the South was probably the most dramatic aspect of the modernization and physical transformation of the region. Urban growth in most southern states outstripped the section's increase in general population between 1840 and 1860. Yet by 1900 southern states averaged only about 15 percent to 19 percent urban population. In striking contrast, by the 1970s the urban portion of the southern states averaged from 54 percent to 72 percent. The continuation of World War II prosperity into the postwar years played a large part in the emergence of the "Sunbelt" South as a vital economic, but also urban, force similar to the New West.

The environmental implications of southern urbanization are many. Certainly, technological innovations such as air-conditioning have encouraged the development of large cities and industries in a part of the country annually racked with long spells of heat and humidity. Urban sprawl, suburbanization, congestion, exploitation of available resources, and pollution are characteristic of both southern and northern cities. Competition for water resources has increased among cities and between rural and urban populations. Stream pollution, saltwater intrusion on the coast, and the reduction of water tables threaten a once abundant resource.

Industrialization and urbanization in the South in recent times point to a characteristic not associated with its antebellum past—constant change. The diversity of the southern environment imbedded in the contrast between the Coastal Plains and the Appalachian system has been magnified by the various forms of human modification over the years. In many ways these modifications have produced changes that link the South to the rest of the nation, undermining some of its unique physical characteristics. At the same time, the emergence of a "modern" South through the "Sunbelt" phenomenon suggests a region still in flux and likely to undergo a major physical transformation.

See also AGRICULTURE: Crops; Garden Patch; / Agricultural Extension Services; Boll Weevil; Fertilizer; Pest Control; ETHNIC LIFE: Indian Cultural Contributions; GEOGRAPHY articles; INDUSTRY: / Bulldozer Revolution; MYTHIC SOUTH: Garden Myth; RECREATION: Fishing; Hunting

Martin V. Melosi
University of Houston

Ralph H. Brown, *Historical Geography of the United States* (1948); Thomas D. Clark, *The Greening of the South: The Recovery of Land and Forest* (1984), *Three Paths to the Modern South: Education, Agriculture, and Conservation* (1965); James C. Cobb, *Industrialization and Southern Society, 1877–1984* (1984); Albert E. Cowdrey, *This Land, This South: An Environmental History* (1983); Carl N. Degler, *Place over Time: The Continuity of Southern Distinctiveness* (1977); Robin W. Doughty, *Feather Fashions and Bird Preservation: A Study in Nature Protection* (1975), *Wildlife and Man in Texas: Environmental Change and Conservation* (1984); Peter Farb, *Face of North America:*

The Natural History of a Continent (1963); Gilbert C. Fite, *Cotton Fields No More: Southern Agriculture, 1865–1980* (1984); David R. Goldfield, *Cotton Fields and Skyscrapers: Southern City and Region, 1607–1980* (1982); Sam B. Hilliard, *Hog Meat and Hoecake: Food Supply in the Old South, 1840–1860* (1972); Charles B. Hunt, *Physiography of the United States* (1967); John Brinckerhoff Jackson, *American Space: The Centennial Years, 1865–1876* (1972); Peter Matthiessen, *Wildlife in America* (1959); Martin V. Melosi, *Coping with Abundance: Energy and Environment in Industrial America 1820–1980* (1985); Howard W. Odum, *Southern Regions of the United States* (1936); Almon E. Parkins, *The South: Its Economic-Geographic Development* (1938); Stephen J. Pyne, *Fire in America: A Cultural History of Wildland and Rural Fire* (1982); James Seay, in *The American South: Portrait of a Culture*, ed. Louis D. Rubin, Jr. (1980); Victor E. Shelford, *The Ecology of North America* (1963); Edgar T. Thompson, *Agricultural History* (January 1941); Rupert B. Vance, *Human Geography of the South* (1932). ☆

Air-Conditioning

"Let us begin by discussing the weather, for that has been the chief agency in making the South distinctive." This was the opening line of U. B. Phillips's 1929 classic, *Life and Labor in the Old South.* In Phillips's day, environmental determinism was a powerful force in American social science; it was the age of Ellsworth Huntington and Walter Prescott Webb, when the link between climate and culture was thought to be a simple relationship of cause and effect, when the southern climate in particular was credited with producing everything from plantation slavery to the southern drawl. Such determinist views are no longer fashionable, but the connection between regional culture and climate remains an intriguing subject, one that has taken on a new dimension since the advent of air-conditioning. Ask any southerner over 30 years of age to explain why the South has changed in recent decades, and he may begin with the civil rights movement or industrialization. But sooner or later he will come around to the subject of air-conditioning. For better or worse, the air conditioner has changed the nature of southern life.

The age of air-conditioning, in the broadest sense of the term, was initiated by Dr. John Gorrie, a Florida physician who began experimenting with mechanical cooling in the 1830s. In an attempt to lower the body temperatures of malaria and yellow fever victims, he blew forced air over buckets of ice suspended from a hospital ceiling. Gorrie eventually patented a primitive ice-making machine, but the world's first true air conditioner—a machine that simultaneously cools, circulates, dehumidifies, and cleanses the air—was not invented until 1902, when Willis Haviland Carrier installed an experimental system in a Brooklyn publishing company. Carrier's invention soon spread to the South, thanks to the efforts of two young southern engineers, Stuart Cramer and I. H. Hardeman. Cramer actually coined the term "air-conditioning" in 1906, and later the same year Hardeman helped Carrier design and install the region's first air-conditioning system, at the Chronicle Cotton Mills in Belmont, N.C. By 1920 the new technology was being used as a quality-control device in a number of southern cotton and rayon mills, paper mills, cigar factories, tobacco stemming rooms, breweries, and bakeries. Prior to the 1920s air-conditioning in the South was restricted almost entirely to industrial uses. The major exceptions were a Baltimore hotel and Montgomery's elegant Empire Theatre.

This situation began to change in 1923 when Carrier's invention of the centrifugal compressor ushered in the age of "comfort cooling." By the mid-1930s air-conditioned movie theaters and railway cars had become common. But the movement of air-conditioning into other areas of southern life was more gradual. Although a sprinkling of air-conditioned department stores, office buildings, homes, hospitals, drugstores, barber shops, and restaurants could be found across the region by the late 1930s, air-conditioning remained an oddity until after World War II. During the 1950s air-conditioning became an immutable part of southern life. After the air conditioner invaded the home (the inexpensive, efficient window unit appeared in 1951) and the automobile, there was no turning back. By the mid-1970s air-conditioning had made its way into more than 90 percent of the South's high-rise office buildings, banks, apartments, and railroad passenger coaches; more than 80 percent of its automobiles, government buildings, and hotels; approximately two-thirds of its homes, stores, trucks, and hospital rooms; roughly half of its classrooms; and at least a third of its tractors. The South of the 1970s could claim air-conditioned shopping malls, domed stadiums, greenhouses, grain elevators, chicken coops, aircraft hangars, crane cabs, offshore oil rigs, cattle barns, steel mills, and drive-in movies and restaurants. Even the Alamo had central air, and in Houston alone the cost of air-conditioning in 1980 exceeded the gross national product of several Third-World nations.

Not all southerners live in air-conditioned homes, ride in air-conditioned cars, or work in air-conditioned buildings. Among rural and working-class blacks, poor whites, migrant laborers, and mountaineers, air-conditioned living is not the norm. Nevertheless, in varying degrees virtually all southerners have been affected, directly or indirectly, by the technology of climate control. Air-conditioning has influenced everything from architecture to sleeping habits and has contributed to the erosion of several regional traditions, most notably cultural isolation, agrarianism, romanticism, poverty, neighborliness, a strong sense of place, and a relatively slow pace of life. The net result has been a dramatic decline in regional distinctiveness. In combination with other historical forces—the civil rights movement, advances in communication and transportation technology, and economic and political change—the air conditioner has greatly accelerated what John Egerton has called "the Americanization of Dixie."

To begin with, the air conditioner has helped to reverse an almost century-long southern tradition of net out-migration. It was more than a coincidence that in the 1950s, the decade when air-conditioning first engulfed the South, the region's net out-migration was much smaller than in previous decades; and that in the 1960s, for the first time since the Civil War, the South experienced more in-migration than out-migration. The 1970 census, according to the *New York Times*, was "The Air Conditioned Census." "The humble air conditioner," the *Times* concluded, "has been a powerful influence in circulating people as well as air in this country. . . . Its availability explains why increasing numbers of Americans find it comfortable to live year round in the semitropical heat." The 1960s was only the beginning; between 1970 and 1978, 7 million people migrated to the South, twice the number that left the region. By the end of the decade, the Sunbelt era was in full swing. Abetted by millions of tourists, northern migrants have brought new ideas and new lifestyles to the South, disrupting the region's longstanding cultural isolation. Thanks in part to air-conditioning, the southern population has become increasingly heterogeneous, and the concept of the Solid South—long a bulwark of regional mythology—has all but faded from view.

Air-conditioning has also played a key role in the industrialization of the modern South. In addition to bringing new factories and businesses to the region, it has helped to improve working conditions and increase productivity. Economic growth, partially induced by a better work environment, has led to a rising standard of living for many southern families; per capita income in the South has risen from 52 percent of the national average in 1930 to almost 90 percent today, and air-conditioning is one of the reasons why.

Air-conditioning has also fostered the urbanization of the South: by encouraging industrialization and population growth; by accelerating the development of large public institutions, such as universities, museums, hospitals, sports arenas, and military bases; by facilitating the efficient use of urban space and opening the city to vertical, high-rise development; and by influencing the development of distinctively urban forms of architecture. Without air-conditioning, skyscrapers and high-rise apartments would be less prevalent; urban populations would be smaller; cities would be more spread out; and the physical and architectural differences between inner cities and suburbs would be less striking. Although the region's agrarian legacy is still a force to be reckoned with, in the air-conditioned South the locus of power and activity has moved to Main Street.

In a related development, climate control has altered southern attitudes toward nature and technology. Air-conditioning has taken its toll on the traditional "folk culture," which, as David Potter once pointed out, "survived in the South long after it succumbed to the onslaught of urban-industrial culture elsewhere." The South has always been an elemental land of blood, sweat, and tears—a land where personalism and a curious mixture of romance and realism have prevailed. At the very least, climate control has taken the edge off this romantic element. As the southern climate has been artificially tamed, pastoralism has been replaced by technological determinism. Human interaction with the natural environment has decreased significantly since the advent of air-conditioning. To confirm this point, one has only to walk down almost any southern street on a hot summer afternoon, listen to the whir of compressors, and look in vain for open windows or front porch society.

In many cases, the porch is not simply empty, it is not even there. To the dismay of many southerners, air-conditioning has impinged upon a rich tradition of vernacular architecture. From the "dogtrot cabin" with its central breezeway, to the grand plantation with its wraparound porch, to the tin-roofed "cracker" house up on blocks, traditional southern architecture has been an ingenious conspiracy of passive cooling and cross-ventilation. The catalogue of structural techniques developed to tame the hot, humid southern climate is long and varied: high ceilings, thin walls, long breezeways, floors raised three or more feet off the ground, steeply pitched roofs vented from top to bottom, open porches with broad eaves that blocked the slanting sun, massive doors and windows, which sometimes stretched from floor to ceiling, louvered jalousies, transoms placed above bedroom doors, dormers, groves of shade trees blanketing the southern exposure, houses situated to capture prevailing breezes, and so on. Historically these techniques have been an important element of a distinctively southern aesthetic and social milieu. But with the proliferation of residential air-conditioning, vernacular architecture gave way to the modern tract house, with its low ceilings, small windows, and compact floor plan.

Residential air-conditioning has not only affected architectural form; it has also influenced the character of southern family life. As families have withdrawn into air-cooled private spaces, interaction with grandparents, aunts, uncles, cousins, not to mention friends and neighbors, has often suffered. As more than one observer has noted, the vaunted southern tradition of "visiting" has fallen on hard times in recent years.

The air conditioner has also had an impact on the basic rhythm of southern life. To a significant degree air-conditioning has modulated the daily and seasonal rhythms, which were once an inescapable part of southern culture. Thanks to air-conditioning, the "siesta mentality" has declined, and the summer sun is no longer the final arbiter of daily and yearly planning. In addition to these mundane changes, the declining importance of climatic and seasonal change may have profound long-term consequences, eventually dulling the southerner's sense of time and perhaps even his sense of history.

A more immediate threat is the air-conditioner's assault on the South's strong "sense of place." Southerners, more than most other Americans, have tied themselves to local geography. Their lives and identities have been rooted in a particular county, town, neighborhood, or homestead. Yet in recent years, thanks in part to air-conditioning, the southern landscape has been overwhelmed by an almost endless string of look-alike chain stores, tract houses, glassed-in high-rises, and perhaps most importantly, enclosed shopping malls. The modern shopping mall is the cathedral of air-conditioned culture, and it symbolizes the placelessness of the New South.

See also FOLKLIFE: House Types; / Porches; HISTORY AND MANNERS: Manners

Raymond Arsenault
University of South Florida

Raymond Arsenault, *Journal of Southern History* (November 1984); Raymond B. Becker, *John Gorrie, M. D.: Father of Air Conditioning and Mechanical Refrigeration* (1972); Daniel Boorstin, *The Americans: The Democratic Experience* (1973); Robert Friedman, *American Heritage* (August–September 1984); Margaret Ingalls, *Willis Haviland Carrier: Father of Air Conditioning* (1952). ☆

Animals

The woods and waters of the American South provide a rich habitat for the fauna of its lands, and this varied animal life has nourished the needs of peoples who have lived there. With its large populations of birds, mammals, fish, reptiles, and amphibians, the South was a bountiful wilderness of mixed forests, pine barrens, swamps, grasslands, and fish-bearing streams in the era before settlement. Its extensive coastline provided access to the marine wealth of the Atlantic Ocean and Gulf of Mexico. The growing presence of man in the South altered the biotic capabilities of the area to support wildlife. With Indians and white settlers utilizing the fauna of the region as a major source of food, the populations of specific animal species were subsequently reduced. In the South, as in the rest of the nation, the flora and fauna of an area were a larder of nondomestic foods upon which Indians and white settlers depended.

As white settlement increased its pace in southern states, the face of the land was noticeably altered. The development of agriculture in the South and the consequent clearing of land reduced the habitat for some animals and created new microhabitats for others. Civilization's incessant campaign against coyotes, wolves, bears, and cougars reduced their numbers and permitted the animals upon which they preyed to increase their populations. Deer, rabbit, and quail were frequently helped by the noncontiguous patterns of land clearing and the second growth vegetation that developed. While bears, wolves, and cougars found the presence of humans detrimental, deer found increased food, rabbits dined upon a variety of new crops, and the quail increased their numbers as they fed upon domestic grains. These animals, and others, learned to live with civilization and to be nourished by the fruits of newly planted fields.

Although the buffalo, the American bison, lived in historic times in all the southern states except Florida, by the early 18th century it was becoming rare in the southeastern states and was increasingly confined primarily to western lands. The buffalo did not play the crucial role in the evolution of the South that it played in the development of the trans-Mississippi West. The whitetail deer assumed the role of the buffalo in the South and became an antlered commissary for Indians and settlers. It provided them with meat for food; hides for shirts, moccasins, and gloves; and horns for implements and knife handles. In America from the 16th century to the present the whitetail deer has ranked only below cattle and sheep as an animal useful to man. Its milk contains three times the protein and butterfat of a dairy cow's milk, and vain attempts were made to domesticate deer for milk production. During World War II, the nation consumed millions of pounds of deer meat as America stretched its limited meat rations.

Remarkably adept at increasing its numbers, the whitetail has been estimated to have once reached a population of 40 million throughout its natural ranges on this continent. When tobacco prices declined in the late 17th and early 18th centuries, the trade in deerskins increased, providing substantial economic activity for the developing region.

Trappers and traders in deerskins entered the Mississippi Valley and the lands along the Gulf Coast. From 1765 to 1773 Georgia exported 200,000 pounds of deerskins annually. As with the buffalo in the latter half of the 19th century, they were slain primarily for their hides with most of their meat left rotting upon the ground. Confronted by the reality of a declining resource, Virginia, North Carolina, and South Carolina in the 18th century passed legislation that limited unrestrained hunting. Seasons were closed, dog packs were not permitted, fire and night hunting were forbidden, and the meat of a deer could not be left upon the ground. By the 1770s every southern colony had passed laws protecting game, with deer receiving special attention. Writing of deer, John James Audubon remarked that the "tender, juicy, savoury, and above all digestible qualities of its flesh are well known and venison is held in highest esteem from the camp of the backwoodman to the luxurious tables of the opulent." In the South, the population of whitetail deer was probably more than 6 million in the years immediately prior to the Civil War. With its capacity to adapt itself to a variety of habitats and to increase its numbers through its remarkable fertility, the whitetail will maintain itself in the South as long as states preserve a balanced hunting season for this graceful species.

The capacity of deer populations to exceed the resources of their immediate habitat is well known. The mountain lion, or cougar, or puma, provided an ideal check on deer populations in the South until hunting reduced the numbers of this beautiful animal. Playful and secretive, it once was found in all the southern states. Today it is confined primarily to Florida. In spite of popular belief that it frequently preyed upon humans, its principal food has been deer. When settlers began to introduce pigs, sheep, calves, and horses into the South, those animals fell prey to the mountain lion. Presently an endangered species, this wild animal has an unsure future in the South.

Still common in the forests, swamps, and mountainous areas of all southern states, the black bear has been hunted since the colonial period. Omnivorous in its diet, it is a vegetarian throughout much of the year, although it is always willing to dine upon carrion or any animal it can catch. While agile, it does not usually possess the speed necessary to bring down a deer. Indians and settlers hunted the bear for its meat, oil, and hide. Its lengthy two-year breeding cycle usually produces two cubs, but its low reproductive rate makes it susceptible to overhunting.

Squirrels and rabbits have historically augmented the diets of Indians, blacks, and whites in the South, and in the 18th and 19th centuries they were important additions to southern meals. The gray squirrel with its characteristic white-bordered tail is a favorite target for southern hunters. Among the most agile of the tree squirrels, it prefers a habitat of hardwood forests where it feeds upon acorns and hickory nuts, usually foraging within 200 yards of its den or nest. Audubon observed that the gray squirrel's occasional nocturnal activities made it easy prey to the great horned owl.

The fox squirrel is also common in the South and often shares the same range as the gray squirrel. It is larger than the gray squirrel and varies in color from a reddish, yellowish rust to a gray shade. In the darker phases, it has a white nose the gray squirrel lacks. It is also characterized by its large head and is less graceful than other tree squirrels. Its preferred habitat is old growth forests of oak, longleaf pine, or the fringes of cypress swamps.

The most graceful squirrel of the southern states is the southern flying squirrel. Although it is the smallest and most carnivorous of the tree squirrels, these are not its only distinguishing characteristics. It is nocturnal and sometimes sleeps and eats while hanging by its claws upside down. Stretching the loose skin of its white stomach by extending its four feet, it can glide up to 150 feet. Intrigued by this small gentle animal, southerners have often kept them as pets.

Equally gentle in its habits is the cottontail rabbit. The most common rabbit in America, the Eastern Cottontail played a substantial role in the dietary history of the South. It is the most numerous of all southern game mammals. In the 19th century it was frequently trapped by slaves and became an important addition to their diet. Adapting well to a habitat altered by man, the cottontail continues to prosper in the South although most die before they are a year old.

The opossum, the only marsupial in North America, is an interesting and significant member of the fauna of the South. Living easily in the presence of civilization, it has an omnivorous diet that often includes dead animals and that allows it to maintain itself in various habitats. Seldom exceeding 12 pounds in weight, this nocturnal, gray, coarse-furred animal has a long, scaly, prehensile tail and is easily "treed" by hunters with dogs. When frightened, it feigns death, becomes rigid, and "plays possum." In the 19th and early 20th centuries, opossums were a favorite southern food. Easily captured, they were then caged and fed bread, sweet potatoes, or vegetables to improve their taste before they themselves became the meal.

Birds play an important role in the fauna of the South, gracing the region with the beauty of their songs, color, and activity. More species of birds can be found here than in any other region of the nation, and the South is privileged to bear witness yearly to the pageantry of migration. Numerous species breed regularly in southern states, including wrens, warblers, sparrows, vultures, hawks, owls, woodpeckers, tanagers, vireos, doves, turkeys, and quail. The mockingbird is closely identified with the human culture of the South. Some birds once common in the South, such as the passenger pigeon and Carolina parakeet, have become extinct. Other southern birds—the ivory-billed woodpecker, whooping crane, brown pelican, bald eagle, and Everglade kite—are endangered or threatened species.

The passenger pigeon once filled the skies of some southern states with numbers that defy description. The dedicated Scottish naturalist Alexander Wilson calculated that he saw a flock of passenger pigeons a mile in breadth and 240 miles in length. It took four hours for this great flock to pass before him. While passenger pigeons contributed significantly to the diet of the rural poor in the 18th and 19th centuries, their numbers were somewhat reduced in the Deep South. Pigeons were cooked in a variety of fashions and preserved in fat and by pickling and drying. Their fat was used for cooking and as a base for soap and their feathers were used for mattress ticking. Some pigeons were used as feed for hogs. This 16½-inch bird, which flew so gracefully through the skies, gained for itself the title of "blue meteor." Despite its speed and grace, it was easy prey for hunters. In 1914 the last of the species died. The cattle egret is a species that recently migrated to the South from Africa by way of South America. Each summer their flocks migrate north from Central America and nest in the Deep South. They are frequently seen devouring insects on the backs of cattle, and at times the white-plumed birds fill trees like blossoms.

Wild turkeys and quail are still important southern game birds. The turkey has been pursued for almost three centuries. Reaching a height of up to 40 inches, these gregarious birds roost in trees but nest and feed upon the ground. Early travelers commented upon the indifference these birds showed to human presence, but once they began to be hunted they became among the most wary animals of the South. Their eggs, flesh, and feathers were used by Indians and early settlers. By 1900 the turkey's numbers were quite small, but game management practices, which emphasized seasonal protection and maintenance of habitat, have allowed their numbers to increase in southern states.

Considerably more diminutive, but equally tasty, is the bobwhite quail. Less than 10½ inches in height, it is the smallest of the nation's quail. It often congregates in coveys of up to 30 birds, which explode with a characteristic burst of energy and frenetic fluttering when flushed. In the early 1930s, it has been estimated, 10 million bobwhites were taken each year. Today, they flourish in southern farmlands and scrub areas.

Southern lakes, rivers, bayous, and coastal waters nourish an abundance of marine and aquatic life. In freshwaters, bass, catfish, sunfish, and crappie are important sport fish; in the coastal waters, pompano, tarpon, snook, bonefish, snappers, bluefish, mackerel, shark, and sailfish attract anglers. Commercially, shrimp, oysters, and crabs are still significant products of the Gulf of Mexico.

Although Mark Twain's Huckleberry Finn caught a catfish that was as big as a man and "weighed over two hundred pounds," no documented southern catfish has yet attained this size. A blue cat caught at St. Louis weighed 150 pounds. Although 26 species of catfish may be found in the waters of the South, few reach the size of the blue catfish. Channel cats, bullheads, flatheads, and yellow cats are still pursued eagerly by southern anglers; and both commercially and as sport fish, catfish are important inhabitants of southern waters.

Praised repeatedly for its fighting abilities, the largemouth bass is the most popular freshwater gamefish in the nation. Found in lakes, bayous, and ponds, specimens of over 20 pounds are occasionally caught. Largemouth bass energetically strike artificial lures and are pursued diligently by southern anglers. Many bass tournaments are organized yearly to catch this exciting fish.

In the tropical saltwaters of the Gulf of Mexico, sport and commercial fish appear in large numbers. Great variety exists in the species that can be caught, and each year millions of anglers seek to harvest the products of this marine realm. The most exciting gamefish of the world's waters is the tarpon. Reaching lengths of up to eight feet and weights of over 300 pounds, this fish has long been praised for its strength, skill, agility, and fighting ability. From the west coast of Florida to the waters off south Texas, the explosive leaps of the silver king when hooked have captured the imagination of anglers.

The southern environment has sustained a variety of reptiles and amphibians. The American alligator is found exclusively within the South. It once was common along the Atlantic and Gulf coasts, from North Carolina south to Florida and west to Texas, but hunting for sport and commercial use of its hides has greatly reduced the alligator population. From early frontier days, gator killing was a popular sport. The alligator's large size and menacing shape seemed to make him fair game. The American crocodile has had a more limited range, mainly in south Florida, and was never large in numbers in the South. The Carolina anole is a slender bright green lizard known as the American chameleon because its coloring changes in different situations.

No family of North American salamanders is distinctively southern, yet many species can be found limited to specific regions of the South—the ringed salamander of the Ozark and Ouachita mountains, the flatwoods salamander of the Atlantic and Gulf coasts, and the hellbender of southern rivers. The largest toad in the South (*B. marinus*) is not native to the region but was introduced from South America to help control insects. Frogs found in the South include the leopard frog, the green frog, the eastern spadefoot frog, the carpenter frog, the pig frog, and the river frog. The best-known frog in the South may be the bullfrog since the distinctive call of the male punctuates the southern night. Its legs have been a prized food delicacy, leading to attempts at setting up frog farms. Turtles found in the South include the pond slider (the familiar dime-store turtle), the river cooter, and the common snapping turtle. The alligator snapping turtle is the largest freshwater turtle in the world; its languid movements allow green algae to grow on its shell. The gopher tortoise burrows underground along the southern coasts when temperatures become too high.

Four kinds of venomous snakes reside in the South—rattlesnakes, copperheads, cottonmouths, and coral snakes. Among rattlers, the eastern diamondback, which can reach a length of eight feet, and the canebreak rattler are found only in the South. The copperhead feeds on small animals and is rarely seen by humans, whom it avoids. The cottonmouth is also called the water moccasin. It is an aggressive reptile, found near swamps, rice fields, lakes, and rivers. Its bite is particularly dangerous, and it is fond of climbing trees and then dropping off the limbs when frightened. The eastern coral snake is found in the woods and grasses from the East Coast to Texas. It is among the most colorful of reptiles because of its ringed markings. Most southern snakes are nonvenomous and have been looked upon kindly by humans for keeping down the numbers of animal predators. The eastern indigo snake grows to eight feet in length and is the largest snake in North America. It is frequently seen at roadside snake farms in the Deep South, sometimes advertised as a cobra. The rainbow snake is found in swamps along the coast. Other reptiles found in the South include the redbellied mud snake, the scarlet coral snake, racers, eastern worm snakes, rat snakes, king snakes, water snakes, milk snakes, and hognose snakes.

Since the time of early American Indian societies, animals have profoundly influenced human culture in the South. Animals, especially birds and reptiles, have long been dominant design motifs in native American pottery in the region, reflecting the importance of serpent and bird symbolism in the Indian's belief system. Pottery effigies of the opossum, snake, deer, cougar, and assorted birds appeared in prehistoric Indian cultures in south Georgia, and examples have often been found at burial sites in the Gulf Coast area. Indian shell art in the Southeast included iconographic representations of such animals as rattlesnakes, woodpeckers, and spiders. Animals were central symbols of Indian religion, and objects such as eagle feathers and swan wings had ritual importance. Indian folklore included stories illustrating the personalities of various animals, such as the Choctaw tale "Why the Possum Grins."

Blacks and whites have similarly used animals in the culture they built in the South. Blacks brought to the New World an African tradition of animal tales about lions, elephants, and monkeys; those animals, as well as animals encountered by the slaves in the New World, appeared in black folktales. African omens and signs were altered to fit American fauna. Animals played a role in black folk medicine. The plantation conjurer might wear a snake skin around his neck, or carry a petrified frog in one pocket and a dead lizard in the other. A large body of black folklore related the stories of humanized animals such as Brer Rabbit and Brer Fox. African and American Indian prototypes for these trickster tales have been discovered, but, whatever their origins, most of these animal folktales suggested how clever slaves outsmarted their masters.

There is also a rich tradition among southern blacks, whites, and Indians of folk sayings and beliefs about animals. In Louisiana, for example, if a dog howls with his nose in the earth some people believe a fire will occur; if a rooster crows at the back door, it means death; if animals in the woods and swamps are unusually noisy, then it will rain soon. Black children have even incorporated the snake into a children's game ("Black snake, black snake, where are you hiding?").

In the folk arts and crafts of the whites of southern Appalachia animals emerge, as in Indian and black art, as a major design motif in wood carving, quilting, pottery, basketmaking, and toymaking. Animals are the central figures of Anglo-American folksongs such as "Froggie Went a Courtin'," "Raccoon," "Groundhog," "Little Sparrow," and "Bear Went over the Mountain." Again, as with Indians and blacks, animals fulfilled for mountain and rural whites in the South a variety of practical and symbolic functions. They served as a direct source of food and clothing, as an economic resource from trading in animal products, as an ingredient in the prevention and treatment of disease and illness, and as figures in folk art and lore. One group of Appalachian whites even made serpents the ritual center of a snake handler's religion.

In the modern South animals have figured in the musical and literary traditions of the region. Blues singers, for example, apply animal comparisons to themselves through lyrics such as "the

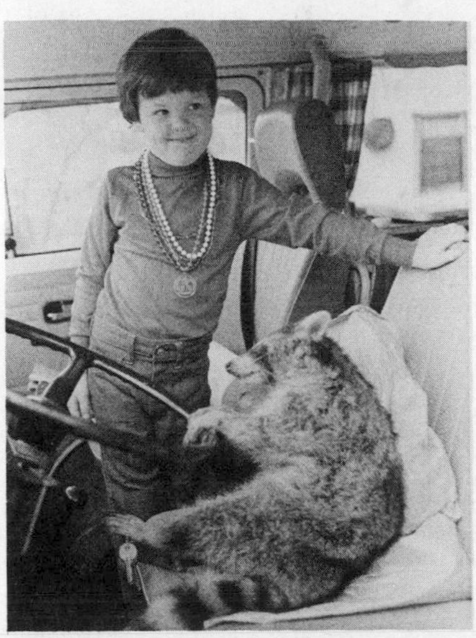

Child and animal friend, Vicksburg, Mississippi, 1977

rattlesnakin' daddy who wants to rattle all the time," the "black wolf that hollers," or the "rootin' ground hog who roots both night and day." Southern writers generally see animals the same way rural people have over the years, as simply part of the land, beings encountered as part of normal living. Their portrayal of animals is rooted in familiarity. Marjorie Kinnan Rawlings raises her hat when she sees the water moccasin, which once refrained from biting her nervous horse. William Faulkner used an animal for what critics regard as one of his most profound tales, "The Bear." He conveyed an almost mystical awareness of the relationship between man and animal in the southern woods, an attitude rooted in American Indian belief. For Faulkner's southern hunters, there is great respect for the animals hunted, because they discover an identity between themselves and their prey. Harry Crews captures the drama of the rattlesnake roundup, a southern subcultural ritual, in his novel *A Feast of Snakes* (1976).

See also FOLKLIFE: Folk Medicine; RECREATION: Fishing; Hunting

Phillip Drennon Thomas
Wichita State University

Henry Hill Collins, *Complete Field Guide to American Wildlife* (1959); Albert E. Cowdrey, *This Land, This South: An Environmental History* (1983); Gilbert C. Fite, *Cotton Fields No More: Southern Agriculture, 1865–1980* (1984); Sam B. Hilliard, *Hog Meat and Hoecake: Food Supply in the Old South, 1840–1860* (1972); David Starr Jordan and Barton Warren Everman, *American Food and Game Fishes* (1902); Howard W. Odum, *Southern Regions of the United States* (1936); Olin Sewall Pettingill, Jr., *A Guide to Bird Finding East of the Mississippi* (1977); Arlie W. Schorger, *The Passenger Pigeon: Its Natural History and Extinction* (1955), *The Wild Turkey: Its History and Domestication* (1966); Walter P. Taylor, ed., *The Deer of North America: The White-Tailed Mule and Black-Tailed Deer, Genus "Odocoileus," Their History and Management* (1956). ☆

Climate and Weather

Scholars and other observers have long seen the South's climate and weather as the key to understanding its people. James McBride Dabbs saw in the violence of southern thunderstorms a parallel for the violence of the region's people, nurturing the tension that demanded release. He called the weather a "demi-god." Wilbur J. Cash portrayed the southern climate creating "a cosmic conspiracy against reality in favor of romance." Clarence Cason, in *90° in the Shade* (1935), used the weather to explain the southerner's slow talk and movement. Sociologist Rupert B. Vance blamed the prevalence of hookworm in the South partly on the warm climate, which encouraged people to go shoeless and thus expose themselves to infection through the feet. He also argued that barns in the South were not as tightly constructed as those in New England because southerners did not have the incentive of the harsh northern winters. Certainly, the architecture of the South—with its use of high ceilings and tall windows, with its porches, galleries, verandas, and dogtrot breezeways, all to promote summer cooling—has testified to the southerner's awareness of the weather's importance in terms of daily living.

The warm, humid climate, long growing season, and abundant moisture of most of the South have indeed had a far-reaching impact on the region's economy and culture. Much of the South's early history involved the raising of agricultural products for export. Even in Texas, where the climate of the northern and western two-thirds of the state differs dramatically from the rest of the South, conditions proved ideal for large livestock operations. The southern climate has helped to make agricultural pursuits profitable. Southerners also have had to work to overcome the disadvantages imposed upon them by their climate. The hot and humid weather that produced unhealthy conditions took many an early southerner's life. Advances in medicine, architecture, and technology have curbed the outbreak of disease, permitted the construction of artificially cooled environments, and helped to create a healthy environment in which to live.

The South is divided into three large climate regions: the southern Plains and Lowlands, the Middle Atlantic Lowlands, and the Appalachian Mountains. The largest of these three is the southern Plains and Lowlands, a vast area including the states of Texas, Georgia, Florida, and South Carolina. The area inland from the Gulf and Atlantic coastlines has a continental climate featuring cold winters, warm to hot summers, and great extremes of temperature. Coastal regions are modified by the warm waters of the Gulf of Mexico and the Atlantic. Winters there are relatively humid and mild, summers very humid and warm. The southern portion of Florida has a special subtropical climate marked by dominating northwest tradewinds that differentiate it from the rest of the South.

As a whole the climate of the southern Plains and Lowlands is influenced by the interaction between strong, cold, and dry polar air masses from the interior and warm, moist maritime air masses from the Atlantic and, especially, from the Gulf. In winter the cold inland air is heavier and is drawn toward the warmer, lighter air over the water. This situation allows cold winter storms to penetrate, at times, as far as the coastal regions. When this occurs there can be freezes as far south as central Florida. In summer the inland air mass is warmer than the one over the ocean, and a reverse flow occurs that carries moist maritime air northward and provides a major source of precipitation for the interior. Along the Atlantic Coast precipitation is carried by southerly and easterly winds off the ocean. The intense summer heat of inland areas helps produce violent tornadoes and thunderstorms. Coastal areas are exposed to hurricanes with strong tides, considerable rain, and high winds.

With the exception of extreme southern Texas and Florida, temperatures in January range from a mean maximum of 70° to a mean minimum of 20° (in north Texas). In general there can be 0 to 30 days along the coast when temperatures fall below 32° and as many as 90 days in more northerly and westerly areas. In southern Texas and Florida temperatures range on average in January from 50° to 80° and days below 32° are very rare. July temperatures for this region range from 70° to 100° inland and from 70° to 90° on the immediate coast. The number of days with temperatures above 90° ranges from 60 to 120. Growing seasons for the most southerly parts of the region have a mean length of 330 days, though the most northern portions of Texas and Arkansas have growing seasons as short as 200 days.

Yearly snowfall accumulations decrease from north to south. In far northern regions three feet of snow is a normal yearly total while it rarely falls in coastal areas. With the exception of Atlantic coastal areas and Texas, yearly precipitation accumulations range from 48″ to 64″ and in scattered locations along the Gulf Coast may reach as high as 100″. Along the Atlantic Coast there is less precipitation with yearly means of 32″ to 48″. In Texas the amount of yearly precipitation decreases from east to west with a high in eastern coastal areas of 56″ and a low of 8″ at El Paso.

Humidity levels are high for this entire region except in western Texas. Winter levels range from 60 to 85 percent and summer readings average over 90 percent. In more northern and western regions humidity levels are somewhat decreased, with El Paso having summer levels of only 60 to 70 percent.

The remaining two climate regions of the South are climatically connected to each other. The Middle Atlantic Lowlands comprise an approximately 200-mile-wide strip along the coastlines of North Carolina and Virginia. The Appalachian Mountain region is an upland area that extends northeastward from Georgia and includes eastern Tennessee and western North Carolina and Virginia. The mountain peaks, averaging from 2,000 to 4,000 feet above sea level, act as a partial barrier to air masses moving in from the west. Although some fronts cross the mountains and head to the coast, others are forced north and east away from the Middle Atlantic Lowlands. Other fronts are pushed South into South Carolina, Georgia, and Florida. When the latter occurs in winter, Atlantic coastal areas in the southern Plains and Lowlands climate region may be colder than coastal Virginia or North Carolina. As air masses approach the mountains from the west, they are forced to rise and often lose their moisture, producing considerable rain and snow for the western slopes. The Atlantic coastal region and the eastern slopes of the Appalachian chain receive their moisture from maritime air masses moving ashore from the Atlantic. Occasionally snow reaches these areas from air masses that pass over the mountain barrier. Coastal areas are exposed to sometimes destructive hurricanes.

Temperatures in these two regions range from annual mean minimums of 20° in winter to summer highs in the 90s. Along the coast there are from 30 to 90 days with temperatures below 32°, whereas in the mountains there may be as many as 150 days with below freezing temperatures. On the coast more humidity is typical (around 90 percent in summer). Humidity levels are relatively low in mountainous areas. Great extremes of both temperature and humidity occur as one moves from mountain valleys to higher elevations. Annual precipitation amounts range from 32″ to 48″ in coastal areas to as much as 64″ in some mountain locations.

Although numerous old weather records are available for the South, no climate reconstructions have been made. However, from studies conducted on other regions of North America, one can deduce the climatic changes that have taken place in the South. Considerable evidence suggests that a period of increased cold weather and variable temperatures and precipitation greeted the first Europeans to reach the American coast. Called the Little Ice Age, it lasted until the last third of the 19th century. In the South this period was probably marked by more outbreaks of cold, freezing weather in Gulf coastal regions and somewhat cooler temperatures in northern, western, and mountain areas. In this century there has been a gradual warming trend and a relative decrease in variable weather, until the late 1940s. Thereafter climatic conditions have remained fairly stable.

Talking about the weather has always been a favorite southern pastime. The region's folklore tradition contains a body of sayings on the weather, geared toward predicting it. The wider the stripes on a caterpillar's back, the colder the winter. A row of dark spots on a goose bone also means a harsh winter. Some of these sayings originated in Africa, some in Europe, and others with American Indians. The thicker an onion skin, the colder the winter is a Deep South regional saying found in Georgia, Mississippi, and Alabama, and similar proverbs about the weather can be found in other subregions of the South.

A thermometer and a cola—southern icons, Reganton, Mississippi, 1975

Southern writers have absorbed this interest in climate. Critic Malcolm Cowley has noted of William Faulkner that "no other American writer takes such delight in the weather," but Faulkner was merely typical of southern writers in this regard. "That's the one trouble with this country," says Dr. Peabody in *As I Lay Dying* (1930), "everything, weather, all hangs on too long." But it was not even just southern writers who noted the weather's importance. Henry Adams wrote in *The Education of Henry Adams* (1907) of his visit to the South, whose people he portrayed negatively but whose climate left him enthralled. He viscerally recalled "the May sunshine and shadow," "the thickness of foliage and the heavy smells," "the sense of atmosphere," and "the brooding indolence of a warm climate and a negro population."

The changing South can be seen in the modern southern attitude toward weather. Historian Francis Butler Simkins once noted that a key change in the South had been "the disappearance of the fear of the hot climate inherited from European ancestors." Technology had much to do with this through the invention of artificial ice and refrigeration; air-conditioning has had a profound role in freeing southerners of the climate's debilitating effects. Climate-related diseases such as malaria, yellow fever, and hookworm have been all but eliminated. Southerners, even more than other Americans, wear light and loose garments. "The South has learned to regard the sun as a beneficent god instead of a cruel tyrant," concluded Simkins. The southern attitude toward beauty and health now emphasizes that a brown skin is more attractive than a fair one. This is a true aesthetic revolution for a people as racially conscious as southern whites, but it also reflects a different attitude toward climate and weather than earlier in southern history.

William R. Baron
Northern Arizona University

John L. Baldwin, *Climates of the United States* (1973); Lorin Blodget, *Climatology of the United States* (1857); James C. Bonner, in *Writing Southern History: Essays in Historiography in Honor of Fletcher M. Green*, ed. Arthur S. Link and Rembert W. Patrick (1965); David Hackett Fischer, *Journal of Interdisciplinary History* (Spring 1980); Hubert H. Lamb, *Climate, History and the Modern World* (1982); W. J. Maunder, *The Value of the Weather* (1970); Edgar T. Thompson, *Agricultural History* (January 1941); U.S. Department of Agriculture, *Climate and Man* (1941). ☆

Endangered Species

Through millions of millennia, the actions of climate, rainfall, and other agents of geological change have sculpted in the American South a rich and diverse topography. From the unique coral islands that form the Florida Keys to the expansive Delta of the Mississippi River with its wilderness of bayous to the great pine forests with their mixed stands of hardwoods, this area's distinctive habitat has nourished a rich and diverse flora and fauna. White settlement in the region led to a gradual but sustained alteration of the natural setting in which southern wildlife maintained itself. The rapid pace of industrialization in the South in the 20th century further altered the habitat. The reduction of virgin forests, alteration of waterways, introduction of domestic prey species, and consumption of land through urban development have encroached decade after decade upon the habitat of the South's wildlife. All of these developments have biologically impoverished the natural environment for every species but man and have demonstrated the fragility of ecosystems.

In every southern state wildlife is under pressure with some species threatened, some endangered, and some extinct. "Endangered species" are those species in danger of becoming extinct in wild, natural environments. "Threatened species" are those species that will become endangered if present conditions are not altered. In the South, as in other regions of the nation, animal species became extinct or endangered through the alteration and destruction of habitat, competition with introduced species, predation, disease, or through the more direct pressure of unrestrained hunting. Although few animals in America have become extinct through the pressures of hunting alone, the demise of the passenger pigeon and the Carolina parakeet were substantially, if not decisively, aided by such activities, and the American alligator's future was threatened.

The passenger pigeon once ranged throughout most of the lands east of the Rocky Mountains and wintered in the southern states. Among the most numerous of all the world's birds, its population was greater than that of any other bird in North America. The noted early American naturalist, Alexander Wilson, recorded that in 1810 he had seen a flock of migrating passenger pigeons whose numbers he estimated at 2,230,272,000. In spite of such numbers, a century later the species was at the threshold of extinction because of a century of unrestricted hunting. In 1914 at the Cincinnati Zoological Garden, Martha, the last known passenger pigeon died.

In the same year, the Carolina parakeet experienced a similar fate. North America's only parrot and a bird once numerous in the southern states, this aggressive yellow, green, and orange bird frequently devoured the fruits and nuts of orchards; consequently it had been hunted since colonial times. The bird's bright plumage attracted milliners and it subsequently fell subject to commercial utilization. Its pattern of behavior made it easy prey for bird catchers and market hunters. With the death of a captive Carolina parakeet in 1914, no verified sightings of this colorful and active bird have been recorded. For the passenger pigeon and Carolina parakeet, the pressures of hunting, habitat destruction, and behavior patterns that limited their dispersal in times of danger led to their extinction.

Other birds have experienced the threat of extinction in the South, and the whooping crane, Mississippi sandhill crane, brown pelican, bald eagle, and Everglade kite are endangered or threatened in all southern states. The whooping crane is North America's tallest extant bird and a survivor from the Pleistocene era. Rare in historic times, it was by the end of the 19th century confined primarily to the region west of the Mississippi River. Hunted for sport, meat, and eggs and experiencing changes in its habitat as the result of agriculture, its numbers declined dramatically. Restricted to a population that numbers less than 75 today, this magnificent bird makes a 2,300-mile migration each spring from its wintering site at the Aransas Refuge in Texas to nesting sites in the Wood Buffalo Park in Canada. The whooping crane is protected by the governments of both the United States and Canada and the energetic advocacy of conservation groups who have made its plight well known. Attempts to improve its breeding cycle have met with some success, and determined efforts have been initiated to maintain this graceful but endangered species. Perhaps even more endangered than the whooping crane is its relative, the Mississippi sandhill crane, which has an even smaller population. This endangered species is now protected at the Mississippi Sandhill Crane Refuge.

Endangered in all southern states but Florida, where it is threatened, the brown pelican is an excellent example of an animal that can become suddenly devastated by the actions of pesticides on an avian species. Until the 1960s the brown pelican existed in abundant numbers, but the increased use of endrin to control the boll weevil, the bollworm, and the sugarcane borer in the Mississippi Delta led to the demise of brown pelicans by directly killing them, destroying their food supplies, and altering their physiological processes. Endrin was responsible for massive fish kills in the Mississippi River in the late 1950s and early 1960s. Brown pelicans have been transplanted from Florida, where the population is stable, to Louisiana to reestablish colonies of this once plentiful bird. In Texas colonies are still limited with the population not yet considered viable.

Overspecialization in a species introduces an element of rigidity in that species' ability to adapt to changing environmental circumstances. America's largest woodpecker, the ivory-billed woodpecker, confronted a limited future because of its dependence upon virgin, old growth forests in the South with their characteristic dead and dying trees. Logging has so reduced its habitat that sightings have become limited and often unverified, and the species may be extinct.

Specialization has also limited the future of the Everglade kite. Until the second decade of this century, this strikingly beautiful hawk was frequently observed soaring above the freshwater marshes of Florida. Its principal food source was the large freshwater apple snail. Dependent upon this one snail, which in turn depended upon the standing water of a marsh for habitat, it had a fragile ecosystem. The progressive draining of wetlands in Florida for agriculture and urban development destroyed the populations of the apple snail and reduced the food supply of the Everglade kite. Today, its severely limited population is confined primarily to the southwestern reaches of Lake Okeechobee with a few small nesting sites at the Loxahatchee National Wildlife Refuge. This graceful and noble bird's future is now tied to the preservation of the apple snail's environment.

The federal government declared the piping plover, a once-common Atlantic and Gulf coastal shore bird, an endangered and threatened species in 1985. Scientists launched a major effort in the 1980s to save another bird, the dusky seaside sparrow, from extinction. The last known example of the species died in captivity in Florida in 1987 despite their efforts.

Because of the habitat alteration and hunting pressures, the American alligator is an endangered species in Alabama, Arkansas, Georgia, Mississippi, North Carolina, South Carolina, and Texas. John Bartram could observe in the mid-18th century that alligators were so thick in Florida's St. Johns River that one could have walked across the river on their heads if they had been harmless; by the middle years of this century, hide hunters had severely reduced their numbers. Legislation that reduced the market for their skins and protected their habitat has permitted their numbers to increase in Florida and Louisiana, and they are no longer endangered in those states. Their situation is more precarious in other southern states.

A more timid and more nocturnal relative of the American alligator, the American crocodile, is also an endangered species in the South. Because of its limited range and specialized habitat, its prospects are less bright than those of the alligator. Confined primarily to the mangrove estuaries of southern Florida, the American crocodile is the only representative of this genera in North America, although its range includes the coastal littoral of Colombia and eastern Venezuela, the Caribbean and West Indies, the Pacific coasts of Ecuador and Colombia and most of the Pacific coast of Central America and Mexico. Protected today and watched carefully in the Everglades National Park and the lower Keys, it is no longer subjected to hide hunters, and habitat encroachment has now been restricted. There is hope that the declining numbers of this fierce-countenanced reptile have been stabilized and that a species that has existed for 140 million years will be able to maintain itself.

The crocodile's relatives, the sea turtles, are also endangered in the southern states. All five genera of sea turtles may be found in the Gulf of Mexico, and all once nested on the sun-caressed beaches of the southern states. Sea turtles are particularly vulnerable to predation and habitat alteration. After spending years at sea, they return to nest on the limited expanse of shore on which they were hatched. Once laid, their eggs are desired by man both as a source of protein and as an aphrodisiac that renews sexual vigor. Sea turtles are easily caught and drowned in trawlers' nets. The green turtle is among the most valuable of all reptiles and was once common to the majority of the world's oceans where temperatures did not drop below 68° F. Classified as an endangered species in the United States, it is still harvested outside of this nation because of the quality of its meat for soup, the skin of its forequarters for shoes, and its oil for cosmetics and soap. The Atlantic hawksbill turtle also serves the needs of fashion as a source for tortoiseshell. It is also harvested for its calipee, a cartilaginous material removed from the bones of the bottom shell, which is used in clear green turtle soup and for leather. Immature hawksbill turtles are often mounted for sale to tourists in Latin American countries.

In the warm waters of Florida and perhaps as far west as Texas in the Gulf of Mexico and as far north as southern Georgia, the docile, slow-breeding, marine herbivore the manatee is attempting to maintain its population against increasing habitat destruction and human intrusion into its domain. This imperfectly studied, large marine mammal, whose nearest relative is the elephant, can reach a length of 12 feet and a weight of 1,200 pounds. During the course of a day, it may consume up to 150 pounds of aquatic plants. It has no natural enemies, unless man is placed in this category, but it is among the most endangered of all marine mammals. Until the end of the 19th century, it was hunted by the Seminole Indians and early settlers because of the veal-like quality of its meat. Its hide made a strong, durable leather; its bones with their ivory appearance were often carved into small objects; and its fat was used for lubrication and light. Declining populations of this tranquil animal encouraged the Florida Legislature to pass in 1893 a bill to protect the manatee. In 1907 additional legislation imposed a $600 fine and a six-month prison term for killing a manatee. Part of a population that is probably less than 1,000, the manatee does not have a secure future. Even in protected waters, manatees are often injured by the propellers of motorboats. Development has restricted their access to warm springs. Highly susceptible to cold weather, they frequently become victims of harsh winters. Protected by state and federal legislation, their future depends upon the stability of their habitat.

Although the manatee is an elusive animal to investigate, even more secretive in its habits is the Florida panther, or eastern cougar. Historically, the cougar, or mountain lion or panther, had the greatest natural range of any terrestrial mammal in the New World, ranging from Tierra del Fuego at the tip of South America to southeastern Alaska in the north. The eastern cougar, or Florida panther, still maintains a limited presence in Florida and other southeastern states. While its present population is difficult to determine, its future is dependent upon the preservation of a protected habitat where it may range widely in pursuit of food. The Everglades National Park and other such large southern preserves may be ultimately the Florida panther's last refuge.

Florida is also the home for the endangered key deer, a small subspecies of the Virginia whitetail deer. With bucks ranging in weight from 60 to 110 pounds, with the does smaller, this dwarf deer of the Florida Keys was constantly hunted by the inhabitants of the area. Reduced in numbers during the 20th century, key deer were protected from hunters by a ban passed by the Florida Legislature in 1939. Poaching and the devastations of fire and hurricane continued to reduce their numbers, and by 1949 their population was estimated to be down to 30. After much political debate, conservationists secured the establishment in 1957 of the Key Deer National Wildlife Refuge. This 7,000 acre refuge, which embraces 16 keys, not only provides a sanctuary for the key deer but also for 11 other endangered or threatened species. The population has increased and presently numbers more than 400.

One of the tragedies of a species approaching the brink of extinction is that their population reaches such low numbers that it becomes very difficult to study the natural history of the animal. The southern red wolf faces such a predicament, and the study of the animal is confronted by countless difficulties. Early colonists in the South frequently confronted a distinctive native wolf population. Although called the red wolf, most members of this species had gray-brown, black, or tawny coats with only a few of them having the distinctive red coat. They were generally larger than a coyote but smaller than their relatives, the gray wolves. The red wolf was perhaps slightly less predatory than the gray wolf, but its natural history was quite similar. Civilization's constant war upon carnivores and increased patterns of settlement reduced the red wolves' range and their numbers. By the 1920s the red wolf had been eliminated from most regions east of the Mississippi River. Populations of red wolves still existed in the Coastal Prairie of Louisiana and Texas, in eastern Oklahoma, and in the Ozark-Ouachita Highlands of Arkansas. Among these animals, there was interbreeding with coyotes, and consequently the gene pool has been degraded by hybridization. In the mid-1960s the red wolf was placed on the rare and endangered species list. The future for this species lies in the protection of the limited number of nonhybridized members of this gene pool, which still reside in the upper Gulf Coast region of Texas.

See also RECREATION: Hunting

Phillip Drennon Thomas
Wichita State University

Albert E. Cowdrey, *This Land, This South: An Environmental History* (1983); Robin W. Doughty, *Wildlife and Man in Texas: Environmental Change and Conservation* (1983); Peter Matthiessen, *Wildlife in America* (1959); Arlie W. Schorger, *The Passenger Pigeon: Its Natural History and Extinction* (1973); Stanley A. Temple, ed., *Endangered Birds: Management Techniques for Preserving Threatened Species* (1978); James A. Tober, *Who Owns the Wildlife?: The Political Economy of Conservation in Nineteenth-Century America* (1981). ☆

Energy Use and Development

The South is richly endowed with energy resources, but it exhibits a complex pattern in its production and use of particular fuels and power sources. The Atlantic coastal regions of the southern states, being energy importers, have committed themselves heavily to nuclear power. The southern Appalachian Mountains contain extensive seams of high quality coal, which has long been exported along the rivers, railroads, and highways that link mines to markets. Many of the rivers flowing out of the mountains have also been harnessed for hydroelectric power, most notably in the Tennessee Valley, and the great hardwood forests that clothe the hills they drain continue to provide fuel wood for domestic and local industrial heat. Petroleum and natural gas are the bonanza fuels of the southwestern states, especially Texas and Louisiana.

Although the South as a whole cannot be considered a cohesive energy region, southern culture, like that of other regions in the nation, has been profoundly affected by the historical experience of developing and utilizing energy resources. Before the 1820s, when new canals began carrying anthracite from northeastern Pennsylvania to the Tidewater ports of the East Coast, soft coal mines near Richmond, Va., served as one of America's few sources of commercial coal. In Alabama coal was shipped down the Coosa River as early as the 1830s and later fueled the ironworks that manufactured munitions for the Confederacy. Coal shipments out of western Virginia grew steadily after the Baltimore and Ohio rail line reached the Ohio River in the 1850s, and Tennessee coal, mined commercially from the 1830s, also gained access to growing markets when the Nashville & Chattanooga Railroad was completed in 1855.

Following the Civil War the South stepped up its laborious efforts to industrialize, a transformation that required much more intensive exploitation and utilization of energy resources. Water power was harnessed to drive machinery in fall line mills and factories at Richmond, Va., and at Augusta and Columbus, Ga. Railroad building also boomed after the war, creating both a demand for coal and iron and the means for satisfying it. The New River coalfield was opened in 1873 when the Chesapeake & Ohio Railroad pushed its lines through the rugged mountains of central West Virginia, and 10 years later the Norfolk & Western began shipping out high quality metallurgical coal from the Pocahontas field of southern West Virginia and southwestern Virginia. In the final decades of the 19th century the iron and steel industry was consolidated in great industrial cities such as Pittsburgh and Chicago; the South has its representative in Birmingham.

The 20th century brought new forms of industrial production and the discovery of new sources of energy. The oil industry, born in the Appalachian hills of western Pennsylvania and West Virginia, experienced explosive growth following the east Texas and Spindletop strikes. The chemical industry also expanded rapidly, especially in the Kanawha and Tennessee river valleys and, as petroleum feed stocks grew in importance, along the Gulf Coast of Texas. Cheap electrical power was used to produce chemical fertilizers, which, together with rural electrification and mechanization, became the mainstays of energy-intensive agriculture. This agricultural revolution in turn led to the great migration of population from the rural South during the middle decades of this century.

Taken as a whole, the South is comparatively rich in fossil fuels, but historically this has been a mixed blessing. Both the coal and the oil industries are unusually prone to cycles of boom and bust. Both industries include major corporations, which seek to reduce their vulnerability to cyclical shifts, and aggressive independent operators poised to reap high profits during times of rising demand. The hard-driving wildcatter depicted in the film *Giant* and the high-rolling strip miner are both southern types. Where the energy resources the independent operators exploit are utilized locally, as is the case in parts of Texas and Louisiana, they appear as marginal figures in a diversified economy. Where the fuels the independent operators mine are shipped out for use elsewhere, as is the case in the coal regions, they are dominant figures in local societies that are unbuffered against the dire consequences of the boom-bust cycle.

The migration of industries from older northern cities to the southern Sunbelt would not have been possible without the development of new types of energy utilization. Southern cities are just as dependent on air-conditioning and automobiles as are the older northern cities on central heating and urban rail systems. The South has used its energy resources shrewdly in the national competition for new industry. Whether southerners will be able to manage successfully the consequences of their energy decisions and how they will evaluate the long-term effects of these decisions on their regional culture remain open questions.

See also AGRICULTURE: / Rural Electrification; GEOGRAPHY: / Mills and Milling; HISTORY AND MANNERS: Railroads; INDUSTRY articles; SCIENCE AND MEDICINE: Technology; SOCIAL CLASS: Appalachia, Exploitation of

Arthur Donovan
Virginia Polytechnic Institute
and State University

Harry M. Caudill, *Night Comes to the Cumberlands* (1962); Louis C. Hunter, *Waterpower: A History of Industrial Power in the United States, 1780–1930* (1979); Ronald L. Lewis, *Coal, Iron, and Slaves: Industrial Slavery in Maryland and Virginia, 1715–1865* (1979); Martin V. Melosi, *Coping with Abundance: Energy and Environment in Industrial America, 1820–1980* (1985); Joseph A. Pratt, *The Growth of a Refining Region* (1980); John A. Williams, *West Virginia and the Captains of Industry* (1976). ☆

Environmental Movements

The South followed, although sometimes tardily, the rest of the nation in its evolution from natural resource conservation to the environmentalism of the 1960s. Cooperative efforts often developed between federal and state governments, but at times various state governments followed federal guidelines only reluctantly. While the South faced conservation problems similar to those throughout the country, its geography, history, and economic and social conditions gave southern conservation activities their own regional characteristics. Just as the environmental movements began to develop in the 1960s, the southern economy lagged. The southern legacy of individualism and resentment of outside authority also affected southern attitudes toward conservation and environmental policy.

Although the Indians were not necessarily the natural ecologists they are often portrayed as being, they were the first humans to begin to change the environment of the South and to learn to live with its characteristics. Early European settlers, less inclined to adapt to the natural environment than the Indian, generally wanted to transform the landscape. England expected its American colonies to produce certain products. In addition to the native tobacco, Europeans introduced other crops such as wheat and rice, thus contributing new flora and fauna as well as new diseases to the southern environment.

Even before the American Revolution, soil exhaustion caused southern planters to become concerned with soil conservation. Both George Washington and Thomas Jefferson evidenced a concern for soil depletion and its consequences in the Tidewater region. While he advocated soil conservation methods, Jefferson realized that most people would solve their soil fertility problem by simply moving to cheaper lands farther west. In all probability the Moravians represented the first group to treat natural resources in a conservationist manner.

Colonials viewed forests ambivalently, as a nuisance to agriculture to be removed as soon as possible and as a useful product for sale or building use. The English crown made some attempts to regulate cutting of the American forests, but most colonists resented such laws and contended that their freedom to cut forests was a right. In fact, it was a practical reality that conditioned future American attitudes toward use of forest resources. Much of the cut timber was wasted, often burned for clearing; thus by the time of the Revolution southern forests had been much modified.

Early European settlers found an abundance of wildlife in the South. Indians had already depleted some forms of wildlife by indiscriminate killing. The colonials killed either for food or to eliminate predators that interfered with agriculture. While they did not eliminate any species, the colonials' actions often created an ecological imbalance. In England, hunting rights had been considered a privilege of the upper class, and attempts to impose restrictions on the colonials created resentment. As with the cutting of trees, the settlers generally believed they had a right to hunt. Such attitudes have persisted, making the contemporary hunting laws in states such as Texas a patchwork of state and local control.

European settlers and travelers took an early interest in the exotic flora and fauna they found in the southern colonies. Planters like Jefferson and William Byrd II as well as other lesser-known settlers provided important accounts of colonial wildlife, laying the groundwork for further study. John Bartram, a Philadelphia botanist, and the English traveler Mark Catesby provided significant information concerning southern wildlife, although Catesby's writings provided misinformation as well.

Prior to the American Revolution both the crown and the colonial legislature passed conservation laws. Some colonial laws restricted the slaughter of deer while others controlled fishing activities. In practice colonials generally ignored conservation laws, but they established the principle, persisting into modern times, that the sovereign had the authority to control natural resources.

Between the American Revolution and the Civil War, movement of population across the Appalachian Mountains and into the Mississippi River Valley had a tremendous impact on southern soils, forests, rivers, and wildlife. Rapid expansion of cotton agriculture between 1790 and 1835 exhausted the soil in the more easterly parts of the South. By the 1830s much of the older

South needed considerable fertilizer to maintain production, setting in motion a cycle that continued to characterize American agriculture. The use of fertilizer to maintain or increase production resulted in the demand for more, and increasingly expensive, fertilizers. Cutting of timber and the destruction of natural ground cover combined with the clean field and row crop cultivation of cotton, corn, and tobacco to accelerate soil erosion. A few advocates of agricultural reform, such as Edmund Ruffin, urged the use of contour plowing and cheaper natural fertilizers. With a seemingly endless abundance of cheap land farther west, few southern farmers heeded the advice of these prophets.

Both national and state governments attempted to control destruction of forests before 1860. The national government reserved certain trees for naval use, while most southern states prohibited burning of trees because of the danger to other property. Only the settlers' capacity to use and sell wood limited the continued exploitation of southern forest resources in the antebellum period.

In the postrevolutionary era, naturalists, particularly John James Audubon, focused attention on the South. Ignoring the development of conservation for aesthetic reasons, and often taking abundance for granted, they were extremely important in providing scientific understanding of southern flora and fauna. Also important to the use of southern resources in the postrevolutionary period was concern for improving navigation and controlling floods on the rivers of the South. Because most southern rivers provided an unreliable means of transportation, local, state, and national governments attempted to transform rivers to make them more navigable. The South's greatest river, the Mississippi, proved both a blessing and a threat. While providing fertile land and an avenue for much southern commerce, it often brought devastating floods. Settlers attempted to hold back the river's rampages with levees. Constriction of the river forced its flood waters to rise higher, requiring further heightening of the levees. Both federal and state governments attempted to improve navigation and to control floods on the Mississippi. Studies and recommendations made prior to the Civil War long influenced government policy toward the Mississippi and its tributaries.

So far as wetlands were concerned, neither antebellum southerners nor other Americans had any understanding of their ecological value, generally regarding them as a nuisance. In 1849 and 1850 the national government turned much of the wetlands over to state control for reclamation through drainage. Although exploitation characterized the general southern (and American) approach to resource use, a small population and limited industrial development moderated the degree of this exploitation prior to the Civil War.

After the Civil War the development of technology created an opportunity for almost unlimited exploitation of southern natural resources. Northern industrialists, Europeans, and some southerners saw in these resources opportunities for quick wealth. Both federal and state governments encouraged railroad construction through land grants. Much of the most valuable publicly owned timber and mineral lands in the South passed to private ownership between 1865 and 1900.

Although southerners played some role in calling for wiser use of natural resources, the impetus for conservation, like much of the force for exploitation, came from outside the South. In particular, government scientists occupied a prominent position in the early conservation movement. They helped establish national parks, forest reserves, and other important programs for natural resource management. Outside leadership focused on conservation of southern resources as part of a larger movement throughout the nation. While contributing some leaders in the struggle, the South more often provided the battleground for conservation controversies.

Agriculture and the extractive industries took the greatest toll on southern resources, ravaging soil, timber, and wildlife. Increased cotton production, fostered by the tenant system, encouraged a single crop economy greater in extent than prior to the Civil War. The use of fertilizers, promoted by agricultural reformers, helped maintain production in the face of a decline in natural soil fertility. A midwesterner who moved to Louisiana in the 1870s made one of the most significant contributions to southern agricultural reform. In 1903, at Terrell, Tex., Seaman A. Knapp introduced the demonstration farm as a means of agricultural education, a concept that became federal law with establishment of the Agricultural Extension Services. The spread of the boll weevil across the South demonstrated problems associated with a cotton monoculture, although little was effectively done about the threat prior to 1900.

The exploitation and conservation of southern forests during the Gilded Age followed an erratic course. Reconstruction government had restricted sale of public lands in the South. With Redemption, southern Democrats supported laws promoting the sale of such land, which included much forested land, although by 1889 southern members of Congress led a campaign to keep the few remaining areas under governmental control. During the period of sale large tracts of southern timber passed to speculators and lumbermen, especially non-southerners, most of whom considered timber a commodity and little understood its relationship to the rest of the environment. Although lumbermen attempted reforestation, in 1873 a committee established by the American Association for the Advancement of Science encouraged federal and state governments to pass laws protecting forests and promoting timber cultivation. Gradually, support grew for development of national and state forest reserves.

The development of scientific forestry began at Yale University, but the first practical demonstration of its principles occurred, serendipitously, in North Carolina. George W. Vanderbilt hired the young forester Gifford Pinchot to manage the forest reserves of his Biltmore estate. In 1898 the Biltmore Forest School opened. Although Pinchot's activities at Biltmore influenced other areas of the South, he was not alone in his concern for southern forest resources. The Mississippi politician L. Q. C. Lamar, in his position as secretary of the interior, supported President Cleveland's call for forest reserves. All these attempts to protect and manage southern forests, however, clashed with the strong American traditions of quick profits and individualism, as well as the southern suspicion of outside interference.

The commercial development of agriculture and forestry along with the fashion trade's desire for fur and feathers sped depletion of southern wildlife.

The passenger pigeon disappeared completely while other species experienced rapid decline. State laws designed to protect favored species such as fish were spottily enforced, if at all. One historian claimed that the imposition of game and hunting laws in the South stemmed partially from southern white determination to maintain control of blacks after Reconstruction. Many blacks had supplied food for their families partly by hunting on unfenced public and private land, so hunting restrictions made the blacks more dependent on white landowners for their employment. Throughout the Gilded Age the American Ornithologists Union (AOU) joined with the Audubon Society to promote passage of model laws listing game birds and protecting nongame species. Although these attempts were often ineffective, their proposal represented a changing attitude among scientists and some sportsmen concerning feathered wildlife. Passage by Congress of the Lacey Act in 1900 spurred more effective state regulation of commercial hunting.

Water projects, both reclamation and flood control, became prominent during the Gilded Age. Southern interest in water projects centered generally on attempts to control floods on the Mississippi River or to improve navigation on southern streams. Responding to a proposal by Louisiana Congressman Randall L. Gibson, President Rutherford B. Hayes signed a bill establishing the Mississippi River Commission (MRC) in 1879—the first time the federal government had agreed to help control floods on an American river. Throughout the Gilded Age both the MRC and government policymakers debated the best technology for controlling floods on the mighty river, as well as the constitutionality of federal aid for flood control. Southern support helped establish the precedent for active federal participation in flood control activities. Ironically, by adopting a "levees only" approach the MRC actually aggravated flooding on the river. Levees constricted the river, forcing floods to rise higher and bringing extensive damage to property in the floodplain.

The period from 1900 to 1930 saw the development of embryonic conservation movements in the South that promised to halt the exploitation of southern resources. Many factors, ranging from the boll weevil pestilence to the influence of agricultural experiment stations, moved southern farmers toward more scientific and modern agricultural methods. In many ways the South responded positively to the Progressive conservation movement. Rational development of natural resources coincided with the New South emphasis on economic development, whether it be forest cultivation, river basin planning, or wildlife management. Following the lead of Theodore Roosevelt, many southern governments began to focus more attention on conservation matters, yet there was still much resistance to centralized control over resources whether from the state or national government. Forest conservation was most often embraced by larger corporations concerned with sustained yield. By the 1920s support for scientific forestry had become widespread throughout the South with establishment of several forestry programs in regional colleges and universities. Concern for wildlife conservation and management grew among certain groups in the South, often with guidance from the Audubon Society. Although more southern states passed game control laws after 1900, enforcement still proved difficult.

Economic developments of the 1920s both challenged and encouraged the southern conservation movements. Settlement in Florida during the 1920s led to attempts to drain swamps, including the Everglades. Looked upon as progressive, such drainage often created long-range problems similar to those associated with use of levees for flood control. Discovery of oil in Texas in 1901 ushered in a new era of opportunity and conservation problems; prior to World War II most efforts to conserve oil were prompted by wise use, rather than pollution concerns. Perhaps no idea so attracted those concerned with southern economic development as did river basin planning. By 1925 the principle of comprehensive river basin development had been embodied in federal law, as demands for new approaches to flood control on the Mississippi gained support. Senator George Norris attracted increased southern support for his plans to transform the Tennessee Valley through scientific planning.

The New Deal had a profound effect on southern conservation and development policy. This effect was nowhere more evident than in the implementation of water projects in the Mississippi and Tennessee valleys. The Corps of Engineers began the impressive Atchafalaya Floodway project to help relieve floods on the lower Mississippi. Engineers were soon to learn that nature had ways of pursuing its goals despite human activities. Some scientists predicted that despite human efforts the Mississippi would eventually change its main channel to the Atchafalaya, leaving New Orleans on a backwater tributary. In no way, however, did the New Deal touch southern resources and influence conservation ideas as it did with establishment of the Tennessee Valley Authority.

New Deal policies influenced southern policies concerning forest and wildlife conservation as well. Most noted of these influences were the reforestation programs carried out by the Civilian Conservation Corps. The federal practice of purchasing cutover and eroded land for development of parks and national forests was emulated by many states. The New Deal also focused attention on the need for soil conservation, important to a region that had some of the most exhausted and eroded soil in the nation. Above all, conservation activities during the New Deal created a greater understanding of the interrelated nature of natural resource use and preservation. The experiences of World War II altered the attitude of many southerners toward conservation. Private organizations, universities, and public bureaus cooperated to provide more effective development of southern resources. Tree farming combined with improved fire prevention methods laid the basis for a sustained yield of southern timber. Critics questioned the wisdom of a timber monoculture, and while cotton remained a significant part of farm production, a revolution occurred in southern agriculture. New crops such as soybeans, improved fertilizers and farming techniques, and the use of insecticides all profoundly affected the nature of southern farming. As with the changes in timber cultivation certain groups began to question whether these changes were all environmentally beneficial.

From 1960 to 1970 Roosevelt-Pinchot concepts of utilitarian conservation gave way to ideas stressing environmental quality. Again the South followed the national trends, not always enthusiastically. The National Environmental Protection Act (1969) was most important in promoting environmental activity at the state level both through its general philosophy and through its direct application in the South. Most southern states began to develop plans to protect public lands and supervise the use of natural resources, often consciously to avoid federal intervention. In addition, some of the first federal actions to enforce environmental protection laws were taken in the South. In 1971, under the Clean Air Act, the federal government obtained its first restraining order for environmental enforcement to control air pollution in Birmingham, Ala. Bringing about a complete, if temporary, stoppage of steel manufacturing in Birmingham, the national government demonstrated the potential power it could exercise to achieve environmental improvement.

Since 1960 local environmental groups in the South have independently or in cooperation with national organizations attempted to influence environmental policy within the southern states. Efforts were made to protect the biologically unique Big Thicket of Texas and to prevent development of expensive and environmentally questionable water projects.

While most southerners continue to consider economic growth more important than environmental protection, some groups increasingly insist that the South's water supply, air quality, coastal areas, and general environment have to be considered as part of the Sunbelt movement. Given the South's advantages for economic growth, such as labor and land costs, taxes, and climate, southerners need no longer fear that industry could be attracted only at the cost of a livable environment.

See also AGRICULTURE: Crops; Diversification; / Agricultural Extension Services; Knapp, Seaman A.; HISTORY AND MANNERS: Frontier Heritage; SCIENCE AND MEDICINE: Technology; / Ruffin, Edmund

J. B. Smallwood
North Texas State University

Nelson M. Blake, *Land into Water—Water into Land: A History of Water Management in Florida* (1980); Thomas D. Clark, *Mississippi Quarterly* (Spring 1972); Albert E. Cowdrey, *This Land, This South: An Environmental History* (1983); Gilbert C. Fite, *Agricultural History* (January 1979); Paul W. Gates, *Agricultural History* (January 1979); Martin Reuss, *Louisiana History* (Spring 1982); Stanley W. Trimble, *Man-induced Soil Erosion on the Southern Piedmont, 1700–1970* (1974). ☆

Flood Control and Drainage

Although most sections of the United States have had to cope with floods, these problems have assumed extraordinary magnitude in two regions of the South—the lower Mississippi River Valley and the Florida peninsula.

The Mississippi River both blesses and curses lower valley residents. Bearing its tremendous burden of water, the river has built up a delta of rich alluvial soil ideal for agriculture, but at times it has also overflowed its banks and taken a tragic toll in lives, homes, and property. Recognizing its threat, the founders of New Orleans ordered a protective embankment to be built. As early as 1727 Governor Étienne de Périer reported construction of an earthen wall a mile long and 18 feet wide. Thus began the type of flood control on which valley residents would have to depend for the next two hundred years. Appropriately, *levée*, the French word for such an earthen embankment, passed into the American language.

From 1718 to 1850 the burden of flood control was mostly carried by individual owners of riverfront property. The French government required each to build and maintain a levee as a condition of his grant; the government intervened only to enforce the requirement and occasionally to inspect the levees. The system established by the French continued after the United States purchased the territory. This early policy resulted in the extension of levees along both banks of the Mississippi as far as they were settled. But the levees provided a frail defense. With one man's levees poorly joined to the next and differing in size and condition, the raging river would frequently break through.

A great flood in 1844 strengthened a growing demand for federal help. Arguing that the destructive waters originated in remote parts of the Union, proponents urged Congress to appropriate funds for building levees just as it provided aid for oceanic commerce. Although strict constructionists opposed any such expenditure, Congress did find a way to provide indirect assistance. In 1849 it transferred to the state of Louisiana all unsold public swampland within its borders; in 1850 it made a similar grant to Arkansas on condition that the state apply the proceeds to reclaiming the land by means of levees and drains. The provisions of the 1850 act were extended to each state where swamp and overflowed land might be situated. Fifteen states received grants totalling almost 64 million acres. The South acquired almost two-thirds of this land: Florida, 20.2 million acres; Louisiana, 9.3 million acres; Arkansas, 7.6 million acres; Mississippi, 2.2 million acres; and Alabama, .4 million acres.

The swampland grants resulted in much state and local governmental activity. Florida's huge share encouraged schemes for draining the Everglades, but reversals of policy, diversions of land to the railroads, and the disruption caused by the Civil War delayed any effective reclamation. The lower Mississippi Valley states made a stronger effort to use the swamplands for the specified purpose. State and local agencies initiated works to prevent floods and provide drainage, but poor management, unsound projects, local jealousies, and fiscal chicanery handicapped the movement. Most of the new structures were swept away by floods in 1858 and 1859, and the whole levee system was devastated by military action and neglect during the Civil War.

A third period marked by renewed state activity and a cautious infusion of federal aid began in 1879 when Congress established the Mississippi River Commission to supervise all federal public works on the river. At first these projects were intended for the benefit of navigation, but the Army Corps of Engineers found indirect ways to help with the flood problem. As early as 1861 Captain Andrew Humphreys and Lieutenant Henry Abbott published an influential report, *Physics and Hydraulics of the Mississippi River*, which analyzed the inadequacies of existing levees. In planning later works for improving navigation, the Army Corps began to design levees that would also protect against floods. Local levee districts still bore the major burden, but the Commission served a vital coordinating function. By 1912 the combined efforts of state, local, and federal agencies had extended the levees along the Mississippi and its tributaries for 1,500 miles—the length of the Great Wall of China.

In Florida the ancient dream of draining the Everglades was revived by Hamilton Disston, heir to a Philadelphia toolmaker's fortune, who in 1881 contracted with the state to reclaim a vast area overflowed by Lake Okeechobee and nearby lakes and rivers. Disston was to receive one-half the drained land. Despite a major effort, the enterprise failed. In 1906 the state itself began to build a system of canals to lower the level of Lake Okeechobee and reclaim Everglades land. Modestly successful in opening up new regions for agriculture and residence, the program involved the state so deeply in debt that it had to be halted during the Great Depression.

The latest period of flood control began about 1928 with the federal government accepting major responsibility. Great floods in 1912, 1922, and 1927 demonstrated the inadequacy of the Mississippi levees. The 1927 flood, the most catastrophic of all, inundated 26,000 square miles of land, took 214 lives, drove 637,000 people from their homes, and ruined $236 million worth of property. Poet William Alexander Percy chronicled it in *Lanterns on the Levee* (1941). Events elsewhere emphasized that the problem had become a national one. In 1926 and 1928 hurricanes drove the waters of Lake Okeechobee through frail local levees and took more than 2,000 lives. California and New England both suffered serious floods, strengthening the call for federal government assistance.

At the request of Congress the Army Corps of Engineers began to study the flood problem on a national basis. In 1928 Lieutenant General Edgar Jadwin, Chief of the Corps, laid out a $300 million program for the Mississippi and its tributaries. In addition to stronger levees, Jadwin advised deepening river channels, establishing floodways, and studying the feasibility of storage reservoirs. In the so-called 308 reports the Corps provided studies of over 200 other rivers, showing how they might be managed to serve multiple purposes—flood control, navigation, irrigation, and power generation.

Congress accepted the federal responsibility in a series of laws. The Reid-Jones Act of 1928 authorized the Corps to proceed with the Jadwin Plan. A 1930 law provided for the construction of Hoover Dike, an 85-mile-long levee around Lake Okeechobee. In 1933 the Tennessee Valley Authority was established with a mandate to build multipurpose dams. The movement culminated in the Flood Control Act of 1936, affirming that flood control was "a proper activity of the Federal Government" and "in the interest of the general welfare." Some 2,111 projects spread over 31 states were approved.

These historic laws, extended by later ones, have resulted in a huge federal flood control program. The Mississippi levees have been strengthened with revetments of cement and steel. To speed the passage of the water, the channel has been deepened and made 152 miles shorter by cutoffs across the bends. Floodways have been provided to release surplus water in times of emergency. Dams across the Yazoo River and other tributaries provide storage reservoirs. The federal government has also spent large sums in Florida. In 1948 Congress authorized the Central and Southern Florida Flood Control Project, a complex system of water management to benefit a large area both north and south of Lake Okeechobee.

Despite general acceptance of the value of flood control, this interference with nature often involved environmental damage. For example, canalizing the Kissimmee River, the principal source of Lake Okeechobee, has helped to create a serious pollution problem in the lake itself. In other places it might have been wiser to regulate development on the floodplain rather than to build dams or alter river courses. Federal budgetary problems may compel a more careful scrutiny of future proposals.

Pare Lorentz's 1937 film *The River*, which was made for the Farm Security Administration, was a striking visual portrait of the Mississippi River, its valleys and tributaries, its exploitation and pollution, and of flood control by levee building along its banks and through reforestation efforts. The vivid memory of southern flooding survives in music through blues songs such as Blind Lemon Jefferson's "Risin' High Water Blues" (1927), Sippie Wallace's "The Flood Blues" (1927), Joe Pullum's "Mississippi Heavy Water Blues" (1935), and Alabama Sam's "Red Cross Blues" (1933).

Nelson M. Blake
Syracuse University

Nelson M. Blake, *Land into Water—Water into Land: A History of Water Management in Florida* (1980); Hodding Carter, *Man and the River: The Mississippi* (1970); Pete Daniel, *Deep'n as It Come: The 1927 Mississippi River Flood* (1977); Robert W. Harrison, *Alluvial Empire: A Study of State and Local Efforts toward Land Development in the Alluvial Valley of the Lower Mississippi River* (1961); William G. Hoyt and Walter B. Langbein, *Floods* (1955); Luna B. Leopold and Thomas Maddock, Jr., *The Flood Control Controversy: Big Dams, Little Dams, and Land Management* (1954); Gary B. Mills, *Of Men and Rivers: The Story of the Vicksburg District* (1978); Dunbar Rowland, *History of Mississippi: The Heart of the South* (1925). ☆

Forests

The Great American Forest is in good part southern. As of 1978 the estimated total commercial forest land in the South equaled 229 million acres, 40 percent of the national total. The South, moreover, contained nearly 60 percent of the nation's industrially owned timberlands. Most of the region is wooded, and virtually all of it can support forests. The southern forest consists of three general woodland types: hardwoods, pine, and various woody assemblages associated with swamps, pocosins (swamplands in an upland coastal region), and understories.

The hardwoods occupy much of the southern Appalachians, bottomlands and floodplains, and riverine environments throughout the Piedmont. Commercial hardwoods amount to about 143 million acres. More than 70 commercially important tree species make up the hardwood complex. In broad terms, the hardwoods divide into two groups—those in perennially wet bottomlands and those in Appalachian uplands. The gradation between hardwood types is subtle, and between hardwoods and pine quite variable, with each interpenetrating the other. Historically, some hardwoods were harvested for saw timber (especially oak for ships); much for furniture and charcoal; and much, in conjunction with drainage, for agricultural reclamation. Thanks to traditional logging practices and the use of fire in clearing land, most of the southern hardwood forest is of poor quality.

The southern pines, however, are flourishing. Commercial pine forests cover some 100 million acres. Four pines are prominent: longleaf and slash

Pine trees, Mississippi coast, postcard, date unknown

along the Coastal Plain, and loblolly and shortleaf across the Piedmont and within interior highlands. The longleaf was the primary sawtimber species, the backbone of the southern lumber industry; the slash, along with the longleaf, was the source for naval stores; and loblolly and shortleaf were secondary sawtimber sources and, in more recent decades, the producers of pulp.

Pine and hardwoods compete for sites, and, without disturbances (principally fire) or deliberate cultivation, the pine will prevail over hardwoods. Fire was the great shaper of the southern forest: its realm was, in turn, dictated by the cultural practices and the geography of standing water. The relative distribution of pine and hardwoods still conforms to this pattern. Currently, hardwoods are being replaced by farms, especially along the Mississippi River floodplain; pocosins and coastal swamps are being transformed into pine plantations; and farm woodlots are being converted into pine, recreational woodlands, and fuelwood groves.

The present geography of the southern forest is the product of its human history. Among the American Indians, land was cleared for cultivation, then maintained as a prairie or a savanna by burning. Nearly everywhere, broadcast fire was used to control the tangle of hardwood saplings, shrubs, palmetto, and grass known as the "rough." If not burned frequently, this dense understory would supplant pine with hardwood. To perpetuate a desirable habitat and reduce fuels available for wildfire, to make travel possible, and to drive game, like deer, during hunting, nearly all naturally drained lands were fired. During droughts, even swamps burned.

Early southern settlers adopted and accelerated Indian practices. Slash and burn agriculture prepared sites for tobacco, corn, and cotton, but the soil was soon depleted of nutrients, and a pattern of shifting cultivation resulted. Agricultural land clearing across the Piedmont was completed during antebellum expansion, although pockets of forest remained in sandy areas, undrained sites, remote hills, and, where farms had been abandoned, in "old field" regeneration. The woods themselves, as long as the understory could be kept in grass, served for hunting and herding; the woods range was kept habitable by the liberal use of fire. Importing European techniques for the reclamation of wetlands, settlers drained low-lying bogs, exposing many sites to logging and fire that were not available to Indian use. They learned to tap resinous pines for sap, which could be processed into naval stores like turpentine. They cut timber for fuelwood and converted hardwoods into charcoal. Eventually, industrial logging moved into the region.

Between 1890 and 1920 the timber industry left the cutover pineries of the Great Lake states for the relatively virgin pineries of the South. Around 1909 national lumber production, concentrated in the southern yellow pine (longleaf), reached its all-time high. Even granted the extravagance of the process, however, the southern forest should have regenerated. That it did not was due, first, to the promiscuous use of fire ("woodsburning") and then, during the late 1920s, due to an overly aggressive suppression of fire. Longleaf pine, in particular, shows peculiar adaptations to heat, and without fire it never recovered its former prominence. Fire practices, abandoned farmland (the result of a depressed farm economy and infestations by the boll weevil), and cutover forests made the South into a wasteland. In 1919 it was estimated that 92 million acres had been cut over and deserted.

Eventually, the forest reestablished itself. Industrial logging in the South coincided with the conservation reforms of the Progressive era and the coming of age of professional forestry. The nation's first forestry school was established at the Biltmore Estate in North Carolina. The U.S. Forest Service became active after the Weeks Act (1911) allowed for the acquisition of land for national forests; it greatly expanded its influence through cooperative programs with state forestry bureaus, themselves stimulated by the Clarke-McNary Act (1924), and quadrupled its holdings during the 1930s, as tax delinquent land accumulated and the Roosevelt Administration pushed major conservation programs. The Forest Service established two research stations, in Louisiana and North Carolina, and a forest fire laboratory in Georgia. Among private landholders, the experiment by Henry Hardtner in Louisiana—sustained production through regeneration—had national repercussions. The Great Southern Lumber Company of Louisiana and the Crosset Lumber Company of Arkansas were models for fire protection and management; and in 1941 the Forest Farmers Association was created as a southern counterpart to the Tree Farm movement of the Northwest. Professional foresters took the torch away from folk practitioners and developed the techniques of prescribed burning—one of the South's great gifts to land management in the United States.

But the crucial event was the development during the 1930s of a pulp industry based on the southern pines. Eventually, the southern forest would produce half the pulp and a third of the paper in this country. Pine plantations for pulp production, based on short rotations and genetically selected species, would become big business, though southern agrarianism resisted its encroachments as it did other forms of industrialization. Thus, industrial logging completed the destruction of the South's First (virgin) Forest; the commercialization of the southern pine for pulp led to the Second Forest; and the Third Forest is now undergoing harvesting and regeneration. The environmental potential of the southern forest is immense. Its limitations are socioeconomic, principally related to ownership patterns. By the 1970s about 10 percent of the southern forest was publicly owned and 20 percent was held by corporations; 70 percent remained in private hands, mostly under the care of farmers. Less than 1 percent of forest land was devoted to parks or wilderness.

See also AGRICULTURE: / Naval Stores; INDUSTRY: / Furniture Industry; Timber Industry; SOCIAL CLASS: / Timber Workers

Stephen J. Pyne
University of Iowa

John W. Barrett, ed., *Regional Silviculture of the United States* (2d ed., 1980); Thomas D. Clark, *The Greening of the South: The Recovery of Land and Forest* (1984); Henry Clepper, *Professional Forestry in the United States* (1971); Stephen J. Pyne, *Fire in America: A Cultural History of Wildland and Rural Fire* (1982); U.S. Forest Service, *Forest Statistics of the U.S.* (annual).

Gardens and Gardening

The South has long been noted for beautiful antebellum homes with lovely gardens, spacious lawns, beautiful large trees, and masses of flowering shrubs. With many beautiful native and introduced plants to use in landscaping and one or more botanical or public display gardens in nearly every southern state offering workshops, the southern gardening tradition continues.

A large proportion of the ornamental plants used throughout the southern states are broadleaf evergreens. These are far more predominant than the deciduous plants or the narrow-leaved evergreens such as junipers and dwarf hemlock pines. Once southern gardens consisted primarily of the magnolia (the handsome large evergreen southern magnolia), camellias, azaleas, boxwood, gardenias, groundcovers of English ivy, liriope, crape myrtle, and daylilies for summer color. This is now changing as gardeners use exciting deciduous and evergreen plants such as elaeagnus, hollies, hydrangeas, flowering quince, and viburnums. Interest in native plants such as native azaleas and many herbacious plants has also increased; some of these are grown by specialty nurseries.

The *Camellia japonica* was introduced to Europe from Asia in the 18th century. An old but popular variety, "Alba Plena," was displayed in Belgium in 1811 and arrived in the northeastern United States in 1880. Throughout the Northeast camellias were grown as tub plants for the greenhouse or conservatory and are still popular for this use. Large collections of camellias were a part of plantation life near port cities in South Carolina, Alabama, Louisiana, and Mississippi. In the late 1840s camellias were planted at Magnolia Gardens near Charleston, S.C. The first plants probably came from greenhouses in Philadelphia and other northern cities. Later they were imported directly from Europe. The glossy foliaged camellias range from large shrubs to small trees and are grown in shaded gardens from North Carolina southward to eastern Texas. The large flowers bloom from October to April and vary from white to pink to red or variegated. The American Camellia Society offices are surrounded by a large camellia garden and greenhouse near Marshallville, Ga. The *Camellia sasanqua*, which flowers in autumn, is also important to the landscape. Despite popular legend, the plant is not as cold hardy as *C. japonica* yet the colorful single to double flowers often suffer little if any fall damage, unlike some of the later flowering *C. japonica*.

Azalea gardens are a spectacular feature of the southern landscape. The large-flowered, evergreen Southern Indian Hybrid azaleas were first introduced from Europe to the United States as Belgian Indian Hybrids. The hybrids were developed in England and Belgium as greenhouse plants from several species native to Japan and China. Like camellias, they were used as tub plants in greenhouses and conservatories in the northeastern states before figuring as landscape plants in the South. In the 1840s they were introduced to Magnolia Gardens and proved to be hardy to the Deep South; they were soon popular throughout the Gulf Coast area. The hardier Belgian Indian Hybrids in the South became known as the Southern Indian Hybrids. The famous Fruitland Nursery in Augusta, Ga., played an important role in introducing azaleas, camellias, and many other ornamental plants to the South. A catalog of 1883 listed over 50 varieties of azaleas; unfortunately many of these old varieties are no longer available.

Southern cities such as Mobile, Savannah, and Charleston are famous for their azalea trails, roadside plantings, and special gardens lined with huge, colorful masses of such Southern Indian azaleas as the purplish-red Formosa, the Fielder's White, and the pink Pride of Mobile.

The small-flowering Kurume azaleas were known in Japan over 300 years ago and were introduced to the United States in 1915. Their hardy plants survive in -5 to -10°F, as far north as Kentucky and Maryland. Over 300 varieties of the Kurume azalea are still known in Japan and some gardens in the South have 50 or more named varieties. Over 20 Kurume azaleas are commonly grown in commercial specialty nurseries. Many of these plants were given English names after their introduction from Japan. Some of the favorites are Christmas Cheer (Imashojo), Hino (Hino degiri), Pink Pearl (Asuma-kagami), Coral Bells (Kirins), Snow, and Salmon Beauty.

Other evergreen or persistent-leaved azaleas are noted in the South for flowering from early spring to May and June. These include the Glenn Dale hybrids (over 400 named varieties), the Back Acres hybrids (over 50 named varieties), and the late-flowering Satsuki hybrids, with over 600 varieties grown in the United States. The interest in growing and hybridizing new azaleas continues throughout the South, and seven chapters affiliated with the American Rhododendron Society and/or the Azalea Society of America exist in the southern states.

The South is also known for its attractive evergreen boxwood hedges and large, compact specimen plants. Two species are frequently discovered in southern gardens. *Boxus sempervirens*, the common box, was introduced from Europe and is especially popular in the South. There are many selected varieties, however. *Suffruticosa* is a popular dwarf plant known as the "true dwarf box" and is prominent in the gardens of Williamsburg and Mount Vernon. *Boxus microphylla*, from Japan, is much hardier and lower in growth, and is fond of the warmer areas of the Gulf states.

The large, handsome *Magnolia grandiflora*, southern magnolia, is typical of the South and native from North Carolina to Texas. A large tree (to 100 feet) with glossy evergreen leaves six to eight inches long, its large white flowers are borne in mid- to late spring and add a delicate fragrance to the garden.

Other broadleaf evergreens noted in

southern gardens include the fragrant gardenia, tea olive, and *Elaeagnus*. Numerous hollies are used, such as the common American holly (*Ilex opaca*), the popular *Ilex cornuta* Burfordii holly, along with Japanese hollies (*Ilex crenata*). Other common broadleaf evergreens include mountain laurel, cherry laurel, leucothe, and osmanthus. Of the many deciduous ornamental plants in the South the crape myrtle is the best known. The crape myrtle (*Lagerstroemia indica*) is a large shrub or small tree known as the "lilac of the South." It is noted for its smooth, strong trunk formation and is frequently used as a street tree. The large pyramidal clusters of white, pink, red, or purple flowers appear in early to late summer. Many named varieties are available, and two favorites are Watermelon Red and Near East, a pale pink.

Other deciduous ornamental shrubs and small trees include the flowering quince or "japonica," *Chaenomeles speciosa* (lagenaria), pearl bush, *Exochorda racemosa*, hydrangeas, Bradford pear, redbud (*Cercis canadensis*), and the beautiful, native flowering dogwood (*Cornus florida*) and its many colorful varieties.

Two outstanding native shrubs are the oakleaf hydrangea and the many species of native azaleas often referred to as "wild honeysuckle." The fragrant native azaleas include the white to pink forms of rhododendron *R. canescens* (Piedmont azalea), *R. periclymenoides* [*nudiflorum*] (Pinxterbloom azalea), *R. alabamense* (Alabama azalea), the pink *R. vaseyi* (Pinkshell azalea), and the white *R. aborescens* (Sweet Azalea), *R. viscosum* (swamp azalea), and the yellow *R. austrinum* (Florida azalea).

The nonfragrant azaleas include the orange to red *R. flammeum* (*specosium*), Oconee azalea, the yellow to deep orange flame azalea (*R. Calendulaceum*), and the rare late-flowering plumleaf azalea (*R. prunifolium*).

The South has a tradition of public gardens, many of them associated with historic places such as Williamsburg, Mount Vernon, Monticello, Middleton, Hermitage, and numerous other plantation locales. Dumbarton Oaks, Biltmore, Bayou Bend, and the Elizabethan Garden represent spectacular gardens on private estates. Other well-known gardens include Callaway, Bellingrath, Cypress, Hodges, Magnolia, and Brookgreen. Botanical gardens at Fairchild in south Florida and the Plant Introduction Station at Savannah experiment with new plants to test their appropriateness to the southern environment.

Flower gardening, at a different level, has always had special meaning for the southern poor. Flowers offered an aesthetic dimension to the sometimes drab rural life, and women as far back as the 1600s set out ceramic flowerpots along porches or on steps in yards. One North Carolina mill town woman, Ida L. Moore, who was interviewed in the 1930s, was probably typical of many women in saying that "no place seems like home without a few flowers." Her husband made flower boxes out of old car gas tanks and painted them red. She grew petunias, phlox, and the simple but popular zinnias. "It's nice settin' on the porch when they's somethin' to look at besides a red, ugly hill," she said.

Writer Alice Walker has perhaps best captured the cultural importance of flower gardening for the poor, especially southern black women. She points out that, although circumscribed in much of what they could do in society, black women in the South expressed their artistic creativity, indeed their human spirituality, through such seemingly simple activities as gardening. In Walker's novel *The Third Life of Grange Copeland* (1970), the character Mem decorates with flowers the rundown houses she has to live in. Walker's own mother in Georgia did the same, ambitiously planting gardens of 50 or so varieties that would bloom from early March until November, bringing color to the lives of her family. "Because of her creativity with her flowers," writes Walker, "even my memories of poverty are seen through a screen of blooms—sunflowers, petunias, roses, dahlias, forsythia, spirea, delphiniums, verbena."

See also AGRICULTURE: Garden Patch

Fred C. Galle
Hamilton, Georgia

James C. Bonner, *Landscape* (Spring–Summer 1977); Ben A. Davis, *The Southern Garden: From the Potomac to the Rio Grande* (1971); Fred C. Galle, *Azaleas* (1974); Catherine Howell, *Landscape Journal* (Spring 1982); William L. Hunt, *Southern Gardens, Southern Gardening* (1982); Felder Rushing, *Gardening Southern Style* (1987); John Wedda, *Gardens of the American South* (1971); Brooks E. Wigginton, *Trees and Shrubs for the Southeast* (1963). ☆

Indians and the Environment

The ecology of the South was well suited to Indian occupation, with large populations inhabiting the river valleys of the interior as well as the coastal plains at white contact in the 16th century. These native people were highly successful at exploiting their ecosystem, drawing subsistence from a combination of hunting, farming, and gathering. When necessary, they purposely changed the environment, employing technologies that scholars only recently began to understand. Such economic diversity made Native American lives relatively secure. The southern Indians possessed an unusually sophisticated understanding of the environment, which provided virtually everything they needed for survival.

The largest concentration of Indian population in the western part of the South was in the Mississippi Delta and along the rivers east of it. Here the ancestors of the modern Choctaws and Chickasaws began building cities centuries before the voyage of Columbus. With the Spanish invasion, disease spread throughout the countryside killing at times 80 percent of the Indian occupants, leaving but a scattered remnant of people by 1600. To the west of the Mississippi River, Caddoan groups survived in well-protected villages, whereas on the river itself the Natchez were the dominant urban dwellers. To the east, Europeans found the Choctaws, living in towns along the Big Black, Pearl, Tombigbee, and Yazoo rivers. And to the north of the Choctaws lived their distant relatives, the Chickasaws. Hunters predominantly, the Chickasaws held the region from north-central Mississippi to the Ohio River, and eastward to the Tennessee and Cumberland rivers.

Farther east, the river valleys of Mississippi and Georgia were occupied by the Creek Nation, a loose confederacy with various subtribes including the Seminoles. The Creeks maintained some 50–60 towns after the initial decline in population brought about by European invasion. Related linguistically to the Chickasaws and Choctaws, the Creek populations were the largest in the eastern half of the South. The lands they occupied were part of an almost unbroken forest, with villages located generally along navigable streams such as the Alabama and Chattahoochee. The Cherokees lived north and east of the Creek towns in the more rugged landscapes of western Georgia, North and South Carolina, and eastern Tennessee. North and west of the Cherokees, in the Upper South, were the Shawnees, hunters of considerable skill, and eastward on the Atlantic Coast smaller tribal groups could be found such as the Virginia tribes, often called Powhatan's Confederacy, the Tuscarora, Catawba, Yamassee, Westos, and finally in Florida, the Timucua.

The forest environment of the South had an important impact on all the nations of the region, fostering unique skills needed for survival. Nearly every southern tribe turned to the hunt in November to begin the subsistence cycle, stalking the white-tailed deer. The herds were approached by hunters during the rutting season when they were less inclined to run; hunters surrounded and killed the deer with bow and arrows. On occasions, thick underbrush and forest were set on fire to flush deer out, creating intermittent parklands across the South that allowed for better browsing. The winter hunt went into January, with large amounts of meat being smoked for later use. Some estimates suggest that deer provided upwards of 50 to 80 percent of the protein used in the diet of southern Indians. Other game animals that contributed were bear and turkey.

The opening of farms followed the hunt in spring, with various varieties of corn, squash, and beans being planted on scattered fields, usually opened in the fertile floodplains of river valleys. Women took charge of the planting after men had cleared the wild cane and trees. This slash and burn agriculture left scars; large trees were seldom removed, but rather girted and left to die. The Indians planted their crops in hills, a practice that limited erosion. Planting sticks and shell hoes were used to break the ground. About half a dozen seeds were placed in each hill, necessitating some thinning when the seedlings came up. Although more food probably came from hunting and gathering, corn was a substantial part of the native diet, and all accounts suggest that yields were high. Because fertilizer was not used, however, towns had to move occasionally in order to find new land capable of sustaining crops.

Gathering provided the third means of subsistence. The list of edible foods found in the South was extraordinary, including nuts and seeds and many species of roots. Some wild plants such as sweet potatoes were semidomesticated, in that natives regularly burned off regions so that they might better compete with the surrounding fauna. Fishing was another form of gathering. Inland tribes depended less on fish for food than did coastal groups, but both stalked catfish, a southern delicacy. The fish were collected in V-shaped rock fishtraps, constructed at considerable effort, in fast-moving streams. The end of the V was pointed downstream so that the current forced fish into the enclosure. The Florida Indians were most adept at fishing and coastal food gathering. Sea life became a primary food source for them and they carried on the hunt for various edible sea creatures throughout the year. Everything from oysters to whales were taken, with men stalking the larger animals and women and children working primarily as gatherers. Even sharks were hunted, although the technique used to take them is still unclear. Apparently, they were clubbed while in shallow water.

The obvious diversity in subsistence forms of southern Indians led to a keen perception of nature and environment. Indian religion and social organization evolved around this economic relationship with nature. Cherokee hunters, for example, carefully disposed of the bones of animals they had taken, not wanting to offend their spirits. Florida tribes also treated with respect the remains of whales and fish. The planting of corn and the harvest were occasions for careful thought and celebration. Southern Indians manipulated the ecosystem to its fullest, changing the natural environment when necessary to suit needs, but living within its bounds more fully than most other civilizations in history.

See also ETHNIC LIFE: Indian Cultural Contributions; GEOGRAPHY: Indians and the Landscape

Gary Clayton Anderson
Texas A&M University

Robert S. Cotterill, *The Southern Indians: The Story of The Civilized Tribes before Removal* (1954); Frederick Hodge, ed., *Handbook of American Indians North of Mexico*, 2 vols. (1971); Charles Hudson, *The Southeastern Indians* (1976); Lewis H. Larson, *Aboriginal Subsistence Technology on the Southeastern Coastal Plain during the Late Prehistoric Period* (1980); Wilcomb E. Washburn, *The Indian in America* (1975); Richard White, *The Roots of Dependency: Subsistence, Environment, and Social Change among the Choctaws, Pawnees, and Navajos* (1983); J. Leitch Wright, Jr., *The Only Land They Knew: The Tragic Story of the American Indians in the Old South* (1981). ☆

Insects

Imagine southerners living in a world without the flicker of the firefly, the chirp of a cricket, the buzz of the honeybee, or the flutter of a swallowtail butterfly. They would probably prefer to live in a world without the bite of a mosquito, the itch of a chigger, the sting of the wasp, or the invasion of cockroaches. Southerners cannot escape the influence of insects. As a group, insects comprise the largest and most diverse form of animal life on earth, a fact southerners can easily believe on summer nights.

Most people enjoy products like silk and honey that are made by insects. Southerners have been especially successful at the business of raising bees. They sell packaged bees—including a queen and her workers—to northerners, whose bees die during the cold winters if left outdoors. A common sight for travelers in the South is people by the side of the road selling jars of such local honey flavors as sourwood, tupelo, and orange blossom.

Shellac and carmine dyes are also products of insects, and many foods are available only because insects pollinate the plants from which they are produced. Although unknown perhaps to most people, significant benefits accrue from the lives of literally hundreds of insect species, which prey on or parasitize other insects.

Throughout history insects have been well known for their ravages of humans and their domesticated animals, to crops and other material possessions. A negative image has resulted. One interested in learning more about how insects have influenced humans through the ages might begin with biblical accounts of swarms of flies or locust (grasshopper) plagues (Exodus 8:24, 10:4, and 10:13), and any text on the history of Europe will give a detailed account of the Black Plague.

American history is equally rich in its accounts of insect-human relationships. Indeed, settlement of many areas of the southern United States was greatly influenced by mosquitoes. Mosquitoes infested the early English colony at Jamestown and contributed to the diseases of the 1608 "starving time," which almost destroyed the colony. Later, southerner Walter Reed discovered that the mosquito (*Aedes aegypti*) transmits the yellow fever virus, and he helped to end a great plague in the region.

The fire ants (*Solenopsis invicta* and *Solenopsis richter*, the red and black imported fire ants) are pests common through the South. The red imported fire ant arrived from Brazil more than 60 years ago, apparently entering the South through wood off a freighter at Mobile. By 1985 these ants had caused nearly $59 million in damage to soybean crops, and one study by the Mississippi Cooperative Extension Service estimated that 744,000 people are stung annually in that state. The Mediterranean fruit fly has periodically endangered the South's citrus fruit industry, the screwworm has been costly for cattle growers to combat, the Texas cattle tick devastated cattle in years past, and the pine bark beetle is currently threatening the region's trees.

Perhaps no insect alien has gained greater notoriety than the boll weevil, originally a native of Mexico and Central America, because of its devastating effect on cotton culture during the early 1900s. In 1919, though, the citizens of Coffee County, Ala., erected a large monument to the boll weevil on the town square of Enterprise as acknowledgment of its influence on the economy of the region. The boll weevil was credited with causing farmers to pursue more profitable ventures like peanuts and livestock in the southern states.

Many insects that humans label as pests became pestiferous because of the alteration of environments to suit human needs. Southerners live in heated homes, thus creating a somewhat tropical habitat for formerly tropical creatures such as cockroaches; southerners drained floodplains and planted them with crops, creating vast "food tables" for literally hundreds of native and imported insect species; and, as Americans learned to travel by wheel, sea, and air, they ignored insect "hitchhikers" like the Hessian fly, the European corn borer, and the smaller European elm bark beetle.

Insects have been the subject matter for a variety of cultural expressions in the South. Insect life is portrayed through folk sayings such as the old rule for planting corn: "One for the cutworm, One for the crow, One to rot, and Two to grow." Because of the sheer numbers of places that insects inhabit, southern language is graced with such expressions as "finer than a gnat's eyeball!" and "snug as a bug in a rug." Vernacular names chosen for many common insects reveal that nonentomologists can be good observers of nature. Such names as devil's horse for the praying mantis, dung roller for the adult dung beetle, snake doctor for any of the numerous species of dragonflies, and chicken choker for the larva of the tiger beetle are not the common names accepted by professional entomologists, but they are accurate statements about each insect's behavior.

On the other hand, certain vernacular names such as waterbug for the Oriental cockroach and locust for the dog-day or 13- and 17-year cicadas have come about from observations, but convey misconceptions about the insect's ecology. Vernacular origins were likely for many of the accepted common names of insects including the tumblebug, hornworm, blisterbug or blister beetle, stink bug, water strider, cabbageworm, ladybug or lady beetle, plant louse, head louse, crab louse, bluebottle fly, house fly, stable fly, horse fly, deer fly, bedbug, mayfly or fishfly, May beetle, and June beetle.

Southern literature and music reflect the human-insect interaction. James Agee recalled in his short vignette, "Knoxville, Summer, 1915," lying in the yard of his family's house, after supper, listening to "the dry and exalted noise of the locusts," and that of the crickets, which was "of the great order of noises." Like many a southern child, he chased fireflies—or lightning bugs, as they are called in the vernacular. Preacher Will Campbell entitled his autobiographical memoir about growing up in Mississippi, *Brother to a Dragonfly*, and used an image of that insect to convey his moving relationship with his brother. In a more humorous vein, Harper Lee made a rollicking scene in *To Kill a Mockingbird*, when Burris Ewell inadvertently disrupted the school classroom by carrying a head louse—a cootie—in his head to school.

"Just looking for a home, just looking for a home" is a verse from the boll weevil ballad, one of the most popular southern folk songs. Kokomo Arnold sang the "Bo-Weevil Blues." Bobbie Gentry's song "Bugs" is a veritable compendium of good-natured human annoyance with insects, evoking images of a "granddaddy long legs" creeping up a screen, boll weevils in the cotton, dirt daubers and red wasps swooping out of the sky, and yellow jackets buzzing around one's head; of shooing flies from the table and avoiding chiggers in the blackberry bushes.

Women in the South made spider leg quilts, in tribute to a close relative of insects; the pattern had 12 to 16 strips arranged like the limbs of a spider. Finally, one university, Georgia Tech, has made an ultimate modern southern tribute to an insect—the mascot for its football team is the Yellow Jacket.

See also AGRICULTURE: / Boll Weevil; Pest Control

T. J. Helms
Mississippi State University

W. J. Holland, *The Moth Book: A Popular Guide to a Knowledge of the Moths of North America* (1903); Maurice T. James and Robert F. Harwood, *Herm's Medical Entomology* (1969); Robert E. Pfadt, ed., *Fundamentals of Applied Entomology* (4th ed., 1985). ☆

Land Use

Approximately 27 percent of the land area of Mississippi, Louisiana, and Arkansas, 26 percent of Texas and Oklahoma, and 16 percent of the Southeast as a whole is used for crops and pasture. These averages, varying from 36 percent in Oklahoma to 11 percent in Florida, place the South behind corn belt states and the northern plains' wheat belt, but ahead of the Northeast, mountain states, and the West as an agricultural region. Former Confederate states account for approximately 20 percent of the nation's cropland harvested.

The large arable area, in relation to its small population, has resulted in two centuries of widespread land exploitation. As historian Lewis C. Gray put it, "Planters bought land as they might buy a wagon—with the expectation of wearing it out"; the wave of farmers that swept from Virginia to Texas planting corn and cotton thus "passed like a devastating scourge." Poor husbandry, stemming from lack of motivation rather than ignorance about fertilizers or crop rotation, brought about soil exhaustion and erosion before the Civil War. In 1850 the South was basically a mixed farming region. Plantations, mostly cotton, represented 18 percent of holdings. The remainder took the form of farms whose size was greater than the national average; improved land was average, but value of holdings fell below the average. Livestock numbers were higher in the South, where 60 percent of U.S. swine, 90 percent of mules, about 50 percent of meat cattle, and a third of the country's sheep were run.

During Reconstruction the character of agriculture remained constant; after 1900, however, diversification and specialization and the shift away from cotton and corn began. Land planted in crops peaked in the 1920s, then declined. Texas, which had the largest harvested acreage, dropped from 30.6 million acres in 1930 to 22.2 million acres in 1960 and 19 million acres in 1970, a 35.5 percent decline. Farm numbers also tumbled 30 percent between 1950–60, and 9 percent in the 1970s to a total of 159,000, or 7 percent of the nation's total. Less cultivation, fewer farms, and more specialized crops have been the trend in many southern states.

Irrigation agriculture has boomed. In the mid-1970s almost one quarter of Texas's harvested cropland was irrigated. Six million acres under cotton and grains in the Panhandle and Coastal Plain represent a sevenfold increase in irrigation since 1939. Florida ranked eighth after Texas with 1.6 million acres irrigated, and Arkansas was 12th with 950,000 acres.

Rice requires heavy drafts of water and is concentrated in the South. Arkansas grows more than 1 million acres, Texas and Louisiana exceed 500,000 acres each, and Mississippi has 200,000 acres in long-grain rice.

Horticulture, drawing upon irrigation, is pronounced. South Carolina ranks second in peaches, and Georgia is third. Florida excels in citrus. Just over 1 million acres nationwide are in grapefruit, oranges, lemons, and other citrus crops. Florida produced six times more than California, and four times more than second-ranked Texas in 1978. Similarly, over 4 times more oranges come from Florida than California and 28 times more than from third-ranked Texas. Large-scale beekeeping to bolster pollination has a strong foothold with the growing season and varied subtropical and warm temperate produce. Florida has the most bee colonies (356 in 1978) after California (504), followed closely by North Carolina (190), Texas (150), and Tennessee (140).

Other specialized crops are tobacco, peanuts, and soybeans. Tobacco has had a southeastern focus where North Carolina's 399,000 acres (in 1978), 8 percent of cropland, were almost double Kentucky's acreage (195,000), followed by Virginia (73,000) and South Carolina (71,000). Yields have rocketed in North Carolina from 12 million pounds in 1850, triple that in 1900, 12.5 times that by 1950. The tobacco yield was 850 million pounds in 1978.

Georgia has 530,000 acres, 11 percent, of cropland in peanuts. Texas is second with 307,000 acres, followed by Alabama (216,000), North Carolina (169,000), and Oklahoma (123,000). Virtually all the 1.5 million acres in peanuts are in nine southern states.

Since 1950 soybean acreage has grown fourfold nationally, and soybeans are a major southern crop. Arkansas has about 4.7 million acres or 65 percent of the cropland. The Midwest dominates in acreage, but Mississippi (3.7 million acres), Louisiana (2.7), Tennessee (2.3), and Alabama (1.6) are important. These four states have a combined 75 percent of their croplands in soybeans.

Grassland pasture, covering 96 million acres or 57 percent of Texas, produced 6 million beef cattle in that state in 1979. Surprisingly, Arkansas, Kentucky, Tennessee, and Florida have over 1 million beef cattle each, or 12 percent of the U.S. total.

Two factors explain the decline in the use of land for agriculture in the 20th century. First, woodland is extensive, accounting for two-thirds of Alabama and Georgia, and over one-half of South Carolina, Florida, Mississippi, Arkansas, Louisiana, and Virginia. These states possess roughly 30 percent of forest area in the nation and have supplied 38 percent of the timber. Peak years of production were in 1916 and 1925, but output declined to a steady 20 percent, mostly softwood timber. Crop intensification, however, has released marginal lands back to native vegetation, and forest development, producing stands of even-age, quick-growing trees, has extended pinelands.

Second, one-third of the American population now resides in the 15 states termed the Sunbelt. Urban and other special use categories have increased to reflect the 22 percent population growth there in the 1970s. Florida and Texas are over 80 percent urban, and neighboring states have sizable urban populations. Over 14 percent of Florida falls into the urban industrial category. The Texas-Louisiana "oil patch," cities in Oklahoma, and the manufacturing belt in the Southeast are expressions of metropolitan land use in the region.

See also AGRICULTURE articles; GEOGRAPHY: Land Use; URBANIZATION: Urban Growth

Robin W. Doughty
University of Texas at Austin

Thomas D. Clark, *The Greening of the South: The Recovery of Land and Forest* (1984); Donald B. Dodd and Wynelle S. Dodd, *Historical Statistics of the South, 1790–1970* (1973); Lewis C. Gray, *History of Agriculture in the Southern United States to 1860*, 2 vols. (1932, 1941); Sam B. Hilliard, *Hog Meat and Hoecake: Food Supply in the Old South, 1840–1860* (1972); U.S. Department of Agriculture, *Agricultural Statistics: 1980* (1980); U.S. Department of Agriculture, Economic Service, *Major Uses of Land in the United States: Summary for 1969* (1969). ☆

Natural Disasters

Natural disasters suddenly convey the vulnerability of human life and the fragility of civilization. They violently disrupt the fabric of society and create human misery as well as social dislocation. In the South most natural disasters are caused by weather-related phenomena—violent thunderstorms, tornadoes, floods, and hurricanes. The complex mechanics of warm, moisture-laden air from the Gulf of Mexico combining with the cool, drier air from the North spark violent thunderstorms that often engender short-lived tornadoes that tear unforgivingly across the landscape. Tropical weather patterns also spawn depressions that often evolve into hurricanes that threaten the Gulf and Atlantic coasts from June to November. Most of the South is also subject to heavy, anomalous rainfalls that push rivers beyond their banks, transforming towns and farms into a surreal watery landscape. The following cases illustrate the capricious forces of nature that often overwhelm the puny efforts of humankind to provide safe, comfortable habitats.

Thunderstorms are common natural occurrences of uncommon power and energy. A typical storm might be three miles across its base, tower 50,000 feet into the air, contain a half-million tons of condensed water, and release 10 times the energy of the atomic bomb dropped on Hiroshima. Tornadoes are the most devastating result of thunderstorms. Although they occur throughout the world, the American South and Midwest experience more tornadoes than anywhere else on earth. Southeastern tornadoes tend to be more deadly than those in the Great Plains and Midwest. Twisters in this region strike more often at night, are usually obscured in clouds and heavy rain, and are less prone to early detection than those that often are observed miles away on the plains. In fact, from 1916 to 1974 more tornado-related deaths occurred in Mississippi than in any other state—1,091.

Tornadoes sometimes break out in large patterns. In the so-called super outbreak of 2–3 April 1974, a record 148 tornadoes swept across the Upper South and Lower Midwest. Entire communities such as Xenia, Ohio; Brandenburg, Ky.; and Guin, Ala., were almost totally devastated. Losses totaled 315 dead, 6,142 injured, and $600 million in property damage. More than 9,600 homes were destroyed and 27,590 families suffered to some degree. The combined length of the tornadoes' paths was an incredible 2,598 miles.

A series of tornadoes also sliced through Mississippi and Georgia on 5–6 April 1936. At Tupelo, Miss., a huge tornado mangled the city's residences and business district, destroyed its municipal water reservoir, killed 216 persons, and injured 1,500. The next morning two tornadoes ripped through Gainesville, Ga., and ignited a large fire. Deaths totaled 203 and injuries from the funnels and fire reached 934. Gainesville, like other communities, suffered multiple tornado strikes. A 1903 twister claimed 28 lives and another in 1944 took 44.

Hurricanes develop over southern portions of the North Atlantic, as well as over the Gulf of Mexico and the Caribbean Sea, usually during the "season" that lasts from 1 June to 31 October. On average, 8 to 10 storms a year are large enough to be named by the U.S. Weather Service and carefully monitored as possible risks to mainland areas. The combination of great size (hurricanes average 100 miles in diameter) and long life compounds their destructive powers. They are the most damaging of all geophysical disasters because they produce heavy rainfall, high winds, flash floods, as well as powerful storm surges and tides.

The first written account of a hurricane in the South recorded the destruction that occurred at Jamestown, Va., on 27 August 1667. The "dreadful Hurry Cane" produced "such violence that it overturned many houses, burying in the ruins much goods and many people . . . the sea swelled twelve foot above the normal height drowning the whole country before it."

Hurricanes occur along the Atlantic Coast, but the seaboard of the Gulf of Mexico is more prone to these violent attacks. Gulf Coast hurricanes usually follow a track toward the northeast and dump heavy precipitation across large areas of the South, causing widespread flash floods.

At the turn of the century, Galveston, Tex., was a thriving, prosperous community that boasted the fastest-growing port in the United States. Much of the city was built on a barrier island, with the highest point only 20 feet above sea level. When a hurricane struck the morning of 8 September 1900, a ship broke from its moorings and crashed through the three bridges to the mainland, cutting off any chance of escape. Tides soon rose 20 feet above normal, tearing apart homes and buildings and reshaping them into a two-story-high mass of debris that was driven inland by the storm surge. An estimated 6,000 of Galveston's 20,000 residents died, a weather catastrophe unequaled before or since. Because of the threat of disease, masses of bodies were piled into trenches and burned—an acrid postlude to the worst natural disaster in the nation's history.

As the Miami, Fla., area developed in the 1920s, the fertile muck lands surrounding Lake Okeechobee became a source of produce for Florida's urbanites. Hundreds of small shantytowns arose near the lakeshore to house fieldworkers, and long mud dikes were built to mitigate flooding. On 16 September 1928 a hurricane with winds estimated at 160 miles per hour drove the lake waters across the flat landscape, collapsing dikes and drowning hundreds of people. The final death toll was estimated between 1,800 and 2,500, the second worst hurricane disaster in American history. After the storm, the federal government funded a massive flood control program for some 12,000 square miles of the Lake Okeechobee Everglades area to prevent future disasters.

Hurricane Camille (14–22 August 1969) was by far the most powerful hurricane of recent times. It devastated the Louisiana, Mississippi, and Alabama Gulf Coast with winds over 170 miles per hour and gusts up to 200. Storm surges reached almost unbelievable proportions, including an estimated 25-foot height at Pass Christian, Miss. (The National Weather Service estimates that storm surges cause 9 of 10 hurricane-related fatalities.) Camille caused 152 deaths in Mississippi and Louisiana and, after passing over the Southeast, dumped unusually heavy rains on the Mid-Atlantic region. Some 21 inches of rain fell within 24 hours over parts of Virginia and West Virginia, causing serious flash floods.

Because of relatively heavy rainfalls, much of the South is prone to flash, general, and backwater flooding. The propensity of people to farm, build, and live upon former floodplains poses hazards to lives and property. Flood control measures such as levees, dams, pumping plants, and channel improvements have reduced these threats in many areas. For example, the Mississippi River and portions of its tributaries are now being controlled by the massive Mississippi River and Tributaries Project authorized by Congress in 1928 and still only 76 percent complete. The project was developed in response to the catastrophic 1927 flood that caused crevasses in levees and sometimes spread out nearly 100 miles. The statistical dimensions of the tragedy were nightmarish: 16.6 million acres flooded; 162,000 homes inundated; as many as 500 killed; and 325,500 people cared for in refugee camps. Then Secretary of Commerce Herbert Hoover headed a relief effort that included 31,000 volunteers.

Some parts of the South have also experienced major seismic activity. The most violent and prolonged series of earthquakes in U.S. history occurred in the supposedly seismically quiet Mississippi Valley, far from the great faults of the West. During the early morning of 16 December 1811, a series of tremors centered near New Madrid, Mo., literally tore apart the landscape. Cabins and houses creaked and groaned, huge waves capsized boats on the Mississippi, trees swayed and snapped, and huge fissures opened in the earth. The shocks were felt over two-thirds of the United States and continued intermittently until 7 February 1812. An estimated 150,000 acres of timberland were destroyed and new lakes were created in Arkansas (Lake Francis) and in Tennessee (Reelfoot Lake). In addition, thousands of acres of farmland were transformed into swamps through settling. So severe was the damage that in 1815 Congress passed the first national disaster relief act, which enabled owners of ruined property to obtain equal tracts of land elsewhere.

The South's other major seismic event occurred near Charleston, S.C., the evening of 31 August 1886. Felt as far away as Boston and Bermuda, the earthquake destroyed or badly damaged most of the city's major buildings, caused more than $5 million damage, and claimed some 111 lives.

In the past quarter century the life-threatening potential of some disasters has been reduced by improved weather forecasting, flood control, hurricane protection projects, and highly effective emergency management programs developed by federal, state, and local agencies. Nevertheless, property damage will probably escalate as the Sunbelt continues to grow.

Michael C. Robinson
U.S. Army Corps of Engineers
Lower Mississippi Valley Division
Vicksburg, Mississippi

Allen H. Barton, *Communities in Disaster: A Sociological Analysis of Collective Stress Situations* (1969); James Cornell, *The Great International Disaster Book* (1976); Gordon E. Dunn and Banner I. Miller, *Atlantic Hurricanes* (1960); Kendrick Frazier, *The Violent Face of Nature* (1979); Gary Jennings, *The Killer Storms: Hurricanes, Typhoons, and Tornadoes* (1970); David Ludlum, *Early American Hurricanes, 1492–1870* (1963); James Penick, Jr., *The New Madrid Earthquakes of 1811–1812* (1976). ☆

Naturalists

Colonial Europeans were overwhelmed by the richness of the flora and fauna they found in the American wilderness. Until the middle of the 19th century and the development of specialization in science, those interested in examining the topography, geology, native peoples, and plant and animal life were amateurs—planters, ministers, teachers, mariners, and physicians—who had limited, if any, scientific training in a specific field of natural history. Most of them were self-taught. They generally focused their energies on the collection of data, the classification of that data into a systematic framework, and the development of a scientific nomenclature that would permit the integration of newly discovered scientific species and phenomena into a larger framework of knowledge. The knowledge they gained on the flora, fauna, peoples, and geography of this continent permitted the development of scientific specialization into distinct scientific disciplines. Although botany was the dominant interest among field naturalists in America until the middle of the 19th century, the most original contributions of Americans to science were in zoology and paleontology.

The American South lacked the libraries, gardens, and herbaria to permit the systematic study of natural history, but its varied topography and rich flora and fauna attracted many naturalists. As early as the 16th century, Thomas Harriot and John White chronicled and illustrated the plants, animals, and native peoples found near Sir Walter Raleigh's ill-fated Roanoke settlement. Harriot's *A briefe and true report of the new found land of Virginia* (London, 1588), which recorded his travels into the interior of Carolina, and possibly Virginia, distinguished between the geology of the Coastal Plain and the Piedmont, identified the mineral resources of the coastal region, commented upon the agricultural practices of the Indians, identified their crops, and recorded 28 species of mammals, 86 species of birds, and the presence of oak, elm, ash, walnut, fir, cedar, maple, witch hazel, willow, beech, and sassafras trees. His description of the American *Cervidae*, with its distinction between the deer of America and Europe, would not be surpassed for two centuries. Nevertheless, Harriot's scientific knowledge was limited, and his work provided generally accurate descriptions but little analysis. John White's delicate watercolors, housed in the British Museum, complemented Harriot's work and became the basis for the engravings that accompanied Harriot's published *Report*, the first work in English to describe the New World's natural history.

In the 17th century, individuals living in Virginia and other southern colonies served as correspondents for the Royal Society of London and provided Europeans with information ranging from the abundance of oyster shells in the soil to the proliferation of nettles, spinach, rattlesnakes, and turkey buzzards. As a result of such communications the *Philosophical Transactions* of the Royal Society began to publish accounts of New World phenomena. John Clayton and John Banister were particularly conscientious in providing English naturalists with field observations from America in the last decades of the 17th century.

John Lawson, Surveyor-General for the Lords Proprietors of the province of North Carolina, traveled widely in North Carolina, and he published the results of his 1700–1701 reconnaissance as a *New Voyage to Carolina* (London, 1709). Two-thirds of this volume examined the natural history of the region and provided a description of 93 birds, 28 mammals, 70 fish, and 4 species of pine. Some of the information he provided was curious, for he classified tortoises, alligators, and snakes among insects, maintained that snakes charmed their victims and their bites could be cured by snake root, recorded that whales seldom washed ashore with their tongues intact, and noted that some American Indians hunted whales by climbing upon a whale's back and plugging up its spout. His ornithological observations and his comments upon Indian life in North Carolina were more carefully prepared and are important sources for that period. Lawson provided James Petiver, a Fellow of the Royal Society and patron of John Banister, with information and specimens from North Carolina. Captured by Tuscarora Indians while on an expedition up the Neuse River, Lawson was slain on 22 September 1711.

Lawson's work was eclipsed by the endeavors of Mark Catesby. English by birth, Catesby had studied under the distinguished naturalist John Ray and became the most experienced naturalist to work in America up to that date. In 1712 he came to Virginia to live with his sister and her family to satisfy, as he notes in the preface to his major work, "a passionate Desire of viewing as well the Animal as Vegetable productions in their native countries; which are strangers in England." For seven years Catesby collected materials in Tidewater Virginia, made trips west into the Blue Ridge Mountains, and voyaged to Jamaica and the islands of Bermuda. He became an experienced field collector before returning to England in 1719. The variety of his collections and the knowledge he had gained of American flora and fauna won support in both England and America for his proposed study on American natural history. In 1722 he returned to America to conduct additional studies. For three more years he conducted field studies, made drawings, and collected specimens from North Carolina to Georgia and Florida and west into the Piedmont. Under conditions of poverty, Catesby labored to complete his work on American natural history. In 1731 his *Natural History of the Carolinas, Florida, and the Bahama Islands* began to appear in sections. The two volumes were completed in 1743. With their colored plates containing 220 illustrations, they became the most attractive works on American natural history published for the next century. Although Catesby's taxonomy was weak, Linnaeus utilized Catesby's work and frequently incorporated Catesby's descriptions and binomial names of birds, fishes, and plants in his work. Catesby's *Hortus Britanno-Americanus*, published in 1737, with its description of 85 southern trees and shrubs, was the first study in English dedicated to the trees of this continent.

As a descriptive ornithologist, Catesby surpassed the standards of his time and concerned himself with enduring problems that are still studied. Although the plates in his work have been criticized as being on occasion too brightly colored, he was a talented and influential scientific illustrator. Catesby developed the practice of portraying on one plate an ornithological, zoological, or botanical specimen in a balanced natural habitat with the appropriate ecological setting of trees, shrubs, grasses, or other animals. Alexander Wilson and John James Audubon followed Catesby's practice of including floral and faunal specimens on one plate. Through his correspondence, his collections, and his magnificent folio volumes, Catesby stimulated an interest in American natural history in America and England and on the continent.

Natural history in the South was further enhanced by the endeavors of the first native-born American naturalist, John Bartram. Praised by Linnaeus as one of the world's greatest natural botanists, this diligent and meticulous field naturalist made numerous expeditions to collect seeds and specimens for his English friend and patron, Peter Collinson. Always interested in the promotion of natural science in America, he established a major botanical garden on the banks of the Schuylkill River, corresponded with numerous European scientists and collectors, suggested to Benjamin Franklin the need for the exploration of the western reaches of the continent, contributed substantively to the understanding of southern flora and fauna, and was honored by King George III with appointment as "Botanist to the King."

With his son William, an able illustrator, naturalist, and author, he journeyed south in 1765 through Georgia and Florida with instructions from the English crown to find the sources of the St. Johns River. In the fall of 1765 they discovered along the banks of the Altamaha River a new species of small tea tree, which they named in honor of Benjamin Franklin, *Gordonia pubescens Franklinia*, today *Franklinia altamaha*. By the end of the 18th century this species was no longer seen in the wild state. The attractive specimens of this flowering tree, which can still be seen today in American gardens, are all descendants from specimens maintained by the Bartrams in their Pennsylvania garden. A new species of anise, *Ilicium parviflorum*, was also discovered on this expedition, and observations were made on soils, trees, fossils, and plants. With his vision declining, this was the 66-year-old Bartram's last expedition. Details of Bartram's experiences were published in 1767 in an *Account of East Florida*.

William Bartram maintained an interest in Florida and in 1773 embarked upon a five-year exploration of the natural history of Georgia, eastern Florida, the Carolinas, and Alabama. Named *Pucpuggy*, the "Flower Hunter," by Indians, he wandered patiently and alone through the southern wilderness studying and observing plants, animals, and Indians. Captivated by the richness and abundance of the area's natural history, he made the first detailed study of the American alligator and provided important early information on the reptiles, amphibians, birds, Indians, and plants of this region. His study contains many elements of a modern ecological survey. While Bartram's *Travels through North and South Carolina, Georgia, East and West Florida* (1791) contributes substantively to southern natural history, the wealth of romantic and exotic imagery in the *Travels* nourished the creative muses of Coleridge, Wordsworth, Chateaubriand, and other authors of the Romantic movement. "Kubla Khan" and "The Rime of the Ancient Mariner," as well as other works, bear the distinct intellectual imprint of the imagery of Bartram's *Travels*.

Science has traditionally developed in cities, and the lack of cities in the South impeded its development there. Charleston's momentary eminence in the development of southern natural history is related to its prominence as an urban area in the late 18th and early 19th centuries. Charleston physicians and planters nourished interest in natural history and provided an intellectual milieu attractive to visiting naturalists. Near Charleston in 1787, the French naturalists André and François Michaux established a nursery. André Michaux had been commissioned by the French monarch Louis XVI to ascertain which of America's trees, particularly the oaks, could be profitably grown in France. In 1801 he published the handsomely illustrated *Histoire des Chènes de l'Amérique*, the first major study of American oaks. From their base near Charleston, André and his son, François, collected specimens in the Carolina mountains, the southern Appalachians, Florida, and the Bahamas. André's posthumously published *Flora Boreali-Americana* (1803) was the first systematic study of North American flora and included valuable information about southern flora.

Thomas Jefferson's *Notes on the State of Virginia* (1785) presented a perceptive assessment of the resources and natural history of that state with clear descriptions of the Indians, animals, plants, minerals, climate, and topography found there. Jefferson took the opportunity to refute French naturalist Comte de Buffon's contention that the same species of animals and humans grew smaller in America than in Europe. Less disciplined than Jefferson in scientific interests, Constantine Rafinesque was as comprehensive as the Virginian in his activities. Born in Constantinople, he became an ardent, if occasionally unfocused, student of this nation's natural history. From 1819 to 1826 he collected specimens and studied plants, fishes, shells, fossils, and Indian mounds while a professor at Transylvania College in Lexington, Ky. Although he traveled widely and published profusely on these topics in a variety of journals, he failed to make a substantive contribution in any specific area.

John James Audubon also led a life of wide wanderings. Born in Santo Domingo, he traveled through many of the southern states in his quest to capture through his paintings the birds of America. Much of his life was characterized by economic failures and frustrations, but he labored almost without ceasing from 1827 to 1838 to complete his monumental *Birds of America*. To obtain specimens for study and to observe birds in their natural habitats, he traveled to South Carolina and Florida and to the Keys in 1831. Friends in Washington provided him with government schooners so that he could more comfortably conduct his studies on the St. Johns River and in the Keys. On this trip he made the sketches and studies for the Great White Heron and Brown Pelican, which appear in his *Birds of America*. In 1837 Audubon journeyed along the Gulf Coast to Galveston, Tex., but few significant studies resulted from this trip.

In the three decades immediately preceding the Civil War, science became more specialized. The economic advantages of natural resources began to be of concern to southern states, and in North Carolina, South Carolina, Tennessee, Virginia, Alabama, Mississippi, Texas, and Florida state geological surveys were established. The increasing pace of scientific advancement and the development of more sophisticated theoretical assumptions about the methodologies of a scientific discipline reduced in the last half of the 19th century the contributions that naturalists and natural historians could make to understanding the natural resources of the South. Although the age of naturalists was waning, the great variety of the South's flora and fauna would continue to attract the attention of scientists.

See also HISTORY AND MANNERS: / Jefferson, Thomas

Phillip Drennon Thomas
Wichita State University

Whitfield J. Bell, *Early American Science: Need and Opportunities for Study* (1955); Albert E. Cowdrey, *This Land, This South: An Environmental History* (1983); Robert Elman, *First in the Field: America's Pioneering Naturalists* (1977); John C. Greene, *American Science in the Age of Jefferson* (1984); Brooke Hindle, *The Pursuit of Science in Revolutionary America* (1956); Kathryn Hall Proby, *Audubon in Florida, with Selections from the Writings of John James Audubon* (1974); William Martin Smallwood and Mabel Sarah Coon Smallwood, *Natural History and the American Mind* (1941); Henry Savage, Jr., *Discovering America, 1700–1875* (1979); Raymond Phineas Stearns, *Science in the British Colonies of America* (1970). ☆

Natural Resources

Because gold and silver are not produced to any degree in the 11 states of the old Confederacy, there is a tendency to consider the South a region short of natural resources. Nothing could be further from the truth. If natural resources are defined as forms of wealth or potential wealth supplied by nature, then the South always has been blessed. Even though some of these treasures have been abused, they remain the region's greatest hope for a bright and prosperous future.

The South's most basic natural resources are high humidity and warm weather. From 45 to 70 inches of rain fall a year, and temperatures reach 90° more than 50 days annually. Most of the region enjoys a nine months' growing season.

In much of the South soils were originally rich and productive. The earliest white Virginians grew tobacco, followed by corn and wheat. South Carolina soil, in combination with large quantities of water, produced rice, and an excellent short-staple cotton was grown above tidewater in the Carolinas, in the Black Belt of Georgia and Alabama, and in the rich Mississippi Delta between the Mississippi and Yazoo rivers. The land was surely abused, leached, eroded, and often made sterile, but with conservation measures and intelligent husbandry, it can and, indeed, has come back. Whether one speaks of the Tidewater South along the Atlantic, the Piedmont above the fall line, the Appalachian Highlands, the Kentucky Bluegrass, the Gulf Coastal Plain, or the red clay hills of north Georgia and Alabama, the land has always borne foodstuffs in abundance.

The first white explorers initially exploited the most prevalent natural resource, the wild game. Deer, bear, buffalo, turkeys, passenger pigeons, bass, catfish, and other game, birds, and fish were killed in abundance. In the late 1600s more than 54,000 deerskins were shipped annually from Charleston, S.C. Even today sportsmen consider the South a paradise for hunters and fishermen.

When pioneer agriculturalists entered the South they exploited the game but also attacked another great natural resource—the great forest covering much of the land with both hardwoods and softer conifers. In the 19th and early 20th centuries much of the hardwood was cut. So favorable was the South to the growth of timber, however, that tree farming of soft woods, especially for papermaking, is today one of the region's major industries. Over 200 million acres are currently forested.

A consequence of the high rainfall is the veining of the southern countryside with deep, sluggish rivers. In the early days settlers were attracted to the river valleys because canebrakes filled them and stretched for hundreds of miles along the stream banks. Settlers' cattle could graze on the leaves of the cornlike stalks, and the destruction of the cane and replacement by fields of grain or cotton was easier than clearing the forest and preparing it for planting.

Rivers range from the Potomac and James in Virginia, the Savannah and Altamaha down the Atlantic, to the Suwannee, Apalachicola, Pearl, and Alabama along the Gulf and, in the Upper South, the Kentucky, Cumberland, and Tennessee. These rivers have always been, and remain, liquid highways of commerce; in the 20th century they have also furnished immense quantities of electric power. Greatest of all is, of course, the mighty Mississippi, immortalized by Samuel Clemens.

The rivers carry rich nutrients into the bays of the Atlantic and the Gulf of Mexico, feeding schools of edible fish and seafood including scallops, oysters, and shrimp. Apalachicola Bay off the north Florida coast is one of the world's richest bodies of water, providing fish and seafood for markets as far away as Japan.

Precious metals are rare in the South—although gold was discovered at Dahlonega, Ga., and in small quantities elsewhere—but other useful minerals have been found. Texas, Arkansas, Louisiana, and Mississippi are leading producers of petroleum and natural gas; some sulphur is also mined. Alabama, Tennessee, and Virginia (including West Virginia) produce bituminous coal. Within the South are found in quantities suitable for exploitation stone, cement, sand and gravel, and phosphates.

See also AGRICULTURE: Crops; INDUSTRY: / Mining; Oil Industry; Timber Industry; RECREATION: Fishing; Hunting

Richard A. Bartlett
Florida State University

Thomas D. Clark, *The Greening of the South: The Recovery of Land and Forest* (1984); Henry H. Collins, *Complete Field Guide to American Wildlife* (1959); Albert E. Cowdrey, *This Land, This South: An Environmental History* (1983); Gilbert C. Fite, *Cotton Fields No More: Southern Agriculture, 1865–1980* (1984); Charles B. Hunt, *Physiography of the United States* (1967); Howard W. Odum, *Southern Regions of the United States* (1936); Stephen J. Pyne, *Fire in America: A Cultural History of Wildland and Rural Fire* (1982). ☆

Parks and Recreation Areas

Although parklands came late to the American South, the region today is renowned for its stunning variety of national, state, and local preserves. Paralleling the motivations for park establishment in the North, Middle West, and West, preservation in the South accelerated rapidly with the development of an urban population in the 20th century. Historically, after all, preservation had its roots in the city. As the noted environmental historian Roderick Nash has so eloquently written, "The literary gentleman wielding a pen, not the pioneer with his axe, made the first gestures of resistance against the strong currents of antipathy."

In this vein Thomas Jefferson was among the first to identify the natural world as a great source of national pride. In 1784, for example, writing his *Notes on the State of Virginia*, he challenged Europeans to concede the grandeur of Harpers Ferry and the Natural Bridge. "The passage of the Patowmac through the Blue ridge is perhaps one of the most stupendous scenes in nature," he wrote. "This scene is worth a voyage across the Atlantic." To the frontiersman, however, wilderness was an obstacle to settlement and commerce, an adversary to subdue rather than appreciate. It followed that most of the South throughout the 19th century was not receptive to the appreciation of the natural world visible in a Thomas Jefferson.

The gardens and common fields of Williamsburg, Va., underscored that appreciation was strongest where people of wealth, leisure, and culture prevailed. "A library, a Garden, a Grove, a Purling stream are the Innocent scenes that divert our Leisure," wrote Colonel William Byrd (1674–1744) of Westover speaking for the planter class. Byrd's emphasis on leisure—on recreation as opposed to the protection of nature for its own sake—was by far the most important catalyst leading to what might be considered the first parks in the South. To be sure, as early as 1832 the federal government set aside the Hot Springs Reservation in Arkansas; its purposes were strictly practical rather than aesthetic. Southerners concerned about their health looked to its waters for cures to common ailments; the preservation of the Hot Springs as a natural area was the last thing on most people's minds in 1832.

The first great scenic park in the United States was Yosemite, which became a state park in 1864 and then a national park in 1890. Yellowstone, the first national park, was established in Wyoming Territory in 1872. In contrast, few Americans recognized the South as naturally distinctive. Instead, adjectives such as "monotonous" and "commonplace" were often used to describe many southern landscapes. The obvious exceptions, such as the Great Smoky Mountains, were by and large outside the mainstream of national development. Equally significant, by the time Americans learned to appreciate the ecological if not the topographical distinctiveness of southern scenery, most areas worthy of park status had long ago passed out of the public domain and into private ownership.

These odds against preservation aside, southerners began making rapid strides in conservation shortly after the turn of the century. As early as 1899, for example, preservationists headquartered in Asheville, N.C., formed the Appalachian National Park Association (ANPA). In the words of the Association, time was running out for "the last of the Eastern wilderness." By "Eastern," of course, the ANPA meant the *southern* Appalachians. Areas of special concern included the Great Smoky Mountains, on the Tennessee-North Carolina border, and the Blue Ridge Mountains, running down the spine of north-central Virginia east of the Shenandoah Valley.

Congressional opposition to the creation of national parks from private lands, coupled with the claims of preservationists elsewhere in the nation that neither area possessed true national significance, frustrated the plans of the Appalachian National Park Association well into the 1920s. Finally, in 1926, Congress authorized both Great Smoky Mountains and Shenandoah national parks, provided that no federal funds would be used to make the actual purchases. Instead, acquisition was the sole responsibility of the states involved in the projects, specifically, Virginia, North Carolina, and Tennessee.

Even during the 1920s, when land values were relatively modest, none of these states had the wherewithal to complete a major undertaking such as the purchase of an entire national park. For this reason, private philanthropy became a crucial component in park acquisition in the South. Southerners were not alone in this effort. John D. Rockefeller, Jr., for example, donated nearly half the $12 million required to purchase Great Smoky Mountains National Park plus a more modest amount toward completion of the Shenandoah National Park.

Even more controversial was the establishment of Everglades National Park, located in the sawgrass and mangrove provinces at the tip of southern Florida. At least the Great Smokies and Blue Ridge Mountains had some topographical significance to link them with the common perception of national parks as scenic masterpieces; in the Everglades the elevation barely exceeded 17 feet above sea level. The Tropic Everglades National Park Association, formed in 1928 by the Miami activist Ernest F. Coe, retorted that the absence of geological uniqueness alone was no justification for denying the region national park status. The purposes of the Everglades were strictly biological: namely, the protection of vanishing forms of bird and animal life in the nation's only subtropical setting. The national parks "have much of interest in bold topography and other uniqueness," Dr. John K. Small of the New York Botanical Garden agreed. "Why not also have a unique area exhilarating by its lack of topography and charming by its matchless vegetation and animal life?"

Gradually, preservationists nationwide rallied to the argument, and in May 1934 Congress authorized Everglades National Park. Once again, however, the park faced crippling delays in the requirement that the state of Florida and private citizens must undertake the actual purchases. As a result, Everglades National Park was not formally dedicated until 1947; still another 10 years elapsed before all the critical parcels in the park had been acquired.

If the establishment of national parks came slowly and painfully, it is not surprising that state park systems in the South also lagged behind the rest of the nation. An important exception was Royal Palm State Park, established by Florida in 1916 at the urging of the Florida Federation of Women's Clubs. Originally only 1,920 acres, the tract later formed the nucleus of Everglades National Park. Another important milestone was achieved in 1924 with calls for the establishment of Cumberland Falls State Park, Ky. In this instance the DuPont family donated $400,000 to make the purchase, thereby saving the area from a proposed hydroelectric project.

Spurred by government relief projects during the Depression, and followed by dramatic increases in population after World War II, state park systems throughout the South posted impressive gains. As late as 1933, for example, Virginia had only one state park; by 1962 her state park system included 20 separate areas totaling nearly 30,000 acres of land and water. Meanwhile, the federal government, shorn of its earlier prejudice against funding parklands from the national treasury, responded to the need for recreation areas through several agencies, especially the U.S. Forest Service, U.S. Army Corps of Engineers, and the Tennessee Valley Authority. The creation of TVA in 1933 not only led to an impressive chain of reservoirs throughout the Tennessee and Cumberland river valleys, but encouraged the use of those reservoirs—as well as tens of thousands of acres of lands bordering the man-made lakes—for a myriad of outdoor activities, including boating, fishing, water skiing, swimming, hiking, and hunting. Undoubtedly the most impressive of these areas is the so-called Land Between the Lakes. Begun in January 1964 by the Tennessee Valley Authority, the 170,000-acre project lies in southwestern Kentucky and northwestern Tennessee, between Kentucky Lake, formed by the great dam just above the mouth of the Tennessee River, and Lake Barkley, created by a dam just above the confluence of the Cumberland and Ohio rivers.

Although such extensive disruptions of the environment have been controversial, preservation itself has made some important gains in the South during the past quarter century. As modern urbanites, more southerners of the 1960s and 1970s came to understand the concerns of Americans who confronted the disrupting influences of industrialization and urbanization a half century earlier. An outstanding example of the new ecological awareness in the South is Big Thicket National Preserve, Texas, authorized in 1974. In the spirit of Everglades National Park, the Big Thicket is purely biological in purpose, designed to protect the approximately 85,000 acres of the rare plant and animal associations once common in eastern Texas and neighboring Louisiana. Similarly, Big Cypress National Preserve, Florida, also authorized in 1974, will protect a critical aquifer northwest of Everglades National Park.

Southerners have taken further pride in their combination of recreational pursuits with preservation needs in the creation of the first national seashore at Cape Hatteras, North Carolina, in 1937. Not only has the idea caught on throughout the South, but along all the nation's coastline. In addition, the 1978 authorization of the Chattahoochee River National Recreation Area, in the heart of Atlanta, Ga., has proven a model for urban parklands across the United States.

Preservationists have not achieved everything they initially thought vital or desirable. They caution, for example, that achievements in recreation, especially recreation areas built around big dams and reservoirs, are not always in the best interest of ecological needs. Considering all the obstacles to preservation, however, especially the need to overcome widespread biases against landscapes lacking topographical distinction, such as those found in the West, environmental reform has indeed made impressive gains in the South during the past 75 years.

See also HISTORY AND MANNERS: / Jefferson, Thomas; RECREATION: Fishing; Hunting; / Colonial Williamsburg

Alfred Runte
University of Washington

North Callahan, *TVA: Bridge over Troubled Water* (1980); Carlos C. Campbell, *Birth of a National Park in the Great Smoky Mountains* (rev. ed., 1978); Hans Huth, *Nature and the American: Three Centuries of Changing Attitudes* (1957); John Ise, *Our National Park Policy: A Critical History* (1961); Roderick Nash, *Wilderness and the American Mind* (3d ed., 1982); Alfred Runte, *National Parks: The American Experience* (1979); Freeman Tilden, *The State Parks: Their Meaning in American Life* (1962). ☆

Plants

To early colonial explorers and settlers accustomed to the relatively low plant diversity of Europe, the plants of the New World were one of its greatest wonders. The immense botanical diversity of the South has played, and continues to play, an important role in both the commerce and the culture of the region. Indeed, no other part of the country has such a strong association of its culture with plants. Native magnolias, Spanish moss, and longleaf pine and introduced plants such as indigo, rice, cotton, tobacco, peanuts, collards, okra, and kudzu elicit historical, political, economic, and culinary associations all of a regional nature.

Although the inland hardwood forests of the southern piedmont and mountains were generally similar in appearance to the deciduous forests of eastern North America and northern Europe, the first colonial settlements were in coastal areas that, in the South, are typified by forests of broad-leaved evergreens—magnolia, bay, live oak, and cherry laurel—which were quite unfamiliar. For the first two centuries after the discovery of America by the Europeans, these exotic evergreen trees, often shrouded in gray wisps of Spanish moss, typified the South. The associations remain even today a part of both actual and legendary southern culture.

Many of the early colonists truly had to "live off the land," and they depended upon the variety of native trees, shrubs, and herbs for basic needs of food, shelter, fuel, and medicine. Some southern plants that maintain a visible role in southern culture and commerce are the pecan (*Carya illinoensis*), persimmon (*Diospyros virginiana*), sassafras (*Sassafras albidum*), and muscadine grape (*Vitis rotundifolia*), all of which provide food and/or beverage; the various species of pine for pulp, timber, and solvents; the white oaks for timber and cooperage; and an array of other native hardwoods for furniture manufacture, paneling, and other specialized use. In addition, a number of native plants, such as magnolia, azalea, rhododendron, bayberry, and holly, are of horticultural value.

During the 18th century naturalists began to collect and describe the wealth of plants available in the South. Among these naturalists were John Clayton (1657–1725) of Virginia whose collections of native plants were carefully studied and published as *Flora Virginia* in 1739–43 by J. F. Gronovius of Holland; Mark Catesby (1682–1749), an English naturalist who spent the years from 1712 to 1726 in Virginia and the Bahamas and then returned to England to publish, in 1731 and 1743, his remarkably illustrated *Natural History of the Carolinas, Florida and the Bahama Islands*; André Michaux (1746–1802), a French botanist who established a garden at Charleston, S.C., and whose botanical explorations of much of eastern

North America were the basis for his *Flora Boreali-Americana* published in 1817–19; the father and son naturalists, John (1699–1776) and William (1739–1823) Bartram of Pennsylvania, whose active botanical exploration, writing, and plant exchange program provided the strongest botanical link between Britain and America during the middle of the 18th century and led to the 1791 publication of William Bartram's classic *Travels through North and South Carolina, Georgia, East and West Florida*; and the English Thomas Walter (1740–88), who settled along the Santee River in South Carolina and from the surrounding area of 500 or so square miles collected the varied plants that formed the basis for his *Flora Caroliniana*, which was published in 1788.

Of special interest to the many professional and amateur European naturalists of the 18th century were the various species of insect-catching or "carnivorous" plants native to the moist, sandy, open Coastal Plain savannas of the South. Indeed, worldwide interest in these interesting and often colorful plants continues even today, and overexploration of the native populations has brought a number of these species to the verge of extinction. The greatest variety of insectivorous plants to be found in North America can still be observed, however, on protected lands in the vicinity of Wilmington, N.C. Here, with diligent searching in appropriate habitats one can find four species of pitcher plant (*Sarracenia* sp.), four species of sundew (*Drosera* sp.), nine species of bladderwort (*Utricularia* sp.), three species of butterwort (*Pinguicula* sp.), and the widely known Venus flytrap (*Dionaea muscipula*), which was first brought to the attention of botanists in 1759 by Governor Arthur Dobbs of North Carolina and which Charles Darwin called "the most wonderful plant in the world."

Wildflowers have long been a beloved part of the southern rural landscape. Tourists and natives alike have frequently commented on their growth along the roadside, in meadows, and in fields. They are hardy plants, adapting to a variety of climate and soil conditions. One sees buttercups in spring, Queen Anne's lace in summer, and goldenrod in fall. There are bloodroots, black-eyed susans, yellow lady's slipper orchids, bee balms, mayapples, atamasco lilies, bird's-foot violets, rue anemones, and jack-in-the-pulpits. In the modern South the natural heritage is reinforced through human efforts. Texas has launched a major program to promote wildflower growth, especially the state's floral emblem, the bluebonnet, making the state's highways more attractive. Regionally oriented magazines such as *Southern Living* and gardening books tell southerners how to cultivate wildflowers as parts of planned suburban gardens. Organizations such as the Plant Rescue Volunteers at the North Carolina Botanical Gardens in Chapel Hill collect endangered plants and grow plants from these specimens.

The southern states acknowledged the cultural significance of plants in the early 20th century when they adopted state flowers—goldenrod (Alabama, 1927, Kentucky, 1926, North Carolina, unofficial), apple blossom (Arkansas, 1901), orange blossom (Florida, 1909), Cherokee rose (Georgia, 1916), magnolia (Louisiana, 1900, Mississippi 1900), yellow or Carolina jessamine (South Carolina, 1924), iris (Tennessee, 1933; earlier the passion flower or maypop), American dogwood (Virginia,

1918), and bluebonnet (Texas, 1901). Florida's nickname is the Flower State because of its abundant plant life.

During the past two centuries natural plant migrations and continued introductions by man have added many additional species to the varied flora of the South. In succession, corn, then cotton, and finally soybeans have been dominant cash crops in the region. Sugar in Louisiana, rice in low-lying terrains of the coast and river areas, tobacco in the Upper South, hemp in Kentucky—all represent cultivated plants of economic importance in specific regions within the South. The study of these native and naturalized plants is still of considerable scientific interest, and their role in commerce and recreation is of growing importance. The wise use and realistic conservation of the South's natural plant resources are issues that are also of growing relevance to the future of the region.

Plants not only add beauty to the environment and interest to a culture but are the world's only renewable resource that can reasonably be expected to supply man's growing needs for food, fuel, and fiber. Because the milder climate, longer growing season, and generally adequate rainfall characteristic of much of the South are often the primary factors in optimal plant growth, the plants of southern fields and forests will likely continue to play an important role in the economy, politics, and culture of the area for many years to come.

See also AGRICULTURE: Crops

C. Ritchie Bell
North Carolina Botanical Gardens
University of North Carolina
at Chapel Hill

William Bartram, *Travels of William Bartram*, ed. Francis Harper (1967); Ben A. Davis, *The Southern Garden: From the Potomac to the Rio Grande* (1971); Blanche E. Dean, Amy Mason, and Joab L. Thomas, *Wildflowers of Alabama and Adjoining States* (1973); Albert E. Radford, Harry E. Ahles, and C. Ritchie Bell, *Manual of the Vascular Flora of the Carolinas* (1968); Harold W. Rickett, *Wildflowers of Southeastern States* (1967); J. K. Small, *Manual of the Southeastern Flora* (1933). ☆

Plant Uses

In addition to making economic use of cultivated plants, southerners have long utilized wild plants in a variety of ways. The pattern was set long ago by southeastern Indians. Plants were an important part of their belief system. The Indians believed that humans, animals, and plants were interrelated and that a balance between these forms should exist to keep nature properly functioning. The boundary between the animal and plant realms was blurred by plants such as the Venus flytrap and the pitcher plant, which trapped and "ate" insects. This kind of anomaly was of particular interest to southerners and took on symbolic significance in their oral traditions, which attributed extraordinary powers to the roots of these plants.

Native Americans made plants part of their ritual life. The cedar, pine, spruce, holly, and laurel ranked at the top of the Cherokee belief system in terms of ritual purity. Tobacco smoking preceded council meetings of chiefs, and "black drink" was a ceremonial beverage regarded as essential for these occasions. The Indians in their own language called it "white drink," because it symbolized purity, happiness, and harmony. The Europeans labeled it "black drink" because of its color. Made from the leaves of a variety of holly (*Ilex vomitoria* Ait.), black drink was a tea with a bitter taste and high caffeine content. To make it, the Indians dried leaves and twigs and parched them over a fire to a deep brown color. The product of this process was then boiled in water, producing a dark brown liquid. It was a stimulant and a diuretic and the Indians also used it as an emetic. Early European colonists used black drink as a stimulant but gave it up after coffee and tea became more available in the later 1600s.

Wild vegetables were important as a food source for southeastern Indians. Women, the elderly, and children gathered vegetables, fruits, berries, seeds, and nuts, all of which were plentiful through much of the Southeast. Roots and tubers were the most valuable wild vegetables in the Indian diet. The big, tuberous roots that grow on various species of a green shrub called *Smilax* L., which twines itself around trees, were especially popular. The taproot of the "wild sweet potato," or wild morning glory (*Ipomoea pandurata* L.), can weigh as much as 20–30 pounds. "Swamp potatoes" were collected in low-lying marshlands from the root of arrowhead (*Sagittaria* L.). The crunchy roots of the Jerusalem artichoke were gathered in fall and winter. The southeastern Indians enjoyed the persimmon and collected muscadine grapes and scuppernongs. They also ate wild cherries, papaws, crab apples, and wild plums. The summer months saw them feasting on gathered blackberries, strawberries, gooseberries, raspberries, and huckleberries, and they picked from trees the black gum berries, mulberries, serviceberries, and palmetto berries. Nuts were especially important in the southeastern Indian diet. In autumn, they collected chestnuts, chinquapins (a small variety of chestnuts), pecans, hickory nuts, black walnuts, and the acorns of the live oak, white oak, chestnut oak, and others. They ground seeds from cockspurgrass (*Echinochloa Beau* V.), the nulumbo, and chenopodium (*Chenopodium ambrosioides* L.) to make meal to be used in cooking.

Herbs were crucial in the Indian medicinal system. The Creeks, for example, used "red root," made from the bark of the root of a willow tree, to treat rheumatism, nausea, fever, malaria, and other health problems. Creeks used "button snakeroot" to treat neuralgia, kidney troubles, snakebite, and as a spring tonic. The roots of ginseng (*Panex quinquefolium* L.) were boiled in water and used as a potion to help with shortness of breath, to heal a wound, and to keep ghosts away. Among the other main Creek herbs were angelica, wormseed, red cedar, spicebush, and horsemint—a typical list for other tribes as well.

The southeastern Indians had a multitude of other uses for wild plants: they made clothing from Spanish moss; used the bottle gourd (*Lagenaria siceraria*) for water vessels, dippers, ladles, cups, bowls, bird houses, rattles, and masks, among other things; and made baskets of bark, grass, and, especially, strips of the outer covering of cane.

Rural southern blacks and whites followed in the paths of the southeastern Indians and used wild plants as food, drink, cosmetics, and medicine, and in their arts and crafts. Much understanding of the uses of plants was also brought from Europe and Africa by early settlers. Medicine has made particular use of plants. Yellow root, tree bark, and sassafras have long been used by southern blacks as home remedies; traditional healers, or "root doctors," are still consulted to cure ailments such as headaches, loss of memory, itching, and exhaustion. Specialists are sought who deal with particular ailments. Among North Carolina root doctors, for example, mint tea is known as the treatment for hysteria, sassafras for stomach pains, and jimson tea for constipation. Allen Eaton, in a 1937 volume on the southern highlands, reported that one local root doctor in Tennessee had a list of 52 herbs that he used. The list included bloodroot, a spring tonic; blacksnake, to calm the stomach; blackberry root, for diarrhea; boneset, for colds; butterfly root, for female troubles; buckeye, for rheumatism; calamas, for an upset stomach; crab apple bark, for asthma; dandelion root, for the blood; heart leaf, good for "weak hearted persons"; larkspur tincture, for hair trouble; mullen for coughs; persimmon bark, a salve; pennyroyal, good for bed bugs and colds; redroot, to ease the bowels; stone root, good to ease kidney stone pain; slippery elm, to treat sore eyes; wild comfort, "a manhood medicine"; and redbud roots, to clean the teeth. In Louisiana sarsaparilla tea was drunk each spring in hopes of purifying the blood; a poultice of wild potato plant leaves was said to relieve boils and inflammation; copal moss, when soaked in hot water with whiskey, was an effective drink for general "miseries."

Rural whites and blacks used extracts from wild plants to color yarns, threads, baskets, and textiles. The most important colors used by Appalachian women were indigo and madder, which provided the blue and red colorings used in many blankets and quilts. Indigo comes from the plant *indigofera*; it produces yellow flowers in late summer and the boiled plant makes a blue dye, which was popular because it was a highly permanent natural dye and also subject to a variety of shades. Madder was both native and cultivated in the mountains, where pioneer women used the huge roots to produce a range of shades, from a deep red to a delicate pink, on both cotton and wool. Other natural vegetable dye colors used by southern blacks and whites included browns, blacks, and grays from walnuts; grays and tans from sumac berries; pinks and lavenders from pokeberries; yellows from hickory bark; yellow and orange from wild coreopsis; pink-yellow from sedge grass; and green from pine needles. The time of the year in which the roots, barks, hulls, fruits, nuts, leaves, seeds, stems, or whole plants are gathered can produce different shades.

During the Civil War, southerners relied on plants in various ways. They used caffeine-bearing holly berries to make tea, and they parched rye, acorns, beets, and sweet potatoes to make a coffee substitute. Chinaberries were used to make a shoe blacking paste, Spanish moss became an ingredient in rope, and cork was made from cypress "knees." Children were set to work puncturing poppies to obtain opium-bearing droplets for use as a medicine for the wounded.

Southerners used plants and their products in folk arts and crafts. Pine needles and straw, white oak strips, palmetto fronds, and other plant materials were essential ingredients in basketry. Mountain women gathered native barks, cones, grasses, seeds, leaves, pods, berries, and acorns to make home decorations for interiors or to sell to tourists and collectors. Gourds were used as sounding boxes for homemade fiddles and banjos, for decorative purposes, and for bird houses.

Southern writers and artists have frequently used plants to establish the sense of a distinctive place. Scholar Earl F. Bargainnier has noted that in literary portrayals of the myth of "moonlight and magnolias," "the aroma of magnolias—or honeysuckle, oleanders, or roses—is thick in the warm evening." William Faulkner entitled a short story "An Odor of Verbena" and described many plants, but his favorite must have been wistaria. "It was a summer of wistaria," says Quentin Compson in *Absalom, Absalom!* (1936). Quentin recalled the "sweet and oversweet" smell of "twice-bloomed wistaria" at Rosa Coldfield's house, and when he was a student at Harvard he still thought of the plant's "odor, the scent." Folk artist Theora Hamblett of Oxford, Miss., painted the calamus vine, recalling later that the morning after her stroke in 1964 she would close her eyes and see a vision of long vines and golden leaves. She had never actually seen a calamus, but she painted her vision and later discovered the actual plant it was. At a more popular level, southerners of all social classes and groups decorate their homes with paintings and ceramics of local flowers: magnolias in Mississippi, bluebonnets in Texas, and orange blossoms in Florida.

See also ETHNIC LIFE: Indian Cultural Contributions; FOLKLIFE: Folk Medicine; WOMEN'S LIFE: Healers, Women

Charles Reagan Wilson
University of Mississippi

Judith Bolyard, *Medicinal Plants and Home Remedies of Appalachia* (1981); Allen Eaton, *Handicrafts of the Southern Highlands* (1937); Wayland Hand, ed., *American Folk Medicine: A Symposium* (1976); Charles Hudson, *The Southeastern Indians* (1976); Clarence Meyer, *American Folk Medicine* (1973); Newbill Niles Puckett, *Folk Beliefs of The Southern Negro* (1926; reprint ed., 1969); Virgil Vogel, *American Indian Medicine* (1970); Eliot Wigginton, *The Foxfire Book* (1972). ☆

Pollution

The southerner's attachment to the land has been a regional cultural axiom. Novelists, scholars, and journalists since early in this century observed an ambivalence, if not apathy, toward the region's natural environment, but poverty has encouraged industrial development irrespective of environmental consequences. Pollution, after all, was preferable to pellagra.

Even before the industrial development campaigns launched by southern states in the 1930s and 1940s, the region's natural resources proved attractive to firms more interested in extracting profits than in preserving the environment for future generations. Because local and state governments not only avoided placing legal obstacles in the path of exploiting companies, but actively supported their efforts, pollution intruded into primeval forests, fields, and cities.

The advancing petrochemical industry along the Texas (and later Louisiana) Gulf Coast during the first three decades of this century produced unparalleled water and air pollution, fouling beaches and rivers. Oil interests so controlled and influenced state government that, as late as the 1960s, the industry was self-policing. Also, the timber industry denuded wide swaths of virgin forest beginning in the late 19th century, causing soil erosion and excessive runoff.

The Nashville Agrarians were among the earliest southerners to point out the potential pollution hazards of industrialization, but such diverse writers as Howard W. Odum, William Faulkner, Robert Penn Warren, and Jonathan Daniels echoed similar themes in the 1930s. Faulkner and Warren noted the scars left by timber companies. Odum generalized from his discussion of the timber industry by observing that "the greater cultural tradition of the South has been one of exploitation of the land and its resources." Or, as Jonathan Daniels quoted a Knoxville newspaperman, "the trouble with the South was that southern people hated the land."

The post–World War II generation of southerners seemed intent on proving these characterizations true, as states offered low-cost labor, attractive financial schemes, and a moratorium on regulatory enforcement to prospective industrial investors. The results of this good business climate were predictable. The once-beautiful Savannah River was buffeted by daily discharges of sulfuric acid from an American Cyanimid plant, mercury from Augusta's Olin Corporation, and nuclear wastes from a Dupont factory. Paper mills have befouled the air and water along Georgia's coastline, in the North Carolina mountains, and the countryside around Selma, Ala., where, by the late 1960s, according to Pat Watters, "the pall and stench of the mill were so heavy that one had to drive ten or twenty miles out of town to escape the low clouds of it." He added that "this is not an uncommon experience in the South."

Despite state and federal regulations, the petrochemical industry continues virtually unabated in its environmental negligence, infiltrating the water systems in Louisiana. One scientist warned in 1972 that the Gulf of Mexico "could become a dead sea," as a result of chemical effluvia. The national craving for fossil fuels has similarly enabled the coal regions of eastern Kentucky to bypass legal restraints. The situation is scarcely better in high consumption areas such as Houston where city highways now rival the ship channel in pollution.

The passage of the federal Clean Air Act of 1970 and the establishment of the Environmental Protection Agency that same year were significant landmarks for southern environmentalists. The federal legislation enabled Washington to intervene in especially egregious pollution cases (as in the Birmingham steel mills in 1971), and it inspired companion legislation throughout the South. More than that, by establishing uniform air and water quality standards, it removed the fear of environmentally minded states that unilateral pollution controls would frighten potential industrial investors away. Or, as journalist Joel Garreau colorfully put it, "The EPA's existence allows an Alabama mayor to say to a developer 'Now Fred, you know how much I'd like to let you dump your purple widget waste right into the drinking water here, and if it were up to me, Lord knows we could work something out, but it isn't. You know those damn boys in Washington would be all over me.' "

But "those damn boys in Washington" change with changing administrations. The historically lenient attitude of southern states toward potential polluters requires uniform and consistent enforcement of federal legislation. A vigorous Environmental Protection Agency inspired similar organizations and legislation in the South in the early 1970s, especially in Florida and Alabama, but a weak, inconsequential federal environmental presence would likely give succor to growth-at-any-cost enthusiasts, especially in the era of relatively high unemployment. If southerners were required to choose between jobs and clean air, polls indicate that a slight majority would opt for the former. Improved technology and uniform enforcement of existing legislation might render such choices unnecessary.

Increasing vigilance over environmental contamination will be necessary in the future as the toxicity of pollutants increases. The South, for example, is the region most dependent upon nuclear energy, and questions are arising about the disposal of nuclear wastes and about the safety of the nuclear plants themselves. There are some indications that carcinogenic substances from a Savannah River nuclear power plant may have seeped into the Tuscaloosa aquifer, a major southeastern water source. Moreover, cities are struggling against the costs and logistics of disposing of solid wastes, growing geometrically with population increases. Finally, an insidious visual pollution is creeping into the rural and suburban landscapes with billboards, fast-food emporia, and service stations dotting the once serene countryside. As Robert Penn Warren catalogued the lost landscape in his novel *Flood*, "the trouble was not so much what was not there. It was what was there."

There are some encouraging indications that the states are beginning to take the initiative in environmental protection as federal efforts lag. Florida has made belated attempts to protect its threatened natural water supply. Mississippi recently rescued a timber-company-threatened swamp that sustains natural life in the Pascagoula region. In the spring of 1983, in an unprecedented move, the state of South Carolina sued the federal government to clean up DuPont's Savannah River nuclear reactor, which has operated under federal contract since the 1950s. As South Carolina Attorney General Travis Medlock observed, "We sued 'em [the U.S. Energy Department] and they were shocked beyond belief. South Carolina has been very hospitable to these folks. But I think the hospitality had probably gone too far."

Indeed, the welcome mat is no longer automatic. Southern cities are appropriately shocked by the specter of the automobile-dependent, air-polluted Houston lurking in their midst and are promoting mass transit. Chambers of Commerce are discovering that clean environments are attractive to potential investors, tourists, and retirees, as that elusive "quality of life" becomes an increasingly important part of the lifestyle equation. Finally, if southerners have paid heed to environmental amenities—the carefully cultivated azaleas, the gracious and spacious parks, the proximity of the countryside, however eroded by suburban subdivision—the time is appropriate for that tradition to emerge from the shadows and replace environmental exploitation as a regional characteristic. Enough of the beauty and solace of the region's natural heritage remains to secure its enjoyment and protection for this and future generations.

See also INDUSTRY articles; MYTHIC SOUTH: / Agrarians, Vanderbilt

David R. Goldfield
University of North Carolina
at Charlotte

Nelson M. Blake, *Land into Water—Water into Land: A History of Water Management in Florida* (1980); James C. Cobb, *The Selling of the South: The Southern Crusade for Industrial Development, 1936–1980* (1982); Ray Jones, *Southern Living* (January 1983); Linda L. Liston, *Industrial Development* (September–October 1971); Joseph A. Pratt, *Business History Review* (Spring 1978); William Reynolds, *Southern Exposure* (Winter 1979); Suzanne Rhodes, *Southern Exposure* (Winter 1979); Frank E. Smith, in *You Can't Eat Magnolias*, ed. H. Brandt Ayers and Thomas H. Naylor (1972). ☆

Reclamation and Irrigation

Reclamation is a term more common to the West than the South. It usually denotes bringing former wastelands into production through the application of water. In the more humid South, the term has a broader usage. In most areas, settlement and expansion involved some major transformation of the land by clearing, providing drainage, and building flood control works. This process began with the first settlers of the Atlantic and Gulf coasts and continues to the present. Irrigation was first used extensively during the 17th century in Georgia and the Carolinas to support the production of rice. For over 200 years, from 1685 to 1890, rice production centered in the South Atlantic states. Then gradually a shift occurred, and by 1970 some 94 percent of the United States crop was produced in Arkansas, Louisiana, Texas, and California. The use of irrigation for other crops in the South, however, lagged until after World War II.

Unlike in the arid West, a chief problem of southern settlers was to keep water off rather than apply it to agricultural lands. This was especially true of the alluvial valley of the Mississippi River and its major tributaries—the focus of drainage, flood control, and other reclamation efforts since the early 18th century.

Land reclamation was largely in private hands until passage of the Swamp Lands Acts of 1849 and 1850, the first important federal legislation relating to land reclamation. Under their provisions, "swamp and overflowed" lands were given to the states on the condition that revenues from land sales be used to build levees and provide drainage. For the following 30 years, states undertook extensive flood control and drainage programs that were beset with failures, frauds, and scandals. Nevertheless, the experience gained from 1850 to 1880 contributed to later successful reclamation efforts by public and private interests.

The drainage programs launched in the late 19th and early 20th centuries were part of a nationwide reclamation and land-development movement. Following the end of the Civil War, most southern states created immigration agencies to attract settlers to undeveloped lands. After a boom in the timber industry from 1870 to 1890, large acreages of cutover lands were released by lumber companies, particularly in the Mississippi Valley. Consequently, the local economies based on lumber milling began to regress, and promoters came forth with schemes to transform barren areas as well as swamps and marshes into productive agricultural lands.

These efforts were, in part, a response to the closing of the western frontier. To many prospective farmers, the undeveloped wetlands of the South and the dry lands that required irrigation seemed the final opportunity to obtain productive farms. Many of these home seekers were recent immigrants and second-generation Americans who originally settled in the midwestern states. Their reputation for hard work and farming small acreages in an intensive manner attracted the attention of reclamation promoters. These boosters viewed the corn belt and Great Lake states as a key source for latter-day pioneers who would settle the reclaimed Everglades, the lower Louisiana marshes, and the swamps of Mississippi, Arkansas, and later Missouri. The hardscrabble hill farmers of Kentucky, Tennessee, Mississippi, and Arkansas were also viewed as prospective residents on reclaimed alluvial land in the lower Mississippi Valley. A vast pamphlet literature developed describing the ease of reclaiming southern land, the feasibility of harvesting two crops during the long growing season, and the comfort and attractiveness of the "good life" in the lower Mississippi Valley.

Lumber companies, with large, relatively worthless acreages of cutover lands, joined with the railroads in elaborate plans to provide transportation for potential buyers. Land offices were established in Chicago to advertise the fertility of Delta and coastal marsh soils. The companies advertised largely in the Midwest and obtained cooperation from city commercial interests in forming a regional promotional association. The land, offered in tracts of 40 acres or more, was touted as suitable for dairy farming as well as cotton and all staple crops grown in the corn belt. In some cases, groups of prospective purchasers were brought to reclamation projects where land auctions were held. Land selling for $8 to $10 per acre in the 1880s was selling for $75 to $100 by 1920. In southeastern Missouri, property within newly organized drainage districts was fetching $125 per acre prior to World War I.

Drainage districts played an important role in the development of southern agriculture. They were organized under a variety of laws and local customs, with the peak of activity from 1907 to 1927. The districts continued the prevailing concept of drainage as a local problem—jurisdiction remained with county or other units of local government and the projects were administered by local officials. State legislation relating to drainage and reclamation had three principal purposes: (1) to standardize cooperation among landowners; (2) to define methods of apportioning drainage costs among property owners; and (3) to authorize financing and payment for drainage improvements.

Despite the fact that reclamation is generally regarded as a phenomenon of the arid West, an extensive drainage program took place in the South concurrently under private auspices. The undertakings varied from marshland pump-reclamation projects requiring large capital investments to more common gravity-drainage projects of areas with higher elevations. The larger projects in Arkansas, Mississippi, Missouri, and the marshlands of Louisiana were organized to develop land that could be sold in small tracts to prospective farmers. However, most of the 400 to 500 gravity drainage districts developed in the Mississippi Valley were organized to improve the lands of existing owners.

The drainage movement was assisted by both state and federal agencies. The states promoted settlement and established the legal basis for special improvement districts. The federal government, especially the Department of Agriculture, conducted investigations of drainage problems and provided technical assistance in the planning of many projects. Federal funds were made available for reclamation of the arid lands of the West, and a strong desire existed throughout the South for federal support of the drainage movement. In the 1920s a strong effort was made to expand the Bureau of Reclamation's land development to the South and to regions of the country other than the West. A blue-ribbon panel of "Special Advisers on Reclamation and Rural Development" was created by Congress and issued a report in 1926 calling for a national effort to redeem southern agriculture. The group's views went unheeded.

With the onset of the Depression, drainage districts were hard hit and became heavily indebted. Tax delinquency became chronic in many areas, and farmers became disillusioned with many of the programs. Some relief was provided by the Reconstruction Finance Corporation and other New Deal programs. An important new element was added by the 1944 Flood Control Act, which, for the first time, enabled the U.S. Army Corps of Engineers to engage in drainage work not directly related to levee building and other flood control projects. With passage of the 1954 Watershed Protection and Flood Prevention Act, the drainage activities of the Department of Agriculture entered a new phase. It enabled the department to give technical and financial assistance in planning and conducting small watershed projects, in which drainage was a part. This landmark law bridged the gap between the work of the Soil Conservation Service on local farms and flood control, and major drainage projects carried out by the Corps of Engineers in cooperation with state and local interests.

Louisiana was the only state that inaugurated a large state-sponsored drainage program. In 1940 the state established a far-reaching program for rebuilding the existing drainage system and extending drainage to large undeveloped areas. The program served as a coordinating link between local organizations and the federal government.

Much of the reclamation effort undertaken after World War II has been land clearing by private farmers. This development has been prompted by growing demands for rice, soybeans, cotton, and livestock. Former timbered areas, in addition to swamplands, have been transformed into tillable acreages and pastures. For example, estimates are that large-scale agribusinesses rather than family farmers have cleared at least 70 percent of the land that has been cleared in the Mississippi Alluvial Valley since the close of World War II. The transformation of southern agriculture from tenancy and subsistence farming to increasingly larger operations also affected the development of irrigation. The postwar development of rice growing and the use of irrigation for crops such as soybeans have led to large amounts of land receiving supplemental water. In 1950 a total of 5,056 acres in Mississippi were irrigated; by 1982 the total had risen to 430,901 acres. Problems have arisen, however, with the drawdown of aquifers resulting from extensive pumping of groundwater. Thus, a new challenge has been added to the problems of flood control, drainage, and land clearing—the three additional elements in the reclamation of forested swamp and other so-called wastelands in the South.

See also INDUSTRY: / Timber Industry

Michael C. Robinson
U.S. Army Corps of Engineers
Lower Mississippi Valley Division
Vicksburg, Mississippi

Quincy C. Ayers and Daniels Scoates, *Land Drainage and Reclamation* (1939); Albert E. Cowdrey, *This Land, This South: An Environmental History* (1983); Robert W. Harrison, *Alluvial Empire* (1961); George W. Pickels, *Drainage and Flood-Control Engineering* (1941). ☆

River Life

If southerners are "tied to the land" as many historians and cultural thinkers have argued, many are also tied to the water. One must not overlook the influence—occupational, economic, and environmental—that the freshwater streams and rivers have played and continue to play in southern life and culture. Just as many depend on the land as the prime sustainer and stabilizer of the traditional southern community, others choose a river way of life that offers occupational freedom and economic diversity. River culture here refers to the lives and methods of those who choose to work independently on the water—fishing, rafting logs, or musseling.

"Shantyboat" or houseboat life has all but died out as a widespread tradition on the navigable rivers of the region. Up until the 1950s one could find families living seminomadic lives on houseboats along the Mississippi, Tennessee, Cumberland, Yazoo, and other rivers and tributaries of the South. Often portrayed in the popular media as impoverished, lawless "water gypsies," these river folk made conscious choices to pursue lives of freedom and independence. In the Depression years the ranks of the water dwellers swelled as many southerners were forced through economic hardship to find alternative sources of survival.

Typically a houseboat family would tie up near fertile land, perhaps at the mouth of a small tributary, thus shielding themselves from disturbance by larger river traffic. A garden planted in the late spring provided summer food and vegetables to can for winter. Fish was the staple food, and catfish the most common. If the landing was suitable a family might stay for years; if not, perhaps only a few months, moving on with the aid of a small motorboat or simply drifting with the current.

More common today, however, are families who live on small pieces of land near the banks of freshwater streams or rivers. Commercial fishing, usually for catfish, buffalo, or spoonbill (sometimes called "shovelbill"), small farming, and hunting or logging form the economic base for a river family. In Tennessee, southern Kentucky, Arkansas, and Alabama river families also dig for mussel shells, a common occupation after German immigrants located pearl button factories on the Mississippi River in the late 1800s. Until the 1940s river men tied logs together to make log rafts and floated them down the river to a sawmill. Such work, generally done in the spring of the year, supplemented fishing, musseling, and farm income.

Commercial fishing is the center of the river economy. Commercial fishing families may at once be fisher folk, boat builders, net makers, bait-line box makers, small-engine repair specialists, trappers, and small farmers. Fishing tackle used in the South is largely built by hand within the community. Bait lines or trot lines are commonly set in the evening and checked each morning. Other common tackle includes hoop nets or barrel nets, snag lines, gill nets, trammel nets, and wooden and wire fish traps.

Musseling, today an important occupation on the rivers of the Upland South, has very early origins. Oral tradition in the lower Tennessee Valley suggests that musselers were active by the early 1900s. From Paducah, Ky., to Florence, Ala., there was musseling around 1910, and in 5 to 10 years an increasing number of men turned to shells for their income. Prior to 1900 there was a market for pearls, but very little demand for the shell itself, the "mother of pearl." With a growing pearl button industry in the United States, shells were in high demand.

Mussel shells are "dug" in a variety of ways. Toe digging, or feeling for the shells in shallow water with one's feet, is still a popular way to dig for shells. The most common historically, however, is brailing, a system of dragging a long wooden or steel pole (called a brail) on the bottom of the river. All along the brail, groups of mussel hooks are suspended from short pieces of string. When the brail gets heavy the musseler knows he has many shells and raises the brail. Brailing continues today assisted since 1920 by gasoline-powered motors and winches.

Among younger river men, diving for mussels has become a popular occupation. An air compressor on an 18–24-foot boat provides the lifeline to divers as they work—sometimes as deep as 50 feet—with an air hose in their mouths, feeling for shells on the dark, muddy river bottom. A good day can bring as much as $300 when the price per pound is up. The freedom of the work hours, the independence from supervisors, and the possibility of earning the equivalent of a week's pay in one day lead many to take up mussel diving. Today, companies like the Tennessee Shell Company, located in Camden, Tenn., regularly buy shells to sell to Japanese companies in the cultured pearl industry.

Like rivers themselves, traditional river culture constantly evolves, adapting to changing environmental conditions, new laws, and new technologies. In parts of the South the farm-raised catfish industry threatens to destroy the independent commercial fisherman, and in others water pollution threatens the fish and mussel populations. These pressures will change the culture of the river family, but its reliance on the river, both spiritually and economically, will continue.

Tom Rankin
Southern Arts Federation

Ernest T. Hiller, *Houseboat and River-Bottoms People* (1939); Harlan Hubbard, *Shantyboat: A River Way of Life* (1953). ☆

Rivers and Lakes

From the Potomac to the Rio Grande, the South is blessed with rivers flowing, with few exceptions, to the Atlantic and Gulf coasts. Fed by an average annual rainfall of 40 to 50 inches, with even greater amounts in the Appalachians and along the Gulf Coast east of New Orleans, the rivers of the South have bountiful flows except in drier west Texas, and the warm southern climate keeps the streams free of ice during most of the year. Because the rains fall abundantly in the winter and spring, however, the rivers often flood during those seasons, and they sometimes dwindle to trickles during summer and autumn droughts. Although uneven flows have at times hampered their usefulness, rivers provide southerners, in varying regional proportions, with fertile floodplains for agriculture, convenient routes for trade and travel, power to turn mills and produce electricity, water to drink, and many fish and waterfowl for dietary variety. The history of southern rivers has been marked by cooperative efforts to make the rivers better serve those purposes, and it is in the field of water resource development that the South has most eagerly sought federal assistance.

Along the Atlantic Coast, Virginia has the Potomac, James, and Rappahannock rivers; North Carolina the Roanoke, Neuse, and Cape Fear; South Carolina the Pee Dee, Santee, and Edisto; Georgia the Savannah and Altamaha; and Florida the St. Johns River; all except the latter have sources in the mountainous western sections of the states. Estuarine near their mouths and easily navigated to the head of tidal influences, the rivers were ascended by explorers and colonists penetrating through the forests, into the interior. The earliest plantations and settlements were located along the lower reaches of the rivers where the colonists cooperated in the construction of wharves and later in port development to maintain trade and contact with their homelands by water. Port cities such as Charleston and Savannah arose there. At the fall line dividing the Atlantic Coastal Plain from the hilly piedmont and marking the head of navigation for larger vessels, water power for mills was available for manufacturing, and the transfer of commodities from small craft navigating the upper rivers to larger vessels was necessary. Cooperative efforts to develop that water power and to transfer the commodities from one vessel to another around the falls often contributed to the founding of cities at the fall line; Alexandria and Georgetown on the Potomac, Richmond on the James, and Augusta on the Savannah River are examples.

In the absence of railroads and highways, rivers became the southern arteries of travel and commerce, vital for the transport of bulky commodities—hogsheads of tobacco, sacks of rice and sugar, bales of cotton—to settlements at the falls and mouths of the rivers for use or for sale in foreign markets. Some of the earliest legislation enacted by colonial and state governments was therefore aimed at preventing the obstruction of navigable rivers and in some cases providing for cooperative efforts to remove those obstructions.

Pioneers pushing west from the coastal settlements also followed the rivers, ascending to their sources and crossing the Appalachians through water gaps to rivers leading farther west. In western Virginia the pioneers followed the Clinch and Holston and New rivers and in western North Carolina the French Broad and Little Tennessee. Those streams funneled the pioneer migration northwest into Tennessee, Kentucky, and the Ohio Valley, but not directly west into Alabama and Mississippi. This explains in part why Kentucky and Tennessee were settled earlier than Alabama and Mississippi, though factors such as Indian resistance were perhaps more significant.

A similar settlement pattern developed along the Gulf Coast, explored by the Spanish and French who planted their first settlements at Pensacola, Mobile, Biloxi, and New Orleans near the mouths of rivers flowing into the Gulf and then ascended the streams for exploration and Indian trade. In addition to the great Mississippi River in Louisiana, the major rivers emptying into the Gulf are the Suwannee, Apalachicola, Choctawhatchee, and Escambia in the Florida Panhandle, the Mobile and Alabama river system, the Pearl and Pascagoula rivers of Mississippi, and the Sabine, Neuces, Trinity, Brazos, and Rio Grande of Texas. Only Arkansas and Tennessee in the Old South had no direct outlet to the Gulf or Atlantic coasts, but they used the Cumberland and Tennessee rivers and the Arkansas, St. Francis, and White rivers flowing to the Mississippi as their outlets to markets.

The Mississippi River, draining a 1,245,000-square-mile area covering all or parts of 31 states and two Canadian provinces, is the largest river in North America. Together with its tributaries, it funneled commercial navigation downstream to New Orleans from western New York state on the east to Montana on the west and Minnesota at the north. The lower Mississippi, the thousand miles of serpentine channel downstream of Cape Girardeau, Mo., was bordered by a 35,460-square-mile alluvial floodplain, initially settled by the French and Spanish at Natchez and New Orleans before Americans crossed the Appalachians into the central South. Called the "Father of Waters" by Indians, the Mississippi had a central role in the socioeconomic and cultural history of the South.

Log rafting, Levisa Fork of the Big Sandy River, Johnson County, Kentucky, c. 1910

After settlements and plantations had been established in the fertile floodplains where ample water supply and fish and wildlife were available, southern pioneers built mills at falls on the streams for grinding grain, sawing lumber, and other manufacturing purposes. They marketed the products of those mills and the produce of the floodplains via the waterways using unpowered craft at first and after 1811, when the first steamboat reached New Orleans, adapting the steamboat to shallow river navigation. Able to rely chiefly on rivers for transport, southern states seldom undertook the elaborate canal and turnpike projects of the sort built in the North in the early 19th century, the significant exception being Virginia where the falls on the Potomac and James rivers were bypassed by canals extending upriver. More common were local cooperative projects to clear the rivers of snags and boulders and the organization of port authorities to dredge and improve harbors at such ports as Charleston, Mobile, and New Orleans.

The southern concern for waterways navigation was reflected in Congress. Although southern statesmen often questioned the propriety of federal funding for road and canal projects, they tended to support such aid for river and harbor improvements. During the presidential administrations of Andrew Jackson of Tennessee, John Tyler of Virginia, and Zachary Taylor of Kentucky and Louisiana, substantial federal appropriations were approved for clearing the channels of inland rivers, the Ohio and Mississippi especially, and for dredging the coastal entrances to the mouths of rivers. Southerners after the Civil War avidly sought federal waterways project funding; small indeed was the southern river that was not improved for navigation during the late 19th century.

Vigorous southern support for navigation projects continued in the 20th century. Both the Gulf and Atlantic coasts were lined with intracoastal waterways, and elaborate systems of locks and dams to provide navigation uninterrupted by droughts and low-water flows were built on many rivers, making possible navigation by powerful diesel towboats and barge tows. Locks and dams on the Arkansas and Red rivers, for instance, opened Arkansas and Louisiana to barge navigation into Oklahoma, and locks and dams on the Cumberland and Tennessee rivers supported barge traffic in northern Alabama and Tennessee to the western slope of the Appalachians. A canal for the movement of towboats and barges from the Tennessee River to Mobile, Ala., known as the Tennessee-Tombigbee Waterway and ranking in size with the Panama Canal, established a route other than the Mississippi River for shipment of commodities from the Upper South to the Gulf.

The pioneers settling in the floodplains also undertook cooperative efforts at an early date to protect their settlements and plantations from inundation by flooding, especially along the Mississippi River, where the first levee for flood protection was constructed by the French at New Orleans in 1727. Southerners organized local- and state-funded levee districts in the early 19th century and lined the Mississippi and other streams with earthen walls to hold out floods. Contending that flooding was a national problem because the Mississippi poured northern floodwater onto southern lands, southern statesmen ushered through Congress the 1850 Swamp Lands Act, used to assist levee construction, and the 1879 act establishing the Mississippi River Commission, which would assist local levee districts with levee construction. With vigorous southern support Congress enacted flood control legislation in 1917, 1928, and 1936, authorizing federal participation in an immense program for building levees and also for creating floodways and constructing multipurpose reservoirs for flood control, hydroelectric power generation, water supply, and recreation. That program converted the South into a land of lakes.

Because the South was unglaciated, it had far fewer natural freshwater lakes than the North and none comparing with the Great Lakes except Florida's Lake Okeechobee, a shallow lake in the Everglades covering 730 square miles and ranking second to Lake Michigan as the largest lake entirely within the borders of the United States. Lakes Pontchartrain and Borgne near New Orleans are brackish embayments of the Gulf rather than freshwater lakes. The other natural southern lakes are chiefly ponding areas in swamps, oxbows of abandoned river meanders, lakes in the Florida limestone region, and Reelfoot Lake in Tennessee created by the 1811 earthquake.

By the 1980s, however, cooperative water resource development along the South's rivers had dotted the map of the South with many lakes, some built by private power and utility companies for hydroelectric power production and water supply but most constructed by the Tennessee Valley Authority in the Tennessee River basin and by the U.S. Army Corps of Engineers throughout the remainder of the South. Those lakes harnessed rivers for many purposes, impounding flooding to protect downstream areas, furnishing pools for commercial navigation, producing economical hydroelectric power, supplying water for community and industrial uses, and offering recreational opportunities equal to those of the natural lakes of the North. Southern lakes, especially those built near the inland Atlanta, Nashville, and Dallas–Fort Worth urban areas, consistently ranked tops in the nation in terms of their use for recreation.

The Old South stereotypes in fiction and film portraying the plantation aristocracy and chattels greeting steamboats at the landings, or picturing heroic struggles to save mansions and cotton fields from crevasses in the levees, do not reflect the diversity of southern experience, yet they properly illustrate the paramount role of rivers in the history of the South. The relationship of rivers to exploration and settlement patterns and to the agricultural, urban, and industrial development of the South is noteworthy. Equally significant is the cooperative effort of southerners to improve and manage their rivers, for that effort belies the image of the South as the bastion of individualism and states' rights. At early dates, southerners cooperated to improve their rivers for navigation and to achieve a measure of flood protection, eagerly seeking federal assistance even before the Civil War and acquiring it in full measure during the Reconstruction years and afterwards. As a result, southern rivers have been developed to an extent exceeding that of any other section of the United States.

Leland R. Johnson
Hermitage, Tennessee

Stanley J. Folmsbee, *Sectionalism and Internal Improvements in Tennessee, 1796–1845* (1939); Robert H. Haveman, *Water Resource Investment and the Public Interest: An Analysis of Federal Expenditures in Ten Southern States* (1965); Institute for Water Resources, *National Waterways Roundtable: Proceedings, History, Regional Development, Technology, A Look Ahead* (1981); Leland R. Johnson, *Engineers on the Twin Rivers: A History of the U.S. Army Engineers, Nashville District* (1978); Charles L. White, Edwin J. Foscue, and Tom L. McKnight, *Regional Geography of Anglo-America* (1974). ☆

Roads and Trails

From preindustrial times to the automobile age, elaborate networks of roads and trails have crisscrossed the South and made commerce, political activity, and cultural exchange possible. The locations of these routes were determined in many cases not entirely by men and women who built them, but by previous inhabitants who had already carved their own trails out of the landscape. These ancient trails served as a blueprint for later road-building efforts, and an unmistakable continuity exists between the trails established by early Native American residents of the South and the roads and highways built later by whites.

Long before humans inhabited the South, however, animals had worn a permanent system of trails to food supplies, watering holes, and all-important salt deposits. Salt licks like those in Mason and Boone counties, Ky., for example, attracted countless buffaloes and other animals, which, over thousands of years, tramped lasting routes to these locations. These particular trails served 18th-century white settlers who crossed the frontier south of the Ohio River to establish interior settlements in Kentucky. Animal trails were also a part of the elaborate arterial network of Indian traces throughout the South.

Indian trails paralleled water routes like the Alabama, Altahama, Apalachicola, Mississippi, Mobile, Pascagoula, Santee, Savannah, Tennessee, and Tombigbee rivers. Others avoided parts of the terrain that were either too rugged, dense with undergrowth, or swampy. These overland trails stretched across the South for hundreds of miles and made trade possible with Native American cultures in remote parts of the region, as well as other reaches of the country. The Natchez Trace, which ran from central Tennessee to Chickasaw towns in northern Mississippi, and the Great Indian Warpath, which began in the Creek country of Alabama and Georgia, traversed Cherokee settlements in eastern Tennessee, and, after dividing near Kingsport, Tenn., branched off to the northeast through Virginia and into Pennsylvania, were two of the more famous. Some Indian trails, notably the Natchez Trace in Tennessee and Mississippi and the famous Warriors' Path in Kentucky, served whites who used them for exploration, trade, and as military and wagon roads. Spaniards Navarez, De Vaca, De Soto, and De Luna explored parts of the 16th-century South over Indian trails. In his invasion of Creek territory in 1813, Andrew Jackson also made use of existing Indian trails, as did other American militiamen about that time, who constructed a series of outposts along the Georgia and Alabama frontiers to protect white settlers.

As white pioneers pushed into the South, both animal and Indian trails provided the beginnings for the construction of wagon roads, private turnpikes, post roads, and railroad rights-of-way. Although Daniel Boone built most of the historic Wilderness Road, which ran from Moccasin Gap in southwestern Virginia through the Appalachian Mountains to the fertile Bluegrass region of central Kentucky, portions of the route followed old Indian trails. Within the state of Kentucky, animal and Indian trails determined many lines of transportation and settlement patterns. In the construction of the Cincinnati, New Orleans & Texas Pacific Railway in Tennessee and southern Kentucky, the Tennessee Central Railroad from Rockwood to Cookeville, Tenn., as well as the Western & Atlantic Railroad from Chattanooga south to the Chattahoochee River, engineers followed parts of extant animal and Indian trails.

Post roads, which the federal government began constructing during the early 1800s, also facilitated the settlement of the South. After the United States acquired the Louisiana Territory, interest in opening a line of communication between the District of Columbia and New Orleans developed. A 1,500-mile circuitous route over the Appalachian and Blue Ridge mountains to Knoxville, Nashville, and on to New Orleans across the unsettled wilderness west of the Georgia frontier already existed. Congress decided to continue use of this route rather than build a shorter one, but not before Isaac Briggs, a government surveyor, had laid out a road to New Orleans through southern Alabama and Mississippi, which early 19th-century settlers used extensively. Despite Indian hostilities, post-road construction continued in the South until by 1823 a network of routes radiated from six mail distribution points located at Augusta, Ga.; Savannah, Ga.; Creek Agency, Ga.; St. Stephens, Ala.; Huntsville, Ala.; and Natchez, Miss. And once mail service began over these and other post roads, the South became more attractive to settlers.

Aside from post roads, the federal government did not commit itself until 1921 to public road construction on a large scale within the United States. After the 1820s, southerners had adamantly opposed federal aid for internal improvements. Spokesmen for the South argued that Congress had no right of eminent domain or police powers necessary to build bridges, canals, or roads. They claimed that the Constitution specifically authorized only post-road construction and that any attempt on the part of Washington to engage in road building would violate the rights of individual states. This states' rights point of view prevailed throughout the 19th century, and, except for post roads built after 1896 in conjunction with the Rural Free Delivery program, the only roads constructed in the United States before 1921 were built either privately or by state and local governments.

Long-distance travel in the 19th-century South took place over post roads, privately built and maintained turnpikes, and stagecoach roads. By 1850, for example, there were approximately 180 turnpikes in Virginia; and a network of stagecoach roads, with Milledgeville as its hub, linked Georgia with neighboring states. These roads were good enough to accommodate Civil War cavalry and foot soldiers, but they proved completely inadequate for 20th-century automobile travel.

Poor roads were a nemesis to automobile travel in the South throughout much of the first half of the 20th century. Before the end of World War I, few automobilists braved the uncertainty of travel over the South's treacherous roads. R. H. Johnson, an Ohio automobile executive, was one of the earliest to do so. In 1908 Johnson blazed two motor routes over the largely unmapped and often impassable roads of the South. His first trek lasted 25 days and took him from Ohio south to Lexington, Louisville, Nashville, Huntsville, Chattanooga, Atlanta, and finally Savannah. To determine the correct directions between towns, Johnson relied on information he gleaned from Civil War documents. His second trip in 1908 opened an auto route that connected the cities of Savannah, Atlanta, Anderson, Spartanburg, Charlotte, Winston-Salem, Roanoke, Staunton, Philadelphia, and New York. Johnson mapped these routes and published them commercially as the first official automobile guides to the South.

As automobile ownership increased in the United States, more and more Americans chose to vacation in the "Sunny South." Southerners responded by developing a system of motor routes, which, like the ancient Indian trails, connected their region with the rest of the nation. By the early 1920s, 12 officially recognized automobile highways ran through the South to Florida from various parts of the country. They included the Dixie Highway, the (Robert E.) Lee Highway, the (Andrew) Jackson Highway, the Dixie Overland Highway, the Mississippi River Scenic Highway, and the Old Spanish Trail. When the federal government, as a result of the Federal Aid Highway Act of 1921, assumed the responsibility for building and maintaining a national network of highways, these roads lost much of their regional identity. The Dixie Highway, for example, which connected Sault Sainte Marie, Mich., and Miami, Fla., became U.S. 41 and U.S. 441. The Bankhead Highway, named after the Alabama senator who had persistently advocated federalization of highways in the United States, became U.S. 29; and the old Capital Highway, the first north-south interstate route to be proposed that connected the national capital with the state capitals of Virginia, North Carolina, and South Carolina, received the distinction of becoming U.S. 1.

The construction of these first interstate automobile highways linked parts of post roads, county highways, and privately built turnpikes, which had comprised the 19th-century network of roads in the South. Some automobile highways, like much of the motor route from Augusta, Ga., to Petersburg, Va., were originally trails and roads used by Indians and early white settlers. During the automobile age, however, as road-building technology improved, construction engineers were able to ignore the established well-traveled routes of earlier generations. Speed of movement became the premium, and it was as technologically feasible to build a highway through a mountain as around one. Witness the modern four-lane superhighways that now shuttle travelers in and out of the South. In 1956 Congress set up the highway trust fund to pay for 90 percent of the interstate highway system, and today 97 percent of the 42,500-mile system is complete.

These modern interstate highways have erased the continuity that existed between generations of road builders in the South, and they have so homogenized travel that much of the uniqueness of the South has been exchanged for a uniformity manifest in motel accommodations and fast-food restaurants. Although earlier roads and trails in the South helped export southern culture to other parts of the nation, the modern superhighway has done much to destroy it. To be sure, some roads have enduring regional significance because national and regional culture celebrates them. Country music and trucking lore paint images of I-40 going into Nashville; labor union literature refers to I-85, or the "Textile Highway," in North Carolina; and blues singers and even Bob Dylan have celebrated Highway 61, which runs through the Mississippi Delta, north to Chicago. Nonetheless, perhaps more than any other medium, interstate-highway travel has eroded sectional differences and helped forever nationalize the South.

Highway 61 between Clarksdale and Tunica in the Mississippi Delta, 1968

See also AGRICULTURE: Good Roads Movement; / Rural Free Delivery; ETHNIC LIFE: Indian Cultural Contributions; GEOGRAPHY: Indians and the Landscape; HISTORY AND MANNERS: Automobiles; Railroads

Howard L. Preston
Spartanburg, South Carolina

Peter A. Brannon, *Alabama Highways* (April 1927); Robert F. Hunter, *Technology and Culture* (Spring 1963); Wheaton J. Lane, in *Highways in Our National Life: A Symposium*, ed. Jean Labatut and Wheaton J. Lane (1950); William E. Myer, "Indian Trails of the Southeast," *42nd Annual Report of the Bureau of American Ethnology, 1924–25* (1928); U. B. Phillips, *The History of Transportation in the Eastern Cotton Belt to 1860* (1908); Douglas L. Rights, *North Carolina Historical Review* (October 1931); Randle B. Truett, *Trade and Transportation around the Southern Appalachians before 1830* (1935). ☆

Soil and Soil Conservation

Intertwined physical, climatic, economic, and cultural factors brought on severe soil erosion in the South. The Piedmont, the loessial bluff lands east of the Mississippi River, and the red clay hills of Alabama and Mississippi have been the areas of severest erosion. Farming steep slopes with cultivated row crops was the main cause, but soil characteristics also contributed to the erosiveness of these areas. Geologic processes washed the soil particles from the Piedmont uplands to form the Coastal Plain. The erosion plus the intense weathering process left the Piedmont with thin topsoils having little water-holding capacity. Impermeable clay-rich subsoils hastened erosion of topsoil.

The South has the highest annual precipitation in the United States, and the predominance of cultivated staple crops, especially tobacco and cotton, exposed the soil to intense summer thunderstorms. The use of close-growing grain crops, such as wheat and oats, and pasture and hay to support meat and dairying enterprises would have reduced erosion, but such crops held a minor place in southern agriculture. Availability of new lands to the west and south inhibited development of intensive agriculture employing fertilizers and conservation measures. An alternative to moving was to let fields rest for a few years and then extract the accumulated fertility in the organic matter. It was, and still is, a system prevalent in climates where high temperatures and rainfall accelerate leaching and decomposition of organic material, thus creating soils of low fertility and high erodibility.

In the 19th century southerners developed most of their means of contending with erosion. Thomas Jefferson observed horizontal plowing (contour farming) in France. He and his son-in-law Thomas Mann Randolph introduced the method in Virginia. A Jefferson correspondent, William Dunbar, popularized the method in the Natchez District of Mississippi. Another Mississippian, Joseph Gray, invented a level for precision layout of contour rows. By 1850 horizontal plowing was common in the South. In the two decades preceding the Civil War the hillside ditch—forerunner of the terrace—was widely used as an adjunct to horizontal plowing. Nicholas Sorsby devised the most elaborate of these systems and popularized his ideas through a series of publications on "Level Culture."

Several influential southerners, notably John Taylor and Edmund Ruffin, perceived conservation of the soil as necessary to the preservation of southern agrarian life. Ruffin, more than any predecessor, emphasized lime and drainage of level bottom lands. Adoption of Ruffin's teachings had an impact in the Tidewater of Virginia, where the use of green manures, fertilizers, and rotations restored depleted tobacco fields.

After the Civil War short-term sharecropping and rental arrangements aggravated the erosion problem. Piedmont farmers increasingly turned to commercial fertilizers as an alternative to resting fields. Structural measures of erosion control evolved into terracing. The Mangum Terrace, designed about 1885 by Priestly Mangum of Wake Forest, N.C., came into general use. Between 1880 and 1920 most farmers on steep lands in the Piedmont and upper Coastal Plain installed some type of terrace. Faulty design and construction as well as poor maintenance limited their value and occasionally created additional erosion problems.

The present programs of soil conservation began with the crusade of Hugh Hammond Bennett. A native of Anson County, N.C., Bennett proposed using vegetative controls and good land use, along with structural controls in a coordinated conservation plan designed specifically for each farm. Bennett became the first chief of the Soil Erosion Service (SES) in 1933. In 1934 the new agency conducted a reconnaissance erosion survey to ascertain the extent and conditions of soil erosion in Virginia, Tennessee, the Carolinas, Georgia, Florida, Alabama, Mississippi, Louisiana, and Arkansas.

The SES's successor, the Soil Conservation Service, moved from working on demonstration projects to cooperation with local conservation districts organized under state laws. The South became the national leader in organizing conservation districts. The obvious need for conservation and Bennett's evangelistic style and moral persuasion appealed to the farmers. District supervisors served without pay and set priorities for the conservationists supplied by SCS. The conservationist relied on an ever-expanding body of knowledge concerning structural design, the value of vegetation, and planting and tillage techniques to assist farmers.

In addition to improved technical expertise, the decline of cotton under the tenant system, mechanization of agriculture, and land use changes have influenced conservation since the 1930s. For example, tractors allowed frequent and deeper plowings that readied the soil for erosion, and large farm equipment was incompatible with the traditional serpentine terraces. As farmers eliminated these terraces, conservationists assisted farmers in installing parallel ones. Such land use changes in the last 50 years have both reshaped the southern landscape and benefited soil conservation.

Animal disease control, purebred cattle, and the introduction and spread of annual pasture grasses by SCS and other federal and state agencies expanded the cattle industry and brought pasture acreage from 19.5 million acres in 1929 to 44 million acres in 1977. High soybean and grain prices and a drop in cattle prices in the early 1970s reversed this trend, but livestock continues to be a major enterprise.

Pine tree occupancy of unprofitable hilly fields is no longer a nuisance to farmers, and expanded forest acreage results in part from developments in forest products technology and higher prices. Artificial regeneration through

Table 1. *Conditions of Southern Soil Erosion, 1934*

Erosion Condition	Acres	Percentage of Total
Total area (exclusive of large cities and water)	300,967,150	100
Area with little or no erosion	147,256,748	48.9
Total area affected by sheet erosion	130,226,130	43.3
One-fourth to three-fourths of topsoil lost	94,415,128	31.4
Over three-fourths of topsoil lost	35,801,001	11.9
Total area affected by gullying	127,880,121	42.5
Occasional gullies	110,527,582	36.7
Severe gullies	16,073,713	5.3
Destroyed by gullies	1,548,826	.5

Source: Natural Resources Board, *Soil Erosion: A Critical Problem in American Agriculture* (1935).

planting seedlings has replaced natural reforestation. Under one federal program, the Soil Bank (1956–64), landowners in South Carolina, Georgia, and Alabama planted acres of the 2,154,428 acres of cropland reforested in the United States.

Cropland shrank from 65.5 million acres in 1929 to 53 million acres in 1977. Erosion-inducing row crops still predominate over close-growing crops, particularly because soybeans occupy much of the acreage formerly devoted to cotton. Regionally, farmers have shifted row crops to the gentler slopes of the lower Coastal Plain, deltas, and bottom lands. With the increase in fertilizer usage, the lower fertility of many Coastal Plain soils, compared to the Piedmont, is no longer a deterrent. Drainage systems, however, are necessary on many of the level fields. Southerners artificially drained 11.3 million acres by 1930 and 36.7 million acres by 1978. The rush to convert the fertile, easily farmed, bottom land hardwood areas to cropland is causing concern among some southerners who want to preserve portions of the area for its aesthetic, historical, recreational, and scientific value.

Along with farmers throughout the United States, southern farmers have increased acreage planted with conservation tillage systems that utilize herbicides to eliminate weed competition. In 1979 farmers used conservation tillage on 22 percent of the cropland, a figure that rose to 35 percent in 1981. In addition to retarding erosion and providing humus to the soil, the system permits double cropping in the southern climate. In traditional small farm areas of the South, where farmers rent widely scattered tracts of farm land, the time saved is a major inducement.

Southern farmers continue to cite soil erosion as their major resource problem.

Soil erosion, Natchitoches Parish, Louisiana, 1967

Twenty-two million of the 54 million cropland acres erode at a rate greater than soil formulation. The fertile, heavily farmed, loessial bluffs erode at four times that rate. But the 32 million acres of cropland on which soil erosion is negligible represents an evolution from an extractive, pioneering ethos to a permanent agriculture.

See also AGRICULTURE: Crops; Diversification; Garden Patch; / Agricultural Extension Services; HISTORY AND MANNERS: / Jefferson, Thomas; SCIENCE AND MEDICINE: / Ruffin, Edmund

Douglas Helms
Washington, D.C.

Arthur R. Hall, "Soil Erosion and Agriculture in the Southern Piedmont" (Ph.D. dissertation, Duke University, 1948); John Hebron Moore, *Agriculture in Ante-Bellum Mississippi* (1958); Arthur F. Raper, *Preface to Peasantry: A Tale of Two Black Belt Counties* (1936); *Soil Erosion: A Critical Problem in American Agriculture* (1935); U.S. Department of Agriculture, Soil Conservation Service, *Early American Soil Conservationists*, Misc. Pub. 449 (1941), *Soil, Water and Related Resources in the United States: Part I* (1981); Rupert B. Vance, *Human Geography of the South* (1932); Frank B. Vinson, "Conservation and the South" (Ph.D. dissertation, University of Georgia, 1971). ☆

Streams and Steamboats

Waterways help explain much of the demographic, econonomic, and social history of the South. The Potomac, Ohio, and Missouri rivers formed a rough boundary for the slave states and the Confederacy. Seven thousand miles of the Mississippi River system with its tributaries from the Ohio and Tennessee southward to the Big Black and the Red rivers flow through the central agricultural region of the South. Smaller river systems from the Trinity at Galveston Bay, to the Alabama at Mobile Bay and the Suwannee in Florida drain the Gulf Coast states. On the Atlantic Seaboard, 20 river systems from the York and James to the Cape Fear, from the Pee Dee to the Broad, and from the Savannah to the St. Johns have offered transportation from fall line towns to tidewater ports. Few southerners in the past acknowledged that the Ashley and Cooper rivers joined at Charleston Harbor to form the Atlantic Ocean, but almost all farmers recognized the opportunities existing in fertile river valleys. *Niles Weekly Register* reported in 1818 that two-thirds of South Carolina's farm exports were grown within five miles of a river and that all of the market crops were produced within 10 miles of navigable water.

More than 12,000 miles of navigable rivers flowed through the South. Henry Hall, reporting on American boat building in the *Tenth Census* (1880), noted that southern rivers were seldom closed by snow or ice, and that the "noble" Tennessee alone provided a transportation route of more than 800 miles. Although most southern rivers were "subject to variations in depth," Hall emphasized that they were "all good highways." He could have added that captains of small boats, boasting that their steamer could make way on a "heavy dew" or on the "foam from a barrel of beer," converted innumerable shallow streams into back roads, if not good highways.

Rafts, flatboats, and keelboats transported farm produce downstream from the early colonial period to the mid-19th century. Only an occasional keelboat on narrow rivers or a sailing vessel on broader sheets challenged the currents until the steamboat *New Orleans* reached her name city in 1811, and thereby inaugurated a new era in transportation. Steamboats, whether the grand floating palace or the meanest little workaday "trade boat" peddling notions and necessities along shallow rivers, served the South for more than a hundred years. Regardless of size or opulence, steamers brought the sound of modernity to southerners along the meandering rivers. The loud puffing of the tall chimneys, the clanging bell, the steam whistle, and an occasional calliope interrupted the quiet farm life and transformed sleepy river towns and landings into centers of excitement and activity.

The commercial activity associated with steamboats in New Orleans is well known. But the same activity, although reduced in scale, occurred at thousands of landings. The antebellum cotton port of Apalachicola, Fla., is representative of the excitement. Sail and steam vessels brought cargoes to Apalachicola merchants in the late summer and early fall. As autumn changed into winter, the Apalachicola *Commercial Advertiser* (1844) dreamed of the "busy scenes which will ensue when the [steamboats] come booming down the river with their tall chimneys just peeping over the bales of cotton." When winter rains raised the Chattahoochee River, the newspaper announced that "*the river is riz*—the boat bells are ringing, ships are loading, draymen swearing, Negroes singing, clerks marking, captains busy, merchants selling, packages rolling, boxes tumbling, wares rumbling, and everybody appears up to his eyes in business." During the remainder of the cotton season, "steamboat follows steamboat—each wharf has its pile—every merchant his business—every clerk his duty—loafers are out of fashion." The "River News" column of newspapers throughout the South reported similar activity. Steamboats provided farms and plantations, river towns and rural hamlets, with news, gossip, and accommodations for travelers; boats came loaded with necessities, tools, and luxury goods and backed from the landing loaded with outgoing farm produce. The steamers provided a way to the outside world and brought the sights and sounds of the outside to the river valleys.

The everyday business of steamboating sometimes became dramatic. During the 1836 Creek Indian War, the little frontier settlement of Roanoke, a few miles south of Columbus, Ga., was attacked by Indians. The steamer *Georgian* touched at the landing, rescued the settlers, and escaped when the crew threw sides of bacon into the fires to get up steam and speed. During the 1848 Christmas season, William and Ellen Craft, making an exciting escape from slavery, traveled in disguise aboard steamboats from Savannah to Charleston and then to Wilmington, N.C., in their successful bid for freedom. During the Civil War, Robert Smalls, a slave pilot in Charleston Harbor, escaped to freedom by taking a Confederate steamer, the *Planter*, to the Union fleet standing offshore. During flood seasons throughout the South, steamers rescued stranded farmers from dangerous situations, and in a yellow fever epidemic along the Yazoo River steamboats brought medicine and supplies to ravaged towns and took panic-stricken citizens to safer ports. Steamboat fires and explosions saddened southerners when they lost relatives, friends, cargoes, or just a favorite boat. The worst steamboat disaster, the explosion of the *Sultana* in 1865 with more than 1,500 casualties, shocked the nation. Accidents and disasters only temporarily diminished southern reliance on, or affection for, the glamour and excitement of steamboats.

Many boats on southern rivers, especially steamers in the St. Louis to New Orleans trade, were floating palaces. Historian Louis C. Hunter described the elegance as "steamboat gothic" and regarded it as an "aesthetic experience" for many backwoods farmers. He noted that the *Eclipse* (363′ × 36′) was built for the lower Mississippi River in 1852, and offered an elegance surpassing "many of the best hotels in the country." By 1850 steamers had adopted a standard arrangement for passenger service. The main cabin of large steamers was 150 to 200 feet long, with staterooms of 50 to 100 square feet flanking each side. The ever present barroom, the boat's office, and the pantry were at the fore end, with the ladies' cabin aft. The main cabin was the showpiece. Often richly decorated with white paneling, gilded decorations, richly colored carpets, ornate chandeliers, stained glass skylights, polished furniture, gleaming tableware, and snow white linen, the saloon was the center of social activity, providing dining facilities for as many as 200 passengers. Smaller boats engaged in passenger service tried to offer a comparable degree of elegance, reduced only in scale.

The decade beginning in 1850 constituted the Golden Age of American steamboating, but the Golden Age for steamers in the southern passenger and cotton trade came after the Civil War. Some of the fastest, the most luxurious, and the largest boats steamed between New Orleans and St. Louis. The *R. E. Lee* raced the *Natchez* in 1870 with both boats making about 17 miles an hour on the lower Mississippi. Henry Hall reported on two "remarkably handsome vessels," which made their maiden trip to New Orleans in 1878. The *Ed. Richardson* (303′ × 48.5′) cost $125,000, while the *J. M. White*, (321′ × 48′) cost $220,000. The 233′ main cabin of the *J. M. White*, flanked by staterooms, with a polished bar forward, and the ladies' cabin overlooking the stern, could seat 250 guests for dinner. In addition to cabin passengers, this fine steamer could transport 2,600 tons of freight, or 10,000 bales of cotton. Everything about the boat seemed oversized: the magnificent bell weighed 2,500 pounds.

When such fine steamers as the *Natchez*, or the *J. M. White*, and hundreds of smaller boats faced increased competition from southern railroads, steamboats changed to meet the challenge. The foredeck of steamers was first squared to accommodate barges; then the bow was further changed to handle larger tows. As tows increased, speed and passenger service diminished, and once steamboats completed the change to towboats, the magic was gone. In 1902 the giant *Sprague* (276′ × 61′), with a tow of 67,000 tons in 60 barges covering nearly seven acres, could not generate the excitement of the grand packets of the Golden Age of southern steamboats. Even before the Howard Boatyards at Madison, Ind., built their last steamboat in 1934, railroads, towboats, and the internal combustion engine ended the Age of Steamboats on southern rivers. Today only two steamboats—the *Delta Queen* and the *Mississippi Queen*—continue to travel the Mississippi.

See also RECREATION: / Showboats

Harry P. Owens
University of Mississippi

Charles P. Fishbaugh, *From Paddle Wheels to Propellers: The Howard Ship Yards of Jeffersonville in the Story of Steam Navigation on the Western Rivers* (1970); Charles H. Fitch, "Report on Marine Engines and Steam Vessels in the United States Merchant Service," *Tenth Census of the United States* (1880); Henry Hall, "Report on the Ship-Building Industry of the United States," *Tenth Census of the United States* (1880); Forrest P. Holdcamper, ed., *Merchant Steam Vessels of the United States 1807–1868* (1952); Louis C. Hunter, *Steamboats on the Western Rivers: An Economic and Technological History* (1949); T. C. Purdy, "Report on Steam Navigation in the United States," *Tenth Census of the United States* (1880); George Rogers Taylor, *The Transportation Revolution, 1815–1860* (1951). ☆

Tennessee Valley Authority (TVA)

The 50th anniversary of the signing of the TVA Act by President Franklin D. Roosevelt was 18 May 1983. In that half century the Tennessee Valley Authority played a major role in transforming one of the most underdeveloped and poverty-stricken areas in the nation into one centrally involved with critical problems besetting the South, the nation, and the world in the waning years of the 20th century. Senator George Norris's vision of "taking the Tennessee River as a whole and developing it systematically, as one great enterprise, to bring about the maximum control of navigation, of flood control, and of the development of electricity" was realized along with other major environmental accomplishments before his death in 1944. And by the end of World War II the agency already was involved with matters that transcended the initial vision of its creators.

On 8 October 1945 President Harry Truman dedicated Kentucky Dam, the last of the on-river dams to be constructed and the 16th dam built by TVA within the seven states (Tennessee, Alabama, Georgia, Kentucky, Mississippi, North Carolina, and Virginia) encompassed by the drainage system of the Tennessee River, an area roughly the size of Scotland and England. The president in his remarks quoted those spoken by Roosevelt on 18 April 1933: "The usefulness of the entire Tennessee River . . . transcends mere power development; it enters the wide fields of flood control, soil erosion, reforestation, elimination from agricultural use of marginal lands, and distribution and diversification of industry." Truman then made the obvious point that Roosevelt's prophecy had been fulfilled, "for in the TVA the Congress has provided for a tying together of all things that go to make up a well-rounded economic development." With the goal of well-rounded economic development in mind, TVA in its first decade, through planned development, modified the environment in remarkable ways to achieve its mission.

In 1933 throughout the valley unemployment was endemic, mountains had been slashed and burned, a barter economy was widespread, and spring flooding was taken for granted. By constructing 16 dams within 12 years TVA put thousands of people to work and provided untold opportunities for the development of skills among a largely untutored rural work force. To further assist its work force, TVA encouraged the establishment of unions and collective bargaining with its employees. It also pursued a policy of working with landowners to increase the production and use of trees in ways that would assist in erosion control and watershed protection. And, as it generated electricity, rates came down so that electricity became easily available.

Through the Electric Home and Farm Authority, TVA facilitated the purchase of low-cost appliances. Before the advent of TVA 97 percent of the people had no electricity; within three decades thereafter it was universally available. In helping to ease the lives of an undernourished, deprived, rural population, TVA helped create opportunities for a better life that agency officials as well as many in government hoped could be emulated elsewhere.

TVA also pioneered in the development of rural regional libraries and helped to improve county school systems and to create parks throughout the region. Plans, ordinances, and codes developed in villages constructed by TVA at various dam sites were usually adopted by the councils of these communities as they were absorbed into the structure of county government. Many practices, notably TVA's emphasis on uniform accounting, were adopted by municipalities and other local and state government agencies.

One of the notable changes TVA accomplished, initially through the slight raising and lowering of water levels at various dams, was the eradication of malaria, previously considered endemic throughout a large portion of the valley. Before TVA came to the valley at least a third of the people there suffered from malaria. By making the river navigable, by providing a nine-foot channel from Knoxville to Paducah, where it entered the Ohio River, and by providing cheaper electricity, TVA helped to make cities and surrounding areas attractive to commercial and industrial ventures, furthering the economic development of the valley states. Moreover, research conducted at the TVA National Fertilizer Development Center at Muscle Shoals developed and encouraged the use of inexpensive phosphate fertilizers, thereby assisting farmers in the valley, throughout the nation, and in other countries as well to increase their yields and to combat erosion of their soils. TVA through various programs encouraged valley farmers in organizing cooperatives to bring electricity to their farms and in weaning them away from an agriculture largely based on cotton and corn.

The devastating flooding that occurred throughout the Ohio and Mississippi river valleys in 1937 brought to national attention the fact that flood control on the Tennessee River was already quite effective. At that time only three dams and reservoirs were in operation. By 1980 there were 9 dams on the Tennessee River itself, 5 major dams on headstreams, 12 smaller impoundments, 7 steam plants, and an equal number of nuclear plants in operation or in various stages of construction. The dams and impoundments provided the Tennessee River Valley with the nation's most effective flood control system. Moreover, the various TVA structures—dams, powerhouses, bridges, and generators—were widely proclaimed as magnificent functional structures. In most instances they blended harmoniously with the environment, imaginatively utilized building materials, and successfully coordinated the science of engineering with the art of architecture. They quickly gained national and worldwide attention as models of public architecture, a successful team effort in one of the largest construction projects in the world.

With the outbreak of World War II and America's participation in it, TVA put increased emphasis on the production of electricity to assist plants in the valley manufacturing aluminum for aircraft and for the installation at Oak Ridge utilizing uranium 235 to produce atomic weapons. The Muscle Shoals fertilizer program was set aside for the production of phosphates and nitrates for munitions. During these years the capacity of TVA's power system more than doubled from a little less than a million kilowatts in 1940 to more than 2.5 million in 1946. By 1980 TVA installations had a generating capacity of over 100 billion kilowatts.

The last figure indicates that TVA in the postwar years continued to play a leading role in the economic development and transformation of the valley. During these years TVA focused its attention on tributary area development and enhanced energy production, including nuclear energy. As a result by 1980 Decatur, Ala., for example, had 20 Fortune 500 companies within the Tennessee River environs. Barges on the river were moving more than 30 million tons of freight. A more balanced economy, agricultural and urban, had been established in large part through the efforts of TVA. In a half-century the valley had been transformed from a deprived, eroded, flooded area where the per capita annual income was $168, to a modern region with an income nearly 80 percent of the national average. The towns of the region, in contrast to those of neighboring central Appalachia, had an air of solid brick-built prosperity.

All these changes did not come easily, and in the postwar years TVA was the butt of increasing criticism. At the outset blacks found much to complain about in the racism and discriminatory practices of the agency, some of which went beyond those prevailing in various parts of the valley. Black leaders noted that little rehabilitation for blacks was included in the programs and policies espoused by TVA. In addition, population removal was a serious problem as almost a million acres were flooded by TVA reservoirs. The agency, after several years, developed procedures to provide adequate compensation for displaced people. These became models for emulation in other parts of the country. Whenever possible TVA rebuilt or replaced roads, bridges, and other structures. It tried to move churches and cemeteries. But not everyone was satisfied. Farm families not owning the land on which they lived received no compensations and were placed in dire straits.

Moreover, TVA was never exempt from political pressures, legal challenges, and internal controversies. Investor-owned utilities at first challenged its constitutionality and later succeeded in preventing any expansion of the area TVA could serve. In the postwar years, as the institutional apparatus of the states and counties throughout the Tennessee Valley became more sophisticated, some resentment against TVA developed as various agencies of state and local government claimed that their prerogatives had been usurped or ignored.

In the late 1960s environmentalists in the valley and throughout the nation criticized various aspects of TVA's operations. They successfully challenged TVA's purchasing most of its coal for its 63 coal-burning steam-generating plants from strip-mine operators in eastern Kentucky. They correctly charged TVA with being one of the worst despoilers and polluters in the region and prompted the agency to mend its ways by installing scrubbers to reduce the emission of sulphur from its coal-fired plants as well as cooling towers to lower the temperature from its coal-fired and nuclear plants. Their interest in a then endangered species, the snail-darter, delayed the completion of Tellico Dam on the Little Tennessee River. By the next decade, however, TVA's concern for conservation had markedly improved.

As inflation and escalating interest rates became more evident and as energy costs increased in the 1970s (by 119 percent between 1973 and 1983), TVA raised its rates and many of the almost 3 million hard-pressed consumers throughout the valley became increasingly critical of the agency. Its attempts to produce nuclear energy and thereby lower utility rates have resulted in dismal failure and exacerbation of the situation. TVA planned to build 17 nuclear generating plants, but as of January 1986 the agency had abandoned eight of the projects and had halted work at the remaining nine because of construction or safety problems. In the face of Nuclear Regulatory Commission citations for over 1,000 violations plus legislative rumblings regarding restructuring of the agency, TVA has hired new top-level personnel to untangle managerial and operational problems with its nuclear projects. Current TVA chairman Charles Dean foresees gradual reopening and full operating of the existing reactors. Successful operation of the nuclear plants would enable TVA once again to provide cheap power, thus encouraging industry, especially the paper and aluminum companies, to remain in the valley. TVA has already made a tremendous impact on industrial growth. In the fiscal year 1982, in a recessionary economy, there were 273 announcements from industries planning to build new facilities or expand existing ones. Since 1933 the number of manufacturing plants in the region has increased by 400 percent.

See also AGRICULTURE: / Fertilizer; / Rural Electrification; INDUSTRY: / Mining; Nuclear Industry

Richard Lowitt
Iowa State University

North Callahan, *TVA: Bridge over Troubled Waters* (1980); Wilmon H. Droze, *High Dams and Slack Waters: TVA Rebuilds a River* (1965); Erwin Hargrove and Paul Conkin, eds., *TVA: Fifty Years of Grassroots Bureaucracy* (1983); David E. Lilienthal, *TVA: Democracy on the March* (1944); Michael McDonald and John Muldowny, *TVA and the Dispossessed: The Resettlement of Population in the Norris Dam Area* (1982); R. C. Martin, ed., *TVA: The First Twenty Years* (1956); John Robert Moore, ed., *The Economic Impact of TVA* (1967); Martha E. Munzer, *Valley of Vision: The TVA Years* (1969); Philip Selznick, *TVA and the Grass Roots: A Study in the Sociology of Formal Organization* (1949); TVA, *Annual Reports* (1934–). ☆

Trees

William Faulkner's story "Delta Autumn" talks of Mississippi Delta land that is an "impenetrable jungle of water-standing cane and cypress, gum and holly and oak and ash." Trees have been both a natural and a cultural resource for southerners. A great forest has covered much of the South since the region's human history began. Pine forests paralleled the Atlantic and Gulf coasts, hardwoods were found in the uplands, mixed pine-hardwood growth occurred in the low-lying swamps and river valleys, and the mountains produced appropriate high altitude hardwoods. The slopes of the Appalachian Mountains and the Ozarks have been especially rich with tree life.

Oaks found in the South include the chestnut oak (*Quercus acuminata*) in the Mississippi River Valley, the cinnamon oak from North Carolina to Texas, Durand's oak from Alabama to Texas, the laurel oak (*Q. laurifolia*) from Virginia to Florida, the swamp white oak along southern creeks and river banks, and the myrtle oak from South Carolina to Florida. Strips of white oak are used by Deep South basketmakers, and the bark from red oaks is commonly used by rural southerners to make a tea believed to cure backache, rheumatism, diarrhea, toothache, and chills and fever. The live oak, which figures prominently in southern literature and regional imagery, has been an important source for the American shipbuilding industry and is popular in landscape design throughout the region.

Evergreens are coniferous trees, with tough, needle-like leaves; they remain verdant throughout the winter months. The yellow or shortleaf pine (*Pinus echinata*) grows naturally in the Coastal Plain of the South, as does the longleaf, or Georgia, pine (*P. palustrisis*), which is hardy from Tampa Bay west to the Mississippi River and north to Virginia. The loblolly pine can grow to 170 feet in its native southern habitat, where it can adapt to either swampland or more barren highlands. The red spruce keeps to the uplands of the Carolinas and Georgia, whereas the white cedar (sometimes called a juniper) ranges along the Atlantic and Gulf coasts, growing up to 80 feet in height. One also sees the Carolina hemlock, the cherry laurel, and the evergreen magnolia. The Cherokee Indians regarded the red cedar, an aromatic wood resistant to the damp southeastern climate, as the most sacred of all trees. The litters on which their honored dead were carried were made from cedar wood. It also has been important to the regional furniture industry.

In 1936 Howard W. Odum pointed out that the South grew over a third of all the peach trees in the nation, a third of the orange trees, and four-fifths of the grapefruit trees. Today, delicious apples are abundantly grown in North Carolina and Virginia, the Japanese plum is found throughout the South, and the fig tree can be grown as far north as southern Virginia, with Florida, Georgia, South Carolina, Louisiana, Texas, and Mississippi among the largest producers of figs in the nation. The South grows a variety of pears as well. In terms of nut trees, the pecan is native throughout the Mississippi River Valley, but its special home is Texas, which adopted it as the state tree in 1927. The English walnut (*Juglans regia*) also thrives in the Southeast.

The southern Appalachians are noted for their hardwoods. The sweet gum (*Liquidambar styraciflua*), which is also called red gum in places, has massive branches, a light-gray bark, and is seen from the Upper South down to the Gulf of Mexico. In autumn, it is a glorious sight, with brilliant colors, described by one naturalist as running "the gamut in hues from kingly yellow, through bright orange and red, and on to a deep bronze." Hickories are abundant in the South, sturdy, tough trees, which gave a nickname to President Andrew Jackson, who lived among them in the uplands.

The South has always had a number of flowering trees that have captivated the southern imagination. In particular the dogwood (*Cornus florida*) is identified with the imagery of the region. In Atlanta a million dogwoods were once planted in a campaign to beautify the city. Red and white flowering dogwoods grow wild through most of the region and can reach 30 feet tall. They are slow growers, and their leaves are glossy, pointed, grayish-green in color, turning to a deep red in autumn. Dogwood festivals throughout the South attest to its popularity among southerners. Other flowering trees include the Texas ash and tulip trees.

Other trees in the South that are particularly associated with the region include the black willows, the red birch, the yellow birch, palm trees in Florida and along the Gulf Coast, and the blue ash (seen to best effect in the Great Smoky Mountains). The mimosa, or silk tree, is a somewhat fragile-looking tree that grows as far north as northern North Carolina. It has attractive colorings and delicate foliage. It belongs to the Mimosaceae family, is native to warm, tropical regions, and can grow to 40 feet. When flowering, it shows an array of whites, yellows, and reds. Chinaberry trees (*Melia azedarach*) are popular throughout much of the Deep South as flowering shade trees. They bear in the early spring, producing a pale-pink flower, slightly tinged with purple. Members of the Lester family in Erskine Caldwell's *Tobacco Road* were frequently lurking behind a chinaberry tree, and the tree crushed to death a character in Eudora Welty's "Curtain of Green."

See also INDUSTRY: / Timber Industry

Charles Reagan Wilson
University of Mississippi

William C. Coker, *Trees of the Southeastern States, including Virginia, North Carolina, South Carolina, Georgia, and Northern Florida* (1937); Charlotte H. Green, *Trees of the South* (1939); Ellwood S. Harrar and J. George Harrar, *Guide to Southern Trees* (1962); F. Schuyler Mathews, *Familiar Trees and Their Leaves* (1903); Gary O. Robinette, *Trees of the South: Collected and Organized by Gary O. Robinette* (1985); John K. Small, *Florida Trees: A Handbook of the Native and Naturalized Trees of Florida* (1913). ☆

Water Use

Stretching from the soggy Dismal Swamp of Virginia to the semiarid Llano Estacado of western Texas, the diverse southern geography and the associated climatic differences create the need for a variety of approaches to the utilization and management of southern water resources. Found in lakes, streams, and aquifers, these resources have both blessed and cursed the South. Watercourses provided the means by which early European settlers moved westward to settle the southern coastal plains and piedmont. Traversing the Appalachian Mountains, other pioneers sought the fertile valleys of the Tennessee and

Cumberland rivers, and the access they gave to farther movement westward. Representing a temporary impediment to westward movement, the Mississippi River became the chief waterway to the southern states. Crossing the "Father of Waters," settlers moved up its lush and boggy tributaries until they reached the drier areas that foretold of the arid West.

As the settlers moved westward from the Atlantic Coast they discovered that southern rivers did not provide a reliable means of transportation. Periodic low water alternated with floods to make water transportation difficult, while rapids and other impediments added to the difficulty and danger of southern waterways. Early southerners focused on making southern streams more navigable. During the Monroe Administration, Secretary of War John C. Calhoun gave serious consideration to the Muscle Shoals rapids as an obstruction to navigation on the Tennessee River. After the administration of Andrew Jackson such projects were considered primarily state rather than federal responsibility.

Both the federal and state governments, however, struggled with improving navigation and controlling floods on the Mississippi River. In the antebellum era a government engineer, Charles Ellet, emphasized the need for scientific data on water flow and suggested that a relationship existed between stream flow and other conditions within a river's watershed. In suggesting the construction of tributary reservoirs to regulate the river's flow for navigation as well as to control floods, Ellet anticipated later engineering principles. The concepts of another pair of engineers, Andrew A. Humphreys and Henry L. Abbot, had a more immediate influence on attempts to control Mississippi waters by stressing the use of levees, outlets, and cutoffs.

As far as swamps and coastal wetlands were concerned, few people prior to the Civil War had much understanding of their value. In the Swamp Lands Acts of 1849 and 1850 the federal government ceded much of this area to the states to be reclaimed by drainage.

During the Gilded Age the attempts to reclaim wetlands and to prevent flooding in the Mississippi basin continued as a practical matter. Only later in that period did such attempts merge as part of the conservationists' river basin development concept, with its implications for federal action on a regional basis. Responding to projects he had seen in Europe, Louisiana Congressman Randall L. Gibson proposed in 1876 to establish a commission for supervising developments on the Mississippi. When President Rutherford B. Hayes signed Gibson's bill in 1879 he implicitly committed the federal government for the first time to flood control on an American river.

In the following decades members of the Mississippi River Commission debated not only the best technology for controlling floods on the Mississippi but also the question of the constitutionality of federal aid for flood control. When the commission adopted a "levees only" policy as the primary solution for Mississippi flooding, the results often aggravated problems of control. The constriction caused by levees not only forced the river to rise higher during flood stage but levees encouraged expensive developments in the floodplain. Some scholars, particularly the geographer George P. Marsh, pointed to the dangers inherent in relying solely on levees for flood control. He considered headwater reservoirs of equal importance in solving the complicated problem of flooding.

During that same period both geographers and other social scientists developed the philosophy of approaching a river basin as an ecological unit for planning purposes. Advocates of this concept readily incorporated the idea of reservoir control as part of their philosophy. Among the promoters of the regional planning philosophy was the Scot, Patrick Geddes, whose ideas influenced American conservationists and politicians. John Wesley Powell and W. J. McGee of the Geological Survey promoted the principle of treating a river system as a unit, finding strong support for their ideas with politicians such as Gifford Pinchot and Theodore Roosevelt. Congressional approval of the Reclamation Act of 1902 reinforced the idea of multipurpose water developments under federal authority. In establishing the Inland Waterway Commission President Roosevelt instructed the group to consider a comprehensive plan for all the watersheds in the United States as well as the integration of varied water uses. Perhaps Roosevelt's most important single contribution to the future development of the nation's water resources was his resounding veto whenever Congress attempted to allow private development of water power sites without proper government supervision. His boldest statement of the government's duty to protect the public interest in power development came in the James River (Missouri) Dam veto of 1909, thus reserving a southern river for federally supervised development. Passage of the Weeks Act in 1911 recognized the association between forest conservation and watershed protection, an important element of river basin planning. The federal government took a major step toward acceptance of the idea of comprehensive watershed planning with passage of the Federal Water Power Act of 1920.

The first extensive proposal for multipurpose water planning within a river basin was made for a southern river, the Tennessee. Concerned primarily with establishing federal responsibility for water development and interested in public power development, Senator George Norris of Nebraska proposed that the government continue to develop the hydroelectric potential at Muscle Shoals, Ala., on the Tennessee River. Although government support for developing electric power at Muscle Shoals had been associated with the nation's war effort, Norris proclaimed that the government should retain the project to produce cheap electricity for the region and cheap fertilizer for the farmer. Eventually the senator incorporated into his proposal the multipurpose and river basin planning ideas that had already become current in some bureaucratic and academic circles. The noted North Carolina geologist and engineer Joseph H. Pratt recognized the need for an interchange system of electricity, and he also envisioned the possibilities for development that hydroelectric production offered the South. Beginning in 1917 George Norris consistently favored financing of reservoirs on the Missouri River, claiming they would contribute to flood control on the lower Mississippi, and would also provide irrigation water for parts of the arid West from whence the senator came. As early as 1913 he endorsed federal development of hydroelectric power on the Potomac River.

The congressional debates over Muscle Shoals continued throughout the 1920s. While Congress deliberated over government control of Muscle Shoals, it passed other legislation significant to water resource development. Significantly, the River and Harbors Bill passed by Congress in February 1925 embodied many of the principles of multiple use of water resources, which implied the need for integrated planning in developing each watershed.

The congressional debate about disposal of the Muscle Shoals property revealed that power production would be the project's primary importance. As this fact became more evident Norris gained greater support from southern congressional representatives. Progressive politicians from the arid West who supported government operation of the Boulder Dam project joined in support of government ownership of Muscle Shoals. Norris's campaign for multipurpose river development also gained support as a result of disastrous floods on the Mississippi River in the spring of 1927. Ironically, the Corps of Engineers' report a year earlier had ignored concepts of tributary control and had maintained that all was well with the levees and channel works on the lower reaches of the river.

The year 1928 proved to be a crucial one for advocates of water resource development. In May Congress passed a flood control act providing for a comprehensive study of water resources of the nation's major streams for purposes of flood control, irrigation, power, and navigation. The act included many of the ideas of comprehensive and integrated water resource management, although on the same day Congress approved a plan for flood prevention on the lower Mississippi which completely ignored tributary control.

In late May 1928 Congress passed Norris's bill calling for government ownership and operation of the Muscle Shoals property for purposes of improving navigation and controlling floods on the Tennessee as well as for producing electric power, but President Calvin Coolidge failed to sign the bill. By the beginning of the special session of Congress in the spring of 1929, many groups in the South more openly and firmly supported the comprehensive development of the Tennessee Valley by the central government as best for the economic and social well-being of the region. With a few minor changes, Norris reintroduced his bill for government ownership and distribution of power in May 1929. After intense debate in both houses of Congress and in conference committee, Congress approved a compromise version in February 1931. The bill allowed the president either to choose Norris's concept of government operation or to lease the property to a private chemical company. Southern congressmen and legislatures urged Hoover to sign the legislation. On March 3 the president issued a resounding veto of the bill, basing his rejection primarily on opposition to government distribution of power.

During the Muscle Shoals debate another controversy arose concerning a southern river that held great significance in settling the larger question of the government's right to promote comprehensive development of navigable streams and their tributaries. The issue arose when the Appalachian Electric Power Company asked for a "minor part" license to build a power dam on the New River, a tributary of the Kanawha, located in Virginia. Although Virginia granted permission the Federal Power Commission (FPC) refused to approve the request in 1927. The question arose as to whether the federal government had jurisdiction over a nonnavigable tributary of a navigable river located entirely within one state. In 1931 the courts upheld FPC jurisdiction over the New River under the Water Power Act. Eventually in the 1970s President Gerald Ford incorporated the

New River as a part of the National Wild and Scenic Rivers System, ending a decades-long conflict between conservationists and development groups.

When the principles of planning and regionalism became more widely known and supported, the Muscle Shoals debate took on new vigor. Whereas previously it had been backed almost entirely by conservationists and public power advocates, by 1932 professional planners paid more attention to it as an opportunity for practical application of many of their theories. Franklin D. Roosevelt's nomination as the Democratic candidate for president in 1932 proved crucial to achieving Norris's goals for the Muscle Shoals project. An ardent conservationist, Roosevelt already understood the interrelationship of various conservation measures, such as reforestation, water control, and soil erosion.

The economic emergency of 1932 aided in creating a favorable atmosphere for the acceptance of Norris's proposal for integrated water resource development and Roosevelt's broader concepts of planning. During his campaign Roosevelt endorsed the Norris proposal for multipurpose development, declaring that conditions in the Tennessee Valley offered an opportunity to set an example of planning for the whole country. Roosevelt's election to the presidency resulted in the launching of an experiment in river basin planning as embodied in the Tennessee Valley Authority Act signed on 18 May 1933.

Most southern states established agencies to collect data concerning water resources but such agencies seldom had authority to develop or enforce water plans. By the end of the 1920s some southern states had begun to experiment with the river basin concept of water resource planning. In 1929 Texas established the Brazos River Conservancy and Reclamation District. The New Deal further spurred interest in water development and management throughout the South. With encouragement from the federal government some southern states developed river basin projects and established water planning agencies.

The Mississippi River continued to receive attention from both state and national governments during the 1930s and 1940s. The destructive flood of 1927 brought demands for action. The Corps of Engineers responded by deepening the Atchafalaya tributary, which left the main channel near its joining with the Red River. Acting as a safety valve for the Mississippi floods, the Atchafalaya channeled excess waters into the swamplands surrounding its course. In the process of deepening and straightening the Atchafalaya, the Corps blocked drainage into 22 tributary bayous, thus restricting the Atchafalaya's capacity to absorb Mississippi floodwaters. Eventually the Corps constructed an extensive, complicated levee system to hurry floodwaters through the Atchafalaya to the Gulf. This constriction of the floodwaters raised the ground level within the levees higher than that of the surrounding basin, reducing the capacity of the basin to absorb floods while creating a greater potential for disaster if the levees were ever breached. Controversy raged over this project, intensifying in the environmental debates of the 1970s and 1980s. Environmentalists not only questioned the effectiveness of the system as a flood control measure but condemned the ecological changes it wrought.

Pressure created by rapid expansion of water use during World War II highlighted the need for coherent water plans in the southern states. During the war both federal authorities and state governments attempted to develop desirable water policies in the South, but many southerners remained suspicious of federal efforts except when directly affected by floods or when water developments promised immediate economic benefits.

The period from the end of World War II until passage of the National Environmental Protection Act of 1969 represents a significant stage in the history of southern water development. As in other areas of the United States the 1950s and 1960s saw southerners evolve from the older conservation ethic to new principles of environmentalism, with their emphasis on quality of life as well as wise use of resources for development purposes. In the post–World War II period older concepts of water management were increasingly challenged by new environmental coalitions.

Like most other Americans, the majority of southerners tended to believe that there would always be an adequate supply of water. Throughout its history most water had been managed for developmental use. During the 1950s and 1960s, for the first time, conflict developed in many areas of the South over priority of water use, since the usable water supply was no longer adequate to accommodate all demands. Little thought was given to environmental protection until the 1970s, when it was supported by actions of the federal government such as passage of the National Environmental Protection Act and the Water Quality Act. As a result, many southern states established water development and water quality boards, but the thrust of their efforts has often been more toward development than protection. Some state boards, such as Georgia's, made serious efforts to protect water quality while others, such as the Texas Water Quality Board, did little that might retard economic growth. In 1973 one study indicated that at least 60 major industrial sources were contaminating the waters of the lower Mississippi with significant quantities of 89, often highly toxic, organic compounds.

Since 1969 environmental groups have challenged many of the traditional water projects in the South, especially the grandiose, very expensive ones funded by the federal government and enthusiastically supported by local development groups. Each region of the South had advocates of such projects. In the Arkansas Valley politicians and local support groups promoted development of a navigable waterway that would make Tulsa, Okla., a port city. Its critics called it wasteful and unprofitable. When Texans attempted to get the national government to fund channelization of the Trinity River for barge traffic to Dallas and Fort Worth, a decades-long controversy ensued. Local environmental groups combined with fiscal conservatives to defeat the project for ecological and financial reasons. In Mississippi and Alabama a similar controversy raged around the Tennessee-Tombigbee Waterway.

One of the most spectacular proposals that engendered intense support and opposition was the plan in Texas to pump water from the wet regions of the east to the arid regions of the west. Severe water depletion on the High Plains threatened the irrigated agriculture of that area. The plan recommended taking water from as far east as the Mississippi River and transferring it more than a thousand miles westward. This suggestion not only encountered opposition from Louisiana and Arkansas but also from local environmentalists and fiscal conservatives, a combination that again stalled action on the plan. Even the Tennessee Valley Authority came under scrutiny by environmental groups.

The wetlands of the South, especially the coastal areas, have increasingly engaged the attention of environmentalists. Humans have made numerous demands on nature's resources in many of these areas. Traditionally, Americans viewed swampy and marshy lands as undesirable areas to be altered for the benefit of man. By the 1890s, scientists and others had become aware of the crucial nexus that this transitional area between land and sea represents. The federal government encouraged action in preserving the ecology of the South's coastal regions with passage in 1972 of the Federal Coastal Zone Management Act. With federal urging many southern states established coastal management programs.

The conditions in southern Florida represent the complexity of water resource management in the wetlands and coastal zones of the South. In 1971 21,000 acres of land south of Lake Okeechobee burned simultaneously. This situation resulted from decades of alteration by humans of the water conditions in southern Florida. The lake acted as a great reservoir for maintaining the marshes and swamps of the Everglades, essential to survival of the wildlife and the ecological balance of the region. Settlers in the area considered the wetland unproductive unless drained so that the fertile muck that remained could be cultivated. When dry, however, the muck was also flammable.

Canals were dug in the region to service the growing tourist centers of the east and west coasts of Florida, further altering the ecology of the wetlands. Some envisioned canals cutting across the state to shorten the barge route around the peninsula. In 1971 President Nixon halted construction by the Corps of Engineers on the Cross Florida Barge Canal project, the first time a president had ever stopped work on a public works project for environmental reasons. The state of Florida also turned away from its policy of encouraging drainage and canal building. With toughened laws the state inaugurated a program to protect and preserve its remaining wetlands.

The water problems of the Florida coast have parallels throughout the South: in South Carolina, where citizens prevented the construction of a chemical plant on their coast; in Savannah, Ga., where the people have demanded that polluting industries alter their practices; along the Texas coast where environmental groups insist on balancing clean water and air with industrial development. In 1982 the South still possessed more undeveloped islands and more productive wetlands than any region in the contiguous United States. The question for the future was how would resort and industrial developments affect the wildlife, commercial fishing industry, recreational opportunities, and the existing culture of these vital and attractive areas of the South.

J. B. Smallwood
North Texas State University

Nelson M. Blake, *Land into Water—Water into Land: A History of Water Management in Florida* (1980); Albert E. Cowdrey, *This Land, This South: An Environmental History* (1983); James M. Fallows et al., *The Water Lords: Ralph Nader's Study Group Report on Industry and Environmental Crisis in Savannah, Georgia* (1971); Donald E. Green, *Land of the Underground Rain: Irrigation on the Texas High Plains, 1910–1970* (1972); Martin Reuss, *Louisiana History* (Spring 1982); Thomas J. Schoenbaum, *The New River Controversy* (1979); *Southern Exposure* (May–June 1983). ☆

Wetlands

Southern wetlands—those low-lying, swampy areas with high soil moisture—have played a role in the region's economy, recreation, and imaginative life. The vast expanses of wetlands inhibited extensive reclamation until this century, and the continued existence of Louisiana's bayous, Virginia's Dismal Swamp, Georgia's Okefenokee Swamp, and Florida's Everglades encouraged awareness of nature's intrinsic values. Southern seaboard districts are currently among the region's most densely populated and fastest growing areas. Once considered useless, disease-ridden wastes, wetlands there, and especially southern estuarine marshes, have become the richest nurseries for commercial fisheries and wildlife, surpassing other ecosystems in productivity. The most recent 20-year survey of the U.S. Fish and Wildlife Service revealed, however, significant losses of wetlands in every southern coastal state except Virginia; Louisiana, Mississippi, Arkansas, Florida, the Carolinas, and Georgia led the nation in the destruction of the wetlands. Without wetlands to recharge underground aquifers with fresh water for cities, critical water shortages will become another burden for already polluted rivers and estuaries. By maintaining biologically healthy wetlands, the natural sanitizing function of rivers is enhanced, fisheries flourish, and wildlife thrives.

Reclamation, drainage, and dredging remain the primary strategies in conserving the resources of wetlands. Biologically productive wetlands are an essential facet, like rivers and aquifers, in the region's water supply, but no comprehensive program on the scale of the Tennessee Valley Authority (TVA) has emerged to wisely use, in perpetuity, the fisheries of the Atlantic and Gulf coasts. Southern oyster, shrimp, crab, and bass fisheries, so dependent on wetlands, water quality, and stream flow, employ over 10,000 fishermen in an industry annually worth more than $100 million.

The river valleys of the Atlantic and Gulf shores scour the Coastal Plain, carrying water, silt, and nutrients to many estuaries, which are bordered by numerous tidal marshes, sloughs, swamps, and overflowed woodlands or grasslands. Abundant wildlife thrives because of fecund soils, year-round plant growth, recycled nutrients, and plentiful water associated with both backcountry swamps and the marshes of the ocean shore.

Wetlands are transitional areas between deep-water habitats and dry uplands, and they are usually distinguished according to the causes, duration, and extent of submergence. Tidelands lying astride estuaries merge with swamplands that are inundated by seasonal river floods. Above the tide line inland swamps also nourish innumerable deer, turkey, turtle, and bear; rare, uncut hardwood forests; and endangered species including clapper rails, cranes, herons, and bald eagles. Wildlife managers have classified 17 varieties of wetlands according to soils, vegetation, and water conditions. Periodic inundation, sedimentation, and water chemistry can substantially influence the character of wetland soils and vegetation. Indigenous southern wetland habitats associated with freshwater cypress and saltwater mangrove forests and with alligators and manatees are particularly rare public interest lands of world significance requiring national protection.

The oldest economy sustained by southern wetlands derived from fishing and hunting. These activities encouraged dense Native American populations along coastal shores before prolonged European epidemics in the 15th and 16th centuries. Indigenous peoples relied on grasses for basketry, matting, and thatch; on clam and oyster shells for tools, ornaments, or building materials for mounds; and on hides, feathers, and trees for canoes. Pelts from muskrats, raccoons, rabbits, and otters were plentiful. For the peoples of the Powhatan Confederation, Chesapeake Bay linked and supported a diverse culture. The same was true of wetlands associated with Pamlico, Yamassee, Guale, Colusa, Chitimacha, and Natchez cultures indigenous to the coastal or river bottom lands of the Atlantic Seaboard and Gulf. Numerous remains of middens, mounds, and stilt villages still can be found along southern lake, river, and coastal shores.

Commerce among Native Americans thrived near the South's numerous estuaries or river mouths thanks to the back-and-forth tidal currents in protected bays. Countless broad rivers still meander down to the sea, depositing sediments behind coastal barrier islands, where productive wetlands once nourished indigenous cultures and fostered European imperial rivalry. After the initial Spanish missions, plantations and trade dominated the European uses of wetlands. Colonists relied on marshes and wetlands not only for fishing and hunting but also for cattle grazing, cultivating rice, and milling. Wetlands also supplied oyster shells for construction, marl for fertilizer, reeds for thatch, and mallow for confectionery. Sugar and rice plantations required the drainage and dredging of channels, while tobacco cultivation greatly added to erosion and consequent siltation of harbors.

Their diversity, extent, and location of southern wetlands nourished original cultures while simultaneously tying a common regional culture to national and international events. Slave cultures on the plantations, including the Sea Island Gullah and Louisiana Creole peoples, survived amid coastal wetlands. Isolated wetlands became enclaves for runaway slaves, French Acadians, and Seminole peoples. At the same time burgeoning trade led people in the South's busiest ports of Baltimore, Charleston, and New Orleans to try to reclaim wetlands. Such reclamation efforts were bolstered by both religious faith in the human duty to steward God's creation and the advent of steam technology.

The modern uses of wetland resources evolved in three stages of landscape alteration, from preindustrial to agra-industrial to modern modifications. Shifting economic demands in each case required a resynthesis of laws, knowledge, and values from uncontrolled use, to picturesque admiration, and eventually to recreational and ecological protection. During each phase private-property rights, federalism, states' rights, and community interest underwent redefinition.

During the colonial, or preindustrial, era economic reliance on wetlands for subsistence made the mouths of rivers a nexus of southern plantation and maritime development. Maryland's extensive tobacco crops increased the siltation and obstruction of the northern

Chesapeake Bay's navigation channels. However, Virginia's Tidewater tobacco farmers avoided wetland soils except for cattle grazing despite the House of Burgesses's encouragement of agricultural reclamation. Diked wetlands and salt marshes flooded for rice cultivation promoted the plague of malarial mosquitoes in South Carolina, while tidal energy ran grist mills throughout the seaboard region. Early investors, George Washington among them, unsuccessfully planned the drainage of the Dismal Swamp to connect Pamlico Sound and the Chesapeake Bay.

Colonial accounts of wildlife in wetlands by Robert Beverly and John and William Bartram provided the foundation for preservationist sentiments during the second, or agra-industrial, phase of wetlands alteration. Throughout the 19th century agriculturalists like Edmund Ruffin, engineers like Charles Ellet, poets like Sidney Lanier, and landscape architects like Frederick Law Olmsted fashioned a more sophisticated appreciation of wetlands' physical, scenic, and public aspects. Ruffin, a soil-conservation advocate, systematically described the North Carolina Outer Banks, recognized the increased incidence of malaria due to freshwater flooding of South Carolina rice fields, and inveighed against downstream flooding caused by upstream levees and drainage. Independent of Ruffin, Ellet, after surveying the Mississippi River Delta, criticized the Swamp Lands Acts (1849–50) as giveaways of wetlands to states. He believed that unplanned upstream reclamation was destroying valuable downstream farms in Louisiana. Ellet recommended a federal river conservation program to improve the navigability and regulate the flow of the Mississippi River, thereby avoiding damage to fisheries and commerce that might result from excessive flooding caused by disturbance of the river's natural floodplain.

With the Civil War and federal capture of southern rivers and coasts, the problems encountered by army engineers constructing canals, providing for sanitation, and housing homeless slaves encouraged national planning and experimentation. Georgia's Sea Islands, abandoned by loyal Confederate planters, were temporarily turned over to freedmen's families, who built their economy around the resources of the wetlands. Free blacks in the Upper South, often landless, had supported their families before the war by relying on wetland fishing and hunting.

Olmsted spoke favorably of health "resorts," which had emerged near wetlands in the Deep South before the war and afterward had grown in popularity because of improved transportation. Olmsted's landscape plans for urban parks also used wetlands and rivers as natural drainage basins. The picturesque qualities ascribed to the coast from Charleston to Saint Augustine by William Cullen Bryant were also reflected in Lanier's poem "The Marshes of Glynn." Despite the growing industrial and commercial demands for the reclamation of wetlands, southern tidal marshes became metaphors for the sublime and peaceful freedom embodied in wild landscapes.

Southern ambivalence about whether to convert wetlands to further farming and commerce or to preserve the marshland beauty through protected hunting, fishing, and recreation fostered conflicting national programs. The third phase of wetlands alteration—that of suburban modifications—began in the 20th century. Fisheries laboratories were constructed on the Carolina Outer Banks and Florida Keys, while Pelican

Island, Fla., became the first National Wildlife Refuge in 1905 and Cape Hatteras the first National Seashore in 1937. Houston rose out of Buffalo Bayou and Miami Beach usurped Biscayne Bay's barrier islands, confirming the New South's ongoing reliance on wetland real estate. After World War II, suburban growth, automobile accessibility, and increasing per capita demands for resources jeopardized the uneasy balance between the use and preservation of wetlands.

The protection afforded wildlife and fisheries by the creation of the Everglades National Park in 1947 represented a departure from an older and narrower view of parks for recreation to an ecologically broader desire to protect the biological integrity of water, energy, and land. Studies of the Texas and Gulf shrimp fisheries by Gordon Gunther, and Eugene Odum's productivity experiments on Sapelo Island tidal marshes have challenged the utility versus beauty arguments for reclaiming wetlands. The accumulated ecological evidence now suggests that far from being disease-infested wastelands, wetlands are productive, transitional vegetation zones capable of sustaining fisheries, recharging groundwater supplies, protecting uplands from flooding, and decomposing biodegradable wastes. Ecologists have argued that merely preserving landscape is inadequate to protect the numerous public benefits provided by wild wetlands. Instead, the delicately functioning balances between growing plants, migratory wildlife, and impeccably high water quality must be surveyed, monitored, and guaranteed.

See also BLACK LIFE: / Sea Islands; ETHNIC LIFE: / Cajuns and Creoles; HISTORY AND MANNERS: / Beverley, Robert; LAW: River Law; RECREATION: Fishing; Hunting; SCIENCE AND MEDICINE: / Ruffin, Edmund

Joseph V. Siry
Solano Community College
Suisun, California

Nelson M. Blake, *Land into Water—Water into Land: A History of Water Management in Florida* (1980); Alexander C. Brown, *Dismal Swamp Canal* (1946); Archie Carr, *The Everglades* (1973); Malcolm L. Comeaux, *Atchafalaya Swamp Life: Settlement and Folk Occupations* (1972); Albert E. Cowdrey, *This Land, This South: An Environmental History* (1983); Cecile H. Matschat, *Suwannee River: Strange Green Land* (1938); Joseph V. Siry, *Marshes of the Ocean Shore: The Development of an Ecological Ethic* (1984). ☆

ALLIGATORS AND CROCODILES

The American alligator (*Alligator mississipiensis*), one of only two remaining species of alligator, inhabits the rivers, swamps, and marshes of the southeastern United States as far west as Texas. The name "alligator" is an Anglicization of the Spanish *el legarto*, "the lizard." The American crocodile (*Crocodylus acutus*), an extremely endangered species, is limited to the southern tip of Florida.

Eighteenth-century accounts and drawings by explorers and naturalists in the American South elevated the alligator to a symbol representing America in European cartography and art. William Bartram's *Travels through North and South Carolina, Georgia, East and West Florida* (1791) and his drawings of "the alegator of St. Johns" burned into both American and European imaginations the image of a fearsome, aggressive, bellowing man-eater.

E. W. Kemble drawing, "A Live Capture," in **Harper's Weekly,** *1890*

White southerners have alternately hunted and been hunted by the alligator. Up until the Civil War, alligator hunting was a sport common enough to decimate the alligator population in the lower Mississippi. The use of alligator hides for shoes, belts, and purses began in the 1850s and for the next century accelerated the hunt, as the value of the hides grew astronomically. In the 1940s the southern states outlawed the killing and trapping of alligators, and the 1970 U.S. Endangered Species Act banned the international sale of hides and products. Despite continued poaching, the protected alligator population had so replenished itself that in 1981 it became legal once more to sell the hides.

Stories of encounters with alligators, especially deadly attacks upon children and dogs, have been common throughout the South since the 18th century. The belief that alligators are especially prone to attack blacks began in early slave ship accounts and persists as a motif in white southern fiction and humor, and on postcards and souvenirs from the early decades of this century.

The attitudes of southern blacks and Native Americans toward alligators are quite mixed. Afro-American folktales portray the alligator as the victim of a trickster animal such as the rabbit with whom blacks identified. The Seminole Indians of Florida have had a relationship to alligators something like that of the Plains Indians to the bison. Alligator wrestling that has thrilled tourists since the 1920s at alligator farms and at dozens of smaller roadside attractions never was a Seminole native custom.

Blacks and Native Americans have incorporated the alligator into their foodways. Southern magical medicine employs alligator teeth and oil in treatments for pain, as antidotes for poison, and as charms against witches. A Cajun superstition alleges that an alligator crawling under one's house is a portent of death. Most southerners, it seems, attribute great power to the alligator.

Jay Mechling
University of California, Davis

Dick Bothwell, *The Great Outdoors Book of Alligators and Other Crocodilia* (n.d.); Sherman A. Minton, Jr., and Madge Rutherford Minton, *Giant Reptiles* (1973); Wilfred T. Neill, *The Last of the Ruling Reptiles: Alligators, Crocodiles, and Their Kin* (1971). ☆

APPALACHIAN COAL REGION

The Appalachian coalfields stretch from northern Pennsylvania to Alabama, with major southern sites in West Virginia, southwestern Virginia, western Kentucky and Tennessee, and northern Alabama. As a group, the Appalachian coal-producing areas comprise one of seven major coalfields in the United States. The mountainous topography and the industrial history of the Appalachian coalfields have uniquely shaped the inhabitants' lives, producing a sense of otherness within the fabric of southern culture.

The southern Appalachians were sparsely settled by self-sufficient mountain families before the coming of the railroad. The coal in their hills, however, was of great value to America's burgeoning industrial economy in the 19th century, so mining operations proliferated. Company towns were built, and mine workers were brought in from other states and many nations. Sharing more with the propertyless wage earners of the industrial cities of the North than with the sharecropping farmers of the South, the miners suffered through the ups and downs of an exceedingly unstable industry by clinging to visions of both militant unionism and individual success. Outsiders have found it easiest to attribute their stridency, pride, and recurring poverty to the fierce, if ignorant, independence of the mountaineer. This perception of the beliefs and problems of those who live in the coal regions turns a blind eye to the underlying industrial causes of Appalachian backwardness.

The development of the coalfields as an economic resource reflected technological and business innovation. Modern methods of exploiting fields of bituminous coal were applied to Appalachia beginning in the 1880s. Coal output rose from 6 million tons in 1880 to 26 million tons by 1890 and 52 million tons in 1900. Coal companies such as the Virginia Iron, Coal, and Coke Company, Western Kentucky Coal, and the Peabody Coal Company became giants of the American energy industry, controlling land and deposits of coal, limestone, oil, and gas.

Exploitation of the coalfields has left its mark on the Appalachian environment and on the region's inhabitants. The high sulfur content of coal has meant widespread pollution of air and a blackened landscape. Until the 1950s, miners worked primarily underground, gathering coal in deep-shaft mines. Mine explosions were common, and the death rate for miners was the highest in the industrial world. Strip mining became increasingly common after 1960, thanks to the development of huge new earth-moving machinery. "Big Muskie" is the world's largest piece of heavy machinery, broad as an eight-lane road, and it is used in Appalachian coalfields. Contour strip mining scars the region's hillsides, promoting erosion and flooding. Protest songs and folksongs—such as John Prine's "Paradise," which tells of the Peabody Coal Company in Muhlenberg County, Ky.—have chronicled the story of the Appalachian coalfields and the hardships of coal miners and their families, seldom the beneficiaries of the wealth they have helped reap.

See also INDUSTRY: / Mining; MYTHIC SOUTH: / Appalachian Myth; SOCIAL CLASS: / Coal Miners

Arthur Donovan
Virginia Polytechnic Institute and State University

David A. Corbin, *Life, Work, and Rebellion in the Coal Fields: The Southern West Virginia Miners, 1880–1922* (1981); Ronald D. Eller, *Miners, Millhands, and Mountaineers: The Modernization of the Appalachian South, 1880–1930* (1981); Henry D. Shapiro, *Appalachia on Our Mind: The Southern Mountains and Mountaineers in the American Consciousness, 1870–1920* (1978); David E. Whisnant, *All That Is Native and Fine: The Politics of Culture in an American Region* (1983). ☆

APPALACHIAN MOUNTAINS

This extended mountain system stretches from the St. Lawrence Valley in Canada to central Alabama. It includes a series of ranges, and those in the South include the Allegheny Mountains, the Blue Ridge, the Black Mountains, the Great Smoky Mountains, and the Cumberland Plateau. Composed of sedimentary rock, the beds of insoluble material in the southern mountains have resisted erosion, resulting in the South's having the highest ranges of the series. Mount Mitchell (6,684 feet) in the Black Mountains is the highest peak in the Appalachians. The Blue Ridge Mountains run upward into Pennsylvania and represent the eastern escarpment of the southern Appalachians. They are a maze of coves, hills, and spurs, resulting from gradual erosion of a mound of irregular rock. The Appalachian Valley lies between the Blue Ridge Mountains on the east and the Great Smoky Mountains on the west. It is a series of river valleys, including the Coosa, Tennessee, Shenandoah, and Cumberland.

The Appalachian Mountains represented a barrier to the advance of the frontier in the colonial era, but were being crossed by the time of the American Revolution. Folksongs such as "The Cumberland Gap" and stories of Daniel Boone and other frontiersmen preserve the memory of this phase of southern history. Comparatively small and diffuse coves, gorges, basins, and hollows developed population centers that remained isolated until the late 19th century. The mountains were a source of Unionist sentiments in the South during the Civil War, and the Great Valley of Virginia was the scene of General Philip Sheridan's raids, one of the most dramatic chapters of the military struggle. In the late 19th century commercial interests began the exploitation of such mountain resources as coal, gas, petroleum, iron, and timber found abundantly in the mountains. The area has in the 20th century been the scene for some of the nation's worst poverty, with Lyndon B. Johnson's War on Poverty including special programs aimed at southern mountain economic and social development. The Appalachian Mountains' natural resources support tourism and recreational sports. Aaron Copland's "Appalachian Spring" conveys in music the beauties and mysteries of the mountains, and photographer Eliot Porter's *Appalachian Wilderness* (1973) captures their rhythms in visual images.

See also INDUSTRY: / Mining; MYTHIC SOUTH: / Appalachian Myth; SOCIAL CLASS: / Coal Miners

Charles Reagan Wilson
University of Mississippi

Thomas L. Connelly, *Discovering the Appalachians: What to Look for from the Past and in the Present along America's Eastern Frontier* (1968); Thomas R. Ford, ed., *The Southern Appalachian Region: A Survey* (1962); Karl B. Raitz and Richard Ulack, *Appalachia: A Regional Geography: Land, People, and Development* (1984); Charlotte T. Ross, ed., *Bibliography of Southern Appalachia* (1976). ☆

ARMADILLO

The armadillo is an armored mammal about 30 inches long, including a tail of about 12 inches, usually weighing about 10 pounds. The body is enclosed by a three-sectioned shell. One section in the front protects the shoulders; another section in the rear protects the pelvic region. In the middle section between these two are a number of movable bands. The vulnerable underside is without armor, but it is protected by a tough skin covered with coarse hair.

Collectively, armadillos are distributed throughout South America and north to Texas and into the Deep South. Because the early explorers had not seen the animal before in Europe, it was natural for them to identify the "New Animal" with the "New World." Gradually this identification became so fixed that the armadillo took on the nature of a symbol. It was widely used in such symbolic contexts as decorative map frames in the 1500s and 1600s.

In 20th century America there has been special interest in a single species—the nine-banded armadillo, which is known formally as *Dasypus novemcinctus mexicanus*, or informally as the Texas Armadillo. In modern times the nine-banded armadillo has become identified with Texas just as strongly as the armadillo once was identified with America. This identification is somewhat emotional and symbolic because in fact the armadillo is not at all confined to present-day Texas. Indeed, there are large numbers of armadillos in Louisiana, Mississippi, and Florida.

The armadillo usually comes out only at night. It lives on insects and worms. The animal is basically harmless to people and does not put up a fight when captured. In fact, its peaceful nature invited its use by antiwar protestors as a symbol during the 1960s. In 1968 self-styled hippie artist Jim Franklin, asked to come up with a design for a poster for a free concert in a park in Austin, drew an armadillo smoking a marijuana cigarette, and after that the armadillo became the visual symbol of the Texas youth culture.

In the early 1970s a group of counterculture businessmen started an Austin music hall called the Armadillo World Headquarters in an abandoned armory. The music hall became the center of "redneck rock," a fusion of country and western with rock and roll.

The popularity of the new music catapulted the armadillo into high status at the University of Texas. The armadillo was soon rendered in orange and white, the university's colors. In 1971 the student senate voted to change the school's mascot from the longhorn to the armadillo, but the change was never made official.

The armadillo became familiar in Austin through the musical scene and was reinforced by posters and handbills, stories, and jokes. The connection between the armadillo and Texas youth culture may fade since the last concert at the Armadillo World Headquarters was on 31 December 1980. The building has since been torn down.

Angus K. Gillespie
Rutgers—The State University of New Jersey

Larry L. Smith and Robin W. Doughty, *The Amazing Armadillo* (1984). ☆

ATCHAFALAYA BASIN SWAMP

The Atchafalaya Basin Swamp is a large swamp in south Louisiana located between the high natural levees of Bayou Teche on the west and south, and those of the Mississippi River and Bayou Lafourche on the east. This basin is about 100 miles long and 30 miles wide. It is a forested region laced with rivers, lakes and bayous. The Atchafalaya River, a tributary of the Mississippi, traverses the swamp and brings high floods in late winter and early spring.

Early French settlers avoided swamps and settled rich agricultural lands along rivers. After the Louisiana Purchase southern plantation owners migrated to Louisiana and began acquiring the farms of the small French farmers, who then moved onto small ridges of high land in nearby swamps. Floods were not a problem in the Atchafalaya Swamp in the early 19th century, but by mid-century they had become severe, and all agriculture in the Atchafalaya Swamp ended by 1875.

A swamp culture slowly evolved as farmers adjusted to a new and alien way of life. Certain swamp products such as Spanish moss, cypress lumber, and various foodstuffs (crawfish and frogs) were always in demand by French speakers surrounding the swamp, and these ex-farmers began to exploit the swamp, selling its products to surrounding peoples. English-speaking fishermen drifted into the Atchafalaya from the upper Mississippi River and introduced houseboats and new fishing gear. By 1900 the Atchafalaya Swamp had become the most productive swamp in the world, producing fish, crawfish, Spanish moss, alligators, frogs, turtles, game animals, crabs, pelts, lumber, and other swamp products (and today oil). It remains very productive.

All swamp dwellers are white. This is not unique, as there are few black commercial fishermen in the entire Mississippi River System. French- and English-speaking fishermen exchanged ideas about fishing and swamp life, but they occupied distinct portions of the Atchafalaya Swamp, and because of religious, linguistic, and cultural differences little mixing took place between them. Today, those who exploit the swamp live in small communities where they have access to the outside world, and they commute to their hunting, fishing, and trapping grounds by boat.

Malcolm L. Comeaux
Arizona State University

Malcolm L. Comeaux, *Atchafalaya Swamp Life: Settlement and Folk Occupations* (1972); Harold N. Fisk, *Geological Investigation of the Atchafalaya Basin and the Problem of Mississippi River Diversion* (1949); Charles Fryling, Jr., *Ozark Society Bulletin* (Autumn 1978). ☆

AUDUBON, JOHN JAMES

(1785–1851) Naturalist and artist.

Although Audubon's observations of wildlife extended from Labrador to the Florida Keys and from New Jersey to the Missouri River country, his works are particularly rich in material gathered in Kentucky, Louisiana, Mississippi, and Florida. During the years when these southern frontiers abounded in birds, he was able to compile an extraordinary record in paintings and journals.

The illegitimate son of Captain Jean Audubon and Jeanne Rabine, a French servant, Audubon was born 26 April 1785 on his father's plantation in Aux Cayes, Santo Domingo. Brought up in Nice, France, as the adopted son of Captain Audubon and his legal wife, the boy received very little formal schooling, but did have some instruction in painting and music. In 1804 the 18-year-old Audubon came to America where he lived for a time on a Pennsylvania farm belonging to his father. From 1808 to 1819 he attempted to make a living as a frontier trader in Kentucky. He had some success operating a store and sawmill in Henderson, but had to declare himself bankrupt in 1819. After this failure he concentrated most of his energies on hunting and painting birds, activities in which he had spent his happiest hours since first coming to America. He occasionally earned a few dollars practicing taxidermy, painting portraits, and teaching drawing and music, but his remarkable wife, Lucy Bakewell, often had to support herself and their two sons by tutoring while Audubon was ranging the wilderness. He traveled extensively in the Mississippi Valley and lived briefly in New Orleans and West Feliciana Parish, La.

In 1826 Audubon's portfolios contained some 400 paintings of birds, done in watercolor and pastel. Unsuccessful in getting support for his work in America, Audubon carried his appeal to the British Isles where he managed to interest important savants and wealthy people. With this backing he was able to arrange for the reproduction of his paintings in color by Robert Havell, a skillful London engraver. Through persistent effort Audubon signed up enough subscribers for the publication of *The Birds of America* (1827–38) in four beautiful volumes, "double elephant" or 39½ by 29½ inches in size. No more than 200 complete sets were issued, and surviving copies now command very high prices in the rare book market.

Audubon's restless energy found many outlets. In 1831–32 he extended his knowledge of the South by hunting birds in the St. Augustine region and the Florida Keys. With the help of scientific collaborators and his own artist sons, John and Victor, he published *Ornithological Biography* (5 vols., 1831–39), a cheaper edition of *The Birds of America* (7 vols., 1840–44), and *The Vivaporous Quadrupeds of North America* (2 vols., 1845–46). He died 17 January 1851 at Minnie's Land, his estate on Manhattan Island near the Hudson River.

During his lifetime Audubon had to contend with the jealousy of other naturalists, and he defended himself vigorously against charges of plagiarism and mendacity. Modern critics have applauded the originality, general accuracy, and beauty of his work, including his documentation of an important phase of southern wildlife. Contemporary southern authors such as Eudora Welty and Robert Penn Warren have celebrated Audubon in their own works as a significant southern artist.

Nelson M. Blake
Syracuse University

Alice Ford, *John James Audubon* (1964); Francis H. Herrick, *Audubon the Naturalist: A History of His Life and Time* (1938); Kathryn Hall Proby, *Audubon in Florida: with Selections from the Writings of John James Audubon* (1974). ☆

AZALEA

This is the name for a group of colorful deciduous shrubs, now usually classified with their evergreen relatives in the genus *Rhododendron.* Although native primarily to the acid soils and more temperate climates of the southeastern United States and southeastern Asia, many of its botanical species and horticultural varieties are widely grown in other areas of the world that have comparable soils and climates. Indeed, although azaleas were among the first North American shrubs to be sent back to England in the early days of colonial exploration, their general association with the South stems primarily from the extensive plantings of horticultural forms in some of the major southern show gardens during the early to mid-20th century. Many of the varieties now grown in the South were introduced from Asia.

From the impact generated by colorful spring displays at such gardens as Bellingrath, near Mobile, Ala., Orton, near Wilmington, N.C., and the Magnolia and Middleton gardens near Charleston, S.C., azaleas have come to be associated with the South. The association is greatly strengthened by the brilliant spring display of the native flame azalea (*Rhododendron calendulaceum*) along the Blue Ridge Parkway in Virginia and North Carolina and by the intense, spicy fragrance of swamp honeysuckle (*R. viscosum*), another attractive native shrub, which grows in bogs and along stream margins over much of the South. The azalea has become a resource for luring tourists. Mobile annually sponsors its Azalea Trail; Lafayette, La., has an Azalea Tour; and Charleston greets spring with its Azalea Festival.

C. Ritchie Bell
North Carolina Botanical Gardens
University of North Carolina
at Chapel Hill

Charles Reagan Wilson
University of Mississippi

Ben A. Davis, *Azaleas, Camellias, Gardenias* (1950), *The Southern Garden: From the Potomac to the Rio Grande* (1971); Fred C. Galle, *Azaleas* (1974); William L. Hunt, *Southern Gardens, Southern Gardening* (1982). ☆

BIG THICKET

A biological and historical subregion of southeast Texas, the Big Thicket once covered approximately 3 million acres, from the Louisiana border across the lower Neches and Trinity river basins westward to the San Jacinto River and its tributaries. This dense wilderness is now reduced to approximately 300,000 acres, in Hardin and surrounding counties.

Biologically the Big Thicket is the southwesternmost extension of the Southern Evergreen Forest. Proximity to both the Gulf of Mexico and the dry Texas prairies accounts for the incursion of western and tropical species into its otherwise deep-southern ecology. Roadrunner and alligator, prickly pear cactus and water tupelo, sagebrush and subtropical orchids can be found there within sight of one another. Many of its rare, scarce, or endangered bird, plant, and animal species are now protected in the 84,550-acre Big Thicket (National) Preserve. Biologists have described the region as zoologically and botanically the most diverse area of its size in the Western Hemisphere.

Historically the Big Thicket has long been famous as a refuge. Early pioneers entering southeast Texas in the 1820s found their way blocked by dense vegetation along innumerable streams. They detoured around the area, which they termed the "Big Thicket." Though it was never an unbroken jungle, civilization tended to bypass the Thicket. During the Civil War deserters and conscientious objectors from Texas and nearby southern states hid there, pursued without success by conscription forces. During World Wars I and II descendants of some of these original fugitives hid there for the duration of the conflict. As late as the 1950s prisoners from nearby state prisons were said to have a good chance of escape if they could reach the Thicket ahead of their pursuers.

Pete A. Y. Gunter
North Texas State University

Geyata Ajilvsgi, *Wildflowers of the Big Thicket, East Texas, and Western Louisiana* (1979); Pete A. Y. Gunter, *The Big Thicket: A Challenge for Conservation* (1971); Campbell and Lynn Loughmiller, *Big Thicket Legacy* (1977). ☆

BLUE RIDGE

The Blue Ridge is a long mountain barrier, a part of the Appalachians, running from southwestern North Carolina northeast some 1,400 miles to the vicinity of Gettysburg, Penn. The southern section is massive with peaks over 5,000 feet and a breadth of over 50 miles. North of Boone, N.C., the highlands become less broad and are interrupted by numerous gaps. The Indians called the mountain "the long divide," but early European colonists named it "blue" because of the blue haze hanging over it (the transpiration of water from the forest below the ridge creates the haze).

In colonial times the ridge became a temporary frontier between the plantation economies to the east and the Indians to the west. During the late 1700s English, German, and Celtic settlers moved into the area and intermingled. They formed a self-sufficient small farm society with almost no dependence on the African slave labor that dominated older southern societies.

During the 1930s a scenic highway (the Blue Ridge Parkway opened in 1933) was built along portions of the ridge. This highway now extends 470 miles from the Great Smoky Mountains to Front Royal, Va. The Appalachian Trail uses the ridge in its route from the Great Smokies to Maine. It attracts thousands of hikers every year.

The Blue Ridge thus serves as a prominent physical feature of the Appalachian region, a historical boundary between two major cultural hearths of the Americans, and a contemporary mecca for recreation.

Richard S. Little
West Virginia University

William A. Bake, *The Blue Ridge* (1977); Harley E. Jolley, *The Blue Ridge Parkway* (1960); Jean Thomas, *Blue Ridge Country* (1942); Richard A. Williams, Jr., "The Regional Impact of the Blue Ridge Parkway in Virginia" (Ph.D. dissertation, Virginia Polytechnic Institute and State University, 1981). ☆

CATFISH

Southerners have never aligned themselves as closely with any cold-blooded creature as they have with the feline-looking catfish. Catfish are found elsewhere, to be sure. There are some 2,000 species throughout the world and more than two dozen in the United States alone. Southerners, though, have claimed the freshwater cat as their own. They have written the bewhiskered fish into their literature and sung songs and spun tales around it. And they have argued among themselves for years about which one tastes best and how it should be cooked.

The three major kinds, all of the family *Ictaluridae*, are the blue, the channel, and the flathead. Names change with locale, but none of the fish are particularly attractive. The flathead, in fact, looks like its head has been slammed in a car door. For long years, too, all three have suffered from the image of being a trash fish that would eat anything. Catfish were considered a lazy man's fish, a poor man's fish, a black man's fish. Still, the size and exploits of the catfish—and catfisherman—have become legend below the Mason-Dixon line, and their image is beginning to change.

Reports still exist from the 19th century of catfish weighing 150 to 200 pounds or more regularly surfacing at the major fishmarkets along the Mississippi River. It has been a century since Huck Finn and Jim pulled a catfish as big as a man out of the Mississippi. Roughly the same amount of time has passed since Mark Twain also reported that a gargantuan catfish bumped into Marquette's canoe, almost prompting the French explorer to believe what Indians had told him about the river's roaring demon.

Today's equivalent is the omnipresent tale about car-sized catfish lurking below the dams of the South's major rivers, but, like Twain's frequent references, facts of these sightings have never been verified. Still, the catfish's association with the South persists—enough so that catfish were the subject of one rollicking song from a 1982 Broadway musical, "Pump Boys and Dinettes," set somewhere near Frog Level, Ga.

Although sizes are not consistently documented, plenty of catfish are caught—and bragged about—yearly by southern anglers. In earlier times, dynamite was sometimes used to kill a mess of cats. So was "telephoning" or electric-shocking, but both these practices are strictly illegal. Big, old catfish, however, are still caught in a variety of ways in the South, many of them a legacy from the old days.

There are those who continue to work the banks with a cane pole, sinker, and handful of worms. A brave few carry on the practice of handgrabbing in the warmer, sluggish rivers of late spring or summer. Sometimes called grabbling or noodling, it consists of reaching into a submerged, hollow log, grabbing a resident blue or flathead by the lower jaw, and hauling it out by hand like a suitcase.

Many fishermen use trotlines to hook cats. "Jugging" is a mobile version of trotlining. Anglers simply take a piece of line, tie a jug on one end and a baited hook on the other, and then follow the jug as it bounces the bait along river's bottom. Snagging consists of just hooking the fish any way possible with bare treble hooks. It is not too sporting, admittedly, but it has brought in some flatheads weighing 130 pounds or more from Arkansas rivers.

The rod-and-reel fisherman in search of a good fight and a good meal began to modernize the image of the South's catfish. Casting with heavy rigs below the dams and using electronic equipment, southern fishermen are netting prize blues and flatheads of 38 to 55 pounds and more.

The channel catfish, too, has made another significant step toward revamping the tarnished image. Based in the South and Southwest, channel catfish farming is the nation's leading aquaculture industry. Since 1960 soybean and cotton fields in Mississippi, Alabama, Arkansas, and other southern states have been converted into catfish ponds. Fed on grain and carefully nurtured, the grown fish are trucked live from the ponds to processing plants, from which they are shipped out across the country. Supplying some 65 percent of the United States production, Mississippi currently leads the industry, which annually yields an estimated 200 million pounds of farm-raised catfish. Industry spokesmen swear that catfish is the best thing to hit the South since cotton.

Experts cite several reasons for the fish's growing popularity. Research is constantly improving the product, creating better strains of fish that are easier to raise. The channel cat's white, flaky-clean flesh is high in protein and low in fat and calories—a plus in an increasingly diet-conscious culture.

Recipes for dishes like soufflé-stuffed catfish, catfish amandine, and catfish kiev-style are appearing more and more often in magazines such as *Southern Living*, one of the South's self-proclaimed culinary bibles. A National Farm-Raised Catfish Cooking Contest, held in Mississippi, garners almost 1,000 recipe entries each year. One of the country's better-known fast-food chains, Church's Fried Chicken, has opted to add catfish to its standardized menu. When fried catfish was served to the world's leaders at the 1983 Williamsburg Summit Conference, not a single piece of the entree, according to observers, remained as leftovers. The South's lowly catfish has finally swum uptown.

New image and all, however, the catfish will probably never leave behind its down-home connections. Every southern state proclaims at least one "catfish capital of the world." To name but a few, Mississippi boasts Belzoni; Tennessee has Paris; and Arkansas declares Toad Suck as *the* spot for catfish. Most of these places and many more still hold annual festivals to celebrate their own hometown favorite—the catfish. They batter and fry huge amounts of the fish and serve it swimming in catsup on plates heaped high with hushpuppies, coleslaw, and french fries, usually all to the beat of local bluegrass or country music. Most of these are all-you-can-eat affairs, meant to be social occasions rather than gourmet experiences. Despite its changing image, the catfish's place as an excuse for a traditional southern celebration is not likely to change anytime soon.

Dianne Young
Southern Living

Kenneth D. Carlander, *Handbook of Freshwater Fishery Biology*, vols. 1 and 2 (1969, 1977); John Madson, *Smithsonian* (September 1984); Dianne Young, *Southern Living* (July 1984). ☆

CHESAPEAKE BAY

This is the largest estuary in North America, stretching 200 miles in length, from southern Virginia to northern Maryland, and ranging from 3 to 35 miles in width. The bay includes 4,300 square miles of water and covers 8,100 miles of shoreline. There are 170 miles of channel connecting the bay to the island seaport of Baltimore. The area has historically nurtured a distinctive culture of the Upper South and today continues to provide an economic and environmental context for many southerners.

The Chesapeake Bay was the site of

the first permanent English colony in North America and gave rise to a cohesive society in the colonial South. Jamestown was founded in 1607 on the lower bay, on the James River. Captain John Smith called it "a faire Bay." "Heaven and earth never agreed better to frame a place for man's habitation," he wrote. Some 200 Algonkian Indian villages were already in the area when the settlers arrived, and the Native American influence survives in the names of such rivers as the Potomac, Patuxent, Patapsco, Rappahannock, Nanticoke, and Wicomico. More than 10 major waterways feed into the bay, as well as 140 other rivers, creeks, and streams. The Susquehanna River is the bay's main artery.

Tobacco early became the dominant economic factor in the Chesapeake. The long shoreline and extensive system of navigable waterways encouraged the growing and exportation of staple crops, especially tobacco, for trade. In 1775 tobacco represented 75 percent of the total value of export from the Chesapeake area, was worth $4 million, and accounted for 60 percent of the colonies' total exports to England. Shipbuilding, another important economic activity dating back to the 1600s, reached a high point before the Civil War. The construction of canals in the 1820s and railroads in the 1830s and 1840s provided a foundation for the region's economic expansion during the 19th century. The Chesapeake became part of a Middle Atlantic industrial seaboard area, with its ports in Baltimore, Norfolk, and Hampton Roads serving as centers of international commerce.

The Chesapeake Bay has immense environmental importance. It gives life to 2,700 species of animals, especially fish and shellfish. Clams, crabs, eels, sea trout, flounder, bluefish, croakers, shad, and herring are found in the bay, which produces 33 percent of the United States oyster catch and 50 percent of its blue crabs. Crisfield, Md., the self-styled crab capital of the world, sponsors an end-of-summer hard crab derby and a Miss Crustacean Beauty Pageant. Geese, ducks, swans, and other waterfowl can be seen in the bay, as part of their winter migration from the North. Baltimore journalist H. L. Mencken called the bay "a great big protein factory" because of its animal resources. The environment there also supports recreational activities for sport fishermen and others from the surrounding areas.

The Chesapeake region has grown enormously in recent decades, now supporting almost 9 million people, with a 50 percent population increase from 1950 to 1984 in the bay's drainage area of six states (Virginia, Maryland, Pennsylvania, New York, Delaware, and West Virginia). This increased concentration of population, along with pollution from the factories and farms of the area, has brought a deteriorating environment and rising fear for its future. The Susquehanna empties chemical pollutants from Pennsylvania industries into the bay, the Patapsco in Maryland carries refinery contaminants, and the James River holds waste from Richmond and Norfolk. Fertilizer runoff from farms is considered perhaps an even greater threat than industrial pollution. A significant decline of sea life has resulted. In the mid-1970s the bay produced over 6 million pounds of striped bass yearly, but that had declined to 600,000 by the mid-1980s. The federal government and the Chesapeake states announced a major cleanup program in September of 1985.

See also LANGUAGE: / Chesapeake Bay Dialect

Charles Reagan Wilson
University of Mississippi

Carl Bridenbaugh, *Myths and Realities: Societies of the Colonial South* (1963); Ernest M. Eller, *Chesapeake Bay in the American Revolution* (1982); Carolyn Ellis, *Fisher Folk: Two Communities on the Chesapeake Bay* (1986); William C. McCloskey, *National Wildlife* (April–May 1984); Arthur P. Middleton, *Tobacco Coast: A Maritime History of Chesapeake Bay in the Colonial Era* (1984); Thad W. Tate and David L. Ammerman, eds., *The Chesapeake in the Seventeenth Century: Essays on Anglo-American Society* (1979); William W. Warner, *Beautiful Swimmers: Watermen, Crabs, and the Chesapeake Bay* (1976). ☆

COLLARD GREENS

Collard greens grow throughout the South and, probably more than any other food, delineate the boundaries of the Mason-Dixon line. Some claim greens kept Sherman's scorched-earth policy from totally starving the South into submission; many today are living testament to surviving Depression winters with greens, fatback, and corn bread. Southern childhood memories often focus on collard greens: either the pleasant, loving connection of grandma's iron pot and steaming pot likker, or the traumatizing effects engendered from the first whiff of the unmistakable odor for which greens are famous. Writing in the Charlotte, N.C., *Observer* in 1907, J. P. Caldwell explained, "The North Carolinian who is not familiar with pot likker has suffered in his early education and needs to go back and begin it over again." Particularly among rural and poor southerners, collard greens have endured as a dietary staple.

Sometimes defined as headless cabbages, collards are best when prepared just after the first frost, though they are eaten year round. They should always be harvested before the dew dries. First, they are "crapped," then "looked," then cooked; that is, cut at the base of a stalk, searched for worms, and then cooked "till tender" on a low boil, usually with fatback, or neck or backbone, added. The resultant "mess o' greens" topped with a generous helping of vinegar can easily make a meal in itself. If they are summer greens (and much tougher), the tenderizing could take two hours or more; after first frost, it may take less than an hour. A whole pecan in the pot should eliminate the pungent and earthy smell. Pot likker, the juice left in the pot after the greens are gone, is a southern version of nectar from the gods, and is valued both as a delicacy—particularly when sopped with corn bread—and for its alleged aphrodisiacal powers. Greens combine well with the black-eyed peas and hog jowl in the traditional New Year's Day meal. To ensure good fortune, one should either eat lots of greens, or tack them to the ceiling. In fact, a collard leaf left hanging over one's door can ward off evil spirits all year long.

Nutritionally, collards are good sources of vitamin A. They seem to have unique laxative qualities, though the resultant gas is often troublesome. Folk legends claim a fresh collard leaf placed on the forehead should cure a headache. The same remedy can be applied to nervous afflictions plaguing women, though it works best on such cases when the leaf is still wet with dew and the woman just rising. The roots bound on arthritic joints ease pain, and a poultice prepared from collard leaves has been recommended as a cure for cancers on the face, boils, and festering sores.

Though collard greens are grown throughout the South and Southwest (Indians call them "quelites"), they are most prevalent in the Deep South and the eastern plains of North and South Carolina. The exporting of collards to displaced southerners in the Northeast is big business for Texas and Arizona, but Georgia is easily the top exporter of whole, fresh greens. From the last week of October through May, seven firms around Cairo, Ga., ship 315 tons of collards a week to all the major northeastern metropolitan areas, though over half of that amount goes to New York City alone. The greens are cut and banded with rubber bands, then packed in bundles on ice, about 25 pounds per box.

Collards are usually grown for utilitarian purposes, but southerners have been known to decorate a particularly brilliant plant as a Christmas tree. Thelonious Monk, the jazz great born in Rocky Mount, N.C., wore a collard leaf in his lapel while playing New York club dates. Greens were first officially celebrated in 1950, when the North Carolina playwright Paul Green led a "Collards and Culture" symposium in Dunn, N.C. According to Sam Ragan, North Carolina's poet laureate, Green "urged us all to move out of the commonplace and bring a new dimension to our collard lives."

Flannery O'Connor's Ruby Hill, in "A Stroke of Good Fortune," takes a different view of greens. When her brother, home from the European Theater, asks her to cook him some, she complies grudgingly: " 'Collard greens!' she said, spitting the word from her mouth as if it were a poisonous seed."

Collard greens are presently celebrated in two annual festivals—in Gaston, S.C., and in Ayden, N.C. In celebration of its 10th annual event, in 1984 the Ayden Collard Festival published the first volume of collard poetry, *Leaves of Greens: The Collard Poems*, and staged the first-ever collard poetry reading. Over 500 entries in the poetry contest were submitted from poets in 32 states and three European countries.

The world's record for eating collards was claimed at the 1984 Ayden festival when C. Mort Hurst ate 7½ pounds in 30 minutes, and kept them down just long enough to claim his prize.

Alex Albright
East Carolina University

Alex Albright and Luke Whisnant, eds., *Leaves of Greens: The Collard Poems* (1984); "Collard Files," Folklore Archives, English Department, East Carolina University, Greenville, N.C.; Greenville, N.C., *Daily Reflector* (9 September 1984); Flannery O'Connor, "A Stroke of Good Fortune," *The Complete Stories* (1971); Sam Ragan, "Southern Pines," *N.C. Pilot* (12 July 1984); *The State* (July 1984). ☆

CYPRESS

Author Willie Morris, looking back on his childhood in the Mississippi Delta, recalled a vivid memory of the "cypresses, bent down like wise men trying to tell us something." The bald cypress (*Taxodium distichum R.*) is a common image in the literary and visual works of southerners who are well acquainted with the tree that grows in the Coastal Plain of the Gulf and Atlantic coasts, along inland swamps and rivers, and in pine-barren ponds. It is submerged during much of the year, often providing nearly total forest coverage of large wetland areas. Spanish moss is frequently seen draped over the cypress's heavy branches, and herons and water turkeys sometimes nest in its limbs.

Unlike most coniferous trees, the cypress sheds its foliage, leaving its gray trunk and its branches bare in winter months. This can create an eerie—and Gothic, in the mind of a romanticist—impression during the winter and early spring seasons. Known as the "wood eternal," it has survived since the ice age. The cypress can grow to be 100 foot high, but it grows slowly, typically expanding its radius by only one inch every 30 years. A stump of eight feet in diameter was once found 30 feet underground in Florida. Such trees, which have been preserved in mud, are known as "Choctaw" cypress and are highly valued for their color and resistance to water. The cypress's distinctive "knees" are conical-shaped appendages rising into the air from the main roots; they help aerate the tree.

Cypress has played an important role in the economy of the Deep South. Its wood is highly durable and resists the humid climate of the Southeast. Builders value it for use as roof beams, flooring, and shingles. Southerners made cisterns, coopers' staves, and rail fences from it, and it was an essential material for the shipbuilding industry. As a result of the Swamp Lands Acts (1849–50), the region's best cypress lands near the Atchafalaya, Mississippi, and Red rivers ended up in the hands of lumbermen. They gained it through fraud involving surveyors and land agents and then proceeded to cut the land and to illegally clear nearby public land as well. After the Civil War, the cypress lands of the South were even more fully exploited, as the center of the nation's lumber industry moved south. Developers built railroads into swampy areas, giving access for sawmills and disturbing the entire ecology of areas. They produced "pecky" cypress, which is charred and brushed with acids to produce an antique effect, and it became popular for use as interior beams, paneling, and doors.

Charles Reagan Wilson
University of Mississippi

William C. Coker, *Trees of the Southeastern States, including Virginia, North Carolina, South Carolina, Georgia, and Northern Florida* (1937); E. S. Harrar and J. G. Harrar, *Guide to Southern Trees* (1962); Nollie Hickman, *Mississippi Harvest: Lumbering in the Longleaf Pine Belt, 1840–1915* (1962); John Hebron Moore, *Andrew Brown and Cypress Lumbering in the Old Southwest* (1968). ☆

EVERGLADES

The Everglades comprise a wilderness area in southern Florida, unique in the profusion and variety of vegetation and wildlife. Before 20th-century encroachments the Everglades extended from Lake Okeechobee to the tip of the Florida peninsula, a distance of 100 miles, and stretched halfway across the state, some 50 to 70 miles. This entire region, an ancient seabed, is almost flat. Most of it is covered with water, overflow from Lake Okeechobee and incremental rainfall, that moves sluggishly southward until it finally discharges into Florida Bay and the Gulf of Mexico. In this water, varying in depth with the seasons, tough sawgrass, sometimes growing to a height of 12 feet, stands waving in the breezes, dominating the landscape. Here and there so-called hammocks rise out of the water. On these island trees, shrubbery, ferns, and flowering plants grow in profusion. The climate is subtropical, and much of the vegetation, particularly in the southern Everglades, is exotic. Indigenous to the West Indies, such species as royal palms, gumbo limbo and mahogany trees, and strangler figs may have sprung from seeds brought to the Florida wilderness by hurricanes or migrating birds.

In this unique and isolated terrain wildlife abounds. Where the water is not too deep, small brown deer and other common animals are found. Alligators multiply throughout the Everglades; rare American crocodiles and manatees still survive in the mangrove swamps and the coastal waters. The warm damp environment fosters the growth of snakes, turtles, and snails. Vultures, buzzards, and occasional bald eagles and kites soar over the sawgrass, and herons, cranes, egrets, and ibises wade through the waters. Also to be seen are such unusual birds as roseate spoonbills, wood storks, brown pelicans, and anhingas.

Twentieth-century development has reduced the Everglades to half their original size. Vast farms now grow sugarcane and winter vegetables south and east of Lake Okeechobee; housing developments and shopping malls stand on drained land once part of the eastern Everglades. Still more disruptive is the wholesale interference with the natural flow of the water, resulting from the construction of canals, levees, pumping stations, and conservation areas. Engineers now control the passage of the life-bearing stream.

Alarmed by the threat of encroaching development, nature lovers organized the campaign that led to the establishment of Everglades National Park in 1947. Located in the southern extremity of the state and containing almost 1.4 million acres, this is one of the largest national parks. Thousands of visitors annually walk its paths or boat upon its streams, marveling at the subtropical vegetation and the unusual birds and animals. But the park faces continual danger. Too much or too little water can destroy its fragile ecology, and the water must come from the northern Everglades. Accused of favoritism toward agriculture, the water managers at first appeared neglectful of the park, but the state is now committed to restoring a more natural flow. This is vital not only to protect the park, but to preserve the Biscayne Aquifer upon which the southeastern cities depend for their water supply.

Nelson M. Blake
Syracuse University

Archie Carr, *The Everglades* (1973); Patricia Caulfield, *Everglades: Selections from the Writings of Peter Matthiessen* (1970); Marjory Stoneman Douglas, *The Everglades: River of Grass* (1947). ☆

GREAT SMOKY MOUNTAINS

Located in the southeastern United States, near the junction of the Carolinas, Georgia, and Tennessee, the Great Smokies is a mountain range of some 80 peaks over 5,000 feet. Mount Mitchell (6,684 feet) is the highest peak in the eastern United States. The Smokies form an ellipse with the long axis running from southwest to northeast about 140 miles and the short axis about 70 miles. The name "Smoky Mountains" comes from the haze and clouds hanging over the peaks. Annual rainfall in this humid area is 83 inches.

Three distinct periods of human occupation have occurred in the mountains since the 1500s. Until the early 1800s Cherokee Indians occupied the surrounding region. They hunted in the mountains and considered them sacred. In 1980 Jackson and Swain counties, which include the Cherokee Reservation on the east side of the National Park, listed an Indian population of about 4,700. Most of the Indian population (over 35,000) in North Carolina is in Robeson County, south of Fayetteville on the Coastal Plain.

The appearance of Europeans represented the second stage of settlement. Spanish explorers, including possibly De Soto, came from the south in the 1540s. Some evidence suggests they conducted mining operations in the 1600s. French and English traders penetrated the region in the late 1600s. The third phase of development came when American colonists arrived in the 1770s. Indian culture was modified immensely during this time, changing from a relatively self-sufficient economy (with limited trade in seashells from the Gulf, copper from the Upper Great Lakes, and other high value goods) to a commercial gathering economy for the European fur markets. Deerskins from Cherokee traders were shipped to Charleston, S.C., by the tens of thousands in the colonial period.

The Great Smoky Mountains are a naturalist's delight. The first published reference to the mountains was by the French botanist, Michaux, in 1793. John Muir visited the area and wrote in the 1860s of the "cool, clear brooks" he saw every few miles. Botanists have identified between 1,500 and 2,000 specimens of plant life in the mountains. The azalea and laurel are in profusion in May and June, the rhododendron in June, and the wild tiger lilies on summits in August. Blazing autumn colors come from the extensive hardwood forest. Wildlife is also abundant. Bird aficionados, for example, have identified over 260 species from Knoxville east to the summits of the mountains. Over 50 mammals are indigenous to the area, including the giant black bear. The Appalachian Trail provides hiking across the crest of the mountains, and it is only the most famous of many paths. Geological interest in the region dates from Joseph Le Conte, the 19th-century Georgia botanist who traced the Smokies' geological history. The mountains were selected as the site for a national park in 1926, although it was not officially established until 1934.

In view of the dynamic changes in recent centuries, measuring the influence of the mountains on human cultural evolution is difficult. They have played a prominent part in regional literature, serving as a favorite setting for the local color writing of the late 19th century, and in song (the folksong "On Top of Old Smoky," for example). The American settlers tended to be people who sought isolation and often had a history of separation from the mainstreams of events. The people in the mountains were isolated until their "discovery" after the Civil War. Charles E. Craddock (Mary N. Murphree) was the first writer to portray the image of the mountaineer in the Smokies. The immense investment in transportation systems and the growth of major urban centers surrounding the mountains have transformed the area. The 1920s launched a new period of federal ownership of the region with a national park and national forests. Today, the permanent population is greatly augmented by seasonal influxes of tourists.

Richard S. Little
West Virginia University

Elizabeth Bowman, *Land of High Horizons* (1938); Alberta and Carson Brewer, *Valley so Wild: A Folk History* (1975); Carlos S. Campbell, *Birth of a National Park in the Great Smoky Mountains* (1978); Michael Frome, *Strangers in High Places: The Story of the Great Smoky Mountains* (1966); Roderick Peattie, *The Great Smokies and the Blue Ridge* (1943). ☆

HOMER, WINSLOW

(1836–1910) Painter.

Among the 19th century's most prominent artists, Winslow Homer has been praised for his engravings, genre paintings, and marine oils. Although the details of Homer's reclusive life and career are well known, his deep attachment to the South, its people, and its scenes is less frequently acknowledged. He was the quintessential New England Yankee, but his development as an artist was complemented by the incorporation of southern and tropical themes in his work. His bright, expressive, and energetic watercolors in particular reveal the impact of his southern experiences and differ substantively in color and mood from his famous marine paintings.

Homer's works began to appear in *Harper's Weekly* in the 1860s. One of his earliest engravings was of Abraham Lincoln shortly before his inauguration. With the outbreak of the Civil War, Homer became a special artist for *Harper's*; and for a brief period, he was with the Army of the Potomac during the early phases of the Peninsular campaign. Numerous sketches were made of the Union forces in the field with Homer frequently illustrating the monotony of military life. Essentially genre paintings of daily incidents in a soldier's camp life, the sketches and notes that he made of the early phases of the Civil War provided him with the themes for his first oil paintings. Of these 20 paintings, only one focused upon a battle. Homer exhibited selections of these early military paintings at the National Academy in 1863, 1864, 1865, and 1866. The most distinguished of these initial oils was Homer's *Prisoners from the Front*, which was exhibited at the Paris International Exposition of 1867 and later at Brussels and Antwerp.

During the Civil War, Homer became interested in blacks as a subject. He was one of the earliest American painters to portray blacks in a series of oil paintings. His *Upland Cotton*, *Sunday Morning in Virginia* and *Visit from the Old Mistress* demonstrate his skill in painting such subjects in a graceful, dignified, noncomic manner. His later watercolors from the Bahamas rejoiced in the physical abilities of the black fishermen of those waters and document his ability to define in art the human anatomy. In his most famous painting, *The Gulf Stream*, he captures the raw energy of human conflict with the sea as a black seaman drifts on a dismasted sloop circled by sharks.

Although his Florida watercolors are less graphic in the depiction of man confronting the elements, nature is still a fundamental theme. Homer traveled to Florida in the winters of 1885–86, 1890, 1903–04, and 1908. On each occasion he prepared watercolors of the area he visited from the St. Johns River to the Homosassa River to Key West.

The most striking and graceful of his Florida watercolors are those he painted at Key West. Key West was a favorite place for Homer to work, and his marine watercolors reveal his enthusiasm for this region. In his beautiful depiction of schooners and fishing boats at Key West, he demonstrated his mastery of the technical and pictorial skills appropriate to the medium and justified his recognition as one of the nation's premier watercolorists.

Phillip Drennon Thomas
Wichita State University

Philip C. Beam, *Winslow Homer* (1975), *Winslow Homer's Magazine Engravings* (1979); James Thomas Flexner, *The World of Winslow Homer, 1836–1910* (1966); Lloyd Goodrich, *Winslow Homer* (1944); Patti Hannaway, *Winslow Homer in the Tropics* (1973). ☆

KUDZU

Kudzu is a weedy vine (*Pueraria lobata*) with often rampant invasive growth (a foot or more in a single day), which, if not controlled, soon covers anything in its path—shrubs, trees, automobiles, or even small buildings. A native of Asia, kudzu has been a useful plant to Orientals for 2,000 years. The Chinese made a medicinal tea from its roots and used it to treat dysentery and fever, and fibers from the vine were used to make cloth and paper. The Japanese as far back as the 1700s used starches from the plant's roots to make cakes. Kudzu powder is still used as a thickening ingredient in cooking and as a coating for fried foods. It is widely available in health food stores in the South.

Kudzu was introduced into this country at the Philadelphia Centennial Exposition of 1876, and it became known in the South through the Japanese pavilion at the New Orleans Exposition (1884–86). It was first used in the South as a shade plant on porches and arbors, but by the early 20th century some southern farmers were buying kudzu seeds and cuttings and planting them. Alabama Polytechnic Institute (Auburn University) led in the study of kudzu in this era.

Florida farmer C. E. Pleas, beginning in 1902, devoted 50 years to singing kudzu's praises. He wrote a pamphlet, *Kudzu—Coming Forage of the South*, in 1925, and after his death a bronze plaque was erected near his agricultural center, announcing "Kudzu Was Developed Here."

The United States Department of Agriculture in the 1930s imported kudzu to help control erosion on bare banks and fallow fields throughout the South. The federal government paid as much as $8 per acre for farmers to plant kudzu, which became so popular during the ensuing years that kudzu festivals were held and kudzu beauty queens crowned. Georgia farmer Channing Cope, sometimes called the "father of kudzu," wrote about it in the Atlanta *Constitution* from 1939 on, formed the Atlanta-based Kudzu Club of America in 1943, and published the *Front Porch Farmer* in 1949, urging southern farmers to plant the crop. "Cotton isn't king here anymore," he once announced. "Kudzu is king!"

Because the plant is a member of the bean family (*Fabaceae*), the bacteria in the roots fix atmospheric nitrogen and thus help increase soil fertility. Although the vines are killed by frost, the deep roots easily survive the relatively mild winters of the South and produce a new and larger crop of vines each growing season. They bloom in late summer, but the clusters of purple or magenta, wistaria-like flowers, which have the fragrance of grapes, are usually hidden beneath the large, three-lobed leaves. Kudzu is rich in protein and is sometimes used as fodder for livestock in times of drought. When animals graze on it regularly, though, they tend to kill it. Kudzu today has become a danger to timberland, because its vine will envelop a tree and eventually choke it to death by shutting out the sun. Kudzu is now categorized as a weed, and it covers 2 million acres of forestland in the South.

Whatever kudzu's current practical value to the South, it has assumed almost mythic cultural sigificance. James Dickey's poem "Kudzu" portrays it as a mysterious invader from the Orient, hinting at foreign domination, scientific misjudgment, and the ineptitude of a federal government that encouraged its use among unsuspecting southerners. The poem is filled with a sense of danger, as the vine he portrays kills hogs and cows, hides snakes, and threatens humans. "In Georgia, the legend says / That you must close your windows / At night to keep it out of the house. / The glass is tinged with green, even so. . . ." Marjie Short's 1976 film *Kudzu* is an informative and amusing documentary film, containing a scientific discussion of the weed by botanist Tetsuo Kyama, Dickey reading from his poem and referring to the plant as the "vegetable form of cancer," and interviews with Jimmy Carter about his memories of the vine in south Georgia, Atlanta resident James H. Jordan ("kudzu, city life, and mosketeers go hand in hand to make your life miserable"), and Athens, Ga., newspaper columnist Tifton Merritt, who suggests that the government may eventually subsidize kudzu and then pay farmers not to grow it. There is also a visit with the 1930s Kudzu Queen of Greensboro, Ala. (Martha Jane Stuart Wilson), who said she was continuing the kudzu tradition "by spreading out in all directions."

There has been a southern rock band called Kudzu, a film entitled *Kurse of the Kudzu Kreature*, and an underground counterculture newspaper from Birmingham, Ala., named *Kudzu*. Finally, Doug Marlette chose Kudzu as the name for his comic strip dealing with the South.

C. Ritchie Bell
North Carolina Botanical Gardens
University of North Carolina
at Chapel Hill

Charles Reagan Wilson
University of Mississippi

William Shurtleff and Akiko Aoyagi, *The Book of Kudzu: A Culinary and Healing Guide* (1977); Larry Stevens, *Smithsonian* (December 1976); John J. Winberry and D. M. Jones, *Southeastern Geographer* (November 1973); Henry Woodhead, Atlanta *Journal and Constitution* (19 September 1976). ☆

LIGHTWOOD

Pronounced "light'ood"—the *w*, particularly in the Deep South, having lost sound altogether—lightwood is the resin-saturated, naturally dried trunks, limbs, and knots of pine trees. It is important as a building and kindling material in areas of the South heavily forested with conifers. Not subject to replication by any known process, lightwood occurs only in nature. More often than not it begins with still-standing trunks of large trees killed by lightning strikes in the late spring, after sap has risen. Typically, an ensuing hot summer dries the moisture from the tree, leaving the resins free to permeate the wood before they solidify, a process that takes many years. The resulting material is extremely hard and brittle, practically impervious to bacterial rot or insect attacks, and readily ignitable, even when wet, by as little heat as that of a simple match. Similar in quality and color—dark red-black—to heart pine, lightwood differs from it in including the entire corpus of the tree, heart and pulp, all save the bark, thus providing much larger building members.

Found only rarely now, lightwood once served as a major product in the South. Trunks were used only whole or in short sections called "drums," for lightwood was too hard to rip lengthwise into boards or beams, though it can be cross-sawed. Lightwood drums, stood upright or laid on their sides (the preferred method, for in that position they were even less prone to deterioration), provided excellent, cheap, and convenient piers for log-and-frame structures, houses, and service buildings. Larger, finer houses in areas of the South where lightwood was easily available frequently had lightwood drums supporting the inner, unseen portions of the substructure, though they might have brick or stone piers on the periphery of the structure. Though whole lightwood tree trunks were sometimes used as sills for simple log houses and outbuildings, sills were usually hewn from the heartwood of new-felled trees. More often, whole lightwood trunks were stood upright in the ground to form tall pillars supporting whole structures, often quite large barns, storehouses, carriage houses, sheds, and shelters, as well as early "open-side" churches.

Lightwood as kindling was almost as important as its use in building. Limbs sawed into 1-foot sections could, because of their brittle nature, be easily split into half-inch-square splinters. Lightwood splinters, tied in small 8- to 10-inch bundles, were long a standard commodity in southern grocery, hardware, and seed stores. Lightwood knots, cut out of limbs or found in the woods where they had fallen, were too hard to split—hence the expression "hard as a lightwood knot." The knots were left for the country poor—or in antebellum times, slaves, and later, tenants and sharecroppers—to pick up, cart, or carry into town and peddle to the urban poor for important extra cash.

Jerah Johnson
University of New Orleans

Nicholas Minov, *The Genus Pinus* (1967). ☆

LIVE OAK

Few trees are as closely linked to southern culture as the live oak, or Virginia Live Oak (*Quercus virginiana*). This native tree grows along the Atlantic coastal area from southeast Virginia to south Florida and along the Gulf Coast from Florida to central Texas. A variety in central Texas and other southwestern locales called Texas Live Oak (var. *fusiformis*) has slightly different leaves and acorns. Called live oak because of its evergreen foliage, it is as tenacious as it is stately. It can be found growing in the driest sands of the Coastal Plain as a dwarf tree, or in the rich fertile soils of hardwood hammocks as a Spanish moss-ladened dominant tree.

Highly resistant to salt spray and hurricane force winds, the tree is ideally suited to the climate and geography of its range. The low-spreading tree rarely tops 50 feet in total height but can stretch 125 feet in crown spread. The trunk diameter can grow to eight feet.

The tree produces vast quantities of acorns that are highly desired by squirrels, turkeys, bears, and other small animals. It is not uncommon for squirrels to bury the acorns, forget them, and thus plant future live oaks. This unique association helps both animal and tree.

Indians are said to have derived a sweet oil from the acorn and then used it to cook hominy, rice, and other foods. They would also roast the acorns in hot coals before eating them. It is also claimed that the Indians used the acorns to produce an imitation of cocoa.

Because of the live oak's great tensile strength, resistance to rot, tightly grained wood, and naturally curved branches, it became a highly prized timber for use in building this nation's early wooden sailing fleets. Shipwrights, called "live-oakers," would travel to the South each winter to cut and form live oak timber needed by the northern shipbuilding industry.

Heavy harvesting during this period forced the U.S. government to purchase over a quarter of a million acres of live oak forest preserves in Florida, Alabama, Mississippi, and Louisiana. Some of these acreages are still owned by the government. With the decline of the wooden shipbuilding industry, the live oak had no other commercial value. Its wood was not straight enough for lumber and was too hard to work.

Today, the live oak's main value is as an ornamental tree. In many of the South's coastal cities, long avenues of live oaks can be found planted along street rights-of-way, parks, and in homeowners' lawns. This relationship with the live oak has had a direct effect on the identity of many areas. There is a "Live Oak Street" in every southern coastal state. There is a city in Florida named Live Oak Manor, while both Louisiana and Texas have towns named Live Oak. And the state tree of Georgia is the live oak.

W. Neil Letson
Montgomery, Alabama

Elbert L. Little, *The Audubon Society Field Guide to North American Trees, Eastern Region* (1980); William Trelease, *The American Oaks* (1924); William D. Weekes, *American Forests* (February 1979); Virginia S. Wood, *Live Oaking: Southern Timber for Tall Ships* (1981). ☆

MAGNOLIA

In an otherwise grim portrait of life in the segregated South of the early 20th century, Mississippian Richard Wright in *Black Boy* (1945) remembered from his youth "the drenching hospitality in the pervading smell of sweet magnolias." More than any other plant, the magnolia, a large tree with lustrous, dark green leaves and spectacular white, fragrant flowers, is associated with the South.

The southern magnolia (*Magnolia grandiflora*), sometimes also known as "bull bay," is native to the southern Coastal Plain from Virginia to Texas. Of somewhat wider, but still essentially coastal, distribution is the closely related sweet bay (*Magnolia virginia*), which is also an evergreen tree but has smaller leaves and flowers. Among other, and less known, native magnolias are three species with deciduous leaves: the umbrella tree (*M. macrophylla*), which has thin, pale green leaves up to three feet long and flowers over one foot in diameter; the cucumber tree (*M. acuminata*) with attractive yellow flowers; and the mountain or Fraser magnolia (*M. fraseri*). In addition, two very attractive horticultural species from Asia have been widely planted in the South. These shrubs or small trees are the star magnolia (*M. stellata*) and the Japanese magnolia (*M. X soulangeana*). The attractive and commercially valuable tulip poplar, or tulip tree (*Liriodendron tulipifera*), of southern forests is not a true poplar but is rather a member of the magnolia family.

The magnolia is one of the prime symbols for the romanticized South of the plantation. The phrase "moonlight and magnolias" describes one of the South's central myths—the story of the charmed and graceful society of the Old South. It is an image that appears frequently in literature and in visual portrayals of the region. It has come to suggest an unrealistic attitude toward life, of a people blinded by beauty. Paul Oliver, a blues scholar, has written that blues lyrics are unsentimental, and magnolias do not appear in them. A group of liberal southerners chose *You Can't Eat Magnolias* for the title of a book of 1971 essays urging reform in the region.

The magnolia image is frequently applied to southern women. Words typically used to describe the southern lady are those also applied to the magnolia—"beautiful and graceful," "delicate," "a fragrant beauty," "neatness, grace, and beauty," and "a showy flower." The sensual aspect of the magnolia is also sometimes noted and applied to the South and its women. A *Time* magazine article on the South in 1977 mentioned, for example, "the aphrodisiac-soporific magnolia, more potent by far in midnight bloom than overblown fiction can convey." The region's environment, then, nurtured its sensual women.

The magnolia is particularly associated with the Deep South. It was officially adopted as the state flower of Louisiana and Mississippi in 1900; in the latter, school children were allowed to determine the choice through a statewide vote (the magnolia won with 12,745 votes, to 4,171 for the cotton blossom, and 2,484 for the cape jasmine).

C. Ritchie Bell
North Carolina Botanical Gardens
University of North Carolina
at Chapel Hill

Charles Reagan Wilson
University of Mississippi

Pearl Cleage, *Southern Magazine* (June 1987); F. Schuyler Mathews, *Familiar Trees and Their Leaves* (1903); Brooks E. Wigginton, *Trees and Shrubs for the Southeast* (1963). ☆

MISSISSIPPI RIVER

The largest river in North America, the Mississippi River was named by Indians the "Father of Waters" and created the central South both literally and figuratively. The lower Mississippi over geologic eons built a fertile valley and delta to which it adds even now from a drainage area of 1,245,000 square miles including all or parts of 31 states and two Canadian provinces. The river system severed soil from the slopes of the Appalachians and Rockies, from prairies and plains, and carried it downstream eventually to become the croplands, forests, and swamps of an alluvial valley with a 35,460-square-mile area bordering the 1,000 miles of the Mississippi downstream of Cape Girardeau, Mo.

Celebrated in fiction, film, and music, the Mississippi was the setting for many Old South stereotypes: of crinolined belles and riverboat dandies, of cheerful roustabouts toting bales to steamboats at the levees, and of colonnaded mansions and cotton fields saved by heroic fights against floods. Steamboat transport, starting with the *New Orleans* in 1811, once was vital to the economy of the central South, and there were indeed belles, dandies, roustabouts, and mansions; yet, the stereotypes did not convey the richness of the cultures blended by the river—the Native American, the Spanish, French, British, and African threads that are part of the rococo fabric of the southern heritage.

The history of the river falls into two phases: efforts to secure strategic control of the stream and its hinterlands followed by efforts to control the river itself through engineering. In 1541 conquistador Hernando de Soto became the first European to see the Mississippi, and he later was buried in it; the French first settled the valley, building the first levee for protection against flooding in 1717. Through byzantine diplomacy and military raids, the Europeans wrested control of the river from the native tribes and from each other, the Spanish taking New Orleans and the British occupying Natchez after the French and Indian War in 1763. The Spanish and the Americans drove the British from its banks during the American Revolution, and the Americans purchased full control of the river from Napoleon in 1803, subsequently repulsing an effort by the British to retake it at New Orleans in 1815.

Through construction of levees, Americans then wrested croplands from the rich floodplain, establishing an agricultural system made possible not only by the soils brought south by the river, but also by flatboats crammed with midwestern foodstuffs and manufactures, barges of Pittsburgh coal for sugar refineries and steamship fuel, and thousands of steamboats funneling downriver the commerce of a network of waterways reaching as far north as St. Paul, Minn., as far west as Fort Benton, Mont., and as far east as Olean, N.Y.

The Mississippi also brought less welcome guests south: northern soldiers in ironclad steamboats breaking the chain the Confederacy placed across the river, scalawags and rascals, and the floodwater from its immense watershed. Southerners lost the fights against both the soldiers and the floods, but, through formation of the Mississippi River Commission in 1879, enlisted some of those soldiers in the efforts to control flooding and maintain navigation. Supplemented by floodways to sap the river's strength and by reservoirs to stop floods where they originated, the levee system was fortified after the 1927 flood. By 1972, 1,683.8 miles of the proposed 2,193.7 miles of levees had been completed, and they successfully withstood the record 1973 flooding.

Powerful diesel towboats pushing barges supplanted steamboats after 1930. The 1,832-mile navigation channel maintained between Baton Rouge and Minneapolis and the 12,350-mile network of connecting waterways bore a tonnage far larger than that carried by steamboats. The barges moved through the Illinois River to the Great Lakes and via the Gulf Intracoastal Waterway west to Houston and east to Tampa. The Tennessee-Tombigbee Waterway offers an alternative to the Mississippi for barge traffic, but it is not expected that tonnage moving on the Mississippi will significantly diminish.

Leland R. Johnson
Hermitage, Tennessee

Benjamin A. Botkin, *A Treasury of Mississippi River Folklore* (1955); Hodding Carter, *Lower Mississippi* (1942); Marquis William Childs, *Mighty Mississippi: Biography of a River* (1982); Pete Daniel, *Deep'n as It Come: The 1927 Mississippi River Flood* (1977); Normal R. Moore, *Improvement of the Lower Mississippi River and Tributaries, 1931–1972* (1972). ☆

MOCKINGBIRD

Atticus Finch in *To Kill a Mockingbird* (1960) told his children "it's a sin to kill a mockingbird," because, as Miss Maudie explained to them, mockingbirds "don't do one thing but sing their hearts out for us." The mockingbird has been, indeed, particularly tied to the imagery of the South. It is as close to being an official southern bird as any; five southern states (Arkansas, Florida, Tennessee, Mississippi, and Texas) have adopted it as their state bird. The legislative resolution in Florida naming the mockingbird as the avian emblem of the state referred to it as a "bird of matchless charm." "Song of Louisiana," which was adopted as the official song of that state in 1932, speaks of the "singing of the mocking bird, and of the blossoms of the flowers" in describing the natural wonders found there.

The mockingbird, whose Latin name, *Mimus polyglottos*, means "many tongued," has been a prominent part of the environmental landscape of the South. Discovered over 250 years ago by naturalist Mark Catesby, who called it the "Mock-Bird of Carolina," it is now found from the eastern United States to California, but it is still particularly identified with the South. A noted songbird, the mockingbird is an unequaled mimic, noted, as an Audubon Society writer says, for "rapturous singing on moonlight nights among magnolias and moss-covered live oaks of the South." The male sings by day or night, repeating a phrase several times before striking a new one. Its "whisper song" is particularly soft and haunting, but its call notes tend to be harsh, grating noises. It can mimic 39 bird songs, 50 call notes, as well as the cackling of chickens, creaking of wheelbarrows, croaking of frogs, barking of dogs, and tinkling of a piano.

The appearance of the mockingbird is not particularly striking or colorful. Its predominant look is a dull gray, together with a faded white on its underside. It is slimmer than a robin and has long legs and a constantly twitching tail. It lives year-round in trees, shrubs, and on the edge of woods, pastures, rail fences, and farm hedges. In the Southwest, it nests in sage and cactus. Found in both suburban and rural gardens, the mockingbird feeds on insects (especially grasshoppers and beetles), seeds, and wild and cultivated berries.

Mockingbirds are aggressive by nature. Males are belligerent and courageous, especially while courting. They tolerate no one intruding on their territory, and they quickly attack anyone or anything seen as a threat. Males challenge each other through a highly ritualized dance, squaring off and rapidly bouncing sideways like boxers sparring, with heads held high and wings arched defiantly.

Charles Reagan Wilson
University of Mississippi

Southern Living (September 1985); John K. Teres, *The Audubon Society Encyclopedia of North American Birds* (1980). ☆

NATCHEZ TRACE

Originating as one of many narrow lanes beaten through the brush between the Great Lakes and the Gulf of Mexico, the Natchez Trace ran roughly north and south some 600 miles from the loess bluffs of the Natchez Indians into the game-filled hunting grounds of the Cumberland River Valley. As the native tribes that bordered the path settled and cultivated their land, the trace became an essential link in a network of commerce. When Europeans first forged their way into the tribal lands, they too used the well-worn path. Hernando de Soto traveled it on his way to the Mississippi River, while French explorers established trading posts at its extremities—Natchez and Nashville—in the early 18th century. During the American Revolution the road served as a path of freedom as colonists fled southwest.

The importance of the trace expanded with the new American Republic. White settlers who pushed past the Appalachian Mountains took their products downstream to market, sold their crude boats as lumber in New Orleans, and then proceeded back up the trace laden with gold. Poised to prey upon these hapless travelers were dense swamps, swirling rivers, and notorious highwaymen who lay in wait for the easy pickings on this thoroughfare of hunted and hunters.

Aside from rogues and plunderers, a motley array of other adventurers traversed the road: traders, medicine peddlers, pioneer mothers with their families, frontier tarts headed for Natchez-under-the-Hill, gentlemen and ladies from the East Coast, trains of slaves, circuit-riding evangelists, and fortune hunters—a diverse company of proud, predatory, courageous, land-hungry Americans.

The government also recognized the path's potential for public services. The trace was designated as a mail route in 1800 and then was cleared and widened to serve as a military road. Using the road in this capacity Major General Andrew Jackson earned for himself the nickname "Old Hickory" and marched up it victoriously after the battle of New Orleans.

The end of the short, rambunctious heyday of the trace was sounded with the whistle of the steamboat, which defied the Mississippi's current and thus eliminated the need for overland travel homeward. Gradually the road began to revert to nature, though it experienced a brief revival as a strategic artery during the Civil War.

Modern interest in the trace began in 1909 as the Daughters of the American Revolution initiated a program to mark the route of the Old Trace. Several years later a Natchez Trace Association was organized, but not until 1934 did the Department of the Interior, through the National Park Service, authorize a survey of the trace. It later initiated the construction of the Natchez Trace Parkway. Since that time three generations of local supporters have worked to generate interest and funding for the project, which, after 50 years, is nearing completion.

Lucie R. Bridgforth
Memphis State University

Patti Carr Black, *The Natchez Trace* (1985); Julian Bretz, *Mississippi Valley Historical Review* (June 1926); Jonathan Daniels, *The Devil's Backbone* (1962); L. M. Jamison, *Journal of Mississippi History* (April 1939); Dawson A. Phelps, *Journal of Mississippi History* (January 1949, July 1953), *Tennessee Historical Quarterly* (September 1954). ☆

NUCLEAR POLLUTION

Attracted by the promise of money and jobs for the region, the South began actively courting the nuclear industry in the early 1950s. Soon the federal government responded to southern invitations and opened military-related facilities in the area, and southern utilities cooperated to exploit nuclear power for commercial uses. These developments led to the growth of the nuclear equipment industry in the South, which provides the necessary turbine generators, pressurizers, steam generators, and fabricated fuel for the nation's reactors.

In the 1960s the South also became the home for the radioactive waste generated by the nuclear industry. By 1980 well over one-half of the nation's commercial low-level nuclear wastes were stored in southern facilities, while approximately 30 percent of the nation's high-level military wastes and 40 percent of the low-level military wastes were also stored in the South. While recent disclosures about the potential dangers of stored waste due to leaks and inadequate plans for long-term storage have turned some southern policymakers against the continued growth of the region's reliance on and support of the nuclear industry, the promise of jobs and the threat of energy shortages have been enough to allow the industry to retain its hold on the region's economy.

The major nuclear waste storage facilities in the South are the Oak Ridge National Laboratory at Oak Ridge, Tenn., the Maxey Flats facility near Morehead, Ky., the Savannah River Plant near Aiken, S.C., and the Chem-Nuclear plant at Barnwell, S.C. In addition to the major facilities, smaller radioactive dumpsites are located in the South, including ones in Kentucky, Tennessee, Texas, and North Carolina. The Chem-Nuclear plant in South Carolina is the only currently operating low-level waste facility on the East Coast. The Chem-Nuclear plant alone now holds over one-half of the nation's existing commercial low-level waste, and each year it receives about 85 percent of all the low-level wastes commercially produced in the United States. Business at the Chem-Nuclear plant steadily increased in the late 1970s, as some other sites were either temporarily or permanently closed due to safety problems.

Doug Marlette editorial cartoon on nuclear pollution, 1986

South Carolina officials grew concerned about the increased number of shipments from outside the region and the possibility that the Barnwell facility would fill up quickly and be abandoned, creating a severe financial drain on the state for its perpetual maintenance. Concerned state officials proposed to reduce the flow of waste into Barnwell and help protect the state financially by raising the state's fees from Chem-Nuclear 600 percent.

High-level radioactive wastes are generated through the process of reprocessing spent fuel rods. In reprocessing, the still-usable uranium and plutonium are extracted, leaving only liquid high-level radioactive waste. Various options for the disposal of high-level waste have been investigated by the Department of Energy (DOE). Deep-earth burial has received the most attention, and one of the first federal attempts at implementing such a plan involved the Savannah River Plant in South Carolina between 1951 and 1972. According to the plans for this type of storage, the liquid waste is solidified and stored in double-walled steel tanks and then buried underground. The salt-dome formations in Louisiana, Texas, and Mississippi have been suggested as possible burial sites. Citizens in these areas have mobilized in opposition to locating a nuclear waste repository in their areas, and Louisiana has banned the disposal of radioactive waste in the state's salt mines. This opposition is leading the DOE to consider other possible sites; however, the federal government has the right to mandate the location of nuclear waste sites through the right of eminent domain regardless of state laws.

Other possible burial sites reportedly considered by the DOE include granite deposits, found in all the Appalachian mountain states, clay-based rocks found in the Piedmont region of the Carolinas and Virginia, and the sedimentary rocks in the Coastal Plain of the Carolinas. Until the DOE finalizes plans and activates a burial site, the majority of the high-level liquid waste will remain at the Savannah River Plant, which has already been rejected as a safe permanent depository, and in the temporary storage tanks of individual reactors.

One of the greatest concerns among southerners about nuclear waste is the transportation of radioactive materials through the region. Critics have said that the transport of irradiated fuel elements ("spent fuel") from nuclear reactors to storage sites is particularly dangerous. Furthermore, spent fuel from nuclear ships is carried from shipyards in Charleston, S.C., and Norfolk, Va., to reprocessing facilities in Idaho. Critics also complain that officials along the shipment routes have no prior notice as to when and where the shipments will take place and that vehicles carrying the hazardous materials are not marked with appropriate warnings. In response to what they see as limited safety efforts by the federal government, individual southern communities and environmental and pacifist groups have called for local and state regulation of the transport of radioactive materials. In 1978 the Louisiana Legislature passed a law banning the transport of high-level radioactive wastes through the state. Such measures have prompted the federal government to propose its own regulations of the transports which would preempt local authority, but which, some local officials charge, would not provide supervision equal to that demanded by local citizens.

See also INDUSTRY: / Nuclear Industry

Karen M. McDearman
University of Mississippi

Betty Brink, *Southern Exposure* (Fall 1981); Beth Damon Coonan, *Southern Exposure* (January–February 1985); Stephen Hoffius, *Southern Exposure* (March–April 1984); John W. Johnson, *Insuring against Disaster: The Nuclear Industry on Trial* (1986); *Southern Exposure* (Winter 1979); Joanne Thompson and Debra Castaldo, *Southern Changes* (April–May 1986). ☆

OIL POLLUTION

The discovery of the Spindletop field on the Texas Gulf Coast in 1901 ushered in a new era for the American petroleum industry, characterized by the shift of major producing zones from the East to the Southwest and the emergence of giant firms such as Texaco and Gulf. It also introduced new threats to the southern environment. The "gusher" was the most visible ecological problem, as uncontrolled flush production led to massive drain-offs of crude that soaked the ground. The rapid removal of oil from subsurface strata resulted in the introduction of brine into the Gulf region's water system as well as into underground reservoirs of oil. Frequent oil spills at plants and terminals saw periodic floods wash much of this oil into rivers and streams. Oil particulates entered lakes and ultimately the Gulf of Mexico, joining oil spilled during the loading of tankers and the contaminated ballast those same vessels dumped at sea. Hydrocarbon vapors from poorly constructed transportation and storage equipment and sulphur fumes emitted from refineries also polluted the air.

The development of offshore drilling in the South, which increased dramatically after World War II, presented another environmental threat. In 1970, for example, the extinguishing by explosives of a fire on the Chevron Oil Company's platform-C, 12 miles off the Louisiana coast, resulted in a spreading oil slick that grew at a rate of 600–1,000 barrels a day.

As in earlier decades, oil spills are not limited to the ocean; pipelines break, refinery tanks rupture, and barges run into bridges. In January 1973 a barge struck a bridge pier over the Mississippi River near Helena, Ark., spilling 19,000 barrels of oil into the river. There have also existed instances of conscious polluting of rivers and groundwater by commercial firms, as in the case of the Union Camp Bag Company of Savannah, Ga., which was prosecuted in 1969 and 1970 for releasing oil into the Savannah River. In 89 documented cases of groundwater contamination before 1981 in South Carolina (a state that shares its main aquifer with Georgia and Florida), petroleum products were involved in the majority of the incidents.

A growing environmental consciousness in the South has tapped a historical tradition that is both sentimental about the natural ecology and wary of the exploitation of southern resources by outsiders. This was evidenced in the wake of the 1973 energy crisis when Louisiana openly criticized those northeastern states that blocked offshore drilling on their coasts for environmental reasons but that were all too willing to import natural gas produced off the coast of the Bayou state. There is clearly a trade-off between the search for new energy and protection of the environment, but the South in the latter 20th century is attempting to balance the two in a rational way.

See also INDUSTRY: / Oil Industry; SOCIAL CLASS: Oil Workers

August W. Giebelhaus
Georgia Institute of Technology

John R. Holum, *Topics and Terms in Environmental Problems* (1977); Joseph A. Pratt, *The Growth of a Refining Region* (1980); Veronica I. Pye, Ruth Patrick, and John Quarles, *Groundwater Contamination in the United States* (1983). ☆

OPOSSUM ("POSSUM")

Over 70 species can be found in the opossum family, ranging from South America northward to Canada, but the Virginia opossum (*Didelphis virginia*) once resided only in the Southeast and is still identified closely with the region's culture. It is the only marsupial (a mammal that carries its newborn young in an abdominal pouch for weeks) found north of Mexico and the largest of the opossum family. It weighs from 4 to 15 pounds and is from 25 to 40 inches long. Captain John Smith, leader of the early Virginia settlement, described the female opossum in 1608: "An opossum hath a head like a Swine, and a taile like a Rat, and is of the bigness of a Cat. Under her belly she hath a bagge wherein she lodgeth, carrieth, and sucketh her young."

In the South opossums are brown and black. The head, face, and throat are whitish, and the dark ears have pinkish tips. They have short legs, an opposable thumb-like toe on their back feet, and sharp claws on their forelegs. The opossum's tail is long (9 to 13 inches) and unadorned. Good tree climbers and mostly active at night, opossums are omnivorous, consuming insects, frogs, birds, eggs, snakes, earthworms, and small animals; they also eat grains, seeds, and fruits such as apples and persimmons. They are scavengers, eating any and everything including carrion. They live mostly in wooded areas, but are frequently seen in suburbs and have even been found in urban areas. Garbage dumps attract them, and farmers have charged them with invading chicken yards. Many are killed by automobiles, as the small creatures are attracted to other animals dead on the side of the road. When threatened, an opossum will roll over and play dead. It gives a convincing performance, as it goes semirigid, mouth open and drooling, tongue extended, and eyes open but glazed. Scientists have discovered that this is an actual catatonic state brought on by fear. The phrase "playing possum" has come, nonetheless, to mean feigning sleep or death.

The opossum is generally not considered the most intelligent of animals (25 small white beans would fit in the brain cavity of an adult male opossum's skull; 150 would be needed for the brain cavity of a raccoon of the same size). Its life expectancy is short, but it has shown what can be described as a Faulknerian sense of endurance, surviving since the age of dinosaurs. It has evolved numerous survival mechanisms. Feigning death is a device against danger. It spends most of its time lolling about in isolated, lazy seclusion in trees or in underground burrows, avoiding occasions for direct conflict with predators. It has a well-developed sense of smell that is useful for foraging, and its 50 small teeth—more than any other mammal in North America—provide protection. It is extremely fertile, with females in the South bringing forth two to three litters of 8 to 18 young ones in a year, with around 7 normally surviving the early phase of life in the pouch. The opossum has changed little since prehistoric times and now thrives in spite of evolving conditions.

The opossum has long figured prominently in human culture in the South. Stories of this critter's activities were told by Native Americans and blacks. The Choctaws' "Why the Possum Grins" was one such tale, and a Cherokee legend explains that the opossum's tail is naked because he burned it in a fire, trying to make his white tail black. A southern black version of this story has a ghost skinning all the hair off his tail when Possum, along with Fox and Rabbit, tries to steal corn from a graveyard. The Mississippi Delta has a story of the opossum that was killed and put in to cook, but ate all the sweet potatoes and gravy in the roasting pan, jumping out and escaping when the oven door was opened. Pottery effigies of the opossum from as far back as prehistoric times have been found in south Georgia burial sites, and poor southern blacks and whites have hunted the opossum for its fur and flesh. Roy Blount, Jr., after tasting the animal, wrote that "possum was sort of like dark meat of chicken, only stronger-tasting and looser on the bone, and stringy, like pork." It has also been described as somewhat greasy.

Opossum, male and female, with their young

The opossum has been a prominent contemporary southerner. The Pogo comic strip featured the animal. Wausau, Fla., annually holds a Possum Festival in August, and a possum cult appeared in the South in the 1970s. The Possum Growers and Breeders Association of America, Incorporated, sponsored a national meeting in 1971 in Clanton, Ala., and from that beginning the group has expanded to include 40,000 members, who receive bumper stickers saying "Eat More Possum." It sponsors an annual gathering, including a Miss Possum pageant for female humans and an opossum judging contest, awarding the most worthy candidate of the latter the designation of "Beauregard." Frank Basil Clark, who manages the Clanton Drive-In Theatre and lives in a mobile home he calls the Big C Possum Ranch, was the guiding spirit behind the movement, and at one point he had plans to breed "superpossums" of giant size to provide protein for the world's hungry. Roy Blount, Jr., wrote an article on possums for *Sports Illustrated* (1 March 1976) and then featured the possum cult prominently in his *Crackers* (1980). *Possum Opossum* was an award-winning film by Greg Killmaster chronicling, with tongue firmly in cheek, the possum cult's activities.

Charles Reagan Wilson
University of Mississippi

Wayne King, *New York Times* (16 March 1975); Stanley Klein, *Encyclopedia of North American Wildlife* (1983). ☆

OUTER BANKS

The Outer Banks are low, extremely narrow islands running from near Norfolk, Va., south for 175 miles to Cape Hatteras, N.C., and ending near Cape Lookout. They are separated from the mainland by the shallow Pamlico and Albemarle sounds. In 1524 Giovanni de Verrazzano landed on the Outer Banks and thought he was off the coast of China. The real history of the islands began, though, in 1584 when Sir Walter Raleigh chose Roanoke Island, which was between the Outer Banks and the North Carolina coast, as the site for the first attempted English colony in North America. A fort was built but the colony remained unstable, and its inhabitants had mysteriously disappeared by the time a supply ship arrived in 1590. The "Lost Colony" is the subject of Paul Green's outdoor dramatic presentation, which is staged each summer in Manteo, N.C., and the Fort Raleigh National Historic Site now includes a reconstruction of the early fort.

Captain Edward Teach—the infamous Blackbeard—was the most famous of a number of pirates who used the sounds and bays behind the Outer Banks as a hiding place in the 1700s. Most of the island inhabitants have been less exotic, though: mainly farmers, stockmen, fishermen, boatmen, marines, and pilots. Because of the relatively consistent winds in the area, Orville and Wilbur Wright picked a 100-foot-high hill near Kitty Hawk, N.C., as the locale for their first successful airplane flight in 1905. The Wright Brothers National Memorial was set up in 1927 and has become a center for a growing tourist industry on the islands. The Cape Hatteras National Seashore Recreation Area, established in 1937 as a public beach and campsite, provides access to the natural wonders of the Outer Banks.

The Outer Banks are an environmental treasure. Beach grass and sedges grow there, but sea oats is the most typical grass, growing in clumps and serving as an effective sand binder. Wax myrtle and yaupons (or Sea Island holly) are widespread, and one can find American holly, laurel oaks, and loblolly pines in the woods. Live oaks have been especially important to these islands. Near the shore of a sound, the wind makes them small and twisted, but several hundred yards away, they grow straight and tall and are hung with Spanish moss.

The Sea Island National Wildlife Refuge has almost 6,000 acres of beach, dunes, and marshes. Nearly 26,000 acres in the waters of Pamlico Sound are off limits to hunters. Estimates are that 265 species of birds visit or live at the refuge. One sees gulls and sandpipers, but migratory waterfowl are the most frequently sighted birds, with snow and Canadian geese common in the late fall. Brown pelicans can be seen in the summer, and peregrine falcons and other species live there year round.

At Cape Hatteras the cold waters from the north meet the warm currents from the Gulf Stream, making for turbulent navigation. The cape contains the tallest lighthouse in the United States—a 208-foot-high, black-and-white monument. The area's changing currents and dense fogs have resulted in more than 500 ships foundering near the cape, earning it the reputation of the "Graveyard of the Atlantic." The first lighthouse there was built in 1803, and the present landmark dates from 1870.

See also LANGUAGE: / Outer Banks Dialect

Charles Reagan Wilson
University of Mississippi

Charlton Ogburn, *The Winter Beach* (1971); Caleb Pirtle III, *Southern Living* (April 1975); John T. Starr, *American Forests* (April 1979). ☆

PALM TREES

"Florida is the land of Palms," wrote horticulturist Henry Nehrling. "Avenues of Palms in our cities! Forests of Palms beside our streams and lakes! Thickets of Palms in our woods! Groves of Coconut Palms on the East Coast! Majestic Royal Palms in the south Everglades!" His enthusiasm was unbounded but appropriate because the palm has been one of the preeminent cultural-environmental symbols of the semitropical South, from the promotional advertising of Henry Flagler luring tourists south, to the contemporary lyrics of Jimmy Buffet songs and the visual images of television's *Miami Vice*.

The main physical feature of the palm is the cylindrical trunk, which supports a leaf-crown. Its drooping leaves can be 100 feet off the ground. The leaves are either plume-like (pinnate) or fan shaped (palmate). The South's native palmettos belong to the second group, whereas the royal, coconut, and date palms have plume-like leaves. About 14 species of palms are native to Florida and 2 or 3 can be found as far north as North Carolina. The palmetto is the official tree of South Carolina, where it is used by blacks to make distinctive Sea Islands baskets. Many imported tropical palms do well in south Florida, and subtropical varieties thrive along the beaches of the Gulf Coast down into the south Texas valley.

The cabbage palmetto (*Sabal palmetto*) is the most common palm in Florida and the one growing most frequently in other areas of the South. It is often found growing in groups with hundreds of plants standing close together. The early settlers named this tree the cabbage palmetto because of its heart, which they consumed like cabbage.

The coconut palm and the royal palm are conspicuously displayed, popular palms in Florida. One horticulturist called them "the exclamation points in the poetry of tropical landscape." The royal palm grows straight as a column, while the coconut will bend gracefully. The coconut palm grows in nearly all tropical coast regions of the world, but is never found growing naturally inland. The winter resort of Palm Beach gained its name from the stands of coconut trees growing there. When settlement in south Florida increased in the early 20th century, people planted inexpensive coconut palms in droves, further reinforcing the area's association with the plant. The royal palms are majestic looking in their hammocks, which are seen to best effect in the southern Everglades. Of the five species of its genus, one—the *Oreodoxa regia*—is native to south Florida. It is confined naturally to Biscayne Bay, the Keys, and several hammocks of south Florida. Royal Palm State Park (formerly Paradise Key) is in Dade County, with many trees there at least 100 feet tall.

Date palms also thrive in Florida, south Texas, and along the Gulf Coast. The genus *Phoenix* is Asian and African in origins. The date palms have pinnate leaves, which may be either soft and glossy or, in other species, hard. Many of these were introduced into the Southwest in the early 20th century. Other of the many palms found in Florida include the blue palmetto (*Rhapidophyllum hystrix*), the bamboo palm (*Rhapis flabelliformis*), and the silver palm (*Thrinax floridana*).

Charles Reagan Wilson
University of Mississippi

Henry Nehrling, *The Plant World in Florida*, ed. Alfred and Elizabeth Kay (1933). ☆

RED RIVER EXPEDITION

When the Louisiana Purchase was acquired by the United States in 1803, no true scientific surveys had been done in the West, and many geographical details were unclear. Thus President Thomas Jefferson conceived and put into the field two major exploring expeditions to examine Louisiana. That of Meriwether Lewis and William Clark into the northern Purchase was the most successful and is the best known. The second, intended to survey similarly the geography and natural history of the southern regions of the Purchase, only partially accomplished that task, because of Spanish opposition. On the expedition, however, was a young University of Pennsylvania naturalist named Peter Custis, the first American naturalist in the West. His reports are a principal source in determining the "virgin" conditions of the Red River Valley and parts of Louisiana, Arkansas, and Texas.

The plan for the exploration, formulated by Jefferson early in 1804, called for an ascent of the Red River "to the tops of the mountains" and a descent of the Arkansas. When at last attempted, in 1806, the 50-man expedition was terminated by a Spanish army after four months, at a location 615 miles above the mouth of the Red. The early termination (near today's Oklahoma border) prevented expedition leader/geographer Thomas Freeman from making many new geographical discoveries. His field courses were drawn into a definitive map of the lower Red River Valley by Nicholas King and appeared on Anthony Nau's 1807 map of the West based on American exploration. The map represents outstanding topographical features, game and trading paths, and Indian villages and sacred places.

The work done by naturalist Custis was of greater significance. He was the last-minute choice in a search that featured an offer of the position to the world-famous William Bartram and included applications by C. S. Rafinesque and Alexander Wilson. Custis's training under Benjamin Smith Barton was sound, but he was inexperienced and his small reference library was inadequate. He closely followed the directions of Jefferson and expedition supervisor William Dunbar. The result was a wide-ranging survey: he collected minerals and botanical specimens, kept a meteorological chart, and compiled natural history data on 80 birds and animals and nearly 190 plants. He offered eight new scientific names, three of which are currently recognized.

Jefferson's southern exploration failed in its larger objectives, but the data accumulated were important to environmental study. The explorers portrayed an organic environment in a state of change, a valley that European plants were already invading and whose waters were yearly modified by the growth of the immense logjam called the Great Raft. The prairies they saw and the relative absence of undergrowth in the towering virgin forest were, they believed, the result of Indian-set fires. Above all, they were most impressed with the beauty and richness of the river valley wilderness: "The Valley of the Red River is one of the richest and most beautiful imaginable," Freeman wrote in his journal, and Custis added that, "were the Rafts removed . . . this country would become the Paradise of America. . . . in point of beauty, fertility, and salubrity there is not its equal in America, nay in the world."

Daniel L. Flores
Texas Tech University

Daniel L. Flores, ed., *The Freeman & Custis Account of the Red River: The Chronicle of Jefferson's Southwestern Exploration* (1983); Donald Jackson, *Thomas Jefferson and the Stony Mountains: Exploring the West from Monticello* (1981); Conrad Morton, *Journal of the Arnold Arboretum* (1967). ☆

SHELLFISH

The South has both recreational and industrial shellfish resources, all of which have been exploited as far back as the earliest aboriginal inhabitants. Shellfish may be categorized as mollusks or crustaceans found in either fresh or salt waters. Important mollusks include clams, mussels, oysters, scallops, and snails. Valuable crustaceans are crabs, freshwater crayfish, shrimps, and spiny lobsters.

Aboriginal settlements are often located by the presence of shell mounds, or middens, adjacent to inland rivers. Indians ate copious quantities of mussels and coveted those with pearls and lustrous mother-of-pearl inner shells for ornaments. European settlers ate few mussels but exploited them for the mother-of-pearl used in buttons. Even today, many tons of southern mussel shells are shipped to the Orient, where small pieces are used for nuclei of cultured pearls. In estuarine areas surrounding the South inhabitants have used clams and oysters as foodstuffs and their shells for building materials. Many mollusks, especially in Florida waters, are so beautiful that they are the subject of world-famous shell-collecting industries. Major offshore scallop resources have provided sustained yields of the sweet-meated bivalves. Mollusks are also valuable. In 1984 over 40 million pounds of oyster meats worth over $66 million were taken from southern waters, while scallop harvests accounted for at least 40 million pounds of meat worth in excess of $30 million.

Oysters deserve special attention. Most are cultivated in what represents the oldest form of American mariculture. Today's oysterman commonly relies on natural nursery beds where larval oysters settle. These so-called spat attach to old shells. Nursery beds are usually located in less productive, low salinity waters so that the spat must be moved to prime high-salinity growing beds. Low, squat white oyster boats are constantly relocating and/or harvesting oysters in Gulf coastal waters. In the Chesapeake Bay, sail-powered skipjack oyster boats relocate and harvest oysters in waters where rival oystermen from

Maryland and Virginia fought pitched sea battles over oyster grounds in the late 1800s. Fresh oysters are available in all months, but quality is somewhat poorer in warm months when they spawn. Oyster dishes vary from salted, raw, and live oysters on the half shell to savory stews and the always-popular fried oysters, including oysters en brochette (wrapped with bacon and fried). The New Orleans oyster "po-boy" sandwich on french bread is a favorite of oyster lovers who visit the Crescent City.

All southern coastal states have major shrimp and crab fisheries. White, brown, and pink shrimp spawn at sea, but larvae are nurtured in the fragile coastal wetlands before returning to sea to mature and spawn. Shrimp boats with high masts festooned with trawl nets are common sights along all coasts, and annual blessings of local fleets are gala festivities. Blue crabs generally remain in estuaries, growing, as do all crustaceans, by shedding their hard shells periodically. The crab boil is a southern coastal tradition, but soft-shelled crabs command the highest prices and are cultivated throughout the region. Spiny lobsters are a legacy of south Florida and are so valuable that the fishery is intensively regulated. Prawns, pandalid shrimps, are important as fish bait, especially the one- to two-inch grass, or glass, shrimp. Thriving fisheries once existed for the clawed, lobster-like langostina species in estuarine areas, but these have been largely displaced by pollution, habitat destruction, and man-made changes in hydrology. In fresh water, crayfish are the crustacean kings. Although exploited throughout the South by Indian communities, they became important food sources only in French Louisiana. There the inventive Acadians, or Cajuns, have even learned to cultivate the "ecrevisse" in earthen ponds during the cool months, often in a unique rotation with rice, which is grown in the warm months.

In 1984 the marine shrimp harvest in south Atlantic waters was 19.2 million pounds worth $34 million, but this was dwarfed by a harvest of 254.3 million pounds in the Gulf of Mexico worth $439.2 million. The southern blue crab harvest in 1984 was 201.6 million pounds worth $56 million. While the spiny lobster catch was only 6.3 million pounds in 1984, it was worth $17.3 million. Southern crayfish production exceeded 70 million pounds in 1984 and was valued at more than $35 million.

Southern shellfish resources are threatened. Stream channelization, draining of wetlands, and pollution have destroyed many productive freshwater shellfish habitats. All southern coastal waters are polluted to some degree. Each state monitors edible mollusks for signs of sewage pollution to avoid health problems like hepatitis, which is contracted by eating raw, contaminated mollusks. Estuaries are especially hard-hit by all forms of water pollution because contaminants are dropped there when freshwater runoff reaches the sea. The problems of suffocating silt and toxic chemicals are obvious, but inorganic fertilizers and organic matter fuel microbial activity that strips bottom waters of oxygen and severely restricts habitat and productivity in once-fertile waters. Coastal development in the form of recreational centers and fossil-fuel exploitation has destroyed thousands of acres of productive marshes. Vigilance and environmental education are beginning to show significant and measurable improvement of conditions in southern waters and must continue to insure that future generations will share in the South's bountiful shellfish resources.

Jay V. Huner
Center for Small Farm Research
Southern University

R. Tucker Abbott, *Seashells of North America: A Guide to Field Identification* (1968); Jay V. Huner and E. Evan Brown, eds., *Crustacean and Mollusk Aquaculture in the United States* (1985); James A. Michener, *Chesapeake* (1979); Fred Ward, *National Geographic* (February 1985). ☆

SHENANDOAH VALLEY

Located in northern Virginia, the Shenandoah Valley is approximately 6,500 square miles in area, 180 miles long, and 10 to 24 miles wide. It is drained by the Shenandoah River, which has played an important role in the valley's development as a rich agricultural area.

The Shenandoah Valley was settled in the early 1700s by Germans, Dutch, Scotch-Irish, and English. The valley was an important route for the westward pioneer movement in the early 19th century. Its population at the time of the Civil War was predominantly white and rural.

The valley was the site of an extraordinary Civil War battle in 1862. The residents' loyalties were divided between the Union and the Confederacy, and the area was strategically important to both sides. In an effort to divert Union General George B. McClellan's attack on the Confederate capital of Richmond, Confederate General Thomas J. "Stonewall" Jackson launched the successful "valley campaign" against the Union armies designated to join McClellan's. With an inferior number of troops, Jackson brilliantly used his interior lines of communication and tactics of strategic diversion to repel the Union forces.

Another successful defense of the valley came at the battle of New Market in 1864 under the command of General John C. Breckinridge. The battle, in which young cadets from the Virginia Military Institute fought, inspires one of the nation's largest Civil War reenactments each May at the site. The Union had its revenge for the losses, however, when General Philip Sheridan's army laid waste the region, wrecking railroad lines, burning factories, and destroying farms and supplies.

After Reconstruction the valley's economy was primarily agricultural, although many small manufacturing plants were established in the late 1800s. Resort spas and summer homes flourished after 1890, and the area became a popular tourist attraction. Today, the valley's rolling plains, stone farmhouses, quaint colonial inns, and a smalltown southern lifestyle intrigue visitors from throughout the nation. Each May the valley is the site of festivals and historic commemorations such as the Shenandoah Apple Blossom Festival in Winchester, Va. A Museum of American Frontier Culture proposed for construction in Staunton, Va., in 1987 will feature 18th-century farm buildings from England, Northern Ireland, Germany, and Appalachia.

The Shenandoah National Park, established in 1935, encompasses over 195,000 acres with tree-covered mountains, trails, streams, waterfalls, and trout-filled pools. The Skyline Drive north-south highway extends for 105 miles through the park and offers an opportunity to view the scenic valley as well as the Blue Ridge Mountains, the

Massanutten Mountain, and the Allegheny Mountains.

Some Shenandoah Valley residents are concerned that the rural, small-town aspect of their region is disappearing. In 1985 the Adolph Coors Company began construction on a $70 million packaging and distribution center and announced plans for a brewery in the area by 1990. The valley's underground limestone aquifers will provide an excellent water source for the plant. Controversy surrounded the announcement of Coors's coming, and critics cited moral objections to alcoholic beverages and possible environmental problems. As early as the 1960s, concern over new developments spawned historic preservation societies in the area. These groups have been successful in restoring and improving over 100 buildings and residences.

Karen M. McDearman
University of Mississippi

William Couper, *History of the Shenandoah Valley* (1952); Julie Davis, *The Shenandoah* (1945); Gary D. Ford, *Southern Living* (May 1986). ☆

SPANISH MOSS

Spanish moss is a soft, silver-gray, tropical herb (*Tillandsia usneoides*) with slender leaves and stems that grow on the branches of trees, often oak or other hardwoods, in the low woodlands and swamp forests of the southern Coastal Plain from Virginia to Texas. It is an epiphyte, using tree limbs for mechanical support, but drawing its nutrients from the air. Epiphytes never injure the host plant as do parasites. The long pendant strands may reach a length of 10 to 20 feet and sway with the slightest movement of the humid coastal air.

It is not a true moss but a member of the pineapple family, *Bromeliaceae*. The small, solitary, yellowish-green flowers and the brown, cylindrical, three-parted seed capsules that mark these as true flowering plants and not a moss are seldom noticed. However, a number of other species of epiphytic bromeliads, such as the quill-leaf (*Tillandsia fasciculata*) of peninsular Florida, have very colorful flower spikes. Spanish moss was a major fiber plant of the American Indians and was used to make skirts for Indian women, the French in south Louisiana once used it as a decoration at Christmas, and later it had limited commercial use as a packing and bedding material, but its primary cultural role has been as a botanical trademark for the Lowland South.

Journalist James Kilpatrick sees Spanish moss as a metaphor for the South, "an indigenous, an indestructible part of the Southern character; it blurs, conceals, softens, wraps the hard limbs of hard times in a fringed shawl." It is particularly associated with Gothic imagery of the Deep South, suggesting romantic, mysterious, and sometimes menacing events.

C. Ritchie Bell
North Carolina Botanical Gardens
University of North Carolina
at Chapel Hill

Charles Reagan Wilson
University of Mississippi

Fred B. Kniffen and Malcolm L. Comeaux, *Melanges*, vol. 12 (1979). ☆

Spanish moss swaying in front of an old plantation home, south Louisiana, 1930s

TENNESSEE–TOMBIGBEE WATERWAY

The Tennessee-Tombigbee Waterway, also known as "Tenn-Tom," is a man-made, 234-mile-long inland water route connecting the Gulf of Mexico with the Tennessee River in northeast Mississippi. This regionally significant and bold engineering project constructed by the U.S. Army Corps of Engineers links over 16,000 miles of inland navigable waterways, thus providing commercial users in at least 14 states an alternate route for shipping ores, chemicals, farm products, and many other commodities between ports along the Ohio River, the western tributaries of the upper Mississippi River, and the Gulf. By shortening distances that would ordinarily be traveled by water between the port of Mobile and such important commercial centers as Pittsburgh, Cincinnati, Louisville, Kansas City, and Chicago, the Tennessee-Tombigbee offers substantial savings in transportation costs. This benefit to commercial users has long been one of the most important justifications for its construction.

The idea of a navigable route connecting the Gulf and the Tennessee River is thought to have been originally proposed in the early 1700s by Jean-Baptiste Le Moyne, Sieur de Bienville (1680-1768). For nearly 250 years the idea surfaced and then faded in response to changes in American politics, economy, public opinion, and technological development. Finally, in July 1946, Congress passed legislation authorizing construction of the waterway. However, no funds were allocated directly for this purpose until October 1970, when President Richard Nixon signed a bill authorizing expenditure of the first million dollars in construction costs. The project was controversial, with critics charging it was a political pork barrel measure to channel federal money to the Deep South. Environmental lawsuits also slowed development of the waterway. When the project finally was completed in December 1984, total costs reached approximately $1.992 billion.

The high total cost of the Tennessee-Tombigbee Waterway relates to many factors, including inflation, delays, legal expenses, environmental study expenses, and increased labor costs. It is also related to the complexity of its own engineering requirements, for the waterway truly is a unique hydraulic structure. The project makes use of the existing channel of the Tombigbee River in portions of Alabama and Mississippi, a man-made canal that parallels the river course in northeast Mississippi, and a "divide cut" through a high ridge of land in Mississippi's Tishomingo County. Throughout most of its length the waterway is maintained at 300 feet wide and 9 feet deep. There is also a drop of 341 feet in elevation between its northern and southern points, requiring the presence of five dams and 10 locks. Each lock along the route is 110 feet wide and 600 feet long and capable of accommodating a towboat and eight standard barges. These facilities are maintained year-round by the U.S. Army Corps of Engineers. In all, over 307 million cubic yards of earth were excavated when building Tenn-Tom—more material than was excavated during construction of the Panama Canal.

W. Lee Minnerly
Chicago, Illinois

James Williams Jones, "An Analytical History of the Tennessee-Tombigbee Waterway" (M.A. thesis, University of Mississippi, 1982); Tennessee-Tombigbee Waterway Development Authority, *The Tennessee-Tombigbee Waterway Story* (1969); U. S. Army Corps of Engineers, *Tennessee-Tombigbee Waterway, Alabama and Mississippi: Background and History* (1978); John P. Worsham, *The Tennessee-Tombigbee Waterway: A Chronological Bibliography in Report Form* (1976). ☆

INDEX OF CONTRIBUTORS

Albright, Alex, 650
Allison, Clinton B., 514
Anderson, Gary Clayton, 579
Andrews, William L., 346
Antin, Doris H., 518
Arsenault, Raymond, 545
Atkins, Leah Rawls, 462

Bailey, Guy, 332
Bailey, Ronald, 309, 364
Baker, Eleanor J., 382
Baker, Eugene W., 465
Baker, Paul S., 423
Barlow, Bill, 368
Baron, William R., 555
Barr, Alwyn, 369
Bartlett, Richard A., 592
Bell, C. Ritchie, 598, 644, 656, 659, 675
Berry, Jason, 373
Bethel, Elizabeth Rauh, 339
Blake, Nelson M., 571, 643, 652
Blight, David W., 351
Boles, John B., 510
Bowman, Shearer Davis, 491
Boyer, Horace Clarence, 374
Bradford, M. E., 527
Brandon, Betty, 479
Brazil, Wayne D., 505
Bridgforth, Lucie R., 663
Brown, D. Clayton, 74
Brown, Norman D., 516
Bryan, John Morrill, 215
Byrd, Rudolph P., 380

Calvert, Robert A., 62
Cangelosi, Robert J., 101, 138, 169, 171
Carson, Clayborne, 270
Cates, Gerald L., 494
Cell, John W., 323
Chappell, Edward A., 99
Chitty, Arthur Ben, 521
Clark, Thomas D., 7, 16
Cobb, William H., 477
Comeaux, Malcolm L., 642
Cone, Carl, 496
Coté, Joseph A., 31, 63, 71
Cripps, Thomas, 262

Dabney, Virginius, 524
Daniel, Pete, 56, 74, 82
Darling, Marsha Jean, 286
Dethloff, Henry C., 28, 517
Dewey, Thomas, 105
Dickerson, Dennis C., 378, 383
Dittmer, John, 394
Donovan, Arthur, 562, 639
Doughty, Robin W., 583
Dozier, Richard K., 239
Durden, Robert F., 480
Dyer, Thomas G., 408

Edelstein, Tilden G., 302
Ellis, Ann Wells, 349

Fabre, Geneviève, 337
Fazio, Michael W., 129, 132
Ferriss, Abbott L., 428
Fincher, Cameron, 443
Fiser, Jack, 498
Fleming, Thomas, 419
Flores, Daniel L., 671
Foner, Philip S., 341
Foy, Jessica, 345, 359, 486
Fraser, Walter J., Jr., 473
Fuller, Wayne E., 76
Fullinwider, S. P., 395

Galle, Fred C., 577
Garrow, David J., 371, 381
Gavins, Raymond, 361, 375
Giebelhaus, August W., 666
Gifford, James M., 416, 465
Gillespie, Angus K., 53, 641
Goldfield, David R., 604
Golding, Alan, 466
Goodenow, Ronald K., 256
Greene, J. Lee, 294
Griffith, Benjamin W., 470
Grossman, James, 300
Guice, John D. W., 39
Gumbert, Edgar B., 431
Gunter, Pete A. Y., 645
Guth, James, 467

Hair, William I., 297
Hardeman, Nicholas P., 54
Harlan, Louis R., 391
Harley, Sharon, 343, 393
Harrison, Alferdteen, 507
Hart, R. Douglas, 41
Hazel, Forest, 276
Heitmann, John A., 79
Hellwig, David J., 281
Helms, Douglas, 52, 70, 619
Helms, T. J., 581
Hine, Darlene Clark, 312
Hollis, Daniel W., 513
Holt, Elvin, 363
Holt, Thomas C., 228
Hood, Davyd Foard, 116, 202
Hudson, Berkley, 354
Huner, Jay V., 673

Jenkins, Robert L., 501
Johnson, Clifton H., 360
Johnson, Jerah, 657
Johnson, Leland R., 612, 661
Joyner, Charles, 248, 264

King-Hammond, Leslie, 210
Kingsley, Karen, 216, 220
Kirby, Jack Temple, 44
Kirschke, Amy, 217
Kolb, Carolyn Goldsby, 385

Langer, Sandra, 157
Letson, W. Neil, 658
Lewis, Shelby, 440
Lisenby, William Foy, 460
Little, Richard S., 645, 654
Long, Huey, 412
Lord, J. Dennis, 46
Lowitt, Richard, 625
Lupold, John S., 135

McCorkle, James L., Jr., 83
McDearman, Karen M., 344, 463, 486, 497, 665, 674
McGehee, Elizabeth, 197, 522
McMath, Robert C., Jr., 488
McMillen, Neil R., 347
McMurry, Linda O., 51
McNeil, W. K., 470
Mahar, William J., 306
Makowski, Elizabeth M., 77, 357, 432, 478
Martin, Julia, 525
Masson, Frank W., 112, 212
Mechling, Jay, 638
Mellard, James M., 388
Melosi, Martin V., 541
Mertz, Paul E., 50, 58
Miletich, Patricia, 523
Minnerly, W. Lee, 676
Mitchell, Theodore R., 452
Morrison, Keith A., 242
Mullikin, Kent, 502

Napier, John Hawkins, III, 426, 439
Neverdon-Morton, Cynthia, 377
Newman, Joseph W., 453
Norrell, Robert J., 519

Odom, E. Dale, 57
Ogilvie, Charles F., 411
Owen, Dennis E., 471
Owens, Harry P., 622

Payne, Ladell, 368
Pennington, Estill Curtis, 219
Pepe, Marie Huper, 196
Perry, Percival, 65, 66, 67
Piehl, Charles K., 209
Poesch, Jessie, 91, 94, 141, 143, 148, 198
Powell, William S., 490, 503
Preston, Howard L., 36, 616
Proctor, Samuel, 484
Pruitt, Elaine Doerschuk, 504
Pyne, Stephen J., 574

Raboteau, Albert J., 326
Rampersad, Arnold, 353
Rankin, Tom, 608
Rasmussen, Wayne D., 78
Reel, Jerome V., Jr., 474
Rhodes, Lelia G., 493
Richardson, Joe M., 483
Rickels, Patricia K., 358
Roberts, Randy, 335
Robinson, Michael C., 586, 607
Rogosin, Donn, 379
Roper, John Herbert, 355, 528
Rosenberg, Bruce A., 314
Runte, Alfred, 595
Rushing, Felder, 61

Sanders, Taylor, 526
Sansing, David, 376, 500
Savitt, Todd L., 279
Scanlon, James Edward, 509
Schweninger, Loren, 329
Sharp, Sharon A., 252, 350, 387, 492
Sheridan, Richard C., 59
Simms, L. Moody, Jr., 203, 218
Siry, Joseph V., 637
Smallwood, J. B., 568, 633
Smith, Mark, 506
Snadon, Patrick A., 125, 129
Stewart, Rick, 155, 200, 205, 206, 207, 214
Suggs, Henry Lewis, 317
Synnott, Marcia G., 422, 463

Terry, Marshall, 514
Thomas, Phillip Drennon, 552, 560, 591, 655
Thompson, Edgar T., 25
Tischler, Nancy M., 289
Tucker, Mary Louise, 166, 203, 208, 211, 213
Turner, Newell, 495
Turner, William H., 235
Twining, Mary Ann, 380

Upton, Dell, 109, 120, 191, 194
Urban, Wayne J., 458

Vlach, John Michael, 231, 272

Weare, Walter B., 245, 266
Webb, George E., 456
Werner, Craig, 390
White, Arthur O., 511
Whitehead, Tony L., 259, 276
Whittenburg, James P., 475
Whitwell, W. L., 180
Wiggins, Sarah Woolfolk, 460
Wigginton, B. Eliot, 485
Williams, Walter L., 283
Willingham, Robert M., Jr., 436
Wilson, Charles Reagan, 21, 34, 72, 186, 199, 365, 393, 416, 448, 489, 601, 627, 640, 644, 649, 651, 656, 659, 662, 667, 669, 670, 675
Wilson, Francille Rusan, 367
Winborne, Lee, 180
Wynes, Charles E., 372

Young, Dianne, 647
Young, James Harvey, 481

Index

Boldface page numbers refer to main articles
Italic page numbers refer to illustrations

Abele, Julian, 238
Abernathy, Ralph D., 383
Adams, Henry, 555
Aerospace industry, 455–56
African influences: black English, 330; black life, **230–31**; creolization, **245–48**; dance, 249–50; folklore, 263; gardens, 32; painting, 240–41; preachers, 313; religion, black, 263, 323–24
Afton Villa, 122, *123*
Agee, James, 163, 581; on gardens, 33
Agrarianism, 61–62, 70–71, 429–30
Agrarians, Vanderbilt, 149, 458
Agribusiness, **17–21**, 45
Agricultural Adjustment Administration (AAA), 49, 56, 73, 80
Agriculture, **3–7**; agribusiness, **17–21**, 45; animal life and, 546; aquaculture, 646–47; architecture of buildings and houses, **106–9**, *109*, 118–20; black farmers, 15, 19, 284–85, 286; climate and, 532, 553; crops, **26–28** (*see also* specific crops); diversification, 19, **28–31**, 51–52, 74; education, **448–52**, 454; environmental impact, 6, 538–39, 563–64, 565; extension services, **50–51**, 62–63; fertilizers, **58–59**, 563–64; forest clearing, 537, 572; government involvement in, 18, 21, 30, 50, 56, 57–58, 73, 80–81; irrigation, 582, 606–7; land use, **581–83**; mechanization, 19, 27, **39–41**, *41*, 50, 56, 73–74, 81; organic farming, 33–34; pest control, 33, 52, **67–70**, 557; reclamation projects, **604–6**; soil conservation, **616–19**; truck farming, **82–83**; TVA and, 623; urbanization and, 20. *See also* Livestock; Plantations; Sharecroppers and tenants
Aiken, D. Wyatt, 61
Ailey, Alvin, 251
Air-conditioning, 87–88, **542–45**, 555
Alabama: agriculture, 40, 45, 46, 51, 66, 583; black life, 255, 297, 311, 315–16, 340; Citizens' Councils, 347; education, 255, 401, 438; energy resources, 561; flood control, 569; pollution, 602
Alabama, University of, 424, 425, 439, **459–60**, 462
Albrizio, Conrad, 149
Alexander, Will W., 58, 348
Alexander v. *Holmes County Board of Education* (1969), 421
Allen, James Lane, 14
Alligators, 549–50, 558, **637–38**
American Agriculture Movement, 21
American Federation of Arts, 147
American Federation of Labor (AFL), 340
American Federation of Teachers (AFT), 453
American Teachers Association (ATA), 453
Ames, Jessie Daniel, 296, 348
Amisano, Joseph, **195–96**
Amphibians, 549–50
Anderson, Walter, 153, **196–97**
Angelou, Maya, 334
Animal carvings, 184
Animals and animal life, **545–52**, 634, 635, 648, 652; destruction of wildlife, 537–38, 565–66; endangered species, **556–60**; trails, 613. *See also* specific animals
Anoles, 550
Antrobus, John, 143
Ants, fire, 70, 580
Apalachicola, Fla., 620
Appalachia and Appalachians: animals and, 551; blacks, **231–35**; Campbell's work in, 469; Civil War, 640; coalfields, **630–32**; poverty, 234, 640
Appalachian Mountains, 533–34, 554, **639–40**, 645
Appalachian National Park Association, 593–94
Apples, 60–61
Aquaculture, 646–47
Architecture, **87–91**; art deco, 137, 171, 178; beaux arts classicism, 136; black, **235–39**; California style, 169–70; climate and, 128, 552; Colonial Revival, **99–101**; columnar, 126–27; commercial style, 136; of country stores, 24; craftsman style, 170; decorative brick style, 136–37; Eastlake, **168–69**; energy conservation and, 91; farm buildings and houses, **106–9**, *109*, 118–20; Federal-style, 125–26; French, **110–12**; Georgian Revival, **112–16**, *114*, 201–2; German, **116–20**; Gothic Revival, **120–25**, 135; Greek revival, 121, **125–29**, *126*, 173, 417; historiography of, 127–28, **129–32**; industrial 19th century, **132–35**; international style, 171; Johnston's photographs of, 211; neoclassicism, 136; neo-Italianate, 171; nonresidential 20th-century, **135–38**; prairie style, 170–71; Queen Anne, **167–68**; Renaissance revival, 171; residential 20th-century, **169–71**; resort, **172–80**; slavery and, 126–27, 128–29; storefront modern style, 137; streamline moderne, 137–38, 171; stripped-down classicism, 136; Tudor style, 171; TVA and, 623–24; Williamsburg historic preservation, 90, **94–99**, 114–15. *See also* House types; specific architects
Architecture, vernacular styles, 89, 91, 98; air-conditioning and, 544–45; Lowland South, **186–91**; Upland South, **191–94**
Arkansas: agriculture, 20, 27, 40, 45, 46, 60, 72, 73, 582; black life, 297, 299, 311; flood control, 569; military schools, 437; wetlands, 634
Arkansas, University of, **460**
Armadillos, **640–41**
Armstrong, Louis, 266, 306
Armstrong, Samuel C., 450, 491
Art. *See* Visual arts
Artistic organizations, 147, 150, 213, 216–17
Atchafalaya Basin Swamp, **641–42**

Atchafalaya Floodway project, 567, 631
Atheist movement, 447
Atlanta, Ga., 76, 341, 435; Amisano's buildings, 195–96; educational system, 442, 457, 458
Atlanta University, 240, 253; Du Bois and, 352
Attaway, William, 292
Auburn University, **460–62,** *461*
Audubon, John James, 94, 143, 547, 564, 588, 590, **642–43**
Augusta, Ga., 134, 609
Automobiles, 35, 614–15
Azaleas, 575, 576, **643–44**

Baldwin, Calvin B., 58
Baldwin, James, 321
Baldwin, Joseph Glover, 13
Baltimore, Md., 89
Banjo, 230, 234
Baptists: blacks and, 324, 325; education and, 409, 444, 445, 446, 447, 448
Barnard, Frederick A. P., 158, 418, *462,* **462–63**
Barnard, George N., 159
Barnett, Ross, 376, 499
Barnett-Aden Gallery, 240
Barnhill, William A., 163
Barns, 106–7, 118–19
Bartram, John, 563, 589, 597
Bartram, William, 94, 589, 597, 637
Baseball, blacks in, 333, 334, **378–79**
Basketball, 334, 414
Basketmaking, 263
Bass, largemouth, 549
Baylor University, 447, **463–65**
Beach resorts, 179–80
Bearden, Romare, 152, **198–99,** 241
Bears, black, 547
Beck, George, 143
Bees, 582
Belmead (plantation house), 121–22
Bennett, Hugh Hammond, 617
Benton, Thomas Hart, 149, 213
Berea College, 234, 253, **465,** 485
Bethune, Mary McLeod, **342–43**
Bethune-Cookman College, 342–43
Big Thicket, 595, **644–45**
Bilbo, Theodore G., 499
Binford, Julien, 152, **199–200**
Birds, 548–49, 556–58, 566, 643, 660–61
Birmingham, Ala., 561, 568
Birth of a Race, The (film), 260
Black drink, 598–99
Black English, **329–32**
Black Mountain College, 153–54, **465–66**
Black Panther party, 386
Black Patch War, 6
Blacks, **223–28;** African influences, **230–31;** agriculture, 15, 19, 50–51, 284–85, 286; alligators and, 638; animals and, 551; Appalachians, **231–35;** architecture, **235–39;** artisans, 235–36, 243, 339–40; businesses, **242–45;** in cities, 225, 298, 299–300, **306–9;** clothing of, 247–48; communism and, 309; country stores and, 24; creolization of, **245–48;** dance, **248–52,** *249;* film images of, **259–62;** folklore, 230, 246, **262–64,** 328; foodways, 247, 264; fraternal orders and mutual benefit societies, 227, **265–66,** 343; funerary customs, **271, 271–72,** health, **276–79;** illiteracy, 427, 428; immigrants and, **279–81;** Indians and, **281–83;** interracial cooperation, **347–49,** 366; Juneteenth, **369;** kinship networks, 233, 257; landownership, 257–58, **283–86;** literary portrayals of, **286–89;** lynchings, **294–97,** *296,* 302, 321, 348, 392; Mardi Gras Indians, **372–73,** *373;* migration, 233, 259, 285–86, **297–300,** 306–9, 325; miners, 232–33, *233,* 340; miscegenation, 288, **300–2;** naming patterns, 246; newspapers, **314–17,** 350, 351, 392; opossums and, 667; painters, 151–52, 198–99, 207, 209–10, 239–42; paintings of, 142, 143, 145, 151, 152, 210, 286–87, 654; "passing," 302; "pet Negro system," 362; photographers, 163, 164; politics, **310–12,** 360, 364, 371–72; racism and, **318–23;** Sea Islands and, **379–81;** sharecroppers and tenants, 223–25, 318; speech patterns, 227–28, 230–31, 245–46, 262, 327–28, **329–32;** in sports, **333–35,** 378–79; teachers, 453; towns, **337–39;** TVA and, 624; women, 244, 266, 316, 343; workers, 225, 307–8, **339–42.** *See also* Civil rights movement; Education, black; Family, black; Literature, black; Music, black; Religion, black; Segregation; Slavery; Slaves
Block Gay, 166
Blount, Roy, Jr., 667
Blueberries, 60
Blue Ridge Mountains, **645**
Blues music, 234, 263, 305, 308, 368, 571
Bob Jones University (BJU), **466–67**
Boca Raton, Fla., 216
Boca Raton Club, 177–78
Boley, Okla., 338
Boll weevil, 18, **51–52,** 55–56, 68, 69, 580
Bond, Julian, **343–44,** 386
Bonner, James C., 131
Bontemps, Arna, 290, 292, **344–45,** 482
Boone, Daniel, 613
Bottomley, William Lawrence, 113, **201–2**
Boxing, blacks in, 333–34
Boxwood hedges, 575
Brady, Mathew, 158, 159
Breckinridge, John C., 673
Brer Rabbit and the Wolf tale, 328
Bridges, Charles, 139
Brooks, Cleanth, 498
Brown, H. Rap, 293
Brown, John, 234
Brown, Sterling, 228, 290, 308
Brown, Tony, 234
Brown, William Wells, 291, 293
Brown v. *Board of Education* (1954), 254, 255, 310, 323, 378, 421, 423
Bryant, Paul "Bear," 415
Budworm, 69
Buffalo (American bison), 546
Bungalows, 169–70
Burgess, Ned, 184
Business. *See* Industry and business
Busing, **467–68**
Butler, Benjamin, 337
Butler, Eugene, 72
Butler, Tait, 71–72
Byrd, William, II, 563, 593

Cabins, 192–93
Cable, George Washington, 14

Caldwell, Erskine, 14, 30, 288, 627
Calhoun, John C., 628
Camellias, 574
Cameron, James, 143
Campbell, John C., **469–70**
Campbell, Will, 581
Camphene, 63–64
Canals, 610, 611, 675–76
Candler, Warren A., 457–58, 481
Cane (Toomer), 387
Cape Hatteras, 668–69
Capote, Truman, 287
Carawan, Guy, 393
Carmichael, Stokely, *229*, 270, 386
Carson, Rachel, 70
Carter's Grove (mansion), 114
Carver, George Washington, 66, 211, 454, 519
Cash, W. J., 287, 552
Cason, Clarence, 531, 552
Catesby, Mark, 94, 140, 563, 588–89, 596, 661
Catfish, 549, **645–47**
Catlin, George, 142–43
Cattle. *See* Livestock
Cellars, 188
Cemeteries, 11, 272
Central Lowlands, 534
Chairs, 102–3, 104
Chapel Hill, N.C., 114
Chapman, Conrad Wise, 144, **202–3**
Charleston, College of, 418
Charleston, S.C., 101, 265, 304, 609; architecture, 89, 90, 133; Chapman's paintings of, 202–3; The Citadel and, 472–73; earthquake, 586; education, 417–18, 432, 433, 434; furniture industry, 103–4; naturalists and, 589–90
Chautauqua movement, **470–71**
Chemical industry, 561
Chem-Nuclear plant, 663–64
Cherokees, 282, 578, 579, 598, 626, 653
Chesapeake Bay, **647–49,** 672
Chesnutt, Charles W., 291, 292, **345–46**
Chest of drawers, 105
Chickasaws, 37, 282, 577
Chickens, 44–46; chicken "factory," *18*
Childress, Alice, 291, 292
Chinaberry trees, 627
Choctaws, 282, 577
Christenberry, William, 166, **203**
Church of Christ, 409, 445
Church of God in Christ, 374
Citadel, The, 437, 438, 439, **472–73**
Citizens' Councils, **347–48**
Citrus groves, 60
Civil Rights Act of 1964, 354, 370, 421
Civil rights movement: in Appalachia, 234; black-Indian relations and, 283; freedom movement and, **267–70,** *270;* origins of, 226, 322–23; Selma march of 1965, 269, **381;** "We Shall Overcome," 393. *See also* specific leaders and organizations
Civil War: Douglass and, 351; environmental impact, 539–40; military school faculty in, 438; paintings of, 202, 654; peanuts and, 65; photography of, 159–60; in Shenandoah Valley, 640, 673–74
Clague, Richard, 145
Claiborne, Herbert, Sr., 115
Clark, Thomas D., 25, 413, 454
Classical tradition: architecture, **125–29,** 136; education, **416–19;** Gildersleeve and, 488–89
Clayton, Ga., 484
Clean Air Act of 1970, 568, 602
Clemens, Samuel Langhorne (Mark Twain), 79, 120–21, 211, 646
Clemson University, **473–74**
Climate and weather, 128, **552–56;** air-conditioning and, 542; air masses and, 536; culture of South and, 531–32; natural disasters, 584–86; rainfall, 534–35, 536
Clinton, Tenn., 234
Cloar, Carroll, 153, **203–5**
Clogging, 234
Clothing, of blacks, 247–48
Coal, 561, **638–39**
Coal carvings, 184–85
Coastal Plains, 533
Coe, Richard, 149–50
Cogdell, John, 181
Collard greens, **649–50**
Colleges and universities: academic freedom, 409; adult education, 412; in antebellum society, 399–400, 406–7; architecture, 125; athletics programs, 335, 416; classical tradition, **416–19;** in colonial era, 399; denominational ties, 409; desegregation of, 421–22; doctoral programs, 404–5; fraternities and sororities, **424–26,** 495; innovation at, 431, 457–58; junior colleges, **493–95;** in late 1800s, 401–2; libraries, 433, 434, 435; military schools, **436–39;** post-World War II period, 403, 405; regionalism and, 407–8; religious training, 443–44; technological education, **453–56.** *See also* specific institutions
Colonial era: agriculture, 26, 31–32, 36–37; decorative arts, 102–3; education, 399; environmentalism, 563; miscegination, 300–1; painters, 139–41; wetlands use, 635–36
Colonial Williamsburg. *See* Williamsburg, Va.
Colored National Labor Union, 340
Commission on Interracial Cooperation (CIC), **347–49**
Committee on Appeal for Human Rights, 344
Commonwealth College, **475–77**
Communal farms, **52–53,** 266
Communism, blacks and, 309
Conference on Education and Race Relations, (CERR), 348
Confessons of Nat Turner, The (Styron), 388
Congress of Industrial Organizations, 341
Congress of Racial Equality (CORE), 268, 311, **349–50,** 363
Conjure, 324
Conroy, Pat, 473
Cook, George Smith, 158–59
Cook, Howard, 150
Corn, 3, 26, 28, **54**
Cottages, raised, 89
Cotton, 3, 4, 5, 6, *8*, 19, 26, *27*, **55–56;** country stores and, 23; diversification and, 29, 30; environmental impact, 539, 565; fertilizer use and, 58, 59; history of, 27; mechanization and, 40; neoplantations and, 44; slavery and, 339. *See also* Boll weevil
Couch, W. T., 14, **477–78**
Council of Federated Organizations, 269
Country stores, 12–13, **21–26,** *26*
County seat, 12

Cowboys, 37
Crabs, 672–73
Cracker-barrel philosophy, 25
"Crackers," 37
Cramer, Stuart, 542
Crape myrtle, 576
Crawford, Ralston, 154
Crayfish, 672–73
"Creationism," 410
Credit, 5, 6, 12, 22, 47, 225, 318
Creek nation, 577–78, 599
Creole music, 306
Creolization, **245–48**
Cress, George, 154
Crews, Harry, 76, 552
"Cribs," freestanding, 107
Crocodiles, 558, **637–38**
Crop dusting, 68
Crop-lien system, 5, 22, 47, 318
Cubans, 279
Cumberland Falls State Park, 594
Curry, J. L. M., **478–79**
Custis, Peter, 670, 671
Cypress, **650–51**

Dabbs, James McBride, 552
Daingerfield, Elliot, 146
Dairy industry, **56–57**
Dallas, Tex., 76, 151
Dance, black, **248–52,** *249*
Davidson, Donald, 148, 149, 418, 458
Davis, Angela, 234
Davis, Jefferson, 437, 463
Davis Bend, Miss., 337
Death, black attitudes toward, 271–72
De Batz, Alexandre, 140
De Bry, Théodore, 138, 139
Decorative arts, **101–5,** *105*
Decoys, 184
Deer: key, 559–60; whitetail, 546–47
Delta Airlines, 68
Delta and Pine Land Company, 20
De Mille, Agnes, 249
Democratic party, 300, 310, 360
Dickey, James, 536, 656
Disciples of Christ, 445
Disease, 68, 276–79, 623
Dismal Swamp, 533, *533*
Dixon, George "Little Chocolate," 333
Dixon, Thomas, Jr., 287
Dodd, Lamar, 150, **205–6,** 217
Dogwood trees, 627
Dorsey, Thomas A., 308–9
Douglas, Aaron, 151–52, 207, 240
Douglass, Frederick, 280, 291, **350–51,** *351*
Downing, Andrew Jackson, 122
Drayton Hall, 88, *92*
Du Bois, W. E. B., 151, 288, **352–53;** education and, 254, 492; on fraternal orders, 265, 266; NAACP and, 377; on religion, 326; segregation, response to, 226, 322
Duke, James B., 480
Duke University, 125, **479–80,** *480*, 501
Dureau, George, 166
Durham, N.C., 244

Earl, Ralph E. W., 141, 142
Earthquakes, 586
Eastlake, Charles Locke, 168–69
Eaton, John, 337
Ecology of the South, 534–36
Edmondson, William, 184
Education, **399–408;** academic freedom, **408–11;** adult education, **411–13,** 427–28; agrarianism and, 429–30; agricultural, **448–52,** 454; athletics and, **413–16;** "big school" consolidation, 16, 414; Chautauqua movement, **470–71;** Christian academies, **471–72;** classical tradition in, **416–19;** "dangers" of, 450; expenditures on, 423, 442, 449; federal-state relations, **422–24;** *Foxfire* and, **484–85;** home teaching, *403;* illiteracy and, 411–12, **426–29;** industry and, 442; innovations in, **429–31,** 457–58; learned societies, **431–32;** libraries, **432–36,** *434;* military, 407, **443–48;** philanthropy and, 402, 451, 478, 485–86; politics of, **439–41;** populism and, 429; preprimary programs, 441; quality of education, **441–43;** racial attitudes and, 401, 402–3; reform movements, 402, 406, 429–31; religion and, 324, 408–10, **443–48;** rural, 13, **448–52;** Sears catalog and, 76; "southern" outlook, 406–7; teachers and teaching, 401, 403, 442, **452–53;** textbook adoptions, 448; urbanization and, **457–59;** women's, 400, 440. *See also* Colleges and universities
Education, black, **252–56,** 401, 402–3; academic freedom and, 410–11; architectural training, 237, 238; arts education, 239–40; dance training, 251; fraternities at colleges, 425; General Education Board and, 485–86; medical training, 253–54, 278; opposition to, 450; philanthropy and, 402; politics of, 440; religiously supported schools, 324, 445; technological education, 454. *See also* specific schools and educators
Education, desegregation of, 255, 405–6, **420–22,** 458; athletics and, 415; busing, **467–68;** Meredith and, 375–76; segregated conditions, 253–55, 320, 422–23
"Educational trains," 448–49
Edwards, Jay D., 159
Eggleston, William, 165, **207–8**
Egrets, 548–49
Eisenhower, Dwight D., 255, 311
Elder, John Adams, 144–45
Elder, Lee, 335
Electrification, **74,** 623, 629
Ellet, Charles, 628, 636
Elliot Society of Natural History, 432
Ellison, Ralph, 288, 292, 293
Emery, Lynne Fauley, 249, 250, 251
Emory University, 457–58, **480–81,** 504
Energy resources, **560–62**
Environment, **531–42;** agriculture and, 6, 538–39, 563–64, 565; Appalachian Mountains, 554, **639–40,** 645; Big Thicket, 595, **644–45;** Blue Ridge Mountains, **645;** energy resources, **560–62;** Great Smoky Mountains, 593, 594, **652–54;** human modification of, 536; Indians and, 562, **577–79;** insecticides and, 69–70; natural disasters, **583–86;** naturalists and, 140, 143, **586–91,** 596–97, 642–43; natural resources, **591–92;** plants, **596–98;** Shenandoah Valley, **673–74.** *See also* Animals and animal life; Climate and weather; Forests; Pollution; Water resources

Environmentalism, **562–68;** forests and, 573; parks and recreation areas, **592–96,** 652; pollution, response to, 603; soil conservation, **616–19;** water projects and, 624–25, 629, 631, 632–33
Environmental Protection Agency (EPA), 602
Episcopalianism, 123–24, 446
Ervin, Sam, 419
Evangelicalism, 325, 446
Evans, Walker, 163, 203
Everglades, 569–70, 594, **651–52**
Evers, Medgar, **353–54**
Evolutionism, 409–10

Family: air-conditioning and, 545; migration and, 259; reunions, 258, 275; rural life, 11
Family, black, **256–59;** adoption, informal, 273; genealogy, **273–76;** kinship networks, 233, 257; slave families, 327; urban life and, 309
Farm, The (communal farm), 53
Farm buildings and houses, **106–9,** *109*, 118–20
Farmers' Cooperative Demonstration Work program, 50, 62–63
Farm Security Administration (FSA), 49, **57–58,** 163, 348
Faulkner, William, 148, 536; animals, portrayal of, 552; black characters, 287, 288, 289, 314; climate, descriptions of, 555; plants, use of, 601; on pollution, 602; on rural life, 14, 30; on trees, 625–26
Federal Aid Highway Act of 1921, 36, 615
Federal Aid Road Act of 1916, 35
Fee, John, 465
Fences and walls, 109
Fertilizers, **58–59,** 563–64
Festivals: blacks and, 263; for collard greens, 650; Juneteenth, **369;** for opossums, 667
Film, 261; blacks, images of, **259–62**
Fish, 549
Fisk University, 151–52, 207, 240, 253, **481–83;** Johnson, Charles S., and, 365–66
Fitz, Henry, Jr., 157
Fitzpatrick, Kelly, 150
Flack, Roberta, 234
Flagler, Henry M., 176, 177
Flaxman, Theodore, 137
Flood control. *See under* Water resources
Florida: agriculture, 20, 60, 66, 79, 82, 582; Bethune's work in, 342–43; black migration, 297; communal farms, 52; education, 401, 494, 510–11; endangered species, 557, 558, 559–60; Everglades, 569–70, 594, **651–52;** Mizner's buildings, 215–16; painters in, 146, 654–55; palm trees, 669–70; parks, 594; pollution, 603; resort business, 176–78; vegetation, 535; water resource management, 569–70, 633, 634
Florida, University of, **483–84**
Flowers, 597–98
Folk art: black, 263–64; plants used for, 600–1; sculpture, 180–81, 183–85
Folklore: animals and, 551; black, 230, 246, **262–64,** 328; boll weevil and, 51; climate and, 555; insects and, 580–81; of rural life, 12; of slaves, 328; trickster tales, 246, 262, 328
Foodways: of blacks, 247, 264; catfish, 645–47; collard greens, 649; gardens and, 33; of Indians, 578–79; pecans, 67; of sharecroppers and tenants, 48–49
Football: blacks in, 334; college, 416; high school, 413–14
Forests, 535, **571–74,** 592, 596; exploitation of, 64, 536–38, *537*, 564; reforestation, 567, 617–18; reforestation programs, 567; trees, **625–27.** *See also* Timber industry
Forman, James, 386
Fort Maurepas, 110
Fortress Monroe, Va., 337
Foxfire magazine and books, **484–85**
Fragmented plantations, 43
Franklin, Aretha, 314
Franklin, C. L., 314
Franklin, John Hope, **354–55,** 372, 438
Fraser, Charles, 142
Fraternal orders, black, **265–66**
Fraternities and sororities, **424–26,** 495
Free African Society, 265
Freedmen's Bureau, 275, 278, 284, 422, 452
Freedom movement, **267–70,** *270*
Freedom Rides, 268–69, 349, 386
Freedom's Journal (newspaper), 314–15
Freeman, Roland L., 164
Freeman, Thomas, 671
Free Southern Theater (FST), 336, **355–57**
Frogs, 550
Fruit, **59–61,** 82, 582, 599, 626
Fugitive group, 148
Fundamentalism, religious, 446, 466–67; Christian academies, **471–72**
Funerary customs, black, *271*, **271–72**
Furniture, **101–5,** *105*

Gaines, Ernest J., 164, 292, **357–58**
Gainesville, Ga., 46, 584
Galveston, Tex., 585
Gardens, 115; flower and shrub, **574–77;** vegetable, **31–34**
Gardner, Alexander, 159
Garvey, Marcus, 309, 322
Gaskin, Stephen, 53
Genealogy, 11, 16; black, **273–76**
General Education Board, 63, 451, **485–86**
Genthe, Arnold, 162
Georgia: agriculture, 20, 27, 28, 37, 40, 45, 46, 51, 60, 66, 67, 80, 582, 583; black life, 255, 297, 301, 336, 340; Bond's political career, 344; communal farms, 52; Dodd's paintings of, 205–6; energy resources, 561; illiteracy, 427–28; libraries, 433, 435; lynchings, 295, 296; military schools, 438; plantations, 41; pollution, 602; roads and trails, 614; wetlands, 634
Georgia, University of, 150, 205, **486–87,** 504
Georgia Institute of Technology, **487–88,** 581
Gildersleeve, Basil L., 418, **488–89**
Giovanni, Nikki, 234
Gist, Eloyce, 261
Glasgow, Ellen, 14
Golf, 179, 335
Good roads movement, 7, **34–36**
Gorrie, John, 542
Gospel music, 262–63, 308, 325
Gothic sensibility of Southerners, 120–21
Grady, Henry W., 15, 451
Graham, Frank Porter, *489*, **489–90**

Grange, The, **61–62,** 76, 500
Grapes, 59–60
Great Depression, 6, 49. *See also* New Deal
Great Georgian Houses of America, 115–16
Great Indian Warpath, 613
Great Smoky Mountains, 593, 594, **652–54**
Greensboro, N.C., 268
Griffin, Marvin, 335
Grimké, Thomas, 417
Gullah (creole language), 245–46, 327–28, 380
Gum trees, 626–27
Guy, Francis, 143
Gwathmey, Robert, 152, **208–9**

Haley, Alex, 273, 293, *358,* **358–59**
Halsey, William, 154
Hamblett, Theora, 601
Hamer, Fannie Lou, **359–61,** 386
Hampden-Sydney College, **490–91**
Hampton, Wade, III, 43
Hampton Institute, 251, 253, 450, 451, **491–92**
Hancock, Gordon Blaine, 361
Hardeman, I. H., 542
Harlem Renaissance arts movement, 289–90
Harrington, William H., 158
Harriot, Thomas, 587
Harris, Alex, 164–65
Harris, Joel Chandler, 14, 211, 230, 287
Harrison, Benjamin, 371
Hartwig, E. E., 78
Hayden, Palmer, 240–41
Heade, Martin J., 146
Hearsey, Henry J., 296
Hellman, Lillian, 289
Henderson, George W., 293
Henry, Patrick, 42, 490
Herbicides, 69
Herring, James, 239–40
Hesselius, John and Gustavus, 139
Highlander Folk School, 393
Hill, Daniel H., 438
Hine, Lewis, 162–63
Historic preservation, 89–90; at Williamsburg, 90, **94–99,** 114–15
Historiography: of architecture, 127–28, **129–32; black historians, 354–56; Phillips and, 505–6; of visual arts, 93–94; Woodward and, 527–28**
Homer, Winslow, 144, 145, 146, 654–55
Hooks, Benjamin L., 378
Hookworm, 74
Hoover, Herbert, 630
Horse racing, blacks in, 333
Horses. *See* Livestock
Horton, Myles, 234
Hot Springs, Va., 175
House types, *190;* bungalows, 169–70; cabins, 192–93; central-passage-plan, 194; Colonial Revival, **99–101;** Creole cottage, 190; creolization process, 248; dogtrot, 193–94; double-pen, 193; Eastlake, **168–69;** Georgian-plan, 189; Georgian Revival, **112–16,** *114,* 201–2; German, 117–18, 119–20; Greek Revival, 128; I houses, 189; log construction, 187–88, 191–92; masonry construction, 192; post-built, 186–87; Quaker-plan, 194; Queen Anne, **167–68;** saddlebag, 193; shotgun, 231, 248, 264; southern frame, 187; T-plan, 190–91; 20th-century architecture, **169–71;** vernacular (Lowland South), **186–91;** vernacular (Upland South), **191–94**
Houston, Charles Hamilton, 420
Houston, Tex., 602, 603
Howard University, 238, 239–40, 253, 254, 425
Howell, Claude, 154
Hughes, Langston, 228, 260, 289–90, 291
Hull, Marie, 150
Humidity levels, 554
Hunting: animal populations and, 546–47, 549, 556, 557, 565–66; popular attitudes toward, 563
Hurricanes, 553, 584–85
Hurston, Zora Neale, 288, 290, 293, **362–63**

Illiteracy, 401, 411–12, **426–29**
Immigrants, blacks and, **279–81**
Incest, 274
Independent Order of St. Luke, 266
Indianola, Miss., 256
Indians: animals and, 546, 547, 550–51, 637, 638; blacks and, **281–83;** discrimination against, 282–83; environment and, 562, 572, **577–79,** 635; foodways, 578–79; gardens, 31; livestock, 37; oaks, use of, 658; paintings of, 138, 141–42; photographs of, 158; plants, beliefs about, 598–99; slavery and, 282; trails, 613. *See also* specific tribes
Indigo, 3, 26, 27, 600
Industrialization, 540–41
Industrial Workers of the World, 340
Industry and business: agribusiness, **17–21;** air-conditioning and, 542–43, 544; architecture of industrial buildings, **132–35;** black businesses, **242–45;** education and, 442; energy resources and, 561–62; environmentalism and, 566; photography of, 161, 164; pollution, **601–4;** racial issues, 279–80, 320; slavery and, 339; technological education, **453–56.** *See also* specific industries
Insecticides, 33, 52, 68–70, 557
Insectivorous plants, 597
Insects, **579–81**
Insurance industry, blacks and, 244
Ironwork sculpture, 185
Island resorts, 178

Jackson, Andrew, 42, 181, 215, 613, 662
Jackson, Jesse, 311–12, 314, **363–64**
Jackson, Kiefer, 261
Jackson, Michael, 252
Jackson, Miss., 268–69, 354, 374
Jackson, Thomas "Stonewall," 144–45, 438, 525, 673
Jackson State University, **492–93**
Jamestown, Va., 80
Jazz, 263, 305–6; Storyville and, 385
Jefferson, Thomas, 20, 42, 175, 214; architectural style, 125–26; education and, 417, 434, 494; as naturalist, 590, 593; Red River expedition, 670; soil conservation, 563, 616; University of Virginia, 523, 524
Jekyll Island, 178
Jewell, J. D., 46
Jews, blacks and, 325
Jim Crow laws, **364–65**
Johnson, Andrew, 224
Johnson, Bushrod R., 438
Johnson, Charles S., **365–67,** 482

Johnson, Jack, 334
Johnson, James Weldon, 207, 228, 288, 289, 290, 292, 326, **367–68,** 482
Johnson, Joshua, 142, 239
Johnson, Lyndon B., 269, 311
Johnson, R. H., 614
Johnson, Robert, **367–69**
Johnson, William Henry, 151, **209–10,** 241
Johnston, Frances Benjamin, 162, **210–11**
Johnston, Henrietta, 139
Jones, John T., 61
Jordan, Barbara, 311
Jordan, David Starr, 493–94
Jordon, Clarence, 52
Journal of Industry (newspaper), 315
Jubilee (Walker), 389–90
Julio, Everett B. D. Fabrino, 144
Juneteenth, 369

Kappa Alpha Order, *495,* **495–96**
Kelley, Oliver H., 61
Kennedy, John F., 311, 354, 447
Kennedy, Robert F., 268
Kentucky: agriculture, 4, 6, 28, 108, 583; basketball, 414; black migration, 297; military schools, 437; plantations, 42; pollution, 602; religion, 10; roads and trails, 613; stone walls, 109
Kentucky, University of, **496–97**
"Kentucky homosexuals," 414
Kentucky Military Institute (KMI), 437
Key, V. O., Jr., **497**
Kilpatrick, James J., 414, 675
King, Horace, 133, 236
King, Martin Luther, Jr., *229,* 309, 326, **369–71,** *370,* 375, 528; freedom movement and, 267–68, 269; Jackson, Jesse, and, 363; preaching style, 314; SCLC and, 383; Selma march, 381
Kirkland, James H., 447, 458
Kites, Everglade, 558
Knapp, Seaman A., 18, 30, 50, **62–63,** 450, 565
Knights of Labor, 340
Knox, Samuel, 417
Koch, Richard, **211–12**
Koinonia Farms, 52–53
Kudzu, **655–56**
Kühn, Justus Engelhardt, 139
Ku Klux Klan, the Grange and, 62
Kuspit, Donald, 93
Kwilecki, Paul, 165

Labor, organized, 232, 340–41, 453, 476
Labov, William, 331
Lakes, 611–12
Lamar, L. Q. C., 565
Land Between the Lakes, 595
Landry, Pierre Joseph, 183
Langston, Okla., 338
Lankford, John A., 237
Latrobe, J. H. B., 174
Laughlin, Clarence John, 125, 164, **212–13**
Lawson, John, 587–88
League of American Wheelmen, 34
Learned societies, **431–32**
Ledbetter, Huddie "Leadbelly," 51
Lee, Harper, 581
Lee, Robert E., 159, 219; mausoleum, 217–18; Washington and Lee University, 495, 526
Lee, Umphrey, 513
Legaré, Hugh S., 417
Leland, Mickey, 311
Le Moyne de Morgues, Jacques, 138, 140
Libraries, **432–36,** *434*
Lightwood, **656–57**
Lion, Jules, 157
Literature: animals, portrayal of, 552; blacks, portrayal of, **286–89;** classical themes, 419; climate, descriptions of, 555; insects and, 581; magnolias and, 659; plants used in, 601; racism in, 321–22; rural life, portrayal of, 13–14. *See also* specific writers
Literature, black, 228, **289–91;** autobiographical material, 293; blacks portrayed in, 288; double entendres, 291; drama, 290–91, 335–37; novels, 292–93; oral literature, 230–31, 246; poetry, 289–90; proverbs, 246; short stories, 291–92. *See also* specific writers
Livestock, 4, 6, 19, **36–39,** 617; dairy industry, **56–57;** pest control, 68, 69; poultry, **44–46**
Lobsters, 672–73
Locke, Alain, 151, 207
Logan, Alexis F., 493–94
Log rafting, 607–8, *610*
Long, Huey P., 138, 498
Lost Cause myth, in art, 144–45, 182
Louis, Joe, 334
Louisiana: agriculture, 27, 39, 51, 67, 72, 73, 79, 583; animal folklore, 551; architecture, 110–12, 128; black life, 297, 299, 329, 336; Citizens' Councils, 347; endangered species, 557, 558; energy resources, 561; flood control, 568–69; furniture, 104; illiteracy, 427, 428; lynchings, 295, 296; photography of, 164; plantations, 42; pollution, 602, 664; wetlands, 606, 634, 641–42
Louisiana State Capitol, 121, *121,* 138, 149
Louisiana State University, 438, **497–98**
Louisiana Sugar Planters' Association, 79
Lumbees, 283
Lynch, John Roy, **371–72**
Lynching, **294–97,** *296,* 302, 321; anti-lynching movements, 348, 392
Lytle, Andrew, 17

McCabe, Edward P., 338
McCrady, John, 150–51, 213–14
McCullers, Carson, 287
McIntosh, William, 143
MacKenzie, Roderick, 149
Macomber, Walter, 96, 98
Macon, Ga., *8*
McPherson, James A., 292, 293
McPherson, William D., 160
Madison, James, 42, 490
Magnolia-maritime region, 535
Magnolia trees, 575, **658–59**
Mail service, rural, **75–76**
Malaria, 623
Mallard, Prudent, 105
Manatees, 559
Mantels, 111–12
Mardi Gras Indians, **372–73,** *373*
Marshall, George C., 525

Marshall, Thurgood, 420
Maryland, 41, 109, 116, 635–36
Mason, Charles Harrison, **373–74**
Matthews, Kate, 162
Mays, Benjamin E., 323, 361, **374–75**
Meatyard, Ralph Eugene, 165
Medicine and health: blacks, **276–79;** country stores and, 25; medical education, 253–54, 278; plants used for medicines, 599, 600, 649–50
Meharry Medical College, 253, 254
Memphis, Tenn., 76, 458, 468
Mencken, H. L., 180, 648
Meredith, James, **375–76,** 499
Methodism: blacks and, 324, 325; education and, 444, 445, 446, 447, 522–23
Metoyer, Louis, 236
Miami, Fla., 89, 178, 279
Michaux, André and François, 590, 596–97
Micheaux, Oscar, 260
Migration: by agricultural workers, 18–19, 49, 50; air-conditioning and, 543–44; by blacks, 233, 259, 285–86, **297–300,** 306–9, 325; family and, 259
Miley, Michael, 159
Military education, 407, **443–48.** *See also* specific schools
Mills, Robert, **214–15**
Mimosa trees, 627
Mineral resources, 535, 592
Mineral springs, 172–76, *174*
Miners and mining, 561–62; blacks, 232–33, *233*, 340; coalfields, **638–39**
Minstrelsy, 250, 382
Miscegenation, 274, 288, **300–2,** 321
Mississippi: agriculture, 27, 40, 45, 46, 51, 82, 583, 606; black life, 297, 311, 316–17; boxing, 333; Citizens' Councils, 347; Evers's work in, 353–54; flood control, 569; freedom movement, 268–69; Hamer's work in, 359–60; lynchings, 295, 296; Lynch's political career, 371–72; military schools, 437; plantations, 42; segregation laws, 365; wetlands, 634
Mississippi, University of, 353–54, 424, 429, **498–500,** *499;* Barnard and, 463; Meredith and, 375–76
Mississippi Freedom Democratic party (MFDP), 269, 360, 386
Mississippi River, 533, 610, **659–61;** flood control, 564, 566, 568–69, 570, 571, 586, 611, 628–29, 630, 631
Mississippi River Commission (MRC), 566
Mississippi State University, **500–1**
Mitchell, Clarence, 378
Mitchell, Margaret, 287
Mizner, Addison, 100, 177–78, **215–16**
Mobile, Ala., 304
Mockingbirds, **661–62**
Monroe, N.C., 394
Montgomery, Ala., 267–68
Montgomery, Isaiah, 338
Moral Majority, 447–48
Moravian buildings, 118
Moravian furniture, 104
Morehouse College, 375
Moses, Gilbert, 355, 356
Mosler, Henry, 144
Mosquitoes, 580
Motley, Archibald, 240
Moton, Robert R., 519
Mound Bayou, Miss., 243, 338
Mountain lions, 547, 559
Mount Vernon, 90, 116, *142*
Mulattoes, 301, 302
Murphree, Mary Noailles, 14
Murphy, Isaac, 333
Murray, Pauli, **376–77**
Muse, Clarence, 260
Museum of Early Southern Decorative Arts (MESDA), 101–2
Music, animals and, 551–52, 581
Music, black, **303–6;** creolization, 247; folklore and, 262–63; religious influences, 314; Silas Green show, **381–83;** slave music, 328; urban life and, 308; vocal techniques, 304–5; "We Shall Overcome," **393–94.** *See also* specific forms
Muslims, 325
Musseling, 608
Myers, Isaac, 340

Nashoba (communal farm), 52
Natchez, Miss., 88–89
Natchez Trace, 613, **662–63**
National Association for the Advancement of Colored People (NAACP), 254, 268, 310, 311, 316, 322, **377–78;** desegregation of schools, 420–21; Du Bois and, 352; Evers and, 354
National Council of Negro Women, 343
National Education Association (NEA), 453
National Humanities Center, **501–2**
National Negro Finance Corporation (NNFC), 244
Nation of Islam, 308
Native Americans. *See* Indians
Natural disasters, **583–86**
Naturalists, 140, 143, **586–91,** 596–97, 642–43
Naval stores industry, **63–65**
Negro baseball leagues, **378–79**
Neoplantations, 43–44
Nettles, Bea, 166
Newcomb College, 105, 146, 518
New Deal: agricultural policies, 56, 57–58; arts programs, 149, 200; environmentalism and, 567; sharecroppers and tenants, impact on, 49. *See also* specific agencies
New Madrid, Mo., 586
New Orleans, La.: architecture, 89, 90, 111, 211–12; boxing, 333; dance, black, 250; flood control, 568; Free Southern Theater, 356; furniture, 105; Mardi Gras, 250, 372–73; music, 304; roads, 613–14; Storyville, **384–85**
New River controversy, 630–31
New South, classical tradition and, 418
New Southern Group, 213
Newspapers, 13, 14, 296; black, **314–17,** 350, 351, 392
"Nine, The" (artists' group), 151
Nixon, Nicholas N., 65
Norfolk, Va., 65, 468
Norfolk *Journal and Guide*, 316, 317
Norris, George, 622, 629, 630
North Carolina: agriculture, 27, 40, 45, 46, 60, 65, 66, 80, 108, 583; black life, 255, 297, 311; education, 255, 401, 494; gardens, 31; libraries, 435; naval stores industry, 63–64; Outer Banks, **668–69;** plantations, 42; pollution, 602; religion, 10; road construction, 35; statuary, 181; wetlands, 634

North Carolina, University of, 501, **502–3;** Odum and, 504; Press, 477–78
North Carolina School of the Arts, **503–4**
North Carolina State University, 71, 501
Northern cities, blacks in, **306–9**
Nuclear power, 603, 625; pollution from, **663–65**

Oak-hickory region, 535
Oak trees, 626; live oak, 657–58
O'Connor, Flannery, 30, 289, 650
Odetta, 234
Odum, Howard W., 14, 15, 150, *504*, **504–5;** CIC and, 348; on foodways, 33; on pollution, 602; on trees, 626; Vance and, 521
Office of Roads Inquiry (ORI), 34
Ogden, Robert C., 451
O'Hair, Madalyn Murray, 447
Oil industry, 164, 561–62; pollution, 601–2, **665–66**
Okeechobee, Lake, 570, 571, 585, 611, 633
Oklahoma, 40, 66, 299, 338, 583
Olmsted, Frederick Law, 179, 181, 236, 636
O'Neal, John, 336, 355, 356
Operation Breadbasket, 363–64
Operation PUSH, 364
Opossums, 548, **666–68,** *667*
Oranges, 60
Osceola, 143
Outer Banks, **668–69**
Owens, Jesse, 334
Oxford, Miss., 137
Oysters, 672

Painting: 1564–1790, **138–41;** 1790–1860, **141–43;** 1860–1920, **144–48;** 1920–60, **148–55;** 1960–80, **155–57;** artistic organizations, 147, 150, 213, 216–17; black images, 142, 143, 145, 151, 152, 210, 286–87, 654; landscapes, 143, 145; Lost Cause myth and, 144–45; modernist styles, 93, 154; portraiture, 141–43; regionalism, 93, 145–46, 148–51, 155–57. *See also* specific painters
Palm Beach, Fla., 177, 215, 216
Palm trees, **669–70**
Parakeets, Carolina, 556–57
Parks, Rosa, 267, 323
Parks and recreation areas, **592–96,** 652
Patterson, Frederick D., 519
Peaches, 60
Peale, Charles Willson, 139
Peale, Rembrandt, 139–40
Peanuts, 30, **65–66,** 583
Pears, 60
Pecans, **66–67**
Pelicans, brown, 557
Pentecostalism, 325, 409
Perry, William G., 95–96
Petersburg *Lancet*, 316
Phillips, U. B., **505–6,** 542
Photography, **157–66,** *160*
Physiography of the South, 532–34
Piedmont, 533, 617
Pigeons, passenger, 548, 556, 566
Pinchot, Gifford, 565, 629
Pinehurst, N.C., 179
Pine trees, 571–72, *572*, 626
Piney Woods Country Life School, **506–7,** *507*
Pittman, Hobson, 153
Pittman, William, 238
Plant, Henry B., 176
Plantations, 4–5, **41–44;** agribusiness and, 20; architecture, 120–21, 127, 188–89, 235–36; black ownership, 236; climate and, 532; diversification and, 29; gardens, 32; livestock, 38; pest control, 67–68; Phillips's works on, 506. *See also* Slavery; Slaves
Plants, **596–98;** uses for, **598–601.** *See also* specific plants
Pleasants, J. Hall, 93
Plessy v. *Ferguson* (1896), 253, 320, 365, 420, 423
Plumbe, John, Jr., 157–58
Pocketknives, 183
Poe, Clarence H., 30, **70–71,** 71–72
Politics: black, **310–12,** 360, 364, 371–72; of education, **439–41;** segregation in, 319–20
Polk, Leonidas L., **70–71**
Polk, Prentice Hall, 163
Pollard, Edward, 120
Pollution, 541, **601–4,** 648, 673; nuclear, **663–65;** oil, **665–66**
Ponce de Leon Hotel, 177
Populism, 319, 429
Post roads, 613–14
Pot likker, 649
Pottery, 103, 105, 185
Poultry, **44–46**
Poverty: in Appalachia, 234, 640; of sharecroppers and tenants, 48, 49
Powers, Hiram, 181
Powhatan, Va., 200
Pratt, Joseph H., 629
Preachers and preaching, 44; blacks, **312–14,** 324–25, 373–74; religious training, 444, 446
Precipitation, 553–54
Presbyterians, 444, 445, 446, 447
Presley, Elvis, 263
Processing and storage buildings, 107–9
Proctor, Gloria, 234
Progressive Farmer, 30, 70, **71–72**
Prostitution, 384–85
Proverbs, 246
Pulp industry, 573

Quail, 549
Quilts, 581, 600

Rabbits, 547, 548
Rabun Gap-Nacoochee School, 412, 484
Rafinesque, Constantine, 590
Ragtime music, 305
Railroad Brotherhoods, 340
Railroads, 161, 176–78, 561, 613
Railroad stations, architecture of, 133–34
Raleigh, Sir Walter, 668
Randolph, A. Philip, 317
Randolph-Macon College, **508–9**
Ransom, John Crowe, 148
Rape, lynching and, 295
Raper, Arthur, 348, 349
Rawlings, Marjorie Kinnan, 552
Rawls, Lou, 314
Rayfield, Wallace, 237–38
Reclamation, **604–6**
Reconstruction: black towns, 337–38; education and, 400–1; land resettlement, 284

Red River expedition, **670–71**
Refrigeration, 74
Religion, black, 227, 263, **323–26;** creolization, 247; family and, 258; in northern cities, 308; preachers and preaching, **312–14,** 324–25, 373–74; slaves, 324, 327
Religion: camp meetings, 10, 312–13; Christian academies, **471–72;** church architecture, 123–24, *124,* 195; education and, 324, 408–10, **443–48;** film and, 261; illiteracy and, 427; rural life and, 10, 12; sports and, 413. *See also* specific denominations
Reptiles, 549–50, 558–59
Republican and Civil Rights Advocate, 316
Republican party, 371–72
Resorts, **172–80**
Rice, 3, 6, 26, 62, **72–74;** history of, 27; irrigation and, 582, 606; mechanization and, 39; neoplantations and, 44
Rice, T. D., 250
Rice mills, 133
Rice University, **509–10**
Richards, T. Addison, 143
Richmond, Va.: libraries, 434; mansions, 113, 115, 201; as river port, 609; statuary, 182, 217–18
Rickey, Branch, 334
River life, **607–8**
Rivers and lakes, **608–12,** 619–20
Roads and highways, **612–16,** *615;* good roads movement, 7, **34–36;** Natchez Trace, 613, **662–63**
Roanoke Island, 668
Robinson, Bill, 250–51
Robinson, Jackie, 334
Rockbridge Alum Springs, Va., 175–76
Rolfe, John, 26
Roman Catholicism, 123, 124, 324, 325, 444
Roosevelt, Franklin D., 57–58, 317, 343, 622, 631
Roosevelt, Theodore, 629
Root doctors, 600
Roots (Haley), 359
Rosin, 63, 64, 65
Royal Palm State Park, 594
Royal Poinciana Hotel, 177
Rucker, Sparky, 234
Ruffin, Edmund, 29, 617, 636
Rural Electrification Administration (REA), **74**
Rural life, **8–16;** country stores, **21–26,** *26;* education and, **448–52;** electrification, **74,** 623, 629; good roads movement, **34–36;** mail service, **75–76;** photography of, 163; racism and, 318; on rivers, **607–8;** Sears catalog, **76–77**
Rutledge, Anna Wells, 93–94

Salamanders, 550
Salesmen, traveling, 24
Sandy, George, 417
Savannah, Ga., 64, 90, 133–34, 609
Savannah River, 602, 603
Saxon, Rufus, 337
Scopes Trial, 410
Scott, Sir Walter, 120, 121
Scottsboro case, 317
Screwworm, 69
Sculpture, **180–86;** by blacks, 241
Sea Island, Ga., 178
Sea Islands, 337, **379–81**
Sears, Roebuck catalog, **76–77**
Seaside, Fla., 179–80
Sebron, Hippolyte, 143
Sectional and regional views of the South, 531
Segregation: blacks' response to, 225–27, 322–23, 390–91; Citizens' Councils, **347–48;** civil rights movement and, 322–23; country stores and, 23–24; creation of segregationist system, 318–19; in industry, 320; Jim Crow laws, **364–65;** moderates' support for, 322; in northern cities, 307; in politics, 319–20; in sports, 333–35; ubiquity of, 320–21; violence and, 321. *See also* Education, desegregation of
Selma march of 1965, 269, **381**
Seminoles, 37, 281–82, 638
"Separate-but-equal" principle, 253, 320, 365, 420–21, 423
Sexuality: black sexuality, whites' fear of, 287, 295, 301; incest, 274; miscegenation, 274, 288, **300–2,** 321
Shakers, 52
Shannon, Charles, 152
Shape-note singing, 234
Sharecroppers and tenants, *2,* 6, 15, 29, 30, **46–50,** *47, 48;* blacks, 223–25, 318; cotton and, 55, 56; credit for, 225; fragmented plantations and, 43; gardens, 32–33; history of, 223–25; job actions, 224; rice growing, 73
Shaw, Richard Norman, 167
Shawnees, 578
Sheats, William N., **510–11**
Sheet metal sculpture, 185
Shellfish, 608, **671–73**
Shenandoah National Park, 593, 594
Shenandoah Valley, 640, **673–74**
Sherman, William Tecumseh, 438
Shopping malls, 87, 195
Shreveport, La., 137–38, 219–20
Shrimp, 672
Silas Green show, **381–83**
Silverware, 103, 104
Simms, William Gilmore, 419, 434
Slavery, 223; architecture and, 126–27, 128–29; "classical" defense of, 418; cotton and, 339; Douglass' efforts against, 350–51; genealogy and, 273–74, 275–76; Indians and, 282; industry and, 339; miscegenation, 300–1; naval stores industry, 64; plantations and, 42–43; "quasifreedom," 329; racism and, 318; task system, 55; Turner's case, 388
Slaves: clothing, 247; culture of, **326–29;** dance, *249,* 240–50; death, attitude toward, 271; economic underground, 242; education for, 252; family life, 258, 327; fraternal orders, 265; gardens, 32; health of, 277; livestock-tending, 37; migration, 297; religion, 324, 327; revolts, 328–29; running away, 328; stereotypes of, 287
Smith, Capt. John, 648, 666
Smith, Lillian, 375
Snakes, 550
Snowfall, 553–54
Social class, 9, 43
Soils, 535, 591; erosion and conservation, 538–39, **616–19**
Sound and the Fury, The (Faulkner), 314
South Carolina: agriculture, 27, 37, 40, 51, 60, 65, 80, 582, 583; black-Indian relations, 281; black life, 297, 311, 338; Citizens' Councils, 347; fertilizer production, 58–59; lynchings, 295, 296; military schools, 437; Mills's buildings, 214–15; plantations, 41;

South Carolina (*cont.*)
pollution, 603, 663–64; religion, 10; segregation laws, 365; slaves, 327; statuary, 181; wetlands, 634, 636
South Carolina, University of, **511–13**
South Carolina College, 434
South Carolina Opportunity School, 412
Southern Baptist Theological Seminary, *444*
Southern Christian Leadership Conference (SCLC), 311, 381, **383–84;** CORE and, 349; founding of, 268; freedom movement, 268, 269; Jackson and, 363; King and, 370
Southern Commission on the Study of Lynching (SCSL), 348
Southern Education Board, 451
Southern Methodist University (SMU), **513–14**
Southern Regional Council, 348, 375
Southern Review, 498
Southern States Art League, 147, **216–17**
Southern Tenant Farmers' Union (STFU), 49, 476
Soybeans, 19, 26, 30, **77–78**, 583
Space exploration, art based on, 206
Spanish moss, *669*, **674–75**
Spencer, Anne, 290
Sports: blacks in, **333–35**, 378–79; education and, **413–16;** religion and, 413; women in, 415–16
Squirrels, 547–48
States' rights, road construction and, 614
Steamboats, **620–22**
Stereotypes: of blacks, 214, 287; blacks' satires on, 240–41
Stevens, Will Henry, 153
Stone Mountain, Ga., 182
Storyville, **384–85**
Strawberries, 60
Stribling, T. W., 14, 288
Stryker, Roy Emerson, 163, 164
Stuart, Gilbert, 141
Student Nonviolent Coordinating Committee (SNCC), 268, 311, 344, 349, **385–87**
Styron, William, 288, 388
Suffolk, Va., 65
Sugarcane, 6, 26, 39–40, **78–79**
Sullivan, Louis, 179
Sully, Thomas, 141–42, 218
"Sunbelt" phenomenon, 531, 541
Sunday schools, 448
Swann v. *Charlotte-Mecklenburg Board of Education* (1971), 467
Sweet Springs, Va., 175

Tables, gateleg, 102
Talmadge, Eugene, 77
Tampa Bay Hotel, 176–77
Tandy, Vertner A., 238
Tap dancing, 250–51
Tar, 63
Tarpons, 549
Tate, Allen, 148–49
Tate, Willis M., 513
Taylor, L. O., 163
Taylor, Robert R., 237
Teachers and teaching, 401, 403, 442, **452–53**
Technological education, **453–56**
Teed, Cyrus R., 52
Telephones, country stores and, 24–25
Television, blacks in, 261
Temperate Deciduous Forest Biome, 534–36
Temperatures, 553, 554
Tenant farming. *See* Sharecroppers and tenants
Tennessee: academic freedom, 410; agriculture, 4, 27, 60, 583; black life, 297, 311; communal farms, 52, 53; energy resources, 561; libraries, 435; military schools, 438; segregation laws, 365
Tennessee, University of, **514–15**
Tennessee Capitol, 88
Tennessee-Tombigbee Waterway, 611, 632, **675–76**
Tennessee Valley Authority (TVA), 59, 541, 567, 570, 595, 612, **622–25;** legislative background, 629–31
Tennis, blacks in, 334
Texas: agriculture, 20, 21, 27, 28, 39, 40, 51, 66, 72, 82, 582, 583; armadillos, 641; Big Thicket, 644–45; black life, 297, 299, 311; education, 401, 438, 494; endangered species, 557, 560; energy resources, 561; German immigrants, 119–20; Juneteenth, **369;** lynchings, 294, 295, 296; sports, 414, 415; water projects, 632–33; white primary, 310
Texas, University of, 426, 435, *515*, **515–16**, 641
Texas A&M University, 438–39, **516–17**
Texas Christian University, 445
Textile mills, architecture of, 134–35
Theater, black, 290–91, **335–37;** Free Southern Theater, **355–57**
Theüs, Jeremiah, 140
Thomas, James "Son," 185
Thomas, Rufus, 252
Thunderstorms, 584
Tidewater, 98, 106, 107, 617
Tillman, Benjamin R., 512
Timber industry, 537–38, 565, 573, 592; cypress and, 651; pollution, 602; reclamation and, 604–5; tree farming, 567
Toads, 550
Tobacco, 3, 6, 26, *81*, 582–83, 648; diversification and, 29; fertilizer use and, 58, 59; flue-cured, **80–82**, 108; history of, 26; mechanization and, 40–41; pest control and, 68; soil exhaustion and, 538; storage areas for, 106, 108–9
Toomer, Jean, 288, 290, 292, **387–88**
Tornadoes, 553, 584
Track-and-field, blacks in, 334
Tractors, 19, 40
Transportation: good roads movement, 7, **34–36;** rivers for, 609, 610–11, 619–20; roads and trails, **612–16**, *615*, 662–63
Trees, **625–27**. *See also* specific trees
Trinity Episcopal Church (Mobile), 123, *124*
Troye, Edward, 143
Truck farming, **82–83**
Truman, Harry S, 490, 622
Trumbull, John, 142
Tulane University, 105, 146, **517–18**
Tupelo, Miss., 584
Turkeys, 549
Turner, Michael, 165
Turner, Nat, **388–89**, 437
Turpentine, 63, 64, 65
Turtles, 550, 558–59
Tuskegee Air Base, 238
Tuskegee Institute, 51, 163, 211, 237, 253, 390, 454, **518–19**
Twin Oaks (communal farm), 53

Ullman, Doris, 163
Underground Railroad, 234
Universal Negro Improvement Association, 309
University of the South, 407, 445, **519–21**
Upjohn, Richard, 99, 123–24
Urbanization, 20, 165; air-conditioning and, 544; blacks in cities, 225, 298, 299–300, **306–9;** black towns, **337–39;** education and, **457–59;** environmental implications, 541; racism and, 318–19

Valentine, Edward Virginius, 182, **217–18**
Vance, Rupert B., 14, **521–22,** 552
Vanderbilt University, 409, 445, 458, **522–23**
Vaughan, A. J., 61
Vaughn, Sarah, 314
Vegetables, 31–34, 82, 599
Violence, 11–12, 321. *See also* Lynching
Virginia: agriculture, 26, 27, 60, 65, 66, 82, 108, 583; black politics, 311; communal farms, 53; energy resources, 561; furniture industry, 103; gardens, 31; libraries, 435; mansions, 113, 114, 116; New River controversy, 630–31; plantations, 41, 42; religion, 10; roads and trails, 614; slaves, 326; statuary, 181; wetlands, 636
Virginia, University of, 88, 417, 418, **523–24**
Virginia Beach, Va., 178
Virginia Capitol, 88
Virginia Military Institute (VMI), 437, 438, 439, **524–25**
Visual arts, **92–94;** art museums, **197–98;** black artists, **239–42;** decorative arts, **101–5,** *105;* photography, **157–66,** *160;* sculpture, **180–86,** 241. *See also* Folk art; Painting
Von Reck, Philip Georg Friedrich, 140–41
Voodoo, 250
Voting rights, 310–11, 370, 381

Walker, Alice, 288, 293, 363, 576–77
Walker, Madame C. J., 244
Walker, Maggie Lena, 227, 266
Walker, Margaret, 290, 292, *389,* **389–90,** 493
Walking canes, 184
Wallace, George, 226, 468
Walter, Thomas, 597
Warm Springs, Ga., 175, 176
Warren, Robert Penn, 148, 498, 643; black characters, 289; on pollution, 602, 603; rural life, depiction of, 30
Washington, Booker T., 211, 226, 234, **390–91,** *391;* accommodation philosophy, 253; business movement, 243; on extermination of Indians, 322; Hampton Institute and, 492; on immigrants, 280; newspapers and, 316; segregation, response to, 322; Tuskegee Institute and, 237, 518–19
Washington, D.C., 157–58, 215
Washington, George, 42, 141–42, 173, 181, 187, 526
Washington, William D., 144
Washington and Lee University, 218, 445, 495, *495,* **525–27**
Washington Monument (Baltimore), 214
Washington Monument (Washington, D.C.), 215
Waterman, Thomas Tileston, 96, 97, 113
Water power, 561
Water resources, 535–36, 592; flood control and drainage, 564, 566, 567, **568–71,** 585–86, 604–6, 611, 618, 623, 628–29, 630, 631, 636, 660; river life, **607–8;** rivers and lakes, **608–12,** 619–20; utilization and management, **627–34.** *See also* Tennessee Valley Authority (TVA); specific bodies
Waud, Alfred, 145
Waverley (plantation house), 121
Weather. *See* Climate and weather
Weaver, Richard M., **527**
Wells-Barnett, Ida, 226, 296, **391–93**
Welty, Eudora, 627, 643; black characters, 289; photography, 164; rural life, depiction of, 14, 30
"We Shall Overcome" (song), **393–94**
West, Benjamin, 139
West, William Edward, **218–19**
Wetlands, 564, 633, **634–37,** 651–52
Wheat, 27
White, John, 94, 138, 140, 432–33, 587
Whitehurst, Jesse H., 158
White primary, 310
White Sulphur Springs, *174,* 174–75
Whittling, 183
Whooping cranes, 557
Wiener, Samuel G., **219–20**
Wilderness Road, 613
Wilkins, Roy, 378
William and Mary, College of, 97, 399, 424, 433, 443, **474–75,** *475*
Williams, Robert F., **394–95**
Williams, Samm-Art, 291
Williams, Spencer, 261
Williams, Tennessee, 289
Williamsburg, Va., *95,* 103, 475, 593; historic preservation, 90, **94–99,** 114–15
Wilmington, N.C., 65, 346
Winemaking, 60
Winston-Salem, N.C., 90
Withers, Bill, 234
Wolfe, Thomas, 14
Wollaston, John, 139
Wolves, 560
Women: blacks, 244, 266, 316, 343; education for, 400, 440; magnolias and, 659; painters, 146; photographers, 162, 163, 166, 210–11; rural life, *10,* 10–11; sororities, **425–26;** in sports, 415–16; teachers, 452
Woodburning, 536–37
Woodpeckers, 557–58
Woodruff, Hale, 240
Woodson, Carter G., 234, 237, **395**
Woodward, C. Vann, 365, **527–28**
Woodward, Ellsworth, 145–46, 147, 216, 217
Workers: blacks, 225, 307–8, **339–42;** immigrants, 279–80
World War I, 35, 182, 316
World War II, 40, 317, 455, 624
Wright, Frances, 52
Wright, Frank Lloyd, 170–71, 179
Wright, Orville and Wilbur, 668
Wright, Richard, 288, 291–92, 293, 658; on gardens, 33; on migration, 300

X, Malcolm, 309, 358–59

Yellow fever, 68
Yeoman farmers, 3, 4, 9, 20, 21–22
Young, Andrew, 311
Young, P. B., 316, 317

Picture Credits

Agriculture

Page

1 William Ferris Collection, Archives and Special Collections, University of Mississippi Library, Oxford

8 Ann Rayburn Paper Americana Collection, Archives and Special Collections, University of Mississippi Library, Oxford

10 Photographic Archives, University of Louisville (Kentucky)

15 Arthur Rothstein, Library of Congress (LC-USW-3-4061-D), Washington, D.C.

18 Cold Kist Corporation, Atlanta, Georgia

26 William Ferris Collection, Archives and Special Collections, University of Mississippi Library, Oxford

27 Georgia Department of Archives and History, Atlanta

39 William Ferris Collection, Archives and Special Collections, University of Mississippi Library, Oxford

41 Marion Post Wolcott, Library of Congress (LC-USF-34-53810D), Washington D.C.

47 Walker Evans, Library of Congress (LC-USF-342-8147-A), Washington, D.C.

58 Marion Post Wolcott, Library of Congress (LC-USF-51099E), Washington, D.C.

72 Jack Delano, Library of Congress (LC-USF-34-440054D), Washington, D.C.

81 Howard Odum Papers, Southern Historical Collection, University of North Carolina, Chapel Hill

Art and Architecture

85 Brooks Museum of Art, Memphis, Tennessee

92 National Trust for Historic Preservation, Washington, D.C.

95 Colonial Williamsburg, Inc., Virginia File, Library of Congress (LC-USW-33-26180-ZC), Washington, D.C.

105 Jack Delano, Library of Congress (LC-USF-34-44484-D), Washington, D.C.

109 William Ferris Collection, Archives and Special Collections, University of Mississippi Library, Oxford

114 Valentine Museum, Richmond, Virginia

121 David J. Kaminsky, photographer, Historic American Buildings Survey, Library of Congress, Washington, D.C.

123 Photographer not given, Historic American Buildings Survey, Library of Congress, Washington, D.C.

124 Trinity Episcopal Church, Mobile, Alabama

126 Marion Post Wolcott, Library of Congress (LC-USF-34-54827-D), Washington, D.C.

142 Benjamin Henry Latrobe Collection, Maryland Historical Society, Baltimore

146 Cook Collection, Valentine Museum, Richmond, Virginia

153 Walter Anderson Family, Ocean Springs, Mississippi

160 Marion Post Wolcott, Library of Congress (LC-USF-33-30740-M3), Washington, D.C.

162 Frances Benjamin Johnston, Library of Congress (number unavailable) Washington, D.C.

163 Todd Webb, Historic New Orleans Collection (1978.90.13), New Orleans, Louisiana

174 The Greenbrier, White Sulphur Springs, West Virginia

190 M. B. Newton, Baton Rouge, Louisiana

203 William Christenberry, University Museums, University of Mississippi, Oxford

209 Patrons Art Fund, 1944, Carnegie Museum of Art, Pittsburgh, Pennsylvania

Black Life

221 William Ferris Collection, Archives and Special Collections, University of Mississippi Library, Oxford

227 William Ferris Collection, Archives and Special Collections, University of Mississippi Library, Oxford

229 Ernest C. Withers, photographer, Memphis, Tennessee

233 Victor Howard Collection, Archives and Special Collections, University of Mississippi Library, Oxford
249 *The Century Magazine*, vol. 31, February 1886, p. 525
261 Film Stills Archives, Museum of Modern Art, New York, New York
270 Birmingham (Alabama) *News*
271 William Ferris Collection, Archives and Special Collections, University of Mississippi Library, Oxford
272 William Ferris Collection, Archives and Special Collections, University of Mississippi Library, Oxford
296 Georgia Department of Archives and History, Atlanta
302 Film Stills Archives, Museum of Modern Art, New York, New York
303 Cheryl Thurber, photographer, Memphis, Tennessee
320 Archives and Manuscripts, Birmingham (Alabama) Public Library
351 Sophia Smith Collection, Smith College, Northampton, Massachusetts
358 Robert Jordan, photographer, University of Mississippi, Oxford
365 Esther Bubley, Library of Congress (LC-USW3-37939-E), Washington, D.C.
370 William Ferris Collection, Archives adn Special Collections, University of Mississippi Library, Oxford
373 Michael P. Smith, photographer, Brazos Films/Arhoolie Records, Los Cerrito, California
389 William Ferris Collection, Archives and Special Collections, University of Mississippi Library, Oxford
391 Photographer and number unavailable, Library of Congress, Washington, D.C.

Education

397 R. G. Potter Collection, Photographic Archives, University of Louisville (Kentucky)
403 Russell Lee, Library of Congress (number unavailable), Washington, D.C.
407 William Ferris Collection, Archives and Special Collections, University of Mississippi Library, Oxford
434 Archives and Manuscripts, Birmingham (Alabama) Public Library
444 Photographic Archives, University of Louisville (Kentucky)
461 Auburn (Alabama) University Archives
462 Archives and Special Collections, University of Mississippi Library, Oxford
475 University Archives, Swem Library, College of William and Mary, Williamsburg, Virginia
480 Duke University Archives, Durham, North Carolina
489 Southern Historical Collection, University of North Carolina, Chapel Hill
495 William Garver, Kappa Alpha Order, Lexington, Virginia
499 E. C. Boynton, photographer, Archives and Special Collections, University of Mississippi Library, Oxford
504 North Carolina Collection, University of North Carolina, Chapel Hill
507 Ann Rayburn Paper Americana Collection, Archives and Special Collections, University of Mississippi Library, Oxford
515 Barker Texas History Center, University of Texas at Austin

Environment

529 Virginia Museum of Fine Arts, Richmond
533 Maier Museum of Art, Randolph-Macon Woman's College, Lynchburg, Virginia
537 William Ferris Collection, Archives and Special Collections, University of Mississippi Library, Oxford
551 William Ferris Collection, Archives and Special Collections, University of Mississippi Library, Oxford
555 William Feris Collection, Archives and Special Collections, University of Mississippi Library, Oxford
572 Ann Rayburn Paper Americana Collection, Archives and Special Collections, University of Mississippi Library, Oxford
610 Photographic Archives, University of Louisville (Kentucky)
615 William Ferris Collection, Archives and Special Collections, University of Mississippi Library, Oxford
618 Soil Conservation Service, U.S. Department of Agriculture, Washington, D.C.
638 Historic New Orleans Collection (1979.338i-vi), New Orleans, Louisiana
663 Doug Marlette, Atlanta (Georgia) *Journal-Constitution*
667 Uncredited engraving in A. B. Strong, editor and compiler, *Illustrated Natural History of the Three Kingdoms* (1849)
675 Marion Post Wolcott, Library of Congress (LC-USF-34-54302-D), Washington, D.C.